P9-CJF-599

Western Hemisphere

Multiple images from satellites *Terra*, *Aqua*, *Radarsat*, and *Defense Meteorological Satellite*, and from Space Shuttle *Endeavor's* radar data of topography, all merge in a dramatic composite to show the Western Hemisphere and Eastern Hemisphere of Earth. What indications do you see on these images that tell you the time of year? These are part of NASA's Blue Marble Next Generation image collection.

[NASA images by Reto Stöckli, based on data from NASA and NOAA.]

Eastern Hemisphere
50°N
40°N
30°N
20°N
10°N
0°
10°S
20°S
30°S
40°S
50°S
60°S
70°S
40°E
50°E
60°E
70°E
80°E
90°E
100°E
110°E
120°E
130°E
140°E
150°E
160°E
170°E

So Many Options for Your Physical Geography Class!

Students today want options when it comes to their textbooks. *Elemental Geosystems* gives students the flexibility they desire, offering a wide range of formats for the book and a large array of media and online learning resources. Find a version of the book that works best for YOU!

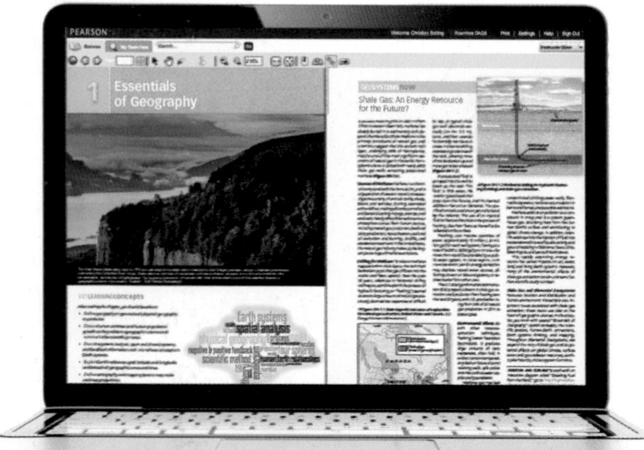

Whether it's on a laptop, tablet, smartphone, or other wired mobile device, *Elemental Geosystems* lets students access media and other tools for learning physical geography.

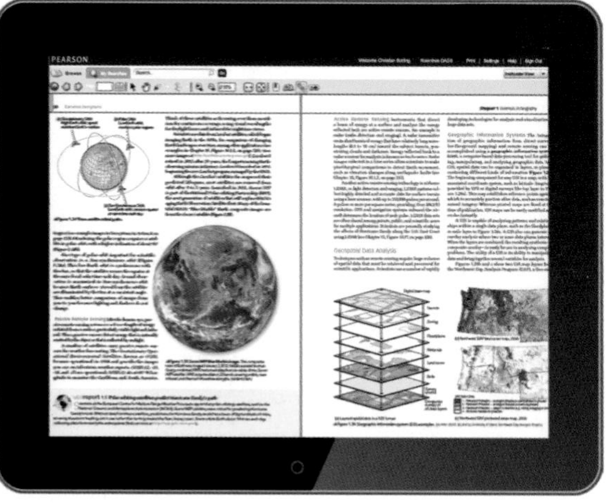

Elemental Geosystems* Plus *MasteringGeography with eText
ISBN 0-321-99470-1/978-0-321-99470-7

Available at no additional charge with MasteringGeography, the Pearson eText version of *Elemental Geosystems,* 8th Edition, gives students access to the text whenever and wherever they are online. Features of Pearson eText:

- Now available on smartphones and tablets.
- Seamlessly integrated videos and other rich media.
- Fully accessible (screen-reader ready).
- Configurable reading settings, including resizable type and night reading mode.
- Instructor and student note-taking, highlighting, bookmarking, and search.

***Elemental Geosystems* CourseSmart eTextbook**
ISBN 0-321-99431-0/978-0-321-99431-8

CourseSmart eTextbooks are an alternative to purchasing the print textbook, where students can subscribe to the same content online and save up to the 40% off the suggested list price of the print text.

***Elemental Geosystems* Books à La Carte**
ISBN 0-321-98782-9/978-0-321-98782-2

Books à la Carte features the same exact content as *Elemental Geosystems* in a convenient, three-hole-punched, binder-ready, loose-leaf version. Books à la Carte offers a great value for students—this format costs 35% less than a new textbook package.

Pearson Custom Library:
You Create Your Perfect Text
http://www.pearsoncustomlibrary.com

Elemental Geosystems is available on the Pearson Custom Library, allowing instructors to create the perfect text for their courses. Select the chapters you need, in the sequence you want. Delete chapters you don't use: students pay only for the materials chosen.

MasteringGeography Student Study Area

No matter the format, with each new copy of the text, students will receive full access to the Study Area in MasteringGeography™, providing a wealth of Interactive Animations, Videos, MapMaster™ Interactive Maps, *In the News* readings, Flashcards, Practice Quizzes, and much more.

A Virtual Field Trip Through Earth's Dynamic Systems

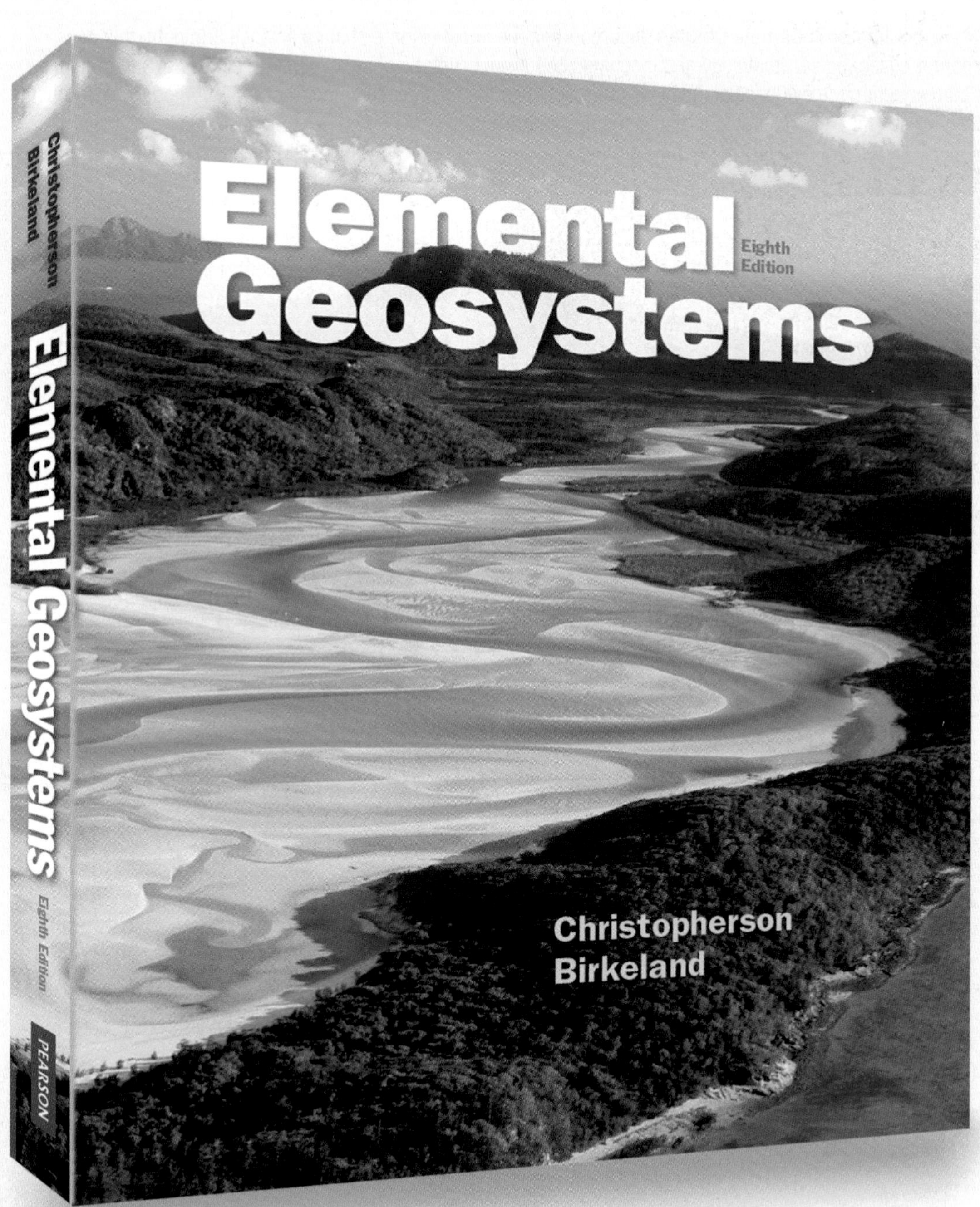

Exploring Earth's Dynamic Systems

Elemental Geosystems is organized around the natural flow of energy, materials, and information, presenting subjects in the same sequence in which they occur in nature—an organic, holistic Earth systems approach that is unique in this discipline. Offering current examples and modern science, *Elemental Geosystems* combines a structured learning path, student-friendly writing, current applications, outstanding visuals, and a strong multimedia program for a truly unique physical geography experience.

▼ NEW! Chapter 8: **Climate Change.** Incorporating the latest climate change science and data, this new chapter covers paleoclimatology and mechanisms for past climatic change, climate feedbacks and the global carbon budget, the evidence and causes of present climate change, climate forecasts and models, and actions that we can take to moderate Earth's changing climate.

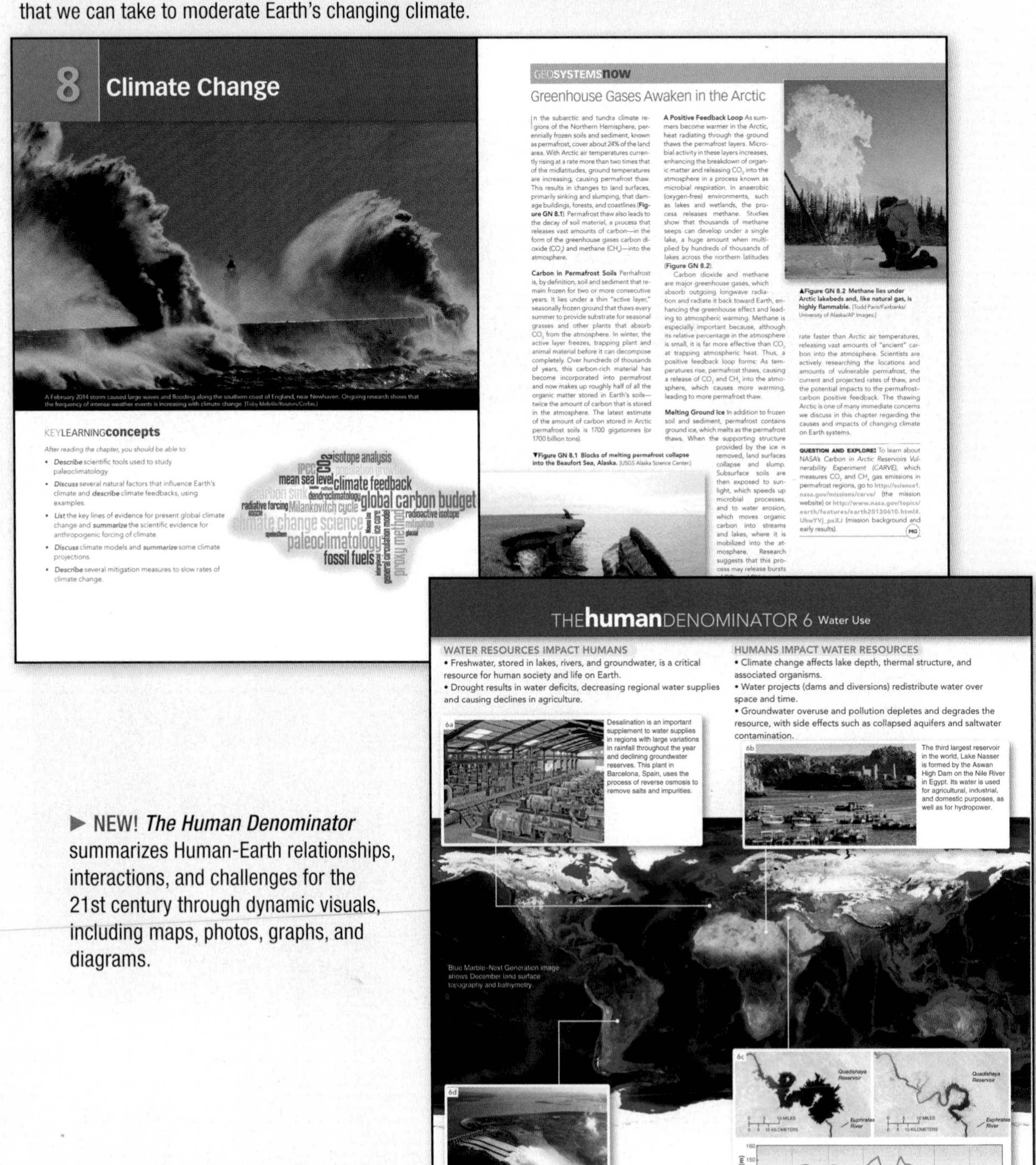

▶ NEW! *The Human Denominator* summarizes Human-Earth relationships, interactions, and challenges for the 21st century through dynamic visuals, including maps, photos, graphs, and diagrams.

Visualizing Processes & Landscapes

▼ NEW! ***Geosystems in Action*** provide highly-visual presentations of core physical processes and critical chapter concepts.

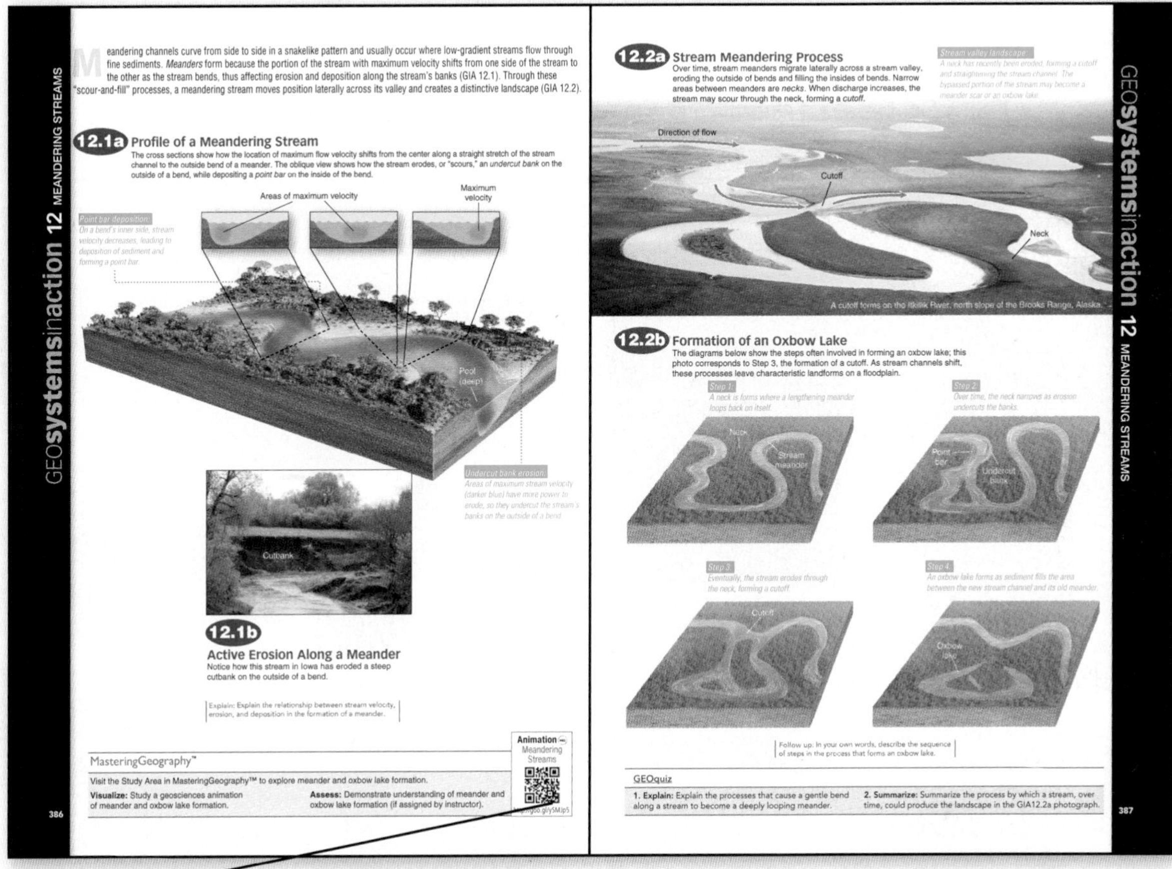

GEOsystemsinaction 12 MEANDERING STREAMS

Meandering channels curve from side to side in a snakelike pattern and usually occur where low-gradient streams flow through fine sediments. *Meanders* form because the portion of the stream with maximum velocity shifts from one side of the stream to the other as the stream bends, thus affecting erosion and deposition along the stream's banks (GIA 12.1). Through these "scour-and-fill" processes, a meandering stream moves position laterally across its valley and creates a distinctive landscape (GIA 12.2).

12.1a Profile of a Meandering Stream

The cross sections show how the location of maximum flow velocity shifts from the center along a straight stretch of the stream channel to the outside bend of a meander. The oblique view shows how the stream erodes, or "scours," an *undercut bank* on the outside of a bend, while depositing a *point bar* on the inside of the bend.

12.1b Active Erosion Along a Meander

Notice how this stream in Iowa has eroded a steep cutbank on the outside of a bend.

Explain: Explain the relationship between stream velocity, erosion, and deposition in the formation of a meander.

MasteringGeography™

Visit the Study Area in MasteringGeography™ to explore meander and oxbow lake formation.

Visualize: Study a geosciences animation of meander and oxbow lake formation.

Assess: Demonstrate understanding of meander and oxbow lake formation (if assigned by instructor).

Animation Meandering Streams http://goo.gl/ySMJp5

386

12.2a Stream Meandering Process

Over time, stream meanders migrate laterally across a stream valley, eroding the outside of bends and filling the insides of bends. Narrow areas between meanders are *necks*. When discharge increases, the stream may scour through the neck, forming a *cutoff*.

12.2b Formation of an Oxbow Lake

The diagrams below show the steps often involved in forming an oxbow lake; this photo corresponds to Step 3, the formation of a cutoff. As stream channels shift, these processes leave characteristic landforms on a floodplain.

Follow up: In your own words, describe the sequence of steps in the process that forms an oxbow lake.

GEOquiz

1. Explain: Explain the processes that cause a gentle bend along a stream to become a deeply looping meander.

2. Summarize: Summarize the process by which a stream, over time, could produce the landscape in the GIA12.2a photograph.

387

Geosystems in Action include links to mobile-ready media and MasteringGeography, as well as GeoQuizzes and integrated active learning tasks that ask students to analyze, explain, infer, or predict based on the information presented.

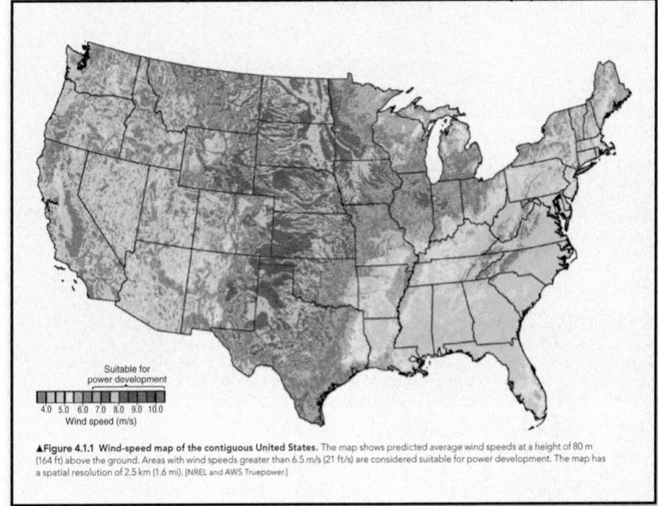

▲**Figure 4.1.1 Wind-speed map of the contiguous United States.** The map shows predicted average wind speeds at a height of 80 m (164 ft) above the ground. Areas with wind speeds greater than 6.5 m/s (21 ft/s) are considered suitable for power development. The map has a spatial resolution of 2.5 km (1.6 mi). [NREL and AWS Truepower.]

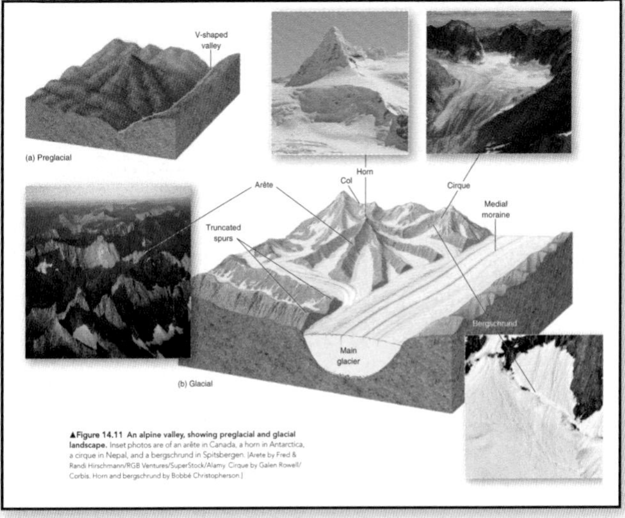

▲**Figure 14.11 An alpine valley, showing preglacial and glacial landscape.** Inset photos are of an arête in Canada, a horn in Antarctica, a cirque in Nepal, and a bergschrund in Spitsbergen. [Arete by Fred & Randi Hirschmann/RGB Ventures/SuperStock/Alamy. Cirque by Galen Rowell/Corbis. Horn and bergschrund by Bobbé Christopherson.]

▲ An unparalleled visual program includes a variety of illustrations, maps, photographs, and composites, providing authoritative examples and applications of physical geography and Earth systems science.

Real World Applications

Elemental Geosystems **integrates current real events and phenomena and presents the most thorough and integrated treatment of systems trends and climate change science, giving students compelling reasons for learning physical geography.**

▼ ***Geosystems Now*** open each chapter with interesting, current applications of physical geography and Earth systems science. New **Geosystems Now Online** features direct students online to related resources.

GEOSYSTEMSnow

Sand Dunes Protect Coastlines during Hurricane Sandy

During the winter of 2013, several months after Hurricane Sandy, many residents along New Jersey's coastline added their discarded Christmas trees to carefully stacked lines of trees acting as "seeds" for new sand dune formation along several area beaches. The trees were intended to catch windblown sand to begin the dune formation process, in one of many such restoration efforts along the Atlantic coast. In the face of Sandy's winds, houses and neighborhoods with protective dunes in place experienced less damage than those that were more exposed to and closer to the ocean.

Dune Protection versus Ocean Views The effectiveness of dune systems as protection from wave erosion and storm surge during Hurricane Sandy, far from being a subtle statistical phenomenon, was easily observed by local residents. However, the fostering of large and sometimes obtrusive sand dunes near the shoreline is controversial in coastal communities with million-dollar homes. For such dunes to function as barriers to erosion, they must sit between oceanfront property and the sea, thus blocking ocean views and decreasing property values (**Figure GN 13.1**). For many landowners, establishing dunes for storm protection means financial loss in the short term, even if long-term protection is the result.

Video The Making of a Superstorm http://goo.gl/k6HaNa

Coastal Dune Geomorphology Coastal sand dunes consist of sediment supplied by the work of ocean waves and by fluvial processes that move sediment onto deltas and estuaries. Once sand is deposited on shore, it is reworked by wind processes into the shape of dunes. Dunes along seacoasts are either *foredunes*, where sand is pushed up the seaward-facing slope, or *backdunes*, which form farther away from the beach and are protected from onshore winds (blowing toward the beach); backdunes are more stable and may be hundreds of years old. Most areas of coastal dunes are relatively small in size (especially when compared with desert dune fields that may cover large portions of continents).

Along the Atlantic coast, foredunes are moving inland as sea level rises and storm energy increases with climate change. In developed areas, this landward retreat of foredunes impinges on human development. When storms occur, dune movement is intensified, and either dune erosion or sand deposition, or both, occurs within the developed area of the coast (**Figure GN 13.2**).

Dune Restoration Efforts The establishment of new foredunes replenishes the sand supply and protects structures and infrastructure, making this a potentially worthwhile investment of money and effort for communities along the New Jersey shoreline. Many experts point out that dunes are *not* a guarantee of storm protection and that Sandy's winds and storm surge were strong enough to erode some large natural dune systems along the Atlantic Seaboard. However, in Bradley Beach, New Jersey, where the storm eroded several miles of restored dunes about 4.6 m (15 ft) in height, the community still escaped excessive damage, since the dunes absorbed much of the storm's impact.

Thus, many local communities are supporting dune restoration, as evidenced by the 2013 Christmas tree initiative. Because vegetation is important for dune stabilization, the planting of grasses is another protective strategy being embraced by New Jersey residents. In this chapter, we discuss coastal systems, wind processes, and dune formation.

QUESTION AND EXPLORE For information and links to research on dunes in New Jersey and along the Atlantic coast, see http://marine.rutgers.edu/geomorph/geomorph/_pages/dunes.html. More on coastal dune geomorphology is at http://www.nature.com/scitable/knowledge/library/coastal-dunes-geomorphology-25822000. MG

Video Hurricane Sandy http://goo.gl/Yj3FWj

▲**Figure GN 13.2 Coastal damage from Sandy in Mantoloking, New Jersey.** View looking west before and after Hurricane Sandy. The yellow arrow points to the same feature in each image. [USGS.]

◀**Figure GN 13.1 Constructed dunes.** Restored sand dunes shield homes in Mantoloking, New Jersey, from an incoming nor'easter a few weeks after Hurricane Sandy. [Sharon Karr/FEMA.]

▼ ***Focus Studies*** present detailed discussions of critical physical geography topics, emphasizing the applied relevance of physical geography today.

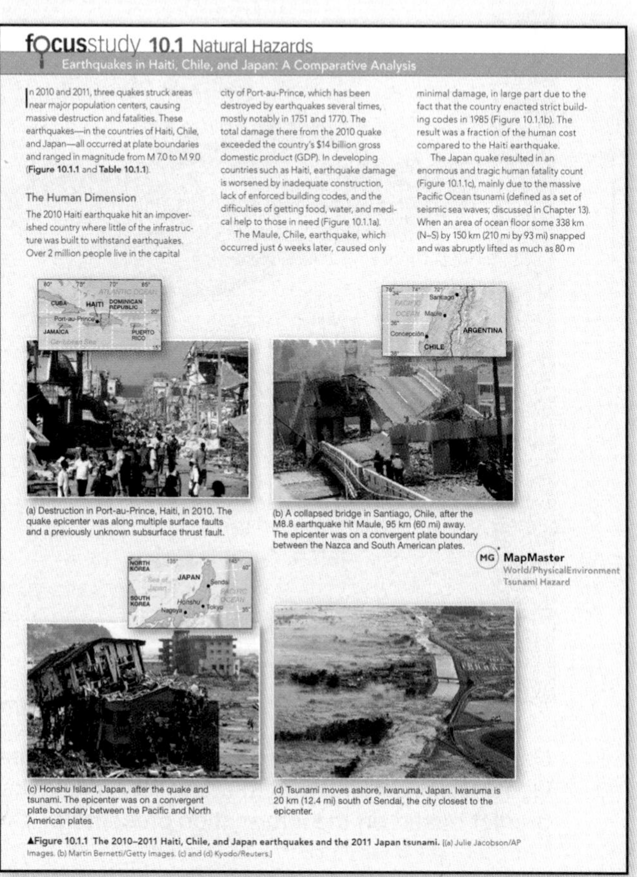

focusstudy 10.1 Natural Hazards

Earthquakes in Haiti, Chile, and Japan: A Comparative Analysis

In 2010 and 2011, three quakes struck areas near major population centers, causing massive destruction and fatalities. These earthquakes—in the countries of Haiti, Chile, and Japan—all occurred at plate boundaries and ranged in magnitude from M 7.0 to M 9.0 (**Figure 10.1.1** and **Table 10.1.1**).

The Human Dimension

The 2010 Haiti earthquake hit an impoverished country where little of the infrastructure was built to withstand earthquakes. Over 2 million people live in the capital city of Port-au-Prince, which has been destroyed by earthquakes several times, mostly notably in 1751 and 1770. The total damage there from the 2010 quake exceeded the country's $14 billion gross domestic product (GDP). In developing countries such as Haiti, earthquake damage is worsened by inadequate construction, lack of enforced building codes, and the difficulties of getting food, water, and medical help to those in need (Figure 10.1.1a).

The Maule, Chile, earthquake, which occurred just 6 weeks later, caused only minimal damage, in large part due to the fact that the country enacted strict building codes in 1985 (Figure 10.1.1b). The result was a fraction of the human cost compared to the Haiti earthquake.

The Japan quake resulted in an enormous and tragic human fatality count (Figure 10.1.1c), mainly due to the massive Pacific Ocean tsunami (defined as a set of seismic sea waves; discussed in Chapter 13). When an area of ocean floor some 338 km (N–S) by 150 km (210 mi by 93 mi) snapped and was abruptly lifted as much as 80 m

(a) Destruction in Port-au-Prince, Haiti, in 2010. The quake epicenter was along multiple surface faults and a previously unknown subsurface thrust fault.

(b) A collapsed bridge in Santiago, Chile, after the M8.8 earthquake hit Maule, 95 km (60 mi) away. The epicenter was on a convergent plate boundary between the Nazca and South American plates.

MG MapMaster World/PhysicalEnvironment Tsunami Hazard

(c) Honshu Island, Japan, after the quake and tsunami. The epicenter was on a convergent plate boundary between the Pacific and North American plates.

(d) Tsunami moves ashore, Iwanuma, Japan. Iwanuma is 20 km (12.4 mi) south of Sendai, the city closest to the epicenter.

▲**Figure 10.1.1 The 2010–2011 Haiti, Chile, and Japan earthquakes and the 2011 Japan tsunami.** [(a) Julie Jacobson/AP Images. (b) Martin Bernetti/Getty Images. (c) and (d) Kyodo/Reuters.]

▶ ***GeoReports*** offer a wide variety of brief interesting facts, examples, and applications to complement and enrich the chapter reading.

GEOreport 5.2 Mountains cause record rains

Mount Waialeale, on the island of Kaua'i, Hawai'i, rises 1569 m (5147 ft) above sea level. On its windward slope, rainfall averaged 1234 cm (486 in., or 40.5 ft) a year for the years 1941–1992. In contrast, the rain-shadow side of Kaua'i received only 50 cm (20 in.) of rain annually. If no islands existed at this location, this portion of the Pacific Ocean would receive only an average 63.5 cm (25 in.) of precipitation a year. (These statistics are from established weather stations with a consistent record of weather data; several stations claim higher rainfall values, but do not have dependable measurement records.)

Cherrapunji, India, is 1313 m (4309 ft) above sea level at 25° N latitude, in the Assam Hills south of the Himalayas. Summer monsoons pour in from the Indian Ocean and the Bay of Bengal, producing 930 cm (366 in., or 30.5 ft) of rainfall in 1 month. Not surprisingly, Cherrapunji holds the all-time precipitation record for a single year, 2647 cm (1042 in., or 86.8 ft), and for every other time interval from 15 days t

GEOreport 13.3 Ocean acidification impacts corals

As the oceans absorb more excess carbon dioxide, their acidity increases and potentially damages coral formations, an interaction that scientists are actively researching. A 2013 study examined Mediterranean red coral (*Corallium rubrum*) colonies under more acidic conditions in a laboratory and discovered reduced growth rates of 59% and abnormal skeleton development when compared with colonies growing under current ocean conditions. The test conditions were at a pH of 7.8 (which would occur w

GEOreport 16.1 Sea turtles navigate using Earth's magnetic field

The fact that birds and bees can detect the abiotic influence of Earth's magnetic field and use it for finding direction is well established. Small amounts of magnetically sensitive particles in the skull of the bird and the abdomen of the bee provide compass directions. Recently, scientists found that sea turtles detect magnetic fields of different strengths and inclinations (angles). This means that the turtles have a built-in navigation system that helps them find certain locations on Earth. Loggerhead turtles hatch in Florida, crawl into the water, and spend the next 70 years traveling thousands of miles between North America and Africa around the subtropical high-pressure gyre in the Atlantic Ocean. The females return to where they were hatched to lay their eggs. In turn, the hatchlings are imprinted with magnetic data unique to the location of their birth and then develop a more global sense of position as they live a life swimming across the ocean.

A Refined Learning Path

Elemental Geosystems **provides a structured learning path that helps students achieve a deeper understanding of physical geography through active learning.**

KEYLEARNING**concepts**

After reading the chapter, you should be able to:

- *Sketch* a basic drainage basin model and *identify* different types of drainage patterns by visual examination.
- *Explain* the concepts of stream gradient and base level and *describe* the relationship between stream velocity, depth, width, and discharge.
- *Explain* the processes involved in fluvial erosion and sediment transport.
- *Describe* common stream channel patterns and *explain* the concept of a graded stream.
- *Describe* the depositional landforms associated with floodplains and alluvial fan environments.
- *List* and *describe* several types of river deltas and *explain* flood probability estimates.

▲ ***Key Learning Concepts*** at the beginning of every chapter help students identify the key knowledge and skills they will acquire through study of the chapter.

▼ ***Key Learning Concepts Reviews*** at the end of each chapter feature summaries, narrative definitions, a list of key terms with page numbers, and review questions.

KEYLEARNING**conceptsreview**

Sketch a basic drainage basin model and *identify* different types of drainage patterns by visual examination.

Fluvial processes are stream-related. The basic fluvial system is a **drainage basin**, or *watershed*, which is an open system. *Drainage divides* define the catchment (water-receiving) area of a drainage basin. In any drainage basin, water initially moves downslope in a thin film of **sheetflow**, or *overland flow*. This surface runoff concentrates in *rills*, or small-scale downhill grooves, which may develop into deeper *gullies* and a stream course in a valley. High ground that separates one valley from another and directs sheetflow is an *interfluve*. Extensive mountain and highland regions act as **continental divides** that separate major drainage basins. Some regions, such as the Great Salt Lake Basin, have *internal drainage* that does not reach the ocean, the only outlets being evaporation and subsurface gravitational flow.

Drainage density is determined by the number and length of channels in a given area and is an expression of a landscape's topographic surface appearance. **Drainage pattern** refers to the arrangement of channels in an area as determined by the steepness, variable rock resistance, variable climate, hydrology, relief of the land, and structural controls imposed by the landscape. Seven basic drainage patterns are generally found in nature: dendritic, trellis, radial, parallel, rectangular, annular, and deranged.

fluvial (p. 374)
drainage basin (p. 374)
sheetflow (p. 375)
continental divide (p. 375)
drainage pattern (p. 377)

1. Define the term *fluvial*. What is a fluvial process?
2. What role is played by rivers in the hydrologic cycle?
3. What are the five largest rivers on Earth in terms of discharge? Relate these to the weather patterns in each area and to regional potential evapotranspiration (PE) and precipitation (P)—concepts discussed in Chapter 6.
4. What is the basic organizational unit of a river system? How is it identified on the landscape? Define the several relevant key terms used.
5. In Figure 12.3, follow the Allegheny–Ohio–Mississippi river system to the Gulf of Mexico.

level occurs when something interrupts the stream's ability to achieve base level, such as a dam or a landslide that blocks a stream channel.

Discharge, a stream's volume of flow per unit of time, is calculated by multiplying the velocity of the stream by its width and depth for a specific cross section of the channel. Streams may have *perennial*, *ephemeral*, or *intermittent* flow regimes. Discharge usually increases in a downstream direction; however, in rivers in semiarid or arid regions, discharge may decrease with distance downstream as water is lost to evapotranspiration and water diversions.

A graph of stream discharge over time for a specific place is called a **hydrograph**. Precipitation events in urban areas result in higher peak flows during floods. In deserts, a torrent of water that fills a stream channel during or just after a rainstorm is a **flash flood**.

gradient (p. 379)
base level (p. 379)
discharge (p. 379)
hydrograph (p. 380)
flash flood (p. 381)

7. Explain the base level concept. What happens to a stream's base level when a reservoir is constructed?
8. What was the impact of flood discharge on the channel of the San Juan River near Bluff, Utah? Why did these changes take place?
9. Differentiate between a natural stream hydrograph and one from an urbanized area.

Explain the processes involved in fluvial erosion and sediment transport.

Water dislodges, dissolves, or removes surface material and moves it to new locations in the process of **erosion**. Sediments are laid down by the process of **deposition**. **Hydraulic action** is the erosive work of water caused by hydraulic squeeze-and-release action to loosen and lift rocks and sediment. As this debris moves along, it mechanically erodes the streambed further through a process of **abrasion**. Streams may deepen their valley by channel incision, they may lengthen in the process of headward erosion, or they may erode a valley laterally in the process of meandering.

When stream energy is high, particles move downstream in the process of **sediment transport**. The sedi-

▼ ***Critical Thinking*** activities integrated throughout chapter sections give students an opportunity to stop, check, and apply their understanding.

CRITICAL**thinking 12.1**

Locate Your Drainage Basin

Determine the name of the drainage basin within which your campus is located. Where are its headwaters? Where is the river's mouth? If you are in the United States or Canada, use Figure 12.3 to locate the larger drainage basins and divides for your region, and then take a look at this region on Google Earth™. Does any regulatory organization oversee planning and coordination for the drainage basin you identified? Can you find topographic maps online that cover this region?

CRITICAL**thinking 12.2**

Identifying Drainage Patterns

Examine the photograph in **Figure CT 12.2.1**, where you see two distinct drainage patterns. Of the seven types illustrated in Figure 12.5, which two patterns are most like those in the aerial photo? Looking back to Figure 12.1a, which drainage pattern is prevalent in the area around Mount Mismi in Brazil? Explain your answer. The next time you fly in an airplane, look out the window to observe the various drainage patterns across the landscape.

▲Figure CT 12.2.1 Two drainage patterns dominate this scene from central Montana, in response to rock structure and local relief. [Bobbé Christopherson.]

MasteringGeography™

Continuous learning before, during, & after class

MasteringGeography™ delivers engaging, dynamic learning opportunities—focusing on course objectives and responsive to each student's progress—that are proven to help students absorb geography course material and understand challenging physical processes and geographic concepts.

BEFORE CLASS

Pre-Class Assignments Provide Students with a Preview of What's to Come

▼ NEW! ***Mobile-Enabled Media*** Quick Response (QR) Codes integrated throughout each chapter empower students to use their mobile devices to learn as they read, providing instant access to over 80 Animations and Videos of real-world physical geography phenomena and visualizations of key physical processes. All media can be assigned with quizzes in MasteringGeography.

Video MG
Superstorm Sandy
http://goo.gl/k6HaNa

Sandy then took a sharp left turn into the New Jersey and New York coasts
01:30 / 03:06

▶ **Pearson eText** in MasteringGeography gives students access to *Elemental Geosystems, 8th Edition* whenever and wherever they are online. The eText includes powerful interactive and customization features:

- Now available on smartphones and tablets.
- Seamlessly integrated videos and other rich media.
- Fully accessible (screen-reader ready).
- Configurable reading settings, including resizable type and night reading mode.
- Instructor and student note-taking, highlighting, bookmarking, and search.

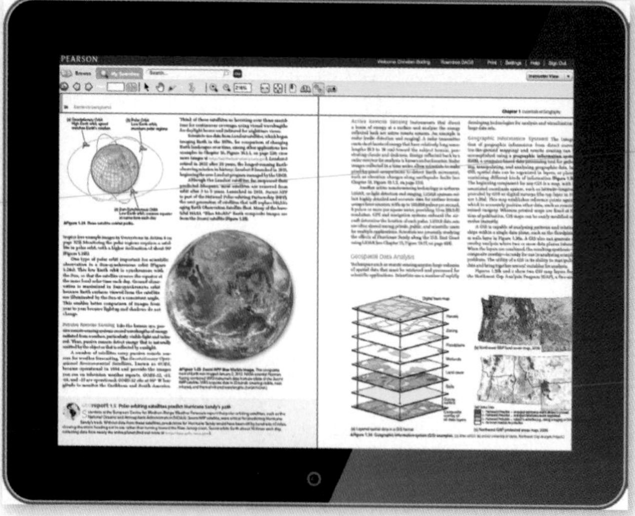

Pre-Lecture Reading Quizzes are Easy to Customize and Assign.

NEW! ***Reading Quiz Questions*** in MasteringGeography ensure that students complete the assigned reading before class and stay on track with reading assignments. Reading Quizzes are 100% mobile ready and can be completed by students on their mobile devices.

DURING CLASS
Learning Catalytics

"My students are so busy and engaged answering Learning Catalytics questions during lecture that they don't have time for Facebook." (Declan De Paor, Old Dominion University)

What has teachers and students excited? Learning Catalytics, a "bring your own device" student engagement, assessment, and classroom intelligence system, allows students to use their smartphone, tablet, or laptop to respond to questions in class. With Learning Catalytics, teachers can:

- Assess students in real-time using open-ended question formats to uncover student misconceptions and adjust lecture accordingly.
- Automatically create groups for peer instruction based on student response patterns to optimize discussion productivity.

Enrich Lecture with Dynamic Media

Teachers can incorporate dynamic media into lecture, such as Geoscience Animations, Videos, and MapMaster Interactive Maps.

AFTER CLASS

Easy-to-Assign, Customizable, Media-Rich, and Automatically-Graded Assignments

The breadth and depth of media content available in MasteringGeography are unparalleled, allowing teachers to quickly and easily assign homework to reinforce key concepts.

▶ **Encounter Activities** provide rich, interactive Google Earth explorations of physical geography concepts to visualize and explore Earth's landscape and physical processes. Available with multiple-choice and short answer questions. All Explorations include corresponding Google Earth KMZ media files, and questions include hints and specific wrong-answer feedback to help coach students toward mastery of the concepts.

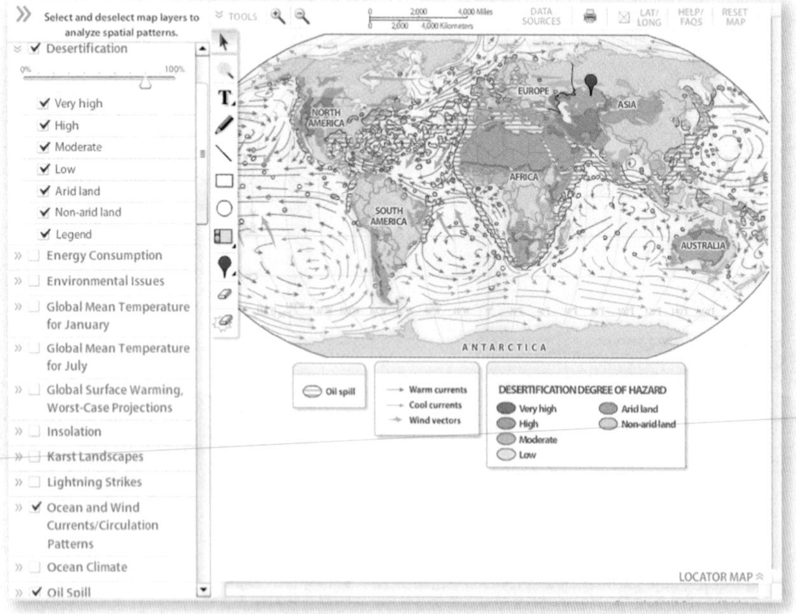

◀ **MapMaster Interactive Map Activities** are inspired by GIS, allowing students to layer various thematic maps to analyze spatial patterns and data at regional and global scales. This tool includes zoom and annotation functionality, with hundreds of map layers leveraging recent data from sources such as NOAA, NASA, USGS, United Nations, and the CIA.

Student Study Area Resources in MasteringGeography include:

- Animations, Videos, MapMaster™ interactive maps
- Practice quizzes, Glossary flashcards
- "In the News" RSS feeds
- Optional Pearson eText and more

▶ **Geoscience Animations** help students visualize the most challenging physical processes in the physical geosciences with schematic animations that include audio narration.

Animations include assignable multiple-choice quizzes with specific wrong-answer feedback to help guide students toward mastery of these core physical process concepts.

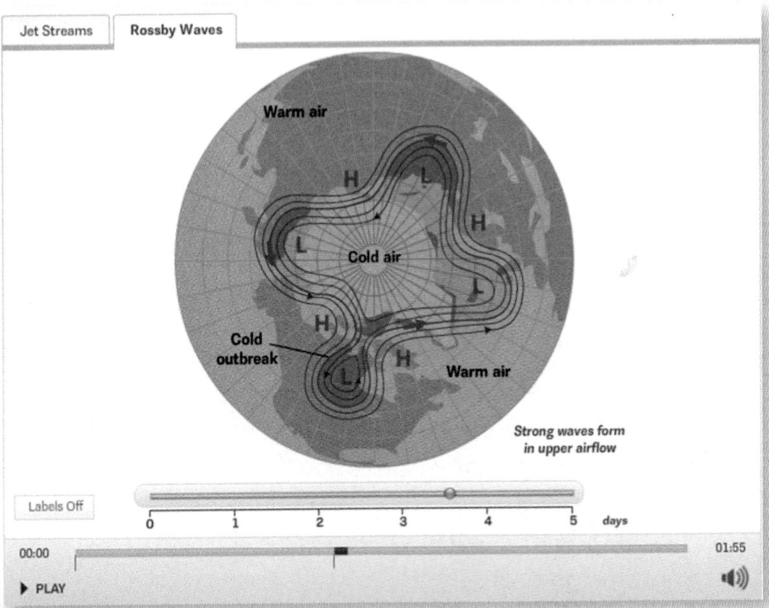

◀ **NEW! Videos** from such sources as the BBC and the *Financial Times* are now included in addition to the videos from Television for the Environment's *Life and Earth Report* series in MasteringGeography. These videos provide students with applied real-world examples of physical geography in action, a sense of place, and allow them to explore a range of locations and topics.

▶ **GeoTutor Coaching Activities** help students master the toughest physical geoscience concepts with highly visual, kinesthetic activities focused on critical thinking and application of core geoscience concepts.

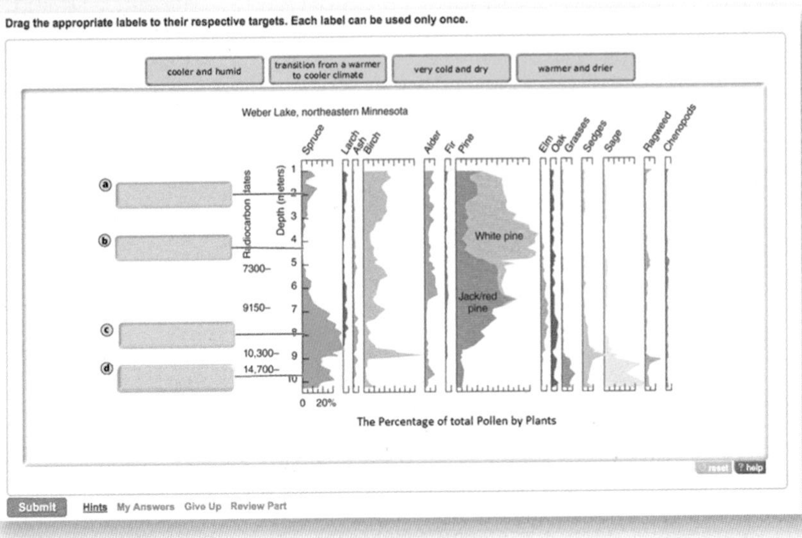

Elemental Geosystems

Eighth Edition

Robert W. Christopherson

Ginger H. Birkeland

PEARSON

Senior Geography Editor: Christian Botting
Executive Marketing Manager: Neena Bali
Program Manager: Anton Yakovlev
Project Manager: Connie Long
Editorial Assistant: Amy De Genaro
Director of Development: Jennifer Hart
Development Editor: Moira Lerner-Nelson
Art Development Editor: Jay McElroy
Senior Project Manager, Text and Images: Tim Nicholls
Text Permissions Specialist: Mark Schaeffer, Lumina Datamatics
Program Management Team Lead: Kristen Flathman
Project Management Team Lead: David Zielonka
Production Management/Composition: Suganya Karuppasamy/Cenveo Publisher Services
Design Manager: Marilyn Perry
Interior and Cover Designer: Jeanne Calabrese
Illustrators: Precision Graphics and International Mapping
Photo Researcher: Lauren McFalls, Lumina Datamatics
Operations Specialist: Maura Zaldivar-Garcia

Cover Photo Credit: Aerial shot of Whitehaven Beach, Whitsunday Island, Great Barrier Reef, Queensland. Gerhard Zwerger-Schoner/Imagebroker/Age Fotostock.

Credits and acknowledgments for materials borrowed from other sources and reproduced, with permission, in this textbook appear on the appropriate page within the text or on p. C-1.

Dedication Quote Credit: B. Kingsolver, *Small Wonder* (New York: Harper Collins Publishers, 2002) p.39

Library of Congress Cataloging-in-Publication Data

Christopherson, Robert W.
Elemental geosystems / Robert W. Christopherson, Ginger H. Birkeland. -- Eighth edition.
pages cm
Includes index.
ISBN 978-0-321-98501-9 -- ISBN 0-321-98501-X
1. Physical geography. I. Birkeland, Ginger H. II. Title.
GB54.5.C47 2016
910'.02--dc23
2014045751

2 3 4 5 6 7 8 9 10—V011—18 17 16 15

Student edition ISBN 10: 0-321-98501-X; ISBN 13: 978-0-321-98501-9
Instructor's Review Copy ISBN 10: 0-321-99507-4; ISBN 13: 978-0-321-99507-0

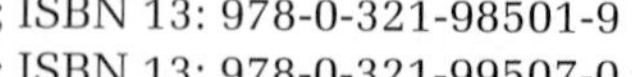

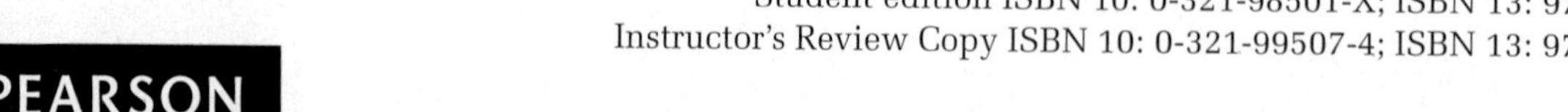

www.pearsonhighered.com

dedication

To the students and teachers of Earth, and to all the children and grandchildren, for it is their future and home planet.

The land still provides our genesis, however we might like to forget that our food comes from dank, muddy Earth, that the oxygen in our lungs was recently inside a leaf, and that every newspaper or book we may pick up is made from the hearts of trees that died for the sake of our imagined lives. What you hold in your hands right now, beneath these words, is consecrated air and time and sunlight.

—Barbara Kingsolver

Brief Contents

Contents

4 Atmospheric and Oceanic Circulations 106

PART II The Water, Weather, and Climate Systems 140

5 Atmospheric Water and Weather 142

10 Tectonics, Earthquakes, and Volcanism 310

11 Weathering, Karst Landscapes, and Mass Movement 346

12 River Systems 372

13 Oceans, Coastal Systems, and Wind Processes 404

14 Glacial and Periglacial Landscapes 438

PART IV Soils, Ecosystems, and Biomes 470

15 The Geography of Soils 472

16 Ecosystem Essentials 502

17 Terrestrial Biomes 530

MasteringGeography™
Mobile-Ready Animations & Videos

Elemental Geosystems, 8th edition includes Quick Response links to over 80 mobile-ready animations and videos, which students can access using mobile devices. These media are also available in the Study Area of MasteringGeography.

1 Essentials of Geography

Video
- The Changing Face of Earth

Geoscience Animation
- Map Projections

2 Solar Energy, Seasons, and the Atmosphere

Geoscience Animations
- Nebular Hypothesis
- Earth Sun Rotations, Seasons
- Ozone Breakdown, Ozone Hole

3 Atmospheric Energy and Global Temperatures

Geoscience Animations
- Global Warming, Climate Change
- Earth-Atmosphere Energy Balance
- The Gulf Stream

4 Atmospheric and Oceanic Circulations

Videos
- The Thermohaline Circulation
- North Atlantic Deep Water Circulation

Geoscience Animations
- Coriolis Force
- Wind Pattern Development
- Global Patterns of Pressure
- Global Atmospheric Circulation
- Cyclones and Anticyclones
- Jet Streams, Rossby Waves
- Ocean Circulation
- El Niño and La Niña

5 Atmospheric Water and Weather

Videos
- Hurricane Hot Towers
- Superstorm Sandy

Geoscience Animations
- Water Phase Changes
- Atmospheric Stability
- Cold Fronts
- Warm Fronts
- Midlatitude Cyclones
- Tornado Wind Patterns

6 Water Resources

Geoscience Animations
- Earth's Water and the Hydrologic Cycle
- The Water Table
- Groundwater Cone of Depression

7 Earth's Climatic Regions

Video
- Supercomputing the Climate

Geoscience Animations
- Global Patterns of Precipitation

8 Climate Change

Videos
- Keeping up with Carbon
- Taking Earth's Temperature

Geoscience Animations
- Global Warming, Climate Change
- Earth-Sun Relations

9 The Dynamic Planet

Geoscience Animations
- Applying Relative Dating Principles
- Foliation of Metamorphic Rock
- Plate Motions Through Time
- Seafloor Spreading, Subduction
- Motion at Plate Boundaries
- Correlating Processes and Plate Boundaries
- Forming a Divergent Boundary
- India Collision with Asia
- Transform Faults
- Hot-Spot Volcano Tracks
- Convection and Plate Tectonics

10 Tectonics, Earthquakes, and Volcanism

Geoscience Animations
- Terrane Formation
- Fold, Anticlines, and Synclines
- Fault Types, Transform Faults, Plate Margins
- Subduction Zones
- Plate Boundaries
- Seismograph, How It Works
- P and S Waves, Seismology
- Elastic Rebound
- Forming Types of Volcanoes
- Debris Avalanche and Eruption of Mt. St. Helens

11 Weathering, Karst Landscapes, and Mass Movement

Geoscience Animations
- Mass Movements
- Physical Weathering

12 River Systems

Geoscience Animations
- Meandering Streams
- Stream Processes, Floodplains, Oxbow Lake Formation
- Stream Terrace Formation

13 Oceans, Coastal Systems, and Wind Processes

Videos
- Making of a Superstorm
- Hurricane Sandy

Geoscience Animations
- Multilatitude Productivity
- Monthly Tidal Cycles
- Wave Motion and Wave Refraction
- Beach Drift, Coastal Erosion
- Coastal Stabilization Structures
- Movement of Barrier Island in Response to Rising Sea Level
- How Wind Moves Sand
- Dune Formation and Cross-Bedding

14 Glacial and Periglacial Landscapes

Videos
- A Tour of the Cyrosphere
- Operation IceBridge

Geoscience Animations
- Global Processes
- Flow of Ice Within a Glacier

15 The Geography of Soils

Video
- The Soil Moisture Active Passive (SMAP) Mission

Geoscience Animation
- Soil Science of America

16 Ecosystem Essentials

Video
- The Ocean's Green Machines

17 Terrestrial Biomes

Videos
- Plant Productivity in a Warming World
- Amazon Deforestation

Geoscience Animation
- End of Last Ice Age

Preface

Welcome to the Eighth Edition of *Elemental Geosystems.* This edition marks the addition of Dr. Ginger Birkeland as a coauthor to Robert Christopherson. This Eighth Edition features significant revision, with a new chapter on climate change, new features, updated content, and many new photos and illustrations. We continue to build on the success of the first seven editions, as well as the companion texts, *Geosystems*, now in its ninth edition, and *Geosystems, Canadian Edition*, Third Edition. Students and teachers appreciate the systems organization, scientific accuracy, integration of figures and text, clarity of the summary and review sections, and overall relevancy to what is happening to Earth systems in real time. *Elemental Geosystems* continues to tell Earth's story in student-friendly language.

The goal of physical geography is to explain the spatial dimension of Earth's dynamic systems—its energy, air, water, weather, climate, tectonics, landforms, rocks, soils, plants, ecosystems, and biomes. Understanding human–Earth relations is part of physical geography as it seeks to understand and link the planet and its inhabitants. Welcome to physical geography!

New to the Eighth Edition

Nearly every page of *Elemental Geosystems*, Eighth Edition, presents updated material, new content in text and figures, and new features. A sampling of new features includes:

- A **new chapter on climate change**. Although climate change science affects all systems and is discussed to some extent in every chapter of *Elemental Geosystems*, we now present a stand-alone chapter covering this topic—Chapter 8, Climate Change. This chapter covers paleoclimatology and mechanisms for past climatic change (expanding on topics covered in Chapter 13 in previous editions), climate feedbacks and the global carbon budget, the evidence and causes of present climate change, climate models and projections, and actions that we can take to moderate Earth's changing climate. This new Chapter 8 expands on the climate change discussion that was formerly part of Chapter 7, Climate Systems and Climate Change, in previous editions.
- A new ***Geosystems in Action*** feature focusing on key topics, processes, systems, or human–Earth connections. In every chapter, *Geosystems in Action* is a one- to two-page highly visual presentation of a topic central to the chapter, with active learning questions and links to media in *MasteringGeography*™, as well as a GeoQuiz to aid student learning. Throughout each part of the *Geosystems in Action* figure, students are asked to analyze, explain, infer, or predict based on the information presented. Topics include Earth–Sun Relations (Chapter 2), Earth–Atmosphere Energy Balance (Chapter 3), The Global Carbon Budget (Chapter 8), Glaciers as Dynamic Systems (Chapter 14), and Biological Activity in Soils (Chapter 15).
- A new feature, ***The Human Denominator***, linking chapter topics to human examples and applications. At the end of Chapters 2 through 17, this new feature includes maps, photos, graphs, and other diagrams to provide visual examples of many human–Earth interactions. This feature replaces and expands on the content of Chapter 17 in previous *Elemental Geosystems* editions, called Earth and the Human Denominator.
- **New and revised illustrations and maps** to improve student learning. More than 250 new photos and images bring real-world scenes into the classroom. Our photo and remote sensing program, updated for this edition, exceeds 500 items, integrated throughout the text.
- **New integrated mobile media**, where students use mobile devices to scan Quick Response (QR) codes throughout the book to view over 100 animations and videos.
- **Learning Catalytics**, a "bring your own device" student engagement, assessment, and classroom intelligence system, integrated with *MasteringGeography*™.

Continuing in the Eighth Edition

- Fifteen *Focus Studies*, with either updated or new content, explore relevant applied topics in greater depth and are a popular feature of the *Elemental Geosystems* texts. In the Eighth Edition, these features are grouped by topic into five categories: Pollution, Climate Change, Natural Hazards, Sustainable Resources, and Environmental Restoration. Nine new Focus Study topics include:
    - Hurricanes Katrina and Sandy: Development, Effects, and Links to Climate Change (Chapter 5)
    - Global Climate Feedback Mechanisms (Chapter 8)
    - Earthquakes in Haiti, Chile, and Japan: A Comparative Analysis (Chapter 10)
    - Human-Caused Mass Movement at the Kingston Steam Plant, Tennessee (Chapter 11)
    - Stream Restoration: Merging Science and Practice (Chapter 12)
    - The 2011 Japan Tsunami (Chapter 13)
    - Thawing Methane Hydrates—Another Arctic Methane Concern (Chapter 14)

- Wildfire and Fire Ecology (Chapter 16)
- Global Conservation Strategies (Chapter 17)

- The chapter-opening *Geosystems Now* case study feature presents current issues in geography and Earth systems science. These original, unique applications, updated for the Eighth Edition, immediately draw readers into the chapter with relevant, real-world examples of physical geography. New *Geosystems Now* topics in the Eighth Edition include shale gas as an energy resource in the United States (Chapter 1), California's Santa Ana winds (Chapter 4), the Oso, Washington, landslide (Chapter 11), the effects of proposed dams on rivers in China (Chapter 12), and coastal erosion caused by Hurricane Sandy (Chapter 13). Many of these features emphasize linkages across chapters and Earth systems, exemplifying the *Elemental Geosystems* approach.
- *GeoReports* continue to describe timely and relevant events or facts related to the discussion in the chapter, provide student action items, and offer new sources of information. The 26 *GeoReports* in the Eighth Edition, placed along the bottom of pages, are updated, with many new to this edition. Example topics include:
  - Did light refraction sink the Titanic? (Chapter 3)
  - Satellite *GRACE* enables groundwater measurements (Chapter 6)
  - Tropical climate zones advance to higher latitudes (Chapter 7)
  - Surprise waves flood a cruise ship (Chapter 13)
  - Will species adapt to climate change? (Chapter 16)
  - Overgrazing effects on Argentina's grasslands (Chapter 17)
- *Critical Thinking* exercises are integrated throughout the chapters. These carefully crafted action items bridge students to the next level of learning, placing students in charge of further inquiry. Example topics include:
  - Applying Energy-Balance Principles to a Solar Cooker
  - What Causes the North Australian Monsoon?
  - Identify Two Kinds of Fog
  - Consider Your Carbon Footprint
  - Compare Two Mass-Movement Events
  - Tropical Forests: A Global or Local Resource?
- *Key Learning Concepts* appear at the outset of each chapter, many rewritten for clarity. Each chapter concludes with *Key Learning Concepts Review*, which summarizes the chapter using the opening objectives.
- *Elemental Geosystems* continues to embed Internet URLs within the text. More than 150 appear in this edition. These allow students to pursue topics of interest to greater depth, or to obtain the latest information about weather and climate, tectonic events, floods, and the myriad other subjects covered in the book.
- The *MasteringGeography*™ online homework and tutoring system delivers self-paced tutorials that provide individualized coaching, focus on course objectives, and are responsive to each student's progress. Instructors can assign activities built around Geoscience Animations, *Encounter* Google Earth™ activities, MapMaster™ interactive maps, *Thinking Spatially and Data Analysis* activities, new *GeoTutors* on the most challenging topics in the physical geosciences, end-of-chapter questions, Test Bank questions, and more. Students now have access to new *Dynamic Study Modules* that provide each student with a customized learning experience. Students also have access to a text-specific Study Area with study resources, including a Pearson eText version of *Elemental Geosystems*, Geoscience Animations, MapMaster™ interactive maps, new videos, additional content to support materials for the text, photo galleries, *In the News* readings, web links, career links, physical geography case studies, flashcard glossary, quizzes, and more—all at www.masteringgeography.com.

Author Acknowledgments

After all these years, the strength of a publishing team remains ever essential. Continuing thanks to President Paul Corey for his leadership since 1990 and to Frank Ruggirello, Senior Vice-president and Editorial Director for Geosciences, for his vision. Thanks to Senior Geography Editor Christian Botting for his guidance and insightful dialogue and for the attention devoted to the *Geosystems* texts; and to Program Manager Anton Yakovlev, a real strength on our team, and Editorial Assistant Amy De Genaro for her careful attention. Maya Gomez, Image Management, is a great addition to the team and a help to us. Thanks to Project Manager Connie Long and Director of Development Jennifer Hart for their skills and continuing support.

Our appreciation goes to designers Marilyn Perry and Jeanne Calabrese for such skill in a complex book design. Thanks to the late Randall Goodall for his design work over the years on the previous several editions of *Geosystems* and *Elemental Geosystems*. Thanks also to Neena Bali, Executive Marketing Manager; Ami Sampat, Marketing Assistant; and the many publisher representatives who spend months in the field communicating the *Geosystems* approach. Our gratitude is extended to the entire "*Geosystems* Team" for allowing us to participate in the publishing process.

Our sincere appreciation for production coordination goes to Editorial Director for Higher Education Cindy Miller of Cenveo LLC for our friendship and sustaining care through eight books, and to Senior Project Manager Suganya Karuppasamy for her ability to respond to our feedback as she oversees manuscript, copy editing, complex compositing, and page proofs. With so many changes in this edition, her skills make it work. To photo researcher Lauren McFalls, copy editor Sherry Goldbecker, proofreader Jeff Georgeson, and indexer Robert Swanson we give thanks for quality work. We offer special thanks to development editor Moira Lerner Nelson for her advice, suggestions, and attention to detail. Our appreciation also goes to Jay McElroy and Jonathan Cheney for their creative talent in helping develop the new *Geosystems in Action* features and to Jay for his detailed work improving the art program.

Thanks to all the colleagues who served as reviewers on one or more editions of each book or who offered helpful suggestions in conversations at our national and regional geography meetings. Thanks to the accuracy reviewers of all Eighth Edition chapters: Kara Kuvakas, formerly of *Hartnell College*; Lisa DeChano–Cook, *Western Michigan University*; And thanks for special reviews for the new Chapter 8 in this edition from Donald Wuebbles, *University of Illinois, Urbana–Champaign*; Marshall Shepherd, *University of Georgia*; Scott Mandia, *Suffolk County Community College, Long Island*.

We are grateful for the generosity of ideas and sacrifice of time. Thanks to all reviewers who have provided valuable feedback on the *Geosystems* texts over the years:

Michael Allen, *Kent State University*
Philip P. Allen, *Frostburg State University*
Ted J. Alsop, *Utah State University*
Ward Barrett, *University of Minnesota*
Steve Bass, *Mesa Community College*
Stefan Becker, *University of Wisconsin–Oshkosh*
Daniel Bedford, *Weber State University*
David Berner, *Normandale Community College*
Trent Biggs, *San Diego State University*
Franco Biondi, *University of Nevada, Reno*
Peter D. Blanken, *University of Colorado, Boulder*
Patricia Boudinot, *George Mason University*
Anthony Brazel, *Arizona State University*
David R. Butler, *Southwest Texas State University*
Mary-Louise Byrne, *Wilfred Laurier University*
Janet Cakir, *Rappahannock Community College*
Ian A. Campbell, *University of Alberta–Edmonton*
Randall S. Cerveny, *Arizona State University*
Fred Chambers, *University of Colorado, Boulder*
Philip Chaney, *Auburn University*
Muncel Chang, *Butte College,* Emeritus
Jordan Clayton, *Georgia State University*
Philip Clinton, *Ventura College*
Andrew Comrie, *University of Arizona*
C. Mark Cowell, *Indiana State University*
Richard A. Crooker, *Kutztown University*
Stephen Cunha, *Humboldt State University*
Armando M. da Silva, *Towson State University*
Dirk H. de Boer, *University of Saskatchewan*
Dennis Dahms, *University of Northern Iowa*
J. Michael Daniels, *University of Denver*
Shawna Dark, *California State University, Northridge*
Andrew Day, *University of Louisville*
Stephanie Day, *University of Kansas*
Lisa DeChano-Cook, *Western Michigan University*
Mario P. Delisio, *Boise State University*
Joseph R. Desloges, *University of Toronto*
Lee R. Dexter, *Northern Arizona University*
Don W. Duckson, Jr., *Frostburg State University*
Daniel Dugas, *New Mexico State University*
Kathryn Early, *Metropolitan State College*
Christopher H. Exline, *University of Nevada–Reno*
Todd Fagin, *Oklahoma University*
Michael M. Folsom, *Eastern Washington University*
Mark Francek, *Central Michigan University*
Glen Fredlund, *University of Wisconsin–Milwaukee*
Dorothy Friedel, *Sonoma State University*
William Garcia, *University of North Carolina–Charlotte*
Doug Goodin, *Kansas State University*
Mark Goodman, *Grossmont College*
David E. Greenland, *University of North Carolina–Chapel Hill*
Duane Griffin, *Bucknell University*
Barry N. Haack, *George Mason University*
Roy Haggerty, *Oregon State University*
John W. Hall, *Louisiana State University–Shreveport*
Vern Harnapp, *University of Akron*
John Harrington, *Kansas State University*
Blake Harrison, *Southern Connecticut University*
Jason "Jake" Haugland, *University of Colorado, Boulder*
James Hayes, *California State University, Northridge*
Gail Hobbs, *Pierce College*
Thomas W. Holder, *University of Georgia*
David H. Holt, *University of Southern Mississippi*
Robert Hordon, *Rutgers University*
David A. Howarth, *University of Louisville*
Patricia G. Humbertson, *Youngstown State University*
David W. Icenogle, *Auburn University*
Philip L. Jackson, *Oregon State University*
J. Peter Johnson, Jr., *Carleton University*
Gabrielle Katz, *Appalachian State University*
John Keyantash, *California State University, Dominguez Hills*
Guy King, *California State University–Chico*
Ronald G. Knapp, *SUNY–The College at New Paltz*
Peter W. Knightes, *Central Texas College*
Jean Kowal, *University of Wisconsin, Whitewater*
Thomas Krabacher, *California State University–Sacramento*
Hsiang-te Kung, *University of Memphis*
Kara Kuvakas, *Hartnell College*
Steve Ladochy, *California State University, Los Angeles*
Charles W. Lafon, *Texas A & M University*
Paul R. Larson, *Southern Utah University*
Robert D. Larson, *Southwest Texas State University*
Derek Law, *University of Kentucky*

Elena Lioubimtseva, *Grand Valley State University*
Joyce Lundberg, *Carleton University*
Taylor E. Mack, *Louisiana Tech University*
W. Andrew Marcus, *Montana State University*
Giraldo Mario, *California State University, Northridge*
Brian Mark, *Ohio State University*
Nadine Martin, *University of Arizona*
Elliot G. McIntire, *California State University, Northridge*
Norman Meek, *California State University, San Bernardino*
Leigh W. Mintz, *California State University–Hayward, Emeritus*
Sherry Morea-Oaks, Boulder, CO
Debra Morimoto, *Merced College*
Patrick Moss, *University of Wisconsin, Madison*
Steven Namikas, *Louisiana State University*
Lawrence C. Nkemdirim, *University of Calgary*
Peter R. Nkhoma, *University of South Florida*
Andrew Oliphant, *San Francisco State University*
John E. Oliver, *Indiana State University*
Bradley M. Opdyke, *Michigan State University*
Richard L. Orndorff, *University of Nevada, Las Vegas*
FeiFei Pan, *University of North Texas*
Patrick Pease, *East Carolina University*
James Penn, *Southeastern Louisiana University*
Rachel Pinker, *University of Maryland, College Park*
Greg Pope, *Montclair State University*
Robin J. Rapai, *University of North Dakota*
Philip Reeder, *University of South Florida*
Philip D. Renner, *American River College*
William C. Rense, *Shippensburg University*
Leslie Rigg, *Northern Illinois University*
Dar Roberts, *University of California–Santa Barbara*
Wolf Roder, *University of Cincinnati*
Robert Rohli, *Louisiana State University*
Bill Russell, *L.A. Pierce College*
Dorothy Sack, *Ohio University*
Erinanne Saffell, *Arizona State University*
Randall Schaetzl, *Michigan State University*
Glenn R. Sebastian, *University of South Alabama*
Daniel A. Selwa, *Coastal Carolina University*
Debra Sharkey, *Cosumnes River College*
Peter Siska, *Austin Peay State University*
Lee Slater, *Rutgers University*
Thomas W. Small, *Frostburg State University*
Daniel J. Smith, *University of Victoria*
Richard W. Smith, *Hartford Community College*
Stephen J. Stadler, *Oklahoma State University*
Michael Talbot, *Pima Community College*
Paul E. Todhunter, *University of North Dakota*
Susanna T.Y. Tong, *University of Cincinnati*
Liem Tran, *Florida Atlantic University*
Suzanne Traub-Metlay, *Front Range Community College*
Alice V. Turkington, *The University of Kentucky*
Jon Van de Grift, *Metropolitan State College*
David Weide, *University of Nevada–Las Vegas*
Forrest Wilkerson, *Minnesota State University, Mankato*
Thomas B. Williams, *Western Illinois University*
Catherine H. Yansa, *Michigan State University*
Brenton M. Yarnal, *Pennsylvania State University*
Keith Yearwood, *University of Maryland*
Stephen R. Yool, *University of Arizona*
Don Yow, *Eastern Kentucky University*
Susie Zeigler-Svatek, *University of Minnesota*

From Robert: I thank my family for believing in this work, especially considering the next generation: Chavon, Bryce, Payton, Brock, Trevor, Blake, Chase, Téyenna, and Cade. When I look into our grandchildren's faces, I see why we work toward a sustainable future.

I give special gratitude to all the students during my 30 years teaching at American River College, for it is in the classroom crucible that the *Geosystems* books were forged. Special continued thanks to Charlie Thomsen for his creative work and collaboration on *Encounter Geosystems*, the *Applied Physical Geography* lab manual, *MasteringGeography*™ media and assessments, and ancillaries. Thanks and admiration go to the many authors and scientists who published research that enriches this work. Thanks for all the dialogue received from students and teachers shared with me through e-mails from across the globe.

I offer a special thanks to Ginger Birkeland, Ph.D., my new coauthor on this edition and the ninth edition of *Geosystems*, and previous collaborator and developmental editor, for her essential work, attention to detail, and geographic sense. The challenge of such a text project is met by her strengths and talents. She is truly a valuable colleague and partner in this enterprise and makes the future of the *Geosystems* franchise a certainty as we view the path ahead. She has worked as a river guide operating boats on the Colorado River, and at times I felt her at the helm of *Geosystems*!

As you read this book, you will learn from more than 300 content-specific, beautiful photographs made by my wife, nature photographer Bobbé Christopherson. Her contribution to the success of the *Geosystems* texts is obvious. Please visit the photo galleries at *MasteringGeography*™ and learn more from her camera work. Bobbé is my expedition partner, colleague, wife, and best friend.

From Ginger: Many thanks to my husband, Karl Birkeland, for his ongoing patience, support, and inspiration throughout the many hours of work on this book. I also thank my daughters, Erika and Kelsey, for their sense of humor and understanding in enduring my frequent absences from family activities. The love, laughs, and lively discussions shared by our family help me see the world through their eyes and know that the future is bright. My gratitude also goes to the many river guides and scientists who taught me about rivers and the Grand Canyon and inspired my love of all things related to physical geography.

Most importantly, I offer special thanks to Robert Christopherson, who took a leap of faith to bring me on this *Geosystems* journey. I am honored to work with him, and I hope our raft runs smoothly and stays upright on the voyage ahead!

From us both: Physical geography teaches us a holistic view of the intricate supporting web that is Earth's environment and our place in it. Dramatic global change is under way in human–Earth relations as we alter physical, chemical, and biological systems. Our attention to climate change science and applied topics is in response to the impacts we are experiencing and the future we are shaping. All things considered, this is a critical time for you to be enrolled in a physical geography course! The best to you in your studies—and ***carpe diem!***

Robert W. Christopherson
P. O. Box 128
Lincoln, California 95648-0128
E-mail: bobobbe@aol.com

Ginger H. Birkeland
Bozeman, Montana

Digital & Print Resources

For Students and Teachers

MasteringGeography*™ *with Pearson eText. The *Mastering* platform is the most widely used and effective online homework, tutorial, and assessment system for the sciences. It delivers self-paced tutorials that provide individualized coaching, focus on course objectives, and are responsive to each student's progress. The *Mastering* system helps teachers maximize class time with customizable, easy-to-assign, and automatically graded assessments that motivate students to learn outside of class and arrive prepared for lecture. MasteringGeography™ offers:

- **Assignable activities** that include MapMaster™ interactive map activities, *Encounter* Google Earth™ Explorations, video activities, Geoscience Animation activities, map projections activities, GeoTutor coaching activities on the toughest topics in geography, Dynamic Study Modules that provide each student with a customized learning experience, end-of-chapter questions and exercises, reading quizzes, *Test Bank* questions, and more.
- **A student Study Area** with MapMaster™ interactive maps, videos, Geoscience Animations, web links, glossary flashcards, "In the News" readings, chapter quizzes, PDF downloads of outline maps, an optional Pearson eText and more.

Pearson eText gives students access to the text whenever and wherever they can access the Internet. Features of Pearson eText include:

- Now available on smartphones and tablets.
- Seamlessly integrated videos and other rich media.
- Fully accessible (screen-reader ready).
- Configurable reading settings, including resizable type and night reading mode.
- Instructor and student note-taking, highlighting, bookmarking, and search.

www.masteringgeography.com

***Television for the Environment Earth Report Geography Videos,* DVD** (0321662989). This three-DVD set helps students visualize how human decisions and behavior have affected the environment and how individuals are taking steps toward recovery. With topics ranging from the poor land management promoting the devastation of river systems in Central America to the struggles for electricity in China and Africa, these 13 videos from Television for the Environment's global *Earth Report* series recognize the efforts of individuals around the world to unite and protect the planet.

***Geoscience Animation Library,* 5th edition, DVD** (0321716841). Created through a unique collaboration among Pearson's leading geoscience authors, this resource offers over 100 animations covering the most difficult-to-visualize topics in physical geology, physical geography, oceanography, meteorology, and earth science. The animations are provided as Flash files and preloaded into PowerPoint® slides for both Windows and Mac.

Practicing Geography: Careers for Enhancing Society and the Environment by Association of American Geographers (0321811151). This book examines career opportunities for geographers and geospatial professionals in the business, government, nonprofit, and education sectors. A diverse group of academic and industry professionals shares insights on career planning, networking, transitioning between employment sectors, and balancing work and home life. The book illustrates the value of geographic expertise and technologies through engaging profiles and case studies of geographers at work.

Teaching College Geography: A Practical Guide for Graduate Students and Early Career Faculty by Association of American Geographers (0136054471). This two-part resource provides a starting point for becoming an effective geography teacher from the very first day of class. Part One addresses "nuts-and-bolts" teaching issues. Part Two explores being an effective teacher in the field, supporting criticalthinking with GIS and mapping technologies, engaging learners in large geography classes, and promoting awareness of international perspectives and geographic issues.

Aspiring Academics: A Resource Book for Graduate Students and Early Career Faculty by Association of American Geographers (0136048919). Drawing on several years of research, this set of essays is designed to help graduate students and early career faculty start their careers in geography and related social and environmental sciences. *Aspiring Academics* stresses the interdependence of teaching, research, and service—and the importance of achieving a healthy balance of professional and personal life—while doing faculty work. Each chapter provides accessible, forward-looking advice on topics that often cause the most stress in the first years of a college or university appointment.

For Students

***Applied Physical Geography—Geosystems in the Laboratory,* Ninth Edition** by Charlie Thomsen and Robert Christopherson (0321987284). A variety of exercises provides flexibility in lab assignments. Each exercise includes key terms and learning concepts linked to *Geosystems*. The Ninth Edition includes new exercises on climate change, soils, and rock identification, a fully updated exercise on basic GIS using ArcGIS online, and more integrated media, including Google Earth™ and Quick Response (QR) codes linking to Pre-Lab videos. Supported by a website with media resources needed for exercises, as well as a downloadable Solutions Manual for teachers.

Companion website for *Applied Physical Geography: Geosystems in the Laboratory*. The website for the lab manual provides online worksheets as well as KMZ files for all of the Google Earth™ exercises found in the lab manual. www.mygeoscienceplace.com

***Goode's World Atlas*, 23rd Edition** (0133864642). *Goode's World Atlas* has been the world's premiere educational atlas since 1923—and for good reason. It features over 250 pages of maps, from definitive physical and political maps to important thematic maps that illustrate the spatial aspects of many important topics. The 23rd Edition includes over 160 pages of digitally produced reference maps, as well as thematic maps on global climate change, sea-level rise, CO_2 emissions, polar ice fluctuations, deforestation, extreme weather events, infectious diseases, water resources, and energy production.

Pearson's Encounter Series provides rich, interactive explorations of geoscience concepts through Google Earth™ activities, covering a range of topics in regional, human, and physical geography. For those who do not use *MasteringGeography*™, all chapter explorations are available in print workbooks, as well as in online quizzes at www.mygeoscienceplace.com, accommodating different classroom needs. Each exploration consists of a worksheet, online quizzes whose results can be emailed to teachers, and a corresponding Google Earth™ KMZ file.

- *Encounter Physical Geography* by Jess C. Porter and Stephen O'Connell (0321672526)
- *Encounter World Regional Geography* by Jess C. Porter (0321681754)
- *Encounter Human Geography* by Jess C. Porter (0321682203)

***Dire Predictions: Understanding Global Climate Change* 2nd Edition** by Michael Mann, Lee R. Kump (0133909778). Periodic reports from the Intergovernmental Panel on Climate Change (IPCC) evaluate the risk of climate change brought on by humans. But the sheer volume of scientific data remains inscrutable to the general public, particularly to those who may still question the validity of climate change. In just over 200 pages, this practical text presents and expands upon the essential findings of the *IPCC's 5th Assessment Report* in a visually stunning and undeniably powerful way to the lay reader. Scientific findings that provide validity to the implications of climate change are presented in clear-cut graphic elements, striking images, and understandable analogies.

For Teachers

Learning Catalytics is a "bring your own device" student engagement, assessment, and classroom intelligence system. With Learning Catalytics, you can:

- Assess students in real time, using open-ended tasks to probe student understanding.
- Understand immediately where students are and adjust your lecture accordingly.
- Improve your students' critical-thinking skills.
- Access rich analytics to understand student performance.
- Add your own questions to make Learning Catalytics fit your course exactly.
- Manage student interactions with intelligent grouping and timing.

Learning Catalytics is a technology that has grown out of twenty years of cutting-edge research, innovation, and implementation of interactive teaching and peer instruction. Available integrated with *MasteringGeography*™.

***Instructor Resource Manual* (Download)** (0321992687). The manual includes lecture outlines and key terms, additional source materials, teaching tips, and a complete annotation of chapter review questions. Available from www.pearsonhighered.com/irc and in the Instructor Resources area of *MasteringGeography*™.

***TestGen® Test Bank* (Download)** by Todd Fagin (0321995066). TestGen® is a computerized test generator that lets you view and edit *Test Bank* questions, transfer questions to tests, and print tests in a variety of customized formats. This *Test Bank* includes around 3,000 multiple-choice, true/false, and short answer/essay questions. All questions are correlated against the National Geography Standards, textbook key learning concepts, and Bloom's Taxonomy. The *Test Bank* is also available in Microsoft Word® and importable into Blackboard. Available from www.pearsonhighered.com/irc and in the Instructor Resources area of *MasteringGeography*™.

Instructor Resource DVD (0321992679). The *Instructor Resource DVD* provides a collection of resources to help teachers make efficient and effective use of their time. All digital resources can be found in one well-organized, easy-to-access place. The IRDVD includes:

- All textbook images as JPEGs, PDFs, and PowerPoint™ Presentations
- Pre-authored Lecture Outline PowerPoint® Presentations which outline the concepts of each chapter with embedded art and can be customized to fit teachers' lecture requirements
- CRS "Clicker" Questions in PowerPoint™
- The TestGen software, *Test Bank* questions, and answers for both Macs and PCs
- Electronic files of the *Instructor Resource Manual* and *Test Bank*

This *Instructor Resource* content is also available online via the Instructor Resources section of *MasteringGeography*™ and www.pearsonhighered.com/irc.

about our sustainability initiatives

Pearson recognizes the environmental challenges facing this planet and also acknowledges our responsibility in making a difference. This book is carefully crafted to minimize environmental impact. The binding, cover, and paper come from facilities that minimize waste, energy consumption, and the use of harmful chemicals. Pearson closes the loop by recycling every out-of-date text returned to our warehouse.

Along with developing and exploring digital solutions to our market's needs, Pearson has a strong commitment to achieving carbon-neutrality. As of 2009, Pearson became the first carbon- and climate-neutral publishing company. Since then, Pearson has remained strongly committed to measuring, reducing, and offsetting our carbon footprint.

The future holds great promise for reducing our impact on Earth's environment, and Pearson is proud to be leading the way. We strive to publish the best books with the most up-to-date and accurate content, and to do so in ways that minimize our impact on Earth. To learn more about our initiatives, please visit **www.pearson.com/social-impact.html**.

1 Essentials of Geography

The Vista House observatory, built in 1918 as a rest stop for travelers and a memorial to the Oregon pioneers, sits on a dramatic promontory overlooking the Columbia River Gorge. Rivers serve as corridors of movement and transportation, physical and political boundaries, sites for recreation, and sources of hydropower. The ongoing interaction of humans with their environment is one of the essential themes in geographic science, discussed in Chapter 1. [Erik Harrison/Shutterstock.]

KEYLEARNING**concepts**

After reading the chapter, you should be able to:

- ***Define*** geography in general and physical geography in particular.
- ***Discuss*** human activities and human population growth as they relate to geographic science and ***summarize*** the scientific process.
- ***Describe*** systems analysis, open and closed systems, and feedback information and ***relate*** these concepts to Earth systems.
- ***Explain*** Earth's reference grid: latitude and longitude and latitudinal geographic zones and time.
- ***Define*** cartography and mapping basics: map scale and map projections.
- ***Describe*** modern geoscience techniques—the Global Positioning System (GPS), remote sensing, and geographic information systems (GIS)—and ***explain*** how these tools are used in geographic analysis.

GEOSYSTEMSnow

Shale Gas: An Energy Resource for the Future?

In an area stretching 965 km (600 mi) from Ohio to western New York, methane lies deeply buried in a sedimentary rock deposit, the Marcellus Shale. Methane is the primary constituent of natural gas, and scientists suggest that this ancient rock layer, underlying 60% of Pennsylvania, may be one of the most significant reservoirs of natural gas in the world. Pennsylvania alone is dotted with nearly 6000 shale gas wells extracting pressurized methane (**Figure GN 1.1**).

Sources of Methane Methane is a chemical compound with the formula CH_4 and is a by-product of several natural processes: digestive activity of animals (cattle, sheep, bison) and termites; burning associated with wildfires; melting of arctic permafrost; and bacterial activity in bogs, swamps, and wetlands. Nearly 60% of the methane in our atmosphere comes from human sources, including natural gas production, beef and dairy production, rice cultivation, coal and oil extraction and burning, landfills, and wastewater treatment. In the United States, the natural gas industry makes up the largest percentage of methane emissions.

Drilling for Methane To release methane trapped within shale layers, the rock must be broken up so that gas diffuses into the cracks and flows upward. Over the past 20 years, advances in horizontal drilling techniques, combined with the process of hydraulic fracturing, or "fracking," opened access to large amounts of natural gas previously deemed too expensive or difficult to tap. A typical shale gas well descends vertically 2.4 km (1.5 mi), turns, and then extends horizontally into the rock strata. Horizontal drilling exposes a greater area of the rock, allowing more of it to be broken up and more gas to be released (**Figure GN 1.2**).

A pressurized fluid is pumped into the well to break up the rock. This fluid is 90% water, 9% sand or glass beads that prop open the fissures, and 1% chemical additives that act as lubricants. The specific chemicals used are as yet undisclosed by the industry. This use of an injected fluid to fracture the shale is the process of fracking. Gas then flows up the well to be collected at the surface.

Fracking uses massive quantities of water: approximately 15 million L (4 million gal) for each well system, flowing at a rate of 16,000 L (4200 gal) per minute—far more than could be provided by a public water system. In some regions, such intensive water use for energy extraction may deplete natural water sources, affecting stream or lake ecosystems, or redirect water from other uses.

The U.S. Energy Information Administration (EIA) projects a boom in shale gas extraction and production from fracking over the next 20 years, with U.S. production rising from 34% of all natural gas production in 2011 to 50% in 2040.

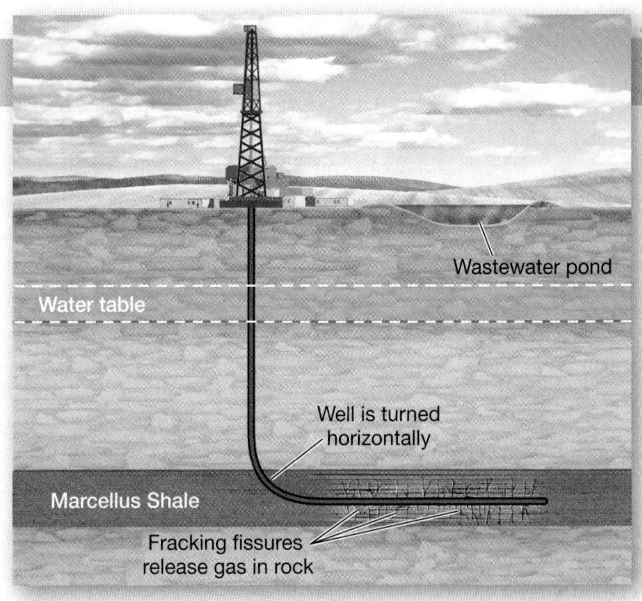

▲**Figure GN 1.2 Horizontal drilling for hydraulic fracturing (fracking) and shale gas extraction.**

Environmental Effects As with other resource-extraction techniques, fracking leaves hazardous by-products. It produces large amounts of toxic wastewater, often held in wells or containment ponds. Any leak or failure of pond retaining walls spills pollutants into surface water supplies and groundwater.

Methane gas may leak around well casings, which tend to crack during the fracking process. Leaks can cause buildup of methane in groundwater, leading to contaminated drinking water wells, flammable tap water, methane accumulation in barns and homes, and possible explosions.

Methane adds to air pollution as a constituent in smog and is a potent greenhouse gas, absorbing heat from the Sun near Earth's surface and contributing to global climate change. In addition, scientific evidence links the injection of fluid into wastewater wells to earthquake activity and ground instability in Oklahoma, Texas, Ohio, West Virginia, and parts of the Midwest.

This rapidly expanding energy resource has varied impacts on air, water, land, and living Earth systems. However, many of the environmental effects of shale gas extraction remain unknown; further scientific study is critical.

Shale Gas and *Elemental Geosystems* Resource location and distribution and human–environment interactions are important issues associated with shale gas extraction; these issues are also at the heart of geographic science. In this chapter, you work with several "Essentials of Geography": spatial concepts, the scientific process, human–Earth connections, Earth systems thinking, and mapping. Throughout *Elemental Geosystems*, we expand the story of shale gas and its potential effects on global climate, surface water and groundwater resources, earthquake hazards, and ecosystem functions.

QUESTION AND EXPLORE To work with an interactive diagram called "Breaking Fuel from the Rock," go to http://ngm.nationalgeographic.com/2012/12/methane/lavelle-text. For another perspective, go to http://www.energyfromshale.org/shale-extraction-process. Should the United States and other countries expand shale gas as an energy resource for the future? MG

▼**Figure GN 1.1 Shale deposits and areas of exploration for natural gas extraction, United States and Canada.** [U.S. Energy Information Administration.]

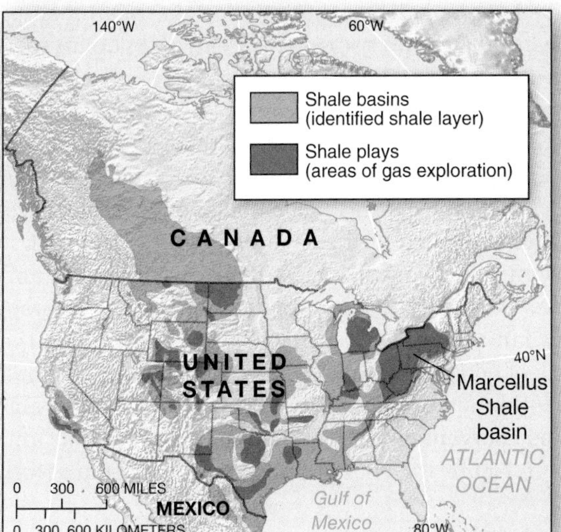

Welcome to the Eighth Edition of *Elemental Geosystems* and the study of physical geography! In this text, we examine the powerful Earth systems that influence our lives and the many ways humans impact those systems. Physical geography involves the study of Earth's environments, including the systems that form the landscapes, seascapes, atmosphere, and ecosystems on which humans depend. In this second decade of the 21st century, our natural world is changing, and the scientific study of Earth and its environments is more crucial than ever.

Physical geography uses a spatial perspective to examine processes and events happening at specific locations and follow their effects across the globe.

Consider as examples the following events and the questions they raise for the study of Earth's systems and physical geography. This text provides tools for answering these questions and addressing the underlying issues.

- In October 2012, Hurricane Sandy made landfall along the U.S. East Coast, hitting New York and New Jersey at high tide with hurricane-force winds and record storm surges. The storm cost 110 human lives and over $42 billion in New York State alone, approaching $100 billion in damages overall. What atmospheric processes explain the formation and movement of this storm? Why the unprecedented size and intensity? How does this storm relate to record air and ocean temperatures?
- In March 2011, a magnitude 9.0 earthquake and resultant 10- to 20-m (33- to 66-ft) tsunami devastated Honshu Island, Japan—at US$309 billion, Earth's most expensive natural disaster so far. Why do earthquakes occur in particular locations across the globe? What produces tsunami, and how far and fast do they travel? How have prevailing winds and ocean currents dispersed tsunami debris across the Pacific?
- In 2014, the U.S. National Park Service finished the deconstruction of two dams on the Elwha River in Washington—the largest dam removals in the world to date. The project will restore a free-flowing river for fisheries and associated ecosystems. How do dams change river environments? Can rivers be restored after dam removal?
- In 2011, the world released 2.4 million pounds of carbon dioxide (CO_2) into the atmosphere every second, mainly from the burning of fossil fuels. This "greenhouse gas" contributes to climate change by trapping heat near Earth's surface. Each year atmospheric CO_2 levels rise to a new record, altering Earth's climate. What are the effects on Earth systems?

Physical geography uses a *spatial* perspective to examine processes and events happening at specific locations and follow their effects across the globe. Why does the environment vary from equator to midlatitudes and between tropical and polar regions? What produces the patterns of wind, weather, and ocean currents? How does solar energy influence the distribution of trees, soils, climates, and human populations? In this book, we explore those questions, and more, through geography's unique perspective.

Perhaps more than any other issue, climate change has become an overriding focus of the study of Earth systems. The past decade experienced the highest air temperatures over land and water in the instrumental record. In response, the extent of sea ice in the Arctic Ocean continues to decline to record lows. At the same time, melting of the Greenland and Antarctica Ice Sheets is accelerating; together, they now lose more than three times the ice they lost annually 20 years ago. As sea ice and ice sheets melt, sea level is rising. Elsewhere, intense weather events, drought, and flooding continue to increase. In presenting the state of the planet, *Elemental Geosystems* surveys climate change evidence and considers its implications. In every chapter, we present up-to-date science and information to help you understand our dynamic Earth systems. Welcome to an exploration of physical geography!

In this chapter: We begin with a look at the science of physical geography, which uses an integrative spatial approach, guided by the scientific process, to study Earth systems. The role of humans is an increasingly important focus of physical geography, as are questions of global sustainability as Earth's population grows.

Physical geographers study the environment by analyzing air, water, land, and living systems. Therefore, we discuss systems and the feedback mechanisms that influence system operations. We then consider location on Earth as determined by the coordinated grid system of latitude and longitude, and the determination of world time zones. Next, we examine maps as critical tools that geographers use to display physical and cultural information. This chapter concludes with an overview of technologies that are adding exciting new dimensions to geographic science: the Global Positioning System, remote sensing from space, and geographic information systems.

The Science of Geography

Geographic science is concerned with much more than place names. **Geography** (from *geo*, "Earth," and *graphein*, "to write") is the science that studies the relationships among natural systems, geographic areas, and human society and culture, and the interdependence of all of these, *over space*. These last two words are key, for geography is a science that is in part defined by its method—a special way of analyzing phenomena over space. In geography, the term **spatial** refers to the nature and character of physical space, its measurement, and the distribution of things within it.

Geographic concepts pertain to distributions and movement across Earth and how these processes interact with human actions. Given this spatial perspective, the concerns of geographic science are traditionally divided into five themes: **location**, **region**, **human–Earth relationships**, **movement**, and **place**, each illustrated and defined in Figure 1.1. These themes provide a framework

Place
No two places on Earth are exactly alike. Place describes the characteristics – both human and physical – of a location. Untracked powder attracts skiers in the backcountry near Mount Hutt.
Location
Location identifies an absolute or relative position on Earth. Mount Cook is the highest point in New Zealand, located at 43°35' S latitude and 170°8' E longitude.
Region
A region is an area defined by uniform physical or human characteristics. The West Coast region between the Southern Alps and the Tasman Sea is dominated by a marine west coast climate, cool and moist.
Movement
Movement includes communication, migration, and diffusion across Earth's surface in our interdependent world. New Zealand receives 2.5 million international visitors each year; Milford Sound is a major attraction; Mitre Peak appears in the background.
Human–Earth Relationships
Natural hazards are one type of human–environment connection. An equipment shed stands in ruins after being hit by an avalanche at Ohau Ski Field in 2009.

▲**Figure 1.1 Five themes of geographic science.** Drawing from your own experience, can you think of examples of each theme? This satellite image shows New Zealand's South Island. [Photos by Karl Birkeland, except Movement by Ian Dagnall/Alamy. *Terra* MODIS image, NASA/GSFC.]

for understanding geographic concepts and asking geographic questions. How does solar energy influence the distribution of climates, soils, and living organisms in particular places and across regions? How do natural systems affect human populations, and, in turn, what impact are humans having on natural systems?

Although geography is not limited to place names, maps and location are central to the discipline and are important tools for conveying geographic data. Evolving technologies such as geographic information systems and the Global Positioning System are widely used for scientific applications and in today's society as hundreds of millions of people access maps and locational information every day on computers and mobile devices.

In response to increasing globalization and environmental change, the geography education guidelines—updated by the National Council for Geographic Education (NCGE)—have now redefined the essential elements (or themes) of geography, expanding their number to six: *the spatial world, places and regions, physical systems, human systems, environment and society,* and *uses of geography in today's society.* These categories emphasize the spatial and environmental perspectives within the discipline and reflect the growing importance of human–environment interactions.

The Geographic Continuum

Because many subjects can be examined geographically, geography is an eclectic science that integrates subject matter from a wide range of disciplines. Even so, it splits broadly into two primary fields: *physical geography,* comprising specialty areas that draw largely on the physical and life sciences; and *human geography,* comprising specialty areas that draw largely on the social and cultural sciences (**Figure 1.2**). The growing complexity of the human–Earth relationship in the 21st century has shifted the study of geographic processes even farther toward the center of the continuum, resulting ultimately in a more balanced, more holistic perspective—such is the thrust of *Elemental Geosystems.*

Within physical geography, research now emphasizes human influences on natural systems in all specialty areas, effectively moving this end of the continuum closer to the middle. For example, physical geographers monitor air pollution, examine the vulnerability of human populations to climate change, study impacts of human activities on forest health and the movement of invasive species, study changes in river systems caused by dams and dam removal, and examine the response of glacial ice to changing climate.

Geographic Analysis

As mentioned earlier, the science of geography is unified more by its method than by a specific body of knowledge. The method is **spatial analysis**. Geographers view phenomena as occurring across spaces, areas, and locations. The language of geography—territory, zone, pattern, distribution, place, location, region, sphere, province, and distance—reflects this spatial view. Geographers analyze the differences and similarities between places.

Process, a set of actions or mechanisms that operate in some special order, is a central concept of geographic analysis. Among the examples you encounter in *Elemental Geosystems* are the numerous processes involved in Earth's vast water–atmosphere–weather system, in continental crust movements and earthquake occurrences, in ecosystem functions, and in river channel dynamics. Geographers use spatial analysis to examine how Earth's processes interact through space or over areas.

Therefore, **physical geography** is the spatial analysis of all the physical elements, processes, and systems that make up the environment: energy, air, water, weather, climate, landforms, soils, animals, plants, microorganisms, and Earth itself. Today, in addition to its place in the geographic continuum, physical geography encompasses the field of **Earth systems science**, the area of study that seeks to understand Earth as a complete entity, an interacting set of physical, chemical, and biological systems. With these definitions in mind, we now discuss the general process and methods used by scientists, including geographers.

The Scientific Process

The process of science consists of observing, questioning, testing, and understanding elements of the natural world. The **scientific method** is the traditional recipe of a scientific investigation; it can be thought of as simple, organized steps leading toward concrete, objective conclusions (**Figure 1.3**). There is no single, definitive method for scientific

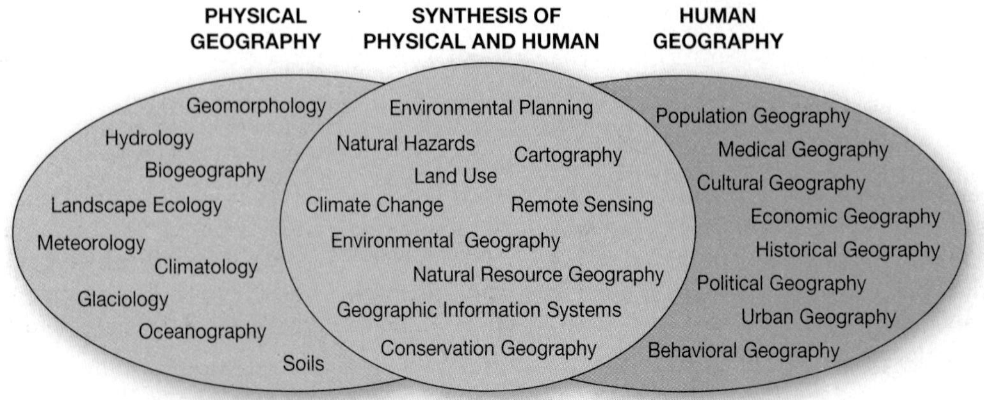

◀Figure 1.2 The geographic continuum. Geography combines Earth topics and human topics, blending ideas from many different sciences. This book focuses on physical geography, but integrates pertinent human and cultural content for a whole-Earth perspective.

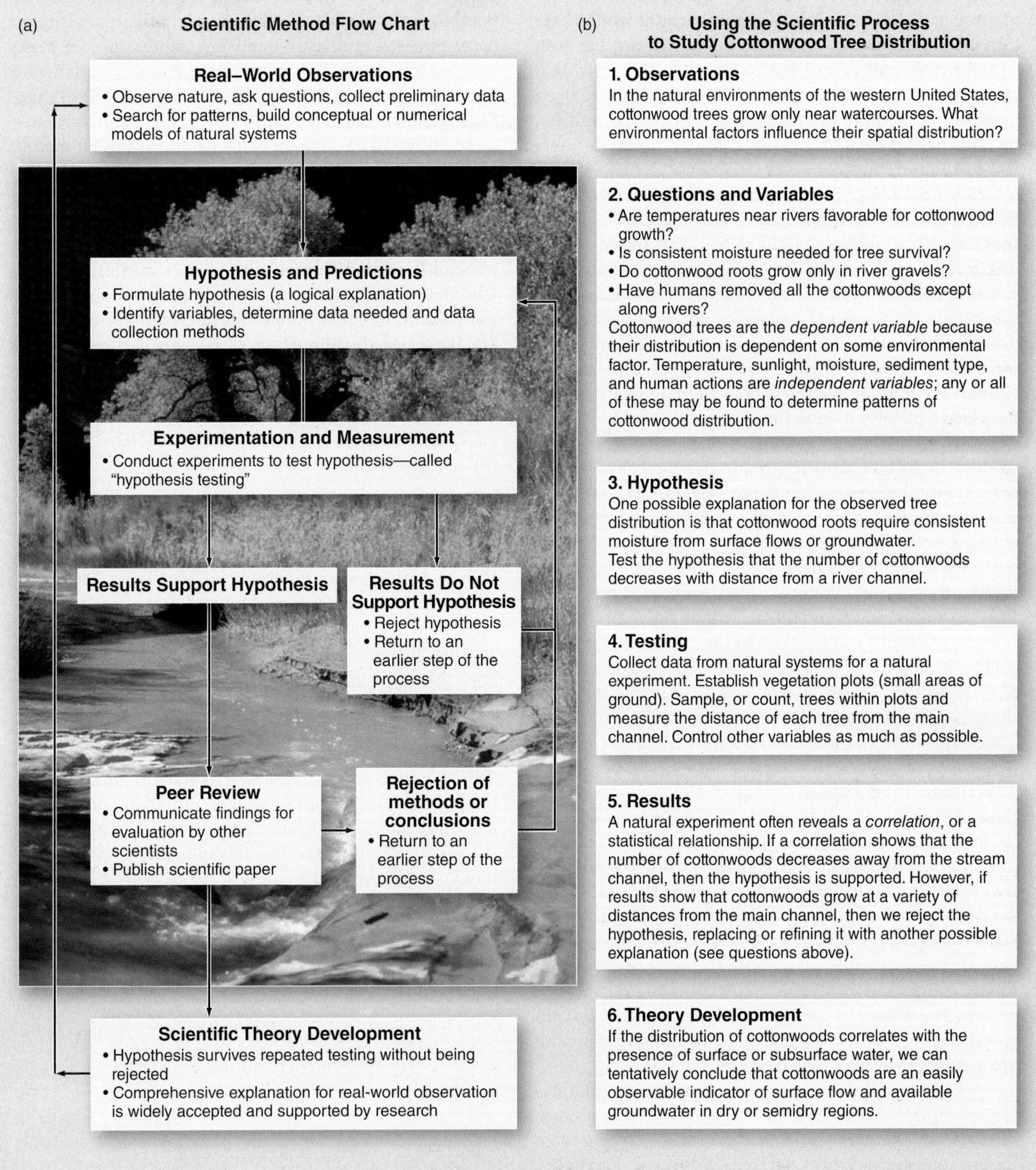

(a) Scientific Method Flow Chart
Real–World Observations
• Observe nature, ask questions, collect preliminary data
• Search for patterns, build conceptual or numerical models of natural systems
Hypothesis and Predictions
• Formulate hypothesis (a logical explanation)
• Identify variables, determine data needed and data collection methods
Experimentation and Measurement
• Conduct experiments to test hypothesis—called "hypothesis testing"
Results Support Hypothesis
Results Do Not Support Hypothesis
• Reject hypothesis
• Return to an earlier step of the process
Peer Review
• Communicate findings for evaluation by other scientists
• Publish scientific paper
Rejection of methods or conclusions
• Return to an earlier step of the process
Scientific Theory Development
• Hypothesis survives repeated testing without being rejected
• Comprehensive explanation for real-world observation is widely accepted and supported by research
(b) Using the Scientific Process to Study Cottonwood Tree Distribution
1. Observations
In the natural environments of the western United States, cottonwood trees grow only near watercourses. What environmental factors influence their spatial distribution?
2. Questions and Variables
• Are temperatures near rivers favorable for cottonwood growth?
• Is consistent moisture needed for tree survival?
• Do cottonwood roots grow only in river gravels?
• Have humans removed all the cottonwoods except along rivers?
Cottonwood trees are the *dependent variable* because their distribution is dependent on some environmental factor. Temperature, sunlight, moisture, sediment type, and human actions are *independent variables*; any or all of these may be found to determine patterns of cottonwood distribution.
3. Hypothesis
One possible explanation for the observed tree distribution is that cottonwood roots require consistent moisture from surface flows or groundwater.
Test the hypothesis that the number of cottonwoods decreases with distance from a river channel.
4. Testing
Collect data from natural systems for a natural experiment. Establish vegetation plots (small areas of ground). Sample, or count, trees within plots and measure the distance of each tree from the main channel. Control other variables as much as possible.
5. Results
A natural experiment often reveals a *correlation*, or a statistical relationship. If a correlation shows that the number of cottonwoods decreases away from the stream channel, then the hypothesis is supported. However, if results show that cottonwoods grow at a variety of distances from the main channel, then we reject the hypothesis, replacing or refining it with another possible explanation (see questions above).
6. Theory Development
If the distribution of cottonwoods correlates with the presence of surface or subsurface water, we can tentatively conclude that cottonwoods are an easily observable indicator of surface flow and available groundwater in dry or semidry regions.

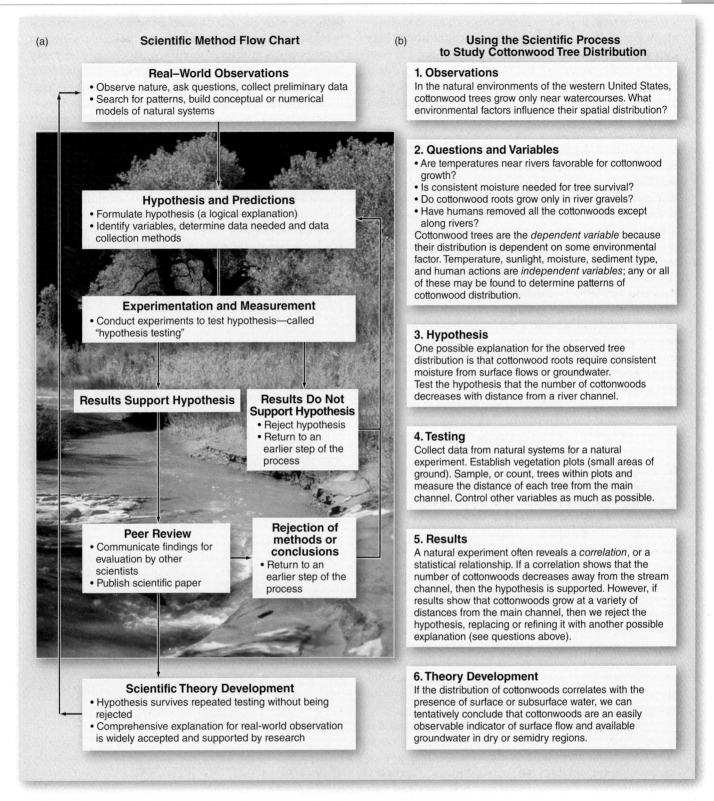

▲**Figure 1.3 Scientific method flow chart and example application.** [Ginger Birkeland.]

inquiry; scientists in different fields and even in different subfields of physical geography may approach their scientific testing in different ways. However, the end result must be a conclusion that is reproducible by other scientists, and that can be tested repeatedly and possibly shown as true or as false. Without this characteristic, it is not science.

Using the Scientific Method Scientists who study the physical environment begin with the clues they see in nature, followed by an exploration of the relevant published scientific literature on their topic. Brainstorming with others, continued observation, and preliminary data collection may occur at this stage.

In the next step, scientists use questions and observations to identify variables, which are the conditions that change in an experiment or model. They often seek to reduce the number of variables when formulating a *hypothesis*—a tentative explanation for the phenomena observed. Since natural systems are complex, controlling or eliminating variables helps simplify research questions and predictions.

Scientists test hypotheses using experimental studies in laboratories or natural settings. The methods used for these studies must be reproducible so that repeat testing can occur. Results may support or disprove the hypothesis, or predictions made according to the hypothesis may prove accurate or inaccurate. If the results disprove the hypothesis, the researcher will need to adjust data-collection methods or refine the hypothesis statement. If the results support the hypothesis, repeated testing and verification may lead to its elevation to the status of a *theory.*

Reporting research results is also part of the scientific method. For scientific work to reach other scientists and eventually the public at large, it should be described in a scientific paper and published in one of the many scientific journals. When a scientist submits a paper to a scientific journal, that journal sends it out for *peer review.* During this critical process, other members of the scientific or professional community critique the methods and interpretation of results set out in the paper. This process also helps detect any personal or political bias on the part of the scientist. The reviewers may recommend rejecting the paper or accepting and revising it for publication. Once a number of papers are published with similar results and conclusions, the building of a theory begins.

A scientific *theory* is an explanation constructed on the basis of several extensively tested hypotheses and can be reevaluated or expanded according to new evidence. Thus, a scientific theory is not absolute truth; the possibility always exists that the theory could be proved wrong. However, theories can be expanded to represent truly broad general principles—unifying concepts that tie together the laws that govern nature. Examples include plate tectonics theory and the theory of evolution, discussed in Chapters 9 and 16. The value of a scientific theory is that it stimulates continued observation, testing, understanding, and pursuit of knowledge within scientific fields.

While the scientific method is of fundamental importance in guiding scientific investigation, the real process of science is more dynamic and less linear, leaving room for questioning and thinking "out of the box." Flexibility and creativity are essential to the scientific process, which may not always follow the same sequence of steps or use the same methods for each experiment or research project.

Applying Scientific Results Scientific studies described as "basic" are designed largely to help advance knowledge and build scientific theories. Other research is designed to produce "applied" results tied directly to real-world problem solving. Applied scientific research may advance new technologies, affect natural resource policy, or directly impact management strategies. Scientists share the results of both basic and applied research at conferences as well as in published papers, and they may take leadership roles in developing policy and planning. For example, the awareness that human activity is producing global climate change places increasing pressure on scientists to participate in decision making. Numerous editorials in scientific journals have called for such practical scientific involvement.

Science is objective by nature and does not make value judgments. Instead, pure science provides people and their institutions with objective information on which to base their own value judgments. Social and political judgments about the applications of science are increasingly important as Earth's natural systems respond to the impacts of modern civilization.

Human–Earth Interactions in the 21st Century

Issues surrounding the growing influence of humans on Earth systems are central concerns of physical geography; we discuss them in every chapter of *Elemental Geosystems.* Human influence on Earth is now pervasive. The global human population passed 6 billion in August 1999 and continued to grow at the rate of 82 million per year, adding another billion by 2011, when the 7 billionth human was born. More people are alive today than at any previous moment in the planet's long history, unevenly distributed among 193 countries and numerous colonies. Virtually all new population growth is in the less-developed countries (LDCs), which now possess 81% (about 5.75 billion) of the total population. Over the span of human history, billion-mark milestones occurred at ever closer intervals through the sixth-billion milestone; the interval is now slightly increasing (**Figure 1.4**).

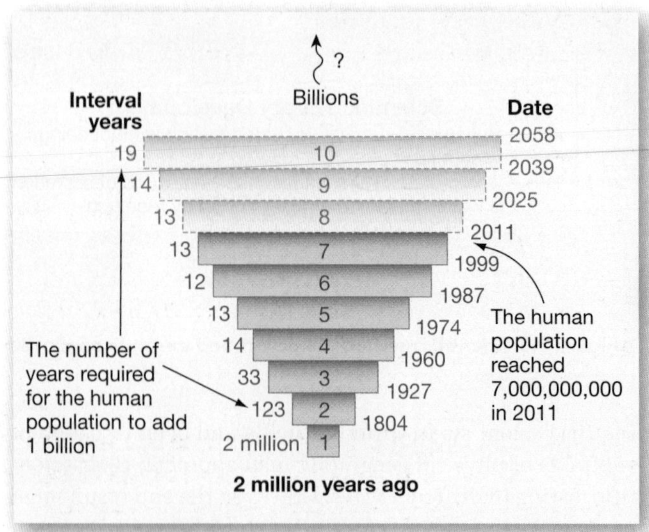

▲**Figure 1.4 Human population growth.** Note the population forecasts through 2058.

The Human Denominator We consider the totality of human impact on Earth to be the *human denominator.* Just as the denominator in a fraction tells how many parts a whole is divided into, so the growing human population and its increasing demand for resources and rising planetary impact suggest the stresses on the whole Earth system that must support us. Yet Earth's resource base—the numerator in this fraction—remains relatively fixed.

The population in just two countries makes up 37% of Earth's human count: 19.1% live in China and 17.9% in India—2.63 billion people combined. Considered overall, the planetary population is young, with some 26% still under the age of 15 years.*

Population in most of the more-developed countries (MDCs) is no longer increasing. In fact, some European countries are actually declining in growth or are near replacement levels. However, people in these developed countries have a greater impact on the planet per person and therefore constitute a population impact crisis. The United States and Canada, with about 5% of the world's population, produce about 25% ($16.2 trillion and $1.8 trillion in 2012, respectively) of the world's gross domestic product (GDP). These two countries use more than 2 times the energy per capita of Europeans, more than 7 times that of Latin Americans, 10 times that of Asians, and 20 times that of Africans. Therefore, the impact of this 5% on the state of Earth systems, natural resources, and sustainability of current practices in the MDCs is critical.

Global Sustainability Recently, **sustainability science** emerged as a new, integrative discipline, broadly based on concepts of sustainable development related to functioning Earth systems. Geographic concepts are fundamental to this new science, with its emphasis on human well-being, Earth systems, and human–environment interactions.

Dr. Carol Harden, past president of the Association of American Geographers, pointed out the important role of geographical concepts in sustainability science in 2009. She wrote that the idea of a human "footprint," representing the human impact on Earth systems, relates to sustainability and geography. When the human population of over 7 billion is taken into account, the human footprint on Earth is enormous in terms of both its spatial extent and the strength of its influence. Shrinking this footprint ties to sustainability science in all of its forms—for example, sustainable development, sustainable resources, sustainable energy, and sustainable agriculture. Geographers are now part of the effort to articulate this emerging field, which seeks to directly link science and technology with sustainability.

If we consider some of the key issues for this century, many of them fall beneath the umbrella of sustainability science, such as global food supply, energy supplies and demands, climate change, loss of biodiversity, and air and water pollution. These are issues that should be addressed in new ways if we are to achieve sustainability for both human and Earth systems. Understanding Earth's physical geography and geographic science informs your thinking on these issues.

*Data for 2013 from the Population Reference Bureau (http://www.prb.org) and the U.S. Census Bureau's *POPClock Projection* (http://www.census.gov/popclock).

Earth Systems Concepts

The word *system* is in our lives daily: "Check the car's cooling system"; "A weather system is approaching." *Systems analysis* techniques in science began with studies of energy and temperature (thermodynamics) in the 19th century. Today, systems methodology is an important analytical tool. In this book's 4 parts and 17 chapters, the content is organized along logical flow paths consistent with systems thinking.

Systems Theory

Simply stated, a **system** is any set of ordered, interrelated components and their attributes, linked by flows of energy and matter, as distinct from the surrounding environment outside the system. The elements within a system

CRITICAL**thinking** 1.1

What Is Your Footprint?

The concept of an individual's "footprint" has become popular—ecological footprint, carbon footprint, lifestyle footprint. The term has come to represent the costs of affluence and modern technology to our planetary systems. Footprint assessments are gross simplifications, but they can give you an idea of your impact and even an estimate of how many planets it would take to sustain that lifestyle and economy if everyone lived like you. Calculate your carbon footprint online at **http://www.epa.gov/climatechange/ghgemissions/ind-calculator.html**, one of many such websites, for housing, transportation, or food consumption. How can you reduce your footprint at home, at school, at work, or on the road? How does your footprint compare to the U.S. and worldwide average footprints?

GEO**report** 1.1 Welcome to the Anthropocene

The human population on Earth reached 7 billion in 2011. Many scientists now agree that the *Anthropocene*, a term coined by Nobel Prize–winning scientist Paul Crutzen, is an appropriate name for the most recent years of geologic history, when humans have influenced Earth's climate and ecosystems. Some scientists mark the beginning of agriculture, about 5000 years ago, as the start of the Anthropocene; others place the start at the dawn of the Industrial Revolution, in the 18th century. To see a video charting the growth of humans as a planetary force, go to **http://www.anthropocene.info**.

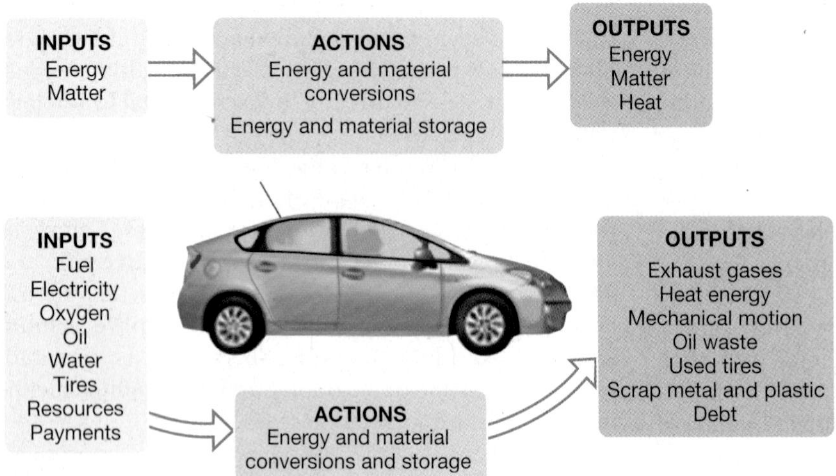

▲**Figure 1.5 An open system.** In an open system, inputs of energy and matter undergo conversions and are stored or released as the system operates. Outputs include energy, matter, and heat energy (waste). After considering how the various inputs and outputs listed here are related to the operation of the car, expand your thinking to the entire system of auto production, from raw materials to assembly to sales to car accidents to junkyards. Can you identify other open systems that you encounter in your daily life?

may be arranged in a series or intermingled. A system may comprise any number of subsystems. Within Earth's systems, both matter and energy are stored and retrieved, and energy is transformed from one type to another. (*Matter* is mass that assumes a physical shape and occupies space; *energy* is a capacity to change the motion of, or to do work on, matter.)

Open Systems Systems in nature are generally not self-contained: Inputs of energy and matter flow into the system, and outputs of energy and matter flow from the system. Such a system is an **open system** (**Figure 1.5**). Within a system, the parts function in an interrelated manner, acting together in a way that gives each system its operational character. Earth is an open system in terms of energy because solar energy enters freely and heat energy leaves, going back into space.

Within the Earth system, many subsystems are interconnected. Free-flowing rivers are open systems: Inputs consist of solar energy, precipitation, and soil and rock particles; outputs are water and sediments to the ocean. Changes to a river system may affect the nearby coastal system; for example, an increase in a river's sediment load may change the shape of a river mouth or spread pollutants along a coastline. Most natural systems are open in terms of energy. Examples of open atmospheric subsystems include hurricanes and tornadoes.

Earth systems are dynamic—active and energetic— because of the tremendous infusion of radiant energy from the Sun. As this energy passes through the outermost edge of Earth's atmosphere, it is transformed into various kinds of energy that power terrestrial systems, such as kinetic energy (of motion), potential energy (of position), and chemical or mechanical energy—setting the fluid atmosphere and ocean in motion. Eventually, Earth radiates this energy back to space as heat energy.

Closed Systems A system that is shut off from the surrounding environment so that it is self-contained is a **closed system**. Although such closed systems are rarely found in nature, Earth is essentially a closed system in terms of physical matter and resources—air, water, and material resources. The only exceptions are the slow escape of lightweight gases (such as hydrogen) from the atmosphere into space and the input of frequent, but tiny, meteors and cosmic dust. The fact that Earth is a closed material system makes recycling efforts inevitable if we want a sustainable global economy.

Natural System Example A forest is an example of an open system (**Figure 1.6**). Through the process of photosynthesis, trees and other plants use sunlight as an energy input and water, nutrients, and carbon dioxide as material inputs. The photosynthetic process converts these inputs to stored chemical energy in the form of plant

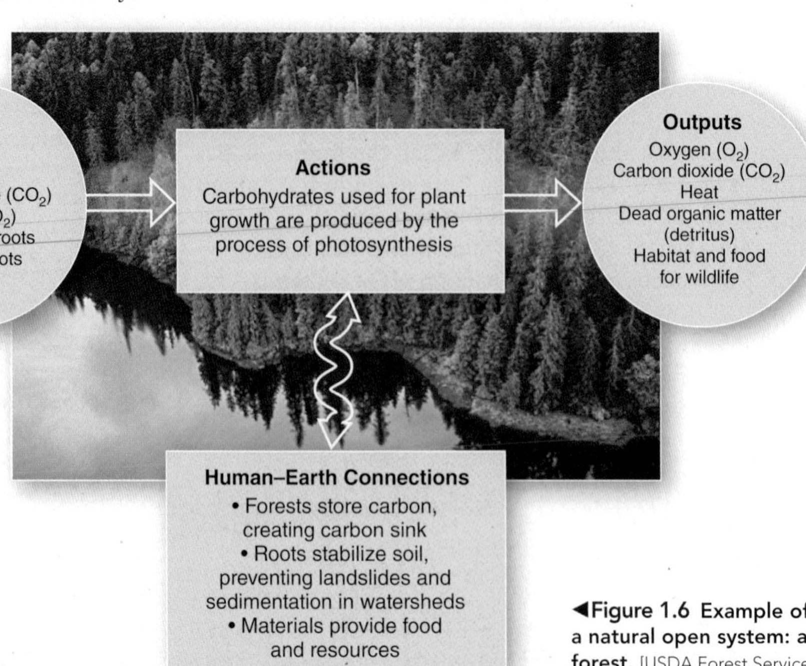

◄**Figure 1.6 Example of a natural open system: a forest.** [USDA Forest Service.]

Earth's Four "Spheres" Earth's surface is a vast area of 500 million km² (193 million mi²) where four immense open systems interact. The three **abiotic**, or nonliving, systems overlap as the framework for the realm of the **biotic**, or living, system. The abiotic spheres are the *atmosphere*, *hydrosphere*, and *lithosphere*. The biotic sphere is the *biosphere*. Together, these spheres form a simplified model of Earth systems.

- **Atmosphere (Part I, Chapters 2–4)** The **atmosphere** is a thin, gaseous veil surrounding Earth, held to the planet by the force of gravity. Formed by gases arising from within Earth's crust and interior and the exhalations of all life over time, the lower atmosphere is unique in the Solar System. It is a combination of nitrogen, oxygen, argon, carbon dioxide, water vapor, and trace gases.
- **Hydrosphere (Part II, Chapters 5–8)** Earth's waters exist in the atmosphere, on the surface, and in the crust near the surface. Collectively, these waters form the **hydrosphere**. That portion of the hydrosphere that is frozen is the **cryosphere**—ice sheets, ice caps and fields, glaciers, ice shelves, sea ice, and subsurface ground ice. Water of the hydrosphere exists in three states: liquid, solid (the frozen cryosphere), and gaseous (water vapor). Water occurs in two general chemical conditions, fresh and saline (salty).
- **Lithosphere (Part III, Chapters 9–14)** Earth's crust and a portion of the upper mantle directly below the crust form the **lithosphere**. The crust is quite brittle compared with the layers deep beneath the surface, which move slowly in response to an uneven distribution of heat energy and pressure. In a broad sense, the term *lithosphere* sometimes refers to the entire solid planet. The soil layer is the *edaphosphere* and generally covers Earth's land surfaces. In this text, soils represent the bridge between the lithosphere (Part III) and biosphere (Part IV).
- **Biosphere (Part IV, Chapters 15–17)** The intricate, interconnected web that links all organisms with their physical environment is the **biosphere**, or **ecosphere**. The biosphere is the area in which physical and chemical factors form the context of life. The biosphere exists in the overlap of the three abiotic, or nonliving, spheres, extending from the seafloor, the upper layers of the crustal rock, to about 8 km (5 mi) into the atmosphere. Life is sustainable within these natural limits. The biosphere evolves, reorganizes itself at times, undergoes extinctions, and manages to flourish.

Within each part, the sequence of chapters generally follows a systems flow of energy and materials. Each of the four part-opening page spreads summarizes the main system linkages; these diagrams are presented together in Geosystems in Action 1. As an example of our systems organization, Part I, "The Energy–Atmosphere System," begins with the Sun (Chapter 2). The Sun's energy flows across space to the top of the atmosphere and through the atmosphere to Earth's surface, where it is balanced by outgoing energy from Earth (Chapters 2 and 3). Then we look at system outputs of temperature (Chapter 3) and winds and ocean currents (Chapter 4). Note the same logical systems flow in the other three parts of this text.

Mount Pinatubo—Global System Impact A dramatic example of interactions between Earth systems in response to a volcanic eruption illustrates the strength of the systems approach used throughout this textbook. Mount Pinatubo in the Philippines erupted violently in 1991, injecting 15–20 million tons of ash and sulfuric acid mist into the upper atmosphere (see photos in GIA 1). This was the second greatest eruption during the 20th century; Mount Katmai in Alaska in 1912 was the only one greater. The eruption materials from Mount Pinatubo affected Earth systems in several ways, as noted on the map. For comparison, the 2010 eruption of Eyjafjallajökull in Iceland was about 100 times smaller in terms of the volume of material ejected, with debris reaching only the lower atmosphere.

As you progress through this book, you see the story of Mount Pinatubo and its implications woven through six chapters: Chapter 1 (discussion of systems theory), Chapter 3 (effects on energy budgets in the atmosphere), Chapter 4 (satellite images of the spread of debris by atmospheric winds), Chapter 8 (temporary effect on global atmospheric temperatures), Chapter 10 (volcanic processes), and Chapter 16 (effects on net photosynthesis). These discussions help us see the linkages and global impacts of such a volcanic explosion.

Location and Time on Earth

Earth's *sphericity*, or roundness, was first determined more than two millennia ago by the Greek mathematician and philosopher Pythagoras (ca. 580–500 B.C.). The idea of a spherical rather than a flat Earth was generally accepted by the educated populace as early as the first century A.D. Christopher Columbus, for example, knew he was sailing around a sphere in 1492; this is one reason why he thought he had arrived in the East Indies.

Until 1687, the spherical-perfection model was a basic assumption of **geodesy**, the science that determines

(*text continues on page 14*)

GEOreport 1.2 Earth's unique hydrosphere

The hydrosphere on Earth is unique among the planets in the Solar System: Only Earth possesses surface water in such quantity, some 1.36 billion km³ (0.33 billion mi³). Subsurface water exists on other planets and their satellites—on the Moon and on the planets Mercury and Mars, on Jupiter's moon Europa, and on Saturn's moons Enceladus and Titan. The *Curiosity* rover in 2012 landed in an area of Mars that billions of years ago was flooded with waist-deep water.

Earth's four "spheres"—the atmosphere, hydrosphere, lithosphere, and biosphere—are the open systems that form the part structure for *Elemental Geosystems*: The Energy–Atmosphere System; Water, Weather, and Climate Systems; The Earth–Atmosphere Interface; and Soils, Ecosystems, and Biomes. In each part, the chapter sequence generally follows the system inputs, actions, and outputs. Human–Earth connections are an integral part of all Earth systems and their interactions.

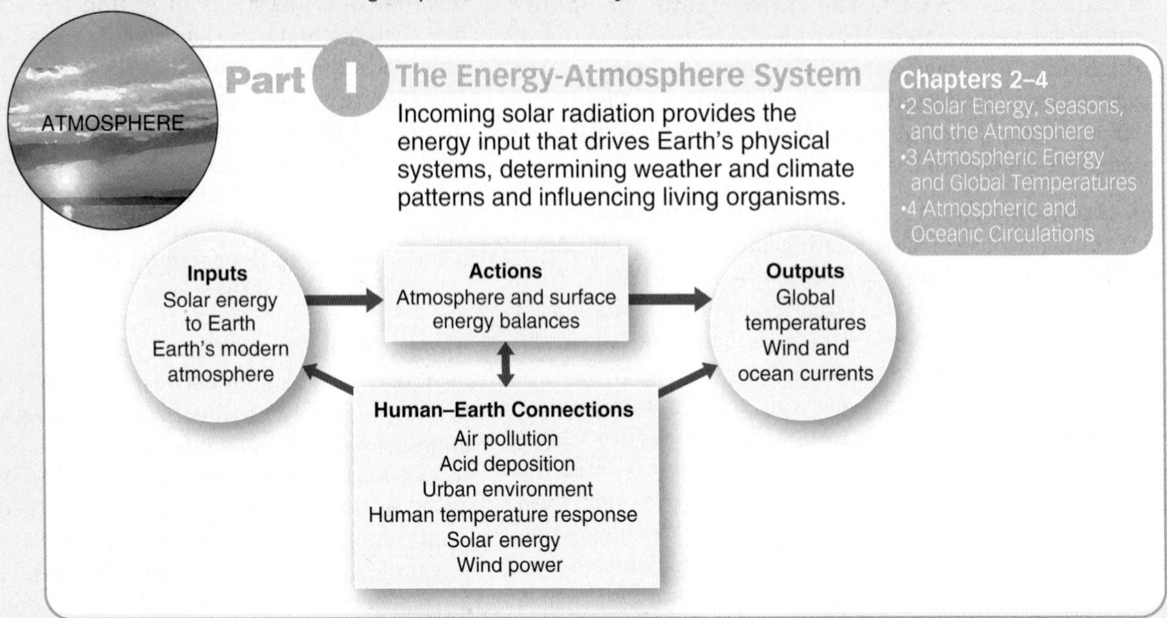

Throughout *Elemental Geosystems*, we discuss the linkages and global impacts of the Mount Pinatubo volcanic explosion. Begin in southeast Asia, and follow the effects counterclockwise around the map.

Aerosol cloud causes colorful twilight and dawn skies worldwide, and increases atmospheric reflectivity (albedo) by 1.5%.

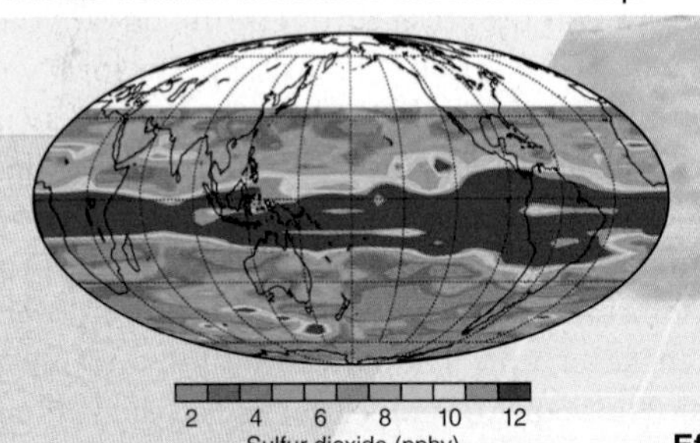

A thin aerosol cloud affects 42% of globe (20° S to 30° N)

Effects on Earth systems: Reduced sunlight at Earth's surface decreases average temperatures in the Northern Hemisphere by 0.5 C° (0.9 F°)

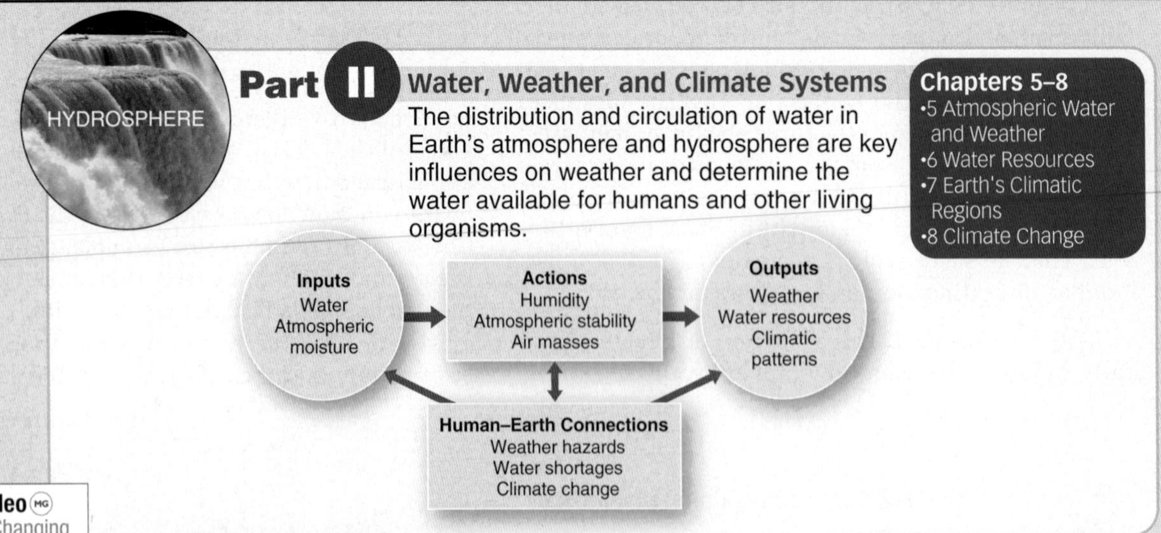

HYDROSPHERE
Part II
Water, Weather, and Climate Systems
The distribution and circulation of water in Earth's atmosphere and hydrosphere are key influences on weather and determine the water available for humans and other living organisms.
Chapters 5–8
•5 Atmospheric Water and Weather
•6 Water Resources
•7 Earth's Climatic Regions
•8 Climate Change
Inputs
Water
Atmospheric moisture
Actions
Humidity
Atmospheric stability
Air masses
Outputs
Weather
Water resources
Climatic patterns
Human–Earth Connections
Weather hazards
Water shortages
Climate change

Video The Changing Face of Earth

http://goo.gl/yevJeg

MasteringGeography™

Visit the Study Area in MasteringGeography™ to explore Earth systems.

Visualize: Study geosciences animations of Earth's radiation balance, the hydrologic cycle, and the rock cycle.

Assess: Demonstrate understanding of Earth-system interactions (if assigned by instructor).

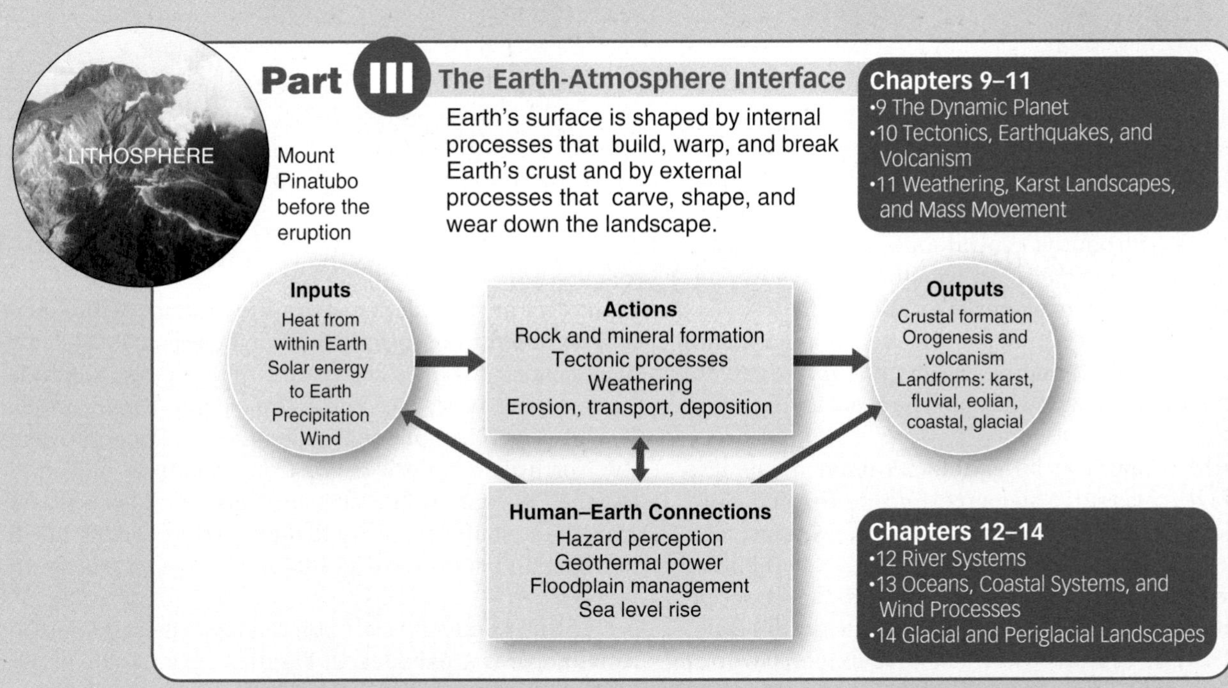

On June 15, 1991, Mount Pinatubo blasted 15–20 million tons of ash and sulfuric acid mist into the atmosphere.

Winds spread the ash cloud westward

15° N 120° E

Mount Pinatubo, a year after the eruption with new lake in the caldera.

Effects on Earth systems: Diffuse sunlight increases, causing a slight enhancement of photosynthesis and plant growth

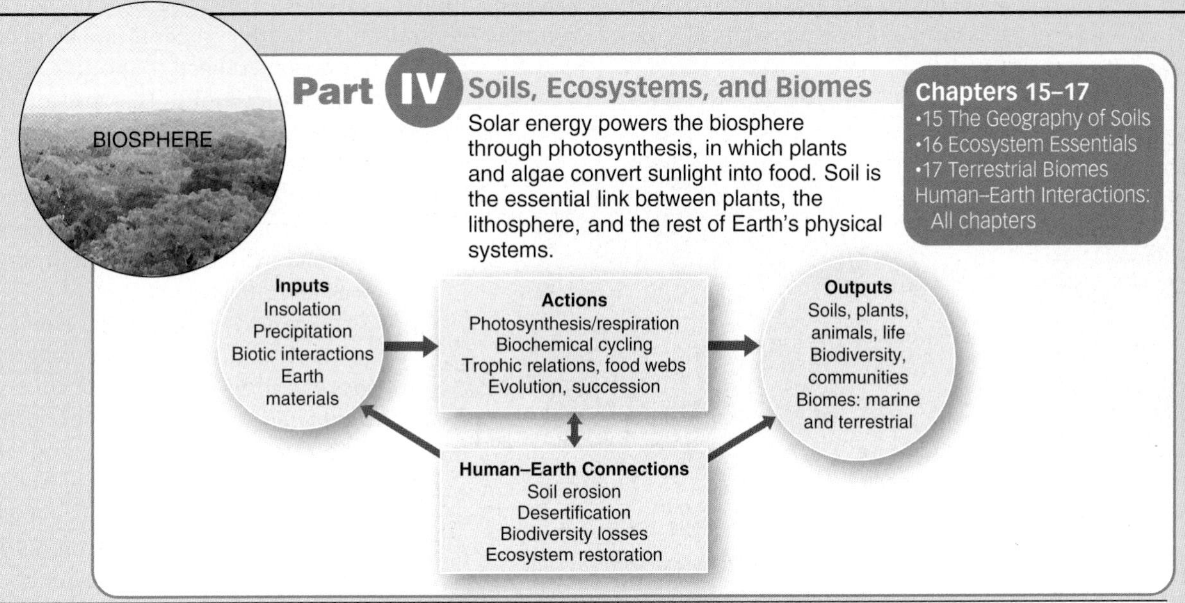

GEOquiz

1. Explain: Which spheres represent Earth's abiotic environment? How are these spheres distinct from one another?

2. Summarize: What were the overall effects of the Mount Pinatubo eruption on Earth's systems?

Earth's shape and size by surveys and mathematical calculations. But in that year, Sir Isaac Newton postulated that Earth, along with the other planets, could not be perfectly spherical. Newton reasoned that the more rapid rotational speed at the equator—the part of the planet farthest from the central axis and therefore the fastest moving—produces an equatorial bulge as centrifugal force pulls Earth's surface outward. He was convinced that Earth is slightly misshapen into an *oblate spheroid*, or, more correctly, an *oblate ellipsoid* (*oblate* means "flattened"), with the oblateness occurring at the poles.

Earth's equatorial bulge and its polar oblateness are today universally accepted and confirmed with tremendous precision by satellite observations. The unique, irregular shape of Earth's surface, coinciding with mean sea level and perpendicular to the direction of gravity, is described as a **geoid**. Imagine Earth's geoid as a constant sea-level surface that extends worldwide, beneath the continents. Both heights on land and depths in the oceans measure from this hypothetical surface. Think of the geoid surface as a balance among the gravitational attraction of Earth's mass, the distribution of water and ice upon its surface, and the outward centrifugal pull caused by Earth's rotation. **Figure 1.9** gives Earth's polar and equatorial circumferences and diameters.

To determine location on our not-quite-spherical planet, we use a coordinated grid system that is internationally accepted. The terms *latitude* and *longitude* for the lines of this grid were in use on maps as early as the first century A.D., with the concepts themselves dating to earlier times.

The geographer, astronomer, and mathematician Ptolemy (ca. A.D. 90–168) contributed greatly to the development of modern maps, and many of his terms are still used today. Ptolemy divided the circle into 360 degrees (360°), with each degree having 60 minutes (60′) and each minute having 60 seconds (60″) in a manner adapted from the ancient Babylonians. He located places using these degrees, minutes, and seconds. However, the precise length of a degree of latitude and a degree of longitude remained unresolved for the next 17 centuries.

Latitude

Latitude is an angular distance north or south of the equator, measured from the center of Earth (**Figure 1.10a**). On a map or globe, the lines designating these angles of latitude run east and west, parallel to the equator (**Figure 1.10b**). Because Earth's equator divides the distance between the North Pole and the South Pole exactly in half, it is assigned the value of 0° latitude. Thus, latitude increases from the equator northward to the North Pole, at 90° north latitude, and southward to the South Pole, at 90° south latitude.

A line connecting all points along the same latitudinal angle is a **parallel**. In Figure 1.10, an angle of 49° north latitude is measured, and, by connecting all points at this latitude, we have the 49th parallel. Thus, *latitude* is the name of the angle (49° north latitude), *parallel* names the line (49th parallel), and both indicate distance north of the equator.

To pinpoint location more precisely, we divide degrees into 60 minutes and minutes into 60 seconds. For example, Mount Cook, South Island, New Zealand, in Figure 1.1 sits at 43 degrees, 35 minutes, 42 seconds (43° 35′ 42″) south latitude. Alternatively, many geographic information systems and Earth visualization programs such as Google Earth™ use decimal notation for latitude and longitude degrees (an online conversion is at http://www.csgnetwork.com/gpscoordconv.html). In decimal units, Mount Cook is at −43.5950° latitude—the negative sign is for south latitude; a positive sign indicates north latitude.

"Lower latitudes" are those nearer the equator, whereas "higher latitudes" are those nearer the poles. You may be familiar with other general names describing regions related to latitude, such as "the tropics" and "the Arctic." Such terms refer to natural environments that differ dramatically from the equator to the poles. These differences result from the amount of solar energy received, which varies by latitude and season of the year.

Figure 1.11 displays the names and locations of the *latitudinal geographic zones* used by geographers: *equatorial* and *tropical*, *subtropical*, *midlatitude*, *subarctic* or *subantarctic*, and *arctic* or *antarctic*. These generalized latitudinal zones are useful for reference and comparison, but they do not have rigid boundaries; rather, think of them as transitioning one to another. We discuss specific lines of latitude, such as

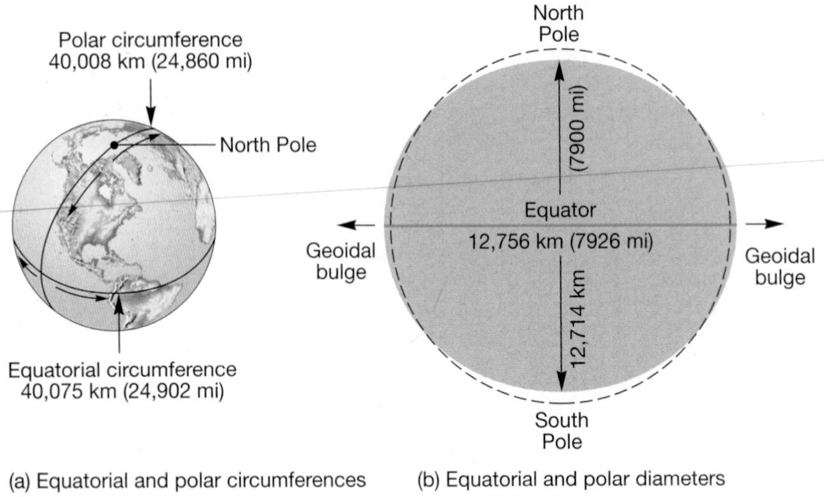

▲**Figure 1.9 Earth's dimensions.** The dashed line is a perfect circle for comparison to Earth's geoid.

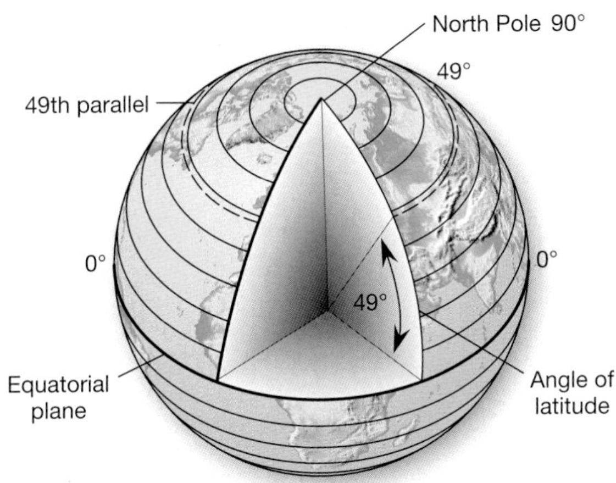

(a) Latitude is measured in degrees north or south of the Equator (0°). Earth's poles are at 90°. Note the measurement of 49° latitude.

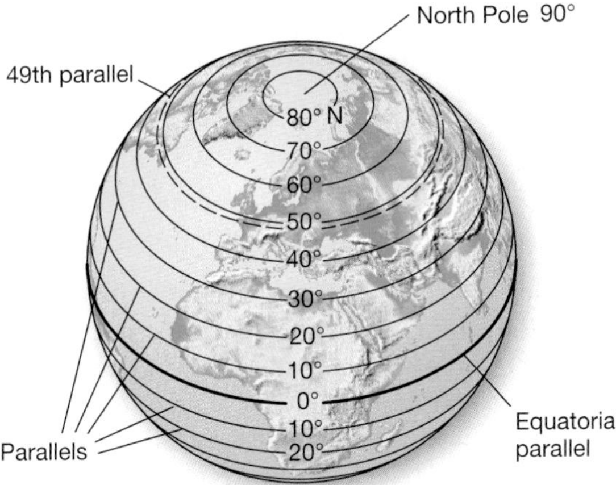

(b) These angles of latitude determine parallels along Earth's surface.

▲**Figure 1.10 Parallels of latitude.** Do you know your present latitude?

the Tropic of Cancer and the Arctic Circle, in Chapter 2 as we learn about the seasons.

Longitude

Longitude is an angular distance east or west of a point on Earth's surface, measured from the center of Earth (**Figure 1.12a**). On a map or globe, the lines designating these angles of longitude run north and south (**Figure 1.12b**). A line connecting all points along the same longitude is a **meridian**. In the figure, a longitudinal angle of 60° E is measured. These meridians run at right angles (90°) to all parallels, including the equator.

Thus, *longitude* is the name of the angle, *meridian* names the line, and both indicate distance east or west of an arbitrary **prime meridian**—a meridian designated as 0° (Figure 1.12b). Earth's prime meridian passes through the old Royal Observatory at Greenwich, England, as set by an 1884 treaty; this is the *Greenwich prime meridian.* Because meridians of longitude converge toward the poles, the actual distance on the ground spanned by

CRITICAL**thinking** 1.2

Latitudinal Geographic Zones and Temperature

Refer to the graph in Figure 3.14, which plots annual temperature data for five cities from near the equator to beyond the Arctic Circle. Note the geographic location for each of the five cities on the latitudinal geographic zone map in Figure 1.11. In which zone is each city located? Roughly characterize changing temperature patterns through the seasons as you move away from the equator. Describe what you discover.

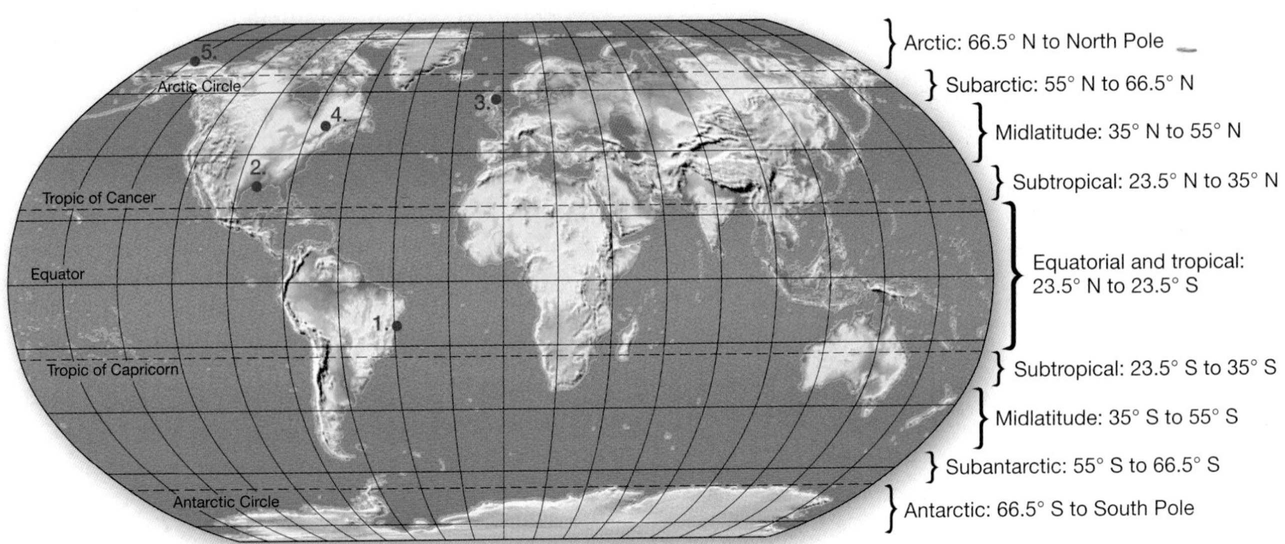

▲**Figure 1.11 Latitudinal geographic zones.** Geographic zones are generalizations that characterize various regions by latitude. Numbered cities (see Critical Thinking 1.2): 1. Salvador, Brazil; 2. New Orleans, Louisiana; 3. Edinburgh, Scotland; 4. Montreal, Quebec; 5. Barrow, Alaska.

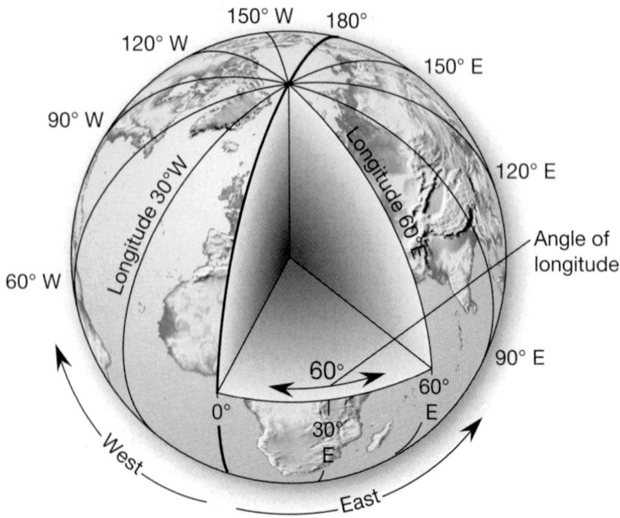

(a) Longitude is measured in degrees east or west of a 0° starting line, the prime meridian. Note the measurement of 60° E longitude.

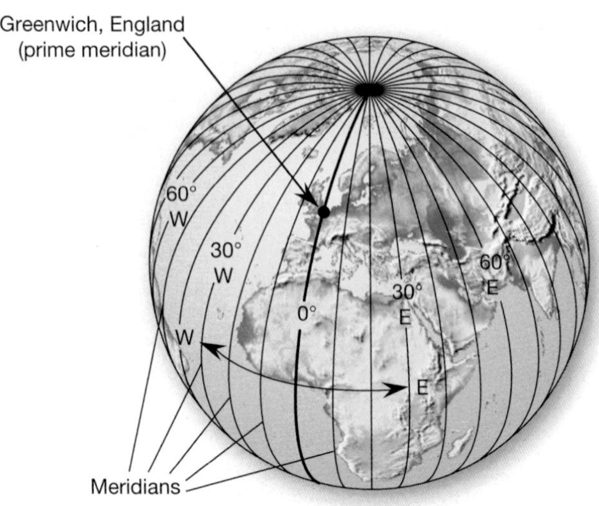

(b) Angles of longitude measured from the prime meridian determine other meridians. North America is west of Greenwich; therefore, it is in the Western Hemisphere.

▲**Figure 1.12 Meridians of longitude.** Do you know your present longitude?

a degree of longitude is greatest at the equator (where meridians separate to their widest distance apart) and diminishes to zero at the poles (where meridians converge). As with latitude, longitude is expressed in degrees, minutes, and seconds or in decimal degrees. Mount Cook in Figure 1.1 is located at 170° 8′ 32″ east longitude, or +170.1421°; east longitude has a positive decimal value, while west longitude is negative.

Figure 1.13 combines latitude and parallels with longitude and meridians to illustrate Earth's complete coordinate grid system. Note the red dot that marks 49° N and 60° E, a location in western Kazakhstan. Next time you look at a world globe, follow the parallel and meridian that converge on your location.

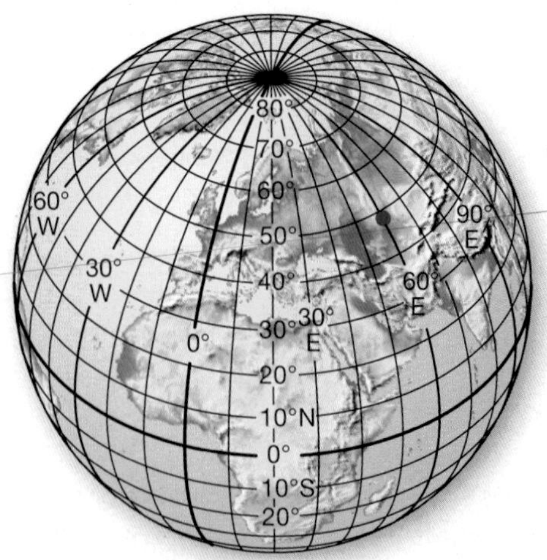

▲**Figure 1.13 Earth's coordinate grid system.** Latitude and parallels and longitude and meridians allow us to locate all places on Earth precisely. The red dot is at 49° N latitude and 60° E longitude.

Great Circles and Small Circles

Great circles and small circles are important navigational concepts that help summarize latitude and longitude (**Figure 1.14**). A **great circle** is any circle of Earth's circumference whose center coincides with the center of Earth. An infinite number of great circles can be drawn on Earth. Every meridian is one-half of a great circle that passes through the poles. On flat maps, airline and shipping routes appear to arch their way across oceans and landmasses. These are *great circle routes*, tracing the shortest distances between two points on Earth (see Figure 1.20).

In contrast to meridians, only one parallel is a great circle—the *equatorial parallel*. All other parallels diminish in length toward the poles and, along with any other non–great circles that one might draw, constitute **small circles**. These circles have centers that do not coincide with Earth's center.

Meridians and Global Time

A worldwide time system is necessary to coordinate international trade, airline schedules, business and agricultural activities, and daily life. Our time system

CRITICAL**thinking** 1.3

Where Are You?

Select a location (for example, your campus, home, or workplace or a city) and determine its latitude and longitude—both in degrees, minutes, and seconds and as decimal degrees. Describe the resources you used to gather this geographic information, such as an atlas, website, Google Earth™, or GPS measurement.

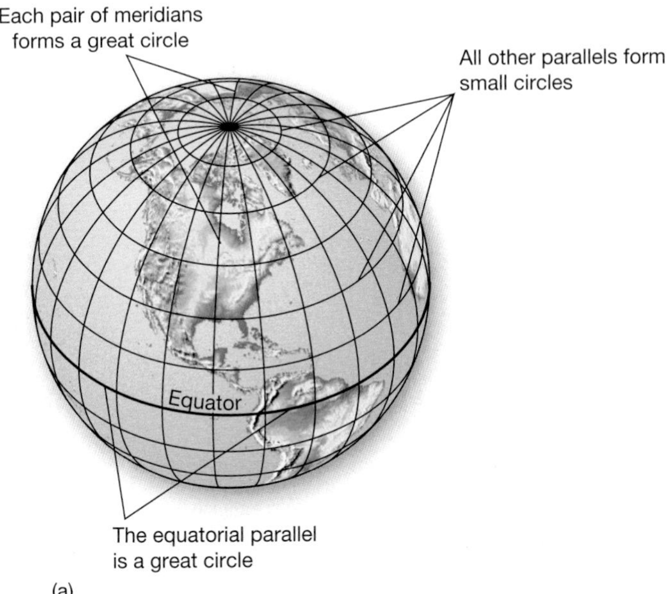

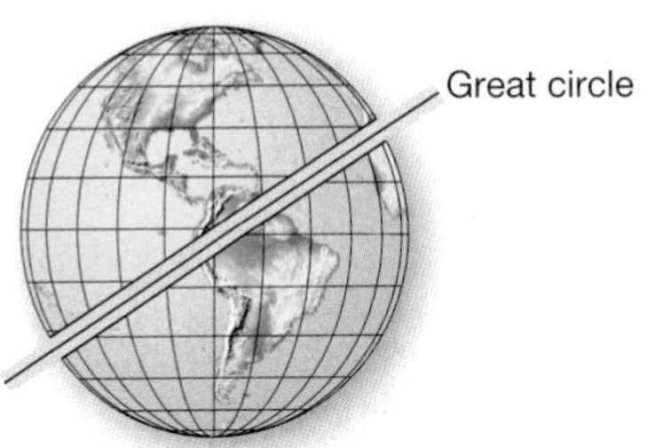

(b) A plane intersecting the globe along a great circle divides the globe into equal halves and passes through its center.

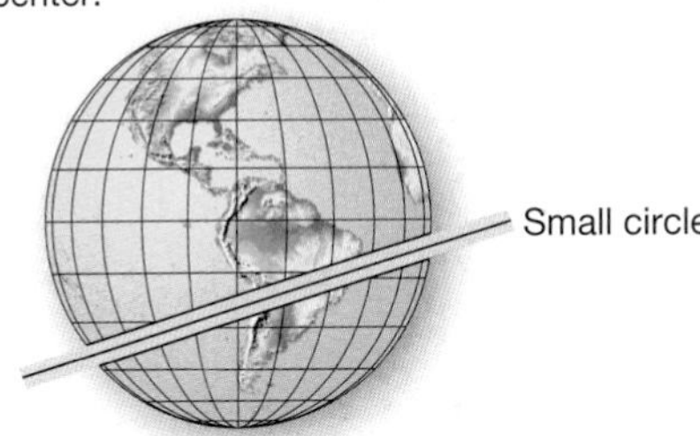

(c) A plane that intersects the globe along a small circle splits the globe into unequal sections—this plane does not pass through the center of the globe.

▲**Figure 1.14 Great circles and small circles.**

is based on longitude, the prime meridian, and the fact that Earth rotates on its own axis, revolving 360° every 24 hours, or 15° per hour (360° ÷ 24 = 15°).

In 1884 at the International Meridian Conference in Washington, DC, a prime meridian was set as the official standard for the world time zone system—**Greenwich Mean Time (GMT)** (see http://wwp.greenwichmeantime.com/). This standard time system established 24 standard meridians around the globe at equal intervals from the prime meridian, with a time zone of 1 hour spanning 7.5° on either side of each of these *central meridians*. Before this universal system, time zones were problematic, especially in large countries. In 1870, railroad travelers going from Maine to San Francisco made 22 adjustments to their watches to stay consistent with local time! Today, only three adjustments are needed in the continental United States—from Eastern Standard Time to Central, Mountain, and Pacific—and four changes across Canada (**Figure 1.15**).

Using the international time zones in Figure 1.15, you can determine that when it is 9:00 P.M. in Greenwich, then it is 4:00 P.M. in New York (–5 hr), 3:00 P.M. in Chicago (–6 hr), 2:00 P.M. in Denver (–7 hr), 1:00 P.M. in Seattle and Los Angeles (–8 hr), noon in Anchorage (–9 hr), and 11:00 A.M. in Honolulu (–10 hr). To the east, it is midnight in Riyadh, Saudi Arabia (+3 hr). The designation A.M. is for *ante meridiem*, "before noon," whereas P.M. is for *post meridiem*, "after noon." A 24-hour clock avoids the use of these designations: 3 A.M. is 3:00 hours; 3 P.M. is 15:00 hours.

Figure 1.15 also shows that national or state boundaries and political considerations distort time boundaries. For example, China spans four time zones, but its government decided to keep the entire country operating at the same time. Thus, in some parts of China clocks are several hours off from what the Sun is doing. In the United States, parts of Florida and west Texas are in the same time zone.

Coordinated Universal Time For decades, GMT was determined using the Royal Observatory's astronomical clocks and was the world's standard for accuracy. However, Earth rotation, on which those clocks were based, varies slightly over time, making it unreliable as a basis for timekeeping. For example, 150 million years ago, a "day" was 22 hours long, and, 150 million years in the future, a "day" will be approaching 27 hours in length.

The invention of a quartz clock in 1939 and atomic clocks in the early 1950s improved the accuracy of measuring time. In 1972, the **Coordinated Universal Time (UTC)*** time-signal system replaced GMT and became the legal reference for official time in all countries. UTC is based on average time calculations from atomic clocks collected worldwide. You might still see official UTC referred to as GMT or Zulu time.

International Date Line An important corollary of the prime meridian is the 180° meridian on the opposite side of the planet. This meridian is the **International Date Line (IDL)**, which marks the place where each day

*UTC is in use because agreement was not reached on whether to use the English word order, CUT, or the French order, TUC. UTC was the compromise and is recommended for all timekeeping applications; use of the term *GMT* is discouraged.

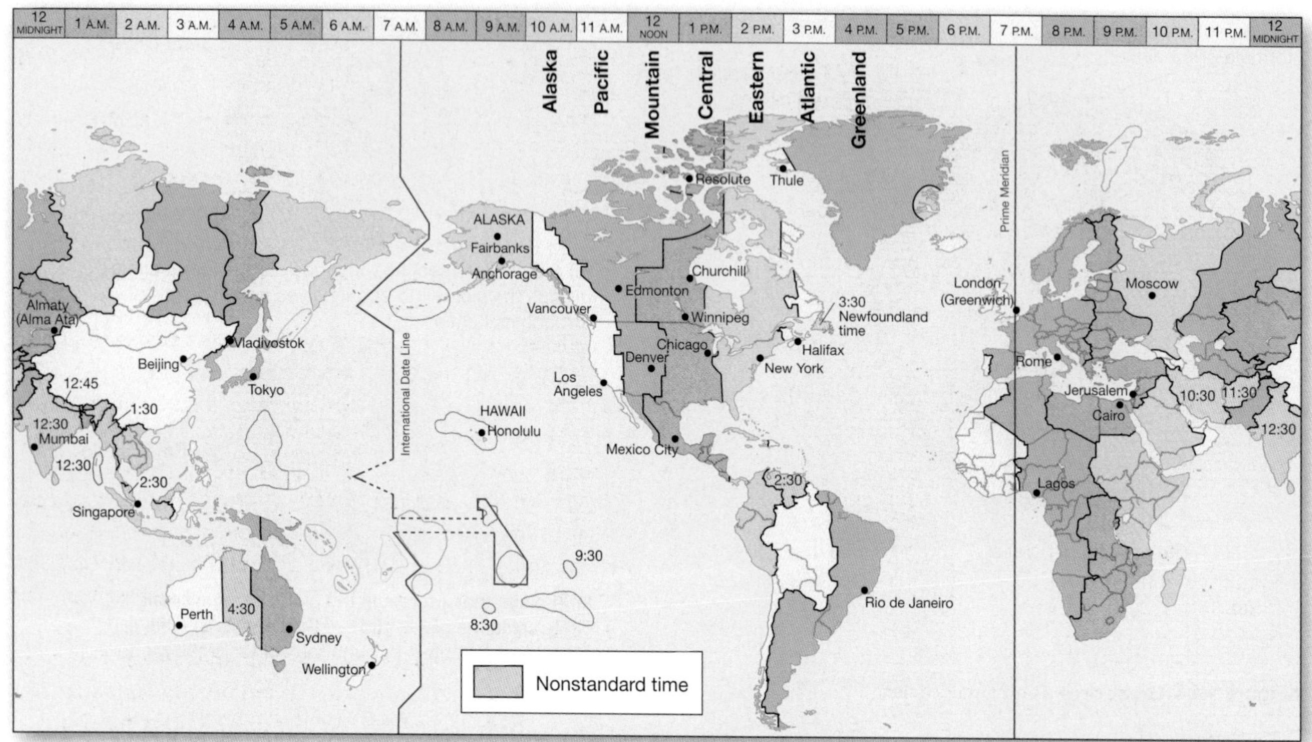

▲**Figure 1.15 Modern international standard time zones.** If it is 7 P.M. in Greenwich, determine the present time in Moscow, London, Halifax, Chicago, Winnipeg, Denver, Los Angeles, Fairbanks, Honolulu, Tokyo, and Singapore. [Adapted from Defense Mapping Agency; see http://aa.usno.navy.mil/faq/docs/world_tzones.html.]

officially begins (at 12:01 A.M.). From this "line," the new day sweeps westward. This *westward* movement of time is created by Earth's turning *eastward* on its axis. Locating the date line in the sparsely populated Pacific Ocean minimizes most local confusion (**Figure 1.16**).

At the IDL, the west side of the line is always one day ahead of the east side. No matter what time of day it is when the line is crossed, the calendar changes a day. Note in the illustration the departures from the IDL and the 180° meridian; this deviation is due to local administrative and political preferences.

Daylight Saving Time In 70 countries, mainly in the temperate latitudes, time is set ahead 1 hour in the spring and set back 1 hour in the fall—a practice known as **daylight saving time**. The idea to extend daylight for early evening activities at the expense of daylight in the morning, first proposed by Benjamin Franklin, was not adopted until World War I and again in World War II, when Great Britain, Australia, Germany, Canada, and the United States used the practice to save energy (1 less hour of artificial lighting needed).

In 1986 and again in 2007, the United States and Canada extended the number of weeks of daylight saving time. Currently, time "springs forward" 1 hour on the second Sunday in March and "falls back" 1 hour on the first Sunday in November, except in a few places that do not use daylight saving time (Hawai'i, Arizona, and Saskatchewan). In Europe, the last Sundays in March and October mark the beginning and ending of the "summer-time period.*"

Maps and Cartography

For centuries, geographers have used maps as tools to display spatial information and analyze spatial relationships. A **map** is a generalized view of an area, usually some portion of Earth's surface, as seen from above and greatly reduced in size. A map usually represents a specific

*see http://webexhibits.org/daylightsaving.

GEOreport 1.3 The world's most accurate clock

The National Institute for Standards and Technology (NIST), U.S. Department of Commerce, operates the world's most accurate clock. The NIST-F1 cesium atomic clock, housed in Boulder, Colorado, will not gain or lose a second in nearly 20 million years. For accurate time in the United States, see http://www.time.gov, operated by NIST and the U.S. Naval Observatory. In Canada, the Institute for Measurement Standards, National Research Council Canada, participates in determining UTC; see http://time5.nrc.ca/webclock_e.shtml.

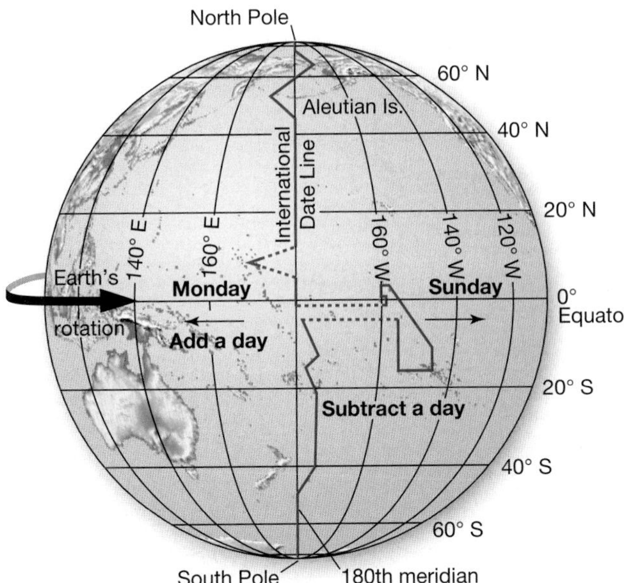

▲**Figure 1.16 International Date Line.** The IDL location is approximately along the 180th meridian (see the IDL location on Figure 1.15). The dotted lines on the map show where island countries have set their own time zones, but their political control extends only 3.5 nautical miles (4 mi) offshore. Officially, you gain one day crossing the IDL from east to west.

characteristic of a place or area, such as rainfall, airline routes, or political features such as state boundaries and place names. **Cartography** is the science and art of mapmaking, often blending aspects of geography, engineering, mathematics, computer science, and art. It is similar in ways to architecture, in which aesthetics and utility combine to produce a useful product.

We all use maps to visualize our location in relation to other places, or maybe to plan a trip, or to understand a news story or current event. Maps are wonderful tools! Understanding a few basics about maps is essential to our study of physical geography.

The Scale of Maps

Architects, toy designers, and mapmakers have something in common: They all represent real things and places with the convenience of a model; examples are a drawing; a pretend car, train, or plane; a diagram; and a map. In most cases, the model is smaller than the reality. For example, an architect renders a blueprint of a structure to guide the building contractors, preparing the drawing so that a centimeter (or inch) on the blueprint represents so many meters (or feet) on the proposed building. Often, the drawing is 1/50 or 1/100 real size.

The cartographer does the same thing in preparing a map. The ratio of the image on a map to the real world is the map's **scale**; it relates the size of a unit on the map to the size of a similar unit on the ground. A 1:1 scale means that any unit (for example, a centimeter) on the map represents that same unit (a centimeter) on the ground, although this is an impractical map scale, since the map is as large as the area mapped! A more appropriate scale for a local map is 1:24,000, in which 1 unit on the map represents 24,000 identical units on the ground.

Cartographers express map scale as a representative fraction, a graphic scale, or a written scale (**Figure 1.17**). A *representative fraction* (*RF*, or *fractional scale*) is expressed with either a colon or a slash, as in 1:125,000 or 1/125,000. No actual units of measurement are mentioned because any unit is applicable as long as both parts of the fraction are in the same unit: 1 cm to 125,000 cm, 1 in. to 125,000 in., or even 1 arm length to 125,000 arm lengths.

A *graphic scale*, or *bar scale*, is a bar graph with units to allow measurement of distances on the map. An important advantage of a graphic scale is that, if the map is enlarged or reduced, the graphic scale enlarges or reduces along with the map. In contrast, written and fractional scales become incorrect with enlargement or reduction. As an example, if you shrink a map from 1:24,000 to 1:63,360, the written scale "1 in. to 2000 ft" is no longer correct. The new correct written scale is "1 in. to 5280 ft (1 mi)."

Scales are *small* or *large*, depending on the ratio described. In relative terms, a scale of 1:24,000 is a large scale, whereas a scale of 1:50,000,000 is a small scale. The greater the denominator in a fractional scale (or the number on the right in a ratio expression), the smaller the scale of the map. Small-scale maps show a greater area in less detail; a small-scale map of the world is little help in finding an exact location, but works well for illustrating global wind patterns or ocean currents. Large-scale maps show a smaller area in more detail and are useful for applications needing precise location or navigation over short distances.

Map Projections

A globe is not always a helpful map representation of Earth. When you go on a trip, you need more-detailed information than a globe can provide. To provide local

CRITICAL**thinking** 1.4

Find and Calculate Map Scales

Find globes or maps in the library or geography department, and check the scales at which they were drawn. See if you can find examples of fractional, graphic, and written scales on wall maps, on highway maps, and in atlases. Find some examples of small- and large-scale maps, and note the different subject matter they portray.

Look at a world globe that is 61 cm (24 in.) in diameter (or adapt the following values to whatever globe you are using). We know that Earth has an equatorial diameter of 12,756 km (7926 mi), so the scale of such a globe is the ratio of 61 cm to 12,756 km. To calculate the representative fraction for the globe in centimeters, divide Earth's actual diameter by the globe's diameter (12,756 km ÷ 61 cm). (*Hint:* 1 km = 1000 m, and 1 m = 100 cm; therefore, Earth's diameter of 12,756 km represents 1,275,600,000 cm, and the globe's diameter is 61 cm.) In general, do you think a world globe is a small- or a large-scale map of Earth's surface?

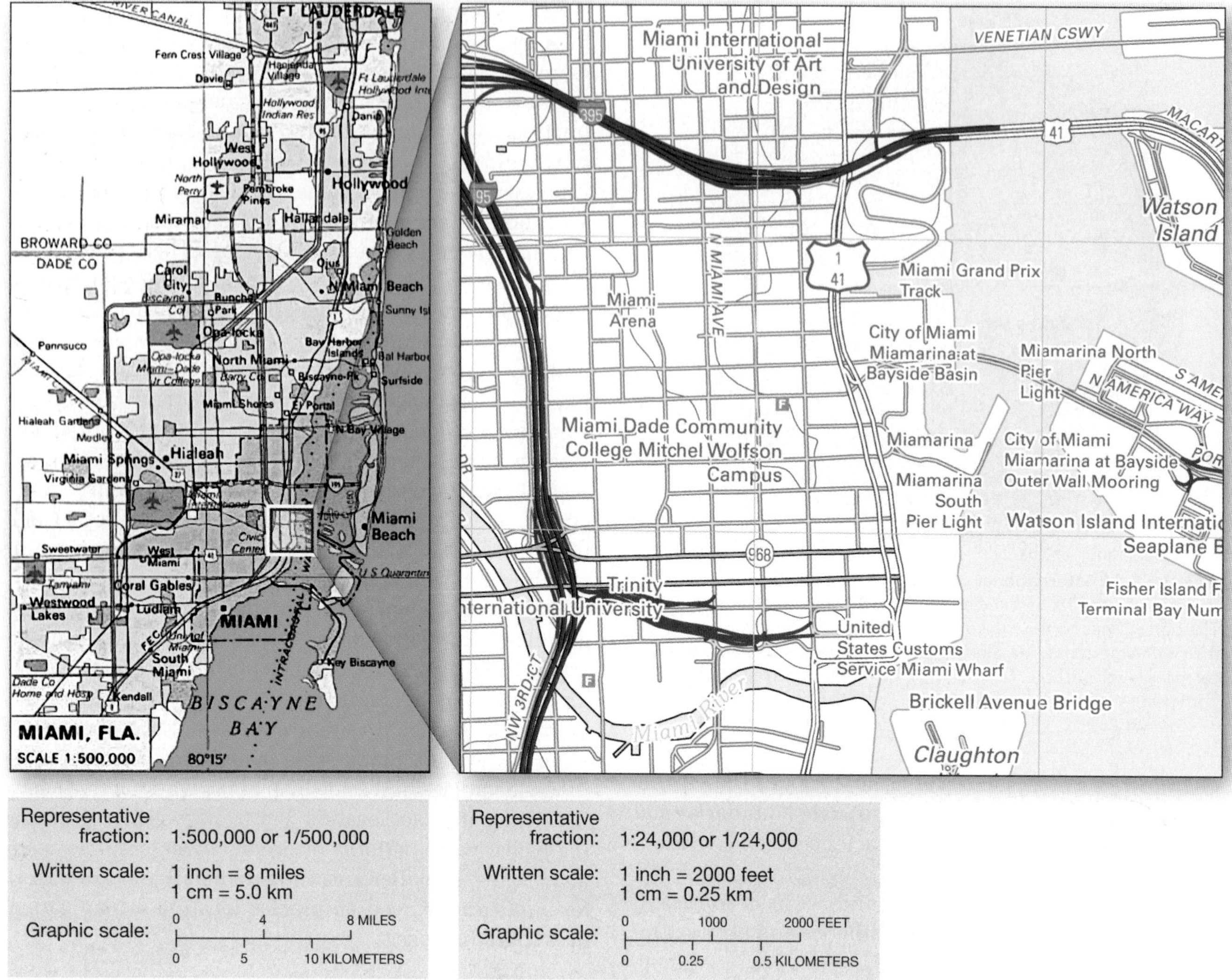

(a) Relatively small scale map of Miami area shows less detail.

(b) Relatively large scale map of the same area shows a higher level of detail.

▲Figure 1.17 Map scale. Examples of maps at different scales, with three common expressions of map scale—representative fraction, written scale, and graphic scale. Both maps are enlarged, so only the graphic scale is accurate. [USGS. Courtesy of University of Texas Libraries, University of Texas at Austin.]

detail, cartographers prepare large-scale *flat maps*, which are two-dimensional representations (scale models) of our three-dimensional Earth. Unfortunately, such conversion from three dimensions to two causes distortion.

A globe can provide a fairly good representation of *distance, direction, area, shape,* and *proximity* on Earth. A flat map distorts these properties. Therefore, in preparing a flat map, the cartographer must decide which characteristics to preserve, which to distort, and how much distortion is acceptable. To understand this problem, consider these important properties of a globe:

- Parallels always are parallel to each other, always are evenly spaced along meridians, and always decrease in length toward the poles.
- Meridians always converge at both poles and always are evenly spaced along any individual parallel.
- The distance between meridians decreases toward the poles, with the spacing between meridians at the 60th parallel equal to one-half the equatorial spacing.
- Parallels and meridians always cross each other at right angles.

The problem is that all these qualities cannot be reproduced simultaneously on a flat surface. Simply taking a globe apart and laying it flat on a table illustrates the challenge faced by cartographers (**Figure 1.18**). You can see the empty spaces that open up between the sections, or gores, of the globe. This reduction of the spherical Earth to a flat surface is a **map projection**, and no flat map projection of Earth can ever have all the features of a globe. Flat maps always possess some degree of distortion—much less for large-scale maps representing a few kilometers; much more for small-scale maps covering individual countries, continents, or the entire world.

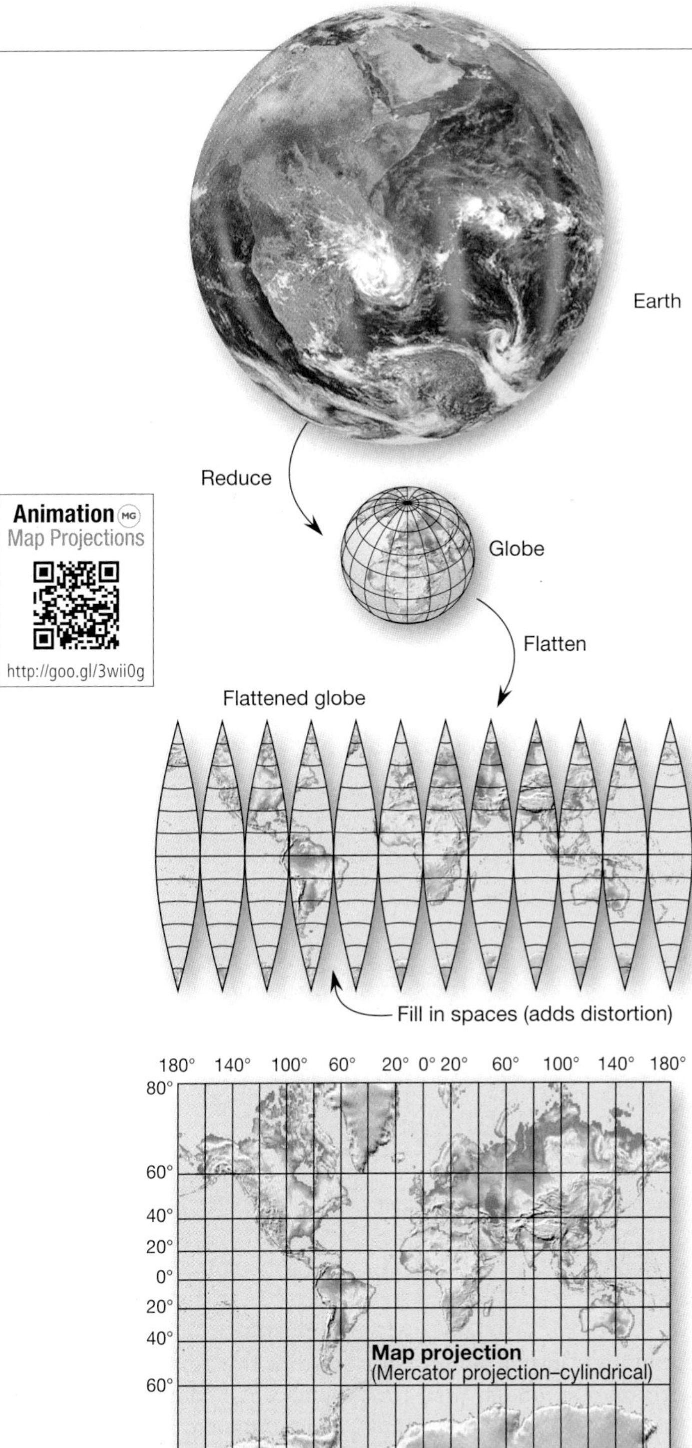

▲**Figure 1.18 From globe to flat map.** Conversion of the globe to a flat map projection requires a decision about which properties to preserve and the amount of distortion that is acceptable. [NASA/NOAA/GSFC/Suomi NPP/VIIRS/Norman Kuring.]

Equal Area or True Shape? The best map projection is always determined by the intended use of the map. The major decisions in selecting a map projection involve the properties of **equal area** (equivalence) and **true shape** (conformality). A decision favoring one property sacrifices the other, for they cannot be shown together on the same flat map.

If a cartographer selects equal area as the desired trait—for example, for a map showing the distribution of world climates—then true shape must be sacrificed by stretching and shearing, which allow parallels and meridians to cross at other than right angles. On an equal-area map, a coin covers the same amount of surface area no matter where you place it on the map. In contrast, if a cartographer selects the property of true shape, such as for a map used for navigational purposes, then equal area must be sacrificed, and the scale will actually change from one region of the map to another.

Classes of Projections Figure 1.19 illustrates four classes of map projections and the perspective from which each class is generated. Despite the fact that modern cartographic technology uses mathematical constructions and computer-assisted graphics, we still use the word *projection*. The term comes from times past, when geographers actually projected the shadow of a wire-skeleton globe onto a geometric surface, such as a *cylinder*, *plane*, or *cone*. The wires represented parallels, meridians, and outlines of the continents. A light source casts a shadow pattern of these lines from the globe onto the chosen geometric surface.

The main map projection classes include the cylindrical, planar (also called azimuthal), and conic. Another class of projections, which cannot be derived from this physical-perspective approach, is the nonperspective oval shape. Still other projections derive from purely mathematical calculations.

With projections, the contact line or contact point between the wire globe and the projection surface—a *standard line* or *standard point*—is the only place where all globe properties are preserved. Thus, a *standard parallel* or *standard meridian* is a standard line true to scale along its entire length without any distortion. Areas away from this critical tangent line or point become increasingly distorted. Consequently, this line or point of accurate spatial properties should be centered by the cartographer on the area of interest.

The commonly used **Mercator projection** (invented by Gerardus Mercator in 1569) is a cylindrical projection (Figure 1.19a). The Mercator is a conformal projection, with meridians appearing as equally spaced straight lines and parallels appearing as straight lines that are spaced closer together near the equator. The poles are infinitely stretched, with the 84th N parallel and 84th S parallel fixed at the same length as that of the equator. Note in Figures 1.18 and 1.19a that the Mercator projection is cut off near the 80th parallel in each hemisphere because of the severe distortion at higher latitudes.

Unfortunately, Mercator classroom maps present false notions of the size (area) of midlatitude and poleward landmasses. A dramatic example on the Mercator projection is Greenland, which looks bigger than all of South America. In reality, Greenland is an island only one-eighth the size of South America and is actually 20% smaller than Argentina alone.

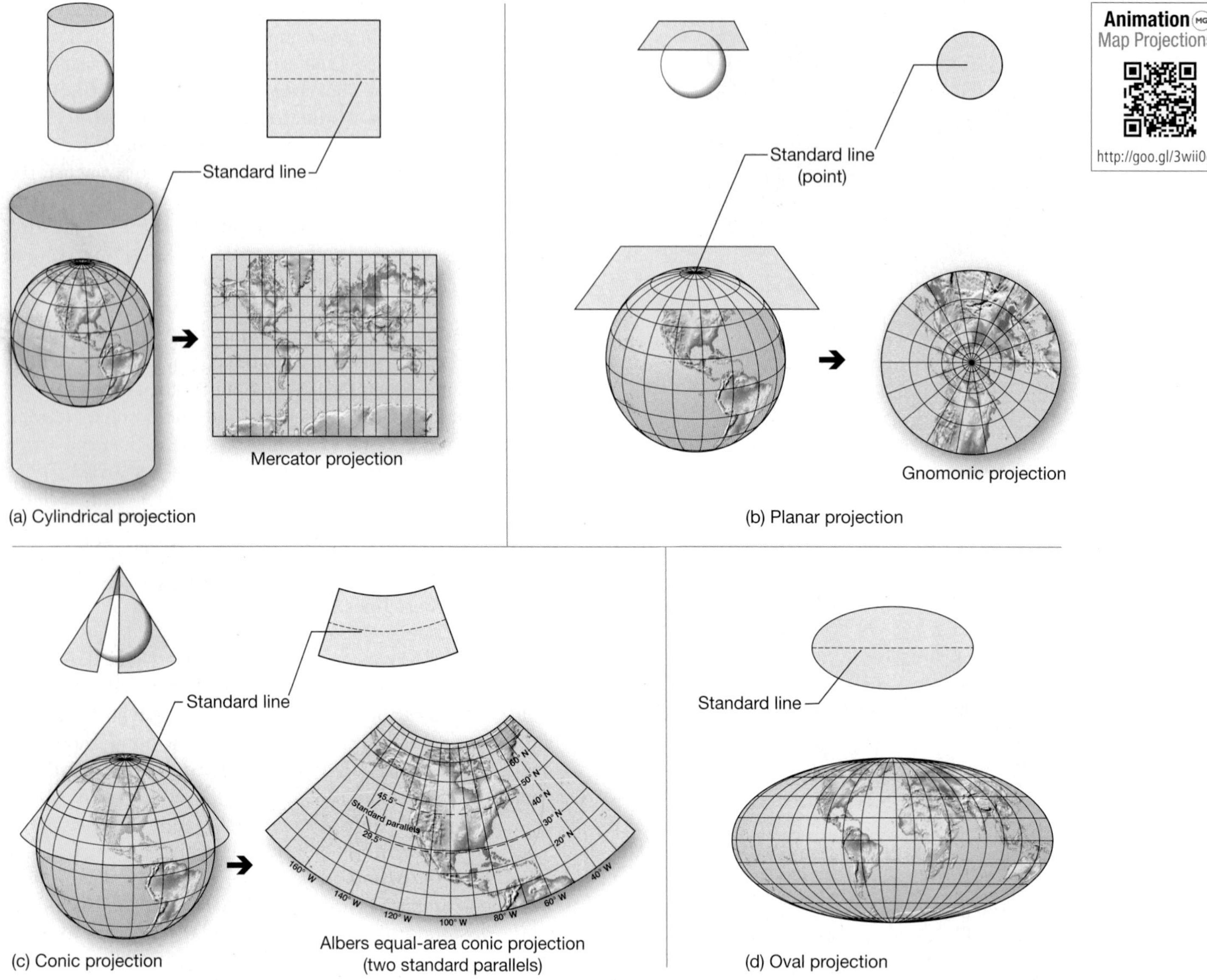

▲**Figure 1.19 Classes of map projections.**

The advantage of the Mercator projection is that a line of constant direction, known as a **rhumb line**, is straight and therefore facilitates plotting directions between two points (**Figure 1.20**). Thus, the Mercator projection is useful in navigation and is standard for nautical charts prepared by the National Ocean Service.

The *gnomonic projection* in Figure 1.19b is a type of planar (azimuthal) projection generated by projecting a light source at the center of a globe onto a plane that is tangent to (touching) the globe's surface. The resulting severe distortion prevents showing a full hemisphere on one projection. However, a valuable feature is derived: All great circle routes, which are the shortest distance between two points on Earth's surface, are projected as straight lines (Figure 1.20a). The great circle routes plotted on a gnomonic projection then can be transferred to a true-direction projection, such as the Mercator, for determination of precise compass headings (Figure 1.20b).

For more information on maps used in this text and standard map symbols, turn to Appendix A, "Maps in This Text and Topographic Maps." Scientists use topographic maps for landscape analysis, since such maps add a vertical component to the landscape. Travelers and others using the outdoors use these maps for navigation. The U.S. Geological Survey (USGS) *National Map* (available at http://nationalmap.gov/) provides downloadable digital topographic data for the entire United States.

Modern Tools and Techniques for Geoscience

Geographers and Earth scientists analyze and map Earth using a number of relatively recent and evolving technologies—the Global Positioning System (GPS), remote

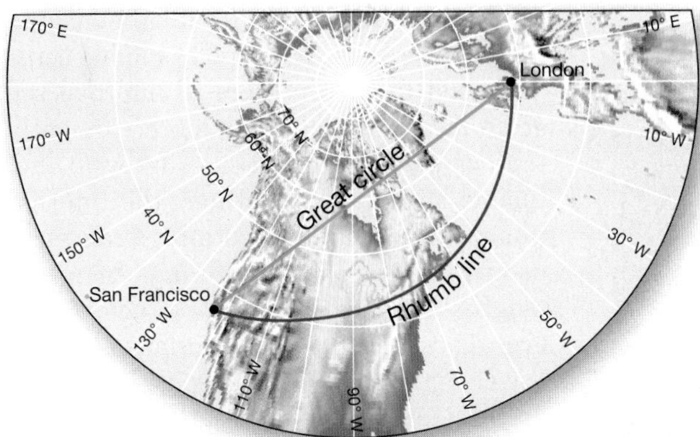

(a) The gnomonic projection is used to determine the shortest distance (great circle route) between San Francisco and London because on this projection the arc of a great circle is a straight line.

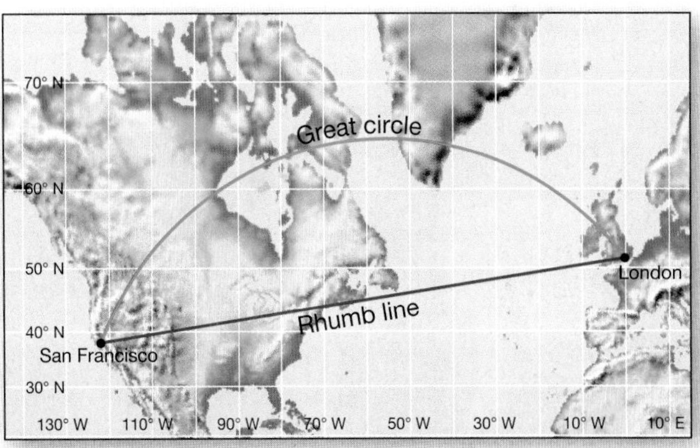

(b) The great circle route is then plotted on a Mercator projection, which has true compass direction. Note that straight lines or bearings on a Mercator projection (rhumb lines) are not the shortest route.

▲**Figure 1.20 Determining great circle routes.**

sensing, and geographic information systems (GIS). GPS relies on satellites in orbit to provide precise location and elevation. Remote sensing utilizes spacecraft, aircraft, and ground-based sensors to provide visual data that enhance our understanding of Earth. GIS is a means for storing and processing large amounts of spatial data as separate layers of geographic information; geographic information science is the geographic subfield that uses this technique.

Global Positioning System

The **Global Positioning System (GPS)** uses radio signals from satellites to accurately determine latitude, longitude, and elevation anywhere on or near the surface of Earth. The system comprises at least 27 orbiting satellites, in six orbital planes, that transmit navigational signals to Earth-bound receivers (backup GPS satellites are in orbital storage as replacements). Think of the satellites as a constellation of navigational beacons with which you can interact to determine your unique location. As we know, every possible square meter of Earth's surface has its own address relative to the latitude–longitude grid.

A GPS receiver senses signals from at least four satellites—a minimum of three satellites for location and a fourth to determine accurate elevation. The distance between each satellite and the GPS receiver is calculated using clocks built into each instrument that time radio signals traveling at the speed of light between them (**Figure 1.21**). The receiver calculates its true position—latitude, longitude, and elevation—using trilateration (determining a position using the distance from three known points). GPS units also report accurate time to within 100 billionths of a second. This allows GPS base stations to have perfectly synchronized timing, essential to worldwide communication, finance, and many industries.

GPS receivers are built into many smartphones, wristwatches, and motor vehicles and can be bought as

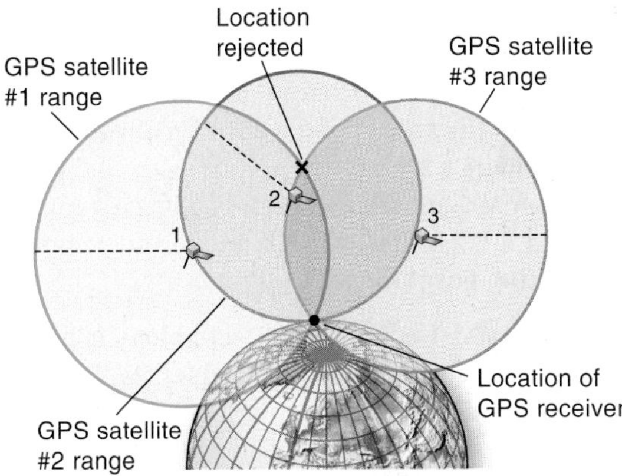

▲**Figure 1.21 Using satellites to determine location through GPS.** Imagine a ranging sphere around each of three GPS satellites. These spheres intersect at two points, one easily rejected because it is some distance above Earth and the other at the true location of the GPS receiver. In this way, signals from three satellites can reveal the receiver's location; adding a fourth satellite determines elevation.

handheld units. Standard cell phones not equipped with a GPS receiver determine location based on the position of cell phone towers—a process not as accurate as GPS measurement.

The GPS is useful for diverse applications. For example, commercial airlines use the GPS to improve accuracy of routes flown and thus increase fuel efficiency. Scientific applications of GPS technology are extensive. Consider these examples:

- In geodesy, GPS helps refine knowledge of Earth's exact shape and how this shape is changing.
- Scientists used GPS technology in 1998 to accurately determine the height of Mount Everest in the Himalayan Mountains, raising its elevation by 2 m (6 ft).
- On Mount St. Helens in Washington, a network of GPS stations measure ground deformation associated with earthquake activity. In southern California, a similar

(a) Students deploy a "drifter" (with GPS unit attached to the top of the mast) in the Gulf of Mexico in 2010.

▼**Figure 1.22 GPS application in the Gulf of Mexico.** [(a) Monty Graham, Dauphin Island Sea Lab. (b) NOAA.]

(b) Movement of the drifters with surface currents helped scientists track and predict the movement of oil.

GPS system can record fault movement as small as 1 mm (0.04 in.).

- GPS units attached to buoys in the Gulf of Mexico helped track the spread of the 2010 *Deepwater Horizon* oil spill (**Figure 1.22**).
- In Virunga National Park, Rwanda, Africa, rangers use handheld GPS units to track and protect mountain gorillas from poaching.

For scientists, this important technology is both convenient and precise, reducing the need for traditional land surveys that require point-to-point line-of-sight measurements on the ground. In your daily life and travels, have you ever used a GPS unit? How did GPS assist you?

Remote Sensing

The acquisition of information about distant objects without having physical contact is **remote sensing**. In this era of observations from satellites outside the atmosphere, from aircraft within it, and from remote submersibles in the oceans, scientists obtain a wide array of remotely sensed data (**Figure 1.23**). Remote sensing is nothing new to humans; we do it with our eyes as we scan the environment, sensing the shape, size, and color of objects from a distance by registering energy from the visible-wavelength portion of the electromagnetic spectrum (discussed in Chapter 2). Similarly, when a camera intercepts the wavelengths for which its film or sensor is designed, it remotely senses energy that is reflected or emitted from a scene.

Aerial photographs from balloons and aircraft were the first type of remote sensing, used for many years to improve the accuracy of surface maps more efficiently than can be done by on-site surveys. Later, remote sensors on satellites, the International Space Station, and other craft were used to sense a broader range of wavelengths beyond the visible range of our eyes. These sensors can be designed to "see" wavelengths shorter than visible light (such as ultraviolet) and wavelengths longer than visible light (such as infrared and microwave radar). As examples, infrared sensing produces images based on the temperature of objects on the ground, microwave sensing reveals features below Earth's surface, and radar sensing shows land-surface elevations, even in areas that are obscured by clouds.

Satellite Imaging During the last 50 years, satellite remote sensing has transformed Earth observation. Physical elements of Earth's surface emit radiant energy in wavelengths that are sensed by satellites and other craft and sent to receiving stations on the ground. The receiving stations sort these wavelengths into specific bands, or ranges. A scene is scanned and broken down into pixels (*pic*ture *el*ements), each identified by coordinates named *lines* (horizontal rows) and *samples* (vertical columns). For example, a grid of 6000 lines and 7000 samples forms 42,000,000 pixels, providing a detailed image when the pixels are matched to the wavelengths they emit.

A single remotely sensed image requires a large amount of data, which are recorded in digital form for later processing, enhancement, and image generation. Digital data are processed in many ways to enhance their utility: with simulated natural color, "false" color to highlight a particular feature, enhanced contrast, signal filtering, and different levels of sampling and resolution.

Satellites can be set in specific orbital paths (**Figure 1.24**) that affect the type of data and imagery produced. Geostationary (or geosynchronous) orbits, typically at an altitude of 35,790 km (22,239 mi), are *high Earth orbits* that effectively match Earth's rotation speed so that one orbit is completed in about 24 hours. Satellites can therefore remain "parked" above a specific location, usually the equator (Figure 1.24a). This "fixed" position means that satellite antennas on Earth can be pointed permanently at one position in the sky where the satellite is located;

GEOreport 1.4 GPS origins

The GPS devices commercially available worldwide were originally devised in the 1970s by the U.S. Department of Defense for military purposes. In 2000, the Pentagon shut down its Pentagon Selective Availability security control, making commercial resolution the same as military applications. Additional frequencies were added in 2003 and 2006, which increased accuracy significantly, to less than 10 m (33 ft). *Differential GPS (DGPS)* achieves accuracy of 1 to 3 m by comparing readings with another base station (reference receiver) for a differential correction. For a GPS overview, see http://www.gps.gov/.

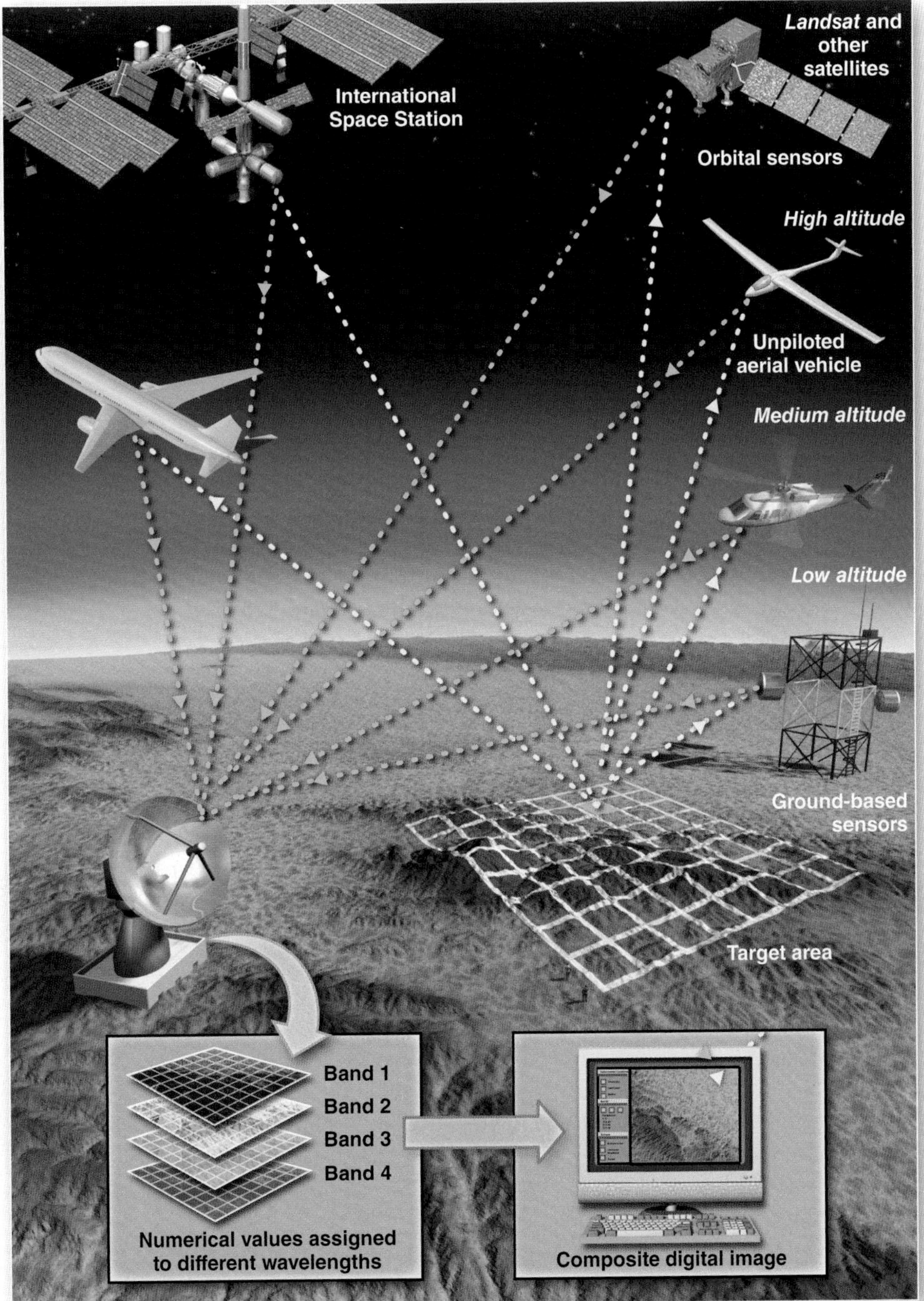

A sample of orbital platforms:

CloudSat: Studies cloud extent, distribution, radiative properties, and structure.

ENVISAT: ESA environment-monitoring satellite; 10 sensors, including next generation radar.

GOES: Weather-monitoring and forecasting; *GOES-12*, *-13*, *-14*, and *-15*.

GRACE: Accurately maps Earth's gravitational field.

JASON-1, -2: Measure sea-level heights.

Landsat: *Landsat-1* in 1972 to *Landsat-7* in 1999 and *Landsat-8* in 2013; have provided millions of images for Earth systems science and study of global change.

NOAA: First in 1978 through *NOAA-15*, *-16*, *-17*, *-18*, and *-19* now in operation; global data gathering, short- and long-term weather forecasts.

RADARSAT-1, -2: Synthetic Aperture Radar in near-polar orbit, operated by Canadian Space Agency.

SciSat-1: Analyzes trace gases, thin clouds, atmospheric aerosols with Arctic focus.

SeaStar: Carries the *SeaWiFS* (Sea-Viewing Wide Field-of-View Sensor) to observe Earth's oceans and microscopic marine plants.

***Terra* and *Aqua*:** Environmental change, error-free surface images, cloud properties, through five instrument packages.

TOMS-EP: Total Ozone Mapping Spectrometer, monitoring stratospheric ozone; similar instruments on *NIMBUS-7* and *Meteor-3*.

***TOPEX-POSEIDON*:** Measures sea-level heights.

***TRMM*:** Tropical Rainfall Measuring Mission, includes lightning detection and global energy budget measurements.

For more information, see: http://www.nasa.gov/centers/goddard/missions/index.html

▲**Figure 1.23 Remote-sensing technology.** Remote-sensing technology measures and monitors Earth's systems from orbiting spacecraft, aircraft, and ground-based sensors. Various wavelengths (bands) are detected by sensors; computers process these data and produce digital images for analysis. A sampling of remote-sensing platforms is listed along the side of the illustration. Also, see the "Remote-Sensing Status Report" on the *MasteringGeography* website.

many communications and weather satellites use these high Earth orbits.

Some satellites orbit at lower altitudes. The pull of Earth's gravity means that the closer to Earth they are, the faster their orbiting speed is. For example, GPS satellites, at altitudes of about 20,200 km (12,552 mi), have *medium Earth orbits* that move more quickly than high Earth orbits. *Low Earth orbits*, at altitudes less than 1000 km (621 mi), are the most useful for scientific monitoring. Several of the National Aeronautics and Space Administration (NASA) environmental satellites in low Earth orbit are at altitudes of about 700 km (435 mi), completing one orbit every 99 minutes.

The angle of a satellite's orbit in relation to Earth's equator is its *inclination*, another factor affecting remotely sensed data. Some satellites orbit near the equator to monitor Earth's tropical regions; this low-inclination orbit acquires data only from low latitudes. An example is the *Tropical Rainfall Measuring Mission* (*TRMM*) satellite, which provides data for mapping rainfall patterns in the

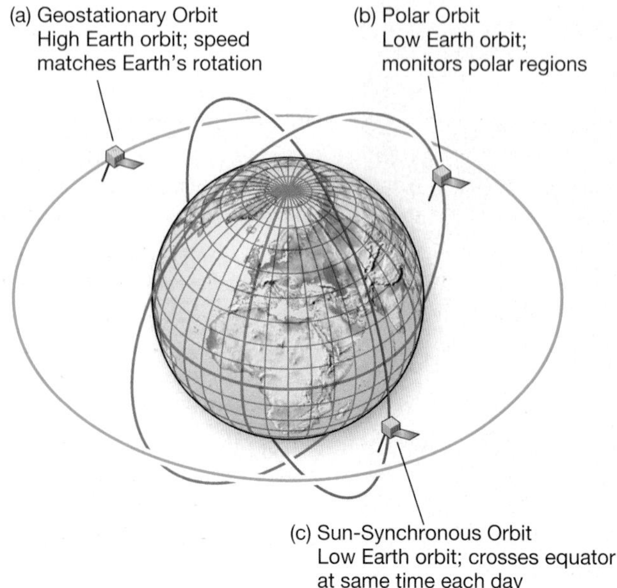

▲**Figure 1.24 Three satellite orbital paths.**

tropics (see example images in Geosystems in Action 4 on page 121). Monitoring the polar regions requires a satellite in polar orbit, with a higher inclination of about 90° (Figure 1.24b).

One type of polar orbit important for scientific observation is a Sun-synchronous orbit (Figure 1.24c). This low Earth orbit is synchronous with the Sun, so that the satellite crosses the equator at the same local solar time each day. Ground observation is maximized in Sun-synchronous orbit because Earth surfaces viewed from the satellite are illuminated by the Sun at a consistent angle. This enables better comparison of images from year to year because lighting and shadows do not change.

Passive Remote Sensing Like the human eye, passive remote-sensing systems record wavelengths of energy radiated from a surface, particularly visible light and infrared. Thus, passive sensors detect energy that is naturally emitted by the object or that is reflected by sunlight.

A number of satellites carry passive remote sensors for weather forecasting. The *Geostationary Operational Environmental Satellites*, known as *GOES*, became operational in 1994 and provide the images you see on television weather reports. *GOES-12*, *-13*, *-14*, and *-15* are operational; *GOES-12* sits at 60° W longitude to monitor the Caribbean and South America. Think of these satellites as hovering over these meridians for continuous coverage, using visual wavelengths for daylight hours and infrared for nighttime views.

Scientists use data from *Landsat* satellites, which began imaging Earth in the 1970s, for comparison of changing Earth landscapes over time, among other applications (see examples in Chapter 13, Visual Analysis 13, on page 437; view more images at http://earthobservatory.nasa.gov). *Landsat-5* retired in 2012 after 29 years, the longest-running Earth-observing mission in history; *Landsat-8* launched in 2013, beginning the new *Landsat* program managed by the USGS.

Although the *Landsat* satellites far surpassed their predicted lifespans, most satellites are removed from orbit after 3 to 5 years. Launched in 2011, *Suomi NPP* is part of the National Polar-orbiting Partnership (NPP), the next generation of satellites that will replace NASA's aging Earth Observation Satellite fleet. Many of the beautiful NASA "Blue Marble" Earth composite images are from the *Suomi* satellite (**Figure 1.25**).

▲**Figure 1.25 *Suomi NPP* Blue Marble image.** This composite view of Earth was imaged January 2, 2012. NASA scientist Norman Kuring combined VIIRS instrument data from six orbits of the *Suomi NPP* satellite. VIIRS acquires data in 22 bands covering visible, near-infrared, and thermal infrared wavelengths. [NASA/NOAA.]

GEOreport 1.5 Polar-orbiting satellites predict Hurricane Sandy's path

Scientists at the European Centre for Medium-Range Weather Forecasts report that polar-orbiting satellites, such as the National Oceanic and Atmospheric Administration (NOAA) *Suomi NPP* satellite, were critical for predicting Hurricane Sandy's track. Without data from these satellites, predictions for Hurricane Sandy would have been off by hundreds of miles, showing the storm heading out to sea rather than turning toward the New Jersey coast. *Suomi* orbits Earth about 14 times each day, collecting data from nearly the entire planet (find out more at http://npp.gsfc.nasa.gov/).

Active Remote Sensing Instruments that direct a beam of energy at a surface and analyze the energy reflected back are active remote sensors. An example is *radar* (*ra*dio *d*etection *a*nd *r*anging). A radar transmitter emits short bursts of energy that have relatively long wavelengths (0.3 to 10 cm) toward the subject terrain, penetrating clouds and darkness. Energy reflected back to a radar receiver for analysis is known as *backscatter*. Radar images collected in a time series allow scientists to make pixel-by-pixel comparisons to detect Earth movement, such as elevation changes along earthquake faults (see Chapter 10, Figure 10.1.2, on page 333).

Another active remote-sensing technology is airborne LiDAR, or *li*ght *d*etection *a*nd *r*anging. LiDAR systems collect highly detailed and accurate data for surface terrain using a laser scanner, with up to 150,000 pulses per second, 8 pulses or more per square meter, providing 15-m (49.2-ft) resolution. GPS and navigation systems onboard the aircraft determine the location of each pulse. LiDAR data sets are often shared among private, public, and scientific users for multiple applications. Scientists are presently studying the effects of Hurricane Sandy along the U.S. East Coast using LiDAR (see Chapter 13, Figure 13.17, on page 424).

Geospatial Data Analysis

Techniques such as remote sensing acquire large volumes of spatial data that must be retrieved and processed for scientific applications. Scientists use a number of rapidly developing technologies for analysis and visualization of large data sets.

Geographic Information Systems The integration of geographic information from direct surveys (on-the-ground mapping) and remote sensing can be accomplished using a **geographic information system (GIS)**, a computer-based data-processing tool for gathering, manipulating, and analyzing geographic data. In a GIS, spatial data can be organized in layers, or planes, containing different kinds of information (**Figure 1.26**). The beginning component for any GIS is a map, with its associated coordinate system, such as latitude–longitude provided by GPS or digital surveys (the top layer in Figure 1.26a). This map establishes reference points against which to accurately position other data, such as remotely sensed imagery. Whereas printed maps are fixed at the time of publication, GIS maps can be easily modified and evolve instantly.

A GIS is capable of analyzing patterns and relationships within a single data plane, such as the floodplains or soils layer in Figure 1.26a. A GIS also can generate an overlay analysis where two or more data planes interact. When the layers are combined, the resulting synthesis—a *composite overlay*—is ready for use in analyzing complex problems. The utility of a GIS is its ability to manipulate data and bring together several variables for analysis.

Figures 1.26b and c show two GIS map layers from the Northwest Gap Analysis Program (GAP), a five-state

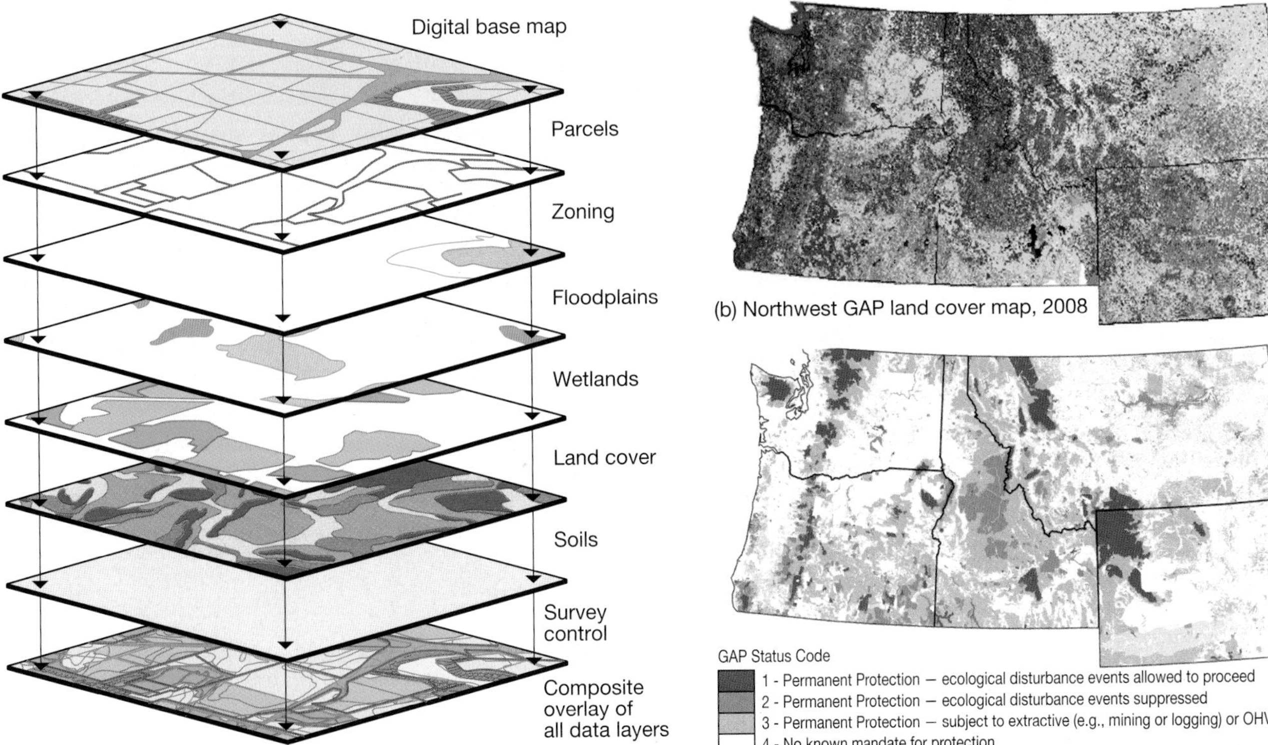

(a) Layered spatial data in a GIS format

(b) Northwest GAP land cover map, 2008

(c) Northwest GAP protected areas map, 2008

▲**Figure 1.26 Geographic information system (GIS) examples.** [(a) After USGS. (b) and (c) University of Idaho, Northwest Gap Analysis Project.]

assessment of terrestrial species and habitat, land stewardship, and management status that began in 2004. The Northwest GAP is part of a nationwide GAP environmental quality assessment by the USGS for species conservation; critical data layers are vegetation type, species range, and land ownership, among other environmental variables. (See http://gapanalysis.usgs.gov/ or http://gap.uidaho.edu to read a project overview and to access interactive maps.)

Geographic information science (GISci) is the field that develops the capabilities of GIS technology for use within geography and other disciplines. GISci analyzes Earth and human phenomena over time. This can include the study and forecasting of diseases, the population displacement caused by Hurricane Sandy, the destruction from the Japan earthquake and tsunami in 2011, and the status of endangered species and ecosystems, to name a few examples.

GIS technology is widely used in the creation of maps with a three-dimensional perspective. These maps are produced by combining *digital elevation models* (DEMs), which provide the base elevation data, with satellite-image overlays (see examples in Chapter 10). Through GIS technology, these data are available for multiple displays, animations, and other scientific analyses.

Visualization Technologies Google Earth™ and similar programs that can be downloaded from the Internet provide three-dimensional viewing of the globe and related geographic information. Google Earth™ allows the user to zoom in on landscapes and features of interest, using satellite imagery and aerial photography at varying resolutions. Users can select layers, as in a GIS model, depending on the task at hand and the composite overlay displayed. NASA's World Wind software is another open-source browser with access to high-resolution satellite images and multiple data layers suitable for scientific applications.

Geovisualization is a set of technologies for adjusting geospatial data sets in real time, so that users can instantly make changes to maps and other visual models. Geovisual tools are important for translating scientific knowledge into resources that nonscientists can use for decision making and planning. For example, scientists at East Carolina University, in partnership with state, local, and nonprofit organizations, are developing geovisual tools to assess the effects of sea-level rise along the North Carolina coast (see http://www.ecu.edu/renci/Technology/GIS.html).

Access to GIS technology, geovisualization tools, and large scientific data sets is expanding and becoming more user-friendly. Numerous open-source GIS software packages are now available. These are usually free, have online support systems, and are updated frequently (see http://opensourcegis.org/). In addition, public access to large remote-sensing data sets for analysis and display is now available, without the need to download large amounts of data (see examples of research applications at http://disc.sci.gsfc.nasa.gov/).

KEYLEARNINGconceptsreview

Here is a handy summary designed to help you review the Key Learning Concepts listed on this chapter's title page. The recap of each concept concludes with a list of the key terms from that portion of the chapter, their page numbers, and review questions pertaining to the concept. Similar summary and review sections follow each chapter in the book.

Define geography in general and physical geography in particular.

Geography combines disciplines from the physical and life sciences with disciplines from the human and cultural sciences to attain a holistic view of Earth. Geography's **spatial** viewpoint examines the nature and character of physical space and the distribution of phenomena within it. Geographic science integrates a wide range of subject matter traditionally categorized into five major themes: **location**, **region**, **human–Earth relationships**, **movement**, and **place**. Methods of **spatial analysis** unify this diverse field, focusing on the interdependence among geographic areas, natural systems, society, and cultural activities over space. The analysis of **process**—a set of actions or mechanisms that operate in some special order—is also central to geographic understanding.

Physical geography applies spatial analysis to all the physical components and process systems that make up the environment: energy, air, water, weather, climate, landforms, soils, animals, plants, microorganisms, and Earth itself. Physical geography is an essential aspect of **Earth systems science**. The science of physical geography is uniquely qualified to synthesize the spatial, environmental, and human aspects of our increasingly complex relationship with our home planet—Earth.

geography (p. 2)
spatial (p. 2)
location (p. 2)
region (p. 2)
human–Earth relationships (p. 2)
movement (p. 2)
place (p. 2)
spatial analysis (p. 4)
process (p. 4)
physical geography (p. 4)
Earth systems science (p. 4)

1. On the basis of information in this chapter, define physical geography and review the approach that characterizes the geographic sciences.
2. Suggest a representative example for each of the five geographic themes; for instance, an example of the movement theme might be oceanic circulation spreading debris from the Japan tsunami.

3. Have you made decisions today that involve geographic concepts discussed within the five themes presented? Explain briefly.
4. In general terms, how might a physical geographer analyze water pollution in the Great Lakes?

Discuss human activities and human population growth as they relate to geographic science and *summarize* the scientific process.

Understanding the complex relations between Earth's physical systems and human society is important to human survival. Hypotheses and theories about the Universe, Earth, and life are developed through the scientific process, which relies on a general series of steps that make up the **scientific method**. Results and conclusions from scientific experiments can lead to basic theories as well as applied uses for the general public.

Awareness of the human denominator, the role of humans on Earth, has led to physical geography's increasing emphasis on human–environment interactions. Recently, **sustainability science** has become an important new discipline, integrating sustainable development and functioning Earth systems.

scientific method (p. 4)
sustainability science (p. 7)

5. Sketch a flow diagram of the scientific process and method, beginning with observations and ending with the development of theories and laws.
6. Summarize population-growth issues: population size, the impact per person, and future projections. What strategies do you see as important for global sustainability?

Describe systems analysis, open and closed systems, and feedback information and *relate* these concepts to Earth systems.

A **system** is any ordered set of interacting components and their attributes, as distinct from their surrounding environment. Systems analysis is an important organizational and analytical tool used by geographers. Earth is an **open system** in terms of energy, receiving energy from the Sun, but it is essentially a **closed system** in terms of matter and physical resources.

As a system operates, "information" is returned to various points in the operational process via pathways of **feedback loops**. If the feedback information discourages change in the system, it is **negative feedback**. Further production of such feedback opposes system changes. Such negative feedback causes self-regulation in a natural system, stabilizing the system. If feedback information encourages change in the system, it is **positive feedback**. Further production of positive feedback stimulates system changes. Unchecked positive feedback in a system can create a runaway ("snowballing") condition. When the rates of inputs and outputs in the system are equal and the amounts of energy and matter in storage within the system are constant (or when they fluctuate around a stable average), the system is in **steady-state equilibrium**. A system showing a steady increase or decrease in some operation over time (a trend) is in **dynamic equilibrium**. A **threshold**, or tipping point, is the moment at which a system can no longer maintain its character and lurches to a new operational level. Geographers often construct a simplified **model** of natural systems to better understand them.

Four immense open systems powerfully interact at Earth's surface: three **abiotic**, or nonliving, systems—the **atmosphere**, **hydrosphere** (including the **cryosphere**), and **lithosphere**—and a **biotic**, or living, system—the **biosphere**, or **ecosphere**.

system (p. 7)
open system (p. 8)
closed system (p. 8)
feedback loop (p. 9)
negative feedback (p. 9)
positive feedback (p. 9)
steady-state equilibrium (p. 9)
dynamic equilibrium (p. 9)
threshold (p. 10)
model (p. 10)
abiotic (p. 11)
biotic (p. 11)
atmosphere (p. 11)
hydrosphere (p. 11)
cryosphere (p. 11)
lithosphere (p. 11)
biosphere (p. 11)
ecosphere (p. 11)

7. Define systems theory as an analytical strategy. What are open systems, closed systems, and negative feedback? When is a system in a steady-state equilibrium condition? What type of system (open or closed) is the human body? A lake? A wheat plant?
8. Describe Earth as a system in terms of both energy and matter; use simple diagrams to illustrate your description.
9. What are the three abiotic spheres that make up Earth's environment? Relate these to the biotic sphere, the biosphere.

Explain Earth's reference grid: latitude and longitude and latitudinal geographic zones and time.

The science that studies Earth's shape and size is **geodesy**. Earth bulges slightly through the equator and is oblate (flattened) at the poles, making its surface a misshapen spheroid, or **geoid**. Absolute location on Earth is described with a specific reference grid of **parallels** of **latitude** (measuring distances north and south of the equator) and **meridians** of **longitude** (measuring distances east and west of a prime meridian). A historic breakthrough in navigation occurred with the establishment of an international **prime meridian** (0° through Greenwich, England). A **great circle** is any circle of Earth's circumference whose center coincides with the center of Earth. Great circle routes are the shortest distance between two points on Earth. **Small circles** are those whose centers do not coincide with Earth's center.

The prime meridian provided the basis for **Greenwich Mean Time (GMT)**, the world's first universal time system. Today, **Coordinated Universal Time (UTC)** is the worldwide standard and the basis for international time zones. A corollary of the prime meridian is the 180° meridian, the **International Date Line (IDL)**, which marks the place where each day officially begins. **Daylight saving time** is a seasonal change of clocks by 1 hour in summer months.

geodesy (p. 11)	**small circle (p. 16)**
geoid (p. 14)	**Greenwich Mean Time (GMT) (p. 17)**
latitude (p. 14)	**Coordinated Universal Time (UTC) (p. 17)**
parallel (p. 14)	**International Date Line (IDL) (p. 17)**
longitude (p. 15)	**daylight saving time (p. 18)**
meridian (p. 15)	
prime meridian (p. 15)	
great circle (p. 16)	

10. Draw a simple sketch describing Earth's shape and size.
11. Define latitude and parallel and define longitude and meridian using a simple sketch with labels.
12. Define a great circle, great circle routes, and a small circle. In terms of these concepts, describe the equator, other parallels, and meridians.
13. Identify the various latitudinal geographic zones that roughly subdivide Earth's surface. In which zone do you live?
14. What does timekeeping have to do with longitude? Explain this relationship. How is Coordinated Universal Time (UTC) determined on Earth?
15. What and where is the prime meridian? How was the location originally selected? Describe the meridian that is opposite the prime meridian on Earth's surface.

Define cartography and mapping basics: map scale and map projections.

A **map** is a generalized depiction of the layout of an area, usually some portion of Earth's surface, as seen from above and greatly reduced in size. **Cartography** is the science and art of mapmaking. For the spatial portrayal of Earth's physical systems, geographers use maps. **Scale** is the ratio of the image on a map to the real world; it relates a unit on the map to a corresponding unit on the ground. When creating a **map projection**, cartographers select the class of projection that is the best compromise for the map's specific purpose. Compromise is always necessary because Earth's roughly spherical three-dimensional surface cannot be exactly duplicated on a flat, two-dimensional map. Relative abilities to portray **equal area** (equivalence), **true shape** (conformality), true direction, and true distance are all considerations in selecting a projection. The **Mercator projection** is in the cylindrical class; it has true-shape qualities and straight lines that show constant direction. A **rhumb line** denotes constant direction and appears as a straight line on the Mercator.

map (p. 18)	**equal area (p. 21)**
cartography (p. 19)	**true shape (p. 21)**
scale (p. 19)	**Mercator projection (p. 21)**
map projection (p. 20)	**rhumb line (p. 22)**

16. Define cartography. Explain why it is an integrative discipline.
17. Assess your geographic literacy by examining atlases and maps. What types of maps have you used: Political? Physical? Topographic? Do you know what map projections they employed? Do you know the names and locations of the four oceans, the seven continents, and most individual countries? Can you identify the new countries that have emerged since 1990?
18. What is map scale? In what three ways may it be expressed on a map?
19. State whether the following ratios are large scale or small scale: 1:3,168,000; 1:24,000; 1:125,000.
20. Describe the differences between the characteristics of a globe and those that result when a flat map is prepared.
21. What type of map projection is used in Figure 1.13? In Figure 1.17? (See Appendix A.)

Describe modern geoscience techniques—the Global Positioning System (GPS), remote sensing, and geographic information systems (GIS)—and *explain* how these tools are used in geographic analysis.

Latitude, longitude, and elevation are accurately measured using **Global Positioning System (GPS)** instrumentation that reads radio signals from satellites. Orbital and aerial **remote sensing** obtains information about Earth systems from great distances without the need for physical contact. Satellites do not take photographs, but instead receive radiant-energy data that are then transmitted to Earth-based receivers. Satellite data are recorded in digital form for later processing, enhancement, and image generation.

Geospatial data may be analyzed using **geographic information system (GIS)** technology. Computers process geographic information from direct ground surveys and remote sensing in complex layers of spatial information. Digital elevation models are three-dimensional products of GIS technology. Open-source GIS is increasingly available to scientists and the public for many applications, including spatial analysis in geography and the better understanding of Earth's systems.

Global Positioning System (GPS) (p. 23)	**geographic information system (GIS) (p. 27)**
remote sensing (p. 24)	

22. What is a GPS and how does it assist you in finding location and elevation on Earth? Give several examples of GPS technology used for scientific purposes.
23. What is remote sensing? What are you viewing when you observe a weather satellite image on TV or in the newspaper? Explain.
24. If you were in charge of planning the human development of a large tract of land, how would GIS methodologies assist you? How might planning and zoning be affected if a portion of the tract in the GIS was a floodplain or prime agricultural land?

VISUALanalysis 1 Remote Sensing

Go to a NASA (http://landsat.visibleearth.nasa.gov/), USGS (http://eros.usgs.gov/), or ESA (European Space Agency; http://www.esa.int/Our_Activities/Observing_the_Earth) website and view some remotely sensed images. Then examine this image. [NASA.]

1. Was the image made by an aircraft, a ground-based sensor, or a satellite?
2. Is this a natural-color or false-color image? What do the colors represent?
3. Can you identify the location, the land and water bodies, and other physical features?
4. Based on your research and examples in this text, can you determine the specific source (LiDAR aircraft, *GOES* or *Landsat* satellite, etc.) of the data that made this image?

USGS

http://goo.gl/a4bKWh

ESA

http://goo.gl/rD5e4X

NASA

http://goo.gl/GTuapW

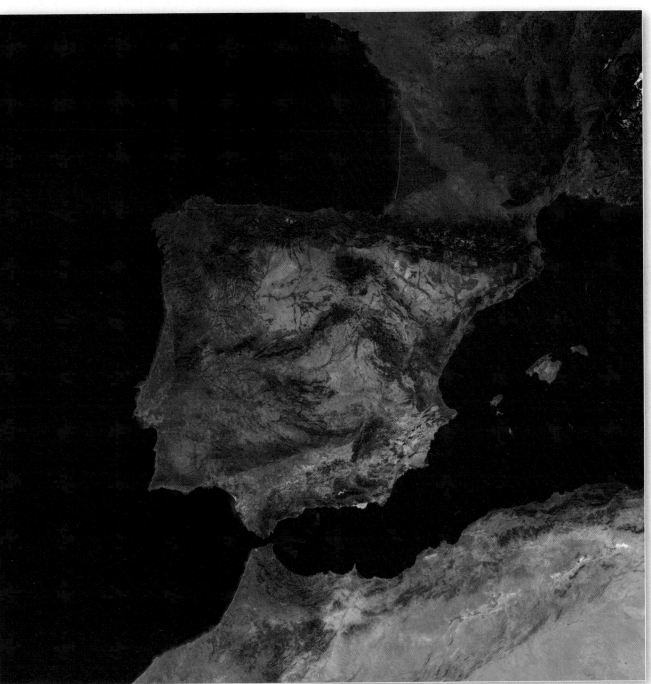

MasteringGeography™

Looking for additional review and test prep materials? Visit the Study Area in *MasteringGeography*™ to enhance your geographic literacy, spatial reasoning skills, and understanding of this chapter's content by accessing a variety of resources, including **MapMaster** interactive maps, geoscience animations, videos, *In the News* RSS feeds, flashcards, web links, self-study quizzes, and an eText version of *Elemental Geosystems*.

PART 1 The Energy–Atmosphere System

For more than 4.6 billion years, solar energy has traveled across interplanetary space to Earth, where a small portion of the solar output is intercepted. This radiant energy from the Sun powers our planet and our lives. Because of Earth's curvature, the arriving energy is unevenly distributed at the top of the atmosphere, creating energy imbalances over Earth's surface—the equatorial region experiences surpluses, receiving more energy than it emits; the polar regions experience deficits, emitting more energy than they receive. Also, the annual pulse of seasonal change varies the distribution of energy during the year.

Earth's atmosphere acts as an efficient filter, absorbing most harmful radiation, charged particles, and space debris so that they do not reach Earth's surface. In the lower atmosphere, the unevenness of daily energy receipt gives rise to global patterns of temperature and the circulation of wind and ocean currents, driving weather and climate. Each of us depends on these interacting systems that are set into motion by energy from the Sun. These are the systems of Part I.

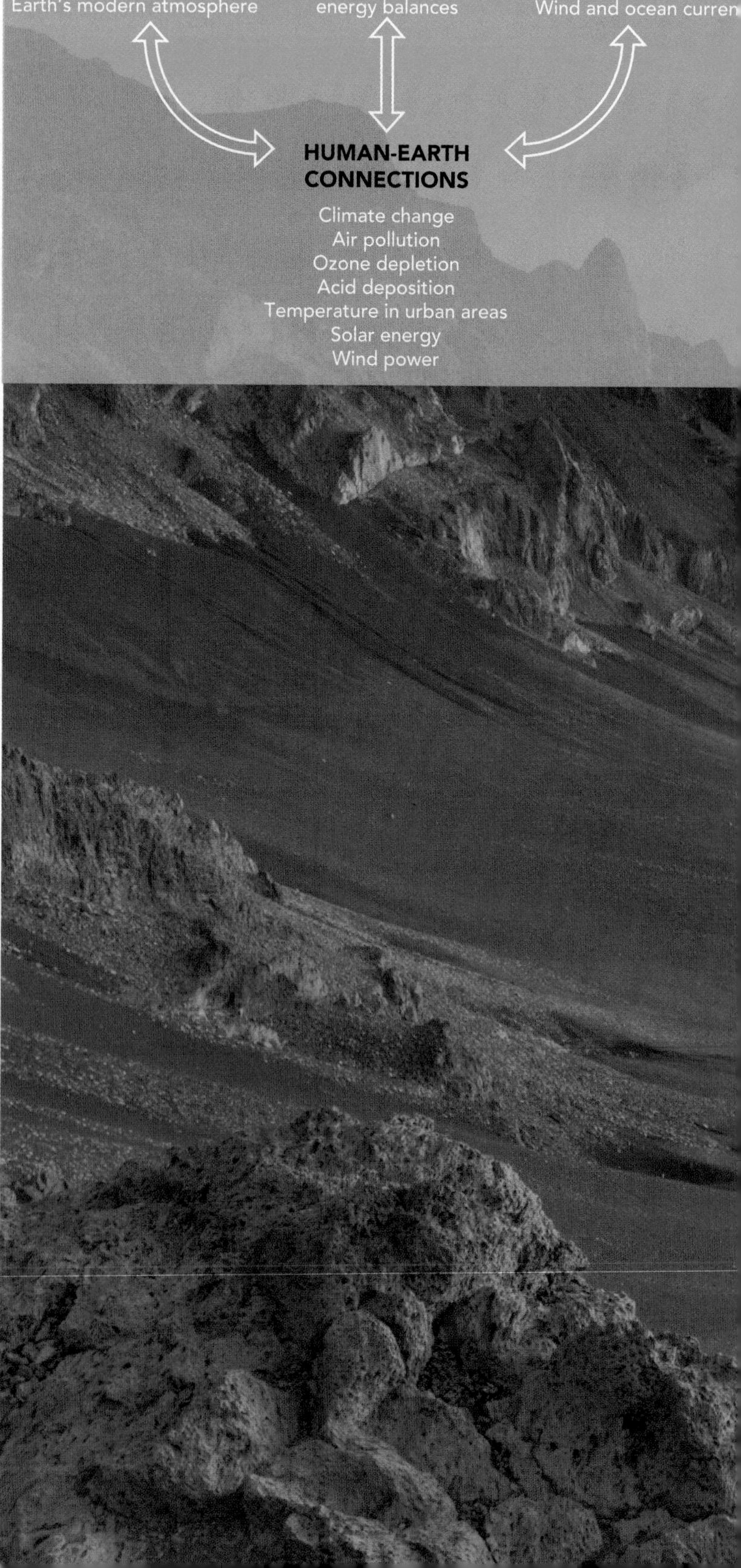

Sunset and a sea of clouds over Haleakalā crater, elevation over 3,000 m (10,000 ft), and the Pacific Ocean, Haleakala National Park, Maui, Hawai'i. [SuperStock/Getty Images.] ▶

Atmosphere
Biosphere
Lithosphere
Hydrosphere

2 Solar Energy, Seasons, and the Atmosphere

Global climate change is affecting seasonal rhythms in the biosphere. In the Rocky Mountains, higher spring temperatures and earlier snowmelt mean that spring wildflowers are producing their first blooms earlier in the year, and continuing to bloom later in the summer, prolonging the flowering season by a month. [Johnny Adolphson/Shutterstock.]

KEYLEARNING**concepts**

After reading the chapter, you should be able to:

- ***Describe*** our Solar System, ***summarize*** the origin of Earth, and ***reconstruct*** Earth's annual orbit about the Sun.
- ***Explain*** the characteristics of the solar wind and the electromagnetic spectrum of radiant energy and ***illustrate*** the interception of solar energy at the top of the atmosphere.
- ***Define*** solar altitude, solar declination, and daylength and ***describe*** the annual variability of each—Earth's seasonality.
- ***Draw*** a diagram showing atmospheric structure based on three criteria for analysis—composition, temperature, and function.
- ***Describe*** conditions within the stratosphere—specifically, the function and status of the ozonosphere, or ozone layer.
- ***Distinguish*** between natural and anthropogenic pollutants in the lower atmosphere and ***construct*** simple diagrams illustrating pollution from photochemical reactions in motor vehicle exhaust and from industrial smog.

troposphere NO_2 ecliptic
Arctic Circle insolation
lapse rate energy solstice
stratosphere speed of light
circle of illumination equinox
Tropic of Cancer gravity
aurora axial tilt wavelength UV
air pressure temperature inversion daylength
solar constant ozone layer aerosols subsolar point
anthropogenic atmosphere
revolution & rotation

Humans Explore the Atmosphere

The atmosphere is a unique reservoir of gases that protects life on Earth from harmful radiation from the Sun. For humans to venture away from the lower regions of the atmosphere, they must wear elaborate spacesuits that replicate the services that the atmosphere performs for us all the time.

For example, astronaut Mark Lee, on a spacewalk from the Space Shuttle *Discovery* in 1994 at 241 km (150 mi) altitude above Earth's surface, was in orbit beyond the protective shield of the atmosphere (**Figure GN 2.1**). He was traveling at 28,165 kmph (17,500 mph), almost nine times faster than a high-speed rifle bullet, the vacuum of space all around him. Where the Sun hit his spacesuit, temperatures reached +120°C (+248°F); in the shadows, they dropped to –150°C (–238°F). Radiation and solar wind struck his pressure suit. To survive at such an altitude is an obvious challenge, one that relies on the ability of NASA spacesuits to duplicate Earth's atmosphere.

Protection in a Spacesuit For human survival, a spacesuit must block radiation and particle impacts, as does the atmosphere. It must protect the wearer from thermal extremes. Spacesuits must also replicate Earth's oxygen–carbon dioxide processing systems as well as fluid-delivery and waste-management systems.

Such a suit must maintain an internal air pressure against the space vacuum; for pure oxygen, this is 4.7 psi (32.4 kPa), which roughly equals the pressure that oxygen, water vapor, and CO_2 gases combined exert at sea level. The modern NASA spacesuit has 18,000 parts to protect the wearer.

▼**Figure GN 2.1 Astronaut Mark Lee, untethered, on a spacewalk.** [NASA.]

Kittinger's Record-Setting Jump In an earlier era, before orbital flights, scientists didn't know how a human could survive in space or how to produce an artificial atmosphere inside a spacesuit. Yet humans pushed the boundaries of survival at the edge of space despite these limitations. In August 1960, Air Force Colonel Joseph Kittinger, Jr., made a historic leap from a small, unpressurized compartment dangling from a helium-filled balloon at 31.3 km (19.5 mi) altitude for an experimental reentry into the atmosphere (**Figure GN 2.2**). He carried only an instrument pack on his seat, his main chute, and pure oxygen for his breathing mask.

The air pressure at his jump altitude was barely measurable—marking what is considered the beginning of space in experimental-aircraft testing. Initially frightened, he heard nothing, no rushing sound, for there was not enough air to produce any sound. The fabric of his pressure suit did not flutter, for there was not enough air to create friction against the cloth. His speed was remarkable, quickly accelerating to 988 kmph (614 mph)—nearly the speed of sound at sea level—owing to the lack of air resistance in the stratosphere.

When his free fall reached the stratosphere and its ozone layer, the frictional drag of denser atmospheric gases slowed his body. He then dropped into the lower atmosphere, finally falling below airplane flying altitudes.

Kittinger's free fall lasted 4 minutes and 37 seconds to the opening of his main chute at 5500 m (18,000 ft). The parachute lowered him safely to Earth's surface. This remarkable 13-minute, 35-second voyage through 99% of the atmospheric mass remained a record for 52 years.

Recent Jumps Break the Record On October 14, 2012, Felix Baumgartner ascended by helium balloon to 39.0 km (24.3 mi) altitude and then jumped (**Figure GN 2.3**). Guided by Colonel Kittinger's voice from mission control, Baumgartner survived an out-of-control spin early in his fall, reaching a top free-fall speed of 1342 kmph (834 mph). Watched live online by millions around the globe, his fall lasted 4 minutes, 20 seconds—faster than Kittinger's free fall by 17 seconds.

▲**Figure GN 2.2 A remotely triggered camera captures a stratospheric leap into history.** [National Museum of the U.S. Air Force.]

On October 24, 2014, computer scientist Alan Eustace set a new free-fall height record of 41.4 km (25.7 mi), an altitude more than halfway to the top of the stratosphere. Eustace survived using a special pressure suit developed during 3 years of preparation by his scientific support team.

The experiences of these men illustrate the evolution of our understanding of upper-atmosphere survival. From events such as Kittinger's dangerous leap of discovery, the now routine spacewalks of astronauts such as Mark Lee, and the 2012 and 2014 record-breaking jumps, scientists have gained important information about the atmosphere. This chapter explores solar energy, the seasons, and our current knowledge of the atmosphere as it protects Earth's living systems.

QUESTION AND EXPLORE Go to http://www.redbullstratos.com/ and http://vimeo.com/109992331 to watch highlights of the Baumgartner and Eustace jumps. Do you think these recent feats make Kittinger's accomplishment less important?

MG

▲**Figure GN 2.3 Felix Baumgartner's 2012 jump set free-fall height and speed records.** Alan Eustace set a new height record in 2014. [Red Bull Stratos/AP Images.]

The Universe is populated with at least 125 billion galaxies. One of these is our own Milky Way Galaxy, and it contains about 300 billion stars. Among these stars is an average-size yellow star, the Sun, although the dramatic satellite image in Figure 2.2 seems anything but average! Our Sun radiates energy in all directions and upon its family of orbiting planets. Of special interest to us is the solar energy that falls on the third planet, our immediate home.

On its way to Earth, solar energy passes through the atmosphere, a unique reservoir of life-sustaining gases, the product of 4.6 billion years of development. Some of the gases are crucial components in biological processes; some protect us from hostile radiation and particles from the Sun and beyond. Humans interact with the atmosphere on many levels, including each breath we take, our energy consumption, and the products and materials we buy. Human activities now have critical implications for our global atmosphere, for they are influencing the atmospheric composition of the future.

Human activities now have critical implications for our global atmosphere, for they are influencing the atmospheric composition of the future.

In this chapter: Incoming solar energy arrives at the top of Earth's atmosphere, establishing the pattern of energy input that drives Earth's physical systems and influences our daily lives. This solar energy input to the atmosphere, combined with Earth's tilt and rotation, produces daily, seasonal, and annual patterns of changing daylength and Sun angle. The Sun is the ultimate energy source for most life processes in our biosphere.

We examine the modern atmosphere using the criteria of composition, temperature, and function. We look at some of the effects of human activities on our atmosphere, including stratospheric ozone losses and the formation of acid deposition. Our look at the atmosphere concludes with a discussion of the spatial impacts of natural and human-produced air pollution.

The Solar System, Sun, and Earth

Our Solar System is located on a remote, trailing edge of the **Milky Way Galaxy**, a flattened, disk-shaped collection of stars in the form of a barred-spiral—a spiral with a slightly barred, or elongated, core (**Figures 2.1a and b**). Our Solar System is embedded more than halfway out from the galactic center, in one of the Milky Way's spiral arms—the Orion Spur of the Sagittarius Arm. A super-massive black hole some 2 million solar masses in size, named *Sagittarius A** (pronounced "Sagittarius A Star"), sits in the galactic center. Our Solar System of eight planets, four dwarf planets, and asteroids is some 30,000 light-years from this black hole at the center of the Galaxy and about 15 light-years above the plane of the Milky Way.

Solar System Formation

According to prevailing theory, our Solar System condensed from a large, slowly rotating and collapsing cloud of dust and gas, a *nebula*. **Gravity**, the mutual attraction exerted by every object upon all other objects in proportion to their mass, was the key force in this condensing solar nebula. As the nebular cloud organized and flattened into a disk shape, the early *protosun* grew in mass at the center, drawing more matter to it. Small eddies of accreting material swirled at varying distances from the center of the solar nebula; these were the *protoplanets*.

The **planetesimal hypothesis**, or *dust-cloud hypothesis*, explains how suns condense from nebular clouds. In this hypothesis, small grains of cosmic dust and other solids accrete to form planetesimals that may grow to become protoplanets and eventually planets; these formed in orbits about the developing Solar System's central mass.

Astronomers study this formation process in other parts of the Galaxy, where planets are observed orbiting distant stars. In fact, by 2013, astronomers had discovered more than 4400 candidate exoplanets orbiting other stars; nearly 1000 have been confirmed. Initial results from the orbiting Kepler telescope estimate the number of planets in the Milky Way at 50 billion, with some 500 million planets in habitable zones (with moderate temperatures and liquid water).

Dimensions and Distances

The **speed of light** is 300,000 kmps (kilometers per second), or 186,000 mps (miles per second)*—in other words, about 9.5 trillion kilometers per year, or nearly 6 trillion miles per year. This is the tremendous distance captured by the term *light-year*, used as a unit of measurement for the vast Universe.

For spatial comparison, our Moon is an average distance of 384,400 km (238,866 mi) from Earth, or about 1.28 seconds in terms of light speed; for the *Apollo* astronauts, this was a 3-day space voyage. Our entire Solar System is approximately 11 hours in diameter, measured by light speed (**Figure 2.1c**). In contrast, the Milky Way is about 100,000 light-years from side to side, and the known Universe that is observable from Earth stretches approximately 12 billion light-years in all directions. (See a Solar System simulator at http://space.jpl.nasa.gov/.)

Earth's average distance from the Sun is approximately 150 million km (93 million mi), which means that light reaches Earth from the Sun in an average of 8 minutes and 20 seconds. Earth's orbit around the Sun is presently elliptical—a closed, oval path (**Figure 2.1d**). At **perihelion**, which is Earth's closest position to the Sun,

*In more precise numbers, light speed is 299,792 kmps, or 186,282 mps.

Top view

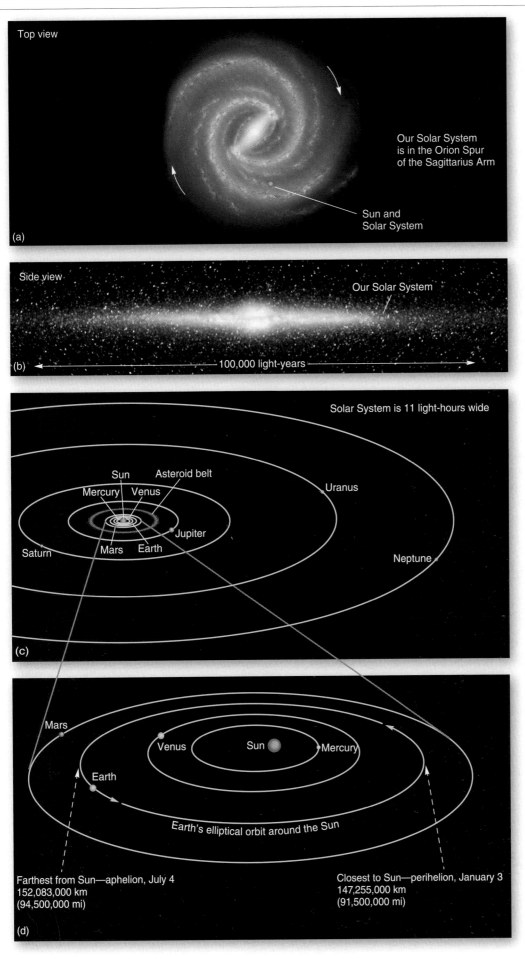

Our Solar System is in the Orion Spur of the Sagittarius Arm

Sun and Solar System

(a)

Side view

Our Solar System

(b) 100,000 light-years

Solar System is 11 light-hours wide

Sun

Asteroid belt

Mercury

Venus

Uranus

Jupiter

Saturn

Mars

Earth

Neptune

(c)

Mars

Venus

Sun

Mercury

Earth

Earth's elliptical orbit around the Sun

Farthest from Sun—aphelion, July 4
152,083,000 km
(94,500,000 mi)

Closest to Sun—perihelion, January 3
147,255,000 km
(91,500,000 mi)

(d)

◄**Figure 2.1 Milky Way Galaxy, Solar System, and Earth's orbit.** (a) The Milky Way Galaxy viewed from above in an artist's conception. (b) An image of the Milky Way Galaxy in cross-section side view. (c) All of the planets have orbits closely aligned to the plane of the ecliptic. Pluto, considered the ninth planet for over 70 years, was reclassified as a dwarf planet, part of the Kuiper asteroid belt, in 2006. (d) The four inner terrestrial planets and the structure of Earth's elliptical orbit, illustrating perihelion (closest) and aphelion (farthest) positions during the year. Have you ever observed the Milky Way Galaxy in the night sky? [(a) and (b) NASA/JPL.]

Animation (MG)
Nebular Hypothesis

http://goo.gl/alti7U

occurring on January 3 during the Northern Hemisphere winter, the Earth–Sun distance is 147,255,000 km (91,500,000 mi). At **aphelion**, which is Earth's farthest position from the Sun, occurring on July 4 during the Northern Hemisphere summer, the distance is 152,083,000 km (94,500,000 mi). This seasonal difference in distance from the Sun causes a slight variation in the solar energy incoming to Earth, but is not an immediate reason for seasonal change.

Solar Energy: From Sun to Earth

Our Sun is average in temperature, size, and color when compared with other stars in the Galaxy, yet it is the ultimate energy source for most life processes in our biosphere. In the entire Solar System, the Sun is the only object having the enormous mass needed to sustain a nuclear reaction in its core and produce radiant energy. The solar mass produces tremendous pressure and high temperatures deep in its dense interior. Under these conditions, the Sun's abundant hydrogen atoms are forced together, and pairs of hydrogen nuclei are joined in the process of **fusion**, liberating enormous quantities of energy.

Solar activity is indicated by surface disturbances that we can observe from Earth. The Sun's principal outputs consist of the *solar wind* and of radiant energy spanning portions of the *electromagnetic spectrum*; both move across space to Earth.

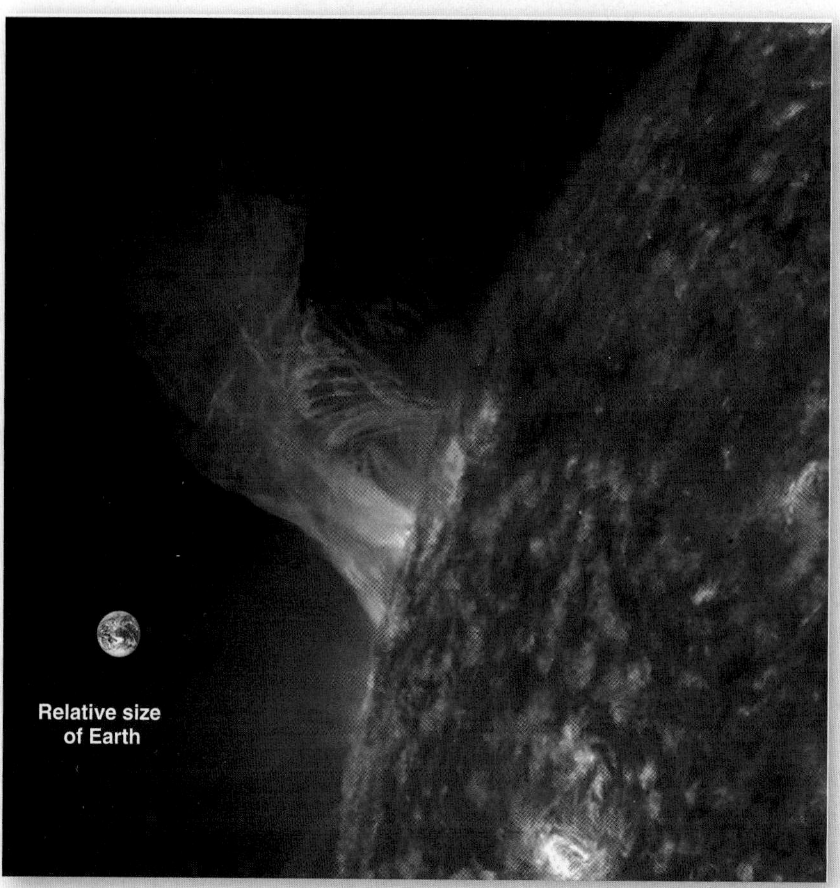

(a) Solar eruption, December 31, 2012

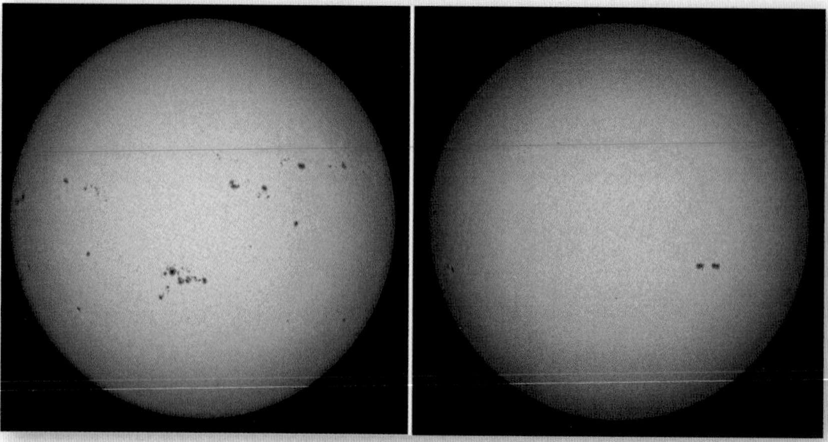

(b) (left) Strong sunspot maximum, July 2000; (right) weak maximum, February 2013

▲**Figure 2.2 Image of the Sun and sunspots.** The prominence eruption rising into the Sun's corona was captured by NASA's Solar Dynamics Observatory. This relatively minor 2012 eruption was about 20 times the diameter of Earth, shown for scale. Earth is actually far smaller than the average sunspot. [(a) NASA/SDO/Steele Hill, 2012. (b) SOHO/EIT Consortium (NASA and ESA).]

Solar Activity and Solar Wind

Telescopes and satellite images reveal solar activity to us in the form of sunspots and other surface disturbances. The *solar cycle* is the periodic variation in the Sun's activity and appearance over time. Since telescopes first allowed sunspot observation in the 1800s, scientists have used these solar surface features to define the solar cycle (**Figure 2.2**).

Sunspots The Sun's most conspicuous features are large **sunspots**, surface disturbances caused by magnetic storms. Sunspots appear as dark areas on the solar surface, ranging in diameter from 10,000 to 50,000 km (6200 to 31,000 mi), with some as large as 160,000 km (100,000 mi), more than 12 times Earth's diameter.

A *solar minimum* is a period of years when few sunspots are visible; a *solar maximum* is a period during which sunspots are numerous. Over the last 300 years, sunspot occurrences have cycled fairly regularly, averaging 11 years from maximum to maximum (Figure 2.2b). A minimum in 2008 and a small maximum in 2013 roughly maintain the average.

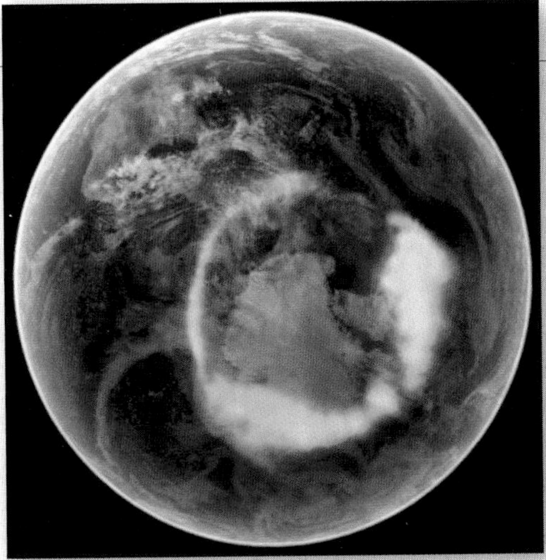

(a) *Aurora australis* as seen from orbit.

(b) *Aurora borealis* over Whitehorse, Yukon, Canada, caused by solar activity. On August 31, 2012, a coronal mass ejection (CME) erupted from the Sun into space. The CME glanced off Earth's magnetosphere, causing this aurora 4 days later.

▲**Figure 2.3 Auroras from orbital and ground perspectives.** [(a) Image Spacecraft GSFC/NASA; (b) David Cartier, Sr., courtesy of GSFC/NASA.]

The present solar cycle began in 2008 and carries the name *Cycle 24*. (For more on the sunspot cycle, see http://solarscience.msfc.nasa.gov/SunspotCycle.shtml.)

Activity on the Sun is highest during solar maximum. *Solar flares*, magnetic storms that cause surface explosions, and *prominence eruptions*, outbursts of gases arcing from the surface, often occur in active regions near sunspots (Figure 2.2a; for videos and news about recent solar activity, go to http://www.nasa.gov/mission_pages/sunearth/news/). Although much of the material from these eruptions is pulled back toward the Sun by gravity, some moves into space as part of the solar wind.

Solar Wind Effects The Sun constantly emits clouds of electrically charged particles (principally, hydrogen nuclei and free electrons) that surge outward in all directions from the Sun's surface. This stream of energetic material travels more slowly than light—at about 50 million km (31 million mi) a day—taking approximately 3 days to reach Earth. This phenomenon is the **solar wind**, originating from the Sun's extremely hot solar corona, or outer atmosphere. The corona is the Sun's rim, observable with the naked eye from Earth during a solar eclipse.

As the charged particles of the solar wind approach Earth, they first interact with Earth's magnetic field. This **magnetosphere**, which surrounds the Earth and extends beyond Earth's atmosphere, is generated by dynamo-like motions within our planet. The magnetosphere deflects the solar wind toward both of Earth's poles, so that only a small portion of it enters the upper atmosphere.

In addition, massive outbursts of charged material, referred to as *coronal mass ejections* (CMEs), contribute to the flow of solar wind material from the Sun into space. CMEs that are aimed toward Earth often cause spectacular **auroras** in the upper atmosphere near the poles. These lighting effects, known as the *aurora borealis* (northern lights) and *aurora australis* (southern lights), occur 80–500 km (50–300 mi) above Earth's surface through the interaction of the solar wind with the upper layers of Earth's atmosphere. They appear as folded sheets of green, yellow, blue, and red light that undulate across the skies of high latitudes poleward of 65° (**Figure 2.3**; see http://www.swpc.noaa.gov/Aurora/ for tips on viewing auroras). In 2012, auroras were visible as far south as Colorado and Arkansas.

Electromagnetic Spectrum of Radiant Energy

The essential solar input to life is electromagnetic energy of various wavelengths, traveling at the speed of light to Earth. Solar radiation occupies a portion of the **electromagnetic spectrum**, which is the spectrum of all possible wavelengths of electromagnetic energy. A **wavelength** is the distance between corresponding points on any two successive waves. The number of waves passing a fixed point in 1 second is the *frequency*. Note the wavelength plot below the chart in **Figure 2.4**.

The Sun emits radiant energy composed of 8% ultraviolet, X-ray, and gamma-ray wavelengths; 47% visible light wavelengths; and 45% shortwave infrared wavelengths. Figure 2.4 shows a portion of the electromagnetic spectrum, with wavelengths increasing from the left to the right side of the illustration. Note the wavelengths at which various phenomena and human applications of energy occur.

An important physical law states that all objects radiate energy in wavelengths related to their individual surface temperatures: The hotter the object, the shorter the wavelengths emitted. This law holds true for the Sun and Earth. **Figure 2.5** shows that the hot Sun radiates shorter wavelength energy, concentrated around 0.5 μm (micrometer).

The Sun's surface temperature is about 6000 K (6273°C, 11,459°F), and its emission curve is similar to that predicted for an idealized surface, or *blackbody radiator*, at 6000 K (shown in Figure 2.5).* A blackbody is

*The Kelvin scale for measuring temperature starts at absolute zero temperature, or 0 K, so that measurements on the scale are proportional to the actual kinetic energy in the material. On this scale, the melting point for ice is 273 K; the boiling point for water is 373 K.

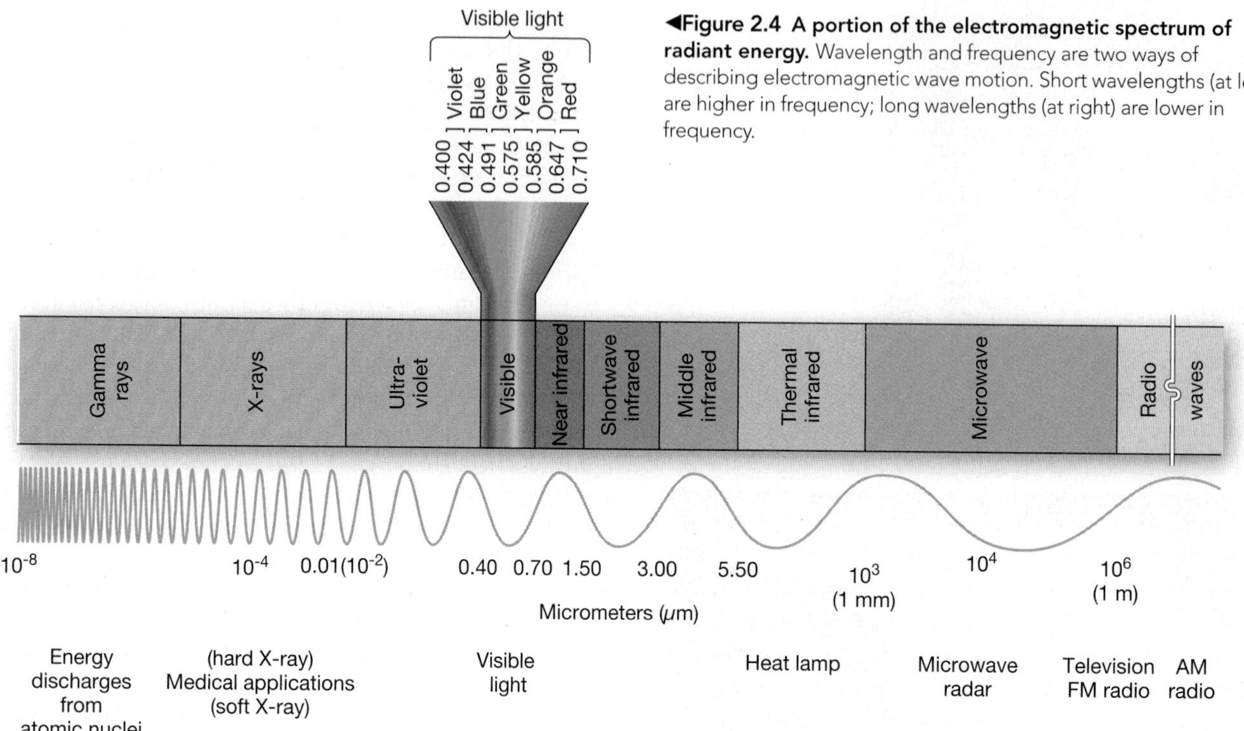

◄Figure 2.4 A portion of the electromagnetic spectrum of radiant energy. Wavelength and frequency are two ways of describing electromagnetic wave motion. Short wavelengths (at left) are higher in frequency; long wavelengths (at right) are lower in frequency.

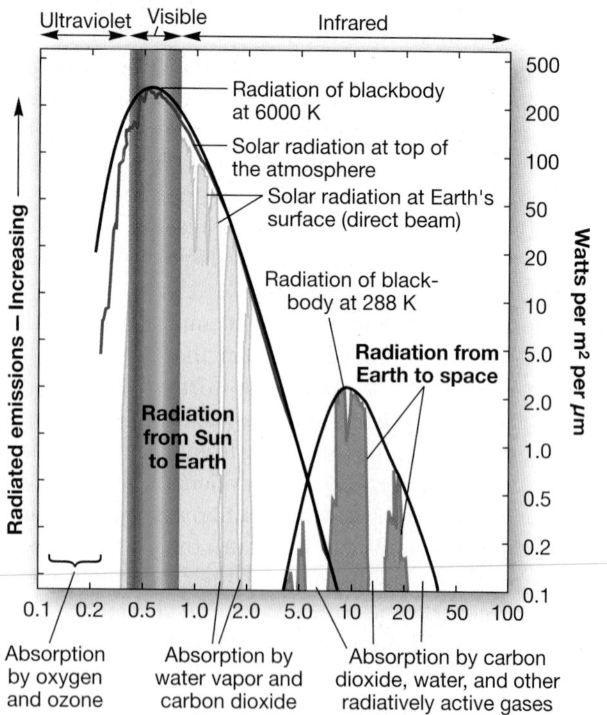

▲Figure 2.5 Solar and terrestrial energy distribution by wavelength. A hotter Sun radiates shorter wavelengths, whereas a cooler Earth emits longer wavelengths. Dark lines represent ideal blackbody curves for the Sun and Earth. The dropouts in the plot lines for solar and terrestrial radiation represent absorption bands of water vapor, water, carbon dioxide, oxygen, ozone (O_3), and other gases. [Adapted from W. D. Sellers, *Physical Climatology* (Chicago: University of Chicago Press), p. 20. Used by permission.]

a perfect absorber of radiant energy; it absorbs and subsequently emits all the radiant energy that it receives. A hotter object like the Sun emits a much greater amount of energy per unit area of its surface than does a similar area of a cooler object like Earth. Shorter wavelength emissions are dominant at these higher temperatures.

Although cooler than the Sun, Earth also acts as a blackbody, radiating nearly all that it absorbs (see **Figure 2.6**). Because Earth is a cooler radiating body, it emits longer wavelengths, mostly in the infrared portion of the spectrum, centered around 10.0 μm. Atmospheric gases, such as carbon dioxide and water vapor, vary in their response to radiation received, being transparent to some wavelengths, while absorbing others.

To summarize, energy flows into and out of Earth systems (Figure 2.6). The Sun's radiated energy is *shortwave radiation* that peaks in the short, visible wavelengths, whereas Earth's radiated energy is *longwave radiation* concentrated in infrared wavelengths. In Chapter 3, we see that Earth, clouds, sky, ground, and all things that are terrestrial radiate longer wavelengths in contrast to the Sun, thus maintaining the overall energy budget of the Earth and atmosphere.

Incoming Energy at the Top of the Atmosphere

The region at the top of the atmosphere, approximately 480 km (300 mi) above Earth's surface, is the **thermopause** (see Figure 2.12). It is the outer boundary of Earth's energy system and provides a useful point at which to assess the arriving solar radiation before it is diminished by scattering and absorption as it passes through the atmosphere.

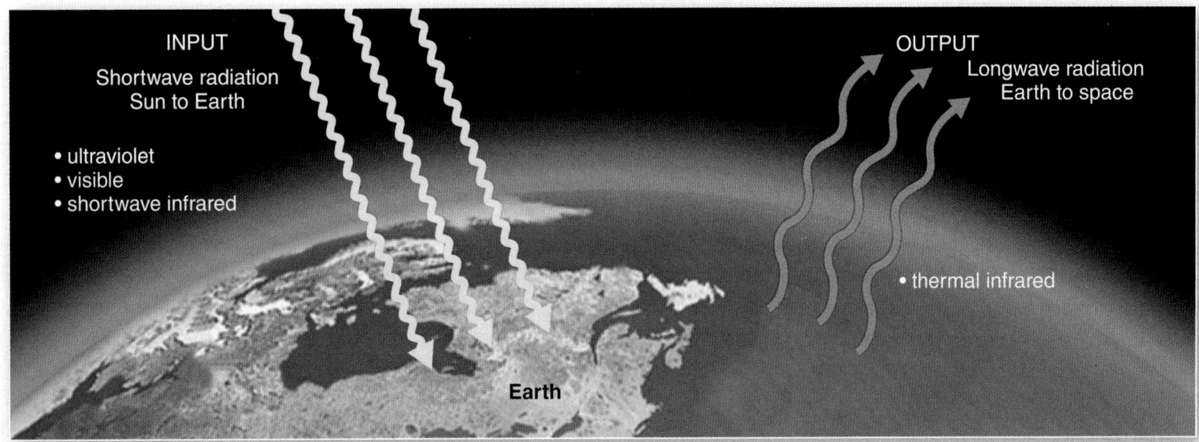

▲**Figure 2.6 Earth's energy budget simplified.**

Earth's distance from the Sun results in its interception of only two-billionths of the Sun's total energy output. Nevertheless, this tiny fraction of energy from the Sun is an enormous amount of energy flowing into Earth's systems. Solar radiation that is intercepted by Earth is **insolation**, derived from the words *in*coming *sol*ar radi*ation*. Insolation specifically applies to radiation arriving at Earth's atmosphere and surface; it is measured as the rate of radiation delivery to a horizontal surface—specifically, as watts per square meter (W/m^2).*

Solar Constant Knowing the amount of insolation incoming to Earth is important to climatologists and other scientists. The **solar constant** is the average insolation received at the thermopause when Earth is at its average distance from the Sun, a value of 1372 W/m^2. As we follow insolation through the atmosphere to Earth's surface (discussed in Chapter 3), we see that its amount is reduced by half or more through reflection, scattering, and absorption of shortwave radiation.

*A *watt* is equal to 1 joule (a unit of energy) per second and is the standard unit of power in the International System of Units (SI). (See the conversion tables in Appendix C of this text for more information on measurement conversions.) In nonmetric *calorie* heat units, the solar constant is expressed as approximately 2 calories per square centimeter per minute, or 2 *langleys* per minute (a langley being 1 cal/cm^2). A calorie is the amount of energy required to raise the temperature of 1 gram of water (at 15°C) 1 degree Celsius and is equal to 4.184 joules.

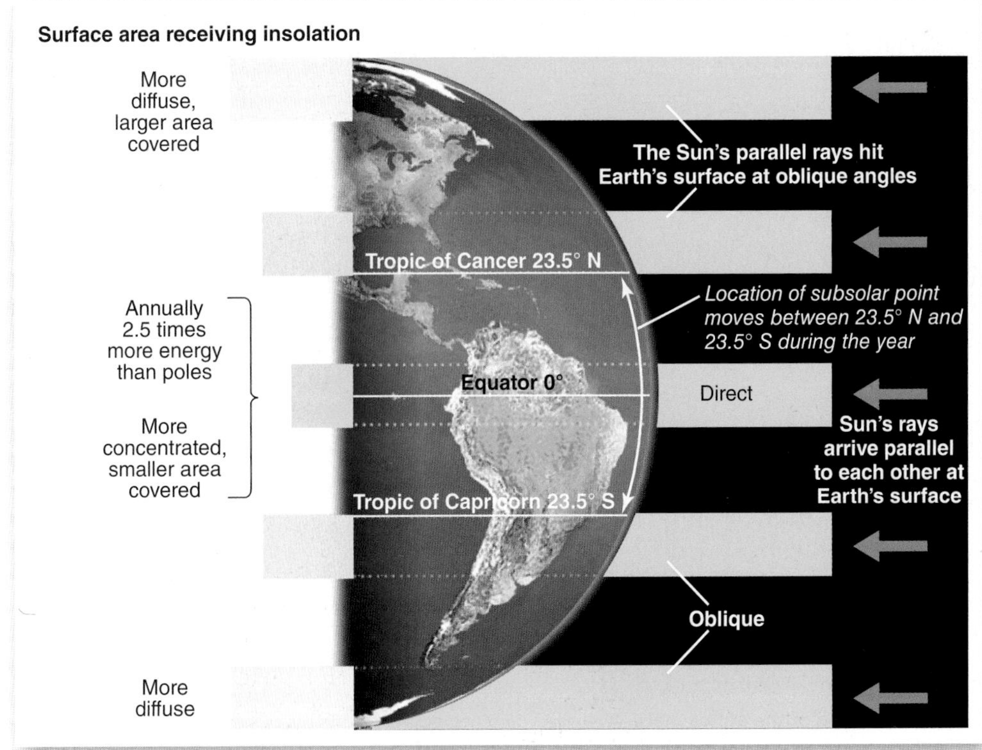

◀**Figure 2.7 Insolation receipts and Earth's curved surface.** The angle at which insolation arrives from the Sun determines the concentration of energy receipts by latitude. The subsolar point, where the Sun's rays arrive perpendicular to Earth, moves between the tropics during the year.

Uneven Distribution of Insolation Earth's curved surface presents a continually varying angle to the incoming parallel rays of insolation (**Figure 2.7** on page 41). Differences in the angle at which solar rays meet the surface at each latitude result in an uneven distribution of insolation and heating. The only point where insolation arrives perpendicular to the surface (hitting it from directly overhead at a 90° angle) is the **subsolar point**.

During the year, this point occurs only at lower latitudes, between the tropics (about 23.5° N and 23.5° S), and as a result, the energy received there is more concentrated. All other places, away from the subsolar point, receive insolation at an angle less than 90° and thus experience more diffuse energy; this effect becomes more pronounced at higher latitudes.

The thermopause above the equatorial region receives 2.5 times more insolation annually than the thermopause above the poles. Of lesser importance is the fact that, because they meet the Earth at a lower angle, the solar rays arriving toward the poles must pass through a greater thickness of atmosphere, resulting in greater losses of energy due to scattering, absorption, and reflection.

Global Net Radiation **Figure 2.8** shows patterns of *net radiation*, which is the balance between incoming shortwave energy from the Sun and all outgoing radiation from Earth and the atmosphere—energy inputs minus energy outputs. The map uses *isolines*, or lines connecting points of equal value, to show radiation patterns. Following the line for 70 W/m² on the map shows that the highest positive net radiation is in equatorial regions, especially over oceans.

Note the latitudinal energy imbalance in net radiation on the map—positive values in lower latitudes and negative values toward the poles. In middle and high latitudes, poleward of approximately 36° N and 36° S latitude, net radiation is negative. This occurs in these higher latitudes because Earth's climate system loses more energy to space than it gains from the Sun, as measured at the top of the atmosphere. In the lower atmosphere, these polar energy deficits are offset by flows of energy from tropical energy surpluses (as we see in Chapters 3 and 4). The largest net radiation values, averaging 80 W/m², are above the tropical oceans along a narrow equatorial zone. Net radiation minimums are lowest over Antarctica.

The Sahara Desert region of North Africa shows a strong negative net radiation pattern of –20 W/m². Here, typically clear skies—which permit great longwave radiation losses from Earth's surface—and light-colored reflective surfaces work together to reduce net radiation values at the thermopause. In other regions, clouds and atmospheric pollution in the lower atmosphere also affect net radiation patterns at the top of the atmosphere by reflecting more shortwave energy to space.

This latitudinal imbalance in energy is critical because it drives global circulation in the atmosphere and the oceans, as discussed in later chapters. Having examined the flow of solar energy to the top of Earth's atmosphere, let us now look at how seasonal changes affect the distribution of insolation as Earth orbits the Sun during the year.

The Seasons

Earth's periodic rhythms of warmth and cold, the timing of dawn and twilight, and the length of daylight and night have fascinated humans for centuries.

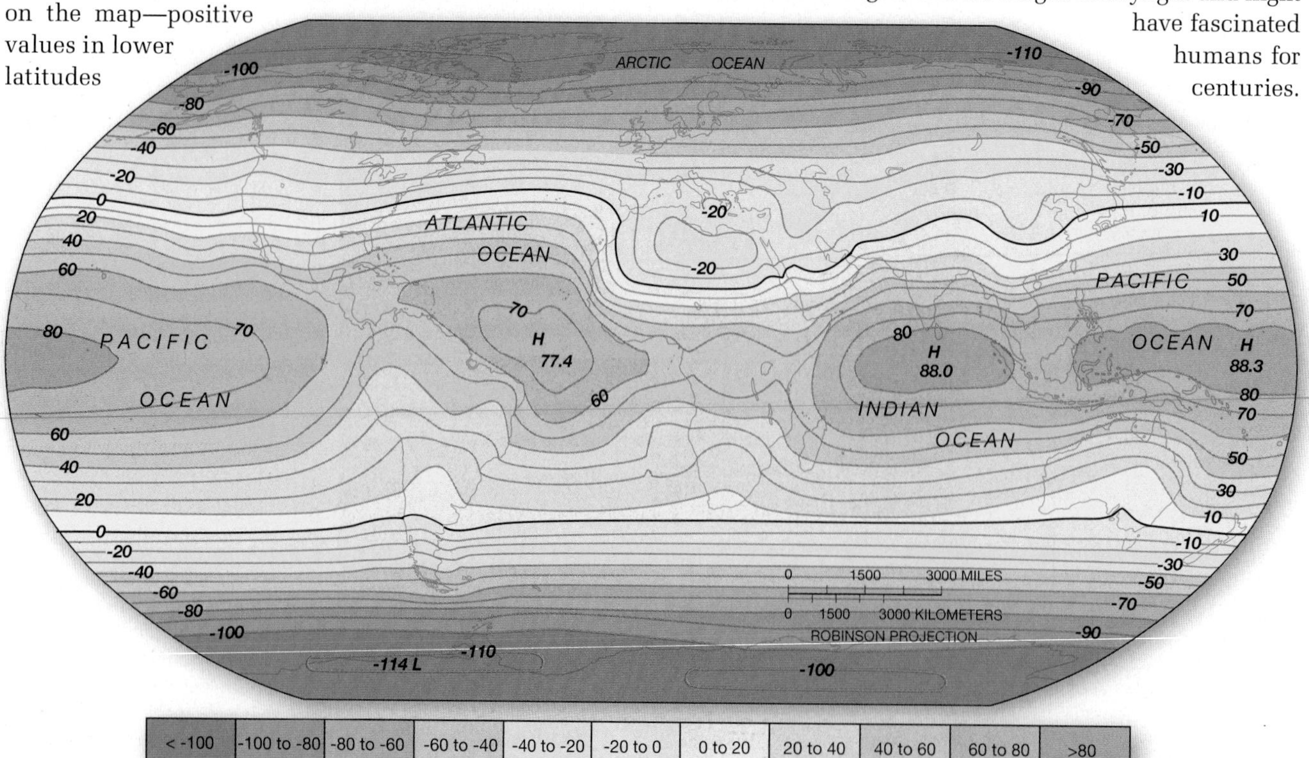

▲**Figure 2.8 Daily net radiation patterns at the top of the atmosphere.** Averaged daily net radiation flows measured at the top of the atmosphere by the Earth Radiation Budget Experiment (ERBE). Units are W/m². [Data for map courtesy of GSFC/NASA.]

In fact, many ancient societies demonstrated an intense awareness of seasonal change and formally commemorated these natural energy rhythms with festivals, monuments, ground markings, and calendars (**Figure 2.9**). Such seasonal monuments and calendar markings are found worldwide, including thousands of sites in North America, demonstrating an ancient awareness of seasons and astronomical relations. Many seasonal rituals and practices persist in this modern era.

Seasonality

Seasonality refers both to the seasonal variation of the Sun's position above the horizon and to the changing daylengths during the year. Seasonal variations are a response to changes in the Sun's **altitude**, or the angle between the horizon and the Sun. At sunrise or sunset, the Sun is at the horizon, so its altitude is 0°. If during the day the Sun reaches halfway between the horizon and directly overhead, it is at 45° altitude. If the Sun reaches the point directly overhead, it is at 90° altitude.

The Sun is found directly overhead (90° altitude, or *zenith*) only at the subsolar point, where insolation is at a maximum. At all other surface points, the Sun is at a lower altitude angle, producing more diffuse insolation.

The Sun's **declination** is the latitude of the subsolar point. Declination annually migrates through 47° of latitude, moving between the Tropic of Cancer and Tropic of Capricorn latitudes. Although it passes through Hawai'i, which is between 19° N and 22° N latitude, the subsolar point does not reach the continental United States or Canada; all other states and provinces are too far north.

The duration of exposure to insolation is **daylength**, which varies during the year, depending on latitude. The equator always receives equal hours of day and night: If you live in Ecuador, Kenya, or Singapore, every day and night is 12 hours long, year-round. People living along 40° N latitude (Philadelphia, Denver, Madrid, Beijing) or 40° S latitude (Buenos Aires, Cape Town, Melbourne) experience about 6 hours' difference in daylight between winter (9 hours) and summer (15 hours). At 50° N or S latitude (Winnipeg, Paris, Falkland, or Malvinas Islands), people experience almost 8 hours of annual daylength variation.

Reasons for Seasons

Seasons result from variations in the Sun's *altitude* above the horizon, the Sun's *declination* (latitude of the subsolar point), and *daylength* during the year. These, in turn, are created by several physical factors that operate in concert: Earth's *revolution* in orbit around the Sun, its daily *rotation* on its axis, its *tilted* axis, the unchanging *orientation of its axis*, and its *sphericity* (summarized in **Table 2.1**). Of course, the essential ingredient is having a single source of radiant energy—the Sun. We now look at each of these factors individually. As we do, note the distinction between revolution—Earth's travel around the Sun—and rotation—Earth's spinning on its axis (**Figure 2.10**).

Revolution Earth's orbital **revolution** about the Sun is shown in Figures 2.1d and 2.10. Earth's speed in orbit averages 107,280 kmph (66,660 mph). This speed, together with Earth's distance from the Sun, determines the time required for one revolution around the Sun and therefore the length of the year and duration of the seasons. Earth completes its annual revolution in 365.2422 days. This number is based on a *tropical year*, measured from equinox to equinox, or the elapsed time between two crossings of the equator by the Sun.

▼Figure 2.9 Solar observatory at Chankillo, Peru. The Thirteen Towers are part of the Chankillo temple complex built in coastal Peru over 2000 years ago, the oldest known solar observatory in the Americas (see **http://www.wmf.org/project/chankillo**). Sunrise aligns with certain towers at different dates during the year, as illustrated in Geosystems in Action 2, just ahead. [Ivan Ghezzi/Reuters.]

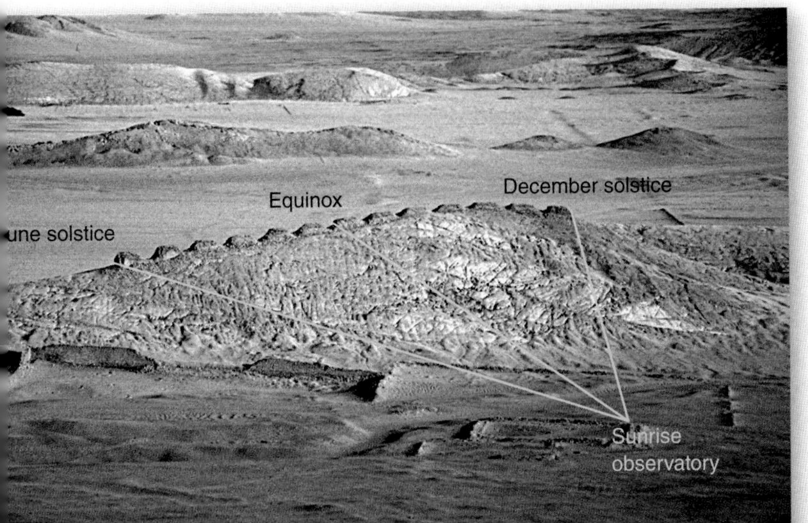

CRITICAL**thinking** 2.1

A Way to Calculate Sunrise and Sunset

Sunrise is the moment when the disk of the Sun first appears above the horizon in the east; *sunset* is the moment when it totally disappears below the horizon in the west. For a useful sunrise and sunset calculator for any location, go to **http://www.esrl.noaa.gov/gmd/grad/solcalc/sunrise.html**, select a city near you or select "Enter lat/long" and enter your coordinates, enter the difference ("offset") between your time and UTC and whether you are on daylight saving time, and enter the date you are checking. Then click "Calculate" to see the solar declination and times for sunrise and sunset. Give this a try. Make a note of your finding; then revisit this site over the course of a full year, and see the change that occurs where you live.

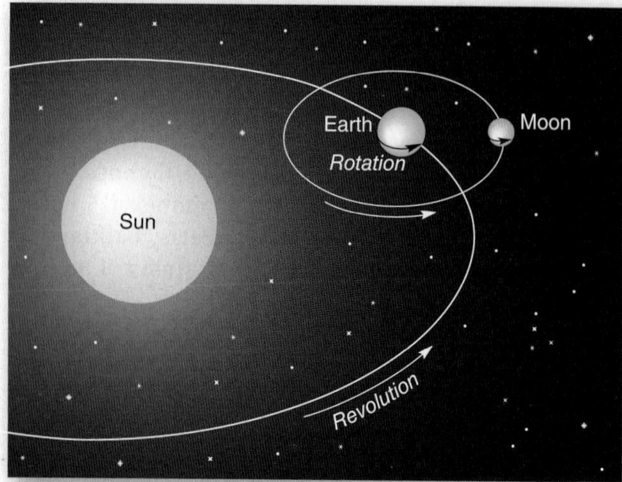

▲**Figure 2.10 Earth's revolution and rotation.** Earth's revolution about the Sun and rotation on its axis, viewed from above Earth's orbit. Note the Moon's rotation on its axis and revolution are counterclockwise as well.

Rotation Earth's **rotation**, or turning on its axis, is a complex motion that averages slightly less than 24 hours in duration. Rotation determines daylength, creates the apparent deflection of winds and ocean currents, and produces the twice-daily rise and fall of the ocean tides in relation to the gravitational pull of the Sun and the Moon.

When viewed from above the North Pole, Earth rotates counterclockwise about its *axis*, an imaginary line extending through the planet from the geographic North Pole to the South Pole. Viewed from above the equator, Earth rotates west to east, or eastward. This eastward rotation creates the Sun's *apparent* westward daily journey from sunrise in the east to sunset in the west. Of course, the Sun actually remains in a fixed position in the center of our Solar System.

Although every point on Earth takes the same 24 hours to complete one rotation, the linear velocity of rotation at any point on Earth's surface varies dramatically with latitude. The equator is 40,075 km (24,902 mi) long; therefore, rotational velocity at the equator must be approximately 1675 kmph (1041 mph) to cover that distance in one day. At 60° latitude, a parallel is only half the length of the equator, or 20,038 km (12,451 mi) long, so the rotational velocity there is 838 kmph (521 mph). At the poles, the velocity is 0. This variation in rotational velocity establishes the effect of the Coriolis force, discussed in Chapter 4.

Earth's rotation produces the diurnal (daily) pattern of day and night. The dividing line between day and night is the **circle of illumination** (as illustrated in Geosystems in Action 2). Because this day–night-dividing circle of illumination intersects the equator (and because both the circle of illumination and the equator are great circles and any two great circles on a sphere bisect one another), *daylength at the equator is always evenly divided*—12 hours of day and 12 hours of night. All other latitudes experience uneven daylength through the seasons, except for the two equinoxes.

Tilt of Earth's Axis To understand Earth's **axial tilt**, imagine a plane (a flat surface) that intersects Earth's elliptical orbit about the Sun, with half of the Sun and Earth above the plane and half below. Such a plane, touching all points of Earth's orbit, is the **plane of the ecliptic**. Earth's tilted axis remains fixed relative to this plane as Earth revolves around the Sun. The plane of the ecliptic is important to our discussion of Earth's seasons. Now, imagine a perpendicular (at a 90° angle) line passing through the plane. From this perpendicular, Earth's axis is tilted about 23.5°. It forms a 66.5° angle from the plane itself (**Figure 2.11**). The axis through Earth's two poles points just slightly off Polaris, which is named, appropriately, the *North Star*.

The tilt angle is "about" 23.5° because Earth's axial tilt changes over a complex 41,000-year cycle (see Figure 8.13). The axial tilt ranges roughly between 22° and 24.5° from a perpendicular to the plane of the ecliptic. The present tilt is 23.45°. For convenience, this is rounded off to a

CRITICAL**thinking** 2.2

Astronomical Factors Vary over Long Time Frames

The variability of Earth's axial tilt and orbit about the Sun, as well as a wobble to the axis, is described in Chapter 8, Figure 8.13. Refer to this figure on page 258, and compare these changing conditions to the information in Table 2.1 and the related figures in this chapter.

What do you think the effect on Earth's seasons would be if the tilt of the axis was decreased? Or if the tilt was increased a little? Or if Earth was lying on its side? You can take a ball or piece of round fruit, mark the poles, and then move it around a lightbulb as if you are revolving it around the Sun. Note where the light falls relative to the poles with no tilt and then with a 90° tilt to help complete your analysis. Now, what if Earth's orbit was more circular as opposed to its present elliptical shape? Earth's elliptical orbit actually does vary throughout a 100,000-year cycle. (Check the answer at the end of the Key Learning Concepts Review.)

GEO**report** 2.1 Measuring Earth's rotation

A slight "wobble" along Earth's rotating axis causes it to migrate irregularly along a circular path with a radius up to about 9 m (30 ft). The accuracy of modern navigation systems such as GPS relies on measuring this "wobble." Scientists at the International Earth Rotation Service track Earth's rotation indirectly by monitoring fixed objects in space using radio telescopes (see http://www.iers.org/). In 2011, a research group made the first accurate direct measurements of Earth's annual rotation using two counter-rotating lasers stored deep underground. The next goal is to precisely measure changes in Earth's rotation over a single day.

TABLE 2.1 Five Reasons for Seasons

Factor	Description
Revolution	Orbit around the Sun; requires 365.2422 days to complete at 107,280 kmph (66,660 mph)
Rotation	Earth turning on its axis; takes approximately 24 hours to complete
Tilt	Alignment of axis at about 23.5° angle from perpendicular to the plane of the ecliptic (the plane of Earth's orbit)
Axial parallelism	Unchanging (fixed) axial alignment, with Polaris directly overhead at the North Pole throughout the year
Sphericity	Oblate spheroidal shape lit by Sun's parallel rays; the geoid (described in Chapter 1)

23.5° tilt (or 66.5° from the plane) in most usage. Scientific evidence shows that the angle of tilt is currently lessening in its 41,000-year cycle.

Axial Parallelism Throughout our annual journey around the Sun, Earth's axis *maintains the same alignment* relative to the plane of the ecliptic and to Polaris and other stars. You can see this consistent alignment in Geosystems in Action 2, Figure GIA 2.2. If we compared the axis in different months, it would always appear parallel to itself, a condition known as **axial parallelism**.

Sphericity Even though Earth is not a perfect sphere, as discussed in Chapter 1, we can still refer to Earth's *sphericity* as contributing to seasonality. Earth's approximately spherical shape causes the parallel rays of the Sun to fall at uneven angles on Earth's surface. As we saw in Figure 2.7, Earth's curvature means that insolation angles and net radiation received vary between the equator and the poles.

All five reasons for seasons—revolution, rotation, tilt, axial parallelism, and sphericity—are summarized in Table 2.1. Now, considering all these factors operating together, we explore the march of the seasons.

Annual March of the Seasons

During the march of the seasons on Earth, daylength is the most obvious way of sensing seasonal changes at latitudes away from the equator. The extremes of daylength occur in December and June. The times around December 21 and June 21 are *solstices*. Strictly speaking, the solstices are specific points in time at which the Sun's declination is at its position farthest north at the **Tropic of Cancer** or south at the **Tropic of Capricorn**. "Tropic" is from *tropicus*, meaning a turn or change, so a tropic latitude is where the Sun's declination appears to stand still briefly (Sun stance, or *sol stice*) and then "turn" and head toward the other tropic.

During the year, places on Earth outside of the equatorial region experience a continuous, but gradual shift in daylength, a few minutes each day, and the Sun's altitude increases or decreases a small amount. You may have noticed that these daily variations become more pronounced in spring and autumn, when the Sun's declination changes at a faster rate.

Geosystems in Action 2 on the following pages summarizes the annual march of the seasons and Earth's relationship to the Sun during the year, using a side view (Figure GIA 2.1) and a top view (Figure GIA 2.2). On December 21 or 22, at the moment of the **December solstice**, or Northern Hemisphere *winter solstice* ("winter sun stance"), the circle of illumination excludes the North Pole region from sunlight, but includes the South Pole region. The subsolar point is about 23.5° S latitude, the Tropic of Capricorn parallel. The Northern Hemisphere is tilted away from these more direct rays of sunlight—our northern winter—thereby creating a lower angle for the incoming solar rays and thus a more diffuse pattern of insolation.

For locations between about 66.5° N and 90° N (the North Pole), the Sun remains below the horizon the entire day. The parallel at about 66.5° N marks the **Arctic Circle**; this is the southernmost parallel (in the Northern Hemisphere) that experiences a 24-hour period of darkness. During this period, twilight and dawn provide some lighting for more than a month at the beginning and end of the Arctic night.

During the following 3 months, daylength and solar angles gradually increase in the Northern Hemisphere as Earth completes one-fourth of its orbit. The moment of the **March equinox**, or *vernal equinox* in the Northern Hemisphere, occurs on March 20 or 21. At that time, the circle of illumination passes through both poles, so that all locations on Earth experience a 12-hour day and a 12-hour night. People living around 40° N latitude (New York, Denver) have gained 3 hours of daylight since the December solstice. At the North Pole, the Sun peeks above the

(*text continued on page 48*)

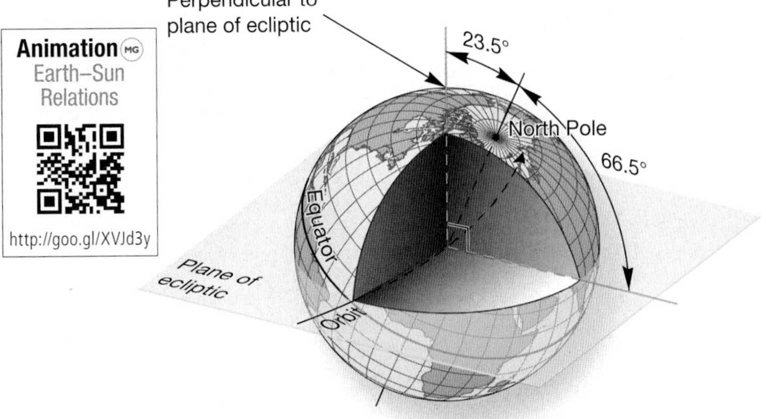

▲**Figure 2.11 The plane of Earth's orbit—the ecliptic—and Earth's axial tilt.** Note on the illustration that the plane of the equator is inclined to the plane of the ecliptic at about 23.5°.

Midnight Sun over Arctic Ocean, June

During the year, outside of the equatorial regions, the Sun's altitude changes slightly each day, and daylength gradually increases and decreases. These changes affect the amount of insolation received, which drives weather and climate. Taken together, these variations in Earth's relationship to the Sun produce the annual "march" of the seasons.

2.1 Earth's Orientation at Solstices and Equinoxes

As Earth (seen in side view) orbits the Sun, the 23.5° tilt of Earth's axis remains constant. As a result, the area covered by the circle of illumination changes, along with the location of the subsolar point (red dot).

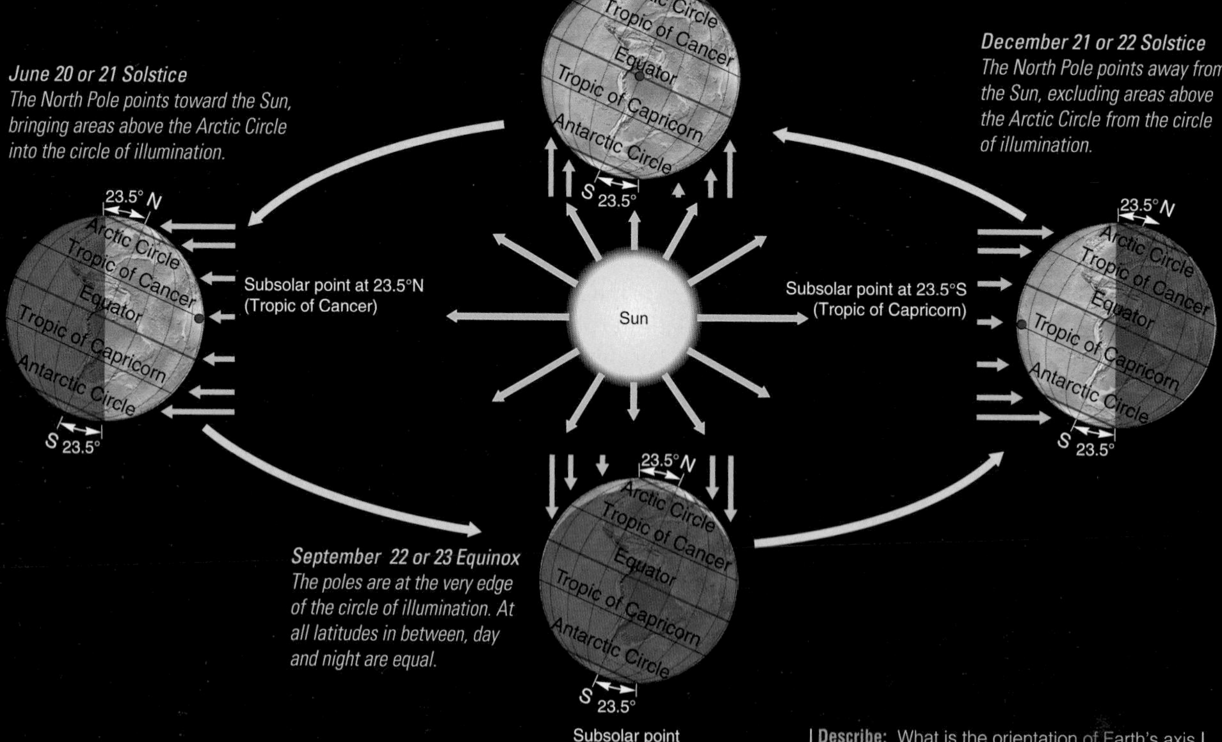

March 20 or 21 Equinox
The poles are at the very edge of the circle of illumination. At all latitudes in between, day and night are equal.
Subsolar point at 0° (Equator)
June 20 or 21 Solstice
The North Pole points toward the Sun, bringing areas above the Arctic Circle into the circle of illumination.
Subsolar point at 23.5°N (Tropic of Cancer)
December 21 or 22 Solstice
The North Pole points away from the Sun, excluding areas above the Arctic Circle from the circle of illumination.
Subsolar point at 23.5°S (Tropic of Capricorn)
September 22 or 23 Equinox
The poles are at the very edge of the circle of illumination. At all latitudes in between, day and night are equal.
Subsolar point at 0° (Equator)
Sun
23.5° N
S 23.5°
Arctic Circle
Tropic of Cancer
Equator
Tropic of Capricorn
Antarctic Circle

Describe: What is the orientation of Earth's axis with respect to the Sun on the March equinox?

Animation Earth–Sun Relations

http://goo.gl/XVJd3y

MasteringGeography™

Visit the Study Area in MasteringGeography™ to explore Geosystems in Action.

Visualize: Study a geosciences animation of the Earth–Sun relations.

Assess: Demonstrate understanding of Earth–Sun relations (if assigned by instructor).

2.2 March of the Seasons

As Earth (visualized from above the North Pole) orbits the Sun, the 23.5° tilt of its axis produces continuous changes in daylength and Sun angle.

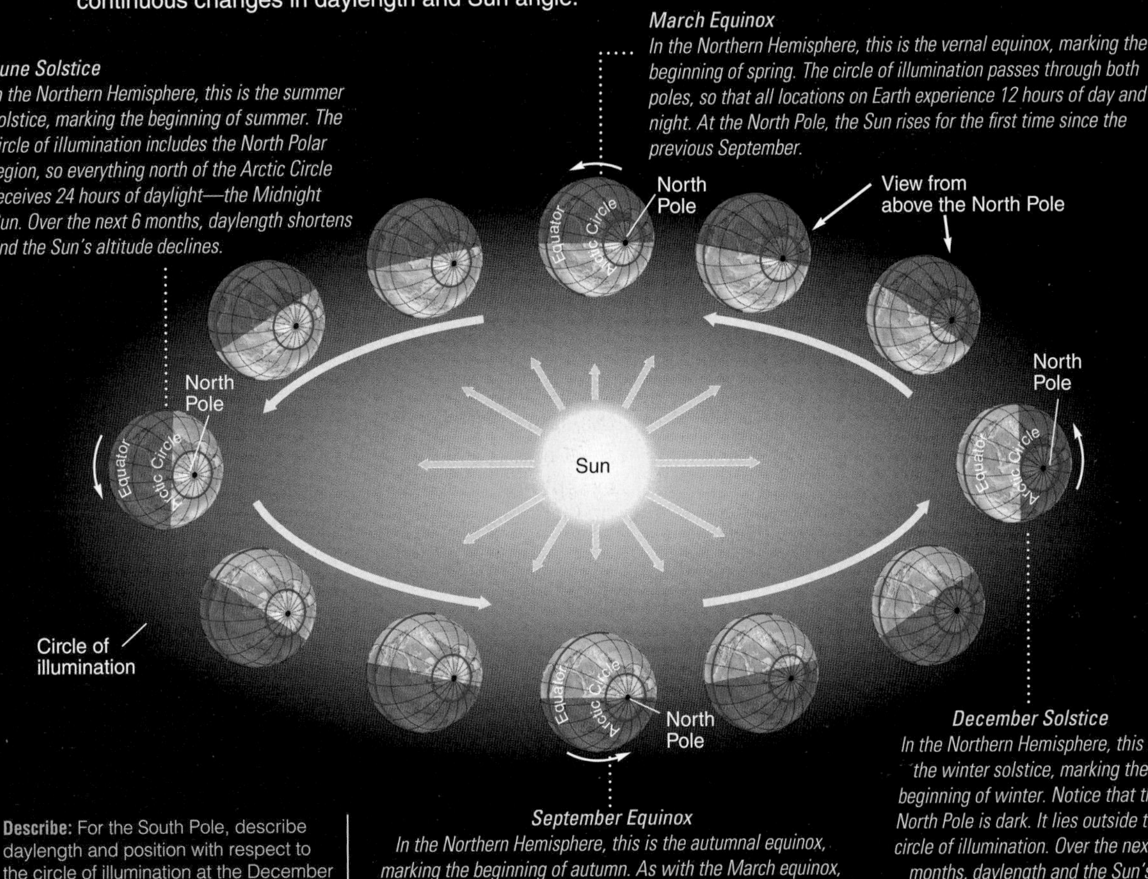

March Equinox
In the Northern Hemisphere, this is the vernal equinox, marking the beginning of spring. The circle of illumination passes through both poles, so that all locations on Earth experience 12 hours of day and night. At the North Pole, the Sun rises for the first time since the previous September.

June Solstice
In the Northern Hemisphere, this is the summer solstice, marking the beginning of summer. The circle of illumination includes the North Polar region, so everything north of the Arctic Circle receives 24 hours of daylight—the Midnight Sun. Over the next 6 months, daylength shortens and the Sun's altitude declines.

September Equinox
In the Northern Hemisphere, this is the autumnal equinox, marking the beginning of autumn. As with the March equinox, days and nights are of equal length.

December Solstice
In the Northern Hemisphere, this is the winter solstice, marking the beginning of winter. Notice that the North Pole is dark. It lies outside the circle of illumination. Over the next 6 months, daylength and the Sun's altitude increase.

Describe: For the South Pole, describe daylength and position with respect to the circle of illumination at the December solstice and the March equinox.

2.3 Observing Sun Direction and Altitude

As the seasons change, the Sun's altitude, or angle above the horizon, also changes, as does its position at sunrise and sunset along the horizon (illustrtated below from the viewpoint of an observer).

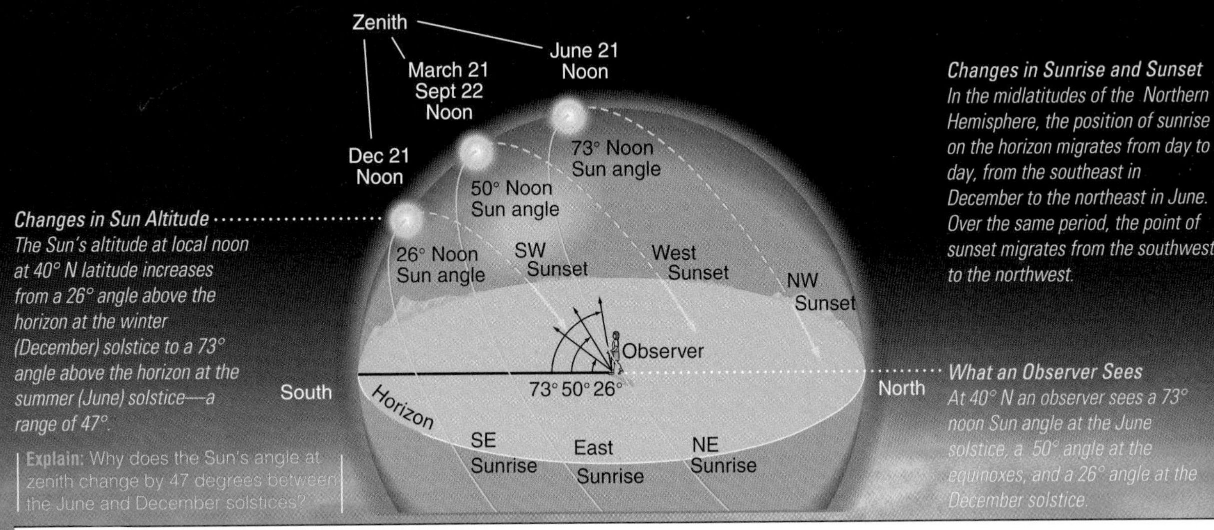

Changes in Sun Altitude
The Sun's altitude at local noon at 40° N latitude increases from a 26° angle above the horizon at the winter (December) solstice to a 73° angle above the horizon at the summer (June) solstice—a range of 47°.

Explain: Why does the Sun's angle at zenith change by 47 degrees between the June and December solstices?

Changes in Sunrise and Sunset
In the midlatitudes of the Northern Hemisphere, the position of sunrise on the horizon migrates from day to day, from the southeast in December to the northeast in June. Over the same period, the point of sunset migrates from the southwest to the northwest.

What an Observer Sees
At 40° N an observer sees a 73° noon Sun angle at the June solstice, a 50° angle at the equinoxes, and a 26° angle at the December solstice.

GEOquiz

1. Apply Concepts: Ushuaia, Argentina, is located at 55° S latitude near the southern tip of South America. Describe the march of the seasons for Ushuaia, explaining changes in daylength, Sun altitude, and the position of sunrise and sunset.

2. Explain: What happens to the amount of insolation an area on Earth's surface receives as you move away from the equator? What role does this play in producing the seasons?

Antarctic sunset, December 11:30 pm

horizon for the first time since the previous September; at the South Pole, the Sun is setting—a dramatic 3-day "moment" for the people working the Amundsen–Scott South Pole Station.

From March, the seasons move on to June 20 or 21 and the moment of the **June solstice**, or *summer solstice* in the Northern Hemisphere. The subsolar point migrates from the equator to 23.5° N latitude, the Tropic of Cancer. Because the circle of illumination now includes the North Polar region, everything north of the Arctic Circle receives 24 hours of daylight—the *Midnight Sun*. In contrast, the region from the **Antarctic Circle** to the South Pole (66.5°–90° S latitude) is in darkness. Those working in Antarctica call the June solstice *Midwinter's Day*.

September 22 or 23 is the time of the **September equinox**, or *autumnal equinox* in the Northern Hemisphere, when Earth's orientation is such that the circle of illumination again passes through both poles, so that all parts of the globe experience a 12-hour day and a 12-hour night. The subsolar point returns to the equator, with days growing shorter to the north and longer to the south. Researchers stationed at the South Pole see the disk of the Sun just rising, ending their 6 months of darkness. In the Northern Hemisphere, autumn arrives, a time of many colorful changes in the landscape, whereas in the Southern Hemisphere it is spring.

Throughout the annual changing of the seasons, the position of the Sun on the horizon at sunrise and sunset, as well as the Sun's altitude—the angle above the horizon—varies, as shown in Figure GIA 2.3. In the midlatitudes of the Northern Hemisphere, the position of sunrise on the horizon migrates from day to day, from the southeast in December to the northeast in June. Over the same period, the point of sunset migrates from the southwest to the northwest. The Sun's altitude at local noon at 40° N latitude increases from a 26° angle above the horizon at the winter (December) solstice to a 73° angle above the horizon at the summer (June) solstice—a range of 47°.

Seasonal change reflected in temperature, weather, and vegetation is quite noticeable across landscapes away from the equator. Recently, the timing of seasonal patterns in the biosphere is shifting with global climate change. In the middle and high latitudes, spring and leafing out are occurring as much as 3 weeks earlier than in previous human experience. Likewise, fall is happening later. Ecosystems are changing in response (look back to the chapter-opening photo).

Atmospheric Composition, Temperature, and Function

The modern atmosphere probably is the fourth general atmosphere in Earth's history. A gaseous mixture of ancient origin, it is the sum of all the exhalations and inhalations of life interacting on Earth throughout time (see GeoReport 2.2). The principal substance of this atmosphere is air, the medium of life as well as a major industrial and chemical raw material. *Air* is a simple mixture of gases that is naturally odorless, colorless, tasteless, and formless, blended so thoroughly that it behaves as if it were a single gas.

As a practical matter, we consider the top of our atmosphere to be around 480 km (300 mi) above Earth's surface, the same altitude we used for measuring the solar constant and insolation received. Beyond that altitude is the **exosphere**, which means "outer sphere," where the rarefied, less dense atmosphere is nearly a vacuum. It contains scarce lightweight hydrogen and helium atoms, weakly bound by gravity as far as 32,000 km (20,000 mi) from Earth.

Atmospheric Profile

Think of Earth's modern atmosphere as a thin envelope of imperfectly shaped concentric "shells" or "spheres" that grade into one another, all bound to the planet by gravity. To study the atmosphere, we view it in layers, each with distinctive properties and processes. **Figure 2.12** charts the atmosphere in a vertical cross-section profile, or side view. Scientists use three atmospheric criteria—*composition*, *temperature*, and *function*—to define layers for distinct analytical purposes. As you read the criteria discussions ahead, note that they repeatedly follow the path of incoming solar radiation as it travels through the atmosphere to Earth's surface.

Air pressure changes throughout the layers of the atmospheric profile. Air molecules create **air pressure** through their motion, size, and number, exerting a force on all surfaces they come in contact with. The pressure of the atmosphere (measured as force per unit area) pushes in on all of us. Fortunately, that same pressure also exists inside us, pushing outward; otherwise, we would be crushed by the mass of air around us.

Earth's atmosphere also presses downward under the pull of gravity and therefore has weight. Gravity

GEOreport 2.2 Earth's evolving atmosphere

The first atmosphere on Earth was probably formed from *outgassing*, or the release of gases trapped within Earth's interior. We still see outgassing today in the form of volcanic activity. This atmosphere was high in sulfuric gases, low in nitrogen, and devoid of oxygen. The second atmosphere formed when Earth cooled and water vapor condensed to form clouds and rain. Oceans formed, nitrogen increased, but oxygen was still not present in the atmosphere. As oceanic life evolved, bacteria began the process of photosynthesis, using the Sun's energy to convert atmospheric carbon dioxide to oxygen. Oxygen became significant in the atmosphere about 2.2 billion years ago, but it took another billion years before atmospheric oxygen levels were stable. Our modern atmosphere formed when oxygen molecules absorbed sunlight and formed ozone, the protective layer in the stratosphere that shields all life from ultraviolet radiation.

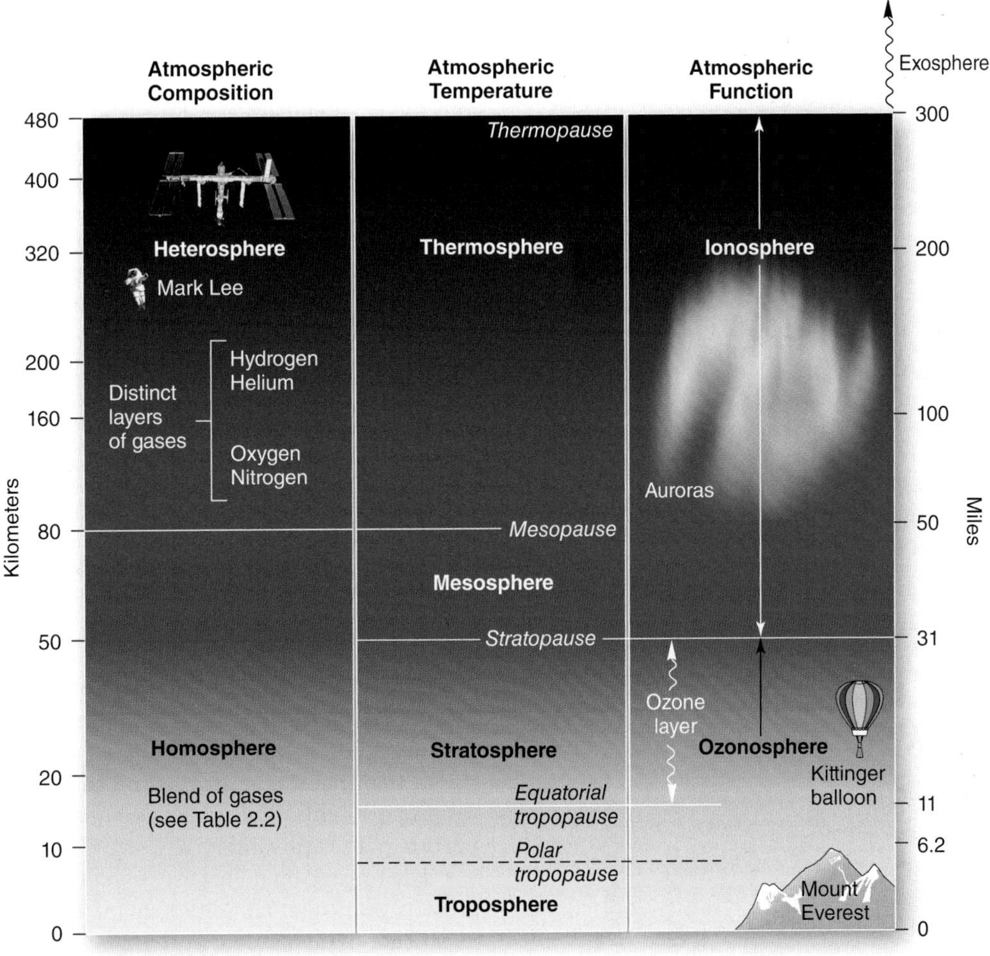

▲**Figure 2.12 Profile of the modern atmosphere.** Note the small astronaut (upper left) and balloon (lower right) showing the altitudes achieved by astronaut Mark Lee and by Joseph Kittinger, discussed in Geosystems Now 2.

compresses air, making it denser near Earth's surface (**Figure 2.13**). At sea level, the atmosphere exerts an average pressure equivalent to that of a 1-kg weight resting on 1 cm² of area. With increasing altitude, density and pressure decrease—this is the "thinning" of air that humans feel on high mountain summits as less oxygen is carried in each breath a person takes. This makes breathing more difficult at the top of Mount Everest (Figure 2.12), where air pressure is about 30% of that on Earth's surface. More information on air pressure and the role it plays in generating winds appears in Chapter 4.

Over half the total mass of the atmosphere, compressed by gravity, lies below 5.5 km (3.14 mi, or 18,000 ft) altitude. Only 0.1% of the atmosphere remains above an altitude of 50 km (31 mi), as shown in the pressure profile in Figure 2.13b (percentage column is farthest to the right).

At sea level, the atmosphere exerts a pressure of 1013.2 mb (millibars, a measure of force per square meter of surface area), or 29.92 in. of mercury (symbol, Hg), as measured by a barometer. In Canada and certain other countries, normal air pressure is expressed as 101.32 kPa (kilopascals; 1 kPa = 10 mb). (See Chapter 4 for further discussion.)

Atmospheric Composition Criterion

By the criterion of chemical *composition*, the atmosphere divides into two broad regions (Figure 2.12), the *heterosphere* (80 to 480 km altitude) and the *homosphere* (Earth's surface to 80 km altitude).

GEOreport 2.3 Outside the airplane

Next time you are in an airplane, think about the air pressure outside. Few people are aware that in routine air travel they are sitting above 80% of the total atmospheric volume and that the air pressure at that altitude is only about 10% of surface air pressure. Only 20% of the atmospheric mass is above you. If your plane is at about 11,000 m (36,090 ft), think of the men who jumped from stratospheric heights, described in Geosystems Now 2; Felix Baumgartner started another 28 km (17 mi) higher in altitude than your plane!

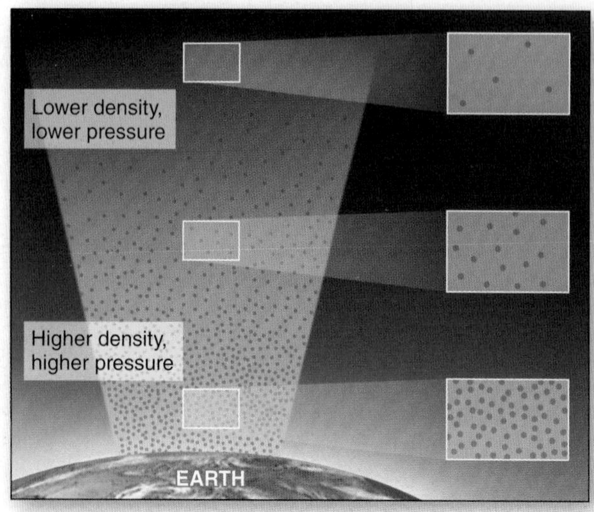

(a) Atmospheric density is higher nearer Earth's surface and decreases with altitude.

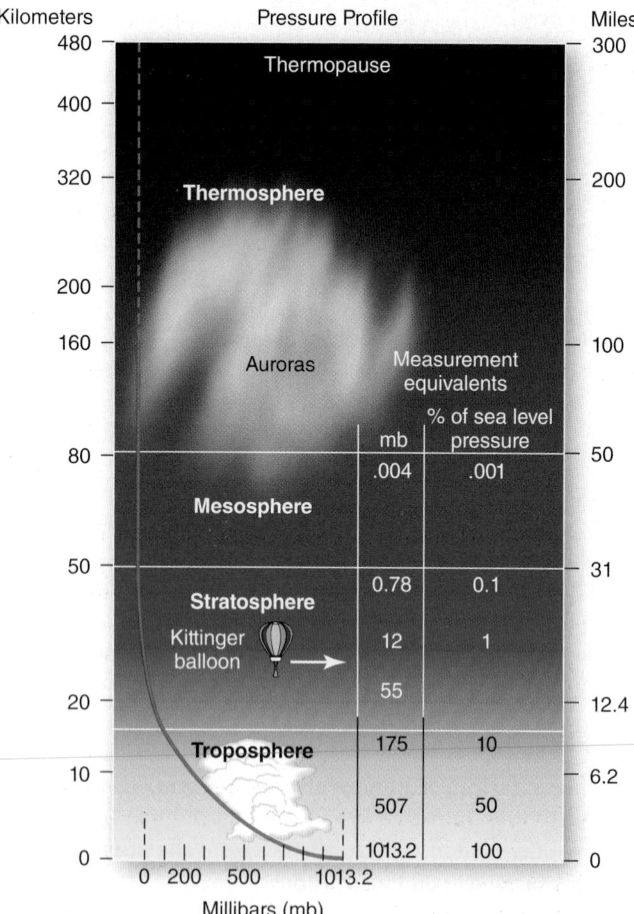

(b) Pressure profile plots the decrease in pressure with increasing altitude. Pressure is in millibars and as a percentage of sea-level pressure. Note that the troposphere holds about 90% of the atmospheric mass (far-right % column).

▲**Figure 2.13 Density decreasing with altitude.** Have you experienced pressure changes that you could feel on your eardrums? How high above sea level were you at the time?

Heterosphere The **heterosphere** is the outer atmosphere in terms of composition. It begins at about 80 km (50 mi) altitude and extends outward to the exosphere and interplanetary space. Less than 0.001% of the atmosphere's mass is in this rarefied region. The International Space Station (ISS) orbits in the middle to upper heterosphere (note the ISS altitude in Figure 2.12).

As the prefix *hetero-* implies, this region is not uniform—its gases are not evenly mixed. Gases in the heterosphere occur in distinct layers sorted by gravity according to their atomic weight, with the lightest elements (hydrogen and helium) at the margins of outer space and the heavier elements (oxygen and nitrogen) dominant in the lower heterosphere. This distribution is quite different from the blended gases we breathe in the homosphere, near Earth's surface.

Homosphere Below the heterosphere is the **homosphere**, extending from an altitude of 80 km (50 mi) to Earth's surface. Even though the atmosphere rapidly changes density in the homosphere—increasing pressure toward Earth's surface—the blend of gases is nearly uniform throughout. The only exceptions are the concentration of ozone (O_3) in the "ozone layer," from 19 to 50 km (12 to 31 mi) above sea level, and the variations in water vapor, pollutants, and some trace chemicals in the lowest portion of the atmosphere.

The present blend of gases evolved approximately 500 million years ago. **Table 2.2** lists by volume the gases that constitute dry, clean air in the homosphere, divided into *constant gases* (showing little or no change over time) and *variable gases* (present in small, but variable amounts).

The air of the homosphere is a vast reservoir of relatively inert *nitrogen*, originating principally from volcanic sources. A key element of life, nitrogen integrates into our bodies not from the air we breathe, but through compounds in food. In the soil, nitrogen-fixing bacteria incorporate nitrogen from air into compounds that can be used by plants; later, the nitrogen returns to the atmosphere through the work of denitrifying bacteria that remove nitrogen from organic materials (see further discussion in Chapter 16).

Oxygen, a by-product of photosynthesis, also is essential for life processes. The percentage of atmospheric oxygen varies slightly over space and time with changes in photosynthetic rates of vegetation with latitude, season, and the lag time as atmospheric circulation slowly mixes the air. Although it makes up about one-fifth of the atmosphere, oxygen forms compounds that compose about half of Earth's crust. Oxygen readily reacts with many elements to form these materials. Both nitrogen and oxygen reserves in the atmosphere are so extensive that, at present, they far exceed human capabilities to disrupt or deplete them.

The gas *argon*, constituting less than 1% of the homosphere, is completely inert (an unreactive "noble" gas) and unusable in life processes. All the argon present in

TABLE 2.2 Composition of the Modern Homosphere

Gas (Symbol)	Percentage by Volume	Parts per Million (ppm)
Constant Gases (little to no variation over time)		
Nitrogen (N_2)	78.084%	780,840
Oxygen (O_2)	20.946	209,460
Argon (Ar)	0.934	9,340
Neon (Ne)	0.001818	18
Helium (He)	0.000525	5.2
Krypton (Kr)	0.00010	1.0
Xenon (Xe)	Trace	~0.1
Variable Gases (change over time and space)		
Water vapor (H_2O)	0%–4% (max. at tropics, min. at poles)	
Carbon dioxide (CO_2)*	0.0402	402
Methane (CH_4)	0.00018	1.8
Hydrogen (H)	Trace	~0.6
Nitrous oxide (N_2O)	Trace	~0.3
Ozone (O_3)	Variable	

*May 2014 average CO_2 measured at Mauna Loa, Hawai'i (see ftp://aftp.cmdl.noaa.gov/products/trends/co2/co2_mm_mlo.txt).

the modern atmosphere comes from slow accumulation over millions of years. Because industry has found uses for inert argon (in lightbulbs, welding, and some lasers), it is extracted or "mined" from the atmosphere, as are nitrogen and oxygen, for commercial, medical, and industrial uses.

Of the variable atmospheric gases in the homosphere, we examine carbon dioxide in the next section, and we discuss ozone later in this chapter (water vapor is covered in Chapter 5 and methane in Chapter 8). The homosphere also contains variable amounts of *particulates*, solids and liquid droplets that enter the air from natural and human sources. These particles, also known as aerosols, range in size from the relatively large liquid water droplets, salt, and pollen visible with the naked eye to relatively small, even microscopic, dust and soot. These particles affect Earth's energy balance (see Chapter 3) as well as human health (discussed later in the chapter).

Carbon Dioxide *Carbon dioxide (CO_2)* occurs naturally in the atmosphere as part of the Earth's carbon cycle (discussed in Chapters 8 and 16). It is a natural by-product of life processes, a variable gas that is increasing rapidly. Although its present percentage in the atmosphere is small, CO_2 is important to global temperatures.

The study of past atmospheres trapped in samples of glacial ice reveals that the present levels of atmospheric CO_2 are higher than at any time in the past 800,000 years. Over the past 200 years, and especially since the 1950s, the CO_2 percentage increased as a result of human activities, primarily fossil-fuel combustion for energy and transportation, and deforestation. The main sources of U.S. CO_2 emissions are electric power plants (40%) and transportation (31%; see http://www.epa.gov/climatechange/ghgemissions/). In 2011, China led the world in overall CO_2 emissions, producing 28% of the total. However, the United States still leads in per capita (per person) CO_2 emissions.

This increase in atmospheric CO_2 is accelerating (see the graphs for atmospheric CO_2 concentrations in Chapter 8). If it continues, scientists warn that we may reach a threshold, or tipping point, beyond which the warming associated with increased levels of atmospheric CO_2 will bring rising temperatures that cause irreversible ice-sheet and species losses. Chapter 8 discusses the role of carbon dioxide as an important greenhouse gas and the implications of CO_2 increases for global climate change.

Atmospheric Temperature Criterion

By the criterion of temperature, the atmospheric profile can be divided into four distinct zones—thermosphere, mesosphere, stratosphere, and troposphere (labeled in Figure 2.12). We begin with the zone that is highest in altitude.

Thermosphere The **thermosphere** ("heat sphere") roughly corresponds to the heterosphere (from 80 km out to 480 km, or 50–300 mi). The upper limit of the thermosphere is the *thermopause* (the suffix *-pause* means "to change"). During periods of a less active Sun, with fewer sunspots and eruptions from the solar surface, the thermopause may decrease in altitude from the average 480 km (300 mi) to only 250 km (155 mi). During periods of a more active Sun, the outer atmosphere increases to an altitude of 550 km (340 mi), where it can create frictional drag on satellites in low orbit.

The temperature profile in **Figure 2.14a** (yellow curve) shows that temperatures rise sharply in the thermosphere, to 1200°C (2200°F) and higher. Despite such high temperatures, however, the thermosphere is not "hot" in the way you might expect. Temperature and heat are different concepts. The intense solar radiation in this portion of the atmosphere excites individual molecules (principally nitrogen and oxygen) to high levels of vibration. This **kinetic energy**, the energy of motion, is the vibrational energy that we measure as *temperature*. (Temperature is a measure of the average kinetic energy of individual molecules in matter.)

In contrast, *heat* is created when kinetic energy is transferred between molecules—and thus between bodies or substances. Heat is therefore dependent on the density or mass of a substance; where little density or mass exists, the amount of heat will be small. The thermosphere is not "hot" in the way we are familiar with because the density of molecules is so low there that little actual heat is produced. (Temperature and heat are discussed further in Chapter 3.)

Mesosphere The **mesosphere** is the area from 50 to 80 km (31 to 50 mi) above Earth and is within the homosphere. As Figure 2.14a shows, the mesosphere's outer boundary, the *mesopause*, is the coldest portion of the atmosphere, averaging −90°C (−130°F), although that temperature may vary considerably (by 25–30 C°, or 45–54 F°). Note in Figure 2.13b the extremely low pressures (low molecule densities) in the mesosphere.

Stratosphere The **stratosphere** extends from about 18 to 50 km (11 to 31 mi) above Earth's surface. Temperatures increase with altitude throughout the stratosphere, from −57°C (−70°F) at 18 km to 0°C (32°F) at 50 km, the stratosphere's outer boundary, called the *stratopause*. The stratosphere is the location of the ozone layer. Measurements over the past 25 years show that ozone concentrations in the stratosphere are decreasing, causing problems discussed later in this chapter. Greenhouse gases are on the increase in the troposphere below; a noted stratospheric cooling is the response.

Troposphere The **troposphere** is the final layer encountered by incoming solar radiation as it surges through the atmosphere to the surface. This atmospheric

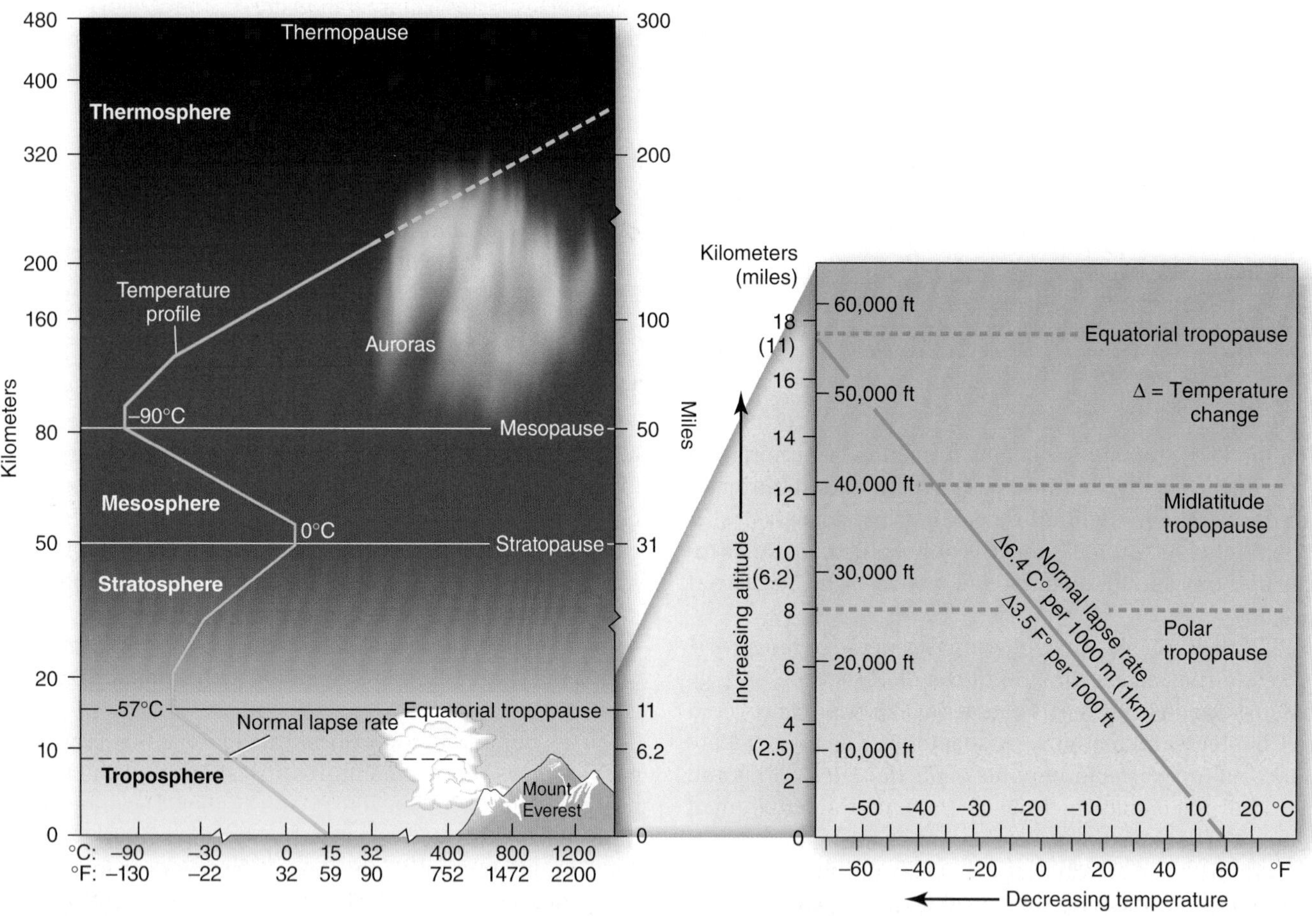

(a) Temperature profile plots temperature changes with altitude.

(b) Temperature decreases with increased altitude at the *normal lapse rate*.

(c) A sunset from orbit shows a silhouetted cumulonimbus thunderhead cloud topping out at the tropopause.

▲**Figure 2.14 Temperature profile of the atmosphere, highlighting the troposphere.** [NASA.]

layer supports life—the biosphere—and is the region of principal weather activity.

Approximately 90% of the total mass of the atmosphere and the bulk of all water vapor, clouds, and air pollution are within the troposphere. An average temperature of −57°C (−70°F) defines the *tropopause*, the troposphere's upper limit, but its exact altitude varies with the season, latitude, and surface temperatures and pressures. Near the equator, because of intense heating from the surface, the tropopause occurs at 18 km (11 mi); in the middle latitudes, it occurs at an average of 12 km (8 mi); and at the North and South Poles, it averages only 8 km (5 mi) or less above Earth's surface (**Figure 2.14b**). The marked warming with increasing altitude in the stratosphere above the tropopause causes the tropopause to act like a lid, generally preventing whatever is in the cooler (denser) air below from mixing into the warmer (less dense) stratosphere (**Figure 2.14c**).

Figure 2.14b illustrates the normal temperature profile within the troposphere during daytime. As the graph shows, temperatures decrease rapidly with increasing altitude at an average of 6.4 C° per km (3.5 F° per 1000 ft), a rate known as the **normal lapse rate**.

The normal lapse rate is an average. The actual lapse rate may vary considerably because of local weather conditions and is called the *environmental lapse rate*. This variation in temperature gradient in the lower troposphere is central to our discussion of weather processes in Chapter 5.

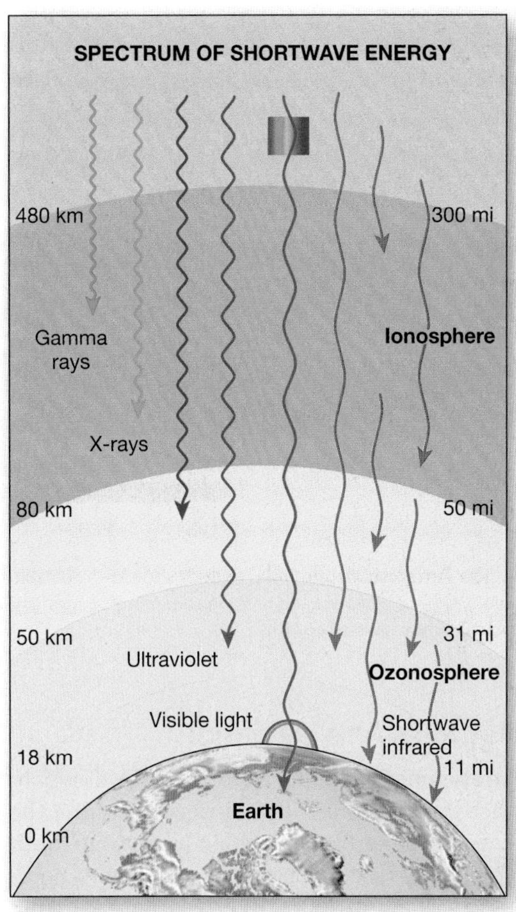

▲Figure 2.15 Absorption of wavelengths above Earth's surface. As shortwave solar energy passes through the atmosphere, the shortest wavelengths are absorbed. Only a fraction of the ultraviolet radiation reaches Earth's surface, as does most of the visible light and shortwave infrared.

Animation Ozone Breakdown, Ozone Hole

http://goo.gl/V8JNt3

Atmospheric Function Criterion

According to our final atmospheric criterion of function, the atmosphere has two specific zones, the ionosphere and the ozonosphere (ozone layer), which together remove most of the harmful wavelengths of incoming solar radiation and charged particles. **Figure 2.15** gives a general depiction of the absorption of radiation by these functional layers of the atmosphere.

Ionosphere The outer functional layer, the **ionosphere**, extends throughout the thermosphere and into the mesosphere below (Figure 2.12). The ionosphere absorbs cosmic rays, gamma rays, X-rays, and shorter wavelengths of ultraviolet (UV) radiation. During this process, atoms change to positively charged ions, giving the ionosphere its name. The glowing auroral lights discussed earlier occur principally within the ionosphere.

Ozonosphere That portion of the stratosphere that contains a high concentration of ozone relative to other layers is the **ozonosphere**, or **ozone layer**. Ozone is a highly reactive oxygen molecule made up of three oxygen atoms (O_3) instead of the usual two atoms (O_2) that make up oxygen gas. Ozone absorbs the shorter wavelengths of UV radiation. In the process, UV energy is converted to heat energy, safeguarding life on Earth by "filtering" some of the Sun's harmful rays.

Scientists have monitored the ozone layer from ground stations since the 1920s and using satellite instruments since 1978. For the past 35 years, increasingly accurate data show stratospheric ozone losses and the formation of an "ozone hole" (an area of severe ozone loss) over Antarctica for part of every year (**Figures 2.16** and **2.17a**; also, see http://ozonewatch.gsfc.nasa.gov/). The depletion has surpassed the changes expected due to natural processes, and scientists have identified human causes for the ozone losses.

CRITICAL**thinking** 2.3

Where Is Your Tropopause?

On your next flight, as the plane reaches its highest altitude, see if you can learn what the temperature is outside the plane. (Some planes display it on video screens, or the flight attendant may have time to check it for you.) By definition, the tropopause is wherever the temperature −57°C (−70°F) occurs. Depending on the season of the year, altitude and temperature make an interesting comparison. Is the tropopause at a higher altitude in summer or winter?

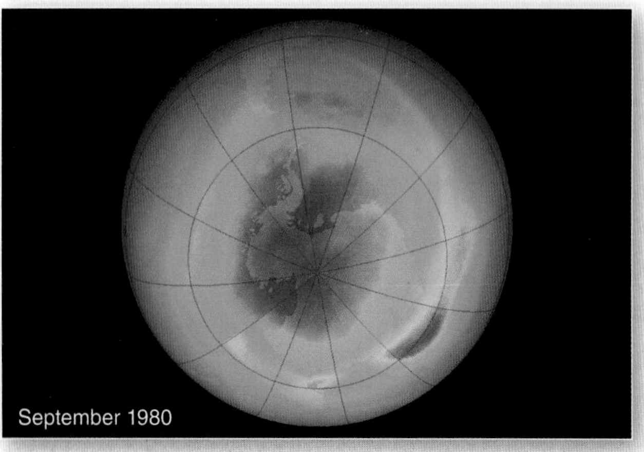

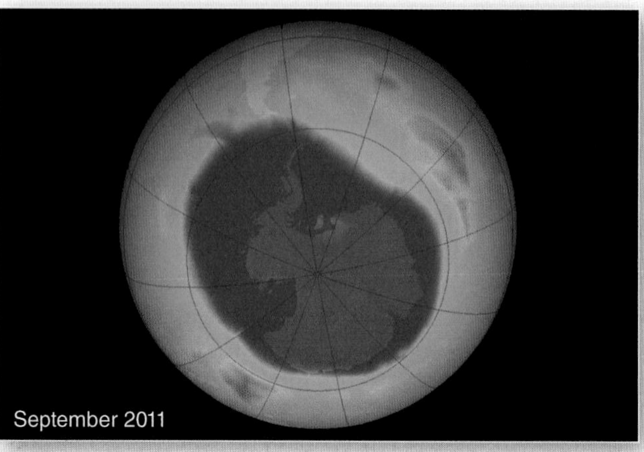

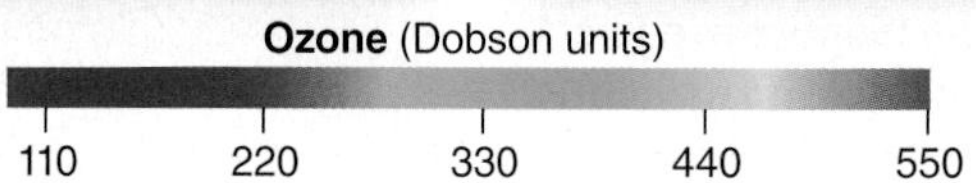

▲**Figure 2.16 The Antarctic ozone hole.** Images show the areal extent of the ozone "hole" in 1980 and 2011. Blues and purples show low ozone (the "hole"); greens, yellows, and reds denote more ozone. [NASA; 1979 to 2011 yearly images are at **http://earthobservatory.nasa.gov/Features/WorldOfChange/ozone.php**.]

Stratospheric Ozone Depletion

If all the stratospheric ozone were brought down to Earth's surface and compressed to surface pressure, the ozone layer would be only 3 mm thick (about one-tenth inch). This relatively thin layer was in steady-state equilibrium for several hundred million years, permitting life to proceed safely on Earth. However, in the 1960s, experts began to express concern that human-made chemicals in the atmosphere may affect ozone. In 1974, two atmospheric chemists, F. Sherwood Rowland and Mario Molina, hypothesized that some synthetic chemicals were releasing chlorine atoms that decompose stratospheric ozone. These **chlorofluorocarbons**, or **CFCs**, are synthetic molecules containing chlorine, fluorine, and carbon.

Ozone Breakdown Process CFCs are stable, or inert, under conditions at Earth's surface, and they possess remarkable heat properties. Both qualities made them valuable as propellants in aerosol sprays and as refrigerants. Also, some 45% of CFCs were used as solvents in the electronics industry and as foaming agents. Being inert, CFC molecules do not dissolve in water and do not break down in biological processes. (In contrast, chlorine compounds derived from volcanic eruptions and ocean sprays are water soluble and rarely reach the stratosphere.)

Researchers Rowland and Molina hypothesized that stable CFC molecules slowly migrate into the stratosphere, where intense UV radiation splits them, freeing chlorine (Cl) atoms. This process produces a complex set of reactions that breaks up ozone molecules (O_3) and leaves oxygen gas

(a) At the South Pole, scientists monitor ozone using a balloonsonde, which carries instruments to 32 km (20 mi) altitude.

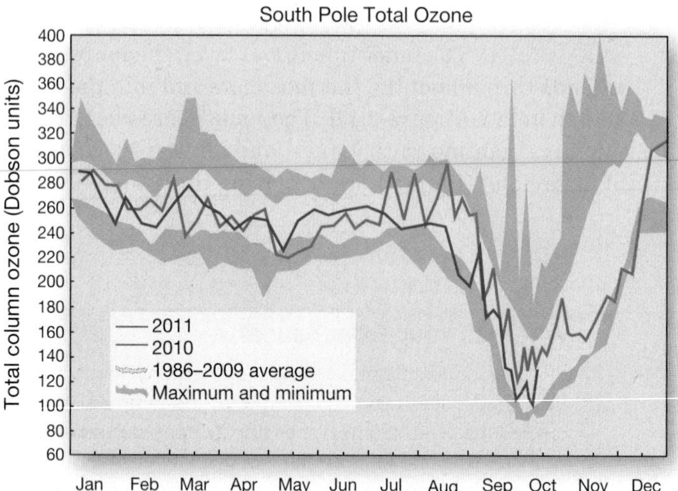

(b) Significant seasonal ozone depletion still occurs over Antarctica, despite decreases in ozone-depleting chemicals.

▲**Figure 2.17 Timing and extent of ozone depletion over Antarctica.** [(a) NOAA. (b) Ozonesonde data courtesy of NOAA. **http://www.noaanews.noaa.gov/stories2011/20111020_ozone.html**.]

molecules (O_2) in their place. The effect is severe, for a single chlorine atom can decompose more than 100,000 ozone molecules. For their work, Doctors Rowland (who passed away in 2012) and Molina and another colleague, Paul Crutzen, received the 1995 Nobel Prize for Chemistry.

The long residence time of chlorine atoms in the ozone layer (40 to 100 years) means the chlorine already in place is likely to have long-term consequences. Tens of millions of tons of CFCs were sold worldwide since 1950 and subsequently released into the atmosphere. The effects of ozone-depleting substances will be with us for the rest of this century.

Ozone Losses over the Poles In the 1980s, satellite measurements confirmed a large ozone "hole" above Antarctica from September through November (the Antarctic spring). In 2006, the largest areas of ozone depletion over Antarctica on record occurred. Although many CFCs are produced in the Northern Hemisphere, the ozone hole forms over the South Pole because chlorine freed in the Northern Hemisphere midlatitudes concentrates over Antarctica through the work of atmospheric winds. Persistent cold temperatures during the long, dark winter create a tight atmospheric circulation pattern—the polar vortex—that remains in place for several months. Chemicals and water in the stratosphere freeze out to form thin, icy *polar stratospheric clouds*.

Within these clouds, ice particle surfaces allow the chemicals to react, releasing chlorine. The chlorine cannot destroy ozone without the addition of UV light, which arrives with the spring in September. UV light sets off the reaction that depletes ozone and forms the ozone hole. As the polar vortex breaks up and temperatures warm, ozone levels return to normal over the Antarctic region (**Figure 2.17b**).

Over the North Pole, stratospheric conditions and temperatures differ from those in the Antarctic. Arctic ozone depletion, first recorded in the 1980s, is smaller in scale than in the Antarctic region, though ozone losses increase each year. The Arctic ozone hole in 2011 was the largest on record (see **http://earthobservatory.nasa.gov/IOTD/view.php?id=49874**).

A complicating factor for ozone loss is rising global temperature and its associated effects on weather. In 2012, scientists reported that intense summer storms over the United States are increasing atmospheric water vapor in the lower stratosphere, causing chemical reactions that deplete ozone. Climate change is driving the more frequent occurrence of these storms.

The Montreal Protocol The United States banned selling and production of CFCs in 1978. However, sales increased again when a 1981 presidential order permitted the export and sale of banned products. CFC sales hit a new peak in 1987 of 1.2 million metric tons (1.32 million tons), at which point an international agreement—the *Montreal Protocol on Substances That Deplete the Ozone Layer* (1987)—halted further sales growth. With 189 signatory countries, the protocol, which aims to reduce and eliminate all ozone-depleting substances, is regarded as the most successful international agreement in history (see **http://ozone.unep.org/new_site/en/index.php**).

CFC sales declined until all production of harmful CFCs ceased in 2010, although concern remains over some of the substitute compounds and a robust black market for banned CFCs. In 2007, the protocol instituted an aggressive phasedown of HCFCs, or *hydrochlorofluorocarbons*, one of the CFC-replacement compounds. If not for this treaty, Earth's atmosphere might already have lost two-thirds of the stratospheric ozone. Instead, if the protocol is fully enforced, scientists estimate that the stratosphere will return to more normal conditions in a century.

The UV Index

UV radiation can be subdivided by wavelength into UVA, UVB, and UVC, each absorbed to a different degree by the ozonosphere. The ozone layer absorbs all the UVC, at 100–290 nm, and most of the UVB, at 290–320 nm.* The longer wavelengths of UVA, 320–400 nm, are not absorbed by ozone and make up about 95% of all UV radiation that reaches Earth.

The health effects of declining ozone vary according to the wavelength of UV radiation. UVC is absorbed by both oxygen and ozone, meaning that small changes in ozone concentrations do not affect UVC levels at Earth's surface. However, UVB is absorbed only by ozone; for every 1% decrease in stratospheric ozone levels, an estimated 1% increase in UVB occurs at Earth's surface. This UVB radiation increase has detrimental effects on human health, plants, and marine ecosystems. In humans, UVB causes skin cancer, cataracts (a clouding of the eye lens),

*Nanometer (nm) = one-billionth of a meter; 1 nm = 10^{-9} m. For comparison, a micrometer, or micron (μm) = one-millionth of a meter; 1 μm = 10^{-6} m. A millimeter (mm) = one-thousandth of a meter; 1 mm = 10^{-3}.

CRITICAL**thinking** 2.4

Finding Your Local Ozone

Total column ozone is the total amount of ozone in a column from the surface to the top of the atmosphere. To determine the total column ozone at your present location, go to "What was the total ozone column at your house?" at **http://ozoneaq.gsfc.nasa.gov/ozone_overhead_all_v8.md**.

Select a point on the map or enter your latitude and longitude, and choose the date you want to check. The ozone column is currently measured by the Ozone Monitoring Instrument (OMI) sensor aboard the *Aqua* satellite and is mainly sensitive to stratospheric ozone. (Note also the limitations listed on the extent of data availability.) If you check for several different dates, when do the lowest values occur? The highest values? Briefly explain and interpret the values you found.

and a weakening of the immune system and is the chief cause of skin reddening and sunburn. UVB alters plant physiology in complex ways that lead to decreased agricultural productivity. In marine ecosystems, scientists have documented 10% declines in phytoplankton productivity in areas of ozone depletion around Antarctica—these organisms are the primary producers that form the basis of the ocean's food chain.

Longer wavelength UVA, which is not absorbed by ozone, is also a concern. It is less intense than UVB, but it penetrates human skin more deeply, causing significant damage in the basal (lowest) part of the epidermis, the outer layer of skin, where most skin cancers occur. UVA levels are fairly constant throughout the year during daylight hours and can penetrate glass and clouds, whereas UVB intensity varies by latitude, season, and time of day as well as by the presence and condition of the ozone layer.

In response to changing UV radiation levels and their associated health impacts, standardized reporting of UV to the public began in the 1990s. Today, weather reports regularly include the *UV Index*, or *UVI*, in daily forecasts to alert the public of the need to use sun protection, especially for children. (Remember, skin damage accumulates, and it may be decades before you experience the ill effects triggered by this summer's sunburn.) The UVI is a simple way of describing the daily danger of solar UV-radiation intensity, using a scale from 1 to 11+ (**Table 2.3**). A higher number indicates a greater risk of UV exposure; an index of 0 indicates no risk, such as at night. Higher risk means that UV damage to skin and eyes can occur over a shorter time period. See http://www2.epa.gov/sunwise/uv-index for the UVI at U.S. locations; in Canada, go to http://ec.gc.ca/uv/default.asp?lang=En&n=396B9A58-1.

Pollutants in the Atmosphere

At certain times or places, the troposphere contains natural and human-caused gases, particles, and other substances in amounts that are harmful to humans or cause environmental damage. Study of the spatial aspects of these atmospheric **pollutants** is an important application of physical geography, with far-reaching human-health implications.

Air pollution is not a new problem. Historically, air pollution has collected around population centers and been closely linked to human production and consumption of energy and resources. For example, Romans complained more than 2000 years ago about the air of their cities, befouled with the stench of open sewers, smoke from fires, and fumes from smelters (furnaces) that converted ores into metals.

Solutions to air-quality issues require regional, national, and international strategies because the pollution sources often are distant from the observed impact. Pollution crosses political boundaries and even oceans. Regulations to curb human-caused air pollution have had great success, although much remains to be done. Before discussing these topics, we examine natural pollution sources.

Natural Sources of Air Pollution

Natural sources produce greater quantities of air pollutants—nitrogen oxides, carbon monoxide, hydrocarbons from plants and trees, and carbon dioxide—than do sources attributable to humans. Volcanoes, forest fires, and dust storms are the most significant sources, based on the volume of smoke and particulates produced and blown over large areas (**Table 2.4**). However, pollen from crops, weeds, and other plants can also cause high amounts of particle pollution, triggering asthma as well as other adverse human health effects. As noted earlier, the particulates produced by these events are known as **aerosols** and include liquid droplets and suspended solids that range in size from visible water droplets and pollen to microscopic dust. (Aerosols produced from human sources are discussed in the next section.)

The 1991 eruption of Mount Pinatubo in the Philippines (discussed in Chapter 1) was a dramatic natural

TABLE 2.3 UV Index*

Exposure Risk Category	UVI Range	Comments
Low	Less than 2	Low danger for average person. Wear sunglasses on bright days. Watch out for reflection off snow.
Moderate	3–5	Take covering precautions, such as sunglasses, sunscreen, hats, and protective clothing, and stay in shade during midday hours.
High	6–7	Use sunscreens with SPF ratings of 15 or higher. Reduce time in the Sun between 11 A.M. and 4 P.M. Use protections listed above.
Very high	8–10	Minimize Sun exposure from 10 A.M. to 4 P.M. Use sunscreens with SPF ratings of over 15. Use protections listed above.
Extreme	11+	Unprotected skin is at risk of burn. Apply sunscreen every 2 hours if outdoors. Avoid direct Sun exposure during midday hours. Use protections listed above.

*The National Weather Service (NWS) and Environmental Protection Agency (EPA) began reporting the UVI in 1991. A revision in 2004 aligned the UVI with guidelines adopted by the World Health Organization (WHO) and World Meteorological Organization (WMO).

TABLE 2.4 Sources of Natural Pollutants

Source	Contribution
Volcanoes	Sulfur oxides, particulates
Forest fires	Carbon monoxide and dioxide, nitrogen oxides, particulates
Plants	Hydrocarbons, pollens
Decaying plants	Methane, hydrogen sulfides
Soil	Dust and viruses
Ocean	Salt spray, particulates

source of air pollution, injecting nearly 20 million tons of sulfur dioxide (SO_2) into the stratosphere. The spread of these emissions is shown in a sequence of satellite images in Chapter 4, Figure 4.1.

Wildfires are another source of natural air pollution and occur frequently on several continents (**Figure 2.18**). Wildfire smoke contains particulates (dust, soot, ash), nitrogen oxides, carbon monoxide, and volatile organic compounds (discussed in the next section), which damage human health. In southern California, recent wildfire smoke was linked to respiratory problems and increased hospital admissions as well as to lower birth weight for babies born to women living in smoke-exposed areas. Wind patterns spread the pollution from the fires to nearby cities, closing airports and forcing evacuations to avoid the health-related dangers. Satellite data show smoke plumes traveling horizontally for distances up to 1600 km (1000 mi). Particulates can be propelled vertically as high as the stratosphere.

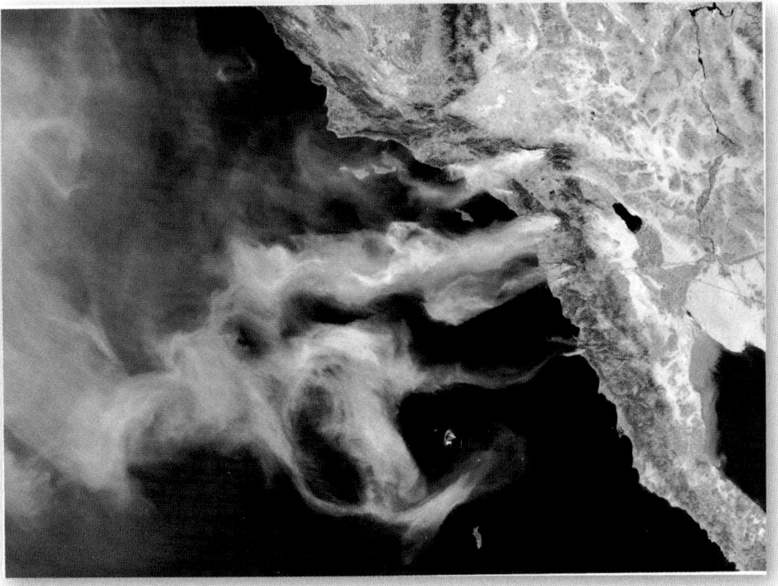

▲**Figure 2.18 Smoke from California wildfires.** Wildfires related to drought and high temperatures in southern California burned more than 136,000 hectares (336,000 acres) in October and November 2007. Over half a million people were evacuated from their homes during these fires. Similar evacuations were repeated during wildfires in subsequent years. [*Terra* MODIS, NASA/GSFC.]

During the past decade, scientists have linked increasing wildfire occurrence in the western United States with climate change, which is causing higher spring and summer temperatures and earlier snowmelt, resulting in a longer fire season. These connections occur across the globe, as in drought-plagued Australia, where thousands of wildfires burned millions of hectares in recent years.

Anthropogenic Air Pollution

The natural events that produce atmospheric contaminants, such as volcanic eruptions and wildfires, have occurred throughout human evolution on Earth. However, they are relatively infrequent events, even though their effects can cover large areas. In contrast, humans have only recently experienced the consistently high concentrations of *anthropogenic* (human-caused) contaminants now present in our metropolitan regions. Currently, our species is contributing significantly to the creation of the **anthropogenic atmosphere**, a tentative label for Earth's next atmosphere (recall GeoReport 2.2).

As in earlier times, anthropogenic air pollution is most prevalent in urbanized regions. Over half the world's population now lives in metropolitan regions, some one-third with unhealthful levels of air pollution. As urban populations continue to grow, the exposure to air pollution represents a potentially massive public-health issue. According to the World Health Organization, urban outdoor air pollution caused an estimated 1.3 million deaths worldwide in 2012. In the United States, although air quality is improving in many places, 41% of the population (over 127 million people) lives with unhealthful levels of air pollution.

Most urban air pollutants result from combustion of fossil fuels in transportation—specifically, cars and light trucks (**Table 2.5**). For example, **carbon monoxide (CO)** results from incomplete combustion, the failure of a carbon-based fuel to burn completely because of insufficient oxygen. The toxicity of carbon monoxide is due to its affinity for blood hemoglobin, as explained in GeoReport 2.5. The main anthropogenic source of carbon monoxide is vehicle emissions.

Motor vehicle transportation is still the largest source of air pollution in the United States and Canada, despite improvements in vehicle emissions over the past 30 years. Reducing air pollution from the transportation sector involves available technologies that result in monetary savings for consumers and lead to significant health benefits—yet still we are slow in achieving better fuel efficiency. Further improvements in fuel efficiency and reductions in fuel emissions, through either technological innovation or promotion of other forms of transportation, are critical for reducing air pollution.

Stationary pollution sources, such as electric power plants and industrial plants that use fossil fuels, contribute the most sulfur oxides and particulates. Concentrations are focused in the Northern Hemisphere, especially over eastern China and northern India.

TABLE 2.5 Major Pollutants over Urban Areas

Name	Symbol	Sources	Description and Effects
Carbon monoxide	CO	Incomplete combustion of fuels, mainly vehicle emissions	Odorless, colorless, tasteless gas. Is toxic due to affinity for hemoglobin; displaces O_2 in bloodstream. 50 to 100 ppm cause headaches and vision and judgment losses.
Nitrogen oxides	NO_x (NO, NO_2)	Agricultural practices, fertilizers, and high-temperature/-pressure combustion, mainly from vehicle emissions	Reddish-brown choking gas. Inflames respiratory system; destroys lung tissue. Leads to acid deposition.
Volatile organic compounds	VOCs	Incomplete combustion of fossil fuels such as gasoline; cleaning and paint solvents	Prime agents of surface ozone formation.
Ozone	O_3	Photochemical reactions related to motor vehicle emissions	Highly reactive, unstable gas. Ground-level ozone irritates human eyes and respiratory systems. Damages plants.
Peroxyacetyl nitrates	PANs	Photochemical reactions related to motor vehicle emissions	Irritates human eyes and respiratory systems. Causes major damage to plants, forests, and crops.
Sulfur oxides	SO_x (SO_2, SO_3)	Combustion of sulfur-containing fuels	Colorless, but with irritating smell. Impairs breathing and taste threshold; causes human asthma, bronchitis, and emphysema. Leads to acid deposition.
Particulate matter	PM	Industrial activities, fuel combustion, vehicle emissions, agriculture	Complex mixture of solid and liquid particles including dust, soot, salt, metals, and organics. Dust, smoke, and haze affect visibility. Black carbon may have a critical role in climate change. Various health effects: bronchitis, pulmonary function.
Carbon dioxide	CO_2	Complete combustion of fossil fuels	Principal greenhouse gas (see Chapter 8).

Photochemical Smog Although not generally present in human environments until the advent of the automobile, photochemical smog is now the major component of anthropogenic air pollution; it is responsible for the hazy sky and reduced sunlight in many of our cities. **Photochemical smog** results from the interaction of sunlight and the combustion products in automobile exhaust, primarily nitrogen oxides and *volatile organic compounds* (VOCs) such as hydrocarbons that evaporate from gasoline. Although the term *smog*—a combination of the words *sm*oke and f*og*—is generally used to describe this pollution, it is a misnomer.

The high temperatures in automobile engines produce **nitrogen dioxide (NO_2)**, a chemical also emitted to a lesser extent from power plants. NO_2 is involved in several important reactions that affect air quality:

- Interactions with water vapor to form nitric acid (HNO_3), a contributor to acid deposition by precipitation, the subject of Focus Study 2.1.
- Interactions with VOCs to produce **peroxyacetyl nitrates**, or **PANs**, pollutants that irritate human eyes and respiratory tracts and damage agricultural crops and forests.
- Interactions with oxygen (O_2) and VOCs to form *ground-level ozone*, the principal component of photochemical smog.

Car exhaust is converted into photochemical smog by a photochemical reaction in which UV radiation liberates atomic oxygen (O) and a nitric oxide (NO) molecule from the NO_2 (**Figure 2.19**). The free oxygen atom combines with an oxygen molecule, O_2, to form the oxidant ozone, O_3. The ozone in photochemical smog is the same gas that is beneficial to us in the stratosphere in absorbing UV radiation. However, ground-level ozone is a reactive gas that damages biological tissues and has a variety of detrimental human health effects, including lung irritation, asthma, and susceptibility to respiratory illnesses.

For several reasons, children are at greatest risk—one in four children in U.S. cities may develop health problems from ozone pollution. This ratio is significant; it means that more than 12 million children are

GEOreport 2.4 Carbon monoxide—the colorless, odorless pollutant

As your car idles at a downtown intersection or you walk through a parking garage, you may be exposed to between 50 and 100 ppm of carbon monoxide without being aware of inhaling this colorless, odorless gas. In the burning ash of a smoking cigarette, CO levels reach 42,000 ppm. No wonder secondhand smoke affects CO levels in the blood of anyone breathing nearby, producing measurable health effects. What happens physiologically? CO combines with the oxygen-carrying hemoglobin of human blood, displacing the oxygen. The result is that the hemoglobin no longer transports adequate oxygen to vital organs such as the heart and brain; too much exposure to CO causes sudden illness and death (see http://www.cdc.gov/nceh/airpollution/).

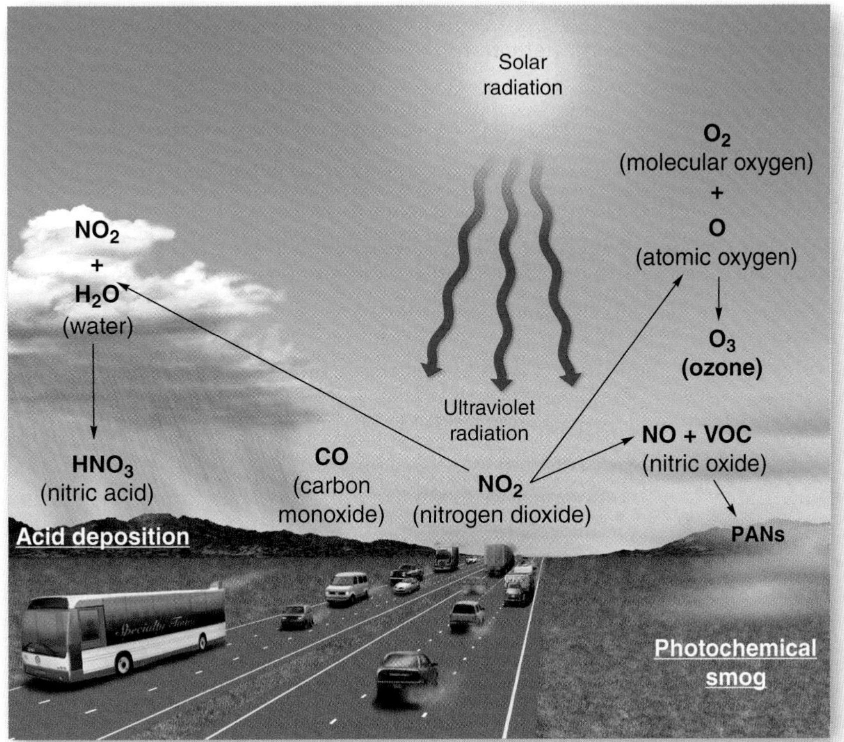

▲**Figure 2.19 Photochemical reactions and pollutants from car exhaust.**

vulnerable in those metropolitan regions with the highest ground-level ozone (Los Angeles, Bakersfield, Fresno, and other California cities; Houston; Washington, DC–Baltimore; Las Vegas). For more information and city rankings of the worst and the best, see http://www.lung.org (enter "city rankings" in the website search box).

Industrial Smog and Sulfur Oxides

Over the past 300 years, except in some developing countries, coal slowly replaced wood as society's basic fuel to provide the high-grade energy needed to run machines. The Industrial Revolution led to the conversion from *animate* energy (from animal sources, such as animal-powered farm equipment) to *inanimate* energy (from nonliving sources, such as coal, steam, and water). Pollution generated by industry and coal-fired electrical generation differs from that produced by transportation.

Air pollution associated with coal-burning industries is known as **industrial smog**. The term *smog*, mentioned earlier, was coined by a London physician in 1900 to describe the combination of fog and smoke containing sulfur gases (sulfur is an impurity in fossil fuels); in the case of industrial air pollution, the use of *smog* is correct.

Industrial pollution has high concentrations of carbon dioxide, particulates (discussed just ahead), and sulfur oxides (**Figure 2.20**). Once in the atmosphere,

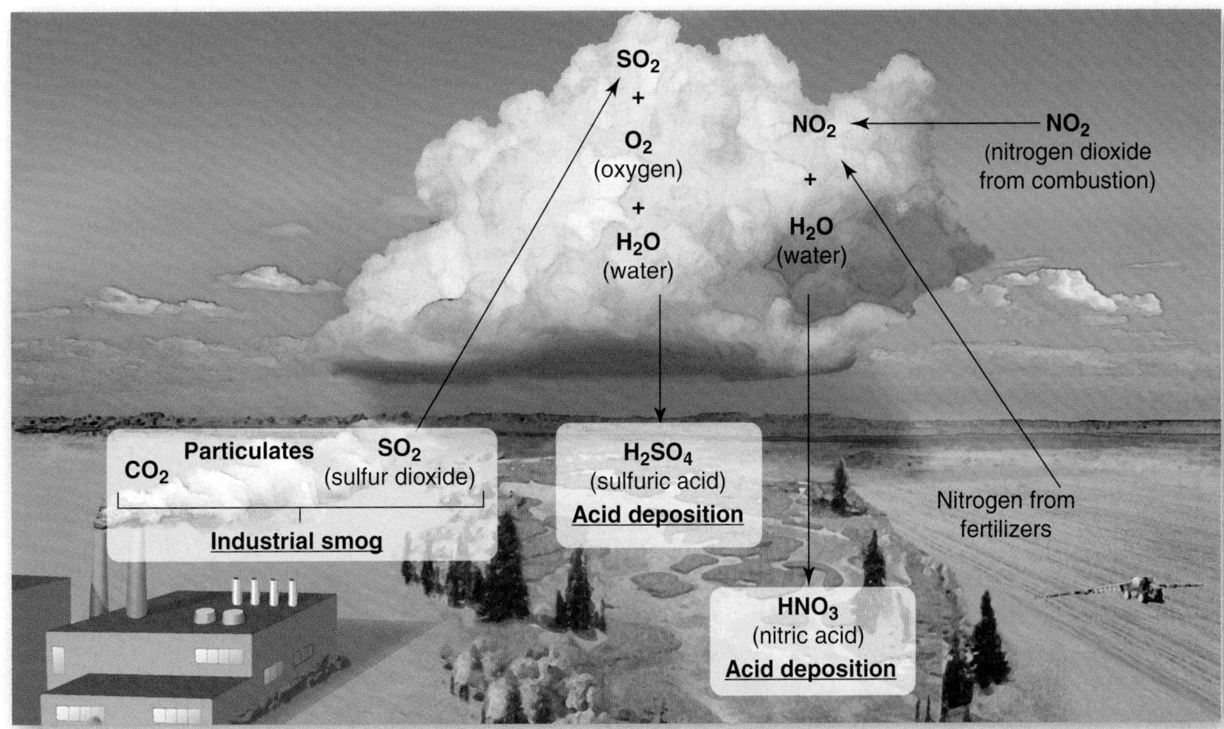

▲**Figure 2.20 Chemical reactions and pollutants from industrial smog.**

sulfur dioxide (SO_2) reacts with oxygen (O) to form sulfur trioxide (SO_3), which is highly reactive and, in the presence of water or water vapor, forms tiny particles known as *sulfate aerosols*. Sulfuric acid (H_2SO_4) can also form, even in moderately polluted air at normal temperatures. Coal-burning electric utilities and steel manufacturing are the main sources of sulfur dioxide.

Sulfur dioxide–laden air is dangerous to health, corrodes metals, and accelerates the deterioration of stone building materials. Sulfuric acid deposition combines with nitric acid deposition to cause environmental problems that have increased in severity since first described in the 1970s. Focus Study 2.1 discusses this important atmospheric issue.

Particulate Matter The diverse mixture of fine particles, both solid and liquid, that pollutes the air and affects human health is referred to as **particulate matter (PM)** by meteorologists and regulatory agencies such as the U.S. Environmental Protection Agency. Other scientists refer to these particulates as aerosols. Examples are haze, smoke, and dust, which are visible reminders of particulates in the air we breathe. Remote sensing now provides a global portrait of such aerosols—look ahead to the background image in The Human Denominator 2.

The effects of PM on human health vary with the size of the particle. $PM_{2.5}$ is the designation for particulates 2.5 microns (2.5 μm) or less in diameter; these pose the greatest health risk. Sulfate aerosols are an example, with sizes about 0.1 to 1 μm in diameter. For comparison, a human hair can range from 50 to 70 μm in diameter. These fine particles, such as combustion particles, *organics* (biological materials such as pollens), and metallic aerosols, can get into the lungs and bloodstream. Coarse particles (PM_{10}) are of less concern, although they can irritate a person's eyes, nose, and throat.

New studies are implicating even smaller particles, known as *ultrafines* at a size of $PM_{0.1}$, as a cause of serious health problems. These are many times more potent than the larger $PM_{2.5}$ and PM_{10} particles because they can get into smaller channels in lung tissue and cause scarring, abnormal thickening, and damage called *fibrosis*. Asthma prevalence has nearly doubled since 1980 in the United States, a major cause being motor vehicle-related air pollution—specifically, ozone, sulfur dioxide, and fine particulate matter.

Natural Factors That Affect Pollutants

The problems resulting from both natural and anthropogenic atmospheric contaminants are made worse by several important natural factors. Among these, wind, local and regional landscape characteristics, and temperature inversions in the troposphere dominate.

Winds Winds gather and move pollutants, sometimes reducing the concentration of pollution in one location while increasing it in another. Dust, defined as particles less than 62 μm, or 0.0025 in., travels easily in winds, sometimes in dramatic episodes that form dust storms (discussed in Chapter 13). Scientists can track the source area of dust using chemical analysis. Dust from Africa, traveling on the prevailing winds, contributes to the soils of South America and Europe (**Figure 2.21**). Texas dust can end up across the Atlantic.

Winds make the atmosphere's condition an international issue. For example, prevailing winds transport air pollution from the United States to Canada, necessitating negotiation between the two governments in response to Canadian complaints. Pollution from North America adds to European air problems. In Europe, the cross-boundary drift of pollution is common because of the small size and proximity of many countries, a factor in the formation of the European Union (EU).

Arctic haze is a term from the 1950s, when pilots noticed decreased visibility in the Arctic region, either on the horizon ahead or when looking down at an angle from their aircraft. Haze is a concentration of microscopic particles and air pollution that diminishes air clarity. Since there is no heavy industry at these high latitudes and only sparse population, this seasonal haze is the product

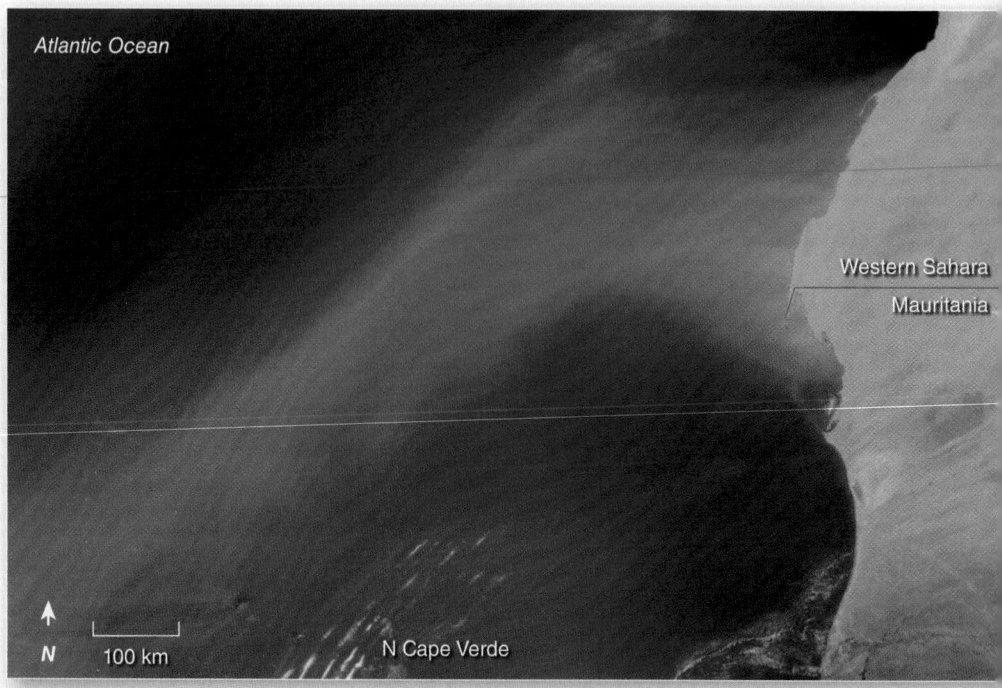

▶Figure 2.21 Winds carrying dust in the atmosphere. Dust moves westward off the African coast in October 2012 over the Cape Verde islands and across the Atlantic. [LANCE MODIS Rapid Response Team, NASA GSFC.]

of industrialization elsewhere in the Northern Hemisphere, especially Eurasia. Recent increases in wildfires in the Northern Hemisphere and agricultural burning in the midlatitudes contribute to Arctic haze. There is no comparable haze over the Antarctic continent. Based on the above discussion, can you think of why Antarctica lacks such a condition?

Local and Regional Landscapes Local and regional landscapes are another important factor affecting the movement and concentration of air pollutants. Mountains and hills can form barriers to air movement or can direct the movement of pollutants from one area to another. Some of the worst air quality results when local landscapes trap and concentrate air pollution.

Places with volcanic landscapes, such as Iceland and Hawai'i, have their own natural pollution. During periods of sustained volcanic activity at Kīlauea, some 2000 metric tons (2200 tons) of sulfur dioxide are produced a day. Concentrations are sometimes high enough to merit broadcast warnings about health concerns, as occurred in 2011, 2012, and 2013. The resulting acid rain and volcanic smog, called *vog* by Hawaiians (for *v*olcanic sm*og*), cause losses to agriculture as well as other economic impacts.

Temperature Inversions Vertical differences in temperature and atmospheric density in the troposphere also can worsen pollution conditions. A **temperature inversion** occurs when the normal temperature, which usually decreases with altitude (normal lapse rate), reverses trend and begins to increase at some point. This can happen at any elevation from ground level to several thousand meters.

Figure 2.22 compares a normal temperature profile with that of a temperature inversion. In the normal profile (Figure 2.22a), air at the surface rises because it is warmer (less dense) than the surrounding air. This ventilates the valley and moderates surface pollution by allowing air at the surface to mix with the air above. When an inversion occurs, colder (more dense) air lies below a warmer air layer (Figure 2.22b) that halts the vertical mixing of pollutants with other atmospheric gases. Thus, instead of being carried away, pollutants are trapped under the inversion layer. Inversions most often result from certain weather conditions, discussed in Chapter 5, or from topographic situations such as when cool mountain air drains into valley bottoms at night (see the discussion of local winds in Chapter 4).

Benefits of the Clean Air Act

The concentration of many air pollutants declined over the past several decades because of Clean Air Act (CAA) legislation (1970, 1977, 1990), saving trillions of dollars in health, economic, and environmental losses. Despite this well-documented relationship, air pollution regulations are subject to a continuing political debate.

(a) A normal temperature profile.

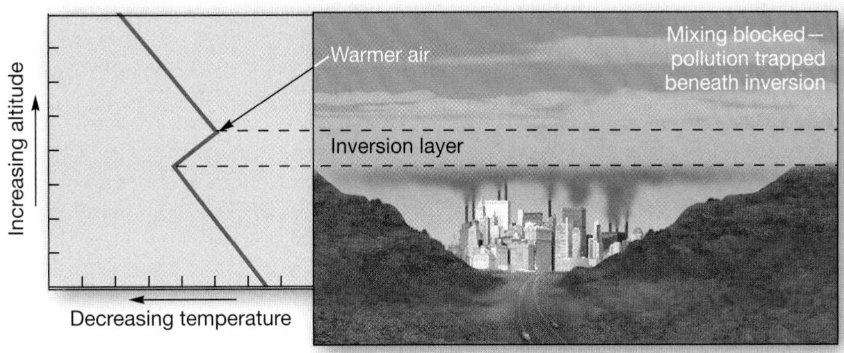

(b) A temperature inversion in the lower atmosphere prevents the cooler air below the inversion layer from mixing with air above. Pollution is trapped near the ground.

Inversion layer

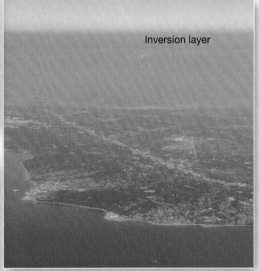

(c) The top of an inversion layer is visible in the morning hours over a landscape.

▲**Figure 2.22 Normal and inverted temperature profiles.** [(c) Bobbé Christopherson.]

focusstudy 2.1 Pollution

Acid Deposition: Damaging to Ecosystems

Acid deposition is a major environmental issue in some areas of the United States, Canada, Europe, and Asia. Such deposition is most familiar as "acid rain," but it also occurs as "acid snow," and in dry form as dust or aerosols. Government estimates of damage from acid deposition in the United States, Canada, and Europe exceed $50 billion annually.

Acid deposition damages buildings, sculptures, and historic artifacts and is causally linked to serious environmental problems: declining fish populations and fish kills, widespread forest damage, and changes in soil chemistry. Regions that have suffered most are the northeastern United States, southeastern Canada, Sweden, Norway, Germany, much of eastern Europe, and China.

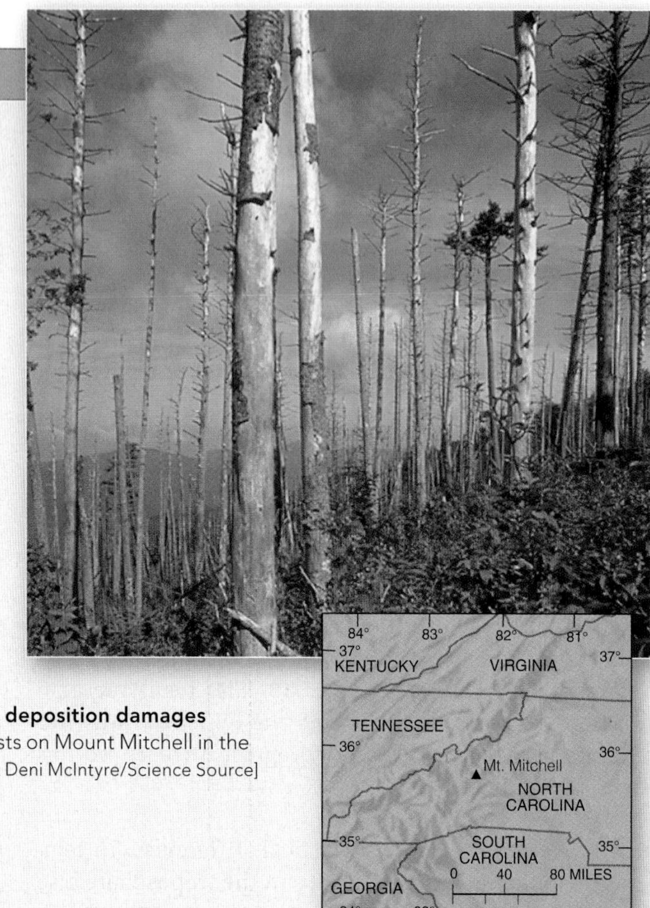

►**Figure 2.1.1 Acid deposition damages trees.** Stressed forests on Mount Mitchell in the Appalachians. [Will & Deni McIntyre/Science Source]

Acid Formation

The problem begins when sulfur dioxide and nitrogen oxides are emitted as by-products of fertilizers and fossil-fuel combustion. Winds may carry these gases many kilometers from their sources. Once in the atmosphere, the chemicals are converted to nitric acid (HNO_3) and sulfuric acid (H_2SO_4). These acids are removed from the atmosphere by wet and dry deposition processes, falling as rain or snow or attached to other particulate matter. The acid then settles on the landscape and eventually enters streams and lakes, carried by runoff and groundwater flows.

The acidity of precipitation is measured on the pH scale, which expresses the relative abundance of free hydrogen ions (H^+) in a solution—these are what make an acid corrosive, for they easily combine with other ions. The pH scale is logarithmic: Each whole number represents a tenfold change. A pH of 7.0 is neutral (neither acidic nor basic). Values less than 7.0 are increasingly acidic, and values greater than 7.0 are increasingly basic, or alkaline. (See Figure 15.8 for a graphic representation of the scale.)

Natural precipitation dissolves carbon dioxide from the atmosphere to form carbonic acid. This process releases hydrogen ions and produces an average pH reading for precipitation of 5.65. The normal range for precipitation is 5.3–6.0. Thus, normal precipitation is always slightly acidic. Scientists have measured precipitation as acidic as pH 2.0 in the eastern United States, Scandinavia, and Europe. By comparison, vinegar and lemon juice register slightly less than 3.0. In lakes, aquatic plant and animal life perishes when pH drops below 4.8.

Effects on Natural Systems

More than 50,000 lakes and some 100,000 km (62,000 mi) of streams in the United States and Canada are at a pH level below normal (that is, below pH 5.3), with several hundred lakes incapable of supporting any aquatic life. Acid deposition causes the release of aluminum and magnesium from clay minerals in the soil, and both of these are harmful to fish and plant communities.

In addition, relatively harmless mercury deposits in lake-bottom sediments convert in acidified lake waters to form highly toxic *methylmercury*, which is deadly to aquatic life and moves throughout biological systems. Local health advisories are regularly issued in two Canadian provinces and 22 U.S. states to warn hunters and fishermen of the methylmercury problem.

Acid deposition affects soils by killing microorganisms and causing a decline in soil nutrients. In New Hampshire's Hubbard Brook Experimental Forest (**http://www.hubbardbrook.org/research/vegetation/templer06.shtml**), ongoing research has found significant leaching of calcium and magnesium base cations from the soil; excess acids are the cause of the nutrient depletion.

The deficiencies in soil nutrients caused by acid deposition have detrimental effects on forests. The most advanced impact is seen in forests in eastern Europe, principally because of the area's long history of burning coal and the density of industrial activity. In Germany and Poland, up to 50% of the forests are dead or damaged.

In the eastern United States, some of the worst forest decline has occurred in the spruce and fir forests of North Carolina and Tennessee (**Figure 2.1.1**). In the Adirondacks, red spruce and sugar maples have been especially hard hit. Affected trees are susceptible to winter cold, insects, and droughts. In red spruce, decline is evidenced by poor crown condition, reduced growth shown in tree-ring analyses, and unusually high levels of tree mortality. For sugar maples, an indicator of forest damage is the reduction by almost half of the annual production of U.S. and Canadian maple sugar.

Nitrogen Oxides: A Worsening Cause

In the United States, the problem of acid deposition appeared to be solved with the passage of the 1990 Clean Air Act amendments, which targeted industrial emissions of sulfur dioxide and nitrogen oxides. From 1990 to 2008, sulfur emissions from power plants decreased almost 70%, and wet sulfate deposition rates dropped across the eastern region (**Figure 2.1.2**)—a real success story for science and public policy. However, nitrogen emissions declined little and in some areas have increased. Nitric oxide (NO) emissions come from three main sources: agricultural operations (specifically, fertilizers and animal-feeding operations, which produce nitrogen and ammonia), motor vehicles, and coal-combustion power plants.

Europe shows similar trends: Several studies have recently found areas with high levels of atmospheric nitrogen oxides in Switzerland and northern Italy, presumably associated with intensive agriculture and fossil-fuel burning, as well as in Norway, where acid deposition in streams could have impacts on the economically important salmon industry. However, 49 European countries began regulating nitrogen emissions in 1999, resulting in a regional decrease in nitrogen emissions of about one-third.

In China, overuse of nitrogen fertilizers (an increase of 191% from 1991 to 2007) has led to acid deposition in soils, lessening crop production by 30% to 50% in some regions. If this trend continues, scientists fear that soil pH could drop as low as 3.0, far below the optimal level of 6.0 to 7.0 required for cereals such as rice.

Acid deposition is an issue of global spatial significance. Because wind and weather patterns are international, efforts at addressing the problem also must be international in scope. Reductions in acid-causing emissions are closely tied to energy conservation and therefore directly related to production of greenhouse gases and global climate-change concerns. Recent research pinpointing nitrogen as the leading cause of acid deposition links this issue to food production and global sustainability issues as well.

1. How are the environmental effects of acid snow potentially different from those of acid rain? (Hint: Think of the timing and impacts on lakes and streams.)
2. Assess the degree to which your region experiences acid rain and acid deposition. Describe any state or regional or local actions designed to mitigate the impacts.

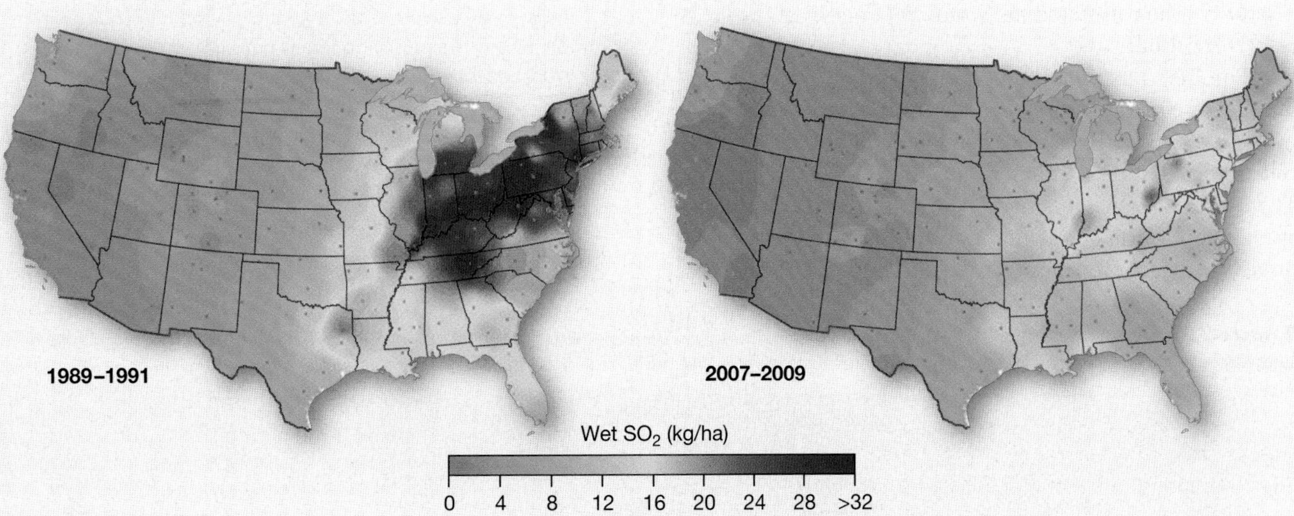

▲**Figure 2.1.2 Improvement in U.S. annual average wet sulfate deposition.** Spatial portrayal of wet sulfate deposition on the landscape, within two separate 3-year periods, in kilograms per hectare, shows a marked decrease since 1989 in the sulfate that falls as rain, snow, or fog. Improvements resulted from combined Canadian and U.S. regulatory action on emissions that add acids to the environment. [National Atmospheric Deposition Program, 2010.]

Since 1970 and the CAA, significant reductions have occurred in atmospheric concentrations of carbon monoxide (–82%), nitrogen dioxide (–52%), volatile organic compounds (–48%), PM_{10} particulates (–75%), sulfur oxides (–76%; see Focus Study 2.1, Figure 2.1.2), and lead (–90%). Prior to the CAA, lead added to gasoline was emitted in exhaust and dispersed over great distances, finally settling in living tissues, especially in children. The 1990 CAA amendment mandated the elimination of lead from all U.S. motor fuel. These remarkable reductions in pollutants show the successful linking of science and public policy.

For abatement (mitigation and prevention) costs to be justified, they must not exceed the financial benefits derived from reducing pollution damage. Compliance with the CAA affected patterns of industrial production, employment, and capital investment. Although the expenditures were investments that generated benefits, the dislocation and job loss in some regions caused hardships—reductions in high-sulfur coal mining and cutbacks in polluting industries such as steel, for example.

In 1990, Congress therefore asked the EPA to analyze the overall health, ecological, and economic benefits of the CAA compared with the costs of implementing the law. In response, the EPA's 1997 report, *The Benefits of the Clean Air Act, 1970 to 1990*, presented an exhaustive cost–benefit analysis of the CAA. The analysis found a 42-to-1 benefit-over-cost ratio and provides a good lesson in cost–benefit analysis, valid to this day. The *total direct cost* to implement all the federal, state, and local CAA rules from 1970 to 1990 was *$523 billion* (in 1990 dollars). This cost was borne by businesses, consumers, and government entities. The estimate of *direct economic benefits* from the CAA from 1970 to 1990 falls into the range of $5.6 to $49.4 trillion, with a central mean of $22.2 trillion. Therefore, the estimated *net financial benefit* of the CAA is $21.7 trillion!

The EPA has ongoing econometric studies to measure these continuing benefits. In 2010, the CAA saved U.S. society $110 billion and some 23,000 lives, whereas related costs of implementation in 2010 were $27 billion. The benefits to society, directly and indirectly, are widespread across the entire population, including improved health and environment, less lead to harm children, lowered cancer rates, and less acid deposition. These CAA benefits were achieved during a period in which the U.S. population grew by 22% and the economy expanded by 70%. Political efforts to weaken CAA regulations seem counterproductive to the progress made so far.

As you reflect on this chapter and our modern atmosphere, the treaties to protect stratospheric ozone, and the benefits from the CAA, you should feel encouraged. Scientists did the research, and society made decisions, took action, and reaped enormous economic and health benefits (**Figure 2.23**). Decades ago scientists learned to sustain and protect Astronaut Mark Lee by designing a spacesuit that served as an "atmosphere." Today, we must learn to sustain and protect Earth's atmosphere to ensure our own survival.

In Chapter 1, we emphasized the impacts of humans and their activities on Earth systems and processes. In turn, Earth systems affect humans in numerous ways. The Human Denominator feature illustrates important examples of human–Earth interactions, with summary text highlighting the influences in each direction. For example, the atmosphere affects humans by protecting them from harmful radiation. Humans are affecting the atmosphere through urban air pollution. Throughout *Elemental Geosystems*, similar illustrations review human interactions with the systems and processes presented in each chapter.

CRITICAL**thinking** 2.5

Evaluating Costs and Benefits

In the scientific study *The Benefits of the Clean Air Act, 1970 to 1990*, the EPA determined that the Clean Air Act provided health, social, ecological, and economic benefits 42 times greater than its costs. In 2010 alone, estimated benefits exceeded costs at a ratio of 4 to 1. In your opinion, why is the public generally unaware of these details? What are the difficulties in informing the public?

Do you think a similar benefit pattern results from laws such as the Clean Water Act, or hazard zoning and planning, or action on global climate change and the Endangerment Finding by the EPA? Take a moment and brainstorm recommendations for action, education, and public awareness on these issues.

▼Figure 2.23 Improved air quality in U.S. cities. In 2013, New York City reported its cleanest air in 50 years, a result of dramatic reductions in sulfur dioxide and soot as part of the city's long-term sustainability blueprint, known as PlaNYC. [Andy Selinger/Alamy.]

SEASONS/ATMOSPHERE IMPACTS HUMANS

- Solar energy drives Earth systems.
- Seasonal change is the foundation of many human societies; it determines rhythm of life and food resources.
- Earth's atmosphere protects humans by filtering harmful wavelengths of light, such as ultraviolet radiation.
- Natural pollution from wildfires, volcanoes, and wind-blown dust are detrimental to human health.

2a

As summers get longer in Alaska, moose migrations no longer coincide with the hunting seasons of native people, who depend on the meat. Shifting animal migrations and vegetation patterns will affect ecosystems across the globe.

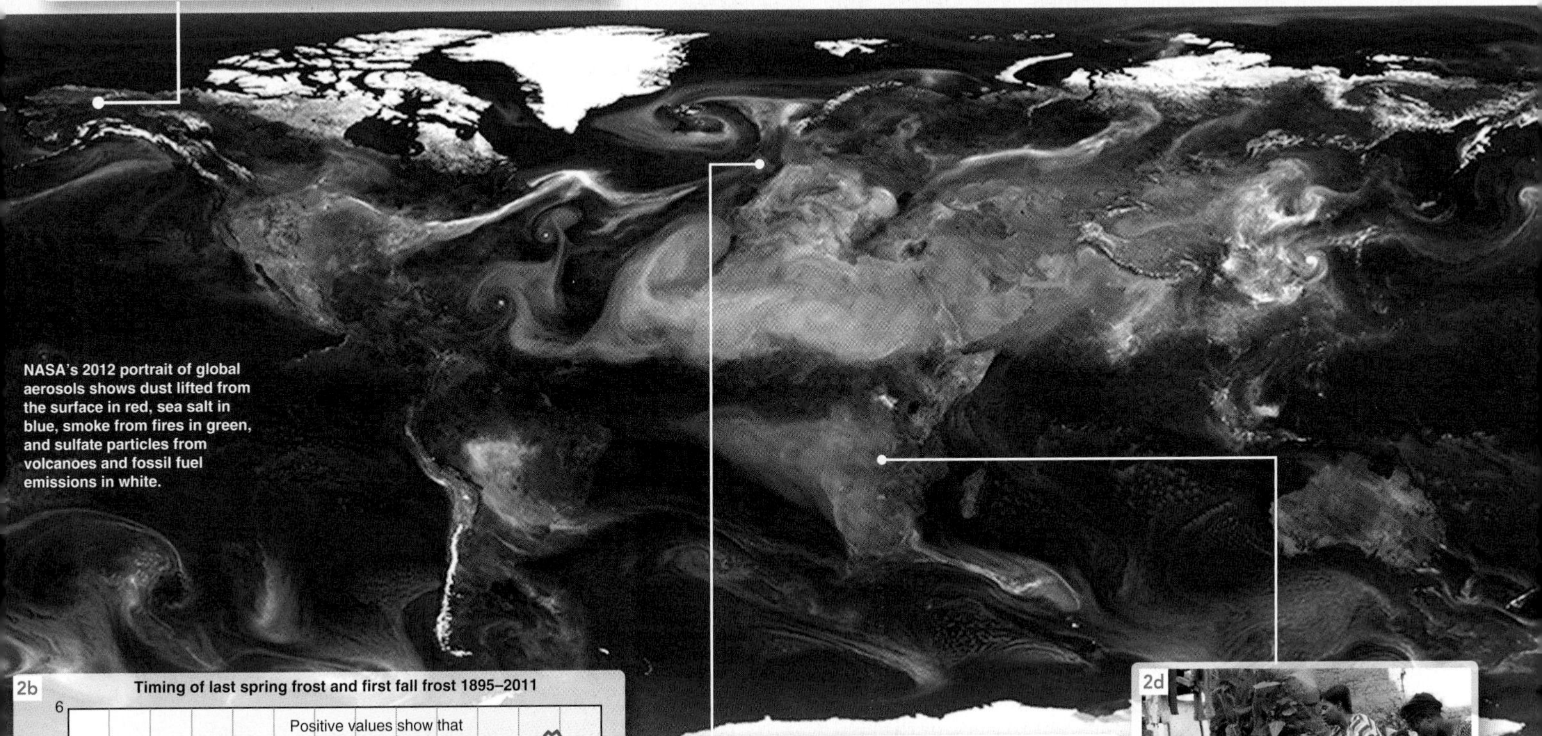

HUMANS IMPACT SEASONS/ATMOSPHERE

- Climate change affects timing of the seasons. Changing temperature and rainfall patterns mean spring is coming earlier and fall is starting later. Prolonged summer temperatures heat water bodies and affect seasonal ice cover, alter animal migrations, and shift vegetation patterns to higher latitudes.
- Human-made chemicals deplete the ozone layer. Winds concentrate these pollutants over Antarctica, where the ozone hole is largest.
- Anthropogenic air pollution collects over urban areas, reaching dangerous levels in some regions, such as northern India and eastern China; other regions have improved air quality, as in the Los Angeles metropolitan area.

NASA's 2012 portrait of global aerosols shows dust lifted from the surface in red, sea salt in blue, smoke from fires in green, and sulfate particles from volcanoes and fossil fuel emissions in white.

2b

Timing of last spring frost and first fall frost 1895–2011

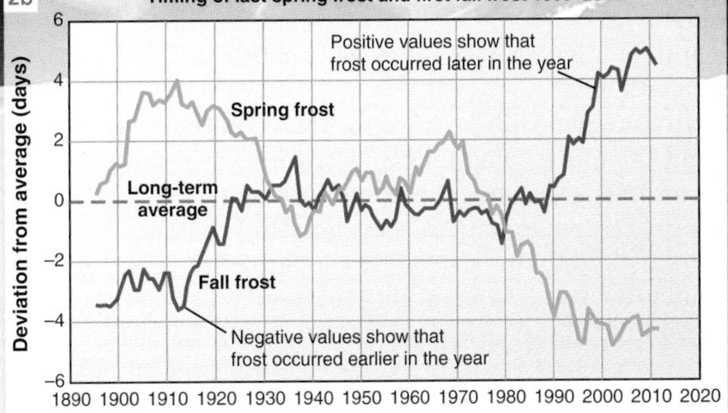

Data for the contiguous United States show an overall trend toward a longer growing season, with a longer fall and an earlier spring.

2c

London implemented new low emissions standards for diesel vehicles in 2012. Owners must comply or face a daily penalty fee. Stricter regulation is one strategy to control increasing air pollution from the transportation sector.

2d

Clean burning cooking stoves will reduce the amount of fine particulates such as black carbon in developing countries. Several international initiatives are working toward this goal (see http://www.projectsurya.org/).

ISSUES FOR THE 21ST CENTURY

- Ongoing climate change is altering Earth systems. Societies will need to adapt their resource base as timing of seasonal patterns changes.
- Human-made emissions must be reduced to improve air quality in Asia. Air pollution will continue to improve in regions where emissions are regulated, such as in Europe, the United States, and Canada.
- Alternative, clean energy sources are vital for reducing industrial pollution worldwide.
- Fuel efficiency, vehicle-emissions regulations, and alternative and public transportation are crucial for reducing urban pollution and CO_2 emissions that drive climate change.

KEY LEARNING concepts review

Describe our Solar System, *summarize* the origin of Earth, and *reconstruct* Earth's annual orbit about the Sun.

Our Solar System—the Sun and eight planets—is located on a remote, trailing edge of the **Milky Way Galaxy**, a flattened, disk-shaped collection of stars. **Gravity**, the mutual attraction exerted by every object upon all other objects in proportion to their mass, is an organizing force in the Universe. The **planetesimal hypothesis** describes the formation of solar systems as a process in which stars (like our Sun) condense from nebular dust and gas, with planetesimals and then protoplanets forming in orbits around these central masses.

The Solar System, planets, and Earth began to condense from a nebular cloud of dust, gas, debris, and icy comets approximately 4.6 billion years ago. The vast distances in space are expressed using the **speed of light** (300,000 kmps, or 186,000 mps, which is about 9.5 trillion km, or nearly 6 trillion mi, per year). In its orbit, Earth is at **perihelion** (its closest position to the Sun) during our Northern Hemisphere winter (January 3 at 147,255,000 km, or 91,500,000 mi). It is at **aphelion** (its farthest position from the Sun) during our Northern Hemisphere summer (July 4 at 152,083,000 km, or 94,500,000 mi). Earth's average distance from the Sun is approximately 8 minutes and 20 seconds in terms of light speed.

Milky Way Galaxy (p. 36)
gravity (p. 36)
planetesimal hypothesis (p. 36)
speed of light (p. 36)
perihelion (p. 36)
aphelion (p. 38)

1. Describe the Sun's status among stars in the Milky Way Galaxy. Describe the Sun's location, size, and relationship to its planets.
2. If you have seen the Milky Way at night, briefly describe it. Use specifics from the text in your description.
3. Compare the locations of the eight planets of the Solar System.
4. Briefly describe Earth's origin as part of the Solar System.
5. How far is Earth from the Sun in terms of light speed? In terms of kilometers and miles?
6. Briefly describe the relationship among these entities: Universe, Milky Way Galaxy, Solar System, Sun, Earth, and Moon.
7. Diagram in a simple sketch Earth's orbit about the Sun. How much does it vary during the course of a year?

Explain the characteristics of the solar wind and the electromagnetic spectrum of radiant energy and *illustrate* the interception of solar energy at the top of the atmosphere.

The **fusion** process—hydrogen nuclei forced together under tremendous temperature and pressure in the Sun's interior—generates incredible quantities of energy. **Sunspots** are magnetic disturbances on the solar surface; solar cycles are fairly regular, 11-year periods of sunspot activity. Solar energy in the form of charged particles of **solar wind** travels out in all directions from magnetic disturbances and solar storms. Solar wind is deflected by Earth's **magnetosphere**, producing various effects in the upper atmosphere, including spectacular **auroras**, the northern and southern lights, that surge across the skies at higher latitudes.

Radiant energy travels outward from the Sun in all directions, representing a portion of the total **electromagnetic spectrum** made up of different energy wavelengths. A **wavelength** is the distance between corresponding points on any two successive waves. Electromagnetic radiation from the Sun passes through Earth's magnetic field to the top of the atmosphere—the **thermopause**, at approximately 500 km (300 mi) altitude. Incoming solar radiation is **insolation**, measured as energy delivered to a horizontal surface area over some unit of time. The **solar constant** is a general measure of insolation at the top of the atmosphere: The average insolation received at the thermopause when Earth is at its average distance from the Sun is approximately 1372 W/m^2 (2.0 cal/cm^2/min; 2 langleys/min).

Eventually, radiant solar energy reaches Earth's surface. The place on Earth, or on any planet, receiving maximum insolation is the **subsolar point**, where solar rays are perpendicular to the surface (radiating from directly overhead). All other locations away from the subsolar point receive slanting rays and more diffuse energy.

fusion (p. 38)
sunspot (p. 38)
solar wind (p. 39)
magnetosphere (p. 39)
aurora (p. 39)
electromagnetic spectrum (p. 39)
wavelength (p. 39)
thermopause (p. 40)
insolation (p. 41)
solar constant (p. 41)
subsolar point (p. 42)

8. How does the Sun produce such tremendous quantities of energy?
9. What is the sunspot cycle? At what stage was the cycle in the year 2013?
10. Describe Earth's magnetosphere and its effects on the solar wind and the electromagnetic spectrum.
11. Describe the various segments of the electromagnetic spectrum, from shortest to longest wavelength. What are the main wavelengths produced by the Sun? Which wavelengths does Earth radiate to space?
12. What is the solar constant? Why is it important to know?
13. If Earth were flat and oriented at right angles to incoming solar radiation (insolation), what would be the latitudinal distribution of solar energy at the top of the atmosphere?

Define solar altitude, solar declination, and daylength and *describe* the annual variability of each—Earth's seasonality.

The angle between the Sun and the horizon is the Sun's **altitude**. The Sun's **declination** is the latitude of the subsolar point. Declination annually migrates between the Tropic of Cancer at about 23.5° N latitude (June) and the Tropic of Capricorn at about 23.5° S latitude (December). Seasonality means an annual pattern of change in the Sun's altitude and changing **daylength**, or duration of exposure to insolation.

Earth's distinct seasons are produced by interactions of **revolution** (annual orbit about the Sun) and **rotation** (Earth's turning on its *axis*, an imaginary line extending through the planet from the geographic North Pole to the South Pole). As Earth rotates, the boundary that divides daylight and darkness is the **circle of illumination**. Other reasons for seasons include **axial tilt** (at about 23.5° from a perpendicular to the **plane of the ecliptic**, an imaginary plane touching all points of Earth's orbit), **axial parallelism** (the parallel alignment of the axis throughout the year), and *sphericity*.

The **Tropic of Cancer** parallel marks the farthest north the subsolar point migrates during the year, about 23.5° N latitude. The **Tropic of Capricorn** parallel marks the farthest south the subsolar point migrates during the year, about 23.5° S latitude. Throughout the march of the seasons, Earth experiences the **December solstice**, **March equinox**, **June solstice**, and **September equinox** (illustrated in Geosystems in Action 2). At the moment of the December solstice, the area above the **Arctic Circle** at about 66.5° N latitude is in darkness for the entire day. At the June solstice, the area from the **Antarctic Circle** to the South Pole (66.5°–90° S latitude) experiences a 24-hour period of darkness.

altitude (p. 43)
declination (p. 43)
daylength (p. 43)
revolution (p. 43)
rotation (p. 44)
circle of illumination (p. 44)
axial tilt (p. 44)
plane of the ecliptic (p. 44)
axial parallelism (p. 45)
Tropic of Cancer (p. 45)
Tropic of Capricorn (p. 45)
December solstice (p. 45)
Arctic Circle (p. 45)
March equinox (p. 45)
June solstice (p. 48)
Antarctic Circle (p. 48)
September equinox (p. 48)

14. The concept of seasonality refers to what two specific phenomena? How do these two aspects of seasonality change during a year at 0° latitude? At 40°? At 90°?
15. Differentiate between the Sun's altitude and its declination at Earth's surface.
16. For the latitude at which you live, how does daylength vary during the year? How does the Sun's altitude vary? Does your local newspaper publish a weather calendar containing such information?
17. List the five physical factors that operate together to produce seasons.
18. Describe Earth's revolution and rotation, and differentiate between them.
19. What is the angle of Earth's present axial tilt? Does the axial tilt change as Earth orbits about the Sun?
20. Describe seasonal conditions at each of the four key seasonal anniversary dates during the year. What are the solstices and equinoxes, and what is the Sun's declination at these times?

Draw a diagram showing atmospheric structure based on three criteria for analysis—composition, temperature, and function.

The principal substance of Earth's atmosphere is air—the medium of life. *Air* is naturally odorless, colorless, tasteless, and formless.

Above an altitude of 480 km (300 mi), the atmosphere is rarefied (nearly a vacuum) and is called the **exosphere**, which means "outer sphere." The weight (force over a unit area) of the atmosphere, exerted on all surfaces, is **air pressure**. It decreases rapidly with altitude.

By *composition*, we divide the atmosphere into the **heterosphere**, extending from 480 km (300 mi) to 80 km (50 mi) above the Earth's surface, and the **homosphere**, extending from 80 km to Earth's surface. The blend of gases (by proportion) in the homosphere is nearly uniform, has evolved slowly, and includes constant gases, with concentrations that have remained stable over time, and variable gases, which change over space and time. The homosphere is a vast reservoir of relatively inert nitrogen; oxygen, a by-product of photosynthesis; completely inert argon; and *carbon dioxide*, a natural by-product of life processes and fuel combustion.

Using *temperature* as a criterion, we identify the **thermosphere** as the outermost layer, corresponding roughly to the heterosphere in location. Its upper limit, the *thermopause*, is at an altitude of approximately 480 km. **Kinetic energy**, the energy of motion, is the vibrational energy that we measure as temperature. *Heat* is the flow of kinetic energy between molecules and from one body to another because of a temperature difference between them. The amount of heat actually produced in the thermosphere is very small because the density of molecules is so low there. Nearer Earth's surface, the greater number of molecules in the denser atmosphere transmits their kinetic energy as *sensible heat*, meaning that we can feel it as a change in temperature.

In the homosphere, temperature criteria define the **mesosphere**, **stratosphere**, and **troposphere**. The top of the troposphere is wherever a temperature of −57°C (−70°F) is recorded, a transition known as the *tropopause*. The normal temperature profile within the troposphere during the daytime decreases rapidly with increasing altitude at an average of 6.4 C° per km (3.5 F° per 1000 ft), a rate known as the **normal lapse rate**. The actual lapse rate at any particular time and place may deviate considerably because of local weather conditions and is called the *environmental lapse rate*.

The outermost region we distinguish by function is the **ionosphere**, extending through the heterosphere and partway into the homosphere. It absorbs cosmic rays, gamma rays, X-rays, and shorter wavelengths of ultraviolet radiation and converts them into kinetic energy. A functional region within the stratosphere is the **ozonosphere**, or **ozone layer**, which absorbs life-threatening ultraviolet radiation, subsequently raising the temperature of the stratosphere.

exosphere (p. 48)
air pressure (p. 48)
heterosphere (p. 50)
homosphere (p. 50)
thermosphere (p. 51)
kinetic energy (p. 51)
mesosphere (p. 52)
stratosphere (p. 52)
troposphere (p. 52)
normal lapse rate (p. 53)
ionosphere (p. 53)
ozonosphere, ozone layer (p. 53)

21. What is air? Where generally did the components in Earth's present atmosphere originate?
22. What three distinct criteria are employed in dividing the atmosphere for study?
23. Describe the two divisions of the atmosphere on the basis of composition.
24. Name the four most prevalent stable gases in the homosphere. Where did each originate? Is the amount of any of these changing at this time?
25. Describe the overall temperature profile of the atmosphere, and list the four layers defined by temperature.
26. What are the two primary functional layers of the atmosphere, and what does each do?

Describe conditions within the stratosphere—specifically, the function and status of the ozonosphere, or ozone layer.

The overall reduction of the stratospheric ozonosphere, or ozone layer, during the past several decades represents a hazard for society and many natural systems and is caused by chemicals introduced into the atmosphere by humans. Since World War II, quantities of human-made **chlorofluorocarbons (CFCs)** have made their way into the stratosphere. The increased ultraviolet light at those altitudes breaks down these stable chemical compounds, thus freeing chlorine atoms. These atoms act as catalysts in reactions that destroy ozone molecules.

chlorofluorocarbon (CFC) (p. 54)

27. Why is stratospheric ozone so important? Describe the effects created by increases in ultraviolet light reaching the surface.
28. Summarize ozone conditions over the poles, and describe treaties to protect the ozone layer.

Distinguish between natural and anthropogenic pollutants in the lower atmosphere and *construct* simple diagrams illustrating pollution from photochemical reactions in motor vehicle exhaust and from industrial smog.

Within the troposphere, both natural and human-caused **pollutants**, defined as gases, particles, and other chemicals in amounts that are harmful to human health or cause environmental damage, are part of the atmosphere. Volcanoes, fires, and dust storms are sources of smoke and particulates, also known as **aerosols**, consisting of suspended solids and liquid droplets such as pollens, dust, and soot from natural and human sources. We coevolved with natural "pollution" and thus are adapted to it. But we are not adapted to cope with our own anthropogenic pollution. It constitutes a major health threat, particularly where people are concentrated in cities. Earth's next atmosphere may be described most accurately as the **anthropogenic atmosphere** (human-influenced atmosphere).

Transportation is the major human-caused source for carbon monoxide and nitrogen dioxide. Odorless, colorless, and tasteless, **carbon monoxide (CO)** is produced by incomplete combustion (burning with limited oxygen) of fuels or other carbon-containing substances; it is toxic because it deoxygenates human blood.

Photochemical smog results from the interaction of sunlight and the products of automobile exhaust, the single largest contributor of air pollution over urban areas in the United States and Canada. The *nitrogen dioxide* and *volatile organic compounds* (VOCs) from car exhaust, in the presence of ultraviolet light in sunlight, convert into the principal photochemical by-products—*nitric acid, peroxyacetyl nitrates* (PANs), and ground-level ozone. The VOCs, including hydrocarbons not only from gasoline, but also from surface coatings such as paint and electric utility combustion, are important factors in ozone formation.

Nitrogen dioxide (NO_2) inflames human respiratory systems, destroys lung tissue, and damages plants. Nitric oxides participate in reactions that produce nitric acid (HNO_3) in the atmosphere, forming both wet and dry acidic deposition. **Peroxyacetyl nitrates (PANs)** affect human eyes and respiratory systems and are particularly harmful to plants, including both agricultural crops and forests. Ground-level ozone (O_3) has negative effects on human health and kills or damages plants.

The distribution of human-produced **industrial smog** over North America, Europe, and Asia is related to coal-burning power plants. Such pollution contains **sulfur dioxide (SO_2)**, which reacts in the atmosphere to produce *sulfate aerosols*, which, in turn, produce sulfuric acid (H_2SO_4) deposition. This deposition has detrimental effects on living systems when it settles on the landscape. **Particulate matter (PM)** consists of dirt, dust, soot, and ash from industrial and natural sources.

Vertical temperature and atmospheric density distribution in the troposphere can worsen pollution conditions. A **temperature inversion** occurs when the normal temperature decrease with altitude (normal lapse rate) reverses and temperature begins to increase at some altitude. This can cause cold air and pollutants to be trapped near Earth's surface, temporarily unable to mix with the air above the inversion layer.

pollutant (p. 56)
aerosol (p. 56)
anthropogenic atmosphere (p. 57)
carbon monoxide (CO) (p. 57)
photochemical smog (p. 58)
nitrogen dioxide (NO_2) (p. 58)
peroxyacetyl nitrate (PAN) (p. 58)
industrial smog (p. 59)
sulfur dioxide (SO_2) (p. 60)
particulate matter (PM) (p. 60)
temperature inversion (p. 61)

29. Describe two types of natural air pollution. What regions of Earth commonly experience this type of pollution?
30. What are pollutants? What is the relationship between air pollution and urban areas?
31. What is the difference between industrial smog and photochemical smog?
32. Describe the relationship between automobiles and the production of ozone and PANs in city air. What are the principal negative impacts of these gases?

33. How are sulfur impurities in fossil fuels related to the formation of acid in the atmosphere and acid deposition on the land?

34. In summary, what are the cost–benefit results from the first 20 years under Clean Air Act regulations?

Answer for Critical Thinking 2.2: Hypothetically, if Earth were tilted on its side, with its axis parallel to the plane of the ecliptic, we would experience a maximum variation in seasons worldwide. In contrast, if Earth's axis were perpendicular to the plane of its orbit—that is, with no tilt—we would experience no seasonal changes, with something like a perpetual spring or fall season, and all latitudes would experience 12-hour days and nights.

VISUALanalysis 2 The Atmosphere

Temperature inversions such as the one shown in this photo occur frequently in Salt Lake City, Utah, often causing high levels of particulate pollution. [Marli Miller/Visuals Unlimited, Inc./Getty images]

1. During a temperature inversion, where is the layer of warm air relative to the layer of cold air? Can you identify each layer in this photo?
2. In what ways does a temperature inversion worsen an air pollution episode? What human activities contribute to air pollution during the winter months?

MasteringGeography™

Looking for additional review and test prep materials? Visit the Study Area in *MasteringGeography*™ to enhance your geographic literacy, spatial reasoning skills, and understanding of this chapter's content by accessing a variety of resources, including MapMaster interactive maps, geoscience animations, videos, *In the News* RSS feeds, flashcards, web links, self-study quizzes, and an eText version of *Elemental Geosystems*.

3 Atmospheric Energy and Global Temperatures

The "green roof" on top of City Hall in Chicago, Illinois, helps mitigate the urban heat island effect, an energy balance phenomenon that causes temperatures in cities to be warmer than those of surrounding regions. This type of living roof provides insulation for the building below, reducing heating and cooling costs by as much as 20%. The roof also absorbs less insolation than one made of black asphalt, lessening the overall warming of city temperatures. [Diane Cook And Len Jenshel/National Geographic/Getty images.]

KEYLEARNING**concepts**

After reading the chapter, you should be able to:

- *Define* energy and heat and *explain* four types of heat transfer: radiation, conduction, convection, and advection.
- *Identify* alternative pathways for solar energy on its way through the troposphere to Earth's surface—transmission, scattering, refraction, and absorption—and *review* the concept of albedo (reflectivity).
- *Explain* the greenhouse concept as it applies to Earth, *analyze* the effect of clouds and aerosols on atmospheric heating and cooling, and *review* the Earth–atmosphere energy balance.
- *Define* the concept of temperature and *review* the principal temperature controls that produce global temperature patterns.
- *Interpret* the pattern of Earth's temperatures from their portrayal on January and July temperature maps and on a map of annual temperature ranges.
- *List* typical urban heat island conditions and their causes and *discuss* heat waves and human heat response.

Melting Sea Ice Opens Arctic Shipping Lanes; However...

Sought for hundreds of years by explorers trying to navigate the icy waters of the Arctic, the Northwest Passage is a sea route connecting the Atlantic and Pacific Oceans through the inland waterways of the Canadian Arctic Archipelago. The Northern Sea Route, or "Northeast Passage," is another Arctic sea route, traversing the Russian coast and linking Europe and Asia. These northern passages offer ships shorter alternatives to the long routes through the Panama and Suez Canals (Figure GN 3.1).

During most years, Arctic Ocean sea ice blocked these sea routes, making them unavailable for shipping—that is, until recently. With a large ice melt in the summer of 2007, the Northwest Passage opened along its entire length for 36 days. In 2009, two German container ships completed the first commercial navigation of the Northern Sea Route. Higher ocean and air temperatures associated with climate change cause the ice losses that opened these northern passages. The 2012 summer sea-ice melt was the largest on record since 1979, allowing over 40 vessels, including freighters and tankers, to traverse the Northern Sea Route. In 2013, the first commercial cargo ship traveled the Northwest Passage (Figure GN 3.2).

Albedo and Sea-Ice Melting In Chapter 1, we described the positive feedback loop between sunlight and the reflectivity of sea-ice surfaces. Lighter surfaces reflect sunlight and remain cooler, whereas darker surfaces absorb sunlight and heat up. Snow- and ice-covered surfaces are natural reflectors; in fact, sea ice reflects about 80%–95% of the solar energy it receives. The ocean surface is darker, reflecting only an average of about 10% of insolation. This percentage is *albedo*, the reflective value of a surface. As the ice-covered area in the Arctic retreats, darker water or land receives direct sunlight and absorbs more heat, which decreases albedo and adds to warming—a positive feedback.

Particulates from the atmosphere appear to decrease albedo even further. Scientists now have evidence that surface accumulations of black carbon (soot) and other atmospheric particulates are significant causes of glacial snow and ice losses across the Himalayas. Also, black carbon accumulation from distant wildfires may be a major factor in the darkening of interior surfaces on the Greenland Ice Sheet, where the percentage of darkened ice surfaces reached record levels in 2014. Thus, soot and particulate matter in the Arctic atmosphere that settles on ice surfaces darkens the color, decreases albedo, and accelerates melting, with far-ranging effects on global climate.

▲**Figure GN 3.2 U.S. and Canadian Coast Guard icebreakers in the Arctic Ocean.** [Jessica K. Robinson/USGS.]

Sea Ice and Arctic Shipping The prospect of an Arctic Ocean with long ice-free periods for freighter and oil-tanker traffic is triggering commercial excitement as use of the Northern Sea Route increases. But while the Arctic shipping lanes save time and money in the transport of goods, their use has potentially huge environmental costs—air pollution, ice loss, climate impacts, oil spills, and risk of ship groundings. The stack emissions from new freighter and tanker traffic will add particulates to the atmosphere. When this material settles on sea ice, snow-covered glaciers, and ice shelves, it will darken their surfaces and worsen albedo-reducing feedback loops that drive climate change.

Computer models now show that with continued significant losses of sea ice, the Arctic Ocean could be ice-free during the summer within a decade. As shipping traffic increases, these losses may occur sooner through impacts of air pollution on surface albedos and surface energy budgets, some of the topics of this chapter.

▼**Figure GN 3.1 Arctic summer sea-ice extent, 2012.** [NASA/GSFC.]

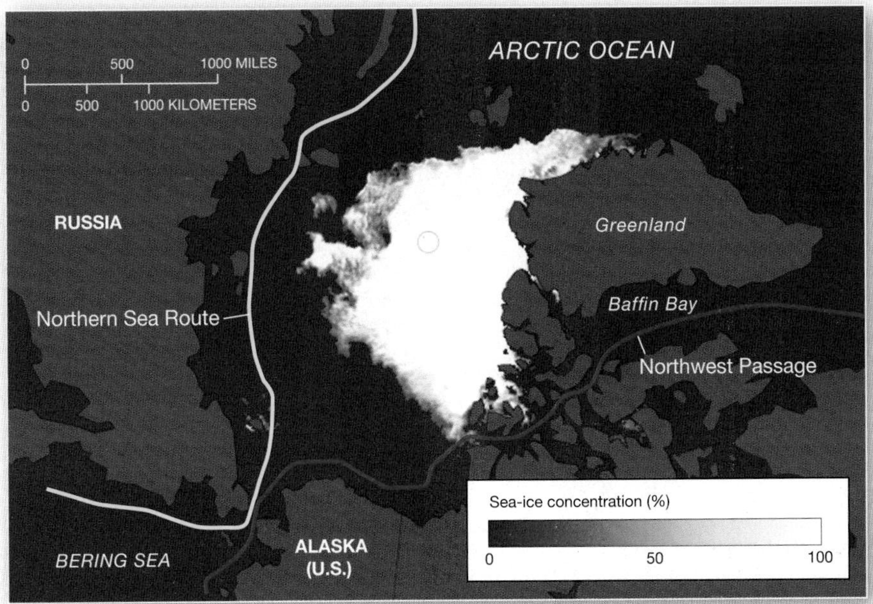

QUESTION AND EXPLORE For daily updates on the status of sea ice, go to the National Snow and Ice Data Center website at http://nsidc.org/arcticseaicenews/. How does sea ice differ from glacial ice and icebergs? See the discussion in Chapter 14, or go to http://nsidc.org/cryosphere/sotc/sea_ice.html. MG

Solar energy cascading through the atmosphere from the Sun to Earth is the engine for the functioning systems on Earth—it heats Earth's surface, drives wind and ocean currents, and impels moisture into the atmosphere to form clouds and precipitation. These energy and moisture exchanges between Earth's surface and its atmosphere are essential elements of weather and climate, discussed in later chapters.

Air temperature plays a role in human life at all levels, affecting not only personal comfort, but also environmental processes across Earth. Understanding temperature concepts is critical for Earth systems science and physical geography, since the variations in average air and water temperatures have far-ranging effects on Earth systems.

... variations in average air and water temperatures have far-ranging effects on Earth systems.

In this chapter: We follow solar energy through the troposphere to Earth's surface, looking at processes that affect insolation pathways. We discuss the balance between solar radiation inputs and outputs from Earth—the energy balance in the atmosphere—and apply the "greenhouse" concept to Earth. We also examine surface energy and daily radiation patterns, analyzing the transfer of net radiation that maintains Earth's energy balance. Focus Study 3.1 discusses applications for solar energy, a renewable energy resource of great potential.

The temperature concepts presented in this chapter provide the foundation for our study of weather and climate systems. We first examine the principal temperature controls of latitude, altitude and elevation, cloud cover, and land–water heating differences as they interact to produce Earth's temperature patterns. We then look at a series of temperature maps illustrating Earth's temperature patterns and discuss current temperature trends associated with global warming. The chapter concludes with a look at the energy environment in our cities and the effect of high air temperatures and humidity on the human body, including a look at heat waves and their increasing occurrence across the globe.

Energy-Balance Essentials

In Chapter 2, we introduced the concept of Earth's energy balance between shortwave solar radiation to Earth and shortwave and longwave radiation to space (please review Figure 2.6). This energy balance is analogous to a *budget* that balances energy income and expenditure. For Earth, energy income is insolation, and energy expenditure is radiation to space, with an overall balance maintained between the two.

Transmission refers to the uninterrupted passage of shortwave and longwave energy through either the atmosphere or water. Our Earth–atmosphere energy budget comprises *inputs* of shortwave radiation (ultraviolet light, visible light, and near-infrared wavelengths) and *outputs* of shortwave and longwave radiation (reflected light and thermal infrared wavelengths) that pass through the atmosphere by transmission. Since solar energy is unevenly distributed by latitude and fluctuates seasonally, the energy budget is not the same at every location on Earth's surface, even though the overall energy system remains in steady-state equilibrium (see a simplified diagram in **Figure 3.1** and the discussion ahead; a more detailed illustration of energy balance is in Geosystems in Action 3 on pages 80 and 81).

Energy and Heat

For the purpose of studying Earth's energy budget, *energy* can be defined as the capacity to do *work*, or move matter. (*Matter* is mass that assumes a physical shape and occupies space.) *Kinetic energy* is the energy of motion, produced when you run or ride a bicycle; it is the vibrational energy of molecules that we measure as temperature. *Potential energy* is stored energy (stored

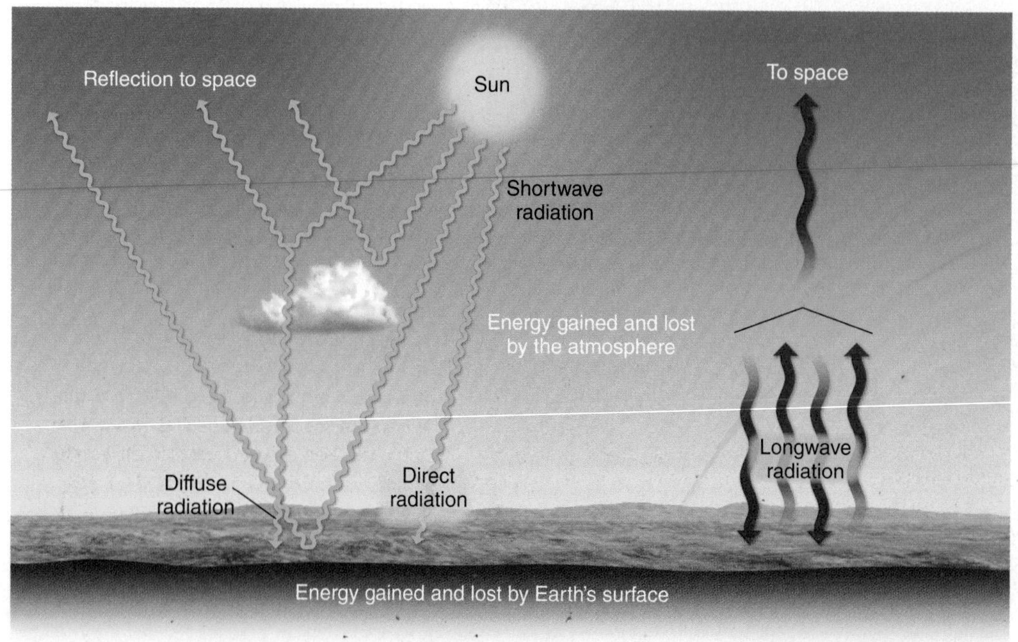

◀**Figure 3.1 Simplified view of the Earth–atmosphere energy system.** Energy gained and lost by Earth's surface and atmosphere includes incoming and reflected shortwave radiation, energy absorbed at Earth's surface, and outgoing longwave radiation. Refer back to this diagram as you read about energy pathways and principles in the atmosphere. A more complete illustration of the Earth–atmosphere energy balance is in Figure GIA 3.

Animation Global Warming, Climate Change

http://goo.gl/cTHCHK

Animation Earth–Atmosphere Energy Balance

http://goo.gl/7UYgTM

due to either composition or position) that has the capacity to do work under the right conditions. Petroleum, for example, has potential energy that is released when a car engine burns gasoline. Water in a reservoir above a hydropower dam has potential energy that is released when the pull of gravity impels it through the turbines and into the river downstream. (Potential energy is converted into kinetic energy in both these examples.)

Types of Heat In Chapter 2, we mentioned that **heat** is the flow of kinetic energy between molecules and from one body or substance to another resulting from a temperature difference between them. Heat always flows from an area of higher temperature into an area of lower temperature; an example is the transfer of heat when you wrap your warm hand around a snowball or a piece of ice, and it melts. Heat flow stops when the temperatures—that is, when the amounts of kinetic energy—become equal.

Two types of heat energy are important for understanding Earth–atmosphere energy budgets. **Sensible heat** can be "sensed" by humans as temperature because it comes from the kinetic energy of molecular motion. **Latent heat** ("hidden" heat) is the energy gained or lost when a substance changes from one state to another, such as from water vapor to liquid water (gas to liquid) or from water to ice (liquid to solid). Latent heat transfer differs from sensible heat transfer in that as long as a physical change in state is taking place, the substance itself does not change temperature (although in Chapter 5 we see that the surroundings do gain or lose heat).

▲**Figure 3.2 Heat-transfer processes.** Infrared energy *radiates* from the burner to the saucepan and the air. Energy *conducts* through the molecules of the pan and the handle. The water physically mixes, carrying heat energy by *convection*. Latent heat is the energy absorbed when liquid water changes to steam (water vapor).

Methods of Heat Transfer Heat energy can be transferred in a number of ways throughout Earth's atmosphere, land, and water bodies. *Radiation* is the transfer of heat in electromagnetic waves, such as that from the Sun to Earth or as that from a fire or a burner on the stove (**Figure 3.2**). The temperature of the object or substance determines the wavelength of radiation it emits; the hotter an object, the shorter the wavelengths that are emitted. Waves of radiation do not need to travel through a medium, such as air or water, in order to transfer heat.

Conduction is the molecule-to-molecule transfer of heat energy as it diffuses through a substance. As molecules warm, their vibration increases, causing collisions that produce motion in neighboring molecules, thus transferring heat from warmer to cooler material. An example is energy conducted through the handle of a pan on a kitchen stove. Different materials (gases, liquids, and solids) conduct sensible heat directionally from areas of higher temperature to those of lower temperature. This heat flow transfers energy through matter at varying rates, depending on the conductivity of the material—Earth's land surface is a better conductor than air; moist air is a slightly better conductor than dry air.

Gases and liquids also transfer energy by **convection**, the transfer of heat by mixing or circulation. An example is a convection oven, in which a fan circulates heated air to uniformly cook food, or the movement of boiling water on a stove. In the atmosphere or in bodies of water, warmer (less dense) masses tend to rise, and cooler (denser) masses tend to sink, establishing patterns of convection. This physical mixing usually involves a strong vertical motion. When horizontal motion dominates, the term **advection** applies.

Energy Pathways and Principles

Insolation, or incoming solar radiation, is the single energy input driving the Earth–atmosphere system, yet it is not equal at all surfaces across the globe (**Figure 3.3**). Consistent daylength and high Sun altitude produce fairly consistent insolation values (about 180–220 watts per square meter, or W/m^2) throughout the equatorial and tropical latitudes. Insolation decreases toward the poles, from about 25° latitude in both the Northern and the Southern Hemispheres. In general, greater insolation at the surface (about 240–280 W/m^2) occurs in low-latitude deserts worldwide because of frequently cloudless skies. Note this energy pattern in the subtropical deserts in both hemispheres (for example, the Sonoran Desert in the American Southwest, the Sahara in North Africa, and the Kalahari in South Africa).

Scattering and Diffuse Radiation Insolation encounters an increasing density of atmospheric molecules as it travels toward Earth's surface. These atmospheric gases, as well as dust, cloud droplets, water vapor, and pollutants, physically interact with insolation to redirect radiation, changing the direction of the light's movement

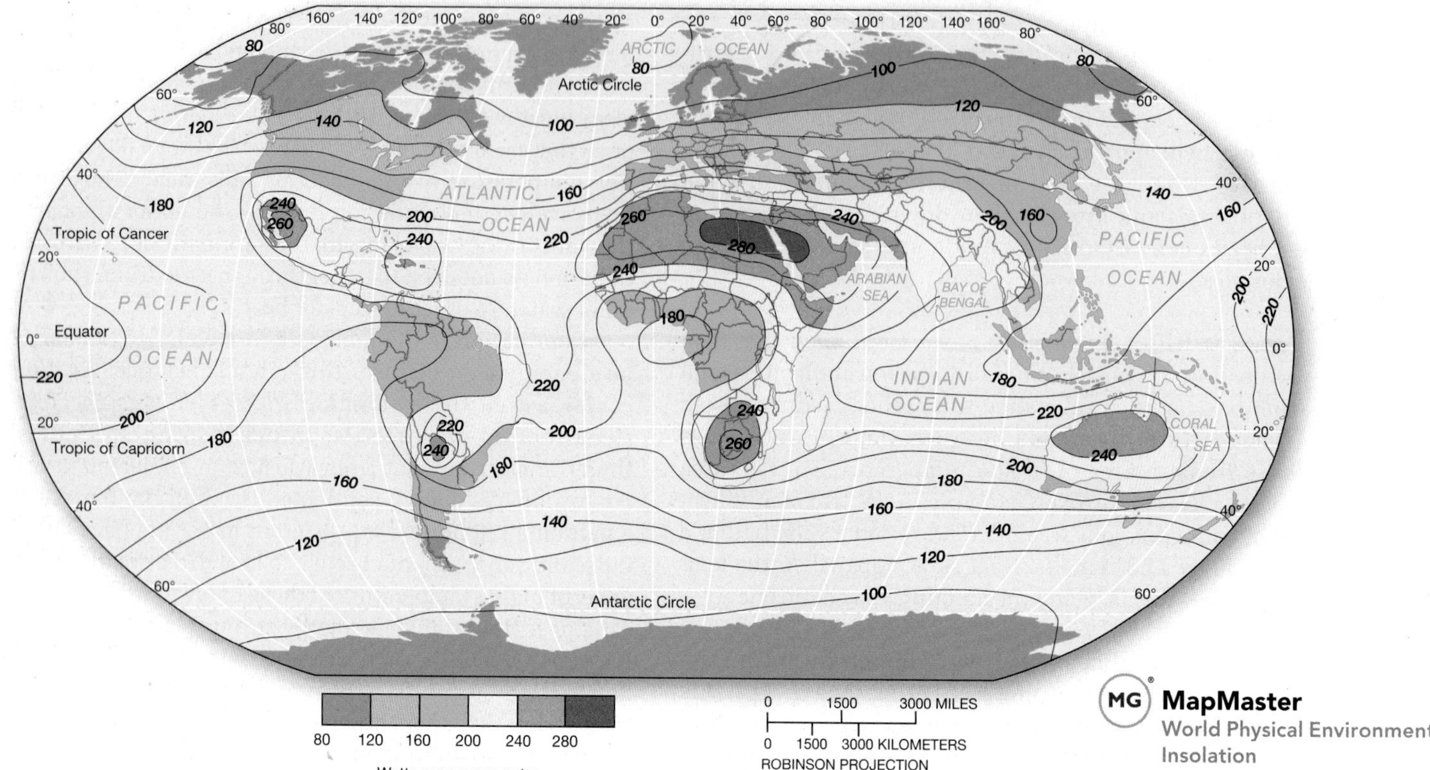

▲**Figure 3.3 Insolation at Earth's surface.** Average annual solar radiation received on a horizontal surface at ground level in watts per square meter (100 W/m^2 = 75 kcal/cm^2/year). [Based on M. I. Budyko, *The Heat Balance of the Earth's Surface* (Washington, DC: U.S. Department of Commerce, 1958).]

without altering its wavelengths. **Scattering** is the name for this phenomenon, which accounts for a percentage of the insolation that does not reach Earth's surface, but is instead reflected back to space.

Incoming energy that reaches Earth's surface after scattering occurs is **diffuse radiation** (labeled in Figure 3.1). This weaker, dispersed radiation is composed of waves traveling in different directions and thus casts shadowless light on the ground. In contrast, *direct radiation* travels in a straight line to Earth's surface without being scattered or otherwise affected by materials in the atmosphere. (The values on the surface-insolation map in Figure 3.3 combine both direct and diffuse radiation.)

Have you wondered why Earth's sky is blue? And why sunsets and sunrises are often red? These common questions are answered using a principle known as Rayleigh scattering (named for English physicist Lord Rayleigh). This principle applies to radiation scattered by small gas molecules and relates the amount of scattering in the atmosphere to wavelengths of light—shorter wavelengths are scattered more, whereas longer wavelengths are scattered less.

Looking back to Chapter 2, Figure 2.4, we see that blues and violets are the shorter wavelengths of visible light. According to the Rayleigh scattering principle, these wavelengths are scattered more than longer wavelengths such as orange or red. When we look at the sky with the sun overhead, we see the wavelengths that are scattered the most throughout the atmosphere. Although both blues and violets are scattered, our human eye perceives this color mix as blue, resulting in the common observation of a blue sky.

For atmospheric particles larger than the wavelengths of light (such as many pollutants), the Rayleigh scattering principle does not apply. *Mie scattering* is the process that works on these particles. In a sky filled with smog and haze, the larger particles scatter all wavelengths of visible light evenly, making the sky appear almost white.

The altitude of the Sun determines the thickness of the atmosphere through which its rays must pass to reach an observer. Direct rays (from overhead) pass through less atmosphere and experience less scattering than do low, oblique-angle rays, which must travel farther through the atmosphere. When the Sun is low on the horizon at sunrise or sunset, shorter wavelengths (blue and violet) are scattered out, leaving only the residual oranges and reds to reach our eyes.

Refraction As insolation enters the atmosphere, it passes from one medium to another, from virtually empty space into atmospheric gases. A change of medium also occurs when insolation passes from air into water. Such transitions subject the insolation to a change of speed, which also shifts its direction—this is the bending action of **refraction**. In the same way, a crystal or prism refracts light passing through it, bending different wavelengths to different angles, separating the light into its component colors to display the spectrum. A rainbow is created when

▲**Figure 3.4 A rainbow.** Raindrops—and in this photo, moisture droplets from the Niagara River—refract and reflect light to produce a primary rainbow. Note that in the primary rainbow the colors with the shortest wavelengths are on the inside and those with the longest wavelengths are on the outside. In the secondary bow, note that the color sequence is reversed because of an extra angle of reflection within each moisture droplet. [Bobbé Christopherson.]

visible light passes through raindrops and is refracted and reflected toward the observer at a precise angle (**Figure 3.4**). Another example of refraction is a *mirage*, an image that appears near the horizon when light waves are refracted by layers of air at different temperatures (and consequently of different densities).

Refraction produces the atmospheric distortion of the setting Sun (**Figure 3.5**). When the Sun is low in the sky, light must penetrate more air than when the Sun is high; thus, light is refracted through air layers of different densities on its way to the observer. This distortion means that we see the Sun's refracted image for about 4 minutes before the Sun actually peeks over the horizon in the morning and for about 4 minutes after the Sun sets in the evening. The extra 8 minutes of daylight caused by refraction vary with atmospheric temperature, moisture, and pollutants.

Reflection and Albedo A portion of arriving energy bounces directly back into space—this is **reflection.** The reflective quality, or intrinsic brightness, of a surface is **albedo**, an important control over the amount of insolation that reaches Earth. We report albedo as the percentage of insolation that is reflected—0% is total absorption; 100% is total reflectance.

In terms of visible wavelengths, darker-colored surfaces (such as asphalt) have lower albedos, and lighter-colored surfaces (such as snow) have higher albedos (**Figure 3.6**). On water surfaces, the angle of the solar rays also affects albedo values: Lower angles produce more reflection than do higher angles. In addition, smooth surfaces increase albedo, whereas rougher surfaces reduce it.

Individual locations can experience highly variable albedo values during the year in response to changes in cloud and ground cover. Satellite data reveal that albedos average 19%–38% for all surfaces between the tropics (23.5° N to 23.5° S latitude), whereas albedos for the polar regions may be as high as 80% as a result of ice and snow. Tropical forests with frequent cloud cover are characteristically low in albedo (15%), whereas generally cloudless deserts have higher albedos (35%).

Earth and its atmosphere reflect 31% of all insolation when averaged over a year. The glow of Earth's albedo, or the sunshine reflected off Earth, is called *earthshine*. By comparison, a full Moon, which is bright enough to read by under clear skies, has only a 6%–8% albedo value.

Absorption Insolation, both direct and diffuse, that is not part of the 31% reflected from Earth's surface and atmosphere is absorbed, either in the atmosphere or by

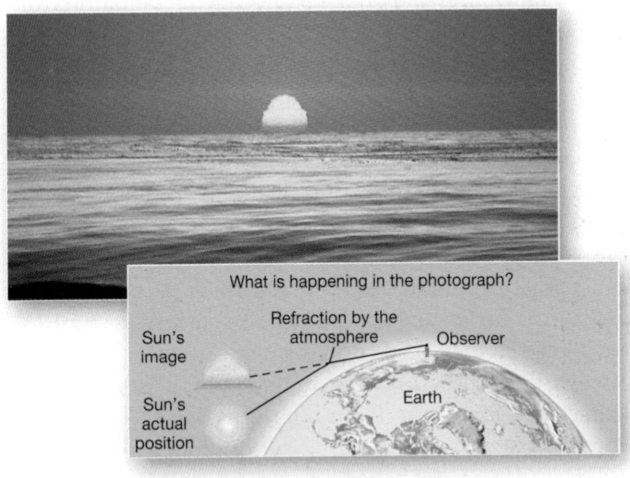

▲**Figure 3.5 Sun refraction.** The distorted appearance of the Sun as it sets over the ocean is produced by refraction of the Sun's image in the atmosphere. Have you ever noticed this effect? [Robert Christopherson.]

GEOreport 3.1 Did light refraction sink the Titanic?

An unusual optical phenomenon called "super refraction" may explain why the *Titanic* struck an iceberg in 1912 and why the *California* did not come to her aid during that fateful April night. Recently, a British historian combined weather records, survivors' testimony, and ships' logs to determine that atmospheric conditions were conducive to a bending of light that causes objects to be obscured in a mirage in front of a "false" horizon. Under these conditions, the *Titanic*'s lookouts could not see the iceberg until too late to turn, and the nearby *California* could not identify the sinking ship. Read the full story at http://www.smithsonianmag.com/science-nature/Did-the-Titanic-Sink-Because-of-an-Optical-Illusion.html.

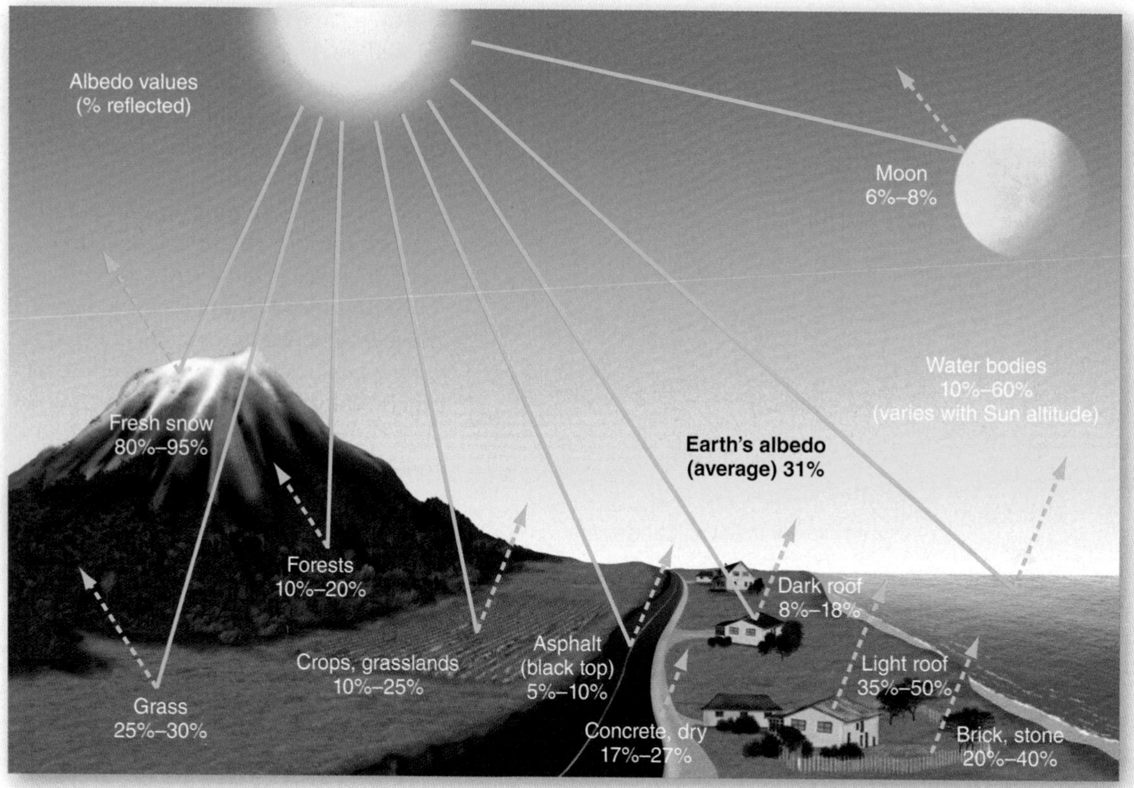

▲**Figure 3.6 Various albedo values.** In general, light surfaces are more reflective than dark surfaces and thus have higher albedo values.

Earth's surface. **Absorption** is the assimilation of radiation by molecules of matter, converting the radiation from one form of energy to another. Solar energy is absorbed by land and water surfaces (about 45% of incoming insolation) as well as by atmospheric gases, dust, clouds, and stratospheric ozone (together about 24% of incoming insolation). It is converted into either longwave radiation or chemical energy (the latter by plants, in photosynthesis). The process of absorption raises the temperature of the absorbing surface.

The atmosphere does not absorb as much radiation as Earth's surface because gases are selective about the wavelengths they absorb. For example, oxygen and ozone effectively absorb ultraviolet radiation in the stratosphere. None of the atmospheric gases absorbs the wavelengths of visible light, which pass through the atmosphere to Earth as direct radiation. Several gases—water vapor and carbon dioxide, in particular—are good absorbers of longwave radiation emitted by Earth. These gases absorb heat in the lower troposphere, a process that explains why Earth's atmosphere is warmer at the surface, acting like a natural greenhouse.

Clouds, Aerosols, and Atmospheric Albedo Clouds and aerosols are unpredictable factors in the tropospheric energy budget. The presence or absence of clouds may make a 75% difference in the amount of energy that reaches the surface. Clouds reflect shortwave insolation, so that less insolation reaches Earth's surface, and they absorb longwave radiation leaving Earth (**Figure 3.7**). Longwave radiation trapped by an insulating cloud layer can create a warming of Earth's atmosphere as part of the *greenhouse effect* (discussed in the next section).

As discussed in Chapter 2, air pollutants from both natural and anthropogenic sources affect atmospheric albedo. Stratospheric aerosols from the 1991 eruption of Mount Pinatubo in the Philippines, shown in Figure 4.1, resulted in an increase in global atmospheric albedo and a temporary average cooling of 0.5 C° (0.9 F°). Scientists have correlated similar cooling trends with other large volcanic eruptions throughout history. Industrial pollutants such as sulfate aerosols are today increasing the reflectivity of the atmosphere, cooling Earth's surface. However, some aerosols (especially black carbon) readily absorb radiation and reradiate heat back toward Earth—with warming effects. Recent research indicates that black carbon, or soot, from human sources plays a more important role in recent global warming than previously thought.

Global stratospheric aerosols increased 7% from 2000 to 2010. An overview of the effects of aerosols is at http://earthobservatory.nasa.gov/Features/Aerosols/page1.php; information about aerosol monitoring is at http://www.esrl.noaa.gov/gmd/aero/.

Global dimming is the general term describing the pollution-related decline in insolation reaching Earth's surface. This process is difficult to incorporate into climate models, although evidence shows that it is causing

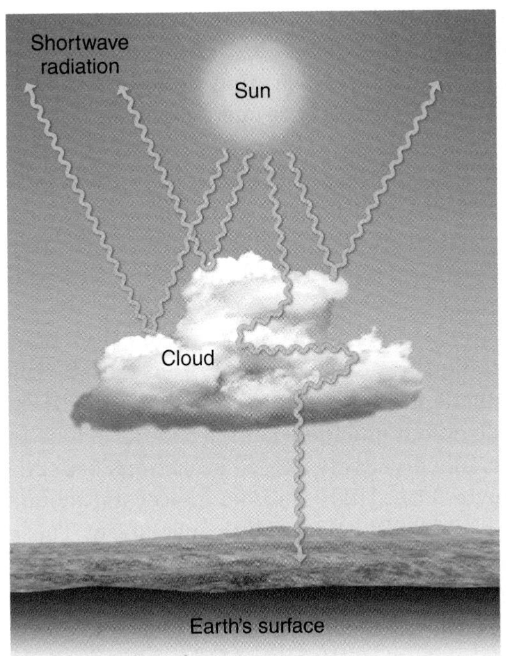

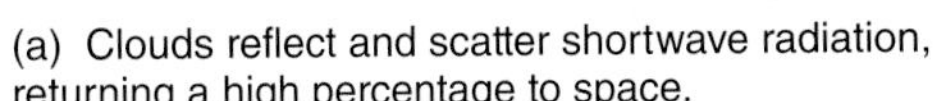

(a) Clouds reflect and scatter shortwave radiation, returning a high percentage to space.

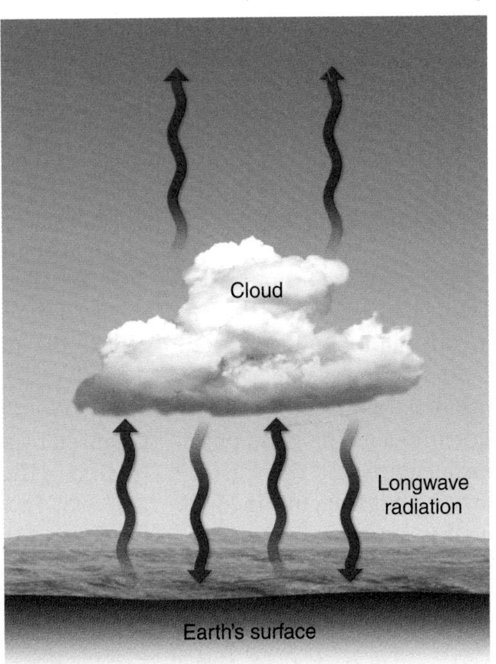

(b) Clouds absorb and reradiate longwave radiation emitted by Earth; some longwave energy is lost to space and some moves back toward Earth's surface.

◄**Figure 3.7 The effects of clouds on shortwave and longwave radiation.**

an underestimation of the actual amount of warming happening in Earth's lower atmosphere.

Energy Balance in the Troposphere

The Earth–atmosphere energy system naturally balances itself in a steady-state equilibrium. The inputs of shortwave energy to Earth's atmosphere and surface from the Sun are eventually balanced by the outputs of shortwave energy reflected and longwave energy emitted from Earth's atmosphere and surface back to space. During times when this balance is not achieved, Earth can undergo a period of temporary warming or cooling that affects the overall climate (discussed further in Chapter 8).

Certain gases in the atmosphere effectively delay longwave energy losses to space and act to warm the lower atmosphere. In this section, we examine this "greenhouse" effect and then develop an overall, detailed energy budget for the troposphere.

The Greenhouse Effect and Atmospheric Warming

In Chapter 2, we characterized Earth as a cooler blackbody radiator than the Sun, emitting energy in longer wavelengths from its surface and atmosphere toward space. However, some of this longwave radiation is absorbed by carbon dioxide, water vapor, methane, nitrous oxide,

CRITICAL**thinking 3.1**

A Kelp Indicator of Surface Energy Dynamics

In Antarctica, on Petermann Island off the Graham Land Coast, a piece of kelp (a seaweed) was dropped by a passing bird. When photographed (**Figure CT 3.1.1**), the kelp lay about 10 cm (4 in.) deep in the snow, in a hole about the same shape as the kelp. In your opinion, what energy principles or pathways interacted to make this scene?

Now, expand your conclusion to the issue of mining coal and other deposits in Antarctica. For now, the international Antarctic Treaty blocks mining exploitation. Construct a case for continuing the ban on mining operations based on your energy-budget analysis of the kelp in the snow and information on surface energy budgets in this chapter. Consider the dust and particulate output of mining. On the other hand, what factors can you think of that might favor such mining?

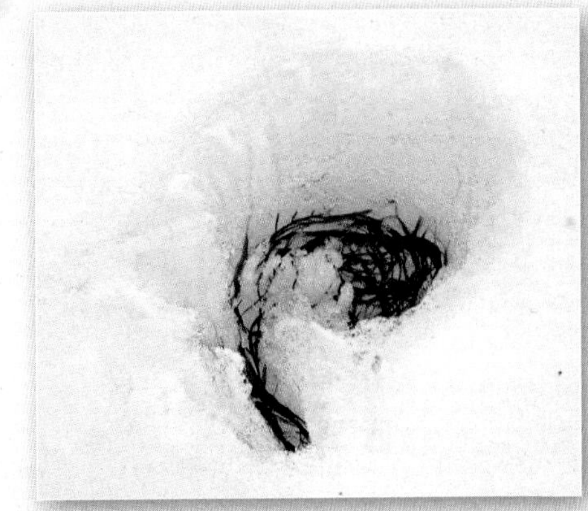

▲**Figure CT 3.1.1** Kelp in Antarctic snow and ice. [Bobbé Christopherson.]

chlorofluorocarbons (CFCs), and other gases in the lower atmosphere and then emitted back, or *reradiated*, toward Earth. This process can raise the temperature of Earth's atmosphere. The rough similarity between this process and the way a greenhouse operates gives the process its name—the **greenhouse effect**. The gases associated with this process are collectively termed **greenhouse gases**.

The "Greenhouse" Concept In a greenhouse, the glass is transparent to shortwave insolation, allowing light to pass through to the soil, plants, and materials inside, where absorption and conduction take place. The absorbed energy is then emitted as longwave radiation, warming the air inside the greenhouse. The glass physically traps both the longer wavelengths and the warmed air inside the greenhouse, preventing it from mixing with cooler outside air. Thus, the glass acts as a one-way filter, allowing the shortwave energy in, but not allowing the longwave energy out except through conduction or, by opening the greenhouse's roof vents, convection. You experience the same process in a car parked in direct sunlight. Opening the car windows allows the air inside to mix with the outside environment, thereby removing heated air physically from one place to another by convection. The interior of a car gets surprisingly hot with the windows closed, even on a day with mild temperatures outside.

Overall, the atmosphere behaves a bit differently. In the atmosphere, the greenhouse analogy does not fully apply because longwave radiation is not trapped as in a greenhouse. Rather, its passage to space is delayed as the longwave radiation is absorbed by certain gases, clouds, and dust in the atmosphere and is reradiated back to Earth's surface. Increasing concentrations of greenhouse gases, especially carbon dioxide, in the lower atmosphere since 1950 have delayed the passage of longwave radiation, thus producing a warming trend and related changes in the Earth–atmosphere energy system.

Clouds and Earth's "Greenhouse" As discussed earlier, clouds sometimes cause cooling and other times cause heating of the lower atmosphere, in turn affecting Earth's climate (Figure 3.7). The effect of clouds is dependent on the percentage of cloud cover as well as cloud type, altitude, and thickness (water content and density). Low, thick stratus clouds reflect about 90% of insolation. The term **cloud-albedo forcing** refers to an increase in albedo caused by such clouds and the resulting cooling of Earth's climate (here, albedo effects exceed greenhouse effects, shown in **Figure 3.8a**). High-altitude, ice-crystal clouds reflect only about 50% of incoming insolation. These cirrus clouds also act as insulation, trapping longwave radiation from Earth and raising minimum temperatures. This is **cloud-greenhouse forcing**, which causes warming of Earth's climate (here, greenhouse effects exceed albedo effects, shown in **Figure 3.8b**).

Jet contrails (condensation trails) produce high cirrus clouds stimulated by aircraft exhaust—sometimes called *contrail cirrus* (**Figure 3.9**). Contrails both cool and warm the atmosphere, and these opposing effects make it difficult for scientists to determine their overall role in Earth's energy budget. Recent research indicates that contrail cirrus trap outgoing radiation from Earth at a slightly greater rate than they reflect insolation, suggesting that their overall effect is a positive radiative forcing, or warming, of climate. When numerous contrails merge and spread in size, their effect on Earth's energy budget may be significant.

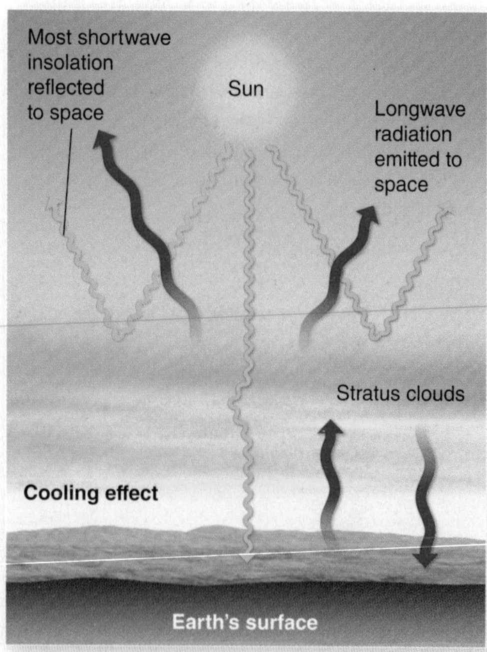

(a) Low, thick clouds lead to cloud-albedo forcing and atmospheric cooling.

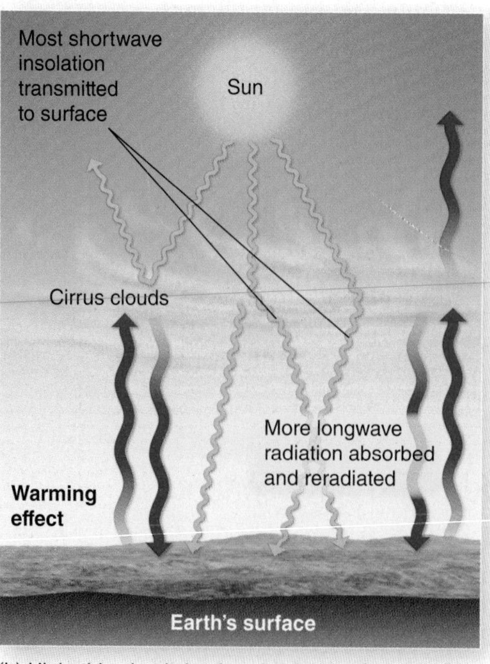

(b) High, thin clouds lead to cloud-greenhouse forcing and atmospheric warming.

◀**Figure 3.8 Energy effects of cloud types.**

Animation MG
Earth–Atmosphere Energy Balance
http://goo.gl/7UYgTM

▲**Figure 3.9 Jet contrails form contrail cirrus.** Older contrails widen to form high cirrus clouds, with an overall warming effect on Earth. [Bobbé Christopherson.]

Earth–Atmosphere Energy Balance

If Earth's surface and its atmosphere are considered separately, neither exhibits a balanced radiation budget in which inputs equal outputs. The average annual energy distribution is positive (an energy surplus, or gain) for Earth's surface and negative (an energy deficit, or loss) for Earth's atmosphere as it radiates energy to space. However, when considered together, these two equal each other, making it possible for us to construct an overall energy balance.

Geosystems in Action 3 summarizes the Earth–atmosphere radiation balance, bringing together all the elements previously discussed by following 100% of arriving insolation through the troposphere. Incoming energy is on the left in the illustration; outgoing energy is on the right.

Summary of Inputs and Outputs Out of 100% of the solar energy arriving at the top of the atmosphere, 31% is reflected back to space—this is Earth's average albedo. This includes scattering (7%), reflection by clouds and aerosols (21%), and reflection by Earth's surface (3%). Another 21% of arriving solar energy is absorbed by the atmosphere—3% by clouds and 18% by atmospheric gases and dust. Stratospheric ozone absorption accounts for another 3%. About 45% of the incoming insolation transmits through to Earth's surface as direct and diffuse shortwave radiation. In sum, Earth's atmosphere and surface absorb 69% of incoming shortwave radiation: 21% (atmosphere heating) + 45% (surface heating) + 3% (ozone absorption) = 69%. Find these pathways in Figure GIA 3.1. Earth eventually emits this 69% as longwave radiation back into space.

Outgoing energy transfers from the surface are both *nonradiative* (involving physical, or mechanical, motion) and *radiative* (consisting of radiation). Nonradiative transfer processes include convection (4%) and the energy released by *latent heat transfer*, the energy absorbed and dissipated by water as it evaporates and condenses (19%). Radiative transfer is by longwave radiation from the surface to the atmosphere and then to space (represented in Figure GIA 3.2 as the greenhouse effect and direct loss to space). Stratospheric ozone radiation to space makes up another 3%.

In total, the atmosphere radiates 58% of the absorbed energy back to space, including the 21% absorbed by clouds, gases, and dust; 23% from convective and latent heat transfers; and another 14% from net longwave radiation that is reradiated to space. Earth's surface emits 8% of absorbed radiation directly back to space, and stratospheric ozone radiation adds another 3%. Note that atmospheric energy losses are greater than those from Earth. However, the energy is in balance overall: 61% atmospheric losses + 8% surface losses = 69%.

Latitudinal Energy Imbalances As stated earlier, energy budgets at specific places or times on Earth are not always the same (see the satellite images in Figure GIA 3). Greater amounts of sunlight are reflected into space by lighter-colored land surfaces such as deserts and snow or by cloud cover. Greater amounts of longwave radiation are emitted from Earth to space in subtropical deserts, where little cloud cover is present over surfaces that absorb heat. Less longwave energy is emitted over the cooler polar regions and over tropical lands covered in thick clouds (in the equatorial Amazon region, in Africa, and in Indonesia).

Figure 3.10 summarizes the Earth–atmosphere energy budget by latitude. Between the tropics, the angle of incoming insolation is high, and daylength is consistent, with little seasonal variation, so more energy is gained than lost—*energy surpluses dominate.* In the polar regions, the Sun is low in the sky, surfaces are light (ice and snow) and reflective, and for up to 6 months during the year, no insolation is received, so more energy is lost than gained—*energy deficits prevail.* At around 36° latitude, a balance exists between energy gains and losses for the Earth–atmosphere system.

The imbalance of energy from the *tropical surpluses* and the *polar deficits* drives a vast global circulation pattern. The meridional (north–south) transfer agents are winds, ocean currents, dynamic weather systems, and other related phenomena. Dramatic examples of such energy and mass transfers are tropical cyclones (hurricanes and typhoons) discussed in Chapter 5. After forming in the tropics, these powerful storms mature and migrate to higher latitudes, carrying with them water and energy that redistribute across the globe.

Energy Balance at Earth's Surface

Solar energy is the principal heat source at Earth's surface; the surface environment is the final stage in the Sun-to-Earth energy system. The radiation patterns at Earth's surface—inputs of diffuse and direct radiation and outputs of evaporation, convection, and radiated longwave energy—are important in forming the environments where we live.

(*text continued on page 82*)

Incoming solar energy in the form of shortwave radiation interacts with both the atmosphere and Earth's surface (GIA 3.1). The surface reflects or absorbs some of the energy, reradiating the absorbed energy as longwave radiation (GIA 3.2). Averaged over a year, Earth's surface has an energy gain, or surplus, while the atmosphere has an energy deficit, or loss. These two amounts of energy equal each other, maintaining an overall balance in Earth's energy "budget."

Identify: Which component of the atmosphere absorbs the most energy? Which reflects the most?

SHORTWAVE ENERGY BUDGET

Reflected and/or scattered	
By atmosphere and clouds	-28
By surface	-3
Total	**-31**
Absorbed	
By atmosphere and ozone	+24
By surface	+45
Total	**+69**
Total solar energy input	+100 units

3.1 Shortwave Radiation Inputs and Albedo

Clouds, the atmosphere, and Earth's surface reflect 31% of the shortwave radiation inputs back to space. Atmospheric gases and dust and Earth's surface absorb 69% of the shortwave energy. Absorbed energy is later emitted as longwave radiation (shown in GIA 3.2).

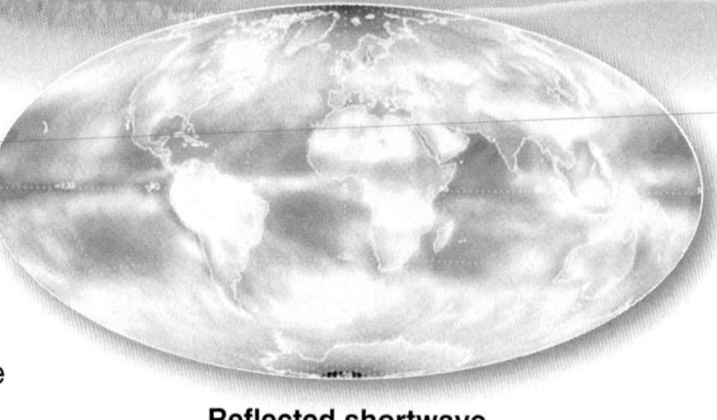

Reflected shortwave radiation, equivalent to Earth's albedo. Note high values (white) over cloudy and snowy regions, and low values (blue) over oceans.

Animation Atmospheric Energy Balance

http://goo.gl/7UYgTM

MasteringGeography™

Visit the Study Area in MasteringGeography™ to explore the Earth–atmosphere energy balance.

Visualize: Study geosciences animations of atmospheric energy balance.

Assess: Demonstrate understanding of the Earth–atmosphere energy balance (if assigned by instructor).

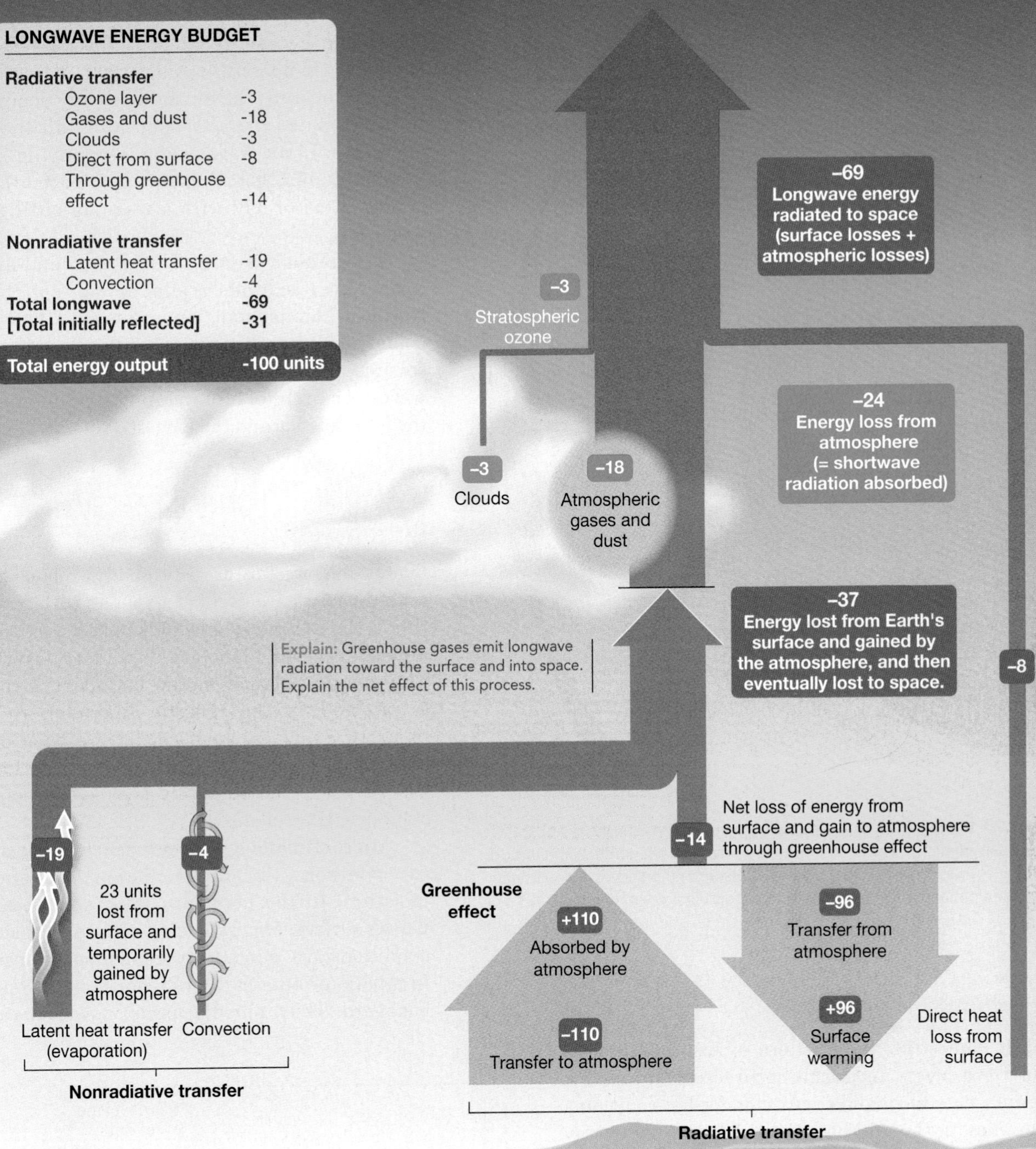

LONGWAVE ENERGY BUDGET

Radiative transfer	
Ozone layer	-3
Gases and dust	-18
Clouds	-3
Direct from surface	-8
Through greenhouse effect	-14
Nonradiative transfer	
Latent heat transfer	-19
Convection	-4
Total longwave	**-69**
[Total initially reflected]	**-31**
Total energy output	**-100 units**

–69 **Longwave energy radiated to space (surface losses + atmospheric losses)**

–3 Stratospheric ozone

–3 Clouds

–18 Atmospheric gases and dust

–24 **Energy loss from atmosphere (= shortwave radiation absorbed)**

–37 **Energy lost from Earth's surface and gained by the atmosphere, and then eventually lost to space.**

–8

Explain: Greenhouse gases emit longwave radiation toward the surface and into space. Explain the net effect of this process.

–19

–4

23 units lost from surface and temporarily gained by atmosphere

Latent heat transfer (evaporation)

Convection

Nonradiative transfer

–14 Net loss of energy from surface and gain to atmosphere through greenhouse effect

Greenhouse effect

+110 Absorbed by atmosphere

–110 Transfer to atmosphere

–96 Transfer from atmosphere

+96 Surface warming

Direct heat loss from surface

Radiative transfer

3.2 Outgoing Longwave Radiation

Over time, Earth emits, on average, 69% of incoming energy to space. When added to the amount of energy reflected (31%), this equals the total energy input from the Sun (100%). Outgoing energy transfers from the surface are both *radiative* (consisting of longwave radiation directly to space) and *nonradiative* (involving convection and the energy released by latent heat transfer).

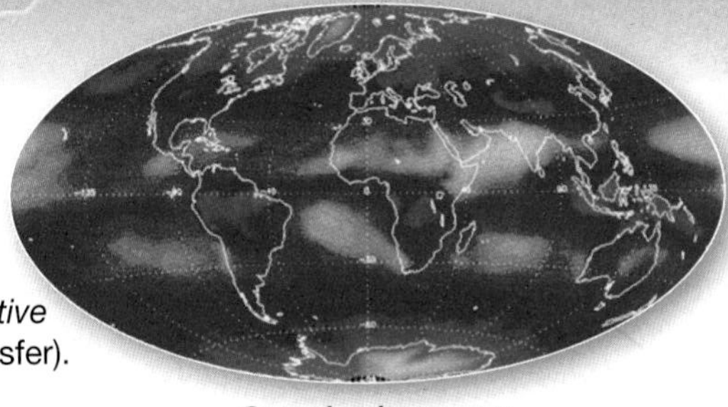

Outgoing longwave radiation emitted from Earth and the atmosphere. Note high values (yellow) over deserts and low values (white and blue) over the polar regions.

GEOquiz

1. Infer: Which is more important in heating Earth's atmosphere: incoming shortwave radiation or outgoing longwave radiation? Explain.

2. Predict: Suppose that latent heat energy is released into the atmosphere as water evaporates from a lake. How is this energy involved in the atmosphere's energy balance and what eventually happens to it?

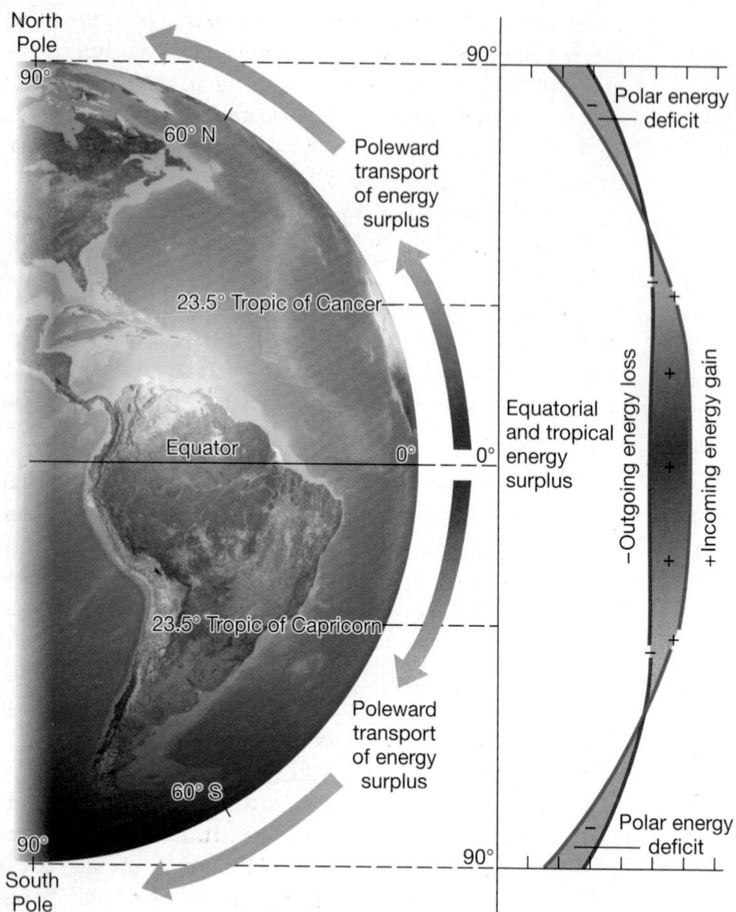

▲**Figure 3.10 Energy budget by latitude.** Earth's energy surpluses and deficits produce the poleward transport of energy and mass in each hemisphere, through atmospheric circulation and ocean currents. Outside of the tropics, atmospheric winds are the dominant means of energy transport toward each pole.

Daily Radiation Patterns

Figure 3.11 shows the daily pattern of absorbed incoming shortwave energy and resulting air temperature. This graph represents idealized conditions for bare soil on a cloudless day in the middle latitudes. Incoming energy arrives during daylight, beginning at sunrise, peaking at noon, and ending at sunset.

The shape and height of this insolation curve vary with season and latitude. The maximum heights for such a curve occur in summer, at the time of the June solstice in the Northern Hemisphere and the December solstice in the Southern Hemisphere. The air-temperature plot also responds to seasons and variations in insolation input. Within a 24-hour day, air temperature generally peaks between 3:00 and 4:00 P.M. and dips to its lowest point right at or slightly after sunrise.

Note that the insolation curve and the air-temperature curve on the graph do not align; there is a *lag* between them. The warmest time of day occurs not at the moment of maximum insolation, but at the moment when a maximum of insolation has been absorbed and emitted to the atmosphere from the ground. As long as the incoming energy exceeds the outgoing energy, air temperature continues to increase, not peaking until the incoming energy begins to diminish as the afternoon Sun's altitude decreases. If you have ever gone camping in the mountains, you no doubt experienced the coldest time of day with a wake-up chill at sunrise.

The annual pattern of insolation and air temperature exhibits a similar lag. For the Northern Hemisphere, January is usually the coldest month, occurring after the December solstice and the shortest days. Similarly, the warmest months of July and August occur after the June solstice and the longest days.

A Simplified Surface Energy Budget

Energy and moisture are continually exchanged with the lower atmosphere at Earth's surface—this is the *boundary layer* (also known as the atmospheric, or planetary, boundary layer). The energy balance in the boundary layer is affected by the specific characteristics of Earth's surface, such as the presence or absence of vegetation and local topography. The height of the boundary layer is not constant over time or space.

Microclimatology is the science of physical conditions, including radiation, heat, and moisture, in the boundary layer at or near Earth's surface. *Microclimates* are local climate conditions over a relatively small area, such as in a park, or on a particular slope, or in your backyard. Thus, our discussion now focuses

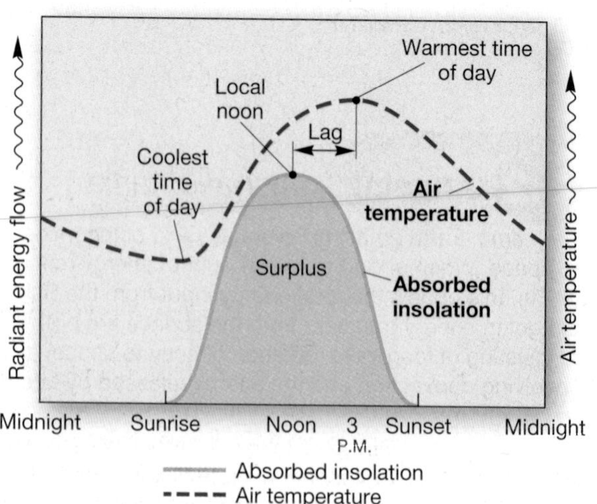

▲**Figure 3.11 Daily radiation and temperature curves.** This sample radiation plot for a typical day shows the changes in insolation (solid line) and air temperature (dashed line). Comparing the curves reveals a lag between local noon (the insolation peak for the day) and the warmest time of day.

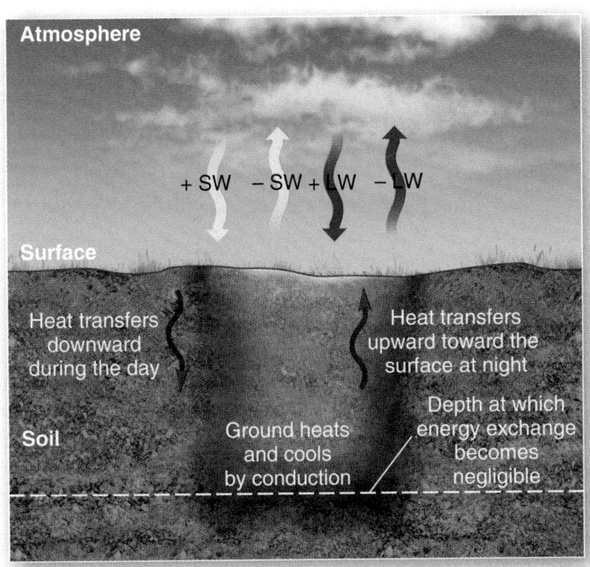

▲**Figure 3.12 Surface energy-budget components over soil column.** Idealized input and output of energy at the surface and within a column of soil (SW = shortwave, LW = longwave).

on small-scale (the lowest few meters of the atmosphere) rather than large-scale (the troposphere) energy-budget components. (See Chapters 7 and 8 for further discussion of climates and climate change.)

The surface in any given location receives and loses shortwave and longwave energy according to the following simple scheme:

$+SW\downarrow$	$-\ SW\uparrow$	$+\ LW\downarrow$	$-\ LW\uparrow$	= NET R
(Insolation)	(Reflection)	(Infrared)	(Infrared)	(Net radiation)

We use SW for shortwave and LW for longwave for simplicity.*

Figure 3.12 shows the components of a surface energy budget over a soil surface. The soil column continues to a depth at which energy exchange with surrounding materials or with the surface becomes negligible, usually less than a meter. Heat is transferred by conduction through the soil, predominantly downward during the day (or in summer) and toward the surface at night (or in winter). Energy moving from the atmosphere into the surface is reported as a positive value (a gain), and energy moving outward from the surface, through sensible and latent heat transfers, is reported as a negative value (a loss) in the surface account.

Net radiation (NET R) is the sum of all radiation gains and losses at any defined location on Earth's surface. NET R varies as the components of this simple equation vary with daylength through the seasons, cloudiness, and latitude. On a daily basis, NET R values are positive during the daylight hours, peaking just after noon with the peak in insolation; at night, values become negative because the shortwave component ceases at sunset and the surface continues to lose longwave radiation to the atmosphere. The surface rarely reaches a zero NET R value—a perfect balance—at any one moment. However, over time, Earth's total surface naturally balances incoming and outgoing energies.

The net radiation available at Earth's surface is the final outcome of the entire energy-balance process discussed in this chapter. As we have learned, in order for the energy budget at Earth's surface to balance over time, areas that have positive net radiation must somehow dissipate, or lose, heat. This happens through nonradiative processes that move energy from the ground into the boundary layer.

- The *latent heat of evaporation* (*LE*) is the energy that is stored in water vapor as water evaporates. Water absorbs large quantities of this *latent heat* as it changes state to water vapor, thereby removing this heat energy from the surface. Conversely, this heat energy releases to the environment when water vapor changes state back to a liquid (discussed in Chapter 5). Latent heat transfer is the dominant expenditure of Earth's entire NET R, especially over water surfaces.
- *Sensible heat* (*H*) is the heat transferred back and forth between air and surface in turbulent eddies through convection and conduction within materials. About one-fifth of Earth's entire NET R is mechanically radiated as sensible heat from the surface, especially over land.
- *Ground heating and cooling* (*G*) is the flow of energy into and out of the ground surface (land or water) by conduction.

Through the processes of latent, sensible, and ground heat transfer, the energy from net radiation is able to do the "work" that ultimately produces the global climate system—work such as raising temperatures in the boundary layer, melting ice, or evaporating water from the oceans. The principles and processes of net radiation at the surface have a bearing on the design and use of solar energy technologies that concentrate shortwave energy for human use. Focus Study 3.1 briefly reviews this direct application of surface energy budgets.

CRITICAL**thinking 3.2**

Applying Energy-Balance Principles to a Solar Cooker

In Focus Study 3.1 on the following pages, you learn about solar cookers (see Figure 3.1.1a). Based on what you have learned about energy balance in this chapter, what principles are most important for making a solar cooker work? Can you diagram the energy flows involved (inputs, outputs, the role of albedo)? How would you position the cooker to maximize its productivity in terms of sunlight? At what time of day is the cooker most effective?

Different symbols are used in the microclimatology literature, such as K for shortwave, L for longwave, and Q for NET R (net radiation).

focusstudy 3.1 Sustainable Resources

Solar Energy Applications

Not only does insolation warm Earth's surface, but also it provides an inexhaustible supply of renewable energy for humanity. The solar energy that Earth receives every hour is enough to meet world power needs for a year. In the United States, the energy produced by fossil fuels in a year arrives in equivalent insolation every 35 minutes.

Sunlight is directly and widely available. In fact, an average commercial building in the United States receives 6 to 10 times more energy from the Sun hitting its exterior than is required to heat the inside. Although collected for centuries using various technologies, sunlight remains underutilized as an energy resource. However, in 2013, solar energy was the fastest-growing renewable energy source in the United States. The recent boom includes rooftop solar installations as well as large solar electric plants.

Collecting Solar Energy

Any surface that receives light from the Sun is a *solar collector*. But the diffuse nature of solar energy received at the surface requires that it be collected, concentrated, transformed, and stored to be most useful.

One of the simplest, most cost-effective solar applications is the solar cooker (Figure 3.1.1). Examples are box cookers that collect insolation through transparent glass or plastic, curved or "parabolic" cookers that reflect and concentrate sunlight, and panel cookers that combine box and parabolic elements. They are simple, yet efficient, reaching temperatures between 107°C and 127°C (225°F and 260°F). With access to solar cookers, people in developing regions of rural Latin America, Africa, and Asia are able to cook meals and sanitize their drinking water without walking long distances to collect wood for cooking fires. See **http://solarcookers.org/** for more information.

Space heating (heating of building interiors) is another simple application of solar energy. It can be accomplished by careful design and placement of windows so that sunlight will shine into a building and be absorbed and converted into sensible heat—an everyday application of the greenhouse effect.

A *passive solar system* captures heat energy and stores it in a "thermal mass," such as a water-filled tank, adobe, tile, or concrete. An *active solar system* heats water or air in a collector and then pumps it through a plumbing system to a tank, where it can provide hot water for direct use or for space heating.

The world's largest operating solar thermal plant is in the Mohave Desert of California about 64 km (40 mi) southwest of Las Vegas, Nevada. The Ivanpah plant, completed in 2014, uses a concentrated solar technology employing heliostat mirrors that track the movement of the Sun from a stationary point. Over 170,000 heliostats reflect sunlight toward receivers in three central towers, each 140 m (459 ft) in height, filled with water; the heat generated creates steam that drives turbines to generate cost-effective electricity (Figure 3.1.2). The facility has a generating capacity of 392 MW (megawatts), enough to power some 140,000 homes.

Solar thermal energy systems can generate heat energy on an appropriate scale for approximately half the present domestic applications in the United States, including space heating and water heating. In marginal climates, solar-assisted water and space heating is feasible as a backup; even in New England and the northern Plains states, solar collection systems prove effective.

Electricity Directly from Sunlight

Photovoltaic (PV) cells were first used to produce electricity in spacecraft in 1958. Today, they are the solar cells in pocket calculators and are also used in rooftop solar panels that provide electricity. When light shines on a semiconductor material in these cells, it stimulates a flow of electrons (an electrical current) in the cell.

(a) These simple cookers collect insolation through transparent glass or plastic and trap longwave radiation in an enclosing box or cooking bag.

(b) A parabolic solar cooker heats water in Periche, Nepal, in 2013.

▲**Figure 3.1.1 Solar cookers.** [(a) Bobbé Christopherson. (b) Peter Barritt/Robert Harding World imagery/PassAge/Corbis.]

▲**Figure 3.1.2 Ivanpah solar thermal plant, California.** [Jim West/Alamy.]

The efficiency of these cells, often assembled in large arrays, has improved greatly, and PV capacity worldwide is more than doubling every 2 years. The residential installation in Figure 3.1.3 features 46 panels, generating 9680 W total, at a 21.5% conversion efficiency. This solar array generates enough surplus energy to run the residential electric meters in reverse and supply electricity to the power grid.

The National Center for Photovoltaics at the National Renewable Energy Laboratory (NREL; **http://www.nrel.gov/ncpv**) coordinates U.S. solar energy research, development, and testing in partnership with private industry. Testing is ongoing at NREL's Outdoor Test Facility in Golden, Colorado, where solar cells have been developed that broke the 40% conversion-efficiency barrier.

In many countries, the cost of rooftop PV electrical installation is now cheaper than power line construction to rural sites. PV roof system installations are increasing and now provide power to hundreds of thousands of homes in Mexico, Indonesia, Philippines, South Africa, India, and Norway. (See the Photovoltaic Home Page at **http://www.eere.energy.gov/solar/sunshot/pv.html**.)

Obvious drawbacks of both solar heating and solar electric systems are periods of cloudiness and night, which inhibit operations. Research is under way to enhance energy storage and to improve battery technology.

The Promise of Solar Energy

Solar energy is a wise choice for the future. It is economically preferable to further development of our decreasing fossil-fuel reserves, further increases in oil imports and tanker and offshore oil-drilling spills, investment in foreign military incursions, or development of nuclear power, especially in a world with security issues. Much of the technology is ready for installation and is cost-effective when all the direct and indirect costs of other energy resources are considered. More information about solar energy technologies (solar-thermal, solar-electric PV cells, solar box cookers, and the like) is available on the *MasteringGeography* website for this chapter.

1. Explain the difference between active and passive solar systems.
2. What kinds of solar technology are available and in use in your area? What are the advantages of these solar applications?

▲**Figure 3.1.3 Solar photovoltaic energy production.** A residence with a 9680-W rooftop solar photovoltaic array that feeds excess electricity to the grid for credits that offset 100% of the home's electric bill as well as producing surplus electricity for charging an electric vehicle. [Bobbé Christopherson.]

Temperature Concepts and Measurement

Earlier, we discussed types of heat and mechanisms of heat transfer, such as conduction, convection, and radiation. Unlike heat, temperature is not a form of energy; however, temperature is related to the amount of energy in a substance. **Temperature** is a measure of the *average* kinetic energy of individual molecules in matter. Thus, temperature is a measure of heat.

Remember that heat always flows from matter at a higher temperature to matter at a lower temperature, and heat transfer usually results in a change in temperature. For example, when you jump into a cool lake, kinetic energy leaves your body and flows to the water, causing a transfer of heat and a lowering of the temperature of your skin. Heat transfer can also occur without a change in temperature, when a substance changes state (as in latent heat transfer, discussed further in Chapter 5).

Temperature Scales

The temperature at which atomic and molecular motion in matter completely stops is *absolute zero*, or *0 absolute temperature*. This value on three commonly encountered temperature-measuring scales is −273° Celsius (C), −459.67 Fahrenheit (F), and 0 Kelvin (K; see **Figure 3.13**). (Formulas for converting among Celsius, SI [Système International], and English units are in Appendix C.)

The Fahrenheit temperature scale, named for German physicist Daniel G. Fahrenheit (1686–1736), places the melting point of ice at 32°F, separated by 180 subdivisions from the boiling point of water at 212°F. Note that ice has only one melting point, but water has many freezing points, ranging from 32°F down to −40°F, depending on its purity, its volume, and certain conditions in the atmosphere.

The Celsius scale (formerly centigrade), named after Swedish astronomer Anders Celsius (1701–1744), places the melting point of ice at 0°C and the boiling temperature of water at sea level at 100°C. The scale divides into 100 degrees using a decimal system.

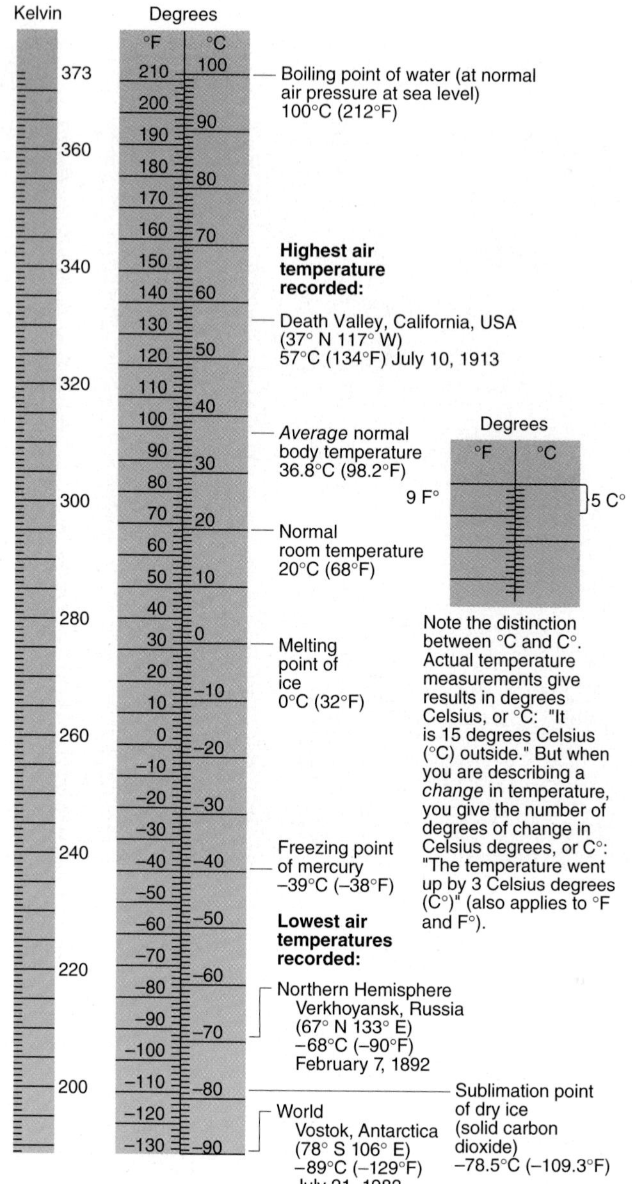

▲Figure 3.13 Temperature scales and temperature records. Scales for expressing temperature in Kelvin (K) and degrees Celsius (°C) and Fahrenheit (°F), including significant temperatures and temperature records. Note the distinction between temperature (indicated by the color gradation on the scale) and units of temperature expression as well as the placement of the degree symbol.

GEOreport 3.2 The hottest temperature on Earth

In 1922, a record-breaking temperature was reported on a hot summer day at Al 'Azīzīya, Libya—an almost unimaginable 58°C (136°F). This record for Earth's hottest temperature was in place for 90 years. Then, in 2012, an international panel of scientists assembled by the World Meteorological Organization (WMO) concluded that the temperature was invalid. After an in-depth investigation, the panel identified several reasons for uncertainty regarding the 1922 measurement, including instrument problems and poor matching of the temperature to nearby locations. Their final decision rejected this temperature extreme, reinstating the 57°C (134°F) temperature recorded in Death Valley, California, in 1913 as the record for hottest temperature ever measured on Earth. The station where this temperature was recorded is one of the lowest on Earth, at −54.3 m, or −178 ft (the minus indicates meters or feet below sea level). One hundred years later on June 29, 2013, the official National Park Service thermometer in Death Valley reached 53.9°C (129°F)—a U.S. record for June, although 2.78 C° (5 F°) lower than 1913. What do you think surface energy budgets were like on that day?

The Kelvin scale, first proposed in 1848 by British physicist Lord Kelvin (born William Thomson, 1824–1907), starts at absolute zero. The Kelvin scale's melting point for ice is 273 K, and its boiling point of water is 373 K, 100 units higher. Therefore, the size of one Kelvin unit is the same size as one Celsius degree. Scientists often use this scale because its temperature readings are proportional to the actual kinetic energy in a material.

Most countries use the Celsius scale to express temperature—the United States is an exception. However, continuing pressure from the international scientific community and other organizations makes adoption of Celsius and SI units inevitable in the United States. This textbook presents Celsius (with Fahrenheit equivalents in parentheses) throughout to help bridge this transition.

Measuring Temperature

A familiar instrument for measuring temperature is a thermometer, a sealed glass tube containing a fluid that expands and contracts according to whether heat is added or removed—when the fluid is heated, it expands; upon cooling, it contracts. Scientists use both *mercury thermometers* and *alcohol thermometers* to measure outdoor temperatures—however, mercury thermometers have the limitation that mercury freezes at –39°C (–38.2°F), making them ineffective for assessing Earth's colder climates. The principle of these thermometers is simple: A thermometer stores fluid in a small reservoir at one end and is marked with calibrations to measure the expansion or contraction of the fluid, which reflects the temperature of the thermometer's environment.

Devices for taking standardized official temperature readings are placed outdoors in small shelters that are white (for high albedo) and louvered (for ventilation) to avoid overheating of the instruments. They are placed at least 1.2–1.8 m (4–6 ft) above the ground surface, usually on turf, and in the shade to prevent the effect of direct insolation.

Temperature readings occur daily, sometimes hourly, at more than 16,000 weather stations worldwide. Some stations also report the duration of a temperature, the rate of temperature rise or fall, and the temperature variation over time throughout the day and night. In 1992, the World Meteorological Organization and other international climate organizations established the Global Climate Observing System to coordinate the reading and recording of temperature and other climate factors among countries worldwide. (For an overview of temperature- and climate-observing stations, go to http://www.wmo.int/pages/prog/gcos/index.php?name=ObservingSystemsandData.)

Three expressions of temperature are common: The *daily mean temperature* is an average of hourly readings taken over a 24-hour day, but may also be the average of the daily minimum–maximum readings. The *monthly mean temperature* is the total of daily mean temperatures for the month divided by the number of days in the month. An *annual temperature range* expresses the difference between the lowest and highest monthly mean temperatures for a given year.

Principal Temperature Controls

Insolation is the single most important influence on temperature variations. However, several other physical controls interact with it to produce Earth's temperature patterns. These include latitude, altitude and elevation, cloud cover, and land–water heating differences.

Latitude

We learned in Chapter 2 that the subsolar point is the latitude where the Sun is directly overhead at noon, and that this point migrates between the Tropic of Cancer at 23.5° N latitude and the Tropic of Capricorn at 23.5° S latitude. Between the tropics, insolation is more intense than at higher latitudes where the Sun is never directly overhead (at a 90° angle) during the year. The intensity of incoming solar radiation decreases away from the equator and toward the poles. Daylength also varies with latitude during the year, influencing the duration of insolation exposure. Variations in these two factors—Sun angle and daylength—throughout the year drive the seasonal effect of latitude on temperature.

Temperature patterns throughout the year for the five cities in **Figure 3.14** demonstrate the effects of latitudinal position. From equator to poles, Earth ranges from continually warm, to seasonally variable, to continually cold.

GEOreport 3.3 Iran desert has highest land-surface temperature

Satellites do not measure air temperature in the same way as thermometers; instead, they measure *land-surface temperature* (LST), or land "skin" temperature, which is the heating of the land surface and is often much hotter than air temperature. You have felt this difference when walking barefoot across hot sand or pavement—the surface under your feet is much hotter than the air around your body above. Data from NASA's MODIS instrument aboard several satellites show that from 2003 to 2009 the Lut Desert of Iran had the highest consistent LST. The highest single LST recorded was 70.7°C (159.3°F) in 2005, hotter than the world record air temperature at Death Valley, California, measured in 1913. Read more at http://earthobservatory.nasa.gov/Features/HottestSpot/page2.php.

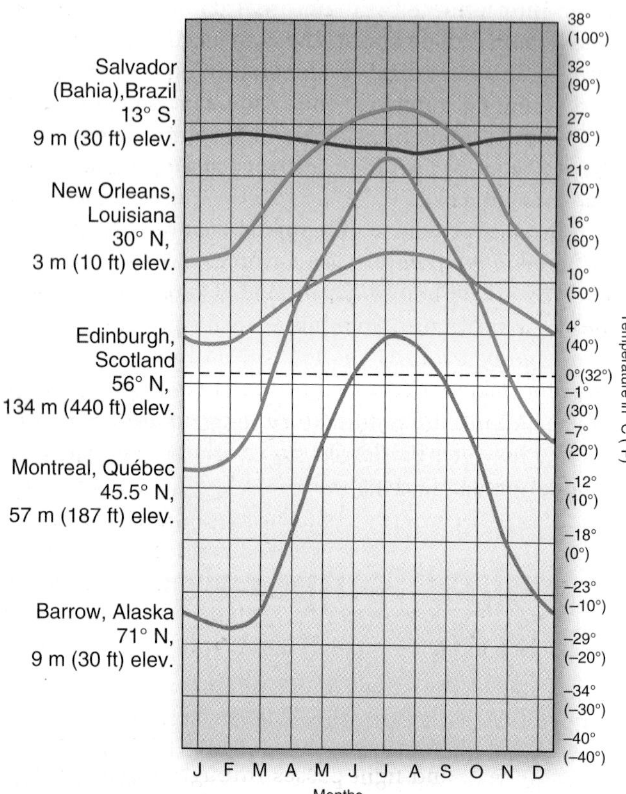

▲**Figure 3.14 Latitudinal effects on temperatures.** A comparison of five cities from near the equator to north of the Arctic Circle demonstrates changing seasonality and increasing differences between average minimum and maximum temperatures with increasing latitude. These cities are located on the map in Figure 1.11.

Altitude and Elevation

From Chapter 2, remember that within the troposphere, temperatures decrease with increasing altitude above Earth's surface. (Recall from Figure 2.14 that the *normal lapse rate* of temperature change with altitude is 6.4 C°/1000 m, or 3.5 F°/1000 ft.) The density of the atmosphere also diminishes with increasing altitude. In fact, the density of the atmosphere at an elevation of 5500 m (18,000 ft) is about half that at sea level. As the atmosphere thins, it contains less sensible heat. Thus, worldwide, mountainous areas experience lower temperatures than do regions nearer sea level, even at similar latitudes.

Two terms, altitude and elevation, are commonly used to refer to heights on or above Earth's surface. *Altitude* refers to airborne objects or heights *above* Earth's surface. *Elevation* usually refers to the height of a point *on* Earth's surface above some plane of reference, such as elevation above sea level. Therefore, the height of a flying jet is expressed as altitude, whereas the height of a mountain ski resort is expressed as elevation.

In the thinner atmosphere at high elevations in mountainous regions or on high plateaus, surfaces lose energy rapidly to the atmosphere. The result is that average air temperatures are lower, nighttime cooling is greater, and the temperature range between day and night is greater than at low elevations.

The *snowline* seen on mountain slopes is the lower limit of permanent snow and indicates where winter snowfall exceeds the amount of snow lost through summer melting and evaporation. The snowline's location is a function both of latitude and of elevation, and to a lesser extent, it is related to local microclimatic conditions. Even at low latitudes, permanent ice fields and glaciers exist on mountain summits, such as in the Andes and East Africa. In equatorial mountains, the snowline occurs at approximately 5000 m (16,400 ft). With increasing latitude, snowlines gradually lower in elevation from 2700 m (8850 ft) in the midlatitudes to lower than 900 m (2950 ft) in southern Greenland.

In the Andes Mountains of South America, the city of La Paz is 4103 m (13,461 ft) above sea level, at a latitude of about 16° S, situated on a high plateau with a cool, dry climate. La Paz has moderate annual temperatures, averaging about 11°C (51.8°F). Despite its high elevation, people living around La Paz are able to grow wheat, barley, and potatoes—crops characteristic of the midlatitudes—in the fertile highland soils (**Figure 3.15**). Compared to the harsh climates at similar elevations in the United States, such as the 4301-m (14,111-ft) summit of Pikes Peak at 38° N in Colorado or the 4392-m (14,410-ft) top of Mount Rainier at 46° N in Washington, La Paz has a mild and hospitable climate resulting from its low-latitude location.

Cloud Cover

At any given moment, approximately 50% of Earth is covered by clouds. We learned that clouds affect the Earth–atmosphere energy balance by reflecting and absorbing radiation and that their effects vary with cloud type, height, and density.

The presence of cloud cover at night has a moderating effect on temperature; you may have experienced the relatively colder temperatures outside on a clear night

▼**Figure 3.15 Effects of latitude and elevation.** In the low-latitude, high-elevation villages of Bolivia, temperatures are moderate throughout the year, averaging about 11°C (52°F). People in these villages grow potatoes and wheat, in view of some of the highest peaks in the Andes Mountains. [Seux Paule/Age Fotostock America, Inc.]

versus a cloudy night, especially before dawn, the coldest time of the day. At night, clouds act as an insulating layer that reradiates longwave energy back to Earth, preventing rapid energy loss to space. Thus, in general, the presence of clouds raises minimum nighttime temperatures. During the day, clouds reflect insolation, lowering daily maximum temperatures; this is the familiar shading effect you feel when clouds move in on a hot summer day. Clouds also reduce seasonal temperature differences as a result of these moderating effects. Clouds are the most variable factor influencing Earth's radiation budget, and studies are ongoing as to their effects on Earth's temperatures.

Land–Water Heating Differences

An important control over temperature is the difference in the ways land and water surfaces respond to insolation. Land and water absorb and store energy differently, with the result that water bodies tend to have more-moderate temperature patterns, whereas continental interiors have more temperature extremes.

The physical differences between land (rock and soil) and water (oceans, seas, and lakes) are the reasons for **land–water heating differences**, the most basic of which is that land heats and cools faster than water. Figure 3.16 summarizes these differences, which relate to the principles and processes of evaporation, transparency, specific heat, and movement. We include ocean currents and sea-surface temperatures in this section because of their effects on temperatures in coastal locations.

Evaporation The process of *evaporation* dissipates significant amounts of the energy arriving at the ocean's surface, much more than over land surfaces where less water is available. An estimated 84% of all evaporation on Earth is from the oceans. When water evaporates, it changes from liquid to vapor, absorbing heat energy in the process and storing it as latent heat.

You experience the cooling effect of evaporative heat loss by wetting the back of your hand and then blowing on the moist skin. Sensible heat energy is drawn from your skin to supply some of the energy for evaporation, and you feel the cooling as a result. As surface water evaporates, it absorbs energy from the immediate environment, resulting in a lowering of temperatures. (Remember that the water and vapor remain the same temperature throughout the process; the vapor stores the absorbed energy as latent heat.) Land temperatures are affected less by evaporative cooling than are temperatures over water.

Transparency Soil and water differ in their transmission of light: Solid ground is opaque; water is transparent. Light striking a soil surface does not pass through, but is absorbed, heating the ground surface. That energy is accumulated during times of sunlight exposure and is rapidly lost at night or when shaded. Maximum and minimum daily temperatures for soil surfaces generally occur at the ground surface level. Below the surface, even at shallow depths, temperatures remain about the same throughout the day.

In contrast, when light reaches a body of water, it penetrates the surface because of water's **transparency**—water is clear, and light passes through it to an average depth of 60 m (200 ft) in the ocean. This illuminated zone occurs in some ocean waters to depths of 300 m (1000 ft). The transparency of water results in the distribution of available heat energy over a much greater depth and volume, forming a larger reservoir of energy storage than that which occurs on land.

Specific Heat The energy needed to increase the temperature of water is greater than for an equal volume of land. Overall, water can hold more heat than can soil or rock. The heat capacity of a substance is **specific heat**. On average, the specific heat of water is about four times that of soil. Therefore, a given volume of water represents a more substantial energy reservoir than does the same volume of soil or rock and consequently heats and cools more slowly. For this reason, day-to-day temperatures near large water bodies tend to be moderated rather than having large extremes.

Movement In contrast to the solid, rigid characteristics of land, water is fluid and capable of movement. The movement

CONTINENTAL
Temperature conditions more extreme—land warms and cools rapidly
Insolation
Less evaporation (lower latent heat)
Surface is **opaque**
Land has a **lower specific heat**
Land has **no mixing** between layers
Land
MARINE
Temperature conditions more moderate—water warms and cools slowly
Insolation
More evaporaton (higher latent heat)
Surface is **transparent**
Water has a **higher specific heat**
Water has **mobility** and mixes in vast ocean currents
Ocean

◀Figure 3.16 Land–water heating differences. The differential heating of land and water produces contrasting marine (more moderate) and continental (more extreme) temperature regimes.

of currents results in a mixing of cooler and warmer waters, and that mixing spreads the available energy over an even greater volume than if the water was still. Surface water and deeper waters mix, redistributing energy in a vertical direction as well. Both ocean and land surfaces radiate longwave radiation at night, but land loses its energy more rapidly than does the moving reservoir of oceanic energy, with its more extensive distribution of heat.

Ocean Currents and Sea-Surface Temperatures

Ocean currents affect land temperatures in different ways, depending on whether the currents are warm or cold. Along midlatitude and subtropical west coasts of continents, cool ocean currents flowing toward the equator moderate air temperatures on land. An example is the effect of the cold Humboldt Current flowing offshore from Lima, Peru, which has a cooler climate than might be expected at that latitude.

The warm current known as the **Gulf Stream** moves northward off the east coast of North America, carrying warm water far into the North Atlantic (**Figure 3.17**). As a result, the southern third of Iceland experiences much milder temperatures than would be expected for a latitude of 65° N, just south of the Arctic Circle (66.5° N). In Reykjavík, on the southwestern coast of Iceland, monthly temperatures average above freezing during all months of the year. The Gulf Stream also moderates temperatures in coastal Scandinavia and northwestern Europe. In the western Pacific Ocean, the warm Kuroshio, or Japan Current, functions much the same as the Gulf Stream, having a warming effect on temperatures in Japan, in the Aleutians, and along the northwestern margin of North America.

Ocean temperatures are typically measured at the surface and recorded as the *sea-surface temperature*, or SST. The maps of global average SSTs measured from satellites in **Figure 3.18** reveal that the region with the highest average ocean temperatures is the *Western Pacific Warm Pool* in the Pacific Ocean, where temperatures are often above 30°C (86°F). Although the difference in SSTs between the equator and the poles is apparent on both maps, note the seasonal changes in ocean temperatures, such as the northward shifting of the Western Pacific Warm Pool in July. The warm Gulf Stream is apparent off the coast of Florida in both images; cooler currents occur off the west coasts of North and South America, Europe, and Africa.

Following the same recent trends as global air temperatures, average annual SSTs increased steadily from 1982 through 2012 to record-high levels. Increasing warmth is measured at depths to 1000 m (3200 ft), and scientists have reported slight increases even in the temperature of deep bottom water. These data suggest that the ocean's ability to absorb excess heat energy from the atmosphere may be nearing its capacity.

Examples of Marine Effects and Continental Effects

The land–water heating differences that affect temperature regimes worldwide can be summarized in terms of continental and marine effects. The **marine effect**, or *maritime effect,* refers to the moderating influences of the ocean and usually occurs in locations along coastlines or on islands. The **continental effect**, or condition of *continentality,* refers to the greater range between maximum and minimum temperatures on both a daily and a yearly basis that occurs in areas that are inland from the ocean or distant from other large water bodies.

The monthly temperatures of San Francisco, California, and Wichita, Kansas, both at approximately 37° N latitude, illustrate these effects (**Figure 3.19**). In San Francisco, only a few days a year have summer maximums that exceed 32.2°C (90°F). Winter minimums rarely drop below freezing. In contrast, Wichita, Kansas, is susceptible to freezing temperatures from late October to mid-April—

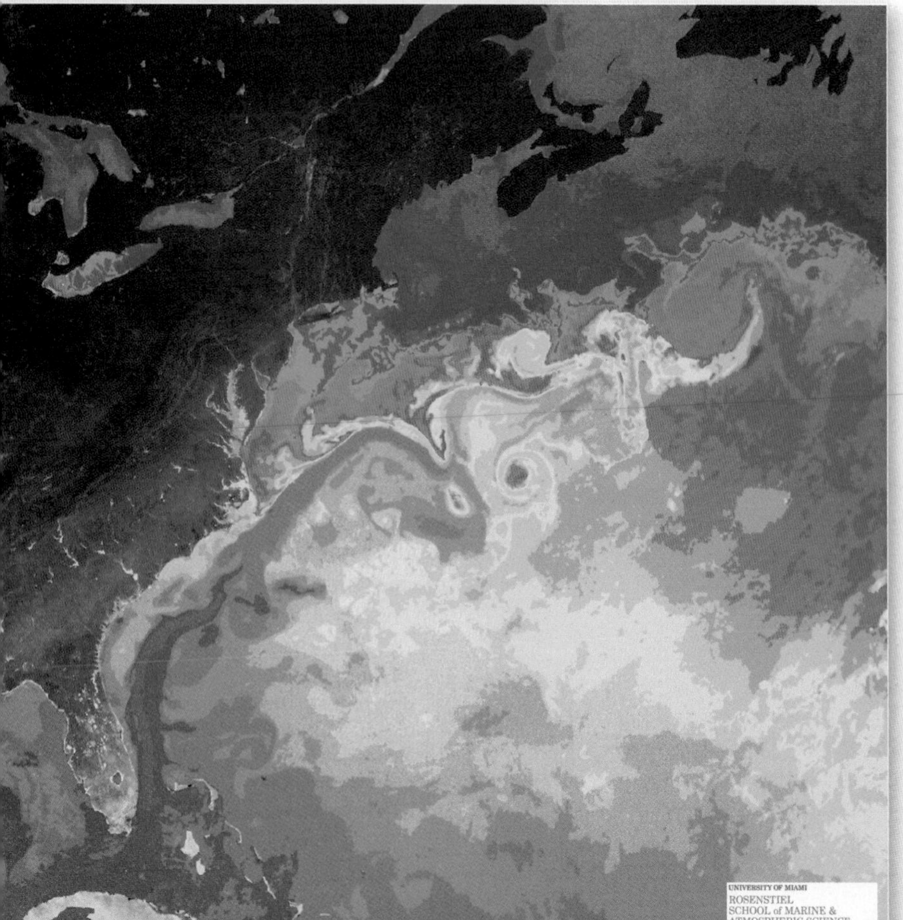

◀Figure 3.17 The Gulf Stream. Satellite instruments sensitive to thermal infrared wavelengths imaged the Gulf Stream. Temperature differences are noted by computer-enhanced false colors: reds and oranges = 25°C to 29°C (76°F to 84°F), yellows and greens = 17°C to 24°C (63°F to 75°F); blues = 10°C to 16°C (50°F to 61°F); purples = 2°C to 9°C (36°F to 48°F). [Imagery by RSMAS, University of Miami.]

Animation The Gulf Stream

http://goo.gl/i2IGHN

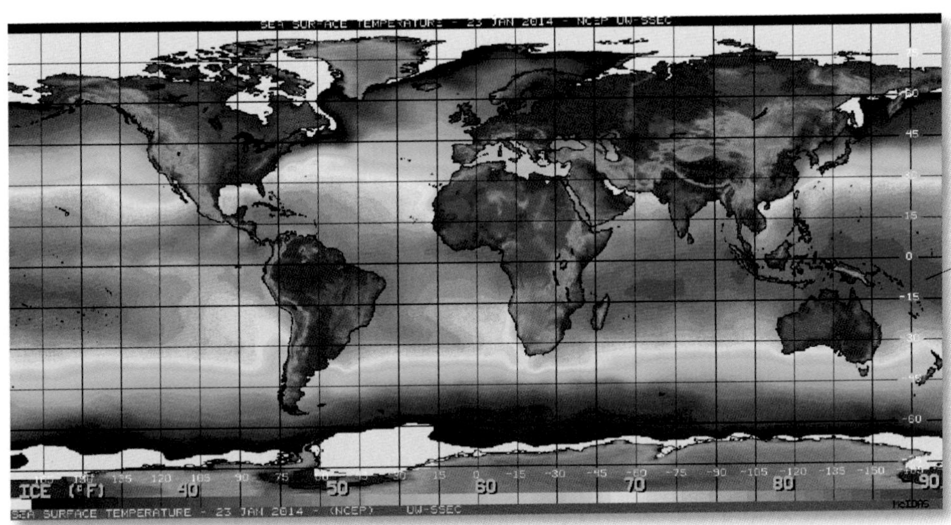

(a) January 23, 2014

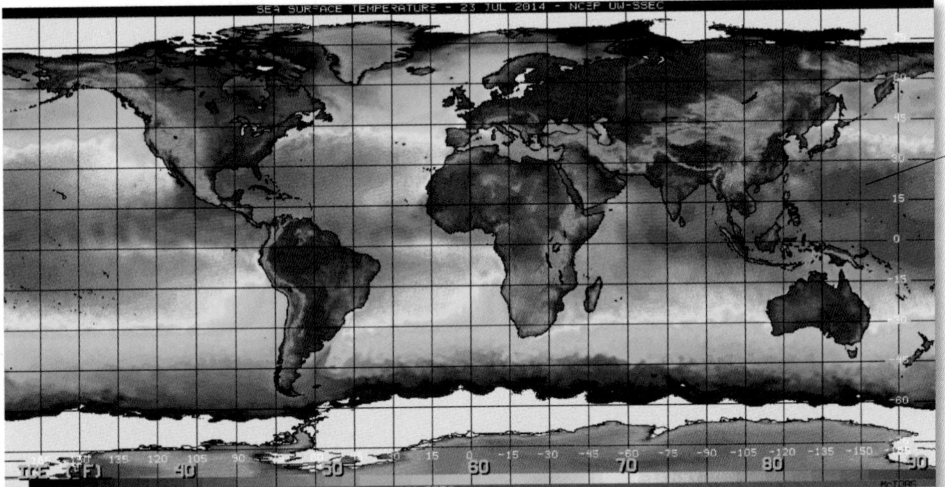

(b) July 23, 2014

◀**Figure 3.18 Average monthly sea-surface temperatures for January and July.** [Satellite data courtesy of Space Science and Engineering Center, University of Wisconsin, Madison.]

the record low temperature is −30°C (−22°F). Wichita's temperature reaches 32.2°C (90°F) or higher more than 65 days each year, with 46°C (114°F) as a record high. During the summer of 2012, temperatures exceeded 38°C (100°F) for a record 53 nonconsecutive days.

In Eurasia, similar trends exist for cities (at similar latitudes and elevations) in marine versus continental locations (**Figure 3.20**). The coastal location of Trondheim, Norway, moderates its annual temperature regime. This city has a 17 C° (30.6 F°) annual temperature range. The lowest minimum and highest maximum temperatures ever recorded in Trondheim are −30°C and +35°C (−22°F and +95°F). In contrast, Verkhoyansk, Russia, with a population of 1400, has a continental location and a 63 C° (113 F°) range in average annual temperatures. Temperature extremes reflect continental effects: Verkhoyansk recorded a record minimum temperature of −68°C (−90°F) in January and a record maximum temperature of +37°C (+98°F) in July—an incredible 105 C° (189 F°) minimum–maximum range for the record temperature extremes!

CRITICAL**thinking** 3.3

Compare and Explain Coastal and Inland Temperatures

Using the map, graphs, and other data in Figure 3.19, explain the effects of San Francisco's marine location on its average monthly temperatures. Why are summer temperatures higher in Wichita relative to those in San Francisco? Why does San Francisco's average monthly temperature peak occur later in the summer than that of Wichita? Is your location subject to marine or continental effects on temperature? (Find the explanation at the end of the Key Learning Concepts Review.)

Earth's Temperature Patterns

Figures 3.21 through 3.25 are a series of maps to help us visualize Earth's temperature patterns: global mean temperatures for January and July, global annual temperature ranges (differences between the averages of the coolest and warmest months), and polar region mean

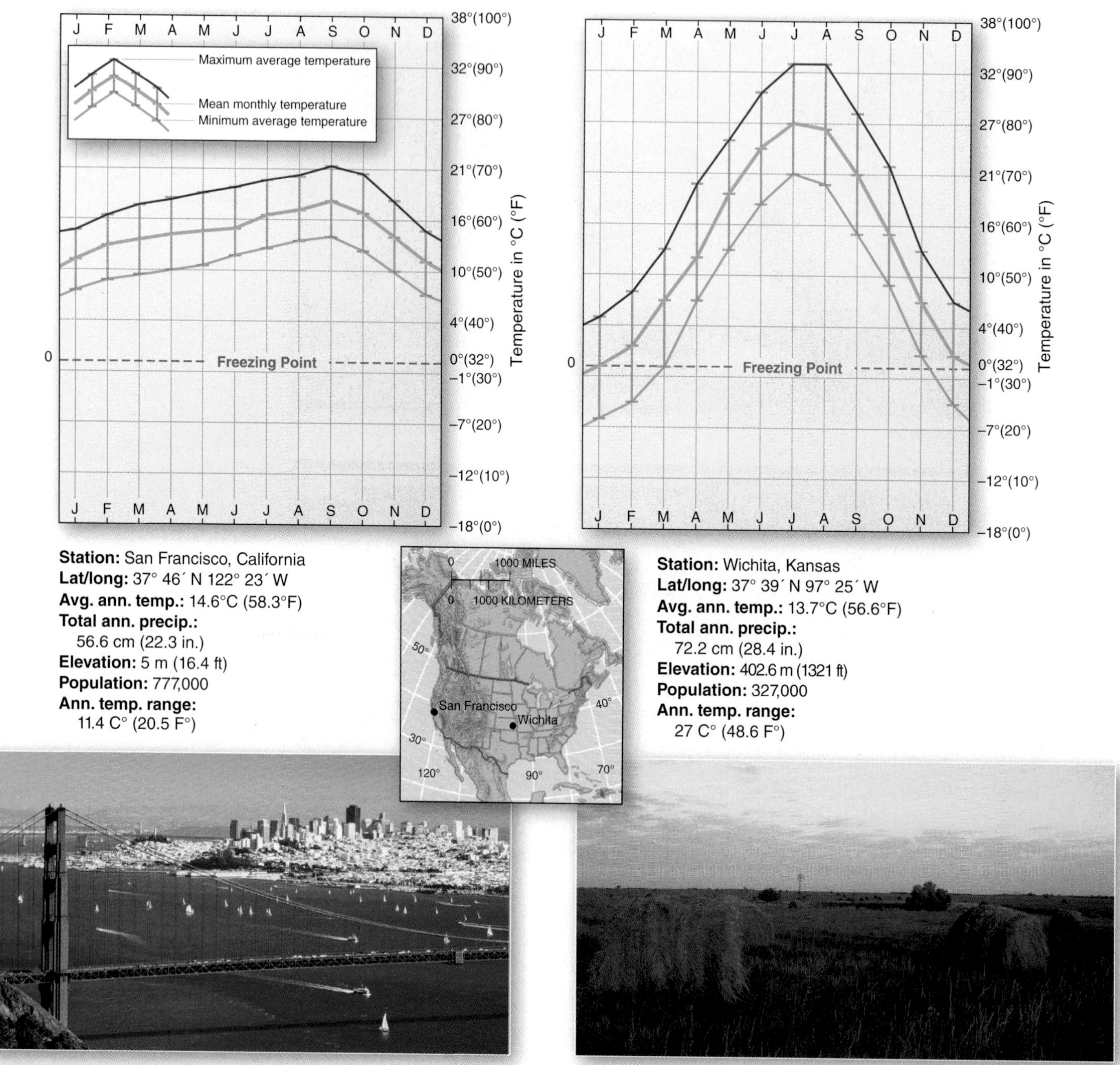

▲**Figure 3.19 Marine and continental cities—United States.** Compare temperatures in coastal San Francisco, California, with those of continental Wichita, Kansas. [kropic1/Shutterstock; RGB Ventures/SuperStock/Alamy.]

temperatures for January and July. Maps are for January and July instead of the solstice months of December and June because of the lag that occurs between insolation received and maximum or minimum temperatures experienced.

The lines on temperature maps are known as *isotherms*. An **isotherm** is an isoline—a line along which there is a constant value—that connects points of equal temperature to portray the temperature pattern, just as a contour line on a topographic map illustrates points of equal elevation. Isotherms are useful for the spatial analysis of temperatures.

Global January and July Temperature Comparison

In January, high Sun altitudes and longer days in the Southern Hemisphere cause summer weather conditions; lower Sun altitudes and shorter days in the Northern Hemisphere are associated with winter. Isotherms on the January average-temperature map mark the general decrease in insolation and net radiation with distance from the equator (**Figure 3.21**). Isotherms generally trend east–west, are parallel to the equator, and are interrupted by the presence of landmasses. This interruption is

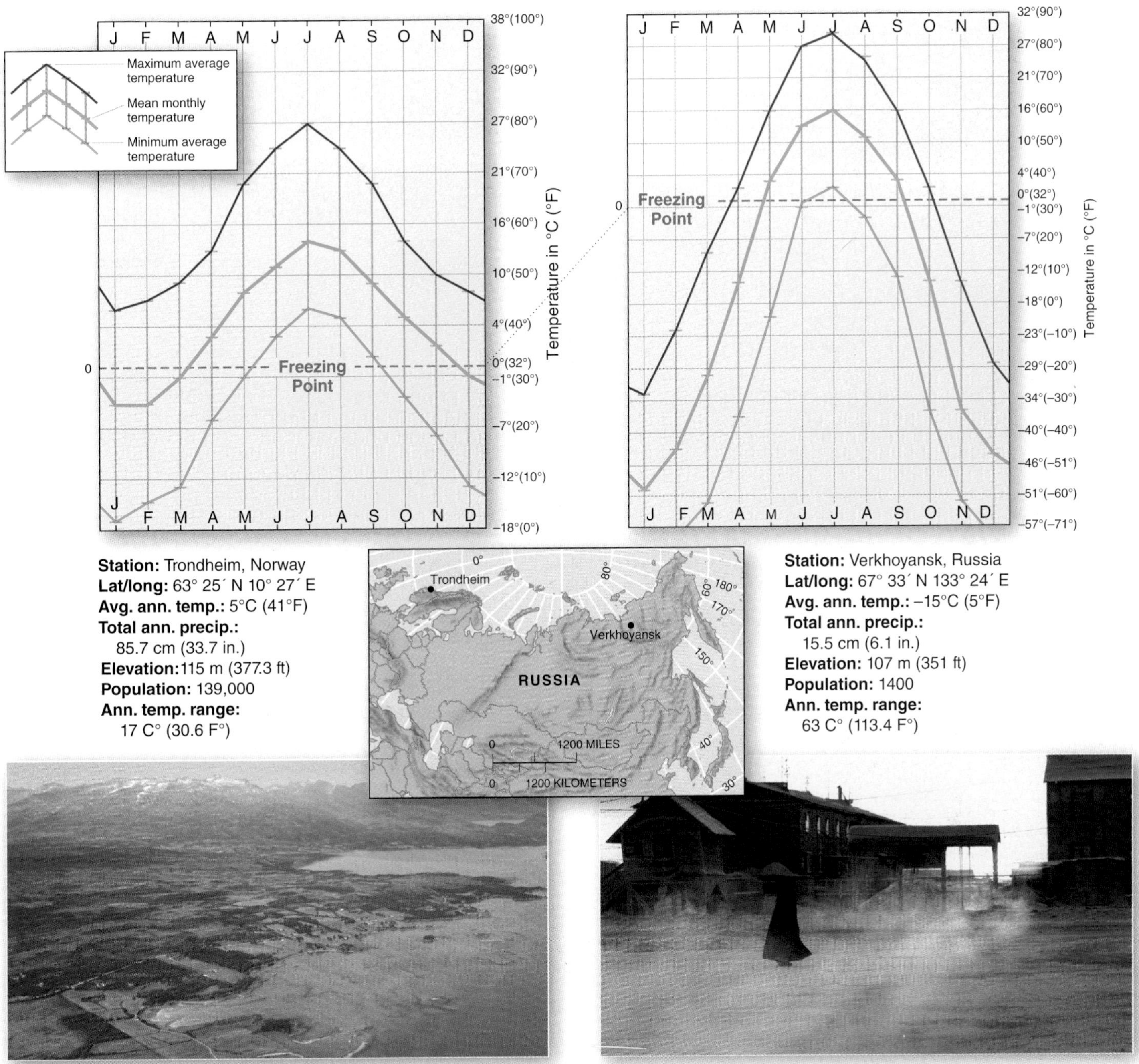

▲**Figure 3.20 Marine and continental cities—Eurasia.** Compare temperatures in coastal Trondheim, Norway, with those of continental Verkhoyansk, Russia. Note that the freezing levels on the two graphs are positioned differently to accommodate the contrasting data. [Bobbé Christopherson; Martin Hartley/The image/Getty Images.]

caused by the differential heating of land and water discussed earlier.

The **thermal equator** is an isotherm connecting all points of highest mean temperature, roughly 27°C (80°F); it trends southward into the interior of South America and Africa, indicating higher temperatures over the interiors of landmasses. In the Northern Hemisphere, isotherms shift toward the equator as cold air chills the continental interiors. More moderate temperatures occur over oceans, with warmer conditions extending farther north than over land at comparable latitudes.

To see the temperature differences over land and water, follow along 50° N latitude (the 50th parallel) in Figure 3.21 and compare isotherms: 3°C to 6°C in the North Pacific and 3°C to 9°C in the North Atlantic, as contrasted with –18°C in the interior of North America and –24°C to –30°C in central Asia. Also, note the orientation of isotherms over areas with mountain ranges and how they illustrate the cooling effects of elevation—check the South American Andes as an example.

For a continental region other than Antarctica, Russia—and specifically, northeastern Siberia—is the

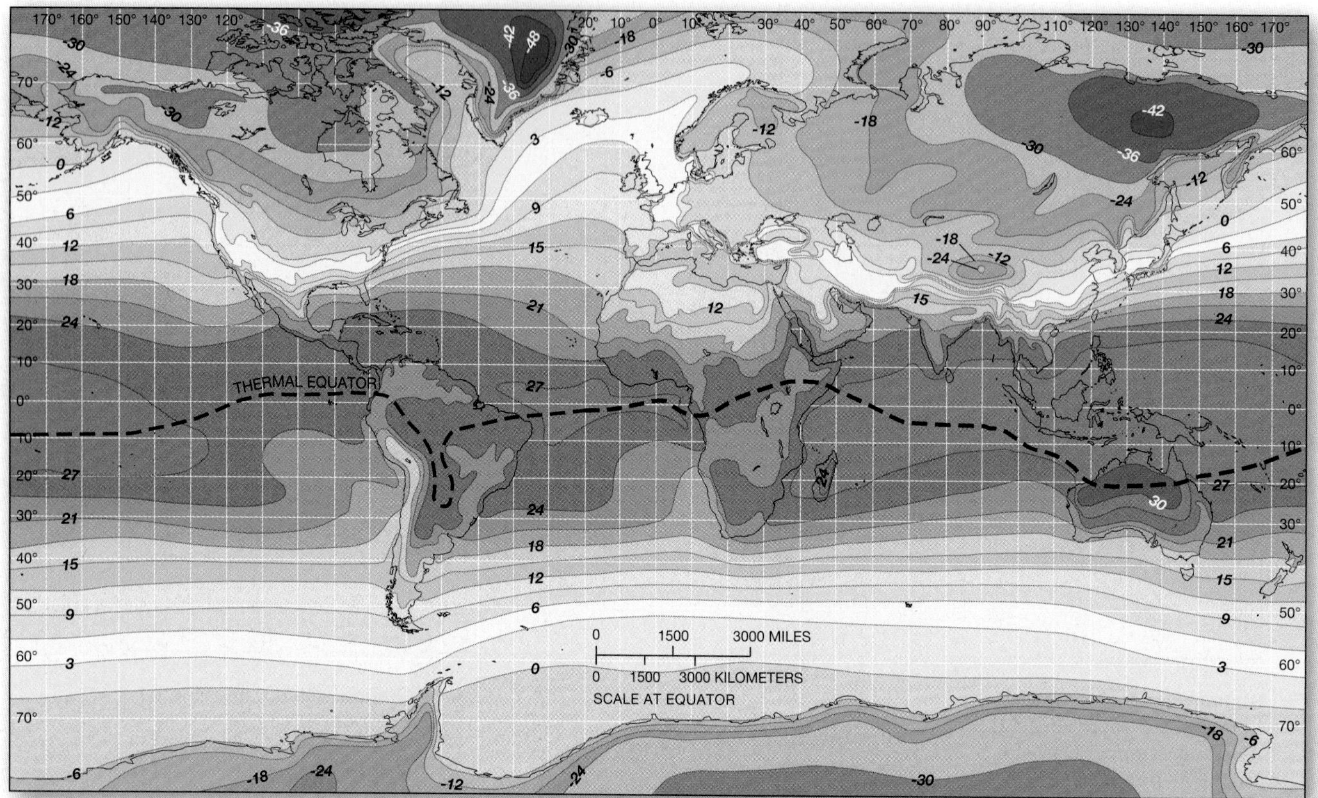

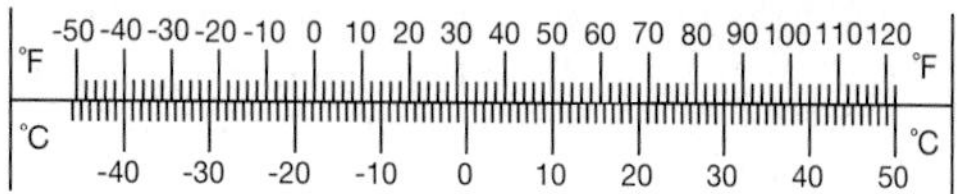

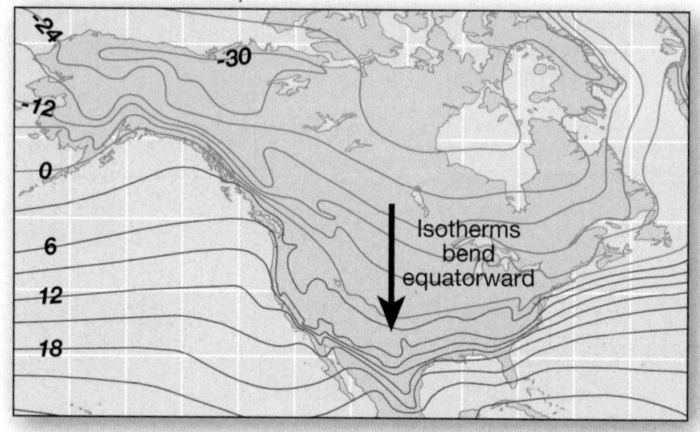

▲Figure 3.21 Global average temperatures for January. Temperatures are in Celsius (convertible to Fahrenheit by means of the scale) as taken from separate air-temperature databases for ocean and land. Note the inset map of North America and the equatorward-trending isotherms in the interior. [Adapted by author and redrawn from National Climatic Data Center, *Monthly Climatic Data for the World*, 47 (January 1994), and WMO and NOAA.]

coldest area (look back to Figure 3.20b). The intense cold results from winter conditions of consistently clear, dry, calm air; small insolation input; and an inland location far from moderating maritime effects. Prevailing global winds prevent moderating effects from the Pacific Ocean to the east.

In July, the longer days of summer and higher Sun altitude are in the Northern Hemisphere (**Figure 3.22**). Winter dominates the Southern Hemisphere, although it is milder than winters north of the equator because continental landmasses, with their greater temperature ranges, are smaller. The thermal equator shifts northward with the high summer Sun and reaches the Persian Gulf–Pakistan–Iran area. The Persian Gulf is the site of the highest recorded sea-surface temperature—an astounding 36°C (96°F).

During July in the Northern Hemisphere, isotherms shift toward the poles over land as higher temperatures dominate continental interiors. The hottest places on Earth occur in Northern Hemisphere deserts during July, caused by clear skies, strong surface heating, virtually no surface water, and limited vegetation. Prime examples are portions of the Sonoran Desert of North America, the Sahara of Africa, and the Lut Desert in Iran.

Annual Temperature Range

Temperature patterns are also indicated by the annual temperature range for a location—that is, the difference between the highest and lowest average annual temperatures for that location. The largest average annual temperature ranges occur at subpolar locations within the

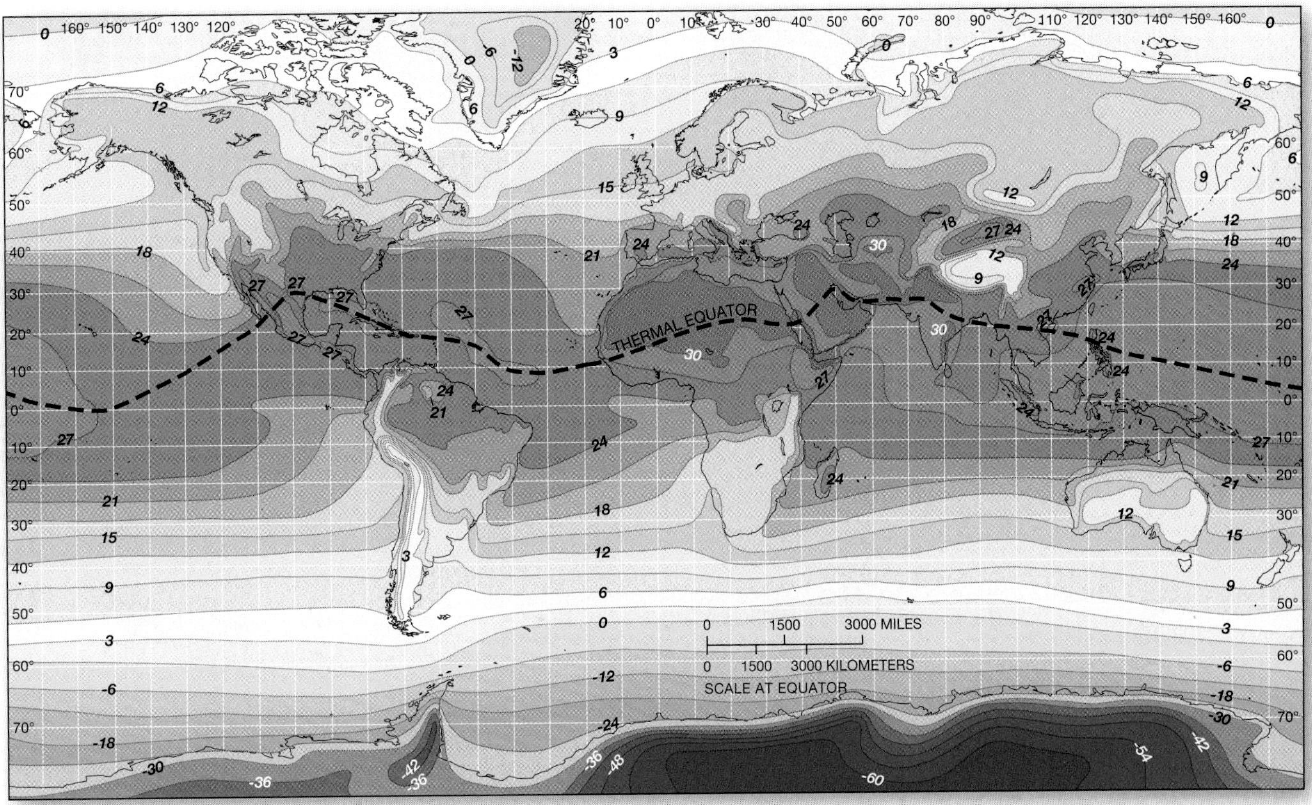

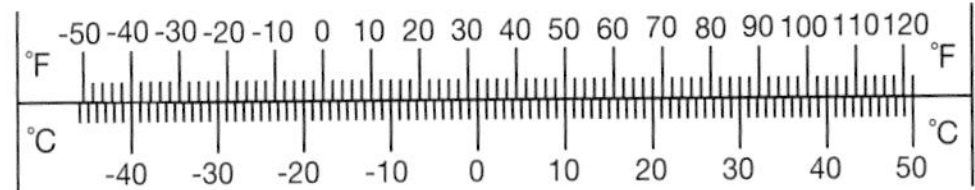

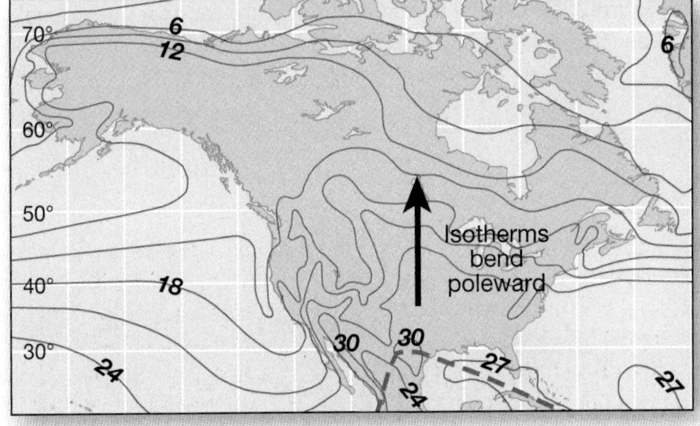

▲**Figure 3.22 Global average temperatures for July.** Temperatures are in Celsius (convertible to Fahrenheit by means of the scale) as taken from separate air-temperature databases for ocean and land. Note the inset map of North America and the poleward-trending isotherms in the interior. [Adapted by author and redrawn from National Climatic Data Center, *Monthly Climatic Data for the World*, 47 (July 1994), and WMO and NOAA.]

continental interiors of North America and Asia (**Figure 3.23**), where average ranges of 64 C° (115 F°) are recorded (see the dark brown area on the map). Smaller temperature ranges in the Southern Hemisphere indicate less seasonal temperature variation owing to the lack of large landmasses and the vast expanses of water to moderate temperature extremes. Thus, continental effects dominate in the Northern Hemisphere, and marine effects dominate in the Southern Hemisphere. The Northern Hemisphere, with greater land area overall, registers a slightly higher average surface temperature than does the Southern Hemisphere.

Polar Region Temperatures

The north polar region is an ocean surrounded by land. The island of Greenland, holding Earth's second largest ice sheet, has a maximum elevation of 3240 m (10,630 ft), the highest elevation north of the Arctic Circle. Two-thirds of the island is north of the Arctic Circle, and its north shore is only 800 km (500 mi) from the North Pole.

The south polar region is the enormous Antarctic ice sheet, covering the Antarctic continent, surrounded by ocean. Antarctica is Earth's coldest and highest landmass (in terms of average elevation).

January Polar Temperatures In January on the Greenland Ice Sheet, the combination of high latitude and interior high elevation produces cold midwinter temperatures (**Figure 3.24a**). In Antarctica (**Figure 3.24b**), December and January are the "summer" months. January average temperatures range from –3°C (26.6°F) on the coast to –28°C (–18.4°F) at the South Pole (elevation 2835 m, or 9301 ft) to –32°C (–25.6°F) at Russia's Vostok Station (elevation 3420 m, or 11,220 ft), the most continental location.

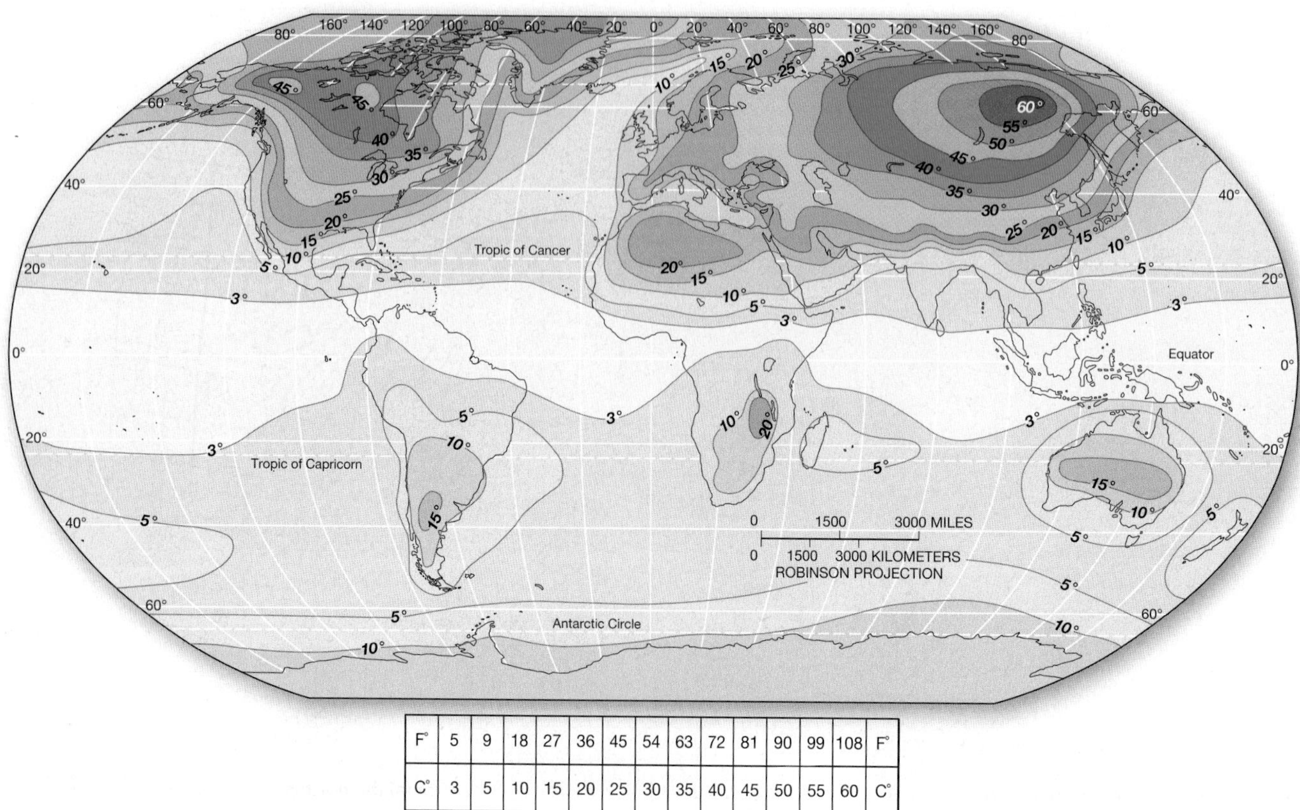

F°	5	9	18	27	36	45	54	63	72	81	90	99	108	F°
C°	3	5	10	15	20	25	30	35	40	45	50	55	60	C°

▲**Figure 3.23 Global annual temperature ranges.** The annual ranges of global temperatures in Celsius degrees (C°), with conversions to Fahrenheit degrees (F°) shown on scale. The mapped data show the difference between average January and July temperature maps.

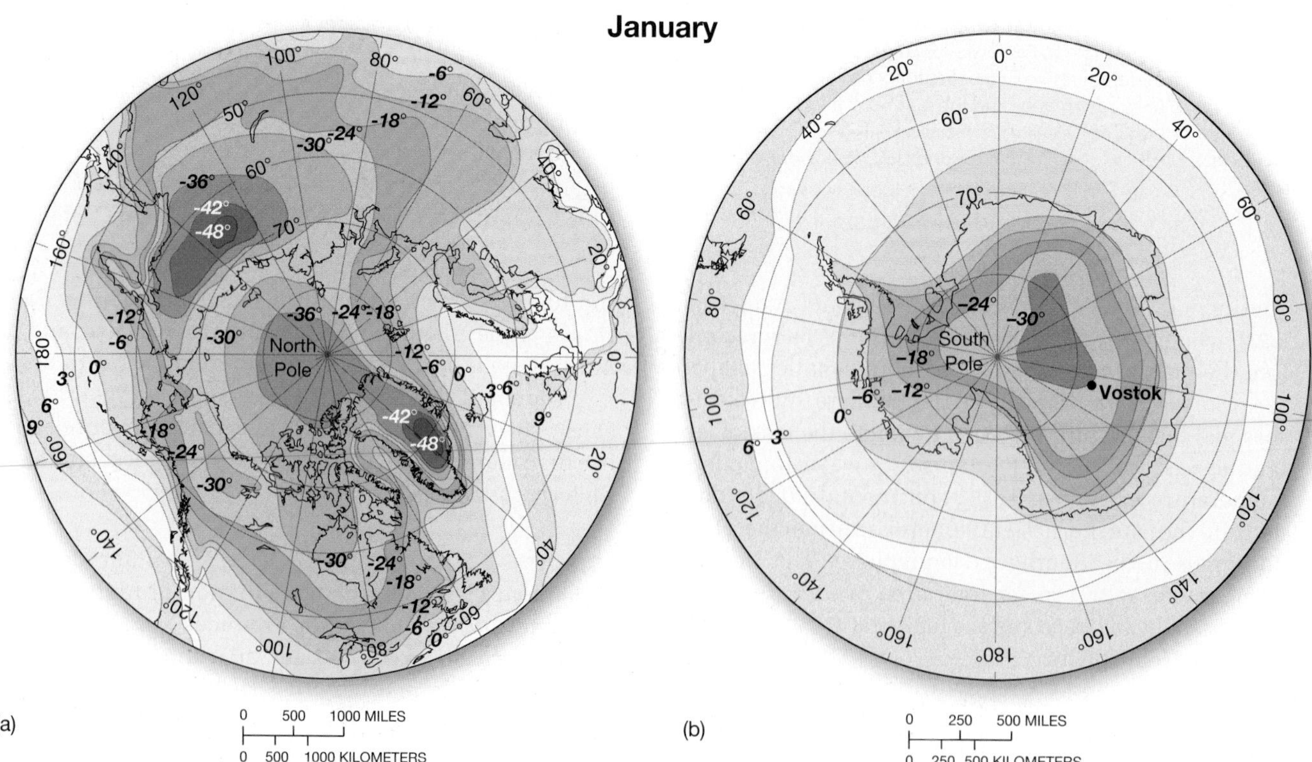

▲**Figure 3.24 January average temperatures for polar regions.** January temperatures in Celsius for (a) the north polar region and (b) the south polar region. Use temperature conversions in Figure 3.21. Note that each map is at a different scale. [Author-prepared maps using same sources as Figure 3.21.]

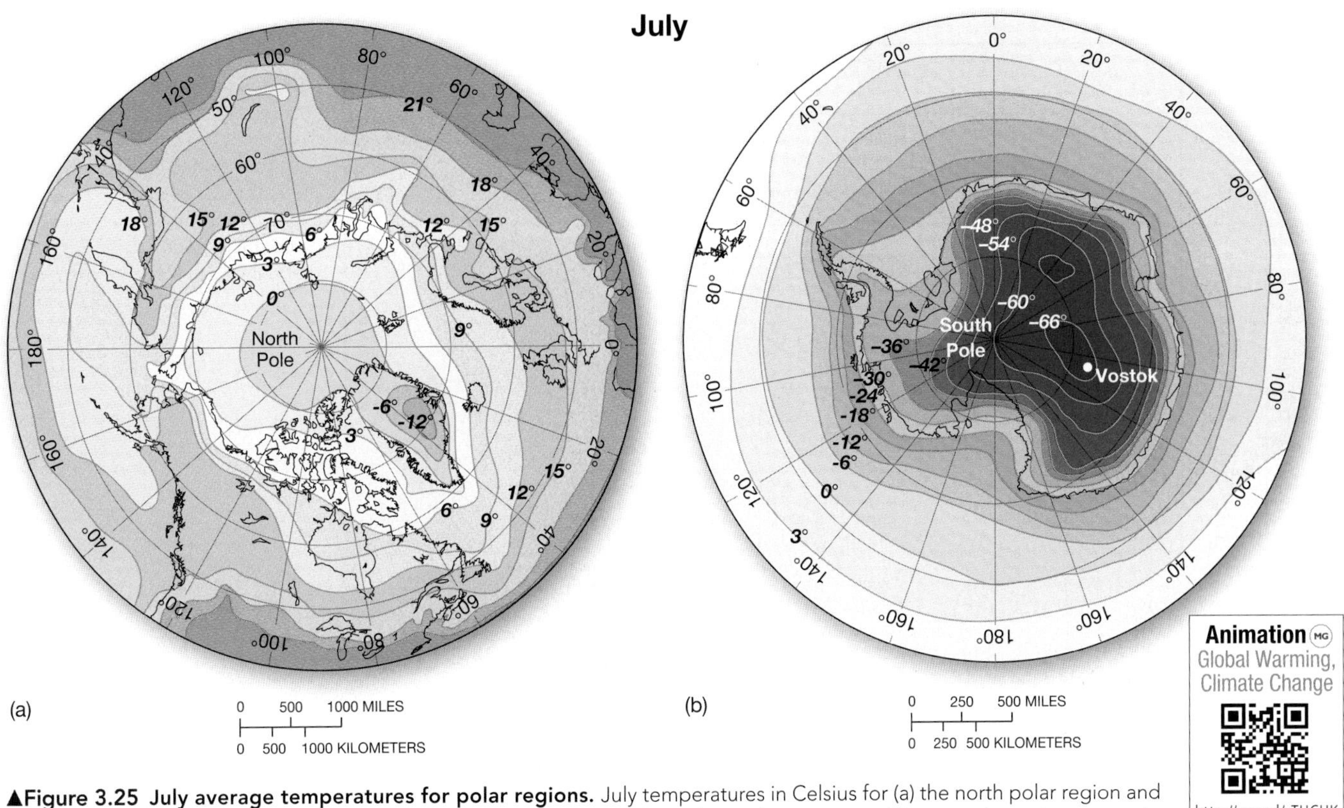

▲Figure 3.25 July average temperatures for polar regions. July temperatures in Celsius for (a) the north polar region and (b) the south polar region. Use temperature conversions in Figure 3.22. Note that each map is at a different scale. [Author-prepared maps using same sources as Figure 3.22.]

Animation Global Warming, Climate Change

http://goo.gl/cTHCHK

July Polar Temperatures July is "summer" in the Arctic Ocean (**Figure 3.25a**), where rising air and ocean temperatures are causing sea-ice melting, as discussed earlier in Geosystems Now. In the Southern Hemisphere, nights in Antarctica are 24 hours long. This lack of insolation results in the lowest natural temperatures reported on Earth. The average July temperature around the Vostok Station is −68°C (−90.4°F; **Figure 3.25b**). However, the record low is a frigid −89.2°C (−128.6°F) recorded on July 21, 1983, at the same location. This temperature is 11 C° (19.8 F°) colder than the freezing point of dry ice (solid carbon dioxide). If the concentration of carbon dioxide was large enough, such a cold temperature would theoretically freeze tiny carbon dioxide dry-ice particles out of the sky.

Wind Chill: Human Response to Cold The extreme cold temperatures of the polar regions pose challenges for human life and work. Although humidity (the water vapor content of the air) affects temperature, wind is a more important influence in cold regions. When strong winds combine with cold temperature, the effects can be deadly.

Apparent temperature is the general term for the outdoor temperature as it is perceived by humans. On a cold, windy day, the air feels colder because wind increases evaporative heat loss from our skin, producing a cooling effect. The *wind-chill factor* quantifies the enhanced rate at which body heat is lost to the air. As wind speeds increase, heat loss from the skin increases, and the wind-chill factor rises. To track the effects of wind on apparent temperature, the National Weather Service (NWS) uses the *wind-chill temperature index*, a chart plotting the temperature we feel as a function of actual air temperature and wind speed. The goal of the chart is to provide a simple, accurate tool for assessing the dangers to humans from winter winds and freezing temperatures. Lower wind-chill values present a serious freezing hazard, called *frostbite*, to exposed flesh.

GEOreport 3.4 Polar regions show greatest rates of warming

Climate change is affecting the higher latitudes at a pace exceeding that in the middle and lower latitudes. Since 1978, warming has increased in the Arctic region at a rate of 1.2 C° (2.2 F°) per decade, which means the last 20 years warmed at nearly seven times the rate of the last 100 years. Since 1970, nearly 60% of the Arctic sea ice has disappeared in response to increasing air and ocean temperatures, with record low levels of ice since 2007. The term *Arctic amplification* refers to the tendency for far northern latitudes to experience enhanced warming relative to the rest of the Northern Hemisphere. This phenomenon is related to the presence of snow and ice and to the positive feedback loops triggered by snow and ice melt (review Figure 1.7 and this chapter's Geosystems Now). Similar warming trends are affecting the Antarctic Peninsula and the West Antarctic Ice Sheet, as ice shelves collapse and retreat along the coast.

Actual Air Temperature in °C (°F)

Wind speed, kmph (mph)									
Calm	4° (40°)	−1° (30°)	−7° (20°)	−12° (10°)	−18° (0°)	−23° (−10°)	−29° (−20°)	−34° (−30°)	−40° (−40°)
8 (5)	2° (36°)	−4° (25°)	−11° (13°)	−17° (1°)	−24° (−11°)	−30° (−22°)	−37° (−34°)	−43° (−46°)	−49° (−57°)
16 (10)	1° (34°)	−6° (21°)	−13° (9°)	−20° (−4°)	−27° (−16°)	−33° (−28°)	−41° (−41°)	−47° (−53°)	−54° (−66°)
24 (15)	0° (32°)	−7° (19°)	−14° (6°)	−22° (−7°)	−28° (−19°)	−36° (−32°)	−43° (−45°)	−50° (−58°)	−57° (−71°)
32 (20)	−1° (30°)	−8° (17°)	−16° (4°)	−23° (−9°)	−30° (−22°)	−37° (−35°)	−44° (−48°)	−52° (−61°)	−59° (−74°)
40 (25)	−2° (29°)	−9° (16°)	−16° (3°)	−24° (−11°)	−31° (−24°)	−38° (−37°)	−46° (−51°)	−53° (−64°)	−61° (−78°)
48 (30)	−2° (28°)	−9° (15°)	−17° (−1°)	−24° (−12°)	−32° (−26°)	−39° (−39°)	−47° (−53°)	−55° (−67°)	−62° (−80°)
56 (35)	−2° (28°)	−10° (14°)	−18° (0°)	−26° (−14°)	−33° (−27°)	−41° (−41°)	−48° (−55°)	−56° (−69°)	−63° (−82°)
64 (40)	−3° (27°)	−11° (13°)	−18° (−1°)	−26° (−15°)	−34° (−29°)	−42° (−43°)	−49° (−57°)	−57° (−71°)	−64° (−84°)
72 (45)	−3° (26°)	−11° (12°)	−19° (−2°)	−27° (−16°)	−34° (−30°)	−42° (−44°)	−50° (−58°)	−58° (−72°)	−66° (−86°)
80 (50)	−3° (26°)	−11° (12°)	−19° (−3°)	−27° (−17°)	−35° (−31°)	−43° (−45°)	−51° (−60°)	−59° (−74°)	−67° (−88°)

Frostbite times: 30 min. 10 min. 5 min.

◀**Figure 3.26 Wind-chill temperature index.** This index uses wind speed and actual air temperature to determine apparent temperature, and was developed by the National Weather Service (http://www.nws.noaa.gov/os/windchill/) and the Meteorological Service of Canada.

Examine the wind-chill temperature index chart in **Figure 3.26.** (or see http://www.nws.noaa.gov/os/windchill/). If the air temperature is −7°C (20°F) and the wind is blowing at 32 kmph (20 mph), what is the wind-chill factor for exposed human skin? Is there a danger of frostbite at this temperature? Even without wind, frostbite is a potential danger in the extreme cold found on high mountain summits and in the polar regions.

Human Impacts on Energy Balance and Temperature

Scientists agree that human activities, principally the burning of fossil fuels, are increasing atmospheric greenhouse gases that absorb longwave radiation, delaying losses of heat energy to space. (We discuss greenhouse gases and present evidence for climate change in Chapter 8.) Thus, human actions are enhancing Earth's natural greenhouse effect, causing the "global warming" phenomenon that is related to complex changes now under way in the lower atmosphere. Temperatures are higher in cities than in surrounding rural areas, a result of pollutants, urban surfaces, lack of plant cover, and output heat from homes, vehicles, and industry.

Global Temperature Increase

One way scientists assess changing temperature patterns is using global temperature anomalies. A temperature *anomaly* is a difference, or irregularity, found by comparing recorded average annual temperatures against the long-term average annual temperature for a time period selected as the *baseline*, or base period (the basis for comparison). Positive anomalies indicate warmer temperatures than average; negative anomalies indicate cooler conditions than average.

Figure 3.27, a study of temperature anomalies since 1880, contains four nearly identical graphs of long-term warming trends as recorded by four independent international scientific agencies. Each agency uses a slightly different base period as a point of reference;

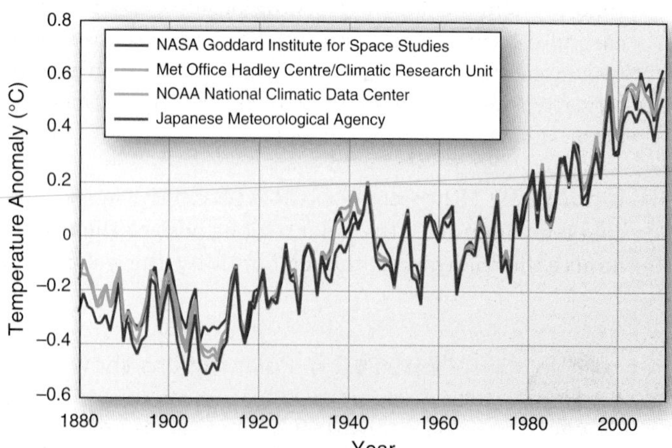

▲**Figure 3.27 Records of global surface air temperatures showing warming trend since 1880.** Four prominent international scientific agencies are in agreement as to recent warming shown by surface-temperature anomalies. Positive anomalies indicate warmer temperatures than the long-term baseline; negative anomalies indicate cooler temperatures. NASA data are from over 6300 stations. [NASA Earth Observatory/Robert Simmon.]

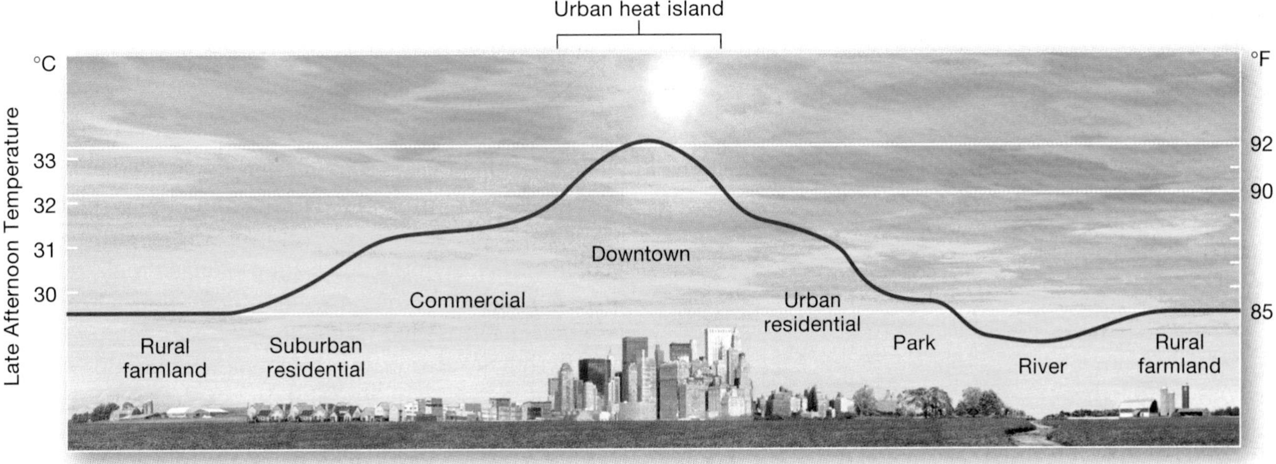

▲**Figure 3.28 Typical urban heat island profile.** On average, urban temperatures may be 1–3 C° (2–5 F°) warmer than nearby rural areas on a sunny summer day. Temperatures are highest at the urban core. Note the cooling over the park and rural areas. [Based on Heat Island, Urban Climatology and Air Quality, available at http://weather.msfc.nasa.gov/urban/urban_heat_island.html.]

for example, NASA uses 1951 to 1980, the United Kingdom Met Office uses 1961 to 1990, and NOAA uses the entire twentieth century. Thus, the numerical values of the anomalies differ slightly from one another. However, the different base periods do not affect the magnitude of temperature rise measured over the past century.

Since 1970, global temperatures have increased an average of 0.17 C° (0.3 F°) per decade. The last 15 years feature the warmest years in the climate record since 1880. As we discuss in detail in Chapter 8, temperatures today are higher than any time during the past 125,000 years, and maybe longer.

However, "global warming" (the recent, ongoing rise in global average surface temperature related to the greenhouse effect) is not the same thing as global climate change, and the two terms should not be considered interchangeable. Climate change (long-term alteration of the climate system, either natural or human-induced) encompasses all the effects of atmospheric warming—these effects vary with location and relate to humidity, precipitation, sea-surface temperatures, severe storms, and many other Earth processes. An example of the effects of global warming is the positive feedback loop created by Arctic sea-ice melting and temperature rise, discussed in this chapter's Geosystems Now. Other impacts will be discussed in chapters ahead—climate change affects almost all Earth systems.

The Urban Environment

Urban microclimates generally differ from those of nearby nonurban areas, with urban areas regularly reaching temperatures as much as 6 C° (10 F°) hotter than surrounding suburban and rural areas. In fact, the surface energy characteristics of urban areas are similar to those of desert locations, mainly because vegetation is lacking in both environments.

The physical characteristics of urbanized regions produce an **urban heat island (UHI)** that has, on average, both maximum and minimum temperatures higher than nearby rural settings (**Figure 3.28**). A UHI experiences higher temperatures toward the downtown central business district and lower temperatures over areas of trees and parks. Sensible heat is less in urban forests than in other parts of the city because of both shading from tree canopies and plant processes such as transpiration that move moisture into the air. In New York City, daytime temperatures average 5–10 C° (9–18 F°) cooler in Central Park than in the greater metropolitan area.

In the average city in North America, heating is increased by modified urban surfaces such as asphalt and glass, building geometry, pollution, and human activity such as industry and transportation. For example, an average car (10 km/l or 25 mpg) produces enough heat to melt a 4.5-kg bag of ice for every km driven (a 14-lb bag of ice for every mile driven). The removal of vegetation and the increase in human-made materials that retain heat are two of the most significant UHI causes. Urban surfaces (metal, glass, concrete, asphalt) conduct up to three times more energy than wet, sandy soil.

CRITICAL**thinking** 3.4

Looking at Your Surface Energy Budget

Given what you now know about reflection, absorption, and net radiation expenditures, assess your wardrobe (fabrics and colors); house, apartment, or dorm (colors of exterior walls, especially south- and west-facing or, in the Southern Hemisphere, north- and west-facing); roof (orientation relative to the Sun and roof color); automobile (color, use of sun shades); bicycle seat (color); and other aspects of your environment to improve your personal energy budget. Are you using colors and materials to save energy and enhance your personal comfort? Do you save money as a result of any of these strategies? What grade do you give yourself? In Chapter 1, you assessed your carbon footprint. How does that relate to these energy-budget considerations (orientation, shade, color, form of transportation)?

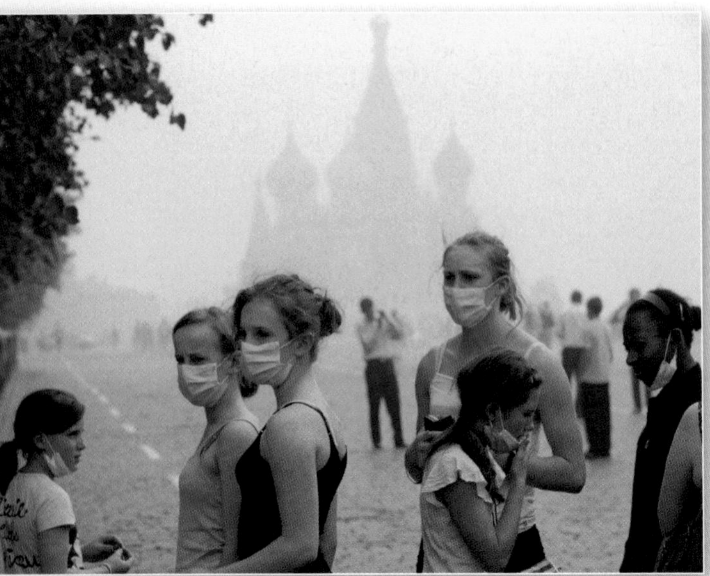

▲**Figure 3.29 Heat wave in Russia, summer 2010.** American tourists in Moscow wear face masks to filter smoke from nearby forest fires as temperatures top 38°C (100°F). The heat wave extended throughout eastern Europe, causing an estimated 55,000 heat-related deaths, massive crop losses, over 1 million hectares (2.5 million acres) of land burned by wildfires, and an overall estimated economic cost of US$15 billion. [Pavel Golovkin/AP images.]

Most major cities also produce a **dust dome** of airborne pollution trapped by certain characteristics of air circulation in UHIs: The pollutants collect with the decrease in wind speed characteristic of urban centers; they then rise as the surface heats and remain in the air above the city, affecting urban energy budgets.

City planners and architects use a number of strategies to mitigate UHI effects, including the planting of vegetation in parks and open space (urban forests), "green" roofs (rooftop gardens), "cool" roofs (high-albedo roofs), and "cool" pavements (lighter-colored materials such as concrete or lighter surface coatings for asphalt). In addition to lowering urban outdoor temperatures, such strategies keep buildings' interiors cooler, thereby reducing energy consumption and greenhouse gases released by fossil-fuel combustion (see the chapter-opening photo of the living roof on Chicago's City Hall). During the hottest day of the 2011 New York City summer, temperature measurements for a white roof covering were 24 C° (42 F°) cooler than those for a traditional black roof nearby. Other studies have shown that for structures with solar panel arrays, the roof temperatures under the shade of the panels dropped dramatically.

With predictions that 60% of the global population will live in cities by the year 2030 and with air and water temperatures rising because of climate change, UHI issues are emerging as a significant concern both for physical geographers and for the public at large. Studies have found a direct correlation between peaks in UHI intensity and heat-related illness and fatalities (more information is at http://www.epa.gov/hiri/). More on UHIs, including further discussion of driving factors and urban climatic response, is on the *MasteringGeography* website.

Heat Waves

One of the challenges humans are facing with the environmental effects of urban landscapes and climate change is an increase in the frequency of heat waves, putting more people at risk from the effects of prolonged high temperatures during the summer season. By definition, a **heat wave** is a prolonged period of abnormally high temperatures, usually, but not always, in association with humid weather.

Heat waves can be fatal in midlatitude regions, where extremes of temperature and humidity can become concentrated over stretches of days or weeks during the warmer months. Those most susceptible to heat-related illness are the young, the elderly, and people with preexisting medical conditions. The deadly effects of high temperatures, especially in cities, result from extreme daily temperature maximums combined with lack of nighttime cooling. Heat waves are also often associated with increased wildfires (**Figure 3.29**).

Human Heat Stress Through several complex mechanisms, the human body maintains an average internal temperature of about 36.8°C (98.2°F)*, although variations occur with exercise, time of day, and method of measurement. Perspiration is the body's first response for maintaining this core temperature under hot conditions.

When exposed to extreme heat and humidity, the human body is at risk of heat-related illness, or *heat stress*. Heat stress in humans takes such forms as heat cramps, heat exhaustion, and heat stroke, which is a life-threatening condition. A person with heat stroke has overheated to the point where the body is unable to cool itself—at this point, internal temperature may have risen to as high as 41°C (106°F) and the sweating mechanism has ceased to function.

Humidity is the presence of water vapor in the air and is commonly expressed as relative humidity (see the full discussion in Chapter 5); the higher the amount of water vapor, the higher the relative humidity. Under humid conditions, the air cannot absorb as much moisture, so perspiration is not as effective a cooling mechanism as in dry environments. The combination of high air temperature, high humidity, and low wind produces the most heat discomfort for humans.

During appropriate months, the NWS reports the *heat index* in its daily weather summaries to indicate how the air feels to an average person—its apparent temperature—and gauge the human body's probable reaction to the combined

*The traditional value for "normal" body temperature, 37°C (98.6°F), was set in 1868 using old methods of measurement. According to Dr. Philip Mackowiak of the University of Maryland School of Medicine, a more accurate modern assessment places normal at 36.8°C (98.2°F), with a range of 2.7 C° (4.8 F°) for the human population (*Journal of the American Medical Association*, September 23– 0, 1992).

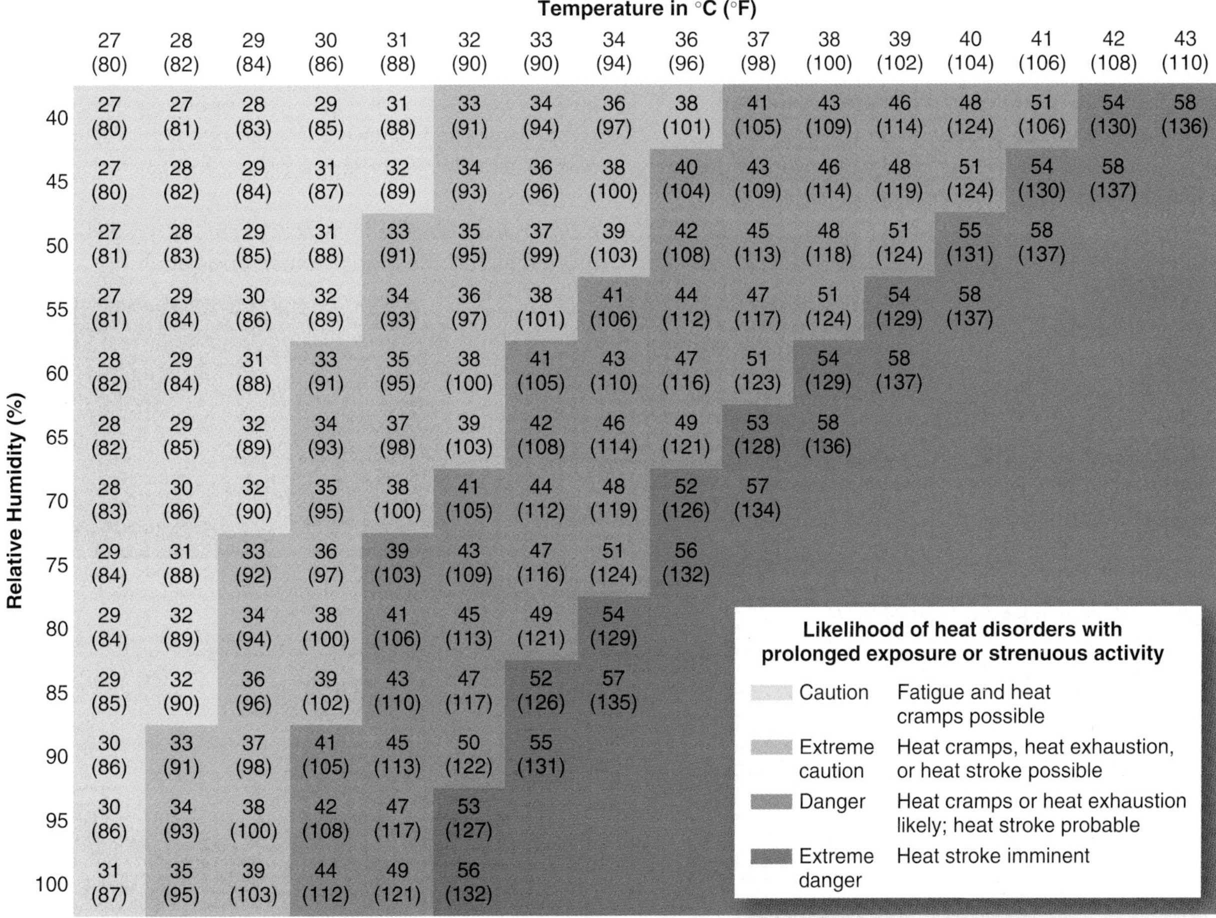

Temperature in °C (°F)

Relative Humidity (%)	27 (80)	28 (82)	29 (84)	30 (86)	31 (88)	32 (90)	33 (90)	34 (94)	36 (96)	37 (98)	38 (100)	39 (102)	40 (104)	41 (106)	42 (108)	43 (110)
40	27 (80)	27 (81)	28 (83)	29 (85)	31 (88)	33 (91)	34 (94)	36 (97)	38 (101)	41 (105)	43 (109)	46 (114)	48 (124)	51 (106)	54 (130)	58 (136)
45	27 (80)	28 (82)	29 (84)	31 (87)	32 (89)	34 (93)	36 (96)	38 (100)	40 (104)	43 (109)	46 (114)	48 (119)	51 (124)	54 (130)	58 (137)	
50	27 (81)	28 (83)	29 (85)	31 (88)	33 (91)	35 (95)	37 (99)	39 (103)	42 (108)	45 (113)	48 (118)	51 (124)	55 (131)	58 (137)		
55	27 (81)	29 (84)	30 (86)	32 (89)	34 (93)	36 (97)	38 (101)	41 (106)	44 (112)	47 (117)	51 (124)	54 (129)	58 (137)			
60	28 (82)	29 (84)	31 (88)	33 (91)	35 (95)	38 (100)	41 (105)	43 (110)	47 (116)	51 (123)	54 (129)	58 (137)				
65	28 (82)	29 (85)	32 (89)	34 (93)	37 (98)	39 (103)	42 (108)	46 (114)	49 (121)	53 (128)	58 (136)					
70	28 (83)	30 (86)	32 (90)	35 (95)	38 (100)	41 (105)	44 (112)	48 (119)	52 (126)	57 (134)						
75	29 (84)	31 (88)	33 (92)	36 (97)	39 (103)	43 (109)	47 (116)	51 (124)	56 (132)							
80	29 (84)	32 (89)	34 (94)	38 (100)	41 (106)	45 (113)	49 (121)	54 (129)								
85	29 (85)	32 (90)	36 (96)	39 (102)	43 (110)	47 (117)	52 (126)	57 (135)								
90	30 (86)	33 (91)	37 (98)	41 (105)	45 (113)	50 (122)	55 (131)									
95	30 (86)	34 (93)	38 (100)	42 (108)	47 (117)	53 (127)										
100	31 (87)	35 (95)	39 (103)	44 (112)	49 (121)	56 (132)										

▲**Figure 3.30** Heat index for various temperatures and relative humidity levels.

effects of air temperature and humidity (**Figure 3.30**). Canada uses the *humidex*, based on a similar formula. (See http://www.nws.noaa.gov/om/heat/index.shtml in the United States; in Canada, go to https://www.ec.gc.ca/meteo-weather/default.asp?lang=En&n=6C5D4990-1#humidex.)

Heat waves can cause human casualties from heat stress. Extreme heat can lead to heart attack or stroke, meaning the heat-wave casualties are often underreported. The Chicago heat wave of July 1995 caused over 700 deaths in the city core, particularly affecting the sick and elderly. The record temperature logged at Midway Airport of 41°C (106°F) was exceeded by the heat-index temperature of 54°C (130°F) in some apartments without air conditioning; such extreme temperatures lasted almost a week. A similar heat wave–related tragedy played out in Europe during the summer of 2003, when temperatures topped 40°C (104°F) in June, July, and August. An estimated 40,000 people died in six western European countries, with the highest number in France.

Recent Heat Records Several recent heat waves are notable for record-breaking temperatures. January 2013 brought weeks of heat in Australia, with temperatures regularly exceeding 45°C (113°F) at several locations. The heat wave registered the highest average temperature ever recorded across the country (40.3°C, or 104.6°F) during the hottest two-day period (January 7–8) in Australia's history. In mid-January, weather forecasters added two new colors to their heat maps to extend the range of temperatures beyond 50°C (122°F) to 54°C (129°F). This heat wave continued a trend of four consecutive months of record-breaking temperatures in Australia.

Temperatures soared across Asia in July and August 2013, setting records and causing heat-related fatalities. In Shanghai, China, with a population of over 23 million, a 3-week heat wave—including a new high temperature of 40.8°C (105.4°F) recorded on August 7—prompted officials to issue the country's first ever weather warning for heat and caused at least 40 reported deaths, although the actual fatalities may be much higher. (More information is at http://earthobservatory.nasa.gov/IOTD/view.php?id=81870.)

In the United States, 2011 and 2012 were the second and third warmest summers on record as of 2013 (the warmest occurred in 1936). The 2011 heat wave was worst in the southern Plains states, centering on Texas and Oklahoma. In 2012, high temperatures were spread over the entire country, with one-third of the nation's population exposed to 10 or more days over 38°C (100°F).

The Human Denominator 3 summarizes some of the key interactions among humans, energy budgets, and global temperatures. The effects of human activities on Earth's energy balance are driving changes in all Earth systems.

TEMPERATURE IMPACTS HUMANS

- The Earth–atmosphere system balances itself naturally, maintaining temperature patterns and planetary systems that support Earth, life, and human society.
- Solar energy is harnessed for power production worldwide, by technology ranging from small solar cookers to large-scale photovoltaic arrays.

HUMANS IMPACT ENERGY BALANCE AND TEMPERATURE

- Humans produce atmospheric gases and aerosols that affect clouds and the Earth–atmosphere energy budget, which, in turn, affect temperature and climate. For example, fossil-fuel burning produces carbon dioxide and other greenhouse gases that warm the lower atmosphere.
- Urban heat island effects accelerate warming in cities, which house more than half the global human population.

3a The International Maritime Organization, made up of 170 countries, is developing policies to improve energy efficiency and reduce diesel ship emissions, especially black carbon. In the Arctic, soot and particulates darken ice surfaces, decrease albedo, and enhance melting.

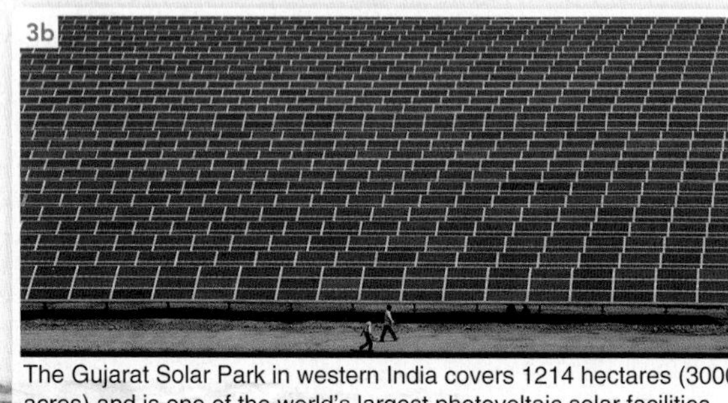

3b The Gujarat Solar Park in western India covers 1214 hectares (3000 acres) and is one of the world's largest photovoltaic solar facilities, with a capacity of 500 MW.

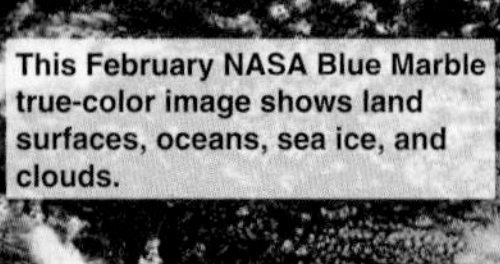

This February NASA Blue Marble true-color image shows land surfaces, oceans, sea ice, and clouds.

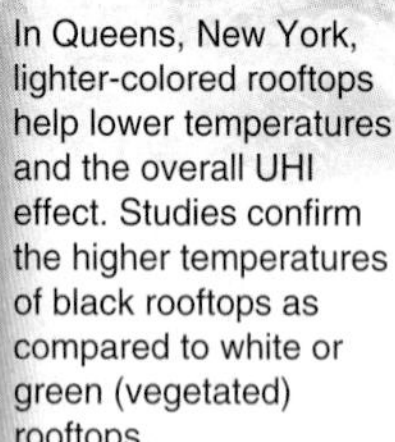

In Queens, New York, lighter-colored rooftops help lower temperatures and the overall UHI effect. Studies confirm the higher temperatures of black rooftops as compared to white or green (vegetated) rooftops.

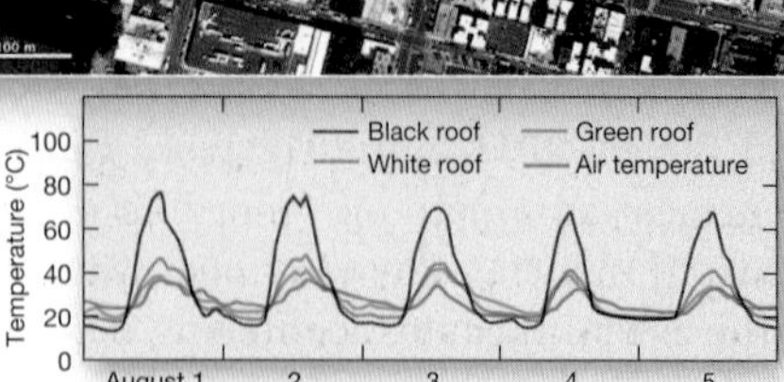

3c Wildfires raged across Australia during the 2013 summer heat wave, fueled by drought and record-breaking high temperatures. Near Hobart, Tasmania, fires destroyed over 80 homes.

ISSUES FOR THE 21ST CENTURY

- Improved energy efficiency and renewable energy sources, such as solar, can reduce the use of energy from fossil fuels, thus slowing the addition of anthropogenic greenhouse gases to the atmosphere.
- Strategies to reduce urban heat island effects can help lessen the dangers of heat waves in cities and slow the general atmospheric warming trend.
- Continued increases in average global air and ocean temperatures will enhance climate change effects worldwide.

KEYLEARNING**concepts**review

Define energy and heat and *explain* four types of heat transfer: radiation, conduction, convection, and advection.

Radiant energy from the Sun that cascades to the surface powers Earth systems. **Transmission** is the uninterrupted passage of shortwave and longwave energy through either the atmosphere or water. Our budget of atmospheric energy comprises *inputs* of shortwave radiation (ultraviolet light, visible light, and near-infrared wavelengths) and *outputs* of shortwave and longwave radiation (reflected light and thermal infrared). *Energy* is the capacity to do work, or move matter. The energy of motion is *kinetic energy*, produced by molecular vibrations and measured as temperature. *Potential energy* is stored energy that has the capacity to do work under the right conditions, such as when an object moves or falls with gravity. The flow of kinetic energy from one body to another resulting from a temperature difference between them is **heat**. Two types are **sensible heat**, energy that we can feel and measure, and **latent heat**, "hidden" heat that is gained or lost in phase changes, such as from solid to liquid to gas and back, while the substance's temperature remains unchanged.

One mechanism of heat transfer is *radiation*, which flows in electromagnetic waves and does not require a medium such as air or water. **Conduction** is the molecule-to-molecule transfer of heat as it diffuses through a substance. Heat also is transferred in gases and liquids by **convection** (physical mixing that has a strong vertical motion) or **advection** (mixing in which the dominant motion is horizontal). In the atmosphere or bodies of water, warmer portions tend to rise (they are less dense), and cooler portions tend to sink (they are more dense), establishing patterns of convection.

transmission (p. 72)
heat (p. 73)
sensible heat (p. 73)
latent heat (p. 73)
conduction (p. 73)
convection (p. 73)
advection (p. 73)

1. Give several examples of each type of heat transfer. Do you observe any of these processes on a daily basis?

Identify alternative pathways for solar energy on its way through the troposphere to Earth's surface—transmission, scattering, refraction, and absorption—and *review* the concept of albedo (reflectivity).

The molecules and particles of the atmosphere may redirect radiation, changing the direction of the light's movement *without altering its wavelengths*. This **scattering** represents 7% of Earth's reflectivity, or albedo. Dust particles, pollutants, ice, cloud droplets, and water vapor produce further scattering. Some incoming insolation is scattered by clouds and atmosphere and is transmitted to Earth as **diffuse radiation**, the downward component of scattered light.

The speed of insolation entering the atmosphere changes as it passes from one medium to another; this change of speed causes a bending action called **refraction**. **Reflection** is the process in which a portion of arriving energy bounces directly back into space without reaching Earth's surface. **Albedo** is the reflective quality (intrinsic brightness) of a surface. Albedo can greatly reduce the amount of insolation that is available for absorption by a surface. We report albedo as the percentage of insolation that is reflected. Earth and its atmosphere reflect 31% of all insolation when averaged over a year. **Absorption** is the assimilation of radiation by molecules of a substance, converting the radiation from one form to another—for example, visible light to infrared radiation.

Clouds, aerosols, and other atmospheric pollutants have mixed effects on solar energy pathways, either cooling or heating the atmosphere. **Global dimming** describes the decline in sunlight reaching Earth's surface owing to pollution, aerosols, and clouds and is perhaps masking the actual degree of global warming.

scattering (p. 74)
diffuse radiation (p. 74)
refraction (p. 74)
reflection (p. 75)
albedo (p. 75)
absorption (p. 76)
global dimming (p. 76)

2. What would you expect the sky color to be at an altitude of 50 km (30 mi)? Why? What factors explain the lower atmosphere's blue color?
3. Define *refraction*. How is it related to daylength? To a rainbow? To the beautiful colors of a sunset?
4. Using Figure 3.6, explain the differences in albedo values for various surfaces. What determines the reflectivity of a surface? Based on albedo alone, which surfaces are cooler? Which are warmer? Why do you think this is?
5. Define the concept of absorption.

Explain the greenhouse concept as it applies to Earth, *analyze* the effect of clouds and aerosols on atmospheric heating and cooling, and *review* the Earth–atmosphere energy balance.

Carbon dioxide, water vapor, methane, and other gases in the lower atmosphere absorb infrared radiation that is then emitted to Earth, thus delaying energy loss to space—this process is the **greenhouse effect**. In the atmosphere, longwave radiation is not actually trapped, as it would be in a greenhouse, but its passage to space is delayed (heat energy is detained in the atmosphere) through absorption and reradiation by **greenhouse gases**.

Cloud-albedo forcing is the increase in albedo, and therefore in reflection of shortwave radiation, caused by clouds, resulting in a cooling effect at the surface. Also, clouds can act as insulation, thus trapping longwave radiation and raising minimum temperatures. An increase in greenhouse warming caused by clouds is **cloud-greenhouse forcing**. Clouds' effects on the heating of the lower atmosphere depend on cloud type, height, and thickness (water content and density). High-altitude, ice-crystal clouds reflect insolation, producing a net cloud-greenhouse forcing (warming); thick, lower cloud cover reflects about 90%, producing a net cloud-albedo forcing (cooling). **Jet contrails**, or condensation trails, are produced by aircraft exhaust, particulates, and water vapor and can form high cirrus clouds, sometimes called *contrail cirrus*.

The Earth–atmosphere energy system naturally balances itself in a steady-state equilibrium. It does so through energy transfers that are *nonradiative* (convection, conduction, and the latent heat of evaporation) and *radiative* (longwave radiation traveling from the surface to the atmosphere and then to space). In the tropical latitudes, high insolation angle and consistent daylength cause more energy to be gained than lost, producing energy surpluses. In the polar regions, an extremely low insolation angle, highly reflective surfaces, and up to 6 months of no insolation annually cause more energy to be lost, producing energy deficits.

Surface energy measurements are used as an analytical tool of **microclimatology**. Air temperature responds to seasons and variations in insolation input. Within a 24-hour day, air temperature peaks between 3:00 and 4:00 P.M. and dips to its lowest point right at or slightly after sunrise. Air temperature lags behind each day's peak insolation. The warmest time of day occurs not at the moment of maximum insolation, but at the moment when a maximum of insolation has been absorbed and emitted to the atmosphere from the ground.

Net radiation (**NET R**) is the value reached by adding and subtracting the energy inputs and outputs at some location on the surface; it is the sum of all shortwave (SW) and longwave (LW) radiation gains and losses. Net radiation is the energy available to do the "work" of running the global climate system, by melting ice, raising temperatures in the atmosphere, and evaporating water from the oceans.

greenhouse effect (p. 78)
greenhouse gases (p. 78)
cloud-albedo forcing (p. 78)
cloud-greenhouse forcing (p. 78)
jet contrail (p. 78)
microclimatology (p. 82)
net radiation (NET R) (p. 83)

6. What are the similarities and differences between an actual greenhouse and the gaseous atmospheric greenhouse? Why is Earth's greenhouse effect changing?
7. Jet contrails affect the Earth–atmosphere balance in what ways? Describe the recent scientific findings.
8. Sketch a simple energy-balance diagram for the troposphere. Label each shortwave and longwave component and the directional aspects of related flows.
9. In terms of surface energy balance, explain the term *net radiation (NET R)*.
10. Why is there a temperature lag between the highest Sun altitude and the warmest time of day? Relate your answer to the insolation and temperature patterns during the day.
11. What are the nonradiative processes for the expenditure of surface net radiation on a daily basis?

Define the concept of temperature and *review* the principal temperature controls that produce global temperature patterns.

Temperature is a measure of the average kinetic energy, or molecular motion, of individual molecules in matter. Heat transfer occurs from object to object when there is a temperature difference between them. Principal controls and influences on temperature patterns include latitude (the distance north or south of the equator), altitude and elevation, cloud cover (reflection, absorption, and radiation of energy), and land–water heating differences.

Altitude describes the height of an object above Earth's surface, whereas *elevation* relates to a position on Earth's surface relative to sea level. Latitude and elevation work in combination to determine temperature patterns in a given location.

Differences in the physical characteristics of land (rock and soil) compared to water (oceans, seas, and lakes) lead to **land–water heating differences** that have an important effect on temperatures. These physical differences, related to *evaporation*, *transparency*, *specific heat*, and *movement*, cause land surfaces to heat and cool faster than water surfaces.

Because of water's **transparency**, light passes through it to an average depth of 60 m (200 ft) in the ocean. This penetration distributes available heat energy through a much greater volume than is possible through land, which is opaque. At the same time, water has a higher **specific heat**, or heat capacity, requiring far more energy to increase its temperature than does an equal volume of land.

Ocean currents and *sea-surface temperatures* also affect land temperature. An example of the effect of ocean currents is the **Gulf Stream**, which moves northward off the east coast of North America, carrying warm water far into the North Atlantic. As a result, the southern third of Iceland experiences much milder temperatures than would be expected for a latitude of 65° N, just below the Arctic Circle (66.5°).

Moderate temperature patterns occur in locations near water bodies, and more extreme temperatures occur inland. The **marine effect**, or maritime effect, usually seen along coastlines or on islands, is the moderating influence of the ocean. In contrast, the **continental effect** occurs in areas that are less affected by the sea and therefore experience a greater range between maximum and minimum temperatures on a daily and yearly basis.

temperature (p. 86)
land–water heating differences (p. 89)
transparency (p. 89)
specific heat (p. 89)
Gulf Stream (p. 90)
marine effect (p. 90)
continental effect (p. 90)

12. What is the difference between temperature and heat?
13. Explain the effects of altitude and elevation on air temperature. Why is air at higher altitudes lower in temperature? Why does it feel cooler standing in shadows at a higher elevation than at a lower elevation?
14. Why is it possible to grow moderate-climate-type crops such as wheat, barley, and potatoes at an elevation of 4103 m (13,460 ft) near La Paz, Bolivia?
15. Describe the effect of cloud cover with regard to Earth's temperature patterns. Review the effects of different cloud types on temperature, and relate the concepts with a simple sketch.
16. List the physical characteristics of land and water that produce their different responses to heating

from absorption of insolation. What is the specific effect of transparency in a medium?

17. Differentiate between temperatures at marine versus continental locations. Give an example of each from the text discussion.

Interpret the pattern of Earth's temperatures from their portrayal on January and July temperature maps and on a map of annual temperature ranges.

Maps for January and July instead of the solstice months of December and June are used for temperature comparison because of the natural lag that occurs between insolation received and maximum or minimum temperatures experienced. Each line on these temperature maps is an **isotherm**, an isoline that connects points of equal temperature. Isotherms portray temperature patterns.

Isotherms generally trend east–west, parallel to the equator, marking the general decrease in insolation and net radiation with distance from the equator. The **thermal equator** (an isoline connecting all points of highest mean temperature) trends southward in January and shifts northward with the high summer Sun in July. In January, it extends farther south into the interior of South America and Africa, indicating higher temperatures over landmasses.

The general term for the outdoor temperature as it is perceived by humans is *apparent temperature*. Under conditions of cold temperature and wind, the *wind-chill factor* indicates the enhanced rate at which body heat is lost to the air. As wind speeds increase, heat loss from the skin increases, decreasing the apparent temperature.

isotherm (p. 92) **thermal equator (p. 93)**

18. What is the thermal equator? Describe its location in January and in July. Explain why it shifts position annually.
19. Observe and compare trends in the pattern of isolines over North America as seen on the January and July average-temperature maps. Why do the patterns shift?
20. Describe and explain the extreme temperature range experienced in north-central Siberia between January and July.
21. Where are the hottest places on Earth? Are they near the equator or elsewhere? Explain. Where is the coldest place on Earth?
22. Compare the maps in Figures 3.24 and 3.25: (a) Describe what you find in central Greenland in January and July; (b) look at the south polar region, and describe seasonal changes there. Characterize conditions along the Antarctic Peninsula in January and July (around 60° W longitude).

List typical urban heat island conditions and their causes and *discuss* heat waves and human heat response.

A growing percentage of Earth's people live in cities and experience a unique set of altered microclimatic effects: increased conduction by urban surfaces, lower albedos, increased water runoff, and heating from transportation and industry. All of these combine to produce an **urban heat island**, where temperatures are higher than surrounding rural areas. Air pollution, including gases, dusts, and aerosols, is greater over urban areas, producing a **dust dome** that adds to the urban heat island effects.

Global climate change is presenting challenges to people across Earth. Recent **heat waves**, prolonged periods of high temperatures lasting days or weeks, have caused fatalities and billions of dollars in economic losses. The *heat index* indicates the human body's reaction to air temperature and water vapor. The level of humidity in the air affects our natural ability to cool through evaporation from skin.

urban heat island (p. 99) **heat wave (p. 100)**
dust dome (p. 100)

23. What observations form the basis for the urban heat island concept? Describe the climatic effects attributable to urban as compared with nonurban environments.
24. Describe strategies to lessen the effects of urban heat islands. How does the green roof in the chapter-opening photo affect Chicago City Hall and the surrounding environment?
25. Discuss recent heat waves in Australia and the United States. How do these events differ from previous heat waves in these regions?
26. On a day when the temperature reaches 37.8°C (100°F), how does a relative humidity reading of 50% affect apparent temperature?

Answer to Critical Thinking 3.3: San Francisco exhibits a smaller temperature range, a marine effect on temperature caused by the cooling waters of the Pacific Ocean and San Francisco Bay, which surround the city on three sides. The slower heating of the ocean helps delay the warmest summer month in San Francisco until September. Wichita has a continental location and therefore a greater annual temperature range. Note that Wichita is also slightly higher in elevation, which has a small effect on daily temperature variations.

MasteringGeography™

Looking for additional review and test prep materials? Visit the Study Area in *MasteringGeography*™ to enhance your geographic literacy, spatial reasoning skills, and understanding of this chapter's content by accessing a variety of resources, including **MapMaster** interactive maps, geoscience animations, videos, *In the News* RSS feeds, flashcards, web links, self-study quizzes, and an eText version of *Elemental Geosystems*.

4 Atmospheric and Oceanic Circulations

Powered by the northeast trade winds, the *Star Flyer* clipper ship sails southwestward across the Atlantic Ocean, along the approximate course of Columbus' fourth voyage to the New World. The bowsprit (shown here) extends forward from the bow, with netting for safety during deployment of the sails. [Bobbé Christopherson.]

KEYLEARNING**concepts**

After reading the chapter, you should be able to:

- ***Define*** the concepts of air pressure and wind and ***describe*** instruments used to measure each.
- ***Explain*** the four driving forces within the atmosphere—gravity, pressure gradient force, Coriolis force, and friction force—and ***locate*** the primary high- and low-pressure areas and principal winds.
- ***Describe*** upper-air circulation and ***define*** the jet streams.
- ***Explain*** several types of local and regional winds, including monsoons.
- ***Sketch*** the basic pattern of Earth's major surface ocean currents and deep thermohaline circulation.
- ***Summarize*** several multiyear oscillations of air temperature, air pressure, and circulation associated with the Arctic, Atlantic, and Pacific Oceans.

California's Santa Ana Winds

In mid-January 2014, dangerously dry conditions in the San Gabriel Mountains outside Los Angeles prompted the National Weather Service (NWS) to issue a Red Flag Warning, the highest alert for fire danger. Soils and vegetation throughout the region were desiccated from a decade-long drought and an extremely dry winter. The fire hazard was worsened by the seasonal Santa Ana winds, downslope winds that concentrate below mountain passes and canyons in the rugged topography of southern California. The Santa Anas can gust over 129 kmph (80 mph) and are notorious for damaging buildings, felling trees, and, most importantly, spreading wildfires (**Figure GN 4.1**).

The Colby Wildfire Just before dawn on January 16, the gusty Santa Ana winds fanned the embers from an illegal campfire near the Colby Trail in the Angeles National Forest into flames. The fire quickly spread into the neighborhoods near Glendora—about 40 km (25 mi) northeast of downtown Los Angeles—where police and firefighters woke residents and asked them to evacuate.

At daybreak, the Santa Anas picked up speed and intensity, blowing the Colby fire downslope toward houses tucked onto steep slopes with difficult access for fighting wildfires. Winds averaged about 42 kmph (26 mph) through the day, with gusts reaching 98 kmph (61 mph). Over the next 5 days, 3700 residents evacuated their homes as the fire burned about 2000 acres.

Causes of the Santa Ana Winds Like most winds, the Santa Anas are driven by an atmospheric pressure gradient, a large difference in pressure between two locations (**Figure GN 4.2**). In winter, high pressure over the relatively cold, high-elevation Great Basin desert region of Nevada and southern Utah contrasts with the lower pressure of the warm, moist southern California coastal areas, forming a pressure gradient.

▼Figure GN 4.1 Glendora, California, during the 2014 Colby fire. [Keith Birmingham/Zuma Press/Alamy.]

As the atmospheric high pressure rotates, this cold air is swept downslope toward the coast, warming as it picks up speed and channels through mountain passes and canyons. With the rise in wind temperature (often at a rate of 10 C°/1000 m [5.5 F°/1000 ft]), the relative humidity drops, resulting in a hot, dry wind in the coastal region. In fact, the hottest day ever recorded in downtown Los Angeles—45°C (113°F) on September 27, 2010—occurred during a Santa Ana wind. These winds can not only spread wildfire flames and embers, but also act as a drying agent for vegetation that fuels the fire on the ground.

The conditions that produce high pressure over the Great Basin desert usually occur between September and March, defining the season for Santa Ana winds. Thus, September typically marks the end of smog season in the Los Angeles Basin, as the winds blow smog out to sea. However, the Santa Anas are most strongly associated with wildfire in October, at the end of the dry summer typical of the southern California climate. Recently, dry winters have made this wind–wildfire association extend longer throughout the year. These winds are now notorious for creating some of the most dangerous wind and wildfire conditions in the United States (**Figure GN 4.3**).

Long-Lasting Effects In March 2014, the first significant rainstorm of the winter season moved into Los Angeles. In Glendora and surrounding neighborhoods, debris flows washed water, soil, and sediment from the fire-ravaged hillslopes onto the city streets and into backyards, swimming pools, and house interiors—another legacy of the Colby fire.

The January wildfire had left hillsides barren of vegetation, having destroyed the canopy that helps intercept rainfall before it hits the ground. Because fire also leaves the ground coated with oils from burned plant material, rainwater flows downslope before it can infiltrate into the soil. In addition, ash accumulation clogs the pore spaces in soil, also inhibiting the infiltration of water. These factors combine to increase the likelihood of flash floods and debris flows, both of which are caused by intense rainfall falling on impermeable soils.

Regional and local winds, such as the Santa Anas in southern California, are atmospheric processes that affect Earth systems, influencing natural ecosystems and human life. In this chapter, we look at the winds and ocean currents that drive Earth's general circulation patterns and produce such local effects.

▲Figure GN 4.2 The Santa Anas blow from an area of high pressure over the Great Basin to one of low pressure over the Pacific coast.

QUESTION AND EXPLORE In Europe, similar pressure-gradient winds are the *Bora*, which blows over the Adriatic Sea, and the *Levante*, which flows through the Strait of Gibraltar. Read about these and other local winds at **http://www.weatheronline.co.uk/reports/wind/** (click on your chosen wind on the right side). MG

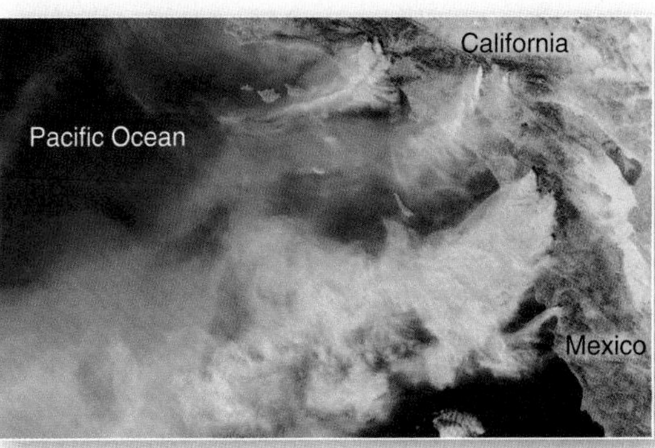

▲Figure GN 4.3 Santa Anas send smoke plumes over the Pacific Ocean. The October 2003 Cedar fire in San Diego was the largest in California's history. [Jacques Descloitres, MODIS Rapid Response Team, NASA/GSFC.]

The global circulation of winds and ocean currents is one of the most important outputs of the Earth–atmosphere energy system. Driven by the imbalance between equatorial energy surpluses and polar energy deficits, Earth's atmospheric circulation transfers both energy and mass on a grand scale, determining Earth's weather patterns and the flow of ocean currents. The atmosphere is the dominant medium for redistributing energy from about 35° latitude to the poles in each hemisphere, whereas ocean currents redistribute more heat in a zone straddling the equator between the 17th parallels in each hemisphere.

... the fluid movement of the atmosphere links humanity more than perhaps any other natural or cultural factor.

More than any other Earth system, our atmosphere is shared by all humanity, as winds move pollutants worldwide, unconfined by political borders. The 1991 eruption of Mount Pinatubo in the Philippines provided a unique opportunity to assess the dynamics of atmospheric circulation as scientists tracked atmospheric contaminants from the volcanic explosion using satellite monitoring (**Figure 4.1a**). The Mount Pinatubo event had tremendous impact, lofting 15–20 million tons of ash, dust, and sulfur dioxide (SO_2) into the atmosphere. As the sulfur dioxide rose into the stratosphere, it quickly formed sulfuric acid (H_2SO_4) aerosols, which concentrated at an altitude of 16–25 km (10–15.5 mi).

In a satellite image from the first few days after the eruption (**Figure 4.1b**), we see the atmospheric aerosols borne by global winds: millions of tons of dust from African soils crossing the Atlantic Ocean, the smoke from Kuwaiti oil well fires set during the first Persian Gulf War, smoke from forest fires in Siberia, and haze off the East Coast of the United States. During the weeks following (**Figures 4.1c** and **d**), Mount Pinatubo's aerosols, mixed with this airborne dust, smoke, and haze, were carried around Earth by atmospheric circulation patterns. This debris increased atmospheric albedo about 1.5%. Some 60 days after the eruption, the aerosol cloud covered about 42% of the globe, from 20° S to 30° N latitude. For almost 2 years, colorful sunrises and sunsets and a small temporary lowering of average temperatures followed.

As aerosols travel freely over Earth, international concerns about transboundary air pollution and nuclear weapons testing illustrate how the fluid movement of the atmosphere links humanity more than perhaps any other natural or cultural factor. The global spread of low-level radioactive contamination from Japan's nuclear disaster associated with the 2011 earthquake and tsunami, which reached the U.S. West Coast in 2014, is another example of this linkage. In our shared global atmosphere, one person's or country's exhalation is another's inhalation.

In this chapter: We begin with a discussion of air pressure and the tools for wind measurement. We examine the driving forces that produce and determine the speed and direction of surface winds: gravity, pressure gradients, the Coriolis force, and friction. We then look at the circulation of Earth's atmosphere: the principal pressure systems, patterns of global surface winds, upper-atmosphere winds, and regional winds, including the seasonally shifting monsoons. Finally, we consider Earth's wind-driven oceanic currents and explain multiyear oscillations in atmospheric and oceanic flows. The energy driving all this movement comes from one source: the Sun.

Atmospheric Pressure and Wind

Air pressure—the weight of the atmosphere described as force per unit area—is key to understanding wind. The molecules that constitute air create **air pressure** through their motion, size, and number, and this pressure is exerted on all surfaces in contact with air. As we saw in Chapter 2, the number of molecules and their motion are also the factors that determine the density and temperature of the air.

Both pressure and density decrease with altitude in the atmosphere. The low density in the upper atmosphere means the molecules are far apart, making collisions between them less frequent and thereby reducing pressure (review Figure 2.13). However, differences in air pressure are noticeable even between sea level and the summits of Earth's highest mountains. The subjective experience of "thin air" at high altitudes is caused by the smaller amount of oxygen available to inhale (fewer air molecules mean less oxygen).

Remember from Chapter 3 that temperature is a measure of the average kinetic energy of molecular motion. When air in the atmosphere is heated, molecular activity increases, and temperature rises. With increased activity, the spacing between molecules increases, so that density is reduced and air pressure decreases. Therefore, warmer air is less dense, or lighter, than colder air and exerts less pressure.

The amount of water vapor in the air also affects its density. Moist air is lighter because the molecular weight of water is less than that of the molecules making up dry air. If the same total number of molecules has a higher

GEOreport 4.1 Blowing in the wind

Dust originating in Africa sometimes increases the iron content of the waters off Florida, promoting the toxic algal blooms (*Karenia brevis*) known as "red tides." In the Amazon, soil samples bear the dust print of these former African soils that crossed the Atlantic. Active research on such dust is part of the U.S. Navy's Aerosol Analysis and Prediction System; see links and the latest navy research at **http://www.nrlmry.navy.mil/7544.html.**

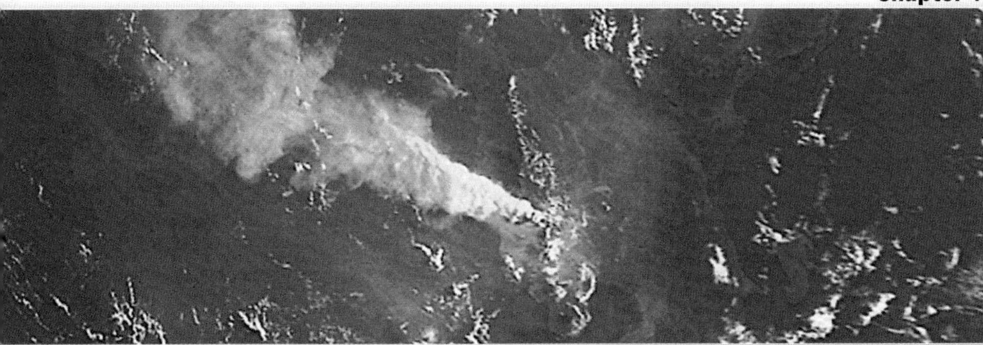

(a) Mount Pinatubo eruption, June 15, 1991. Images below track the movement of aerosols across the globe.

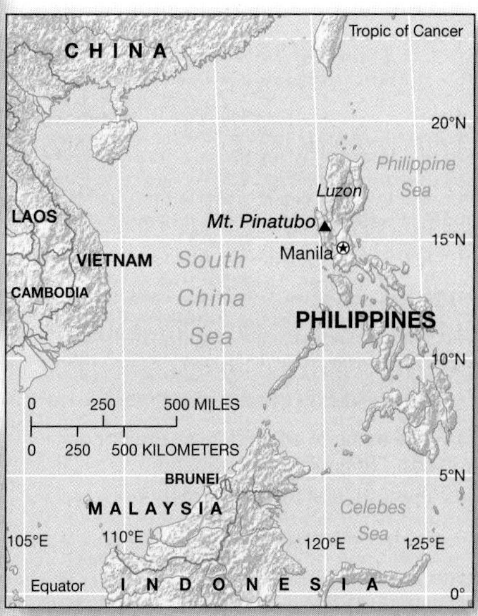

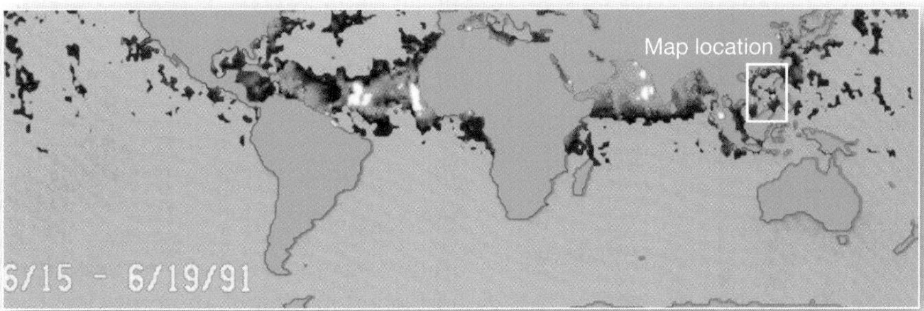

(b) False-color images show aerosol optical thickness: White has the highest concentration of aerosols; yellow shows medium values; and brown shows the lowest values. Note dust, smoke from fires, and haze in the atmosphere at the time of the eruption.

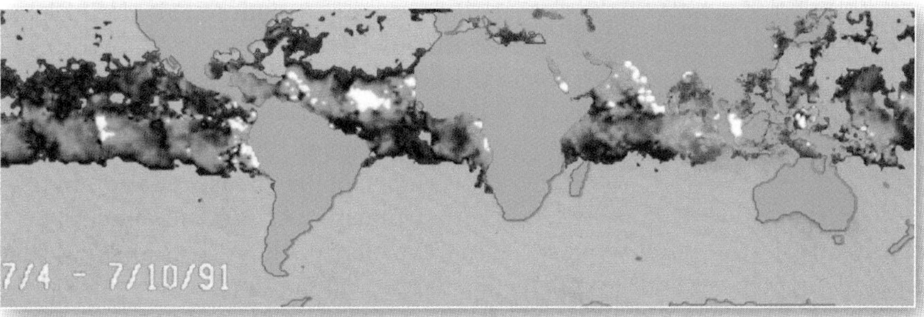

(c) The aerosol layer circles the entire globe 21 days after the eruption.

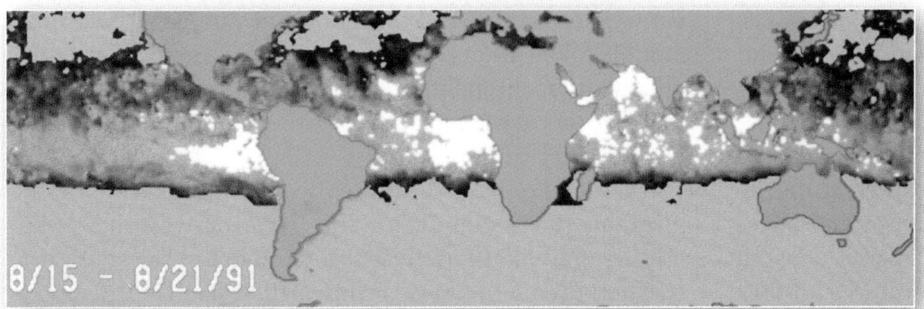

(d) The effects of the eruption cover 42% of the globe after 2 months.

▲**Figure 4.1 Atmospheric effects of the Mount Pinatubo volcanic eruption and global winds.** [(a) USGS. (b–d) AOT images from the advanced very high resolution radiometer (AVHRR) instrument aboard *NOAA-11*; NESDIS/NOAA.]

percentage of water vapor, mass will be less than if the air was dry (that is, less than if it was made up entirely of oxygen and nitrogen molecules). As water vapor in the air increases, density decreases, so humid air exerts less pressure than dry air.

The end result over Earth's surface is that warm, humid air is associated with low pressure and cold, dry air is associated with high pressure. These relationships among pressure, density, temperature, and moisture are important to the discussion ahead.

Air Pressure Measurement

In 1643, work by Evangelista Torricelli, a pupil of Galileo, on a mine-drainage problem led to the first method for measuring air pressure (**Figure 4.2a**). Torricelli knew that pumps in the mine were able to "pull" water upward about 10 m (33 ft), but no higher, and that this level fluctuated from day to day. Careful observation revealed that the limitation was not the fault of the pumps, but a property of the atmosphere itself. He figured out that air pressure, the weight of the air, varies with weather conditions and that this weight determined the height of the water in the pipe.

To simulate the problem at the mine, Torricelli devised an instrument using a much denser fluid than water—mercury (Hg)—and a glass tube 1 m (3.3 ft) high. He sealed the glass tube at one end, filled it with mercury, and inverted it into a dish containing mercury, at which point a small space containing a vacuum was formed in the tube's closed end (**Figure 4.2b**). Torricelli found that the average height of the column of mercury remaining in the tube was 760 mm (29.92 in.), depending on the weather. He concluded that the mass of surrounding air was exerting pressure on the mercury in the dish and thus counterbalancing the weight of the column of mercury in the tube.

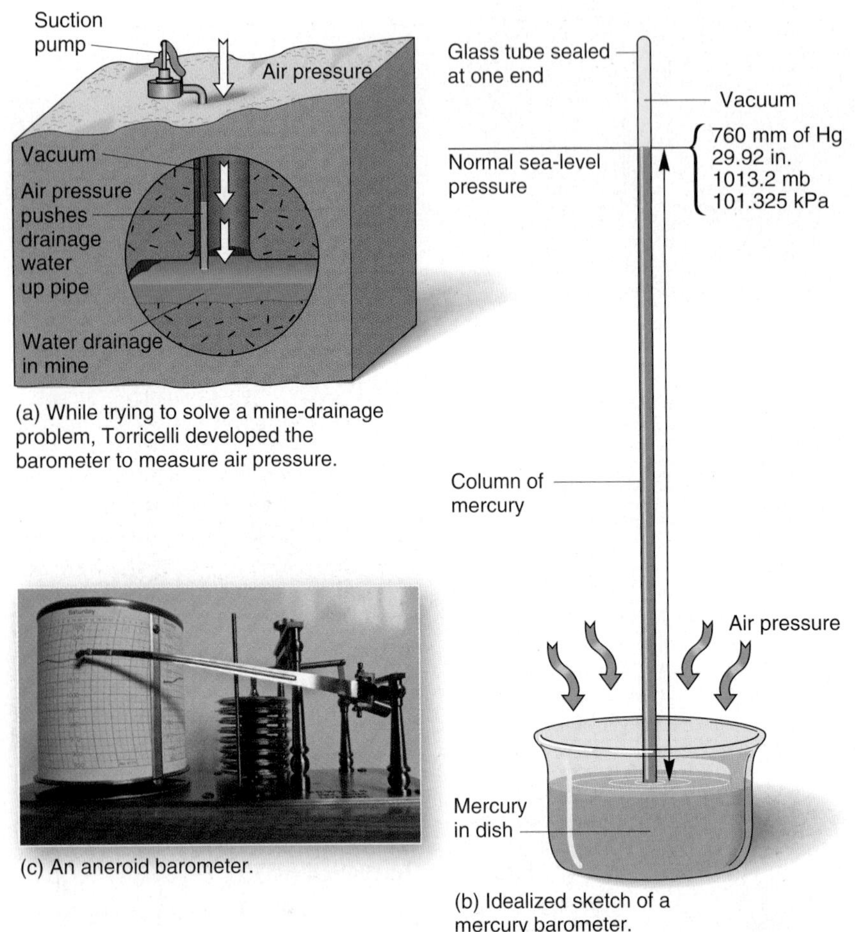

(a) While trying to solve a mine-drainage problem, Torricelli developed the barometer to measure air pressure.

(b) Idealized sketch of a mercury barometer.

(c) An aneroid barometer.

Figure 4.2 Developing the barometer. Have you used a barometer? If so, what type was it? Did you try to reset it using a local weather information source? [(c) Stuart Aylmer/Alamy.]

Any instrument that measures air pressure is a barometer (from the Greek *baros*, meaning "weight"). Torricelli developed a **mercury barometer**. A more compact barometer design, which works without a meter-long tube of mercury, is the **aneroid barometer** (Figure 4.2c). *Aneroid* means "using no liquid." The aneroid barometer principle is simple: Imagine a small chamber, partially emptied of air, that is sealed and connected to a mechanism attached to a needle on a dial. As the air pressure outside the chamber increases, it presses inward on the chamber; as the outside air pressure decreases, it relieves the pressure on the chamber—in both cases causing changes in the chamber that move the needle. An aircraft altimeter is a type of aneroid barometer.

Today, atmospheric pressure is measured at weather stations by electronic sensors that provide continuous measurement over time using millibars (mb, which express force per square meter of a surface area) or hectopascals (1 millibar = 1 hectopascal). To compare pressure conditions from one place to another, pressure measurements are adjusted to a standard of normal sea-level pressure, which is 1013.2 mb or 29.92 in. of mercury (Hg). In Canada and certain other countries, normal sea-level pressure is expressed as 101.325 kilopascals, or kPa (1 kPa = 10 mb). The adjusted pressure is known as *barometric pressure*.

Figure 4.3 shows comparative scales in millibars and inches of mercury for air pressure. Note that the normal range of Earth's atmospheric pressure from strong high pressure to deep low pressure is about 1050 to 980 mb (31.00 to 29.00 in.). The figure also indicates pressure extremes recorded for the United States and worldwide.

Wind: Description and Measurement

Simply stated, **wind** is the generally horizontal motion of air across Earth's surface. Within the boundary layer at the surface, turbulence adds wind updrafts and downdrafts and thus a vertical component to this definition. Differences in air pressure between one location and another produce wind.

Wind's two principal properties are speed and direction, both of which can be measured by simple instruments. An **anemometer** measures wind speed in kilometers per hour (kmph), miles per hour (mph), meters per second (mps), or knots. (A knot is a nautical mile per hour, covering 1 minute of Earth's arc in an hour, equivalent to 1.85 kmph, or 1.15 mph.) A **wind vane** determines wind direction; the standard measurement is taken 10 m (33 ft) above the ground to reduce the effects of local topography on wind direction. (See these instruments at the top of the weather station in Chapter 5, Figure 5.29.)

Winds are named for the direction from which they originate. For example, a wind from the west is a westerly wind (it blows eastward); a wind out of the south is a southerly wind (it blows northward). Figure 4.4 illustrates a simple wind compass, naming 16 principal wind directions used by meteorologists.

Driving Forces within the Atmosphere

Four forces determine both the speed and the direction of winds. The first of these is Earth's *gravitational force*, which exerts a virtually uniform pressure on the atmosphere over all of Earth. Gravity compresses the atmosphere toward Earth's surface, with the density decreasing as altitude increases. The gravitational

Deep low-pressure system

Normal sea-level pressure
1013.2 mb (29.92 in.)

NORMAL RANGE

Decreasing pressure

Increasing pressure

Strong high-pressure system

U.S. record low:
882 mb (26.02 in.)
Hurricane Wilma
(Atlantic/Caribbean)
Oct. 2005

U.S. record high:
1065 mb (31.43 in.)
Barrow, AK
(71° N 156° W)
Jan. 1970

Earth's record low:
870 mb (25.69 in.)
Typhoon Tip
(western Pacific)
Oct. 1979

Earth's record high:
1084 mb (32.01 in.)
Agata, Siberia
(67° N 93° E)
Dec. 1968

850 881 914 948 980 1016 1050 Millibars

25.00 26.00 27.00 28.00 29.00 30.00 31.00 32.00 Inches

mb 850 860 870 880 890 900 910 920 930 940 950 960 970 980 990 1000 1010 1020 1030 1040 1050 1060 1070 1080

in. 25 25.5 26 26.5 27 27.5 28 28.5 29 29.5 30 30.5 31 31.5 32

1. Hurricane Gilbert	**2. Hurricane Rita**	**3. Hurricane Katrina**
888 mb (26.23 in.)	897 mb (26.46 in.)	902 mb (26.61 in.)
Sept. 1988	Sept. 2005	Aug. 2005

Some convenient conversions:
1.0 in. (Hg) = 33.87 mb = 25.40 mm (Hg) = 0.49 lb/in.^{2}
1.0 mb = 0.0295 in. (Hg) = 0.75 mm (Hg) = 0.0145 lb/in.^{2}

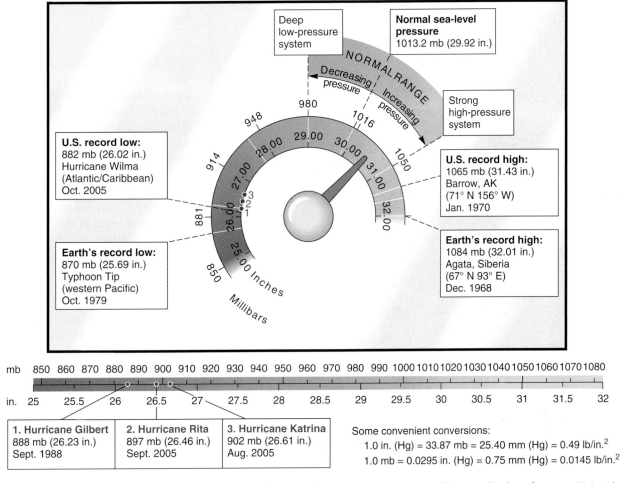

▲**Figure 4.3 Air pressure readings and conversions.** Scales express barometric air pressure in millibars and inches of mercury (Hg), with average air pressure values and recorded pressure extremes. Note the positions of Hurricanes Gilbert, Rita, and Katrina on the pressure dial (numbers 1–3).

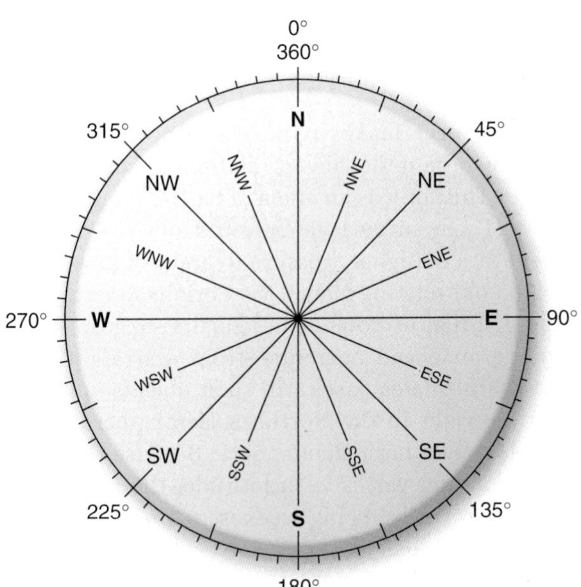

▲**Figure 4.4 Sixteen wind directions identified on a wind compass.** Winds are named for the direction from which they originate. For example, a wind from the west is a westerly wind.

CRITICAL**thinking** 4.1

Measure the Wind

Estimate wind speed and direction as you walk across campus on a day with wind. The Beaufort wind scale presented on the *MasteringGeography* website can assist you with this task. Record your estimates at least twice during the day—more often if you note changing wind patterns. For wind direction, moisten your finger, hold it in the air, and sense evaporative cooling on the side facing the direction from which the wind is blowing. Check the Internet to find a weather station on your campus or at another nearby location, and compare your measurements to actual data. What changes in wind speed and direction do you notice over several days? How did these changes relate to the weather you experienced?

force counteracts the outward centrifugal force acting on Earth's spinning surface and atmosphere. (Centrifugal force is the apparent force drawing a rotating body away from the center of rotation; it is equal and opposite to centripetal, or "center-seeking," force.) Without gravity, there would be no atmospheric pressure—or atmosphere, for that matter.

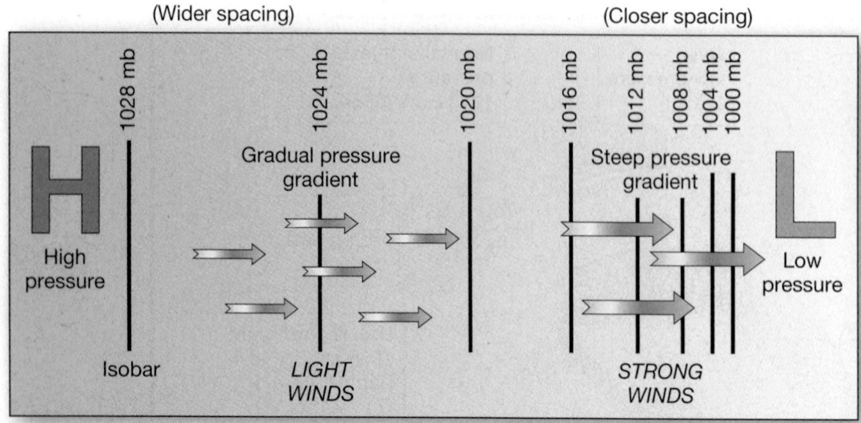

(a) Pressure gradient, isobars, and wind strength.

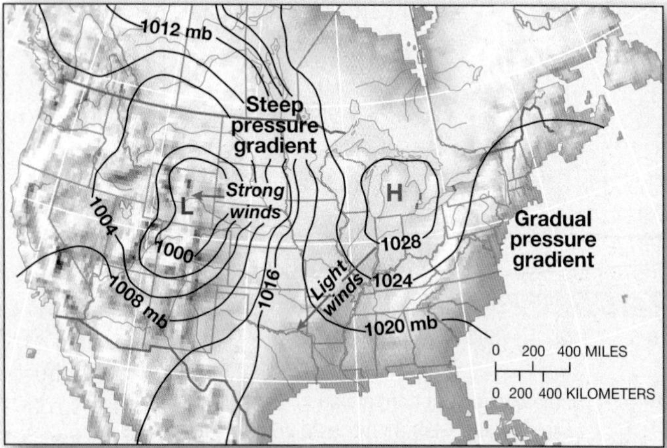

(b) Pressure gradient and wind strength portrayed on a weather map.

◀Figure 4.5 Effect of pressure gradient on wind speed.

The other forces affecting winds are the pressure gradient force, Coriolis force, and friction force. All of these forces operate on moving air and ocean currents at Earth's surface to produce global circulation patterns.

Pressure Gradient Force

The **pressure gradient force** drives air from areas of higher barometric pressure (more-dense air) to areas of lower barometric pressure (less-dense air), thereby causing winds. A *gradient* is the rate of change in some property over distance. Without a pressure gradient force, there would be no wind.

High- and low-pressure areas exist in the atmosphere principally because Earth's surface is unequally heated. For example, cold, dry, dense air at the poles exerts greater pressure than warm, humid, less-dense air along the equator. On a regional scale, high- and low-pressure areas are associated with specific masses of air that have varying characteristics. When these air masses are near each other, a pressure gradient develops that leads to horizontal air movement.

In addition, vertical air movement can create pressure gradients. This happens when air descends from the upper atmosphere and diverges at the surface or when air at the surface converges from different directions and ascends into the upper atmosphere. Strongly subsiding and diverging air is associated with high pressure, and strongly converging and rising air is associated with low pressure. These horizontal and vertical pressure differences establish a pressure gradient force that is a causal factor for winds.

An **isobar** is an isoline (a line along which there is a constant value) plotted on a weather map to connect points of equal pressure. The pattern of isobars provides a portrait of the pressure gradient between an area of higher pressure and one of lower pressure. The spacing between isobars indicates the intensity of the pressure difference, or pressure gradient.

Just as closer contour lines on a topographic map indicate a steeper slope on land and closer isotherms on a temperature map indicate more extreme temperature gradients, so closer isobars denote steepness in the pressure gradient. In **Figure 4.5a**, note the spacing of the isobars. A steep gradient causes faster air movement from a high-pressure area to a low-pressure area. Isobars spaced farther apart from one another mark a more gradual pressure gradient, one that creates a slower airflow. Along a horizontal surface, a pressure gradient force that is acting alone (uncombined with other forces) produces movement at right angles to the isobars, so wind blows across the isobars from high to low pressure. Note the location of steep ("strong winds") and gradual ("light winds") pressure gradients and their relationship to wind intensity on the weather map in **Figure 4.5b**.

Coriolis Force

The **Coriolis force** makes wind traveling in a straight path appear to be deflected in relation to Earth's rotating surface. This force is an effect of Earth's rotation. On a nonrotating Earth, surface winds would move in a straight line from areas of higher pressure to areas of lower pressure. But on our rotating planet, the Coriolis force deflects anything that flies or flows across Earth's surface—wind, an airplane, or ocean currents—from a straight path. Because Earth rotates eastward, such objects appear to curve to the right in the Northern Hemisphere and to the left in the Southern Hemisphere. Because the speed of Earth's rotation varies with latitude, the strength of this deflection varies, being weakest at the equator and strongest at the poles.

Note that we call Coriolis a *force*. In physics, a force operates on an object with mass to change its velocity, direction, or shape and is expressed as mass times acceleration. The Coriolis force is an apparent force that

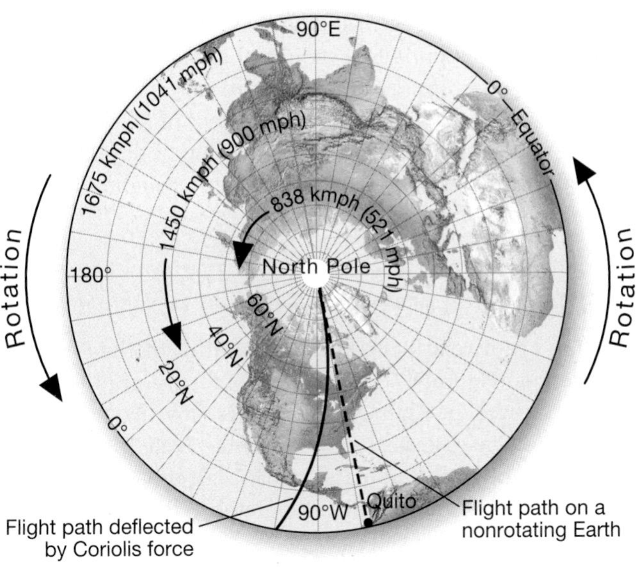

(a) Deflection of a north–south flight path. Note the latitude of Quito, Ecuador, at the equator.

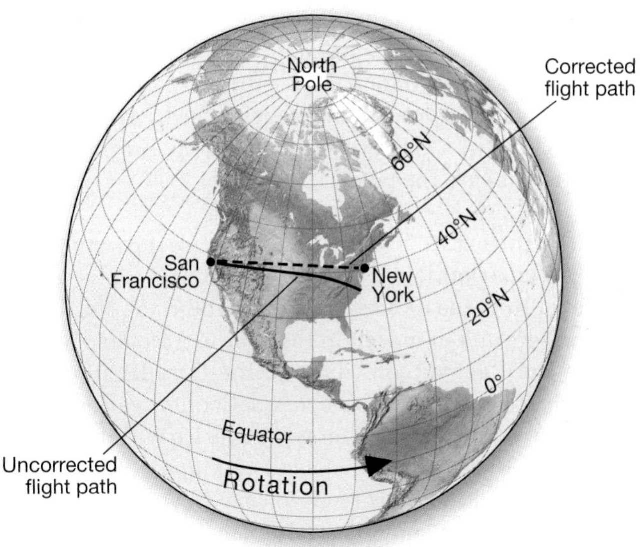

(b) Deflection of an east–west flight path.

◀**Figure 4.6 The Coriolis force—an apparent deflection.**

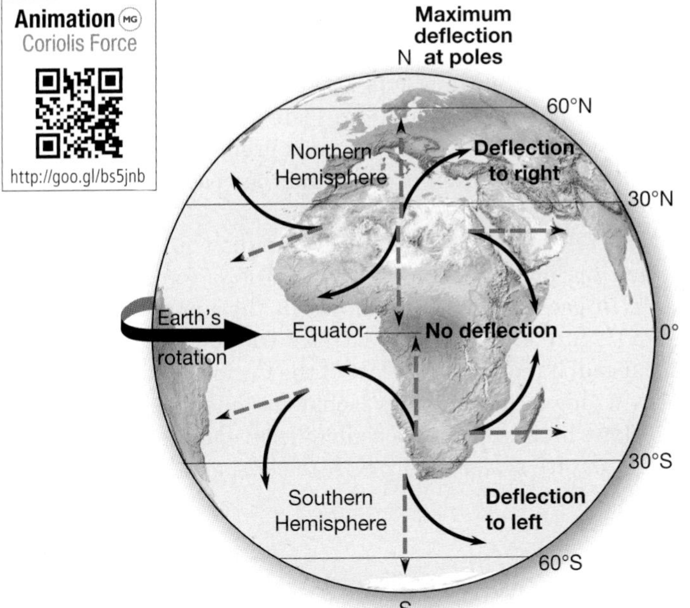

(c) Distribution of the Coriolis force on Earth. Apparent deflection is to the right in the Northern Hemisphere and to the left in the Southern Hemisphere; dashed lines show intended route and solid lines show actual movement.

Animation (MG) Coriolis Force

http://goo.gl/bs5jnb

affects the direction of moving objects. Gaspard Coriolis (1792–1843), a French mathematician and researcher of applied mechanics, first described this force in 1831. For deeper insight into the physics of this phenomenon, go to http://www.real-world-physics-problems.com/coriolis-force.html.

Coriolis Force Example A simple example of an airplane helps explain this subtle, but significant force affecting moving objects on Earth. From the viewpoint of an airplane that is passing over Earth's surface, the surface is seen to rotate slowly below. But, looking from the surface at the airplane, the surface seems stationary, and the airplane appears to curve off course. The airplane does not actually deviate from a straight path, but it appears to do so because we are standing on Earth's rotating surface beneath the airplane. Because of this apparent deflection, the airplane must make constant corrections in flight path to maintain its "straight" heading relative to a rotating Earth (see **Figures 4.6a** and **b**).

Consider a pilot leaving the North Pole and flying due south toward Quito, Ecuador. If Earth were not rotating, the aircraft would simply travel along a meridian of longitude and arrive at Quito. But Earth is rotating eastward beneath the aircraft's flight path. As the plane travels toward the equator, the speed of Earth's rotation increases from about 838 kmph (521 mph) at 60° N to about 1675 kmph (1041 mph) at 0°. If the pilot does not allow for this increase in rotational speed, the plane will reach the equator over the ocean along an apparently curved path, far to the west of the intended destination (Figure 4.6a). On the return flight northward, if the pilot does not make corrections, the plane will end up to the east of the pole, in a right-hand deflection.

This effect also occurs if the plane is flying in an east–west direction. During an eastward flight from California to New York, in the same direction as Earth's rotation, the centrifugal force pulling outward on the plane in flight (Earth rotation speed + plane speed) becomes so great that it cannot be balanced by the gravitational force pulling toward Earth's axis. Therefore, the plane experiences an overall movement away from Earth's axis, observed as a right-hand deflection toward the equator. Unless the pilot corrects for this deflective force, the flight will end up somewhere in North Carolina (Figure 4.6b). In contrast, flying westward on a return flight opposite Earth's rotation direction decreases the centrifugal force (Earth rotation speed – plane speed), so that it is less than the gravitational force. In this case, the plane experiences an overall movement toward Earth's axis, observed in the Northern Hemisphere as a right-hand deflection toward the pole.

Distribution and Significance Figure 4.6c summarizes the distribution of the effects of the Coriolis force on Earth. Note the deflection to the right in the Northern Hemisphere and to the left in the Southern Hemisphere.

Several factors contribute to the Coriolis force on Earth. First, the strength of this deflection varies with the speed of Earth's rotation, which varies with latitude. Remember that rotational speed is 0 kmph at the poles, where Earth's surface is closest to its axis, and 1675 kmph (1041 mph) at the equator, where Earth's surface is farthest from its axis. Thus, deflection is zero along the equator, increases to half the maximum deflection at 30° N and 30° S latitude, and reaches maximum deflection for objects near the poles. Second, the deflection occurs regardless of the direction in which the object is moving and does not change the speed of the moving object. Third, the deflection increases as the speed of the moving object increases; the faster the object's speed, the greater its apparent deflection. Although the Coriolis force affects all moving objects on Earth to some degree, its effects are negligible for small-scale motions that cover insignificant distance and time, such as the flight of a Frisbee or an arrow.

How does the Coriolis force affect wind? As air rises from the surface through the lowest levels of the atmosphere, it leaves the drag of surface friction behind and increases speed (the friction force is discussed just ahead). This increases the Coriolis force, spiraling the winds to the right in the Northern Hemisphere or to the left in the Southern Hemisphere and generally producing upper-air westerly winds from the subtropics to the poles. In the upper troposphere, the Coriolis force just balances the pressure gradient force. Consequently, the winds between higher-pressure and lower-pressure areas in the upper troposphere flow parallel to the isobars, along lines of equal pressure.

Friction Force

In the boundary layer, **friction force** creates drag as the wind moves across Earth's surfaces, but friction force decreases with height above the surface. Without friction, surface winds would simply move in paths parallel to isobars and at high rates of speed. The effect of surface friction extends to a height of about 500 m (around 1600 ft); thus, upper-air winds are not affected by the friction force. At the surface, the effect of friction varies with surface texture, wind speed, time of day and year, and atmospheric conditions. In general, rougher surfaces produce more friction.

Summary of Physical Forces on Winds

Winds are a result of the combination of these physical forces (**Figure 4.7**). When the pressure gradient acts alone, shown in Figure 4.7a, winds flow from areas of high pressure to areas of low pressure. Note the descending, diverging air associated with high pressure and the ascending, converging air associated with low pressure in the side view.

Figure 4.7b illustrates the combined effect of the pressure gradient force and the Coriolis force on air currents in the upper atmosphere, above about 1000 m (3300 ft). Together, they produce winds that do not flow directly from high to low, but that flow around the pressure areas, remaining parallel to the isobars. Such winds are **geostrophic winds** and are characteristic of upper tropospheric circulation. (The suffix *-strophic* means "to turn.") Geostrophic winds produce the characteristic pattern shown on the upper-air weather map in Figure 4.11 on page 122.

Near the surface, friction prevents the equilibrium between the pressure gradient and Coriolis forces that results in geostrophic wind flows in the upper atmosphere (Figure 4.7c). Because surface friction decreases wind speed, it reduces the effect of the Coriolis force and causes winds to move across isobars at an angle. Thus, wind flows around pressure centers form enclosed areas called *pressure systems*, or *pressure cells*, as illustrated in **Figure 4.8**.

High- and Low-Pressure Systems

In the Northern Hemisphere, surface winds spiral out from a *high-pressure area* in a clockwise direction, forming an **anticyclone**, and spiral into a *low-pressure area* in a counterclockwise direction, forming a **cyclone** (Figure 4.7). In the Southern Hemisphere, these circulation patterns are reversed, with winds flowing counterclockwise out of anticyclonic high-pressure cells and clockwise into cyclonic low-pressure cells.

Anticyclones and cyclones have vertical air movement in addition to these horizontal patterns. As air

GEOreport 4.2 Coriolis: Not a force on sinks or toilets

A common misconception about the Coriolis force is that it affects water draining out of a sink, tub, or toilet. Moving water or air must cover some distance across space and time before the Coriolis force noticeably deflects it. Long-range artillery shells and guided missiles do exhibit small amounts of deflection that must be corrected for accuracy. But water movements down a drain are too small in spatial extent to be noticeably affected by this force.

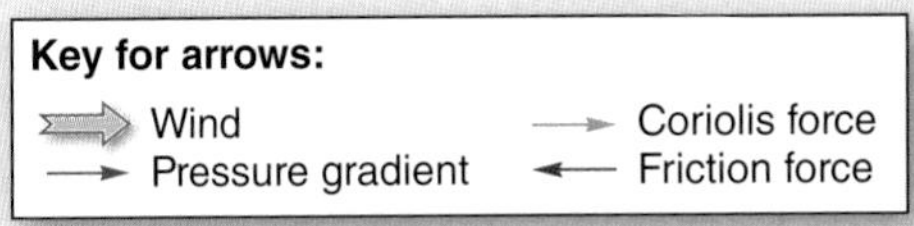

(a) Pressure gradient

Top view and side view of air movement in an idealized high-pressure area and low-pressure area on a nonrotating Earth.

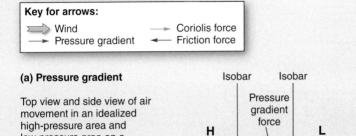

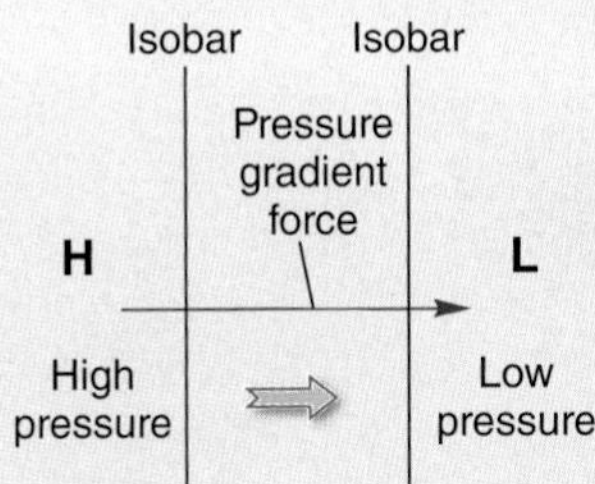

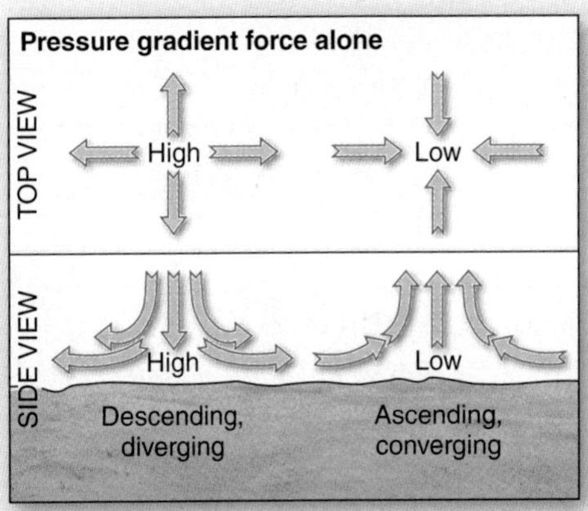

(b) Pressure gradient + Coriolis forces (upper-level winds)

Earth's rotation adds the Coriolis force, giving a "twist" to air movements. High-pressure and low-pressure areas develop a rotary motion, and wind flowing between highs and lows flows parallel to isobars.

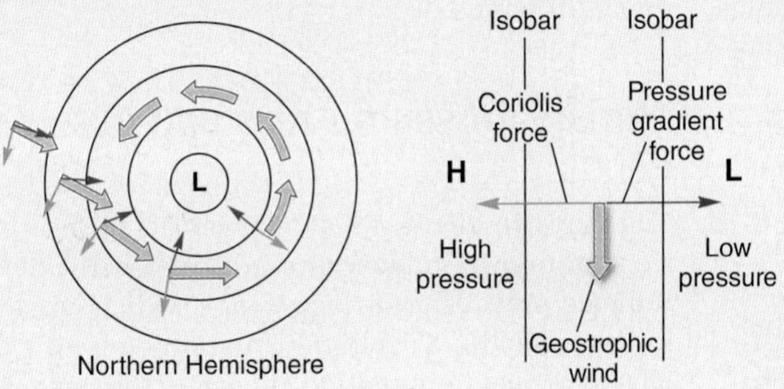

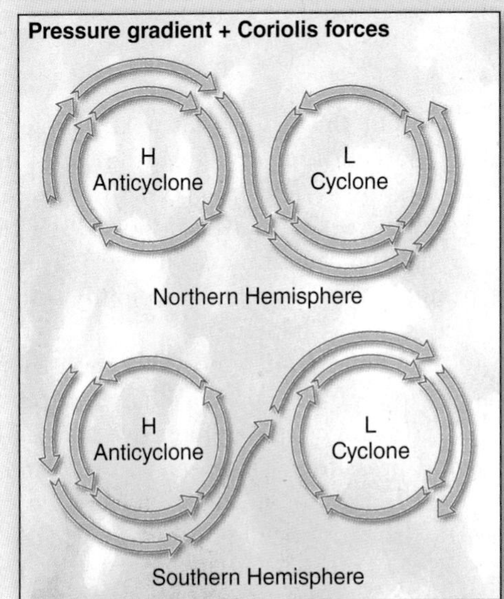

(c) Pressure gradient + Coriolis + friction forces (surface winds)

Surface friction adds a countering force to Coriolis, producing winds that spiral out of a high-pressure area and into a low-pressure area. Surface winds cross isobars at an angle. Air flows into low-pressure cyclones and turns to the left because of deflection to the right.

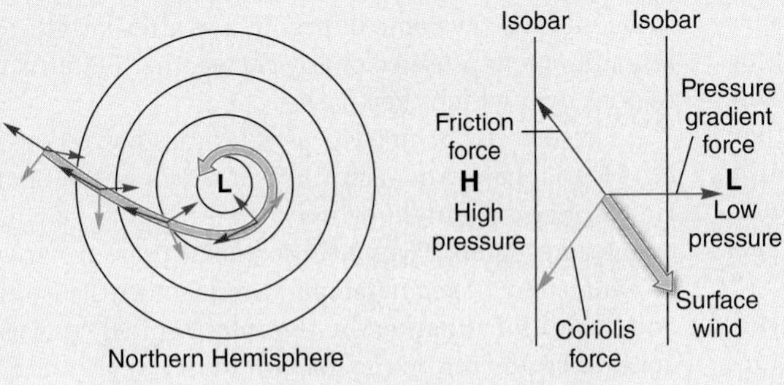

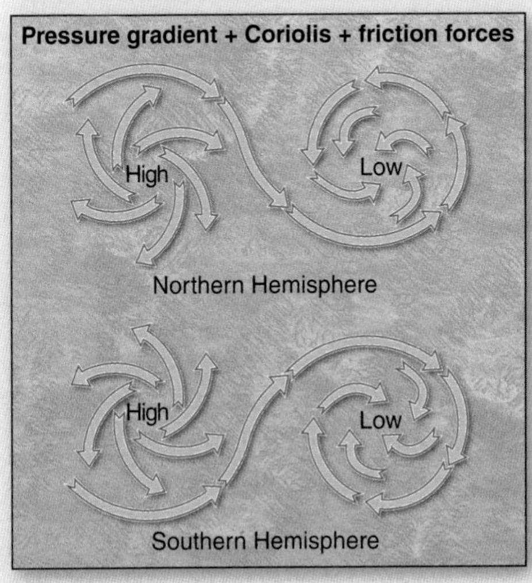

▲**Figure 4.7 Three physical forces that produce winds.** Three physical forces interact to produce wind patterns: (a) pressure gradient force; (b) Coriolis force, which counters the pressure gradient force, producing a geostrophic wind flow in the upper atmosphere; and (c) friction force, which, combined with the other two forces, produces characteristic surface winds.

Animation Wind Pattern Development

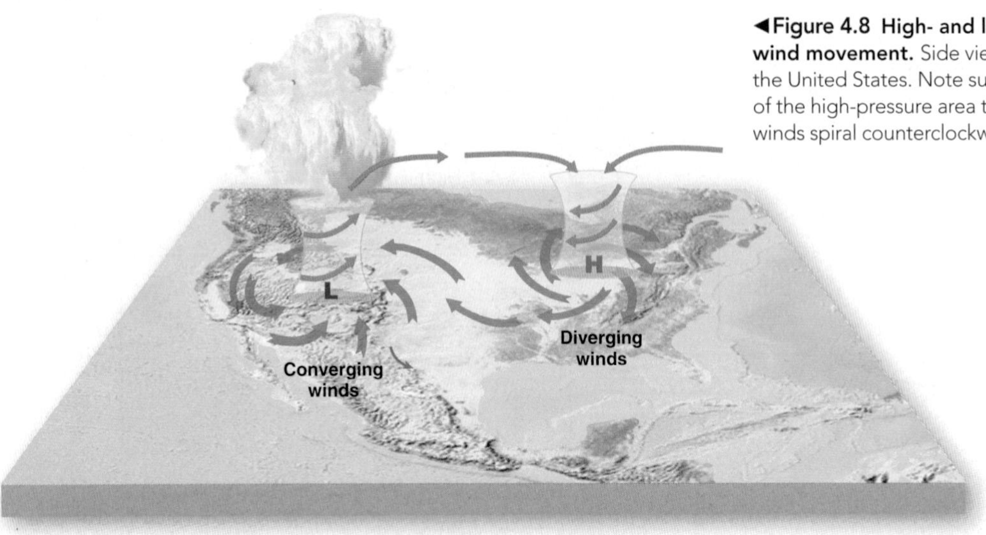

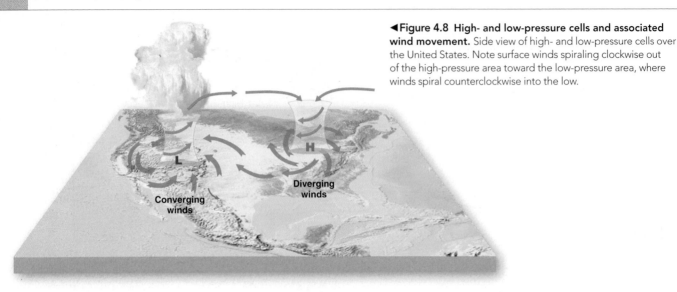

◄**Figure 4.8 High- and low-pressure cells and associated wind movement.** Side view of high- and low-pressure cells over the United States. Note surface winds spiraling clockwise out of the high-pressure area toward the low-pressure area, where winds spiral counterclockwise into the low.

moves away from the center of an anticyclone, it is replaced by descending, or subsiding (sinking), air. These high-pressure systems are typically characterized by clear skies. As surface air flows toward the center of a cyclone, it converges and moves upward. These rising motions promote the formation of cloudy and stormy weather, discussed in Chapter 5.

Figure 4.8 shows high- and low-pressure systems with a side view of the wind movement around and within each pressure cell. You may have noticed that on weather maps, pressure systems vary in size and shape. Often these cells have elongated shapes and are called low-pressure "troughs" or high-pressure "ridges" (illustrated in Figure 4.11 just ahead).

Atmospheric Patterns of Motion

Atmospheric circulation is categorized at three levels: *primary circulation*, consisting of general worldwide circulation patterns; *secondary circulation,* consisting of migratory high-pressure and low-pressure systems; and *tertiary circulation*, including local winds and weather patterns. Winds that move principally north or south along meridians of longitude are *meridional flows.* Winds moving east or west along parallels of latitude are *zonal flows.*

With the concepts related to pressure and wind movement in mind, we are ready to examine primary circulation and build a general model of Earth's circulation patterns. To begin, we should remember the relationships among pressure, density, and temperature as they apply to the unequal heating of Earth's surface (energy surpluses at the equator and energy deficits at the poles). The warmer, less-dense air along the equator rises, creating low pressure at the surface, and the colder, more-dense air at the poles sinks, creating high pressure at the surface. If Earth did not rotate, the result would be a simple wind flow from the poles to the equator, a meridional flow caused solely by pressure gradient. However, Earth does rotate, creating a more complex flow system. On a rotating Earth, the poles-to-equator flow is broken up into latitudinal zones, both at the surface and aloft in the upper-air winds.

Primary Pressure Areas and Associated Winds

The maps in **Figure 4.9** show average surface barometric pressures in January and July. Indirectly, these maps indicate prevailing surface winds, which are suggested by the isobars. The high- and low-pressure areas of Earth's primary circulation appear on these maps as cells or uneven belts of similar pressure that are interrupted by landmasses. Between these areas flow the primary winds. The highs and lows of Earth's secondary circulation form within these primary pressure areas, ranging in size from a few hundred to a few thousand kilometers in diameter and from hundreds to thousands of meters in height. The systems of secondary circulation seasonally migrate to produce changing weather patterns in the regions over which they pass.

Three broad primary pressure areas cover the Northern Hemisphere, and a similar set exists in the Southern Hemisphere. A single primary pressure area covers the equatorial region. Two of these global pressure areas are stimulated by *thermal* (temperature) factors. These are the **equatorial low** (marked by the intertropical convergence zone, or ITCZ, line on the maps) and the weak **polar highs** at the North and South Poles (not shown, as the maps are cut off at 80° N and 80° S latitude). Remember from our discussion of pressure, density, and temperature earlier in the chapter that warmer air is less dense and exerts less pressure. The warm, light air in the equatorial region is associated with low pressure, while the cold, dense air in the polar regions is associated with high pressure. The other pressure areas—the **subtropical highs** (marked with an H on the map) and the **subpolar lows** (marked with an L)—are formed by *dynamic* (mechanical) factors.

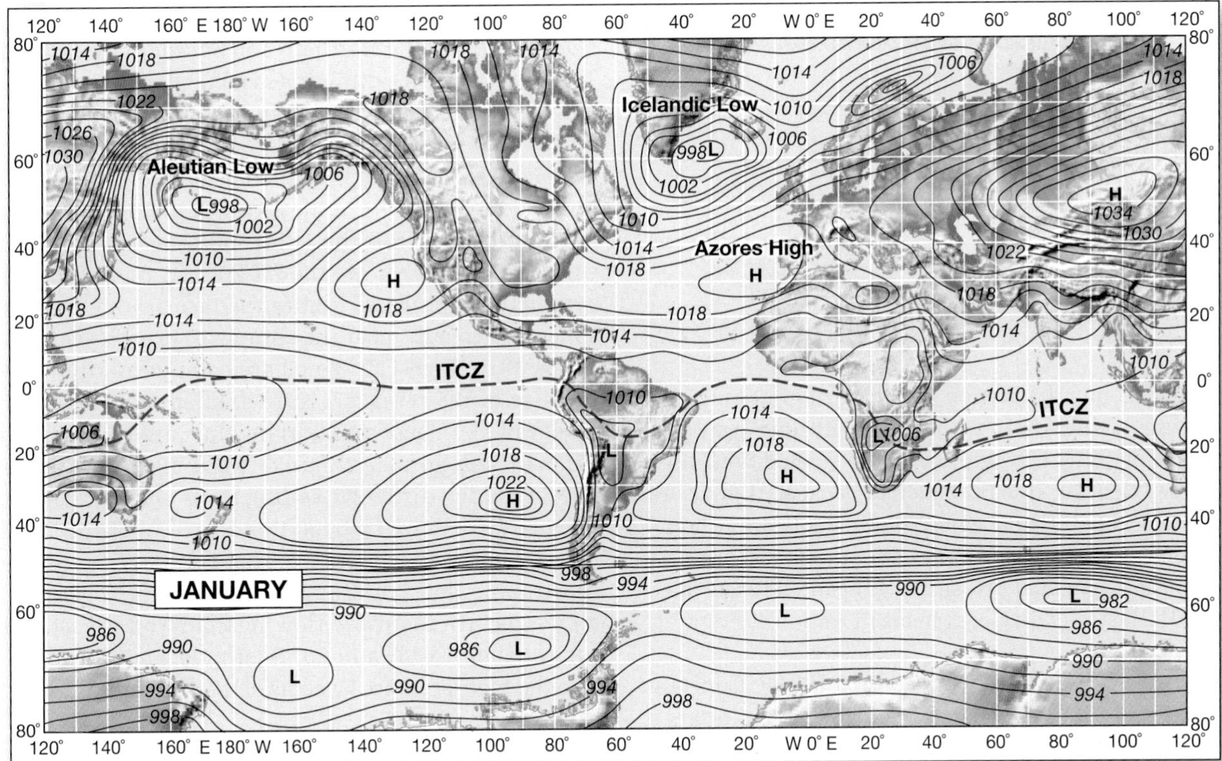

(a) January average surface barometric pressures (millibars); dashed line marks the general location of the intertropical convergence zone (ITCZ).

MG MapMaster
World Physical Environment
Sea Level Pressure January

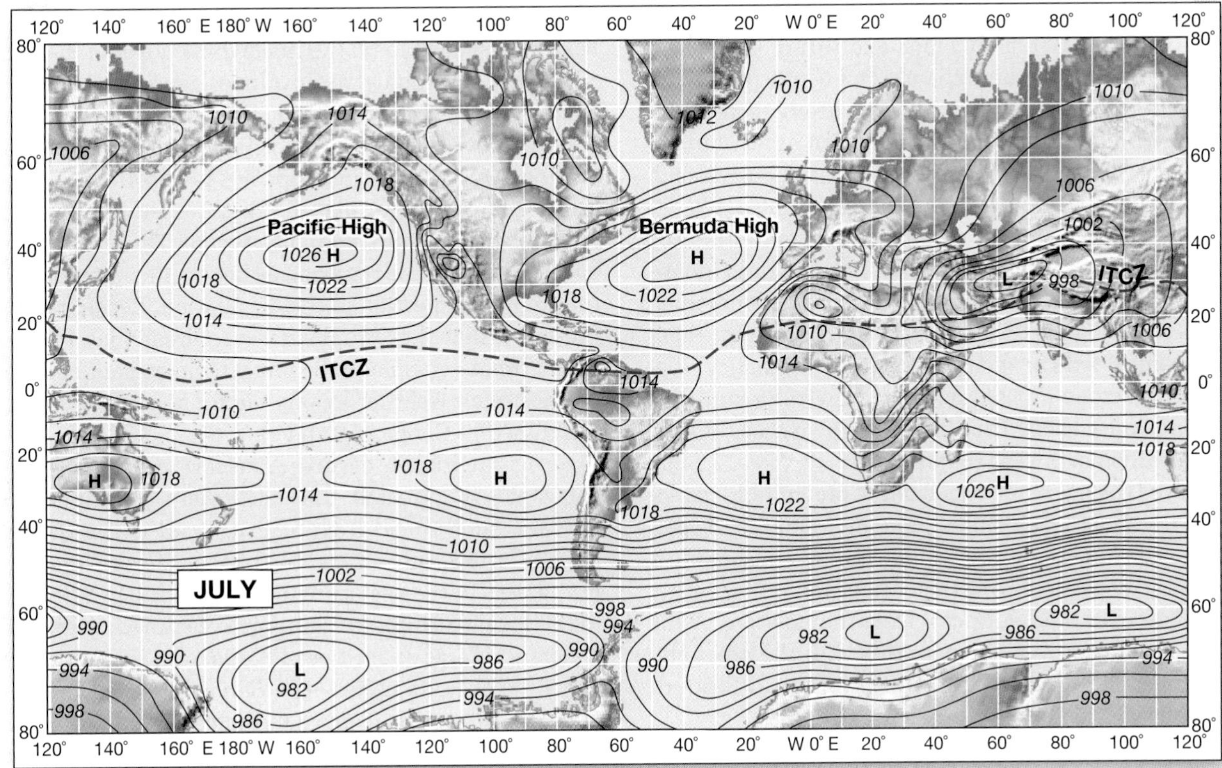

(b) July average surface barometric pressures. Compare pressures in the North Pacific, the North Atlantic, and the central Asian landmass with the January map above.

▲**Figure 4.9 Global barometric pressures for January and July.** [Adapted by author and redrawn from National Climatic Data Center, Monthly Climatic Data for the World, 46 (January and July 1993), and WMO and NOAA.]

TABLE 4.1 Primary Hemispheric Pressure Areas

Name	Cause	Location	Air Temperature/ Moisture
Polar high	Thermal	90° N, 90° S	Cold/dry
Subpolar low	Dynamic	60° N, 60° S	Cool/wet
Subtropical high	Dynamic	20°–35° N, 20°–35° S	Hot/dry
Equatorial low	Thermal	10° N to 10° S	Warm/wet

Remember in our discussion of pressure gradients that converging, rising air is associated with low pressure, whereas subsiding, diverging air is associated with high pressure—these are dynamic factors because they result from the physical displacement of air. **Table 4.1** summarizes the characteristics of these pressure areas. We now examine each principal pressure region and its associated winds, all illustrated in Geosystems in Action 4.

Equatorial Low or ITCZ: Warm and Rainy Constant high Sun altitude and consistent daylength (12 hours a day, year-round) make large amounts of energy available in the equatorial region throughout the year. The warming associated with these energy surpluses creates lighter, less-dense, ascending air, with surface winds converging along the entire extent of the low-pressure trough. This converging air is extremely moist and full of latent heat energy. As it rises, the air expands and cools, producing condensation; consequently, rainfall is heavy throughout this zone (condensation and precipitation are discussed in Chapter 5). Vertical cloud columns frequently reach the tropopause, in thunderous strength and intensity.

The equatorial low, or *equatorial trough*, forms the **intertropical convergence zone (ITCZ)**, which is identified by bands of clouds along the equator and is noted on Figure 4.9 and **Figure GIA 4.1** as a dashed line (representing the central axis of the ITCZ region). In January (Figure 4.9a), the zone crosses northern Australia and dips southward in eastern Africa and South America. In July, the zone shifts northward (Figure 4.9b).

Figure GIA 4.2 shows the band of precipitation associated with the ITCZ on January and July satellite images; precipitation forms an elongated, undulating, narrow band that is consistent over the oceans and only slightly interrupted over land surfaces. Note the position of the ITCZ in Figure 4.9, and compare this with the precipitation pattern captured by the TRMM (Tropical Rainfall Measuring Mission) sensors in Figure GIA 4.2.

Trade Winds The winds converging at the equatorial low are known generally as the **trade winds**, or trades. *Northeast trade winds* blow in the Northern Hemisphere and *southeast trade winds* in the Southern Hemisphere. The trade winds were named during the era of sailing ships that carried merchandise for trade across the seas. These are the most consistent winds on Earth.

Figure GIA 4.1 also shows circulation cells, called *Hadley cells*, in the Northern and Southern Hemispheres. These cells begin with winds rising along the ITCZ, but move in opposite directions in each hemisphere (see the cross-sectional view). The Hadley cells were named for the eighteenth-century English scientist who described the trade winds. Within these cells, air moves northward and southward into the subtropics, descending to the surface and returning to the ITCZ as the trade winds. The symmetry of this circulation pattern in the two hemispheres is greatest near the equinoxes of each year.

Within the ITCZ, winds are calm or mildly variable because of the weak pressure gradient and the vertical ascent of air. These equatorial calms are called the *doldrums* (from an older English word meaning "foolish") because of the difficulty sailing ships encountered when attempting to move through this zone. The rising air from the equatorial low-pressure area spirals upward into a geostrophic flow running north and south. These upper-air winds turn eastward, flowing from west to east, beginning at about 20° N and 20° S latitude, and then descend into the high-pressure systems of the subtropical latitudes.

Subtropical Highs: Hot and Dry Between 20° and 35° latitude in both hemispheres, a broad high-pressure zone of hot, dry air brings clear, frequently cloudless skies over the Sahara and the Arabian Deserts and portions of the Indian Ocean (see Figures 4.9 and Figure GIA 4.2 and the world physical map on the inside back cover of the book).

These subtropical anticyclones generally form as air above the subtropics is mechanically pushed downward and heats by compression on its descent to the surface. Warmer air has a greater capacity to absorb water vapor than does cooler air, making this descending warm air relatively dry (discussed in Chapter 5). The air is also dry because moisture is removed as heavy precipitation along the equatorial portion of the circulation. Recent research indicates that these high-pressure areas may intensify with climate change, with impacts on regional climates and extreme weather events such as tropical cyclones (discussed in Chapters 5 and 8).

Several high-pressure areas are dominant in the subtropics (Figure 4.9). In the Northern Hemisphere, the Atlantic subtropical high-pressure cell is the *Bermuda High* (in the western Atlantic) or the *Azores High* (when it migrates to the eastern Atlantic in winter). The Atlantic subtropical high-pressure area features clear, warm waters and large quantities of *Sargassum* (a seaweed) that gives the area its name—the Sargasso Sea. The *Pacific High*, or *Hawaiian High*, dominates the Pacific in July, retreating southward in January. In the Southern Hemisphere, three large high-pressure centers dominate the Pacific, Atlantic, and Indian Oceans, especially in January, and tend to move along parallels of latitude in shifting zonal positions.

Because the subtropical belts are near 25° N and 25° S latitude, these areas sometimes are known as the "calms of Cancer" and the "calms of Capricorn." These zones of windless, hot, dry desert air, so deadly in the era of sailing ships, earned the name *horse latitudes*. Although the term's true origin is uncertain, it is popularly attributed to becalmed and stranded sailing crews of past centuries who destroyed the horses on board, not wanting to share food or water with the livestock.

The entire high-pressure system migrates with the summer high Sun, fluctuating about 5°–10° in latitude. The eastern sides of these anticyclonic systems are drier and more stable (exhibit less convective activity) and are associated with cooler ocean currents. These drier eastern sides influence climate along subtropical and midlatitude west coasts (discussed in Chapter 7 and shown in **Figure 4.10**). In fact, Earth's major deserts generally occur within the subtropical belt and extend to the west coast of each continent except Antarctica. In Figures 4.10 and 4.17, note that the desert regions of Africa come right to the shore in both hemispheres, with the cool, southward-flowing *Canaries Current* offshore in the north and the cool, northward-flowing *Benguela Current* offshore in the south.

Westerlies Surface air diverging within the subtropical high-pressure cells generates Earth's principal surface winds: the trade winds, which flow toward the equator, and the **westerlies**, which are the dominant winds flowing from the subtropics toward higher latitudes. The westerlies diminish somewhat in summer and are stronger in winter in both hemispheres. These winds are less consistent than the trade winds, with variability resulting from midlatitude migratory pressure systems and topographic barriers that can change wind direction.

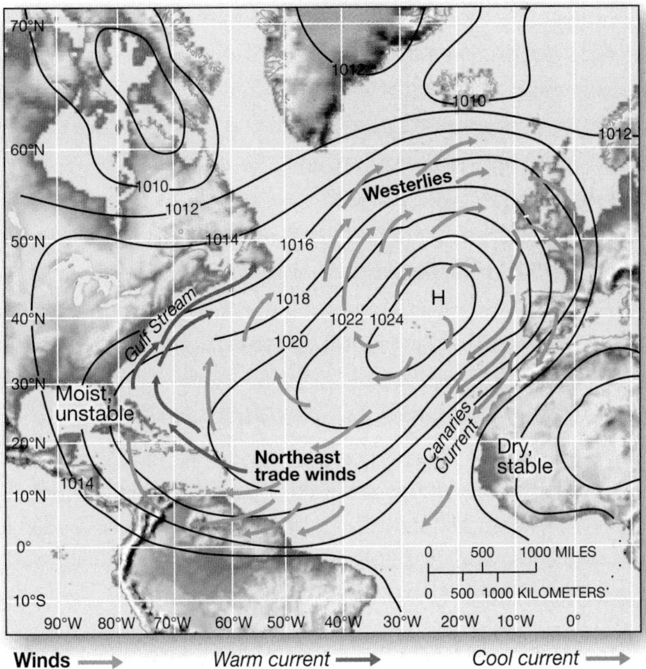

▲Figure 4.10 Subtropical high-pressure system in the Atlantic. Characteristic circulation in the Northern Hemisphere. Note deserts extending to the shores of Africa with offshore cool currents, whereas the southeastern United States is moist and humid, with offshore warm currents.

Subpolar Lows: Cool and Moist In January, two low-pressure cyclonic cells exist over the oceans around 60° N latitude, near their namesake islands: the North Pacific *Aleutian Low* and the North Atlantic *Icelandic Low* (see Figure 4.9a). Both cells are dominant in winter and weaken or disappear in summer with the strengthening of high-pressure systems in the subtropics. The area of contrast between cold air from higher latitudes and warm air from lower latitudes forms the **polar front**, where masses of air with different characteristics meet (air masses and weather are the subjects of Chapter 5). This front encircles Earth, focused in these low-pressure areas.

Figure GIA 4.1 illustrates the polar front, where warm, moist air from the westerlies meets cold, dry air from the polar and Arctic regions. Warm air is displaced upward above the cool air at this front, leading to condensation and precipitation (see the discussion of frontal precipitation in Chapter 5). Low-pressure cyclonic storms migrate out of the Aleutian and Icelandic frontal areas and may produce precipitation in North America and Europe, respectively. Northwestern sections of North America and Europe generally are cool and moist as a result of the passage of these cyclonic systems onshore—consider the weather in British Columbia, Washington, Oregon, Ireland, and the United Kingdom. In the Southern Hemisphere, a discontinuous belt of subpolar low-pressure systems surrounds Antarctica.

Polar Highs: Frigid and Dry Polar high-pressure cells are weak. The polar atmospheric mass is small, receiving little energy from the Sun to put it into motion. Variable winds, cold and dry, move away from the polar region in an anticyclonic direction. They descend and diverge clockwise in the Northern Hemisphere (counterclockwise in the Southern Hemisphere) and form the weak, variable winds of the **polar easterlies** (shown in Figure GIA 4.1).

Of the two polar regions, the Antarctic has the stronger and more persistent high-pressure system, the **Antarctic High**, forming over the Antarctic landmass. Less pronounced is a polar high-pressure cell over the Arctic Ocean. When it does form, it tends to locate over the colder northern continental areas in winter (as the Canadian and Siberian Highs) rather than directly over the relatively warmer Arctic Ocean.

Upper Atmospheric Circulation

Circulation in the middle and upper troposphere is an important component of the atmosphere's general circulation. For surface-pressure maps, we plot air pressure using the fixed elevation of sea level as a reference datum—a *constant height surface*. For upper-atmosphere pressure maps, we use a fixed pressure value of 500 mb as a reference datum and plot its elevation above sea level to produce a **constant isobaric surface** (**Figure 4.11**).

(text continued on page 123)

Earth's atmospheric circulation transfers thermal energy from the equator toward the poles. The overall pattern of the atmospheric circulation (GIA 4.1) arises from the distribution of high- and low-pressure regions, which determines patterns of precipitation (GIA 4.2) as well as winds.

4.1a General Atmospheric Circulation Model

In both the Northern and Southern Hemispheres, zones of unstable, rising air (lows) and stable, sinking air (highs) divide the troposphere into *circulation cells*, which are symmetrical on both sides of the equator.

Subpolar Low-Pressure Cells Persistent lows (cyclones) over the North Pacific and North Atlantic cause cool, moist conditions. Cold, northern air masses clash with warmer air masses to the south, forming the *polar front*. Cause: *Dynamic*

Polar High-Pressure Cells A small atmospheric polar mass is cold and dry, with weak anticyclonic high pressure. Limited solar energy results in weak, variable winds called the *polar easterlies*. Cause: *Thermal*

In the Hadley cells, winds rise along the ITCZ and sweep poleward at high altitude, then sink to the surface in the subtropics and circulate back toward the equator as the trade winds.

In the midlatitudes, the westerlies are the prevailing surface winds, formed where air sinks and diverges along the poleward border of the Hadley cells.

Infer: In what directions would the westerlies and northeast trade winds blow if there were no Coriolis force?

Intertropical Convergence Zone (ITCZ) Lying along the equator, the ITCZ is a trough of low pressure and light or calm winds—the doldrums. Moist, unstable air rises in the ITCZ, causing heavy precipitation year-round. Cause: *Thermal*

Subtropical High-Pressure Cells Persistent highs (anticyclones) produce regions where air is mechanically pushed downward, compressed, and warmed. Earth's major deserts form beneath these cells. Cause: *Dynamic*

Animation Global Atmospheric Circulation

http://goo.gl/9K2Zhw

MasteringGeography™

Visit the Study Area in MasteringGeography™ to explore atmospheric circulation.

Visualize: Study geoscience animations of atmospheric circulation patterns.

Assess: Demonstrate understanding of Earth's atmospheric circulation (if assigned by instructor).

4.1b Cross Section of Atmospheric Circulation

The cross section shows the relationship between pressure cells (rising or sinking air) and the circulation cells and winds.

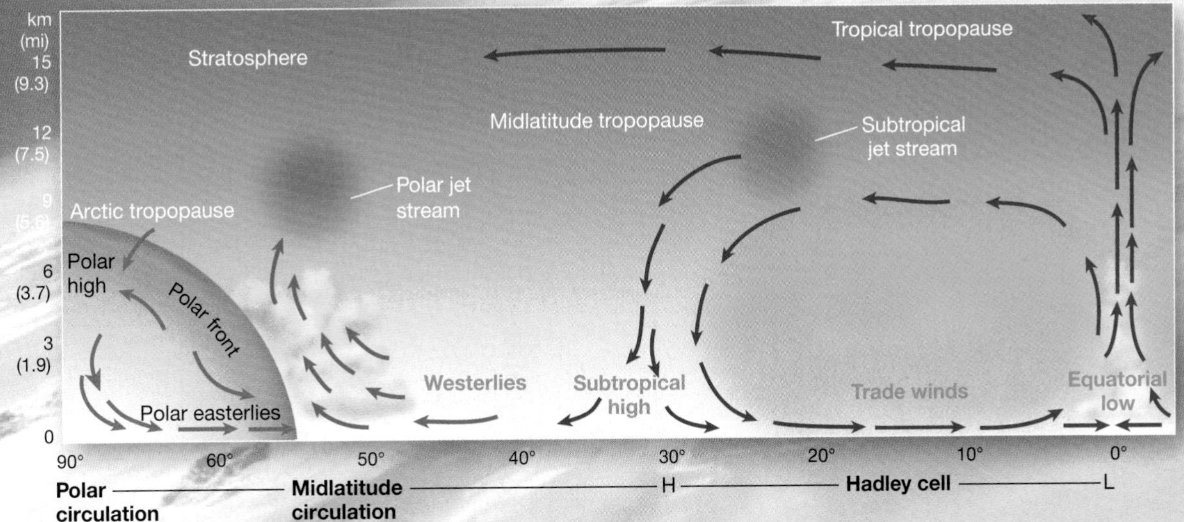

4.2 Precipitation Patterns and Atmospheric Circulation

Areas of higher precipitation in green, yellow, and orange are zones of low pressure and moist, rising air. Areas of lower precipitation, shown in white on the maps, are zones of high pressure, where air sinks and dries out. Notice the band of heavy rainfall along the ITCZ, and how areas of dryness and moisture vary seasonally on both maps [GSFC/NASA].

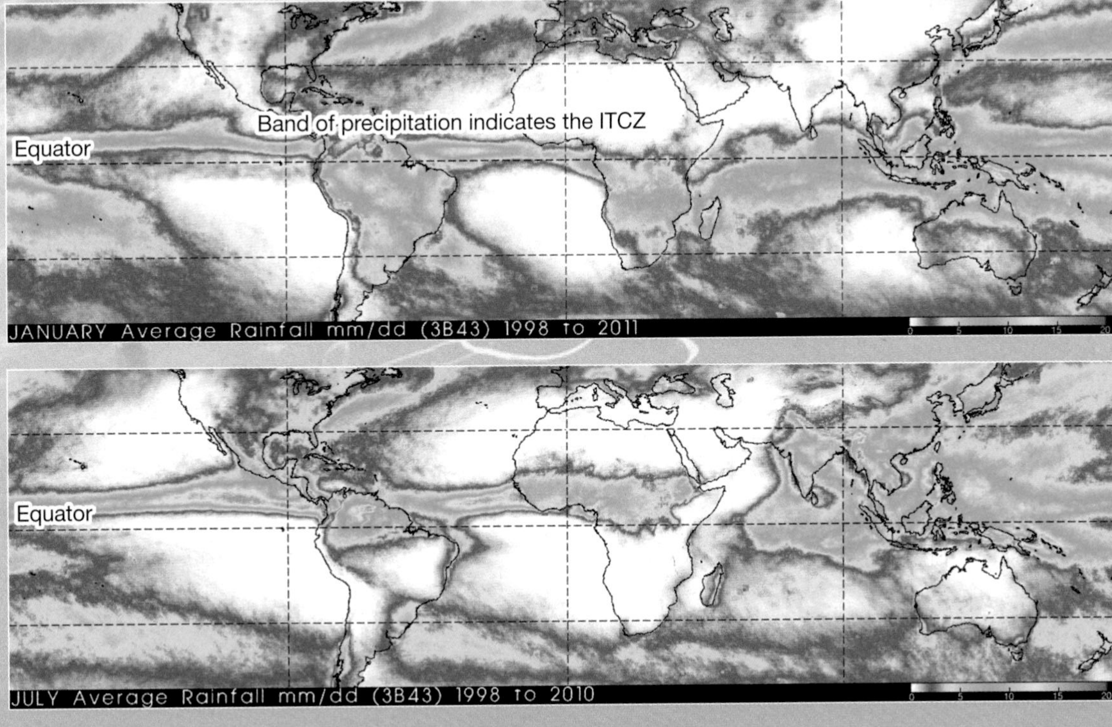

Explain: What causes the difference in precipitation between the dry and rainy seasons?

GEOquiz

1. Explain: The position of subtropical highs and subpolar lows shifts with the seasons. Explain how this shift affects climate patterns of the midlatitudes.

2. Compare: Describe surface air movements where a Hadley cell meets a midlatitude cell and where two Hadley cells meet the ITCZ. How do these movements explain the climate patterns along these boundaries?

Thunderstorms on the Brazilian horizon as seen from the International Space Station (background image).

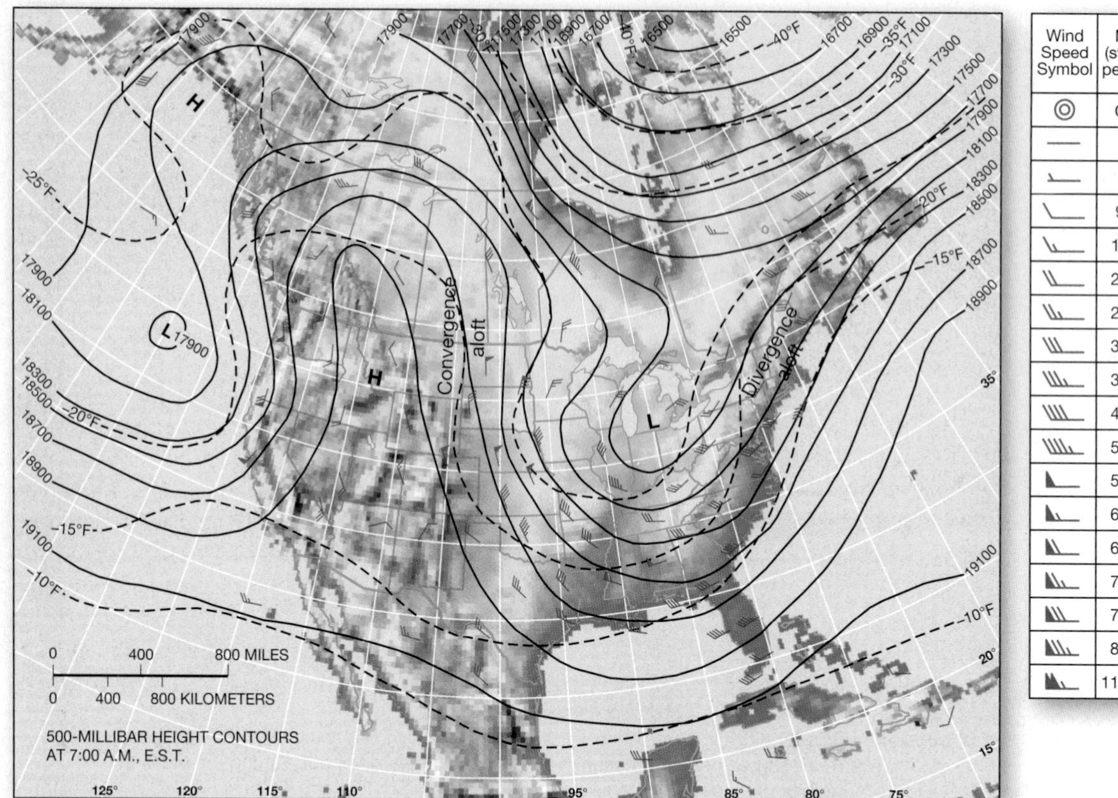

Wind Speed Symbol	Miles (statute) per Hour	Knots
◎	Calm	Calm
	1–2	1–2
	3–8	3–7
	9–14	8–12
	15–20	13–17
	21–25	18–22
	26–31	23–27
	32–37	28–32
	38–43	33–37
	44–49	38–42
	50–54	43–47
	55–60	48–52
	61–66	53–57
	67–71	58–62
	72–77	63–67
	78–83	68–72
	84–89	73–77
	119–123	103–107

(a) Contours show elevation (in feet) at which 500-mb pressure occurs—a constant isobaric surface. The pattern of contours reveals geostrophic wind patterns in the troposphere ranging from 16,500 to 19,100 ft in elevation.

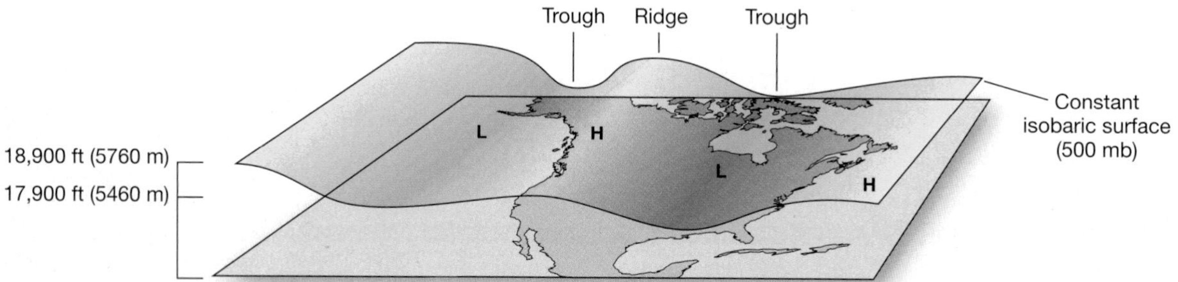

(b) Note the "ridge" of high pressure over the Intermountain West, at an altitude of 5760 m (18,900 ft), and the "trough" of low pressure over the Great Lakes region and off the Pacific Coast, at an altitude of 5460 m (17,900 ft).

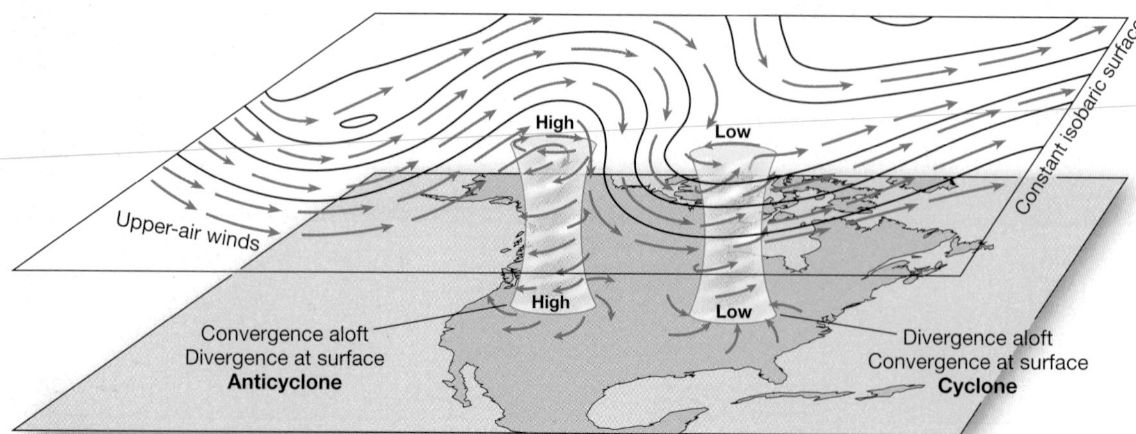

(c) Note areas of convergence aloft (corresponding to surface divergence) and divergence aloft (corresponding to surface convergence).

▲Figure 4.11 Analysis of a constant isobaric surface for an April day.

Animation MG
Cyclones and Anticyclones

http://goo.gl/ZjE1jy

Figures 4.11a and **b** illustrate the undulating surface elevations of a 500-mb constant isobaric surface for an April day. Similar to surface-pressure maps, closer spacing of the height contours indicates faster winds; wider spacing indicates slower winds. On this map, altitude variations in the isobaric surface are ridges for high pressure (with height contours on the map bending poleward) and troughs for low pressure (with height contours on the map bending equatorward).

The pattern of ridges and troughs in the upper-air wind flow is important in sustaining surface cyclonic (low-pressure) and anticyclonic (high-pressure) circulation. Along ridges, winds slow and converge (pile up); along troughs, winds accelerate and diverge (spread out). Note the wind-speed indicators and labels in Figure 4.11a near the ridge (over Alberta, Saskatchewan, Montana, and Wyoming) and compare them with the wind-speed indicators around the trough (over Kentucky, West Virginia, the New England states, and the Maritimes). Also, note the wind relationships off the Pacific Coast.

Figure 4.11c shows convergence and divergence in the upper-air flow. Divergence aloft is important to cyclonic circulation at the surface because it creates an outflow of air aloft that stimulates an inflow of air into the low-pressure cyclone (like what happens when you open an upstairs window to create an upward draft). Similarly, convergence aloft is important to anticyclonic circulation at the surface, driving descending airflows and causing airflow to diverge from high-pressure anticyclones.

Rossby Waves Within the westerly flow of geostrophic winds are great waving undulations, the **Rossby waves**, named for meteorologist Carl G. Rossby, who first described them mathematically in 1938. Rossby waves occur along the polar front, where colder air meets warmer air, and bring tongues of cold air southward, with warmer tropical air moving northward. The development of Rossby waves begins with undulations that then increase in amplitude to form waves (**Figure 4.12**). As these disturbances mature, circulation patterns form in which warmer air and colder air mix along distinct fronts. These wave-and-eddy formations and upper-air divergences support cyclonic storm systems at the surface. Rossby waves develop along the flow axis of a jet stream.

Jet Streams The most prominent movement in the upper-level westerly geostrophic wind flows is the **jet streams**, irregular, concentrated bands of wind occurring at several different locations that influence surface weather systems (Figures 4.13a and GIA 4.1 show jet stream location). The jet streams normally are 160–480 km (100–300 mi) wide by 900–2150 m (3000–7000 ft) thick, with core speeds that can exceed 300 kmph (190 mph; see **Figure 4.13b**). Jet streams in each hemisphere tend to weaken during the hemisphere's summer and strengthen during its winter as the streams shift closer to the equator. The pattern of high-pressure ridges and low-pressure troughs in the meandering jet streams causes variation in jet-stream speeds.

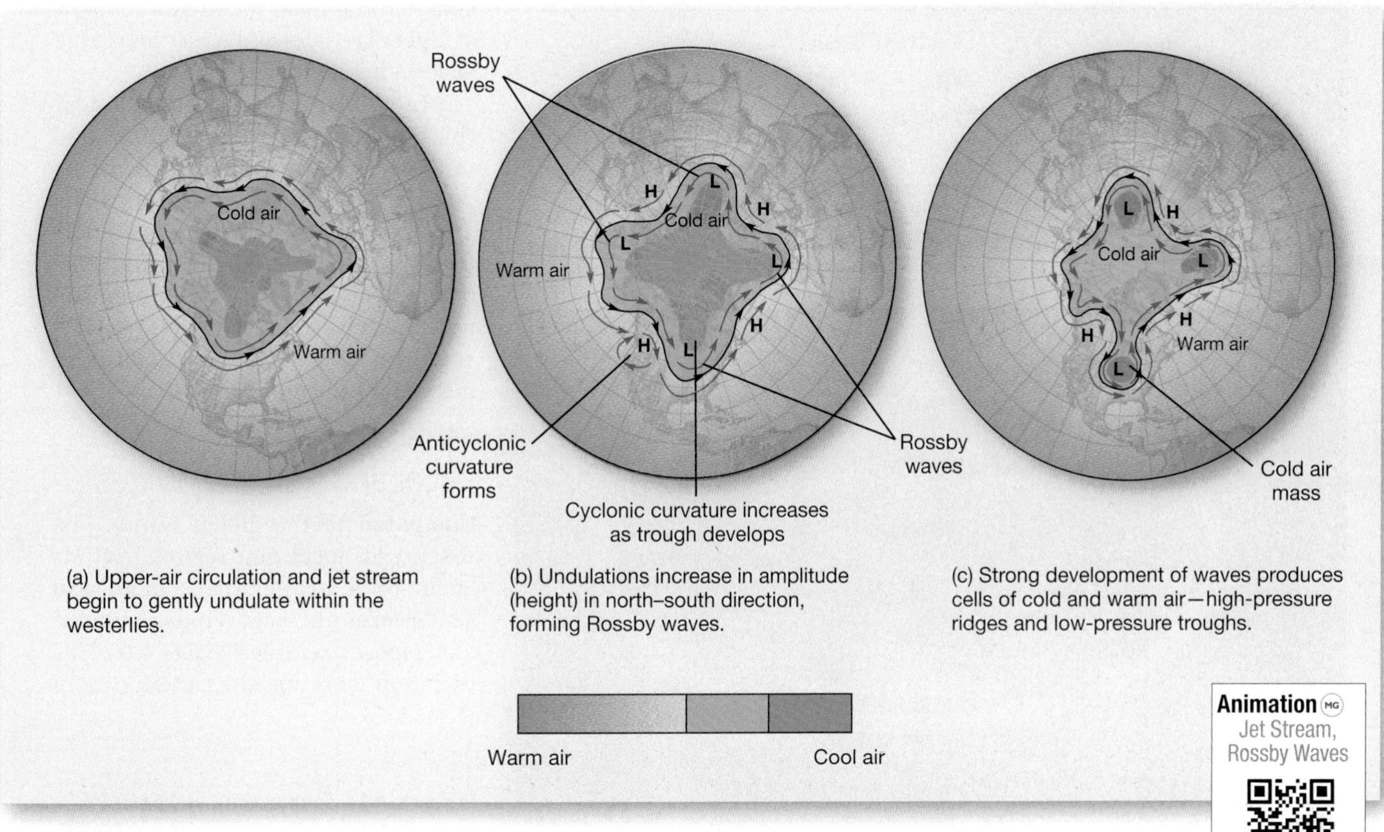

▲**Figure 4.12** Rossby waves in the upper atmosphere.

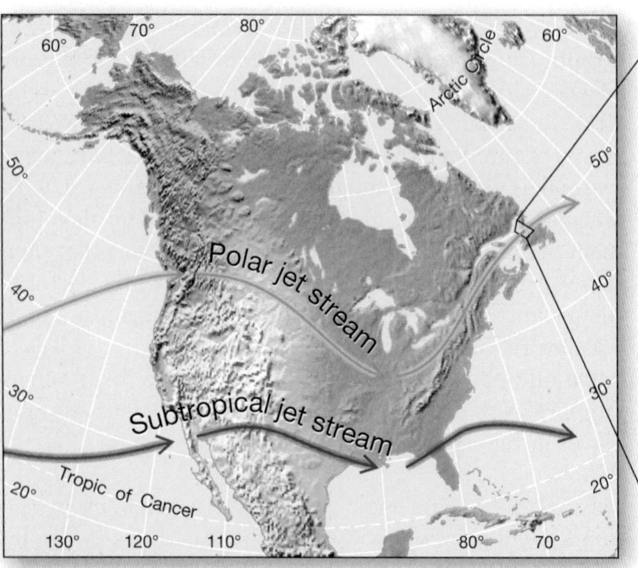

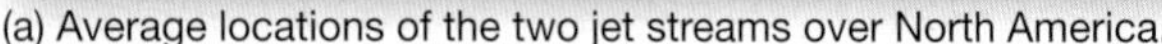
(a) Average locations of the two jet streams over North America.

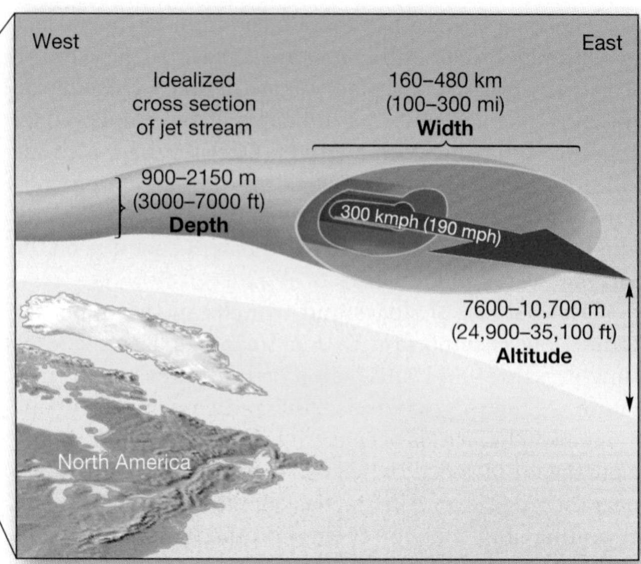

(b) Width, depth, altitude, and core speed of an idealized polar jet stream.

▲Figure 4.13 Jet streams.

The *polar jet stream* meanders between 30° and 70° N latitude, at the tropopause along the polar front, at altitudes between 7600 and 10,700 m (24,900 and 35,100 ft). The polar jet stream can migrate as far south as Texas, steering colder air masses into North America and influencing surface storm paths traveling eastward. In the summer, the polar jet stream remains at higher latitudes and exerts less influence on midlatitude storms.

In subtropical latitudes, near the boundary between tropical and midlatitude air, the *subtropical jet stream* flows near the tropopause. The subtropical jet stream meanders from 20° to 50° N latitude and may occur over North America simultaneously with the polar jet stream—sometimes the two will actually merge for brief episodes.

Local and Regional Winds

Compared to the global winds just discussed, local and regional winds occur on a smaller scale. **Land and sea breezes** are local winds produced along most coastlines (**Figure 4.14**). The different heating characteristics of

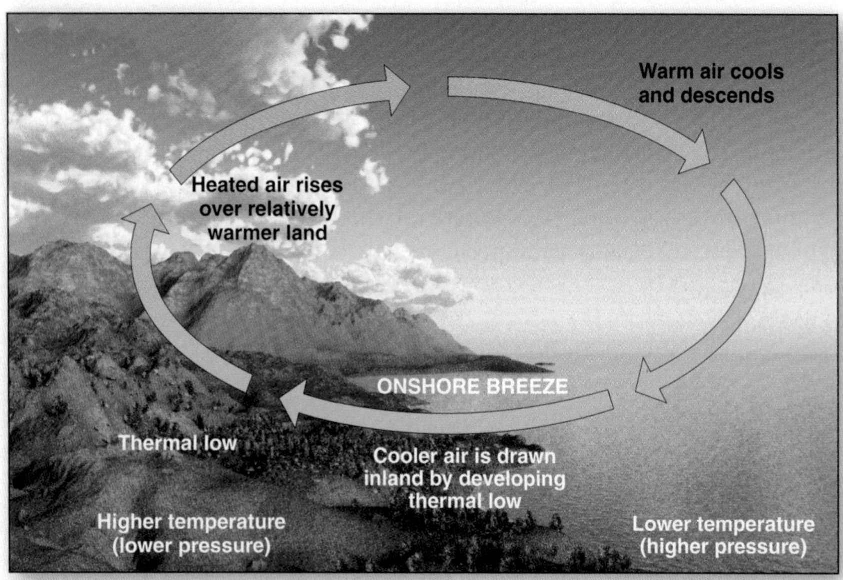

(a) Daytime sea-breeze conditions

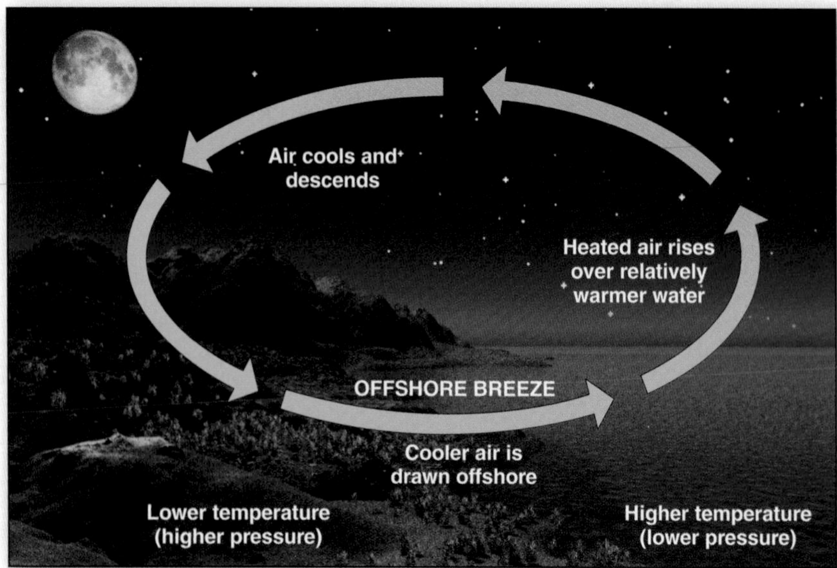

(b) Nighttime land-breeze conditions

◄Figure 4.14 Temperature and pressure patterns for daytime sea breezes and nighttime land breezes.

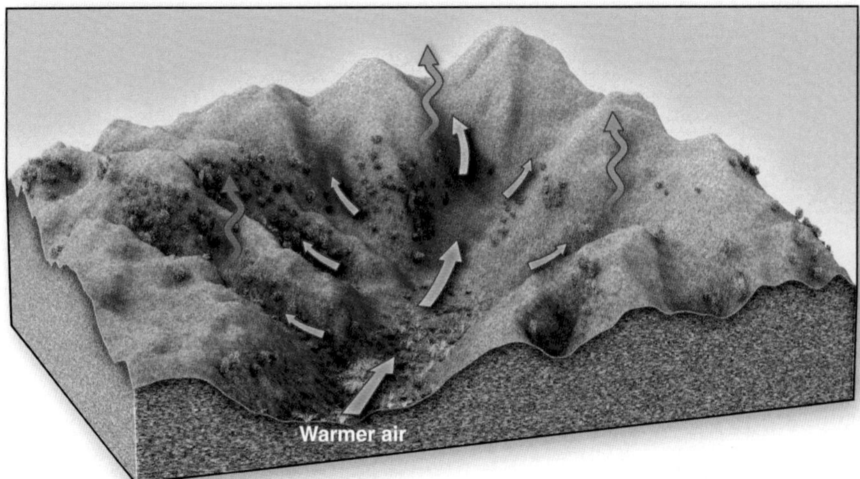

(a) Daytime valley-breeze conditions

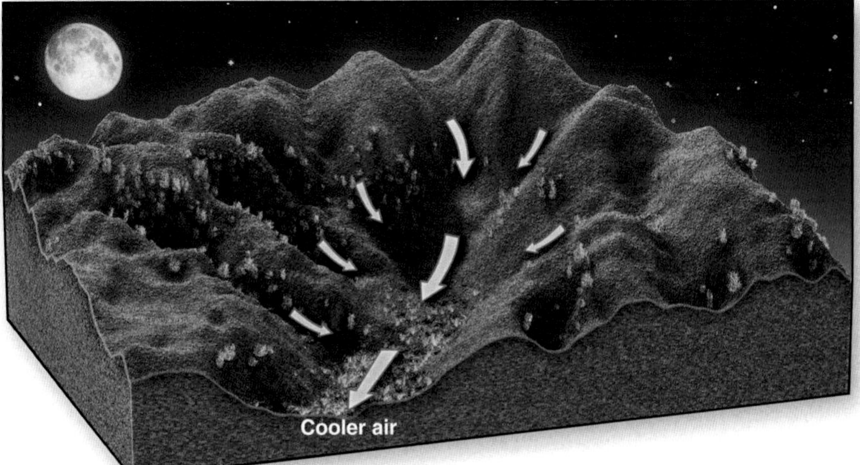

(b) Nighttime mountain-breeze conditions

◀Figure 4.15 Conditions for daytime valley breezes and nighttime mountain breezes.

land and water surfaces create these breezes. Land gains heat energy and warms faster than the water offshore during the day. Because warm air is less dense, it rises and triggers an onshore flow of cooler marine air to replace the rising warm air—the flow is usually strongest in the afternoon, forming a sea breeze. At night, land cools, by radiating heat energy, faster than offshore waters do. As a result, the cooler air over the land subsides (sinks) and flows offshore toward the lower-pressure area over the warmer water, where the air is lifted. This nighttime land-breeze pattern reverses the process that developed during the day.

Mountain and valley breezes are local winds resulting, respectively, when mountain air cools rapidly at night and when valley air gains heat energy rapidly during the day (**Figure 4.15**). Valley slopes are heated sooner during the day than valley floors. As the slopes heat up and warm the air above, this warm, less-dense air rises and creates an area of low pressure. By the afternoon, winds blow out of the valley in an upslope direction along this slight pressure gradient, forming a valley breeze. At night, heat is lost from the slopes, and the cooler air then subsides downslope in a mountain breeze.

As discussed in Geosystems Now, *Santa Ana winds* result from a pressure gradient generated when high pressure builds over the Great Basin of the western United States. A strong, dry wind flows out across this region to southern California coastal areas. Compression heats the air as it flows from higher to lower elevations, and with increasing speed, it moves through constricting valleys to the southwest. These winds bring dust, dryness, and heat to populated areas near the coast and create dangerous wildfire conditions.

Katabatic winds are drainage winds that are of larger regional scale and are usually stronger than local winds. They develop on elevated plateaus or highlands where layers of air at the surface cool, become denser, and flow downslope. Such drainage winds are not specifically related to the pressure gradient. The ferocious winds that can blow off the ice sheets of Antarctica and Greenland are katabatic in nature.

Worldwide, various terrains produce distinct types of regional and local winds that are known by local names. The *mistral* of the Rhône Valley in southern France is a cold north wind that can cause frost damage to vineyards as it moves over the region on its way to the Gulf of Lion and the Mediterranean Sea. The frequently stronger *bora*, driven by the cold air of winter high-pressure systems occurring inland over the Balkans

GEOreport 4.3 Icelandic ash caught in the jet stream

Although smaller than either the Mount St. Helens 1980 eruption or the Mount Pinatubo 1991 eruption, the 2010 eruption of Eyjafjallajökull volcano in Iceland injected about a tenth of a cubic kilometer of volcanic debris into the jet-stream flow. The ash cloud from Iceland was swept toward the European mainland and the United Kingdom. Aircraft cannot risk ingesting volcanic ash into jet engines; therefore, airports were shut down and thousands of flights canceled. People's attention was focused on the guiding jet stream as it impacted their flight schedules and lives. See the ash cloud path in the satellite image in Figure 10.20.

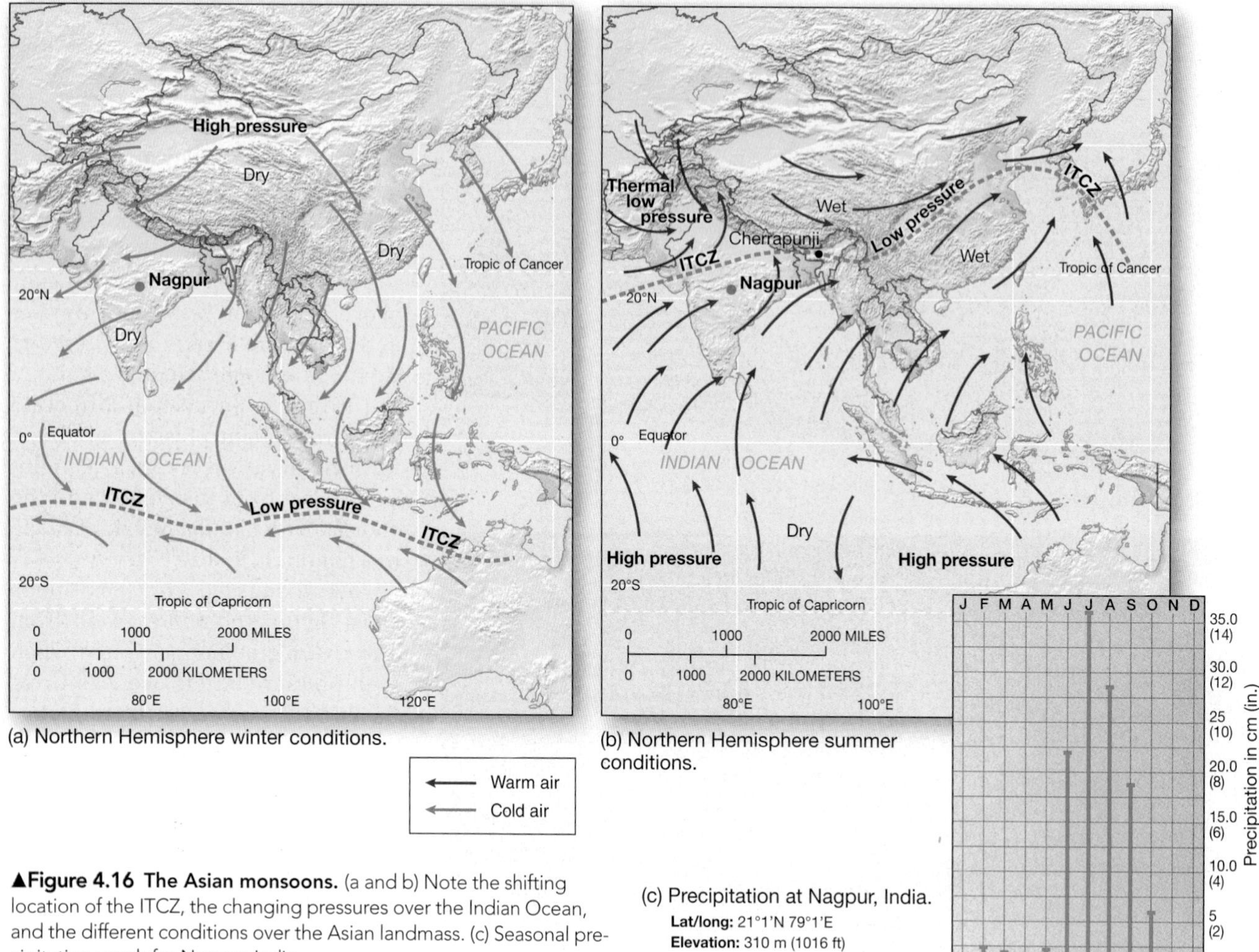

▲**Figure 4.16 The Asian monsoons.** (a and b) Note the shifting location of the ITCZ, the changing pressures over the Indian Ocean, and the different conditions over the Asian landmass. (c) Seasonal precipitation graph for Nagpur, India.

and southeastern Europe, flows across the Adriatic Coast to the west and south. In Alaska, such winds are called the *taku*. In the U.S. West, *chinook winds* are dry, warm downslope winds occurring on the leeward side of mountain ranges such as the Cascades in Washington or the Rockies in Montana.

Regionally, wind represents a significant and increasingly important source of renewable energy. Focus Study 4.1 briefly explores the wind-power resource.

Monsoonal Winds

A number of regional wind systems change direction on a seasonal basis. Such regional wind flows occur in the tropics over Southeast Asia, Indonesia, India, northern Australia, and equatorial Africa; a mild regional flow also occurs in the southwestern United States and in northwest Mexico. These seasonally shifting wind systems are **monsoons** (from the Arabic word *mausim*, meaning "season") and involve an annual cycle of returning precipitation with the summer Sun. Note the changes in precipitation between January and July visible on the TRMM images in Figure GIA 4.2.

The unequal heating between the Asian landmass and the Indian Ocean drives the monsoons of southern and eastern Asia (**Figure 4.16**). This process is heavily influenced by the shifting migration of the ITCZ during the year, which brings moisture-laden air northward during the Northern Hemisphere summer.

A large difference is seen between summer and winter temperatures over the large Asian landmass—a result of the continental effect on temperature discussed in Chapter 3. During the Northern Hemisphere winter, an intense high-pressure cell dominates this continental landmass (see Figure 4.9a and Figure 4.16a). At the same time, the ITCZ is present over the central area of the Indian Ocean. The pressure gradient from about November to March between land and water produces cold, dry winds that flow from the Asian interior over the Himalayas and southward across India. These winds desiccate, or dry out, the landscape, especially in combination with hot temperatures from March through May.

During the Northern Hemisphere summer, the ITCZ shifts northward over southern Asia, and the Asian continental interior develops low pressure associated with high average temperatures (remember the summer warmth in Verkhoyansk, Siberia, from Chapter 3). Meanwhile, subtropical high pressure dominates over the Indian Ocean, causing the warming of sea-surface temperatures (Figure 4.16b). Therefore, the pressure gradient is reversed from the winter pattern. As a result, hot subtropical air sweeps over the warm ocean toward India, producing extremely high evaporation rates.

By the time it reaches India, this air is laden with moisture and clouds, which produce the monsoonal rains from about June to September (Figure 4.16c). These rains are welcome relief from the dust, heat, and parched land of Asia's springtime. World-record rainfalls occur in this region: Cherrapunji, India (Figure 4.16b), holds the record for both the second highest average annual rainfall (1143 cm, or 450 in.) and the highest single-year rainfall (2647 cm, or 1042 in.) on Earth. In the Himalayas, the monsoon brings snowfall.

Although the North American monsoon is not as strong or persistent as the Asian monsoon, it brings episodes of heavy rainfall to Arizona, New Mexico, and western Mexico during the late summer months (**Figure 4.17**). The shift in regional wind patterns is similar to the Asian pattern, as warm summer air creates low pressure over land surfaces and draws moist air from the oceans.

▲**Figure 4.17 The North American monsoon.** Storm clouds and rainfall over Grand Canyon National Park in July 2013 are typical of the monsoon season, which lasts from late June to late September. [Michael Quinn/NPS.]

CRITICAL**thinking 4.2**

What Causes the North Australian Monsoon?

Using your knowledge about global pressure and wind patterns and the maps provided in this chapter and on the back inside cover of the book, sketch a map of the seasonal changes that cause the monsoonal winds over northern Australia. Begin by examining the pressure patterns and associated winds over this continent. How do they change throughout the year? Sketch the patterns for January and July on your map. Where is the position of the ITCZ? Finally, during which months do you expect a rainy season related to monsoonal activity to occur in this region? (Find the answers at the end of the chapter.)

Oceanic Currents

The atmospheric and oceanic systems are intimately connected in that the driving force for ocean currents is the frictional drag of the winds. Also important in shaping ocean currents is the interplay of the Coriolis force, density differences caused by temperature and salinity (the amount of dissolved salts in the water), the configuration of the continents and ocean floor, and the astronomical forces that cause tides.

Surface Currents

Figure 4.18 portrays the general patterns of major ocean currents. Because ocean currents flow over long distances, the Coriolis force deflects them. However, their pattern of deflection is not as tightly circular as that of the atmosphere. Compare this ocean-current map with the map showing Earth's pressure systems (see Figure 4.9), and you can see that ocean currents are driven by the atmospheric circulation around subtropical high-pressure cells in both hemispheres. The oceanic circulation systems are known as *gyres* and generally appear to be offset toward the western side of each ocean basin. Remember, in the Northern Hemisphere, winds and ocean currents move clockwise about high-pressure cells; in the Southern Hemisphere, circulation is counterclockwise, as shown on the map.

Examples of Gyre Circulation In 1992, a child at Dana Point, California (33.5° N), a small seaside community south of Los Angeles, placed a letter in a glass juice bottle and tossed it into the waves, where it entered the vast clockwise-circulating gyre around the Pacific High (**Figure 4.19**). Three years passed as ocean currents carried the message in a bottle to the white sands of Mogmog, a small island in Micronesia (7° N). Imagine the journey of that note from California—traveling through storms and calms, clear moonlit nights and typhoons.

In January 1994, a powerful storm ravaged a container ship from Hong Kong loaded with toys and other goods. One of the containers on board split apart in the wind off the coast of Japan, dumping nearly 30,000 rubber ducks, turtles, and frogs into the North Pacific. Westerly winds and the North Pacific Current swept this floating cargo at up to 29 km (18 mi) a day across the ocean to the coast of Alaska, Canada, Oregon, and California. Other toys drifted through the Bering Sea and into the Arctic Ocean (see the dashed red line in Figure 4.18).

In August 2006, Tropical Storm Ioke formed about 1285 km (800 mi) south of Hawai'i. The storm's track moved westward across the Pacific Ocean as it became one of the strongest tropical cyclones in recorded history—a category 5, discussed in Chapter 5. Turning

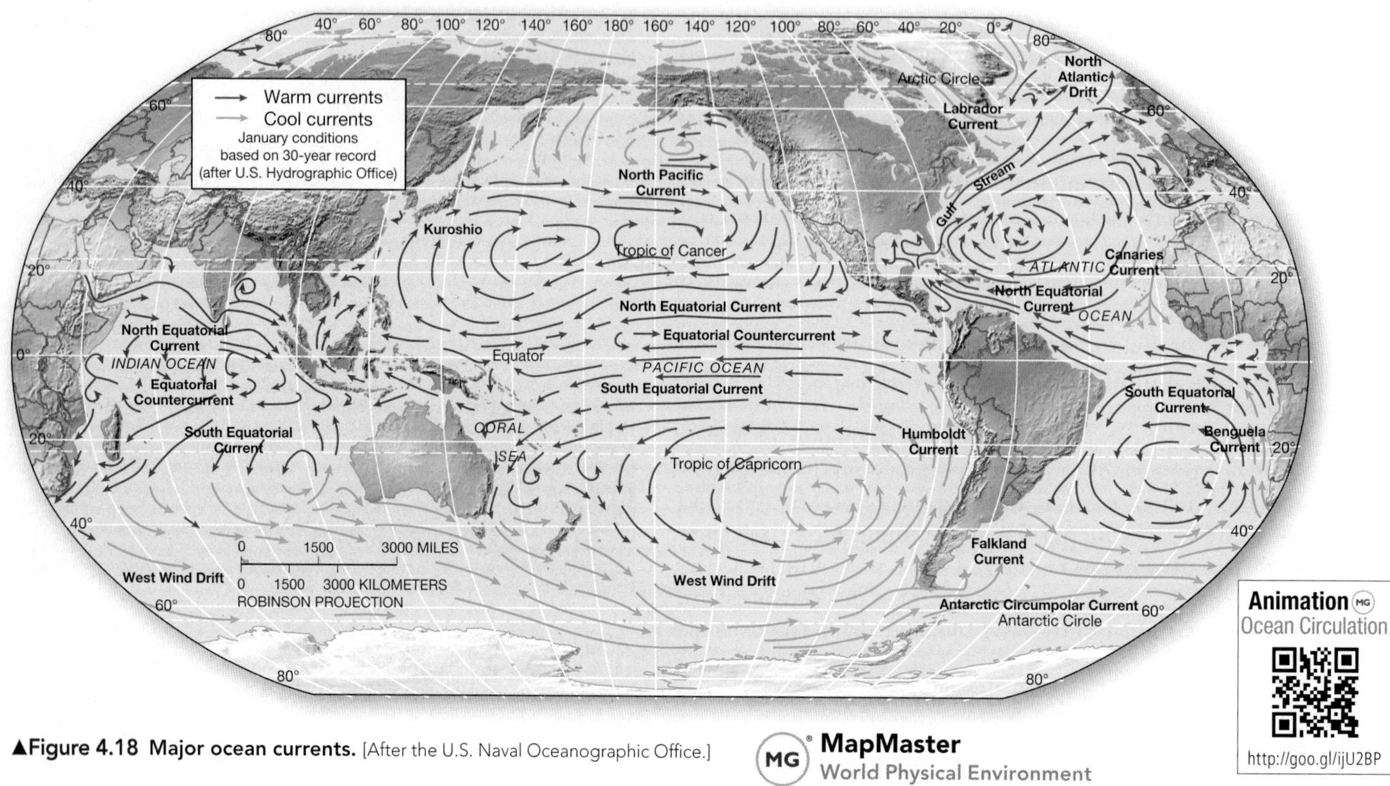

▲Figure 4.18 Major ocean currents. [After the U.S. Naval Oceanographic Office.]

Animation (MG) Ocean Circulation http://goo.gl/ijU2BP

MG MapMaster
World Physical Environment
Ocean and Wind Currents/Circulation Patterns

northward before reaching Japan, the storm moved into higher latitudes around the Pacific gyre. Typhoon Ioke remnants eventually crossed over the Aleutian Islands, reaching 55° N as an extratropical depression. The storm roughly followed the path of the Pacific Gyre as well as the track of the toy rubber duckies.

Marine debris circulating in the Pacific Gyre is the subject of ongoing scientific study. This debris consists predominantly of plastics, especially small-sized plastic fragments, and also includes metals, fishing gear, and abandoned vessels, some remaining in circulation within the gyre and some making landfall. Debris from the 2011 Japan tsunami added more material into the North Pacific; computer models based on winds and currents estimate the extent of the debris, some of which has already washed up on the U.S. coastlines (Figure 4.18). (Go to http://marinedebris.noaa.gov/tsunamidebris for more on the tsunami debris.)

MG MapMaster
World Physical Environment
Ocean and Wind Currents/Circulation Patterns

Equatorial Currents Trade winds drive the ocean surface waters westward in a concentrated channel along the equator (Figure 4.17). These equatorial currents remain near the equator because of the weakness of the Coriolis force, which diminishes to zero at that latitude. As these surface currents approach the western margins of the oceans, the water actually piles up against the eastern shores of the continents. The average height of this pileup is 15 cm (6 in.). This phenomenon is the **western intensification**.

The piled-up ocean water then goes where it can, spilling northward and

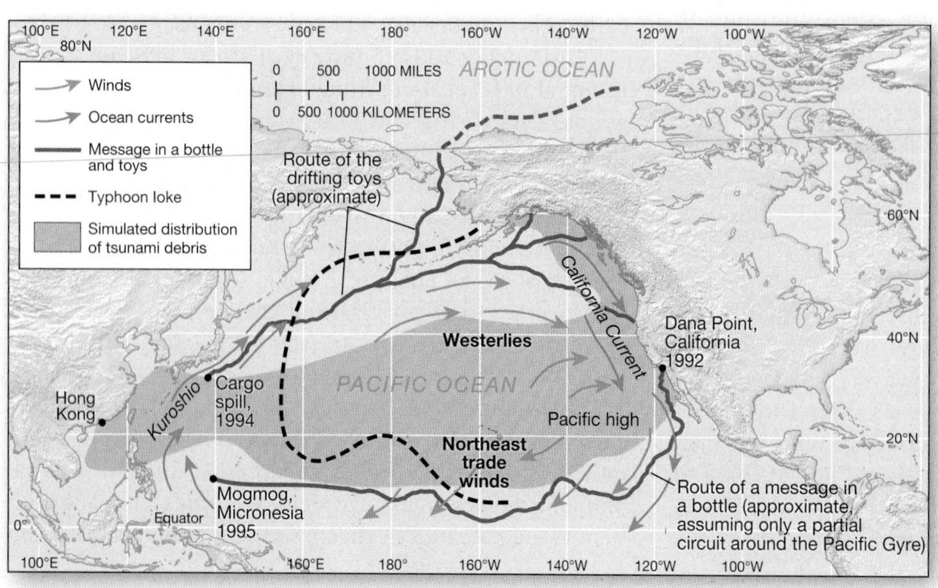

◀Figure 4.19 Transport of marine debris by Pacific Ocean currents. The paths of a message in a bottle, toy rubber duckies, and Typhoon Ioke show the movement of currents around the Pacific Gyre. The distribution of debris from the 2011 Japan tsunami is a computer simulation based on expected winds and currents. [NOAA.]

southward in strong currents, flowing in tight channels along the eastern shorelines. In the Northern Hemisphere, the Gulf Stream and the Kuroshio (a current east of Japan) move forcefully northward as a result of western intensification. Their speed and depth increase with the constriction of the area they occupy. The warm, deep, clear water of the ribbon-like Gulf Stream (Figure 4.17) usually is 50–80 km (30–50 mi) wide and 1.5–2.0 km (0.9–1.2 mi) deep, moving at 3–10 kmph (1.8–6.2 mph). In 24 hours, ocean water can move 70–240 km (40–150 mi) in the Gulf Stream.

Upwelling and Downwelling Flows Where surface water is swept away from a coast, either by surface divergence (induced by the Coriolis force) or by offshore winds, an **upwelling current** occurs. This cool water generally is rich in nutrients and rises from great depths to replace the vacating water. Such cold upwelling currents exist off the Pacific coasts of North and South America and the subtropical and midlatitude west coast of Africa. These areas are some of Earth's prime fishing regions.

In regions with an accumulation of water—such as at the western end of an equatorial current, or in the Labrador Sea, or along the margins of Antarctica—the excess water gravitates downward in a **downwelling current**. These are the deep currents that flow vertically and along the ocean floor and travel the full extent of the ocean basins, redistributing heat energy and salinity over the globe.

Thermohaline Circulation—The Deep Currents

Differences in temperature and salinity produce density differences important to the flow of deep currents on Earth known as the **thermohaline circulation**, or THC (*thermo-* refers to temperature and *-haline* refers to salinity). Traveling at slower speeds than wind-driven surface currents, the thermohaline circulation hauls larger volumes of water. (Figure 13.3 illustrates the ocean's physical structure and profiles of temperature, salinity, and dissolved gases; note that temperature and salinity vary with depth.)

To picture the THC, imagine a continuous channel of water beginning with the flow of the Gulf Stream and the North Atlantic Drift (Figure 4.17). When this warm, salty water mixes with the cold water of the Arctic Ocean, it cools, increases in density, and sinks. The cold water downwelling in the North Atlantic, on either side of Greenland, produces the deep current that then flows southward. Downwelling also occurs in the high southern latitudes as warm equatorial surface currents meet cold Antarctic waters (**Figure 4.20**). As water then moves northward, it warms; areas of upwelling occur in the Indian Ocean and North Pacific. A complete circuit of these surface and subsurface currents may require 1000 years.

Ocean surface waters undergo "freshening" in the polar regions because water releases salt when frozen (the salt is essentially squeezed out of the ice structure) and is then salt-free when it melts. This ocean freshening through the melting of sea ice is currently being accelerated by climate change. Increased rates of glacial and ice-sheet melting are producing fresh, lower-density surface waters that ride on top of the denser saline water. In theory, a large input of fresh water into the North Atlantic could reduce the density of seawater enough that downwelling would no longer occur there—effectively shutting down the THC.

Ongoing scientific research shows the effects of climate change in the Arctic: rising temperatures, melting sea ice, thawing permafrost, melting glaciers, increased runoff in rivers, increased rainfall—all adding to an overall increase in the amount of freshwater entering the Arctic Ocean. Current models suggest that a weakening of the THC is possible by the end of the 21st century.

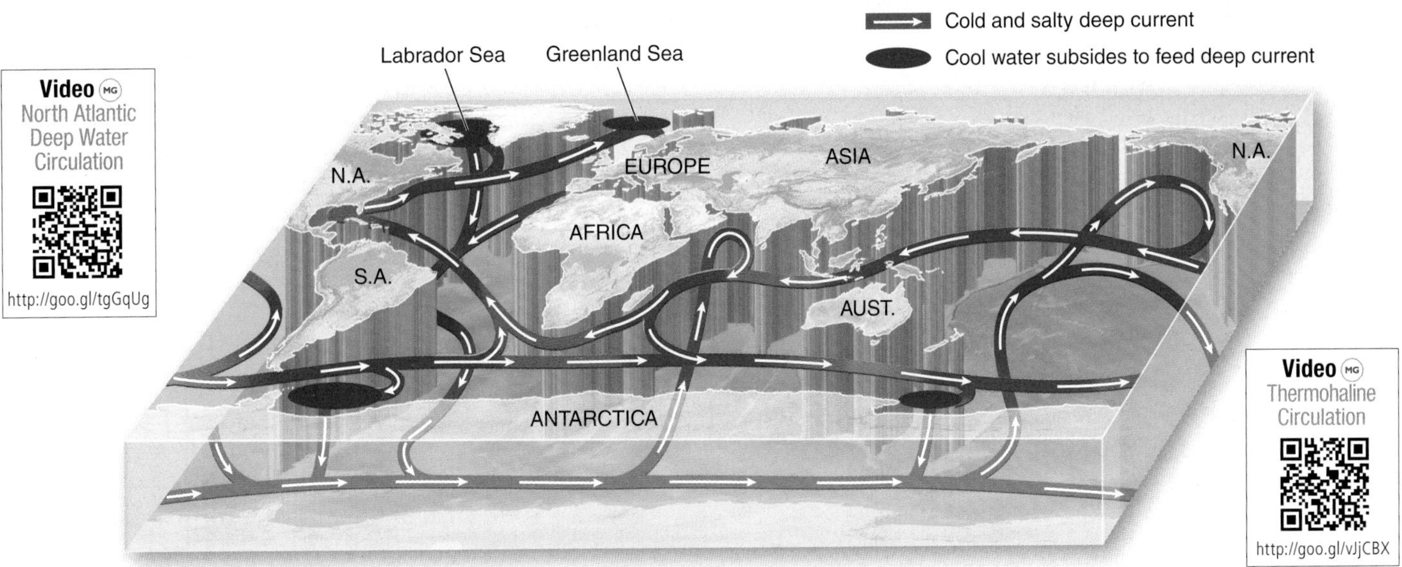

▲**Figure 4.20 Deep-ocean thermohaline circulation.** This vast conveyor belt of water draws heat energy from warm, shallow currents and transports it to higher latitudes for release in the depths of the ocean basins in cold, deep, salty currents. Four areas, colored dark blue, at high latitudes are where surface water cools, sinks, and feeds the deep circulation.

(*text continued on page 132*)

focusstudy 4.1 Sustainable Resources

Wind Power: An Energy Resource for the Present and Future

The principles of wind power are ancient, but the technology is modern, and the benefits are substantial. Scientists estimate that wind as a resource could potentially produce many times more energy than is currently in demand on a global scale. Yet, despite the available technology, wind-power development continues to be slowed, mainly by the changing politics of renewable energy.

The Nature of Wind Energy

Power generation from wind depends on site-specific characteristics of the wind resource. Favorable settings for consistent wind are areas (1) along coastlines influenced by trade winds and westerly winds; (2) where mountain passes constrict air flow and interior valleys develop thermal low-pressure areas, thus drawing air across the landscape; and (3) where localized winds occur, such as an expanse of relatively flat prairies or an area with katabatic or monsoonal winds. Many developing countries are located in areas blessed by such steady winds, such as the trade winds across the tropics. In other areas, local winds are favorable. For example, in the California Coast Ranges, land and sea breezes blow between the Pacific Ocean and Central Valley, peaking in intensity from April to October, which happens to match peak electrical demands for air conditioning and irrigation pumping during the hot summer months.

The potential of wind power in the United States is enormous (**Figure 4.1.1**). In the Midwest, power from the winds of North and South Dakota and Texas alone could meet all U.S. electrical needs. Where winds are sufficient, electricity can be generated by groups of wind turbines (in wind farms) or by individual installations. If winds are reliable less than 25%–30% of the time, only small-scale use of wind power is economically feasible.

Although most U.S. wind power is land-based, offshore wind development has high potential. The proposed Cape Wind Farm near Cape Cod, Massachusetts, was recently approved as the nation's first offshore project. Proponents hope that despite the additional expense of installation, offshore production will increase, especially along the Eastern seaboard, where population centers are close together. At least 12 offshore projects are currently under consideration, most of them on the East Coast.

The appeal of land-based wind-power development is enhanced by the income it brings. Farmers in Iowa and Minnesota receive about $2000 in annual income from electrical production by a leased turbine and about $20,000 a year from electrical production by an owned turbine—requiring only one-quarter acre

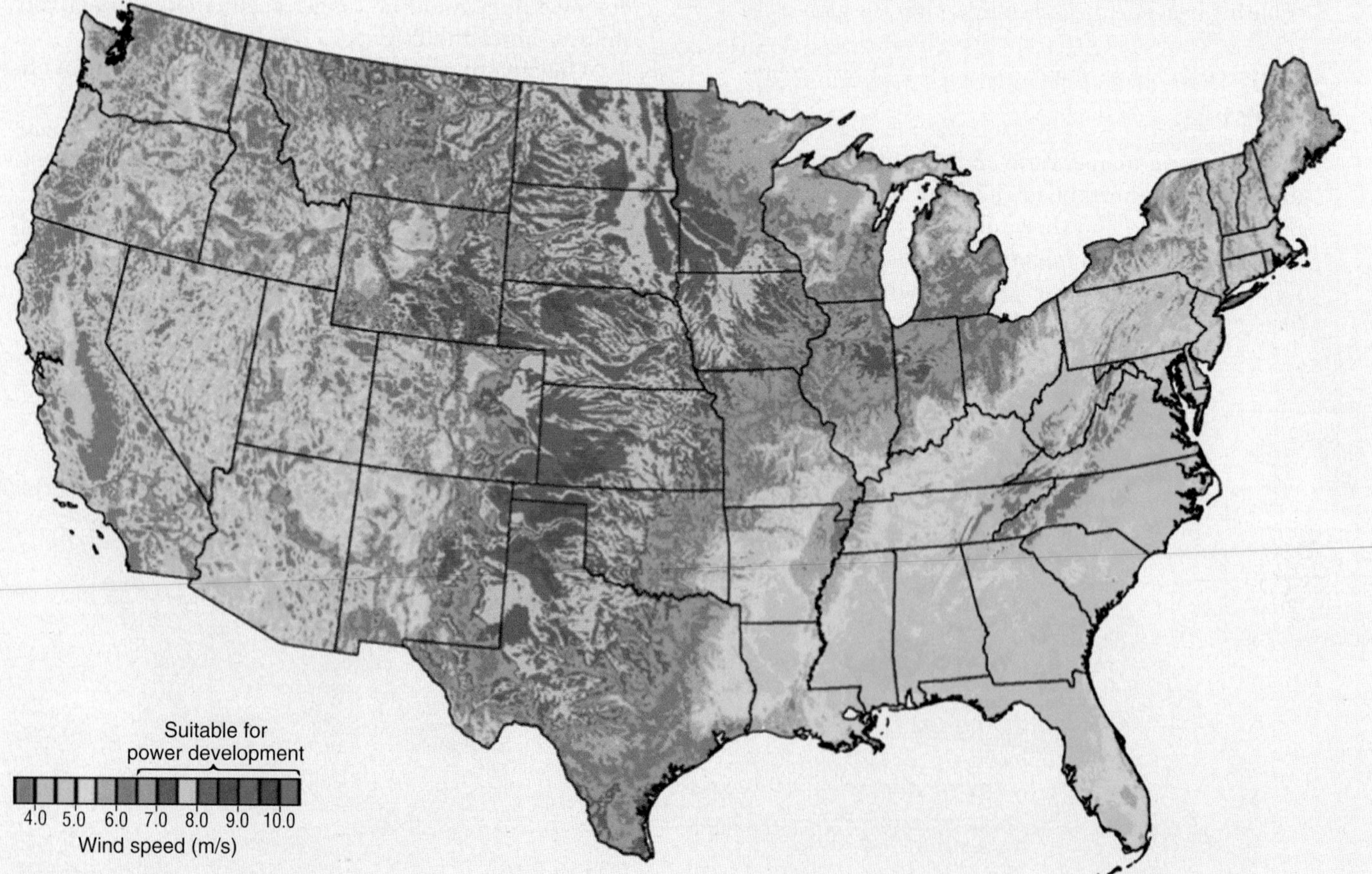

▲**Figure 4.1.1 Wind-speed map of the contiguous United States.** The map shows predicted average wind speeds at a height of 80 m (164 ft) above the ground. Areas with wind speeds greater than 6.5 m/s (21 ft/s) are considered suitable for power development. The map has a spatial resolution of 2.5 km (1.6 mi). [NREL and AWS Truepower.]

▲**Figure 4.1.2 Wind turbines at a former industrial site on Lake Erie.** The "Steel Winds" project began in 2007 and in 2012 achieved a total generating capacity of 35 MW, enough to power about 15,000 homes in western New York. [Ken JP Stucynski.]

to site the wind machine. The Midwest is on the brink of an economic boom if this wind-energy potential is developed and transmission-line capacity installed. In fact, Iowa now ranks third for installed wind-power capacity in the United States.

Wind power can also enhance local economies. In 2007, on the eastern shore of Lake Erie, the "Steel Winds" redevelopment project installed eight 2.5-MW (megawatt) wind-power turbines at the site of the former Bethlehem Steel mill, empty and contaminated with industrial waste since 1995 (**Figure 4.1.2**). The project added six more turbines in 2012, making this 35-MW electrical generation facility the largest urban installation in the country. The former "brownfield" site now supplies enough electricity to power 15,000 homes in western New York. A proposed expansion would add 500 MW from some 167 turbines to be installed offshore in Lake Erie. With the slogan "Turning the Rust Belt into the Wind Belt," this former steel town is using wind power to lift itself out of an economic depression.

Wind-Power Status and Benefits

Wind-generated energy resources are a growing energy technology—capacity has risen worldwide in a continuing trend of doubling every 3 years. Total world capacity approached 282,000 MW, or 282 GW (gigawatts), by the end of 2012, an increase of 19% over 2011. Wind production in 2012 came from installations in over 81 countries, including sub-Saharan Africa's first commercial wind farm in Ethiopia.

In the United States, installed wind capacity exceeded 60 GW through 2012, a 517% increase in 7 years. Installations are operating in 39 states, with the greatest wind-power capacity in Texas, California, Iowa, Illinois, and Oregon. This makes U.S. installed wind capacity the second highest on a global level, behind China's 77 GW, with Germany third.

At the end of 2012, Europe had enough installed capacity to meet 7% of its electricity needs, with Germany leading, followed by Spain, the United Kingdom, Italy, and France. The European Union has a goal of 20% of all energy from renewable sources by 2020.

The economic and social benefits from using wind resources are numerous. With all costs considered, wind energy is cost-competitive and actually cheaper than oil, coal, natural gas, and nuclear power. Wind power is renewable and does not cause adverse human health effects or environmental degradation. The main challenges of wind-generated power are the high initial financial investment required to build the turbines and the cost of building transmission lines to bring electricity from rural wind farms to urban locations.

To put numbers in meaningful perspective, every 10,000 MW of wind-generation capacity reduces carbon dioxide emissions by 33 million metric tons if it replaces coal or by 21 million metric tons if it replaces mixed fossil fuels. If countries rally and create a proposed $600 billion industry by installing 1,250,000 MW of wind capacity by 2020, that would supply 12% of global electrical needs. By the middle of this century, wind-generated electricity, along with other renewable energy sources, could be routine.

1. What is your overall assessment of wind power? Go to **http://www.awea.org/** and **http://www.ewea.org/**, the websites of the American Wind Energy Association and the European Wind Energy Association, respectively, and sample the materials presented. Assess the potential for wind-generated electricity, the reasons for delays in development and implementation, and the economic pros and cons.
2. What do you propose as a brief action plan for the future of this resource?

For more information on this vital research frontier, check http://sio.ucsd.edu/ or http://www.whoi.edu/ for updates (search "thermohaline" at both sites).

Natural Oscillations in Global Circulation

Several regional oscillations in global circulation patterns cause fluctuations in temperature and air pressure that last for multiyear or shorter periods. The most famous of these is the **El Niño–Southern Oscillation (ENSO)** phenomenon, which is a shifting of sea-surface temperatures (SSTs), air pressure, and winds across the equatorial Pacific region. This shift influences marine ecosystems as well as global precipitation and storm movement. Here, we describe ENSO and briefly introduce three other hemisphere-scale oscillations.

El Niño–Southern Oscillation

In the equatorial Pacific, consistent trade winds drag warm surface water away from the South American coast, causing upwelling of colder, nutrient-rich water from below. Yet, for thousands of years, fishermen in this region have observed a periodic warming of coastal ocean temperatures that temporarily lowers the productivity of local fisheries. They named this event *El Niño* ("the boy child"), since it usually happens in December, coinciding with the Christmas holiday. Actually, El Niños can occur as early as spring and summer and persist throughout the year.

In the South Pacific Ocean, the cold Humboldt Current (also called the Peru Current) flows northward off South America's coast, joining the westward movement of the South Equatorial Current near the equator (Figure 4.17). The Humboldt Current is part of the normal counterclockwise circulation of winds and surface ocean currents around the subtropical high-pressure cell dominating the eastern Pacific in the Southern Hemisphere. As a result, the coastal city of Guayaquil, Ecuador, normally receives 91.4 cm (36 in.) of precipitation each year under dominant high pressure and colder SSTs, whereas islands in the Indonesian archipelago receive more than 254 cm (100 in.) under dominant low pressure and warmer SSTs. This normal alignment of pressure and SSTs is shown in **Figure 4.21a.**

El Niño—ENSO's Warm Phase Occasionally, for unexplained reasons, pressure patterns and surface ocean temperatures in the Pacific shift from their usual locations.

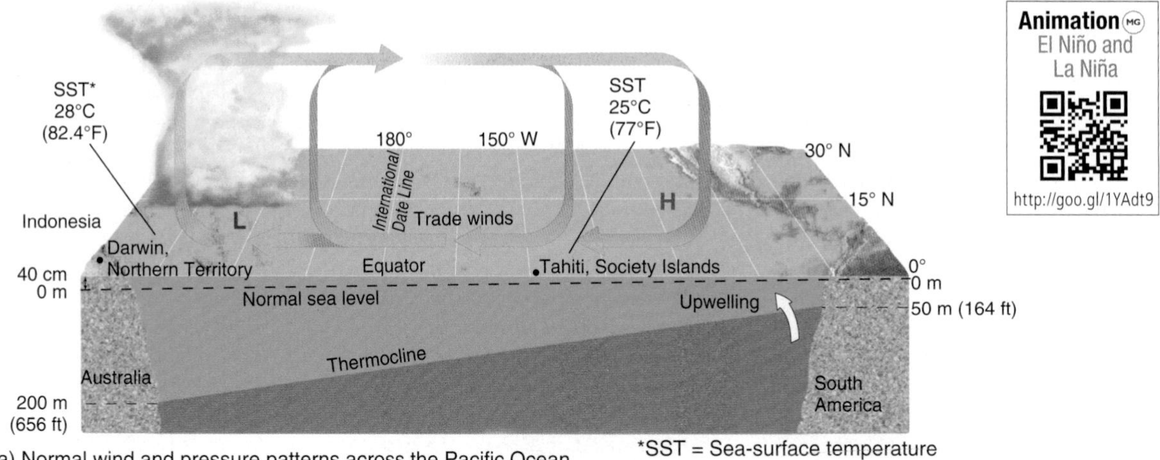

(a) Normal wind and pressure patterns across the Pacific Ocean

Animation El Niño and La Niña
http://goo.gl/1YAdt9

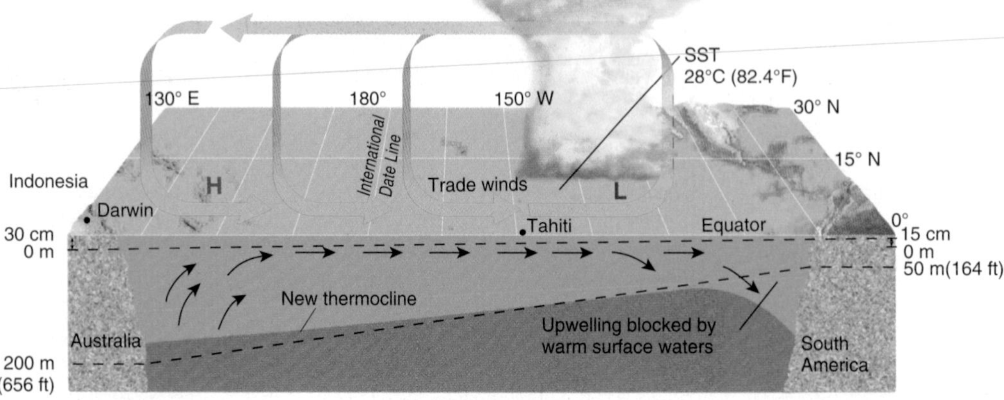

(b) El Niño wind and pressure patterns across the Pacific Ocean.

▲**Figure 4.21 Normal and El Niño conditions in the Pacific.** [Adapted and corrected from C. S. Ramage, "El Niño." © 1986 by *Scientific American, Inc.*]

Higher pressure than normal develops over the western Pacific, and lower pressure develops over the east-central Pacific. Trade winds normally moving from east to west weaken and may be replaced by an eastward (west-to-east) flow (**Figure 4.21b**). The shifting of atmospheric pressure and wind patterns across the Pacific is the *Southern Oscillation.*

As winds and ocean currents no longer pull warm surface waters westward, the *thermocline* (the transition layer between surface water and colder, deeper water beneath it) lowers in depth in the eastern Pacific Ocean, and upwelling stops. The associated loss of nutrients deprives fish, marine mammals, and predatory birds of nourishment.

SSTs may increase to more than 8 C° (14 F°) above normal. Such ocean-surface warming, creating the "warm pool," may extend from South America to the International Date Line. This surface pool of warm water is the El Niño, leading to the designation ENSO, or El Niño–Southern Oscillation.

ENSO events recur roughly every 3 to 7 years, although the interval can range from 2 to 12 years. Each event can last many months, or years, before conditions return to normal. The frequency and intensity of ENSO events increased through the 20th century, a topic of extensive scientific research looking for a link to global climate change. Although recent studies suggest that this phenomenon might be more responsive to global change than previously thought, scientists have found no definitive connection.

The two strongest ENSO events in 120 years occurred in 1982–1983 and 1997–1998 (**Figure 4.22a**). The latest El Niño subsided in May 2010 (**Figure 4.22c**). Although the pattern began to build again in late summer 2012, it resulted in a weak El Niño that ended in early 2013. Neutral conditions returned through the first half of 2014.

La Niña—ENSO's Cool Phase When surface waters in the central and eastern Pacific cool to below normal by 0.4 C° (0.7 F°) or more, the condition is dubbed *La Niña*, Spanish for "the girl." This condition is weaker and less consistent than El Niño; otherwise, there is no correlation in strength or weakness between the two phases. For instance, following the record 1997–1998 ENSO event, the lingering warm water in the Pacific resulted in the subsequent La Niña being not as strong as predicted (**Figure 4.22b**).

In contrast, the 2010–2011 La Niña was one of the strongest on record, according to atmospheric indicators (and correlated with sea-surface height anomalies,

Animation (MG) Ocean Circulation
http://goo.gl/ijU2BP

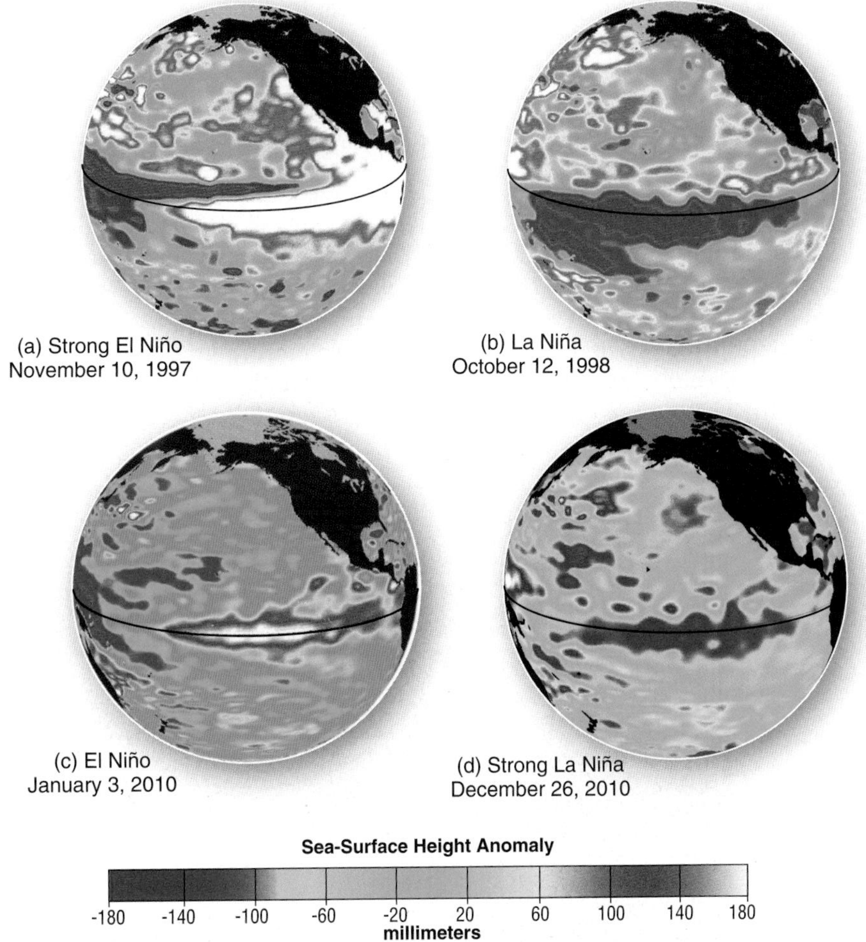

▲**Figure 4.22 Global sea-surface height anomalies during El Niño and La Niña.** Sea-surface heights are used to represent sea-surface temperatures; greater heights indicate warmer temperatures (warm water expands, causing sea level to increase). Sea-surface height anomalies represent the difference between current conditions and average conditions. White indicates the warmest water; blue and magenta indicate the coldest. [(a)–(b) *TOPEX/Poseidon*. (c) *Jason–1*. (d) *OSTM-Jason–2* images courtesy of Jet Propulsion Laboratory, NASA.]

Figure 4.22d). This La Niña intensified again in late 2011, lasting into 2012 (see GeoReport 4.4).

Global Effects Related to ENSO Although this phenomenon was first recognized for its effects on fisheries, scientists have linked ENSO to unusually intense weather and short-term climate effects across the globe. El Niño correlates with droughts in South Africa, southern India, Australia, and the Philippines; strong hurricanes in the Pacific, including Tahiti and French Polynesia; and heavy precipitation in the United States (in the southwestern and mountain states), Bolivia, Cuba, Ecuador, and Peru. In India, every drought for more than 400 years seems linked to this warm phase of ENSO. La Niña often brings wetter conditions throughout Indonesia, the South Pacific, and northern Brazil. The 2010–2011 La Niña corresponded with the wettest December in history in Queensland and across eastern Australia, where months of rainfall led to the country's worst flooding in 50 years (**Figure 4.23**). This prolonged precipitation caused rivers throughout the state to overflow their banks, inundating an area the size of France and Germany combined and causing the evacuation of thousands of people. The Atlantic hurricane season weakens during El Niño years and strengthens during La Niña years. (See http://www.esrl.noaa.gov/psd/enso/ for more on ENSO, or go to NOAA's El Niño Theme Page at http://www.pmel.noaa.gov/toga-tao/el-nino/nino-home.html.)

Pacific Decadal Oscillation

The *Pacific Decadal Oscillation (PDO)* is a pattern of SSTs, air pressure, and winds that shifts between the northern and tropical western Pacific (off the coast of Asia) and the eastern tropical Pacific (along the North American west coast). The PDO, lasting 20 to 30 years, is longer-lived than the 2- to 12-year variation in the ENSO. The PDO is strongest in the North Pacific, rather than in the tropical Pacific, another distinction from the ENSO.

The PDO negative phase, or cool phase, occurs when higher-than-normal temperatures dominate in the northern and tropical regions of the western Pacific and lower temperatures occur in the eastern tropical region; such conditions occurred from 1947 to 1977.

A switch to a positive phase, or warm phase, in the PDO ran from 1977 to the 1990s, when lower-than-normal temperatures were found in the northern and western Pacific and higher-than-normal temperatures dominated the eastern tropical region. This coincided with a time of more intense ENSO events. In 1999, a negative phase began, lasting 4 years, followed by a mild positive phase, lasting 3 years; now, the PDO has been in a negative phase since 2008 (**Figure 4.24**). This PDO negative phase can mean a decade or more of drier conditions in the U.S. Southwest as well as cooler and wetter winters in the U.S. Northwest. Scientists have recently linked cooler sea-surface temperatures associated with a negative PDO to the poleward expansion of subtropical deserts and the shifting of storm tracks to higher latitudes.

The PDO affects fisheries along the U.S. Pacific coast, with more productive regions shifting northward toward Alaska during PDO warm phases and southward along the California coast during cool phases. Causes of the PDO and its cyclic variability over time are unknown. For more information, see http://www.nc-climate.ncsu.edu/climate/patterns/PDO.html.

North Atlantic and Arctic Oscillations

A north–south fluctuation of atmospheric variability marks the *North Atlantic Oscillation (NAO)*, as pressure differences between the Icelandic Low and the Azores High in the Atlantic alternate from a weak to a strong pressure gradient. The NAO is in its positive phase when a strong pressure gradient is formed by a lower-than-normal Icelandic low-pressure system and a higher-than-normal Azores high-pressure cell (review their location

▶**Figure 4.23 Flooding in Queensland, Australia, during La Niña in January 2011.** Flood water covers a section of the Ipswich motorway, west of Brisbane, a result of prolonged rainfall associated with La Niña conditions in the Pacific. [Tim Wimborne/Reuters/Corbis.]

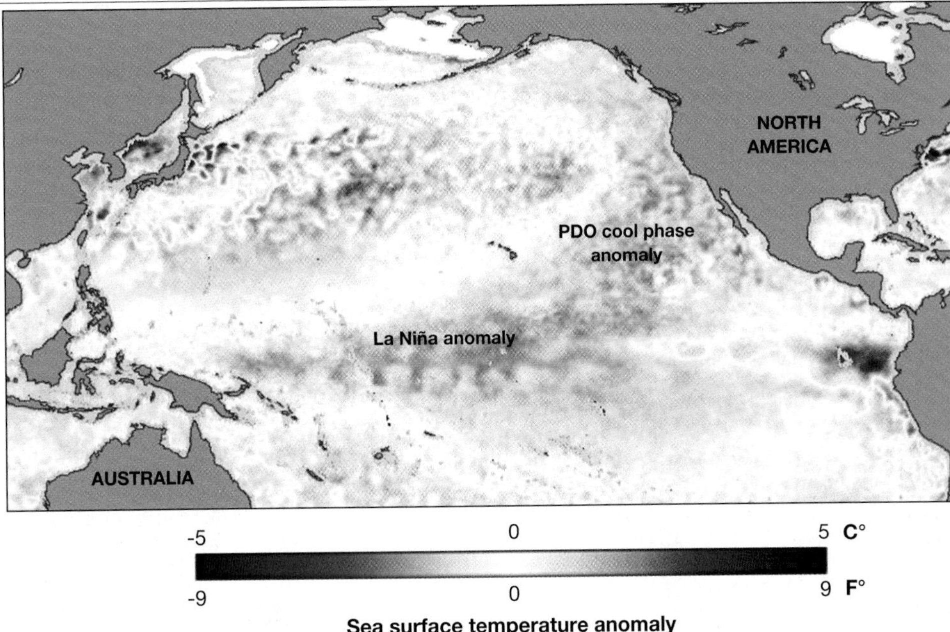

▶Figure 4.24 Sea-surface temperatures in the Pacific Ocean during a PDO negative phase and weakening La Niña. The anomaly map reveals differences in sea-surface temperatures (as measured by satellites) between April 2008 and the baseline period from 1985–1997. Positive anomalies (warmer than average temperatures) are red/orange; negative anomalies (cooler than average temperatures) are blue; average temperatures are white. Unlike ENSO, which shifts every 3 to 7 years, the PDO can remain in the same phase for 2 to 3 decades and can intensify La Niña effects. [*Aqua* AMSR instrument, NASA.]

in Figure 4.9). Under this scenario, strong westerly winds and jet streams cross the eastern Atlantic. In the eastern United States, winters tend to be less severe in contrast to the strong, warm, wet storms hitting northern Europe; however, the Mediterranean region is dry.

In its negative phase, the NAO features a weaker pressure gradient than normal between the Azores and Iceland and reduced westerlies and jet streams. Storm tracks shift southward in Europe, bringing moist conditions to the Mediterranean and cold, dry winters to northern Europe. The eastern United States experiences cold, snowy winters as arctic air masses plunge to lower latitudes.

The NAO flips unpredictably between positive and negative phases, sometimes changing from week to week. From 1980 to 2008, the NAO was more strongly positive; however, through 2009 and into early 2013, the NAO was more strongly negative (see http://www.ncdc.noaa.gov/teleconnections/nao/).

Variable fluctuations between middle- and high-latitude air mass conditions over the Northern Hemisphere produce the *Arctic Oscillation (AO)*. The AO is associated with the NAO, especially in winter, and their phases correlate. In the AO positive, or warm, phase (positive NAO), lower pressure than normal is over the North Pole region, and relatively higher pressures are present at lower latitudes. This sets up stronger westerly winds and a consistently strong jet stream as well as the flow of warmer Atlantic water currents into the Arctic Ocean. Cold air masses do not migrate as far south in winter, whereas winters are colder than normal in Greenland.

In the AO negative, or cold, phase (negative NAO), the pattern reverses. Higher-than-normal pressure is over the polar region, and relatively lower pressure is over the central Atlantic. The weaker zonal wind flow during the winter allows cold air masses into the eastern United States, northern Europe, and Asia. Greenland, Siberia, northern Alaska, and the Canadian Archipelago are all warmer than normal.

The Northern Hemisphere winter of 2009–2010 featured unusual flows of cold air into the midlatitudes. As temperatures dropped in the U.S. Northeast and Midwest, the circumpolar region was experiencing conditions 15 to 20 C° (27 to 36 F°) above average. In December 2009 and again in February 2010, the AO was in its most negative phase since 1970 (see http://nsidc.org/arcticmet/patterns/arctic_oscillation.html).

Recent research shows that melting sea ice in the Arctic region may be forcing a negative AO. As sea ice melts, the open ocean retains heat, which it releases to the atmosphere in the fall, warming the arctic air. This reduces the temperature difference between the poles and the midlatitudes and reduces the strength of the polar vortex, strong wind patterns that trap arctic air masses at the poles. Weakening of the polar vortex causes a weaker jet stream, which then meanders in a north–south direction. This forces a negative AO, leading to mostly colder winters over the Northern Hemisphere and the presence of a blocking high-pressure system over Greenland. The Human Denominator 4 illustrates this phenomenon as well as other examples of interactions between humans and Earth's circulation patterns.

GEOreport 4.4 2010–2011 La Niña breaks records

The *Southern Oscillation Index (SOI)* measures the difference in air pressure between Tahiti and Darwin, Australia, and is one of several atmospheric indexes used to monitor ENSO. In general, the SOI is negative during an El Niño and positive during a La Niña. This index corresponds with SST changes across the Pacific: Negative SOI values coincide with warm SSTs (El Niño), and positive SOI values correlate with cold SSTs (La Niña). During the 2010–2011 La Niña, the SOI reached record levels, coinciding with dramatic weather events in Australia.

ATMOSPHERIC AND OCEANIC CIRCULATION IMPACTS HUMANS

- Wind and pressure contribute to Earth's general atmospheric circulation, which drives weather systems and spreads natural and anthropogenic pollution across the globe.
- Natural oscillations in global circulation, such as ENSO, affect global weather.
- Ocean currents carry human debris and non-native species into remote areas and spread oil spills across the globe.

HUMANS IMPACT ATMOSPHERIC AND OCEANIC CIRCULATION

- Climate change may be altering patterns of atmospheric circulation, especially in relation to Arctic sea-ice melting and the jet stream as well as possible intensification of subtropical high-pressure cells.
- Air pollution in Asia affects monsoonal wind flow; weaker flow could reduce rainfall and affect water availability.

4a In June 2012, a dock washed ashore in Oregon, 15 months after a tsunami swept it out to sea from Misawa, Japan. The dock traveled about 7280 km (4524 mi) on ocean currents across the Pacific.

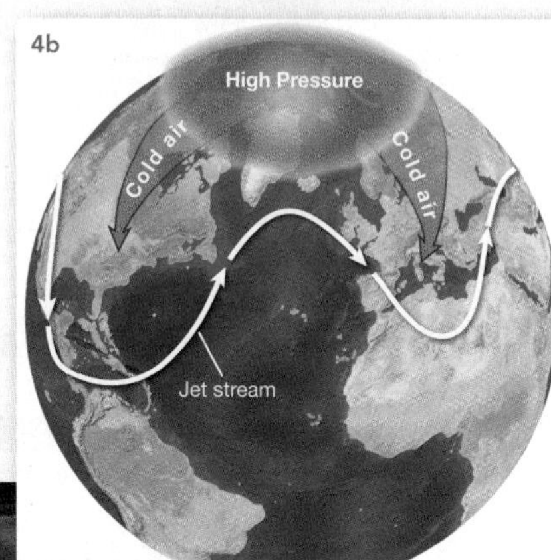

4b High pressure over the polar region associated with the AO negative phase weakens the jet stream, creating large meanders that bring colder conditions to the United States and Europe. High pressure and warmer conditions occur over Greenland.

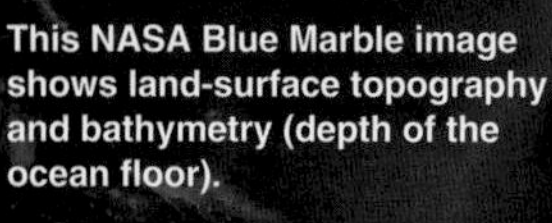

This NASA Blue Marble image shows land-surface topography and bathymetry (depth of the ocean floor).

4c In August 2010, monsoon rainfall caused flooding in Pakistan that affected 20 million people and led to over 2000 fatalities. The rains came from an unusually strong monsoonal flow, worsened by La Niña conditions.

4d Windsurfers enjoy the effects of the mistral winds off the coast of southern France. These cold, dry winds driven by pressure gradients blow southward across Europe through the Rhône River valley.

ISSUES FOR THE 21ST CENTURY

- Wind energy is a renewable resource that is expanding in use.
- Ongoing climate change may affect ocean currents, including the thermohaline circulation as well as natural oscillations in circulation, such as the AO and the PDO.

KEYLEARNINGconceptsreview

Define the concepts of air pressure and wind and *describe* instruments used to measure each.

The weight of the atmosphere in terms of force per unit area is **air pressure**, created by the motion, size, and number of molecules. A **mercury barometer** (mercury in a tube—closed at one end and open at the other, with the open end placed in a vessel of mercury—that changes level in response to pressure changes) measures air pressure at the surface, as does an **aneroid barometer** (a closed cell, partially evacuated of air, that detects changes in pressure).

Wind is the horizontal movement of air across Earth's surface; turbulence adds updrafts and downdrafts, and thus a vertical component, to the definition. Wind speed is measured with an **anemometer** (a device with cups that are pushed by the wind) and its direction with a **wind vane** (a flat blade or surface that is directed by the wind).

air pressure (p. 108)
mercury barometer (p. 110)
aneroid barometer (p. 110)
wind (p. 110)
anemometer (p. 110)
wind vane (p. 110)

1. How does air exert pressure? Describe the basic instrument used to measure air pressure. Compare the operation of two different types of instruments discussed.
2. What is the relationship between air pressure and density and between air pressure and temperature?
3. What is normal sea-level pressure in millimeters? Millibars? Inches? Kilopascals?
4. What is a possible explanation for the beautiful sunrises and sunsets during the summer of 1992 in North America? Relate your answer to global circulation.
5. Explain this statement: "The atmosphere socializes humanity, making the world a spatially linked society." Illustrate your answer with some examples.
6. Define wind. How is it measured? How is its direction determined?

Explain the four driving forces within the atmosphere—gravity, pressure gradient force, Coriolis force, and friction force—and *locate* the primary high- and low-pressure areas and principal winds.

The pressure that Earth's *gravitational force* exerts on the atmosphere is virtually uniform worldwide. The **pressure gradient force** drives winds, as air moves from areas of high pressure to areas of low pressure. Maps portray air pressure patterns using the **isobar**—an isoline that connects points of equal pressure. The **Coriolis force** causes an apparent deflection in the path of winds or ocean currents, owing to the rotation of Earth. This force deflects objects to the right in the Northern Hemisphere and to the left in the Southern Hemisphere. The **friction force** drags winds along Earth's varied surfaces in opposition to the pressure gradient. The pressure gradient and Coriolis force in combination (absent the friction force) produce **geostrophic winds**, which move parallel to isobars, characteristic of winds above the surface frictional layer.

In a high-pressure system, or **anticyclone**, winds descend and diverge, spiraling outward in a clockwise direction in the Northern Hemisphere. In a low-pressure system, or **cyclone**, winds converge and ascend, spiraling upward in a counterclockwise direction in the Northern Hemisphere. (The rotational directions are reversed for each in the Southern Hemisphere.)

The pattern of high and low pressures on Earth in generalized belts in each hemisphere produces the distribution of specific wind systems. These primary pressure regions are the **equatorial low**, the weak **polar highs** (at both the North and the South Poles), the **subtropical highs**, and the **subpolar lows**.

All along the equator, winds converge into the equatorial low, creating the **intertropical convergence zone (ITCZ)**. Air rises in this zone and descends in the subtropics in each hemisphere. The winds returning to the ITCZ from the northeast in the Northern Hemisphere and from the southeast in the Southern Hemisphere produce the **trade winds**.

The subtropical high-pressure cells on Earth are generally located between 20° and 35° in each hemisphere. In the Northern Hemisphere, they include the *Bermuda High*, *Azores High*, and *Pacific High*. Winds flowing out of the subtropics to higher latitudes produce the **westerlies** in each hemisphere.

In January, two low-pressure cells known as the *Aleutian Low* and *Icelandic Low* dominate the North Pacific and Atlantic, respectively. The region of contrast between cold polar air and the warmer air toward the equator is the **polar front**. The weak and variable **polar easterlies** diverge from the high-pressure cells at each pole, the stronger of which is the **Antarctic High**.

pressure gradient force (p. 112)
isobar (p. 112)
Coriolis force (p. 112)
friction force (p. 114)
geostrophic wind (p. 114)
anticyclone (p. 114)
cyclone (p. 114)
equatorial low (p. 116)
polar high (p. 116)
subtropical high (p. 116)
subpolar low (p. 116)
intertropical convergence zone (ITCZ) (p. 118)
trade winds (p. 118)
westerlies (p. 119)
polar front (p. 119)
polar easterlies (p. 119)
Antarctic High (p. 119)

7. What does an isobaric map of surface air pressure portray? Contrast pressures over North America for January and July.
8. Describe the effect of the Coriolis force. Explain how it appears to deflect atmospheric and oceanic circulations.
9. What are geostrophic winds, and where are they encountered in the atmosphere?
10. Describe the horizontal and vertical air motions in a high-pressure anticyclone and in a low-pressure cyclone.
11. Construct a simple diagram of Earth's general circulation; begin by labeling the four principal pressure belts or zones, and then add arrows between these pressure systems to denote the three principal wind systems.

12. How is the intertropical convergence zone (ITCZ) related to the equatorial low? How does the ITCZ appear on the satellite images of accumulated precipitation for January and July in GIA 4.2?
13. Characterize the belt of subtropical high pressure on Earth: Name several specific cells. Describe the generation of westerlies and trade winds and their effects on sailing conditions.
14. What is the relationship among the Aleutian Low, the Icelandic Low, and migratory low-pressure cyclonic storms in North America? In Europe?

Describe upper-air circulation and *define* the jet streams.

A **constant isobaric surface**—a surface that varies in altitude from place to place according to where a given air pressure, such as 500 mb, occurs—is useful for visualizing geostrophic wind patterns in the middle and upper troposphere. The variations in altitude of this surface show the ridges and troughs around high- and low-pressure systems. Areas of converging upper-air winds sustain surface highs, and areas of diverging upper-air winds sustain surface lows.

Vast wave motions in the upper-air westerlies are known as **Rossby waves**. Prominent streams of high-speed westerly winds in the upper-level troposphere are the **jet streams**. Depending on their latitudinal position in either hemisphere, they are termed the *polar jet stream* or the *subtropical jet stream*.

constant isobaric surface (p. 119)
Rossby waves (p. 123)
jet stream (p. 123)

15. What is the relation between wind speed and the spacing of isobars?
16. How is the constant isobaric surface, especially the ridges and troughs, related to surface-pressure systems? To divergence aloft and surface lows? To convergence aloft and surface highs?
17. Relate the jet-stream phenomenon to general upper-air circulation. How is the presence of this circulation related to airline schedules for the trip from New York to San Francisco and for the return trip to New York?

Explain several types of local and regional winds, including monsoons.

The difference in the heating characteristics of land and water surfaces creates **land and sea breezes**. Temperature differences during the day and evening between valleys and mountain summits cause **mountain and valley breezes**. **Katabatic winds**, or gravity drainage winds, are of larger regional scale and are stronger than valley and mountain breezes under some conditions. These winds develop on an elevated plateau or highland where layers of air at the surface cool, become denser, and flow downslope.

Intense, seasonally shifting wind systems occur in the tropics over Southeast Asia, Indonesia, India, northern Australia, equatorial Africa, and southern Arizona. These winds are associated with an annual cycle of returning precipitation with the summer Sun and named using the Arabic word for season, *mausim*, or **monsoon**. The location and size of the Asian landmass and its proximity to the seasonally shifting ITCZ over the Indian Ocean drive the monsoons of southern and eastern Asia.

land and sea breezes (p. 124)
mountain and valley breezes (p. 125)
katabatic wind (p. 125)
monsoon (p. 126)

18. People living along coastlines generally experience variations in winds from day to night. Explain the factors that produce these changing wind patterns.
19. The arrangement of mountains and nearby valleys produces local wind patterns. Explain the day and night winds that might develop.
20. Describe the seasonal pressure patterns that produce the Asian monsoonal wind and precipitation patterns. Contrast January and July conditions.

Sketch the basic pattern of Earth's major surface ocean currents and deep thermohaline circulation.

Ocean currents are primarily caused by the frictional drag of wind and occur worldwide at varying intensities, temperatures, and speeds, both along the surface and at great depths in the oceanic basins. The circulation around subtropical high-pressure cells in both hemispheres is discernible on the ocean-circulation map—these gyres are usually offset toward the western side of each ocean basin.

The trade winds converge along the ITCZ and push enormous quantities of water that pile up along the eastern shore of continents in a process known as the **western intensification**. Where surface water is swept away from a coast, either by surface divergence (induced by the Coriolis force) or by offshore winds, an **upwelling current** occurs. This cool water generally is rich with nutrients and rises from great depths to replace the vacating water. In oceanic regions where water accumulates, the excess water gravitates downward in a **downwelling current**. These currents generate vertical mixing of heat energy and salinity.

Differences in temperatures and salinity produce density differences important to the flow of deep, sometimes vertical, currents; this is Earth's **thermohaline circulation**. Traveling at slower speeds than wind-driven surface currents, the thermohaline circulation hauls larger volumes of water. Scientists are concerned that increased surface temperatures in the ocean and atmosphere, coupled with climate-related changes in salinity, can alter the rate of thermohaline circulation in the oceans.

western intensification (p. 129)
upwelling current (p. 129)
downwelling current (p. 129)
thermohaline circulation (p. 129)

21. Define the western intensification. How is it related to the Gulf Stream and the Kuroshio Current?
22. Where on Earth are upwelling currents experienced? What is the nature of these currents? Where are the four areas of downwelling that feed these dense bottom currents?
23. What is meant by the deep-ocean thermohaline circulation? At what rates do these currents flow? How might this circulation be related to the Gulf Stream in the western Atlantic Ocean?
24. Relative to Question 23, what effects might climate change have on these deep currents?

Summarize several multiyear oscillations of air temperature, air pressure, and circulation associated with the Arctic, Atlantic, and Pacific Oceans.

Several system fluctuations that occur in multiyear or shorter periods are important in the global circulation picture. The most famous of these is the **El Niño–Southern Oscillation (ENSO)** in the Pacific Ocean, which affects interannual variability in climate on a global scale.

The *Pacific Decadal Oscillation (PDO)* is a pattern in which sea-surface temperatures and related air pressure vary back and forth between two regions of the Pacific Ocean: (1) the northern and tropical western Pacific and (2) the northern and tropical eastern Pacific, along the North American west coast. The PDO switches between positive and negative phases in 20- to 30-year cycles.

A north–south fluctuation of atmospheric variability marks the *North Atlantic Oscillation (NAO)*, in which pressure differences between the Icelandic Low and the Azores High in the Atlantic alternate between weaker and stronger pressure gradients. The *Arctic Oscillation (AO)* is the variable fluctuation between middle- and high-latitude air mass conditions over the Northern Hemisphere. The AO is associated with the NAO, especially in winter. During the winter of 2009–2010, the AO was at its most strongly negative phase since 1970.

El Niño–Southern Oscillation (ENSO) (p. 132)

25. Describe the changes in sea-surface temperatures and atmospheric pressure that occur during El Niño and La Niña, the warm and cool phases of the ENSO. What are some of the climatic effects that occur worldwide?
26. What is the relationship between the PDO and the strength of El Niño events? Between PDO phases and climate in the western United States?
27. What phases are identified for the NAO and AO? What winter weather conditions generally affect the eastern United States during each phase? What happened during the 2009–2010 winter season in the Northern Hemisphere?

Answer for Critical Thinking 4.3: The dry season in northern Australia is from about May through October, during the Southern Hemisphere winter. High pressure is over Australia at this time (see the July pressure in Figure 4.9), and the southeast trades blow dry air from the Australian continent northward over the western Pacific toward Indonesia. From about November to April, during the Australian summer, the ITCZ brings moist, warm air over northern Australia (see the January rainfall pattern in Figure GIA 4.2). This is the monsoon season. For more information, go to http://www.environment.gov.au/soe/2001/publications/theme-reports/atmosphere/atmosphere02-1.html and scroll down to "monsoon."

VISUALanalysis 4 Atmospheric Circulation

In 2013, dust plumes rising from the White Sands dune field blew more than 120 km (74 mi) over the Sacramento Mountains of southern New Mexico. [ISS astronaut photograph ISS030-E-174652, NASA/JSC10.]

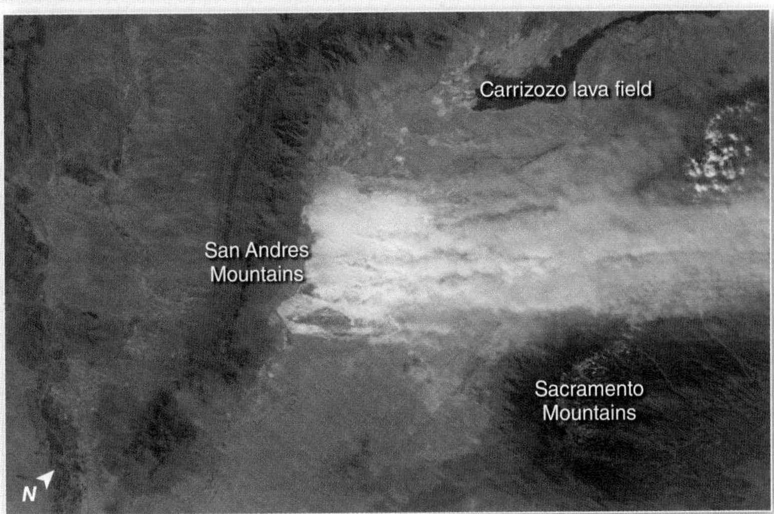

1. Which of Earth's principal surface winds is driving the dust shown in this image? Based on the apparent strength of these winds, during what season did this event occur?
2. Looking back to the images in Figure 2.21, you see dust plumes that are brown, a common color for dust. What characteristic of the landscape makes the dust plumes white in this image? (Note: these plumes are not smoke from wildfires.)

MasteringGeography™

Looking for additional review and test prep materials? Visit the Study Area in *MasteringGeography*™ to enhance your geographic literacy, spatial reasoning skills, and understanding of this chapter's content by accessing a variety of resources, including MapMaster™ interactive maps, geoscience animations, videos, *In the News* RSS feeds, flashcards, web links, self-study quizzes, and an eText version of *Elemental Geosystems.*

PART 2 | The Water, Weather, and Climate Systems

In Part 2, we examine water in the atmosphere, where it produces energy that drives weather, and at Earth's surface, where it is the essential resource needed for life on Earth. Chapter 5 describes the remarkable qualities and properties water possesses and introduces us to atmospheric moisture and weather. We look at the interactions of air masses, the formation of clouds and precipitation, and severe weather phenomena such as thunderstorms, tornadoes, and hurricanes.

Chapter 6 describes the distribution of water on Earth, including water circulation in the hydrologic cycle. We examine the surface water and groundwater resources, outputs of the water–weather system. The quantity and quality of Earth's freshwater supply are emerging as critical issues as human population grows. In Chapter 7, we examine Earth's climates, the output of both the energy–atmosphere and the water–weather systems over time. These climatic patterns interconnect all the system elements from Chapters 2 through 6. Part 2 closes with a discussion of global climate-change science in Chapter 8, including Earth's long- and short-term climate history, present climate conditions, and future climate trends.

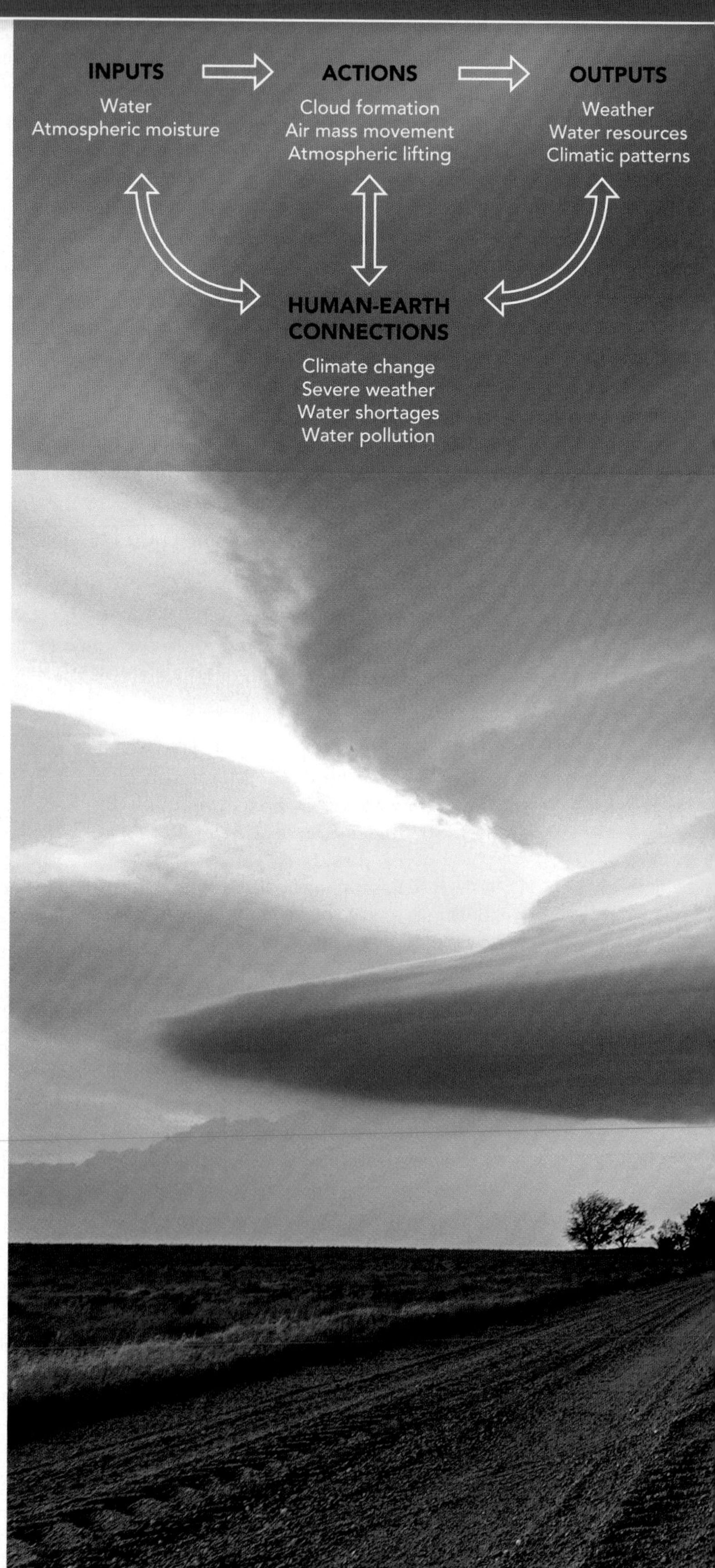

A supercell thunderstorm develops over the Great Plains, June 2013. [Rex/Marko Korosec/Solent News/AP Images.] ▶

Atmosphere
Biosphere
Lithosphere
Hydrosphere

5 Atmospheric Water and Weather

Cold air reaches the dew-point temperature and forms a valley fog in Yosemite Valley, Yosemite National Park, California. [Reimar 4/Alamy.]

KEYLEARNING**concepts**

After reading the chapter, you should be able to:

- ***Describe*** the heat properties of water and ***cite*** the traits of its three phases: solid, liquid, and gas.
- ***Define*** humidity and relative humidity, ***explain*** dew-point temperature, and ***illustrate*** stable and unstable atmospheric conditions.
- ***Identify*** the requirements for cloud formation and ***explain*** the major cloud classes and types, including fog.
- ***Describe*** air masses that affect North America and ***identify*** four types of atmospheric lifting mechanisms.
- ***Describe*** the life cycle of a midlatitude cyclonic storm system and ***list*** several measurable elements that contribute to modern weather forecasting.
- ***Identify*** various forms of violent weather by their characteristics and ***review*** several examples of each.

On the Front Lines of Intense Weather

We frequently see images of violent weather and floods that evoke horror, sadness, and a range of other emotions. Yet most of us are distant from these events and cannot fully imagine what people face on the front lines. As these storms become more intense and destructive, better warning systems reduce human fatalities. However, with population growing in vulnerable areas, recovery becomes increasingly difficult, costly, and demoralizing.

▲Figure GN 5.2 Destroyed houses in a cul-de-sac in a Moore neighborhood. [Tony Gutierrez/AP Images.]

An Oklahoma Tornado On the afternoon of May 20, 2013, as tornado warnings hit media outlets—including Internet weather apps, television, and continuously broadcasting weather radio—the people of Moore, Oklahoma, south of Oklahoma City, retreated into their basements and storm shelters, while schoolchildren huddled in unprotected hallways. Just after 3 P.M., an EF-5–intensity tornado roared in from the southwest with winds over 322 kmph (200 mph).

Spawned by a supercell thunderstorm, a phenomenon discussed in this chapter, the tornado was 2.1 km (1.3 mi) wide as it moved through Moore, devastating a 27-km (17-mile) swath of the city that included two elementary schools (**Figure GN 5.1**; the red line shows the tornado's track). With hundreds at first missing and feared dead, people searched the rubble for friends and family. Days later, officials reported the final death toll at 23 people, with over 200 injured, including 70 children (**Figure GN 5.2**).

The Tornado's Aftermath The U.S. Federal Emergency Management Agency (FEMA) declared the area a federal disaster and mobilized search and rescue personnel as the Oklahoma governor deployed the National Guard. People began the process of applying for disaster assistance, not anticipating the weeks of delay that lay ahead. Residents and volunteers started clearing debris from over 1200 homes destroyed and another 12,000 damaged.

Residents told stories that aired nationwide, but as time passed, the outsiders left, and months rolled by with little media attention. The remains of former neighborhoods of Moore lay piled in a hastily made dump outside of town as the cleanup continued and rebuilding began. How do people on disaster front lines physically and mentally deal with such changes in their lives?

Worldwide, the aftereffects of traumatic events such as these reverberate through local communities—along the Atlantic Seaboard after Hurricane Sandy hit in 2012 (discussed in Focus Study 5.1 in this chapter); across Central Europe since the 2013 floods along the Danube River and its tributaries; and in Joplin, Missouri, hit by an EF-5 tornado in 2011. Contemplate the human dimension as you work through the weather chapter.

▲Figure GN 5.1 The storm system over the U.S. Midwest that spawned the Moore, Oklahoma, tornado on May 20, 2013. [Jeff Schmaltz, LANCE/EOSDIS MODIS Rapid Response Team, NASA/GSFC].

QUESTION AND EXPLORE For links to and information about extreme weather events in the United States and their costs, see http://www.ncdc.noaa.gov/climate-information/extreme-events or http:/www.ncdc.noaa.gov/billions/. To find out more about the Moore tornado and disaster relief, see http://www.srh.noaa.gov/oun/?n=events-20130520 and http://www.defense.gov/home/features/2013/0513_oktornadoes/. MG

Water is everywhere in the atmosphere, in visible forms (clouds, fog, and precipitation) and in microscopic forms (water vapor). Out of all the water present in Earth systems, less than 0.03% is stored in the atmosphere. If this amount fell to Earth as rain, it would cover the surface to a depth of only 2.5 cm (1.0 in.). However, the atmosphere is a key pathway for the movement of water around the globe; in fact, some 495,000 km^3 (118,757 mi^3) of water are cycled through the atmosphere each year.

Water is an extraordinary compound. It is the only common substance that naturally occurs in all three states of matter: liquid, solid, and gas. When water changes from one state of matter to another (as from liquid to gas or solid), the heat energy absorbed or released helps power the general circulation of the atmosphere, which drives daily weather patterns.

When water changes from one state of matter to another (as from liquid to gas or solid), the heat energy absorbed or released helps power the general circulation of the atmosphere, which drives daily weather patterns.

This chapter begins our study of the *hydrologic cycle*, or *water cycle*—the movement of water throughout the atmosphere, hydrosphere, lithosphere, and biosphere. We discuss the surface and subsurface components of the cycle in Chapter 6 and summarize them in Figure 6.4. Although the hydrologic cycle forms a continuous loop, its description often begins with the movement of water through the atmosphere, which includes the formation of clouds and precipitation over land and water. These are the processes that power weather systems on Earth.

Weather is the short-term, day-to-day condition of the atmosphere, contrasted with *climate*, which is the long-term average (over decades) of weather conditions and extremes in a region. Weather is both a "snapshot" of atmospheric conditions and a technical status report of the Earth–atmosphere heat-energy budget.

Meteorology is the scientific study of the atmosphere. (*Meteor* means "heavenly" or "of the atmosphere.") Meteorologists study the atmosphere's physical characteristics and motions; related chemical, physical, and geologic processes; and the complex linkages of atmospheric systems. They also forecast weather. Computers handle the volumes of data from ground instruments, aircraft, and satellites used to accurately forecast near-term weather and to study trends in long-term weather, climates, and climatic change.

In this chapter: We examine the dynamics of atmospheric moisture, beginning with the properties of water in all its states—frozen ice, liquid water, and water vapor in the air. We discuss humidity, saturation, and dew point—all related to water vapor. We study atmospheric conditions of stability and instability and relate them to cloud development and fog.

We follow huge air masses across North America, observe powerful lifting mechanisms in the atmosphere, and examine migrating cyclonic systems with attendant cold and warm fronts. We conclude with a portrait of violent and dramatic weather so often in the news in recent years. The spatial implications of these weather phenomena and their relationship to human activities strongly link meteorology and weather forecasting to the concerns of physical geography.

Water's Unique Properties

Earth's distance from the Sun places it within a most remarkable temperate zone when compared with the positions of the other planets. This temperate location allows all three states of water—ice, liquid, and vapor—to occur naturally on Earth. Two atoms of hydrogen and one of oxygen, which readily bond, make up each water molecule. Once the hydrogen and oxygen atoms join in covalent bonds, they are difficult to separate, thereby producing a water molecule that remains stable in Earth's environment.

The nature of the hydrogen–oxygen bond gives the hydrogen side of a water molecule a positive charge and the oxygen side a negative charge. As a result of this *polarity*, water molecules attract each other: The positive (hydrogen) side of a water molecule attracts the negative (oxygen) side of another—an interaction called *hydrogen bonding*. The polarity of water molecules also explains why water is able to dissolve many substances; pure water is rare in nature because of its ability to dissolve other substances within it. Without hydrogen bonding to make the molecules in water and ice attract each other, water would be a gas at normal surface temperatures.

The effects of hydrogen bonding in water are observable in everyday life, creating the *surface tension* that allows a steel needle to float lengthwise on the surface of water, even though steel is much denser than water. This *surface tension* causes water to bead into droplets on a waxy surface (**Figure 5.1**) and allows you to slightly overfill a glass with water; webs of millions of hydrogen bonds hold the water slightly above the rim.

Hydrogen bonding is also the cause of *capillarity*, which you observe when you "dry" something with a paper towel. The towel draws water through its fibers because hydrogen bonds make each molecule pull on its neighbor. In chemistry laboratory classes, students observe the concave *meniscus*, or inwardly curved surface of the water, that forms in a cylinder or a test tube because hydrogen bonding allows the water to slightly "climb" the glass sides. *Capillary action* is an important component of soil-moisture processes, discussed in Chapter 6.

Phase Changes and Heat Exchange

For water to change from one state to another, heat energy must be added to it or released from it. The amount of heat energy absorbed or released must

◀**Figure 5.1 Surface tension of water.** Surface tension causes water to form beads on a plant leaf. [céline kriébus/Fotolia.]

be sufficient to affect the hydrogen bonds between molecules. This relation between water and heat energy is important to atmospheric processes. In fact, the heat exchanged between physical states of water provides more than 30% of the energy that powers the general circulation of the atmosphere.

Figure 5.2 presents the three states of water and the terms describing each change between states, known as a **phase change**. *Melting* and *freezing* describe the familiar phase changes between solid and liquid. *Condensation* is the process through which water vapor in the air becomes liquid water—this is the process that forms clouds. The process through which liquid water becomes water vapor is *evaporation*—the cooling process discussed in Chapter 3. This phase change is called *vaporization* when water is at boiling temperature.

The phase changes between solid ice and gaseous water vapor may be less familiar. *Deposition* is the process through which water vapor attaches directly to an ice crystal, leading to the formation of *frost*. You may have seen this on your windows or car windshield on a cold morning. It also occurs inside your freezer. **Sublimation** is the process by which ice changes directly to water vapor. A classic sublimation example is the water-vapor clouds associated with the evaporation of dry ice (frozen carbon dioxide) when it is exposed to air. Sublimation is an important contributor to the shrinking of snowpacks in dry, windy environments.

Ice, the Solid Phase As water cools from room temperature, it behaves like most compounds and contracts in volume. At the same time, it increases in density, as the same number of molecules now occupies a smaller space. When other liquids cool, they congeal into the solid state

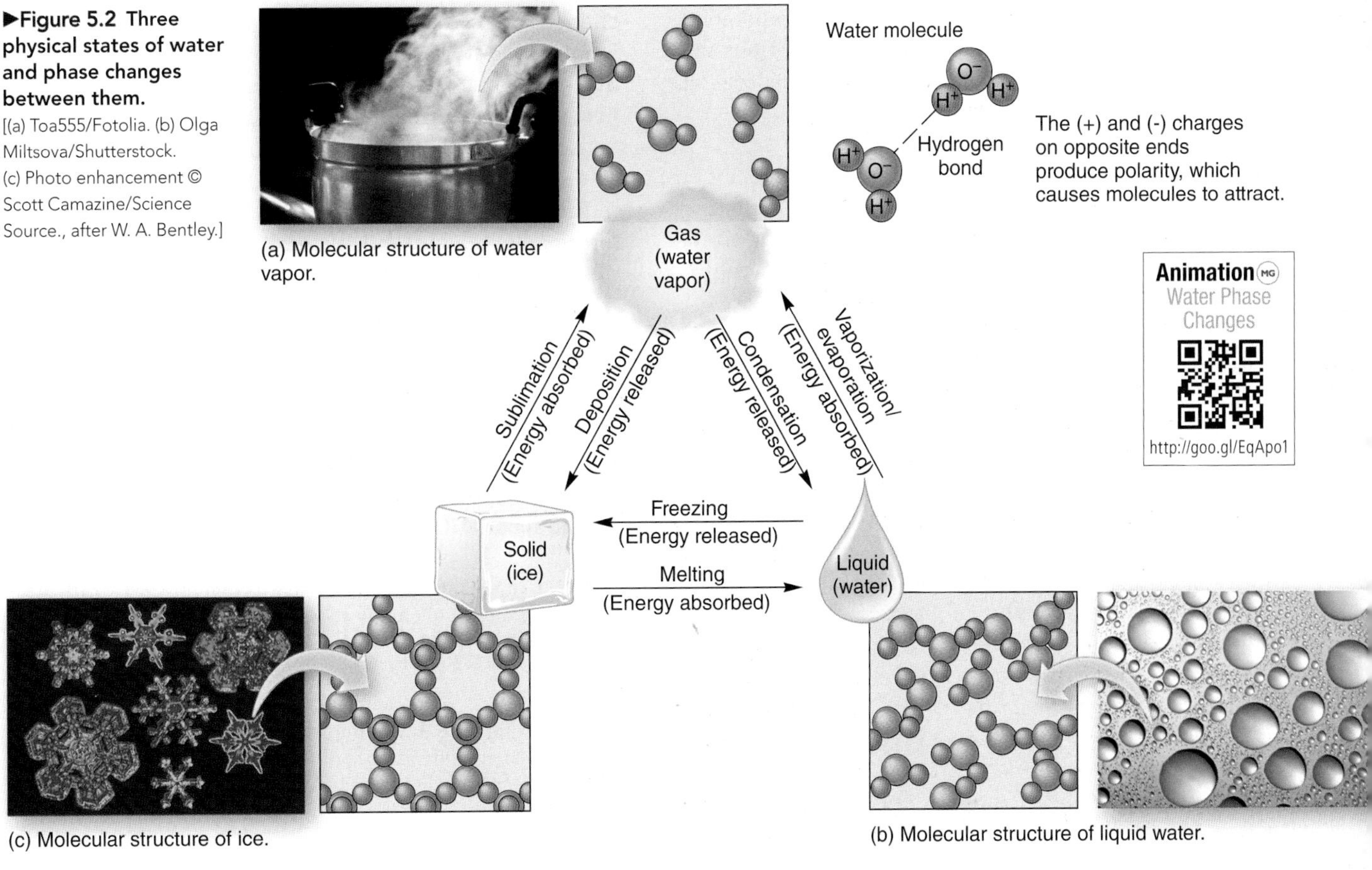

▶**Figure 5.2 Three physical states of water and phase changes between them.** [(a) Toa555/Fotolia. (b) Olga Miltsova/Shutterstock. (c) Photo enhancement © Scott Camazine/Science Source., after W. A. Bentley.]

Water molecule
Hydrogen bond
The (+) and (-) charges on opposite ends produce polarity, which causes molecules to attract.
Gas (water vapor)
Sublimation (Energy absorbed)
Deposition (Energy released)
Condensation (Energy released)
Vaporization/evaporation (Energy absorbed)
Freezing (Energy released)
Melting (Energy absorbed)
Solid (ice)
Liquid (water)

(a) Molecular structure of water vapor.

(b) Molecular structure of liquid water.

(c) Molecular structure of ice.

Animation Water Phase Changes http://goo.gl/EqApo1

by the time they reach their greatest density. However, when water has cooled to the point of greatest density, at 4°C (39°F), it is still in a liquid state. Below a temperature of 4°C (39°F), water behaves differently from other compounds. Continued cooling makes it expand as more hydrogen bonds form among the slowing molecules, creating the hexagonal (six-sided) crystalline structure characteristic of ice (see Figure 5.2c). This six-sided preference applies to ice crystals of all shapes: plates, columns, needles, and dendrites (branching or treelike forms). Ice crystals demonstrate a unique interaction of chaos (all ice crystals are different) and the determinism of physical principles (all have a six-sided structure).

As temperatures descend further below freezing, ice continues to expand in volume and decrease in density to a temperature of −29°C (−20°F)—up to a 9% increase in volume is possible. Pure ice has 0.91 times the density of water, so it floats. Without this unusual pattern of density change, much of Earth's freshwater would be bound in masses of ice on the ocean floor (the water would freeze, sink, and remain in place forever). At the same time, the expansion process just described is to blame for highway and pavement damage and burst water pipes as well as the physical breakdown of rocks known as weathering (discussed in Chapter 11) and the freeze–thaw processes that affect soils in cold regions (discussed in Chapter 14).

In nature, the density of ice varies slightly with age and the air contained within it. As a result, the amount of water that is displaced by a floating iceberg varies, with an average of about one-seventh (14%) of the mass exposed and about six-sevenths (86%) submerged beneath the ocean's surface (**Figure 5.3**). With water temperatures higher than air temperatures, underwater portions melt faster than those above water. Therefore, icebergs are inherently unstable and will overturn.

Water, the Liquid Phase Water, as a liquid, is a noncompressible fluid that assumes the shape of its container. For ice to change to water, heat energy must increase the motion of the water molecules enough to break some of the hydrogen bonds (Figure 5.2b). As discussed in Chapter 3, the heat energy of a phase change is **latent heat** and is hidden within the structure of water's physical state. In total, 80 calories* of heat energy must be absorbed for the phase change of 1 g of ice melting to 1 g of water—this latent heat transfer occurs despite the fact that the sensible temperature remains the same: Both ice and water measure 0°C (32°F; **Figure 5.4a**). When the phase change is reversed and a gram of water freezes, latent heat is released rather than absorbed. The *latent heat of melting* and the *latent heat of freezing* are each 80 cal/g.

To raise the temperature of 1 g of water at 0°C (32°F) to boiling at 100°C (212°F), we must add 100 cal (an increase of 1 C°, or 1.8 F°, for each calorie added). No phase change is involved in this temperature gain.

Water Vapor, the Gas Phase Water vapor is an invisible and compressible gas in which each molecule moves independently of the others (Figure 5.2a). When the phase change from liquid to vapor is induced by boiling, it requires the addition of 540 cal for each gram, under normal sea-level pressure; this amount of energy is the **latent heat of vaporization** (**Figure 5.4**). When water vapor condenses to a liquid, each gram gives up its hidden 540 cal as the **latent heat of condensation**. We see water vapor in the atmosphere after condensation has occurred in the form of clouds, fog, and steam. Perhaps you have felt the release of the latent heat of condensation on your skin from steam when you drained steamed vegetables or pasta or filled a hot teakettle.

In summary, the changing of 1 g of ice at 0°C to water and then to water vapor at 100°C—from a solid to a liquid to a gas—*absorbs* 720 cal (80 cal + 100 cal + 540 cal). Reversing the process, or changing 1 g of water vapor at 100°C to water and then to ice at 0°C, *releases* 720 cal into the surrounding

CRITICAL**thinking** 5.1

Iceberg Analysis

Examine the iceberg in Antarctic waters in Figure 5.3. Fill a clear glass almost to the top with water, and place an ice cube in it. Then estimate the amount of ice above the water's surface compared to the amount below water. Pure ice has 0.91 times the density of water; however, because ice usually contains air bubbles, most icebergs have about 0.86 times the density of water. How do your measurements compare with this range of density?

◀**Figure 5.3 The buoyancy of ice.** A bergy bit (small iceberg) off the coast of Antarctica illustrates the reduced density of ice compared to cold water. [Bobbé Christopherson.]

*Remember, from Chapter 2, that a calorie (cal) is the amount of energy required to raise the temperature of 1 g of water (at 15°C) by 1 degree Celsius and is equal to 4.184 joules.

Animation Water Phase Changes
http://goo.gl/EqApo1

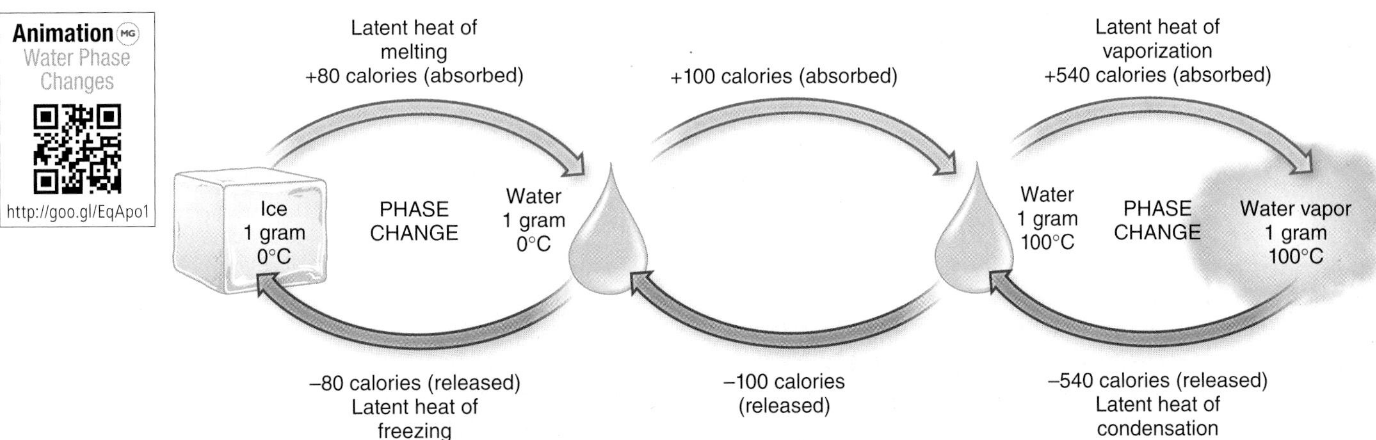

(a) Latent heat absorbed or released in phase changes between ice and water and water vapor. To transform 1 g of ice at 0°C to 1 g of water vapor at 100°C requires 720 cal: 80 + 100 + 540.

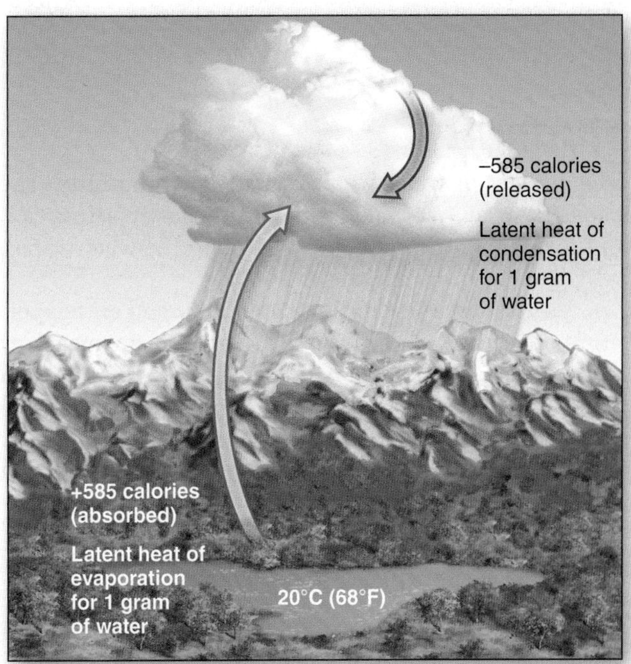

(b) Latent heat exchange between water in a lake at 20°C and water vapor in the atmosphere, under typical conditions.

▲**Figure 5.4 Water's heat-energy characteristics.**

environment. Go to the *MasteringGeography* website for an excellent animation illustrating these concepts.

The **latent heat of sublimation** that is absorbed as a gram of ice transforms into vapor is 680 cal. Water vapor freezing directly to ice releases a comparable amount of energy.

Heat Exchange under Natural Conditions

In a lake or stream or in soil water, at 20°C (68°F), every gram of water that breaks away from the surface through evaporation must absorb from the environment approximately 585 cal as the *latent heat of evaporation* (see Figure 5.4b). This is slightly more energy than would be required if the water were at a higher temperature (if the water is boiling, 540 cal are required). You can feel this absorption of latent heat as evaporative cooling on your skin when it is wet. This latent heat exchange is the dominant cooling process in Earth's energy budget. (Remember from Chapter 4 that the latent heat of evaporation is the most significant nonradiative heat transfer process dissipating positive net radiation at Earth's surface.)

The process reverses when air cools and water vapor condenses back into the liquid state, forming moisture droplets and thus liberating 585 cal for every gram of water as the *latent heat of condensation*. When you realize that a small, puffy, fair-weather cumulus cloud holds 500–1000 tons of moisture droplets, think of the tremendous latent heat released when water vapor condenses to droplets.

Satellites using infrared sensors now routinely monitor water vapor in the lower atmosphere. Water vapor absorbs long wavelengths (infrared), making it possible to distinguish areas of relatively high water vapor from areas of low water vapor (**Figure 5.5**). This technology is important to weather forecasting because it shows the available moisture in the atmosphere and therefore the available latent heat energy and precipitation potential. Water vapor is also an important greenhouse gas in Earth's atmosphere.

GEOreport 5.1 Katrina had the power

Meteorologists estimated that the moisture in Hurricane Katrina (2005) weighed more than 30 trillion tons at its maximum power and mass. With about 585 cal released for every gram as the latent heat of condensation, a weather event such as a hurricane involves a staggering amount of energy. Do the quick math in English units (585 calories times 28 grams to the ounce, times 16 ounces to the pound, times 2000 pounds to the ton, times 30 trillion tons).

◀**Figure 5.5 Global water vapor in the atmosphere.** High water-vapor content is lighter and lower water-vapor content is darker in this February 19, 2013, composite image from the *GOES* (United States), *Meteosat* (European Space Agency), and *MTSAT* (Japan) satellites. [Satellite data courtesy of Space Science and Engineering Center, University of Wisconsin, Madison.]

Humidity

The amount of water vapor in the air is **humidity**. The capacity of air for water vapor is primarily a function of the temperatures of both the air and the water vapor, which are usually the same.

As discussed in Chapter 3, humidity and air temperature determine our sense of comfort. North Americans spend billions of dollars a year to adjust the humidity in buildings, either with air conditioners, which remove water vapor as they cool building interiors, or with air humidifiers, which add water vapor to lessen the drying effects of cold temperatures and dry climates.

Relative Humidity

The most common measure of humidity in weather reports is **relative humidity**, a ratio (expressed as a percentage) of the amount of water vapor that is actually in the air compared to the maximum amount of water vapor that is possible in the air at a given temperature.

Relative humidity varies because of water vapor or temperature changes in the air. The formula to calculate the relative humidity ratio and express it as a percentage places actual water vapor in the air in the numerator and maximum water vapor possible in the air at that temperature in the denominator:

$$\text{Relative humidity} = \frac{\text{Actual water vapor in the air}}{\text{Maximum water vapor possible in the air at that temperature}} \times 100$$

Warmer air increases the evaporation rate from water surfaces, whereas cooler air tends to increase the condensation rate of water vapor onto water surfaces. Because there is a maximum amount of water vapor that can exist in a volume of air at a given temperature, the rates of evaporation and condensation can reach equilibrium at some point; the air is then saturated, and the balance is *saturation equilibrium*.

Figure 5.6 shows changes in relative humidity throughout a typical day. At 5 A.M., in the cool morning air, saturation equilibrium exists, and any further cooling or addition of water vapor produces net condensation. When the air is saturated with maximum water vapor for its temperature, the relative humidity is 100%. At 11 A.M., the air temperature is rising, so the evaporation rate exceeds the condensation rate; as a result, the same volume of water vapor now occupies only 50% of the maximum possible capacity. At 5 P.M., the air temperature is just past its daily peak, so the evaporation rate exceeds condensation by an even greater amount, and relative humidity is at 20%.

Saturation and Dew Point Relative humidity tells us how near the air is to saturation and is an expression of an ongoing process of water molecules moving between air and moist surfaces. At **saturation**, or 100% relative humidity, any further addition of water vapor or any decrease in temperature that reduces the evaporation rate results in active condensation (forming clouds, fog, or precipitation).

The temperature at which a given sample of vapor-containing air becomes saturated and net condensation begins to form water droplets is the **dew-point temperature**. The air is saturated when the dew-point temperature and the air temperature are the same. When temperatures are below freezing, the *frost point* is the temperature at which the air becomes saturated, leading to the formation of frost (ice) on exposed surfaces.

A cold drink in a glass provides a familiar example of these conditions (**Figure 5.7a**). The air near the glass chills to the dew-point temperature and becomes saturated, causing the water vapor in that cooled air to form water droplets on the outside of the glass. **Figure 5.7b** shows active condensation in the saturated air above a cool, wet rock surface. As you walk to classes on some cool mornings, you perhaps notice damp lawns or dew

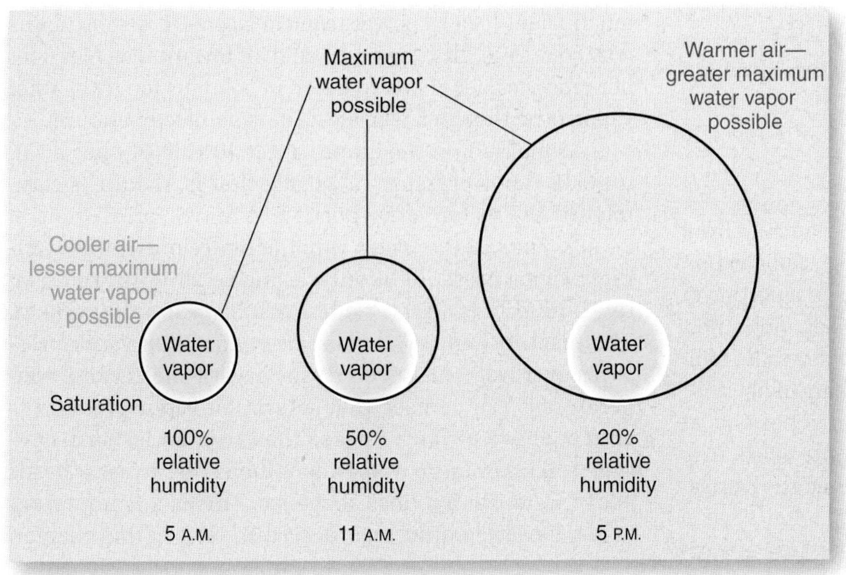

◀**Figure 5.6 Water vapor, temperature, and relative humidity.** The maximum water vapor possible in warm air is greater (net evaporation is more likely) than that possible in cold air (net condensation is more likely), so relative humidity changes with temperature, even though in this example the actual water vapor present in the air stays the same during the day.

on windshields, an indication of dew-point temperature conditions.

Daily Relative Humidity Patterns

An inverse relationship occurs during a typical day between air temperature and relative humidity—as temperature rises, relative humidity falls (**Figure 5.8**). Relative humidity is highest at dawn, when air temperature is lowest. If you park outdoors, you know about the wetness of the dew that condenses on your car or bicycle overnight.

Relative humidity is lowest in the late afternoon, when higher temperatures increase the rate of evaporation. As shown in Figure 5.6, the amount of water vapor actually present in the air may remain the same throughout the day. However, relative humidity changes because the temperature, and therefore the rate of evaporation, varies from morning to afternoon.

(a) When the air reaches the dew-point temperature, water vapor condenses out of the air and onto the glass as dew.

(b) Cold air above the rain-soaked rocks is at the dew point and is saturated. Water evaporates from the rock into the air and condenses in a changing veil of clouds.

▲**Figure 5.7 Dew-point temperature examples.** [Robert Christopherson.]

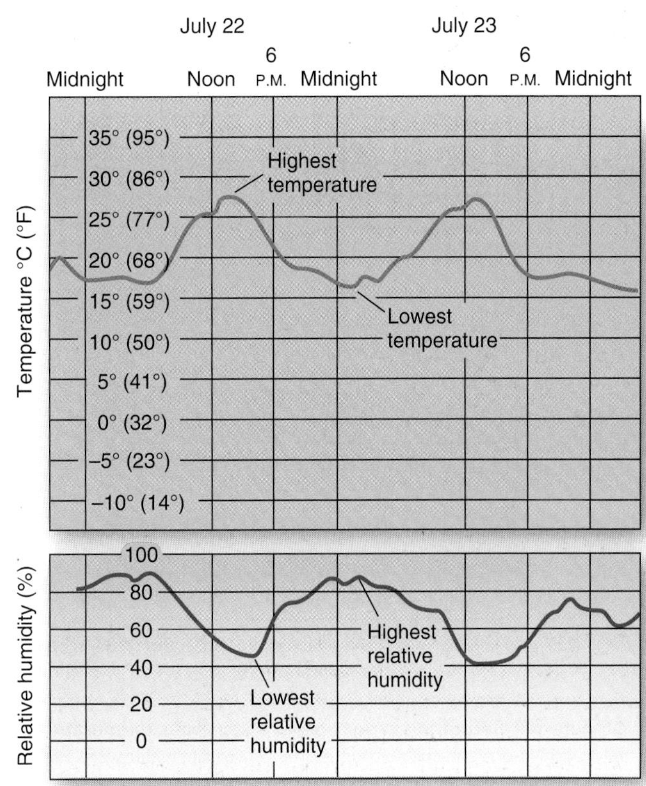

▲**Figure 5.8 Daily relative humidity patterns.** Typical daily variations demonstrate temperature and relative humidity relations.

Specialized Expressions of Humidity

There are several specific ways to express humidity and relative humidity. Each has its own utility and application. Two examples are vapor pressure and specific humidity.

Vapor Pressure As free water molecules evaporate from surfaces into the atmosphere, they become water vapor. Now part of the air, water-vapor molecules exert a portion of the air pressure along with nitrogen and oxygen molecules. The share of air pressure that is made up of water-vapor molecules is **vapor pressure**, expressed in millibars (mb).

Air that contains as much water vapor as possible at a given temperature is at *saturation vapor pressure*. Any temperature increase or decrease will change the saturation vapor pressure.

Figure 5.9 graphs the saturation vapor pressure at various air temperatures. For every temperature increase of 10 C° (18 F°), the saturation vapor pressure in air nearly doubles. This relationship explains why warm tropical air over the ocean can contain so much water vapor, thus providing much latent heat to power tropical storms. It also explains why cold air is "dry" and why cold air toward the poles does not produce a lot of precipitation (it contains too little water vapor, even though it is near the dew-point temperature).

As marked on the graph, air at 20°C (68°F) has a saturation vapor pressure of 24 mb; that is, the air is saturated if the water-vapor portion of the air pressure is at 24 mb. Thus, if the water vapor actually present is exerting a vapor pressure of only 12 mb in 20°C air, the relative humidity is 50% (12 mb ÷ 24 mb = 0.50 × 100 = 50%). The inset in Figure 5.9 compares saturation vapor pressures over water and over ice surfaces at subfreezing temperatures. You can see that saturation vapor pressure is greater above a water surface than over an ice surface—that is, it takes more water-vapor molecules to saturate air above water than it does above ice. This fact is important to condensation processes, described later in this chapter.

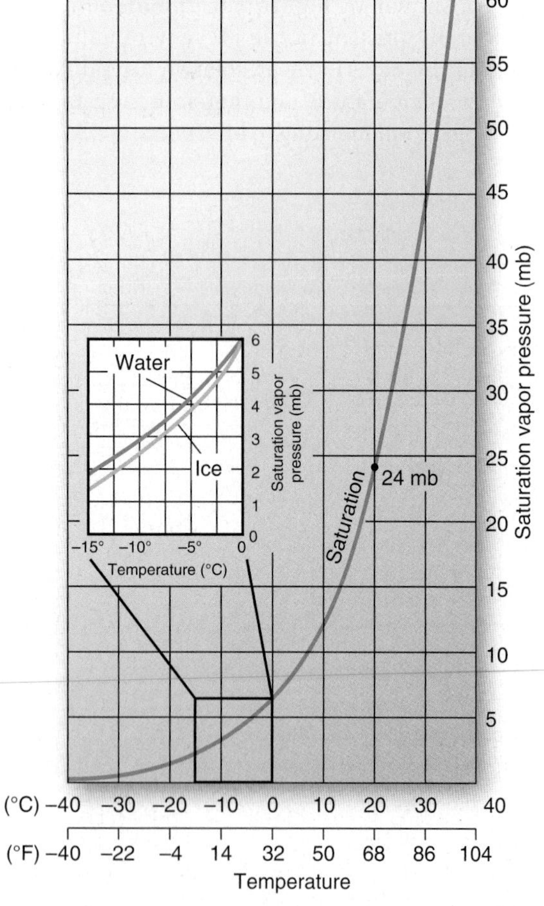

▲**Figure 5.9 Saturation vapor pressure at various temperatures.** Saturation vapor pressure is the maximum possible water vapor, as measured by the pressure it exerts (mb). Inset compares saturation vapor pressures over water surfaces with those over surfaces at subfreezing temperatures. Note the point indicating 24 mb, discussed in the text.

Specific Humidity A useful humidity measure is one that remains constant as temperature and pressure change. **Specific humidity** is the mass of water vapor (in grams) per mass of air (in kilograms) at any specified temperature. Because it is measured in mass, specific humidity is not affected by changes in temperature or pressure, as occur when air rises to higher elevations. Specific humidity stays constant despite volume changes.*

The maximum mass of water vapor possible in a kilogram of air at any specified temperature is the *maximum specific humidity*, plotted in **Figure 5.10**. As noted on the graph, a kilogram of air could hold a maximum specific humidity of 47 g of water vapor at 40°C (104°F), 15 g at 20°C (68°F), and about 4 g at 0°C (32°F). Therefore, if a kilogram of air at 40°C has a specific humidity of 12 g, its relative humidity is 25.5% (12 g ÷ 47 g = 0.255 × 100 = 25.5%). Specific humidity is useful in describing the moisture content of large air masses that are interacting in a weather system and provides information necessary for weather forecasting.

CRITICAL**thinking** 5.2

Using Relative Humidity and Dew-Point Maps

Refer to the discussion of relative humidity, air temperature, dew-point temperature, and saturation on the *MasteringGeography* website. Examine the dew-point temperature map in relation to the map of air temperatures. As you compare and contrast the maps, describe in general terms what relative humidity conditions you find in the Northwest. How about along the Gulf Coast? How does this contrast with the Southeast and with the Southwest? Remember, the closer the air temperature is to the dew-point temperature, the closer the air is to saturation and the possibility of condensation.

*Another similar measure used for relative humidity that approximates specific humidity is the *mixing ratio*—that is, the ratio of the mass of water vapor (in grams) per mass of dry air (in kilograms), as in g/kg.

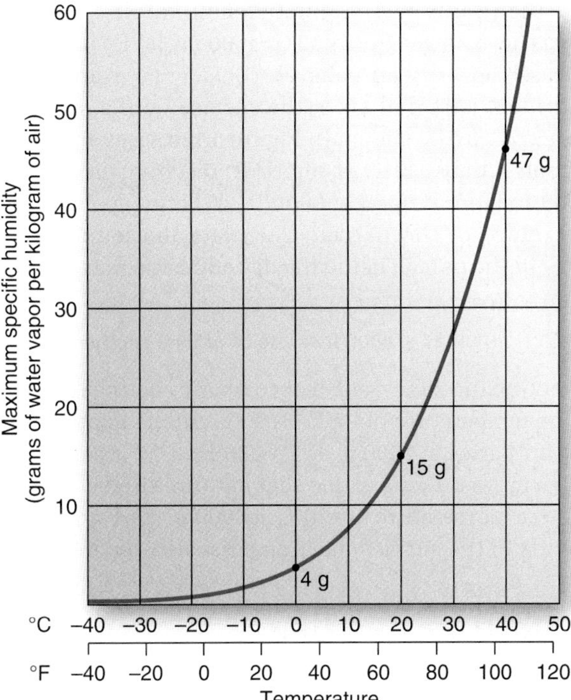
Maximum specific humidity (grams of water vapor per kilogram of air)
60
50
40
30
20
10
47 g
15 g
4 g
°C −40 −30 −20 −10 0 10 20 30 40 50
°F −40 −20 0 20 40 60 80 100 120
Temperature

▲**Figure 5.10 Maximum specific humidity at various temperatures.** Maximum specific humidity is the maximum possible water vapor in a mass of water vapor per unit mass of air (g/kg). Note the points corresponding to 47 g, 15 g, and 4 g mentioned in the text discussion.

Various instruments measure humidity. Examples are the *hair hygrometer*, which uses the principle that human hair changes as much as 4% in length between 0% and 100% relative humidity, and the *sling psychrometer*, which compares the temperatures recorded by side-by-side dry and wet thermometers to determine relative humidity. Go to Chapter 5 on the *MasteringGeography* website for more on the principles behind these instruments and how they work.

Atmospheric Stability

One indicator of weather conditions relates to the vertical movement of air parcels in the atmosphere. Meteorologists use the term *parcel* to describe a body of air, about 300 m (1000 ft) or more in diameter, with specific temperature and humidity characteristics.

Two opposing forces—an upward *buoyant force* and a downward *gravitational force*—decide the vertical position of a parcel of air. A parcel of lower density than the surrounding air is buoyant, so it rises; a rising parcel expands as external pressure decreases. In contrast, a parcel of higher density descends under the force of gravity because it is not buoyant; a falling parcel compresses as external pressure increases. The temperature of the volume of air determines the density of the air parcel—warm air has lower density; cold air has higher density. Therefore, buoyancy depends on density, and density depends on temperature (see Figure 5.12 on page 152).

Stability refers to the tendency of an air parcel either to remain in place or to change vertical position by ascending (rising) or descending (falling). An air parcel is *stable* if it resists displacement upward or, when disturbed, tends to return to its starting place. An air parcel is *unstable* if it continues to rise until it reaches an altitude where the surrounding air has a density and temperature similar to its own. The behavior of a hot-air balloon illustrates these concepts (**Figure 5.11**).

Adiabatic Processes

The stability or instability of an air parcel depends on two temperatures: the temperature inside the parcel and the temperature of the air surrounding the parcel. The difference between these two temperatures determines stability.

The *normal lapse rate*, introduced in Chapter 2, is the average decrease in temperature with increasing altitude, a value of 6.4 C°/1000 m (3.5 F°/1000 ft). This rate of temperature change is for still, calm air, and it can vary greatly under different weather conditions. In contrast, the **environmental lapse rate (ELR)** is the actual lapse rate at a particular place and time. It can vary by several degrees per thousand meters.

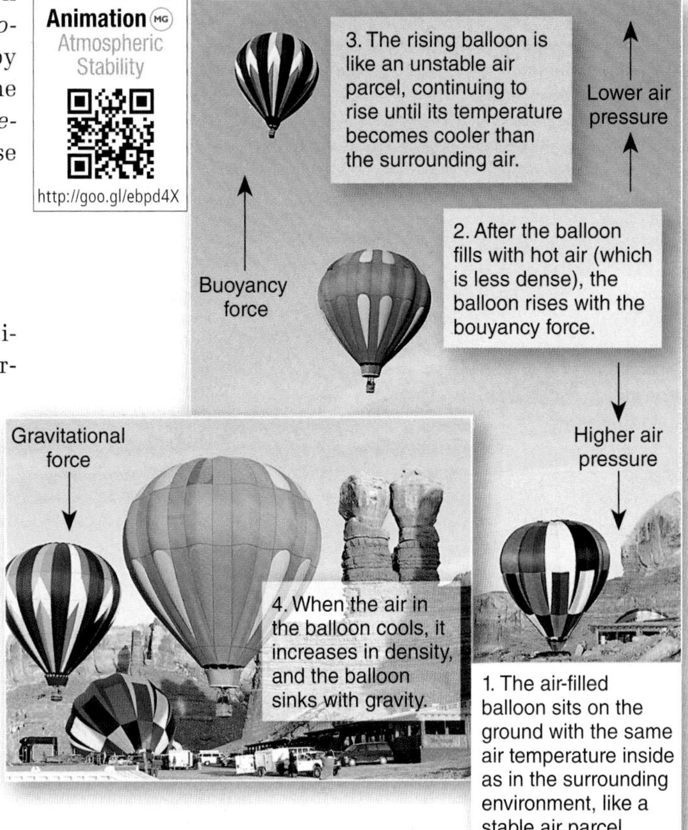
Animation (MG)
Atmospheric Stability
http://goo.gl/ebpd4X
3. The rising balloon is like an unstable air parcel, continuing to rise until its temperature becomes cooler than the surrounding air.
Lower air pressure
Buoyancy force
2. After the balloon fills with hot air (which is less dense), the balloon rises with the bouyancy force.
Gravitational force
Higher air pressure
4. When the air in the balloon cools, it increases in density, and the balloon sinks with gravity.
1. The air-filled balloon sits on the ground with the same air temperature inside as in the surrounding environment, like a stable air parcel.

►**Figure 5.11 Principles of air stability and balloon launches.** Hot-air balloons being launched in southern Utah illustrate the principles of stability. Why do you think these balloon launches are taking place in the early morning? [Steven K. Huhtala.]

Two generalizations predict the warming or cooling of an ascending or descending parcel of air. An ascending parcel of air tends to cool by expansion, responding to the reduced pressure at higher altitudes. In contrast, a descending parcel of air tends to heat by compression. These mechanisms of cooling and heating are adiabatic. *Diabatic* means occurring with an exchange of heat; **adiabatic** means occurring without a loss or gain of heat—that is, without any heat exchange between the surrounding environment and the vertically moving parcel of air. Adiabatic temperature changes are measured with one of two specific rates, depending on moisture conditions in the parcel: dry adiabatic rate (DAR) and moist adiabatic rate (MAR). These processes are illustrated in **Figure 5.12**.

Dry Adiabatic Rate The **dry adiabatic rate (DAR)** is the rate at which "dry" air cools by expansion as it rises or heats by compression as it falls. "Dry" refers to air that is less than saturated (its relative humidity is less than 100%). The average DAR is 10 C°/1000 m (5.5 F°/1000 ft).

To see how dry air behaves, consider an example: an unsaturated parcel of air at the surface with a temperature of 27°C (81°F), shown in Figure 5.12b, rises, expands, and cools adiabatically at the DAR, reaching an altitude of 2500 m (approximately 8000 ft). What happens to the temperature of the parcel? Calculate the temperature change in the parcel, using the dry adiabatic rate:

$$(10\ \text{C}^\circ/1000\ \text{m}) \times 2500\ \text{m} = 25\ \text{C}^\circ \text{ of total cooling}$$

$$(5.5\ \text{F}^\circ/1000\ \text{ft}) \times 8000\ \text{ft} = 44\ \text{F}^\circ \text{ of total cooling}$$

Subtracting the 25 C° (44 F°) of adiabatic cooling from the starting temperature of 27°C (81°F) gives the temperature in the air parcel at 2500 m as 2°C (36°F).

In Figure 5.12d, assume that an unsaturated air parcel with a temperature of –20°C at 3000 m (24°F at 9800 ft) descends to the surface, heating adiabatically. Using the

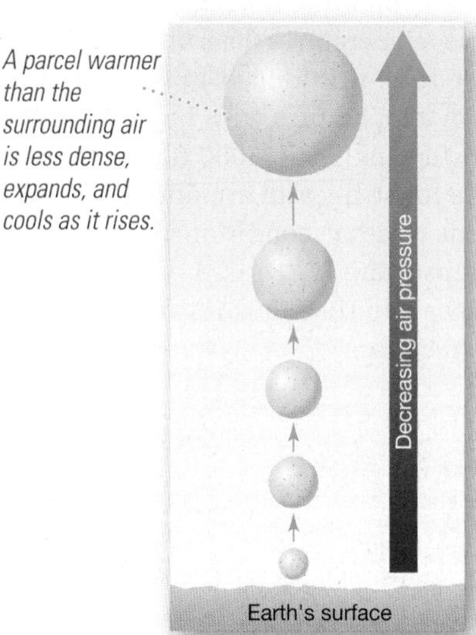

(a) Cooling by expansion

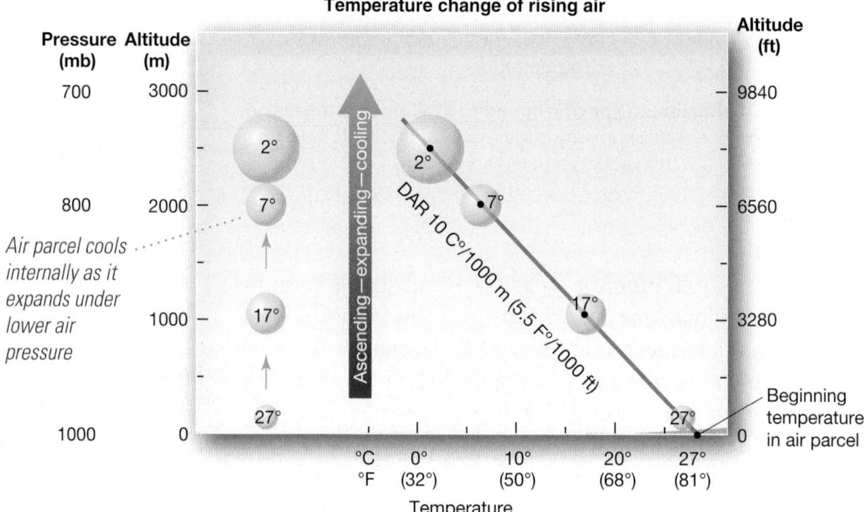

(b) Temperature change as rising air cools adiabatically

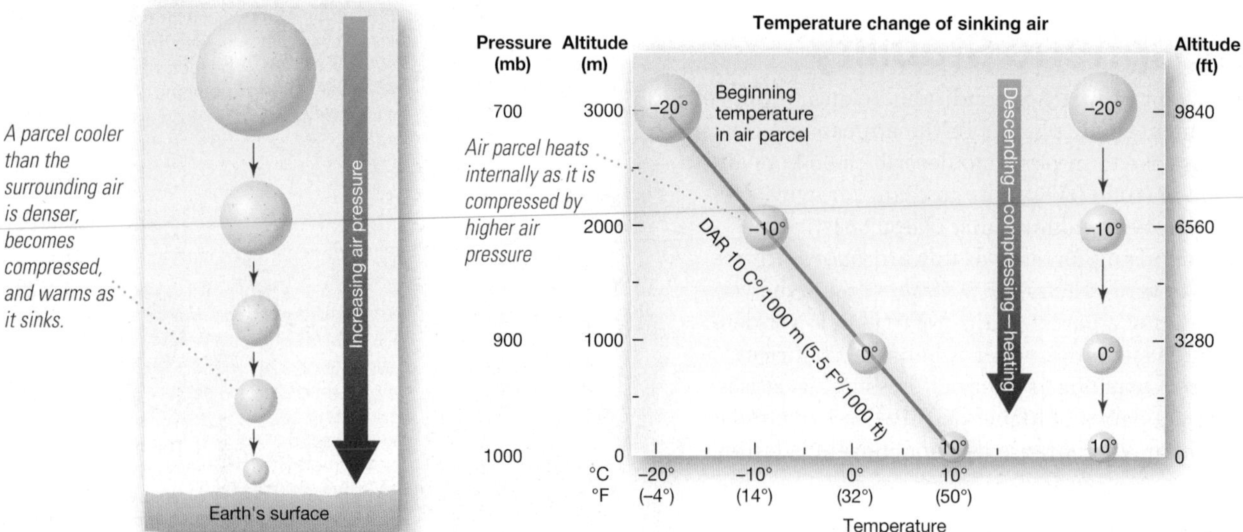

(c) Heating by compression

(d) Temperature change as sinking air heats adiabatically

▲**Figure 5.12 Adiabatic cooling and heating in vertically moving air.** Air that is less than saturated cools (as it rises) and heats (as it sinks) at the dry adiabatic rate.

dry adiabatic lapse rate, we determine the temperature of the air parcel when it arrives at the surface:

(10 C°/1000 m) × 3000 m = 30 C° of total warming

(5.5 F°/1000 ft) × 9800 ft = 54 F° of total warming

Adding the 30 C° (54 F°) of adiabatic warming to the starting temperature of –20°C (–4°F) gives the temperature in the air parcel at the surface as 10°C (50°F).

Moist Adiabatic Rate The **moist adiabatic rate (MAR)** is the rate at which an ascending air parcel that is moist, or saturated, cools by expansion. The average MAR is 6 C°/1000 m (3.3 F°/1000 ft). This is roughly 4 C° (2 F°) less than the dry adiabatic rate. From this average, the MAR varies with moisture content and temperature and can range from 4 C° to 10 C° per 1000 m (2 F° to 5.5 F° per 1000 ft). (Note that a descending parcel of saturated air warms at the MAR as well because the evaporation of liquid droplets, absorbing sensible heat, offsets the rate of compressional warming.)

The cause of this variability, and the reason that the MAR is lower than the DAR, is the latent heat of condensation. As water vapor condenses in the saturated air, latent heat is liberated, becoming sensible heat and thus decreasing the adiabatic rate. The release of latent heat may vary with temperature and water-vapor content. The MAR is much lower than the DAR in warm air, whereas the two rates are more similar in cold air.

Stable and Unstable Atmospheric Conditions

The relationship of the DAR and MAR to the environmental lapse rate, or ELR, at a given time and place determines the stability of the atmosphere over an area. In turn, atmospheric stability affects cloud formation and precipitation patterns, some of the essential elements of weather.

Temperature relationships in the lower atmosphere produce conditions ranging from stable to unstable (**Figure 5.13**, left side). When the ELR is less than the DAR and MAR, the lower atmosphere is stable. When the ELR exceeds the DAR, the atmosphere is unstable. When the ELR is between the DAR and MAR, the atmosphere is neither stable nor unstable, a situation known as conditional instability. Under these conditions, if an air parcel is less than saturated, it will resist upward movement, unless forced. But if the air parcel becomes saturated, it will now be unstable and continue to rise (learn more about conditionally unstable air on the *MasteringGeography* website).

Animation (MG) Atmospheric Stability http://goo.gl/ebpd4X

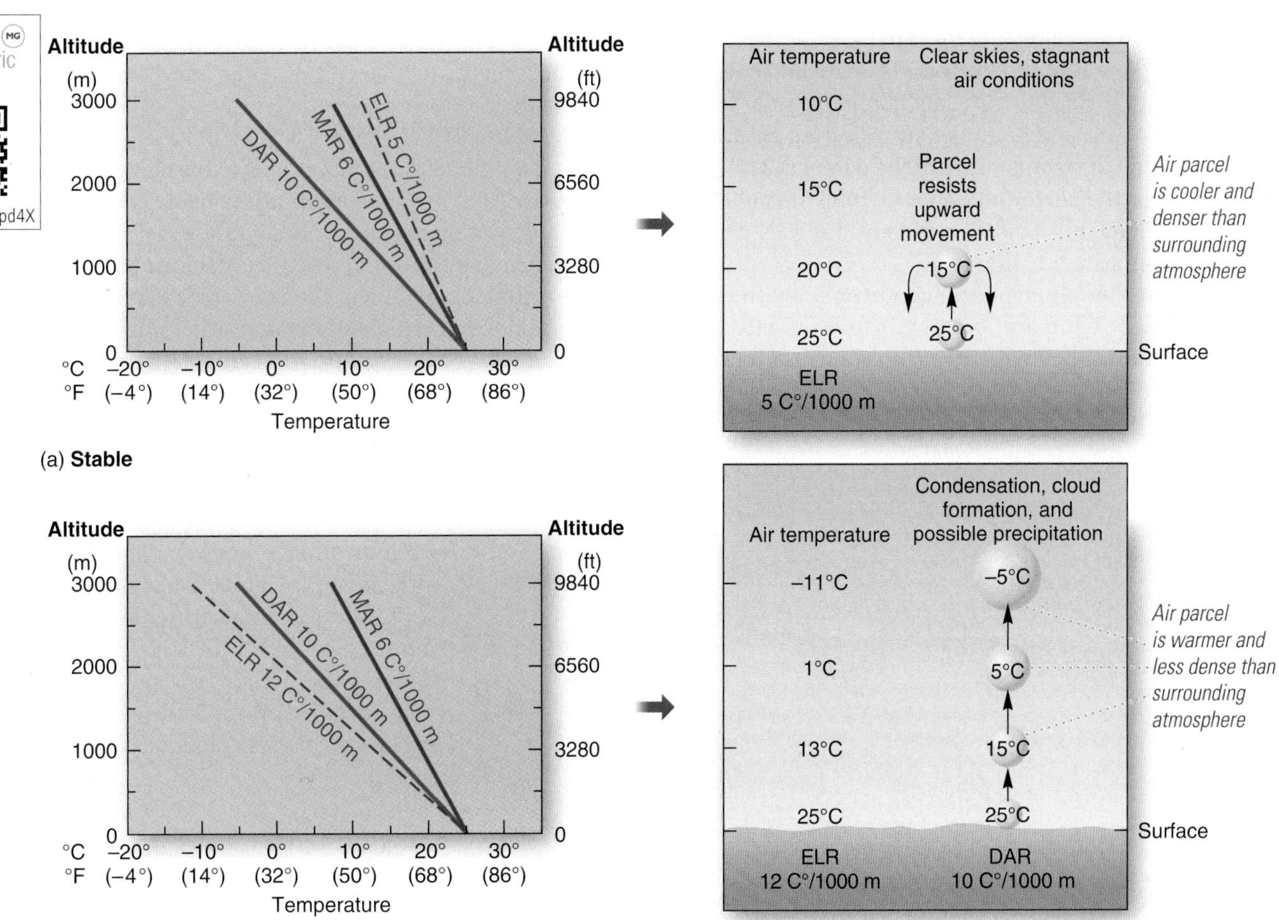

▲**Figure 5.13 Temperature relationships and examples of stable and unstable conditions in the lower atmosphere.** The relationship between dry and moist adiabatic rates and environmental lapse rates produces conditions ranging from stable to unstable. Note the response to these conditions in the air parcel on the right side of each diagram.

Figure 5.13 shows examples of the movement of an air parcel under stable and unstable conditions. For the sake of illustration, both examples begin with an air parcel at the surface at 25°C (77°F). In each example, compare the temperatures of the air parcel and the surrounding environment. Assume that a lifting mechanism, such as surface heating, is present to propel the air parcel upward (we examine lifting mechanisms later in this chapter).

The example in Figure 5.13a shows stable conditions resulting when the ELR is 5 C°/1000 m (3 F°/1000 ft), a rate that is less than both the DAR and the MAR. Under these conditions, the air parcel has a lower temperature (is more dense and less buoyant) than the surrounding environment. The relatively cooler air parcel tends to settle back to its original position—it is *stable*. The air parcel resists lifting, unless forced by updrafts or a barrier, and the sky remains generally cloud-free.

Figure 5.13b shows unstable conditions resulting when the ELR is higher than the DAR and MAR. Under these conditions, the air parcel continues to rise through the atmosphere because it is warmer (less dense and more buoyant) than the surrounding environment. Note that the ELR in this example is 12 C°/1000 m (6.6 F°/1000 ft). That is, the air surrounding the air parcel is cooler by 12 C° for every 1000-m increase (6.6 F° for every 1000-ft increase) in altitude. By 1000 m (3300 ft), the rising air parcel has cooled adiabatically by expansion at the DAR from 25° to 15°C, while the surrounding air has cooled from 25°C at the surface to 13°C. By comparing the temperatures in the air parcel and the surrounding environment, you see that the temperature in the parcel is 2 C° (3.6 F°) warmer than the surrounding air at 1000 m (3300 ft). *Unstable* describes this condition because the less-dense air parcel will continue to lift.

Under unstable atmospheric conditions, as the air parcel continues rising and cooling, it may eventually achieve the dew-point temperature, saturation, and active condensation. This is the *lifting condensation level*, an altitude that you sometimes see in the sky as the flat bottoms of clouds. **Figure 5.14** shows an example of a rising air parcel that cools at the DAR until it reaches the lifting condensation level, at which point it becomes saturated and continues to cool at the MAR. The parcel begins at a temperature of 25°C, within an air mass with a specific humidity of 8 g/kg. The graph in Figure 5.10 shows that air with a specific humidity of 8 g/kg must be cooled to 11°C to achieve the dew-point temperature. Thus, in this example, the rising parcel reaches the dew-point temperature at 1400 m (4600 ft), after 14 C° of adiabatic cooling. Conditions like these frequently occur with surface heating and convectional lifting (discussed later in the chapter), producing clouds and precipitation.

Clouds and Fog

Clouds are fundamental indicators of overall conditions, including stability, moisture content, and weather. A **cloud** is an aggregation of tiny moisture droplets and ice crystals that are suspended in air and are great enough in volume and concentration to be visible. Fog, discussed later in the chapter, is simply a cloud in contact with the ground. Clouds may contain raindrops, but not initially. At the outset, clouds are a great mass of moisture droplets, each invisible without magnification. A **moisture droplet** is approximately 20 μm (micrometers) in diameter (0.002 cm, or 0.0008 in.). It takes a million or more such droplets to form an average raindrop with a diameter of 2000 μm (0.2 cm, or 0.078 in.).

As an air parcel rises, it may cool to the dew-point temperature and 100% relative humidity. (Under certain conditions, condensation may occur at slightly less or more than 100% relative humidity.) More lifting of the air parcel cools it further, producing condensation of water vapor into water. Condensation requires **cloud-condensation nuclei**, microscopic particles that always are present in the atmosphere.

Continental air masses, discussed ahead, average 10 billion cloud-condensation nuclei per cubic meter. These nuclei typically come from dust, soot, and ash from volcanoes and forest fires, and particles from burned fuel, such as sulfate aerosols. The air over cities contains great concentrations of such nuclei. In maritime air masses, nuclei average 1 billion per cubic meter and include sea salts derived from ocean sprays. The lower atmosphere never lacks cloud-condensation nuclei.

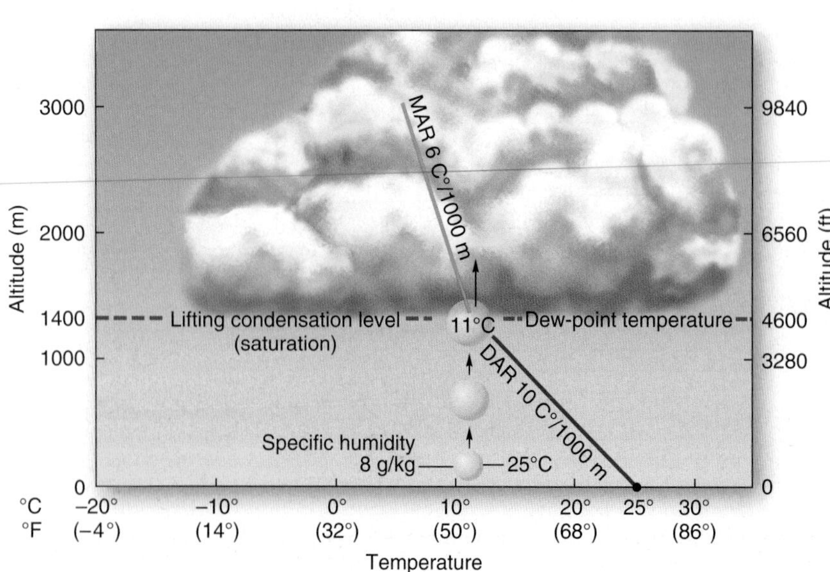

◀**Figure 5.14 Unstable atmospheric conditions.** In this example of unstable conditions, the environmental lapse rate is 12 C°/1000 m. The rising air parcel reaches dew point at 1400 m (4600 ft) after 14 C° of adiabatic cooling. Note that the parcel cools at the DAR when it is less than saturated, changing to the MAR above the lifting condensation level.

Given the presence of saturated air, cloud-condensation nuclei, and cooling (lifting) mechanisms in the atmosphere, condensation occurs. Clouds are a result of these processes.

Cloud Types and Identification

In 1803, English biologist and amateur meteorologist Luke Howard established a classification system for clouds and coined Latin names for them that we still use. *Altitude* and *shape* are key to cloud classification (**Figure 5.15**). Clouds occur in three basic forms—flat, puffy, and wispy—and in four primary altitude classes. Flat and layered clouds with horizontal development are classed as *stratiform*. Puffy and globular clouds with vertical development are *cumuliform*. Wispy clouds, usually quite high in altitude and made of ice crystals, are *cirroform*. The four altitudinal classes are low, middle, high, and clouds vertically developed through the troposphere. Combinations of shape and altitude result in 10 basic cloud types: stratus, stratocumulus, nimbostratus, altostratus, altocumulus, cirrus, cirrostratus, cirrocumulus, cumulus, and cumulonimbus.

Low clouds, ranging from the surface up to 2000 m (6500 ft) in the middle latitudes, are *stratus* or *cumulus* (Latin for "layer" and "heap," respectively). **Stratus** clouds appear dull, gray, and featureless. When they yield precipitation, they become **nimbostratus** (*nimbo-* denotes "stormy" or "rainy"), and their showers typically fall as drizzling rain (Figure 5.15e).

Cumulus clouds appear bright and puffy, like cotton balls. When they do not cover the sky, they float by in infinitely varied shapes. Vertically developed cumulus

▲**Figure 5.15 Principal cloud types and special cloud forms.** Cloud types according to form and altitude (low, middle, high, and vertically developed). [(a), (b), (c), and (h) by Bobbé Christopherson. (d), (e), (f), and (g) by Robert Christopherson.]

clouds can extend beyond low altitudes into middle and high altitudes (illustrated at the far right in Figure 5.15).

Sometimes near the end of the day, patches of lumpy, grayish, low-level **stratocumulus** clouds may fill the sky. Near sunset, these spreading, puffy, stratiform remnants may catch and filter the Sun's rays, sometimes indicating clearing weather.

The prefix *alto-* (meaning "high") denotes middle-level clouds. They are made of water droplets, mixed, when temperatures are cold enough, with ice crystals. **Altocumulus** clouds, in particular, represent a broad category that includes many different styles: patchy rows, wave patterns, a "mackerel sky," or lens-shaped (lenticular) clouds.

Ice crystals in thin concentrations compose clouds occurring above 6000 m (20,000 ft). These wispy filaments, usually white except when colored by sunrise or sunset, are **cirrus** clouds (Latin for "curl of hair"), sometimes dubbed "mares' tails." Cirrus clouds look as though an artist took a brush and made delicate feathery strokes high in the sky. Cirrus clouds can indicate an oncoming storm, especially if they thicken and lower in elevation. The prefix *cirro-*, as in *cirrostratus* or *cirrocumulus*, indicates other high clouds that form a thin veil or have a puffy appearance, respectively.

A cumulus cloud can develop into a towering giant called a **cumulonimbus** cloud (again, *-nimbus* in Latin denotes "rain storm" or "thundercloud"; **Figure 5.16**). Such clouds are known as *thunderheads* because of their shape and associated lightning and thunder. Note the surface wind gusts, updrafts and downdrafts, heavy rain, and ice crystals present at the top of the rising cloud column. High-altitude winds may then shear the top of the cloud into the characteristic anvil shape of the mature thunderhead.

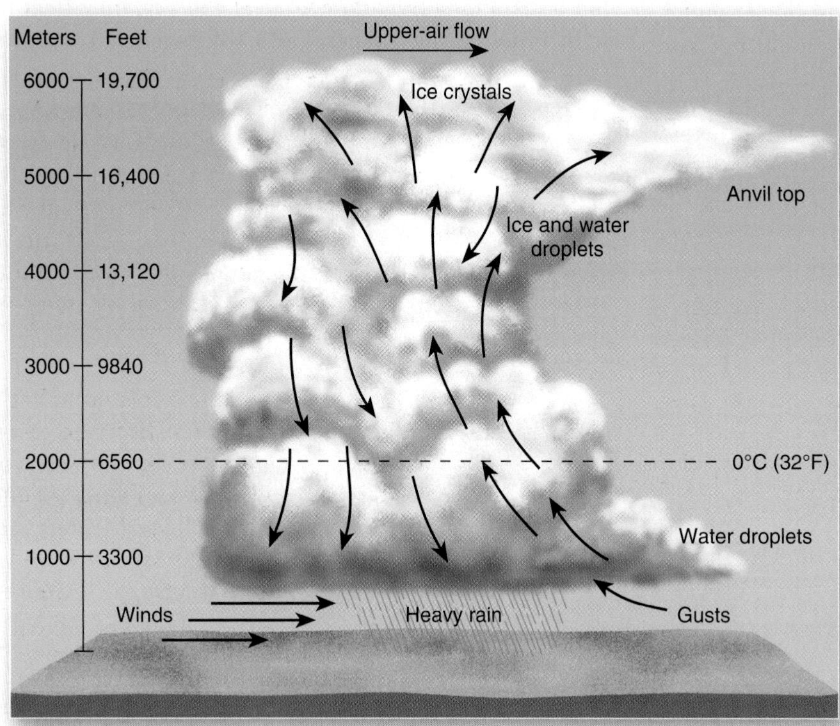

(a) Structure and form of a cumulonimbus cloud. Violent updrafts and downdrafts mark the circulation within the cloud. Blustery wind gusts occur along the ground.

(b) A dramatic cumulonimbus thunderhead over Africa at 13.5° N latitude near the Senegal–Mali border.

◀**Figure 5.16 Cumulonimbus thunderhead.** [(b) ISS Astronaut photograph, NASA.]

Processes That Form Fog

By international definition, **fog** is a cloud layer on the ground, with visibility restricted to less than 1 km (3300 ft). The presence of fog tells us that the air temperature and the dew-point temperature at ground level are nearly identical, indicating saturated conditions. A temperature-inversion layer generally caps a fog layer (warmer temperatures above and cooler temperatures below the inversion altitude), with as much as a 22-C° (40-F°) difference in air temperature between the cooler ground under the fog and the warmer, sunny skies above.

Radiation Fog When radiative cooling of a surface chills the air layer directly above that surface to the dew-point temperature, creating saturated conditions, a **radiation fog** forms. This fog occurs over moist ground, especially on clear nights; it does not occur over water because water does not cool appreciably overnight.

Winter radiation fog is typical in the Central Valley of California, encompassing the Sacramento Valley in the north and the San Joaquin Valley in the south, and is locally known as a *tule fog* (pronounced "toolee") because of its association with the tule (bulrush) plants that line the low-elevation islands and marshes of the Sacramento River and San Joaquin River delta regions (**Figure 5.17**). Tule fog can reduce visibility to 3 m (10 ft) or less and is a leading cause of weather-related traffic accidents in California.

Advection Fog When air in one place migrates to another place where conditions are right for saturation, an **advection fog** forms. For example, when warm, moist air moves over cooler ocean currents, lake surfaces, or snow masses, the layer of migrating air directly above the surface becomes chilled to the dew point, and fog develops. Off all subtropical west coasts in the world, summer fog forms in the manner just described (**Figure 5.18**).

One type of advection fog forms when moist air flows to higher elevations along a hill or mountain. This upslope lifting leads to adiabatic cooling by expansion as the air rises. Eventually, the air reaches the lifting condensation level. The resulting **upslope fog** forms a stratus cloud at the altitude where saturation occurs and condensation begins. Along the Appalachians and the eastern slopes of the Rockies, such fog is common in winter and spring.

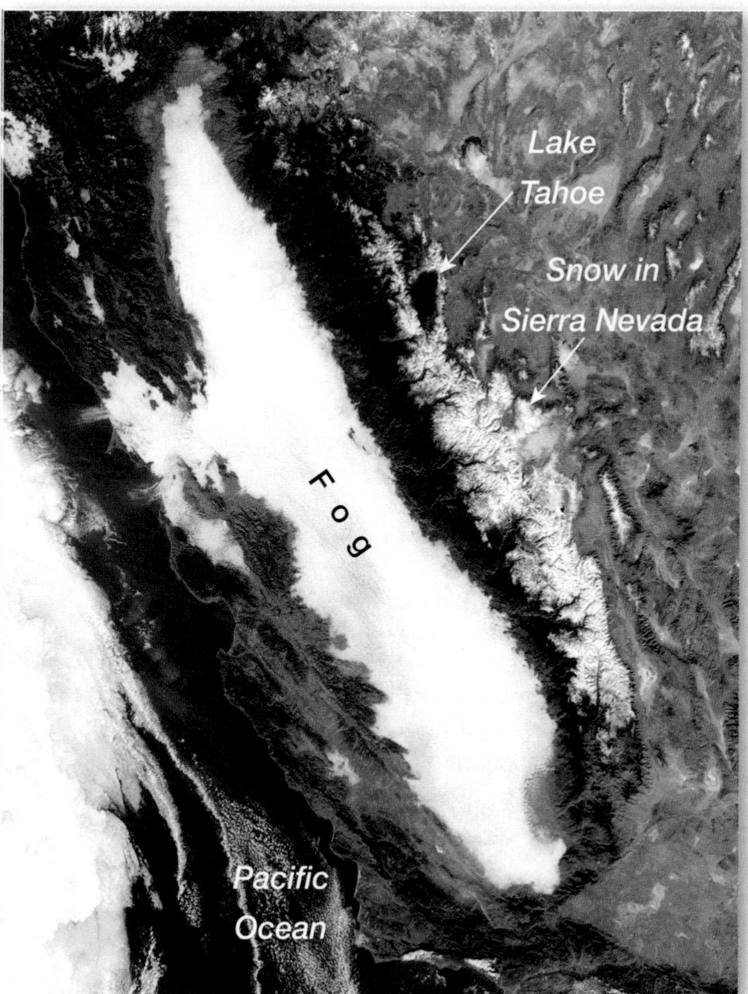

▲**Figure 5.17 Winter radiation fog.** This December 2005 image shows fog in California's Central Valley, trapped by the topographic barriers of the Cascades to the north, the Sierra Nevada to the east, and the Coastal Ranges to the west. Scientists attribute a 46% decline in tule fog events between 1980 and 2014 to regional warming and climate change. [Jeff Schmaltz/*Terra* MODIS image, NASA.]

▲**Figure 5.18 Advection fog.** San Francisco's Golden Gate Bridge is shrouded by an invading advection fog characteristic of summer conditions along a western coast. [Brad Perks Lightscapes/Alamy.]

Another advection fog associated with topography is **valley fog**. Because cool air is denser than warm air, it settles in low-lying areas, producing a fog in the chilled, saturated layer near the ground in the valley (see the chapter opening photo).

Evaporation Fog A type of fog that is related to both advection and evaporation forms when cold air lies over the warm water of a lake, an ocean surface, or even a swimming pool. This wispy **evaporation fog**, or *steam fog*, may form as water molecules evaporate from the water surface into the cold overlying air, effectively humidifying the air to saturation, followed by condensation to form fog (**Figure 5.19**). When evaporation fog happens at sea, it is a shipping hazard called *sea smoke*.

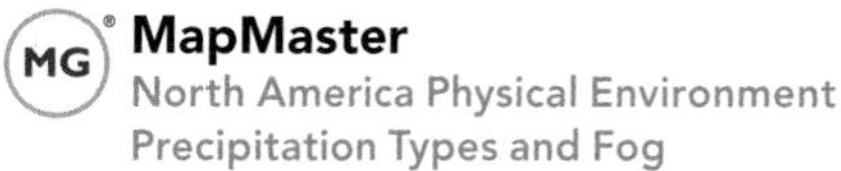

▼**Figure 5.19 Evaporation fog.** Evaporation fog, or sea smoke, highlights dawn on a cold morning at Donner Lake, California. Later that morning as air temperatures rose, what do you think happened to the evaporation fog? [Bobbé Christopherson.]

CRITICAL**thinking** 5.3

Identify Two Kinds of Fog

In **Figure CT 5.3.1**, can you tell which two kinds of fog are pictured? These questions may help: How does the temperature of the river water compare with that of the overlying air, especially beyond the bend in the river? Could the temperature of the moist farmlands have changed overnight, and if so, how? Might that contribute to fog formation? Can you see any evidence of air movement, such as a light breeze? How might this affect the presence of fog? (Find the answers at the end of the Chapter 5 Key Learning Concepts Review.)

▲**Figure CT 5.3.1 Two kinds of fog.** [Bobbé Christopherson.]

Air Masses

Each region of Earth's surface imparts its temperature and moisture characteristics to overlying air. The effect of a region's surface on the air creates a homogenous mix of temperature, humidity, and stability that may extend through the lower half of the atmosphere. Such a distinctive body of air is an **air mass**, and it initially reflects the characteristics of its *source region*. Examples include the "cold Canadian air mass" and "moist tropical air mass" often referred to in weather forecasts. The various masses of air over Earth's surface interact to produce weather patterns.

Air Masses Affecting North America

We classify air masses according to the general moisture and temperature characteristics of their source regions: *Moisture* is designated **m** for maritime (wet) or **c** for continental (dry). *Temperature* is directly related to latitude and is designated **A** for arctic, **P** for polar, **T** for tropical, **E** for equatorial, or **AA** for antarctic. **Figure 5.20** shows the principal air masses that affect North America in winter and summer.

Continental polar (cP) air masses form only in the Northern Hemisphere and are most developed in winter and cold-weather conditions. These cP air masses are major players in middle- and high-latitude weather, as their cold, dense air displaces moist, warm air in their path, lifting and cooling the warm air and causing its vapor to condense. An area covered by cP air in winter experiences cold, stable air; clear skies; high pressure; and anticyclonic wind flow. The Southern Hemisphere lacks the necessary continental landmasses at high latitudes to create such a cP air mass.

Maritime polar (mP) air masses in the Northern Hemisphere sit over the northern oceans. Within them, cool, moist, unstable conditions prevail throughout the year. The Aleutian and Icelandic subpolar low-pressure cells reside within these mP air masses, especially in their well-developed winter pattern (see the January isobaric pressure map in Figure 4.9a).

Two *maritime tropical* (mT) air masses—the mT Gulf/Atlantic and the mT Pacific—influence North America. The humidity experienced in the eastern and midwestern areas of North America is created by the mT Gulf/Atlantic air mass, which is particularly unstable and active from late spring to early fall. In contrast, the mT Pacific is stable to conditionally unstable and generally lower in moisture content and available energy. As a result, the western United States, influenced by this weaker Pacific air mass, receives lower average precipitation than the rest of the country. Review Figure 4.9 and the discussion of subtropical high-pressure cells.

Air Mass Modification

The longer an air mass remains stationary over a region, the more definite its physical attributes become. As air masses migrate from source regions, their temperature and moisture characteristics slowly change to the characteristics of the land over which they pass. For example, an mT Gulf/Atlantic air mass may carry humidity to Chicago and on to Winnipeg, but it gradually loses its initial high humidity and warmth with each day's passage northward.

Similarly, below-freezing temperatures occasionally reach into southern Texas and Florida, brought by an invading winter cP air mass from the north. However, that air mass warms to above the −50°C (−58°F) of its winter source region in central Canada, especially after it leaves areas covered by snow.

Modification of cP air as it moves south and east produces snowbelts to the east of each of the Great Lakes. As below-freezing cP air passes over the warmer Great Lakes, it absorbs heat energy and moisture from the lake surfaces and becomes *humidified*. In what is called the *lake effect*, this enhancement produces heavy snowfall downwind of the lakes, into Ontario, Québec, Michigan, northern Pennsylvania, and New York—some areas receiving in excess of 250 cm (100 in.) in average snowfall a year (**Figure 5.21**). The severity of the lake effect also depends on the presence of a low-pressure system positioned north of the Great Lakes, with counterclockwise winds pushing air across the lakes.

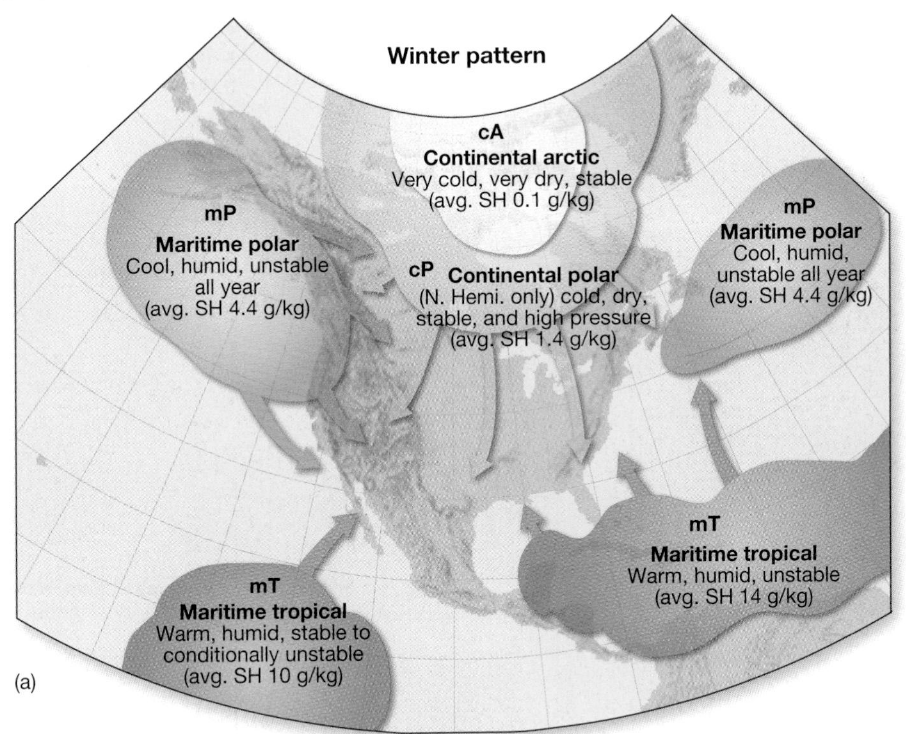

◀**Figure 5.20 Principal air masses affecting North America.** Air masses and their source regions influencing North America during (a) winter and (b) summer. (SH = specific humidity.)

Atmospheric Lifting Mechanisms

When an air mass is lifted, it cools adiabatically (by expansion). When the cooling reaches the dew-point temperature, moisture in the saturated air can condense, forming clouds and perhaps precipitation. Four principal lifting mechanisms, illustrated in **Figure 5.22**, operate in the atmosphere:

- Convergent lifting results when air flows toward an area of low pressure.
- Convectional lifting happens when air is stimulated by local surface heating.
- Orographic lifting occurs when air is forced over a barrier such as a mountain range.
- Frontal lifting occurs as air is displaced upward along the leading edges of contrasting air masses.

Convergent Lifting

Air flowing from different directions into the same low-pressure area is converging, displacing air upward in **convergent lifting** (Figure 5.22a). All along the equatorial region, the southeast and northeast trade winds converge, forming the intertropical convergence zone (ITCZ) and areas of extensive convergent uplift, towering cumulonimbus cloud development, and high average annual precipitation (look back to Geosystems in Action 4).

Convectional Lifting

When an air mass passes from a maritime source region to a warmer continental region, heating from the warmer land surface causes lifting and convection in the air mass. Other sources of surface heating include urban heat islands and the dark soil in plowed fields; the warmer surfaces produce **convectional lifting**. If conditions are unstable, initial lifting continues and clouds develop. Figure 5.22b illustrates convectional action stimulated by local heating, with unstable conditions present in the atmosphere. (Look back to Figure 5.14 for an example of these conditions.)

Florida's precipitation generally illustrates both convergent and convectional lifting mechanisms. Heating of the land produces a convergence of onshore winds from

◀**Figure 5.21 Lake-effect snowbelts of the Great Lakes.** [(a) NCDC's *Climatic Atlas of the United States*, p. 53. (c) *Terra* MODIS image, NASA/GSFC. (d) David Duprey/AP Images.]

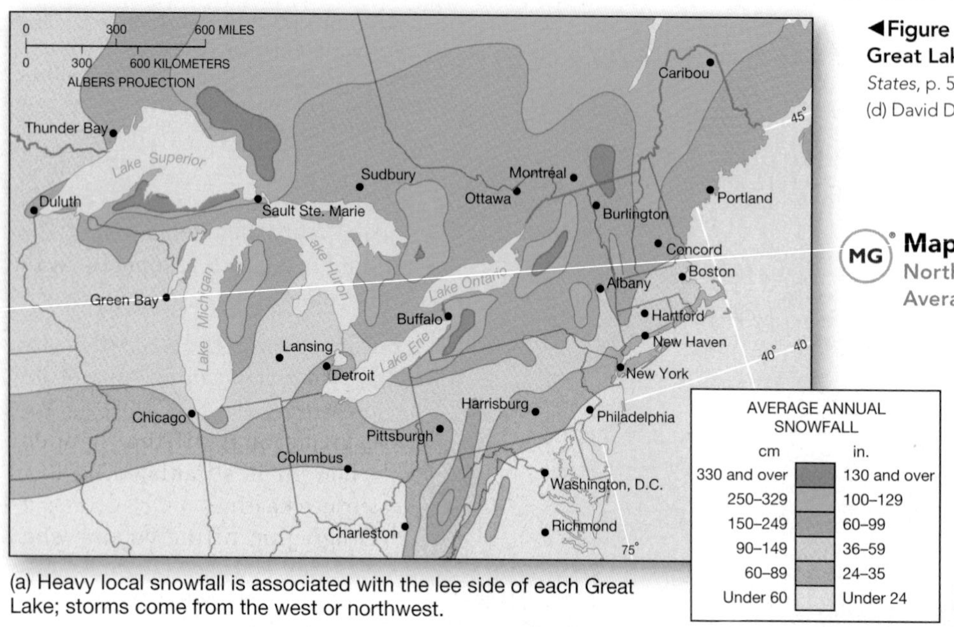

(a) Heavy local snowfall is associated with the lee side of each Great Lake; storms come from the west or northwest.

MG MapMaster
North America Physical Environment
Average Annual Snowfall

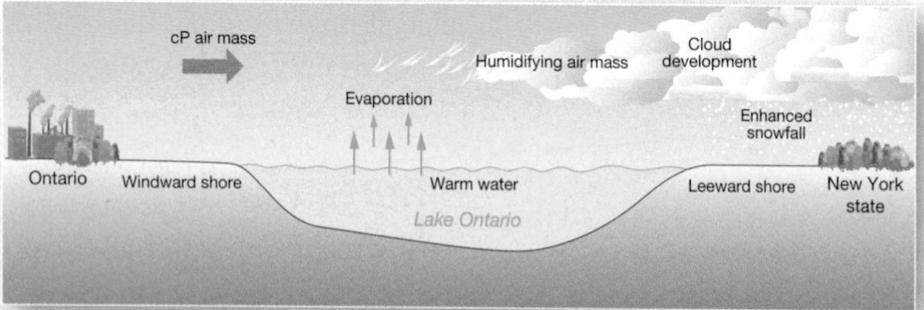

(b) Processes causing lake-effect snowfall are generally limited to about 50 km (30 mi) to 100 km (60 mi) inland.

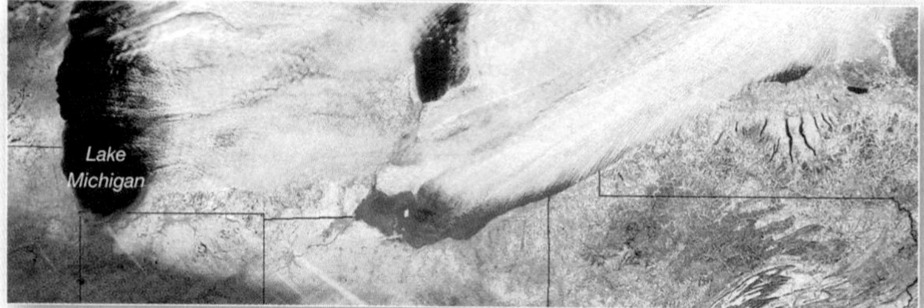

(c) Satellite image shows lake-effect weather in December.

(d) Heavy snowfall buries Buffalo, New York, in December 2010, closing the New York State Thruway.

the Atlantic and the Gulf of Mexico. As an example of local heating and convectional lifting, **Figure 5.23** depicts a day on which the landmass of Florida is warmer than the surrounding Gulf of Mexico and Atlantic Ocean. Because the Sun's radiation gradually heats the land throughout the day and warms the air above it, convectional showers tend to form in the afternoon and early evening. Thus, Florida has the highest frequency of days with thunderstorms in the United States.

Orographic Lifting

The physical presence of a mountain acts as a topographic barrier to migrating air masses. **Orographic lifting** (*oro* means "mountain") occurs when air is forcibly lifted upslope as it is pushed against a mountain (Figure 5.22c). The lifting air cools adiabatically. Stable air forced upward in this manner may produce stratiform clouds, whereas unstable or conditionally unstable air usually forms a line of cumulus and cumulonimbus clouds. An orographic barrier enhances convectional activity and causes additional lifting during the passage of weather fronts and cyclonic systems, thereby extracting more moisture from passing air masses and resulting in *orographic precipitation.*

Figure 5.24 illustrates the operation of orographic lifting under unstable conditions. On the *windward slope* of the mountain, air is lifted and cools, causing moisture to condense and form precipitation; on the *leeward slope*, the descending air mass heats by compression, and any remaining water in the air evaporates. Thus, air beginning its ascent up a mountain can be warm and moist, but finishing its descent on the leeward slope, it becomes hot and dry. The term **rain shadow** is applied to this dry, leeward side of mountains.

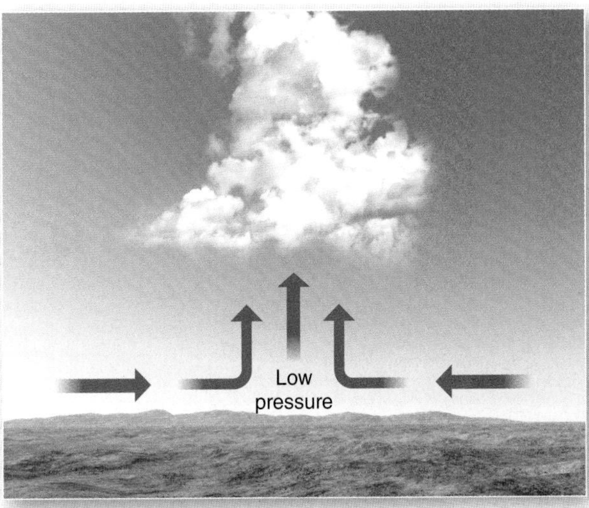

(a) Convergent lifting

(b) Convectional lifting

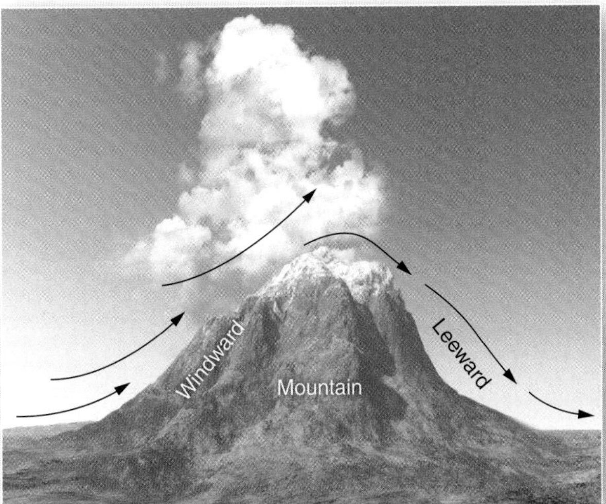

(c) Orographic lifting

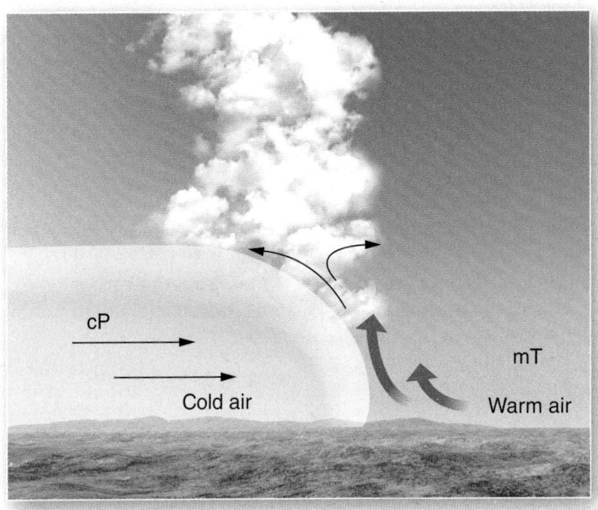

(d) Frontal lifting, cold-front example

▲**Figure 5.22 Four atmospheric lifting mechanisms.**

◀**Figure 5.23 Convectional activity over the Florida peninsula.** Cumulus clouds cover the land, with several cells developing into cumulonimbus thunderheads. [*Terra* MODIS image, NASA/GSFC.]

In North America, the *chinook winds* (called *föhn* or *foehn* winds in Europe) are the warm, downslope airflows characteristic of the leeward side of mountains. Such winds can bring a 20-C° (36-F°) jump in temperature and greatly reduce relative humidity.

In the United States, rain-shadow conditions occur east of the Cascade Range, the Sierra Nevada, and the Rocky Mountains (**Figure 5.25**). The precipitation pattern of windward and leeward slopes is seen worldwide, as confirmed by the precipitation maps for North America (Figure 6.6) and the world (Figure 7.1).

Frontal Lifting (Cold and Warm Fronts)

The leading edge of an advancing air mass is its *front*. Vilhelm Bjerknes (1862–1951) first applied the term while working with a team of meteorologists in Norway during

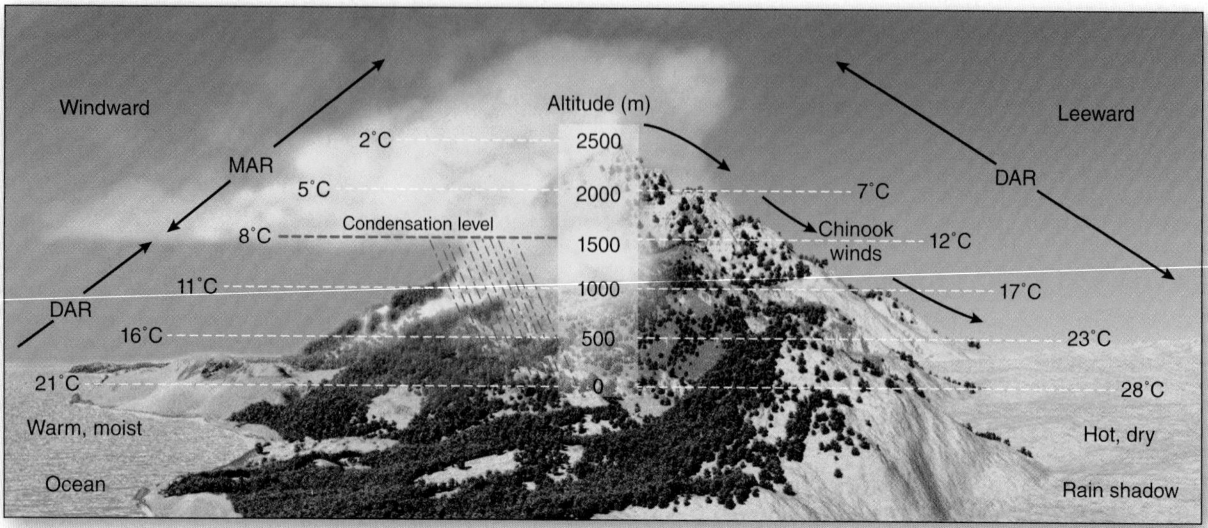

(a) Prevailing winds force warm, moist air upward against a mountain range, producing adiabatic cooling, eventual saturation and net condensation, cloud formation, and precipitation. On the leeward slope, as the "dried" air descends, compressional heating warms it, and evaporation dominates, creating the hot, relatively dry rain shadow.

▲**Figure 5.24 Orographic precipitation, unstable conditions assumed.** Review Figures 5.13 and 5.14 as you work through the temperature changes in part (a). A landscape affected by orographic precipitation is in part (b). [(b) *Terra* MODIS, NASA/GSFC.]

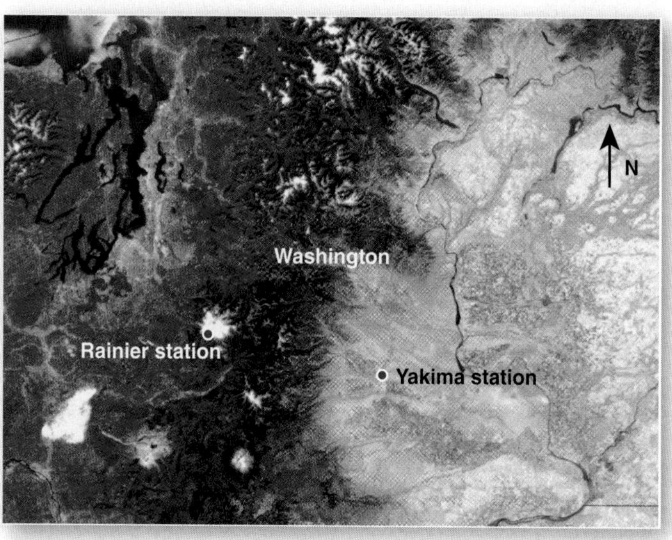

(b) The wetter windward slopes near Rainier station are in contrast to the drier leeward landscapes near Yakima station in Washington.

▼**Figure 5.25 Clouds and rain shadow produced by orographic lifting.** Over the Sierra Nevada in California and Nevada, the rain shadow produced by descending, warming air contrasts with the clouds on the windward side (note the wind direction at the bottom of the photo). [Robert Christopherson.]

World War I. Weather systems seemed to them to be migrating air mass "armies" doing battle along fronts. A front is a place of atmospheric discontinuity, a narrow zone forming a line of conflict between two air masses of different temperature, pressure, humidity, wind direction and speed, and cloud development. The leading edge of a

GEOreport 5.2 Mountains cause record rains

Mount Waialeale, on the island of Kaua'i, Hawai'i, rises 1569 m (5147 ft) above sea level. On its windward slope, rainfall averaged 1234 cm (486 in., or 40.5 ft) a year for the years 1941–1992. In contrast, the rain-shadow side of Kaua'i received only 50 cm (20 in.) of rain annually. If no islands existed at this location, this portion of the Pacific Ocean would receive only an average 63.5 cm (25 in.) of precipitation a year. (These statistics are from established weather stations with a consistent record of weather data; several stations claim higher rainfall values, but do not have dependable measurement records.)

Cherrapunji, India, is 1313 m (4309 ft) above sea level at 25° N latitude, in the Assam Hills south of the Himalayas. Summer monsoons pour in from the Indian Ocean and the Bay of Bengal, producing 930 cm (366 in., or 30.5 ft) of rainfall in 1 month. Not surprisingly, Cherrapunji holds the all-time precipitation record for a single year, 2647 cm (1042 in., or 86.8 ft), and for every other time interval from 15 days to 2 years. The average annual precipitation there is 1143 cm (450 in., 37.5 ft), placing it second only to Mount Waialeale.

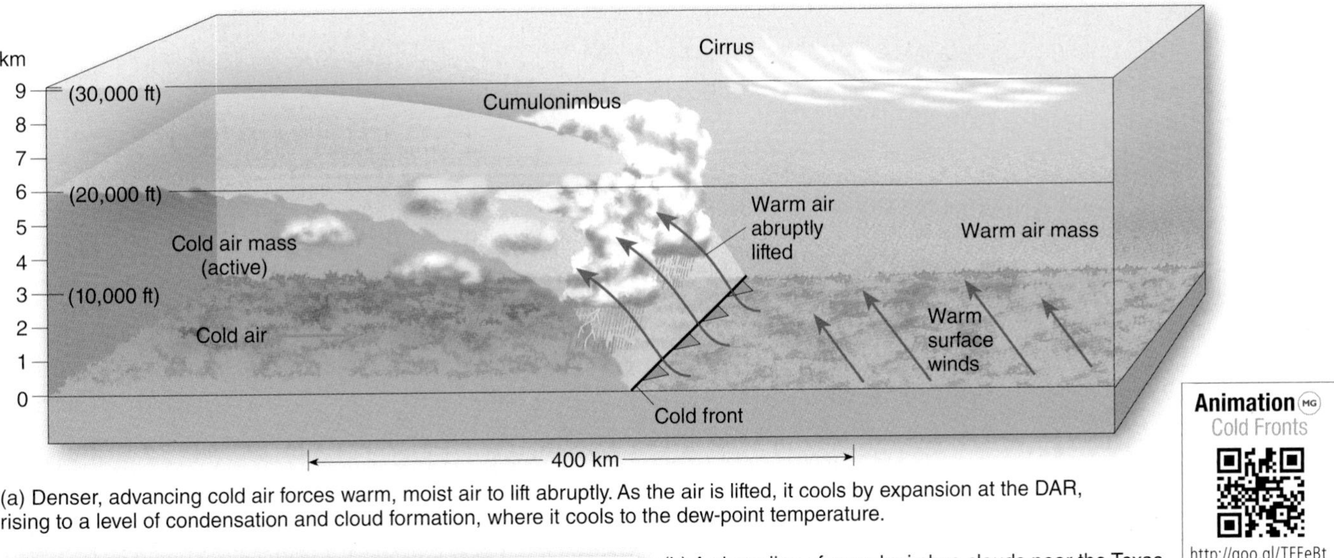

(a) Denser, advancing cold air forces warm, moist air to lift abruptly. As the air is lifted, it cools by expansion at the DAR, rising to a level of condensation and cloud formation, where it cools to the dew-point temperature.

Animation (MG) Cold Fronts http://goo.gl/TFFeBt

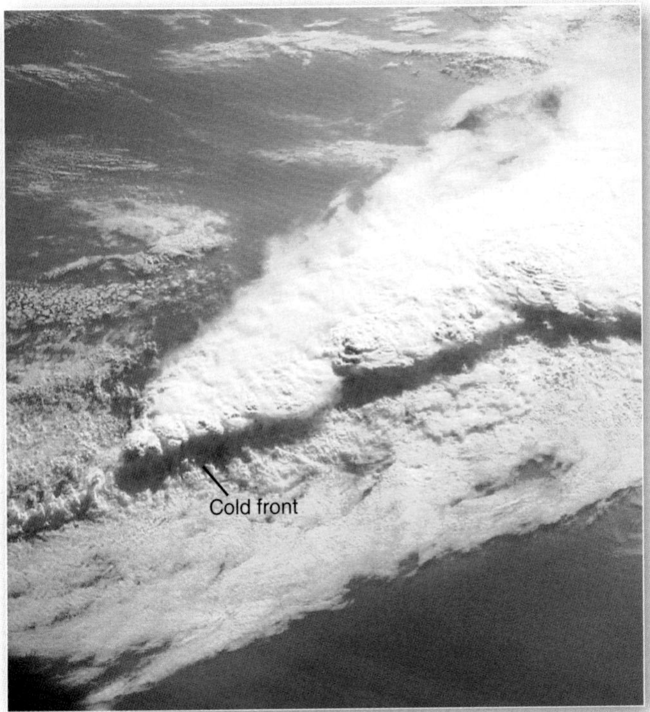

(b) A sharp line of cumulonimbus clouds near the Texas coast and Gulf of Mexico marks a cold front and squall line. The cloud formation rises to 17,000 m (56,000 ft).

▲**Figure 5.26 A typical cold front.** [(b) NASA.]

cold air mass is a **cold front**, whereas the leading edge of a warm air mass is a **warm front** (**Figures 5.26** and **5.27**).

Cold Front The steep face of an advancing cold air mass reflects the ground-hugging nature of cold air, caused by its greater density and more uniform characteristics compared to the warmer air mass it displaces (Figure 5.26a). Warm, moist air in advance of the cold front lifts upward abruptly and experiences the same adiabatic rates of cooling and factors of stability or instability that pertain to all lifting air parcels.

On weather maps, such as in Geosystems in Action 5 on page 166, a cold front is depicted as a line with triangular spikes that point in the direction of frontal movement along an advancing air mass.

A day or two ahead of a cold front's arrival, high cirrus clouds appear. Shifting winds, dropping temperature, and lowering barometric pressure mark the front's advance due to lifting of the displaced warmer air along the front's leading edge. At the line of most intense lifting, usually traveling just ahead of the front itself, air pressure drops to a local low. Clouds may build along the cold front into characteristic cumulonimbus form and may appear as an advancing wall of clouds. Precipitation usually is heavy, containing large droplets, and can be accompanied by hail, lightning, and thunder.

The aftermath of a cold front's passage usually brings northerly winds in the Northern Hemisphere and southerly winds in the Southern Hemisphere as anticyclonic high pressure advances. Temperatures drop, and air pressure rises in response to the cooler, denser air; cloud cover breaks and clears.

A fast-advancing cold front can cause violent lifting, creating a zone known as a **squall line** right along or slightly ahead of the front. (A *squall* is a sudden episode of high winds that is generally associated with bands of thunderstorms.) Along a squall line, such as the one in the Gulf of Mexico shown in Figure 5.26b, wind patterns are turbulent and wildly changing, and precipitation is intense. The well-defined frontal clouds in the photograph rise abruptly, feeding the formation of new thunderstorms along the front. Tornadoes also may develop along such a squall line.

Warm Front Warm air masses can be carried by the jet stream into regions with colder air, such as when an airflow called the "Pineapple Express" carries warm, moist air from Hawai'i and the Pacific into California and the Southwest during July and August. The leading edge of

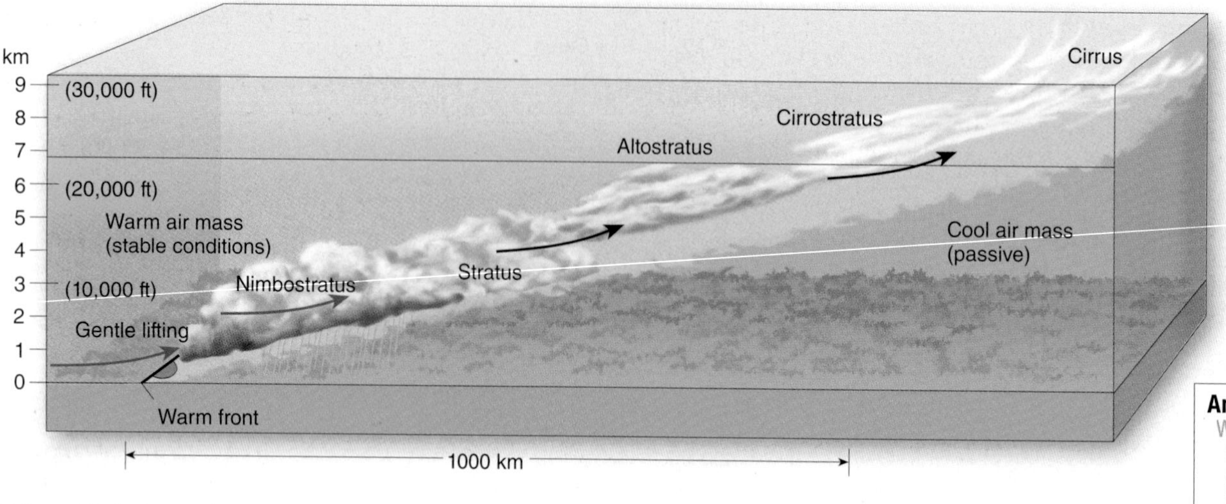

▲**Figure 5.27 A typical warm front.** Note the sequence of cloud development as the warm front approaches. Warm air slides upward over a wedge of cooler, passive air near the ground. Gentle lifting of the warm, moist air produces nimbostratus and stratus clouds and drizzly rain showers, in contrast to the more dramatic cold-front precipitation.

an advancing warm air mass is unable to displace cooler, passive air, which is denser along the surface. Instead, the warm air tends to push the cooler, underlying air into a characteristic wedge shape, with the warmer air sliding up over the cooler air. Thus, in the cooler-air region, a temperature inversion is present, sometimes causing poor air drainage and stagnation.

Figure 5.27 illustrates a typical warm front, in which gentle lifting of mT air leads to stratiform cloud development and characteristic nimbostratus clouds as well as drizzly precipitation. A warm front presents a progression of cloud development to an observer: High cirrus and cirrostratus clouds announce the advancing frontal system; then come lower and thicker altostratus clouds; and, finally, still lower and thicker stratus clouds appear within several hundred kilometers of the front. A line with semicircles facing in the direction of frontal movement denotes a warm front on weather maps (see the map in Figure GIA 5.1 on page 166).

Midlatitude Cyclonic Systems

The conflict between contrasting air masses can develop a **midlatitude cyclone**, also known as a **wave cyclone** or *extratropical cyclone*. Midlatitude cyclones are migrating low-pressure weather systems that occur in the middle latitudes, outside the tropics. They have a low-pressure center with converging, ascending air spiraling inward counterclockwise in the Northern Hemisphere and inward clockwise in the Southern Hemisphere, owing to the combined influences of the *pressure gradient force*, *Coriolis force*, and *surface friction* (see the discussion in Chapter 4). These systems, which can be 1600 km (1000 mi) wide, dominate weather patterns in the middle and higher latitudes. Because of the undulating nature of frontal boundaries and of the jet streams that steer these cyclones across continents, the term *wave* is appropriate. An emerging model of this interactive system characterizes air mass flows as being like "conveyor belts," as described in Figure GIA 5.2, just ahead.

In the United States, midlatitude cyclonic systems known as *nor'easters* are notorious for bringing heavy snows to the northeast and along the Eastern seaboard. The February 2013 nor'easter resulted from the merging of two low-pressure areas off the northeastern coast on February 8, producing record snowfall in Portland, Maine (81 cm, or 32 in.), and a maximum snowfall of 100 cm (40 in.) in Hamden, Connecticut. This precipitation arrived with pressure readings around 968 mb, wind gusts up to 164 kmph (102 mph), and storm surges up to 1.3 m (4.2 ft). Another significant nor'easter occurred in March 2014 (**Figure 5.28**).

The intense high-speed winds of the jet streams guide cyclonic systems, with their attendant air masses, across the continent (review jet streams in Figure 4.13) along *storm tracks* that shift in latitude with the Sun and the seasons. Typical storm tracks crossing North America are farther northward in summer and farther southward in winter. As the storm tracks begin to shift northward in the spring, cP and mT air masses are in their clearest conflict. This is the time of strongest frontal activity, featuring thunderstorms and tornadoes.

Life Cycle of a Midlatitude Cyclone

Geosystems in Action 5 shows the birth, maturity, and death of a typical midlatitude cyclone in several stages, along with an idealized weather map. On average, a midlatitude cyclonic system takes 3–10 days to progress through this life cycle from the area where it develops to the area where it finally dissolves.

- The first stage is *cyclogenesis*, the atmospheric process in which low-pressure wave cyclones develop and strengthen. This process usually begins along the polar front, where cold and warm air masses converge and are drawn into conflict, creating potentially unstable conditions. For a wave cyclone to form along the polar front, a compensating area of divergence aloft must match a surface point of air convergence. Even a slight disturbance along the polar front, perhaps a small change in the path of the jet stream, can initiate the converging, ascending flow of air and thus a surface low-pressure system as in Figure GIA 5.1, Stage 1.

- In the open stage, warm air to the east of the developing low-pressure center of a Northern Hemisphere midlatitude cyclone begins to move northward along an advancing front, while cold air advances southward west of the center (Figure GIA 5.1, Stage 2). As the midlatitude cyclone matures, the counterclockwise flow draws the cold air mass from the north and west and the warm air mass from the south. In the cross section, you can see the profiles of both a cold front and a warm front and each air mass segment.
- Next is the occluded stage (Figure GIA 5.1, Stage 3). Remember the relation between air temperature and the density of an air mass. The colder cP air mass is denser than the warmer mT air mass. This cooler, more unified air mass, acting like a bulldozer blade, moves faster than the warm front. Cold fronts can travel at an average 40 kmph (25 mph), whereas warm fronts average roughly half that, 16–24 kmph (10–15 mph). Thus, a cold front often overtakes the cyclonic warm front and wedges beneath it, producing an **occluded front** (*occlude* means "to close").
- Finally, the dissolving stage of the midlatitude cyclone occurs when its lifting mechanism is completely cut off from the warm air mass that was its source of energy and moisture. Remnants of the cyclonic system then dissipate in the atmosphere, perhaps after passage across the country, as in Figure GIA 5.1, Stage 4.

▼Figure 5.28 A midlatitude cyclonic system off the U.S/Canadian Atlantic coast in 2014. This nor'easter brought blizzard conditions to Massachusetts, Maine, and the Canadian Maritime provinces. [VIIRS instrument aboard Suomi NPP/NOAA.]

Although the actual patterns of cyclonic passage over North America are widely varied in shape and duration, you can apply this general model of the stages of a midlatitude cyclone, along with your understanding of warm and cold fronts, to your reading of the daily weather map.

Weather Maps and Forecasting

Synoptic analysis is the evaluation of weather data collected at a specific time. Building a database of wind, pressure, temperature, and moisture conditions is key to *numerical*, or computer-based, *weather prediction* and the development of weather-forecasting models. Development of numerical models is a great challenge because the atmosphere operates as a nonlinear system, tending toward chaotic behavior. Slight variations in the input data or slight changes in the model's basic assumptions can produce widely varying forecasts. The accuracy of forecasts continues to improve with technological advancements in instruments and software and with our increasing knowledge of the atmospheric interactions that produce weather.

Weather data necessary for the preparation of a synoptic map and forecast include the following:

- Barometric pressure
- Pressure tendency (steady, rising, falling)
- Surface air temperature
- Dew-point temperature
- Wind speed, direction, and character (gusts, squalls)
- Type and movement of clouds
- Current weather
- State of the sky (current sky conditions)
- Visibility; vision obstruction (fog, haze)
- Precipitation since last observation

Environmental satellites are one of the key tools in forecasting weather and analyzing climate. Massive computers handle volumes of data from surface, aircraft, and orbital platforms for accurate forecasting of near-term weather. These data are also used for assessing climatic change. In the United States, the National Weather Service (NWS) provides weather forecasts and current satellite images (see http://www.weather.gov/). Internationally, the World Meteorological Organization coordinates weather information (see http://www.wmo.ch/).

(text continued on page 168)

A midlatitude cyclone is a low-pressure system that forms when a cool air mass (cP) collides with a warm, moist air mass (mT). Steered by the jet stream, these storms typically migrate from west to east. On these pages, a cyclonic system of air mass interactions is represented both in the established Norwegian model (GIA 5.1), and in the new conveyor belt model (GIA 5.2). Remote sensing from satellite platforms is essential for analyzing cyclonic structure (GIA 5.3).

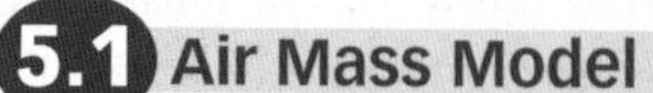

5.1 Air Mass Model

The life cycle of a midlatitude cyclone has four stages that unfold at the meeting point between cold and warm air masses.

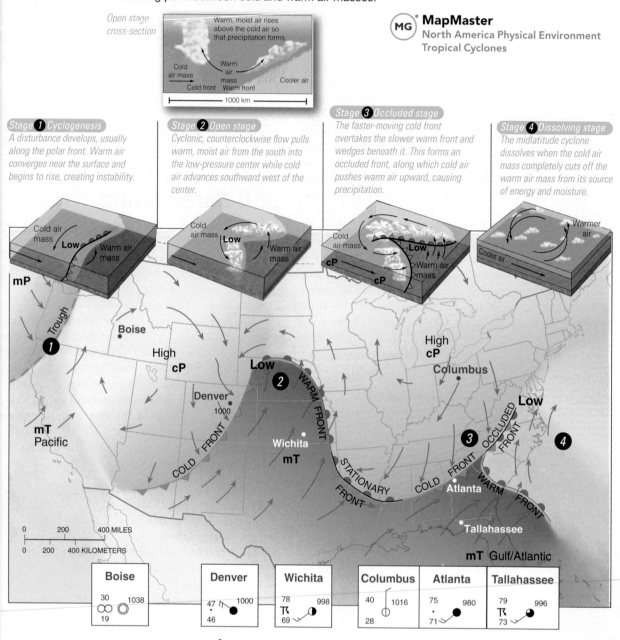

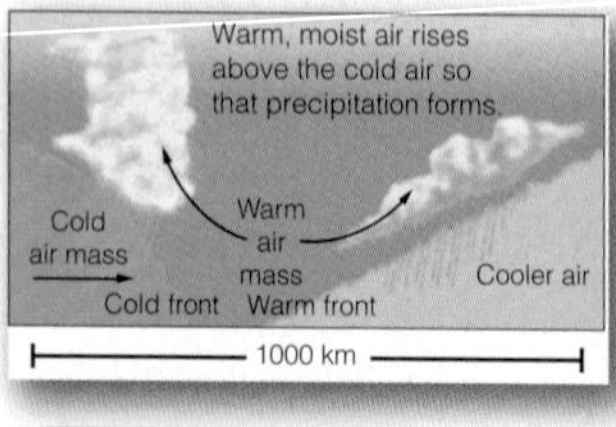

MapMaster
North America Physical Environment
Tropical Cyclones

Open stage cross-section

Warm, moist air rises above the cold air so that precipitation forms.
Cold air mass
Warm air mass
Cooler air
Cold front
Warm front
1000 km

Stage 1 Cyclogenesis
A disturbance develops, usually along the polar front. Warm air converges near the surface and begins to rise, creating instability.

Stage 2 Open stage
Cyclonic, counterclockwise flow pulls warm, moist air from the south into the low-pressure center while cold air advances southward west of the center.

Stage 3 Occluded stage
The faster-moving cold front overtakes the slower warm front and wedges beneath it. This forms an occluded front, along which cold air pushes warm air upward, causing precipitation.

Stage 4 Dissolving stage
The midlatitude cyclone dissolves when the cold air mass completely cuts off the warm air mass from its source of energy and moisture.

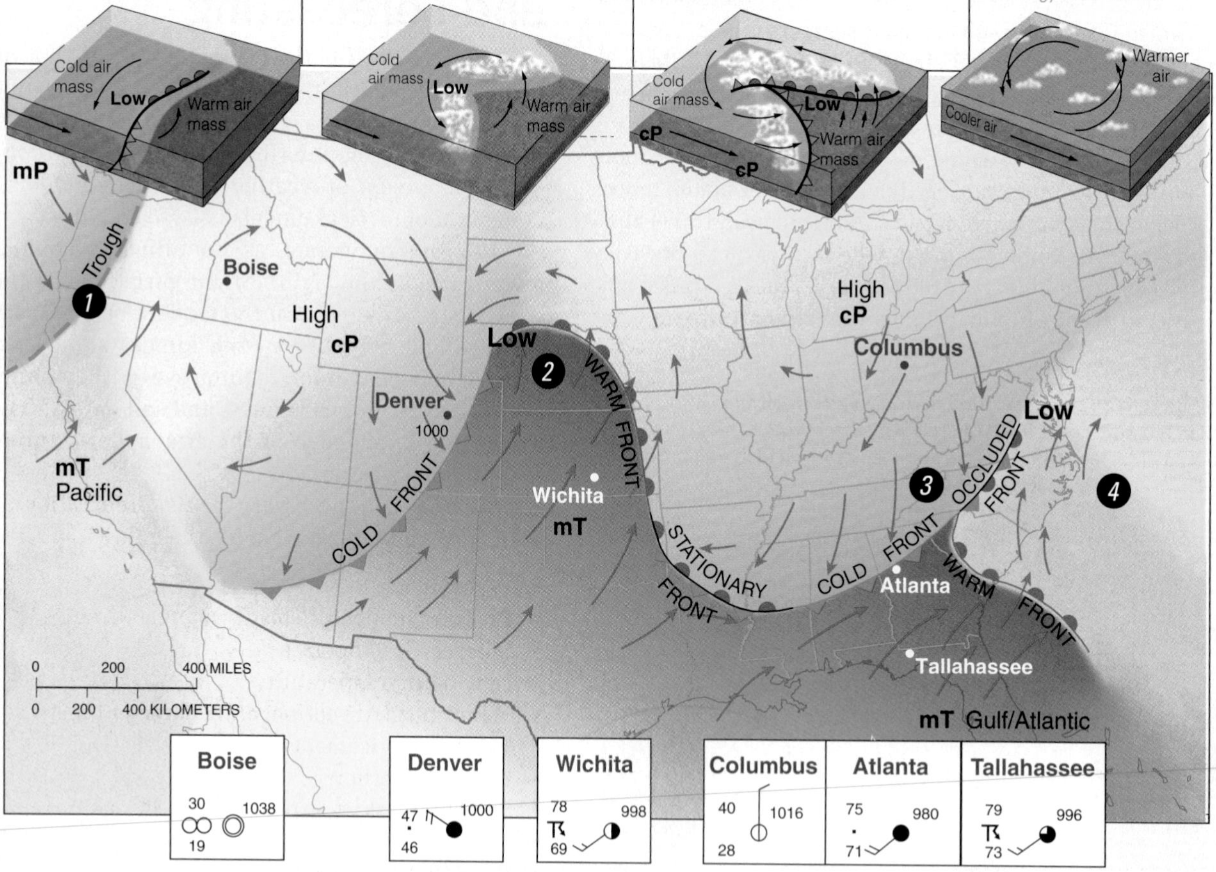

Cold air mass
Low
Warm air mass
Cold air mass
Low
Warm air mass
Cold air mass
cP
Low
Warm air mass
cP
Warmer air
Cooler air

mP
Trough
Boise
High
cP
Low
Denver
1000
WARM FRONT
COLD FRONT
Wichita
mT
mT Pacific
High
cP
Columbus
Low
OCCLUDED FRONT
STATIONARY FRONT
COLD FRONT
Atlanta
WARM FRONT
Tallahassee
mT Gulf/Atlantic
0 200 400 MILES
0 200 400 KILOMETERS

Boise	Denver	Wichita	Columbus	Atlanta	Tallahassee
30 / 19 / 1038	47 / 46 / 1000	78 / 69 / 998	40 / 28 / 1016	75 / 71 / 980	79 / 73 / 996

Key:

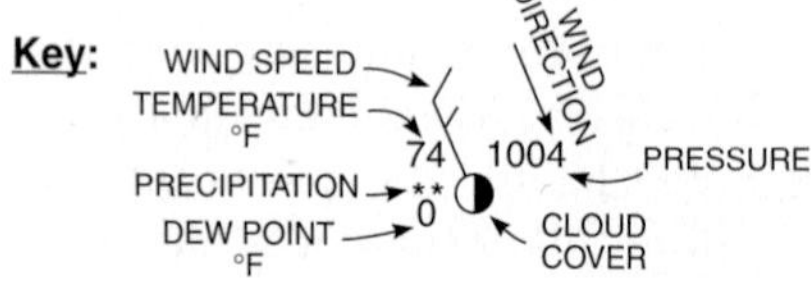

See MasteringGeography™ for a detailed explanation of weather station symbols. See Figure 4.11 for explanation of wind speed symbols.

Describe: Based on the map, what is the weather in Denver and Wichita? How will their weather change as the storm moves east?

Animation Midlatitude Cyclones
http://goo.gl/ZWjpVS

MasteringGeography™ Visit the Study Area in MasteringGeography™ to explore midlatitude cyclones.

Visualize: Study geoscience animations of a midlatitude cyclone.

Assess: Demonstrate understanding of midlatitude cyclones (if assigned by instructor).

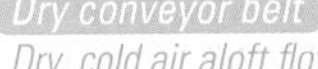

5.2 Conveyor Belt Model

Three conveyors of air and moisture, one aloft and two initially along the surface, interact to produce a midlatitude cyclone and sustain it as a dynamic system.

Dry conveyor belt

Dry, cold air aloft flows from the west, with some descending behind the cold front as clear, cold air. Another branch of this flow moves cyclonically toward the low. This generally cloud-free dry sector can form a "dry slot," separating warm and cold cloud bands, clearly visible on satellite images.

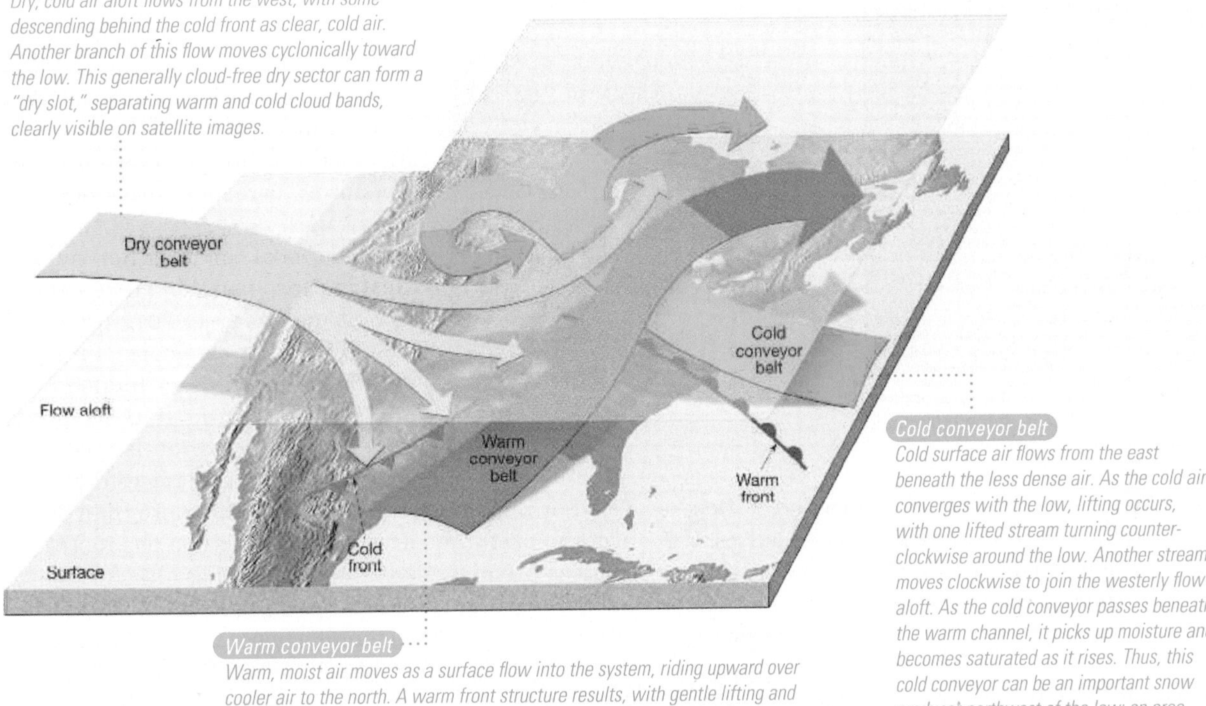

Cold conveyor belt

Cold surface air flows from the east beneath the less dense air. As the cold air converges with the low, lifting occurs, with one lifted stream turning counter-clockwise around the low. Another stream moves clockwise to join the westerly flow aloft. As the cold conveyor passes beneath the warm channel, it picks up moisture and becomes saturated as it rises. Thus, this cold conveyor can be an important snow producer northwest of the low; an area labeled in GIA 5.3a as a "comma head."

Warm conveyor belt

Warm, moist air moves as a surface flow into the system, riding upward over cooler air to the north. A warm front structure results, with gentle lifting and stratus clouds. During its passage, moisture is delivered ahead of the cold front. This flow is the principal moisture source for the frontal systems. Eventually, the warm air conveyor turns eastward and joins the westerly flow aloft.

Explain: How do the conveyor belts interact to produce precipitation north of the warm front?

5.3 Observing a Midlatitude Cyclone

Satellite images reveal the flow of moist and dry air that drives a midlatitude cyclone, as well as how the storm changes over time.

(a) September 26, 2011: Occluded stage. A midlatitude cyclone over the U.S. Midwest.

(b) September 26, 2011: Water vapor image. The cold conveyor belt delivers cold, dry air (in yellow) that will soon cut off the storm's supply of warm, moist air.

GEOquiz

1. Summarize: In your own words, summarize the life cycle of a midlatitude cyclone.

2. Analyze: Which of the three conveyor belts is most critical in maintaining a midlatitude cyclone? Explain.

3. From the sources given in this chapter, find several satellite images of midlatitude cyclones and identify the basic elements described here. List the dates you found.

(a) A radar antenna is within the dome structure of the NWS weather installation at the Indianapolis International Airport.

(b) ASOS weather-instrument station.

◀**Figure 5.29 NWS weather installation and ASOS weather-instrument station.** [Bobbé Christopherson.]

An essential element of weather forecasting is Doppler radar. Using backscatter from two radar pulses, it detects the direction of moisture droplets toward or away from the radar source, indicating wind direction and speed. This information is critical to making accurate severe storm warnings. As part of the Next Generation Weather Radar (NEXRAD) program, the NWS operates 159 Doppler radar systems, mainly in the United States (http://radar.weather.gov/); installations also exist in Japan, Guam, South Korea, and the Azores (**Figure 5.29a**). For links to weather maps, current forecasts, satellite images, and the latest radar, go to the *MasteringGeography* website.

Weather information in the United States comes mainly from the Automated Surface Observing System (ASOS), which is installed at over 900 airports across the country (**Figure 5.29b**). An ASOS instrument array is made up of numerous sensors that supply continuous on-the-ground data concerning weather elements, helping the NWS increase the timeliness and accuracy of its forecasts. The Advanced Weather Interactive Processing System (AWIPS) of the National Oceanic and Atmospheric Administration (NOAA) integrates a variety of data—for example, air pressure, water vapor, humidity, Doppler radar, lightning strikes in real time, and wind profiles—to improve forecast accuracy and severe weather warnings.

Violent Weather

Weather is a continuous reminder that the flow of energy across the latitudes can at times set into motion destructive, violent events. We focus in this chapter on thunderstorms, derechos, tornadoes, and hurricanes.

The cost of weather-related destruction can be staggering—Hurricane Sandy in 2012 produced $65 billion in damages. In 2005, weather-related losses totaled $210 billion; Hurricane Katrina alone produced $146 billion (adjusted to current dollars) in damage that year. Weather-related destruction has risen more than 500% over the past three decades as population has increased in areas prone to violent weather and as climate change intensifies weather anomalies. In the United States, government research and monitoring of violent weather are centered at NOAA's National Severe Storms Laboratory and Storm Prediction Center—see http://www.nssl.noaa.gov/ and http://www.spc.noaa.gov/; consult these sites for each of the topics that follow. Studies estimate that annual weather-related damage losses could exceed $1 trillion by 2040.

Thunderstorms

By definition, a *thunderstorm* is a type of turbulent weather accompanied by lightning and thunder. Such storms are characterized by a buildup of giant cumulonimbus clouds that can be associated with squall lines of heavy rain, including sleet, blustery winds, hail, and tornadoes. Thunderstorms may develop within an air mass, in a line along a front (particularly a cold front), or where mountain slopes cause orographic lifting.

Thousands of thunderstorms occur on Earth at any given moment. Equatorial regions and the ITCZ experience many of them, exemplified by the city of Kampala, Uganda, in East Africa (north of Lake Victoria), which sits virtually

GEOreport 5.3 Kentucky ice storm causes record power losses

According to the NWS, an *ice storm* is a winter storm in which at least 6.4 mm (0.25 in.) of ice accumulate on exposed surfaces. Ice storms occur when a layer of warm air is between two layers of cold air. When precipitation falls through the warm layer into a below-freezing layer of air nearer the ground layer, it may form *sleet*, which is composed of freezing rain, ice glaze, and ice pellets. In late January 2009, an ice storm hit southern Indiana and central Kentucky. Over a 3-day period, precipitation began as freezing rain, later changing to sleet and finally snow. Across Kentucky, the ice-related damage to power lines resulted in 609,000 homes and businesses without power; outages continued for up to 10 days, and area schools were closed for a week. Ice storms of similar intensity blanketed the Midwest, upper South, and Northeast in February 2011.

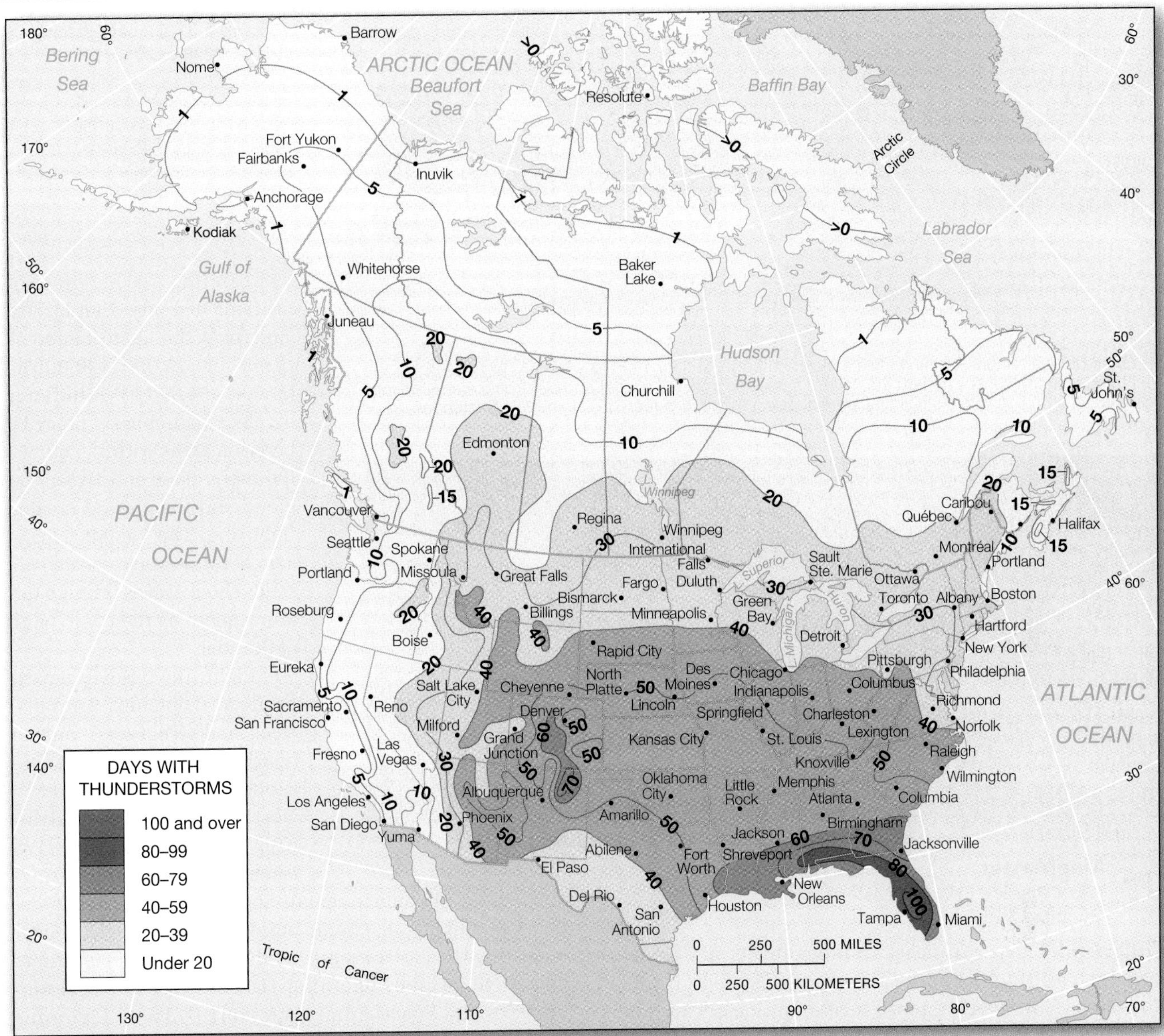

▲**Figure 5.30 Thunderstorm occurrence.** Average annual number of days experiencing thunderstorms. Compare this map with the location of mT air masses in Figure 5.20. [Data courtesy of NWS; *Climatic Atlas of Canada*, Atmospheric Environment Service, Canada.]

MG **MapMaster** North America Physical Environment Thunderstorm Occurence Per Year

on the equator and averages a record 242 days a year with thunderstorms. In North America, most thunderstorms occur in areas dominated by mT air masses (**Figure 5.30**).

A thunderstorm is fueled by the rapid upward movement of warm, moist air. As the air rises, cools, and condenses to form clouds and precipitation, tremendous energy is liberated by the condensation of large quantities of water vapor. This process locally heats the air, causing violent updrafts and downdrafts as rising parcels of air pull surrounding air into the column and as the frictional drag of raindrops pulls air toward the ground (review the illustration of a cumulonimbus cloud in Figure 5.16).

Turbulence and Wind Shear A distinguishing characteristic of thunderstorms is turbulence, which is created by the mixing of air of different densities or by the movement of air layers at different speeds and directions in the atmosphere. Thunderstorm activity also depends on *wind shear*, the variation of wind speed and direction with altitude—high wind shear (extreme and sudden variation) is needed to produce hail and tornadoes, two by-products of thunderstorm activity.

Thunderstorms can produce severe turbulence in the form of *downbursts*, which are strong downdrafts that cause exceptionally strong winds near the ground. Downbursts are classified by size: A *macroburst* is at least 4.0 km (2.5 mi) wide and has winds in excess of 210 kmph (130 mph); a *microburst* is smaller in size and speed. Downbursts are characterized by the dreaded high-wind-shear conditions that can bring down aircraft. Such turbulence events are short-lived and hard to detect. NOAA's forecasting model, launched in 2012, gives hourly updates to improve predictions for severe weather events and aviation hazards (see http://rapidrefresh.noaa.gov/).

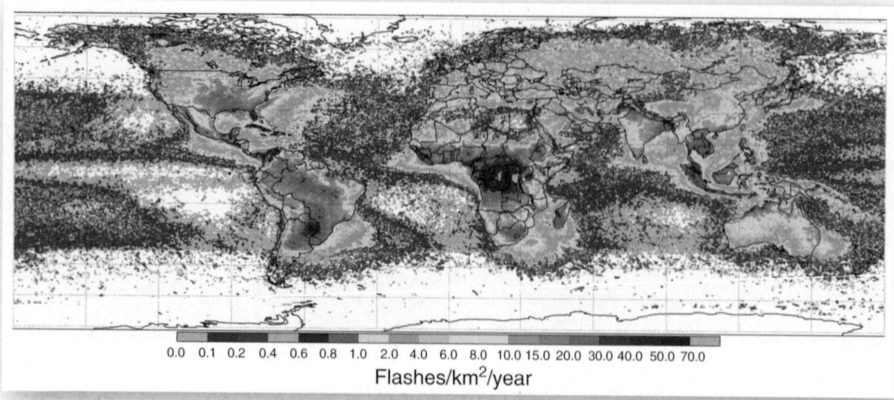

(a) Map of total annual lightning strikes (flashes) from January 1998 to February 2012. The lightning imaging sensor aboard the *TRMM* satellite combines optical and electronic elements that can detect lightning within individual storms, day or night, between 35° N and 35° S latitudes.

(b) Multiple lightning strikes in southern Arizona captured in a time-lapse photo.

◄Figure 5.31 Global lightning strikes, 1998 to 2012. [(a) Lightning Imaging Sensor-Optical Transient Detector (LIS-OTD) global lightning image obtained from the NASA EOSDIS Global Hydrology Resource Center DAAC, Huntsville, AL. Reprinted by permission of Richard Blakeslee. (b) Keith Kent/ Science Source.]

MG MapMaster
World Physical Environment
Lightning Strikes

Supercells The strongest thunderstorms are known as supercell thunderstorms, or *supercells*, and give rise to some of the world's most severe and costly weather events (such as hailstorms and tornadoes). Supercells often contain a deep, persistently rotating updraft called a **mesocyclone**, a spinning, cyclonic, rising column of air associated with a convective storm and ranging up to 10 km (6 mi) in diameter. A well-developed mesocyclone will produce heavy rain, large hail, blustery winds, and lightning; some mature mesocyclones will generate tornado activity (see Figure 5.33 and the discussion ahead).

The conditions conducive to forming thunderstorms and more intense supercells—lots of warm, moist air and strong convective activity—are enhanced by climate change. However, wind shear, another important factor in thunderstorm and supercell formation, will likely lessen in the midlatitudes as Arctic warming reduces overall temperature differences across the globe. Research is ongoing as to which of these effects will be more important for determining severe thunderstorm frequency in different regions of the world.

Lightning and Thunder An estimated 8 million lightning strikes occur each day on Earth. **Lightning** is the term for flashes of light caused by enormous electrical discharges—tens of millions to hundreds of millions of volts—that briefly superheat the air to temperatures of 15,000°–30,000°C (27,000°–54,000°F). A buildup of electrical-energy polarity between areas within a cumulonimbus cloud or between the cloud and the ground creates lightning. The violent expansion of this abruptly heated air sends shock waves through the atmosphere as the sonic bang of **thunder**.

Lightning poses a hazard to aircraft, people, animals, trees, and structures, causing nearly 200 deaths and thousands of injuries each year in North America. When lightning is imminent, the NWS issues *severe storm warnings* and cautions people to remain indoors. People caught outdoors as a lightning charge builds should not seek shelter beneath a tree, as trees are good conductors of electricity and often are hit by lightning. Data from the National Aeronautics and Space Administration's (NASA's) Lightning Imaging Sensor (LIS) show that about 90% of all strikes occur over land in response to increased convection over relatively warmer continental surfaces (**Figure 5.31**; see **http://thunder.msfc.nasa.gov/data/data_nldn.html**).

Hail Ice pellets larger than 0.5 cm (0.20 in.) that form within a cumulonimbus cloud are known as **hail**—or *hailstones*, after they fall to the ground. During hail formation, raindrops circulate repeatedly above and below the freezing level in the cloud, adding layers of ice until the circulation in the cloud can no longer support their weight. Hail may also grow from the addition of moisture on a snow pellet.

Pea-sized hail (0.63 cm, or 0.25 in., in diameter) is common, although hail can range from the size of quarters (2.54 cm, or 1.00 in.) to softballs (11.43 cm, or 4.50 in.). Baseball-sized (6.98 cm, or 2.75 in.) hail fell a half dozen times in 2010 in the United States alone. For larger hail to form, the frozen pellets must stay aloft for longer periods. The largest authenticated hailstone in the world, which fell from a thunderstorm supercell in Aurora, Nebraska, on June 22, 2003, measured 47.62 cm (18.75 in.) in circumference. However, the largest hailstone by diameter and weight fell in Vivian, South Dakota, in July 2010, measuring 20.2 cm (8.0 in.) in diameter and weighing an amazing 0.88 kg (1.9375 lbs).

Hail is common in the United States and Canada, although somewhat infrequent at any given place. Hail occurs perhaps every 1 or 2 years in the highest-frequency areas. Annual hail damage in the United States tops $800 million.

Derechos

Straight-line winds associated with fast-moving, severe thunderstorms can cause significant damage to urban areas as well as crop losses in agricultural regions. Such winds, known as **derechos**—or *plow winds,* in Canada—are produced by the powerful downbursts characteristic of thunderstorms. These strong, linear winds travel in excess of 26 m/s (58 mph) in straight paths fanning out along curved wind fronts over a wide swath of land. The name derives from a Spanish word meaning "direct" or "straight ahead."

Because downbursts occur in irregular clusters, the winds associated with a derecho may vary considerably in intensity along its path. In August 2007, a series of derechos occurred across northern Illinois, with wind gusts exceeding 57 m/s (128 mph)—some of the strongest ever measured. Researchers identified 377 derechos between 1986 and 2003, an average of about 21 per year. Reported derecho wind events have increased since 2000 and may continue to rise as climate change affects precipitation and storm intensity. For more information, see http://www.spc.noaa.gov/misc/AbtDerechos/derechofacts.htm.

Derechos pose distinct hazards to summer outdoor activities by overturning boats, hurling flying objects, and breaking tree trunks and limbs. About 70% of derechos occur between May and August in the U.S. Midwest, from Iowa, to Illinois, and into the Ohio River Valley. In June 2012, a derecho originated near Chicago and traveled southeastward toward Washington, D.C., causing damage and power outages for millions of people as well as several fatalities (**Figure 5.32**). From September through April, areas of derecho activity shift southward toward Texas and Alabama.

In May 2009, a fierce windstorm crossed Kansas, Missouri, and Illinois, reaching wind speeds of 100 mph and creating a path of destruction 100 miles wide. Scientists coined the term *super derecho* to describe this new

(a) A shelf cloud over LaPorte, Indiana, indicates the strong winds of the advancing derecho.

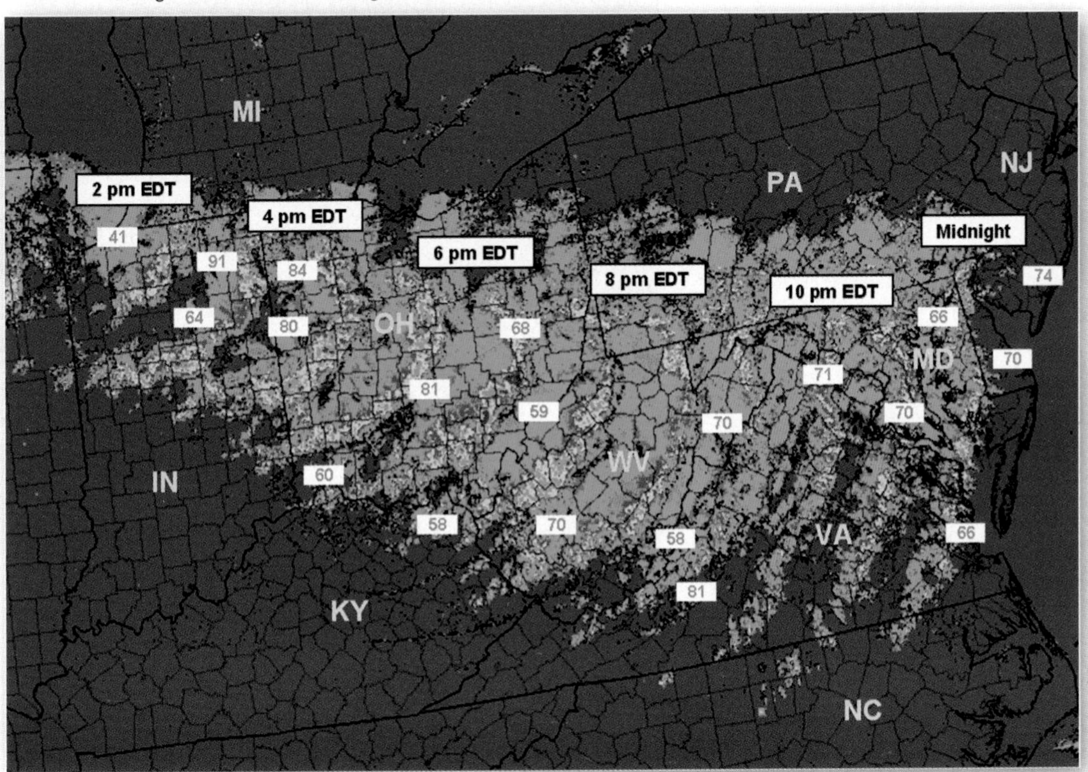

(b) Composite of hourly radar reflectivity imagery shows the development of the June 29, 2012, derecho event, including selected wind gusts (mph), beginning at 2 P.M. Eastern Daylight Time (far left) and ending at midnight (far right).

◀**Figure 5.32 The June 2012 derecho event.** [(a) Courtesy of Kevin Gould, NOAA. (b) Base image by G. Carbin, NOAA Storm Prediction Center.]

phenomenon: a derecho with an eyelike structure similar to a hurricane that spun off 18 tornadoes as it moved across Kansas. Scientists were able to forecast this wind event 24 hours in advance, thus reducing injuries and damage, and are using their forecasting models to investigate the development of this weather phenomenon.

Tornadoes

A **tornado** is a violently rotating column of air in contact with the ground surface, usually visible as a spinning vortex of clouds and debris. A tornado can range from a few meters to more than a kilometer in diameter and can last anywhere from a few moments to tens of minutes.

The updrafts associated with thunderstorm squall lines and supercells are the beginning stages of tornado development (however, fewer than half of supercells produce tornadoes). Figure GN 5.1 in Geosystems Now shows the supercells around Moore, Oklahoma, that spawned the destructive 2013 tornado. As moisture-laden air is drawn up into the circulation of a mesocyclone, energy is liberated by condensation, and the rotation of air increases speed (**Figure 5.33a**). The narrower the mesocyclone, the faster the spin of converging parcels of air being sucked into the rotation; this movement may form a smaller, dark gray **funnel cloud** that pulses from the bottom side of the supercell cloud. This funnel cloud may lower to Earth, resulting in a tornado (**Figure 5.33b**). When tornado circulation occurs over water, surface water is drawn some 3–5 m (10–16 ft) up into the funnel, forming a **waterspout**.

Tornado Measurement Pressures inside a tornado usually are about 10% less than those in the surrounding air. The inrushing convergence created by such a horizontal pressure gradient causes high wind speeds. In 1971, meteorologist Theodore Fujita designed the Fujita Scale, which classifies tornadoes according to wind speed as indicated by related property damage. The 2007 refinement of this scale is the Enhanced Fujita Scale, or EF Scale (**Table 5.1**). To assist with wind estimates, the EF Scale includes damage indicators, representing types of structures and vegetation affected, along with degree of damage ratings, both of which are listed at the URL cited in the table note.

The Storm Prediction Center in Kansas City, Missouri, provides short-term forecasting for thunderstorms and tornadoes to the public and to NWS field offices. Warning times of from 12 to 30 minutes are possible with current technology. From 1950 to 2010 in the United States, tornadoes caused over 5000 deaths (about 85 deaths per year), more than 80,000 injuries, and property damage of over $28 billion. The average annual cost of tornado damage is rising each year. In 2011, Joplin, Missouri, was hit by an EF-5 tornado that killed at least 159 people and cost an estimated $3 billion in damages, the most expensive in U.S. history.

▼Figure 5.33 Mesocyclone and tornado formation. [(b) Photo by Howard Bluestein, all rights reserved.]

Animation MG
Tornado Wind Patterns
http://goo.gl/tlfMNt

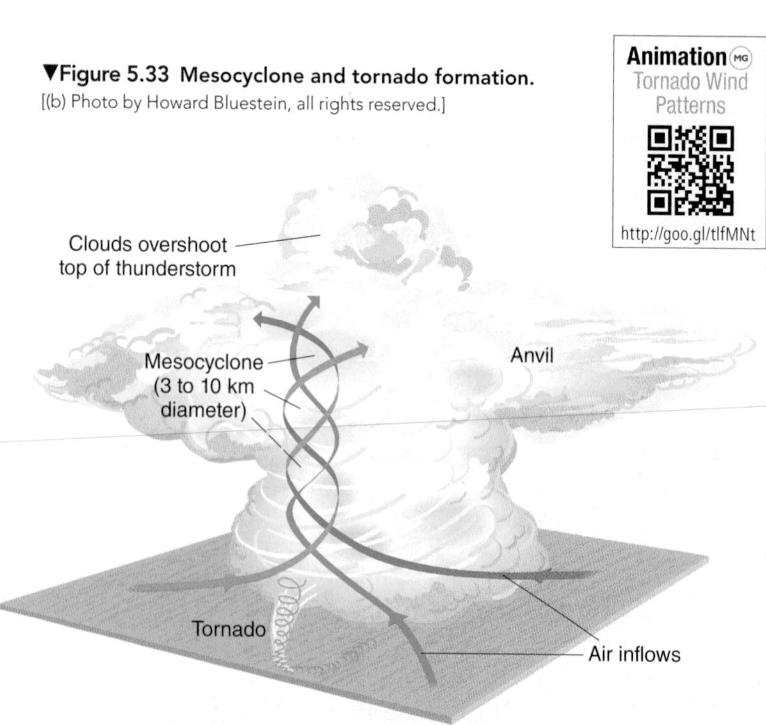

(a) Strong wind aloft establishes spinning, and updraft from thunderstorm development tilts the rotating air, causing a mesocyclone to form as a rotating updraft within the thunderstorm. If one forms, a tornado will descend from the lower portion of the mesocyclone.

(b) A tornado descends from the base of a supercell cloud near Spearman, Texas. Strong hail is falling to the left of the tornado.

TABLE 5.1 The Enhanced Fujita Scale

EF-Number	3-Second-Gust Wind Speed; Damage
EF-0 Gale	105–137 kmph (65–85 mph); *light damage*: branches broken, chimneys damaged.
EF-1 Weak	138–177 kmph (86–110 mph); *moderate damage*: beginning of hurricane wind-speed designation, roof coverings peeled off, mobile homes pushed off foundations.
EF-2 Strong	178–217 kmph (111–135 mph); *considerable damage*: roofs torn off frame houses, large trees uprooted or snapped, boxcars pushed over, small missiles generated.
EF-3 Severe	218–266 kmph (136–165 mph); *severe damage*: roofs torn off well-constructed houses, trains overturned, trees uprooted, cars thrown.
EF-4 Devastating	267–322 kmph (166–200 mph); *devastating damage*: well-built houses leveled, cars thrown, large missiles generated.
EF-5 Incredible	>322 kmph (>200 mph); *incredible damage*: houses lifted and carried distance to disintegration, car-sized missiles fly farther than 100 m, bark removed from trees.

Note: See http://www.spc.noaa.gov/faq/tornado/ef-scale.html for details.

Tornado Frequency North America experiences more tornadoes than anywhere on Earth because its latitudinal position and topography are conducive to the meeting of contrasting air masses and the formation of frontal precipitation and thunderstorms. Tornado occurrence in the United States is highest in Texas and Oklahoma (the southern part of the region known as "tornado alley"), Indiana, and Florida (**Figure 5.34**). Tornadoes have struck all 50 states and all the Canadian provinces and territories. According to records maintained since 1950, May and June are the peak months for tornadoes in the United States.

Although data suggest that the average number of tornadoes per month has increased over the past twenty years, scientists agree that these data are unreliable indicators of actual trends in tornado occurrence. The data more likely correspond with the larger number of people being in the right place to see and photograph tornadoes and with improved communication regarding tornado activity. Any actual increases in tornado occurrence may in part relate to rising sea-surface temperatures with climate change. Warmer oceans increase evaporation rates, which increase the availability of moisture in the mT air masses, thus producing more-intense thunderstorm activity over certain areas of the United States. Other factors in tornado development, such as wind shear, are not as well understood, are difficult to model, and cannot yet be definitively linked to climate change.

Canada experiences an average of 80 observed tornadoes per year, but those in sparsely populated rural areas can go unreported. In the United Kingdom, observers report about 50 per year, all classified less than EF-3. In Europe overall, 330 tornadoes are reported each year, although some experts estimate that as many as 700 occur per year. In Australia, observers report about 16 tornadoes every year. Other continents experience a small number of tornadoes annually.

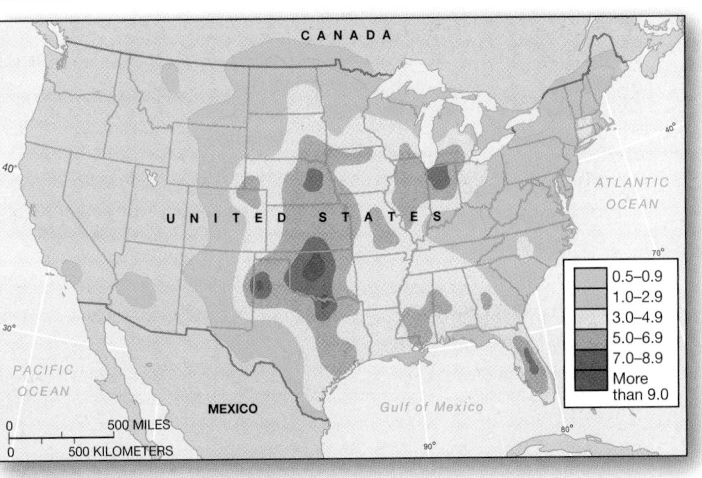

▲**Figure 5.34 Tornado occurrence in the United States.** Average number of tornadoes per 26,000 km² (10,000 mi²). Tornado numbers in Alaska and Hawaii are negligible. [Data courtesy of the Storm Prediction Center, NWS, and NOAA sources.]

MG MapMaster
North America Physical Environment
Tornado Incidence/Tornado Alley (U.S.)

Tropical Cyclones

Originating entirely within tropical air masses, **tropical cyclones** are powerful manifestations of the Earth–atmosphere energy budget. (Remember that the tropics extend from the Tropic of Cancer at 23.5° N latitude to the Tropic of Capricorn at 23.5° S latitude.)

Tropical cyclones are classified according to wind speed; the most powerful are **hurricanes**, **typhoons**, or *cyclones*, which are different regional names for the same type of tropical storm. The three names are based on location: Hurricanes occur around North America, typhoons in the western Pacific (mainly in Japan and the Philippines), and cyclones in Indonesia, Bangladesh, and India. A full-fledged hurricane, typhoon, or cyclone has wind speeds greater than 119 kmph (74 mph, or 64 knots); the wind-speed criteria for tropical storms, depressions, and disturbances are listed in **Table 5.2**. For coverage and reporting, see the National Hurricane Center at http://www.nhc.noaa.gov/ or the Joint Typhoon Warning Center at http://www.usno.navy.mil/JTWC.

In the western Pacific, a strong tropical cyclone is designated a *super typhoon* when winds speeds reach 241 kmph (150 mph, or 130 knots). In November 2013, Super Typhoon Haiyan hit the Philippines with sustained winds at 306–314 kmph (190–195 mph), the strongest ever recorded for a tropical cyclone at landfall (see **Figure 5.35a**).

Storm Development Cyclonic systems forming in the tropics are quite different from midlatitude cyclones

TABLE 5.2 Tropical Cyclone Classification

Designation	Winds	Features
Tropical disturbance	Variable, low	Definite area of surface low pressure; patches of clouds
Tropical depression	Up to 61 kmph (38 mph, 33 knots)	Gale force; organizing circulation; light to moderate rain
Tropical storm	62–118 kmph (39–73 mph, 34–63 knots)	Closed isobars; definite circular organization; heavy rain; assigned a name
Hurricane (Atlantic and East Pacific) Typhoon (West Pacific) Cyclone (Indian Ocean, Australia)	Greater than 119 kmph (74 mph, 64 knots)	Circular, closed isobars; heavy rain, storm surges; tornadoes in right-front quadrant
Super typhoon (West Pacific)	Greater than 241 kmph (150 mph, 130 knots)	

because the air of the tropics is essentially homogeneous, with no fronts or conflicting air masses of differing temperatures. In addition, the warm air and warm seas ensure abundant water vapor and thus the necessary latent heat to fuel these storms. Tropical cyclones convert heat energy from the ocean into mechanical energy in the wind—the warmer the ocean and the atmosphere, the more intense the conversion and the more powerful the storm.

A tropical cyclone begins with the cyclonic motion of a slow-moving easterly wave of low pressure in the trade-wind belt of the tropics. If the sea-surface temperatures exceed approximately 26°C (79°F), a tropical cyclone may form along the eastern (leeward) side of one of these migrating troughs of low pressure, a place of convergence and rainfall. Surface airflow then converges into the low-pressure area, ascends, and flows outward aloft (**Figure 5.35b**). This important divergence aloft acts as a chimney, pulling more moisture-laden air into the developing system. To maintain and strengthen this vertical convective circulation, there must be little or no wind shear to interrupt or block the vertical airflow.

Physical Structure Tropical cyclones have steep pressure gradients that generate inward-spiraling winds toward the center of low pressure—lower central pressure causes stronger pressure gradients, which, in turn, cause stronger winds. However, other factors come into play, so that the storms with the lowest central pressure are not always the strongest or the most damaging. The lowest central pressure for a storm in the Atlantic is 882 mb (26.02 in.), recorded for Hurricane Wilma in 2005.

As winds rush toward the center of a tropical cyclone, they turn upward, forming a wall of dense rain bands called the *eyewall*—this is the zone of most intense precipitation. The central area is designated the *eye* of the storm, where wind and precipitation subside; this is the warmest area of the storm, and although clear skies can appear here, they may not always be present, as commonly believed. The structure of the rain bands, eyewall, and central eye are clearly visible for Typhoon Lekima in **Figure 5.36**, imaged by NASA's TRMM satellite.

▼Figure 5.35 Tropical cyclone structure, top view and oblique view. [(a) NOAA Forecast Systems Laboratory.]

(a) Super Typhoon Haiyan made landfall in the central Phillipines on November 7, 2013, with sustained winds over 306 kmph (190 mph), the strongest ever recorded for a tropical cyclone at landfall using satellite measurements.

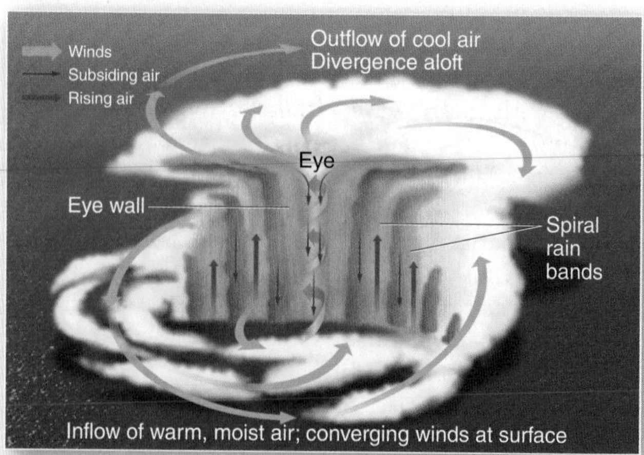

(b) A stylized portrait of a mature hurricane, drawn from an oblique perspective (cutaway view shows the eye, rain bands, and wind-flow patterns).

(a) Precipitation data for Super Typhoon Lekima. Note the lack of rainfall in the eye of the storm.

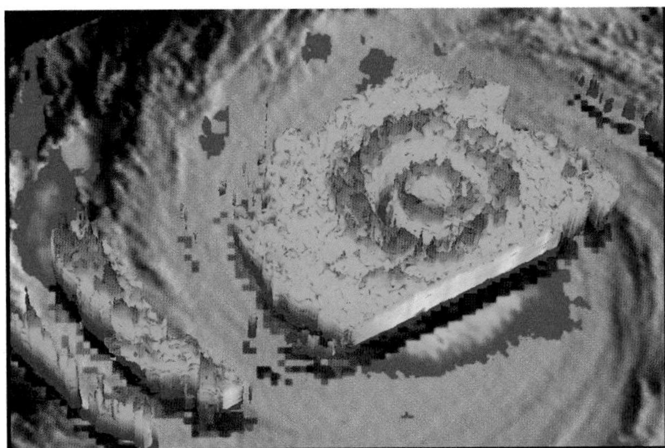

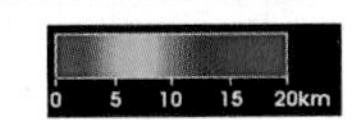

(b) Vertical structure of Lekima shows the well-defined eye and eyewall at the center. In the second, outer eyewall, rain fell at a rate greater than 130 mm/hr (5.2 in./hr).

▲**Figure 5.36 Rainfall and vertical structure of Super Typhoon Lekima over the western Pacific Ocean, October 24, 2013.** Data from TRMM's Microwave Imager (a) and Precipitation Radar instrument (b) are overlaid on infrared images to produce these visualizations. [NASA/GSFC.]

Tropical cyclones range in diameter from a compact 160–1000 km (100–600 mi) to the 1300–1600 km (800–1000 mi) attained by some western Pacific super typhoons. Vertically, a tropical cyclone dominates the full height of the troposphere. These storms move along over water at about 16–40 kmph (10–25 mph). The strongest winds are usually recorded in the storm's right-front quadrant (relative to its directional path). At *landfall*, where the eye moves ashore, dozens of fully developed tornadoes may be located in this high-wind sector.

Damage Potential When you hear meteorologists speak of a "category 4" hurricane, they are using the Saffir–Simpson Hurricane Wind Scale to estimate possible damage from hurricane-force winds. The scale uses sustained wind speed at a certain location to rank hurricanes and typhoons in five categories, from smaller category 1 storms to extremely dangerous category 5 storms (**Table 5.3**). The rating can vary for different locations; for example, Hurricane Charley in 2004 hit the coastal area of Punta Gorda, Florida, with category 4 winds, with the rest of the city experiencing only category 3 winds. Often, the rating category decreases after the storm moves inland. This scale does not address other potential hurricane impacts, such as storm surge, flooding, and tornadoes. Damage depends on the degree of property development at a storm's landfall site, how prepared citizens are for the blow, and the local building codes in effect.

When a tropical cyclone makes landfall, additional hazards arise from storm surge and the flooding associated with heavy rainfall. In fact, the impact of hurricanes on human population centers is as much connected to storm surge as it is to damaging winds. **Storm surge** is the seawater that is pushed inland during a hurricane and can combine with the normal tide to create a *storm tide* of 4.5 m (15 ft) or more in height. The landfall of Hurricane Sandy in 2012 coincided with high tide to create record storm surge in New York City—as high as 4.2 m (13.9 ft) at the southern tip of Manhattan (see Focus Study 5.1). As sea levels rise from melting ice and the expansion of seawater as it warms, storm tides will continue to increase during storm events.

Rainfall and flooding can cause devastation and loss of life, making even a weak, slow-moving tropical cyclone quite dangerous and destructive. In 2011,

TABLE 5.3 Saffir–Simpson Hurricane Wind Scale

Category	Wind Speed	Types of Damage	Recent Atlantic Examples (landfall rating)
1	119–153 kmph (74–95 mph, 65–82 knots)	Some damage to homes	2012 Isaac
2	154–177 kmph (96–110 mph, 83–95 knots)	Extensive damage to homes; major roof and siding damage	2003 Isabel (peaked at cat. 5), Juan; 2004 Francis; 2008 Dolly; 2010 Alex
3	178–208 kmph (111–129 mph, 96–112 knots)	Devastating damage; removal of roofs and gables	2004 Ivan (peaked at cat. 5), Jeanne; 2005 Dennis, Katrina, Rita, Wilma (peaked at cat. 5); 2008 Gustav, Ike (peaked at cat. 4); 2011 Irene; 2012 Sandy
4	209–251 kmph (130–156 mph, 113–136 knots)	Catastrophic damage; severe damage to roofs and walls	2004 Charley; 2005 Emily (peaked at cat. 5)
5	>252 kmph (>157 mph, >137 knots)	Catastrophic damage; total roof failure and wall collapse on high percentage of homes	2004 Ivan; 2007 Dean, Felix. Other notable: 1969 Camille; 1971 Edith; 1979 David; 1988 Gilbert, Mitch; 1989 Hugo; 1992 Andrew

(text continued on page 178)

focusstudy 5.1 Natural Hazards

Hurricanes Katrina and Sandy: Development, Effects, and Links to Climate Change

Hurricane Katrina, devastating the Gulf Coast in 2005, and Hurricane Sandy, slamming the mid-Atlantic coast in 2012, rank as the two most expensive hurricanes in U.S. history. Although both are memorable for destructiveness and human loss, the storms themselves differed greatly. And in the 7-year interval between them, public awareness of the impacts of climate change on global weather events increased.

Katrina and Coastal Flooding

On August 28, 2005, Hurricane Katrina reached category 5 strength over the Gulf of Mexico (Figure 5.1.1). The next day, the storm made landfall near New Orleans as a strong category 3 hurricane, with recorded sustained wind speeds over 200 kmph (125 mph) along the Louisiana coast. Katrina was a textbook tropical cyclone, developed from the warm waters of the tropical Atlantic with a compact low-pressure center and a symmetrical wind field (Figure 5.1.2a).

Hurricane Katrina's landfall was accompanied by high rainfall and storm surges that caused flooding in New Orleans. About half of the city of New Orleans is below sea level in elevation, the result of years of draining wetlands, compacting soils, and overall land subsidence. In addition, a system of canals, built throughout the 20th century for drainage and navigation, runs through the city. As Katrina moved ashore, water moved into the city through the canals. As the level in nearby Lake Pontchartrain rose from rainfall and storm surge, floodwalls and levees (earthen embankments constructed along the banks of waterways to prevent overflow of the channel) either failed or were breached. Some neighborhoods were submerged up to 6.1 m (20 ft); the polluted water remained for weeks. Although the flooding in New Orleans after Hurricane Katrina resulted more from human engineering and construction errors than from the storm itself, the failure of the flood protection system was a valuable lesson. Since Katrina, the Army Corps of Engineers has strengthened levees, floodwalls, floodgates, and pumping stations in preparation for future hurricanes, at a cost of over $12 billion.

Sandy's Unusual Development

As the 2012 Atlantic hurricane season neared its end, Hurricane Sandy began as tropical depression number 18 in the Caribbean Sea, reaching hurricane strength on October 23. Sandy moved northward over Cuba and the Bahamas toward the mid-Atlantic coast, where it became wedged between a stationary cold front over the Appalachian Mountains and a high-pressure mT air mass over Canada. These systems blocked the storm from moving north or east, as it would normally have done, and finally drove it toward the coast. The center of the hurricane hit the New Jersey shoreline just after 11 P.M. on October 29 (Figure 5.1.3).

According to the criteria for storm classification by the National Hurricane Center, Hurricane Sandy transitioned into a *post-tropical*, or *extratropical*, storm just before making landfall. At this point, Sandy departed from the classic tropical cyclone pattern and was instead gathering energy from sharp temperature contrasts between air masses. The storm now exhibited characteristics more closely aligned with nor'easters, midlatitude cyclonic winter storms that typically cover a large area, with strong winds and precipitation far from the center of the storm. Just before landfall, Sandy's wind patterns were asymmetrical, with a broad wind and cloud field shaped like a comma (rather than a circle), but retaining strong, hurricane-force winds (Figure 5.1.2b).

Moving inland, Sandy brought rainfall to low-elevation areas and blizzard conditions to the mountains of West Virginia, North Carolina, and Tennessee. This huge and unusual storm system affected an estimated 20% of the U.S. population, resulted in over 100 fatalities, and cost $75 billion.

Sandy's storm surge broke records along the New York and New Jersey coastlines. It knocked out power for millions of people, destroyed homes, eroded coastlines, and flooded lower Manhattan (see Geosystems Now in Chapter 13). A full moon made tides higher than average; at the height of the storm, a buoy in New York harbor measured a record-setting 10-m (32.5-ft) wave, 2 m (6.5 ft) taller than the 7.6-m (25-ft) wave recorded during Hurricane Irene in 2011.

Hurricanes and Climate Change

Perhaps the most certain causal link between climate change and recent increases in hurricane damage is the effect of rising sea level on storm surge. Sandy's destruction was worsened by recent sea-level rise—as much as 2 mm (0.08 in.) per year since 1950—along the coast from North Carolina to Massachusetts, reflecting

◀**Figure 5.1.1 Hurricane Katrina.** View of Katrina from the *GOES* satellite on August 28, 2005, 20:45 UTC. [NASA/NOAA as processed by SSEC CIMSS, University of Wisconsin–Madison.]

Video (MG) Hurricane Hot Towers

http://goo.gl/1GWjL0

(a) Ocean surface wind map shows Katrina's stronger wind speeds east of the eye, amidst the eyewall, a condition typical of Northern Hemisphere tropical cyclones.

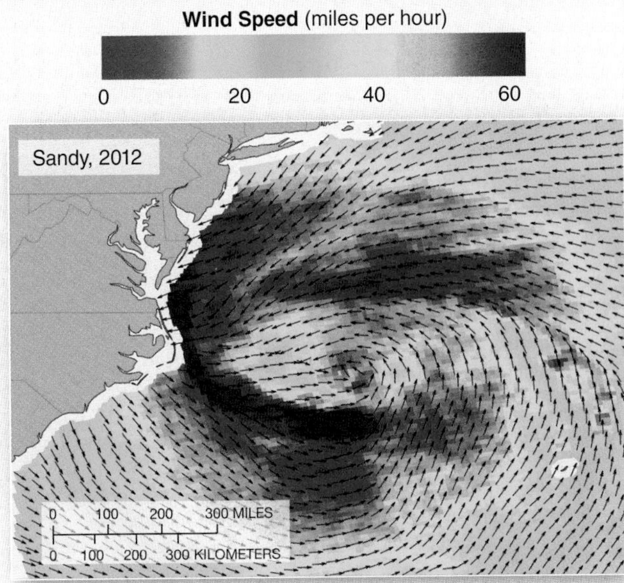

(b) Similar map for Sandy shows weaker winds to the east, indicating the influence of nearby air masses and associated pressure systems.

▲**Figure 5.1.2 Wind-speed maps for Katrina and Sandy.** [(a) *OceanSat-2*, Indian Space Research Organization. (b) *QuickSat*, NASA/JPL.]

both global sea-level rise and shifting ocean currents along the mid-Atlantic shoreline.

Higher sea-surface temperatures caused by climate change are another certain causal link. Research has correlated longer tropical storm lifetimes and greater intensity with rising sea-surface temperatures. As oceans warm, the energy available to fuel tropical cyclones is increasing. This connection is established for the Atlantic basin, where the number of hurricanes has increased over the past 20 years. Models suggest that the number of category 4 and 5 storms in this basin may double by the end of this century (see **http://www.gfdl.noaa.gov/21st-century-projections-of-intense-hurricanes**).

Continued ocean warming combined with the current trend of increasing coastal population will likely result in substantial hurricane-related property losses. Eventually, though, the more-intense storms and rising sea level could lead to shifts in population along U.S. coasts and even to the abandonment of some coastal resort communities, such as those along North Carolina's outer banks and the New Jersey shore.

1. What characteristics of Sandy's development made it unusual? Explain in your own words.
2. Why, in your opinion, did the state of New Jersey, after Hurricane Sandy, suspend its master plan to allow development in vulnerable coastal areas?

Video (MG)
Superstorm Sandy

http://goo.gl/k6HaNa

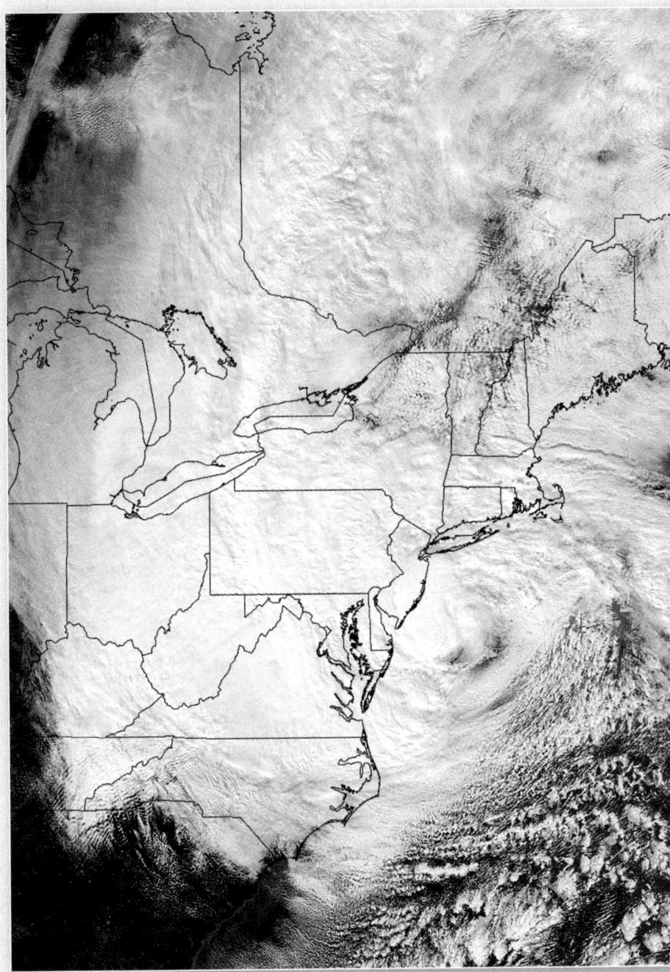

►**Figure 5.1.3 Hurricane Sandy just before landfall.** Sandy's circulation, October 29 at 1:35 P.M. (EDT), with the center southeast of Atlantic City, New Jersey, as the storm moved northward with maximum sustained winds of 150 kmph (90 mph). The storm covered 4.7 million square kilometers (1.8 million square miles), from the mid-Atlantic coast west to the Ohio Valley and the Great Lakes and north into Canada. [VIIRS instrument, *Suomi NPP*, NASA.]

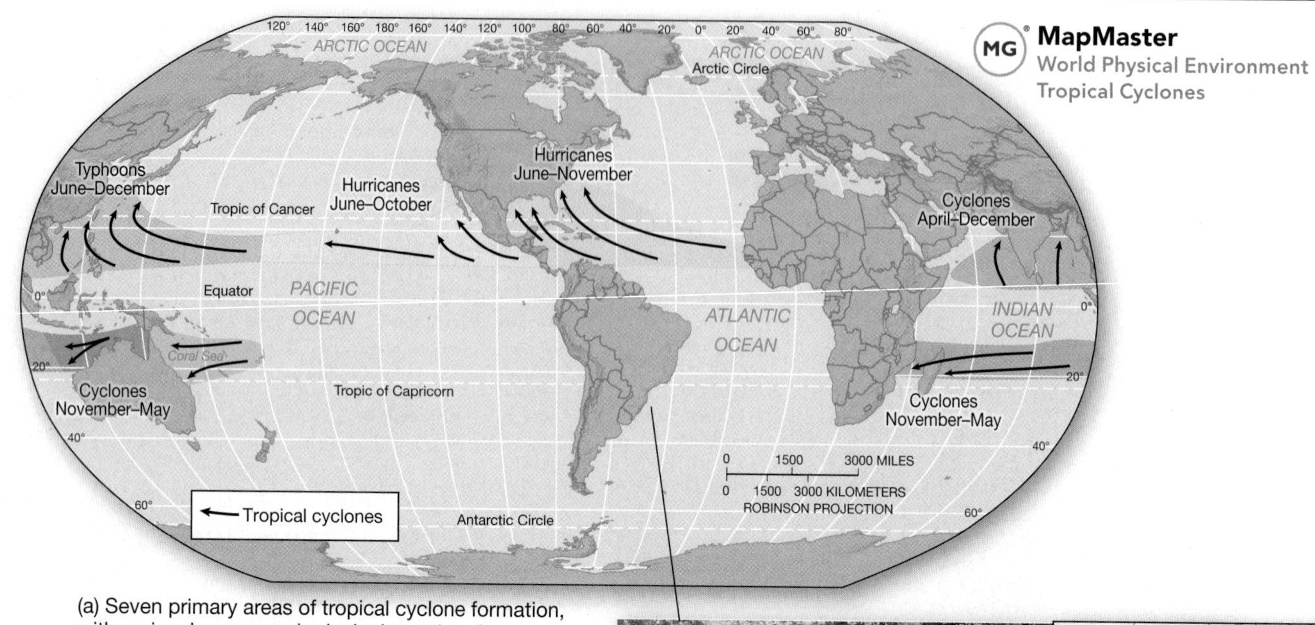

(a) Seven primary areas of tropical cyclone formation, with regional names and principal months of occurrence.

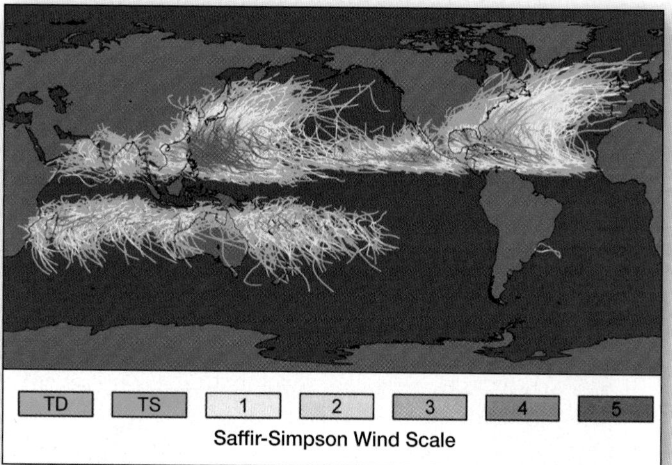

(b) Global tropical cyclone tracks from 1856 to 2006. Note the track of Hurricane Catarina in the South Atlantic.

(c) Hurricane Catarina approaches Brazil's southeastern coast, March 27, 2004—a unique occurrence in recorded history.

▲**Figure 5.37 Worldwide pattern of the most intense tropical cyclones.** [(b) R. Rohde/NASA/GSFC. (c) *Terra* MODIS image, NASA/GSFC.]

heavy rainfall from Hurricane Irene caused flooding from North Carolina's outer banks northward to New England. In 2012, rainfall totals associated with Sandy were greater than 180 mm (7.0 in.) over some coastal areas from South Carolina to New Jersey, and snowfall topped 76 cm (30 in.) in parts of Tennessee and West Virginia.

GEOreport 5.4 Research aircraft dissect Hurricane Karl

In 2010, scientists launched the Genesis and Rapid Intensification Processes (GRIP) mission to study hurricane development using satellites, aircraft, and unmanned aerial vehicles. In September, they sent an aircraft into category 3 Hurricane Karl as it made landfall along the Mexican coast. At 11,277 m (37,000 ft), the plane collected data using nine instruments and launched dropsondes, which record measurements as they fall through the atmosphere to the ocean surface. Another aircraft flew at 17,069 m (56,000 ft), using specialized radiometers to measure rain-cloud systems and surface winds. Meanwhile, the remotely piloted *Global Hawk* flew over the storm for more than 15 hours, sampling the upper reaches of a hurricane for the first time ever. The *Global Hawk* aircraft is being used in the new 5-year Hurricane and Severe Storm Sentinel (HS3) mission that GRIP began in 2012. More information is at **http://www.nasa.gov/mission_pages/hurricanes/missions/grip/main/index.html**.

Formation Areas and Storm Tracks The map in **Figure 5.37a** shows the seven primary formation areas, or "basins," for hurricanes, typhoons, and cyclones and the months during which these storms are most likely to form. **Figure 5.37b** shows the pattern of actual tracks and intensities for tropical cyclones between 1856 and 2006.

In the Atlantic basin, tropical depressions (low-pressure areas) tend to intensify into tropical storms as they cross the Atlantic toward North and Central America. If tropical storms mature early along their track, before reaching approximately 40° W longitude, they tend to curve northward toward the North Atlantic and miss the United States. If a tropical storm matures after it reaches the longitude of the Dominican Republic (70° W), then it has a higher probability of hitting the United States.

The number of Atlantic hurricanes broke records in 2005, including the most named tropical storms in a single year and the highest number of intense hurricanes (category 3 or higher). The 2005 season was also the first time that three category 5 storms (Katrina, Rita, and Wilma) occurred in the Gulf of Mexico (see the discussion of Katrina in Focus Study 5.1). On the *MasteringGeography* website, a map, table, and satellite-image movie detail the storms of this remarkable season.

In the Southern Hemisphere, no hurricane was ever observed turning from the equator into the South Atlantic until Hurricane Catarina made landfall in Brazil in March 2004 (see **Figure 5.37c**). In the satellite image, note the Coriolis force in action, clockwise in the Southern Hemisphere.

Although tropical cyclones are rare in Europe, in October 2005, the remnants of Tropical Storm Vince became the first Atlantic tropical cyclone on record to strike Spain. Likewise, Super Cyclone Gonu in 2007 became the strongest tropical cyclone on record occurring in the Arabian Sea, eventually hitting Oman and the Arabian Peninsula.

An Avoidable Cycle Tropical cyclones are potentially the most destructive storms experienced by humans, claiming thousands of lives each year worldwide. The tropical cyclone that struck Bangladesh in 1970 killed an estimated 300,000 people, and the one in 1991 claimed over 200,000. In Central and North America, death tolls are much lower, but still significant. The Galveston, Texas, hurricane of 1900 killed 6000. Hurricane Mitch (October 26–November 4, 1998) was the deadliest Atlantic hurricane in two centuries, killing more than 12,000 people, mainly in Honduras and Nicaragua. Hurricane Katrina and the associated flooding killed more than 1830 people in Louisiana, Mississippi, and Alabama in 2005. In 2013, Super Typhoon Haiyan, shown in Figure 5.35a, caused 6300 confirmed fatalities, with 1000 people still missing as of April 2014, and left 4 million people homeless.

Despite these statistics, the risk of human fatalities is decreasing in most parts of the world owing to better warning and rescue systems and to ongoing improvements in the forecasting of these storms. At the same time, the damage caused by tropical cyclones is increasing substantially as more and more development occurs along susceptible coastlines.

The history of major hurricanes in the United States reveals a recurrent, yet avoidable, cycle—construction, devastation, reconstruction, devastation—especially in the Gulf Coast, beginning with Hurricane Camille over 45 years ago. The same Gulf Coast towns that Camille washed away in 1969—Waveland, Bay Saint Louis, Pass Christian, Long Beach, and Gulfport, among others—were nearly wiped out again by Hurricane Katrina in 2005. Yet, after each storm, residents vow that "the Gulf Coast will rebuild bigger and better."

No matter how accurate storm forecasts become, coastal and lowland property damage will continue to increase until better hazard zoning and development restrictions are in place. The property insurance industry appears to be taking action to promote these improvements, requiring tougher building standards to qualify for coverage or, in some cases, refusing to insure property along vulnerable coastal lowlands. Given projections for sea-level rise and the increased intensity of tropical storms, the public, politicians, and private sector must become educated about the hazards associated with building along coastlines and change their actions accordingly.

Weather has many consequences for human society, especially as climate change increases the severity of weather events across the globe. For example, according to the May 2014 U.S. National Climate Assessment, *Climate Change Impacts in the United States,* the U.S. Northeast—home to 64 million people—experienced a 71% increase in the amount of precipitation during severe storms between 1958 and 2012. These events included heavy rain, snow, hail, and sleet, all increasing as part of a national trend in climate-change related occurrences. (See http://nca2014.globalchange.gov/ for highlights and the full report.) The Human Denominator 5 summarizes some of the interactions between weather and humans, with a few examples of severe weather events across the globe.

CRITICAL**thinking 5.4**

Hazard perception and planning: What seems to be missing?

Along coasts subject to extreme tropical weather, the cycle of "construction, devastation, reconstruction, devastation" means a cycle of ever-increasing dollar losses to property from tropical storms and hurricanes, even though improved forecasts have resulted in a significant reduction in loss of life. Given rising sea levels along coastlines and the increase in total power dissipation in these tropical storms since 1970, in your opinion, what is the solution to halting this cycle of destruction and increasing losses? How would you implement your ideas?

WEATHER IMPACTS HUMANS

- Frontal activity and midlatitude cyclones bring severe weather that affects transportation systems and daily life.
- Severe weather events—thunderstorms, derechos, tornadoes, and tropical cyclones— and winter storms cause destruction and human casualties.

HUMANS IMPACT WEATHER

- Rising temperatures associated with climate change have caused shrinking spring snow cover in the Northern Hemisphere.
- Sea-level rise is increasing tropical cyclone storm surge on the U.S. East Coast and other locations worldwide.

An ice-covered car sits beside Lake Geneva in Versoix, Switzerland, during a February 2012 arctic cold snap that brought freezing temperatures as far south as North Africa, claiming 300 lives. Ice storms occur when freezing rain and sleet (illustrated at right) cause at least 6.4 mm (0.25 in.) of ice to accumulate on exposed surfaces.

5c

An EF-5 tornado, almost 2 km (1.2 mi) wide at its base, tore across Alabama in April 2011. The tornado hit Tuscaloosa near the University of Alabama, where 44 people died, and continued on to hit the suburbs of Birmingham. As thunderstorms intensify with climate change, tornado frequency may increase.

Blue Marble–Next Generation image shows land surface, ocean, sea ice, and clouds.

In February 2011, 100 cm (39 in.) of snow fell on parts of South Korea's east coast over a 2-day period, the heaviest since record keeping began in 1911. The unusually cold weather may be driven in part by the Arctic Oscillation and in part by the trend toward more extreme snowfall events associated with climate change.

ISSUES FOR THE 21ST CENTURY

- Global snowfall will decrease, with less snow falling during a shorter winter season; however, extreme snowfall events (blizzards) will increase in intensity.
- Increasing ocean temperatures with climate change will strengthen the intensity and frequency of tropical cyclones by the end of the century.

KEYLEARNING**conceptsreview**

Weather is the short-term condition of the atmosphere; **meteorology** is the scientific study of the atmosphere. The spatial implications of atmospheric phenomena and their relationship to human activities strongly link meteorology to physical geography.

weather (p. 144)
meteorology (p. 144)

Describe the heat properties of water and *cite* the traits of its three phases: solid, liquid, and gas.

Water is the most common compound on the surface of Earth, and it possesses unusual solvent and heat characteristics. Water exists naturally in all three states—solid, liquid, and gas. A change from one state to another is a **phase change**. The change from liquid to solid is freezing; from solid to liquid, melting; from vapor to liquid, condensation; from liquid to vapor, vaporization or evaporation; from vapor to solid, deposition; and from solid to vapor, **sublimation**.

The heat energy required for water to change phase is **latent heat** because, once absorbed, it is hidden within the structure of the water, ice, or water vapor. For 1 g of water to become 1 g of water vapor by boiling requires the addition of 540 cal, or the **latent heat of vaporization**. When this 1 g of water vapor condenses, the same amount of heat energy, 540 cal, is liberated and is the **latent heat of condensation**. The **latent heat of sublimation** is the energy exchanged in the phase change from ice to vapor and vapor to ice. Weather is powered by the tremendous amount of latent heat energy involved in the phase changes among the three states of water.

phase change (p. 145)
sublimation (p. 145)
latent heat (p. 146)
latent heat of vaporization (p. 146)
latent heat of condensation (p. 146)
latent heat of sublimation (p. 147)

1. Describe the three states of matter as they apply to ice, water, and water vapor.
2. What happens to the physical structure of water as it cools below 4°C (39°F)? What are some visible indications of these physical changes?
3. What is latent heat? How is it involved in the phase changes of water?
4. Take 1 g of water at 0°C, and follow the changes it undergoes to become 1 g of water vapor at 100°C, describing what happens along the way. What amounts of energy are involved in the changes that take place?

Define humidity and relative humidity, *explain* dew-point temperature, and *illustrate* stable and unstable atmospheric conditions.

The amount of water vapor in the atmosphere is **humidity**. The maximum water vapor possible in air is principally a function of the temperatures of the air and of the water vapor (usually these temperatures are the same). Warmer air produces higher net evaporation rates and maximum possible water vapor, whereas cooler air can produce net condensation and lower the possible water vapor.

Relative humidity is a ratio of the amount of water vapor actually in the air to the maximum amount possible at a given temperature. Relative humidity tells us how near the air is to saturation. Air is said to be at **saturation** when the rate of evaporation and the rate of condensation reach equilibrium; any further addition of water vapor or temperature lowering will result in active condensation (100% relative humidity). The temperature at which air achieves saturation is the **dew-point temperature**.

Among the various ways to express humidity and relative humidity are vapor pressure and specific humidity. **Vapor pressure** is that portion of the atmospheric pressure produced by the presence of water vapor. A comparison of vapor pressure with the saturation vapor pressure at any moment yields a relative humidity percentage. **Specific humidity** is the mass of water vapor (in grams) per mass of air (in kilograms) at any specified temperature. Because it is measured as a mass, specific humidity does not change as temperature or pressure changes, making it a valuable measurement in weather forecasting.

Stability refers to the tendency of an air parcel (a body of air that is homogenous in temperature and humidity), with its water-vapor cargo, either to remain in place or to change vertical position by ascending (rising) or descending (falling). A parcel with warmer air than the surrounding environment has lower density; a parcel with colder air has higher density. An air parcel is *stable* if it resists displacement upward or, when disturbed, tends to return to its starting place. An air parcel is *unstable* if it continues to rise until it reaches an altitude where the surrounding air has a density (air temperature) similar to its own. The decrease in temperature with increasing altitude at a particular place and time is the **environmental lapse rate (ELR)**.

An ascending (rising) parcel of air cools by expansion, responding to the reduced air pressure at higher altitudes. A descending (falling) parcel heats by compression. Temperature changes in ascending and descending air parcels are **adiabatic,** meaning they occur as a result of expansion or compression, without any significant heat exchange between the surrounding environment and the vertically moving parcel of air.

The **dry adiabatic rate (DAR)** is the rate at which "dry" air cools by expansion (if ascending) or heats by compression (if descending). The term *dry* is used when air is less than saturated (relative humidity is less than 100%). The DAR is 10 C°/1000 m (5.5 F°/1000 ft). The **moist adiabatic rate (MAR)** is the average rate at which moist (saturated) air cools by expansion on ascent or warms by compression on descent. The average MAR is 6 C°/1000 m (3.3 F°/1000 ft); however, it varies with moisture content and temperature and can range from 4 to 10 C° per 1000 m (2 to 5.5 F° per 1000 ft).

humidity (p. 148)
relative humidity (p. 148)
saturation (p. 148)
dew-point temperature (p. 148)
vapor pressure (p. 150)
specific humidity (p. 150)
stability (p. 151)
environmental lapse rate (ELR) (p. 151)
adiabatic (p. 152)

dry adiabatic rate (DAR) (p. 152)
moist adiabatic rate (MAR) (p. 153)

5. What is humidity? How is it related to the energy present in the atmosphere? To our personal comfort and how we perceive apparent temperatures?
6. Define relative humidity. What does the concept represent? What is meant by the terms *saturation* and *dew-point temperature*?
7. Using Figures 5.9 and 5.10, derive relative humidity values (vapor pressure/saturation vapor pressure; specific humidity/ maximum specific humidity) for levels of humidity in the air different from the ones presented as examples in the chapter discussion.
8. Differentiate between stability and instability of a parcel of air lifted vertically in the atmosphere.
9. What are the forces acting on a vertically moving parcel of air? How are they affected by the density of the air parcel?
10. How do the adiabatic rates of heating or cooling in a vertically displaced air parcel differ from the normal lapse rate and environmental lapse rate?
11. Why is there a difference between the dry adiabatic rate (DAR) and the moist adiabatic rate (MAR)?
12. What atmospheric temperature and moisture conditions would you experience outside on a day when the weather is unstable? When it is stable?
13. Use the "Atmospheric Stability" animation in the *MasteringGeography*™ Study Area. Try different temperature settings on the sliders to produce stable and unstable conditions.

Identify the requirements for cloud formation and *explain* the major cloud classes and types, including fog.

A **cloud** is an aggregation of tiny **moisture droplets** and ice crystals suspended in the air. A cloud forms when air rises and cools to saturation in the presence of **cloud-condensation nuclei**, microscopic particles in the atmosphere around which water vapor condenses.

Low clouds, ranging from surface levels up to 2000 m (6500 ft) in the middle latitudes, are **stratus** (flat clouds, in layers) or **cumulus** (puffy clouds, in heaps). When stratus clouds yield precipitation, they are **nimbostratus**. Sometimes near the end of the day, lumpy, grayish, low-level clouds called **stratocumulus** may fill the sky in patches. Middle-level clouds are denoted by the prefix *alto-*. **Altocumulus** clouds, in particular, represent a broad category that includes many different types. Clouds at high altitude, principally composed of ice crystals, are called **cirrus**. A cumulus cloud can develop into a towering giant **cumulonimbus** cloud. Such clouds are called *thunderheads* because of their shape and their associated lightning, thunder, surface wind gusts, updrafts and downdrafts, heavy rain, and hail.

Fog is a cloud that occurs at ground level. Radiative cooling of a surface that chills the air layer directly above the surface to the dew-point temperature creates saturated conditions and a **radiation fog**. **Advection fog** forms when air in one place migrates to another place where conditions exist that can cause saturation—for example, when warm, moist air moves over cooler ocean currents. **Upslope fog** is produced when moist air is forced to higher elevations along a hill or mountain. Another fog caused by topography is **valley fog**, formed because cool, denser air settles in low-lying areas, producing fog in the chilled, saturated layer near the ground. Another type of fog resulting from evaporation and advection forms when cold air flows over the warm water of a lake, ocean surface, or swimming pool. This **evaporation fog**, or steam fog, may form as the water molecules evaporate from the water surface into the cold overlying air.

cloud (p. 154)
moisture droplet (p. 154)
cloud-condensation nuclei (p. 154)
stratus (p. 155)
nimbostratus (p. 155)
cumulus (p. 155)
stratocumulus (p. 156)
altocumulus (p. 156)
cirrus (p. 156)
cumulonimbus (p. 156)
fog (p. 156)
radiation fog (p. 156)
advection fog (p. 157)
upslope fog (p. 157)
valley fog (p. 157)
evaporation fog (p. 157)

14. Specifically, what is a cloud? Describe the droplets that form a cloud.
15. Explain the condensation process: What are the requirements?
16. What are the basic forms of clouds? Using Figure 5.15, describe how these cloud forms vary with altitude.
17. Explain how clouds might be used as indicators of atmospheric conditions and of expected weather.
18. List and define the principal types of fog.

Describe air masses that affect North America and *identify* four types of atmospheric lifting mechanisms.

An **air mass** is a regional volume of air that is homogenous in humidity, stability, and cloud coverage and that may extend through the lower half of the troposphere. Air masses are categorized by their moisture content—**m** for maritime (wetter) or **c** for continental (drier)—and their temperature, a function of latitude—designated **A** (arctic), **P** (polar), **T** (tropical), **E** (equatorial), or **AA** (antarctic).

Air masses can rise through **convergent lifting** (airflows conflict, forcing some of the air to lift); **convectional lifting** (air passing over warm surfaces gains buoyancy); **orographic lifting** (air passes over a topographic barrier); and *frontal lifting*. Orographic lifting creates wetter windward slopes and drier leeward slopes situated in the **rain shadow** of the mountain. The physical presence of a mountain acts as a topographic barrier to migrating air masses. Conflicting air masses may produce a **cold front** (and sometimes a zone of strong wind and rain) or a **warm front**. A zone right along or slightly ahead of the front, called a **squall line**, is characterized by turbulent and wildly changing wind patterns and intense precipitation.

air mass (p. 158)
convergent lifting (p. 159)
convectional lifting (p. 159)
orographic lifting (p. 160)
rain shadow (p. 160)
cold front (p. 163)
warm front (p. 163)
squall line (p. 163)

19. How does a source region influence the type of air mass that forms over it? Give specific examples of each basic classification.
20. Of all the air mass types, which are of greatest significance to the United States and Canada? What

happens to them as they migrate to locations different from their source regions? Give an example of air mass modification.

21. Explain why it is necessary for an air mass to be lifted if there is to be saturation, condensation, and precipitation.
22. List and describe the four principal lifting mechanisms that cause air masses to ascend, cool, condense, form clouds, and perhaps produce precipitation.
23. Differentiate between the structure of a cold front and that of a warm front.
24. When an air mass passes across a mountain range, many things happen to it. Describe each aspect of a moist air mass crossing a mountain. What is the pattern of precipitation that results?

Describe the life cycle of a midlatitude cyclonic storm system and *list* several measurable elements that contribute to modern weather forecasting.

A **midlatitude cyclone,** or **wave cyclone,** is a vast low-pressure system that migrates across a continent, pulling air masses into conflict along fronts. These systems are guided by the jet streams of the upper troposphere along seasonally shifting storm tracks. *Cyclogenesis* is the birth of the low-pressure circulation. A midlatitude cyclone then passes through the open stage, followed by the occluded stage—during which an **occluded front** may form as a cold front overtakes a warm front and wedges beneath it—and finally ends in the dissolving stage.

Synoptic analysis involves the collection of weather data at a specific time. Computer-based weather prediction and the development of weather-forecasting models rely on data such as barometric pressure, surface air temperatures, dew-point temperatures, wind speed and direction, clouds, sky conditions, and visibility. On weather maps, these elements appear as specific weather station symbols.

midlatitude cyclone (p. 164)
wave cyclone (p. 164)
occluded front (p. 165)

25. Differentiate between frontal lifting at an advancing cold front and at an advancing warm front, and describe what you would experience with each one.
26. What is meant by cyclogenesis? What is the role of upper-tropospheric circulation in the formation of a surface low?
27. Diagram a midlatitude cyclonic storm during its open stage. Label each of the components in your illustration, and add arrows to indicate wind patterns in the system.
28. How do warm, cold, and dry "conveyors" of air interact in a midlatitude cyclonic system?

Identify various forms of violent weather by their characteristics and *review* several examples of each.

The violent power of some weather phenomena poses a hazard to society. Thunderstorms are fueled by rapid upward movement of warm, moist air and are characterized by turbulence and wind shear. In strong thunderstorms known as *supercells*, a cyclonic updraft—a **mesocyclone**—may form within a cumulonimbus cloud, sometimes rising to the mid-troposphere. Thunderstorms produce **lightning** (electrical discharges in the atmosphere), **thunder** (sonic bangs produced by the rapid expansion of air after intense heating by lightning), and **hail** (ice pellets formed within cumulonimbus clouds). Strong linear winds in excess of 26 m/s (58 mph), known as **derechos**, are associated with thunderstorms and bands of showers crossing a region. These straight-line winds can cause significant damage and crop losses.

A **tornado** is a violently rotating column of air in contact with the ground surface, usually visible as a dark gray **funnel cloud** pulsing from the bottom side of the parent cloud. A **waterspout** forms when a tornado circulation occurs over water.

Within tropical air masses, large low-pressure centers can form along easterly wave troughs to produce a tropical cyclone. A **tropical cyclone** becomes a **hurricane, typhoon**, or *cyclone* when winds exceed 119 kmph (74 mph, or 64 knots). As forecasting of weather-related hazards improves, loss of life decreases, although property damage continues to increase. Great damage occurs to occupied coastal lands when the hurricane makes landfall and when winds drive ocean water inland in **storm surges**.

mesocyclone (p. 170)
lightning (p. 170)
thunder (p. 170)
hail (p. 170)
derecho (p. 171)
tornado (p. 172)
funnel cloud (p. 172)
waterspout (p. 172)
tropical cyclone (p. 173)
hurricane (p. 173)
typhoon (p. 173)
storm surge (p. 175)

29. What constitutes a thunderstorm? What type of cloud is involved? What type of air mass would you expect in an area of thunderstorms in North America?
30. Lightning and thunder are powerful phenomena in nature. Briefly describe how they develop.
31. Describe the formation process of a mesocyclone. How does a mesocyclone develop into a tornado?
32. Evaluate the pattern of tornado activity in the United States. What generalizations can you make about the distribution and timing of tornadoes?
33. What are the different classifications for tropical cyclones? List the various names used worldwide for hurricanes. Have tropical cyclones ever occurred in the South Atlantic?
34. After reading Focus Study 5.1, explain several differences between Hurricanes Katrina and Sandy. How is present climate change affecting hurricane intensity and damage costs?

Answer to Critical Thinking 5.3: The river water is warmer than the cold overlying air, producing an evaporation fog, especially beyond the bend in the river. The moist farmlands have radiatively cooled overnight, chilling the air along the surface to the dew point, resulting in active condensation. Wisps of radiation fog reveal the flow of light air movements from right to left in the photo.

MasteringGeography™

Looking for additional review and test prep materials? Visit the Study Area in *MasteringGeography*™ to enhance your geographic literacy, spatial reasoning skills, and understanding of this chapter's content by accessing a variety of resources, including **MapMaster** interactive maps, geoscience animations, videos, *In the News* RSS feeds, flashcards, web links, self-study quizzes, and an eText version of *Elemental Geosystems*.

6 Water Resources

A section of the Arizona Canal near Scottsdale separates irrigated fields from natural landscapes. Part of the Salt River Project, this is one of nine canals transporting water from reservoirs on the Salt River throughout the Phoenix metropolitan area. The Arizona Canal is tied through an interconnect to the Central Arizona Project, which transfers water from the Colorado River. More than a decade of drought is affecting water deliveries throughout the region (discussed in Focus Study 6.1 in this chapter). [Tim Roberts Photography/Shutterstock.]

KEYLEARNING**concepts**

After reading the chapter, you should be able to:

- ***Describe*** the origin of Earth's waters, ***report*** the quantity of water that exists today, and ***list*** the locations of Earth's freshwater supply.
- ***Illustrate*** the hydrologic cycle with a simple sketch and ***label*** it with definitions for each water pathway.
- ***Construct*** the water-budget equation, ***define*** each of the components, and ***explain*** its use.
- ***Discuss*** water storage in lakes and wetlands and ***describe*** some large water projects involving hydroelectric power production.
- ***Describe*** groundwater and ***define*** the elements of the groundwater environment.
- ***Evaluate*** the U.S. water budget and ***identify*** critical aspects of present and future freshwater supplies.

GEOSYSTEMS**now**

Environmental Change at Earth's Largest Lake

by Debra Sharkey, Cosumnes River College

Russia's Lake Baikal, located in south-central Siberia, is the world's largest (by volume), deepest, oldest, and most biologically diverse lake. Holding 23,600 km³ (5662 mi³) of water, almost as much as all five of the U.S. Great Lakes combined, Baikal contains 20% of the world's liquid freshwater. At its deepest point, the lake descends 1642 m (5387 ft) and is deeper than the Grand Canyon. At nearly 644 km (400 mi) long, this enormous crescent-shaped lake is easily seen in satellite images or on a world map (**Figures GN 6.1** and **GN 6.2**).

Like most of Earth's lakes, Baikal faces increasing threats from human activities. Industrial pollution, agricultural runoff, and development threaten water quality. In addition, climate change is already disrupting lake environments.

Changes in Water Temperature and Ice Cover As annual average air temperature has increased throughout Siberia during the past century, the natural processes and environments of Lake Baikal are changing. Satellite data reveal that Lake Baikal's surface water temperature increased 1.2 C° (2.1 F°) over the past 25 years. Direct measurements of surface lake temperatures since 1946 indicate a similar rate of warming.

The lake's continental location and far northerly latitude produce cold winters during which thick ice covers the lake surface for several months each year. Rising lake temperature affects the timing and characteristics of lake ice: Ice is now forming later in the fall and breaking up earlier in the spring. In addition, over the past 60 years, average annual ice thickness has decreased.

Scientists predict that by the end of this century Baikal's winters will be warmer and wetter, with as much as 25% more winter precipitation than present averages. As air temperatures warm and winter snow increases, the duration and thickness of ice cover will further decrease. Changing snow accumulation, combined with changes in wind patterns that move snow around, will diminish the transparency of the ice. These changes are already affecting Lake Baikal's aquatic ecosystems.

Effects on Biota Over millennia, prolonged seasonal freezing of Lake Baikal has caused most of the lake's flora and fauna to adapt to life on and under the ice. *Phytoplankton*, microscopic organisms that live in fresh- or saltwater environments, are the basis of the lake's food web. Lake Baikal is the only lake in the world in which both the dominant primary producers (phytoplankton) and the top predator (the Baikal seal, locally known as the nerpa) require ice for reproduction.

▲**Figure GN 6.2 Olkhon Island in Lake Baikal.** [Mikhail Markovskiy/Shutterstock.]

Baikal's phytoplankton include green algae, which can grow explosively in "blooms" that may last days or weeks. Ice thickness and transparency determine the amount of light reaching the water, a critical factor for phytoplankton growth. Because these unique algae have adapted to specific under-ice conditions, recent changes in the ice have decreased algae growth rates and slowed spring algal blooms. The effects of this decrease then move up the food chain, from the enormous quantities of tiny crustaceans that eat the algae to the fish that eat the crustaceans to the seals that depend on fish as their main food source.

The Baikal seal (*Pusa sibirica*), smallest of the world's seals and the only species exclusively living in freshwater, mates and gives birth on the lake ice. The seals require ice in early spring for shelter. If ice melt occurs early, the seals are forced into the water, and the extra energy expended affects female fertility and nurturing ability.

From a systems perspective, recent changes in water temperature and ice cover at Lake Baikal exemplify how changes in the atmosphere link to changes in the hydrosphere and biosphere. Many of Earth's other major lakes are experiencing similar warming trends. In this chapter, we examine lakes and other parts of the hydrologic cycle as we assess Earth's water resources.

QUESTION AND EXPLORE Scientists have recently compiled a record of chemical changes in lake water as revealed by hundreds of Baikal seal teeth harvested from lake ice (see http://www.wellesley.edu/news/2014/03/node/42933). For an example of the effects of climate change on U.S. lakes, read about warming temperatures in Lake Superior at http://www.scientificamerican.com/article.cfm?id=lake-superior-a-natural-global-warming-gauge-is-running-a-fever. MG

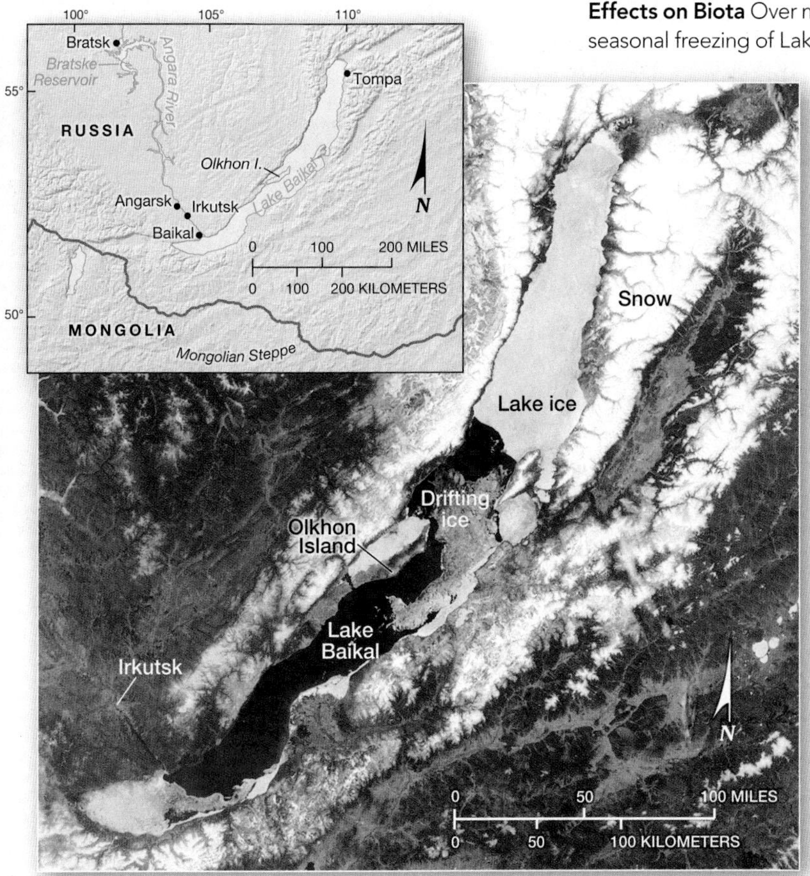

◀**Figure GN 6.1 Ice cover over Lake Baikal, May 10, 2012.** [Jeff Schmaltz, LANCE/EOSDIS Rapid Response/NASA.]

Earth's physical processes are dependent on water, which is the essence of all life. Humans are about 70% water, as are plants and other animals. We use water to cook, bathe, wash clothes, dilute wastes, and run industrial processes. We use water to produce food, from the scale of small gardens to vast agricultural tracts. Water is the most critical resource supplied by Earth systems.

In the Solar System, water occurs in significant quantities only on our planet, covering 71% of Earth by area. Yet water is not always naturally available where and when we want it. Consequently, we rearrange water resources to suit our needs. We drill wells to tap groundwater and dam and divert streams to redirect surface water, either spatially (geographically, from one area to another) or temporally (over time, from one part of the calendar to another). All of this activity constitutes water-resource management. **Hydrology** is the science of water and its global circulation, distribution, and properties—focusing on water at and below Earth's surface.

For many parts of the world, the question of water quantity and quality looms as the most important resource issue in this century.

Fortunately, water is a renewable resource, constantly cycling through the environment in the hydrologic cycle. Even so, some 1.1 billion people lack safe drinking water. People in 80 countries face impending water shortages, either in quantity or in quality, or both. Approximately 2.4 billion people lack adequate sanitary facilities—80% of these in Africa and 13% in Asia. This translates to some 2 million deaths a year due to lack of water and 5 million deaths a year from waterborne infections and disease. Investment in safe drinking water, sanitation, and hygiene could decrease these numbers. During the first half of this century, water availability per person will drop by 74% as population increases and adequate water decreases.

In this chapter: We begin with the origin and distribution of water on Earth. We then examine the hydrologic cycle, which gives us a model for understanding the global water balance. Next, we introduce a water-budget approach to looking at water resources. Similar in many ways to a money budget, it focuses attention on water "receipts" and "expenses" at specific locations. This budget approach can be applied at any scale, from a small garden to a farm to a regional landscape, such as the High Plains Aquifer discussed in this chapter.

We also examine the various types of surface water and groundwater resources and discuss issues concerning water quantity and quality on a national and global basis. The chapter concludes by considering water supply in North America—specifically, the U.S. water budget, including water withdrawal and consumption for irrigation and industrial and municipal uses. For many parts of the world, the question of water quantity and quality looms as the most important resource issue in this century.

Water on Earth

Earth's hydrosphere contains about 1.36 billion cubic kilometers of water (more specifically, 1,359,208,000 km^3, or 326,074,000 mi^3). Much of Earth's water originated from icy comets and from hydrogen- and oxygen-laden debris within the planetesimals that coalesced to form the planet. In 2007, the orbiting Spitzer Space Telescope observed for the first time the presence of water vapor and ice during the formation of new planets in a system 1000 light-years from Earth. Such discoveries prove water to be abundant throughout the Universe. As a planet forms, water from within migrates to its surface and outgasses.

Outgassing on Earth is a continuing process in which water and water vapor emerge from layers deep within and below the crust, 25 km (15.5 mi) or more below the surface, and are released in the form of gas (**Figure 6.1**).

▶**Figure 6.1 Water outgassing from the crust.** Outgassing of water from Earth's crust occurs in geothermal areas such as southern Iceland west of where the Eyjafjallajökull volcano erupted in 2010. [Bobbé Christopherson.]

GEOreport 6.1 The water we use

In terms of direct water usage, urban dwellers in the United States average 680 L (180 gal) of water per person per day, whereas rural populations average only 265 L (70 gal) or less per person per day. (Take a moment to speculate about why there is a difference.) When calculated in overall terms, however, individual water averages are actually much higher than these figures because of indirect use, such as consuming food and beverages made with water-intensive practices. See **http://www.worldwater.org/data.html**, World's Water 2008–2009, Table 19, for more on the amount of water used for everyday foods and other products.

In the early atmosphere, massive quantities of outgassed water vapor condensed and then fell to Earth in torrential rains. For water to remain on Earth's surface, land temperatures had to drop below the boiling point of 100°C (212°F), something that occurred about 3.8 billion years ago. The lowest places across the face of Earth then began to fill with water—first forming ponds, then lakes and seas, and eventually ocean-sized bodies of water. Massive flows of water washed over the landscape, carrying both dissolved and solid materials to these early seas and oceans. Outgassing of water has continued ever since and is visible in volcanic eruptions, geysers, and seepage to the surface.

Worldwide Equilibrium

Today, water is the most common compound on the surface of Earth. The present volume of water circulating throughout Earth's surface systems was attained approximately 2 billion years ago, and this quantity has remained relatively constant even though water is continuously gained and lost. Gains occur as pristine water not previously at the surface emerges from within Earth's crust. Losses occur when water dissociates into hydrogen and oxygen and the hydrogen escapes Earth's gravity to space or when it breaks down and forms new compounds with other elements. The net result of these water inputs and outputs is that Earth's hydrosphere is in a steady-state equilibrium in terms of quantity.

Within this overall balance, the amount of water stored in glaciers and ice sheets varies, leading to periodic global changes in sea level (discussed further in Chapters 8 and 13). The term **eustasy** refers to changes in global sea level caused by changes in the volume of water in the oceans. Such sea-level changes caused specifically by glacial ice melt are *glacio-eustatic* factors (see Chapter 14). During cooler global climatic conditions, when more water is bound up in glaciers (at high latitudes and at high elevations worldwide) and in ice sheets (on Greenland and Antarctica), sea level lowers. During warmer periods, less water is stored as ice, so sea level rises. Today, sea level is rising worldwide at an accelerating pace as higher temperatures melt more ice and, in addition, cause ocean water to thermally expand.

Distribution of Earth's Water Today

From a geographic point of view, ocean and land surfaces are distributed unevenly on Earth. If you examine a globe, it is obvious that most of Earth's continental land is in the Northern Hemisphere, whereas water dominates the surface in the Southern Hemisphere. In fact, when you look at Earth from certain angles, it appears to have an *oceanic hemisphere* and a *land hemisphere* (**Figure 6.2**).

The present distribution of all of Earth's water between the liquid and frozen states, between fresh and saline, and between surface and underground, is shown in **Figure 6.3**. The oceans contain 97.22% of all water, with about 48% of that water in the Pacific Ocean (as measured by ocean surface area). The remaining 2.78% is freshwater (nonoceanic) and is either surface or subsurface water, as detailed in the middle pie chart in the figure. Ice sheets and glaciers contain the greatest amount of Earth's freshwater. Groundwater, either shallow or deep, is the second largest amount. The remaining freshwater, which resides in lakes, rivers, and streams, actually represents less than 1% of freshwater.

The Hydrologic Cycle

Vast currents of water, water vapor, ice, and associated energy are flowing continuously in an elaborate, open, global system. Together, they form the **hydrologic cycle**, which has operated for billions of years, circulating and transforming water throughout Earth's lower atmosphere, hydrosphere, biosphere, and lithosphere to several kilometers beneath the surface.

The water cycle can be divided into three main components: atmosphere, surface, and subsurface. The residence time for a water molecule in any component of the cycle, and its effect on climate, is variable. Water has a short residence time in the atmosphere—an average of 10 days—where it plays a role in temporary fluctuations in regional weather patterns. Water has longer residence times in deep-ocean circulation, groundwater, and glacial ice (as long as 3000–10,000 years), where it acts to moderate

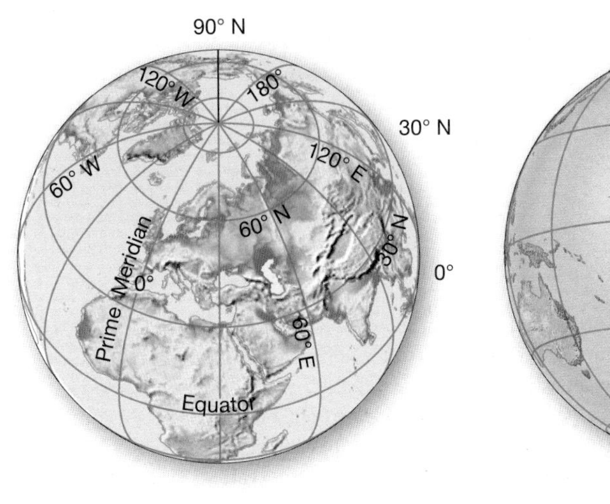

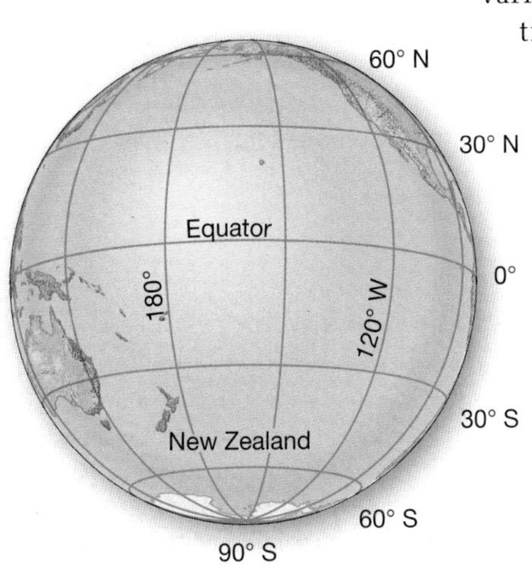

◄**Figure 6.2 Land and water hemispheres.** Two perspectives that roughly illustrate Earth's ocean hemisphere and land hemisphere.

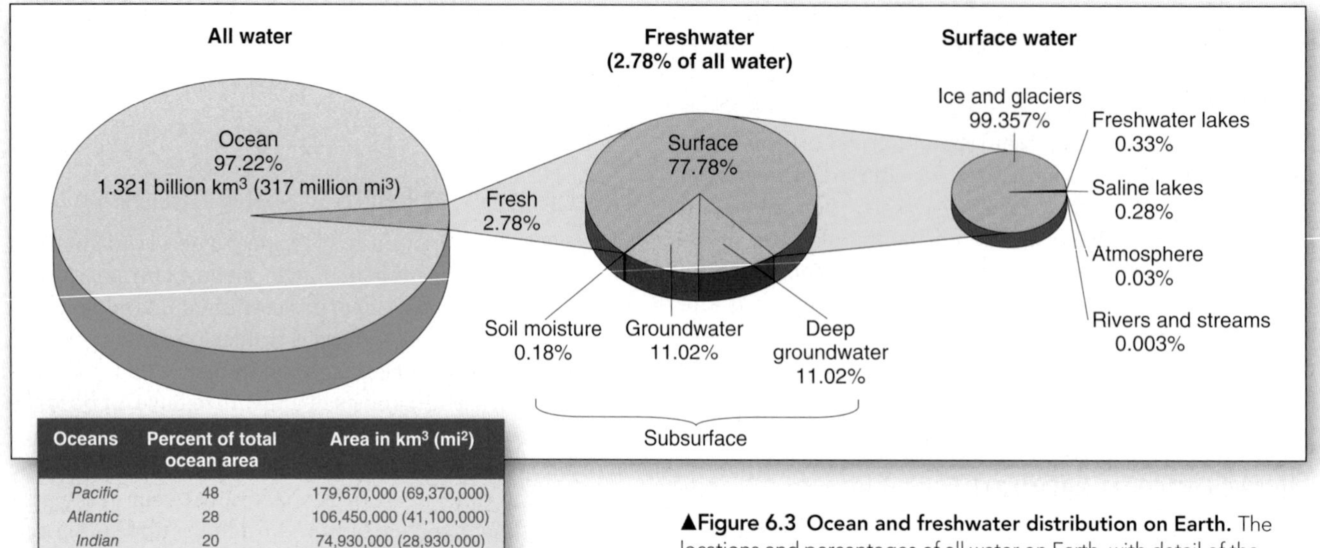

Oceans	Percent of total ocean area	Area in km³ (mi²)
Pacific	48	179,670,000 (69,370,000)
Atlantic	28	106,450,000 (41,100,000)
Indian	20	74,930,000 (28,930,000)
Arctic	4	14,090,000 (5,440,000)

▲**Figure 6.3 Ocean and freshwater distribution on Earth.** The locations and percentages of all water on Earth, with detail of the freshwater portion (surface and subsurface) and a breakdown of the surface water component.

temperature and climatic changes. These slower parts of the hydrologic cycle, the parts where water is stored and released over long periods, can have a "buffering" effect during periods of water shortage.

Water in the Atmosphere

Figure 6.4 is a simplified model of the hydrologic system, with estimates of the volume of water involved in the main pathways (in thousands of cubic kilometers). We use the ocean as a starting point for our discussion, although we could jump into the model at any point. More than 97% of Earth's water is in the oceans, and it is over these water bodies that 86% of Earth's evaporation occurs. As discussed in previous chapters, **evaporation** is the net movement of free water molecules away from a wet surface into air that is less than saturated.

Water also moves into the atmosphere from land environments, including water moving from the soil into plant roots and passing through their leaves to the air. This process is **transpiration**. During transpiration, plants release water to the atmosphere through small openings called stomata in their leaves. Transpiration is partially regulated by the plants themselves, as control cells around the stomata conserve or release water. On a hot day, a single tree can transpire hundreds of liters of water, and a forest, millions of liters. Evaporation and transpiration from Earth's land surfaces together make up **evapotranspiration**, which represents 14% of the water entering Earth's atmosphere in Figure 6.4.

Figure 6.4 also shows that of the 86% of evaporation rising from the oceans, 66% combines with 12% advected (moved horizontally) from the land to produce the 78% of all precipitation that falls over the oceans. The remaining 20% of moisture evaporated from the ocean, plus 2% of land-derived moisture, produces the 22% of all precipitation that falls over land. Clearly, the bulk of continental precipitation comes from the oceanic portion of the cycle. The different parts of the cycle vary over different regions on Earth, creating imbalances that, depending on the local climate, lead to water surpluses in one place and water shortages in another.

Water at the Surface

Precipitation that reaches Earth's surface as rain follows two basic pathways: It either flows overland or soaks into the soil. Along the way, **interception** also occurs, in which precipitation lands on vegetation or other ground cover before reaching the surface. Intercepted water that

GEOreport 6.2 Harvesting fog as a water resource

Sand beetles in the Namib Desert in extreme southwestern Africa harvest water from fog by holding up their wings so condensation collects and runs down to their mouths. As the day's heat arrives, they burrow into the sand, only emerging the next night or morning when the advection fog brings in more water for harvesting. For centuries, coastal villagers in the deserts of Oman collected water drips deposited on trees by coastal fogs. In the Atacama Desert of Chile and Peru, residents stretch large nets to intercept advection fog; moisture condenses on the netting, drips into trays, and then flows through pipes to a 100,000-L (26,000-gal) reservoir. At least 30 countries across the globe experience conditions suitable for this water resource technology. (See http://www.oas.org/dsd/publications/unit/oea59e/ch33.htm.)

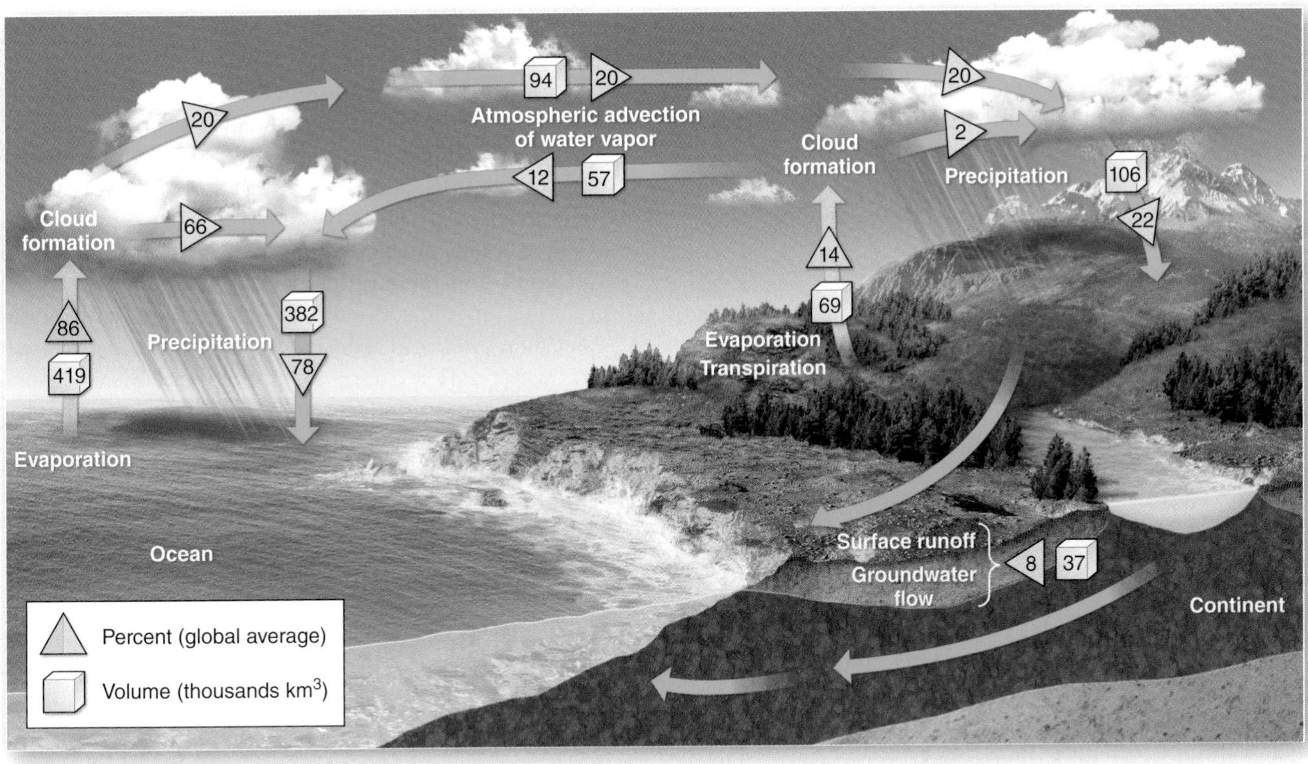

▲**Figure 6.4 The hydrologic cycle model.** Water travels endlessly through the hydrosphere, atmosphere, lithosphere, and biosphere. The triangles show global average values as percentages. Note that all evaporation (86% + 14% = 100%) equals all precipitation (78% + 22% = 100%) and that advection in the atmosphere is balanced by surface runoff and subsurface groundwater flow when all of Earth is considered. (To convert volume, 1 $km^3 \times 0.24 = 1\ mi^3$.)

drains across plant leaves and down their stems to the ground is known as *stem flow*. Precipitation that falls directly to the ground, including drips from vegetation that are not stem flow, is *throughfall*. Precipitation that reaches Earth's surface as snow may accumulate for a period of hours or days before melting, or it may accumulate as part of the snowpack that remains throughout winter and melts in the spring.

After reaching the ground surface as rain, or after snowmelt, water may soak into the subsurface through **infiltration**, or penetration of the soil surface (**Figure 6.5**). If the ground surface is impermeable (does not permit the passage of liquids), then the water will begin to flow downslope as **overland flow**, also known as **surface runoff**. Overland flow will also occur if the soil has been infiltrated to full capacity and is saturated. Excess water may remain in place on the surface in puddles or ponds, or it may flow until it forms channels—at this point, it becomes *streamflow*, a term that describes surface water flow in streams, rivers, and other channels.

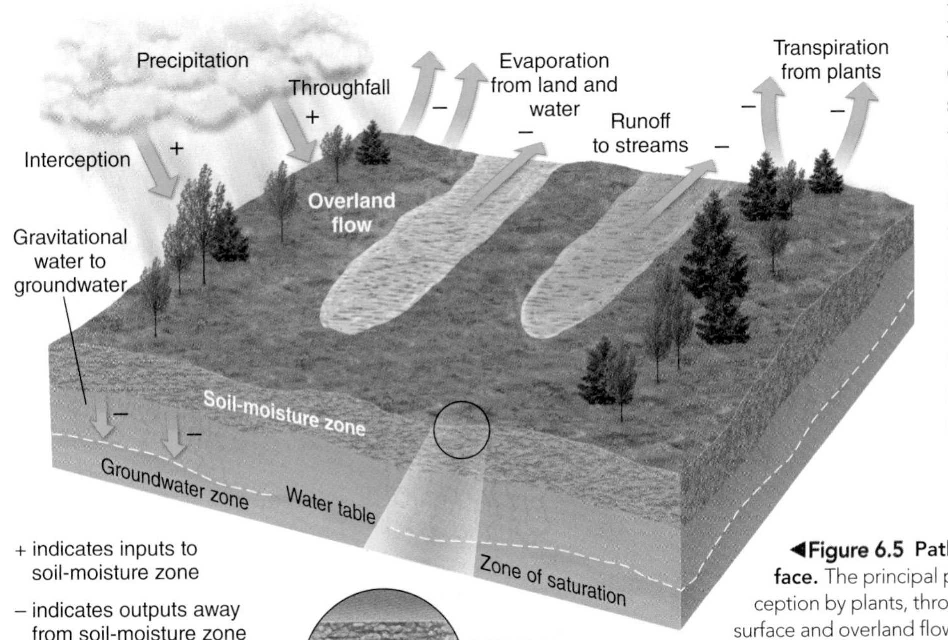

◀**Figure 6.5 Pathways for precipitation on Earth's surface.** The principal pathways for precipitation include interception by plants, throughfall to the ground, collection on the surface and overland flow to streams, transpiration and evaporation from plants, evaporation from land and water, and gravitational water moving to subsurface groundwater.

Figure 6.4 shows that 8% of the water in the cycle is moving on or through land. Most of this movement—about 95%—comes from surface waters that wash across land as overland flow and streamflow. Only 5% of water movement is slow-moving subsurface groundwater. The surface component in rivers and streams is dynamic and fast-moving compared to its sluggish subsurface counterpart.

Water in the Subsurface

Water that infiltrates into the subsurface moves downward into soil or rock by **percolation**, the slow passage of water through a porous substance (shown in Figure 6.5). The **soil-moisture zone** contains the volume of subsurface water stored in the soil that is accessible to plant roots. Within this zone, some water is bound to soil, so that it is not available to plants—this depends on the soil texture (discussed in Chapter 15). An estimated 76% of precipitation over land infiltrates the subsurface, and about 85% of this water returns to the atmosphere either by evaporation from soil or by transpiration from plants.

If the soil is saturated, then any water surplus within the soil body becomes *gravitational water*, percolating downward into the deeper groundwater. The latter defines the *zone of saturation*, where the soil spaces are completely filled with water. The top of this zone is known as the *water table*. At the point where the water table intersects a stream channel, water naturally discharges at the surface, producing **base flow**, which refers to the portion of streamflow that consists of groundwater.

Under natural conditions, streams and groundwater ultimately flow into oceans, thus continuing movement through the hydrologic cycle. In some cases, streams flow into closed lake basins, where water evaporates or soaks into the ground. Many streams flow into reservoirs behind dams, where water is stored until it evaporates or is released into the channel downstream. Groundwater flows slowly toward the sea, intersecting the surface or seeping from underground after reaching the coast, sometimes mixing with seawater in coastal wetlands and estuaries (bodies of water near the mouths of rivers). We discuss groundwater later in the chapter.

Water Budgets and Resource Analysis

An effective method for assessing portions of the water cycle as they apply to water resources is to establish a **water budget** for any area of Earth's surface—a continent, country, region, field, or front yard. A water budget is derived from measuring the input of precipitation and its distribution and the outputs of evapotranspiration, including evaporation from ground surfaces, transpiration from plants, and surface runoff. Also included in this budget is moisture that is stored in the soil-moisture zone. Such a budget can cover any time frame, from minutes to years.

A water budget functions like a money budget: Precipitation is the income that must balance against expenditures for evaporation, transpiration, and runoff. Soil-moisture storage acts as a savings account, accepting precipitation deposits and yielding withdrawals of water. Sometimes all expenditure demands are met, and any extra water results in a **surplus**. This water surplus often becomes surface runoff, feeding surface streams and lakes and recharging groundwater. At other times, precipitation and soil-moisture savings are inadequate to meet demands, and a **deficit**, or water shortage, results. This water deficit occurs when the demands of evaporation and transpiration cannot be satisfied by precipitation inputs, by stored moisture in the soil, or by additional inputs of water by artificial irrigation. Deficits cause drought conditions, discussed ahead in this chapter.

Components of the Water Budget

In its simplest form, a water budget shows that, for any area functioning as the accounting unit, the amount of water flowing into that unit is balanced by rate of water flowing out, plus or minus the change in water storage in the soil. To understand water-budget methodology, we begin by defining terms and concepts relating to water supply, demand, and storage as components of the water-budget equation (presented in Figure 6.9).

Precipitation The moisture supply to Earth's surface is **precipitation** (P) in all its forms, such as rain, sleet, snow, or hail. Precipitation is usually measured with a rain gauge, described on the *MasteringGeography* website. **Figure 6.6** shows precipitation patterns in the United States and Canada; note that patterns on the map relate to air masses and lifting mechanisms presented in Chapter 5. Precipitation data come from regular precipitation measurements at more than 100,000 locations worldwide. For global annual precipitation patterns, see the map in Chapter 7, Figure 7.1.

Evapotranspiration The moisture demand at a given location is evapotranspiration, an actual expenditure of water to the atmosphere. For water budget analyses and other applications, this is called **actual evapotranspiration** (AE).

In contrast, **potential evapotranspiration** (PE) is the amount of water that would evaporate and transpire under optimum moisture conditions when adequate precipitation and soil moisture are present. We can illustrate this concept by filling a bowl with water and letting the water evaporate: When the bowl becomes dry, some degree of evaporation demand remains. If the bowl could be constantly replenished with water, the amount of water that would evaporate given this constant supply is the PE—the total water demand. If the bowl dries out, the amount of PE that is not met is the water deficit.

During the period when PE is greater than AE, the water demand must be met by moisture stored in the soil

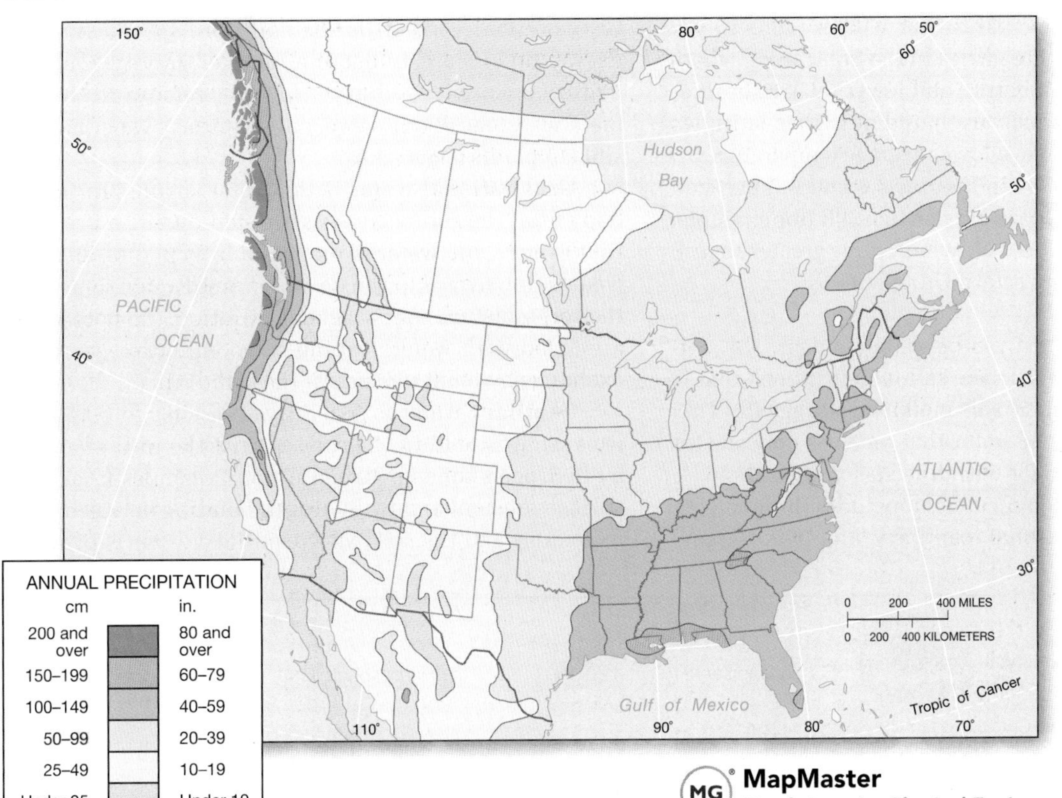

◀**Figure 6.6 Precipitation in North America—the water supply.** [Based on NWS, U.S. Department of Agriculture, and Environment Canada.]

MG® **MapMaster**
North America Physical Environment
Average Annual Precipitation

or by artificial irrigation. A deficit, or moisture shortage, results when PE cannot be satisfied by precipitation inputs, soil moisture storage, or additional inputs of water by irrigation. Under ideal conditions for plants, potential and actual amounts of evapotranspiration are about the same, so plants do not experience a water shortage.

Precise measurement of evapotranspiration is difficult. Methods may use an evaporation pan or the more elaborate *lysimeter*, both discussed on the *MasteringGeography* website. **Figure 6.7** presents PE values for the United States and Canada, derived by geographer Charles Thornthwaite (1899–1963), who pioneered applied water

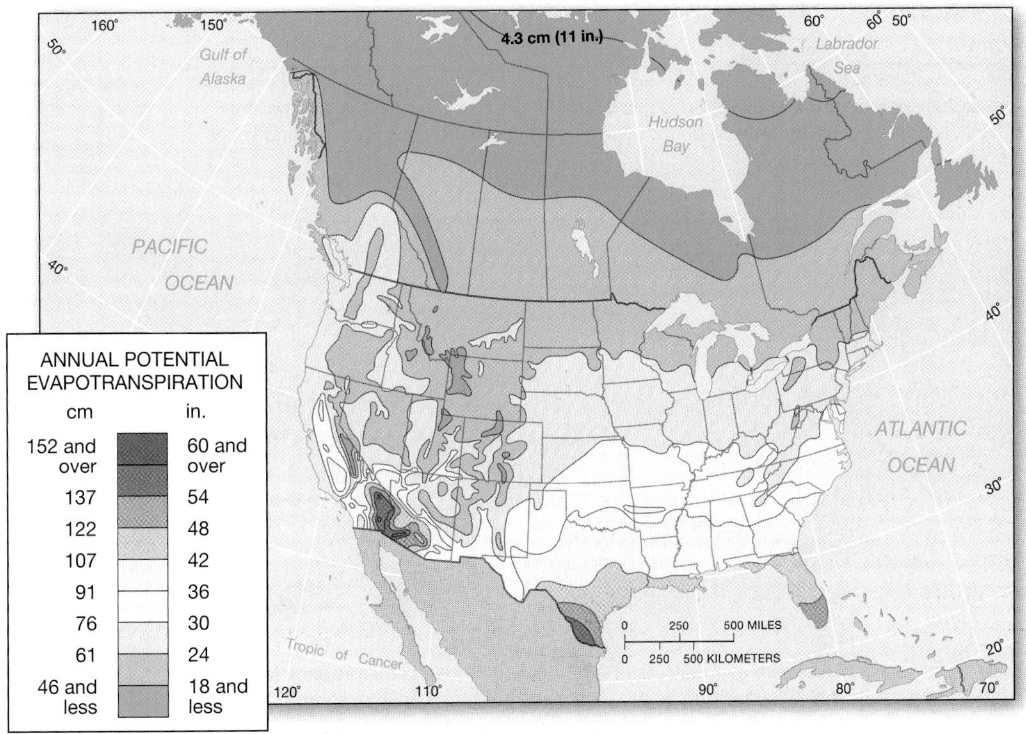

◀**Figure 6.7 Potential evapotranspiration for the United States and Canada—the water demand.** [From C. W. Thornthwaite, "An approach toward a rational classification of climate," *Geographical Review* 38 (1948): 64, © American Geographical Society. Canadian data adapted from M. Sanderson, "The climates of Canada according to the new Thornthwaite classification," *Scientific Agriculture* 28 (1948): 501–517.]

resource analysis. Note that higher values occur in the South, with the highest readings in the Southwest, where higher average air temperature and lower relative humidity exist. Lower PE values are found at higher latitudes and elevations, which have lower average temperatures.

Comparing the maps in Figures 6.6 and 6.7, can you identify regions where P is greater than PE (for example, the eastern United States)? Or where PE is greater than P (for example, the southwestern United States)?

Soil Moisture As part of the water budget, the volume of water in the subsurface soil-moisture zone that is accessible to plant roots is **soil-moisture storage** (S). This is the savings account of water that receives deposits (or recharge) and provides for withdrawals (or utilization).

The soil-moisture environment includes three categories of water—gravitational, capillary, and hygroscopic. Gravitational water fills the soil pore spaces and then drains downward under the force of gravity. Only the hygroscopic and capillary categories remain in the soil-moisture zone; of these two, only capillary water is accessible to plants (**Figure 6.8a**).

Gravitational water is the water surplus in the soil body after the soil becomes saturated during a precipitation event. This water is unavailable to plants, as it percolates downward to the deeper groundwater zone. Once the soil-moisture zone reaches saturation, the pore spaces are filled with water, leaving no room for oxygen or gas exchange by plant roots until the soil drains.

Capillary water is generally accessible to plant roots because it is held in the soil, against the pull of gravity, by hydrogen bonds between water molecules (that is, by surface tension) and by hydrogen bonding between water molecules and the soil. Most capillary water is *available*

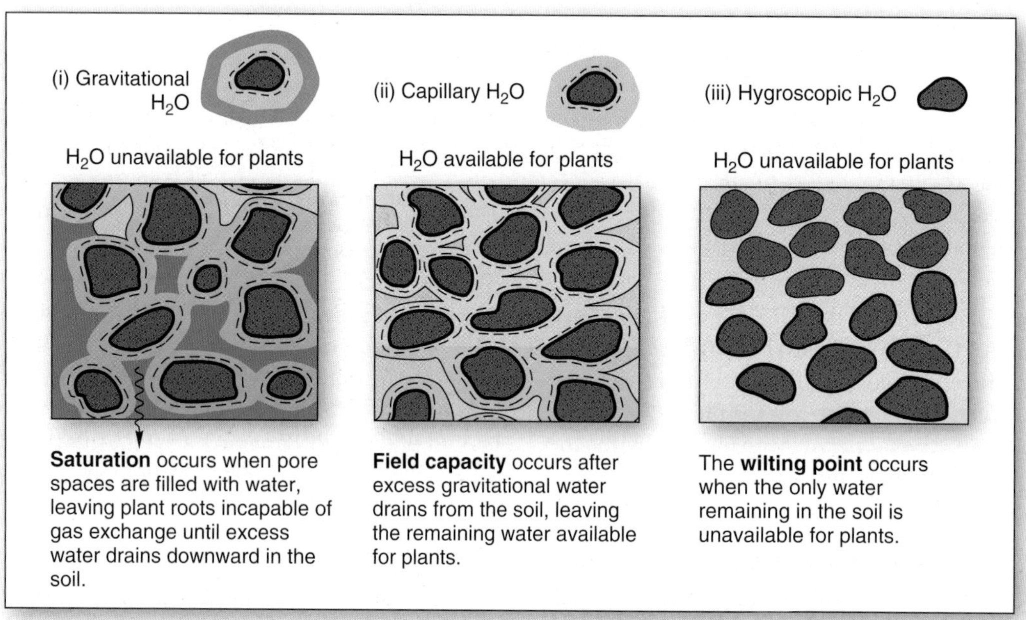

(i) Gravitational H_2O
(ii) Capillary H_2O
(iii) Hygroscopic H_2O
H_2O unavailable for plants
H_2O available for plants
H_2O unavailable for plants
Saturation occurs when pore spaces are filled with water, leaving plant roots incapable of gas exchange until excess water drains downward in the soil.
Field capacity occurs after excess gravitational water drains from the soil, leaving the remaining water available for plants.
The **wilting point** occurs when the only water remaining in the soil is unavailable for plants.

(a) The (i) gravitational, (ii) capillary, and (iii) hygroscopic categories of water exist in the soil moisture environment. Note that some capillary water is bound to hygroscopic water on soil particles and is not available to plants.

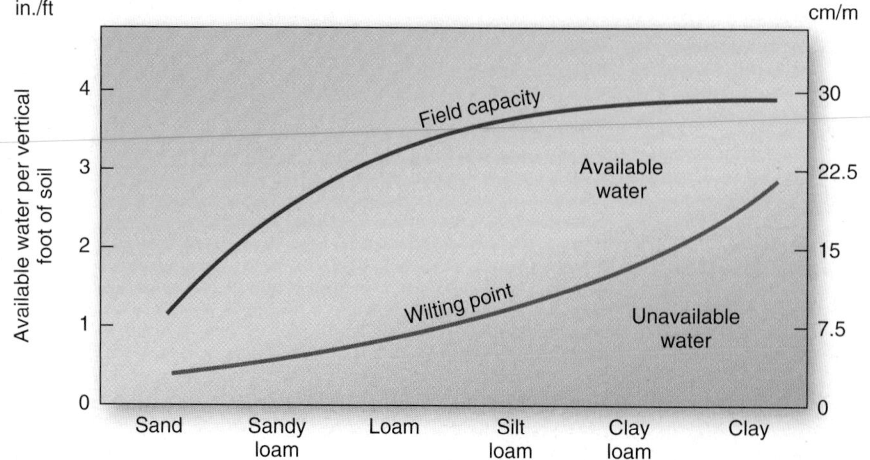

(b) The relationship between soil-moisture availability and soil texture determines the distance between the two curves that show field capacity and wilting point. A loam soil (one-third each of sand, silt, and clay) has roughly the most available water per vertical foot of soil exposed to plant roots.

▲**Figure 6.8 Types and availability of soil moisture.** [(b) After U.S. Department of Agriculture, *1955 Yearbook of Agriculture—Water*, p. 120.]

water in soil-moisture storage. After some water drains from the larger pore spaces, the amount of available water remaining for plants is termed **field capacity**, or storage capacity. This water can meet PE demands through the action of plant roots and surface evaporation. Field capacity is specific to each soil type; the texture and the structure of the soil dictate available pore spaces, or *porosity* (discussed in Chapter 15).

When only a small amount of soil moisture is present, it may be unavailable to plants. *Hygroscopic water* is inaccessible to plants because it is a molecule-thin layer that is tightly bound to each soil particle by the hydrogen bonding of water molecules. Hygroscopic water exists in all climates, even in deserts, but it is unavailable to meet PE demands. Soil moisture is at the **wilting point** for plants when all that remains is this inaccessible water; plants wilt and eventually die after a prolonged period at this degree of moisture stress. In agriculture, farmers use irrigation to avoid a deficit and enhance plant growth with adequate amounts of available water.

Figure 6.8b shows the relation of soil texture to soil-moisture content. Different plant species send roots to different depths and therefore reach different amounts of soil moisture. A soil blend that maximizes available water is best for plants (see the discussion of soil texture in Chapter 15).

When water demand exceeds the precipitation supply, **soil-moisture utilization**—usage by plants of the available moisture in the soil—occurs. As water is removed from the soil, plants have increased difficulty extracting the amount of moisture they need. Eventually, even though a small amount of water may remain in the soil, plants may be unable to use it.

When water infiltrates the soil and replenishes available water, whether from natural precipitation or artificial irrigation, **soil-moisture recharge** occurs. The property of the soil that determines the rate of soil-moisture recharge is its **permeability**, the ability of water to flow through rock or soil, which depends on particle sizes and the shape and packing of soil grains.

Water infiltration is rapid in the first minutes of precipitation and slows as the upper soil layers become saturated, even though the deeper soil may still be dry. Agricultural practices such as plowing and adding sand or manure to loosen soil structure can improve both soil permeability and the depth to which moisture can efficiently penetrate to recharge soil-moisture storage. You may have found yourself working to improve soil permeability for a houseplant or garden—that is, working the soil to increase the rate of soil-moisture recharge.

The Water-Budget Equation

As explained in **Figure 6.9**, the water budget equation states that, for any given location or portion of the hydrologic cycle, the water inputs are equal to the water outputs plus or minus the change in water storage. The delta symbol, Δ, means "change"—in this case, the change in soil-moisture storage, which includes both recharge and utilization.

In summary, precipitation (mostly rain and snow) provides the moisture input. This supply is distributed as actual water undergoing evaporation and plant transpiration, extra water running into streams and subsurface groundwater, and water that moves in and out of soil-moisture storage. As in all equations, the two sides must balance; that is, the precipitation input (left side) must equal the outputs (right side).

Ultimately, the climatic factors of precipitation and temperature (as it affects evapotranspiration) determine the water budget. However, local vegetation, soils, and land use also influence the movement of water through the hydrologic cycle in a given area.

Sample Water Budgets

As an example, study the water-budget graph for the city of Kingsport, in the extreme northeastern corner of Tennessee (36.6° N, 82.5° W) at an elevation of 390 m (1280 ft).

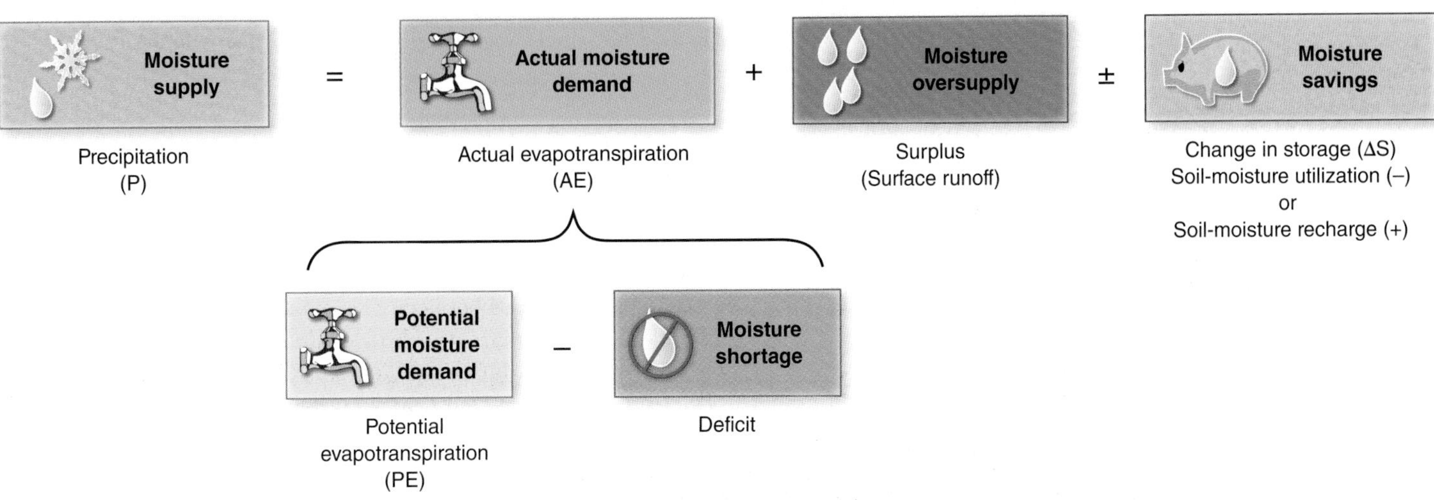

▲**Figure 6.9 The water-budget equation explained.**

Figure 6.10 plots P, AE, and PE, using monthly averages, which smooth out the actual daily and hourly variability. The cooler time from October to May shows a net surplus (blue areas), as precipitation is higher than potential evapotranspiration. The warm days from June to September create a net water demand. If we assume a soil-moisture storage capacity of 100 mm (4.0 in.), typical of shallow-rooted plants, this water demand is satisfied through soil-moisture utilization (green area), with a small summer soil-moisture deficit (orange area).

Kingsport experiences water supply-and-demand patterns typical of a humid continental region. In other climatic regimes, the relationships between water-budget components are different. **Figure 6.11** presents water-budget graphs for the cities of Berkeley, California, which has a summer minimum in precipitation, and Phoenix, Arizona, which has low precipitation throughout the year. Compare the size and timing of the water deficits at these locations with the Kingsport graph.

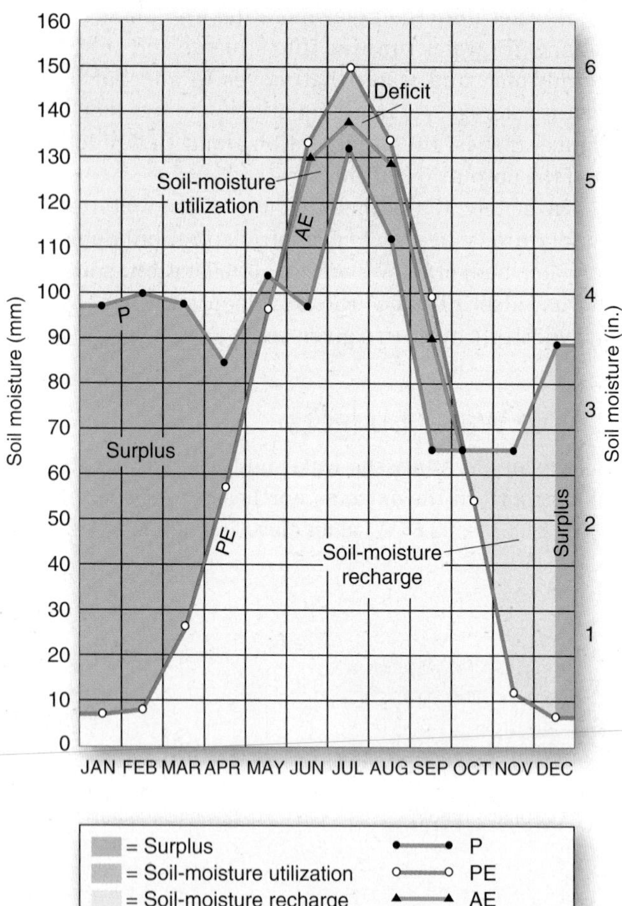

▲Figure 6.10 Sample water budget for Kingsport, Tennessee. Compare the average plots for precipitation inputs and potential evapotranspiration outputs to determine the condition of the soil-moisture environment. A typical pattern for Kingsport exhibits a spring surplus, summer soil-moisture utilization, a small summer deficit, autumn soil-moisture recharge, and a year-ending surplus.

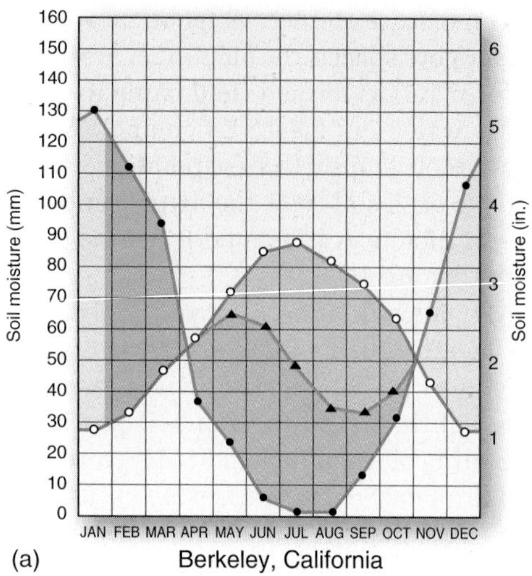

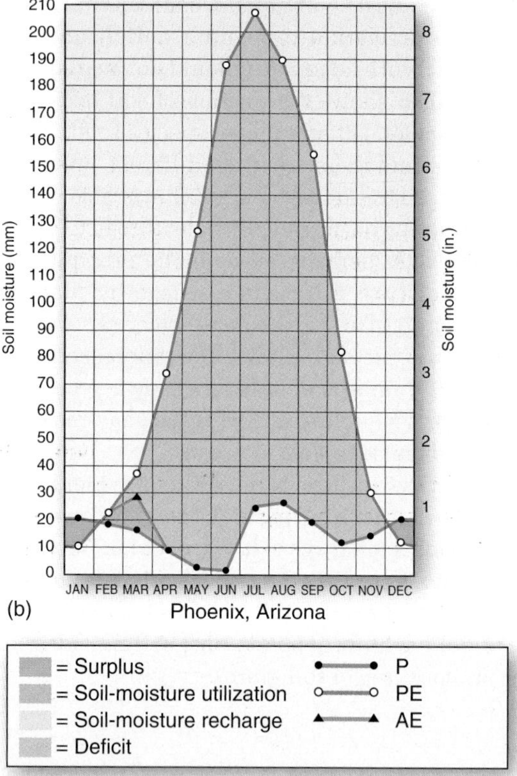

▲Figure 6.11 Sample water budgets for stations near two U.S. cities.

Water budgets can be used to assess water supply and demand for any spatial scale over any period of time (minutes to years to millennia). As human populations grow, balancing the water used by humans with that needed for Earth systems becomes more challenging. Assessing the linkages between components of the water budget helps us understand how changes to one component affect the other components. An example is the extraction of groundwater and its associated effects on streamflow, discussed later in this chapter.

Tropical cyclones provide an interesting application of water-budget analysis. Ironically, sometimes a hurricane is significant not only for damage and fatalities, but also for generally positive effects on regional water resources. Go to the *MasteringGeography* website for maps and a discussion of Hurricane Camille's impact on moisture shortages from the Gulf Coast to the inland regions of the U.S. Southeast.

CRITICAL**thinking 6.1**

Your Local Water Budget

Select an area of interest, such as your campus, your yard, or even a houseplant container, and apply the water-budget concepts to it. Where does the water supply originate—its source? Estimate the ultimate water supply amount and demand for the area you selected. For a general idea of precipitation and evapotranspiration, find your locale on Figures 6.6 and 6.7. Consider the seasonal timing of this supply and demand, and estimate water needs and how they vary as components of the water-budget change.

Drought: The Water Deficit

In simplest terms, **drought** is an extended period of dry conditions caused by lower precipitation and higher temperatures. During a drought, dry conditions last long enough to cause environmental problems, such as fish mortality associated with low streamflow, or socioeconomic problems, such as the financial losses resulting from crop failure. Yet drought is a complex concept because the term is used differently by meteorologists (emphasizing dry weather conditions), farmers (emphasizing soil-moisture shortages as they affect crop yields), and hydrologists (emphasizing snowpack declines, lowered streamflows and reservoir levels, and groundwater removal). Drought also operates on a variety of different time scales, from weeks to months to years. In the United States, scientists and resource managers use the Palmer Drought Indices to assess drought conditions. The *Palmer Z Index* measures short-term drought on a monthly basis, the *Palmer Drought Severity Index* measures long-term meterological (weather) conditions that cause drought, and the *Palmer Hydrological Drought Index* measures long-term effects of drought on streamflow, groundwater, and reservoir levels (see http://www.ncdc.noaa.gov/oa/climate/research/prelim/drought/palmer.html).

In July of 2012, the U.S. Department of Agriculture declared almost one-third of all U.S. counties federal disaster areas owing to drought conditions—the largest natural disaster area ever declared. According to the National Climatic Data Center, 16 of the droughts that occurred from 1980 to 2011 cost over $1 billion each, making drought one of the costliest U.S. weather-related events. (See http://www.drought.unl.edu/ for a weekly Drought Monitor map.)

In early 2014, intensifying drought conditions in California led to conditions so severe that the governor declared a state of emergency, calling for state officials to prepare for depleted water supplies and for all Californians to conserve water. By the end of January, with mountain snowpacks at 12% of normal, reservoirs at less than 50% capacity, and a new record of 52 days without rain during what should be the wettest time of the year, the state reached a water crisis (**Figure 6.12**). On average, a little more than half of California's precipitation falls during the months of December, January, and February. In the fall of 2013, a persistent ridge of high pressure dominated the atmosphere over the U.S. West, remaining in place for almost three months. In the following February and March, a few low-pressure systems moved through the region, with storms producing some precipitation, but not enough to restore water supplies to average conditions.

Drought is a natural and recurrent feature of climate. In the southwestern United States, drought conditions have existed since early 2000, one of several such droughts evident in the region's climatic record over the last 1000 years. However, scientists are finding mounting evidence that this increased aridity, or climatic dryness, links not only to natural factors, but also to global climate change and a poleward expansion of the subtropical dry zones. Thus, human-caused warming is combining with natural climate variability to create a trend toward lasting drought, made worse by steady population growth and ever-increasing demand on regional water supplies. Focus Study 6.1 on pages 200 and 201 discusses this drought and its effects on the Colorado River watershed.

Surface Water Resources

Water distribution over Earth's surface is uneven over space and time. Because humans require a steady water supply, we increasingly rely on large-scale management projects intended to redistribute water resources either geographically, by moving water from one place to another, or through time, by storing water until it is

▲**Figure 6.12 Low reservoir levels caused by drought.** At Bridge Bay, on Shasta Lake in northern California, water levels were 30 m (100 ft) lower than normal full reservoir capacity in January 2014. [Robert Galbraith/Reuters.]

needed. In this way, surpluses are held for later release, and water availability is improved to satisfy natural and human demands.

The freshwater on Earth's surface is found primarily in snow and ice, rivers, lakes, and wetlands. Surface water is also stored in reservoirs, artificial lakes formed by dams on rivers. **Figure 6.13** shows the world's major rivers, lakes, reservoirs, and wetlands, all discussed in this section.

Snow and Ice

The largest amount of surface freshwater on Earth is stored in glaciers, permafrost, and polar ice (review Figure 6.3). Seasonal melting from glaciers and the annual snowpack in temperate regions feeds streamflow, contributing to water supplies. Snowpack melting captured in reservoirs behind dams is a primary water source for humans in many parts of the world.

Glaciers provide a form of water storage, although rising temperatures associated with recent climate change are causing accelerated rates of glacial melting. The residence time of water in glaciers can range between decades and centuries, and the relatively small, but continuous meltwater from glaciers can sustain streamflow throughout the year (Chapter 14 discusses glaciers and ice sheets).

Some scientists estimate that most glaciers will be gone by 2035 if present melt rates continue. On Asia's Tibetan Plateau, the world's largest and highest plateau at 3350 km (11,000 ft) elevation, climate change is causing mountain glaciers to recede at rates faster than anywhere else in the world. More than 1000 lakes store water on this plateau, forming the headwaters for several of the world's longest rivers. Almost half the world's population lives within the watersheds of these rivers; the Yangtze and Yellow Rivers (both flowing eastward through China) alone supply water to approximately 520 million people

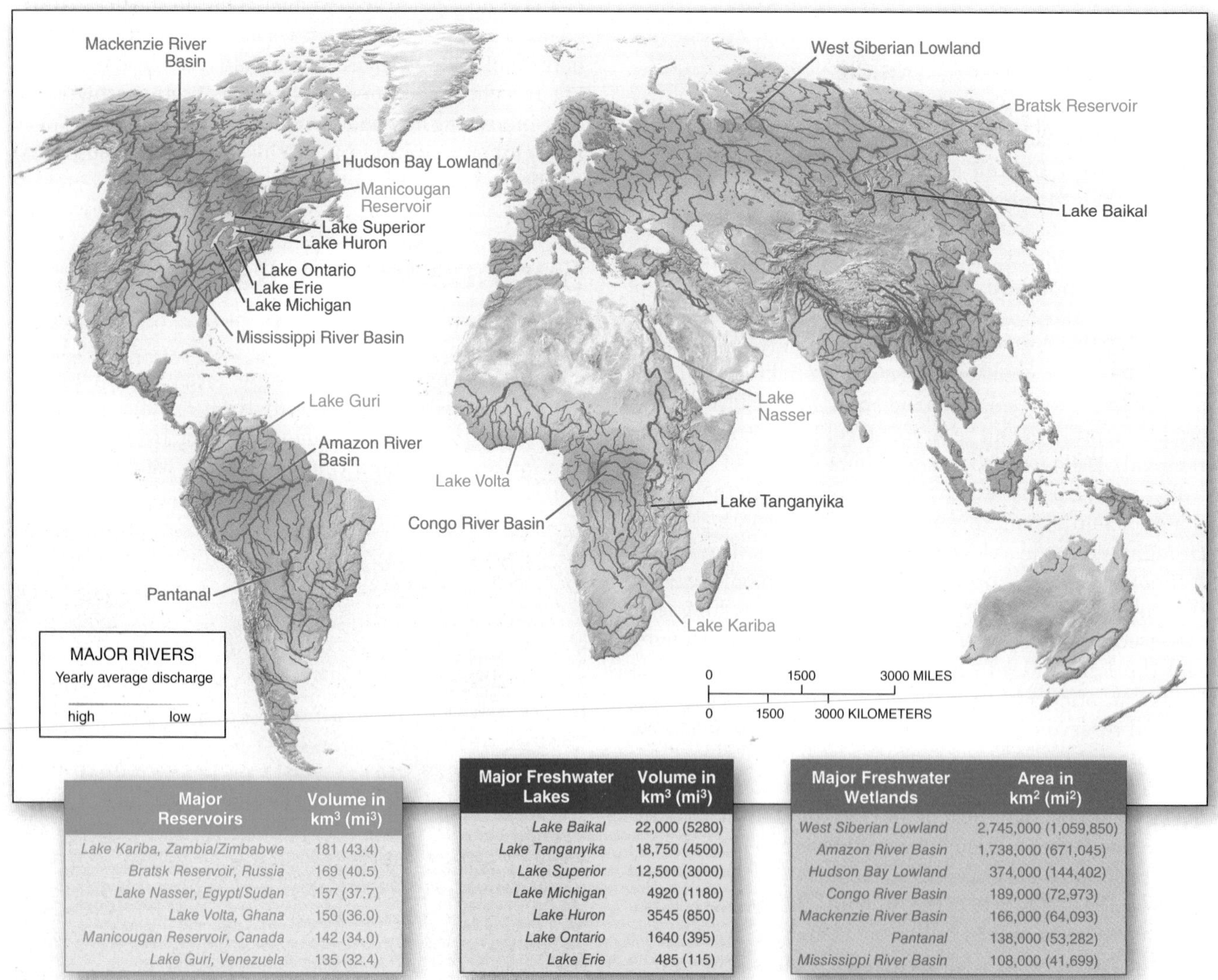

Major Reservoirs	Volume in km³ (mi³)
Lake Kariba, Zambia/Zimbabwe	181 (43.4)
Bratsk Reservoir, Russia	169 (40.5)
Lake Nasser, Egypt/Sudan	157 (37.7)
Lake Volta, Ghana	150 (36.0)
Manicougan Reservoir, Canada	142 (34.0)
Lake Guri, Venezuela	135 (32.4)

Major Freshwater Lakes	Volume in km³ (mi³)
Lake Baikal	22,000 (5280)
Lake Tanganyika	18,750 (4500)
Lake Superior	12,500 (3000)
Lake Michigan	4920 (1180)
Lake Huron	3545 (850)
Lake Ontario	1640 (395)
Lake Erie	485 (115)

Major Freshwater Wetlands	Area in km² (mi²)
West Siberian Lowland	2,745,000 (1,059,850)
Amazon River Basin	1,738,000 (671,045)
Hudson Bay Lowland	374,000 (144,402)
Congo River Basin	189,000 (72,973)
Mackenzie River Basin	166,000 (64,093)
Pantanal	138,000 (53,282)
Mississippi River Basin	108,000 (41,699)

▲**Figure 6.13 The world's major rivers, lakes, and wetlands.** Earth's largest streamflow volumes occur within and just adjacent to the tropics, reflecting the continual rainfall associated with the Intertropical Convergence Zone (ITCZ). Regions of lower streamflow coincide with Earth's subtropical deserts, rain-shadow areas, and continental interiors, particularly in Asia. [Adapted from William E. McNulty, National Geographic Society, based on data from USGS; World Wildlife Fund; State Hydrological Institute, Russia; University of Kassel Center for Environmental Systems Research, Germany.]

in China. Even as glacial melting has increased streamflows, the worsening drought in western China is causing these flows to evaporate or infiltrate into the ground before reaching the largest population centers. Although disappearing glaciers will not significantly change water availability in the lower-elevation regions, which depend on monsoonal precipitation and snowmelt, these changes will affect high-elevation water supplies, especially during the dry season.

Rivers and Lakes

Surface runoff and base flow from groundwater move across Earth's surface in rivers and streams, forming vast arterial networks that drain the continents. Freshwater lakes are fed by precipitation, streamflow, and groundwater and store about 125,000 km^3 (30,000 mi^3), or about 0.33%, of the freshwater on Earth's surface. About 80% of this volume is in just 40 of the largest lakes, and about 50% is contained in just 7 lakes (Figure 6.13).

The greatest single volume of lake water resides in 25-million-year-old Lake Baikal in Siberian Russia, discussed in this chapter's Geosystems Now. This lake contains almost as much water as all five North American Great Lakes combined. Africa's Lake Tanganyika contains the next largest volume, followed by the five Great Lakes. About one-fourth of global freshwater lake storage is in small lakes. More than 3 million lakes exist in Alaska alone; Canada has at least that many in number and has more total surface area of lakes than any country in the world.

Not connected to the ocean are saline lakes and salty inland seas, containing about 104,000 km^3 (25,000 mi^3) of water. They usually exist in regions of interior river drainage (no outlet to the ocean), which allows salts resulting from evaporation over time to become concentrated. Examples of such lakes include Utah's Great Salt Lake, California's Mono Lake and Salton Sea, Southwest Asia's Caspian and Aral Seas, and the Dead Sea between Israel and Jordan.

Lakes Warm with Climate Change Increasing air temperatures are affecting lakes throughout the world. Some lake levels are rising in response to the melting of glacial ice; others are falling as a result of drought and high evaporation rates. Longer, warmer summers change the thermal structure of a lake, blocking the normal mixing between deep and surface waters.

Normally, most lakes exhibit stratification in the summer: Water at the surface, which is warmer, fails to mix with the cooler water down below. This leads to a depletion of nutrients in the shallows by late summer. In the fall, as the surface cools, water sinks, creating a turnover that replenishes surface nutrients throughout the lake. As regional temperatures warm, the summerlike stratification appears earlier in the year and persists later in the fall, and mixing slows or stops. This prolonged stratification can adversely affect phytoplankton, fish, and other organisms in a lake's food web (see further discussion in Chapter 16).

Lake Tahoe in the Sierra Nevada mountain range along the California–Nevada border is warming at about 1.3 C° (2.3 F°) per decade. The rate of warming is highest in the upper 10 m (33 ft), and mixing has slowed. Nonnative, invasive species such as large-mouth bass, carp, and Asian clam are on the rise in warming lakes, while cold-water species decline.

In East Africa, Lake Tanganyika is surrounded by an estimated 10 million people, with most depending on its fish stocks, especially freshwater sardines, for food. Present water temperatures have risen to 26°C (79°F), the highest in a 1500-year climate record revealed by lake-sediment cores. The mixing of surface and deep waters is necessary to replenish nutrients in the upper 200 m (656 ft) of the lake, where the sardines reside. As mixing slows or stops, scientists fear that fish stocks will continue to decline.

Hydroelectric Power Human-made lakes are generally called *reservoirs*, although the term *lake* often appears in their name. Dams built on rivers cause surface water reservoirs to form upstream; the total volume worldwide of such reservoirs is estimated at 5000 km^3 (1200 mi^3). The largest reservoir in the world by volume is Lake Kariba in Africa, impounded by the Kariba Dam on the Zambezi River on the border between Zambia and Zimbabwe. The third and fourth largest are also in Africa (Figure 6.13). The largest U.S. reservoir is Lake Mead on the Colorado River, discussed in Focus Study 6.1.

Although flood control and water-supply storage are two primary purposes for dam construction, an associated benefit is power production. Hydroelectric power, or **hydropower**, is electricity generated using the power of moving water. Currently, hydropower supplies almost one-fifth of the world's electricity and is the most widely used source of renewable energy. However, because it depends on precipitation, hydropower is highly variable from month to month and year to year.

China is the world's leading hydropower producer. The Three Gorges Dam on the Yangtze River in China is 2.3 km (1.5 mi) long and 185 m (607 ft) high, making it the largest dam in the world in overall size, including all related construction at the dam site (**Figure 6.14**). Entire cities were relocated (including more than 1.2 million people) to make room for the 600-km-long (370-mi-long) reservoir upstream from the dam. The immense scale of environmental, historical, and cultural losses associated with the project was the subject of great controversy. Benefits from the project include flood control, water storage for redistribution, and electrical power production, with capacity at 22,000 MW. In October 2012, the reservoir was filled to its design capacity; however, water pollution and landslides along the reservoir banks may force the relocation of an additional 300,000 people.

In the United States in 2013, hydropower accounted for 7% of total electricity production and 50% of the

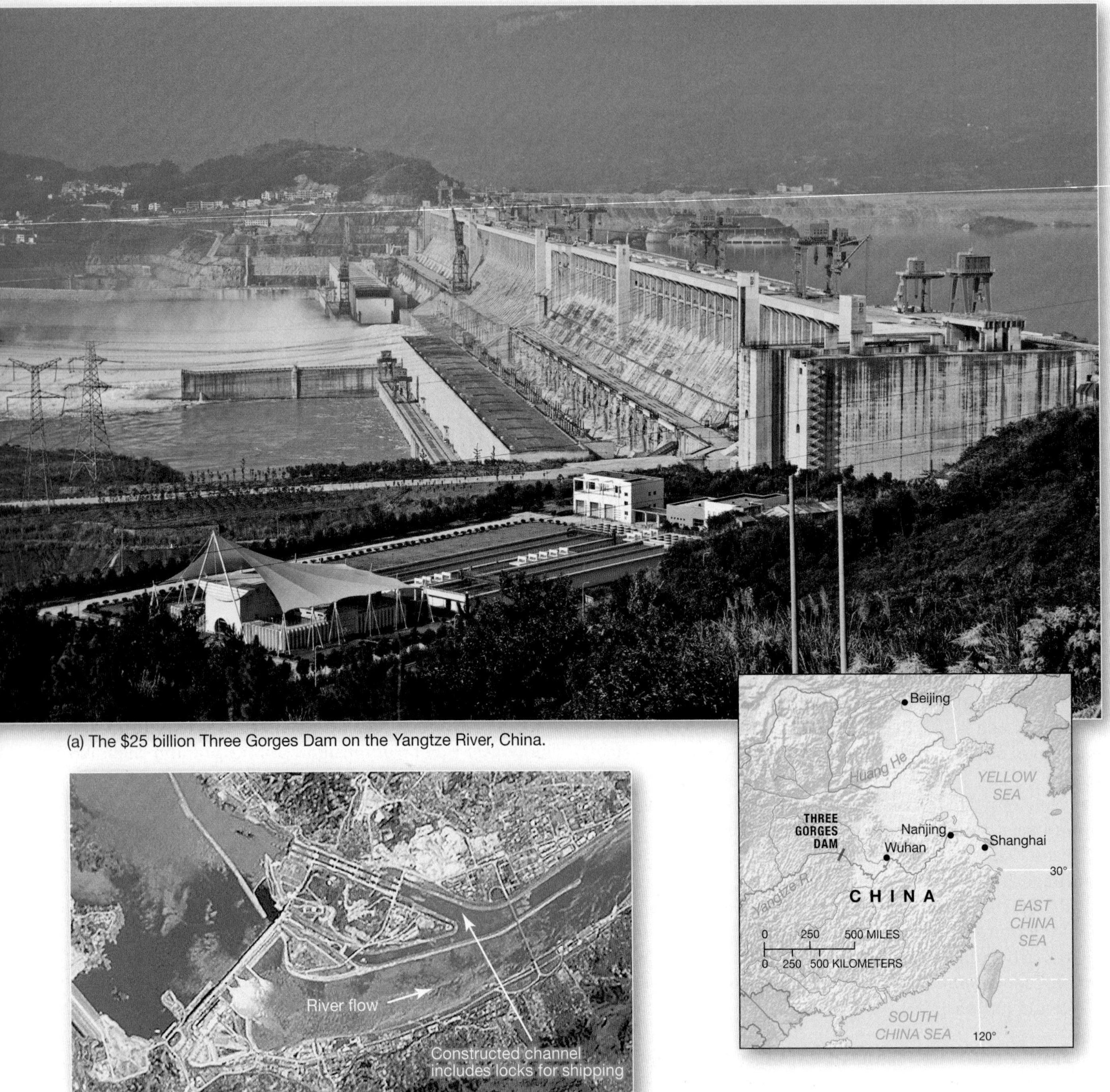

(a) The $25 billion Three Gorges Dam on the Yangtze River, China.

(b) Satellite view shows the dam and shipping channel.

▲**Figure 6.14 Three Gorges Dam in China.** [(a) John Henshall/Alamy. (b) *Terra* ASTER, NASA/GSFC/MITI/ERSDAC/JAROS.]

electricity generation in the Pacific Northwest. The Grand Coulee Dam, on the Columbia River, is the world's fifth largest hydropower plant and the largest in the United States. Power from the dam is marketed by the Bonneville Power Administration, which sells electricity from 31 federally operated hydropower plants in the Columbia River basin.

In the U.S. Southeast, the Tennessee Valley Authority operates 29 dams and hydroelectric facilities in the Tennessee Valley. In the Southwest, the Colorado River is an important, yet threatened, source of hydroelectric power (discussed in Focus Study 6.1).

In the United States, dams have already been built on the best multipurpose dam sites, with numerous detrimental consequences for river environments. Many of the largest hydropower projects are old, and overall production of hydropower is declining. In late 2014, solar, wind, and other renewable energy sources together exceeded hydropower generation, part of an ongoing trend. Chapter 12 examines the environmental effects of dams and reservoirs on river ecosystems and reports on recent dam removals. Worldwide, however, hydropower is increasing; several large projects are proposed and under construction in Brazil alone.

Water Transfer Projects The transfer of water over long distances in pipelines and aqueducts is especially important in dry regions where the most dependable water resources are far away from population centers. The Salt River Project, for example, is a system of aqueducts that move water from the Salt River to the Phoenix metropolitan area (look back to the chapter-opening photo). In western Arizona, the Central Arizona Project canal system moves water from the Colorado River to the cities of Phoenix and Tucson.

The California State Water Project (SWP) is the nation's most extensive water storage and delivery system, including dams, reservoirs, canals, pumping stations, and power plants that provide water for over 25 million people and 750,000 acres of farmland. Water distribution over time is altered by holding back winter runoff for release in summer, and water distribution over space is altered by pumping water from the northern to the southern parts of the state. Completed in 1971, the 1207-km-long (750-mi-long) California Aqueduct is a "river" flowing from the Sacramento River delta to the Los Angeles region, servicing irrigated agriculture in the San Joaquin Valley along the way. In early 2014, during the worst of the winter drought, the California Department of Water Resources cut off their share of the state's water supply, managed as part of the SWP, in order to preserve the remaining water supply for use during the summer months.

Wetlands

A **wetland** is an area that is permanently or seasonally saturated with water and characterized by vegetation adapted to *hydric* soils (soils saturated long enough to develop anaerobic, or "oxygen-free," conditions). The water found in wetlands can be freshwater or saltwater (Chapter 13 discusses saltwater wetlands). Marshes, swamps, bogs, and peatlands (bog areas composed of peat, or partly decayed vegetation) are types of freshwater wetlands that occur worldwide along river channels and lakeshores, in surface depressions such as the prairie potholes in the U.S Great Plains region, and in the cool, lowland, high-latitude regions of Canada, Alaska, and Siberia. Figure 6.13 shows the global distribution of some major wetlands.

Large wetlands are important sources of freshwater and recharge groundwater supplies. When rivers flow over their banks, wetlands absorb and spread out the floodwaters. For example, the Amazon River floodplain is a major wetland that stores water and mitigates flooding within the river system—the river and its associated wetlands provide about one-fifth of the freshwater flowing into the world's oceans. Wetlands are also significant for improving water quality by trapping sediment and removing nutrients and pollutants. In fact, constructed wetlands are increasingly used globally for water purification. (See Chapter 16 for more on freshwater wetlands.)

Groundwater Resources

Although **groundwater** lies beneath the surface, beyond the soil-moisture zone and the reach of most plant roots, it is an important part of the hydrologic cycle. In fact, it is the largest potential freshwater source on Earth—larger than all surface lakes and streams combined. In the region from the soil-moisture zone to a depth of 4 km (13,000 ft) worldwide is an amount of water totaling some 8,340,000 km^3 (2,000,000 mi^3), a volume comparable to 70 times all the freshwater lakes in the world. Groundwater is not an independent source of water; it is tied to surface supplies for recharge through pores in soil and rock. An important consideration in many regions is that groundwater accumulated over millions of years, so care must be taken not to deplete this long-term buildup with excessive short-term demands.

Groundwater provides about 80% of the world's irrigation water for agriculture and nearly half the world's drinking water. Major aquifers occur on every continent except Antarctica (**Figure 6.15**). Groundwater is generally free of sediment, color, and disease organisms, although polluted groundwater conditions are considered irreversible. Where groundwater pollution does occur, it threatens water quality. Overconsumption is another problem, depleting groundwater volume in quantities beyond natural replenishment rates and thus threatening global food security.

About 50% of the U.S. population derives a portion of its freshwater from groundwater sources. In some

(text continued on page 202)

GEOreport 6.3 How is water measured?

In most of the United States, hydrologists measure streamflow in cubic feet per second (ft^3/s); Canadians use cubic meters per second (m^3/s). For large-scale assessments, water managers in the eastern United States use millions of gallons a day (MGD), billions of gallons a day (BGD), or billions of liters a day (BLD). In the western United States, where irrigated agriculture is so important, total annual streamflows are frequently measured in acre-feet per year. One acre-foot is an acre of water, 1 ft deep, equivalent to 325,872 gal (43,560 ft^3, or 1234 m^3, or 1,233,429 L). An acre is an area that is about 208 ft on a side and is 0.4047 hectares. For global measurements, 1 km^3 = 1 billion m^3 = 810 million acre-feet; 1000 m^3 = 264,200 gal = 0.81 acre-feet. For smaller measures, 1 m^3 = 1000 L = 264.2 gal.

focusstudy 6.1 Climate Change

The Colorado River: A System Out of Balance

The most important water resource in the U.S. Southwest is the Colorado River and its tributaries. From its headwaters in a mountain region of water surpluses, the Colorado River travels almost 2317 km (1440 mi) through arid lands toward its outlet in Mexico. At the river's source in the Rocky Mountains, orographic precipitation totaling 102 cm (40 in.) per year falls mostly as snow (**Figure 6.1.1a**). At Yuma, Arizona, near the river's end, annual precipitation is a scant 8.9 cm (3.5 in.), an extremely small amount in a region with high evaporation rates and growing numbers of people adding to water demand.

The Colorado River flows southwestward through Colorado and Utah; into Lake Powell, the reservoir behind Glen Canyon Dam (**Figure 6.1.1b**); and on through the Grand Canyon. The river then turns southward, forming the Arizona–California border. Along this stretch sit Hoover Dam and the major storage reservoir Lake Mead, near Las Vegas (**Figure 6.1.1c**); Davis Dam, built to control the releases from Hoover Dam; Parker Dam, for the water needs of Los Angeles; three more dams for irrigation water (Palo Verde, Imperial, and Laguna); and, finally, Morelos Dam at the Mexican border. Mexico owns the end of the river and whatever water is left. Most years, the river ends as a trickle, kilometers short of its former mouth in the Gulf of California (**Figure 6.1.1d**).

The annual streamflow and suspended sediment load measured for the Colorado River at Yuma, Arizona, declined with the completion of Hoover Dam in the 1930s and additional dams in subsequent years (**Figure 6.1.1e**). By the mid-1960s, streamflow and sediment at Yuma were nearly zero (we discuss the effects of sediment reduction on rivers below dams in Chapter 12).

Overall, the Colorado River basin encompasses 641,025 km^2 (247,500 mi^2) in parts of seven states, all growing in population. (In 2013, Utah, Arizona, Colorado, and Wyoming were ranked among the top 10 fastest-growing U.S. states.) The rapidly expanding urban areas of Las Vegas, Phoenix, Tucson, Denver, San Diego, and Albuquerque all depend on Colorado River water, which supplies nearly 40 million people. The river has played a crucial part in the history of the Southwest and will have a defining role in the future of this dry region.

Allocating the Colorado's Water

As settlement of the U.S. West increased in the late 1800s, irrigation and water storage became important issues in lands where precipitation was not enough to meet water demand. Common thought was that water *reclamation*, the name given to irrigation projects at that time, would "reclaim" the arid lands of the West, making them suitable for human settlement. In 1902, the government established the U.S. Reclamation Service, today known as the Bureau of Reclamation, to develop water projects on federal lands in the West. Because the Colorado River is the region's major water source, allocating its water among potential users was critical for development.

In 1923, six states signed the Colorado River Compact, which divided water allocations in the Colorado River basin between the upper basin and the lower basin, with Lee's Ferry, near the Utah–Arizona border, designated the dividing line (Figure 6.1.1; the seventh basin state, Arizona, signed the compact 21 years later). In 1928, Congress authorized Hoover Dam as the first major reclamation project in the Colorado basin. This multipurpose dam would store water for later use, divert water for irrigation, provide flood control for downstream resources, and generate hydroelectric power. This project included construction of the All-American Canal to carry water for irrigation into the Imperial Valley of California as well as construction of the Imperial Dam to divert water into the canal. Los Angeles then began its project to bring Colorado River water 390 km (240 mi) from still another dam and reservoir on the river to the city.

Eight major dams and numerous canals and diversions are now in place. The last effort to redistribute Colorado River water was the Central Arizona Project (CAP), which carries water to the cities of Phoenix and Tucson.

Variable River Flows

The most notable flaw in long-range planning and water distribution in the Colorado River system relates to the river's highly variable flows, typical of a river that rises in a wet region, but flows mostly through drylands. The government based the terms of the Colorado River Compact on the river's average annual flows from 1914 up to the compact signing in 1923—an exceptionally high 18.8 million acre-feet (maf). That amount was perceived as more than enough to supply the upper and lower basins with 7.5 maf each and, later, to allow Mexico to receive 1.5 maf (as determined by the 1944 Mexican Water Treaty).

Scientific studies since the compact signing now reveal the problems in long-term planning based on data from such a short time period. Climate reconstructions for about the past 1000 years suggest that the only other time Colorado River flows were at the high 1914–1923 level was between 1606 and 1625. Since 1923, average annual river flows have varied from a high of 24.5 maf in 1984 to lows of 5.0 maf or less in 1934, 1977, and 2002. Thus, planners have regularly overestimated river flows, a situation that has created shortfalls as water demand exceeds water supply.

The seven states want rights to Colorado River water that amount to far more than the river contains. Additionally, a 2012 United States–Mexico agreement grants storage rights in Lake Mead to Mexico during times of surplus, although the country must forfeit the storage rights during periods of water shortage. In the present ongoing western drought, no surplus exists in the river's water budget.

Ongoing Drought and Sustainable Water Management

Higher temperatures and evaporation rates, as well as reduced mountain snowpack and earlier spring melt, have caused on ongoing drought in the Colorado River basin since 2000. According to regional tree-ring records, nine droughts have affected the American Southwest since A.D. 1226. However, streamflow reconstructions using tree ring data have revealed that the drought spanning the 14-year period from 2000 to 2014 is the worst in 1200 years and is the first to occur with increasing human demand for water as population growth continues throughout the region.

The period from 2000 to 2010 marked the lowest 10-year-average total flow of the Colorado River in the 103-year record, with 2002 dropping to an all-time record low. Water inflow to Lake Powell is now running at less than one-third of long-term averages (in the lowest year, 2002, it ran at just 25%).

The effects of ongoing drought are evident in declining reservoir levels throughout the Colorado River system. This is the water reserve intended to offset variable Colorado River flows, especially during periods of drought. The largest reservoirs—Lake Mead and Lake Powell—together account for over 80% of total system storage. In mid-2014, the level of Lake Mead behind Hoover Dam dropped to 329 m (1080 ft), far below the 375-m (1229-ft) full capacity of the reservoir reached in July 1983.

In five to seven years, scientists forecast that Lake Mead will drop to the critical 305-m (1000-ft) level below which water cannot enter the intake pipelines for transfers to Las Vegas or to CAP canals. Low reservoir levels also degrade hydropower capability because the efficiency of electrical output depends on the height of the reservoir; higher water means more water pressure, supplying more energy to turn the turbines. Scientists agree that the overall trend of declining snowfall and ongoing drought is likely to continue. Increasing evaporation associated with rising temperatures across the Southwest and increasing human water use will make drought recovery slower than in the past.

In recent years, water users throughout the Colorado River basin have initiated more-sustainable water-management practices, employing conservation strategies (use of less water) and efficiency strategies (more effective use of water) to reduce the tremendous demand for water. For instance, southern Nevada launched a campaign to replace lawns with drought-tolerant xeriscaping (desert landscaping). Las Vegas, which receives 90% of its water from the Colorado River, has implemented mandatory watering schedules, water waste fees, and numerous other conservation strategies resulting in a decrease in water consumption of about 378 L (100 gal) per person per day since 2002.

Lowering water demand, rather than focusing solely on water supply, is the best solution to balance the Colorado River water budget. For more information, see the 2012 Colorado River Basin Water Supply and Demand Study at **http://www.usbr.gov/lc/region/programs/crbstudy.html**.

1. Are the issues concerning dams and hydropower in the U.S. Pacific Northwest the same as those affecting the Colorado River basin? Why or why not? Explain.

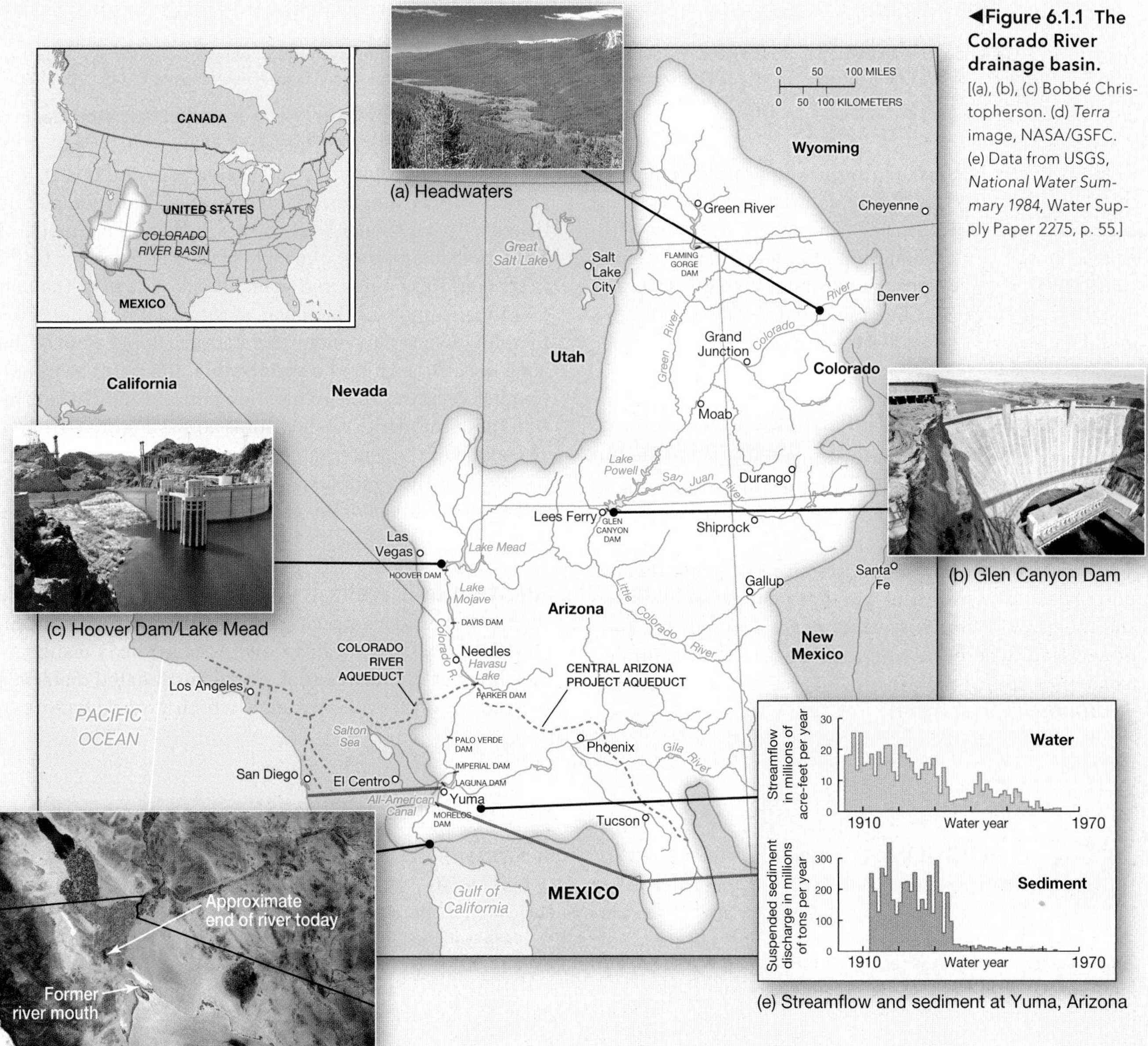

Figure 6.1.1 The Colorado River drainage basin. [(a), (b), (c) Bobbé Christopherson. (d) *Terra* image, NASA/GSFC. (e) Data from USGS, *National Water Summary 1984*, Water Supply Paper 2275, p. 55.]

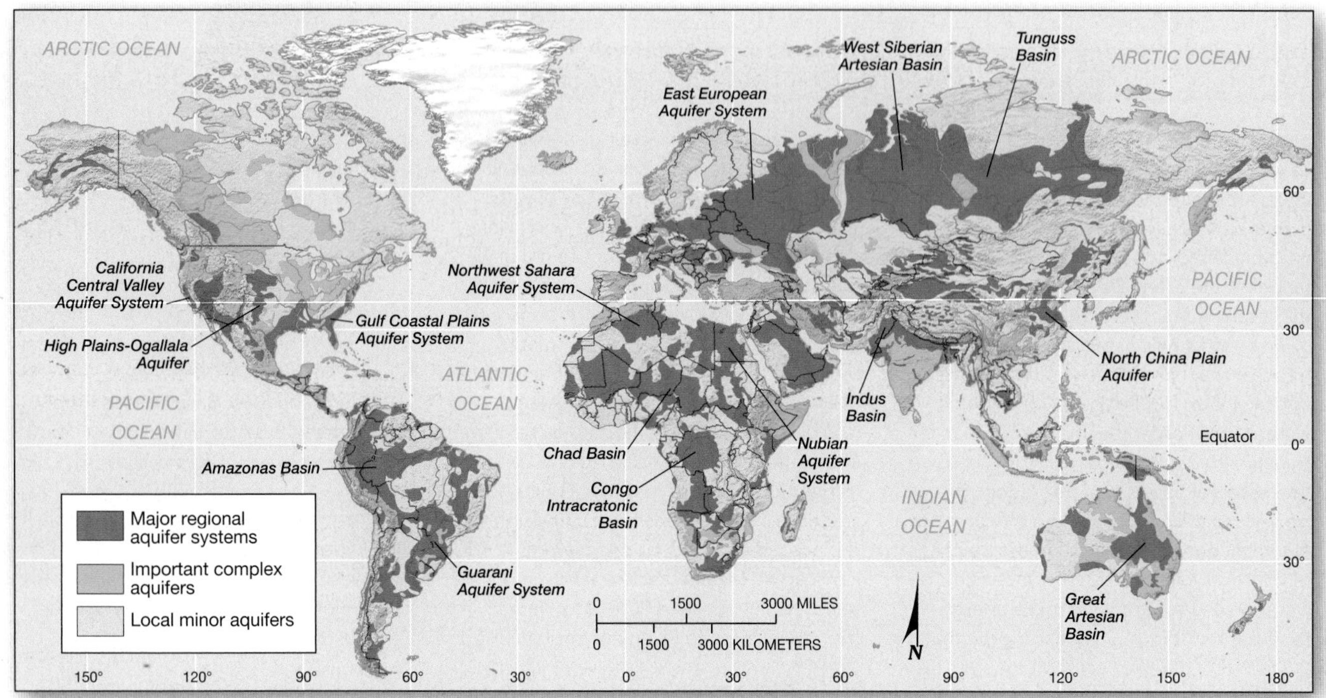

▲**Figure 6.15 Generalized map of global groundwater resources and important regional aquifer systems.** [Adapted from Taylor et al., "Groundwater and climate change," *Nature Climate Change* 3 (2013): 322–329. Simplified map based on Struckmeier, W. et al., *Groundwater Resources of the World (1:25,000,000)*, BGR & UNESCO World-wide Hydrogeological Mapping and Assessment Programme, 2008.]

MG MapMaster: North America Physical Environment: Groundwater Resource Potential

states, such as Nebraska, groundwater supplies 85% of water needs, with that figure as high as 100% in rural areas. Between 1950 and 2000, annual groundwater withdrawal in the United States and Canada increased more than 150%. For the latest research on U.S. groundwater resources, go to http://water.usgs.gov/ogw/gwrp/; for maps and data, see http://groundwaterwatch.usgs.gov/.

The Groundwater Environment

Geosystems in Action 6 brings together many groundwater concepts in a single illustration. Follow its 13 numbers as you read about each part of the groundwater environment.

Precipitation is the main source of groundwater, percolating downward as gravitational water from the soil-moisture zone. This water moves through the **zone of aeration**, where soil and rock are less than saturated (some pore spaces contain air), an area also known as the *unsaturated zone* (GIA #1).

Eventually, gravitational water accumulates in the **zone of saturation**, where soil pore spaces are completely filled with water (GIA #2). Like a hard sponge made of sand, gravel, and rock, the zone of saturation stores water in its countless pores and voids. It is bounded at the bottom by an impermeable layer of rock that obstructs further downward movement of water. The upper limit of the zone of saturation is the **water table**, the point of transition between the zone of aeration and the zone of saturation (note the white dashed lines across Figure GIA 6.1). The slope of the water table, which generally follows the contours of the land surface, drives groundwater movement toward areas of lower elevation and lower pressure (GIA #3).

Aquifers and Wells

As discussed earlier, permeable rock or materials conduct water readily, while impermeable rock obstructs water flow. An **aquifer** is a subsurface layer of permeable rock or unconsolidated materials (silt, sand, or gravels) through which groundwater can

GEOreport 6.4 Satellite *GRACE* enables groundwater measurements

Groundwater is difficult to study and measure because it lies hidden beneath Earth's surface. Scientists are now using NASA's Gravity Recovery and Climate Experiment (*GRACE*) satellites to study changes in groundwater storage using measurements of Earth's gravity field. Water table declines in India—as large as 33 cm (1 ft) between 2002 and 2008—appear to be almost entirely caused by human use, which is depleting the resource more quickly than it can recharge. In the Middle East, *GRACE* data show that reservoir volumes have also declined precipitously, attributed to groundwater pumping. *GRACE* has given scientists a "scale in the sky" that may prove critical for initiating action on water conservation in these regions.

flow in amounts adequate for wells and springs. The blue underground area on the left-hand page of Figure GIA 6.1 is an unconfined aquifer; note the water wells on the left side of that page. An **unconfined aquifer** has a permeable layer above, which allows water to pass through, and an impermeable one beneath (GIA #4). A **confined aquifer** is bounded above and below by impermeable layers of rock or unconsolidated materials (GIA #9). The solid, impermeable layer that forms such a boundary is known as an *aquiclude*. An *aquitard* is a layer that has low permeability, but cannot conduct water in usable amounts. The zone of saturation may include the saturated portion of the aquifer and a part of the underlying aquiclude (GIA #7).

Humans commonly extract groundwater using wells that are drilled downward into the ground until they penetrate the water table. Shallow drilling results in a "dry well" (GIA #6); drilling too deeply will punch through the aquifer and into the impermeable layer below, also yielding little water. The water in a well drilled into an unconfined aquifer is not under pressure and so must be pumped to rise above the water table (GIA #5). In contrast, the water in a confined aquifer is under the pressure of its own weight, creating a pressure level called the *potentiometric surface* to which the water can rise on its own.

The potentiometric surface can be above ground level (GIA #10). Under this condition, **artesian water**, or groundwater confined under pressure, may rise in a well and even flow at the surface without pumping if the top of the well is lower than the potentiometric surface (GIA #11). (These wells are called *artesian* for the Artois area in France, where they are common.) In other wells, however, pressure may be inadequate, and the artesian water must be pumped the remaining distance to the surface.

The size of the *aquifer recharge area*, where surface water accumulates and percolates downward, differs for unconfined and confined aquifers. For an unconfined aquifer, the recharge area generally extends above the entire aquifer; the water simply percolates down to the water table. But in a confined aquifer, the recharge area is far more restricted. Pollution of this limited area causes groundwater contamination; note in Figure GIA 6.1 (#12) the pollution caused by leakage from the disposal pond on the aquifer recharge area, contaminating the nearby well.

Groundwater at the Surface Where the water table intersects the ground surface (GIA #8), water flows outward in the form of springs, streams, lakes, and wetlands. Springs are common in karst environments, in which water dissolves rock (primarily limestone) by chemical processes and flows underground until it finds a surface outlet (we discuss karst in Chapter 11). Hot springs are common in volcanic environments where water is heated underground before emerging under pressure at the surface. In the southwestern United States, a ciénega (the Spanish term for *spring*) is a marsh where groundwater seeps to the surface.

Groundwater interacts with streamflow to provide base flow during dry periods when runoff does not occur. Conversely, streamflow supplements groundwater during periods of water surplus. Figure GIA 6.2 illustrates the relationship between groundwater and surface streams in two different climatic settings. In humid climates, the water table is higher in elevation than the stream channel and generally supplies a continuous base flow to a stream. In this environment, the stream is *effluent* because it receives the water flowing out from the surrounding ground. The Mississippi River is a classic example, among many other humid-region streams. In drier climates, the water table is lower than the stream, causing *influent* conditions in which streamflow feeds groundwater, sustaining deep-rooted vegetation along the stream. Parts of the Colorado River and Rio Grande of the American West are examples of influent streams.

Overuse of Groundwater

As water is pumped from a well, the surrounding water table within an unconfined aquifer might experience **drawdown**, or become lowered. Drawdown occurs if the pumping rate exceeds the replenishment flow of water into the aquifer or the horizontal flow around the well. The resultant lowering of the water table around the well is a **cone of depression** (Figure GIA 6.1, left-hand side).

An additional problem arises when aquifers are overpumped near the ocean or seacoast. Along a coastline, fresh groundwater and salty seawater establish a natural interface, or *contact surface*, with the less-dense freshwater flowing on top. But excessive withdrawal of freshwater can cause this interface to migrate inland. As a result, wells near the shore become contaminated with saltwater, and the aquifer becomes useless as a freshwater source (GIA #13). Pumping freshwater back into the aquifer may halt seawater intrusion, but once contaminated, the aquifer is difficult to reclaim.

Groundwater Mining of the High Plains Aquifer

The utilization of aquifers beyond their flow and recharge capacities is known as **groundwater mining**. In the United States, chronic groundwater overdrafts occur in the Midwest, lower Mississippi Valley, Florida, Central Valley of California, and in the intensely farmed Palouse region of eastern Washington. In many places, the water table or artesian water level has declined more than 12 m (40 ft) since 1950. Groundwater mining is of special concern for the massive High Plains Aquifer, North America's largest known aquifer system.

The High Plains Aquifer underlies a 450,600-km^2 (174,000-mi^2) area shared by eight states and extending from southern South Dakota to Texas. Also known as the Ogallala Aquifer, for the principal geologic unit forming the aquifer system, it is composed mainly of sand and gravel, with some silt and clay deposits. The average thickness of the saturated parts of the aquifer is highest in Nebraska, southwestern Kansas, and the Oklahoma Panhandle

(text continued on page 206)

Groundwater forms when rainfall and snowmelt seep down through the soil and accumulate in the pore spaces in fractured bedrock or sediment. GIA 6.1 shows the structure of groundwater deposits, called *aquifers*, and threats to this resource from pollution and overuse. GIA 6.2 shows how groundwater helps to maintain streamflow.

An artesian spring in Manitoba, Canada

6.1 The Water Table and Aquifers

The water table is a boundary between the zones of aeration and saturation. Beneath the zone of saturation, an impermeable layer of rock blocks further downward movement of water. An aquifer contains groundwater stored in the zone of saturation.

(1) Zone of aeration
In this layer, some pore spaces contain air.

(2) Zone of saturation
In this layer, water fills the spaces between particles of sand, gravel, and rock.

(3) Slope and flow
The water table follows the slope of the land surface above it. The water in an aquifer flows toward areas of lower elevation and lower pressure. A plume of water pollution from septic systems or landfills can flow through an aquifer, contaminating wells.

(4) Unconfined aquifer
An ***unconfined aquifer*** *has a permeable layer above and an impermeable layer beneath.*

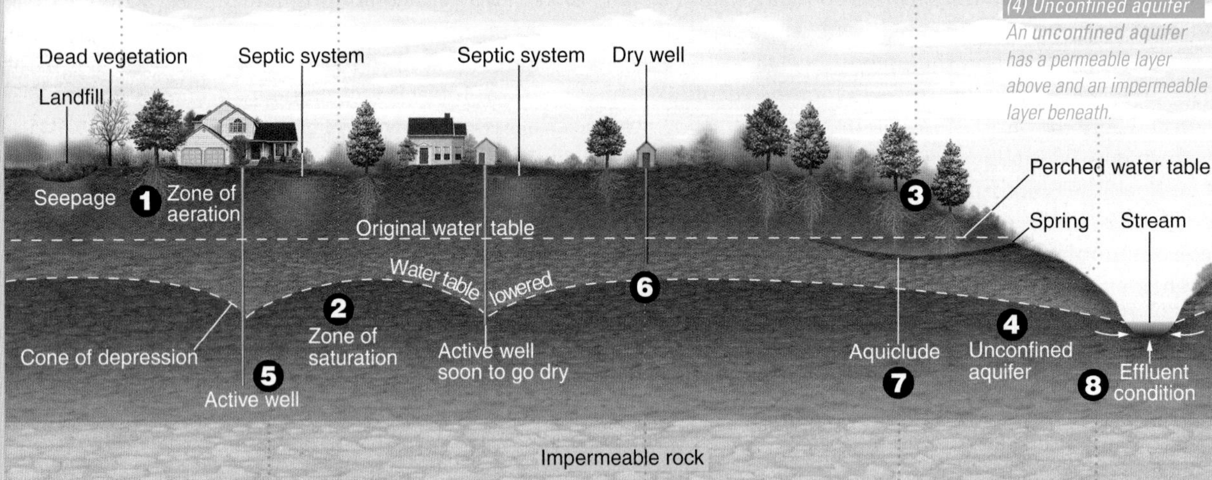

(5) Wells in an unconfined aquifer
The water in an unconfined aquifer is not under pressure and must be pumped to the surface.

(6) Dry wells and aquifer overuse
Wells pump groundwater to the surface, lowering the water table. Overuse, or groundwater mining, occurs when drawdown exceeds an aquifer's recharge capacity. A dry well results if a well is not drilled deep enough or if the water table falls below the depth of the well.

(7) Aquicludes and springs
An ***aquiclude*** *is a layer of impermeable rock or unconsolidated material that prevents water from seeping farther down.* ***Springs*** *form where the perched water table intersects the surface.*

(8) Water table at the surface
Streams, lakes, and wetlands form where the water table intersects the surface.

Infer: In which direction does the water flow in this aquifer? How can you tell?

Animation The Water Table

http://goo.gl/tmd506

MasteringGeography™

Visit the Study Area in MasteringGeography™ to explore groundwater.

Visualize: Study a geoscience animation of groundwater, the water table, and aquifers.

Assess: Demonstrate understanding of groundwater (if assigned by instructor).

6.2 Groundwater Interaction with Streamflow

Runoff and groundwater together supply the water to keep streams flowing. Groundwater can maintain streamflow when runoff does not occur. The diagrams show the relationship of the water table and streamflow in humid and dry climates.

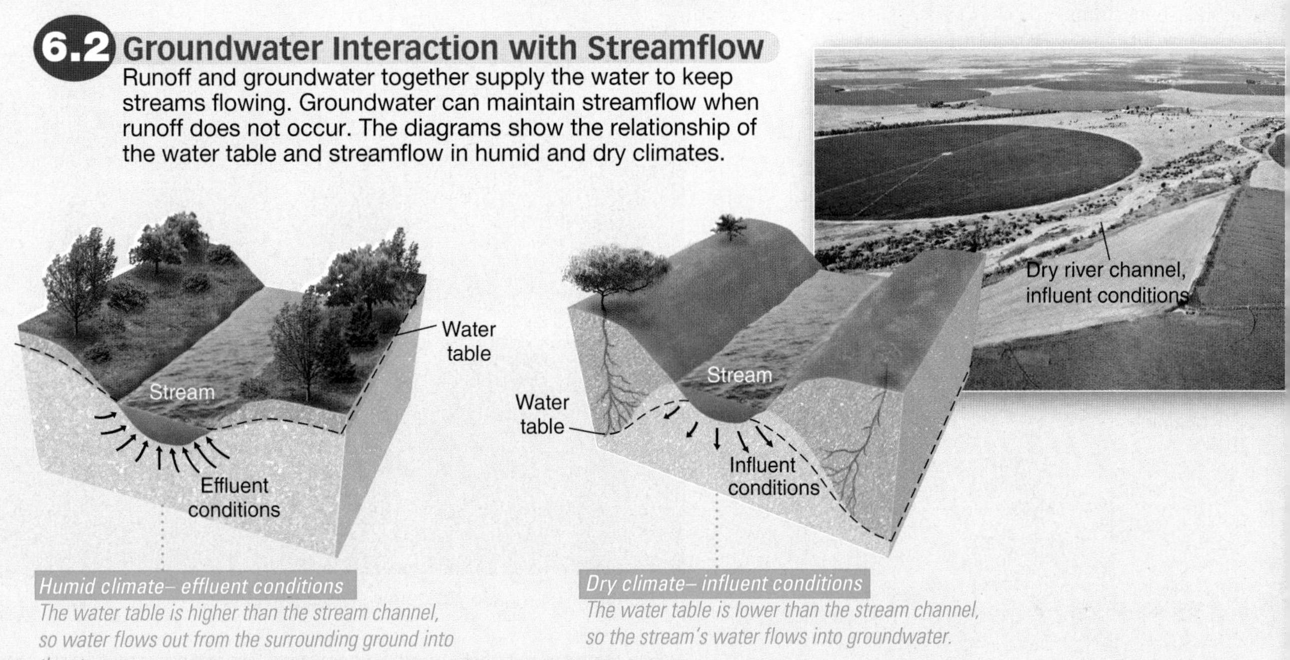

Humid climate– effluent conditions
The water table is higher than the stream channel, so water flows out from the surrounding ground into the stream.

Dry climate– influent conditions
The water table is lower than the stream channel, so the stream's water flows into groundwater.

---

(9) Confined aquifer
A ***confined aquifer*** *is bounded above and below by impermeable layers (aquicludes)*

(10) Potentiometric surface
The ***potentiometric surface*** *is the level to which groundwater under pressure can rise on its own, and can be above ground level.*

(11) Artesian wells
Artesian water *is groundwater in a sloping, confined aquifer where groundwater is under pressure. If the top of a well is lower than the potentiometric surface, artesian water may rise in the well and flow at the surface without pumping.*

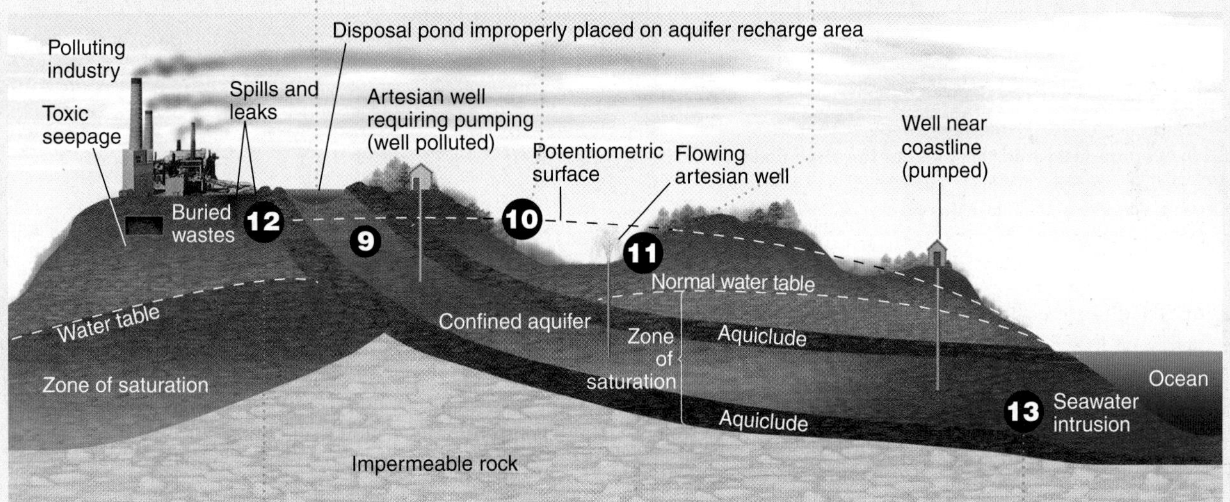

(12) Pollution of aquifer
In industrial areas, spills, leaks, and improper disposal of wastes can pollute groundwater. Notice the improper placement of a disposal pond in the aquifer recharge area.

(13) Seawater intrusion
In coastal areas, overuse of groundwater can cause salty seawater to move inland, contaminating a freshwater aquifer. A rise in sea level can force seawater intrusion, forcing the local water table upward to the surface, with resulting flooding.

Animation (MG)
Groundwater
Core of
Depression

http://goo.gl/rZCYNH

Explain: Suggest steps to prevent such groundwater pollution.

GEOquiz

1. Apply Concepts: Where in Figure GIA 6.1 could you drill a well that was free of pollutants and saltwater contamination? Explain.

2. Predict: What would happen to a stream with influent conditions if runoff were greatly reduced?

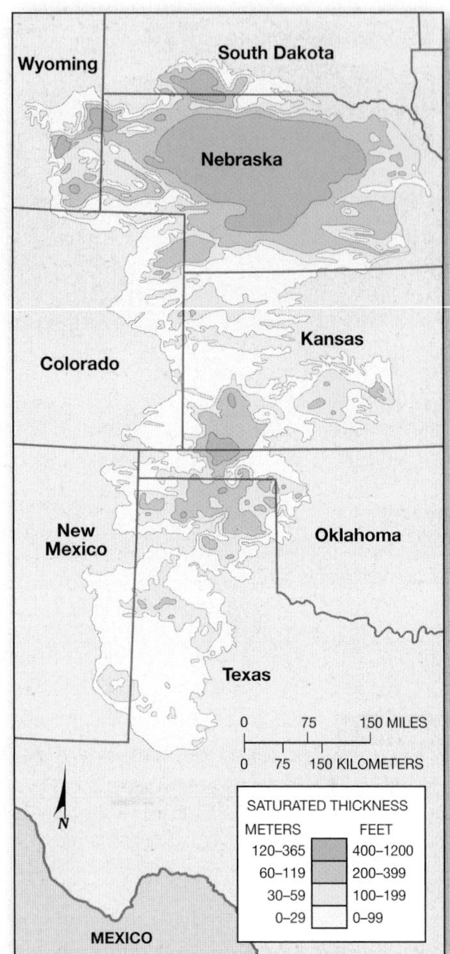

▲**Figure 6.16 Average saturated thickness of the High Plains Aquifer.** [After D. E. Kromm and S. E. White, "Interstate groundwater management preference differences: The High Plains region," *Journal of Geography* 86, no. 1 (January–February 1987): 5.]

(**Figure 6.16**). Throughout the region, groundwater flows generally from east to west, discharging at the surface into streams and springs. Precipitation, which varies widely over the region, is the main source of recharge; annual average precipitation ranges from about 30 cm in the southwest to 60 cm in the northeast (12 to 24 in.). Drought conditions have prevailed throughout the region since 2000.

Heavy mining of High Plains groundwater for irrigation intensified after World War II with the introduction of center-pivot irrigation, in which large, circular devices provide water for wheat, sorghums, cotton, corn, and about 40% of the grain fed to cattle in the United States (**Figure 6.17**). The U.S. Geological Survey (USGS) began monitoring this groundwater mining from a sample of more than 7000 wells in 1988.

The High Plains Aquifer now irrigates about one-fifth of all U.S. cropland, with more than 160,000 wells providing water for 5.7 million hectares (14 million acres). The aquifer also supplies drinking water for nearly 2 million people. Between 1950 and 1980, the annual rate of water pumped from the aquifer increased 300%. By 2000, withdrawals had decreased slightly due to declining well yields and increasing pumping costs, which led to the abandonment of thousands of wells.

(a) Center-pivot irrigation system waters a wheat field.

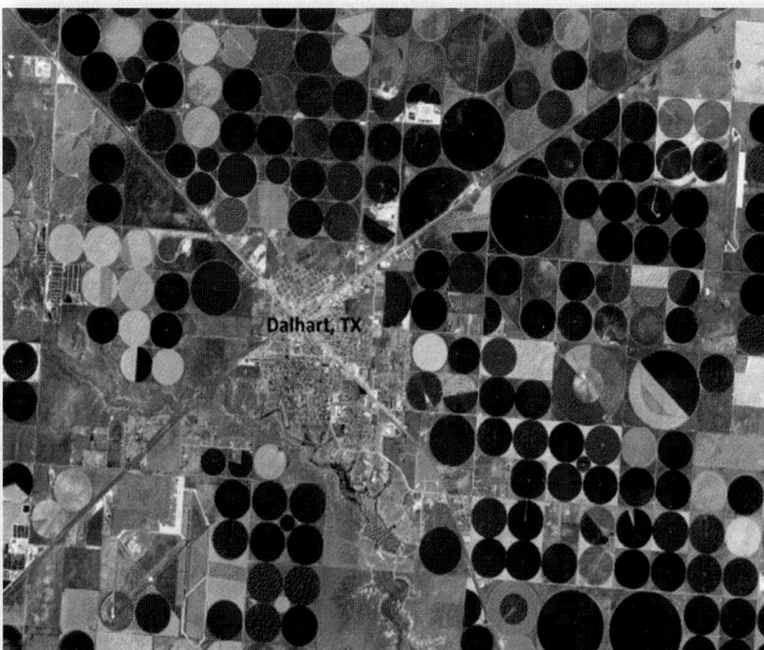

(b) A pattern of quarter-section circular fields results from center-pivot irrigation systems near Dalhart, Texas. In each field, a sprinkler arm pivots around a center, delivering about 3 cm (1.18 in.) of High Plains Aquifer water per revolution.

▲**Figure 6.17 Center-pivot irrigation.** [(a) Gene Alexander, USDA/NRCS. (b) USDA National Agricultural Imagery Program, 2010.]

The overall effect of groundwater withdrawals has been a drop in the water table of more than 30 m (100 ft) in most of the region. Throughout the 1980s, the water table declined an average of 2 m (6 ft) each year. During the period from predevelopment (about 1950) to 2011, the level of the water table declined more than 45 m (150 ft) in parts of northern Texas, where the saturated thickness of the aquifer is least, and in western Kansas (**Figure 6.18**). Rising water levels are noted in Nebraska and in small areas of Texas due to recharge from surface irrigation, a short period of years with above-normal precipitation,

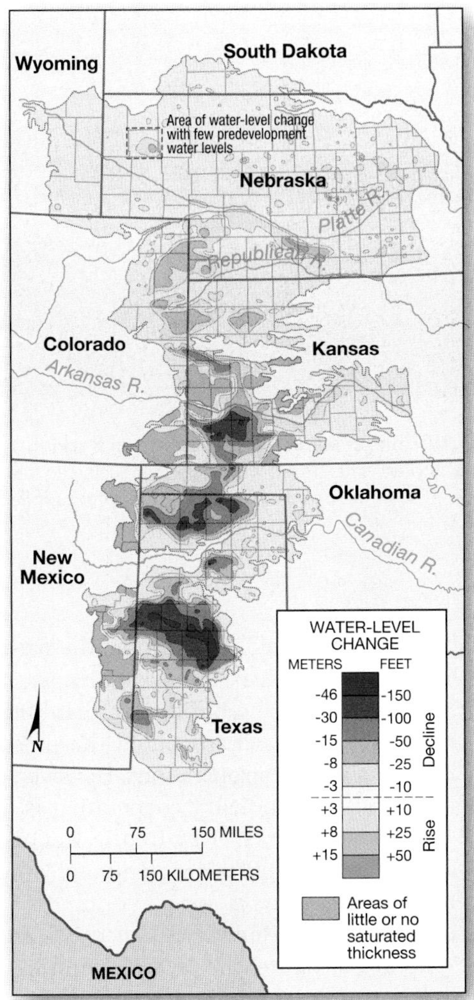

▲**Figure 6.18 Water-level changes in the High Plains Aquifer, 1950 to 2011.** The color scale indicates widespread declines and a few areas of water-level rise. [Adapted from V. L. McGuire, "Water-level and storage changes in the High Plains aquifer, predevelopment to 2011 and 2009–2011," *USGS Scientific Investigations Report 2012-5291*, 2013, Fig. 1; available at http://ne.water.usgs.gov/ogw/hpwlms/.]

and downward percolation from canals and reservoirs. (See http://ne.water.usgs.gov/ogw/hpwlms/.)

Water accumulation in the High Plains Aquifer occurred over millions of years, and recharge today is extremely slow. The USGS estimates that recovery of the aquifer would take at least 1000 years if groundwater mining stopped today. Obviously, billions of dollars of agricultural activity cannot be abruptly halted, but neither can extravagant water mining continue. This issue raises tough questions: How do we best manage cropland? Can extensive irrigation continue? Can the region continue to meet the demand to produce commodities for export and for animal feedstocks? Should we continue high-volume farming of certain crops that are in chronic oversupply?

Scientists now suggest that irrigated agriculture is unsustainable on the southern High Plains. Present irrigation practices, if continued, will deplete 69% of the High Plains Aquifer by 2060. Eventually, farmers will be forced to switch to non-irrigated crops, such as sorghum, and these are more vulnerable to drought conditions (and will also yield smaller economic returns). Add to this the approximate 10% loss of soil moisture due to increased evapotranspiration demand caused by climatic warming for the region by 2050, as forecast by computer models, and we have a portrait of a major regional water problem.

Aquifer Compaction and Collapse A possible effect of removing water from an aquifer is that the ground will lose internal support and collapse as a result (remember that aquifers are layers of rock or unconsolidated material). Water in the pore spaces is not compressible, so it adds structural strength to the rock or other material. If the water is removed through overpumping, air infiltrates the pores. Air is readily compressible, and the tremendous weight of overlying rock may compact or crush the aquifer. The result is *land subsidence*, a settling or sinking of earth materials on the surface. The visible result is cracks in building foundations, changes in surface drainage, and sinkholes (see the photos and discussion in Chapter 11).

In Houston, Texas, the removal of groundwater and crude oil caused land throughout an 80-km (50-mi) radius to subside more than 3 m (10 ft) over the years. In the Fresno area of California's San Joaquin Valley, after years of intensive pumping of groundwater for irrigation, land levels dropped almost 10 m (33 ft) because of a combination of water removal and soil compaction from agricultural activity.

Desalination In areas with declining groundwater reserves, **desalination** of seawater is an increasingly important method for obtaining freshwater. Desalination processes remove organic compounds, debris, and salinity from seawater, brackish (slightly saline) water found along coastlines, and saline groundwater, yielding potable water for domestic uses. More than 14,000 desalination plants are now in operation worldwide; the volume of freshwater produced by desalination worldwide is projected to nearly double between 2010 and 2020.

Approximately 50% of all desalination plants are in the Middle East, where groundwater overuse is severe. The groundwater resources beneath Saudi Arabia, accumulated over tens of thousands of years, consist of "fossil aquifers," so named because they receive little or no recharge in the desert climate that exists in the region today. Thus, increasing withdrawals in Saudi Arabia at present are not being naturally recharged—in essence, groundwater has become a nonrenewable resource.

The world's largest desalination plant is the Jebel Ali Desalination Plant in the United Arab Emirates, capable of producing 636 million L (168 million gal) of desalinated water a day. In Saudi Arabia, 30 desalination plants currently supply 70% of the country's drinking water needs, providing an alternative to further groundwater mining and problems with saltwater intrusion.

In the United States, especially in Florida and along the coast of southern California, desalination use is slowly increasing. Around Tampa Bay–St. Petersburg,

Florida, water levels in the region's lakes and wetlands are declining and land surfaces subsiding as the groundwater drawdown for export to the cities increases. The Tampa Bay desalination plant was finished in 2008, after being plagued with financial and technical problems during its 10-year construction. The plant met final performance criteria for operation in 2013, making it fully operational.

The Carlsbad Desalination Project, including a desalination plant and a water-delivery pipeline, near San Diego, California, will be the largest in the United States when it is finished in 2016. The plant will use *reverse osmosis*, a process that forces water through semipermeable membranes to separate the solutes (salts) from the solvent (water), in effect removing the salt and creating freshwater (see http://carlsbaddesal.com/pipeline for more information). One of the drawbacks to desalination is that concentrated salts must be disposed of in a manner that does not contaminate freshwater supplies. In addition, the desalination process is energy-intensive and expensive.

▲**Figure 6.19 Contaminated wastewater from fracking operations.** Stored water, laced with toxic chemicals, can leak through the lining of the pond into local groundwater supplies. [Jim West/Alamy.]

Pollution of Groundwater

If surface water is polluted, groundwater inevitably becomes contaminated during recharge. Whereas pollution in surface water flushes downstream, slow-moving groundwater, once contaminated, remains polluted virtually forever.

Pollution can enter groundwater from many sources: industrial injection wells (which pump waste into the ground), septic tank outflows, seepage from hazardous-waste disposal sites, industrial toxic waste, agricultural residues (pesticides, herbicides, fertilizers), and urban solid-waste landfills. An example is the suspected leakage from some 10,000 underground gasoline storage tanks at U.S. gasoline stations, thought to be contaminating thousands of local water supplies with cancer-causing gasoline additives. About 35% of groundwater pollution comes from *point sources*, such as a gasoline tank or septic tank; 65% is categorized as having a *nonpoint source*—that is, coming from a broad area, such as runoff from an agricultural field or urban community. Regardless of the spatial nature of the source, pollution can spread over a great distance.

A controversial source of groundwater contamination is shale gas extraction, discussed in the Chapter 1 Geosystems Now. The process of hydraulic fracturing, or fracking, requires that large quantities of water and chemicals be pumped under high pressure into subsurface rock, fracturing it to release natural gas. The wastewater produced is contaminated with chemicals used as lubricants in the fracking process and is often held in wells or containment ponds (**Figure 6.19**). Leaks or spills send toxic wastewater into surface water supplies and groundwater. More than 500,000 such wells already exist in the United States, more than 50,000 of these in Pennsylvania alone, and numbers are increasing. In addition, the natural gas released by fracking can leak into groundwater, causing contamination and methane buildup in drinking water wells—several studies have attributed the presence of methane in wells to fracking operations. However, further research and fossil-fuel industry cooperation is needed, especially since the effects of hydraulic fracturing on groundwater relate to regional geology and other site-specific conditions.

As discussed in GeoReport 6.4, scientists are using satellite data to estimate the overall volume of the groundwater resource. Assessing groundwater quality remains problematic, however, since aquifers are generally inaccessible to measurement and analysis.

Our Water Supply

Human thirst for adequate water supplies, both in quantity and in quality, will be a major issue in this century. Internationally, increases in per capita water use are double the rate of population growth. Since we are so dependent on water, it seems that humans should cluster where good water is plentiful. But accessible water supplies are not well correlated with population distribution or the regions where population growth is greatest.

Table 6.1 provides statistics that, taken together, indicate the unevenness of Earth's water supply. These data include population, land area, annual streamflow, and projected population change for six world regions. The adequacy of Earth's water supply is tied, first, to climatic variability and, second, to water usage, which is, in turn, tied to level of development, affluence, and per capita consumption.

For example, North America's mean annual streamflow is 4310 BGD, and Asia's is 9540 BGD. However, North America has only 6.6% of the world's population,

TABLE 6.1 Regional Comparison of Factors Influencing Global Water Supply

Region	2013 Population (in millions)	Share of Global Population	Land Area in Thousands of km² (mi²)	Share of Global Land Area	Mean Annual Streamflow (BGD)	Share of Annual Streamflow	2050 Population as a Multiple of 2013
Africa	1100	15.4%	30,600 (11,800)	23%	3060	11%	2.2
Asia	4302	60.3%	44,600 (17,200)	33%	9540	34%	1.2
Australia–Oceania	38	0.5%	8,420 (3,250)	6%	1420	5%	1.6
Europe	740	10.4%	9,770 (3,770)	7%	2280	8%	1.0
North America*	469	6.6%	22,100 (8,510)	16%	4310	15%	1.3
Central and South America†	489	6.8%	17,800 (6,880)	13%	7510	27%	1.3
Global (excluding Antarctica)	7137	—	134,000 (51,600)	—	28,100	—	1.4

Population data from *2013 World Population Data Sheet* (Washington, DC: Population Reference Bureau, 2013).
*Includes Canada, Mexico, and the United States.
†Includes the Caribbean region.
Note: BGD, billion gallons per day.

whereas Asia has 60%, with a population doubling time less than half that of North America. In northern China, 550 million people living in approximately 500 cities lack adequate water supplies. For comparison, consider that the 1990 floods cost China $10 billion, whereas water shortages are costing the Chinese economy more than $35 billion a year.

In Africa, 56 countries draw from a varied water-resource base; these countries share more than 50 river and lake watersheds. Population growth that is ever more concentrated in urban areas and the need for increased irrigation during periods of drought are enhancing the water demand. Conditions of water stress (where people have less than 1700 m³ of water per person per year) presently occur in 12 African countries; water scarcity (less than 1000 m³ per person per year) occurs in 14 African countries. Recent research indicates, however, that the total volume of groundwater on the African continent is much larger than previously thought, with substantial reserves below the dry northern countries of Libya, Algeria, and Chad. But with ongoing drought in this region, even these reserves could be quickly depleted.

Water resources are different from other resources in that *there is no substitute for water*. Water shortages increase the probability for international conflict, endanger public health, reduce agricultural productivity, and damage life-supporting ecological systems. Since surface water and groundwater resources do not respect political boundaries, nations must share water resources, a situation that inevitably creates problems. For example, 145 countries of the world share a river basin with at least one other country. Streamflow truly represents a global commons, and water-resource stress related to decreasing quantity and quality will dominate future political agendas.

CRITICAL**thinking** 6.2

Calculate Your Water Footprint

How much water have you used today? From taking showers to brushing our teeth to cooking and cleaning up the dishes to quenching our thirst, our households have a water "footprint" that relates to affluence and technology. Just as you calculated your carbon footprint in Chapter 1, Critical Thinking 1.1, you can calculate your water footprint at http://www.gracelinks.org/1408/water-footprint-calculator. How does your individual water use compare to the average American's? Can you think of ways to reduce your water footprint?

Water Supply in the United States

The U.S. water supply (excluding Alaska and Hawai'i) derives from surface water and groundwater sources that are fed by an average precipitation of 4200 BGD. In terms of space, this input is unevenly distributed across the 48 contiguous states, and in terms of time, it is unevenly distributed throughout the year. (Annual average precipitation across the contiguous U.S states is 76.2 cm, or 30 in.;

GEO**report** 6.5 The water cost of food and necessities

Simply providing the foods we enjoy requires voluminous water. For example, 77 g (2.7 oz) of broccoli requires 42 L (11 gal) of water to grow and process; producing 250 mL (8 oz) of milk requires 182 L (48 gal) of water; producing 28 g (1 oz) of cheese requires 212 L (56 gal); producing 1 egg requires 238 L (63 gal); and producing a 113-g (4-oz) beef patty requires 2314 L (616 gal). And then there are our toilets, the majority of which still flush approximately 4 gal of water.

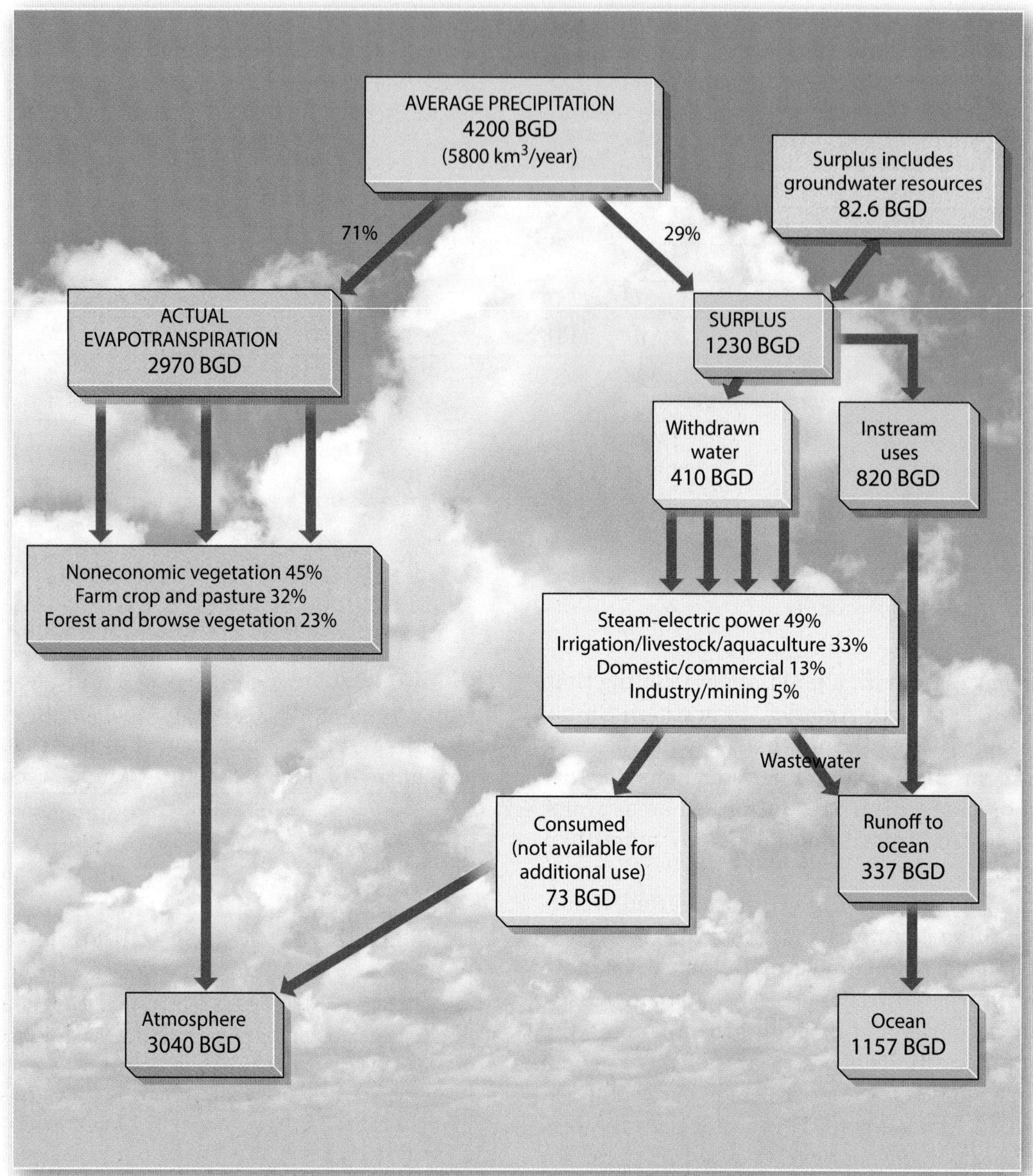

▲**Figure 6.20 Daily water budget for the contiguous 48 U.S. states in billions of gallons a day (BGD).** [Data from J. Kenny, N. Barber, S. Hutson, K. Linsey, J. Lovelace, and M. Maupin, *Estimated Use of Water in the United States in 2005*, USGS Circular 1344, 2005—the latest year for which data are available. Photo: Bobbé Christopherson.]

review the map in Figure 6.6.) For example, New England's water supply is so abundant that only about 1% of available water is consumed each year.

Viewed daily, the national water budget has two general outputs: 71% actual evapotranspiration and 29% surplus (**Figure 6.20**). The 71% actual evapotranspiration occurs over land with nonagricultural vegetation, agricultural crops and pastures, and forest and browse (shrubs and woody vegetation eaten by wildlife). The remaining 29% surplus is what we directly use.

Note that groundwater is considered part of surface freshwater (remember that it is linked to surface supplies). In 2005, about 67% of groundwater withdrawals were for irrigation and 18% for public supply water needs. Accounting for 50% of withdrawals were just six states: California, Texas, Nebraska, Arkansas, Idaho, and Florida, where more than half of the public supply of water is from groundwater.

Water Withdrawal and Consumption

Rivers and streams represent only a tiny percentage (0.003%) of Earth's overall surface water (review Figure 6.3). In terms of volume, they represent 1250 km³ (300 mi³), the smallest of any of the freshwater categories. Yet streamflow represents about four-fifths of all the water making up the surplus 1230 BGD that are available for withdrawal, consumption, and various instream uses.

- **Water withdrawal**, sometimes called *nonconsumptive use* or *offstream use*, refers to the removal or diversion of water from surface water or groundwater supplies followed by the subsequent return of that water to the same supply. Examples include water use by industry, agriculture, and municipalities and in steam-electric power generation. A portion of the water withdrawn may be consumed.

- **Consumptive use** refers to the permanent removal of water from the immediate water environment. This water is not returned and so is not available for a second or third use. Examples include water lost to evapotranspiration, consumed by humans or livestock, and used in manufacturing.
- *Instream use* refers to uses of streamflow while it remains in the channel, without being removed. Examples include transportation, waste dilution and removal, hydroelectric power production, fishing, recreation, and ecosystem maintenance, such as sustaining wildlife.

Water withdrawal provides the opportunity to extend the water resource through reuse. The four main uses of withdrawn water in the United States in 2005 were (1) steam-electric power (49%, about 30% of which is met with saline ocean and coastal water); (2) irrigation, livestock, and aquaculture (33%); (3) domestic and commercial use (13%); and (4) industry and mining (5%; see Figure 6.20). However, when water returns to the stream system, its quality usually is altered—contaminated chemically with pollutants or waste or contaminated thermally with heat energy.

Contaminated or not, returned water becomes a part of all water systems downstream as runoff moves into oceans. In New Orleans, the last city to withdraw municipal water from the Mississippi River, streamflows include diluted and mixed contaminants from the entire Missouri–Ohio–Mississippi River system. These include the effluent from chemical plants, agricultural runoff from fields treated with fertilizer and pesticides, treated and untreated sewage, pollution from oil spills and gasoline leaks, wastewater from thousands of industries, runoff from urban streets and storm drains, and particulates from countless construction sites and from mining, farming, and logging activities. Abnormally high cancer rates among citizens living along the Mississippi River between Baton Rouge and New Orleans have led to the ominous label "Cancer Alley" for the region.

The estimated U.S. withdrawal of water for 2005 was 410 BGD, double the usage rate in 1950, but down 5% from the peak usage in 1980. Increased water prices helped produce the recent downward trend. For studies of water use in the United States and updated USGS Estimated Use of Water reports (available for download), see http://water.usgs.gov/public/watuse/.

Future Considerations

When water supply and demand are examined in terms of water budgets, the limits of water resources become apparent. In the water-budget equation in Figure 6.9, any change in one side (such as increased demand for surplus water) must be balanced by an adjustment in the other side (such as an increase in precipitation). How can we satisfy the growing demand for water? Water availability per person declines as population increases, and individual demand increases with economic development, affluence, and technology. World population growth since 1970 has reduced per capita water supplies by a third. In addition, pollution limits the water-resource base, so that even before quantity constraints are felt, quality problems may limit the health and growth of a region.

However, certain cities and regions are making progress toward a sustainable water balance. In Texas, one of the nation's fastest-growing states in terms of population, a decade of ongoing drought, severe since 2010, caused huge financial losses to the agriculture and cattle industries. The state's official "Water Plan," a comprehensive overview of how the state will handle more people and less water in the future, admits that Texas does not have enough water to meet the current demand. The state plan focuses on future water supplies coming from a combination of reservoirs, groundwater, wastewater treatment, desalinization, and, most importantly, conservation. In the face of decreasing groundwater resources, some cities are working on water efficiency and conservation; for example, the city of San Antonio, despite a growing population, has reduced its water consumption by 42% over the past few decades.

The Human Denominator 6 lists some of the interactions between humans and water resources and some of the water-related issues for the century ahead. One of the greatest challenges for humans will be the projected water shortages connected with climate change.

Clearly, international cooperation is needed, yet we continue toward a water crisis without a concept of a world water economy as a frame of reference. One of the most important questions is, When will more international coordination begin, and which country or group of countries will lead the way to sustain future water resources? The water-budget approach detailed in this chapter is a place to start.

CRITICAL**thinking** 6.3

That Next Glass of Water

You have no doubt had several glasses of water so far today. Where did this water originate? Obtain the name of the water company or agency, determine whether it is using surface water or groundwater to meet demands, and check how the water is metered and billed. If your state or province requires water-quality reporting, obtain a copy from the water supplier of an analysis of your tap water. Read this report, for you always want to know about that "next glass of water."

WATER RESOURCES IMPACT HUMANS

- Freshwater, stored in lakes, rivers, and groundwater, is a critical resource for human society and life on Earth.
- Drought results in water deficits, decreasing regional water supplies and causing declines in agriculture.

HUMANS IMPACT WATER RESOURCES

- Climate change affects lake depth, thermal structure, and associated organisms.
- Water projects (dams and diversions) redistribute water over space and time.
- Groundwater overuse and pollution depletes and degrades the resource, with side effects such as collapsed aquifers and saltwater contamination.

Desalination is an important supplement to water supplies in regions with large variations in rainfall throughout the year and declining groundwater reserves. This plant in Barcelona, Spain, uses the process of reverse osmosis to remove salts and impurities.

The third largest reservoir in the world, Lake Nasser is formed by the Aswan High Dam on the Nile River in Egypt. Its water is used for agricultural, industrial, and domestic purposes, as well as for hydropower.

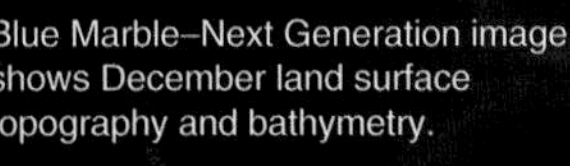

Blue Marble–Next Generation image shows December land surface topography and bathymetry.

The Itaipu Dam and power plant on the Paraná River bordering Brazil and Paraguay produces more electricity annually than the Three Gorges Dam in China. Itaipu Reservoir displaced over 10,000 people and submerged Guaira Falls, formerly the world's largest waterfall by volume.

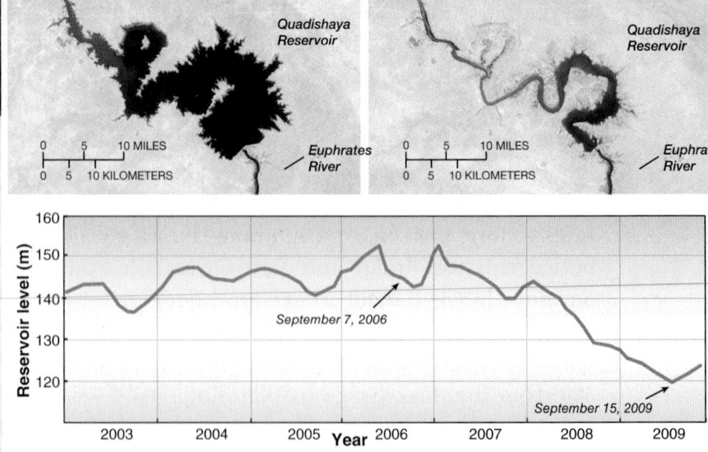

Data from *GRACE* reveal a rapid decline in reservoir levels from 2006 to 2009 along the Euphrates River in the Middle East; Quadishaya Reservoir is an example. The graph shows the surface-level decline, with dates of the images marked. About 60% of the volume loss is attributed to groundwater withdrawals in the region.

ISSUES FOR THE 21ST CENTURY

- Maintaining adequate water quantity and quality will be a major issue. Desalination will increase to augment freshwater supplies.
- Hydropower is a renewable energy resource; however, drought-related streamflow declines and drops in reservoir storage interfere with production.
- Drought in some regions will intensify, with related pressure on groundwater and surface water supplies.

KEYLEARNINGconceptsreview

The science of water at and below Earth's surface, including its global circulation, distribution, and properties, is **hydrology**.

hydrology (p. 186)

Describe the origin of Earth's waters, *report* the quantity of water that exists today, and *list* the locations of Earth's freshwater supply.

Water molecules came from within Earth over a period of billions of years in the **outgassing** process. Water covers about 71% of Earth. Approximately 97% of it is salty seawater, and the remaining 3% is freshwater—most of it frozen.

Earth's hydrosphere is in steady-state equilibrium, with the present volume of water estimated at 1.36 billion km^3 (326 million mi^3), an amount achieved roughly 2 billion years ago. Within this overall quantity, the amount of water stored in glaciers and ice sheets varies, affecting sea level. **Eustasy** refers to worldwide changes in sea level and relates to changes in volume of water in the oceans. Changes in sea level caused specifically by glacial ice melt are described as *glacio-eustatic*.

outgassing (p. 186)
eustasy (p. 187)

1. Approximately where and when did Earth's water originate?
2. If the quantity of water on Earth has been quite constant in volume for at least 2 billion years, how can sea level have fluctuated? Explain.
3. Describe the locations of Earth's water, both oceanic and fresh. What is the largest repository of freshwater at this time? In what ways is this distribution of water significant to modern society?
4. Why would climate change be a concern given this distribution of water?

Illustrate the hydrologic cycle with a simple sketch and *label* it with definitions for each water pathway.

The **hydrologic cycle** is a model of Earth's water system, which has operated for billions of years from the lower atmosphere to several kilometers beneath Earth's surface. **Evaporation** is the net movement of free water molecules away from a wet surface into air. **Transpiration** is the movement of water through plants and back into the atmosphere; it is a cooling mechanism for plants. Evaporation and transpiration are combined into one term—**evapotranspiration**.

Interception occurs when precipitation strikes vegetation or other ground cover. Water soaks into the subsurface through **infiltration**, or penetration of the soil surface. Water may puddle on the surface or flow across the surface toward stream channels. This **overland flow**, also called **surface runoff**, may become *streamflow* as it moves into channels on the surface.

Surface water becomes groundwater when it permeates soil or rock through vertical downward movement called **percolation**. The volume of subsurface water stored in the soil that is accessible to plant roots is contained in the **soil-moisture zone**. Groundwater is the largest potential freshwater source in the hydrologic cycle and is tied to surface supplies. The portion of streamflow that discharges naturally at the surface from groundwater is the **base flow**.

hydrologic cycle (p. 187)
evaporation (p. 188)
transpiration (p. 188)
evapotranspiration (p. 188)
interception (p. 188)
infiltration (p. 189)
overland flow (p. 189)
surface runoff (p. 189)
percolation (p. 190)
soil-moisture zone (p. 190)
base flow (p. 190)

5. Sketch and explain a simplified model of the complex flows of water on Earth—the hydrologic cycle.
6. What are the possible routes that a raindrop may take on its way to and into the soil surface?
7. Compare precipitation and evaporation volumes from the ocean with those over land. Describe advection flows of moisture and the countering flows of surface and subsurface runoff.

Construct the water-budget equation, *define* each of the components, and *explain* its use.

A **water budget** can be established for any area of Earth's surface by measuring the precipitation input and the output of various water demands in the area considered. If demands are met and extra water remains, a **surplus** occurs. If demand exceeds supply, a **deficit**, or water shortage, results. Understanding both the supply of the water resource and the natural demands on the resource is essential to sustainable human interaction with the hydrologic cycle. **Precipitation** (P) is the moisture supply to Earth's surface, arriving as rain, sleet, snow, and hail. The moisture demand at a given location is evapotranspiration, an actual expenditure of water to the atmosphere called **actual evapotranspiration**, or AE. The ultimate demand for moisture is **potential evapotranspiration** (PE), the amount of water that would evaporate and transpire under optimum moisture conditions (adequate precipitation and adequate soil moisture). Unsatisfied PE is a deficit. If PE is satisfied and the soil is full of moisture, then additional water input becomes a surplus.

The volume of water stored in the soil that is accessible to plant roots is the **soil-moisture storage** (S). This is the "savings account" of water that receives deposits and provides withdrawals as water-balance conditions change. When soil is saturated after a precipitation event, surplus water in the soil becomes **gravitational water** and percolates to groundwater. **Capillary water** is generally accessible to plant roots because it is held in the soil by surface tension and hydrogen bonding between water and soil. Almost all capillary water is available water in soil-moisture storage. After water drains from the larger pore spaces, the available water remaining for plants is termed **field capacity**, or storage capacity. *Hygroscopic water* is inaccessible to plants because it is a molecule-thin layer that is tightly bound to each soil particle by hydrogen bonding. As available water is utilized, soil reaches the **wilting point** (all that remains is unextractable water). **Soil-moisture utilization** removes soil water, whereas **soil-moisture recharge** is the rate at which needed moisture enters the soil. The texture and the structure of the soil dictate available pore spaces, or *porosity*. The soil's **permeability** is the degree to which water can flow through it. Permeability depends on particle sizes and the shape and packing of soil grains.

Drought can be simply defined as an extended period of dry conditions caused by lower precipitation and higher temperatures than normal. However, the term has slightly different meanings depending on whether it is used for meteorological, agricultural, or hydrological applications.

water budget (p. 190)
surplus (p. 190)
deficit (p. 190)
precipitation (p. 190)
actual evapotranspiration (p. 190)
potential evapotranspiration (p. 190)
soil-moisture storage (p. 192)
gravitational water (p. 192)
capillary water (p. 192)
field capacity (p. 193)
wilting point (p. 193)
soil-moisture utilization (p. 193)
soil-moisture recharge (p. 193)
permeability (p. 193)
drought (p. 195)

8. What are the components of the water-balance equation? Construct the equation, and place each term's definition below its abbreviation in the equation.
9. Explain how to derive actual evapotranspiration (AE) in the water-balance equation.
10. What is potential evapotranspiration (PE)? How do we go about estimating this potential rate?
11. Explain the difference between soil-moisture utilization and soil-moisture recharge. Include discussion of capillary water and the field capacity and wilting point concepts.
12. In the case of silt loam soil from Figure 6.8, roughly what is the available water capacity? How is this value derived?
13. Use the water-balance equation to explain the changing relation of P to PE in the annual water-balance chart for Kingsport, Tennessee.
14. How does the water-budget concept help your understanding of the hydrologic cycle, water resources, and soil moisture for a specific location? Give a specific example.

Discuss water storage in lakes and wetlands and *describe* some large water projects involving hydroelectric power production.

Surface water is transferred in canals and pipelines for redistribution over space and stored in reservoirs for redistribution over time to meet water demand. Hydroelectric power, or **hydropower**, provides 20% of the world's electricity, and many large projects have changed river systems and affected human populations.

Lakes and wetlands are important freshwater storage areas. A **wetland** is an area that is permanently or seasonally saturated with water and that is characterized by vegetation adapted to *hydric* soils (soils saturated for a long enough period to develop anaerobic, or "oxygen-free," conditions).

hydropower (p. 197)
wetland (p. 199)

15. What changes occur along rivers as a result of the construction of large hydropower facilities?
16. Define wetland, and discuss the distribution of lakes and wetlands on Earth.

Describe groundwater and *define* the elements of the groundwater environment.

Groundwater lies beneath the surface beyond the soil-moisture root zone, and its replenishment is tied to surface surpluses. Excess surface water moves through the **zone of aeration**, where soil and rock are less than saturated. Eventually, the water reaches the **zone of saturation**, where the pores are completely filled with water. The upper limit of the water that collects in the zone of saturation is the **water table**, forming the contact surface between the zones of saturation and aeration.

The permeability of subsurface rocks depends on whether they conduct water readily (higher permeability) or tend to obstruct its flow (lower permeability). They can even be impermeable. An **aquifer** is a rock layer that is permeable to groundwater flow in usable amounts. An **unconfined aquifer** has a permeable layer on top and an impermeable one beneath. A **confined aquifer** is bounded above and below by impermeable layers of rock or unconsolidated material. An *aquiclude* is a solid, impermeable layer that forms such a boundary, while an *aquitard* has low permeability, but cannot conduct water in usable amounts.

Water in a confined aquifer is under the pressure of its own weight, creating a pressure level to which the water can rise on its own. This *potentiometric surface* can be above ground level. Groundwater confined under pressure is **artesian water**; it may rise up in wells and even flow out at the surface without pumping if the head of the well is below the potentiometric surface.

As water is pumped from a well, the surrounding water table within an unconfined aquifer will experience **drawdown**, or become lower, if the rate of pumping exceeds the horizontal flow of water in the aquifer around the well. This excessive pumping causes a **cone of depression**. Aquifers frequently are pumped beyond their flow and recharge capacities, a condition known as **groundwater mining**.

In many areas, especially where groundwater levels are declining, desalination is becoming an increasingly important method for meeting water demands. **Desalination** of seawater and saline groundwater involves the removal of organics, debris, and salinity through distillation or reverse osmosis. This processing yields potable water for domestic uses.

groundwater (p. 199)
zone of aeration (p. 202)
zone of saturation (p. 202)
water table (p. 202)
aquifer (p. 202)
unconfined aquifer (p. 203)
confined aquifer (p. 203)
artesian water (p. 203)
drawdown (p. 203)
cone of depression (p. 203)
groundwater mining (p. 203)
desalination (p. 207)

17. Are groundwater resources independent of surface supplies, or are the two interrelated? Explain your answer.
18. Make a simple sketch of the subsurface environment, labeling the zones of aeration and saturation and the water table in an unconfined aquifer. Then add a confined aquifer to the sketch.
19. At what point does groundwater utilization become groundwater mining? Use the High Plains Aquifer example to explain your answer.
20. What is the nature of groundwater pollution? Can contaminated groundwater be cleaned up easily? What is fracking, and how does it impact groundwater? Revisit Geosystems Now in Chapter 1 to assist with your answer.

***Evaluate* the U.S. water budget and *identify* critical aspects of present and future freshwater supplies.**

The world's water supply is distributed unevenly over Earth's surface. In the United States, water surpluses are used in several ways. **Water withdrawal**, also known as *nonconsumptive use* or *offstream use*, temporarily removes water from the supply, returning it later. **Consumptive use** permanently removes water from a stream. *Instream* use leaves water in the stream channel; examples are recreation and hydropower production. Americans in the 48 contiguous states withdraw approximately one-third of the available water surplus for irrigation, industry, and municipal uses.

water withdrawal (p. 210) **consumptive use (p. 211)**

21. Describe the principal pathways involved in the water budget of the contiguous 48 states. What is the difference between withdrawal and consumptive use of water resources? Compare these with instream uses.
22. Briefly assess the status of world water resources. What challenges exist in meeting the future needs of an expanding population and growing economies?
23. If wars in the 21st century are predicted to be about water availability in the needed quantity and quality, what action could we take to understand the issues and avoid the conflicts?

VISUALanalysis 6 Dryland Agriculture

This false-color image shows irrigated fields in Saudi Arabia; new vegetation is bright green, dry vegetation and fallow fields are dark orange, barren desert surfaces are pink and yellow. [NASA image by Robert Simmon and Jesse Allen using *Landsat* data from USGS.]

1. What is the source of water used to irrigate the fields? Is this source renewable?
2. Describe the irrigation systems used in these fields. What is the evidence for your answer?
3. In your opinion, is irrigated agriculture in this region sustainable?

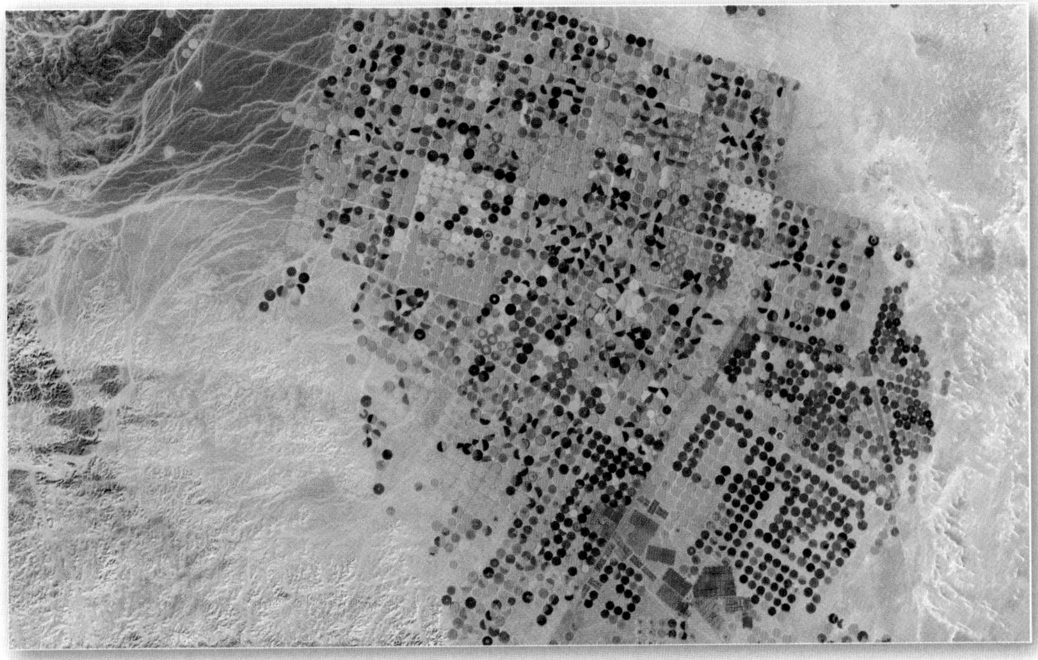

7 Earth's Climatic Regions

Cold winters and mild summers are typical of the continental climate at Emerald Lake in Yoho National Park, Canadian Rockies, British Columbia. [Dolce Vita/Shutterstock.]

KEYLEARNING**concepts**

After reading the chapter, you should be able to:

- ***Define*** climate and climatology and ***review*** the principal components of Earth's climate system.
- ***Describe*** climate classification systems, ***list*** the main categories of world climates, and ***locate*** the regions characterized by each climate type on a world map.
- ***Discuss*** the subcategories of the six world climate groups, including their causal factors.
- ***Explain*** the precipitation and moisture-efficiency criteria used to classify the arid and semiarid climates.

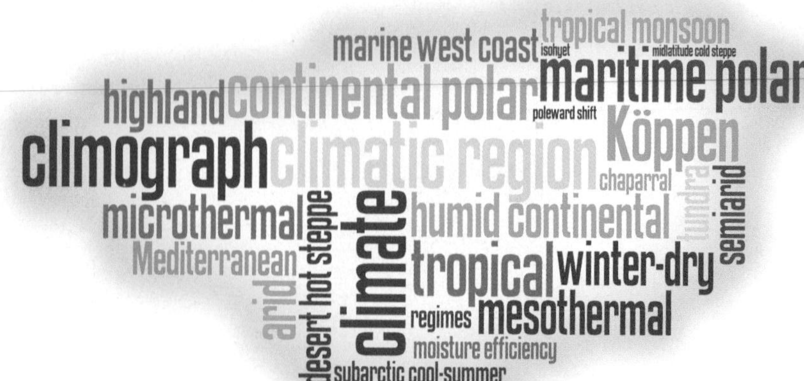

A Close-up Look at New Zealand's Climate

New Zealand's two main islands, known as the North and South Islands, are located in the southwest Pacific Ocean about 2250 km (1400 mi) southeast of Australia. The country stretches over 1500 km (932 mi) from northeast to southwest, extending from 34° S to 47° S latitude. New Zealand's climate—its characteristic weather pattern over many years—is generally categorized as temperate, featuring mild winters and cool summers characteristic of marine west coast climates.

The small-scale world climate map in Figure 7.2, which identifies New Zealand's climate as warm and temperate (mesothermal), shows generalized climate information over broad areas. However, when we "zoom in" to examine specific regions of New Zealand using relatively large-scale precipitation and temperature maps (**Figure GN 7.1**), we see much more variation, including many localized climate types produced by differences in latitude, elevation, and position relative to the windward and leeward sides of the country's mountain ranges. These local climatic variations are reflected in the different types of vegetation across the islands.

Several factors interact to determine New Zealand's climate zones. The ocean moderates temperatures throughout much of the country—an example of the marine effect discussed in Chapter 3. South of the 40th parallel, the country receives the westerly winds of the "roaring forties" latitudes, which blow from southwest to northeast in the Southern Hemisphere. Mountain ranges run north to south on both islands: On the South Island, the Southern Alps rise to 3754 m (12,316 ft); on the North Island, a series of smaller ranges, rarely higher than 1500 m (4920 ft), extend from Wellington north to the East Cape. These ranges form topographic barriers, adding an orographic component to the climate patterns. At higher elevations within these ranges, temperatures are colder, and snow is often present for much of the year.

New Zealand's windward western slopes intercept moisture brought by the westerlies. On the South Island, the West Coast region is the country's wettest, receiving 200 to 1000 cm (79 to 394 in.) of precipitation annually. In contrast, the leeward slopes and coastal plain 100 km (62 mi) to the east, in the rain shadow of the Southern Alps, register the lowest precipitation totals. A similar rainfall pattern occurs on the southern part of the North Island.

Precipitation and temperature combine to produce several climate zones. Subtropical climates (moist all year with a hot summer) occur on the North Island at latitudes lower than about 40° S, where climate is influenced by the trade winds. Temperate climates (with mild winters and cool summers) occur on both islands. Cold winters occur at high elevation in the mountain ranges (classified as highland climates) and in the rain shadow of the Southern Alps on the South Island. As we examine the global distribution of Earth's climates in this chapter, remember the local variation that occurs when we "zoom in" using a larger map scale.

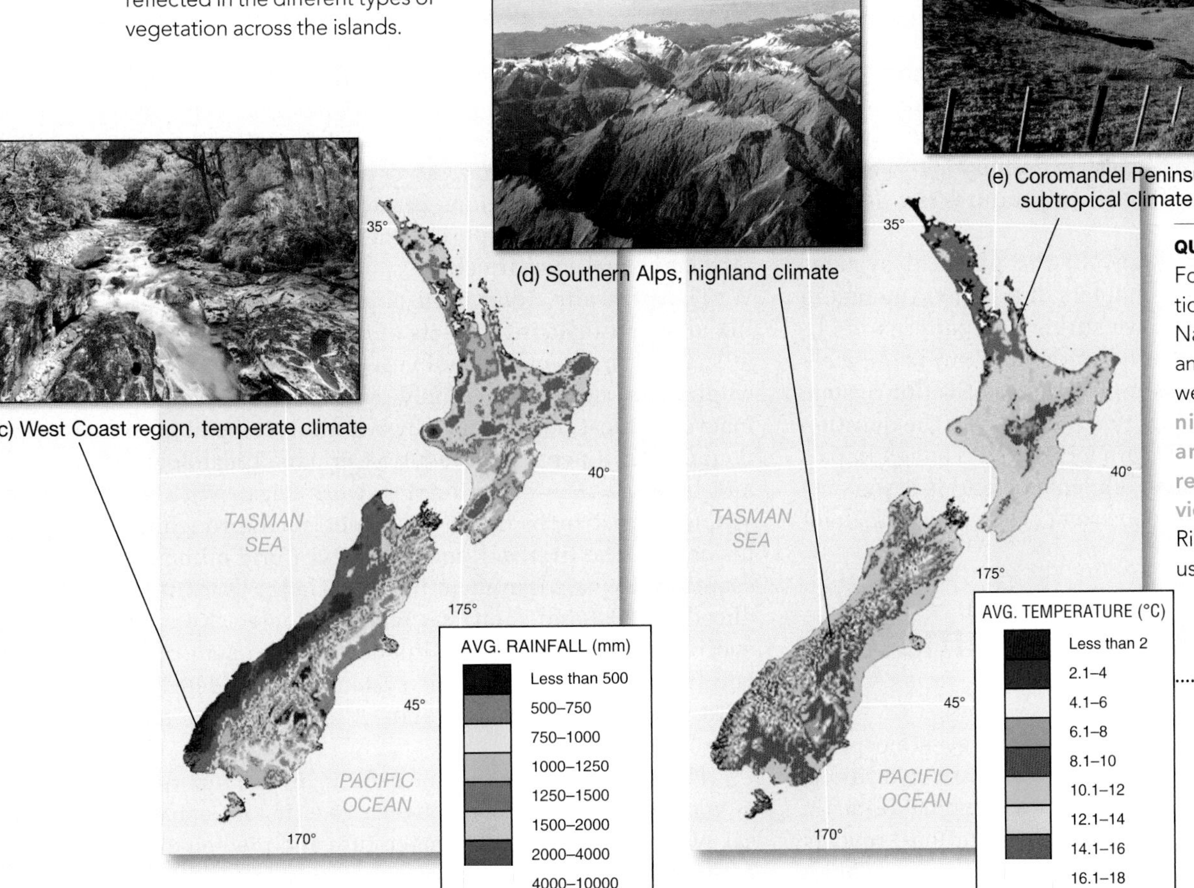

QUESTION AND EXPLORE For more climate information, go to New Zealand's National Institute of Water and Atmospheric Research website at http://www.niwa.co.nz/education-and-training/schools/resources/climate/overview. For a look at Puerto Rico's tropical climates using a large-scale map, go to Chapter 7 on the *MasteringGeography* website. MG

◀**Figure GN 7.1 Precipitation and temperature maps show local climate variability in New Zealand.** [(c) Koroshunova Olga/Shutterstock. (d) David Wall/Alamy. (e) Dmitry Serbin/Shutterstock.]

The climate where you live may be humid with distinct seasons, or dry with consistent warmth, or moist and cool—almost any combination is possible. Some places have rainfall totaling more than 20 cm (8 in.) each month, with monthly average temperatures remaining above 27°C (80°F) year-round. Other places may be rainless for a decade at a time. A climate may have temperatures that average above freezing year-round, yet still pose severe frost problems for agriculture. Students reading *Elemental Geosystems* in Singapore experience precipitation in every month, totaling 228.1 cm (89.8 in.) during an average year, whereas students at the university in Karachi, Pakistan, measure only 20.4 cm (8 in.) of annual rainfall.

Climate is the collective pattern of weather over many years.

Climate is the collective pattern of weather over many years. As we have seen, Earth experiences an almost infinite variety of *weather* at any given time or place. But if we consider a longer time scale, and the variability and extremes of weather over such a time scale, a pattern emerges that constitutes climate. For a given region, this pattern is dynamic rather than static; that is, climate changes over time (we examine this in Chapter 8).

Climatology is the study of climate and its variability, including long-term weather patterns over time (at least 30 years) and space and the controls that produce Earth's diverse climatic conditions. No two places on Earth's surface experience exactly the same climatic conditions; in fact, Earth is a vast collection of microclimates. However, broad similarities among local climates permit their grouping into **climatic regions**, which are areas with similarity in weather statistics. As you see in Chapter 8, the climate designations we study in this chapter are shifting as temperatures rise over the globe.

In this chapter: Many of the physical systems studied in the first six chapters of this text interact to explain climates. Here, we survey the patterns of climate using a series of sample cities and towns. *Elemental Geosystems* uses a simplified classification system based on physical factors that help answer the question "Why are climates in certain locations?" Though imperfect, this method is easily understood and is based on a widely used classification system devised by climatologist Wladimir Köppen.

Review of Earth's Climate System

Several important components of the energy–atmosphere system work together to determine climatic conditions on Earth. Simply combining the two principal climatic components—temperature and precipitation—reveals general climate types, sometimes called *climate regimes*, such as tropical deserts (hot and dry), polar ice sheets (cold and dry), and equatorial rain forests (hot and wet).

Figure 7.1 maps the worldwide distribution of precipitation. These patterns reflect the interplay of numerous factors that should now be familiar to you, including temperature and pressure distributions; air mass types; convergent, convectional, orographic, and frontal lifting mechanisms; and the general energy availability that decreases toward the poles. The principal components of Earth's climate system are summarized in Geosystems in Action 7 on pages 220–21.

Classifying Earth's Climates

Classification is the ordering or grouping of data or phenomena into categories of varying generality. Such generalizations are important organizational tools in science and are especially useful for the spatial analysis of climatic regions. Observed patterns confined to specific regions are at the core of climate classification. When using classifications, we must remember that the boundaries of these regions are *transition zones*, or areas of gradual change. The placement of climate boundaries depends on overall climate patterns rather than precise locations where classifications change.

A climate classification based on *causative* factors—for example, the interaction of air masses—is a **genetic classification**. This approach explores "why" a certain mix of climatic ingredients occurs in certain locations. A climate classification based on *statistics* or other data determined by measurement of observed effects is an **empirical classification**.

Climate classifications based on temperature and precipitation are examples of the empirical approach. One empirical classification system, published by C. W. Thornthwaite, identified climate regions according to moisture, using aspects of water-budget analysis (discussed in Chapter 6) and vegetation types. Another empirical system is the widely recognized Köppen climate classification, designed by Wladimir Köppen (pronounced KUR-pen; 1846–1940), a German climatologist and botanist. His classification work began with an article on heat zones in 1884 and continued throughout his career. The first wall map showing world climates, coauthored with his student Rudolph Geiger, was introduced in 1928 and soon was widely adopted. Köppen continued to refine it until his death. In Appendix B, you find a description of his system and the detailed criteria he used to distinguish climatic regions and their boundaries.

The classification system used in *Elemental Geosystems* is a compromise between genetic and empirical systems. It focuses on temperature and precipitation measurements (and for the desert areas, moisture efficiency)

Animation (MG)
Global Patterns of Precipitations
http://goo.gl/jaH3Zz

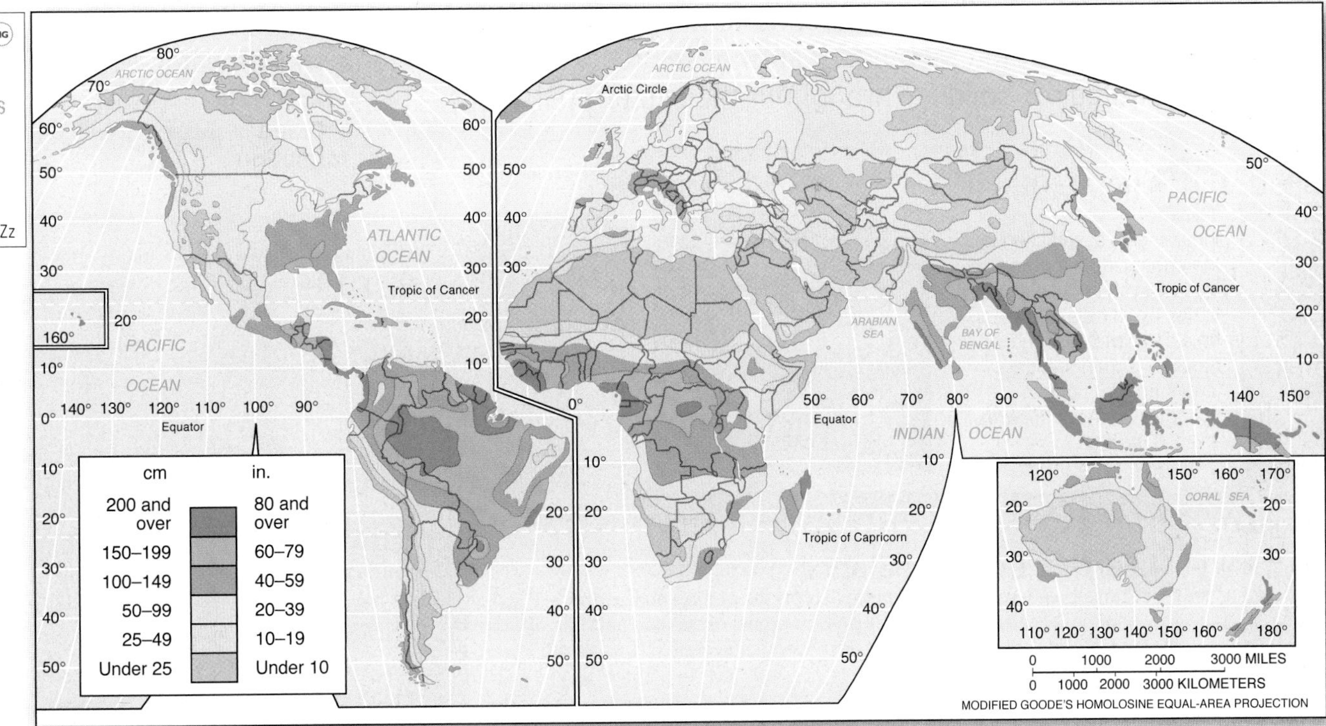

▲**Figure 7.1 Worldwide average annual precipitation.**

(MG) **MapMaster**
World Physical Environment
Average Annual Precipitation

and also on causal factors that produce the climates. World climates are grouped into six primary categories. Four of these climate classifications are based mainly on temperature characteristics:

- Tropical climates: tropical latitudes, winterless
- Mesothermal climates: midlatitudes, mild winters
- Microthermal climates: midlatitudes and high latitudes, cold winters
- Polar and highland climates (high latitudes and polar regions, and high elevations at all latitudes)

Only one primary climate classification is based on both moisture efficiency and temperature characteristics:

- Dry climates: permanent moisture deficits at all latitudes

Each of these climates is divided into subcategories, all of which are presented on the world climate map in **Figure 7.2** (pages 222–23) and described in the following sections. The upcoming discussions include at least one **climograph** for each climate subcategory, showing monthly temperature and precipitation for a representative weather station at a selected city. Listed along the top of each climograph are the dominant weather features that influence that climate's characteristics. A location map and selected statistics—including location coordinates, average annual temperature, total annual precipitation, and elevation—complete the information for each station. For each main climate category, a text box introduces the climate characteristics and causal elements, and includes a world map showing the general distribution of the climate subtypes.

Climates greatly influence *ecosystems*, the natural, self-regulating communities formed by plants and animals in their nonliving environment. On land, the basic climatic regions determine to a large extent the location of the world's major ecosystems. These broad regions, with their associated soil, plant, and animal communities, are called *biomes*; examples include forest, grassland, savanna, tundra, and desert. Discussions of the major terrestrial biomes that fully integrate these global climate patterns appear in Part IV of this text (see Table 17.1). In this chapter, we mention the ecosystems and biomes associated with each climate type.

(*text continued on page 224*)

CRITICAL**thinking 7.1**

Finding Your Climate

Using Figure 7.2, locate your campus and your birthplace and the associated climate descriptions. Then obtain monthly precipitation and temperature data for those places. Briefly describe the information sources you used: library, Internet, teacher, or phone calls to state or provincial climatologists. Next, refer to Appendix B to refine your assessment of climates for the two locations. Begin by identifying your climates at the most general level: A, C, D, E, and B. Then work through the Köppen climate criteria to determine the subgroups within this level, ending with a climate classification for your two cities.

Earth's climate system is the result of interactions among several components. These include the input and transfer of energy from the Sun (GIA 7.1 and 7.2); the resulting changes in atmospheric temperature and pressure (GIA 7.3 and 7.4); the movements and interactions of air masses (GIA 7.5); and the transfer of water—as vapor, liquid, or solid— throughout the system (GIA 7.6).

Cloud formation

Evaporation Transpiration

Runoff

7.1 Insolation

Incoming solar radiation is the energy input for the climate system. Insolation varies by latitude, as well as on a daily and seasonal basis with changing day length and Sun angle. (*Chapter 2; review Figures 2.7, 2.8, and GIA 2*)

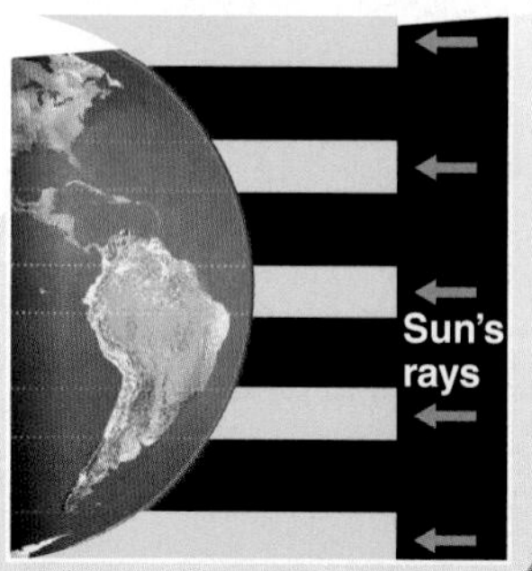

7.2 Earth's Energy Balance

The imbalance created by energy surpluses at the equator and energy deficits at the poles causes the global circulation patterns of winds and ocean currents that drive weather systems. (*Chapter 3; review Figure 3.10*)

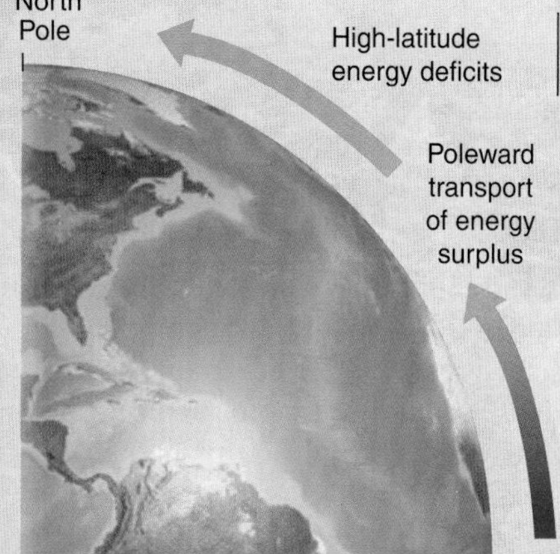

Infer: What is the general pattern of energy flow in the atmosphere? Explain your answer.

7.3 Temperature

Primary temperature controls are latitude, elevation, cloud cover, and land–water heating differences. The pattern of world temperatures is affected by global winds, ocean currents, and air masses. (*Chapter 3; review Figures 3.21 through 3.25*)

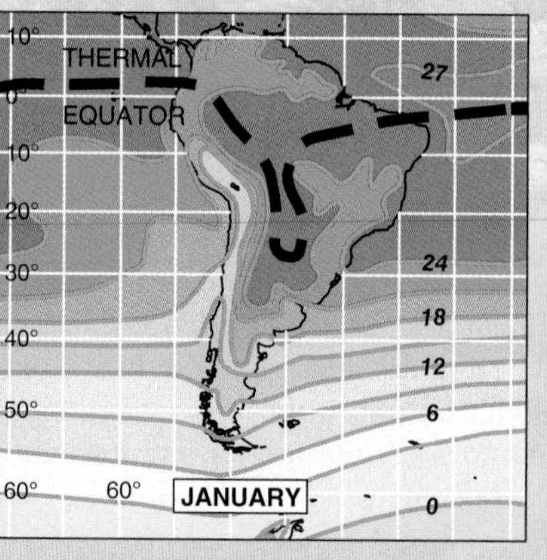

MasteringGeography™

Visit the Study Area in MasteringGeography™ to explore Earth's climate system.

Visualize: Study a NASA video of modeling Earth's climate.

Assess: Demonstrate understanding of Earth's climate system (if assigned by instructor).

Cloud formation

Atmospheric advection of water vapor

Precipitation

Evaporation

7.4 Air Pressure

Winds flow from areas of high pressure to areas of low pressure. The equatorial low creates a belt of wet climates. Subtropical highs create areas of dry climates. Pressure patterns influence atmospheric circulation and movement of air masses. Oceanic circulation and multiyear oscillations in pressure and temperature patterns over the oceans also affect weather and climate. (*Chapter 4; review Figures 4.9 and GIA 4*)

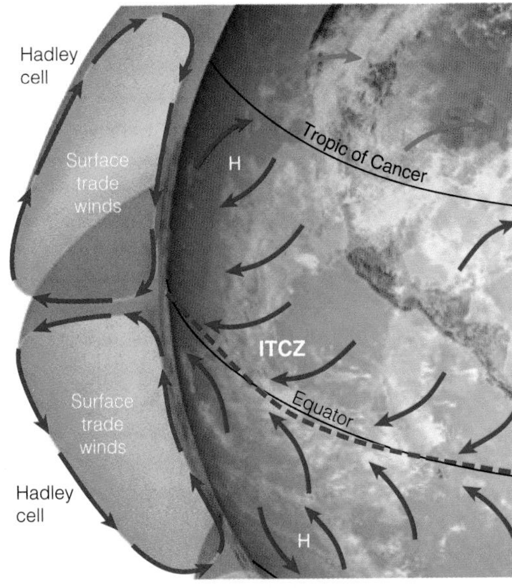

Explain: Where are the trade winds on this view of the globe? Explain and locate areas of warm, wet climates and hot, dry climates in relation to the Hadley cells.

7.5 Air Masses

Vast bodies of homogeneous air form over oceanic and continental source regions, taking on the characteristics of their source region. As these air masses migrate, they carry their temperature and moisture conditions to new regions. (*Chapter 5; review Figure 5.20*)

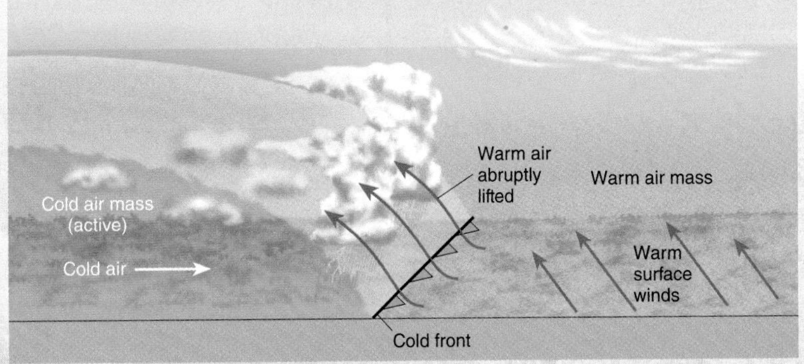

7.6 Atmospheric Moisture

The movement of water through the hydrologic cycle—including the processes of evaporation, transpiration, condensation, and precipitation—affects weather and ultimately determines Earth's climates. (*Chapters 5 and 6; review Figure 6.4*)

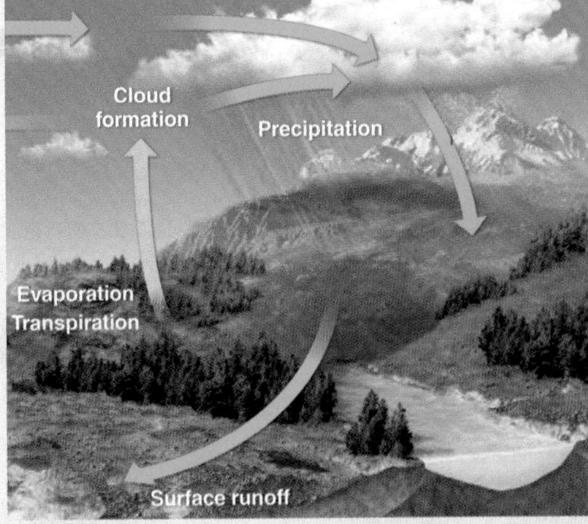

GEOquiz

1. Analyze: How do these six components of Earth's climate system interact to produce the world climates in Figure 7.2?

2. Discuss: Describe the role that each component of the climate system plays in causing precipitation patterns on Earth.

OCEAN CURRENTS (Fig. 4.17)

⟶ Warm current

⟶ Cool current

INTERTROPICAL CONVERGENCE ZONE (Fig. 4.9, GIA 4)

••••• ITCZ July or January

AIR PRESSURE SYSTEMS (Fig. 4.9)

SH Subtropical high

L Aleutian Low, Icelandic Low

AIR MASSES (Fig. 5.20)

mP Maritime polar (cool, humid)

cP Continental polar (cool, cold, dry)

mT Maritime tropical (warm, humid)

cA Continental arctic (very cold, dry)

cT Continental tropical (hot, dry summer only)

mE Maritime equatorial (warm, wet)

MapMaster
World Physical Environment
Climate

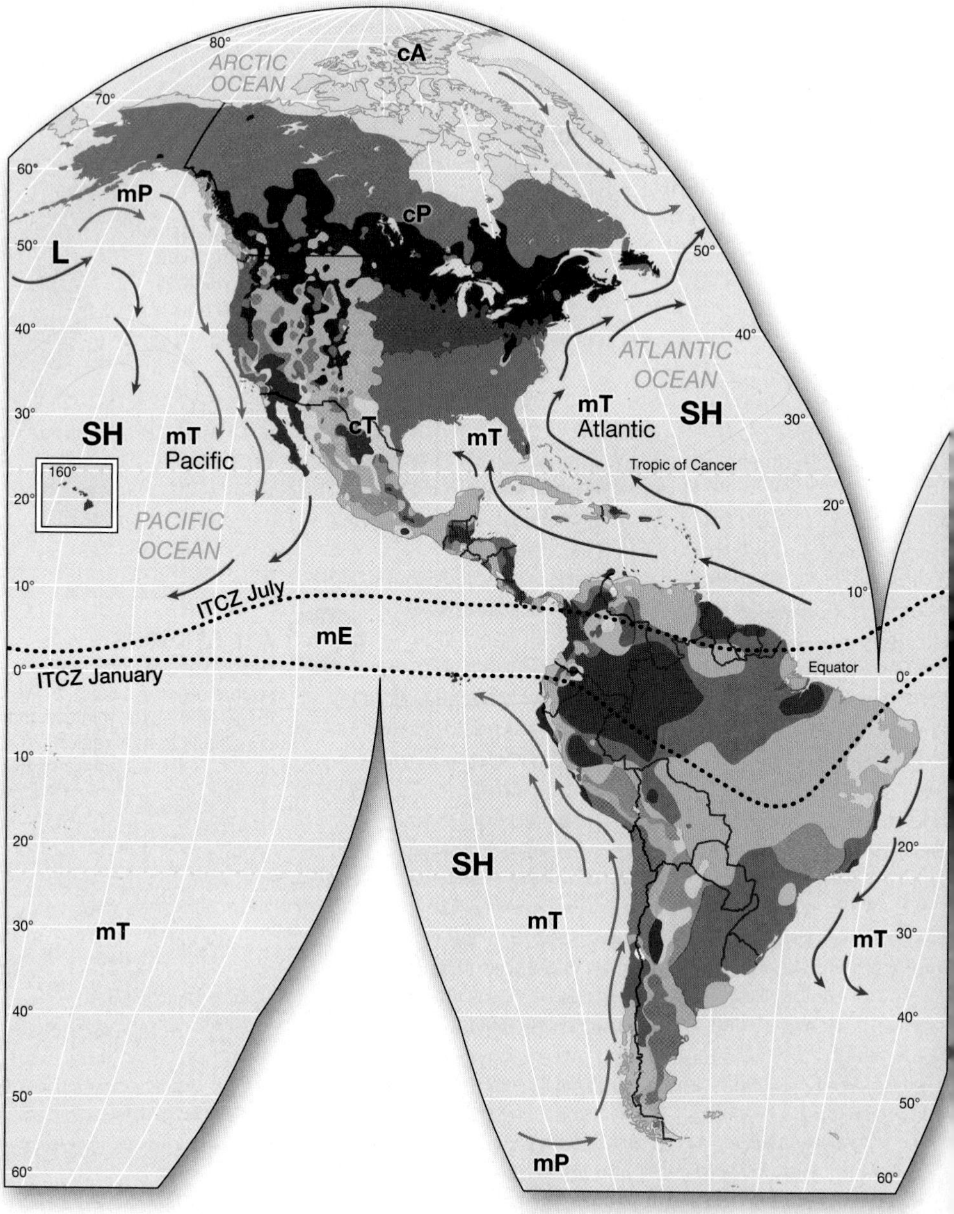

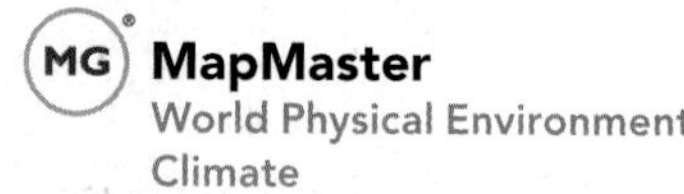

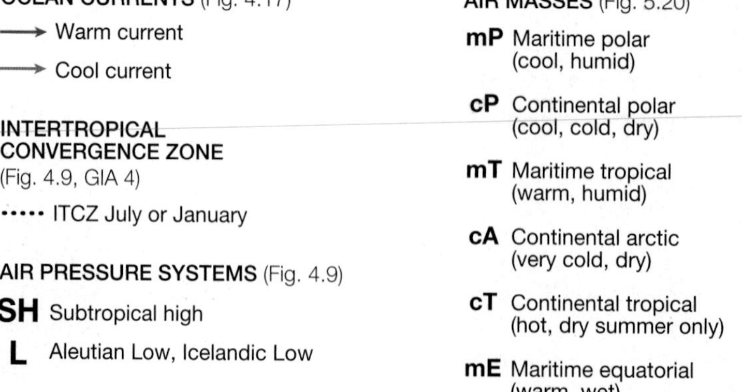

▲**Figure 7.2 World climate classification.** Annotated on this map are selected air masses, nearshore ocean currents, pressure systems, and the January and July locations of the ITCZ. Use the colors in the legend to locate various climate types. [Climate categories based on M. C. Peel, B. L. Finlayson, and T. A. McMahon et al., "Updated world map of the Köppen-Geiger climate classification," *Hydrology and Earth System Sciences* 11 (2007): 1633–1644.]

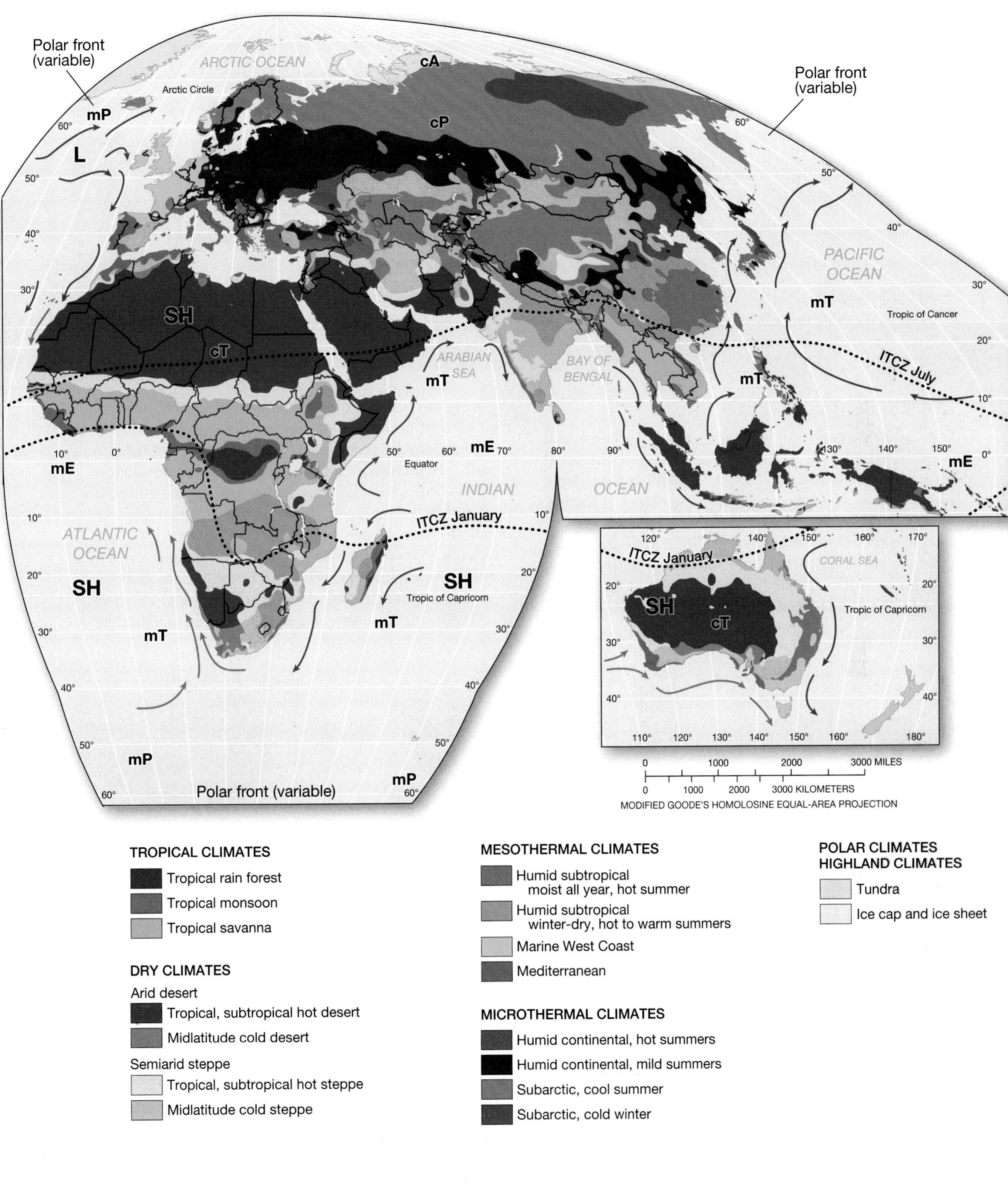

Polar front (variable)
ARCTIC OCEAN
cA
Arctic Circle
mP
cP
L
SH
cT
mT
ARABIAN SEA
BAY OF BENGAL
PACIFIC OCEAN
Tropic of Cancer
ITCZ July
mE
Equator
INDIAN OCEAN
ITCZ January
ATLANTIC OCEAN
Tropic of Capricorn
CORAL SEA
Polar front (variable)
0 1000 2000 3000 MILES
0 1000 2000 3000 KILOMETERS
MODIFIED GOODE'S HOMOLOSINE EQUAL-AREA PROJECTION
TROPICAL CLIMATES
Tropical rain forest
Tropical monsoon
Tropical savanna
DRY CLIMATES
Arid desert
Tropical, subtropical hot desert
Midlatitude cold desert
Semiarid steppe
Tropical, subtropical hot steppe
Midlatitude cold steppe
MESOTHERMAL CLIMATES
Humid subtropical moist all year, hot summer
Humid subtropical winter-dry, hot to warm summers
Marine West Coast
Mediterranean
MICROTHERMAL CLIMATES
Humid continental, hot summers
Humid continental, mild summers
Subarctic, cool summer
Subarctic, cold winter
POLAR CLIMATES
HIGHLAND CLIMATES
Tundra
Ice cap and ice sheet

Tropical Climates (tropical latitudes)

Tropical climates are the most extensive, occupying about 19% of Earth's land surface and about 36% of Earth's total surface (land and water combined). The tropical climates straddle the equator from about 20° N to 20° S latitude, roughly between the Tropics of Cancer and Capricorn—thus, the name. Tropical climates stretch northward to the tip of Florida and to south-central Mexico, central India, and Southeast Asia and southward to northern Australia, Madagascar, central Africa, and southern Brazil. These climates truly are winterless.

Important causal elements include:

- Consistent daylength and insolation, which produce consistently warm temperatures;
- Effects of the intertropical convergence zone (ITCZ), which brings rains as it shifts seasonally with the high Sun;
- Warm ocean temperatures and unstable maritime air masses.

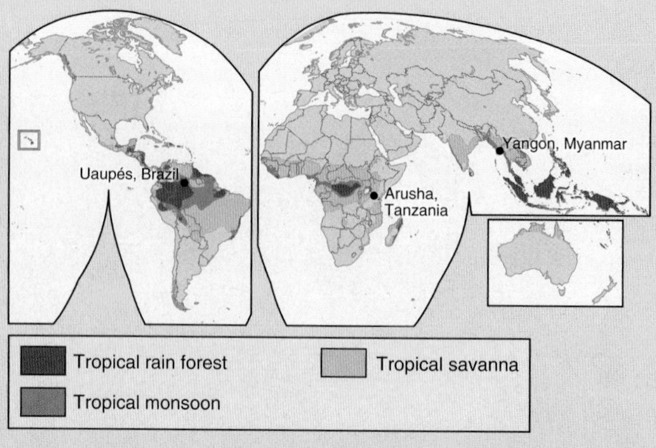

Tropical climates have three distinct regimes: *tropical rain forest* (ITCZ present all year), *tropical monsoon* (ITCZ present 6 to 12 months annually), and *tropical savanna* (ITCZ present less than 6 months).

Tropical Rain Forest Climates

Tropical rain forest climates are constantly moist and warm. Convectional thunderstorms, triggered by local heating and trade-wind convergence, peak each day from midafternoon to late evening inland and earlier in the day along coastlines, where the marine influence is strong. Precipitation follows the migrating ITCZ (review Chapter 4), which shifts northward and southward with the Sun throughout the year, but influences tropical rain forest regions all year long. Not surprisingly, water surpluses in these regions are enormous—the world's greatest streamflow volumes occur in the Amazon and Congo River basins.

High rainfall sustains lush evergreen broadleaf tree growth, producing Earth's equatorial and tropical rain forests. The leaf canopy is so dense that little light diffuses to the forest floor, leaving the ground surface dim and sparse in plant cover. Dense surface vegetation occurs along riverbanks, where light is abundant. (We examine widespread deforestation of Earth's rain forest in Chapter 17.)

Uaupés, Brazil, is characteristic of tropical rain forest. On the climograph in **Figure 7.3**, you can see that the

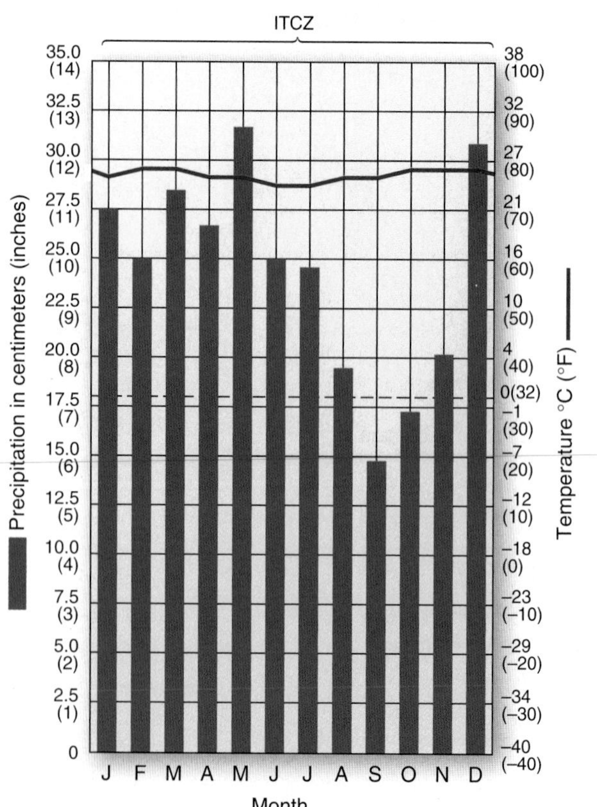

(a) Climograph for Uaupés, Brazil.

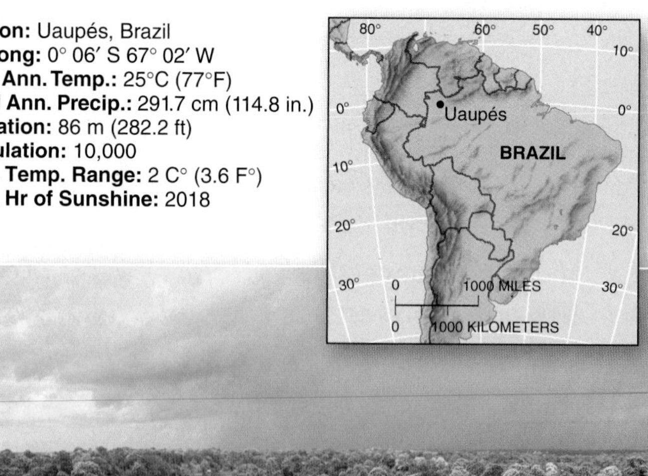

(b) The rain forest along a tributary of the Rio Negro, Amazonas state, Brazil.

▲**Figure 7.3 Tropical rain forest climate.** [(b) Sue Cunnigham Photographic/Alamy.]

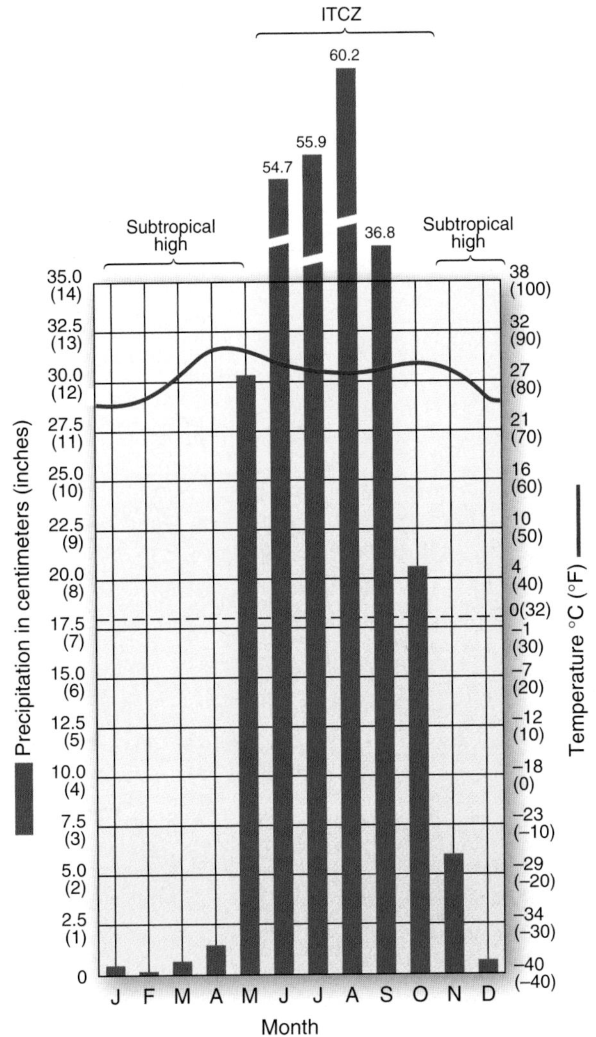

(a) Climograph for Yangon, Myanmar (formerly Rangoon, Burma).

◀Figure 7.4 Tropical monsoon climate. [(b) Shaileshnanal/Shutterstock.]

Station: Yangon, Myanmar*
Lat/long: 16° 47′ N 96° 10′ E
Avg. Ann. Temp.: 27.3°C (81.1°F)
Total Ann. Precip.: 268.8 cm (105.8 in.)
Elevation: 23 m (76 ft)
Population: 6,000,000
Ann. Temp. Range: 5.5 C° (9.9 F°)
*(Formerly Rangoon, Burma)

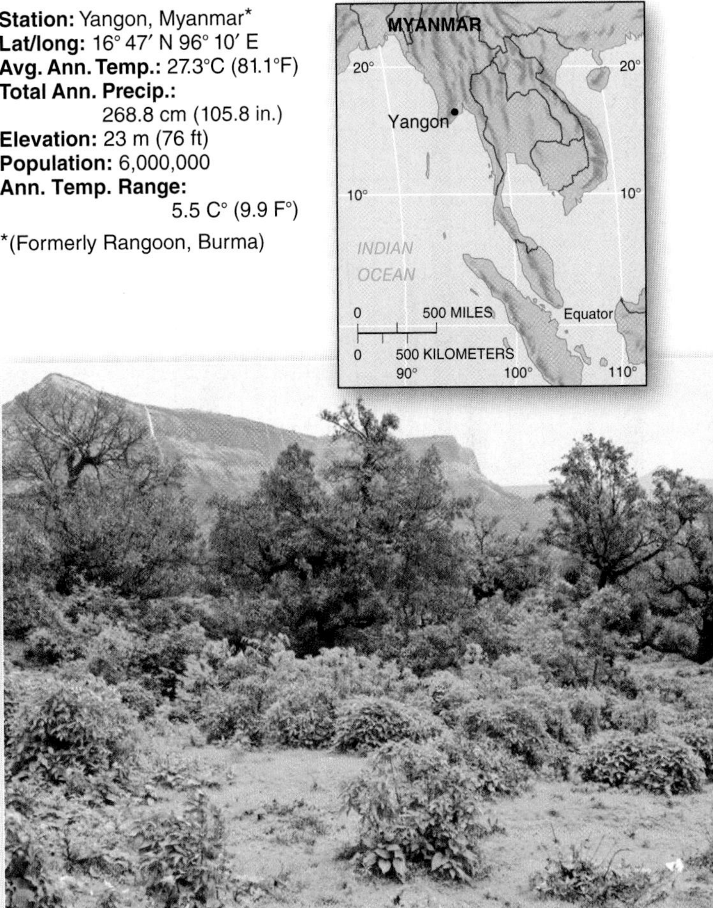

(b) Mixed monsoonal forest and scrub characteristic of the region in eastern India.

month of lowest precipitation receives nearly 15 cm (6 in.) and the annual temperature range is barely 2 C° (3.6 F°). In all such climates, the diurnal (day-to-night) temperature range exceeds the annual average minimum–maximum (coolest to warmest) range: Day–night differences can range more than 11 C° (20 F°), more than five times the annual monthly average range.

The only interruption in the distribution of tropical rain forest climates across the equatorial region is in the highlands of the South American Andes and in East Africa (see Figure 7.2). There, higher elevations produce lower temperatures; Mount Kilimanjaro is less than 4° south of the equator, but at 5895 m (19,340 ft), it has permanent glacial ice on its summit (although this ice has now nearly disappeared due to increasing air temperatures). Such mountainous sites fall within the *highland* climate category.

Tropical Monsoon Climates

Tropical monsoon climates feature a dry season that lasts 1 or more months. Rainfall brought by the ITCZ falls in these areas from 6 to 12 months of the year (whereas in the tropical rain forest regions, the ITCZ brings rain throughout the year). The dry season occurs when the ITCZ has moved away, so that the convergence effects are not present. Yangon, Myanmar (formerly Rangoon, Burma), is an example of this climate type (**Figure 7.4**). Mountains prevent cold air masses from central Asia from moving over Yangon, resulting in its high average annual temperatures.

Tropical monsoon climates lie principally along coastal areas within the tropical rain forest climatic realm and experience seasonal variations of wind and precipitation. Vegetation in this climate type typically consists of evergreen trees grading into thorn forests on the drier margins near the adjoining tropical savanna climates.

Tropical Savanna Climates

Tropical savanna climates exist poleward of the tropical rain forest climates. The ITCZ reaches these climate regions for about 6 months or less of the year as it migrates with the summer Sun. Summers are wetter than winters because convectional rains accompany

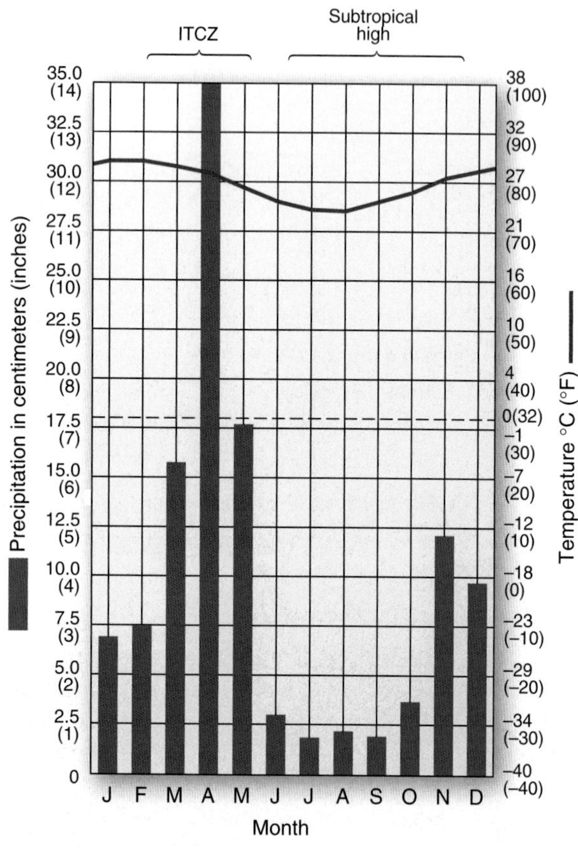

(a) Climograph for Arusha, Tanzania; note the intense dry period.

(b) Characteristic landscape in the Ngorongoro Conservation Area, Tanzania, near Arusha with plants adapted to seasonally dry water budgets.

▲**Figure 7.5 Tropical savanna climate.** [(b) Blaine Harrington III/Terra/Corbis.]

the shifting ITCZ when it is overhead. In contrast, when the ITCZ is farthest away and high pressure dominates, conditions are notably dry. Thus, the moisture demand exceeds the moisture supply in winter, causing water-budget deficits.

Temperatures vary more in tropical savanna climates than in tropical rain forest regions. The tropical savanna regime can have two temperature maximums during the year because the Sun's direct rays are overhead twice—before and after the summer solstice in each hemisphere as the Sun moves between the equator and the tropics. Grasslands with scattered trees, drought resistant to cope with the highly variable precipitation, dominate the tropical savanna regions.

The climate of Arusha, Tanzania, represents tropical savanna conditions (**Figure 7.5**). This metropolitan area is near the grassy plains of the Serengeti, a heavily visited national park that hosts one of the largest annual mammal migrations in the world. Temperatures are consistent with tropical climates, despite the elevation (1387 m, or 4550 ft) of the station. On the climograph, note the marked dryness from June to October, which indicates changing dominant pressure systems rather than annual changes in temperature. This region is near the transition to the drier *desert hot steppe* climates to the northeast (discussed later in the chapter).

GEOreport 7.1 Tropical climate zones advance to higher latitudes

The belt of tropical climates that straddles the equator is getting wider. Recent research suggests that this zone has widened by more than 2° of latitude since 1979, with an overall advance of 0.7° of latitude per decade. Research suggests that the changes are due in part to stratospheric ozone depletion over the Antarctic region and in part to pollutants such as black carbon that absorb sunlight and warm the atmosphere. The southward advance relates to the effect of seasonal ozone depletion on wind patterns, with changes linked to warming temperatures. The northward advance relates to increases in black carbon aerosols and tropospheric (ground-layer) ozone caused by fossil-fuel burning in the Northern Hemisphere. As the tropical climates move poleward, the dry subtropical regions are becoming drier, with more frequent droughts.

Mesothermal Climates (midlatitudes, mild winters)

Mesothermal, meaning "middle temperature," describes these warm and temperate climates, where true seasonality begins. More than half the world's population resides in mesothermal climates, which occupy about 13% of Earth's land surface. The mesothermal climates, and nearby portions of the microthermal climates (cold winters), are regions of great weather variability, for these are the latitudes of greatest air mass interaction.

Causal elements include:

- Latitudinal effects on insolation and temperature, as summers transition from hot to warm to cool moving poleward from the tropics;
- Shifting maritime and continental air masses, guided by upper-air westerly winds;
- Migrating cyclonic (low-pressure) and anticyclonic (high-pressure) systems, bringing changeable weather conditions and air mass conflicts;
- Effects of sea-surface temperatures on air mass strength: Cooler temperatures along west coasts weaken air masses, and warmer temperatures along east coasts strengthen air masses.

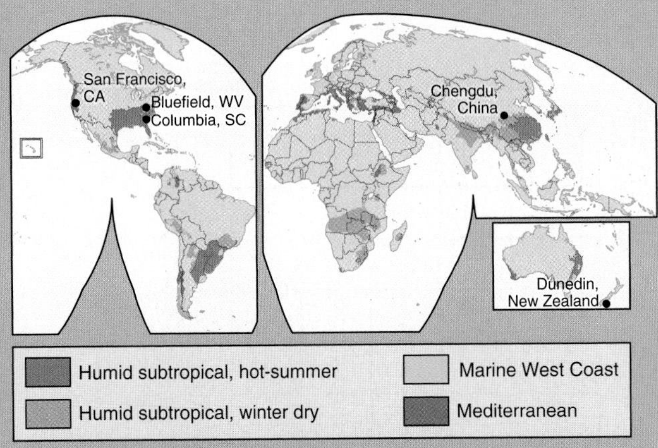

Mesothermal climates are humid, except where subtropical high pressure produces dry-summer conditions. Their four distinct regimes, based on precipitation variability, are *humid subtropical hot-summer* (moist all year), *humid subtropical winter-dry* (hot to warm summers, in Asia), *marine west coast* (warm to cool summers, moist all year), and *Mediterranean dry-summer* (warm to hot summers).

Humid Subtropical Climates

Humid subtropical climates either have hot summers and are moist all year or have hot to warm summers and a pronounced winter-dry period, as occurs in eastern and southern Asia. *Humid subtropical hot-summer* climates are influenced during summer by maritime tropical air masses generated over warm waters off eastern coasts. This warm, moist, unstable air produces convectional showers over land. In fall, winter, and spring, maritime tropical and continental polar air masses interact, generating frontal activity and frequent midlatitude cyclonic storms. These two mechanisms produce year-round precipitation, which averages 100–200 cm (40–80 in.) a year.

In North America, humid subtropical hot-summer climates are found across the southeastern United States. Columbia, South Carolina, is a representative station (**Figure 7.6**), with characteristic winter precipitation from cyclonic storm activity (other examples are Atlanta, Memphis, and New Orleans).

Humid subtropical winter-dry climates are related to the winter-dry, seasonal pulse of the monsoons. They extend poleward from tropical savanna climates and have a summer month that receives 10 times more precipitation than their driest winter month. Chengdu, China, is a representative station in Asia. **Figure 7.7** demonstrates the strong correlation between precipitation and the high summer Sun.

Large numbers of people live in the humid subtropical hot-summer and humid subtropical winter-dry climates, demonstrated by the large populations of north-central India, southeastern China, and the southeastern United States. Although these climates are relatively habitable for humans, natural hazards exist; for example, the intense summer rains of the Asian monsoon cause flooding in India and Bangladesh that affects millions of people. In the U.S. Southeast, dramatic thunderstorms are common, often spawning tornadoes, and rainfall associated with hurricanes can cause seasonal flooding events.

Marine West Coast Climates

Marine west coast climates, featuring mild winters and cool summers, are characteristic of Europe and other middle- to high-latitude west coasts (see Figure 7.2 and refer back to Geosystems Now). In the United States, these climates, with their cooler summers, are in contrast to the humid subtropical hot-summer climate of the Southeast.

Maritime polar air masses—cool, moist, unstable—dominate marine west coast climates. Weather systems forming along the polar front and maritime polar air masses move into these regions throughout the year, making weather quite unpredictable. Coastal fog, annually totaling 30 to 60 days, is a part of the moderating marine influence. Frosts are possible and tend to shorten the growing season.

Marine west coast climates are unusually mild for their latitude. They extend along the coastal margins of the Aleutian Islands in the North Pacific, cover the southern third of Iceland in the North Atlantic and coastal Scandinavia, and dominate the British Isles. Many of us might find it hard to imagine that such high-latitude locations can have average monthly temperatures above freezing throughout the year. Unlike Europe, where the marine west coast regions extend quite far inland, mountains in Canada, Alaska, Chile, and Australia restrict this climate to relatively narrow coastal environs. In the Southern Hemisphere, the marine west coast climate extends across New Zealand (see the maps in this chapter's Geosystems Now). The climograph for Dunedin, New Zealand, demonstrates the moderate temperature patterns and the annual temperature range for this climate type (**Figure 7.8**).

An interesting anomaly occurs in the eastern United States. In portions of the Appalachian highlands, which are in the humid subtropical hot-summer climate region of the continent, increased elevation affects temperatures, producing a cooler summer and an isolated area of marine west coast climate. The climograph for Bluefield, West Virginia (**Figure 7.9**), reveals

(text continued on page 230)

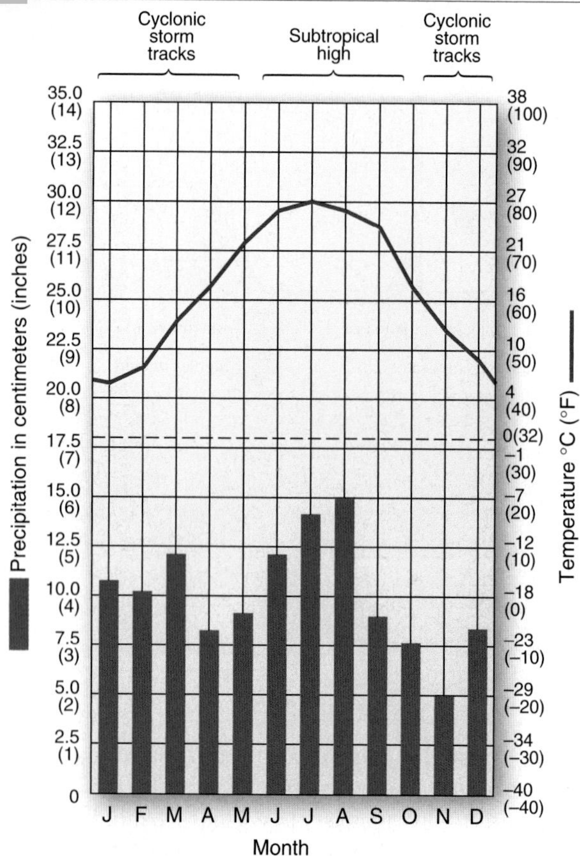

(a) Climograph for Columbia, South Carolina.

Station: Columbia, South Carolina
Lat/long: 34° N 81° W
Avg. Ann. Temp.: 17.3°C (63.1°F)
Total Ann. Precip.: 126.5 cm (49.8 in.)
Elevation: 96 m (315 ft)
Population: 116,000
Ann. Temp. Range: 20.7 C° (37.3 F°)
Ann. Hr of Sunshine: 2800

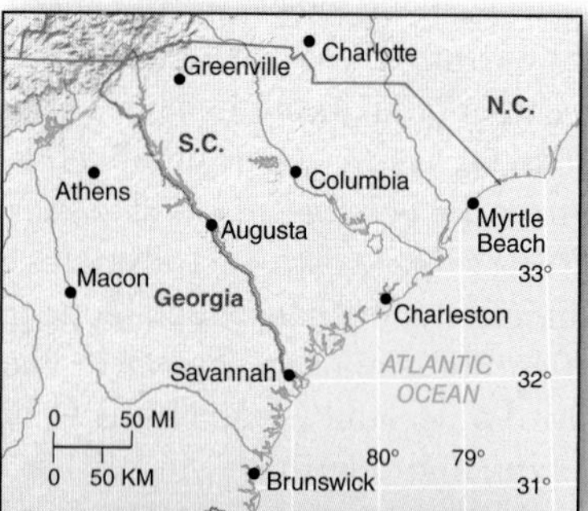

(b) Water lilies and mixed evergreen forest of cypress and pine in southern Georgia.

▲**Figure 7.6 Humid subtropical hot-summer climate.** [(b) Bobbé Christopherson.]

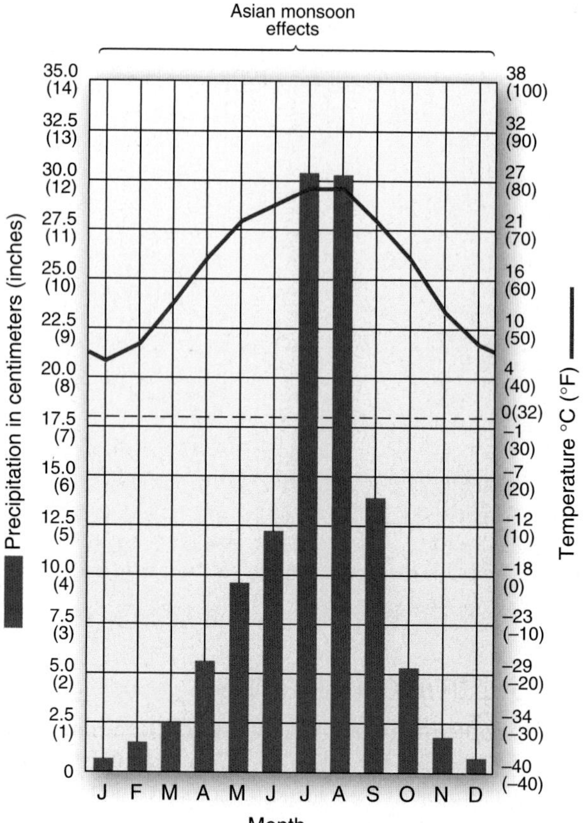

(a) Climograph for Chengdu, China. Note the summer-wet monsoonal precipitation.

Station: Chengdu, China
Lat/long: 30° 40′ N 104° 04′ E
Avg. Ann. Temp.: 17°C (62.6°F)
Total Ann. Precip.: 114.6 cm (45.1 in.)
Elevation: 498 m (1633.9 ft)
Population: 2,500,000
Ann. Temp. Range: 20 C° (36 F°)
Ann. Hr of Sunshine: 1058

(b) Agricultural fields near Chengdu, Sichuaun, China.

▲**Figure 7.7 Humid subtropical winter-dry climate.** [(b) TAO Images Limited/Alamy.]

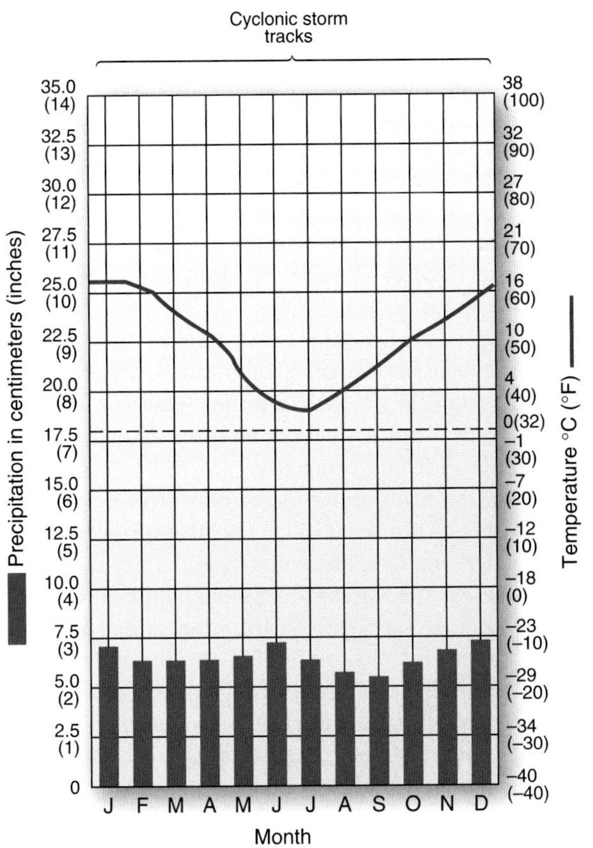

(a) Climograph for Dunedin, New Zealand.

Station: Dunedin, New Zealand
Lat/long: 45° 54′ S 170° 31′ E
Avg. Ann. Temp.: 10.2°C (50.3°F)
Total Ann. Precip.: 78.7 cm (31.0 in.)
Elevation: 1.5 m (5 ft)
Population: 120,000
Ann. Temp. Range: 14.2 C° (25.5 F°)

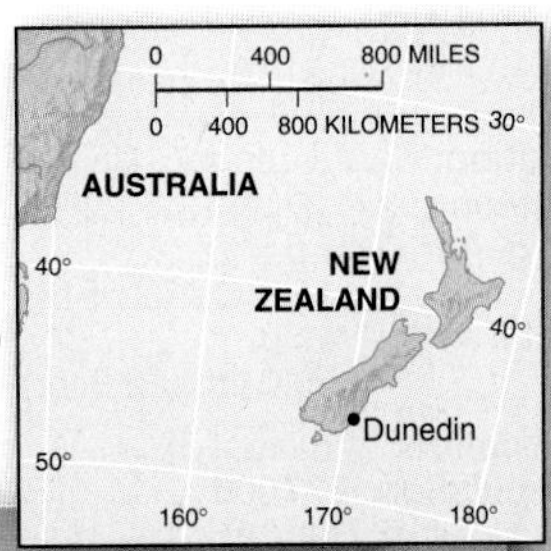

(b) Meadow, forest, and mountains on South Island, New Zealand.

▲Figure 7.8 A Southern Hemisphere marine west coast climate. [(b) Brian Enting/Science Source.]

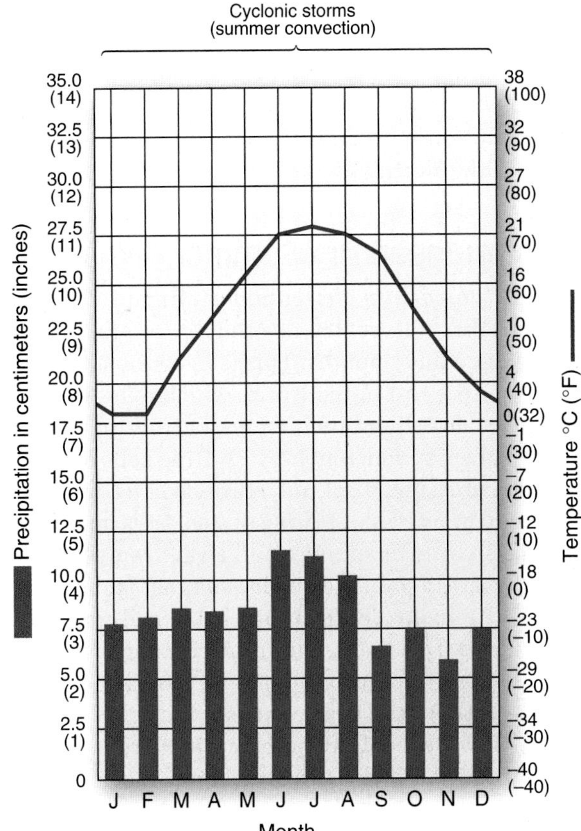

(a) Climograph for Bluefield, West Virginia.

Station: Bluefield, West Virginia
Lat/long: 37° 16′ N 81° 13′ W
Avg. Ann. Temp.: 12°C (53.6°F)
Total Ann. Precip.: 101.9 cm (40.1 in.)
Elevation: 780 m (2559 ft)
Population: 11,000
Ann. Temp. Range: 21 C° (37.8 F°)

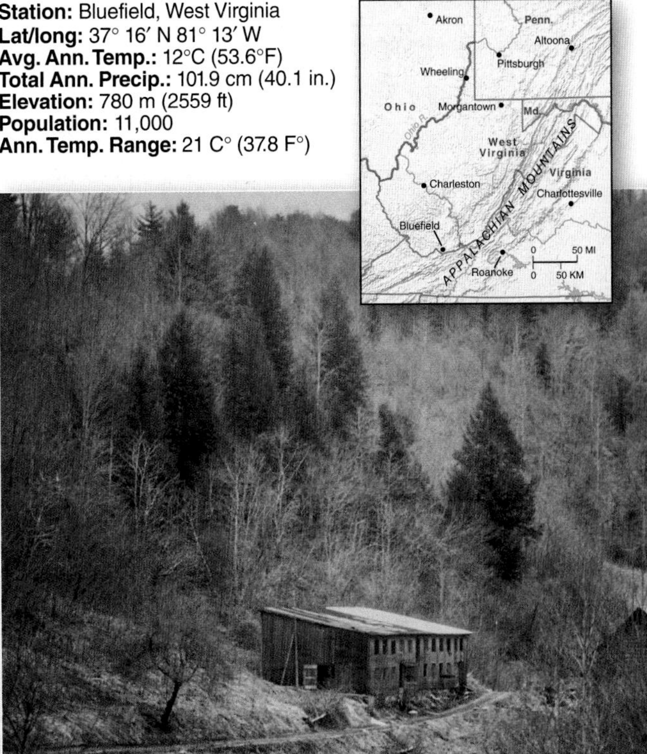

(b) Characteristic mixed forest in Appalachia in winter.

▲Figure 7.9 Marine west coast climate in the Appalachians of the eastern United States. [(b) Robert Christopherson.]

marine west coast temperature and precipitation patterns, despite its continental location in the East. Vegetation similarities between the Appalachians and the Pacific Northwest have enticed many emigrants from the East to settle in these climatically familiar environments in the Northwest.

Mediterranean Dry-Summer Climates

The *Mediterranean dry-summer* climate designation specifies that at least 70% of annual precipitation occurs during the winter months. This is in contrast to climates in most of the rest of the world, which exhibit summer-maximum precipitation. Across narrow bands of the planet during summer months, shifting cells of subtropical high pressure block moisture-bearing winds from adjacent regions. This shifting of stable, warm to hot, dry air over an area in summer and away from that area in winter creates a pronounced dry-summer and wet-winter pattern. For example, in summer the continental tropical air mass over the Sahara in Africa shifts northward over the Mediterranean region and blocks maritime air masses and cyclonic storm tracks.

Worldwide, cool offshore ocean currents (the California Current, Canary Current, Peru Current, Benguela Current, and West Australian Current, shown in Figure 4.17) produce stability in overlying air masses along west coasts, poleward of subtropical high pressure. The world climate map in Figure 7.2 shows Mediterranean dry-summer climates along the western margins of North America, central Chile, and the southwestern tip of Africa as well as across southern Australia and the Mediterranean Basin—the climate's namesake region. Examine the offshore currents along each of these regions on the map.

As discussed in Chapter 3, coastal maritime effects moderate the Mediterranean climate of San Francisco, California, producing a cool summer (**Figure 7.10**). The transition to a hot summer occurs no more than 24–32 km (15–20 mi) inland from the coast.

The Mediterranean dry-summer climate brings summer water-balance deficits. Winter precipitation recharges soil moisture, but water use usually exhausts soil moisture by late spring. Large-scale agriculture in this climate requires irrigation, although some subtropical fruits, nuts, and vegetables are uniquely suited to these conditions. Hard-leafed, drought-resistant vegetation, known locally as *chaparral* in the western United States, is common. (Chapter 17 discusses this type of vegetation in other parts of the world.)

(a) Climograph for San Francisco, California, with a cool, dry summer.

◀Figure 7.10 Mediterranean climate, California. [(b) Bobbé Christopherson.]

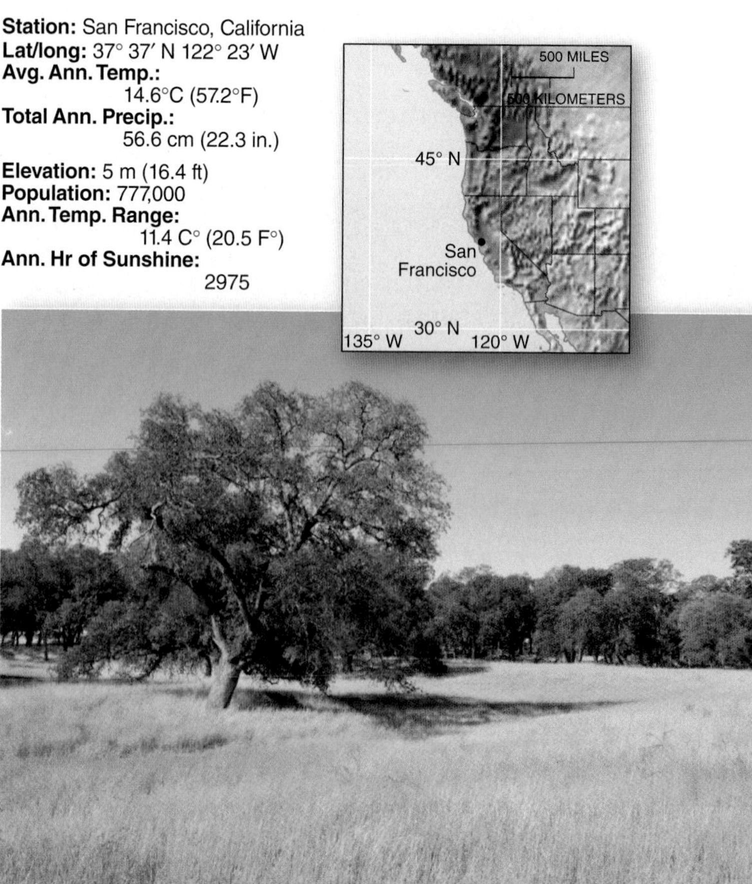

Station: San Francisco, California
Lat/long: 37° 37′ N 122° 23′ W
Avg. Ann. Temp.: 14.6°C (57.2°F)
Total Ann. Precip.: 56.6 cm (22.3 in.)
Elevation: 5 m (16.4 ft)
Population: 777,000
Ann. Temp. Range: 11.4 C° (20.5 F°)
Ann. Hr of Sunshine: 2975
500 MILES
500 KILOMETERS
45° N
San Francisco
30° N
135° W
120° W

(b) Central California Mediterranean landscape of oak savanna.

Microthermal Climates (midlatitudes and high latitudes, cold winters)

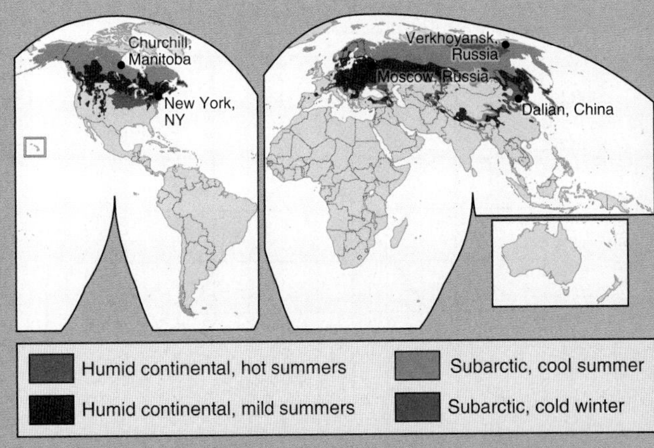

Humid microthermal climates have a winter season with some summer warmth. Here, the term *microthermal* means cool temperate to cold. Approximately 25% of Earth's land surface is influenced by these climates. These climates occur poleward of the mesothermal climates and experience great temperature ranges related to continentality and air mass conflicts. Temperatures decrease with increasing latitude and toward the interior of continental landmasses and result in intensely cold winters. In contrast to moist-all-year regions (the northern tier across the United States, the lower part of Canada, and eastern Europe through the Ural Mountains) is the winter-dry pattern associated with the Asian dry monsoon and cold air masses. In Figure 7.2, note the absence of microthermal climates in the Southern Hemisphere. Because the Southern Hemisphere lacks substantial landmasses, microthermal climates develop only in highlands.

Important causal elements include:

- Increasing seasonality (daylength and Sun altitude) and greater temperature ranges (daily and annually);
- Latitudinal effects on insolation and temperature: summers become cool moving northward, with winters becoming cold to very cold;
- Upper-air westerly winds and undulating Rossby waves, which bring warmer air northward and colder air southward for cyclonic activity, and convectional thunderstorms from maritime tropical air masses in summer;
- Continental interiors serving as source regions for intense continental polar air masses that dominate winter, blocking cyclonic storms;
- Continental high-pressure and related air masses, increasing from the Ural Mountains eastward to the Pacific Ocean, producing the Asian winter-dry pattern.

Microthermal climates have four distinct regimes based on increasing cold with latitude and precipitation variability: *humid continental hot-summer* (Chicago, New York); *humid continental mild-summer* (Duluth, Toronto, Moscow); *subarctic cool-summer* (Churchill); and the formidable extremes of *subarctic cold-winter* (Verkhoyansk and northern Siberia).

Humid Continental Hot-Summer Climates

Humid continental hot-summer climates have the warmest summer temperatures of the microthermal category. In the summer, maritime tropical air masses influence precipitation, which may be consistent throughout the year or may have a distinct winter-dry period. In North America, frequent weather activity is possible between conflicting air masses—maritime tropical and continental polar—especially in winter. New York City and Dalian, China (**Figure 7.11**), exemplify the two types of hot-summer microthermal climates—*moist-all-year* and *winter-dry*. The Dalian climograph demonstrates a winter-dry tendency caused by the intruding cold continental airflow that forces dry monsoon conditions.

In the United States today, the humid continental hot-summer region extends westward to about the 98th meridian (98° W, in central Kansas) and is the location of corn, soybean, hog, feed crop, dairy, and cattle production. To the west, this climate type transitions into the dry climates discussed later in the chapter.

Humid Continental Mild-Summer Climates

Located farther toward the poles, *humid continental mild-summer* climates are slightly cooler. **Figure 7.12** presents a climograph for Moscow, Russia, which is at 55° N, or about the same latitude as the southern shore of Hudson Bay, in Canada. In the United States, this mild-summer climate occurs across the northern plains into the northeast region, from North Dakota to Maine (Figure 7.12c).

Agricultural activity remains important in the cooler microthermal climates and includes dairy, poultry, flax, sunflower, sugar beet, wheat, and potato production. Frost-free periods range from fewer than 90 days in the northern portions of these regions to as many as 225 days in the southern parts. Overall, precipitation is less than in the hot-summer regions to the south; however, snowfall is notably heavier, and its melting is important to soil-moisture recharge. Among various strategies for capturing this snow is the use of fences and tall stubble left standing in fields to create snowdrifts and thus more moisture retention in the soil.

The winter-dry aspect of the mild-summer climate occurs only in Asia, in a far-eastern area poleward of the winter-dry mesothermal climates. A representative of this type of humid continental mild-summer climate along Russia's east coast is Vladivostok, usually one of only two ice-free ports in that country.

Subarctic Climates

Farther poleward, seasonal change becomes greater. The short growing season is more intense during long summer days. The *subarctic* climates include vast stretches of Alaska, Canada, and northern Scandinavia, with their cool summers, and Siberian Russia, with its very cold winters (Figure 7.2).

Areas that receive 25 cm (10 in.) or more of precipitation a year on the northern continental margins and are covered by the so-called snow forests of fir, spruce, larch, and birch are the *boreal forests* of Canada and the *taiga*

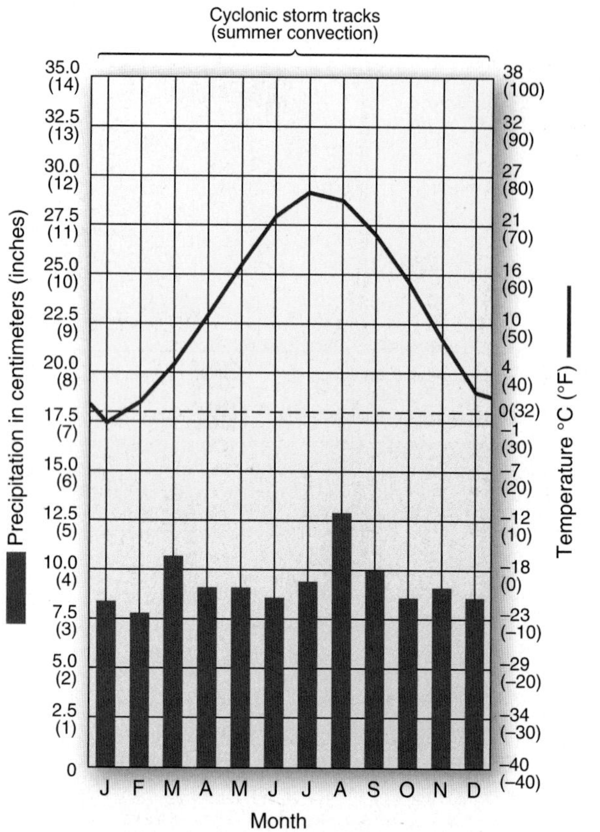

(a) Climograph for New York City (humid continental hot-summer, moist all year).

Station: New York, New York
Lat/long: 40° 46′ N 74° 01′ W
Avg. Ann. Temp.: 13°C (55.4°F)
Total Ann. Precip.: 112.3 cm (44.2 in.)
Elevation: 16 m (52.5 ft)
Population: 8,092,000
Ann. Temp. Range: 24 C° (43.2 F°)
Ann. Hr of Sunshine: 2564

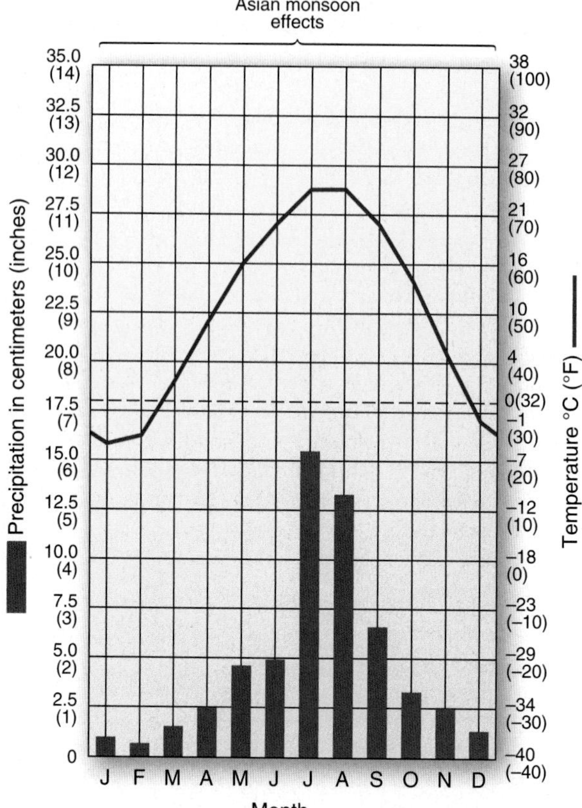

(b) Climograph for Dalian, China (humid continental hot-summer, winter-dry).

Station: Dalian, China
Lat/long: 38° 54′ N 121° 54′ E
Avg. Ann. Temp.: 10°C (50°F)
Total Ann. Precip.: 57.8 cm (22.8 in.)
Elevation: 96 m (314.9 ft)
Population: 5,550,000
Ann. Temp. Range: 29 C° (52.2 F°)
Ann. Hr of Sunshine: 2762

(c) Belvedere Castle, built in 1872, in New York's Central Park; location of weather station from 1919 to 1960.

(d) Dalian, China, cityscape and park in summer.

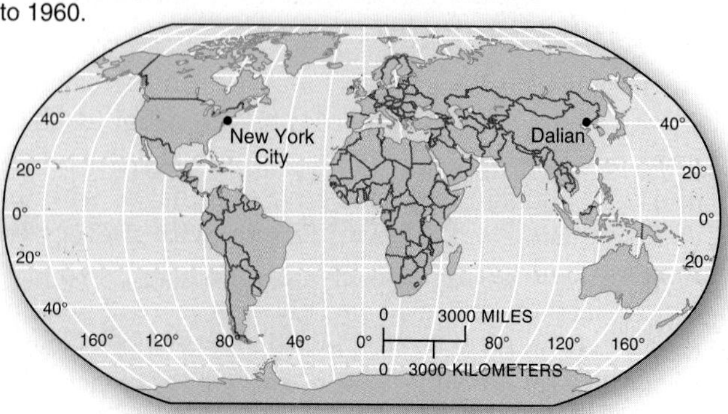

◀**Figure 7.11 Humid continental hot-summer climates, New York and China.** [(c) Bobbé Christopherson. (d) Best View Stock/Alamy.]

of Russia. These forests are in transition to the more open northern woodlands and to the tundra region of the far north. Forests thin out to the north wherever the warmest month drops below an average temperature of 10°C (50°F). Climate models and forecasts suggest that, during the decades ahead, the boreal forests will shift northward into the tundra in response to higher temperatures.

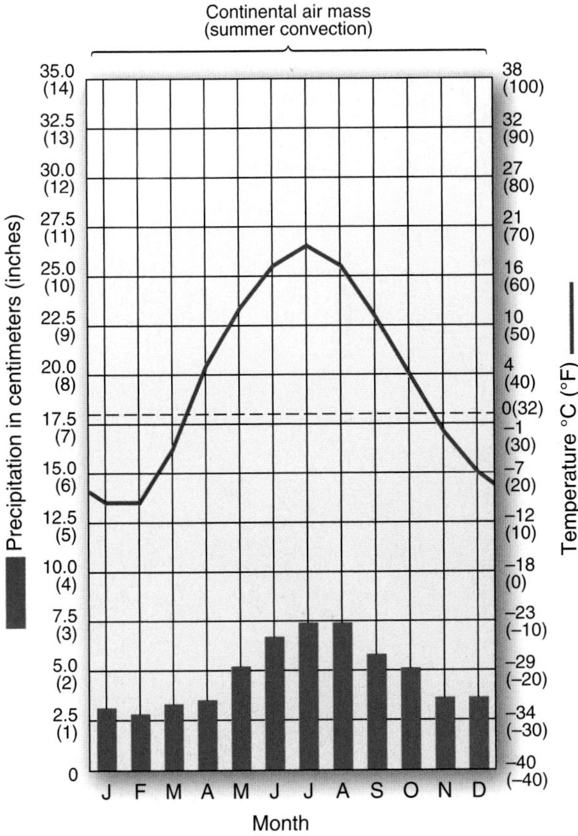

(a) Climograph for Moscow, Russia.

Station: Moscow, Russia
Lat/long: 55° 45′ N 37° 34′ E
Avg. Ann. Temp.: 4°C (39.2°F)
Total Ann. Precip.: 57.5 cm (22.6 in.)
Elevation: 156 m (511.8 ft)
Population: 11,460,000
Ann. Temp. Range: 29 C° (52.2 F°)
Ann. Hr of Sunshine: 1597

0° 180° 80°
Moscow
RUSSIA
0 1200 MILES
0 1200 KILOMETERS

(b) Landscape between Moscow and St. Petersburg along the Volga River.

(c) Winter scene of mixed forest near Brunswick, Maine, in the North American region with this climate type.

▲Figure 7.12 Humid continental mild-summer climate.
[(b) Dave G. Houser/Documentary Value/Corbis. (c) Bobbé Christopherson.]

Precipitation is low, but so is potential evapotranspiration, so soils are generally moist and either partially or totally frozen beneath the surface, a phenomenon known as *permafrost* (discussed in Chapter 13). The Churchill, Manitoba, climograph (**Figure 7.13**) shows average monthly temperatures below freezing for 7 months of the year, during which time light snow cover and frozen ground persist. High pressure dominates Churchill during its cold winter—this is the source region for the continental polar air mass. Churchill is representative of the *subarctic cool-summer* climate, with an annual temperature range of 40 C° (72 F°) and low precipitation of 44.3 cm (17.4 in.).

The subarctic climates that feature a dry and very cold winter occur only within Russia. The intense cold of Siberia and north-central and eastern Asia is difficult to comprehend, for these areas experience an average temperature lower than freezing for 7 months and minimum temperatures of below −68°C (−90°F), as described in Chapter 3. Yet summer-maximum temperatures in these same areas can exceed 37°C (98°F).

An example of this extreme *subarctic cold-winter* climate is Verkhoyansk, Siberia (**Figure 7.14**). For 4 months of the year, average temperatures fall below −34°C (−30°F). Verkhoyansk has probably the world's greatest annual temperature range from winter to summer: a remarkable 63 C° (113.4 F°). In Verkhoyansk, metals and plastics are brittle in winter; people install triple-thick windowpanes to withstand temperatures that render straight antifreeze a solid.

GEO**report** 7.2 Boundary considerations and shifting climates

The boundary between mesothermal and microthermal climates is sometimes placed along the isotherm where the coldest month is −3°C (26.6°F) or lower. That might be a suitable criterion for Europe, but for conditions in North America, the 0°C (32°F) isotherm is considered more appropriate. The distance between the 0°C and −3°C isotherms is about the width of the state of Ohio. In Figure 7.2, you see the 0°C boundary used.

Scientists estimate that climate regions will shift poleward by 150 to 550 km (90 to 350 mi) in the midlatitudes during this century. As you examine North America in Figure 7.2, use the graphic scale to get an idea of the magnitude of these potential shifts.

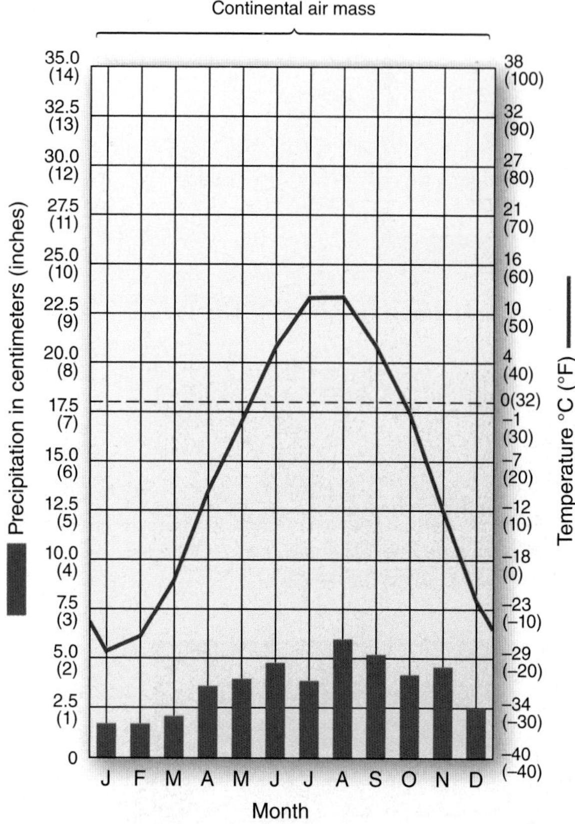

(a) Climograph for Churchill, Manitoba.

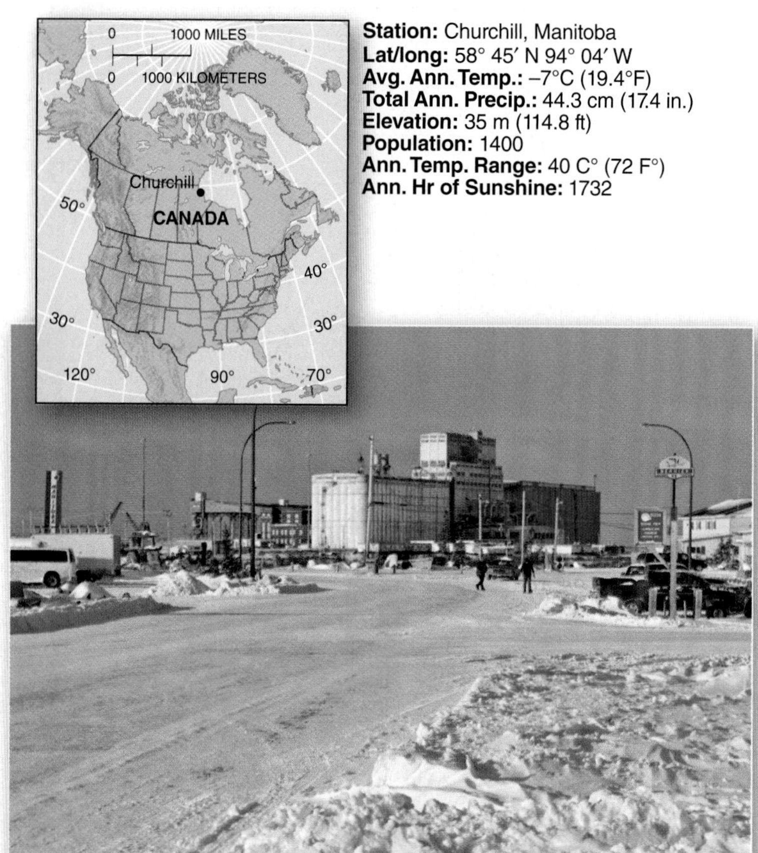

Station: Churchill, Manitoba
Lat/long: 58° 45′ N 94° 04′ W
Avg. Ann. Temp.: −7°C (19.4°F)
Total Ann. Precip.: 44.3 cm (17.4 in.)
Elevation: 35 m (114.8 ft)
Population: 1400
Ann. Temp. Range: 40 C° (72 F°)
Ann. Hr of Sunshine: 1732

(b) Churchill and other port facilities on Hudson Bay may expand with renewed interest in mineral and petroleum reserves in subarctic regions.

▲**Figure 7.13 Subarctic cool-summer climate.** [(b) Bobbé Christopherson.]

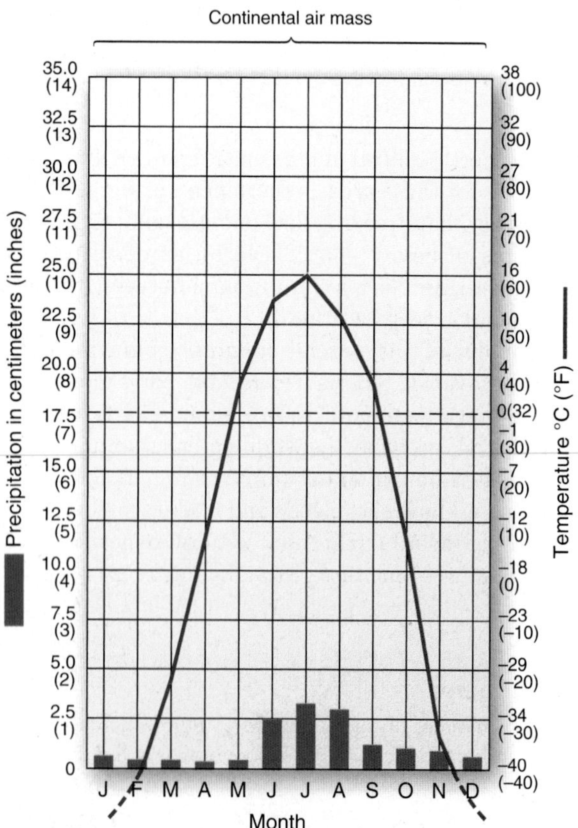

(a) Climograph for Verkhoyansk, Russia.

Station: Verkhoyansk, Russia
Lat/long: 67° 35′ N 133° 27′ E
Avg. Ann. Temp.: −15°C (5°F)
Total Ann. Precip.: 15.5 cm (6.1 in.)
Elevation: 137 m (449.5 ft)
Population: 1500
Ann. Temp. Range: 63 C° (113.4 F°)

(b) A summer scene shows one of many ponds created by thawing permafrost.

▲**Figure 7.14 Extreme subarctic cold-winter climate.** [(b) Dean Conger/Documentary Value/Corbis.]

Polar and Highland Climates

The polar climates occupy about 13% of Earth's land and have no true summer like that in lower latitudes. Overlying the South Pole is the Antarctic continent, surrounded by the Southern Ocean, whereas the North Pole region is covered by the Arctic Ocean, surrounded by the continents of North America and Eurasia. Poleward of the Arctic and Antarctic Circles, daylength increases in summer until daylight becomes continuous, yet average monthly temperatures never rise above 10°C (50°F). These temperature conditions do not allow tree growth. (Review the polar region temperature maps for January and July in Figures 3.24 and 3.25.)

Important causal elements of polar climates include:

- Low Sun altitude even during the long summer days, which is the principal climatic factor;
- Extremes of daylength between winter and summer, which determine the amount of insolation received;
- Extremely low humidity, producing low precipitation amounts—these regions are Earth's frozen deserts;
- Surface albedo impacts, as light-colored surfaces of ice and snow reflect substantial energy away from the ground, thus reducing net radiation.

Polar climates have two primary regimes: *tundra* (at high latitude or high elevation)—including *polar marine* (with an oceanic association and slight moderation of extreme cold)—and *ice cap* and *ice sheet* (perpetually frozen). Also in this climate category are *highland* climates, in which tundra and ice-cap conditions occur at nonpolar latitudes because of the effects of elevation. Highland climates occur on Earth's highest mountains (see Geosystems Now, Figure GN 7.1b). Glaciers on some tropical mountain summits attest to the cooling effects of altitude.

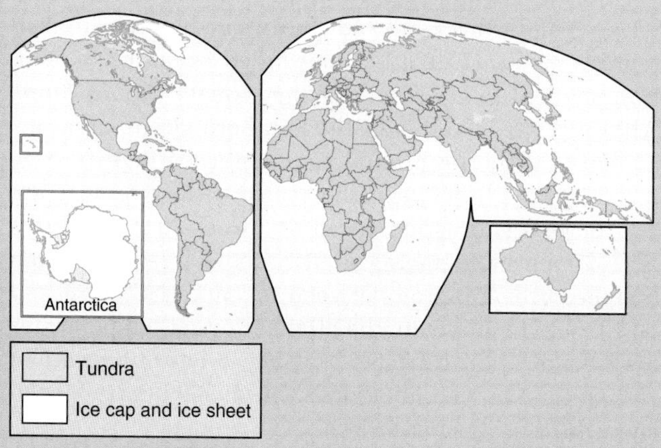

Tundra Climates

The term *tundra* refers to the characteristic vegetation of high latitudes and high elevations, where plant growth is restricted by cold temperatures and a short growing season. In *tundra* climates, land is under some snow cover for 8–10 months, with the warmest month above 0°C (32°F), yet never warming above 10°C (50°F). These climates occur only in the Northern Hemisphere, except for elevated mountain locations in the Southern Hemisphere and a portion of the Antarctic Peninsula. Because of its elevation, the summit of Mount Washington in New Hampshire (1914 m, or 6280 ft) statistically qualifies as a highland tundra climate despite its limited areal extent. In contrast, approximately 410,500 km^2 (158,475 mi^2) of Greenland make up an area of tundra and rock about the size of California.

In spring when the snow melts, numerous plants appear—stunted sedges, mosses, dwarf shrubs, flowering plants, and lichens—and persist through the short summer (**Figure 7.15a**). Some of the dwarf willows (7.5 cm, or 3 in., tall) can exceed 300 years in age. Much of the area experiences permafrost and ground ice conditions; these are Earth's periglacial regions, discussed in Chapter 14.

Within the tundra climates, some areas have a strong marine influence. In 1964, geographer James Shear proposed a separate designation for *polar marine* climates, applying to areas with smaller annual temperature ranges and more moderate winter temperatures than other polar climates, with no month below −7°C (20°F). Overall, polar marine climates are not as warm as tundra climates.

(a) Late September in East Greenland, with fall colors and musk oxen.

(b) An abandoned whaling station at Grytviken; last used 1964.

►**Figure 7.15 Tundra climates.** [Bobbé Christopherson.]

South Georgia Island, made famous as the place where Ernest Shackleton sought rescue help for himself and his men in 1916 after their failed Antarctic expedition, exemplifies a polar marine climate (**Figure 7.15b**). Although the island is in the Southern Ocean and part of Antarctica, the annual temperature range is only 8.5 C° (15.3 F°) between the seasons (the averages are 7°C, or 44.6°F, in January and −1.5°C, or 29.3°F, in July), with 7 months averaging slightly above freezing. Ocean temperatures, ranging between 0°C and 4°C (32°F and 39°F), help to moderate the climate so that temperatures are warmer than expected at its 54°-S-latitude location. Average annual precipitation is 150 cm (59 in.), and it can snow during any month.

Polar marine climates also exist along the Bering Sea, on the southern tip of Greenland, and in northern Iceland and northern Norway; in the Southern Hemisphere, they generally occur over oceans between 50° S and 60° S latitude. For example, Macquarie Island at 54° S in the Southern Ocean, south of New Zealand, is polar marine. Isolated areas of polar marine climate exist in high-elevation mountain regions of New Zealand.

Ice-Cap and Ice-Sheet Climates

An *ice sheet* is a continuous layer of ice covering an extensive continental region. Earth's two ice sheets cover the Antarctic continent and most of the island of Greenland (**Figure 7.16**). An *ice cap* is smaller in extent, roughly less than 50,000 km^2 (19,300 mi^2), but it completely buries the landscape like an ice sheet. The Vatnajökull Ice Cap in southeastern Iceland is an example (see the NASA image in Chapter 14, Figure 14.5).

Most of Antarctica and central Greenland fall within the *ice-cap and ice-sheet* climate category, as does the North Pole, with all months averaging below freezing (the area of the North Pole is actually a sea covered by ice rather than a continental landmass). These regions are dominated by dry, frigid air masses, with vast expanses that never warm above freezing. In fact, minimum temperatures during central Antarctica's winter (July) frequently drop below the temperature of solid carbon dioxide, or "dry ice" (−78°C, or −109°F). Antarctica is constantly snow-covered, but receives less than 8 cm (3 in.) of precipitation each year. However, Antarctic ice has accumulated to several kilometers deep and is the largest repository of freshwater on Earth.

(a) In the Antarctic Sound, between Bransfield Strait and the Weddell Sea, mountains rise from the mist behind a flank of tabular icebergs.

(b) Glaciers move toward the ocean in West Greenland, with the ice sheet on the horizon.

▲**Figure 7.16 Earth's ice sheets—Antarctica and Greenland.** [Bobbé Christopherson.]

GEOreport 7.3 Tundra climates respond to warming

Global warming is bringing dramatic changes to the tundra climate regions, where temperatures in the Arctic are warming at a rate twice that of the global average increase. In parts of Canada and Alaska, near-record temperatures as much as 5 to 10 C° (9 to 18 F°) above average are a regular occurrence. As organic peat deposits in the tundra thaw, vast stores of carbon and methane are released to the atmosphere, further adding to the greenhouse gas problem (more discussion is in Chapters 8, 14, and 15).

Dry Climates (permanent moisture deficits)

To understand the dry climates, we must consider moisture efficiency (both timing and quantity of moisture) along with temperature. These dry regions occupy about 30% of Earth's land area, making it the most extensive climate type. Sparse vegetation leaves the landscape bare; water demand exceeds the precipitation water supply throughout, creating permanent water deficits. The extent of these deficits distinguishes two types of dry climatic regions: *arid deserts*, where the precipitation supply is roughly less than one-half of the natural moisture demand, and *semiarid steppes*, where the precipitation supply is roughly more than one-half of the natural moisture demand. (Review pressure systems in Chapter 4 and temperature controls, including the highest recorded temperatures, in Chapter 3. We discuss desert environments in Chapter 17.)

Important causal elements in these dry lands include:

- The dominant presence of dry, subsiding air in subtropical high-pressure systems;
- Location in the rain shadow (or on the leeward side) of mountains, where dry air subsides after moisture is intercepted on the windward slopes;
- Location in continental interiors, particularly central Asia, which are far from moisture-bearing air masses;

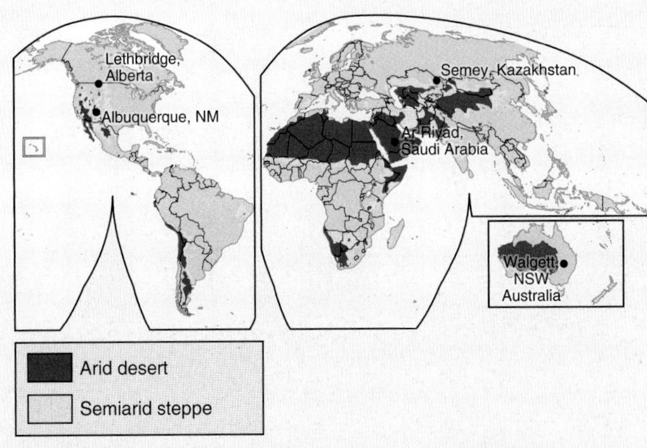

- Location along western continental margins with cool, stabilizing ocean currents;
- Shifting subtropical high-pressure systems, which produce semiarid steppes around the periphery of arid deserts.

Dry climates fall into four distinct regimes, according to latitude and the amount of moisture deficit: arid climates include the *tropical, subtropical hot desert* and *midlatitude cold desert* regimes; semiarid climates include the *tropical, subtropical hot steppe* and *midlatitude cold steppe* regimes.

Characteristics of Dry Climates

Dry climates are subdivided into deserts and steppes according to moisture—deserts have greater moisture deficits than do steppes, but both have permanent water shortages. **Steppe** is a regional term referring to the vast semiarid grassland biome of eastern Europe and Asia (the equivalent biome in North America is shortgrass prairie and in Africa, the savanna; see Chapter 17). In this chapter, we use steppe in a climatic context; a *steppe climate* is considered too dry to support forest, but too moist to be a desert.

The timing of precipitation (winter rains with dry summers, summer rains with dry winters, or even distribution throughout the year) affects moisture availability in these dry lands. Winter rains are most effective because they fall at a time of lower moisture demand. Relative to temperature, the lower-latitude deserts and steppes tend to be hotter with less seasonal change than the midlatitude deserts and steppes, where mean annual temperatures are below 18°C (64.4°F) and freezing winter temperatures are possible.

Earth's dry climates cover broad regions between 15° and 30° latitude in the Northern and Southern Hemispheres, where subtropical high-pressure cells predominate, with subsiding, stable air and low relative humidity. Under generally cloudless skies, these subtropical deserts extend to western continental margins, where cool, stabilizing ocean currents operate offshore and summer advection fog forms. The Atacama Desert of Chile, the Namib Desert of Namibia, the Western Sahara of Morocco, and the Australian Desert each lie adjacent to such a coastline (**Figure 7.17**).

However, dry regions also extend into higher latitudes. Deserts and steppes occur as a result of orographic lifting over mountain ranges, which intercept moisture-bearing weather systems to create rain shadows, especially in North and South America (Figure 7.17). The isolated interior of Asia, far distant from any moisture-bearing air masses, also falls within the dry climate classification.

The world's largest desert, as defined by moisture criteria, is the Antarctic region. The largest nonpolar deserts in surface area are the Sahara in North Africa, the Arabian in western Asia, the Gobi in China and Mongolia, the Patagonian in Argentina, the Great Victoria in Australia, the Kalahari in South Africa, and the Great Basin of the western United States.

Tropical, Subtropical Hot Desert Climates

Tropical, subtropical hot desert climates are Earth's true tropical and subtropical deserts and feature annual average temperatures above 18°C (64.4°F). They generally are found on the western sides of continents, although Egypt, Somalia, and Saudi Arabia also fall within this classification. Rainfall is from local summer convectional showers. Some regions receive almost no rainfall, whereas others may receive up to 35 cm (14 in.) of precipitation a year. A representative subtropical hot desert city is Riyadh, Saudi Arabia (**Figure 7.18**).

Along the Sahara Desert's southern margin in Africa is a drought-prone region called the Sahel, where human populations suffer great hardship as desert conditions

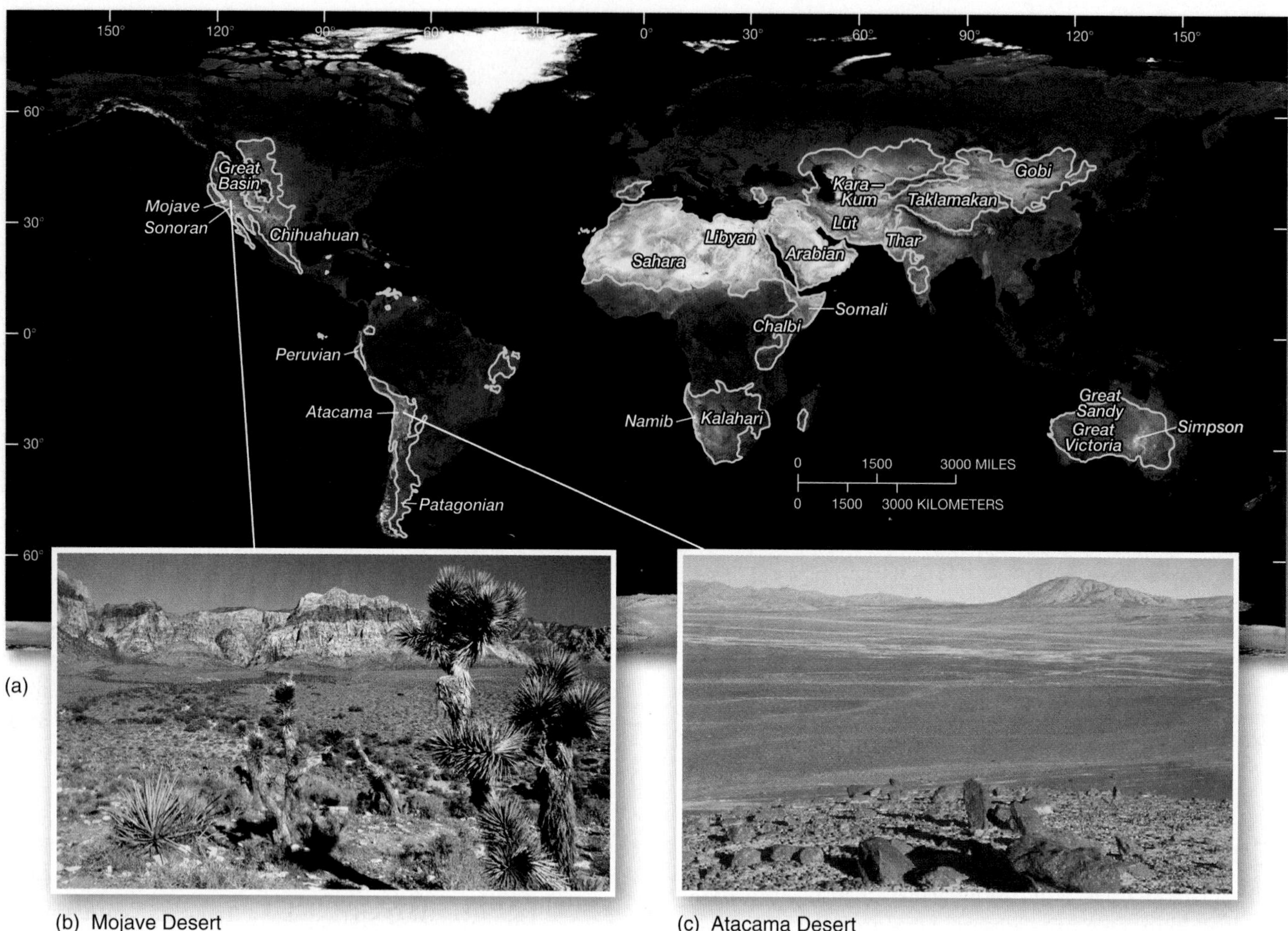

▲**Figure 7.17 Important deserts and steppes.** Worldwide distribution of arid and semiarid climates, with the world's major deserts and steppes labeled. [(a) *Terra* MODIS image, NASA GSFC. (b) Bobbé Christopherson. (c) Jacques Jangoux/Science Source.]

gradually expand over their homelands. Geosystems Now in Chapter 15 examines the process of desertification (expanding desert conditions), an ongoing problem in many dry regions of the world.

Death Valley, in California, holds the record for highest temperature ever recorded—57°C (134°F), during July 1913. Extremely hot summer temperatures occur in other hot desert climates, such as around Baghdad, Iraq, where air temperatures regularly reach 50°C (122°F) and higher in the city. Baghdad records zero precipitation from May to September, as it is dominated by an intense subtropical high-pressure system. In January, averages for Death Valley (11°C, or 52°F) and Baghdad (9.4°C, or 49°F) are comparable. Death Valley is drier, with 5.9 cm (2.33 in.) of precipitation, compared to 14 cm (5.5 in.) in Baghdad; however, both are low amounts.

Midlatitude Cold Desert Climates

Midlatitude cold desert climates cover only a small area: the countries along the southern border of Russia, the Taklamakan Desert, and Mongolia in Asia; the central third of Nevada and areas of the American Southwest, particularly at high elevations; and Patagonia in Argentina. Because of lower temperature and lower moisture-demand criteria, rainfall must be low—in the realm of 15 cm (6 in.)—for a station to qualify as a midlatitude cold desert climate.

A representative station is Albuquerque, New Mexico, with 20.7 cm (8.1 in.) of precipitation and an annual average temperature of 14°C (57.2°F) (**Figure 7.19**). Note the precipitation increase from summer convectional showers on the climograph. This characteristic expanse of midlatitude cold desert stretches across central Nevada, over the region of the Utah–Arizona border, and into northern New Mexico.

Tropical, Subtropical Hot Steppe Climates

Tropical, subtropical hot steppe climates generally exist around the periphery of hot deserts, where shifting subtropical high-pressure cells create variable rainfall throughout the year, with a distinct seasonal wet–dry pattern in some locations. Average annual precipitation in these climates is usually below 60 cm (23.6 in.). Walgett, in interior New South Wales, Australia, provides a Southern Hemisphere example (**Figure 7.20**). This climate is also seen around the Sahara's periphery, in Pakistan and parts of India, in Mexico and northeastern Brazil, and in southern Africa.

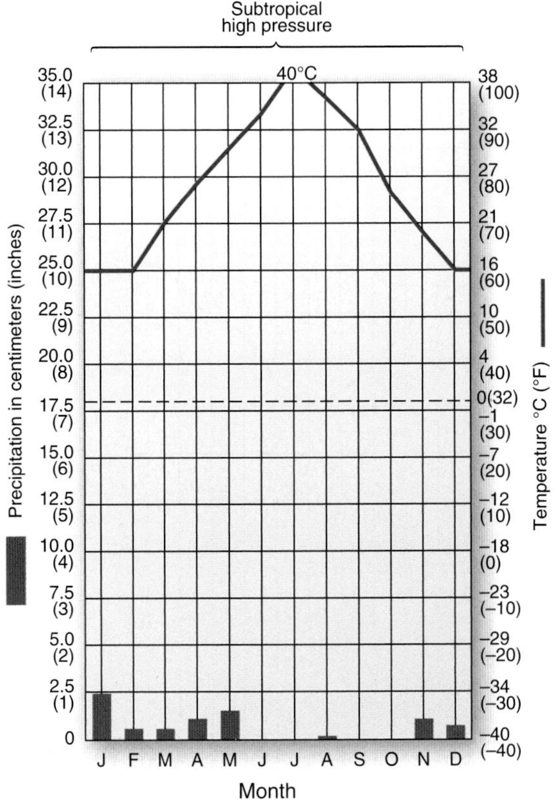

(a) Climograph for Riyadh, Saudi Arabia.

Station: Riyadh, Saudi Arabia
Lat/long: 24° 42′ N 46° 43′ E
Avg. Ann. Temp.: 26°C (78.8°F)
Total Ann. Precip.: 8.2 cm (3.2 in.)
Elevation: 609 m (1998 ft)
Population: 5,024,000
Ann. Temp. Range: 24 C° (43.2 F°)

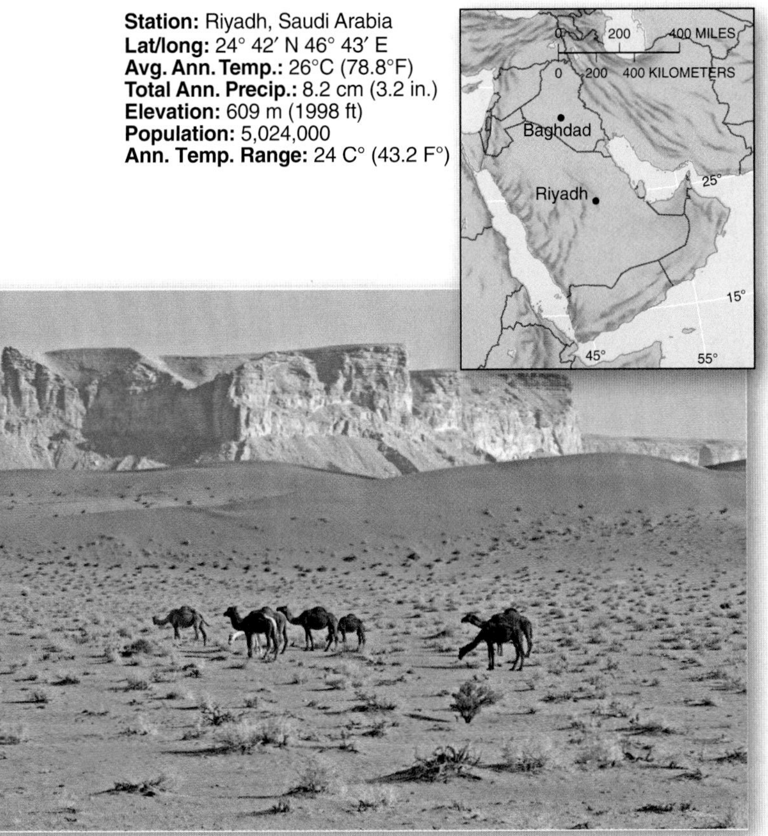

(b) The Arabian desert landscape of Red Sands near Riyadh.

▲**Figure 7.18 Tropical, subtropical hot desert climate.** [(b) Andreas Wolf/Panther Media/Age Fotostock.]

Midlatitude Cold Steppe Climates

The *midlatitude cold steppe* climates occur poleward of about 30° latitude and of the *midlatitude cold desert* climates. As with other dry climate regions, rainfall in the steppes is widely variable and undependable, ranging from 20 to 40 cm (7.9 to 15.7 in.). Not all rainfall is convectional, for cyclonic storm tracks penetrate the continents; however, most storms produce little precipitation. Midlatitude steppes occur in the Southern Hemisphere in the Patagonia region of South America and across southern Australia. In the Northern Hemisphere, the western Great Plains of North America have a midlatitude steppe climate. In Asia, cold steppe climates occur across portions of Kazakhstan, Russia, and Mongolia.

Figure 7.21 presents a comparison between Asian and North American midlatitude cold steppe climates. Semey, Kazakhstan, has more even precipitation throughout the year, with only a slight summer precipitation maximum. Lethbridge, Alberta, in the rain shadow of the Rocky Mountains, has summer-maximum convectional precipitation and is dry in winter. Note the differences in grassland characteristics, due in part to the timing of precipitation through the year, but also in part to soils and other ecological factors.

Climate Regions and Climate Change

The boundaries of climate regions are changing worldwide. The current expansion of tropical climates to higher latitudes means that subtropical high-pressure areas and dry conditions are also moving to higher latitudes. In addition, warming temperatures are making these areas more prone to drought. At the same time, storm systems are being pushed farther into the midlatitudes. In many cases, the evidence for shifting climate regions comes from changes in associated ecosystems—for example, the growth of trees in tundra climate regions or the expanding range of animals to higher latitudes or higher elevations on mountains. More discussion of ecosystems, ranges, and biomes is in Chapters 16 and 17.

CRITICAL**thinking** 7.2

Assessing Impacts as Climate Regions Shift

Recent studies suggest that climate zones are shifting at an accelerated rate as global temperatures rise. As frost areas decrease, deserts expand, and cool-summer climates become hot-summer climates, plants and animals are struggling to adapt or shift their range as climate region boundaries change. Survey the article "More global warming speeds climate shifts" at http://www.scientificamerican.com/article/more-global-warming-speeds-climate-shifts/. In the region where you live, what species or agricultural practices are at risk as climate zones shift? How will climate changes affect your daily life?

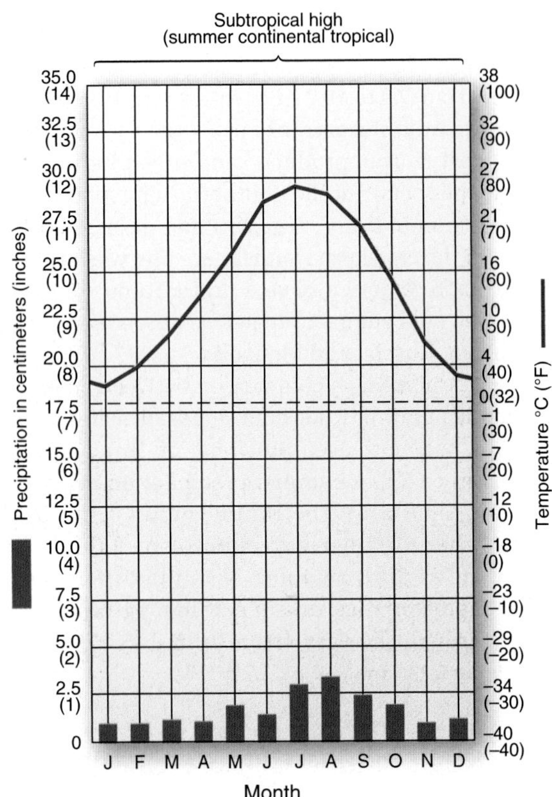

(a) Climograph for Albuquerque, New Mexico.

Station: Albuquerque, New Mexico
Lat/long: 35° 03′ N 106° 37′ W
Avg. Ann. Temp.: 14°C (57.2°F)
Total Ann. Precip.: 20.7 cm (8.1 in.)
Elevation: 1620 m (5315 ft)
Population: 522,000
Ann. Temp. Range: 24 C° (43.2 F°)
Ann. Hr of Sunshine: 3420

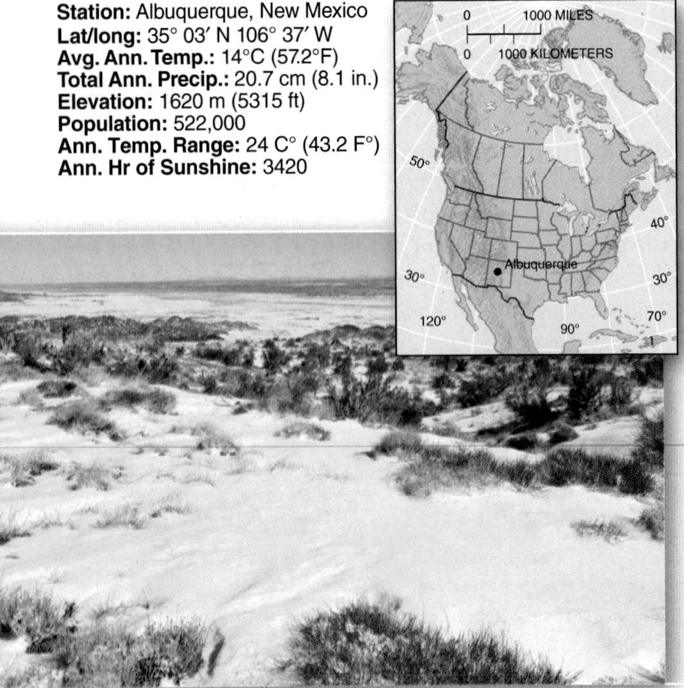

(b) A winter scene near the New Mexico–Arizona border.

▲Figure 7.19 Midlatitude cold desert climate. [(b) Bobbé Christopherson.]

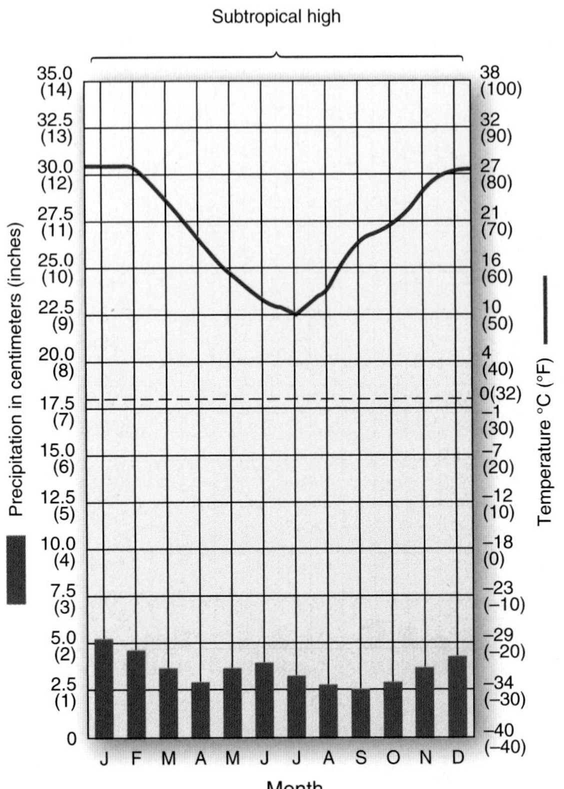

(a) Climograph for Walgett, New South Wales, Australia

Station: Walgett, New South Wales, Australia
Lat/long: 30° S 148° 07′ E
Avg. Ann. Temp.: 20°C (68°F)
Total Ann. Precip.: 45.0 cm (17.7 in.)
Elevation: 133 m (436 ft)
Population: 8200
Ann. Temp. Range: 17 C° (31 F°)

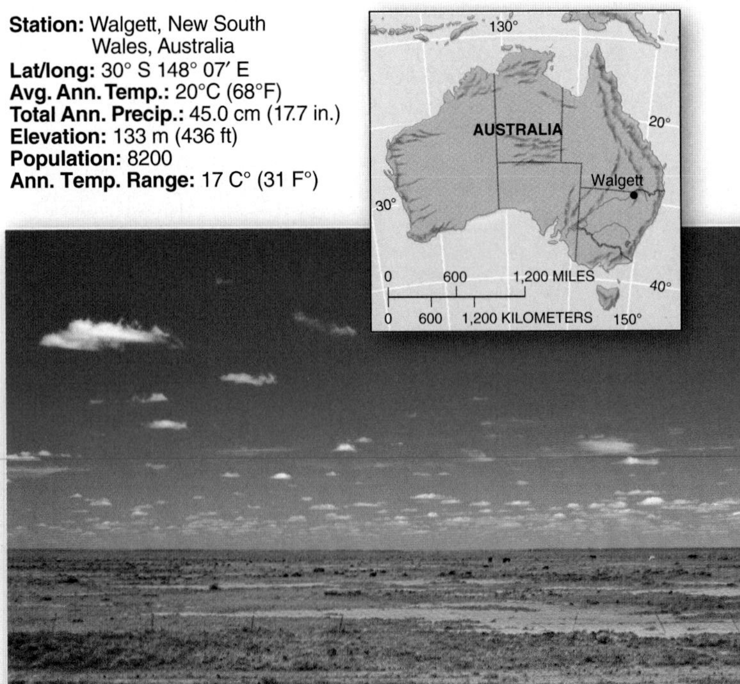

(b) Vast plains characteristic of north-central New South Wales.

▲Figure 7.20 Tropical, subtropical hot steppe climate. [(b) Prisma/SuperStock.]

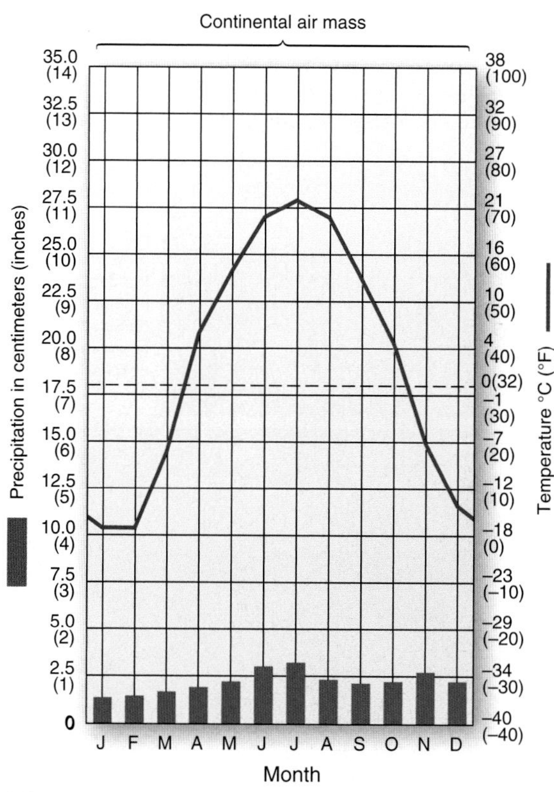

(a) Climograph for Semey (Semipalatinsk), Kazakhstan.

Station: Semey, Kazakhstan
Lat/long: 50° 21′ N 80° 15′ E
Avg. Ann. Temp.: 3°C (37.4°F)
Total Ann. Precip.: 26.4 cm (10.4 in.)
Elevation: 206 m (675.9 ft)
Population: 270,500
Ann. Temp. Range: 39 C° (70.2 F°)

(b) Summer on the cold steppe of eastern Kazakhstan.

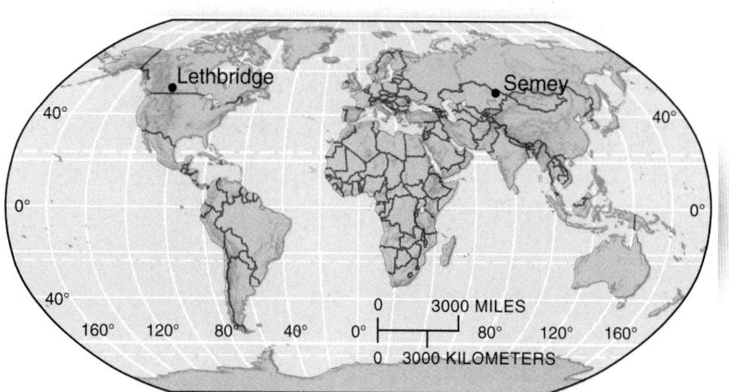

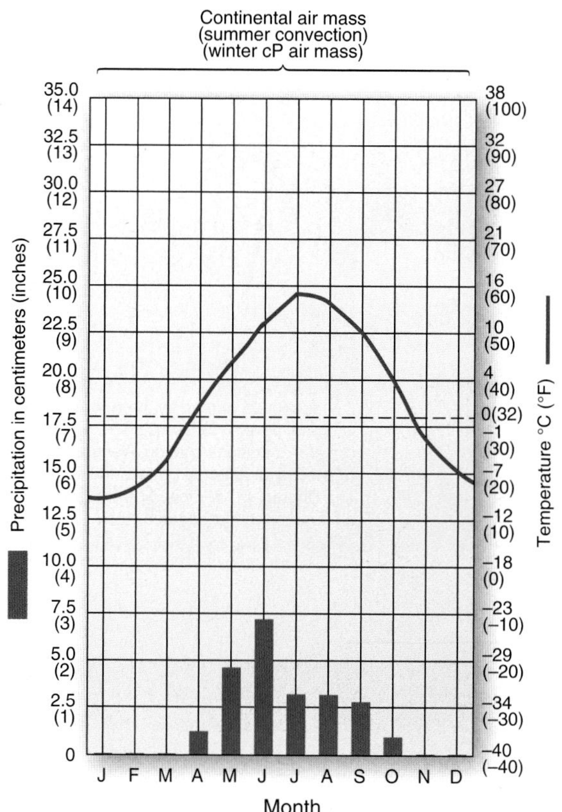

(c) Climograph for Lethbridge, Alberta.

Station: Lethbridge, Alberta
Lat/long: 49° 42′ N 110° 50′ W
Avg. Ann. Temp.: 2.9°C (37.3°F)
Total Ann. Precip.: 25.8 cm (10.2 in.)
Elevation: 910 m (2985 ft)
Population: 73,000
Ann. Temp. Range: 24.3 C° (43.7 F°)

(d) Summer landscape along the Milk River near Lethbridge.

▲**Figure 7.21 Midlatitude cold steppe climates, Kazakhstan and Canada.** [(b) Nadezhda Bolotina/Shutterstock. (d) Bill Brooks/Alamy.]

CLIMATES IMPACT HUMANS

• Climates affect many facets of human society, including agriculture, water availability, and natural hazards such as floods, droughts and heat waves.

7c A 2013 survey revealed that the area covered by polar climate types is shrinking as temperatures rise. In parts of Greenland, ice breakup has increased summer tourism, stimulating the economy, but has made hunting difficult for locals as animals shift their seasonal distributions.

HUMANS IMPACT CLIMATES

• Anthropogenic climate change is altering Earth systems that affect temperature and moisture, and therefore climate.

7a In the Eurasian Arctic tundra, 30 years of warming temperatures have allowed willow and alder shrubs to grow into small trees. This trend may lead to changes in regional albedo as trees darken the landscape and cause more sunlight to be absorbed.

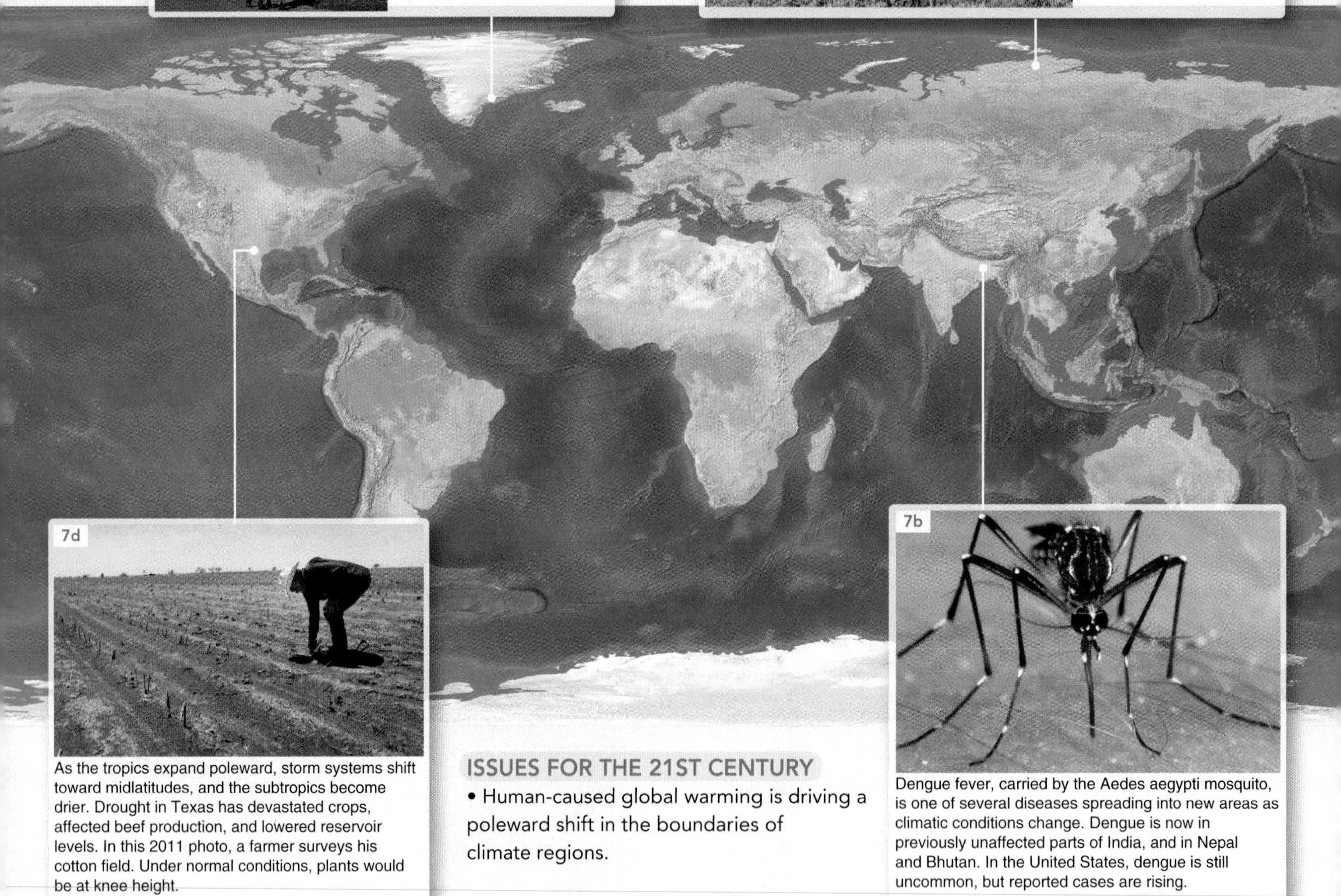

7d As the tropics expand poleward, storm systems shift toward midlatitudes, and the subtropics become drier. Drought in Texas has devastated crops, affected beef production, and lowered reservoir levels. In this 2011 photo, a farmer surveys his cotton field. Under normal conditions, plants would be at knee height.

ISSUES FOR THE 21ST CENTURY

• Human-caused global warming is driving a poleward shift in the boundaries of climate regions.

7b Dengue fever, carried by the Aedes aegypti mosquito, is one of several diseases spreading into new areas as climatic conditions change. Dengue is now in previously unaffected parts of India, and in Nepal and Bhutan. In the United States, dengue is still uncommon, but reported cases are rising.

KEYLEARNINGconceptsreview

Define climate and climatology and *review* the principal components of Earth's climate system.

Climate is a synthesis of weather phenomena at many scales, from planetary to local, in contrast to weather, which is the condition of the atmosphere at any given time and place. **Climatology** is the study of climate and attempts to discern similar weather statistics and identify **climatic regions**. The principal factors that influence climates on Earth include insolation, energy imbalances between the equator and the poles, temperature, air pressure, air masses, and atmospheric moisture (including humidity and precipitation).

climate (p. 218)
climatology (p. 218)
climatic region (p. 218)

1. Define climate, and compare it with weather.

Describe climate classification systems, *list* the main categories of world climates, and *locate* the regions characterized by each climate type on a world map.

Classification is the ordering or grouping of data or phenomena into categories. A **genetic classification** is one based on causative factors, such as the interaction of air masses. An **empirical classification** is one based on statistical data, such as temperature or precipitation. This text analyzes climate using aspects of both approaches. Temperature and precipitation data are measurable aspects of climate and are plotted on **climographs** to display the basic characteristics that determine climate regions.

World climates are grouped into six primary categories—five based mainly on temperature characteristics and one based on moisture efficiency and temperature characteristics:

- Tropical (tropical latitudes)
- Mesothermal (midlatitudes, mild winters)
- Microthermal (midlatitudes and high latitudes, cold winters)
- Polar (high latitudes and polar regions)
- Highland (high elevations at all latitudes)
- Dry (permanent moisture deficits)

classification (p. 218)
genetic classification (p. 218)
empirical classification (p. 218)
climograph (p. 219)

2. What are the differences between a genetic and an empirical classification system?
3. What are some of the climatological elements used in classifying climates? Why is each of these used? Use the approach on the climate classification map in Figure 7.2 in preparing your answer.
4. List and discuss each of the principal climate categories. In which one of these general types do you live? Which category is determined mainly by moisture efficiency?
5. What is a climograph, and how is it used to display climatic information?
6. Which of the major climate types occupies the most land and ocean area on Earth?
7. How do radiation receipts, temperature, air-pressure inputs, and precipitation patterns interact to produce climate types? Give examples from a humid environment and an arid environment.

Discuss the subcategories of the six world climate groups, including their causal factors.

Tropical climates include *tropical rain forest* (rainy all year), *tropical monsoon* (6 to 12 months rainy), and *tropical savanna* (less than 6 months rainy). The shifting ITCZ is a major causal factor for seasonal moisture in these climates. Mesothermal climates include *humid subtropical* (hot to warm summers), *marine west coast* (warm to cool summers), and *Mediterranean* (dry summers). These warm, temperate climates are humid, except where high pressure produces dry-summer conditions. Microthermal climates have cold winters, the severity of which depends on latitude; subcategories include *humid continental* (hot or mild summers) and *subarctic* (cool summers to very cold winters). Polar climates have no true summer and include *tundra* (high latitude or high elevation) and *ice-cap and ice-sheet* (perpetually frozen) climates. The dry climates are subdivided into *tropical, subtropical hot deserts; midlatitude cold deserts; tropical, subtropical hot steppes;* and *midlatitude cold steppes.*

8. Characterize the tropical climates in terms of temperature, moisture, and location.
9. Using Africa's tropical climates as an example, characterize the climates produced by the seasonal shifting of the ITCZ with the high Sun.
10. Mesothermal climates occupy the second largest portion of Earth's entire surface. Describe their temperature, moisture, and precipitation characteristics.
11. Explain the distribution of the humid subtropical hot-summer and Mediterranean dry-summer climates at similar latitudes and the difference in precipitation patterns between the two types.
12. Which climates are characteristic of the Asian monsoon region?
13. Explain how a marine west coast climate can occur in the Appalachian region of the eastern United States.
14. What role do offshore ocean currents play in the distribution of the marine west coast climates?
15. Discuss the climatic conditions for the coldest places on Earth outside the poles.

Explain the precipitation and moisture-efficiency criteria used to classify the arid and semiarid climates.

The dry climates of the tropics and midlatitudes consist of arid deserts, where precipitation (the natural water supply) is less than one-half of the natural water demand, and semiarid steppes, where precipitation, though insufficient, is more than one-half of the natural water demand. A **steppe** is a regional term referring to the vast semiarid grassland biome of eastern Europe and Asia.

steppe (p. 237)

16. How are moisture and temperature used to differentiate the four desert climate subtypes?
17. Describe the factors that contribute to the location of arid and semiarid climates in the western United States. What explains the presence of these climates in northern Africa?

MasteringGeography™

Looking for additional review and test prep materials? Visit the Study Area in *MasteringGeography*™ to enhance your geographic literacy, spatial reasoning skills, and understanding of this chapter's content by accessing a variety of resources, including MapMaster interactive maps, geoscience animations, videos, *In the News* RSS feeds, flashcards, web links, self-study quizzes, and an eText version of *Elemental Geosystems.*

8 Climate Change

A February 2014 storm caused large waves and flooding along the southern coast of England, near Newhaven. Ongoing research shows that the frequency of intense weather events is increasing with climate change. [Toby Melville/Reuters/Corbis.]

KEYLEARNINGconcepts

After reading the chapter, you should be able to:

- ***Describe*** scientific tools used to study paleoclimatology.
- ***Discuss*** several natural factors that influence Earth's climate and ***describe*** climate feedbacks, using examples.
- ***List*** the key lines of evidence for present global climate change and ***summarize*** the scientific evidence for anthropogenic forcing of climate.
- ***Discuss*** climate models and ***summarize*** some climate projections.
- ***Describe*** several mitigation measures to slow rates of climate change.

Greenhouse Gases Awaken in the Arctic

In the subarctic and tundra climate regions of the Northern Hemisphere, perennially frozen soils and sediment, known as permafrost, cover about 24% of the land area. With Arctic air temperatures currently rising at a rate more than two times that of the midlatitudes, ground temperatures are increasing, causing permafrost thaw. This results in changes to land surfaces, primarily sinking and slumping, that damage buildings, forests, and coastlines (**Figure GN 8.1**). Permafrost thaw also leads to the decay of soil material, a process that releases vast amounts of carbon—in the form of the greenhouse gases carbon dioxide (CO_2) and methane (CH_4)—into the atmosphere.

Carbon in Permafrost Soils Permafrost is, by definition, soil and sediment that remain frozen for two or more consecutive years. It lies under a thin "active layer," seasonally frozen ground that thaws every summer to provide substrate for seasonal grasses and other plants that absorb CO_2 from the atmosphere. In winter, the active layer freezes, trapping plant and animal material before it can decompose completely. Over hundreds of thousands of years, this carbon-rich material has become incorporated into permafrost and now makes up roughly half of all the organic matter stored in Earth's soils—twice the amount of carbon that is stored in the atmosphere. The latest estimate of the amount of carbon stored in Arctic permafrost soils is 1700 gigatonnes (or 1700 billion tons).

A Positive Feedback Loop As summers become warmer in the Arctic, heat radiating through the ground thaws the permafrost layers. Microbial activity in these layers increases, enhancing the breakdown of organic matter and releasing CO_2 into the atmosphere in a process known as *microbial respiration*. In anaerobic (oxygen-free) environments, such as lakes and wetlands, the process releases methane. Studies show that thousands of methane seeps can develop under a single lake, a huge amount when multiplied by hundreds of thousands of lakes across the northern latitudes (**Figure GN 8.2**).

Carbon dioxide and methane are major greenhouse gases, which absorb outgoing longwave radiation and radiate it back toward Earth, enhancing the greenhouse effect and leading to atmospheric warming. Methane is especially important because, although its relative percentage in the atmosphere is small, it is far more effective than CO_2 at trapping atmospheric heat. Thus, a positive feedback loop forms: As temperatures rise, permafrost thaws, causing a release of CO_2 and CH_4 into the atmosphere, which causes more warming, leading to more permafrost thaw.

Melting Ground Ice In addition to frozen soil and sediment, permafrost contains ground ice, which melts as the permafrost thaws. When the supporting structure provided by the ice is removed, land surfaces collapse and slump. Subsurface soils are then exposed to sunlight, which speeds up microbial processes, and to water erosion, which moves organic carbon into streams and lakes, where it is mobilized into the atmosphere. Research suggests that this process may release bursts of CO_2 and CH_4 into the atmosphere, in contrast to the slower top-down melting of permafrost.

Permafrost soils are now warming at a rate faster than Arctic air temperatures, releasing vast amounts of "ancient" carbon into the atmosphere. Scientists are actively researching the locations and amounts of vulnerable permafrost, the current and projected rates of thaw, and the potential impacts to the permafrost–carbon positive feedback. The thawing Arctic is one of many immediate concerns we discuss in this chapter regarding the causes and impacts of changing climate on Earth systems.

▲**Figure GN 8.2 Methane lies under Arctic lakebeds and, like natural gas, is highly flammable.** [Todd Paris/Fairbanks/University of Alaska/AP Images.]

▼**Figure GN 8.1 Blocks of melting permafrost collapse into the Beaufort Sea, Alaska.** [USGS Alaska Science Center.]

QUESTION AND EXPLORE To learn about NASA's *Carbon in Arctic Reservoirs Vulnerability Experiment (CARVE)*, which measures CO_2 and CH_4 gas emissions in permafrost regions, go to http://science1.nasa.gov/missions/carve/ (the mission website) or http://www.nasa.gov/topics/earth/features/earth20130610.html#.UhwYVj_pxXJ (mission background and early results). MG

Everything we have learned in *Elemental Geosystems* up to this point sets the stage for our exploration of **climate change science**—the interdisciplinary study of the causes and consequences of changing climate, affecting all Earth systems and the sustainability of human societies. Climate change is one of the most critical issues facing humankind in the 21st century and is today an integral part of physical geography and Earth systems science. Three key elements of climate change science are the study of past climates, the measurement of current climatic changes, and the modeling and projection of future climate scenarios—all of which are discussed in the chapter ahead. We revisit some of the principles of the scientific method as we explore global climate change, and by doing so, we address some of the confusion that complicates the public discussion of this topic.

Climate change is one of the most critical issues facing humankind in the 21st century and is today an integral part of physical geography and Earth systems science.

The physical evidence for recent global climate change is extensive and is observable by scientists and nonscientists alike—record-breaking global average temperatures for air, land surfaces, lakes, and oceans; ice losses from mountain glaciers and from the Greenland and Antarctic Ice Sheets; declining soil-moisture conditions and resultant effects on crop yields; increasing intensity of precipitation events; changing distributions of plants and animals; and the pervasive impact of global sea-level rise, which threatens coastal populations and development worldwide. These are only a fraction of the many complex and far-reaching issues that climate change science must address if we are to understand and mitigate the environmental changes ahead.

In this chapter: We examine techniques used to study past climates, including oxygen isotope analysis of sediment cores extracted from the ocean floor and ice cores extracted from glacial ice, carbon isotope analysis, and dating methods using tree rings, speleothems, and corals. We examine long-term climate trends and discuss mechanisms of natural climate fluctuation, including Milankovitch cycles, solar variability, tectonics, and atmospheric factors. We survey the evidence of accelerating climate change now under way as measured by record-high ocean, land, and atmospheric temperatures; melting glaciers and ice sheets and record losses of Arctic sea ice; accelerating rates of sea-level rise; and the occurrence of severe weather events. We then examine the human causes of contemporary climate change and the climate models that provide evidence and scenarios for future trends. The chapter concludes with a look at the path ahead and the actions that people can take now, on individual, national, and global levels.

Population Growth and Fossil-Fuel Burning—The Setting for Climate Change

As discussed in earlier chapters, carbon dioxide (CO_2) produced from human activities is amplifying Earth's natural greenhouse effect. It is released into the atmosphere naturally from outgassing (discussed in Chapter 6) and from microbial and plant respiration and decomposition on land and in the world's oceans (discussed further in Chapter 16). These natural sources have contributed to atmospheric CO_2 for over a billion years, unaffected by the presence of humans. In recent times, however, the growing human population on Earth has produced significant quantities of atmospheric CO_2. The primary **anthropogenic** source (caused by human activity) is the burning of fossil fuels (coal, oil, and natural gas), which has increased dramatically in the last few centuries and added to greenhouse gas concentrations. To illustrate the increase, **Figure 8.1** shows CO_2 levels for the last 800,000 years, including the steadily rising CO_2 trend since the Industrial Revolution began in the 1800s.

During the 20th century, Earth's human population increased from about 1.6 billion to about 6.1 billion

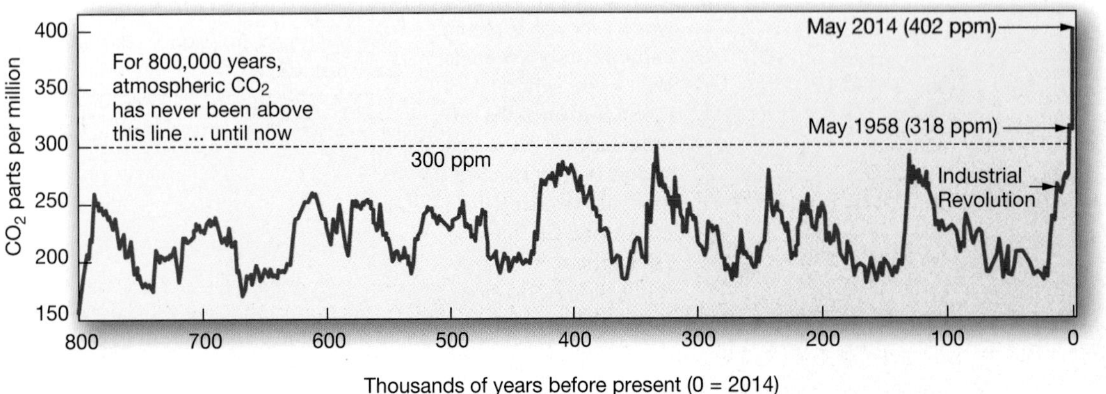

◄Figure 8.1 Carbon dioxide concentrations for the last 800,000 years. Data are from direct CO_2 measurements and from atmospheric samples preserved in ice cores. Note the rise in CO_2 over the past several hundred years since the Industrial Revolution. [NOAA.]

Animation Global Warming, Climate Change http://goo.gl/cTHCHK

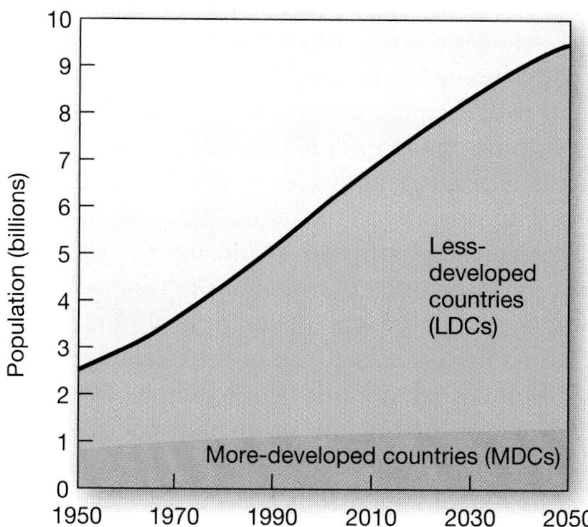

▲**Figure 8.2 Human population growth since 1950 and projected to 2050.** Since 1950, population has increased in LDCs far more than in MDCs, a trend that is expected to increase to 2050. [Reprinted by permission of the Population Reference Bureau from http://www.prb.org/pdf13/2013-population-data-sheet_eng.pdf.]

(review Chapter 1, Figure 1.4, and see **Figure 8.2** for more recent growth figures and projections). At the same time, CO_2 emissions increased by a factor of 10 or more. The burning of fossil fuels as an energy source has contributed to most of this increase, with secondary effects from the clearing and burning of land for development and agriculture. Notice in Figure 8.2 that the majority of population growth is now occurring in the less-developed countries (LDCs). Although the more-developed countries (MDCs) currently emit the greatest share of total greenhouse gases and lead in per capita emissions, this portion is changing. China and India, countries categorized as LDCs with rapidly developing economies, are emitting increasing amounts of CO_2. According to some projections, LDCs will contribute over 50% of global greenhouse gas emissions by 2050.

The rate of population growth increased dramatically after 1950 (see Figure 8.2), and this trend correlates with a dramatic rise in atmospheric CO_2 since that time. In 1953, Charles David Keeling of the Scripps Institute of Oceanography began collecting detailed measurements of atmospheric CO_2 in California. In 1958, he began CO_2 measurements in Hawai'i, producing what is considered by many scientists to be the single most important environmental data set of the 20th century. **Figure 8.3** shows the *Keeling Curve*, a graph of monthly average CO_2 concentrations from 1958 to 2014 as recorded at the Mauna Loa Observatory in Hawai'i.

The uneven line on the graph in Figure 8.3 shows fluctuations in CO_2 that occur throughout the year, with May and October usually being the highest and lowest months, respectively, for CO_2 readings. This annual fluctuation between spring and fall reflects seasonal changes in vegetation cover in the higher latitudes of the Northern Hemisphere. Vegetation is dormant during the Northern Hemisphere winter, allowing CO_2 to build up in

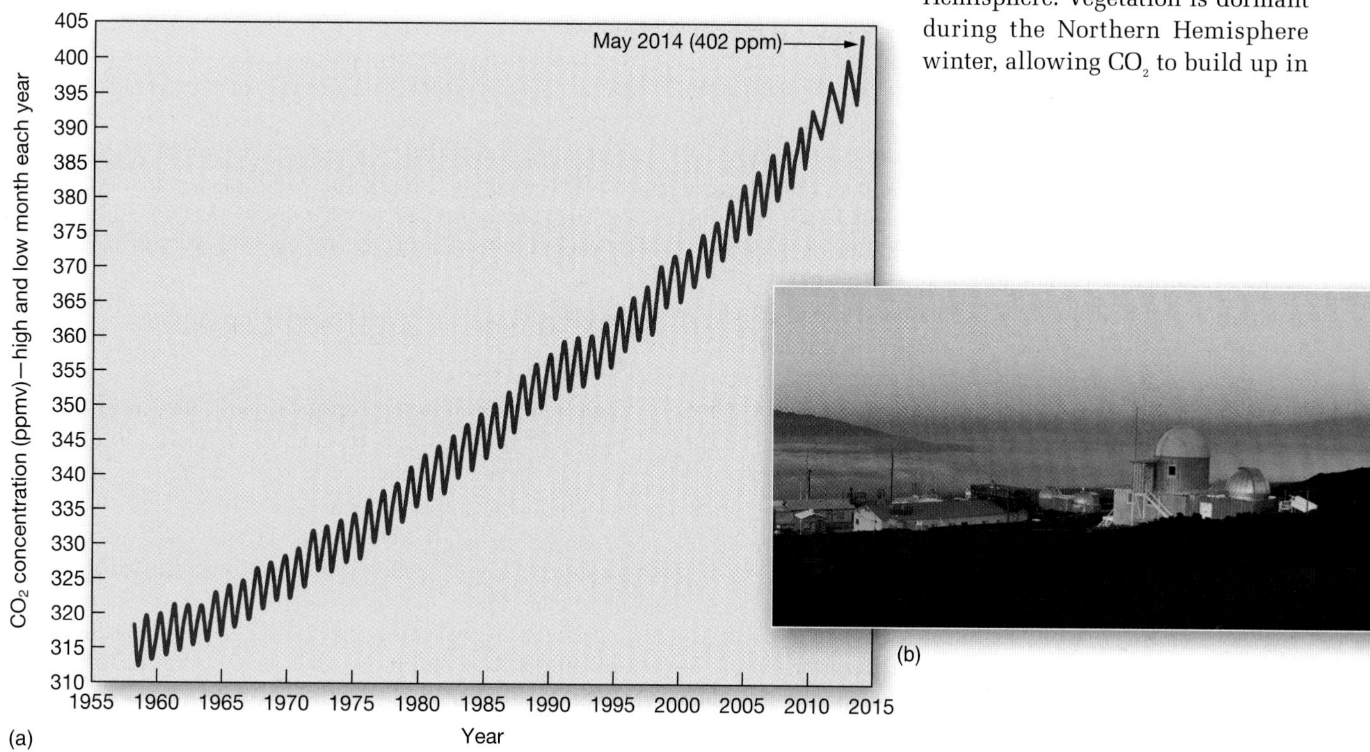

▲**Figure 8.3 The Keeling Curve and Mauna Loa Observatory.** (a) The graph represents 57 years of monthly average CO_2 concentrations measured at the Mauna Loa Observatory, Hawai'i. (b) Located on the north slope of Mauna Loa at 3397 m (11,141 ft) elevation, the station's remote setting minimizes pollution and the effects of vegetation and is above the atmospheric inversion layer, making air-quality data representative of global values. During May 2014, CO_2 concentrations set a new record of more than 402 ppm. [Data from NOAA posted at http://www.esrl.noaa.gov/gmd/ccgg/trends/. Photo: Jonathan Kingston/National Geographic/Getty Images.]

CRITICAL**thinking** 8.1

Crossing the 450-ppm Threshold for Carbon Dioxide

Using the accelerating trend in atmospheric CO_2 concentrations for the past 10 years, shown in Figure 8.3, calculate the year in which we might reach the 450-ppm threshold for atmospheric carbon dioxide. To help stabilize climate change effects, scientists think that we should implement policies to return the level of CO_2 to 350 ppm. By what annual percentage would we need to reduce atmospheric CO_2 concentrations to achieve that goal by 2020?

the atmosphere; in spring, when plant growth resumes, vegetation takes in CO_2 for photosynthesis (discussed in Chapter 16), causing a decline in atmospheric CO_2.

More important than these yearly CO_2 fluctuations, however, is the overall trend: From 1992 to 2012, atmospheric CO_2 increased over 16%. In May 2013, CO_2 concentrations crossed the 400-ppm threshold and by May 2014, reached 402 ppm—a level that is unprecedented during at least the last 800,000 years, and perhaps during the last 1.5 million years, as suggested by recent analyses. These data match records from hundreds of other stations across the globe. The interrelated increases in human population, fossil-fuel usage, and atmospheric CO_2 are the basic ingredients for understanding the causes of present-day climate change and mitigating its effects.

Deciphering Past Climates

To understand present climatic changes, we begin with a discussion of the climates of the past—specifically, how scientists reconstruct climates that occurred before human record-keeping began. Clues to past climates are stored in a variety of environments on Earth. Among these climatic indicators are fossil plankton in ocean-bottom sediments, gas bubbles in glacial ice, fossil pollen from ancient plants, and growth rings in trees, speleothems (mineral formations in caves), and corals. Scientists access these environmental indicators by extracting cores from deep within the various sources and then analyze the materials by various methods to determine age and climate-related characteristics. In this way, scientists can establish a chronology of environmental conditions over time periods of thousands or millions of years.

The study of Earth's past climates is the science of **paleoclimatology**, which tells us that Earth's climate has fluctuated over hundreds of millions of years. To learn about past climates, scientists use **proxy methods** instead of direct measurements. A *climate proxy* is a piece of information from the natural environment that can be used to reconstruct climates that extend back further than our present instrumentation allows. For example, the widths of tree rings indicate climatic conditions that occurred thousands of years before temperature record-keeping began. By analyzing evidence from proxy sources, scientists are able to reconstruct climate in ways not possible using the record of firsthand scientific measurements over the past 140 years or so.

The study of rocks and fossils has provided geologists with tools for understanding and reconstructing past climates over time spans on the order of millions of years (we discuss the geologic time scale and some of the methods for reconstructing past environments in Chapter 9). Geologists study past environments using techniques ranging from simple field observations of the characteristics and composition of rock deposits (for example, whether they are made up of dust, sand, or ancient coal deposits) to complex and costly laboratory analyses of rock samples (for example, mass spectrometry analyzes the chemical makeup of rock and other materials). Fossils of animal and plant material preserved within rock layers also provide important climate clues; for example, fossils of tropical plants indicate warmer climate conditions, and fossils of ocean-dwelling creatures indicate ancient marine environments. The beds of coal that we rely on today for energy were formed of organic matter from plants that grew in warm, wet tropical and temperate climate conditions about 325 million years ago.

Climate reconstructions spanning millions of years show that Earth's climate has cycled between periods that were colder and warmer than today. An extended period of cold (not a single brief cold spell), in some cases lasting several million years, is known as an *ice age*, or *glacial age*. An ice age is a time of generally cold climate that includes one or more *glacials* (glacial periods, characterized by glacial advance) interrupted by brief warm periods known as *interglacials*. The most recent ice age, known as the Pleistocene Epoch (discussed in Chapter 14), lasted from about 2.5 million years ago to about 11,700 years ago. The geologic time scale, which places the Pleistocene within the context of Earth's 4.6-billion-year history, is presented in Chapter 9, Figure 9.1, on page 285.

Methods for Long-Term Climate Reconstruction

Some paleoclimatic techniques yield long-term records that span hundreds of thousands to millions of years. Such records come from cores drilled into ocean-bottom sediments or into the thickest ice sheets on Earth. Once cores are extracted, layers containing fossils, air bubbles, particulates, and other materials provide information about past climates.

The basis for long-term climate reconstruction is **isotope analysis**, a technique that uses the atomic structure of chemical elements—specifically, the relative amounts of their isotopes—to identify the chemical composition of past oceans and ice masses. Using this knowledge, scientists can reconstruct temperature conditions. Remember that the nuclei of atoms of a given chemical element, such as oxygen, always contain the same number of protons, but can differ in the number of neutrons. Each number

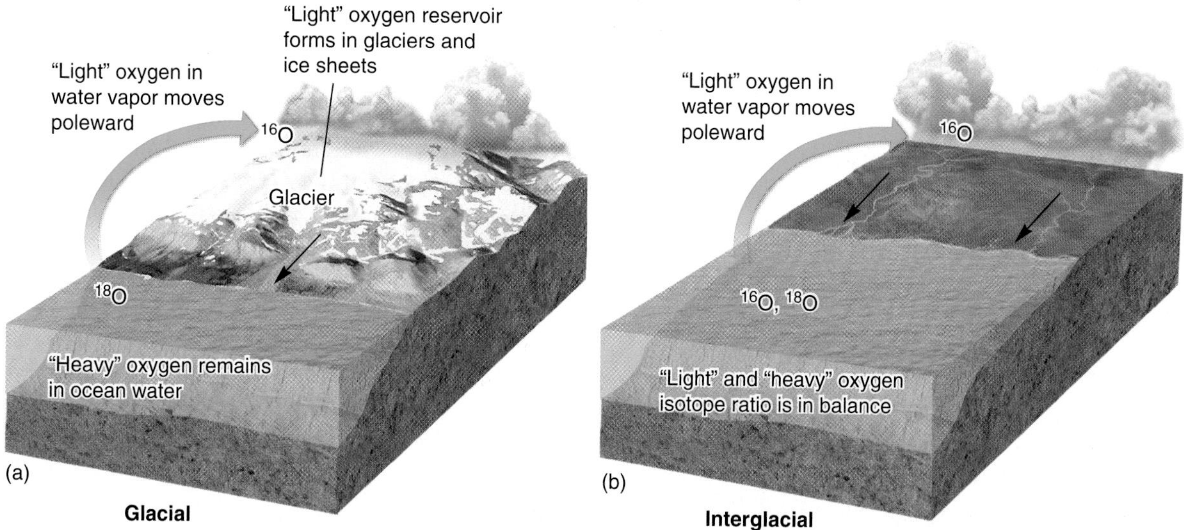

▲**Figure 8.4 Relative oceanic concentrations of ^{16}O and ^{18}O during (a) colder (glacial) and (b) warmer (interglacial) periods.** [Based on *Analysis of Vostok Ice Core Data*, Global Change, available at http://www.globalchange.umich.edu/globalchange1/current/labs/Lab10_Vostok/Vostok.htm.]

of neutrons found in the nucleus represents a different *isotope* of that element. Different isotopes have slightly different masses and therefore slightly different physical properties.

Oxygen Isotope Analysis Oxygen is an element with several isotopes. The most common isotope found in nature is oxygen-16, or ^{16}O ("light" oxygen), which makes up 99.76% of all oxygen atoms. Oxygen-18, or ^{18}O ("heavy" oxygen), comprises only about 0.20% of all oxygen atoms.

Both the ^{16}O and ^{18}O isotopes occur in water molecules. If the water contains "light" oxygen (^{16}O), it evaporates more easily. The opposite is true for water containing "heavy" oxygen (^{18}O), which evaporates less easily. These property differences affect where each of the isotopes is more likely to accumulate within Earth's vast water cycle. As a result, the relative amount, or *ratio*, of heavy to light oxygen isotopes ($^{18}O/^{16}O$) in water varies with climate—in particular, with temperature. Since ^{16}O evaporates more easily, over time the atmosphere becomes relatively rich in "light" oxygen. Eventually, this water vapor condenses and falls to the ground; at higher latitudes, it falls as snow, accumulating in glaciers and ice sheets. At the same time, the oceans become relatively rich in ^{18}O. During periods of colder temperatures, when "light" oxygen is locked up in snow and ice in the polar regions, "heavy" oxygen concentrations are highest in the oceans (**Figure 8.4a**). Thus, a higher ratio of $^{18}O/^{16}O$ in ocean water indicates a colder climate. During warmer periods, when snow and ice melt returns ^{16}O to the oceans, the concentration of ^{18}O in the oceans becomes relatively less—the isotope ratio is essentially in balance (**Figure 8.4b**).

Ocean Sediment Cores Oxygen isotopes are found not only in water molecules, but also in calcium carbonate ($CaCO_3$), the primary component of the exoskeletons, or shells, of marine microorganisms called *foraminifera*. These are some of the world's most abundant shelled marine organisms, living in a variety of environments from the equator to the poles. Upon the death of these organisms, their shells accumulate on the ocean bottom and build up in layers of sediment. By extracting a core of these ocean-floor sediments and comparing the ratio of oxygen isotopes in the $CaCO_3$ shells, scientists can determine the isotope ratio of seawater at the time the shells were formed. Foraminifera shells with a high $^{18}O/^{16}O$ ratio were formed during cold periods; those with low ratios were formed during warm periods. In an ocean sediment core, shells accumulate in layers that reflect these temperature conditions.

Specialized drilling ships have powerful rotary drills able to bore into ocean-bottom rock and sediment, extracting a cylinder of material—a *core sample*—within a hollow metal pipe. Such a core may contain dust, minerals, and fossils that have accumulated in layers over long periods of time on the ocean floor (**Figure 8.5a**). Over the past 50 years, the Integrated Ocean Drilling Program completed about 2000 cores in the ocean floor, yielding more than 35,000 samples for researchers (see http://www.oceandrilling.org/). The international program includes two drilling ships: the U.S. *JOIDES Resolution*, in operation since 1985 (**Figure 8.5b**), and Japan's *Chikyu*, operating since 2007. The *Chikyu* set a new record in 2012 for the deepest hole drilled into the ocean floor—2466 m (8090 ft)—and is capable of drilling 10,000 m (32,800 ft) below sea level and yielding undisturbed core samples. Recent improvements in both isotope analysis techniques and the quality of ocean core samples have led to improved resolution of climate records for the past 70 million years (see Figure 8.7).

Ice Cores In the cold regions of the world, snow accumulates seasonally in layers, and in regions where snow

(a) Core samples of ocean sediments are split open for analysis.

(b) The U.S. *JOIDES Resolution* drilling ship.

▲**Figure 8.5 Ocean-bottom core sample and ocean drilling ship.**
(a) International Ocean Discovery Program. (b) William Crawford/International Ocean Discovery Program.]

is permanent on the landscape, these layers of snow eventually form glacial ice (**Figure 8.6a**). The world's largest accumulations of glacial ice occur in Greenland and Antarctica. Scientists have extracted cores drilled thousands of meters deep into the thickest part of these ice sheets to reconstruct climate. These ice cores provide a climate record for the past 800,000 years, a shorter, but more detailed climatic record than in ocean sediment cores.

Extracted from areas where the ice is undisturbed, ice cores are about 13 cm (5 in.) in diameter and are composed of distinct layers of younger ice at the top and less-defined layering of older ice beneath (**Figure 8.6b**). At the bottom of the core, the oldest layers are deformed from the weight of ice above. In this part of the core, layers can be defined based on horizons of dust and volcanic ash that landed on the ice surface and mark specific time periods. For example, scientists can identify the layers of ash and smoke particulates correlated with the beginning of copper smelting during the Bronze Age—about 3000 B.C.

Within a core, any given year's accumulation consists of a layer of winter ice and a layer of summer ice, each differing in chemistry and texture. Scientists use oxygen isotope ratios to correlate these layers with environmental temperature conditions. However, oxygen isotope ratios in ice have a different relationship to climate than oxygen isotopes in ocean water.

In ice cores, a *lower* $^{18}O/^{16}O$ ratio (less "heavy" oxygen in the ice) suggests colder climates, with more ^{18}O tied up in the oceans and more light oxygen locked into glaciers and ice sheets. Conversely, a *higher* $^{18}O/^{16}O$ ratio (more "heavy" oxygen in the ice) indicates a warmer climate during which more ^{18}O evaporates and precipitates onto ice-sheet surfaces. Therefore, the oxygen isotopes in ice cores are a proxy for air temperature.

Ice cores also reveal information about past atmospheric composition. Within the ice layers, trapped air bubbles reveal concentrations of gases—mainly carbon dioxide and methane—indicative of environmental conditions at the time the bubbles were sealed into the ice (**Figure 8.6c**).

Several ice-core projects in Greenland have produced data spanning more than 250,000 years. In Antarctica, the Dome C ice core (part of the European Project for Ice Coring in Antarctica, or EPICA), completed in 2004, reached a depth of 3270 m (10,729 ft), producing the longest ice-core record at that time: 800,000 years of Earth's past climate history. This record was correlated with a core record of 400,000 years from the nearby Vostok Station and matched with ocean sediment core records to provide scientists with a well-substantiated reconstruction of climate changes throughout this time period. In 2011, American scientists extracted an ice core from the West Antarctic Ice Sheet (WAIS) that will reveal 30,000 years of annual climate history and 68,000 years at resolutions from annual to decadal—a higher time resolution than previous coring projects. (For more information, see the WAIS Divide Ice Core site at http://www.waisdivide.unh.edu/news/.)

Earth's Long-Term Climate History

Climatic reconstructions using fossils and deep-ocean sediment cores reveal long-term changes in Earth's climate, shown on two different time scales in **Figure 8.7**. Over the span of 70 million years, we see that Earth's climate was much warmer in the distant past, during which time tropical conditions extended to higher latitudes than today. Since the warmer times of about 50 million years ago, climate has generally cooled (Figure 8.7a).

A distinct short period of rapid warming occurred about 56 million years ago (known as the Paleocene–Eocene Thermal Maximum, or PETM; see the geologic time scale in Figure 9.1). Scientists think that this temperature maximum was caused by a sudden increase in atmospheric carbon, the cause of which is still uncertain. One prominent hypothesis is that a massive carbon release in the form of methane occurred from the melting of methane hydrates, ice-like chemical compounds—each composed of one methane molecule surrounded by a cage of water molecules—that are stable when frozen under conditions of cold temperature and high pressure. If some

(a) A scientist stands in a snowpit at the West Antarctic Ice Sheet, where layers of snow and ice revealing individual snowfall events are backlit by a neighboring snowpit.

(b) Scientists inspect an ice-core segment at Dome C. A quarter-section of each ice core is kept on site in case an accident occurs during transport to labs in Europe.

(c) Light shines through a thin section from the ice core, revealing air bubbles trapped within the ice that indicate the composition of past atmospheres.

◀**Figure 8.6 Ice-core analysis.** [(a) NASA LIMA. (b) and (c) British Antarctic Survey, http://www.antarctica.ac.uk.]

▼**Figure 8.7 Climate reconstructions using oxygen isotopes (^{18}O) over two timescales.** The vertical axis (y-axis) shows the change in ^{18}O parts per thousand, indicating warmer and colder periods (a) over the past 70 million years and (b) over the past 5 million years. Note the brief, distinct rise in temperature about 56 million years ago during the Paleocene–Eocene Thermal Maximum (PETM). The bottom graph shows alternating periods of warmer and colder temperatures within the 5-million-year time span. [After Edward Aguado and James Burt, *Understanding Weather and Climate*, 7th edition, © 2015 by Pearson Education, Inc. Reprinted and electronically reproduced by permission of Pearson Education, Inc., Upper Saddle River, New Jersey.]

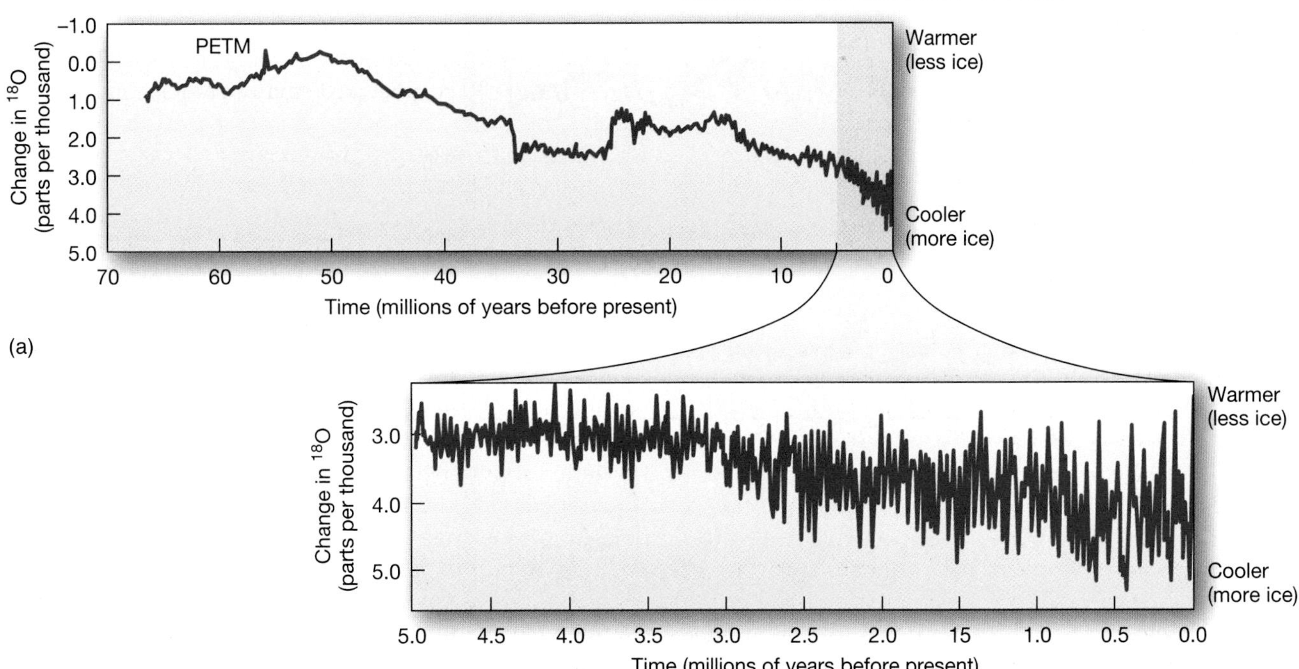

warming event (such as abrupt ocean warming from a sudden change in ocean circulation) caused large amounts of hydrates to melt, the release of large quantities of methane, a short-lived, but potent greenhouse gas, could drastically alter Earth's temperature. (Focus Study 14.1 in Chapter 14 discusses methane hydrates and their potential impacts on present-day warming.)

During the PETM, the rise in atmospheric carbon probably happened over a period of about 20,000 years or less—a "sudden" increase in terms of the vast scale of geologic time. Today's accelerating concentrations of atmospheric CO_2 are building at a more rapid pace. Scientists estimate that the amount of carbon that entered the atmosphere during the PETM is similar to the amount of carbon that human activity would release to the atmosphere with the burning of all Earth's fossil-fuel reserves.

Over the span of the last 5 million years, high-resolution climatic reconstructions using foraminifera from deep-ocean sediment cores reveal a series of cooler and warmer periods (Figure 8.7b). These periods are known as marine isotope stages (MIS), or oxygen isotope stages; many have been assigned numbers that correspond to a specific chronology of cold and warm periods during this time span. These ocean-core data are correlated with ice-core records, which show nearly identical trends.

As discussed earlier, ice cores also provide data on atmospheric composition—specifically, on concentrations of CO_2 and methane, as measured from air bubbles trapped in the ice. **Figure 8.8** shows the changing concentrations of those two greenhouse gases, as well as changing temperature, during the last 650,000 years. Note the close correlation between the two gas concentrations and between the gases and temperature on the graphs. Analyses have shown that the changes in greenhouse gas concentrations lag behind the temperature changes, generally by about 1000 years. This interesting relationship suggests the presence and importance of climate feedbacks, discussed later in the chapter and in Focus Study 8.1.

The last time temperatures were similar to the present-day interglacial period was during the Eemian interglacial about 125,000 years ago, during which time temperatures were warmer than at present (Figure 8.8, bottom graph). The cause for this warm period could relate to variations in solar output, although research is incomplete. Notably, atmospheric carbon dioxide during the Eemian was below 300 ppm, a lower level than expected and one that scientists interpret as resulting from the buffering effect of oceanic absorption of excessive atmospheric CO_2. (We discuss the movement of CO_2 within Earth's carbon budget later in the chapter.)

Methods for Short-Term Climate Reconstruction

Based on the paleoclimatic evidence just discussed, scientists know that Earth has undergone long-term climate cycles that have included conditions that were warmer and colder than today. Using a different set of indicators, they have also determined and verified climatic trends on shorter timescales, on the order of hundreds or thousands of years. The tools for short-term climate analysis consist mainly of radiocarbon dating and the analysis of growth rings of trees, speleothems, and corals.

Carbon Isotope Analysis Like oxygen, carbon is an element with several stable isotopes. Scientists use ^{12}C (carbon-12) and ^{13}C (carbon-13) to decipher past environmental conditions by

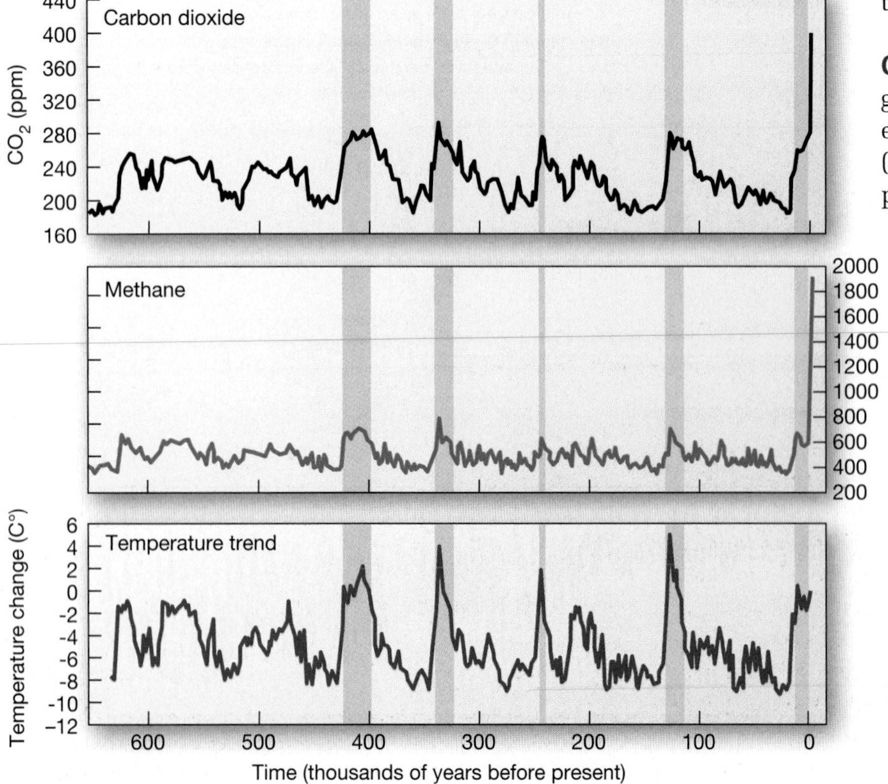

◄**Figure 8.8 The 650,000-year record for carbon dioxide (CO_2), methane (CH_4), and temperature from ice-core data and recent atmospheric measurements.** Temperature trends are based on deuterium concentrations in Antarctic ice-core data. The shaded bands are interglacials, periods of elevated temperature and greenhouse gas concentrations. Adapted from IPCC Fourth Assessment Report, *Climate Change 2007: The Physical Science Basis*, Working Group I, Figure TS-1; available at **http://www.ipcc.ch/publications_and_data/ar4/wg1/en/tssts-2-1-1.html.**]

analyzing the $^{13}C/^{12}C$ ratio in a manner similar to oxygen isotope analysis. In converting light energy from the Sun to food energy for growth, different plants use different types of photosynthesis, each of which produces a different carbon isotope ratio in the plant products. Thus, scientists can use the carbon isotope ratio of dead plant material to determine past vegetation assemblages and their associated rainfall and temperature conditions.

Up to this point, we have discussed "stable" isotopes of oxygen and carbon, in which protons and neutrons remain together in an atom's nucleus. However, certain isotopes are "unstable" because the number of neutrons compared to protons is large enough to cause the isotope to decay, or break down, into a different element. During this process, the nucleus emits radiation. This type of unstable isotope is a **radioactive isotope**.

Atmospheric carbon includes the unstable isotope ^{14}C (carbon-14). The additional neutrons compared to protons in this isotope cause it to decay into a different atom, ^{14}N (nitrogen-14). The rate of decay is constant and is measured as a *half-life*, or the time it takes for half of a sample to decay. The half-life of ^{14}C is 5730 years. This decay rate can be used to date plant material, a technique known as *radiocarbon dating*.

As an example, pollen is a plant material found in ice and lake sediments and is often dated using radiocarbon dating techniques. Since land plants use carbon from the air (specifically, carbon dioxide in photosynthesis), they contain ^{14}C in some amount, as does their pollen. As time passes, this radioactive carbon decays: After 5730 years, half of it will be gone, and, eventually, all of it will be gone. The amount of ^{14}C in the pollen can tell scientists how long ago it was alive. Radioactive isotopes are useful for dating organic material with ages up to about 50,000 years before the present.

Lake Cores The sediments at the bottom of glacial lakes provide a record of climate change extending back as far as 50,000 years. Annual layers of lake sediments, called *varves*, contain pollen, charcoal, and fossils that can be dated using carbon isotopes. The layers are drilled to produce lake sediment cores similar to deep-ocean and ice cores. Materials in the layers reflect variations in rainfall, rates of sediment accumulation, and algal growth, all of which can be used as a proxy for climate.

Tree Rings Most trees outside of the tropics add a growth ring of new wood beneath their bark each year. This ring is easily observed in a cross section of the tree trunk or in a core sample analyzed in a laboratory (**Figure 8.9**). A year's growth includes the formation of earlywood (usually lighter in color with large-diameter cells) and latewood (darker with small-diameter cells). The width of the growth ring indicates the climatic conditions: Wider rings suggest favorable growth conditions, and narrower rings suggest harsher conditions or stress to the tree (often related to moisture or temperature). If a tree-ring chronology can be established for a region, involving cross correlations among a number of trees, then this technique can be effective for assessing climatic conditions in the recent past. The dating of tree rings by these methods is *dendrochronology*; the study of past climates using tree rings is **dendroclimatology**.

To use tree rings as a climate proxy, dendroclimatologists compare tree-ring chronologies with local climate records. These correlations are then used to estimate relationships between tree growth and climate, which in some cases can yield a continuous record over hundreds or even thousands of years. Long-lived species are the most useful for dendroclimatological studies. For example, bristlecone pines in the western United States are some of the oldest organisms on Earth, reaching up to 5000 years in age. Evidence from tree rings in the U.S. Southwest is particularly important for assessing the magnitude of the present drought, as discussed for the Colorado River basin in Chapter 6, Focus Study 6.1.

Speleothems Limestone is a sedimentary rock that is easily dissolved by water (rocks and minerals are discussed in Chapter 9). Natural chemical processes at work on limestone surfaces often form caves and caverns, within which are calcium carbonate ($CaCO_3$) mineral deposits called **speleothems** that take thousands of years to form. Speleothems include *stalactites*, which grow downward from a cave roof, and *stalagmites*, which grow upward from the cave floor. Speleothems form as water drips or seeps from the rock and subsequently evaporates, leaving behind a residue of $CaCO_3$ that builds up over time (**Figure 8.10**).

The rate of growth of speleothems depends on several environmental factors, including the amount of

Wider rings indicate good growing conditions
Narrower rings indicate harsh growing conditions

▲**Figure 8.9 Tree rings in trunk cross section.** Trees generally add one growth ring each year. The size and character of annual growth rings indicate growing conditions. [Dietrich Rose/The Image Bank/Getty Images.]

rainwater percolating through the rocks that form the cave, its acidity, and the temperature and humidity conditions in the cave. Like trees, speleothems have growth rings whose size and properties reflect the environmental conditions present when they formed and that can be dated using uranium isotopes. These growth rings also contain isotopes of oxygen and carbon, whose ratios indicate temperature and the amount of rainfall.

Scientists have correlated speleothem ring chronologies with temperature patterns in New Zealand and Russia (especially in Siberia) and with temperature and precipitation in the U.S. Southwest, among many other places. Some speleothem chronologies date to 350,000 years ago and are often combined with other paleoclimatic data to corroborate evidence of climate change.

Corals Corals are marine invertebrates with a body called a *polyp* that extracts calcium carbonate from seawater and then excretes it to form a calcium carbonate exoskeleton (like the shells found in ocean sediment cores). These skeletons accumulate over time in warm, tropical oceans, forming coral reefs (see the discussion in Chapter 13). X-rays of core samples extracted from coral reefs reveal seasonal growth bands similar to those of trees, yielding information as to the water chemistry at the time the exoskeletons were formed (**Figure 8.11**). Climatic data covering hundreds of years can be obtained this way. Although the process damages polyps living at the surface of the drill site, it does not damage the reef, and drill holes are recolonized by polyps within a few years.

Earth's Short-Term Climate History

The Pleistocene Epoch, Earth's most recent period of repeated glaciations, began 2.5 million years ago. The last glacial period lasted from about 110,000 years ago to about 11,700 years ago, with the *last glacial maximum* (LGM), the time when ice extent in the last glacial period was greatest, occurring about 20,000 years ago. Chapter 14 discusses changes to Earth's landscapes during this time, and Figure 14.25 shows the extent of glaciation during this prolonged cold period. The climate record for the past 20,000 years reveals the period of cold temperatures and little snow accumulation that occurred from the LGM to about 15,000 years ago (**Figure 8.12**).

About 14,000 years ago, average temperatures abruptly increased for several thousand years and then dropped again during the colder period known as the *Younger Dryas*. The abrupt warming about 11,700 years ago marked the end of the Pleistocene Epoch. Note in Figure 8.12 that snow accumulation is less during colder glacial periods. As we learned in Chapter 5, the capacity of cold air to absorb water vapor is less than that of warm air, resulting in decreased snowfall during glacial periods even though a greater volume of ice is present over Earth's surface.

From A.D. 800 to 1200, a number of climate proxies (tree rings, corals, and ice cores) show a mild climatic

▼**Figure 8.10 Speleothems in a cavern and in cross section.** [(a) Chris Howes/Wild Places Photography/Alamy. (b) Pauline Treble/Australian Nuclear Science and Technology Organisation.]

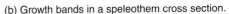

(a) Speloethems in Royal Cave Buchanan, Victoria, Australia.

(b) Growth bands in a speleothem cross section.

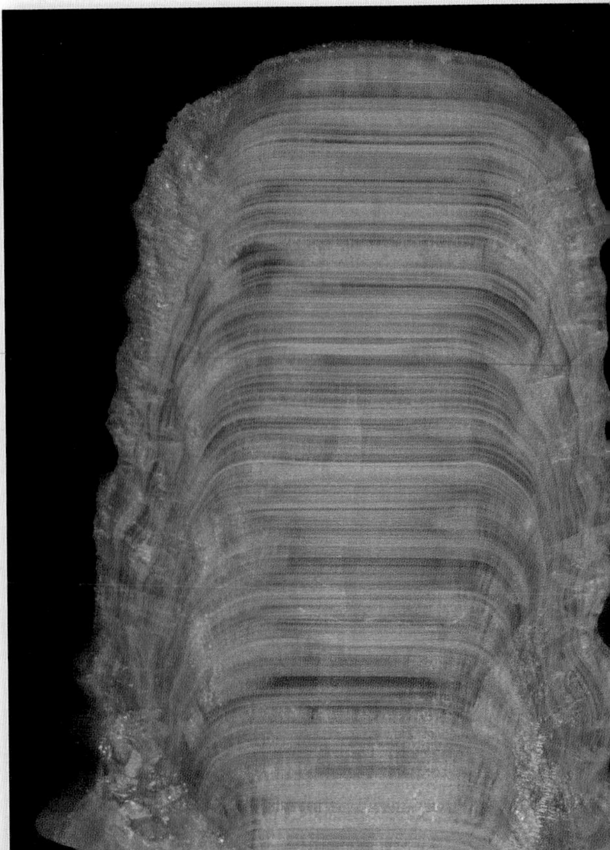

(a) A scientist drills into a coral head in Dry Tortugas National Park, located 112 km (70 mi) west of Key West in the Florida Keys archipelago.

(b) X-ray of core cross section shows banding; each light/dark band indicates one year of growth.

◄**Figure 8.11 Extraction and cross section of coral core samples.** [(a) Hickey, D., Reich, C.D., DeLong, K.L., Poore, R.Z., Brock, J.C., 2013. Holocene core logs and site methods for modern reef and head-coral cores: Dry Tortugas National Park, Florida. Dept. of the Interior, U.S. Geological Survey, Washington DC., p. 27. (b) Thomas Felis, Research Center Ocean Margins, Bremen/NASA.]

episode, now known as the *Medieval Climate Anomaly* (a period during which the Vikings settled Iceland and coastal areas of Greenland). During this time, warmer temperatures—as warm as or warmer than today—occurred in some regions, whereas cooling occurred in other regions. The warmth over the North Atlantic region allowed a variety of crops to grow at higher latitudes in Europe, shifting settlement patterns northward. Scientists think that the cooling in some places during this time is linked to the cool La Niña phase of the El Niño–Southern Oscillation (ENSO) phenomenon over the tropical Pacific.

From approximately A.D. 1250 through about 1850, temperatures cooled globally during a period known as the *Little Ice Age*. Winter ice was more extensive in the North Atlantic Ocean, and expanding glaciers in western Europe blocked many key mountain passes. During the coldest years, snowlines in Europe lowered about 200 m (650 ft) in elevation. This was a 600-year span of somewhat inconsistent colder temperatures, a period that included many rapid, short-term climate fluctuations that lasted only decades and are probably related to volcanic activity and multiyear oscillations in global circulation patterns—specifically, the North Atlantic Oscillation (NAO) and Arctic Oscillation (AO) (see the discussion in Chapter 4). After the Little Ice Age, temperatures steadily warmed, and with growing human population and the onset of the Industrial Revolution, this warming has continued—a trend that is accelerating today.

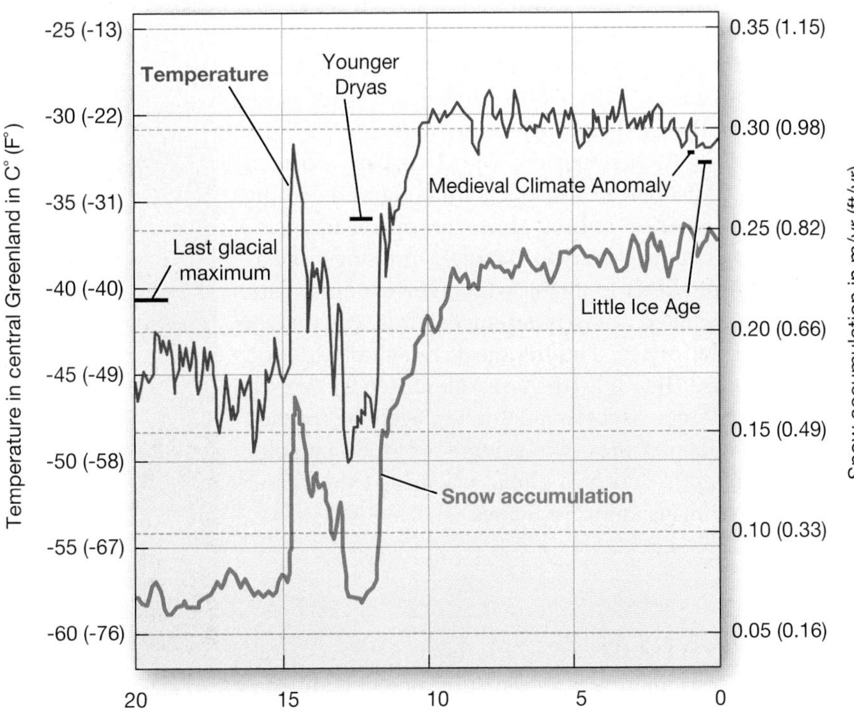

►**Figure 8.12 The past 20,000 years of temperature and snow accumulation.** Evidence from Greenland ice cores shows periods of colder temperatures occurring during the last glacial maximum and the Younger Dryas and an abrupt temperature rise occurring about 14,000 years ago and again about 12,000 years ago at the end of the Younger Dryas. Although this graph uses ice-core data, these temperature trends correlate with other climate proxy records. [From R. B. Alley, "The Younger Dryas Cold Interval as Viewed from Central Greenland," *Quaternary Science Reviews* 19 (January 2000): 213–226; available at http://www.ncdc.noaa.gov/paleo/pubs/alley2000/alley2000.html.]

Mechanisms of Natural Climate Fluctuation

In reviewing climate records on various scales, we see that Earth's climate cycles between warmer and colder periods. When temperature is viewed over certain timescales, such as over periods of about 650,000 years (illustrated in Figure 8.8), patterns are apparent that appear to follow cycles of about 100,000 years, 40,000 years, and 20,000 years. Scientists have evaluated a number of natural mechanisms that affect Earth's climate and might cause these long-term cyclical climate variations.

Solar Variability

As we learned in earlier chapters, energy from the Sun is the most important driver of the Earth–atmosphere climate system. The Sun's output of energy toward Earth, known as *solar irradiance*, varies over several timescales, and these natural variations can affect climate. Over billions of years, solar output has generally increased; overall, it has increased by about one-third since the formation of the solar system. Within this time frame, variations on the scale of thousands of years are linked to changes in the solar magnetic field. Over recent decades, scientists have measured slight variations in the amount of radiation received at the top of the atmosphere using satellite data and have correlated these variations to sunspot activity.

As discussed in Chapter 2, the number of sunspots varies over an 11-year solar cycle. When sunspot abundance is high, solar activity and output increase; when sunspot abundance is low, solar output decreases. Scientists have determined that these relationships are reflected in climatic indicators such as temperature. For example, the record of sunspot occurrences shows a prolonged solar minimum (a period with little sunspot activity) from about 1645 to 1715, during one of the coldest periods of the Little Ice Age. Known as the *Maunder Minimum*, this 70-year period would suggest a causal effect between decreased sunspot abundance and cooling in the North Atlantic region. However, recent temperature increases have occurred during a prolonged solar minimum (from 2005 to 2010), which corresponds with a period of reduced solar irradiance. Thus, the causal effect is not definitive. The Intergovernmental Panel on Climate Change (IPCC) Fifth Assessment Report considers solar irradiance as a climate forcing agent (discussed later in the chapter); however, scientists agree that solar irradiance is not a driver of global warming trends over the past 50 years (as an example, see http://www.giss.nasa.gov/research/news/20120130b/).

Earth's Orbital Cycles

Earth–Sun relationships affect energy receipts and seasonality on Earth and are another possible factor in climate change. These relationships include Earth's distance from the Sun, which varies within its orbital path, and Earth's orientation to the Sun, which varies as a result of the "wobble" of Earth on its axis and Earth's varying axial tilt (review Chapter 2, where we discussed Earth–Sun relations and the seasons).

Milutin Milankovitch (1879–1958), a Serbian astronomer, studied the irregularities in Earth's orbit around the Sun, its rotation on its axis, and its axial tilt and identified regular cycles that relate to climatic patterns (**Figure 8.13**).

- Earth's elliptical orbit about the Sun, known as *orbital eccentricity*, is not constant and changes in cycles over several timescales. The most prominent is a 100,000-year cycle in which the shape of the ellipse varies by more than 17.7 million kilometers (11 million miles), from a shape that is nearly circular to one that is more elliptical (Figure 8.13a).
- Earth's axis "wobbles" through a 26,000-year cycle, in a movement much like that of a spinning top winding down (Figure 8.13b). Earth's wobble, known as *precession*, changes the orientation of hemispheres and landmasses to the Sun.
- Earth's axial tilt, known to astronomers as *obliquity*, at present about 23.5°, varies from 21.5° to 24.5° during a 41,000-year period (Figure 8.13c).

Although many of Milankovitch's ideas were rejected by the scientific community at the time, these consistent orbital cycles, now called **Milankovitch cycles**, are today accepted as influencing Earth's climate system, though their role is still being investigated. Scientific evidence in ice cores from Greenland and Antarctica and in the

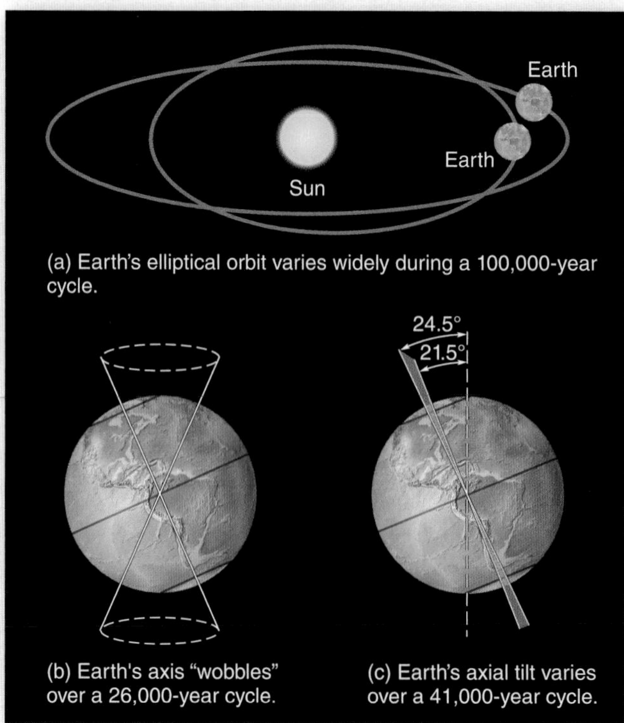

Earth
Earth
Sun
(a) Earth's elliptical orbit varies widely during a 100,000-year cycle.
24.5°
21.5°
(b) Earth's axis "wobbles" over a 26,000-year cycle.
(c) Earth's axial tilt varies over a 41,000-year cycle.

▲**Figure 8.13 Astronomical factors that may affect broad climatic cycles.** Drawings are an exaggeration of actual orbital paths, axis wobble, and axial tilt.

accumulated sediments of Lake Baikal in Russia has confirmed a roughly 100,000-year climatic cycle; other evidence supports the effect of shorter-term cycles of roughly 40,000 and 20,000 years on climate. Milankovitch cycles appear to be an important cause of glacial–interglacial cycles, although other factors probably amplify the effects (such as changes in the North Atlantic Ocean, albedo effects from gains or losses of Arctic sea ice, and variations in greenhouse gas concentrations, discussed just ahead).

Continental Position and Topography

In Chapter 9 and 10, we discuss plate tectonics and the movement of the continents over the past 400 million years. Because Earth's lithosphere is composed of moving plates, continental rearrangement has occurred throughout geologic history (look ahead to Figure 9.11). This movement affects climate, since landmasses have strong effects on the general circulation of the atmosphere. As discussed in previous chapters, the relative proportions of land and ocean area affect surface albedo, as does the position of landmasses relative to the poles or equator. The position of the continents also impacts ocean currents, which are critical for redistributing heat throughout the world's oceans. Finally, the movement of continental plates causes episodes of mountain building and spreading of the seafloor, discussed in Chapter 10. These processes affect Earth's climate system as high-elevation mountain ranges accumulate snow and ice during glacial periods (thus affecting Earth's albedo) and as CO_2 from outgassing enters the atmosphere (from volcanoes) and the oceans (from spreading of the seafloor).

Atmospheric Gases and Aerosols

Natural processes can release gases and aerosols into Earth's atmosphere with varying impacts on climate. Natural outgassing from Earth's interior through volcanoes and vents in the ocean floor is the primary natural source of CO_2 emissions to the atmosphere. Water vapor is a natural greenhouse gas present in Earth's atmosphere, discussed in Focus Study 8.1 with regard to climate feedbacks. Over long time scales, higher levels of greenhouse gases generally correlate with warmer interglacials, and lower levels correlate with colder glacials. As greenhouse gas concentrations change, Earth's surface heats or cools in response. Scientists now know that these gases can cause feedback loops that amplify the climatic trends, discussed in Focus Study 8.1. In cases where huge amounts of greenhouse gases are released into the atmosphere, such as may have happened during the PETM 56 million years ago, these gases can potentially drive climatic change.

In addition to outgassing, volcanic eruptions produce aerosols that scientists have definitively linked to climatic cooling. Accumulations of aerosols ejected into the stratosphere can create a layer of particulates that increases albedo, so that more insolation is reflected and less solar energy reaches Earth's surface. Studies of 20th-century eruptions have shown that sulfur aerosol accumulations affect temperatures on timescales of months to years. For example, the aerosol cloud from the 1982 El Chichón eruption in Mexico lowered temperatures worldwide for several months, and the 1991 Mount Pinatubo eruption lowered temperatures for 2 years (discussed in Chapter 1, Geosystems in Action 1, and Chapter 4, Figure 4.1; also see Figure 8.15 ahead). Scientific evidence also suggests that a series of large volcanic eruptions may have initiated the colder temperatures of the Little Ice Age in the second half of the 13th century.

Climate Feedbacks and the Carbon Budget

Earth's climate system is subject to a number of feedback mechanisms. As discussed in Chapter 1, systems can produce outputs that sometimes influence their own operations via positive or negative feedback loops. Positive feedback amplifies system changes and tends to destabilize the system; negative feedback inhibits system changes and tends to stabilize the system. **Climate feedbacks** are processes that either amplify or reduce climatic trends, toward either warming or cooling.

The Ice–Albedo Feedback

A good example of a positive climate feedback is the *ice–albedo feedback* introduced in Chapter 1 (see Figure 1.7) and discussed in the Chapter 3 Geosystems Now. This feedback is accelerating the current climatic trend toward global warming. However, ice–albedo feedback can also amplify global cooling because lower temperatures lead to more snow and ice cover, which increases albedo, or reflectivity, and causes less sunlight to be absorbed by Earth's surface. Scientists think that the ice–albedo feedback may have amplified global cooling following the volcanic eruptions at the start of the Little Ice Age. As atmospheric aerosols increased and temperatures decreased, more ice formed, further increasing albedo, leading to further cooling and more ice formation. These conditions persisted until the onset of the Industrial Revolution in the 1800s, which led to an influx of anthropogenic greenhouse gases into the atmosphere and an associated global warming trend.

Focus Study 8.1 discusses climate feedbacks, including the permafrost–carbon feedback first introduced in this chapter's Geosystems Now.

Earth's Carbon Budget

Many climate feedbacks involve the movement of carbon through Earth systems and the balance of carbon over time within these systems. The carbon on Earth cycles through atmospheric, oceanic, terrestrial, and living systems

(*text continued on page 260*)

Several processes transfer carbon between the atmosphere, hydrosphere, lithosphere, and biosphere. (GIA 8.1). Over time, the distribution of carbon among the spheres—Earth's carbon budget—has remained roughly in balance. Today, human activities, primarily the burning of fossil fuels (GIA 8.2) and the removal of forests, are increasing the atmospheric concentration of carbon dioxide, altering the carbon budget and affecting Earth's climate.

8.1 Components of Carbon Budget

Numbers are in Gt (gigatonnes, or billions of tons) of carbon per year. White numbers represent natural carbon flows; white boxes indicate carbon sinks, or areas of carbon storage. Red numbers indicate changes in carbon exchange after the onset of the Industrial Era (about 1750).

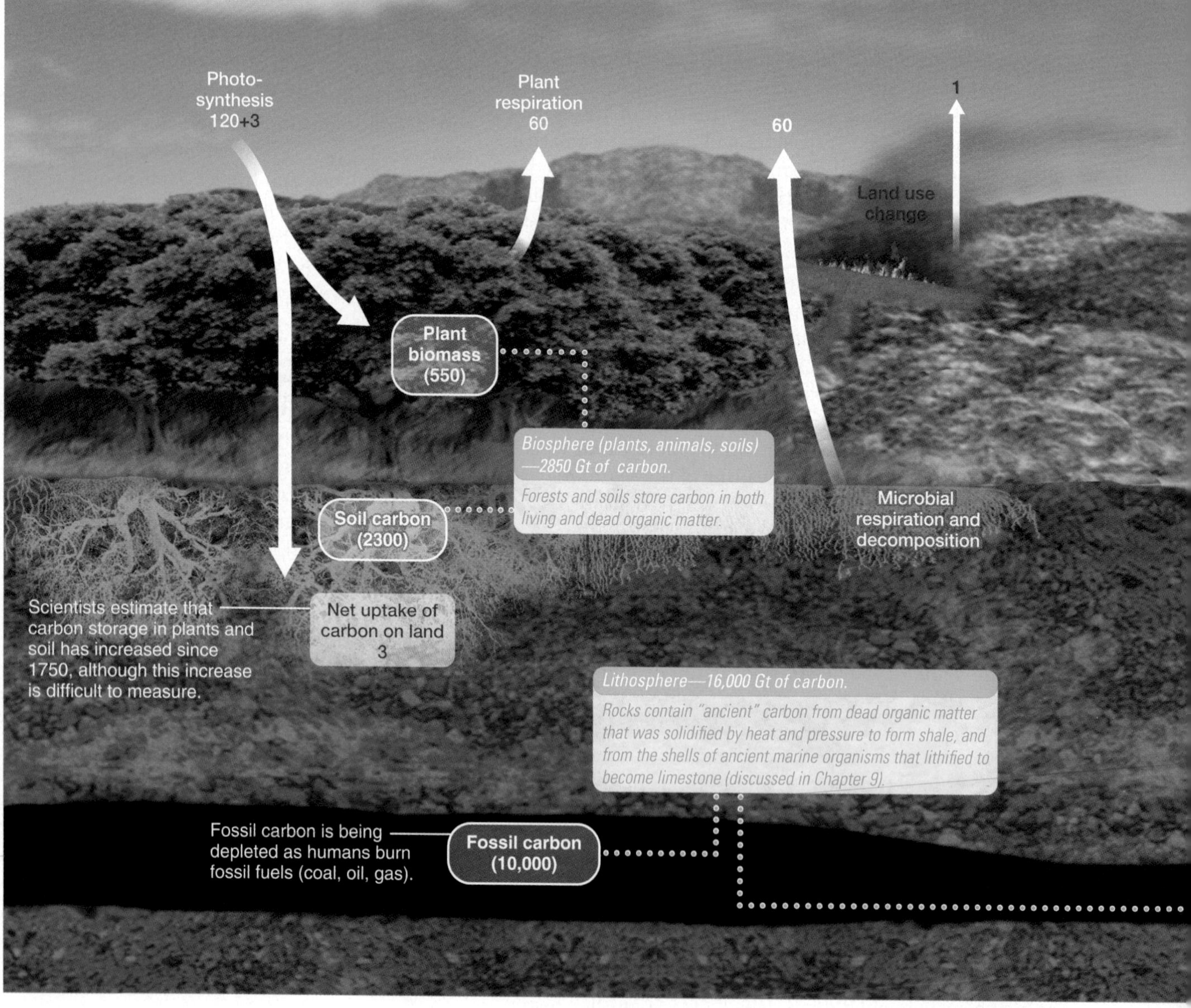

Photo-synthesis 120+3

Plant respiration 60

60

1

Land use change

Plant biomass (550)

Biosphere (plants, animals, soils)—2850 Gt of carbon.

Forests and soils store carbon in both living and dead organic matter.

Soil carbon (2300)

Microbial respiration and decomposition

Scientists estimate that carbon storage in plants and soil has increased since 1750, although this increase is difficult to measure.

Net uptake of carbon on land 3

Lithosphere—16,000 Gt of carbon.

Rocks contain "ancient" carbon from dead organic matter that was solidified by heat and pressure to form shale, and from the shells of ancient marine organisms that lithified to become limestone (discussed in Chapter 9).

Fossil carbon is being depleted as humans burn fossil fuels (coal, oil, gas).

Fossil carbon (10,000)

Video MG Keeping up with Carbon

http://goo.gl/IpQCPX

MasteringGeography™

Visit the Study Area in MasteringGeography™ to explore the carbon budget.

Visualize: Study videos of the carbon cycle and climate modeling.

Assess: Demonstrate understanding of the carbon budget (if assigned by instructor).

Video MG Taking Earth's Temperature

http://goo.gl/qCy4ev

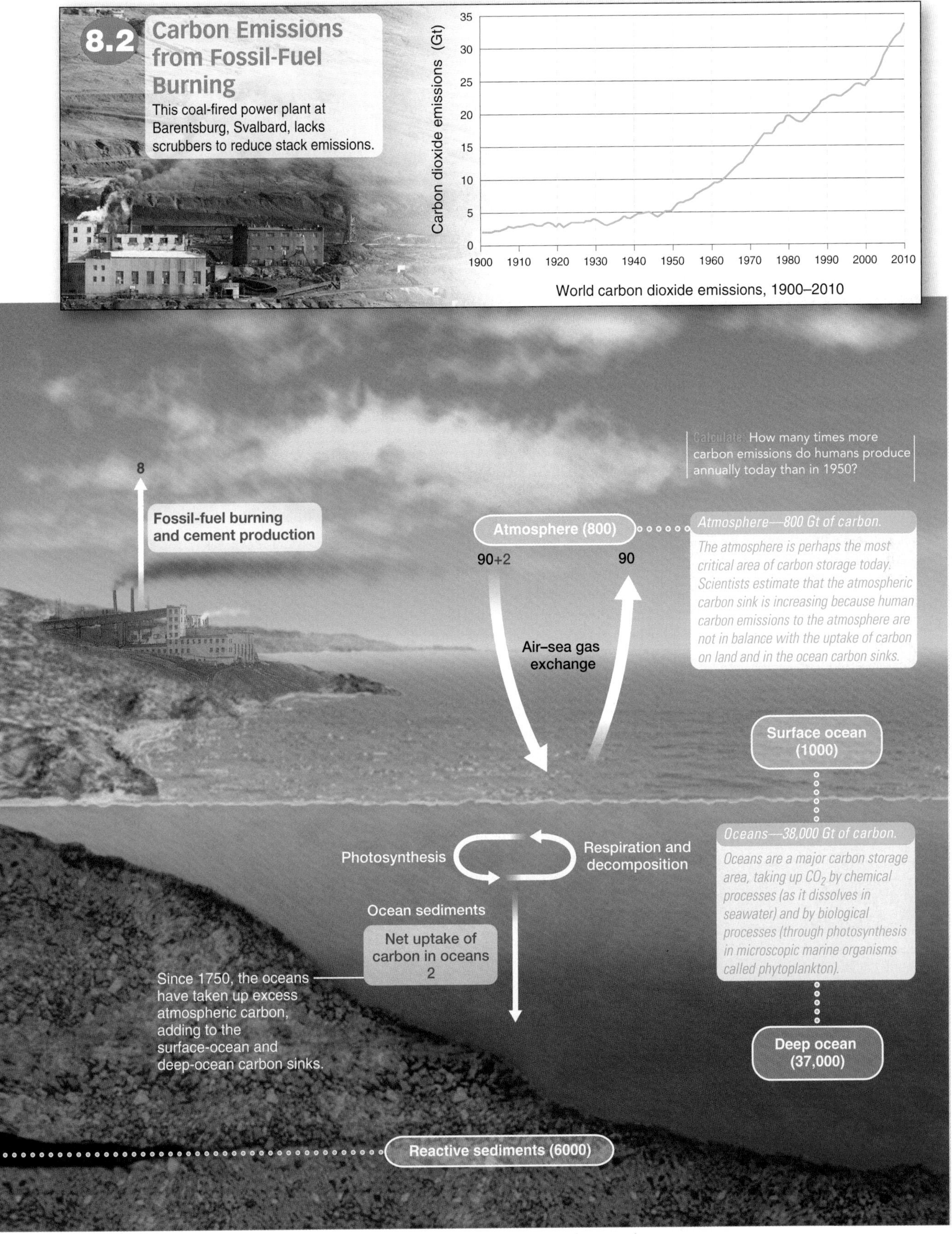
8.2
Carbon Emissions from Fossil-Fuel Burning
This coal-fired power plant at Barentsburg, Svalbard, lacks scrubbers to reduce stack emissions.
Carbon dioxide emissions (Gt)
35
30
25
20
15
10
5
0
1900
1910
1920
1930
1940
1950
1960
1970
1980
1990
2000
2010
World carbon dioxide emissions, 1900–2010
Calculate: How many times more carbon emissions do humans produce annually today than in 1950?
8
Fossil-fuel burning and cement production
Atmosphere (800)
90+2
90
Air–sea gas exchange
Atmosphere—800 Gt of carbon.
The atmosphere is perhaps the most critical area of carbon storage today. Scientists estimate that the atmospheric carbon sink is increasing because human carbon emissions to the atmosphere are not in balance with the uptake of carbon on land and in the ocean carbon sinks.
Surface ocean (1000)
Photosynthesis
Respiration and decomposition
Oceans—38,000 Gt of carbon.
Oceans are a major carbon storage area, taking up CO_2 by chemical processes (as it dissolves in seawater) and by biological processes (through photosynthesis in microscopic marine organisms called phytoplankton).
Ocean sediments
Net uptake of carbon in oceans 2
Since 1750, the oceans have taken up excess atmospheric carbon, adding to the surface-ocean and deep-ocean carbon sinks.
Deep ocean (37,000)
Reactive sediments (6000)

GEOquiz

1. Infer: Some of the 9 Gt of carbon from fossil-fuel burning, cement production, and land-use change is taken up by plants and some is dissolved in the oceans. How much is left to increase CO_2 levels in the atmosphere?

2. Analyze: How much carbon leaves the atmosphere each year through natural and anthropogenic processes on land?

focusstudy 8.1 Climate Change

Global Climate Feedback Mechanisms

Several climate feedbacks influence Earth's global climate system. These feedback mechanisms influence the production and storage of greenhouse gases or affect the movement of carbon through Earth systems—either in the short term (over hundreds of years) or in the long term (over millions of years). We previously discussed the ice–albedo feedback, an important process affecting the present trend of warming climate. Other climate feedbacks include the *water-vapor feedback*, the *permafrost–climate feedback*, and the *CO_2–weathering feedback*, which affects climate only over long time scales.

Water-Vapor Feedback

Water vapor is the most abundant natural greenhouse gas in the Earth–atmosphere system. Water-vapor feedback is a function of the effect of air temperature on the amount of water vapor that air can absorb, a subject discussed in Chapter 5. As air temperature rises, evaporation increases because the capacity to absorb water vapor is greater for warm air than for cooler air. Thus, more water enters the atmosphere from land and ocean surfaces, humidity increases, and greenhouse warming accelerates. As temperatures increase further, more water vapor enters the atmosphere, greenhouse warming further increases, and the positive feedback continues **(Figure 8.1.1)**.

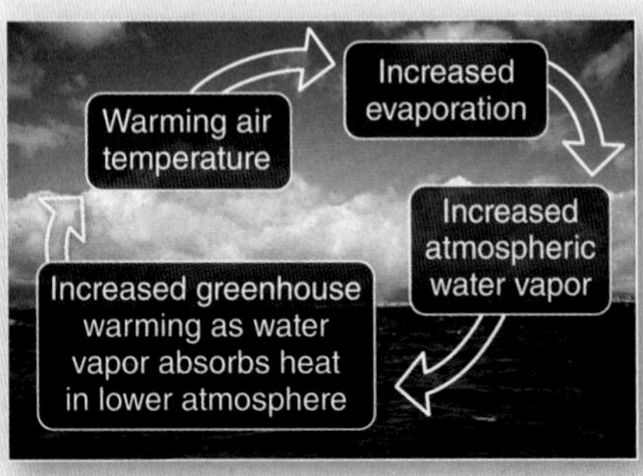

▲**Figure 8.1.1** The water-vapor climate feedback loop, a positive feedback. [NOAA/Historic NWS Collection.]

The water-vapor climate feedback is still not well understood, in large part because measurements of global water vapor are limited, especially when compared to the relatively strong data sets for other greenhouse gases, such as CO_2 and methane. Another complicating factor is the role of clouds in Earth's energy budget. As atmospheric water vapor increases, higher rates of condensation will lead to more cloud formation. Remember from Chapter 3 (Figure 3.8, page 78) that low, thick cloud cover increases the albedo of the atmosphere and has a cooling effect on Earth (cloud albedo forcing). In contrast, the effect of high, thin clouds can cause warming (called cloud greenhouse forcing).

Carbon–Climate Feedback

We saw earlier that over long time periods, CO_2 and methane concentrations track temperature trends, with a slight lag time (Figure 8.8). One hypothesis for this relationship is that warming temperatures caused by changes in Earth's orbital configuration may trigger the release of greenhouse gases (both CO_2 and methane), which then act as a positive feedback mechanism: Initial warming leads to increases in gas concentrations, elevated gas concentrations then amplify warming, and so on.

In this chapter's Geosystems Now, we discussed a similar carbon–climate feedback as it occurs in permafrost areas. Figure 8.1.1 illustrates the *permafrost–carbon feedback* now under way in the Arctic. This process occurs as warming temperatures lead to permafrost thaw, which increases microbial activity and releases more carbon to the atmosphere. Rising atmospheric CO_2 leads to increased plant growth and more abundant microbes, thus releasing even greater amounts of carbon to the atmosphere in a positive feedback that accelerates warming. As permafrost continues to thaw, more stored carbon is released, and the positive feedback continues (**Figure 8.1.2**).

CO_2–Weathering Feedback

Not all climate feedback loops act on short time scales, and not all have a positive, or amplifying, effect on climatic trends. Some feedback is negative, acting to slow the warming or cooling trend. For example, increasing CO_2 stored in the atmosphere increases global warming, which increases the amount of water vapor present in the atmosphere (warm air masses absorb more moisture). Greater atmospheric moisture in a warmer climate generally leads to greater precipitation. With increasing rainfall comes an increase in the breakdown of exposed rock on Earth's surface by chemical weathering processes (discussed in Chapter 11).

The weathering occurs over long time periods as CO_2 in the atmosphere dissolves in rainwater to form a weak acid (carbonic acid, H_2CO_3), which then falls to the ground and works to chemically decompose rocks, releasing calcium, magnesium, potassium, and sodium ions that dissolve in the water. The ions are carried

in a biogeochemical cycle known as the *carbon cycle* (discussed and illustrated in Chapter 16). Areas of carbon release are carbon sources; areas of carbon storage are called **carbon sinks**, or carbon reservoirs. The overall exchange of carbon between the different systems on Earth is the **global carbon budget**, which should naturally remain balanced as carbon moves between sources and sinks. Geosystems in Action 8 illustrates the components, both natural and anthropogenic, of Earth's carbon budget and the areas on Earth that are important carbon sinks.

Humans have impacted Earth's carbon budget for thousands of years, beginning with the clearing of forests for agriculture, which reduces the areal extent of one of Earth's natural carbon sinks (forests) and transfers carbon to the atmosphere. With the onset of the Industrial Revolution, around 1850, the burning of fossil fuels became a large source of atmospheric CO_2 and began the depletion of fossilized carbon stored in rock. These activities have transferred solid carbon stored in plants and rock to gaseous carbon in the atmosphere.

Given the large concentrations of CO_2 currently being released by human activities, scientists have for several decades wondered why the amount of CO_2 in Earth's atmosphere is not higher. Where is the missing carbon? Studies

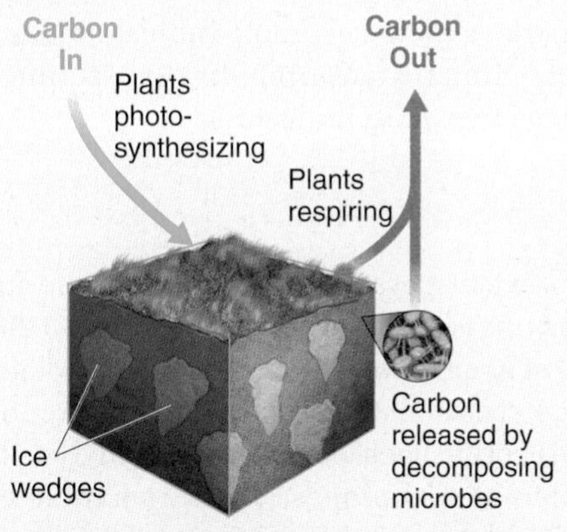

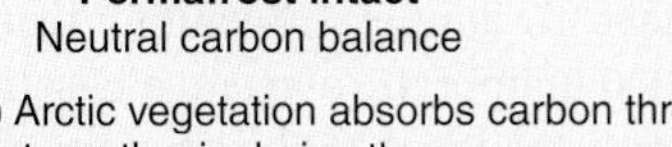

(a) Arctic vegetation absorbs carbon through photosynthesis during the warm summer months. At the same time, vegetation and microbial activity release carbon to the atmosphere by respiration.

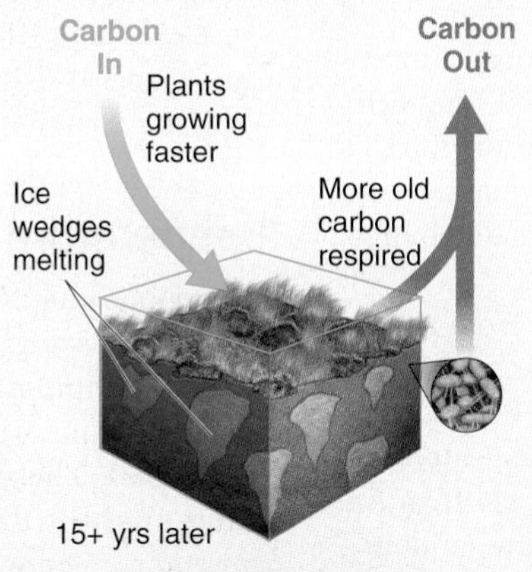

(b) As temperatures warm, the Arctic growing season lengthens, and carbon uptake by vegetation and soils increases. Plant growth accelerates, leading to further carbon uptake. Soil microbes become more abundant and release more stored carbon.

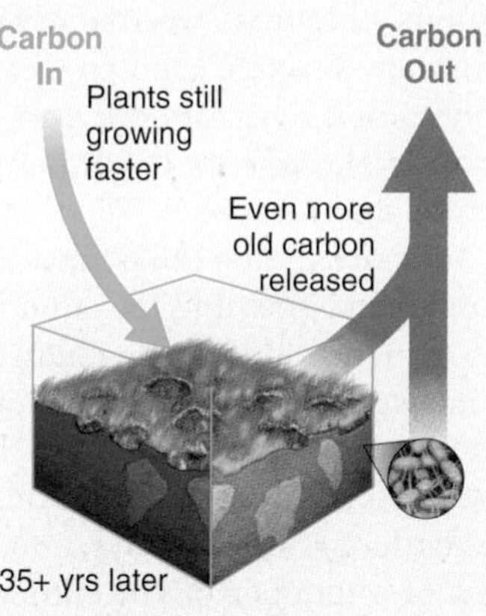

(c) As warming continues, thawing of permafrost and soil allows microbes to flourish and decompose even more organic material, thus releasing large amounts of carbon.

▲**Figure 8.1.2 The permafrost–carbon feedback.** Warming Arctic temperatures thaw permafrost and lead to an increase in carbon emissions, creating a positive feedback between rising air temperature and atmospheric carbon concentrations. [After Zina Deretsky, NSF, based on research by Ted Schuur, University of Florida.]

into rivers and eventually oceans, where the calcium ions react with bicarbonate ions in seawater. This reaction produces calcium carbonate, the material in shelled organisms that accumulate on the ocean bottom after they die. These organisms eventually lithify (are cemented together) to become limestone (see the discussion of sedimentary rocks in Chapter 9).

The carbon in limestone is stored for hundreds of thousands to millions to hundreds of millions of years. In this way, over long time periods, CO_2 is removed from the atmosphere and transferred to the ocean carbon sink. It is a negative climate feedback because its overall effect is to reduce the global warming trend.

This so-called *CO_2–weathering feedback* provides a natural buffer to climatic change over long time scales. For example, if outgassing increases and the level of atmospheric CO_2 rises, global warming will occur. The subsequent increase in precipitation and enhancement of chemical weathering then act to buffer warming by removing CO_2 from the atmosphere and transferring it to the oceans. In contrast, if a change in orbital cycles or oceanic circulation triggers global cooling, then the reduction of precipitation and chemical weathering will leave more CO_2 in the atmosphere, where it works to increase temperatures. Throughout Earth's history, this natural buffer has helped prevent Earth's climate from becoming too warm or too cold. The rapid pace of present climate change, however, is evidently beyond the ability of natural systems to moderate.

1. What is the primary difference between positive and negative feedbacks (see discussion in Chapter 1 for review and clarification)?
2. How do the climate feedbacks, and others discussed in this text, illustrate the complexities of Earth system interactions?

suggest that uptake of carbon by the oceans is offsetting some of the atmospheric increase. When dissolved CO_2 mixes with seawater, carbonic acid (H_2CO_3) forms in a process of *ocean acidification*. The increased acidity affects seawater chemistry and harms marine organisms, such as corals and some types of plankton, that build shells and other external structures from calcium carbonate (discussed in Chapter 13). Scientists estimate that the oceans have absorbed some 28% of the rising concentrations of atmospheric carbon, slowing the warming of the atmosphere. However, as the oceans increase in temperature, their ability to dissolve CO_2 is lessened. Thus, as global air and ocean temperatures warm, more CO_2 will likely remain in the atmosphere, with related impacts on Earth's climate.

Uptake of excess carbon is also occurring in Earth's terrestrial environment, as increased CO_2 levels in the atmosphere enhance photosynthesis in plants. Research suggests that this produces a "greening" effect as plants produce more leaves in some regions of the world (see Chapter 16, Figure HD 16c on page 527). However, many human practices—for example, the overgrazing and poor agricultural practices that lead to soil erosion and the removal of forests for wood products and alternative land use—reduce the capacity of the terrestrial carbon sink.

Evidence for Present Climate Change

In previous chapters, we discussed many aspects of contemporary climate change as we explored Earth's atmosphere and hydrosphere. In subsequent chapters, we examine the effects of climate change on Earth's lithosphere and biosphere. The task of this chapter is to review and consolidate the evidence for climate change, revisiting some issues and introducing others.

The evidence for climate change comes from a variety of measurements showing global trends over the past century—and especially over the past two decades. Data gathered from weather stations, orbiting satellites, weather balloons, ships, buoys, and aircraft confirm the presence of a number of key indicators. New evidence and climate change reports are emerging regularly; a good source for the latest updates on climate change science is the U.S. Global Change Research Program, which in May 2014 published a climate-change impacts report, available at http://nca2014.globalchange.gov/. International climate-change science is coordinated by the IPCC, which issued its Fifth Assessment Report in 2013–2014 (see Summary for Policy Makers for all three Working Groups at http://www.ipcc.ch/).

Figure 8.14 illustrates the measurable indicators that unequivocally show climatic warming. In this section, we discuss each of the five main indicators.

Temperature

In previous chapters, we discussed the rise in atmospheric temperatures during this century. In Chapter 3, Figure 3.26 presents an important graph of data from four independent surface-temperature records showing a warming trend since 1880. These records, each collected and analyzed using slightly different techniques, show remarkable agreement. **Figure 8.15** plots the NASA temperature data of global mean annual surface air temperature anomalies (as compared to the 1951–1980 temperature-average baseline) and 5-year mean temperatures from 1880 through 2012. (Remember from Chapter 3 that temperature anomalies

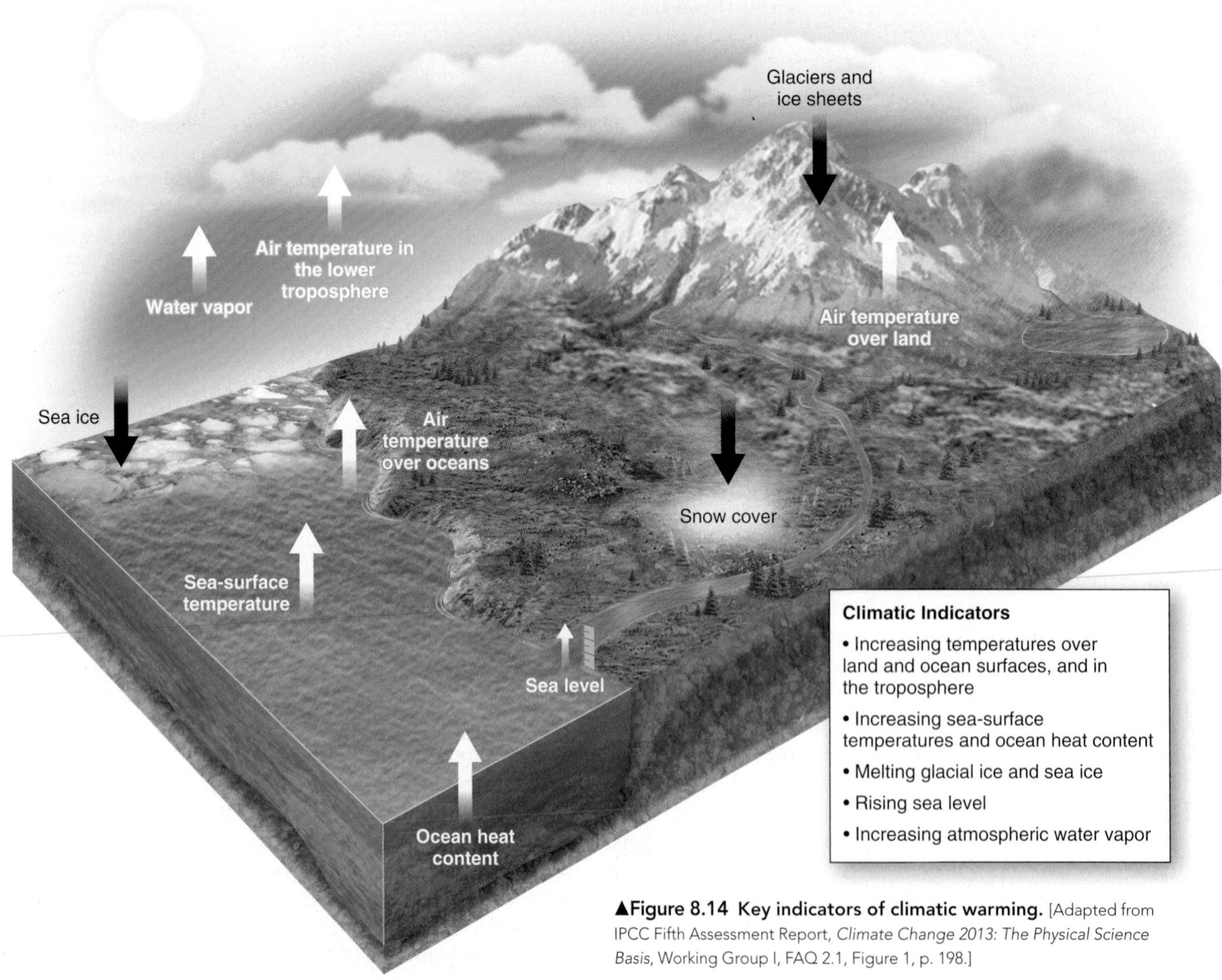

▲**Figure 8.14 Key indicators of climatic warming.** [Adapted from IPCC Fifth Assessment Report, *Climate Change 2013: The Physical Science Basis*, Working Group I, FAQ 2.1, Figure 1, p. 198.]

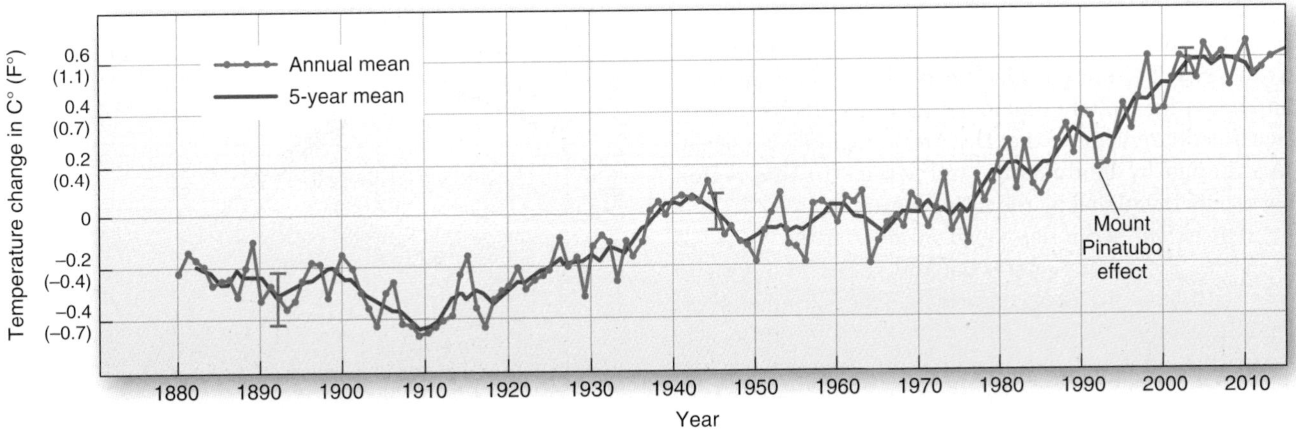

▲**Figure 8.15 Global land–ocean temperature trends, 1880–2013.** The graph shows change in global surface temperatures relative to the 1951–1980 global average. The gray bars represent uncertainty in the measurements. Note the inclusion of both annual average temperature anomalies and 5-year mean temperature anomalies; together, they give a sense of overall trends. [Based on data from NASA/GISS; available at http://climate.nasa.gov/vital-signs/global-temperature/.]

are the variations from the mean temperature during some period of record.)

The temperature data unmistakably show a warming trend. Since 1880, in the Northern Hemisphere, the period from 2000 to 2010 was the warmest decade, and the years with the warmest land-surface temperatures were 2005 and 2010 (a statistical tie). For the Southern Hemisphere, 2009 was the warmest in the modern record. The data from long-term climate reconstructions of temperature point to the present time as the warmest in the last 120,000 years (see Figure 8.8). These reconstructions also suggest that the increase in temperature during the 20th century is *extremely likely* (within a confidence level greater than 95%*) to be the largest to occur in any century over the past 1000 years.

Record-setting summer daytime temperatures are being recorded in many countries (**Figure 8.16**). For example, in August 2013 temperatures in western Japan topped 40°C (104°F) for 4 days, and on August 12, the temperature in Kochi Prefecture reached 41°C (106°F), the highest ever recorded in that country. In the United States, the number of unusually hot summer days has been rising since 1990 (see http://www.epa.gov/climatechange/science/indicators/weather-climate/high-low-temps.html). The year 2012 broke all U.S records (since 1895) by 0.7 C° (1.4 F°), with an average temperature for the year of 12.9°C (55.3°F).

Ocean temperatures are also rising. As discussed in Chapter 3, sea-surface temperatures increased at an average rate of 0.07 C° (0.13 F°) per year from 1901 to 2012 as oceans absorbed atmospheric heat. This rise is reflected in measurements of upper-ocean heat content, which includes the upper 700 m (2296 ft) of ocean (http://www.ncdc.noaa.gov/indicators/, click on "warming climate"). This increasing heat content is consistent with sea-level rise resulting from the thermal expansion of seawater (discussed ahead).

*The IPCC uses the following as standard references to indicate levels of confidence in predictions concerning climate change: *virtually certain* > 99% probability of occurrence; *extremely likely* > 95%; *very likely* > 90%; *likely* > 66%; *more likely than not* > 50%; *unlikely* < 33%; *very unlikely* < 10%; and *extremely unlikely* < 5%.

Ice Melt

The heating of Earth's atmosphere and oceans is causing sea ice and land ice to melt. Chapter 14 discusses the character and distribution of snow and ice in Earth's cryosphere.

Sea Ice In earlier chapters, we discussed the effects of Arctic sea ice on global temperatures. Sea ice is composed of frozen seawater, which forms over the ocean (sea ice does not include ice shelves and icebergs, which are made up of freshwater originating on land). Melting sea ice does

▼**Figure 8.16 Heat wave hits the United Kingdom in 2013.** Temperatures topped 32°C (89.6°F) for over a week in southern England in July 2013, the highest recordings in seven years. [Luke MacGregor/Reuters.]

not contribute appreciably to sea-level rise because the ice almost displaces its own volume in seawater. However, Arctic sea ice, known also as *pack ice*, is especially important for global climate owing to its effects on surface albedo; remember that the Arctic region is an ocean surrounded by landmasses, and sea ice in this region helps cool the planet by reflecting sunlight.

The extent of Arctic sea ice varies over the course of a year, as shown in **Figure 8.17a**, and varies from year to year with local weather conditions. Every summer some amount of sea ice thaws; in winter, the ice refreezes. According to satellite data, Arctic summer sea ice reached its lowest extent in the modern record in 2012 (**Figure 8.17b**). Satellite data also show that the summer sea-ice minimum extent (occurring in September) and winter sea-ice maximum extent (occurring in February or early March) have declined since 1979 (**Figure 8.17c**). September sea ice is declining at a rate of 11% per decade (as compared to the 1979–2000 average). The accelerating decline of summer sea ice, in association with record losses of sea ice in 2007 and 2012, suggests that summer sea ice may disappear sooner than predicted by most models; some scientists estimate an ice-free summer Arctic Ocean within the next few decades, which would accelerate warming and related changes to the global climate system.

Glacial Ice and Permafrost Land ice occurs in the form of glaciers, ice sheets, ice caps, ice fields, and frozen ground. These freshwater ice masses are found at high latitudes and worldwide at high elevations. As temperatures rise in Earth's atmosphere, glaciers are losing mass, shrinking in size in a process known as *glacial retreat* (**Figure 8.18**; also see the discussion in Chapter 14).

Earth's two largest ice sheets, in Greenland and Antarctica, are also losing mass. Summer melt on the Greenland Ice Sheet increased 30% from 1979 to 2006, with about half the surface area of the ice sheet experiencing some melting on average during the summer months. In July 2012, satellite data showed that 97% of the ice sheet's surface was covered by meltwater, the greatest extent in the 30-year record of satellite measurements. Recent studies of the topography of the southern Greenland coastline beneath the ice sheet found deep canyons, extending to depths below sea level and reaching inland up to 96 km (60 mi). Scientists earlier predicted that recent melting would slow as glaciers retreat inland to higher elevations; instead, a greater mass of ice is vulnerable to melting than previously thought.

Recent studies in Antarctica using satellite instruments to assess ice thickness and surface movement show that portions of the West Antarctic Ice Sheet (WAIS) are in an irreversible decline, thinning, losing mass, and flowing more quickly toward the sea. Parts of these glaciers float on the ocean, forming ice shelves that are attached to the grounded continental ice. As ice shelves thin and break up in response to warmer ocean water beneath them, the speed of glacial movement increases (**Figure 8.19**); see the discussion of ice shelf breakup and a map of ice movement speed in Antarctica in Chapter 14. Scientists think that the Amundsen Sea

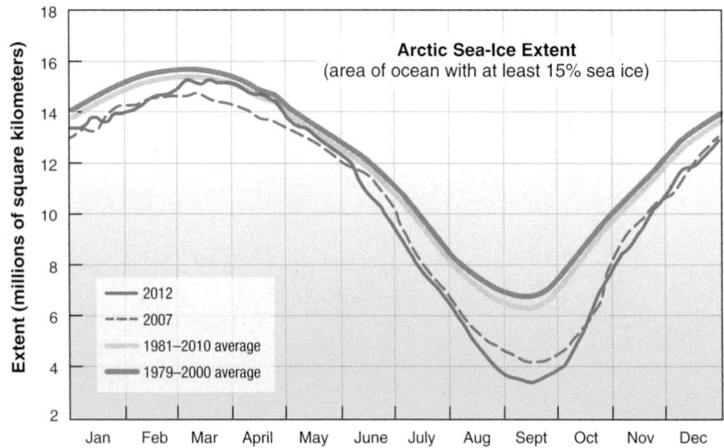

(a) Arctic sea reached its lowest extent in the satellite record in 2007 and 2012.

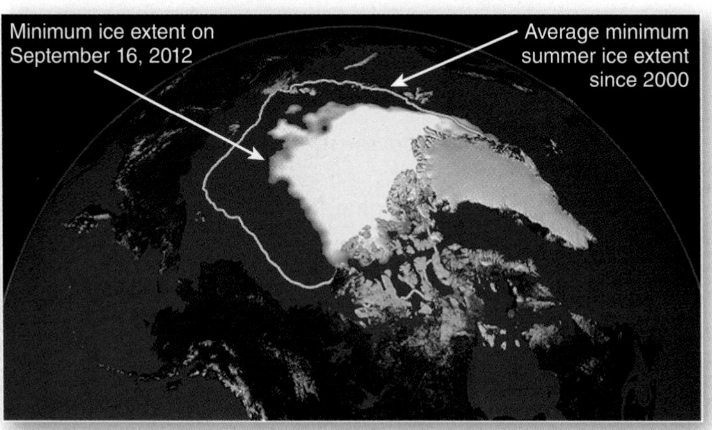

(b) Image shows the 2012 record low compared to the average low since 2000.

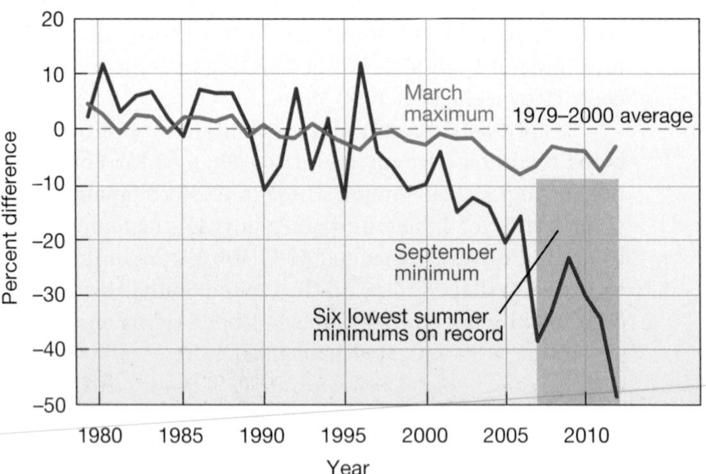

(c) Percent difference between annual March winter maximum (blue line) and September summer minimum (red line) as compared to the 1979–2000 average (dashed line). Note the rapid decrease during the last decade.

▲**Figure 8.17 Recent changes in annual Arctic sea-ice extents.** Continued loss of summer sea ice will accelerate the positive feedback loop as increasing ice melt lowers albedo, causes oceans to absorb more heat, and amplifies atmospheric warming. [(a) National Snow and Ice Data Center. (b) Based on *Arctic Sea Ice Hits Smallest Extent in Satellite Era*, NASA, available at **http://www.nasa.gov/topics/earth/features/2012-seaicemin.html**. (c) Based on *Sea Ice Extents since 1979*, available at **http://www.climate.gov/sites/default/files/seaice1979-2012_final.png**.]

(a) Alaska's Muir Glacier, August 13, 1941.

(b) Muir Glacier, August 31, 2004.

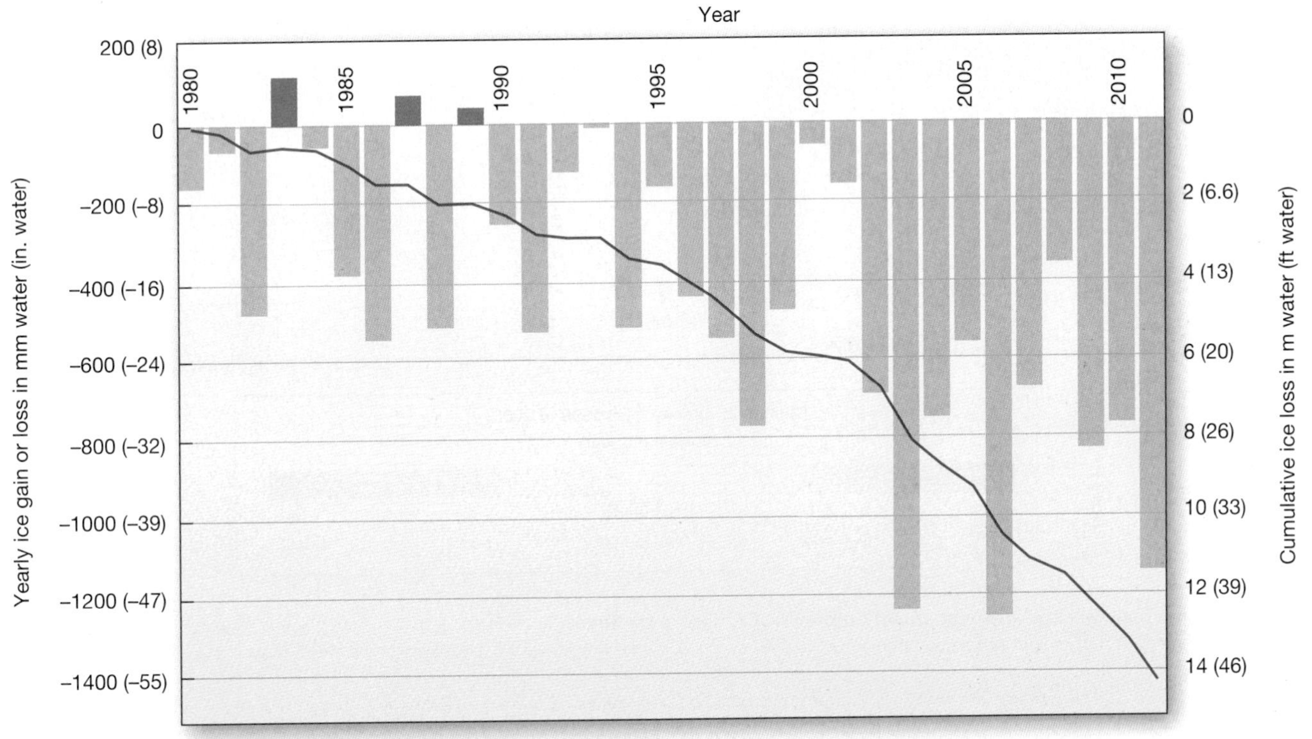

(c) Data from glaciers worldwide show a negative mass balance every year since 1990 (indicated by gray bars). The red line shows the cumulative annual balance.

▲**Figure 8.18 Muir Glacier and worldwide annual glacial mass balance (the gain of snow minus the melt loss) show a net loss of glacial ice.** Glaciers grow when annual winter snowfall exceeds annual summer melt; when snowfall and melting are equal, glacial mass balance is zero (see the discussion in Chapter 14). [(a) and (b) USGS. (c) NOAA graph adapted from *State of the Climate in 2012*, Bulletin of the American Meteorological Society.]

portion of the WAIS, which includes six glaciers, could melt in the next 100 to 200 years, an event that would raise sea level as much as 1.2 m (4 ft). If glacial retreat then destabilizes other areas of the ice sheet, the overall sea-level rise could be much greater. Remember that Antarctic ice is the largest repository of freshwater on Earth.

As discussed in this chapter's Geosystems Now, permafrost (perennially frozen ground) is thawing in the Arctic at accelerating rates. Scientists now estimate that between one- and two-thirds of Arctic permafrost will thaw over the next 200 years, if not sooner; these permafrost reserves took tens of thousands of years to form. Warming land and ocean temperatures may also cause the thaw of methane hydrates stored in permafrost and in deep-ocean sediments on the seafloor (discussed in Focus Study 14.1 on pages 456–457).

Sea-Level Rise

Elevation on Earth is referenced to mean sea level. **Mean sea level (MSL)** is a value based on average tidal levels recorded hourly at a given site over many years. MSL varies globally because of ocean currents and waves, tidal variations, air temperature, pressure differences and

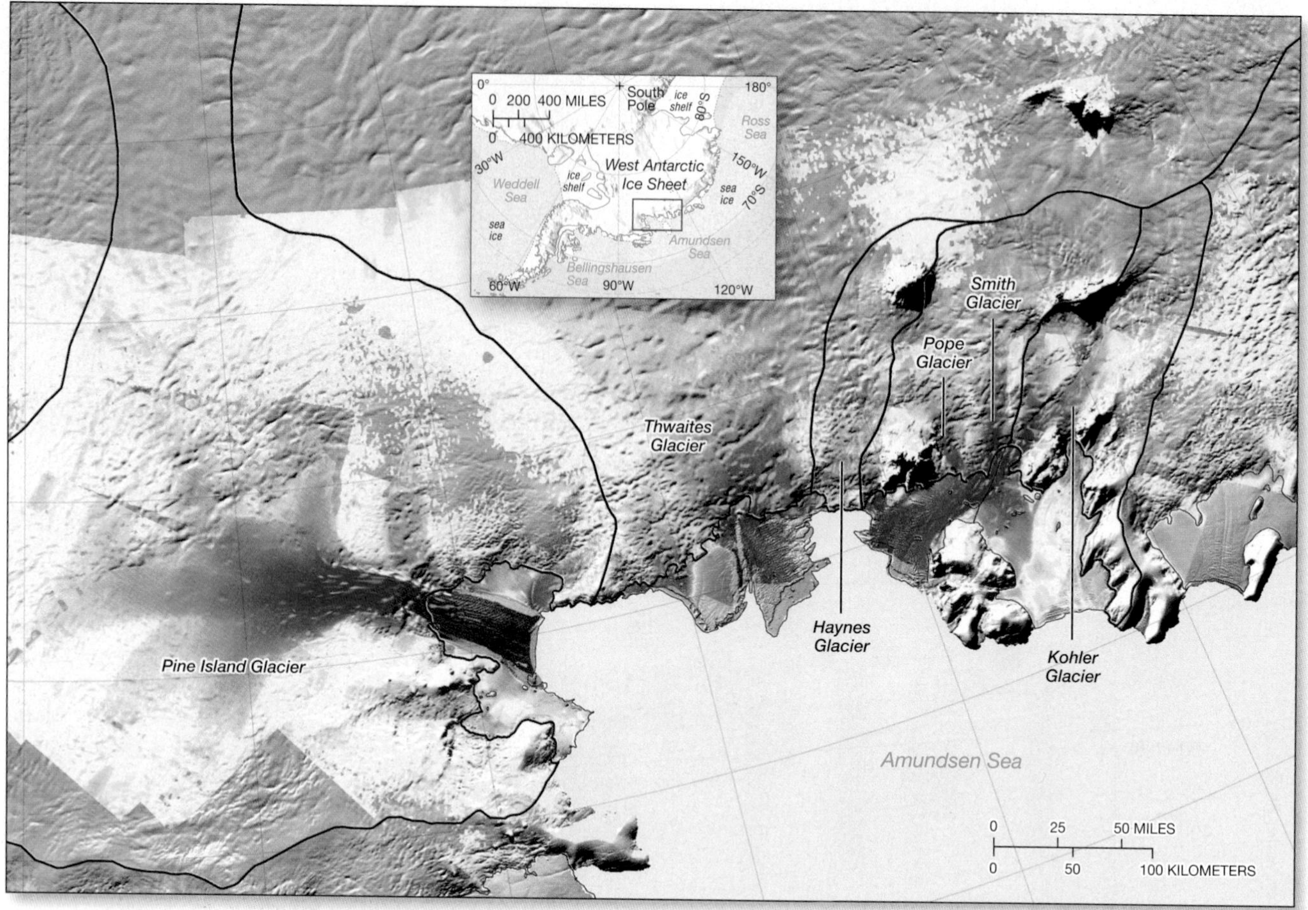

▲**Figure 8.19 Changes in glacial movement on the West Antarctic Ice Sheet.** Studies show that the six glaciers labeled in the image increased their speed of movement toward the sea from 1996 to 2008. These glaciers drain one third of the WAIS, and the accelerated movement is one of multiple indicators that the WAIS is in a state of irreversible decline and will disappear, possibly in the next 100 to 200 years, adding to sea-level rise. [*Landsat*, *ERS*, and *RADARSAT* source images courtesy of Jeremie Mouginot, University of California, Irvine.]

wind patterns, ocean temperature variations, and slight variations in Earth's gravity. However, over the long term, changes in sea level represent changes in the volume of water in the oceans, and these changes relate to temperature. The present sea-level rise is spatially uneven, as is MSL; for instance, the rate of rise along the coast of Argentina is greater than the rate along the coast of France, and the rate of rise along the U.S. East Coast is greater than the rate along the U.S. West Coast (**Figure 8.20**).

Sea level is now rising more quickly than predicted by most climate models, and the rate appears to be accelerating. During the last century, sea level rose 17–21 cm (6.7–8.3 in.), a greater rise in some areas (such as the U.S. Atlantic coast) than at any time during the past 2000 years. From 1901 to 2010, tidal gauge records show that sea level rose 1.7 mm (0.07 in.) per year. From 1993 to 2013, satellite data show that sea level rose 3.16 mm (0.12 in.) per year.

GEOreport 8.1 Rainfall over Australia temporarily halts global sea-level rise

The discovery of complicated interactions and unexpected system responses is common in climate change science. For example, for 18 months beginning in 2010, global sea level dropped by about 7 mm (0.3 in.), temporarily slowing the consistent annual rise in recent decades. New research shows that heavy rainfall over Australia caused vast amounts of water to collect on the continent during 2010 and 2011. The unique topography and soils of interior Australia enable water to collect and eventually evaporate or infiltrate into the soil rather than running off to the ocean. The rain over Australia was generated by an unusual convergence of distinct atmospheric patterns over the Indian and Pacific Oceans. The normal pattern of heavy rainfall over the tropical oceans has since returned, and sea level is rising once again, in line with climate change projections.

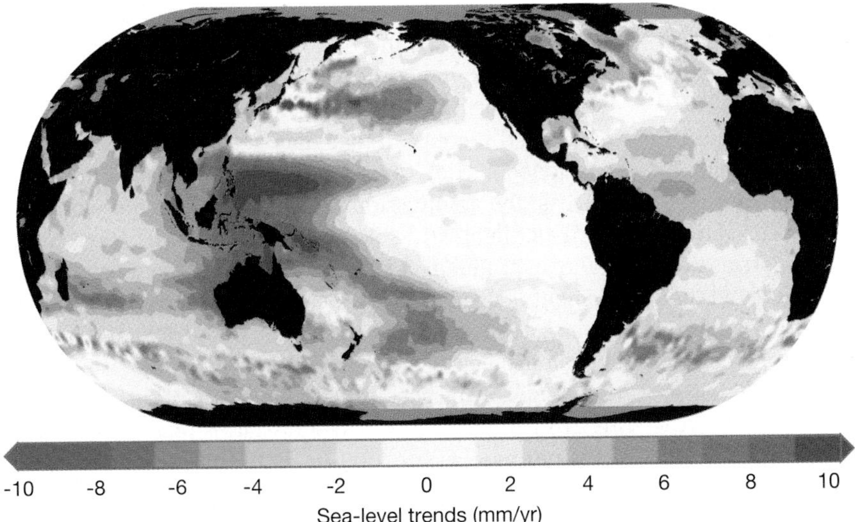

◀**Figure 8.20 Rate of global mean sea-level change, 1992–2013.** Sea-level trends as measured by *TOPEX/Poseidon*, *Jason-1*, and *Jason-2* satellites vary with geographic location. Note the effects of the western intensification in the tropical Pacific, discussed in Chapter 4. [Laboratory for Satellite Altimetry/NOAA.]

Two primary factors are presently contributing to sea-level rise. Roughly two-thirds of the rise comes from the melting of land ice in the form of glaciers and ice sheets. The other third comes from the thermal expansion of seawater that occurs as oceans absorb heat from the atmosphere and expand in volume. Chapter 13 discusses sea level and its measurement; Chapter 14 provides further discussion of ice losses.

Atmospheric Water Vapor and Extreme Events

Since 1973, global average specific humidity has increased by about 0.1 g of water vapor per kilogram of air per decade. This change is consistent with rising air temperatures, since warm air has a greater capacity to absorb water vapor. A greater amount of water vapor in the atmosphere affects weather in a number of ways and can lead to "extreme" events involving temperature, precipitation, and storm intensity. The Annual Climate Extremes Index (CEI) for the United States, which tracks extreme events since 1900, shows such an increase during the past four decades (see the data at http://www.ncdc.noaa.gov/extremes/cei/graph/cei/01-12). Since 1959, precipitation falling during the heaviest rainfall events has increased, especially since 1991 (**Figure 8.21**).

According to the World Meteorological Organization, the decade from 2001 to 2010 showed evidence of a worldwide increase in extreme events—notably, heat waves, increased precipitation, and floods. However, to assess extreme weather trends and definitively link these events to climate change requires data for a longer time frame than is now available.

Causes of Present Climate Change

Scientists agree that rising concentrations of greenhouse gases in the atmosphere are the primary cause of recent worldwide temperature increases. As discussed earlier, CO_2 emissions associated with the burning of fossil fuels—primarily coal, oil, and natural gas—have increased with the growing human population and rising standards of living. We have seen that fluctuations in the concentration of atmospheric CO_2 correlate with fluctuations in Earth's average surface temperature. But how can scientists be sure that the primary source of atmospheric CO_2 over the past 150 years is human activities rather than natural factors?

Scientists track the amount of carbon burned by humans over periods of years or decades by estimating the amount of CO_2 released by different activities. For example, the amount of CO_2 emitted at a particular facility can be computed by estimating the amount of fuel burned multiplied by the amount of carbon in the fuel. Although some large power plants now have devices on smoke stacks to measure exact emission rates, estimation is the more common practice and is now standardized worldwide.

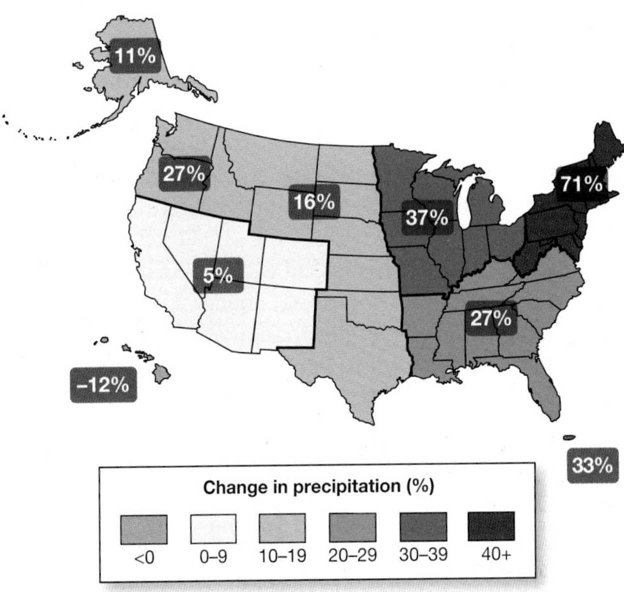

▲**Figure 8.21 Percentage changes in precipitation during very heavy events in the United States, 1958–2012.** "Very heavy events" are defined as the heaviest 1% of all daily events. The trends exceed natural variations for six regions: Northeast, Midwest, Puerto Rico, Southeast, Great Plains, and Alaska. [Adapted and updated from T. R. Karl, J. T. Melillo, and T. C. Peterson, 2009, *Global Climate Change Impacts in the United States*, Cambridge University Press, 189 pp. Updated map available at http://nca2014.globalchange.gov/report/our-changing-climate/heavy-downpours-increasing.]

Recently, scientists have used carbon isotopes to more accurately determine the atmospheric CO_2 emitted from fossil fuels. The basis for this method is the knowledge that fossil carbon—formed millions of years ago from organic matter that now lies deeply buried within layers of rock—contains low amounts of the carbon isotope ^{13}C (carbon-13) and none of the radioactive isotope ^{14}C (carbon-14), with its half-life of 5730 years. This means that as the concentration of CO_2 produced from fossil fuels rises, the proportions of ^{13}C and ^{14}C drop measurably. Scientists first discovered the decreasing proportion of ^{14}C within atmospheric CO_2 in the 1950s; regular measurement of this carbon isotope began in 2003. These data show that most of the CO_2 increase comes from the burning of fossil fuels.

Contributions of Greenhouse Gases

We discussed in Chapter 3 the effect of greenhouse gases on Earth's energy balance. Increasing concentrations of greenhouse gases absorb longwave radiation, delaying losses of heat energy to space and resulting in a warming trend in the atmosphere. Global warming causes complex changes in the lower atmosphere that drive the shifts in climate discussed earlier and examined in the chapters ahead. Today, CO_2 levels far exceed the natural range that has been the norm for hundreds of thousands of years.

The contribution of each greenhouse gas toward warming the atmosphere depends on which wavelengths of energy the gas absorbs and on the gas's *residence time*, the length of time that it resides in the atmosphere. The primary greenhouse gases in Earth's atmosphere are water vapor (H_2O), carbon dioxide (CO_2), methane (CH_4), nitrous oxide (N_2O), and halogenated gases. Of these, water vapor is the most abundant. However, water vapor has a short residence time in the atmosphere (about 9 days) and is subject to phase changes at certain temperatures. Carbon dioxide, in contrast, has a longer residence time in the atmosphere and remains in a gaseous state at a wider range of temperatures.

Carbon Dioxide As discussed earlier and shown in Figures 8.1, 8.3, and 8.8, the present concentration of CO_2 in Earth's atmosphere is higher than at any time in the last 800,000 years, and perhaps longer. The record of that time period up to the Industrial Revolution shows CO_2 ranging between 100 ppm and 300 ppm, while never changing 30 ppm upward or downward in any span of less than 1000 years. After the Industrial Revolution, atmospheric CO_2 rose above 300 ppm, and in May 2014, CO_2 levels reached 402 ppm after rising over 30 ppm in only the last 13 years (having hit 372 in May 2000).

Carbon dioxide has a residence time of 50 to 200 years in the atmosphere; however, rates of uptake vary for different removal processes. For example, the uptake of atmospheric CO_2 into long-term carbon sinks such as marine sediments can take tens of thousands of years. As mentioned earlier, CO_2 emissions come from a number of sources: the combustion of fossil fuels, biomass burning (such as the burning of solid waste for fuel), the removal of forests, industrial agriculture, and cement production. (Cement is used to make concrete, which is used globally for construction, accounting for about 5% of total CO_2 emissions.) Fossil-fuel burning for electricity, transportation, and heating accounts for over 70% of the total. Overall, from 1990 to 1999, CO_2 emissions rose an average of 1.1% per year; from 2000 to 2010, that rate increased to 2.7% per year and is accelerating.

Methane After CO_2, methane is the second most prevalent greenhouse gas with concentrations increasing from human activities. Today, atmospheric methane concentrations are increasing at a rate even faster than those of carbon dioxide. Reconstructions of the past 800,000 years show that methane levels never topped 750 parts per billion (ppb) until relatively modern times, yet in **Figure 8.22a** we see present levels at 1890 ppb.

Methane has a residence time of about 12 years in the atmosphere, much shorter than that of CO_2. However, methane is more efficient at trapping longwave radiation. Over a 100-year timescale, methane is 25 times more effective at trapping atmospheric heat than CO_2, making its global warming potential higher. On a shorter timescale of 20 years, methane is 72 times more effective than CO_2 as a greenhouse gas. After about a decade, methane oxidizes to form water vapor and CO_2 in the atmosphere.

The largest sources of atmospheric methane are anthropogenic, accounting for about two-thirds of the total. Of the anthropogenic methane released, about 20% is from livestock (from waste and from bacterial activity in the animals' intestinal tracts); about 20% is from the mining of coal, oil, and natural gas, including shale gas extraction (discussed in Chapter 1, Geosystems Now); about 12% is from anaerobic ("without oxygen") processes in flooded fields, associated with rice cultivation; and about 8% is from the burning of vegetation in fires. Natural sources include methane released from wetlands (associated with natural anaerobic processes, some of which occur in areas of melting permafrost) and bacterial action inside the digestive systems of termite populations. Finally, scientists suggest that methane is released from permafrost areas and along continental shelves in the

GEOreport 8.2 China leads the world in overall CO_2 emissions

Over the past several years, China took the lead in overall carbon dioxide emissions (29%), with the United States second (16%) and the European Union third (11%). On a per capita basis in 2011, China, with 19.5% of global population, produced 7.2 tonnes per person, on par with the European Union (at 7.5 tonnes per person). The United States, with 4.5% of world population, produced 17.3 tonnes of CO_2 emissions per person. Among the world's major industrialized countries, Australia had the highest per capita CO_2 output at 18.3 tonnes per person in 2011.

Arctic as methane hydrates thaw, potentially a significant source (see Chapter 14, Focus Study 14.1).

Nitrous Oxide The third most important greenhouse gas produced by human activity is nitrous oxide (N_2O), which increased 19% in atmospheric concentration since 1750 and is now higher than at any time in at least the past 10,000 years. Nitrous oxide has a lifetime in the atmosphere of about 120 years—giving it a high global warming potential.

Although nitrous oxide is produced naturally as part of Earth's nitrogen cycle (discussed in Chapter 16), human activities—primarily the use of fertilizer in agriculture, but also wastewater management, fossil-fuel burning, and some industrial practices—also release it to the atmosphere. Scientists attribute the recent rise in atmospheric concentrations mainly to emissions associated with agricultural activities (**Figure 8.22b**).

Halogenated Gases Containing fluorine, chlorine, or bromine, halogenated gases are produced only by human activities. These gases have high global warming potential; even small quantities can accelerate greenhouse warming. *Fluorinated gases*, sometimes called *F-gases*, comprise a large portion of this group. The most important of these are chlorofluorocarbons (CFCs), especially CFC-12 and CFC-11, and hydrochlorofluorocarbons (HCFCs), especially HCFC-22. Atmospheric concentrations of CFC-12 and CFC-11 have decreased in recent years owing to regulations in the Montreal Protocol (**Figure 8.22c**; also see the discussion of stratospheric ozone in Chapter 2). However, hydrofluorocarbons (HFCs), fluorinated gases that are used as substitutes for CFCs and other ozone-depleting substances, have been increasing since the early 1990s. In general, fluorinated gases are the most potent greenhouse gases with the longest atmospheric residence times.

Sources of Radiative Forcing

We learned in Chapter 3 that Earth's energy balance is theoretically zero, meaning that the amount of energy arriving at Earth's surface is equal to the amount of energy eventually radiated back to space. However, Earth's climate has cycled through periods where this balance is not achieved and Earth systems are either gaining or losing heat. The term **radiative forcing**, also called *climate forcing*, describes the amount by which some perturbation causes Earth's energy balance to deviate from zero. A positive forcing indicates a warming condition; a negative forcing indicates cooling.

Anthropogenic Greenhouse Gases Scientists have measured the radiative forcing, quantified in watts of energy per square meter of Earth's surface (W/m²), of greenhouse gases on Earth's energy budget since 1979. **Figure 8.23**, which compares the radiative forcing (RF) exerted by 20 greenhouse gases, shows that CO_2 is the dominant gas affecting Earth's energy budget. On the right side

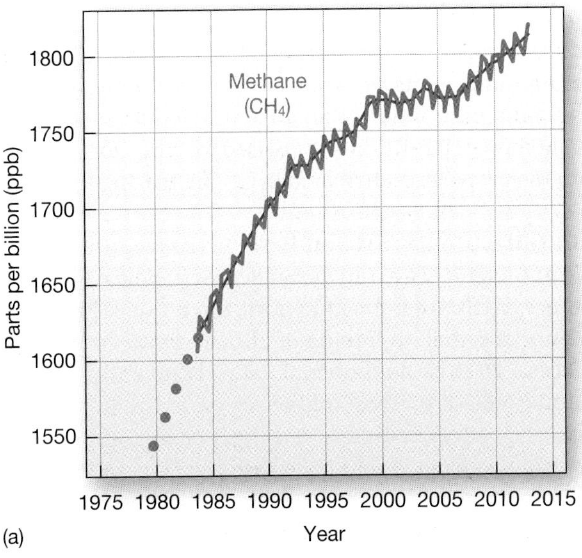

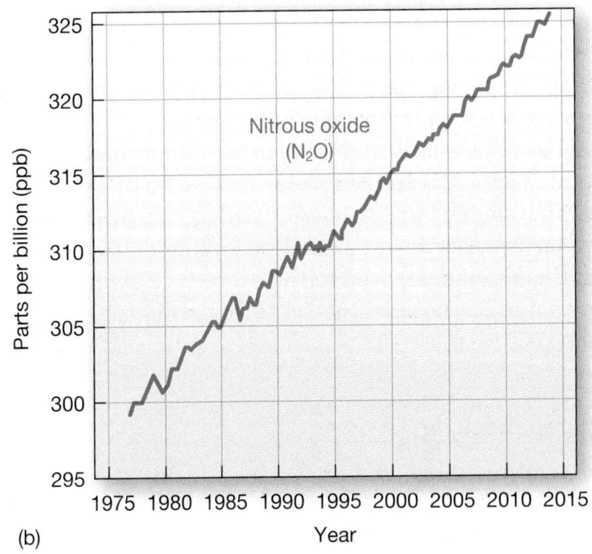

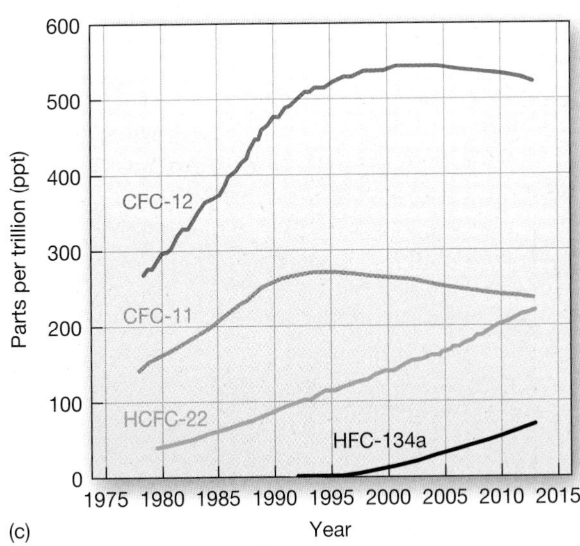

▲**Figure 8.22 Concentrations of methane, nitrous oxide, and fluorinated gases since 1978.** Gas concentrations are in parts per billion (ppb) or parts per trillion (ppt), indicating the number of molecules of each gas per billion or trillion molecules of air. [From *Greenhouse Gases Continue Climbing; 2012 a Record Year*, NOAA, August 2013.]

of the figure is the Annual Greenhouse Gas Index (AGGI), as measured by NOAA, which reached 1.32 in 2012. This indicator converts the total radiative forcing for each gas into an index by using the ratio of the RF for a particular year compared to the RF in 1990 (the baseline year). The graph shows that RF has increased steadily for all gases, with the proportion attributed to CO_2 increasing the most.

Comparison of RF Factors In its report *Climate Change 2013: The Physical Science Basis* (Working Group I, Fifth Assessment Report), the IPCC estimated the amount of radiative forcing of climate between the years 1750 and 2011 for a number of natural and anthropogenic factors (**Table 8.1**). This analysis revealed that by far the highest positive radiative forcing, causing atmospheric warming, is from greenhouse gases, with carbon dioxide responsible for about 60% of the total. The second most important positive forcing factor is tropospheric ozone (in contrast to stratospheric ozone, which has a negative forcing, or cooling, effect on climate). Other factors causing positive forcing are stratospheric water vapor, black carbon on snow, and contrail cirrus clouds. The highest negative forcing of climate is from aerosols.

The IPCC analysis included one important natural forcing factor for climate—solar irradiance (the output of energy from the Sun, discussed earlier). The overall effect of solar irradiance was a positive forcing of 0.05 W/m^2, a small amount compared to the overall 2.3 W/m^2 of forcing caused by the combined anthropogenic factors in the analysis.

TABLE 8.1 Radiative Forcing Factors for Climate, 1750–2011*

	Global Average Radiative Forcing (W/m^2)
Anthropogenic: Greenhouse gases	2.83
Tropospheric ozone	0.40
Stratospheric water vapor	0.07
Surface albedo of black carbon aerosols on ice	0.04
Contrails and contrail cirrus clouds	0.05
Stratospheric ozone	-0.05
Aerosols: Radiation/cloud interactions	-0.90
Surface albedo from land use	-0.15
Total anthropogenic forcing	**2.30**
Natural: Solar irradiance	0.05

* Data from IPCC, Fifth Assessment Report, *Climate Change 2013: The Physical Science Basis*, Working Group I, Table 8.6, p. 696.

Scientific Consensus

The world's climate scientists have reached overwhelming consensus that human activities are causing climate change, agreement that is confirmed throughout the scientific community. Several recent surveys illustrate this consensus; for example, a 2009 survey published in the *Proceedings of the National Academy of Sciences* found that 97 to 98% of actively publishing climate scientists support the conclusion that ongoing climate change is anthropogenic.* Numerous policy statements and position papers from professional organizations (for example, the Association of American Geographers, the American Meteorological Society, the Geological Society of America, and the American Geophysical Union) also support this consensus.

Bringing together leading scientists from an array of disciplines to assess Earth's climate system, the IPCC is the world's foremost scientific entity reporting on climate

*See "William R. L. Anderegg et al., "Expert Credibility on Climate Change," *Proceedings of the National Academy of Sciences*, early ed., 2009. (Available at **http://www.pnas.org/content/early/2010/06/04/1003187107.**)

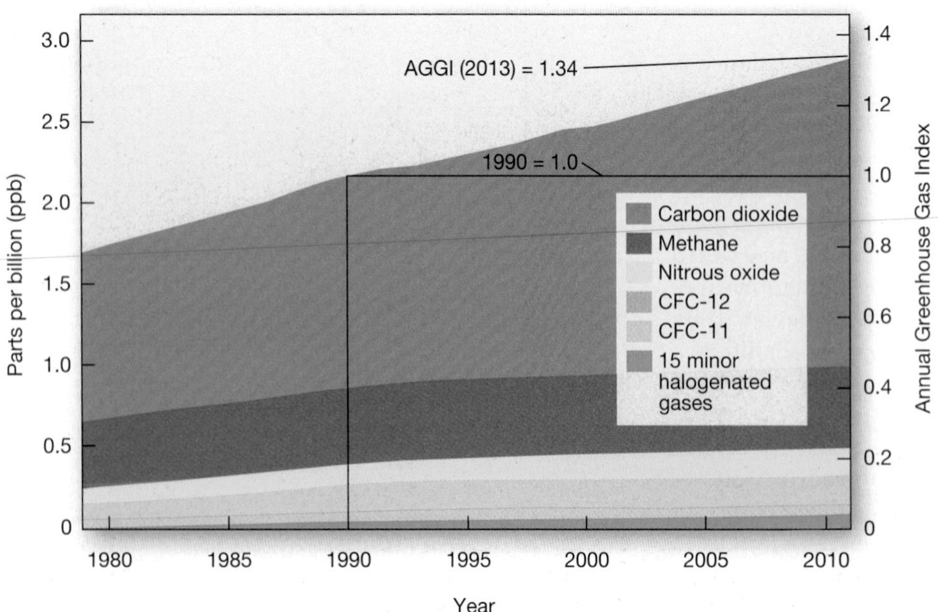

◀Figure 8.23 Greenhouse gases: Relative percentages of radiative forcing. The colored areas indicate the amount of radiative forcing accounted for by each gas, based on the concentrations present in Earth's atmosphere. Note that CO_2 accounts for the largest amount of radiative forcing. The right side of the graph shows radiative forcing converted to the Annual Greenhouse Gas Index (AGGI), set at a value of 1.0 in 1990. In 2013, the AGGI was 1.34, an increase of over 30% in 23 years. [Based on *The NOAA Annual Greenhouse Gas Index (AGGI)*, NOAA, updated summer 2014.]

TABLE 8.2 Summary Points for the Working Groups of the IPCC Fifth Assessment Report*

Working Group I: *The Physical Science Basis*	Working Group II: *Impacts, Adaptation, Vulnerability*	Working Group III: *Mitigation of Climate Change*
Warming of the climate system is unequivocal and it is extremely likely that humans are the dominant cause (95–100% certainty). Many observed changes since the 1950s (warming atmosphere and oceans, melting snow and ice, rising sea level, rising greenhouse gas concentrations) are unprecedented over decades to millennia.	Human interference with the climate system is occurring, and climate change poses risks for human and natural systems. Increasing magnitudes of warming increase the likelihood of severe, pervasive, and irreversible impacts on species, ecosystems, crop yields, human health, natural hazards, and food security.	Effective mitigation of climate change requires collective action at the global scale, because most greenhouse gases (GHGs) accumulate over time and mix globally. International cooperation is needed to effectively mitigate GHG emissions and address other climate change issues.

*The free *Summary for Policy Makers* for each AR5 Working Group is available at https://www.ipcc.ch/report/ar5/.

change. The 2013–2014 IPCC Fifth Assessment Report describes as 95%–100% certain that human activities are the primary cause of present climate change. Specifically, the Fifth Assessment Report concludes with at least 95% certainty that the observed warming from 1951 to 2010 matches the estimated human contribution to warming; in other words, the IPCC found that scientists are 95%–100% certain that humans are responsible for the temperature increase.

The IPCC, formed in 1988 and operating under sponsorship of the United Nations Environment Programme (UNEP) and the World Meteorological Organization (WMO), is a global collaboration of scientists and policy experts that coordinate global climate change research, climate forecasts, and policy formulation. Its reports represent peer-reviewed, consensus opinions among experts in the scientific community concerning the causes of climate change as well as the uncertainties and areas where further research is needed. In 2007, the IPCC shared the Nobel Peace Prize for its two decades of work raising understanding and awareness of global climate change science. **Table 8.2** briefly summarizes some important findings from the 2013–2014 IPCC Fifth Assessment Report.

CRITICAL**thinking** 8.2

Thinking Through an Action Plan to Reduce Human Climate Forcing

Table 8.1 lists some of the many factors that force climate. Let us consider how these variables might inform decision making regarding climate change policy and mitigation. Assume you are a policy maker with a goal of reducing the rate of climate change—that is, reducing positive radiative forcing of the climate system. What strategies do you suggest to alter the extent of radiative forcing or adjust the mix of elements that cause temperature increases? Assign priorities to each suggested strategy to denote the most to least effective in moderating climate change. Try brainstorming and discussing your strategies with others.

Climate Models and Forecasts

In addition to using paleoclimatic records and actual measurements of present-day climatic elements, scientists use computer models of climate to assess past trends and forecast future changes. A climate model is a mathematical representation of the processes and interacting factors that make up Earth's climate systems, including the atmosphere, the oceans, and all land and ice. Some of the most complex computer climate models are **general circulation models (GCMs)**, based on mathematical models originally established for forecasting weather.

The starting point for such a climate model is a three-dimensional "grid box" for a particular location on or above Earth's surface. The atmosphere is divided up vertically and horizontally into such boxes, each having distinct characteristics regarding the movement of energy, air, and water. Within each grid box, physical, chemical, geological, and biological characteristics are represented in equations based on physical laws. All these climatic components are translated into computer codes so that they can "talk" to each other as well as interact with the components of grid boxes on all sides.

GCMs incorporate all climatic components, including climate forcings, to calculate the three-dimensional motions of Earth–atmosphere systems. They can be

GEO**report** 8.3 Causes of extreme weather events in a changing climate

According to the NOAA report "Explaining Extreme Events of 2012 from a Climatic Perspective," *Bulletin of the American Meteorological Society* (volume 94, no. 9), scientific analyses of 12 extreme weather and climate events in 2012 found that anthropogenic climate change was a contributing factor to half the events—to either their occurrence or their outcomes—and that the magnitude and likelihood of each were boosted by climate change. Also important for these extreme events was the influence of natural climate and weather fluctuations, such as ENSO and other global circulation patterns, factors that themselves may be affected by global warming. In 2014, NOAA updated and expanded this report, available at http://www.ncdc.noaa.gov/news/explaining-extreme-events-2013.

programmed to model the effects of linkages between specific climatic components over different time frames and at various scales. Submodel programs for the atmosphere, ocean, land surface, cryosphere, and biosphere may be used within the GCMs. The most sophisticated models couple atmosphere and ocean submodels and are known as **Atmosphere–Ocean General Circulation Models (AOGCMs)**. At least a dozen established GCMs are now in operation around the world.

Radiative Forcing Scenarios

Scientists can use GCMs to determine the relative effects of various climate forcings on temperature (remember that a climate forcing is a perturbation in Earth's radiation budget that causes warming or cooling). One question that scientists have sought to answer is "Does positive radiative forcing of temperature have natural or anthropogenic causes?" In Table 8.1, we saw that greenhouse gases caused the strongest radiative forcing of climate since 1750 and that the estimated positive net radiative forcing of anthropogenic factors was far greater than the positive forcing from solar irradiance. But what is the role of other natural factors on the radiative forcing of temperature?

Figure 8.24 looks at results from two sets of climate simulations as compared to actual global average temperature observations for land and ocean (black line) made from 1906 to 2010. In the graph, the actual temperature data are compared with simulations in which both natural and anthropogenic forcings were included (shaded pink area). These data are also compared with simulations that included natural forcing only, modeled from solar variability and volcanic output alone (shaded blue area).

The model using both natural and anthropogenic forcings (including greenhouse gas concentrations) was the one that produced the closer match to the actual observed temperature averages. Simulations based on natural forcings alone do not match the increasing temperature trend. On the basis of models that combine all the global evidence for climate change, including changes in temperatures, glaciers and sea ice, oceans, and extreme events, the IPCC Fifth Assessment Report concludes that it is *virtually certain* (having a 99% statistical probability) that humans are the strongest drivers of warming since 1950.

Future Temperature Scenarios

GCMs do not predict specific temperatures, but they do offer various scenarios of future global warming. GCM-generated maps correlate well with the observed global warming patterns experienced since 1990, and various AOGCM forecast scenarios are now used to predict temperature change during this century.

Figure 8.25a depicts four temperature scenarios presented in the IPCC Fifth Assessment Report, each with different conditions of radiative forcing. Each Representative Concentration Pathway, or RCP, is identified by the approximate radiative forcing it predicts for the year 2100 as compared to 1750; for example, RCP2.6 denotes

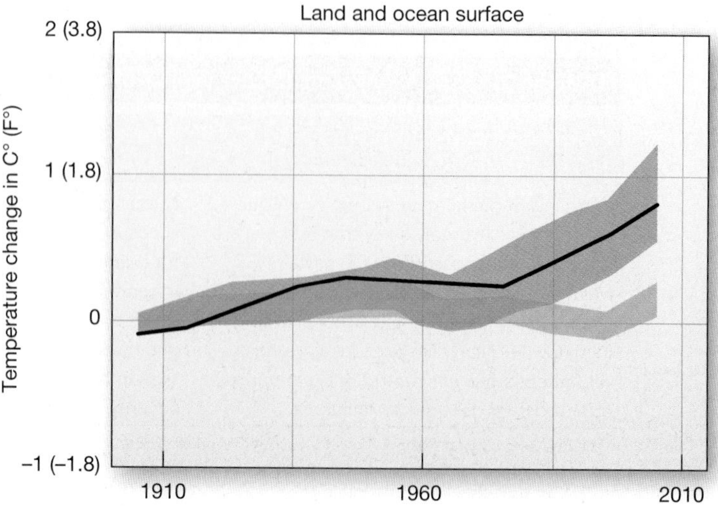

▲**Figure 8.24 Climate model showing the relative effects of natural and anthropogenic forcing.** This computer model tracks the agreement of observed temperature anomalies (black line) with two forcing scenarios: combined natural and anthropogenic forcings (pink shading) and natural forcing only (blue shading). The natural forcing factors include solar activity and volcanic activity, which alone do not explain the temperature increases. [IPCC Fifth Assessment Report, *Climate Change 2013: The Physical Science Basis*, Working Group I, Figure SPM-6, p. 32.]

2.6 W/m^2 of forcing. Each RCP correlates with certain levels of greenhouse gas emissions, land use, and air pollutants that combine to produce the forcing value. For RCP2.6—the lowest level—forcing peaks and declines before 2100. This scenario could occur with major reductions in CO_2 emissions and actions to remove CO_2 from the atmosphere. RCP4.5 represents stabilization of forcing by the year 2100. For RCP6.0 and RCP8.5, high-emission scenarios of continued heavy fossil-fuel use, radiative forcing does not peak by the year 2100. According to these models, continued CO_2 emissions and other human activities that enhance radiative forcing are the scenario that would cause the greatest amount of warming over the 21st century.

Sea-Level Projections

In 2012, NOAA scientists developed scenarios for sea-level rise based on present ice-sheet losses coupled with losses from mountain glaciers and ice caps worldwide. These models project a rise of 0.3 m (1.0 ft) at the low end of the range, under the lowest emission scenarios. On the high end, 1.2 m (4.0 ft) is plausible, with up to 2.0 m (6.6 ft) as the extreme. For perspective, a 0.3-m (1.0-ft) rise in sea level would produce a shoreline retreat of 30 m (98 ft) in some places; a 1.0-m (3.2-ft) rise would displace an estimated 130 million people.

In the United States, sea level is rising more quickly on the East Coast than on the West Coast. **Figure 8.26** shows the area that would potentially be affected by a range of sea-level increases along the U.S. East and Gulf Coasts. The largest areas of inundation at a rise of only 1 meter are around the low-elevation cities of Miami and New Orleans. Many states, including California, presently use a 1.4-m sea-level rise this century as a standard for planning purposes.

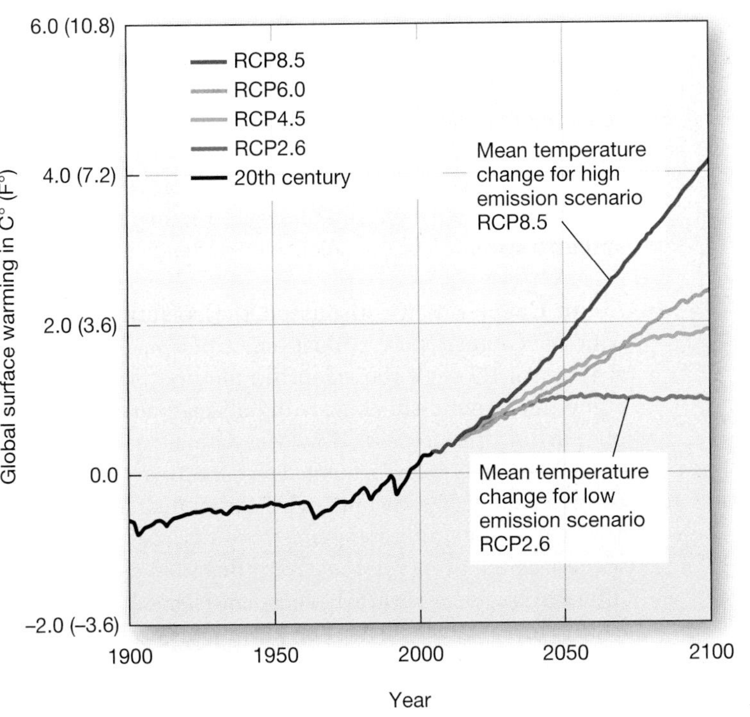

(a) Models suggest that the smallest amount of warming corresponds to the lowest CO_2 emissions scenario (RCP2.6). Warming is greatest under the RCP8.5 scenario, with the highest CO_2 emissions and strongest positive radiative forcing of temperature.

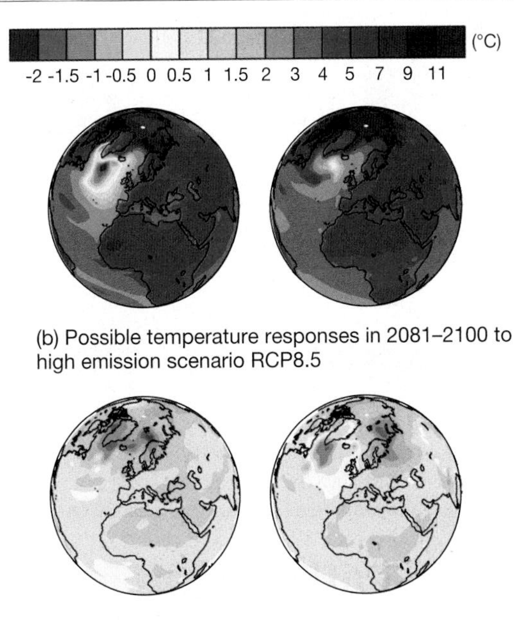

(b) Possible temperature responses in 2081–2100 to high emission scenario RCP8.5

(c) Possible temperature responses in 2081–2100 to low emission scenario RCP2.6

MapMaster
World Physical Environment
Global Surface Warming, Worst-Case Projections

▲Figure 8.25 AOGCM scenarios for surface warming during this century. Temperature change is relative to the 1986–2005 average temperature. [IPCC Fifth Assessment Report, *Climate Change 2013: The Physical Science Basis*, Working Group I, FAQ 12.1, Figure 1, p. 1037.]

The effects of sea-level rise will vary from place to place, with some world regions more vulnerable than others. Even a small sea-level rise would bring higher water levels, higher tides, and higher storm surges to many regions, particularly impacting river deltas, lowland coastal farming valleys, and low-lying mainland areas. Among the densely populated cities most at risk are New York, Miami, and New Orleans in the United States, Mumbai and Kolkata in India, and Shanghai in China, where large numbers of people will have to leave coastal areas. The social and economic consequences especially affect small, low-elevation island states (**Figure 8.27**). For example, in Malé, the capital city of the Maldives archipelago in the Indian Ocean, over 100,000 people reside behind a sea wall at elevations of about 2.0 to 2.4 m (6.7 to 8.0 ft). If the high sea-level rise scenarios occur by 2100, major portions of this island will be inundated. National and international migration—a flood of environmental refugees driven by climate change—would be expected to continue for decades. Sea-level increases will continue beyond 2100, even if greenhouse gas concentrations were to be stabilized today. To see an interactive map of the effects of rising sea level on different areas of the world, go to http://geology.com/sea-level-rise/.

▲Figure 8.26 Coastal inundation caused by a 1-m (3.28-ft) rise in sea level along three portions of U.S. coastline. [Maps prepared by Weiss and Overpeck, Environmental Studies Laboratory, Department of Geosciences, University of Arizona. Used by permission.]

▲**Figure 8.27 Effects of sea-level rise along coastlines.** A house is flooded by a high tide in 2007 on Funafuti Island, Tuvalu, in the South Pacific Ocean. Tuvalu comprises nine small islands, most at or only meters above sea level. [Ashley Cooper/Global Warming Images/Alamy.]

The Path Ahead

Over 26 years ago, in an April 1988 article in *Scientific American*, climatologists described the climatic condition:

> The world is warming. Climatic zones are shifting. Glaciers are melting. Sea level is rising. These are not hypothetical events from a science fiction movie; these changes and others are already taking place, and we expect them to accelerate over the next years as the amounts of carbon dioxide, methane, and other trace gases accumulating in the atmosphere through human activities increase.

In 1997, under the evolving threat of accelerating global warming and associated changes in climate, 84 countries gathered at a climate conference in Kyoto, Japan, and signed the *Kyoto Protocol*, a legally binding international agreement under the United Nations Framework Convention on Climate Change (UNFCCC) that set specific targets to reduce emissions of greenhouse gases. The United States was among the signatory countries; however, it never ratified the treaty. (See http://unfccc.int/kyoto_protocol/items/2830.php.) Since the time of these initial climate warnings and policy actions, climate change science has advanced, and the issue of human-caused climate change has moved from one of scientific and public debate to one of general scientific agreement.

Taking a Position on Climate Change

Despite the consensus among scientists, considerable controversy still surrounds the topic of climate change among the public at large. The disagreement takes two forms: first, disagreement about whether climate change is occurring and, second, disagreement about whether its cause is anthropogenic. The fuel for the continuing "debate" on this topic appears to come, at least partly, from media coverage that at times is biased, alarmist, or factually incorrect. The bias often reflects the influence of special-interest groups, such as corporate interests whose financial gains are at stake if climate change solutions are imposed. In some cases, misinformation campaigns seek to mislead the public about the overwhelming evidence and scientific consensus regaring climate change. In other cases, errors come from simple misinterpretation of the facts, sometimes as interpreted (and frequently sensationalized) by the growing number of blogs and other social media that may present results not yet evaluated by scientific peer review. The bottom line is that having an informed position on climate change requires an understanding of Earth's physical laws and system operations and an awareness of the scientific evidence and ongoing research.

In Chapter 1, we discussed the scientific process, which encourages peer evaluation, criticism, and cautious skepticism through the scientific method. Many would argue that skepticism concerning climate change is simply part of this process. However, climate scientists are overwhelmingly in agreement: The case for anthropogenic climate change has become more convincing as scientists gather new data and complete more research and as we witness actual events in the environment. Even so, as new information becomes available, scientists will constantly need to reevaluate evidence and formulate new hypotheses.

When considering the facts behind climate change, several key questions can help guide you to an informed position based on a scientific approach:

- *Does increasing atmospheric carbon dioxide in the atmosphere cause warming temperatures?*

  Yes. Scientists know that CO_2 acts as a greenhouse gas and that increased concentrations produce warming in the lower atmosphere. Scientists have understood the physical processes related to atmospheric CO_2 for almost 100 years, since well before the effects of global warming became apparent to the scientific community or to the public in general.

- *Does the rise of global temperatures cause global climate change?*

  Yes. Global warming is an unusually rapid increase in Earth's average surface temperature. Scientists know, based on physical laws and empirical evidence, that global warming affects overall climate; for example, it changes precipitation patterns, causes ice melt, lengthens growing seasons, and appears to increase extreme weather events.

- *Have human activities increased the amount of greenhouse gases in the atmosphere?*

  Yes. As discussed earlier, scientists use radioactive carbon isotopes to measure the amount of atmospheric CO_2 that originates from fossil-fuel burning and other human activities. They now know that human sources account for all of the increasing atmospheric CO_2 concentrations.

- *If climate change on Earth has occurred in the past, then why are the present conditions problematic?*

  Carbon dioxide concentrations are today rising more quickly than is seen throughout most of the long-term climate record. This rate of change puts Earth systems in uncharted territory for assessing impacts at a time when Earth's human population exceeds 7.3 billion.

- *Can scientists definitively attribute the changes we are seeing in climate (including extreme events and weather anomalies) to anthropogenic causes alone?*
  Yes, with nearly 100% statistical certainty as ongoing research supports human-forced climate change. Several issues still need further study. One example is the effect of multiyear oscillations in global circulation patterns (such as ENSO) on short- and long-term climate. Scientists also do not yet know the extent to which global warming is driving changes in the intensity of ENSO and other oscillations or whether some observed changes result in part from natural variability.

Climate Change Action: What Can You Do?

Given this scientific knowledge base, taking action on climate change must focus on lowering atmospheric CO_2. As emphasized in numerous scientific and economic assessments pertaining to climate change, opportunities to reduce carbon dioxide emissions are readily available, have additional benefits—called co-benefits—that go beyond slowing climate change, and can be accomplished with little cost to society. For example, the co-benefits from reducing greenhouse gas emissions include improved air quality, with related benefits to human health; reduced oil import costs and related oil-tanker spills; and an increase in renewable and sustainable energy development, with related business opportunities.

Worldwide, many large urban areas are working to reduce greenhouse gas emissions. According to the nonprofit Carbon Disclosure Project (CDP), 110 cities reported in 2013 that actions to mitigate climate change have co-benefits that save money, attract new businesses, and improve the health of residents. (See the CDP report at https://www.cdproject.net/CDPResults/CDP-Cities-2013-Global-Report.pdf.)

From an economic standpoint, delaying action on climate change may be much more costly than taking action now. A study by the U.S. Department of Energy found that the Unites States could meet the carbon-emission reduction targets called for in the Kyoto Protocol with no costs and instead cash savings ranging from \$7 billion to \$34 billion a year. A comprehensive and influential economic analysis by Nicholas Stern, prepared for the British government in 2007 (*Stern Review on the Economics of Climate Change*, Cambridge University Press), stressed that action on a global level, an international response across both developed and developing countries, is needed and that a range of options already exists to cut emissions.

On an individual level, what can you do to address climate change? The principal way to slow the pace of climate change—not only as individuals, but also as an international community—is to reduce carbon emissions, especially the burning of fossil fuels. One way to begin this process is to examine the sustainability of your daily practices and take action to reduce your carbon footprint (review the discussion of an individual's "footprint," whether an ecological footprint, carbon footprint, or lifestyle footprint, in Chapter 1). One goal, discussed in Critical Thinking 8.1, is to reduce atmospheric concentrations of CO_2 to 350 ppm (**Figure 8.28**). Consider these ideas and statistics:

- Driving a vehicle that gets 30 miles per gallon saves 2.9 tons of CO_2 annually over one that gets 20 miles per gallon.
- Replacing incandescent light bulbs with compact fluorescent (CFL) bulbs saves 100 pounds of carbon over the life of each bulb. Using LED bulbs more than doubles this savings.
- Eating less meat reduces demand for animal products; having fewer animals in feedlots reduces atmospheric methane emissions.
- Buying local produce reduces the use of fossil fuels for the transport of goods to supermarkets.
- Planting trees, especially native species, removes CO_2 from the atmosphere; a typical temperate-region tree can store 700 to 7000 pounds of carbon over its lifetime.

All of your actions and decisions have positive and negative consequences for Earth's environment and for our changing climate. Remember that actions taken on an individual level by millions of people can be effective in slowing climate change for present and future generations.

On a collective level, human society must strive to mitigate and adapt to climate change. For example, developers and land managers can change land-use practices to preserve forests and other vegetation. Farmers can use methods that retain more carbon in the soil and plant crop varieties bred to withstand heat, drought, or flood inundation. In coastal areas, landowners can utilize natural shoreline protection, such as sand dunes, and allow for shifting of natural features during storms. Coastal developers must embrace zoning restrictions that account for rising sea level. All societies can promote efficient water use, especially in areas prone to drought.

CRITICAL**thinking** 8.3

Consider Your Carbon Footprint

In Chapter 1, Critical Thinking 1.1 on page 7, you assessed your "footprint" in terms of your impact on Earth systems. (See an example of a carbon footprint calculator at http://coolclimate.berkeley.edu/carboncalculator.) Now, in the context of climate change mitigation, consider how the questions asked in a carbon footprint assessment—for example, what type of lighting, heating or air conditioning, and transportation you use—represent your personal contribution to CO_2 emissions. In other words, given what you now know about atmospheric greenhouse gases and energy budgets, how does your personal energy use and food consumption relate to climate change?

Next, expand your footprint assessment to your campus: Is an energy audit available for your campus? Is a carbon-footprint reduction program in place? Is your college or university cooperating with national efforts to conserve energy and recycle materials, saving money and reducing CO_2 emissions? Do some research to answer these questions, and then get involved in some campus initiatives to promote resource conservation and sustainable lifestyles.

Drive less; walk and bike more
Savings: One lb of carbon for every mile

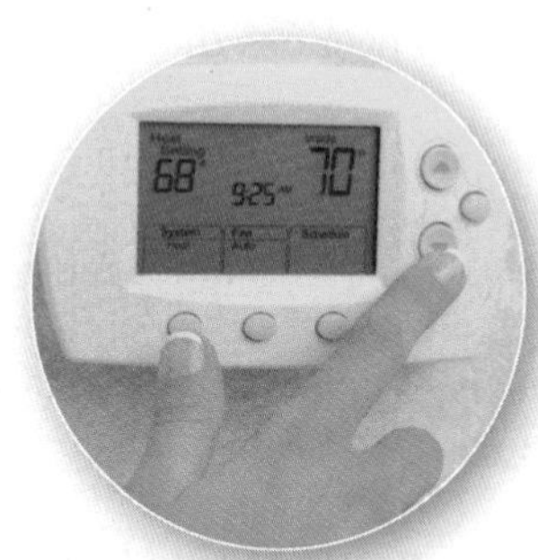

Use energy wisely
Turn down heat and turn up air conditioning settings when you leave the house; insulate your home

Reduce; reuse; recycle
Savings: Every 2 glass bottles recycled saves 2 lbs of carbon

Use Energy Star products
Look for the Energy Star label on appliances, electronics, light bulbs, and heating and cooling equipment

Landscape wisely; plant trees
Plant trees to shade your house. Savings: 200 to 2000 lbs of carbon over the tree's lifetime

Use renewable energy
Purchase renewable energy for your house, or generate your own power using solar or wind

Think globally: act locally
Buy local produce and other food; reduce meat consumption

▲**Figure 8.28 Individual actions to reduce atmospheric CO_2.** Which of these suggested actions are already part of your lifestyle? Can you expand on these possibilities for reducing your personal contribution to greenhouse gas emissions? [(center) NASA. (clockwise from top) William Perugini/Shutterstock; Jordan Tan/Shutterstock; Hgalina/Fotolia; Aerogondo/Fotolia; Esbobeldijk/Shutterstock; Martin Shields/Alamy; Steve Cukrov/Shutterstock.]

These are only a few examples among many for mitigating and adapting to climate change (for links and more information, see http://www.unep.org/climatechange/mitigation/ and http://climate.nasa.gov/solutions).

Both governments and businesses are now planning for climate change impacts. For example, in New York City—in response to the damage from Hurricane Sandy in 2012—over $1 billion is being spent on upgrades to raise flood walls, bury equipment, and assess other changes needed to prevent future damage from extreme weather events. The potential for water scarcity and food shortages in hotter climates with more frequent droughts is emerging as a critical issue for the global community. However, unless greenhouse gas emissions are curbed substantially, the effects of climate change on Earth systems could outpace efforts to adapt.

Present greenhouse gas concentrations will remain in the atmosphere for many decades to come, but the time for action is now. Scientists describe 450 ppm as a possible climatic threshold at which Earth systems would transition into a chaotic mode; with accelerating CO_2 emissions, this threshold could occur in the decade of the 2020s. The goal of avoiding this threshold is a practical start to slowing the rate of change and delaying the worst consequences of our current path. The information presented in this chapter is offered in the hope of providing motivation and empowerment—personally, locally, regionally, nationally, and globally.

THE**human**DENOMINATOR 8 Taking Action on Climate Change

CLIMATE CHANGE IMPACTS HUMANS

- Climate change affects all Earth systems.
- Climate change drives weather and triggers extreme events, such as drought, heat waves, storm surge, and sea-level encroachment, which cause human hardship and fatalities.

HUMANS IMPACT CLIMATE CHANGE

- Anthropogenic activities produce greenhouse gases that alter Earth's radiation balance and induce climate change.
- Cost-effective greenhouse gas reduction strategies are ready and could slow the rate of climate change.

8a

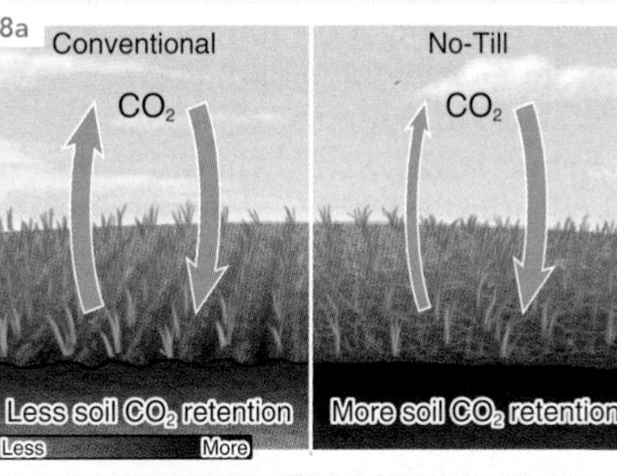

More carbon is retained in soils through no-till agriculture, in which farmers do not plow after a harvest, but instead leave crop residue on the fields. (See the discussion in Chapter 15.) In the photo, a farmer using no-till agriculture in New York plants corn into a cover crop of barley.

8b

Costumed parade participants march in Quezon City, Philippines, during the Global Day of Action against Climate Change on December 8, 2007.

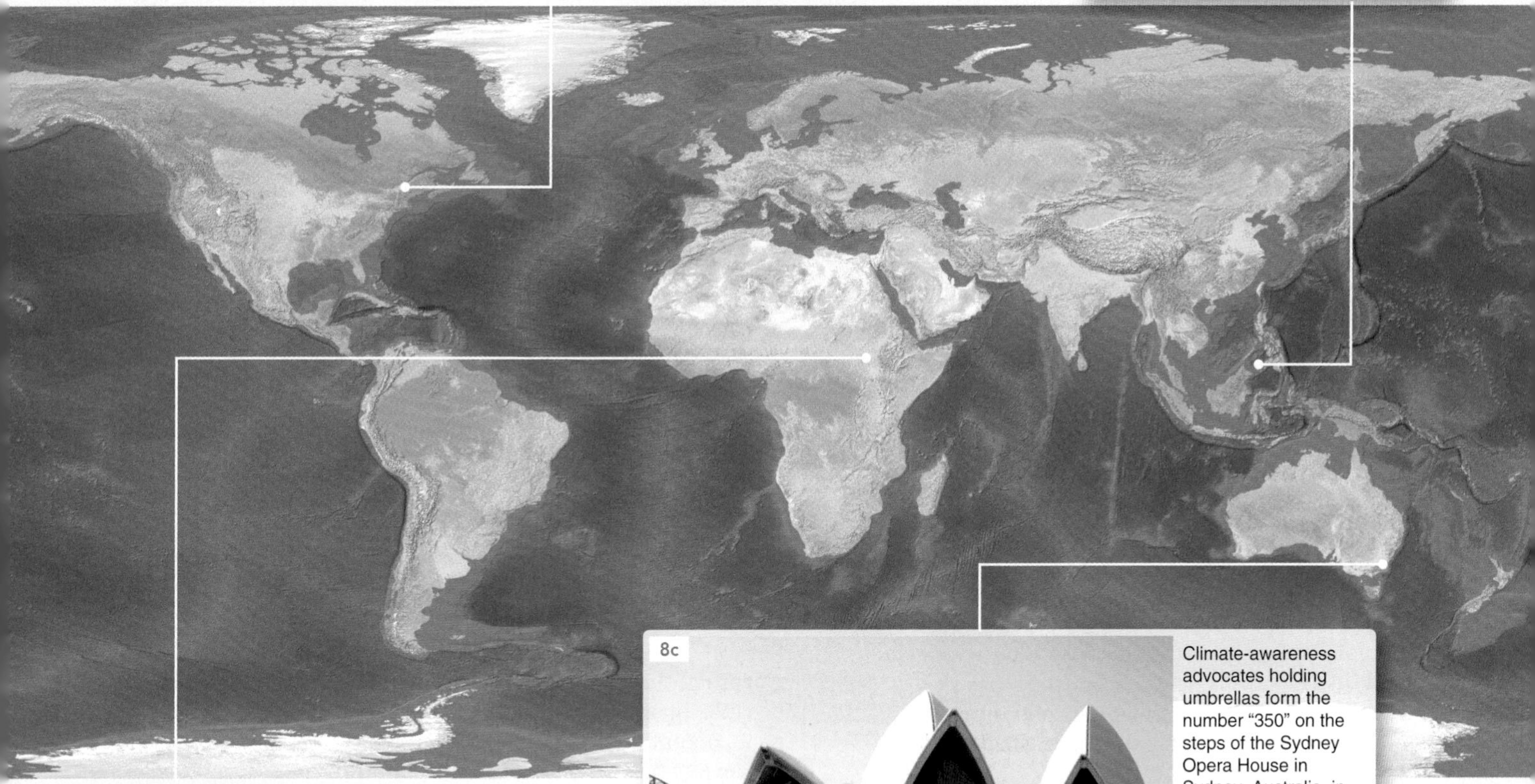

8c

Climate-awareness advocates holding umbrellas form the number "350" on the steps of the Sydney Opera House in Sydney, Australia, in 2009. This number signifies the concentration (in ppm) of atmospheric carbon dioxide that scientists have determined to be sustainable for Earth's climate system. GOAL: 350 ppm CO_2

8d

Through the International Small Group and Tree Planting Program (TIST), subsistence farmers plant trees to reverse deforestation and sequester carbon. The farmers are earning greenhouse gas credits that translate into small cash stipends. Planting trees is a simple and effective way to help combat climate change.

ISSUES FOR THE 21ST CENTURY

How will human society curb greenhouse gas emissions and mitigate change effects? Some examples:

- Using agricultural practices that help soils retain carbon.
- Planting trees to help sequester carbon in terrestrial ecosystems.
- Reducing use of fossil fuels, supporting renewable energy, and changing lifestyles to use fewer resources.
- Protecting and restoring natural ecosystems that are carbon reservoirs.

KEYLEARNINGconceptsreview

Describe scientific tools used to study paleoclimatology.

The study of the causes of changing climate and the consequences for Earth systems is **climate change science**. The growing human population on Earth has led to an accelerating use of natural resources, increasing the release of greenhouse gases—most notably CO_2—into the atmosphere.

The study of natural climatic variability over the span of Earth's history is the science of **paleoclimatology**. Since scientists do not have direct measurements for past climates, they use **proxy methods**, or *climate proxies*—information about past environments that represent changes in climate. Climate reconstructions spanning millions of years show that Earth's climate has cycled between periods both colder and warmer than today. One tool for long-term climatic reconstruction is **isotope analysis**, a technique that uses relative amounts of the isotopes of chemical elements to identify the composition of past oceans and ice masses. **Radioactive isotopes**, such as ^{14}C (carbon-14), are unstable and decay at a constant rate measured as a *half-life* (the time it takes half the sample to break down). The science of using tree growth rings to study past climates is **dendroclimatology**. Analysis of mineral deposits in caves that form **speleothems** and the growth rings of ocean corals can also identify past environmental conditions.

climate change science (p. 246)
paleoclimatology (p. 248)
proxy method (p. 248)
isotope analysis (p. 248)
radioactive isotope (p. 253)
dendroclimatology (p. 253)
speleothem (p. 253)

1. Describe the change in atmospheric CO_2 over the past 800,000 years. What is the Keeling Curve? Where do its measurements put us today in relation to the past 50 years?
2. Describe an example of a climate proxy used in the study of paleoclimatology.
3. Explain how oxygen isotopes can identify glacials and interglacials.
4. What climatic data do scientists obtain from ice cores? Where on Earth have scientists drilled the longest ice cores?
5. How can pollen be used in radiocarbon dating?
6. Describe how scientists use tree rings, corals, and speleothems to determine past climates.

Discuss several natural factors that influence Earth's climate and *describe* climate feedbacks, using examples.

Several natural mechanisms can potentially cause climatic fluctuations. The Sun's output varies over time, but this variation has not been definitely linked to climate change. The *Maunder Minimum*, a solar minimum from about 1645 to 1715, corresponded with one of the coldest periods of the Little Ice Age. However, other solar minimums do not correlate with colder periods. Earth's orbital cycles and Earth–Sun relationships, called **Milankovitch cycles**, appear to affect Earth's climate—especially glacial and interglacial cycles—although their role is still under study. Continental position and atmospheric aerosols, such as those produced by volcanic eruptions, are other natural factors that affect climate.

Climate feedbacks are processes that either amplify or reduce climatic trends toward warming or cooling. Many climate feedbacks involve the movement of carbon through Earth systems between carbon sources, areas where carbon is released, and **carbon sinks**, areas where carbon is stored (carbon reservoirs)—the overall exchange between sources and sinks is the **global carbon budget**. The *permafrost–carbon feedback* and *CO_2–weathering feedback* involve the movement of CO_2 within Earth's carbon budget.

Milankovitch cycles (p. 256)
climate feedback (p. 257)
carbon sink (p. 260)
global carbon budget (p. 260)

7. What is the connection between sunspots and solar output? What happened to sunspot activity during the Maunder Minimum? What was the status of solar activity from 2005 to 2010?
8. What are the three time periods of cyclical variation in Milankovitch cycles?
9. Describe the effect of volcanic aerosols on climate.
10. Name several of the most important carbon sinks in the global carbon budget. What are the most important carbon sources?
11. Define a climate feedback, and sketch an example of a feedback loop.
12. Does the CO_2–weathering feedback described in Focus Study 8.1 work in a positive or negative direction? Explain.

List the key lines of evidence for present global climate change and *summarize* the scientific evidence for anthropogenic forcing of climate.

Several indicators provide strong evidence of climate warming: increasing air temperatures over land and oceans, increasing sea-surface temperatures and ocean heat content, melting glacial ice and sea ice, rising global sea level, and increasing specific humidity. Sea-level rise is measured in terms of changes to **mean sea level (MSL)**, determined by average tide levels recorded hourly at a given site over many years.

The scientific consensus is that present climate change is caused primarily by increased concentrations of atmospheric greenhouse gases resulting from human activities. The primary greenhouse gases produced by human activities are carbon dioxide, methane, nitrous oxide, and halogenated gases, such as chlorofluorocarbons (CFCs) and hydrofluorocarbons (HFCs). The increasing presence of these gases is causing a positive **radiative forcing** (or climate forcing), the amount by which some perturbation causes the Earth–atmosphere energy balance to deviate from zero. Studies show that CO_2 has the largest radiative forcing among greenhouse gases and that this forcing surpasses other natural and anthropogenic factors that force climate.

mean sea level (MSL) (p. 265)
radiative forcing (p. 269)
general circulation model (GCM) (p. 271)
Atmosphere–Ocean General Circulation Model (AOGCM) (p. 272)

13. What is the role of multiyear ice in overall global sea-ice losses? What is the status of this ice today? (Check some websites such as that of the National Snow and Ice Data Center.)
14. What are the two most significant factors currently contributing to global sea-level rise?
15. What are the main sources of carbon dioxide? What are the main sources of atmospheric methane? Why is methane considered to be a more potent greenhouse gas than CO_2?

Discuss climate models and *summarize* some climate projections.

A **general circulation model (GCM)** is a complex computerized climate model used to assess past climatic trends and their causes and to project future changes in climate. The most sophisticated atmosphere and ocean submodels are known as **Atmosphere–Ocean General Circulation Models (AOGCMs)**. Climate models show that positive radiative forcing is caused by anthropogenic greenhouse gases rather than natural factors.

16. What do climate models tell us about radiative forcing and future temperature scenarios?
17. How might we alter future scenarios by changing national policies regarding fossil-fuel usage?

Describe several mitigation measures to slow rates of climate change.

Actions taken on an individual level by millions of people can slow the pace of climate change for us and for future generations. The principal way we can do this—as individuals, as a country, and as an international community—is to reduce carbon emissions, especially in our burning of fossil fuels.

18. What are the actions being taken at present to delay the effects of global climate change? What is the Kyoto Protocol?
19. Take a moment and reflect on possible personal, local, regional, national, and international mitigation actions to reduce climate-change impacts.

VISUALanalysis 8 Wildfire, clouds, climatic regions, and climate change

The King Fire in the central Sierra Nevada of California scorched more than 98,000 acres in September and October 2014, and formed a *pyrocumulus cloud* in which the rising thermal plume is fed by heat from the fire. [Bobbé Christopherson.]

1. What two forms of clouds do you see in the photo? Describe the processes that formed each type.
2. What characteristics of the Mediterranean climate make it prone to the occurrence of wildfire?
3. Given what you have learned about the current state of global temperatures, heat waves, and drought in the first two parts of this textbook, would you expect wildfire occurrence and severity to be increasing, decreasing, or remaining the same as climate changes? See Chapters 16 and 17 for more discussion of wildfire as it relates to ecological processes, climate regions, and climate change.

PART

3 The Earth–Atmosphere Interface

Earth is a dynamic planet whose surface is shaped by active physical agents of change. These arise from two broad systems—endogenic and exogenic—that provide a framework for the organization of Part 3. The *endogenic system* (Chapters 9 and 10) encompasses internal processes that produce flows of heat and material from deep below Earth's crust. Radioactive decay is the principal source of power for these processes. The materials constitute the solid realm of Earth. Earth's surface responds by moving, warping, and breaking, sometimes in dramatic episodes of earthquakes and volcanic eruptions, constructing the crust.

The *exogenic system* (Chapters 11 through 14) consists of external processes at Earth's surface that set into motion air, water, and ice, all powered by solar energy. These media carve, shape, and wear down the landscape. One such process, *weathering*, breaks up and dissolves the crust. *Erosion* picks up these materials; transports them in rivers, coastal waves, winds, and flowing glaciers; and deposits them in new locations. Thus, Earth's surface is the interface between two vast open systems: one that builds the landscape and creates topographic relief and one that tears the landscape down into relatively low-elevation plains of sedimentary deposits.

▲ Slickrock, domes, and canyons surround the sandstone formation known as Pectol's Pyramid in Capitol Reef National Park, Utah. [Alan Majchrowicz/Age fotostock.]

Atmosphere
Biosphere
Lithosphere
Hydrosphere

9 The Dynamic Planet

Karymsky, the most active volcano on Russia's Kamchatka peninsula, erupts in August 2005. [Serguei Fomine/Global Look/Corbis.]

KEYLEARNING**concepts**

After reading the chapter, you should be able to:

- ***Distinguish*** between the endogenic and exogenic systems that shape Earth and ***name*** the driving force for each.
- ***Explain*** the principle of uniformitarianism and ***discuss*** the time spans into which Earth's geologic history is divided.
- ***Depict*** Earth's interior in cross section and ***describe*** each distinct layer.
- ***Describe*** the three main groups of rock and ***diagram*** the rock cycle.
- ***Describe*** Pangaea and its breakup and ***explain*** the physical evidence that crustal drifting is continuing today.
- ***Draw*** the pattern of Earth's major plates on a world map and ***relate*** this pattern to the occurrence of earthquakes, volcanic activity, and hot spots.

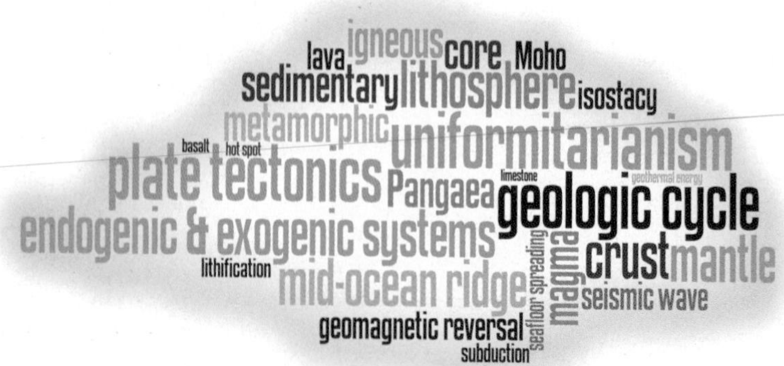

GEOSYSTEMSnow

Earth's Migrating Magnetic Poles

In Chapter 1, we discussed the north geographic pole—the axial pole centered where the meridians of longitude converge. This is *true north* and is a fixed point. Another "north pole" also exists, this one in association with Earth's magnetic field. The *North Magnetic Pole* (NMP) is the pole toward which a compass needle points. Before the Global Positioning System (GPS) was in widespread use, people relied on the compass to find direction, making the location of this pole critical for navigation. Since the location of this pole changes, the NMP must be periodically detected and pinpointed by magnetic surveys.

The deep interior of Earth—the core—has a solid inner region and a fluid outer region. Earth's magnetic field is principally generated by motions in the fluid material of the outer core. Like a bar magnet, the magnetic field has poles with opposite charges. At the NMP, the pull of the magnetic field is directed vertically downward; imagine this pull as an arrow pointing downward, intersecting Earth's surface at the north and south magnetic poles. The movement of the magnetic poles results from changes in Earth's magnetic field.

Magnetic Declination Today, a compass needle does not point to true north. The angular distance in degrees between the direction of the compass needle and the line of longitude at a given location is the *magnetic declination*. Since the NMP is constantly on the move, knowledge of its present location is essential for determining the magnetic declination. Then, to calculate true north from a compass reading, you add or subtract (depending on your longitude relative to the NMP) the magnetic declination appropriate to your location. For example, in 2008, north of San Francisco, California, the declination was 15° west. However, at the junction of the Iowa, Missouri, and Illinois borders, the declination was 0°—at this location, the NMP and true north were aligned. At the same time, in Boston, the declination was 15° east.

Movement of the Poles During the past century, the NMP moved 1100 km (685 mi) across the Canadian Arctic. Presently, the NMP is moving northwest toward Siberia at approximately 55–60 km (34–37 mi) per year. The observed positions for 1831–2013 are mapped in **Figure GN 9.1** and listed in Table GN 9.1. Each day, the actual magnetic pole migrates in a small oval pattern around the average locations given on the map. The Geological Survey of Canada (GSC) tracks the location and movement of the NMP (see http://geomag.nrcan.gc.ca/index-eng.php).

In 2013, the NMP was near 85.9° N by 149° W in the Canadian Arctic. Its *antipode*, or opposite pole, the South Magnetic Pole (SMP), lay off the coast of Wilkes Land, Antarctica. The SMP moves separately from the NMP and is presently headed northwest at just 5 km (3.1 mi) per year (**Figure GN 9.2**). As we explore Earth's interior in this chapter, we discuss the changing intensity of Earth's magnetic field and how the field periodically reverses polarity. We discuss in later chapters the effects of the magnetic field on animal migration and how birds and turtles, among other animals, can read magnetic declination.

TABLE GN 9.1 Approximate North Magnetic Pole Coordinates, 2003 to 2015

Year	Latitude (°N)	Longitude (°W)
2003	82.0	112.4
2004	82.3	113.4
2005	82.7	114.4
2006	83.9	119.9
2007	84.4	121.7
2008	84.2	124.9
2009	84.9	131.0
2010	85.0	132.6
2011	85.1	134.0
2012	85.9	147.0
2013	85.9	148.0
2014	85.9	149.0
2015 (predicted)	86.1	153.0

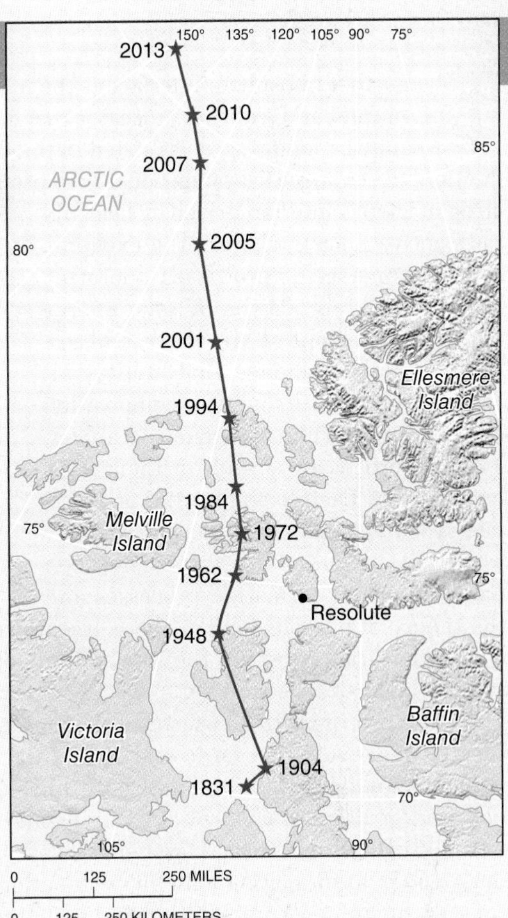

▲**Figure GN 9.1 North Magnetic Pole movement, 1831 to 2013.**

QUESTION AND EXPLORE For more about magnetic declination, go to https://www.ngdc.noaa.gov/geomag/geomag.shtml. Click on the "Declination calculator" on the right to determine the declination for your current location. MG

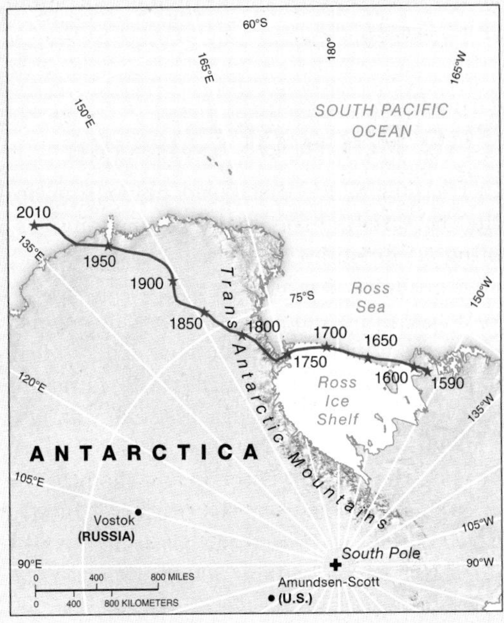

►**Figure GN 9.2 South Magnetic Pole movement, 1590 to 2010.** [Based on Magnetic Field Models, NOAA NGDC.]

The Earth–atmosphere interface is the meeting place of internal and external processes that build up and wear away landscapes. As stated in the Part 3 introduction, the **endogenic system** consists of processes operating in Earth's interior, driven by heat and radioactive decay, whereas the **exogenic system** consists of processes operating at Earth's surface, driven by solar energy and the movement of air, water, and ice. *Geology* is the science that studies all aspects of Earth—its history, composition and internal structure, surface features, and the processes acting on them. Our overview of Earth's endogenic, or internal, system in this chapter covers geology essentials, including the types of rocks on Earth and their formation processes and the theory of plate tectonics. These essentials provide a conceptual framework for the spatial study of the lithosphere in physical geography.

Geology is the science that studies all aspects of Earth—its history, composition and internal structure, surface features, and the processes acting on them.

The study of Earth's surface landforms—specifically, their origin, evolution, form, and spatial distribution—is **geomorphology**, a subfield of both physical geography and geology. Geomorphology is primarily related to the *exogenic*, or external, system; however, our study of Earth's exterior begins with an explanation of Earth's interior, including the basic materials and processes that shape Earth's surface.

In this chapter: Earth's interior is organized as a core surrounded by roughly concentric shells of material. It is unevenly heated by the radioactive decay of unstable elements. A rock cycle produces three classes of rocks through igneous, sedimentary, and metamorphic processes. A tectonic cycle moves vast sections of Earth's crust, called plates, accompanied by the spreading of the ocean floor. Collisions of these plates produce irregular surface fractures and mountain ranges both on land and on the ocean floor. This movement of crustal material results from endogenic forces within Earth; the surface expressions of these forces include earthquakes and volcanic events.

The Pace of Change

In Chapter 8, we discussed paleoclimatic techniques that establish chronologies of past environments, enabling scientists to reconstruct the age and character of past climates. An assumption of these reconstructions is that the movements, systems, and cycles that occur today also operated in the past. This guiding principle of Earth science, called **uniformitarianism**, presupposes that the same physical processes now active in the environment were operating throughout Earth's history. The phrase "the present is the key to the past" describes the principle. For example, the processes by which streams carve valleys at present are assumed to be the same as those that carved valleys 500 million years ago. Evidence from the geologic record, preserved in layers of rock that formed over millennia, supports this concept, which was first hypothesized by geologist James Hutton in the 18th century and later amplified by Charles Lyell in his seminal book *Principles of Geology* (1830).

Although the principle of uniformitarianism applies mainly to the gradual processes of geologic change, it also includes sudden, catastrophic events such as massive landslides, earthquakes, volcanic episodes, and asteroid impacts. These events have geological importance and may occur as small interruptions in the generally uniform processes that shape the slowly evolving landscape. Thus, uniformitarianism means that the natural laws that govern geologic processes have not changed throughout geologic time even though the rate at which these processes operate is variable.

The full scope of Earth's history can be represented in a summary timeline known as the **geologic time scale** (**Figure 9.1**). The scale breaks the past 4.6 billion years down into *eons*, the largest time span (although some refer to the Precambrian as a *supereon*), and then into increasingly shorter time spans of *eras*, *periods*, and *epochs*. Major events in Earth's history determine the boundaries between these intervals, which are not equal in length. Examples are the six major extinctions of life forms in Earth history, labeled in Figure 9.1. The timing of these events ranges from 440 million years ago (m.y.a.) to the ongoing present-day extinction episode caused by modern civilization (discussed in Chapter 16; for more on the geologic timescale, see http://www.ucmp.berkeley.edu/exhibit/geology.html). Geologists assign ages to events or specific rocks, structures, or landscapes using this time scale, based on either relative time (what happened in what order) or numerical time (the actual number of years before the present).

Relative age refers to the age of one feature with respect to another within a sequence of events. Determinations of relative age are based on the general principle of *superposition*, which states that rock and unconsolidated particles are arranged with the youngest layers "superposed" toward the top of a rock formation and the oldest at the base. This principle holds true as long as the materials have remained undisturbed. The horizontally arranged rock layers of the Grand Canyon and many other canyons of the U.S. Southwest are an example. The scientific study of these sequences is **stratigraphy**. Important time clues—for example, *fossils*, the remains of ancient plants and animals—lie embedded within these strata. Since approximately 4.0 billion years ago, life has left its evolving imprint in the rocks.

Numerical age (sometimes called absolute age) is today determined most often using isotopic dating techniques (introduced in Chapter 8) and other scientific methods. The technique of *radiometric dating*, for example, uses the rate of decay for different unstable

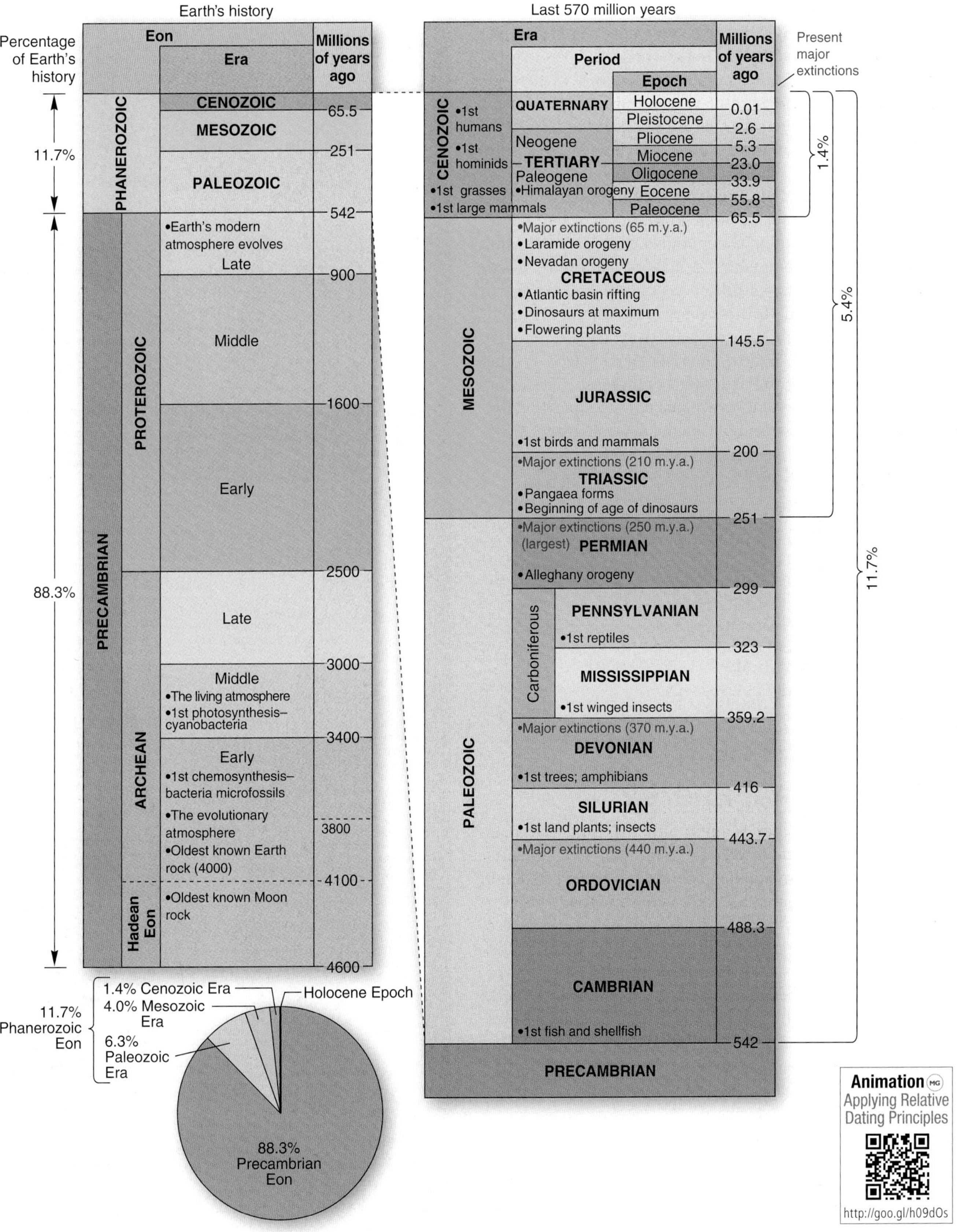

Animation Applying Relative Dating Principles
http://goo.gl/h09dOs

▲**Figure 9.1 Geologic time scale, showing highlights of Earth's history.** Dates appear in m.y.a. (millions of years ago). The scale uses currently accepted names of time intervals, except for the Hadean Eon, the proposed, but as yet unofficial name for the period before the Archean. The six major extinctions or depletions of life forms are shown in red. In the column to the left, note that the Precambrian Eon spans 88.3% of geologic time. [Data from Geological Society of America and *Nature* 429 (May 13, 2004): 124–125.]

isotopes to provide a steady time clock to pinpoint the ages of Earth materials. Precise knowledge of radioactive decay rates allows scientists to determine the date a rock formed by comparing the amount of original isotope in the sample with the amount of decayed end product in the sample. Numerical ages permit scientists to refine the geologic scale and improve the accuracy of relative dating sequences.

The oldest known surface rocks on Earth formed during the Archean Eon, about 4 billion years ago. These rocks are today found in Greenland (3.8 billion years old), northwestern Canada (about 4 billion years old), Western Australia (4.2 to 4.4 billion years old), and northern Quebec, Canada (4.3 billion years old). The most recent epoch in the geologic time scale is the *Holocene*, consisting of the 11,500 years since the last glacial period. As the impacts of humans on Earth systems increase, numerous scientists now agree that we are in a new epoch called the Anthropocene (discussed in Chapter 1, GeoReport 1.1).

CRITICAL**thinking 9.1**

Thoughts about an "Anthropocene Epoch"

Take a moment to explore the idea of naming our current epoch in the geologic time scale for humans. Develop some arguments for doing so that consider landscape alteration, deforestation, and climate change. If we were to designate the late Holocene as the Anthropocene, what do you think the criteria for the beginning date should be?

Earth's Structure and Internal Energy

Along with the other planets and the Sun, Earth is thought to have condensed and congealed from a nebula of dust, gas, and icy comets about 4.6 billion years ago (discussed in Chapter 2). As Earth solidified, gravity sorted materials by density. Heavier, denser substances such as iron gravitated slowly to its center, and lighter, less-dense elements such as silica slowly welled upward to the surface and became concentrated in the outer shell. Consequently, Earth's interior consists of roughly concentric layers (**Figure 9.2**), each distinct in either composition or temperature. Heat energy migrates outward from the center by conduction as well as by convection in the *plastic*, or fluid, layers.

Scientists have direct evidence of Earth's internal structure down to about 2 km (1.2 mi), from sediment cores drilled into Earth's outer surface layer. Below this region, scientific knowledge of Earth's internal layers

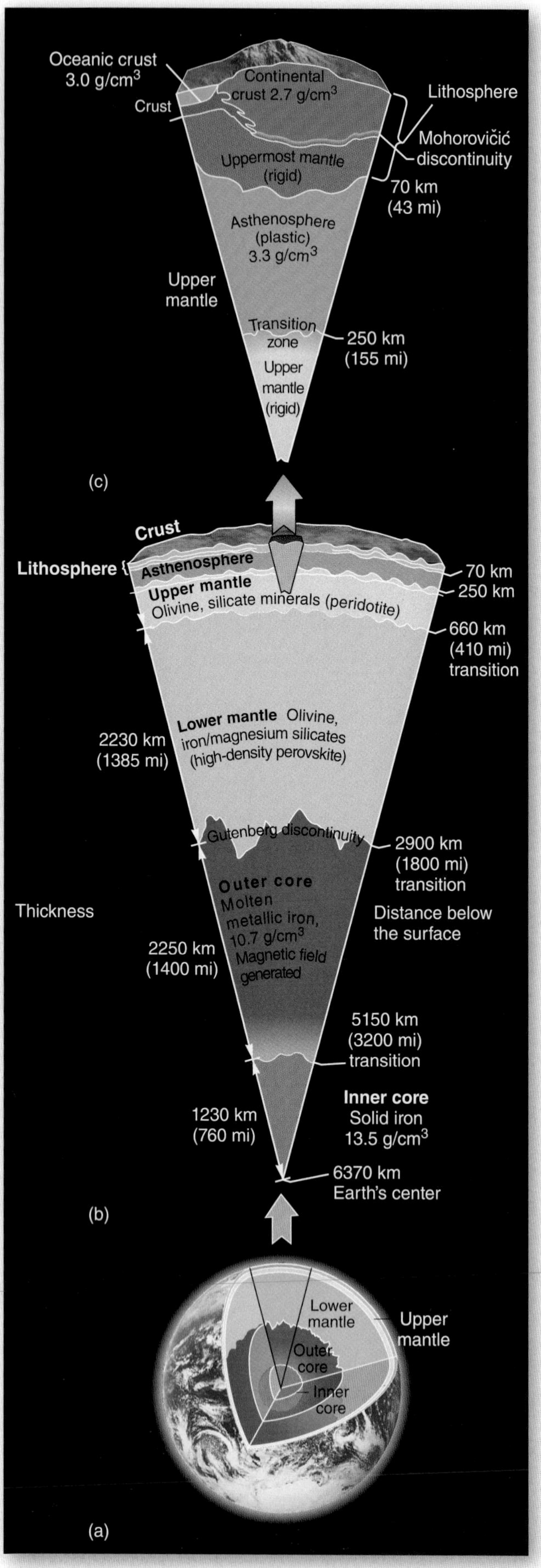

▸**Figure 9.2 Earth in cross section.** (a) Cutaway showing Earth's interior. (b) Earth's interior in cross section, from the inner core to the crust. (c) Detail of the structure of the lithosphere and its relation to the asthenosphere. (For comparison to the densities noted, the density of water is 1.0 g/cm³, and that of mercury, a liquid metal, is 13.0 g/cm³.)

is acquired entirely through indirect evidence. In the late 19th century, scientists discovered that the shock waves created by earthquakes were useful for identifying Earth's internal materials. Earthquakes are the surface vibrations felt when rocks near the surface suddenly fracture, or break (discussed at length in Chapter 10). These fractures generate **seismic waves**, or shock waves, that travel throughout the planet. The speed of the waves varies as they pass through different materials—cooler, more rigid areas transmit seismic waves at a higher velocity than do the hotter, more fluid areas. Plastic zones do not transmit some seismic waves; they absorb them. Waves may also be refracted (bent) or reflected, depending on the density of the material. Thus, scientists are now able to identify the boundaries between different layers within Earth by measuring the depths of changes in seismic wave velocity and direction. This is the science of *seismic tomography*; for animations and information, go to http://www.iris.edu/hq/programs/education_and_outreach/animations/7.

Earth's Core and Mantle

A third of Earth's entire mass, but only a sixth of its volume, lies in its dense core. The **core** is differentiated into two regions—*inner core* and *outer core*—divided by a transition zone several hundred kilometers wide (see Figure 9.2b). Scientists think that the inner core formed before the outer core, shortly after Earth condensed. The inner core is solid iron that is well above the melting temperature of iron at the surface but remains solid because of tremendous pressure. The iron is not pure, but probably is combined with silicon and possibly oxygen and sulfur. The outer core is molten, metallic iron with lighter densities than the inner core. The high temperatures keep the outer core in a liquid state, and the flow of this material generates Earth's magnetic field (discussed just ahead).

Earth's outer core is separated from the mantle by a transition zone several hundred kilometers wide at an average depth of about 2900 km (1800 mi; see Figure 9.2b). This zone is a *discontinuity*, or a place where physical differences occur between adjoining regions in Earth's interior. By studying the seismic waves of more than 25,000 earthquakes, scientists determined that this transition area, the *Gutenberg discontinuity*, is uneven, with ragged peak-and-valley-like formations.

Together, the lower and upper mantles represent about 80% of Earth's total volume. The **mantle** is rich in iron and magnesium oxides and in silicates, which are dense and tightly packed at depth, grading to lesser densities toward the surface. Temperatures are highest at depth and decrease toward the surface; materials are thicker at depth, with higher viscosity, due to increased pressure. A broad transition zone of several hundred kilometers, centered between 410 and 660 km (255 and 410 mi) below the surface, separates the lower mantle from the upper mantle. Rocks in the lower mantle are at high enough temperature that they become soft and are able to flow slowly, deforming over timescales of millions of years.

The boundary between the uppermost mantle and the crust above is another discontinuity, known as the **Mohorovičić discontinuity**, or **Moho** for short. It is named for the Croatian seismologist who determined that seismic waves change at this depth due to sharp contrasts in material composition and density.

Earth's Crust

Above the Moho is Earth's outer layer, the **crust**, which makes up only a fraction of Earth's overall mass and only a small portion of the overall distance from Earth's center to its surface. The thickness of Earth's crust varies over the extent of the planet. Crustal areas beneath mountain masses are thicker, extending to about 50–60 km (31–37 mi), whereas the crust beneath continental interiors averages about 30 km (19 mi) in thickness. Oceanic crust averages only 5 km (3 mi) in thickness. Drilling through the crust and Moho discontinuity (the crust–mantle boundary) into the uppermost mantle remains an elusive scientific goal.

Just eight natural elements make up over 98% of Earth's crust by weight, and just two of these—oxygen and silicon—together account for 74.3% (**Table 9.1**). Oxygen is the most reactive gas in the lower atmosphere, readily combining with other elements. For this reason, the percentage of oxygen is higher in the crust (at 46%) than in the atmosphere, where it makes up 21%. As a result of the internal differentiation process, less-dense elements are nearer the surface, which explains the relatively large percentages of elements such as silicon and aluminum in the crust.

Continental crust differs greatly from oceanic crust in composition and texture, and the difference has a bearing on the dynamics of plate tectonics and continental drift discussed later in the chapter.

- Continental crust is relatively low in density, averaging 2.7 g/cm^3 (or 2700 kg/m^3), and is composed mainly of *granite*. It is crystalline and high in silica, aluminum, potassium, calcium, and sodium. Sometimes continental crust is called *sial*, shorthand for the dominant elements of *si*lica and *al*uminum.

GEOreport 9.1 Radioactive elements drive Earth's internal heat

The internal heat that fuels endogenic processes beneath Earth's surface comes from residual heat left over from the planet's formation and from the decay of radioactive elements—specifically, the radioactive decay of the isotopes potassium-40 (^{40}K), uranium-238 and -235 (^{238}U and ^{235}U), and thorium-232 (^{232}Th).

TABLE 9.1 Common Elements in Earth's Crust

Element	Percentage of Earth's Crust by Weight
Oxygen (O)	46.6
Silicon (Si)	27.7
Aluminum (Al)	8.1
Iron (Fe)	5.0
Calcium (Ca)	3.6
Sodium (Na)	2.8
Potassium (K)	2.6
Magnesium (Mg)	2.1
All others	1.5
Total	100.00

[Quartz: Stefano Cavoretto/Shutterstock.]

A quartz crystal (SiO_2) consists of Earth's two most abundant elements, silicon (Si) and oxygen (O).

- Oceanic crust is denser than continental crust, averaging 3.0 g/cm³ (or 3000 kg/m³), and is composed of *basalt*. It is granular and high in silica, magnesium, and iron. Sometimes oceanic crust is called *sima*, shorthand for the dominant elements of *si*lica and *ma*gnesium.

The Asthenosphere and Lithosphere

The interior layers of core, mantle, and crust are differentiated by chemical composition. Another way to distinguish layers within the Earth is by their rigid or plastic character. A rigid layer will not flow when a force acts on it; instead, it will bend or break. A plastic layer will slowly flow when a force is present. Using this criterion, scientists divide the outer part of Earth into two layers: the **lithosphere**, or rigid layer (from the Greek *lithos*, or "rocky"), and the **asthenosphere**, or plastic layer (from the Greek *asthenos*, meaning "weak").

The lithosphere includes the crust and the uppermost mantle, to about 70 km (43 mi) in depth, and forms the rigid, cooler layer at Earth's surface (Figure 9.2c). Note that the terms *lithosphere* and *crust* are not the same; the crust makes up the upper portion of the lithosphere.

The asthenosphere lies within the mantle from about 70 km to 250 km (43 mi to 155 mi) in depth. About 10% of the asthenosphere is molten in uneven patterns. The movement of convection currents in this zone in part causes the shifting of lithospheric plates, discussed later in the chapter.

Adjustments in the Crust

We discussed the *buoyancy force* in Chapter 5 with regard to parcels of air—if a parcel of air is less dense than the surrounding air, it is buoyant and will rise. In essence, buoyancy is the principle that something less dense, such as wood, floats in something more dense, such as water. The balance between the buoyancy and gravitational forces is the principle of **isostasy**, which explains the elevations of continents and the depths of ocean floors as determined by vertical movements of Earth's crust.

Earth's lithosphere floats on the denser layers beneath, much as a boat floats on water. If a load is placed on the surface, such as the weight of a glacier, a mountain range, or an area of sediment accumulation (rock material that has been transported by exogenic processes), the lithosphere tends to sink, or ride lower in the asthenosphere (**Figure 9.3**). When this happens, the rigid lithosphere bends, and the plastic asthenosphere flows out of the way. If the load is removed, such as when a glacier melts, the crust lifts gradually to ride higher, and the asthenosphere flows back toward the region of uplifting lithosphere. The uplift after removal of surface load is known as *isostatic rebound*. The entire crust is in a constant state of isostatic adjustment, slowly rising and sinking in response to weight at the surface.

In southeast Alaska, scientists have recently measured the most rapid rates of isostatic adjustment on Earth, especially in the area around Glacier Bay. Using an array of GPS receivers, they detected vertical motion averaging 32 mm (1.26 in.) per year, as ongoing uplift

GEOreport 9.2 Deep-drilling the continental crust

The Kola Borehole in Russia, north of the Arctic Circle, is 12.23 km deep (7.6 mi, or 40,128 ft), drilled over a 20-year period purely for exploration and science. This is the deepest drilling attempt for scientific purposes in continental crust; drilling for oil wells has gone deeper—the record is 12.29 km (7.64 mi, or 40,318 ft) in the Al Shaheen oil field in Qatar. The Kola Borehole reached rock 1.4 billion years old at 180°C (356°F) in the Earth's crust and for two decades was the deepest borehole ever drilled (see **http://www-icdp.icdp-online.org/front_content.php?idcat=695**).

Mountain
Oceanic crust
Ocean
Continental crust
Low-density mountain "root"
Lithosphere
Moho
Uppermost mantle (rigid)
Displacement in upper mantle
Asthenosphere (plastic)

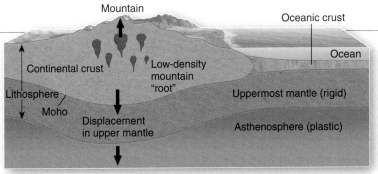

(a) The mountain mass slowly sinks, displacing mantle material.

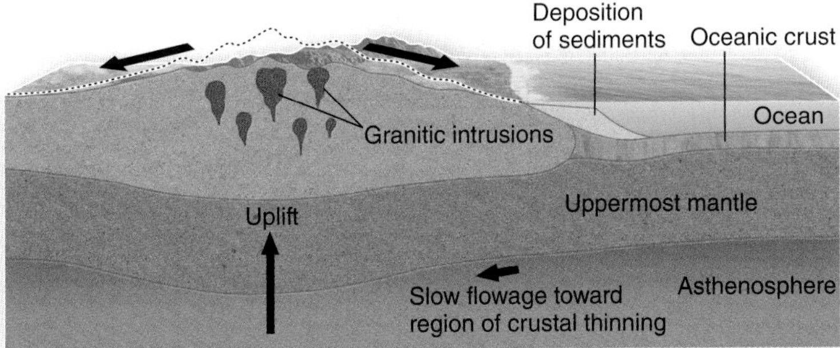

(b) Weathering and erosion transport sediment from land into oceans; as land loses mass, the crust isostatically adjusts upward.

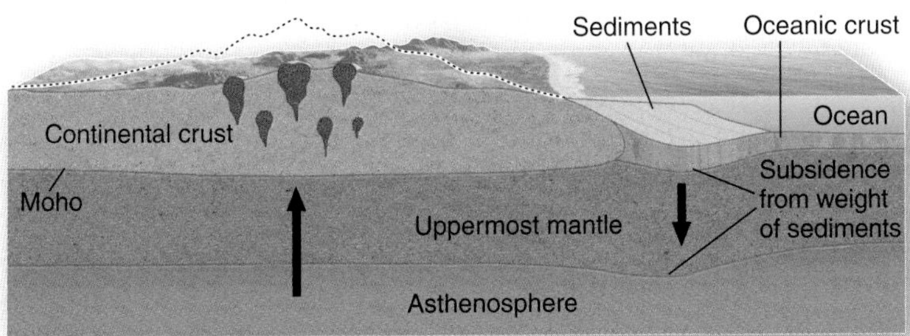

(c) As the continental crust erodes, the heavy sediment load offshore deforms the lithosphere beneath the ocean.

(d) The melting of ice from the last ice age and losses of overlying sediments are thought to produce an ongoing isostatic uplift of portions of the Sierra Nevada batholith.

▲**Figure 9.3 Isostatic adjustment of the crust.** Earth's entire crust is in a constant state of adjustment, as suggested by these three sequential stages. [(d) Bobbé Christopherson.]

counterbalances the removal of weight from the crust that began with the retreat of glacial ice following the last ice age, about 10,000 years ago. Scientists attribute current rates of isostatic rebound to the loss of modern glaciers in the region with ongoing climate change, causing glacial melt and retreat over the past 150 years.

Earth's Magnetism

As mentioned earlier, Earth's fluid outer core generates most (at least 90%) of Earth's magnetic field and the magnetosphere that surrounds and protects Earth from solar wind and cosmic radiation. One hypothesis explains that circulation in the outer core converts thermal and gravitational energy into magnetic energy, thus producing the magnetic field. The locations of the north and south magnetic poles are surface expressions of Earth's magnetic field and migrate as plotted on the map in Geosystems Now for this chapter.

At various times in Earth's history, the magnetic field has faded to zero and then returned to full strength with the polarity reversed (meaning that the north magnetic pole then lies near the south geographic pole, so that a compass needle would point south). In the process, the field does not blink on and off, but instead diminishes slowly to low intensity, perhaps 25% strength, and then rapidly regains full power. This **geomagnetic reversal** has taken place nine times during the past 4 million years and hundreds of times over Earth's history (see Figure 9.13 on page 300). During the transition interval of low strength, Earth's surface receives higher levels of cosmic radiation and solar particles, but not to such an extent as to cause species extinctions. Life on Earth has weathered many of these transitions.

The average period of a magnetic reversal is about 500,000 years, with a range from as short as 20,000 years to as long as 50 million years. Although the cause and timing of these reversals are unknown, they have become a key tool in understanding the evolution of landmasses and the movements of the continents. As rocks cool and solidify from molten material (lava) at Earth's surface, the small magnetic particles (usually iron) in the material align according to the orientation of the magnetic poles at that time, and this alignment locks in place. Thus, rocks of the same age bear identical particle alignments, illustrating global patterns of changing magnetism. Later in this chapter, we see the importance of these magnetic reversals.

Earth Materials and the Rock Cycle

We have already mentioned several types of rocks, such as granite and basalt, and described processes involving rocks and their formation. To understand and classify rocks from a scientific viewpoint, we must begin with minerals, which are the building blocks of rocks. A **mineral** is an inorganic, or nonliving, natural solid compound having a specific chemical formula and usually possessing a crystalline structure. Each mineral has its own characteristic color, texture, crystal shape, and density, among other unique properties. For example, the common mineral *quartz* is silicon dioxide, SiO_2, and has a distinctive six-sided crystal. Ice fits the definition of a mineral, although water does not.

Mineralogy is the study of the composition, properties, and classification of minerals (see http://www.mindat.org/). Of the more than 4200 minerals known, about 30 are the most common components of rocks. Roughly 95% of Earth's crust is made up of *silicates*, one of the most widespread mineral families—not surprising, considering the percentages of silicon and oxygen on Earth and their readiness to combine with each other and with other elements. This mineral family includes quartz, feldspar, clay minerals, and numerous gemstones. Several other groups of minerals are also important: *Oxides* are minerals in which oxygen combines with metallic elements; *sulfides* and *sulfates* are minerals in which sulfur compounds combine with metallic elements; and *carbonates* feature carbon in combination with oxygen and other elements such as calcium, magnesium, and potassium.

A **rock** is an assemblage of minerals bound together (such as granite, a rock containing three minerals), or a mass composed of a single mineral (such as rock salt), of undifferentiated material (such as the noncrystalline glassy obsidian), or even of solid organic material (such as coal). Scientists have identified thousands of different rocks, all of which can be sorted according to three types that depend on the processes that formed them: *igneous* (formed from molten material), *sedimentary* (formed from compaction or chemical processes), and *metamorphic* (altered by heat and pressure). The movement of material through these processes is known as the *rock cycle* and is summarized at the end of this section.

Igneous Processes

An **igneous rock** is one that solidifies and crystallizes from a molten state (*igneous* means "fire-formed" in Latin). Igneous rocks form from **magma**, which is molten rock beneath Earth's surface. When magma emerges at the surface, it is **lava**, although it retains its molten characteristics. Overall, igneous rocks make up approximately 90% of Earth's crust, although sedimentary rocks, soil, or oceans frequently cover them.

Igneous Environments Magma is fluid, highly gaseous, and under tremendous pressure. The result is that it either *intrudes* into crustal rocks, cooling and hardening below the surface to form **intrusive igneous rock**, or it *extrudes* onto the surface as lava and cools to form **extrusive igneous rock**. Extrusive igneous rocks result from volcanic eruptions and flows and are discussed in additional detail in Chapter 10.

The location and rate of cooling determine the crystalline texture of a rock, that is, whether it is made of coarser (larger) or finer (smaller) materials. Thus, the texture indicates the environment in which the rock formed. The slower cooling of magma beneath the surface allows more time for crystals to form, resulting in coarse-grained rocks such as **granite**. Even though this rock cooled below Earth's surface, subsequent uplift of the landscape has exposed granitic rocks (**Figure 9.4a**), some of which form

▼Figure 9.4 Examples of intrusive granite and extrusive basalt. [(a) Egon Bömsch/Imagebroker/SuperStock. (b) Bobbé Christopherson.]

(a) Granite shaped by weathering processes near Joshua Tree National Park, California, the southern region of the extensive California batholith. (We examine weathering in Chapter 11.)

(b) Basaltic lava flows on Hawai'i. The glowing opening is a skylight into an active tube where molten lava flows; the shiny surface is where lava recently flowed out of the skylight.

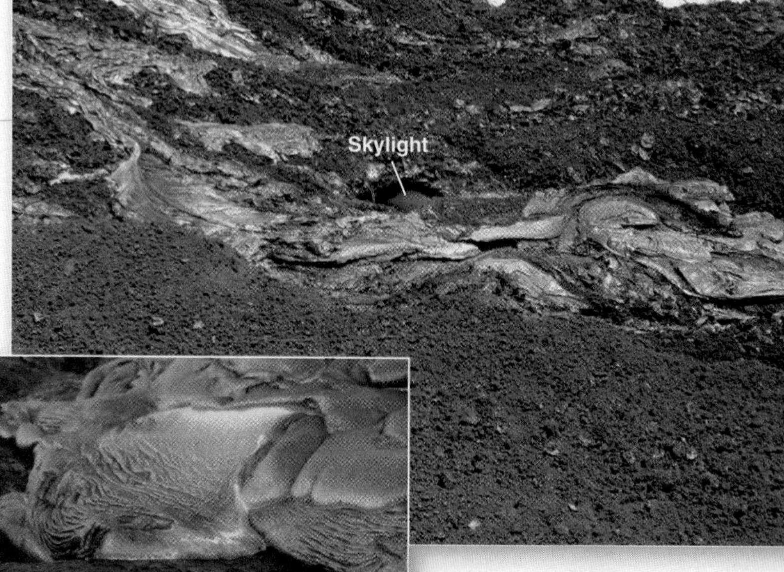

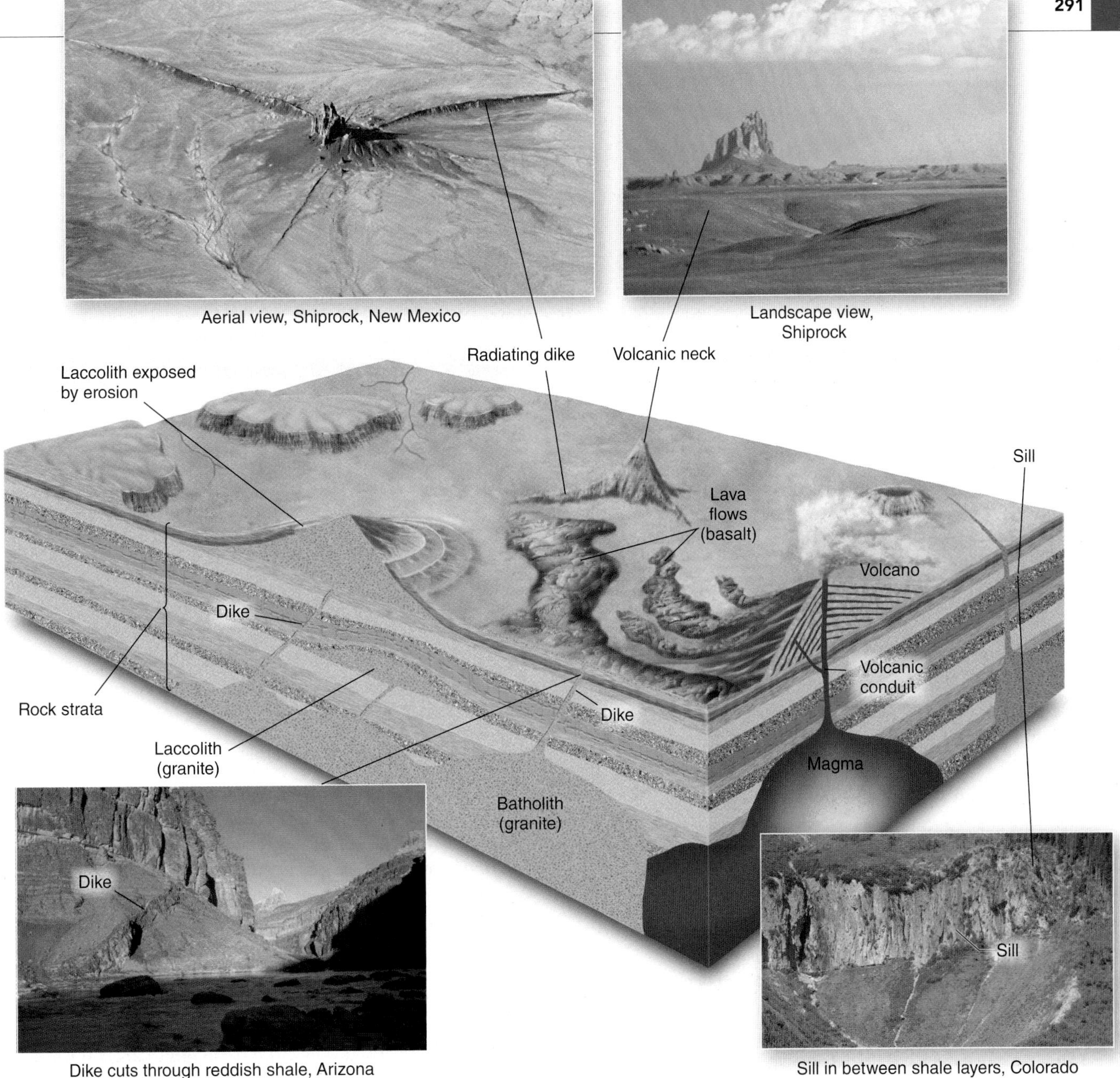

▲**Figure 9.5 Igneous landforms.** Varieties of igneous rocks, both intrusive (below the surface) and extrusive (on the surface), and associated landforms. [Aerial view: Bobbé Christopherson. Landscape view: Robert Christopherson. Dike: NPS. Sill: U.S. Geological Survey.]

the world's most famous cliff faces and rock-climbing destinations—El Capitan and Half Dome in Yosemite Valley, California, and the Great Trango Tower in Pakistan are examples. The faster cooling of lava at the surface forms finer-grained rocks, such as **basalt**, the most common extrusive igneous rock. As discussed later in the chapter, basalt makes up the bulk of the ocean floor, accounting for 71% of Earth's surface, and is actively forming on the Big Island of Hawai'i (**Figure 9.4b**). If cooling is so rapid that crystals cannot form, the result is a glassy rock such as *obsidian*, or volcanic glass.

Igneous Landforms If igneous rocks are uplifted by exogenic processes, the work of air, water, and ice then sculpts them into unique landforms. **Figure 9.5** illustrates the formation environments of several intrusive and extrusive igneous rock types and landforms.

Intrusive igneous rock that cools slowly in the crust forms a **pluton**, the general term for any intrusive igneous body, regardless of size or shape. (The Roman god of the underworld, Pluto, is the namesake.) The largest plutonic form is a **batholith**, usually made up of multiple plutons. When exposed by weathering and erosion, a batholith often has a surface greater than 100 km^2 (40 mi^2). Batholiths form the mass of many large mountain ranges—for example, the Sierra Nevada batholith in California (see Figure 9.3d), the Idaho batholith, and the Coast Range batholith of British Columbia and Washington State.

Smaller plutons include the magma conduits of ancient volcanoes that have cooled and hardened.

(a) Sandstone strata show cross-bedding from ancient sand dune environments, Utah.

(b) Chemical limestone in south-central Indiana.

(c) Biochemical limestone, showing shells and clasts cemented together.

▲**Figure 9.6 Sedimentary rock types.** [Bobbé Christopherson.]

Those that form parallel to layers of sedimentary rock are *sills*; those that cross layers of the rock they invade are *dikes* (Figure 9.5). Magma also can bulge between rock strata and produce a lens-shaped body called a *laccolith*, a type of sill. In addition, magma conduits may solidify in roughly cylindrical forms that stand starkly above the landscape when finally exposed by weathering and erosion. Shiprock volcanic neck in New Mexico is such a feature, rising 518 m (1700 ft) above the surrounding plain; note the radiating dikes in the aerial photo in Figure 9.5.

Sedimentary Processes

Solar energy and gravity drive the processes that form **sedimentary rock**, in which loose *clasts* (grains or fragments) are cemented together (**Figure 9.6**). The clasts that become solid rock are derived from several sources: the weathering and erosion of existing rock (the origin of the sand that forms sandstone), the accumulation of shells on the ocean floor (which make up one form of limestone), the accumulation of organic matter from ancient plants (which forms coal), and the precipitation of minerals from water solution (the origin of the calcium carbonate, $CaCO_3$, that forms chemical limestone). Sedimentary rocks are divided into several categories—clastic, biochemical, organic, and chemical—based on their origin.

Clastic Sedimentary Rocks The formation of clastic sedimentary rock involves several processes. *Weathering*, discussed in detail in Chapter 11, disintegrates and dissolves existing rock into clasts. *Erosion* by gravity, water, wind, and ice then carries these rock particles across landscapes; at this point, the moving material is called **sediment**. Transport occurs from "higher-energy" sites, where the carrying medium has the energy to pick up and move the material, to "lower-energy" sites, where the sediment is deposited. *Deposition* is the process whereby sediment settles out of the transporting medium and results in material dropped along river channels, on beaches, and on ocean bottoms, where it is eventually buried.

Lithification occurs as loose sediment is hardened into solid rock. This process involves *compaction* of buried sediments as the weight of overlying material squeezes out the water and air between clasts and *cementation* as minerals fill any remaining spaces and fuse the clasts—principally quartz, feldspar, and clay minerals—into a coherent mass. The type of cement varies with different environments. Calcium carbonate ($CaCO_3$) is the most common cement, followed by iron oxides and silica. Drying (dehydration) and heating can also unite particles.

The different sediments that make up sedimentary rock range in size from boulders to gravel to sand to microscopic clay particles (**Table 9.2**). After lithification, these size classes, combined with their composition, sorting, and cement characteristics, determine the common sedimentary rock types. For example, pebbles and gravels become conglomerate, silt-sized particles become siltstone or mudstone, and clay-sized particles become shale.

Chemical Sedimentary Rocks Some sedimentary rocks are formed not from pieces of broken rock, but instead from the shells of organisms that contain calcium carbonate (a biochemical process) or from dissolved minerals that precipitate out of water solutions (a chemical process) and build up to form rock. *Chemical precipitation* is the formation of a separate solid substance from a

TABLE 9.2 Clast Sizes and Related Sedimentary Rocks

Clast Size	Sediment Type	Rock Type
80 mm (very coarse)	Boulders, cobbles	Conglomerate (breccia, if pieces are angular)
> 2 mm (coarse)	Pebbles, gravel	Conglomerate
0.5–2.0 mm (medium to coarse)	Sand	Sandstone
0.062–0.5 mm (fine to medium)	Sand	Sandstone
0.004–0.062 mm (fine)	Silt	Siltstone (mudstone)
<0.004 mm (very fine)	Clay	Shale

▲**Figure 9.8 Chemical sediments at a hydrothermal vent.** Black smokers and associated mineral deposits along a mid-ocean ridge in the Pacific. [Image courtesy of MARUM, University of Bremen and NOAA-Pacific Marine Environmental Laboratory.]

solution, such as when water evaporates and leaves behind a residue of salts. This explains the formation of *evaporites*, such as those found in Utah on the Bonneville Salt Flats, created when an ancient salt lake evaporated. These processes are important in oceanic environments, as well as in areas of karst topography (discussed in Chapter 11).

The most common chemical sedimentary rock is **limestone**, and the most common form of limestone is biochemical limestone from marine organic origins. As discussed in Chapter 8, many organisms extract dissolved $CaCO_3$ from seawater to construct solid shells. When these organisms die, the solid shell material builds up on the ocean floor and is then lithified to become limestone (Figure 9.6b).

Limestone is also formed from a chemical process in which $CaCO_3$ in solution is chemically precipitated out of groundwater that has seeped to the surface. This process forms *travertine*, a mineral deposit that commonly forms terraces or mounds near springs (**Figure 9.7**). The precipitation of carbonates from the water of these natural springs is driven in part by "degassing": Carbon dioxide bubbles out of solution at the surface, making the remaining solutes more likely to precipitate. Cave features such as speleothems, discussed in Chapter 8, are another type of travertine deposit.

▼**Figure 9.7 Chemical sedimentary rock.** Travertine, a chemical limestone composed of calcium carbonate, at the natural hot springs of Pamukkale in southwestern Turkey. [Paul Williams/Alamy.]

Hydrothermal deposits, consisting of metallic minerals accumulated by chemical precipitation from hot water, often are found near vents in the ocean floor—often along mid-ocean ridges created by spreading of the seafloor (discussed later in the chapter). As water seeps into the magma below the crust, it becomes superheated and then gushes out of the ocean floor at high speed. Such hydrothermal vents, called "black smokers," belch dark clouds of hydrogen sulfides, minerals, and metals that the hot water (in excess of 380°C, or 716°F) leached from the basalt (**Figure 9.8**). These materials may build up to form towers around the vents that support life forms uniquely suited to the chemical conditions of the vent fluids. The deposits are caused by mineral precipitation, but are closely associated with igneous activity within newly forming crust.

Metamorphic Processes

Any igneous or sedimentary rock may be transformed into a **metamorphic rock** by going through profound physical or chemical changes under pressure and increased temperature (*metamorphic* comes from the Greek "to change form"). Metamorphic rocks generally are more compact than the original rock and therefore are harder and more resistant to weathering and erosion (**Figure 9.9**).

The four processes that can cause metamorphism are heating, pressure, heating and pressure together, and compression and shear. When heat is applied to rock, the atoms within the minerals may break their chemical bonds, move, and form new bonds, leading to new mineral assemblages that develop into solid rock. When pressure is applied to rock, mineral structure may change as atoms become packed more closely. When rock is subject to both heat and pressure at depth, the original mineral assemblage becomes unstable and changes. Finally, rocks may be compressed by overlying weight and subject to shear when

▲**Figure 9.9 Metamorphic rocks.** The Amitsoq Gneiss in Greenland is 3.8 billion years in age, one of the oldest exposed rock formations on Earth. Note the rock's foliated texture. [Kevin Schafer/Corbis.]

one part of the mass moves sideways relative to another part. These processes change the shape of the rock, leading to changes in the mineral alignments within.

Metamorphic rock may form from igneous rocks as the lithospheric plates shift, especially when one plate is thrust beneath another (discussed with plate tectonics, just ahead). *Contact metamorphism* occurs when magma rising within the crust "cooks" adjacent rock; this type of metamorphism occurs adjacent to igneous intrusions and results from heat alone. *Regional metamorphism* occurs when a large areal extent of rock is subject to metamorphism. This can occur when sediments collect in broad depressions in Earth's crust and, because of their own weight, create enough pressure on the bottommost layers to transform the sediments into metamorphic rock. Regional metamorphism also occurs as lithospheric plates collide and mountain building occurs (discussed in Chapter 10).

Metamorphic rocks have textures that are foliated or nonfoliated, depending on the arrangement of minerals after metamorphism (**Table 9.3**). *Foliated* rock has a banded or layered appearance, demonstrating the alignment of minerals, which may appear as wavy striations (streaks or lines) in the rock. *Nonfoliated* rocks do not exhibit this alignment.

The Rock Cycle

Although rocks appear stable and unchanging, they are not. The **rock cycle** is the name for the continuous alteration of Earth materials from one rock type to another (**Figure 9.10**). For example, igneous rock formed from magma may break down into sediment by weathering and erosion and then lithify into sedimentary rock. This rock may subsequently become buried and exposed to pressure and heat deep within Earth, forming metamorphic rock. This may, in turn, break down and become sedimentary rock. Igneous rock may also take a shortcut through that cycle by directly becoming metamorphic rock. As the arrows indicate, there are many pathways through the rock cycle.

Two cyclic systems drive the rock cycle. At and above Earth's surface, the hydrologic cycle, fueled by solar energy, drives the exogenic processes. Below Earth's surface and within the crust, the tectonic cycle, powered by internal heat, drives the endogenic processes. We now discuss plate tectonics theory and the tectonic cycle.

Plate Tectonics

Have you ever looked at a world map and noticed that a few of the continental landmasses appear to have matching shapes like pieces of a jigsaw puzzle—particularly South America and Africa? The reality is that the continental pieces once did fit together. Continental landmasses not only migrated to their present locations, but also are continuing to move today at speeds up to 6 cm (2.4 in.) per year. We say that the continents are *adrift* because convection currents in the asthenosphere and upper mantle provide upwelling and downwelling forces that push and pull portions of the lithosphere. Thus, the arrangement of continents and oceans we see today is not permanent, but is in a continuing state of change. Plate tectonics theory, although at first controversial, now provides the underlying foundation for much of Earth systems science.

Continental Drift

As early mapping gained accuracy, some observers noticed the agreement in the profiles of the continents, particularly those of South America and Africa.

TABLE 9.3 Metamorphic Rocks

Parent Rock	Metamorphic Equivalent	Texture
Shale (clay minerals)	Slate	Foliated
Granite, slate, shale	Gneiss	Foliated
Basalt, shale, peridotite	Schist	Foliated
Limestone, dolomite	Marble	Nonfoliated
Sandstone	Quartzite	Nonfoliated

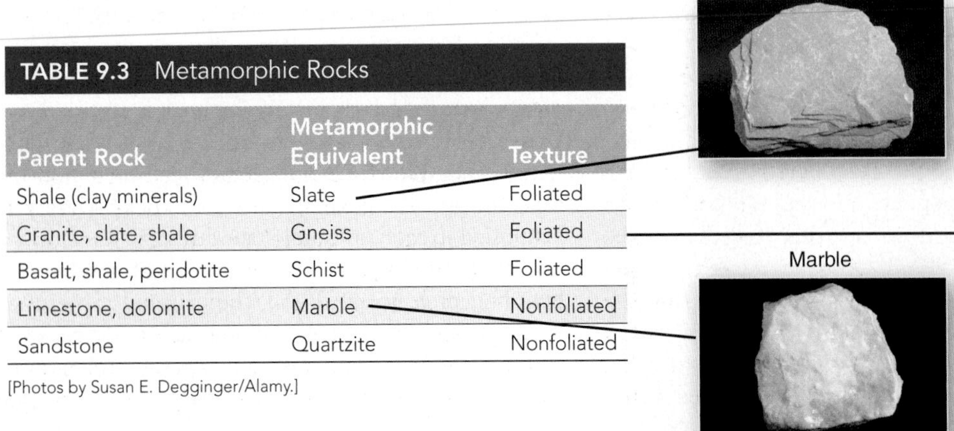

[Photos by Susan E. Degginger/Alamy.]

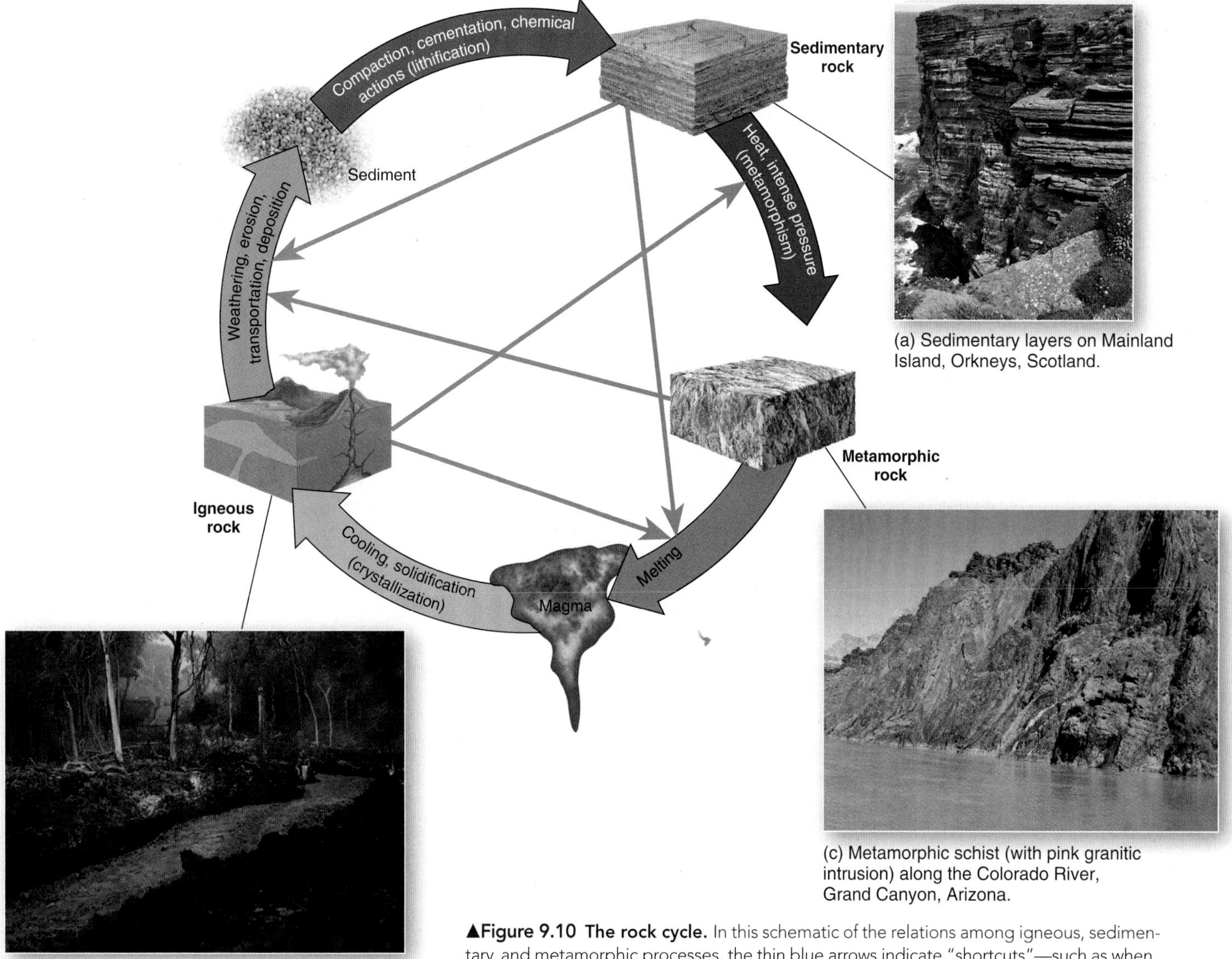

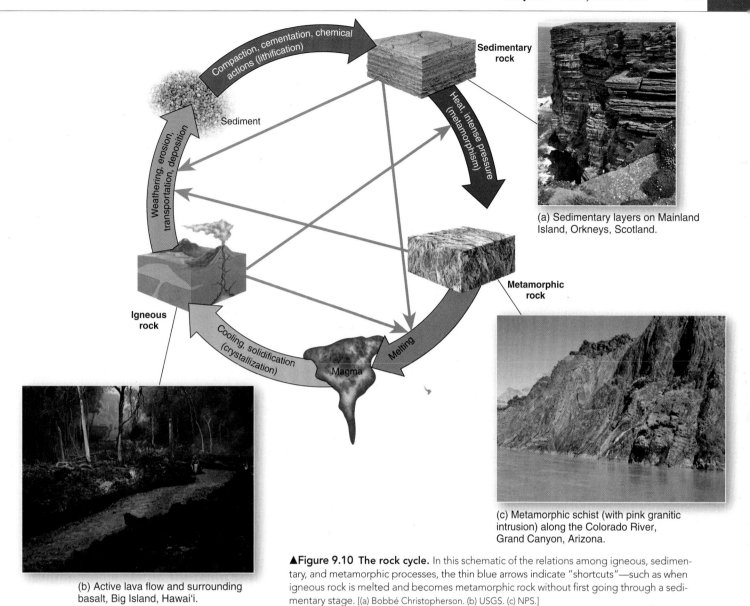

(a) Sedimentary layers on Mainland Island, Orkneys, Scotland.

(b) Active lava flow and surrounding basalt, Big Island, Hawai'i.

(c) Metamorphic schist (with pink granitic intrusion) along the Colorado River, Grand Canyon, Arizona.

▲**Figure 9.10 The rock cycle.** In this schematic of the relations among igneous, sedimentary, and metamorphic processes, the thin blue arrows indicate "shortcuts"—such as when igneous rock is melted and becomes metamorphic rock without first going through a sedimentary stage. [(a) Bobbé Christopherson. (b) USGS. (c) NPS.]

Abraham Ortelius (1527–1598), a geographer, noted the apparent fit of some continental coastlines in his *Thesaurus Geographicus* (1596). In 1620, English philosopher Sir Francis Bacon noted gross similarities between the edges of Africa and South America (although he did not suggest that they had drifted apart). Benjamin Franklin wrote in 1780 that Earth's crust must be a shell that can break and shift by movements of fluid below. Others wrote—unscientifically—about such apparent relationships, but it was not until much later that a valid explanation emerged.

In 1912, German geophysicist and meteorologist Alfred Wegener presented an idea that challenged long-held assumptions in geology and three years later published his book *Origin of the Continents and Oceans*. After studying the geologic record represented in the rock strata, Wegener found evidence that the rock assemblages on the east coast of South America were the same as those on the west coast of Africa, suggesting that the continents were at one time connected. The fossil record provided further evidence, as did the climatic record found in sedimentary rocks. Wegener hypothesized that the coal deposits found today in the midlatitudes exist because these regions were at one time nearer the equator and were covered by lush vegetation that later became the lithified organic material that forms coal. Wegener concluded that all landmasses migrate and that approximately 225 m.y.a. they formed one supercontinent, which he named **Pangaea**, meaning "all Earth."

Today, scientists regard Wegener as the father of plate tectonics, which he first called *continental drift*. However, scientists at the time were unreceptive to Wegener's revolutionary proposal. A great debate began with Wegener's book and lasted almost 50 years. As modern scientific capabilities led to discoveries that built the case for continental drift, the 1950s and 1960s saw a revival of interest in Wegener's concepts and, finally, confirmation. Although his initial model kept the landmasses together too long and his proposal included an incorrect driving mechanism for the moving continents, Wegener's arrangement of Pangaea and its breakup was correct.

Figure 9.11 shows the changing arrangement of the continents, beginning with the pre-Pangaea configuration

▶Figure 9.11 Continents adrift, from 465 m.y.a. to the present. Observe the formation and breakup of Pangaea and the types of motions occurring at plate boundaries (discussed just ahead in the chapter). [(a) From R. K. Bambach, "Before Pangaea: The geography of the Paleozoic world," *American Scientist 68* (1980): 26–38, reprinted by permission. (b–e) From R. S. Dietz and J. C. Holden, *Journal of Geophysical Research 75*, no. 26 (September 10, 1970): 4939–4956, © The American Geophysical Union.]

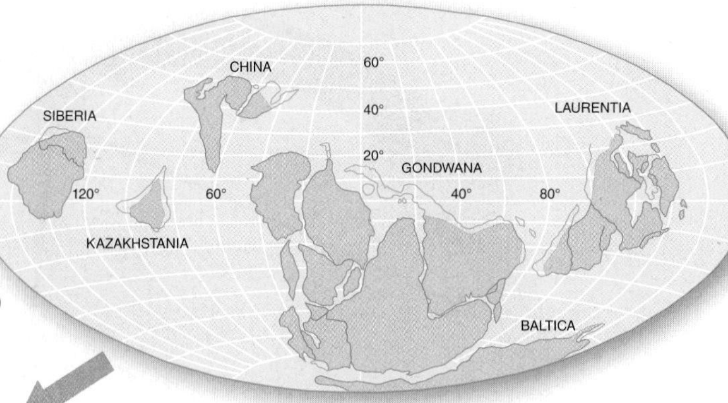

(a) 465 million years ago

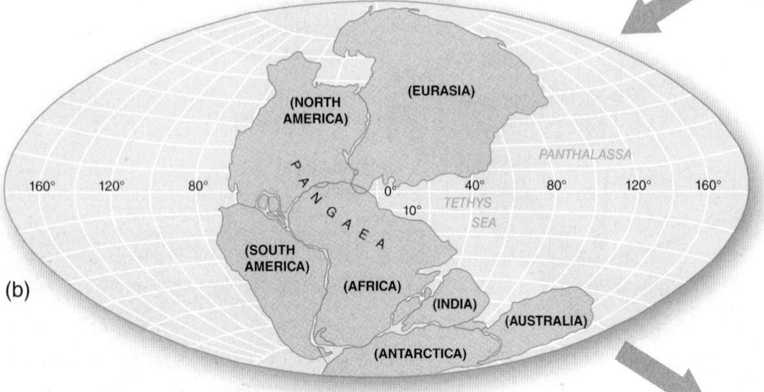

(b) 225 million years ago

At the time of Pangaea ("all Earth"), Africa was connected to North and South America. The Appalachian Mountains in the eastern U.S. and the Lesser Atlas Mountains of northwestern Africa are portions of the same ancestral mountain range. Panthalassa ("all seas") became the Pacific Ocean.

Animation MG
India Collision with Asia
http://goo.gl/pu7HEQ

(c) 135 million years ago

New seafloor is highlighted (purple tint). An active spreading center rifted North America away from landmasses to the east. India moved toward its collision with Asia, a spreading center to the south and a subduction zone to the north.

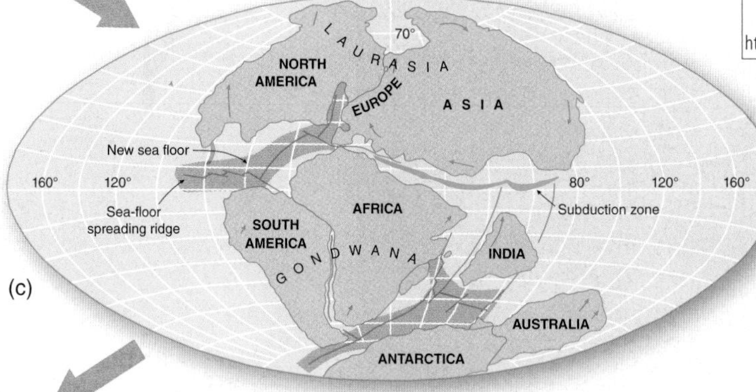

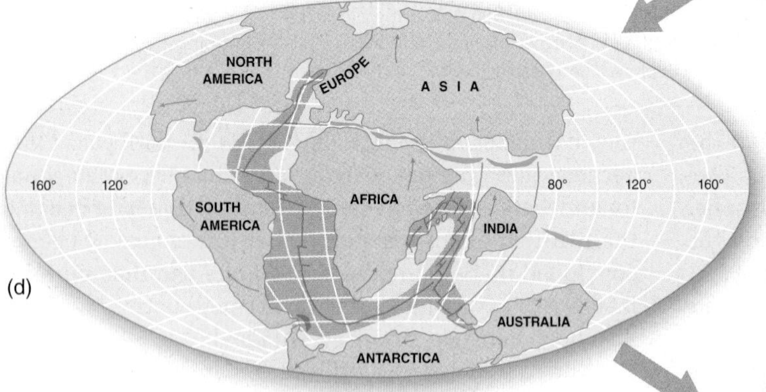

(d) 65 million years ago

Along the Mid-Atlantic Ridge, seafloor spread some 3000 km (almost 1900 mi) in 70 million years. The rifting along where the Red Sea would form began. Of all the major plates, India traveled the farthest—almost 10,000 km.

(e) Today

From 65 m.y.a. until the present, more than half of the ocean floor was renewed. The northern reaches of the India plate underthrust the southern mass of Asia through subduction, forming the Himalayas. Plate motions continue to this day.

Animation MG
Plate Motions Through Time
http://goo.gl/quab8Y

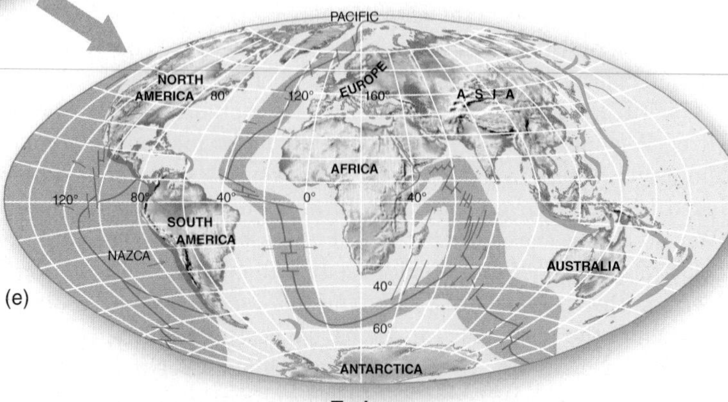

of 465 m.y.a. (during the Middle Ordovician Period; Figure 9.11a) and moving to an updated version of Wegener's Pangaea, 225–200 m.y.a. (Triassic–Jurassic Periods; Figure 9.11b); the configuration that occurred by 135 m.y.a., with the continents of Gondwana and Laurasia (the beginning of the Cretaceous Period; Figure 9.11c); the arrangement 65 m.y.a. (shortly after the beginning of the Tertiary Period; Figure 9.11d); and, finally, the present arrangement in modern geologic time (the late Cenozoic Era; Figure 9.11e).

The word *tectonic*, from the Greek *tektonikùs*, meaning "building" or "construction," refers to changes in the configuration of Earth's crust as a result of internal forces. **Plate tectonics** is the theory that the lithosphere is divided into a number of plates that float independently over the mantle and along whose boundaries occur the formation of new crust, the building of mountains, and the seismic activity that causes earthquakes. Plate tectonics theory describes the motion of Earth's lithosphere; we discuss the various principles of this theory ahead in this section and in Chapter 10.

Seafloor Spreading

The key to establishing the theory of continental drift was a better understanding of the seafloor crust. As scientists acquired information about the bathymetry (depth variations) of the ocean floor, they discovered an interconnected worldwide mountain chain, forming a ridge some 64,000 km (40,000 mi) in extent and averaging more than 1000 km (600 mi) in width (see the opening map in Chapter 10). The underwater mountain systems that form this chain are termed **mid-ocean ridges** (**Figure 9.12**).

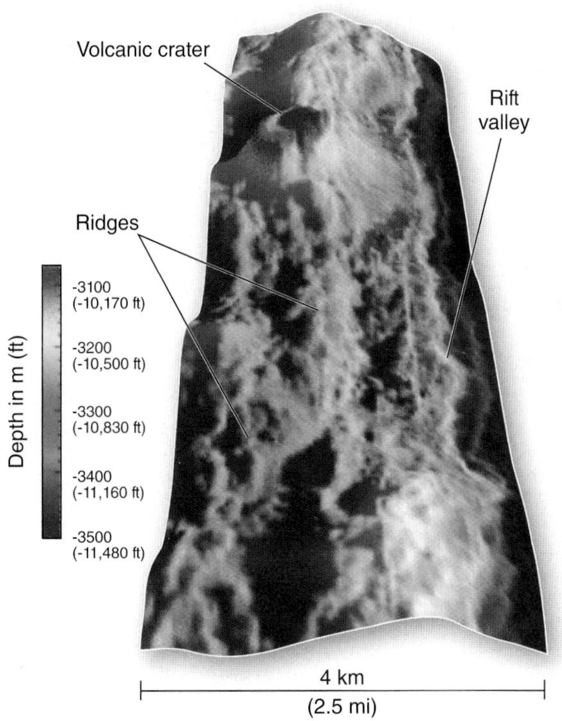

▲**Figure 9.12 The Mid-Atlantic Ridge.** A 4-km-wide image of part of the Mid-Atlantic Ridge shows a volcanic crater, a rift valley, and ridges. The image was taken by the *TOBI* (towed ocean-bottom instrument) at approximately 29° N latitude. [Image courtesy of D. K. Smith, Woods Hole Oceanographic Institute.]

In the early 1960s, geophysicist Harry H. Hess proposed that these mid-ocean ridges are new ocean floor formed by upwelling flows of magma from hot areas in the upper mantle and asthenosphere and perhaps from the deeper lower mantle. While upwelling occurs, the new seafloor moves outward from the ridge as plates pull apart and new crust is formed. This process, now called **seafloor spreading**, is the mechanism that builds mid-ocean ridges and drives continental movement.

Hess and other geologists then faced a new problem: If seafloor spreading and the creation of new crust are ongoing, then old ocean crust must somewhere be consumed; otherwise, Earth would be expanding. Hess and another geologist, Robert S. Dietz, proposed that old seafloor sinks back into the Earth's mantle at deep-ocean trenches and in subduction zones where plates collide.

These hypotheses formed the basis for our current understanding of seafloor spreading. However, scientists now think that the upward movement of material beneath an ocean ridge is a consequence of seafloor spreading rather than the cause. As the plates continue to move apart, more magma rises from below to fill the gaps, accumulating in magma chambers beneath the centerline of the ridge (shown in Figure 9.15). Some of the magma rises and erupts through fractures and small volcanoes along the ridge, forming new oceanic crust. In the areas of ocean basins farthest from the mid-ocean ridges, the oldest sections of oceanic lithosphere are slowly plunging beneath continental lithosphere along Earth's deep-ocean trenches.

Magnetic Reversals Earlier we discussed the history of reversals in Earth's magnetic field. As seafloor spreading occurs and magma emerges at the surface, magnetic particles in the lava orient with the magnetic field in force at the time it cools and hardens. The particles become locked in this alignment as part of the new seafloor, creating an ongoing magnetic record of Earth's polarity. Using isotopic dating methods, scientists have established a chronology for these reversals—that is, the actual years in which the polarity reversal occurred. Ages for materials on the ocean floor proved to be a fundamental piece of the plate tectonics puzzle.

Figure 9.13 shows a record from the Mid-Atlantic Ridge south of Iceland, illustrating the magnetic stripes preserved in the minerals—the colored bands are areas of reversed polarity, the areas between them have normal polarity. The relative ages of the rocks increase with distance from the ridge, and the mirror images that develop on either side of the mid-ocean ridge are a result of the nearly symmetrical spreading of the seafloor. These discoveries were an important step on the way to completing the theory of plate tectonics.

Age of the Seafloor The youngest crust anywhere on Earth is at the spreading centers of the mid-ocean ridges,

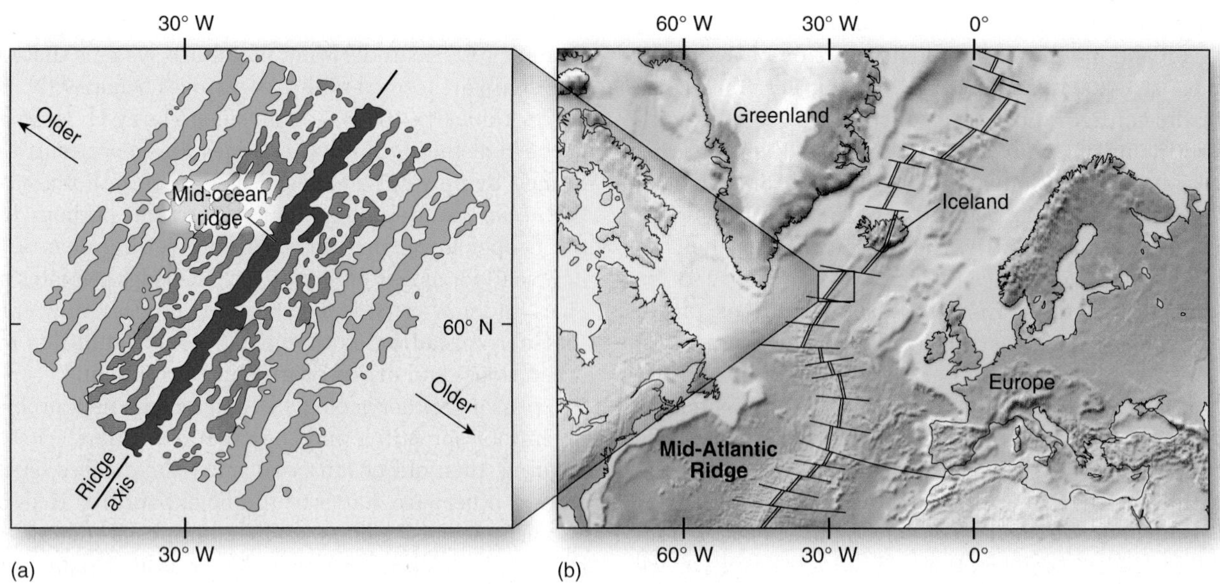

▲**Figure 9.13 Magnetic reversals recorded in a portion of the ocean floor.** (a) Colored bands indicate magnetic stripes on the seafloor with reversed polarity, while the areas between have normal polarity. The mid-ocean ridge (red stripe) is a section of the Mid-Atlantic Ridge south of Iceland, located in (b). Similar colored bands on either side of the ridge indicate symmetrical seafloor spreading, with oldest rock bands farthest from the ridge. [Adapted from J. R. Heirtzler, S. Le Pichon, and J. G. Baron, *Deep-Sea Research 13*, © 1966, Pergamon Press, p. 247.]

and with increasing distance from these centers, the crust gets steadily older (**Figure 9.14**). Overall, the seafloor is relatively young; nowhere is it more than 280 million years old, which is remarkable when you remember that Earth is 4.6 billion years old. In the Atlantic Ocean, the oldest large-scale area of seafloor is along the continental margins, farthest from the Mid-Atlantic Ridge. In the Pacific, the oldest seafloor is in the western region near Japan (dating to the Jurassic Period). Note on the map the distance between this part of the basin and its spreading center in the South Pacific, west of South America. Parts of the Mediterranean Sea contain the oldest seafloor

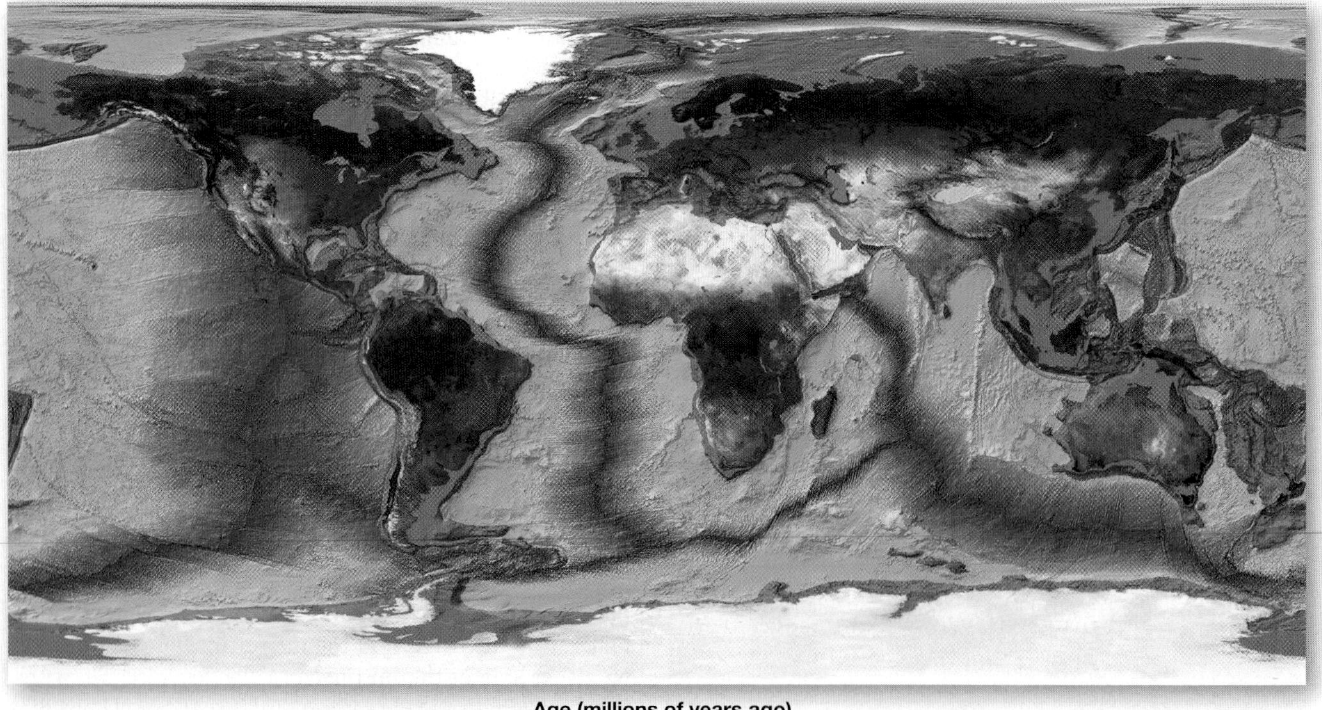

▲**Figure 9.14 Relative ages of oceanic crust.** Compare the width of the red color (young crust) near the East Pacific Rise in the eastern Pacific Ocean with the width of the red color along the Mid-Atlantic Ridge. What does the difference tell you about the rates of plate motion in the two locations? [Image by Elliot Lim, CIRES.]

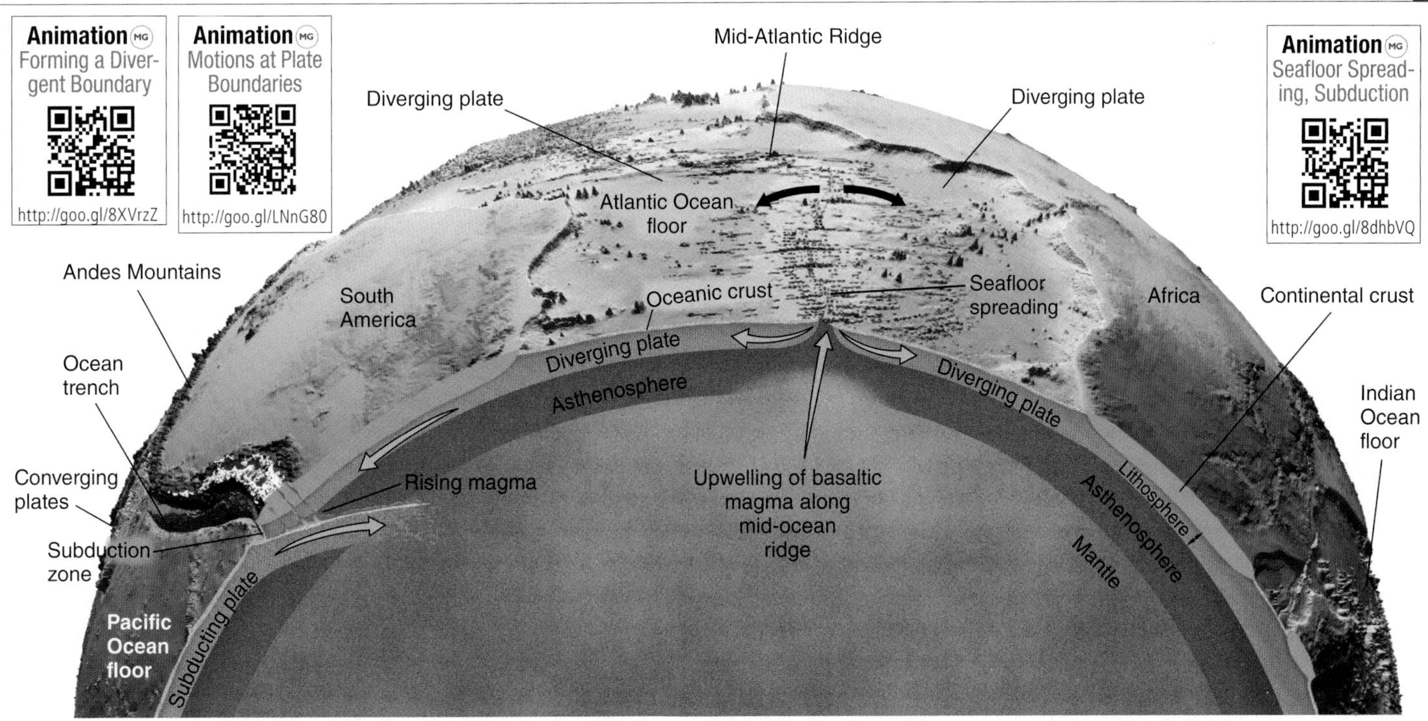

▲**Figure 9.15 Plate movements and seafloor spreading.** Plate movement, seafloor spreading, upwelling magma, and subduction, shown in cross section. Arrows indicate the direction of plate movement.

remnants, which may have been part of the Tethys Sea, dating to about 280 m.y.a (see Figure 9.11).

CRITICAL**thinking** 9.2

Tracking Your Location since Pangaea

Using the maps in this chapter, determine your present location relative to Earth's crustal plates. Now, using Figure 9.11b, identify approximately where your present location was 225 m.y.a.; express it in a rough estimate using the equator and the longitudes noted on the map. Can you track your location throughout parts c and d of Figure 9.11?

Subduction

When one portion of the lithosphere descends beneath another and dives downward into the mantle, the process is called *subduction*, and the area is a **subduction zone**. As discussed earlier, the basaltic ocean crust has an average density of 3.0 g/cm^3, whereas continental crust averages a lighter 2.7 g/cm^3. As a result, when continental crust and oceanic crust slowly collide, the denser ocean floor will grind beneath the lighter continental crust, thus forming a subduction zone (**Figure 9.15**, left side).

The world's deep-ocean trenches coincide with these subduction zones and are the lowest features on Earth's surface. The Mariana Trench near Guam is the deepest, descending below sea level to –11,030 m (–36,198 ft). The Tonga Trench, also in the Pacific, is the next deepest, dropping to –10,882 m (–35,702 ft). For comparison, in the Atlantic Ocean, the Puerto Rico Trench drops to –8605 m (–28,224 ft), and in the Indian Ocean, the Java Trench drops to –7125 m (–23,376 ft).

Subduction occurs where plates are colliding. The subducting slab of crust exerts a gravitational pull on the rest of the plate—a pull now known to be an important driving force in plate motion. The subducted portion travels down into the asthenosphere, where it remelts and eventually is recycled as magma, rising again toward the surface through deep fissures and cracks in crustal rock (left side of Figure 9.15). Volcanic mountains such as the Andes in South America and the Cascade Range from northern California to the Canadian border form inland of these subduction zones as a result of rising plumes of magma. Sometimes the subducting plate remains intact for hundreds of kilometers, whereas at other times it can break into large pieces, thought to be the case under the Cascade Range with its fragmented distribution of volcanoes.

GEO**report** 9.3 Spreading along the East Pacific Rise

The fastest rate of seafloor spreading on Earth occurs along the East Pacific Rise, which runs roughly north–south along the eastern edge of the Pacific plate from near Antarctica to North America. Spreading is occurring at a rate of 6 to 16 cm/yr (2.4 to 6.3 in./yr), depending on location. For perspective, human fingernails grow at a rate of about 4 cm/yr (1.6 in./yr).

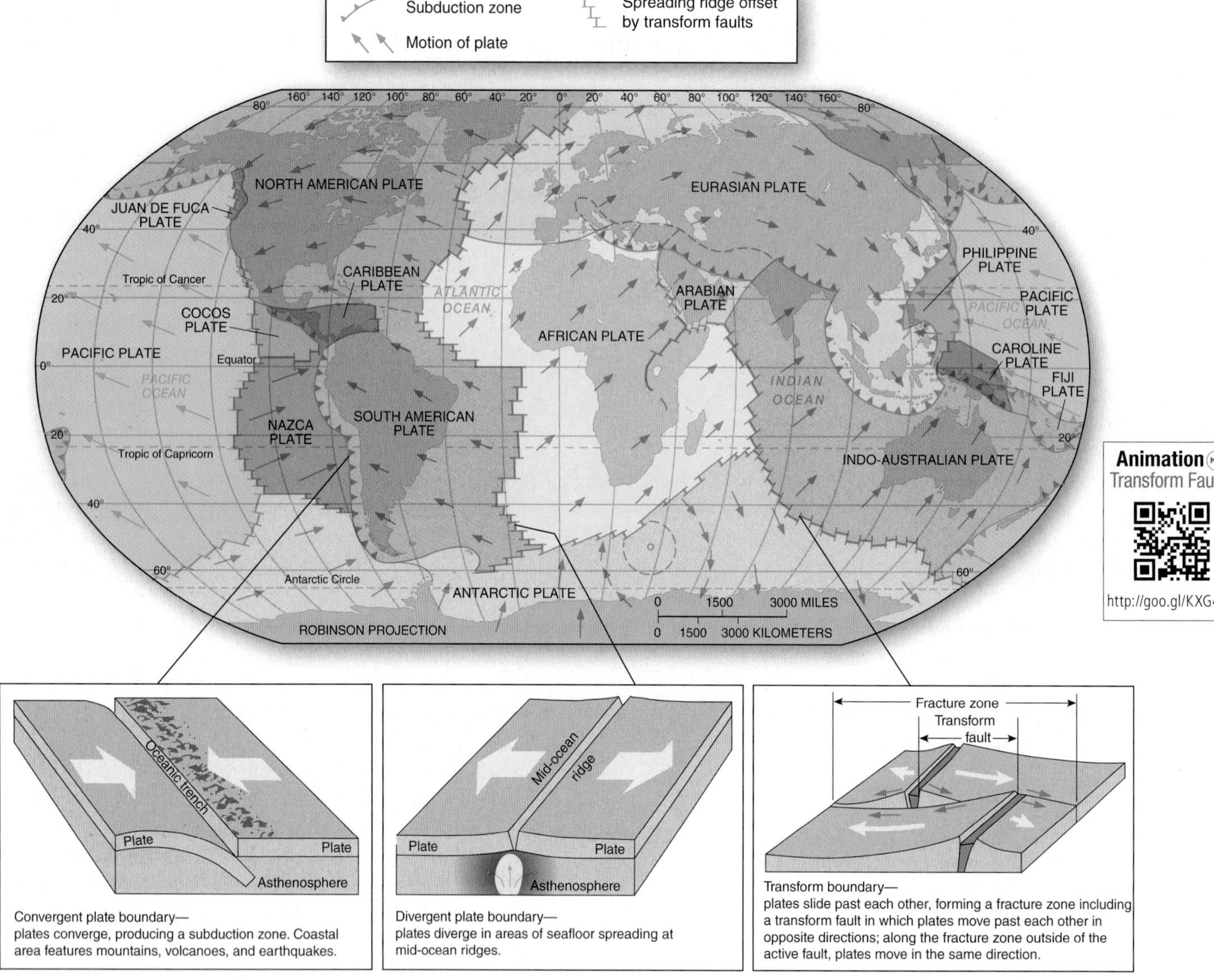

▲**Figure 9.16 Earth's major lithospheric plates and their movements.** Each arrow represents 20 million years of movement. The longer arrows indicate that the Pacific and Nazca plates are moving more rapidly than the Atlantic plates. Compare the length of these arrows with the purple areas on Figure 9.11. [Adapted from U.S. Geodynamics Committee, National Academy of Sciences and National Academy of Engineering.]

Animation (MG) Transform Faults
http://goo.gl/KXG42e

Plate Boundaries

Earth's present crust is divided into at least 14 plates, of which about half are major and half are minor in terms of area (**Figure 9.16**). Hundreds of smaller pieces and perhaps dozens of microplates migrating together make up these broad, moving plates. Arrows in the figure indicate the direction in which each plate is presently moving, and the length of the arrows suggests the relative rate of movement during the past 20 million years.

The boundaries where plates meet are dynamic places when considered over geologic time scales, although slow-moving within human time frames. The block diagrams in Figure 9.16 show the three general types of boundaries and the interacting movements of plates at those locations.

- *Convergent boundaries* occur in areas of crustal collision and subduction. As discussed earlier, where areas of continental and oceanic lithosphere meet, crust is compressed and lost in a destructional process as it moves downward into the mantle. Convergent boundaries form subduction zones, such as off the west coast of South and Central America, along the Aleutian Island trenches (see Figure 9.18 ahead), and along the east coast of Japan, where a magnitude 9.0 earthquake struck in 2011. Convergent boundaries also occur where plates of continental crust collide, such as the collision zone between India and Asia, and where oceanic plates collide, such as along the deep trenches in the western Pacific Ocean.
- *Divergent boundaries* occur in areas of seafloor spreading, where lithospheric plates spread apart and upwelling material from the mantle forms new seafloor in a constructional process. An example is the divergent boundary along the East Pacific Rise, which gives birth to the Nazca plate (moving eastward) and

the Pacific plate (moving northwestward). Whereas most divergent boundaries occur at mid-ocean ridges, a few occur within continents themselves. An example is the Great Rift Valley of East Africa, where continental crust is rifting apart.

- *Transform boundaries* occur where plates slide past one another, usually at right angles to a seafloor spreading center. These are the fractures stretching across the mid-ocean ridge system worldwide, first described in 1965 by University of Toronto geophysicist Tuzo Wilson. As plates move past each other horizontally, they form a type of *fault*, or fracture, in Earth's crust—a *transform fault*.

Along these fracture zones that intersect ridges, a transform fault occurs only along the fault section that lies *between* two segments of the fragmented mid-ocean ridge (Figure 9.16, lower right). Along the fracture zone outside of the transform fault, the crust moves in the same direction (away from the mid-ocean ridge) as the spreading plates. The movement along transform faults is that of horizontal displacement—no new crust is formed or old crust subducted.

These features are *transform* because of the apparent transformation in the direction of fault movement—these faults can be distinguished from other horizontal faults (discussed in Chapter 10) because the movement along one side of the fault line is opposite to the movement along the other side. This unique movement results from the creation of new material as the seafloor spreads.

All the seafloor spreading centers on Earth feature these fractures, which are perpendicular to the mid-ocean ridges. Some are a few hundred kilometers long; others, such as those along the East Pacific Rise, stretch out 1000 km or more (over 600 mi).

Transform boundaries are associated with earthquake activity, especially where they cut across portions of continental crust, such as along the San Andreas fault in California, where the Pacific and North American plates meet, and along the Alpine fault in New Zealand, the boundary between the Indo-Australian and Pacific plates. The San Andreas, running through several metropolitan areas of California, is perhaps the most famous transform fault in the world (see the discussion in Chapter 10).

Earthquake and Volcanic Activity

Plate boundaries are the primary locations of earthquake and volcanic activity, and the correlation of these phenomena is an important aspect of plate tectonics. The massive earthquakes that hit Haiti, Chile, New Zealand, and Japan in 2010 and 2011, as well as the 2010 volcanic eruption in Iceland, focused world attention on these plate boundaries and the principles of plate tectonics. The next chapter discusses earthquakes and volcanic activity in more detail.

Figure 9.17 is a map of earthquake zones, volcanic sites, hot spots, and plate motion. The area surrounding the Pacific basin is known as the "ring of fire," named for the frequent incidence of volcanoes along its margin. The

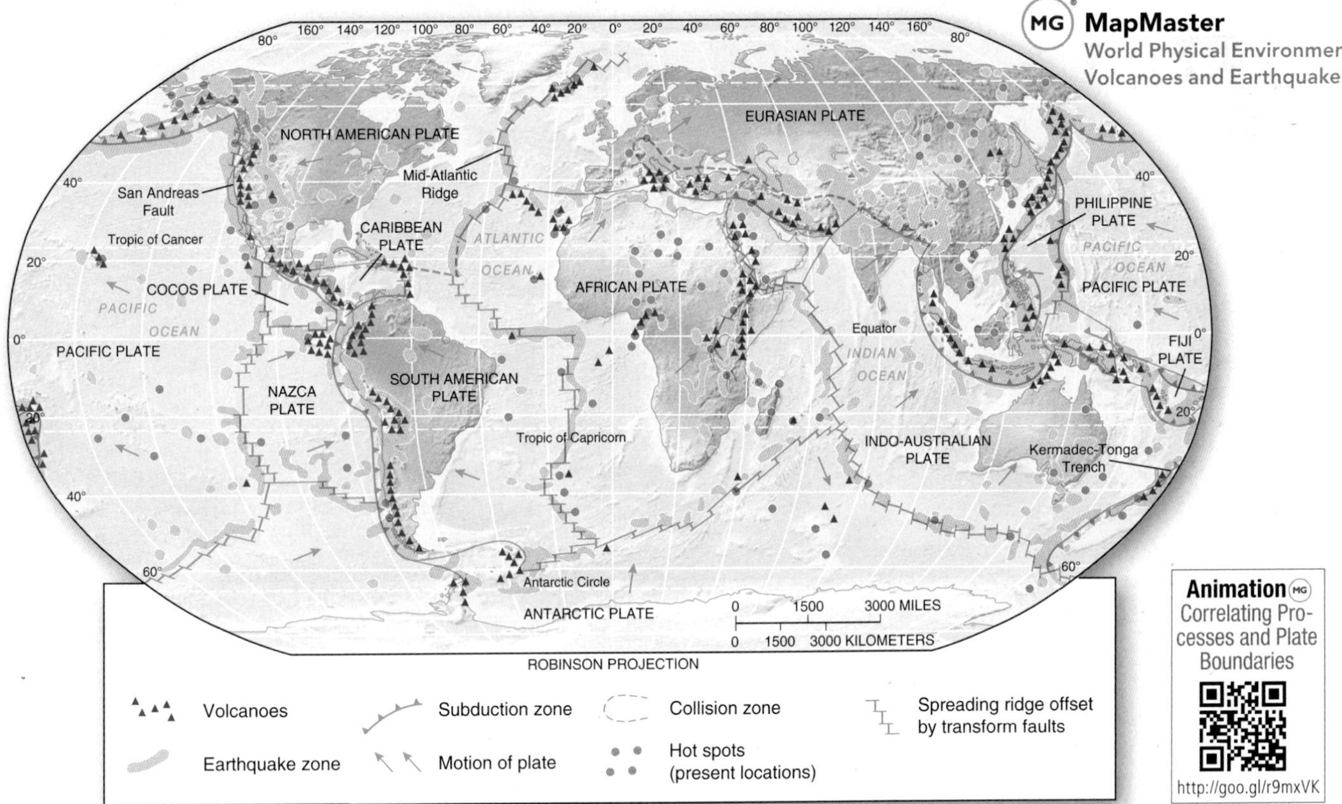

Animation (MG) Correlating Processes and Plate Boundaries

http://goo.gl/r9mxVK

▲**Figure 9.17 Locations of earthquake and volcanic activity.** Earthquake and volcanic activity in relation to major tectonic plate boundaries and principal hot spots. [Earthquake, volcano, and hot-spot data adapted from U.S. Geological Survey.]

features that form this "ring" are caused by the subducting edge of the Pacific plate as it thrusts deep into the crust and mantle and produces molten material that makes its way back toward the surface. The upwelling magma forms active volcanoes along the Pacific Rim. Such processes occur at similar subduction zones throughout the world.

Hot Spots

As mentioned, volcanic activity is often associated with plate boundaries. However, scientists have found an estimated 50 to 100 active sites of upwelling material that exist independent of plate boundaries. These **hot spots** (or hot-spot volcanoes) are places where plumes of magma rise from the mantle, producing volcanic activity as well as thermal effects in the groundwater and crust. Some of these sites produce enough heat from Earth's interior, or **geothermal energy**, to be developed for human uses, as discussed in Focus Study 9.1.

Groundwater that is heated by pockets of magma and other hot portions of the crust may emerge as a hot spring or erupt explosively from the ground as a *geyser*—a spring characterized by intermittent discharge of water and steam. A hot spot below Yellowstone National Park in Montana and Wyoming produces several types of hydrothermal features, including hot springs and geysers (look ahead to The Human Denominator 9, Figure HD 9a).

Hot spots occur beneath both oceanic and continental crust. Some hot spots are anchored deep in the

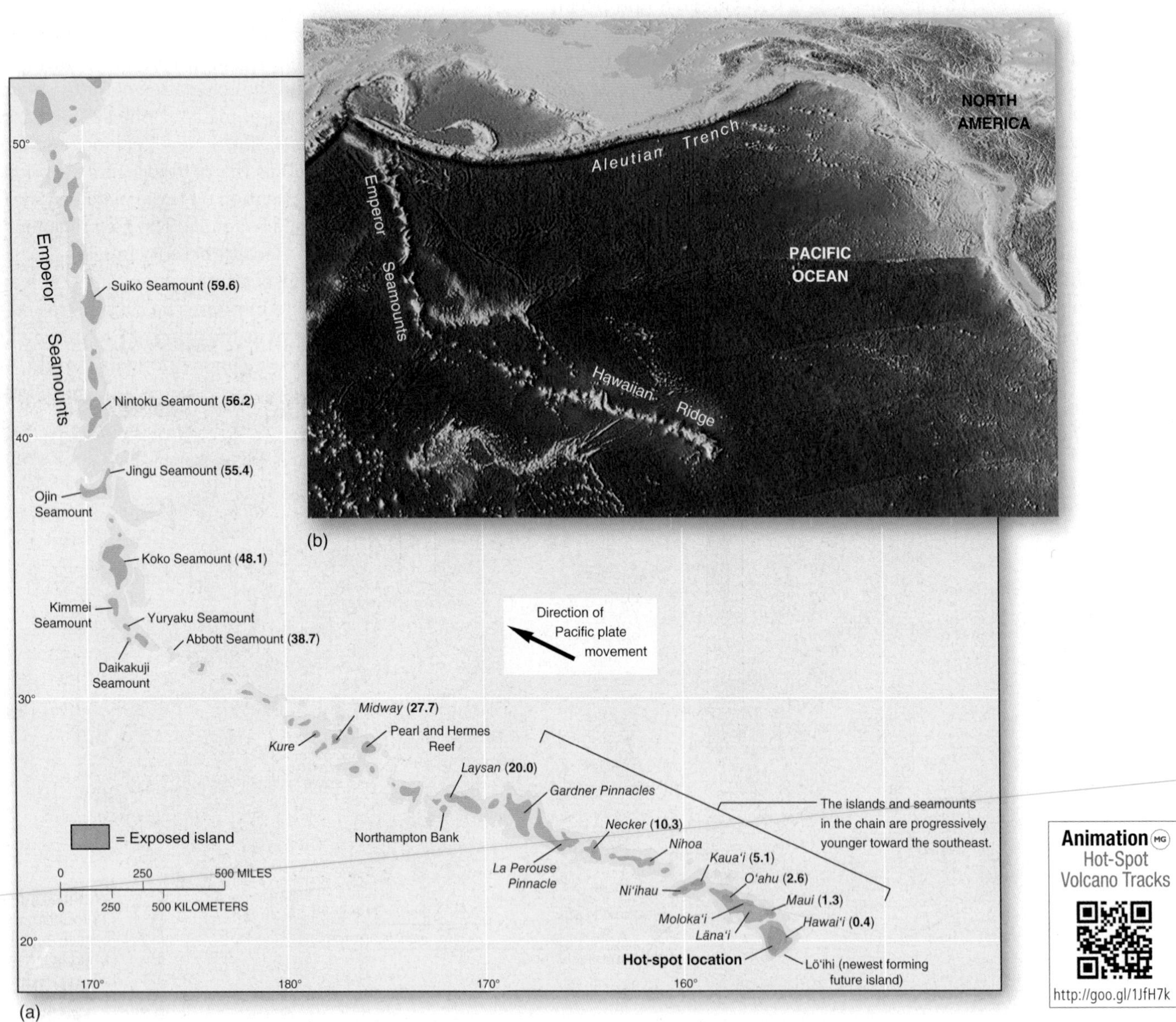

Animation Hot-Spot Volcano Tracks
http://goo.gl/1JfH7k

▲**Figure 9.18 Island and seamount chain formed by a hot spot magma plume.** (a) The volcanic islands and seamounts that make up the Hawaiian Ridge-Emperor Seamount Chain are progressively younger toward the southeast, reflecting the movement of the Pacific plate over a hot spot that is today located near the Big Island of Hawai'i. Ages, in m.y.a., are shown in parentheses. Note that Midway Island is 27.7 million years old, meaning that the site was over the plume 27.7 m.y.a. (b) The Hawaiian-Emperor Chain in the north Pacific Ocean extends from the Big Island of Hawai'i to the Aleutian Trench off Alaska. [(a) After D. A. Clague, "Petrology and K–Ar (Potassium–Argon) ages of dredged volcanic rocks from the western Hawaiian ridge and the southern Emperor seamount chain," *Geological Society of America Bulletin 86* (1975): 991; (b) courtesy of NOAA.]

lower mantle, tending to remain fixed relative to migrating plates; others appear to be above plumes that move by themselves or shift with plate motion. In the case of a fixed hot spot, the area of a plate that passes above it is locally heated for the brief geologic time it remains above that spot (a few hundred thousand or million years), sometimes producing a hot-spot island chain of volcanic features.

A hot spot in the Pacific Ocean produced, and continues to form, the Hawaiian–Emperor Islands chain, including numerous seamounts, which are submarine mountains that do not reach the surface (**Figure 9.18**). The Pacific plate moved across this hot, upward-erupting plume over the last 80 million years, creating a string of volcanic islands and seamounts with ages increasing northwestward away from the hot spot. The oldest island in the Hawaiian part of the chain is Kaua'i, approximately 5 million years old; today, it is weathered and eroded into deep canyons and valleys.

To the northwest of Hawai'i, the island of Midway rises as a part of the same system. From there, the Emperor seamounts spread northwestward and are progressively older until they reach about 40 million years in age. At that point, this linear island chain shifts direction northward. This bend in the chain is now thought to be from both movement in the plume and a possible change in the plate motion itself, a revision of past thinking that all hot-spot plumes remain fixed relative to the migrating plate. At the northernmost extreme, the seamounts that formed about 80 m.y.a. are now approaching the Aleutian Trench, where they eventually will be subducted beneath the Eurasian plate.

The big island of Hawai'i, the youngest in the island chain, actually took less than 1 million years to build to its present stature. The island is a huge mound of lava, formed from magma from several seafloor fissures and volcanoes and rising from the seafloor 5800 m (19,000 ft) to the ocean surface. From sea level, its highest peak, Mauna Kea, reaches an elevation of 4205 m (13,796 ft). This total height of almost 10,000 m (32,800 ft) represents the highest mountain on Earth if measured from the ocean floor.

A new addition to the Hawaiian chain is still a seamount. It rises 3350 m (11,000 ft) from its base, but is still 975 m (3200 ft) beneath the ocean surface. Even though this new island will not experience the tropical Sun for about 10,000 years, it is already named Lo'ihi (noted on the map).

Iceland is another island formed by an active hot spot, this one sitting astride a mid-ocean ridge. It is an excellent example of a segment of mid-ocean ridge rising above sea level. This hot spot continues to generate eruptions from deep in the mantle, the most recent occurring in 2010 and 2011. As a result, Iceland is still growing in area and volume, further evidence that, indeed, Earth is a dynamic planet.

CRITICAL**thinking** 9.3

How Fast Is the Pacific Plate Moving?

Tracing the motion of the Pacific plate shown in Figure 9.18 (note the map's graphic scale in the lower-left corner) reveals that the island of Midway formed 27.7 m.y.a. over the hot spot that today is active under the southeast coast of the big island of Hawai'i. Use the scale of the map to roughly determine the average annual speed of the Pacific plate in centimeters per year for Midway to have traveled this distance. Given your calculation for the plate speed and assuming the directions of movement remain the same, approximately how many years will it take the remnants of Midway to reach 50° N in the upper-left corner of the map?

The Geologic Cycle

We see in this chapter that Earth's crust is in an ongoing state of change, being formed, deformed, moved, and broken down by physical and chemical processes. While the planet's endogenic (internal) system is at work building landforms, the exogenic (external) system is busily wearing them down. This vast give-and-take at the Earth–atmosphere–ocean interface is summarized in the **geologic cycle**. It is fueled from two sources—Earth's internal heat and solar energy from space—while being influenced by the ever-present leveling force of Earth's gravity (see Geosystems in Action 9).

The geologic cycle is itself composed of three principal cycles—the hydrologic cycle, which we summarized in Chapter 6, and the rock and tectonic cycles covered in this chapter (see Figures GIA 9.1 and 9.2). The hydrologic cycle (Figure GIA 9.3a) works on Earth's surface through the exogenic processes of weathering, erosion, and deposition driven by the energy–atmosphere and water–weather systems and represented by the physical action of water, ice, and wind. The rock cycle (Figure GIA 9.3b) produces the three basic rock types found in the crust—igneous, metamorphic, and sedimentary. The tectonic cycle (Figure GIA 9.3c) brings heat energy and new material to the surface and recycles surface material, creating movement and deformation of the crust.

GEO**report** 9.4 The largest volcano on Earth

In 2013, scientists confirmed that the Tamu Massif, located in the Pacific Ocean about 1600 km (1000 mi) east of Japan, is the largest volcano on Earth and one of the biggest in the solar system. Part of the Shatsky Rise, a massive undersea volcanic plateau similar in size to California, the Tamu Massif covers about 310,800 km^2 (120,000 mi^2), an area far larger than Mauna Loa's 5200 km^2 (2000 mi^2) on Hawai'i. Until recently, scientists thought Tamu Massif was a composite of smaller volcanic structures, formed in a manner similar to that of the island of Hawai'i. However, recent research determined that this feature is composed of related materials, formed some 145 m.y.a. above a hot spot that coincides with the boundaries of three tectonic plates. More information is at **http://geology.com/records/largest-volcano/**.

The geologic cycle is a model made up of the hydrologic, rock, and tectonic cycles (GIA 9.1). Earth's exogenic (external) and endogenic (internal) systems, driven by solar energy and Earth's internal heat, interact within the geologic cycle (GIA 9.2). The processes of the geologic cycle create distinctive landscapes (GIA 9.3).

9.1 Interactions Within the Geologic Cycle

The cycles that make up the geologic cycle influence each other. For example, over millions of years, the tectonic cycle slowly leads to the building of mountains, which affects global precipitation patterns, one aspect of the hydrologic cycle.

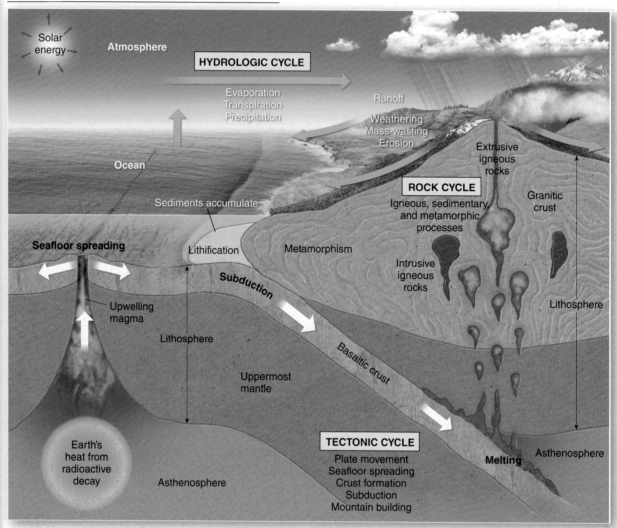

Solar energy
Atmosphere
HYDROLOGIC CYCLE
Evaporation
Transpiration
Precipitation
Runoff
Weathering
Mass-wasting
Erosion
Ocean
Extrusive igneous rocks
ROCK CYCLE
Igneous, sedimentary, and metamorphic processes
Granitic crust
Sediments accumulate
Seafloor spreading
Lithification
Metamorphism
Intrusive igneous rocks
Subduction
Upwelling magma
Lithosphere
Lithosphere
Basaltic crust
Uppermost mantle
Earth's heat from radioactive decay
TECTONIC CYCLE
Plate movement
Seafloor spreading
Crust formation
Subduction
Mountain building
Melting
Asthenosphere
Asthenosphere

9.2 Role of Exogenic and Endogenic Systems

Exogenic processes drive the hydrologic cycle; both endogenic and exogenic processes contribute to the rock cycle; and endogenic processes drive the tectonic cycle.

Give examples: List two additional examples of ways in which the cycles within the geologic cycle could affect each other.

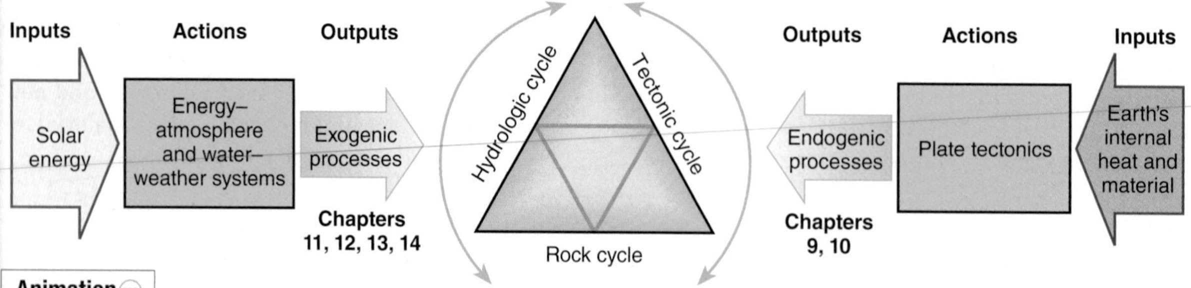

Animation (MG) Convection and Plate Tectonics

http://goo.gl/gUxbH9

MasteringGeography™

Visit the Study Area in MasteringGeography™ to explore the geologic cycle.

Visualize: Study a geosciences animation of convection and plate tectonics.

Assess: Demonstrate understanding of the geologic cycle (if assigned by instructor).

9.3 Processes and Landscapes of the Geologic Cycle

9.3a Hydrologic Cycle

Earth's water cycles continuously among the atmosphere, hydrosphere, lithosphere, and biosphere.

Sources of Energy:
Solar energy provides the heat necessary for water to evaporate. Gravity causes precipitation to fall.

Example of systems interaction:
Water weathers, erodes, and deposits sediments—processes that are part of the rock cycle.

During the monsoon in India, atmospheric moisture flows inland from the Indian Ocean and falls as heavy rains.

9.3b Rock Cycle

The processes that form igneous, sedimentary, and metamorphic rocks operate so that each rock can enter the cycle and be transformed into other rock types.

Sources of Energy:
Solar energy drives the processes involved in weathering, eroding, and transporting sediment. Gravity causes sediment deposition and compaction. Earth's internal heat causes melting of rock.

Example of systems interaction:
Igneous rock forms from the cooling and hardening of molten rock, a process that is part of the tectonic cycle.

These layers of sandstone in Canyonlands National Park, Utah, formed from particles of other rock, pressed and cemented together.

9.3c Tectonic Cycle

Earth's plates diverge, collide, subduct, and slide past each other, changing the continents and ocean basins and causing earthquakes, volcanoes, and mountain building.

Sources of Energy:
Earth's internal heat provides energy that powers plate motions and melts rock to form magma. Gravity drives the subduction of lithospheric plates.

Example of systems interaction:
Volcanic activity releases gases and particles that change the atmosphere and thus affect the hydrologic cycle.

Tectonic processes produced Indonesia's many active volcanoes, including these in Bromo National Park, on the island of Java.

Explain: How could processes in the tectonic cycle contribute to the formation of metamorphic rock in the rock cycle?

GEOquiz

1. Infer: How could mountain building (tectonic cycle) affect weather and climate (hydrologic cycle)?

2. Apply concepts: Describe the role of exogenic and endogenic processes in the rock cycle.

focusstudy 9.1 Sustainable Resources

Heat from Earth—Geothermal Energy

▲**Figure 9.1.1 Svartsengi geothermal power plant on the Reykjavík Peninsula, Iceland.** This geothermal plant produces electricity and provides hot water for homes and businesses. Nearby is the Blue Lagoon Spa, filled with warm geothermal waters. [Eco Images/Universal Images Group/Getty Images.]

Geothermal energy, the tremendous amount of endogenic heat within Earth's interior, can in some places be harnessed for heating and power production by means of wells and pipes that transmit heated water or steam to the surface. Underground reservoirs of hot water at varying depths and temperatures are among the geothermal resources that can be tapped and brought to the surface. Resources of this kind provide *direct geothermal heating*, which uses water at low to moderate temperatures (20°C to 150°C, or 68°F to 302°F) in heat-exchange systems in buildings, commercial greenhouses, fish farms, and other locations.

In Boise, Idaho, which has taken advantage of geothermal resources for decades, the state capitol building uses direct geothermal heating. Most city locations return used geothermal water to the aquifer through injection wells. In Reykjavík, Iceland, the majority of space heating systems (more than 87%) are geothermal. Where available, direct geothermal heating provides energy that is inexpensive and clean.

Geothermal Power Production

Geothermal electricity is produced using steam from a natural underground reservoir to drive a turbine that powers a generator. Because the steam comes directly from Earth's interior (with no burning of fuel to produce it), geothermal electricity is a relatively clean energy. Ideally, groundwater for this purpose should have a temperature of from 180°C to 350°C (355°F to 600°F) and be moving through rock of high porosity and permeability (allowing the water to move freely through connecting pore spaces). The Geysers Geothermal Field in northern California (so named despite the absence of any geysers in the area) is the largest geothermal power production plant using this method in the world.

Today, geothermal applications are in use in 70 countries and include over 200 power plants producing a total output of about 11,000 MW. The top countries for installed geothermal electrical generation are the United States, Philippines, Indonesia, Mexico, Italy, New Zealand, Iceland, and Japan. In Iceland, 30% of total electrical production is generated with geothermal energy (**Figure 9.1.1**).

In the United States, the geothermal industry grew by 5% during 2012, with power now totaling 3300 MW operating in Alaska, California, Hawai'i, Idaho, Nevada, Oregon, Utah, and Wyoming. For more information, see http://www1.eere.energy.gov/geothermal/.

The newest geothermal technology seeks to create conditions for geothermal power production at locations where underground rock temperatures are high, but where water or permeability is lacking. In an *enhanced geothermal system* (EGS), cold water is pumped underground into hot rock, causing the rock to fracture and become permeable to water flow; the cold water, in turn, is heated to steam as it flows through the high-temperature rock.

Several EGS projects are either operational or under development worldwide; the largest of these is in Australia's Cooper Basin. The potential for EGS, as with other geothermal technologies, is highest in the western United States and in areas of the world along plate boundaries that produce upwelling pockets of magma and volcanic activity (**Figure 9.1.2**). In 2013, the Nevada Desert Peak EGS became the first U.S. enhanced geothermal facility to supply electricity to the power grid (see Figure HD 9d).

Geothermal as a Resource

Geothermal power production has many advantages, including only minimal production of carbon dioxide (the extraction of steam emits relatively small amounts of CO_2 compared with the CO_2 generated by burning fossil fuels). Geothermal power can be produced 24 hours a day, an advantage when compared with solar or wind energy, in which the timing of production is linked to daylight or other natural variations in the resource.

Although geothermal is billed as renewable and self-sustaining, research shows that some geysers and geothermal fields are being depleted as the extraction rate exceeds the rate of recharge. In addition, the drilling of wells and the injection or removal of water in connection with geothermal energy projects may produce seismic activity. The environmental impacts of EGS are not yet well understood and compared to the impacts of other geothermal energy technologies may pose the highest risk of *induced seismicity* (that is, minor earthquakes and tremors produced in association with human activity, discussed further in Chapter 10). In Switzerland, geothermal power developers are working on technology to reduce seismic hazards, after several geothermal projects there produced small earthquakes. Research is ongoing to address and mitigate the seismicity issues; if these problems are solved, geothermal is a promising source of clean energy for the future.

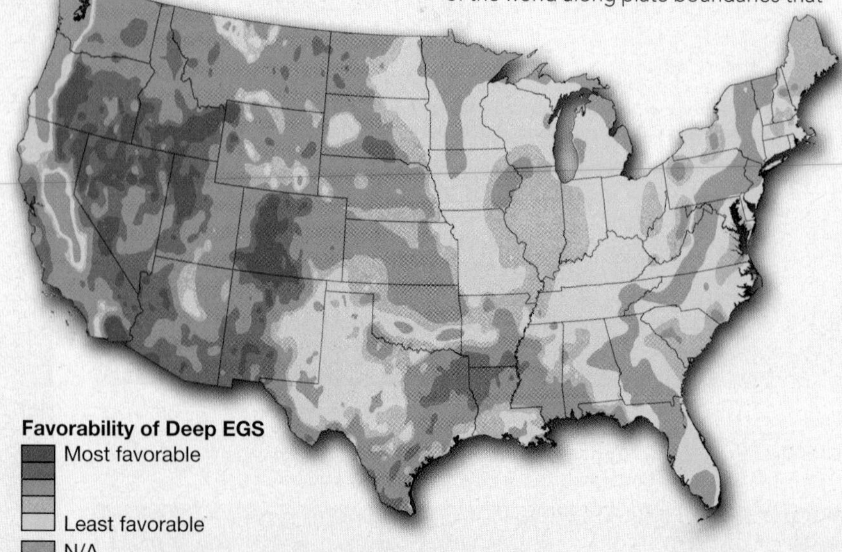

◀**Figure 9.1.2 Potential for development of enhanced geothermal systems.** Favorability ranges from red (most favorable) to yellow (least favorable. [NREL.]

THE**human**DENOMINATOR 9 Earth Materials and Plate Tectonics

ENDOGENIC PROCESSES IMPACT HUMANS

- Endogenic processes cause natural hazards such as earthquakes and volcanic events that affect humans and ecosystems.
- Rocks provide materials for human use; geothermal power is a renewable resource.

HUMANS IMPACT ENDOGENIC PROCESSES

- Wells drilled into Earth's crust in association with oil and gas drilling or for enhanced geothermal systems may cause earthquakes.

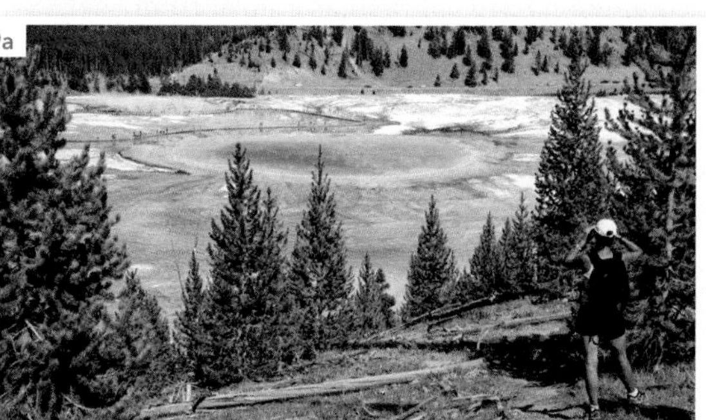

9a

Hydrothermal activity produces hot springs and associated travertine deposits in Yellowstone National Park, Wyoming, which sits above a stationary hot spot in Earth's crust. Grand Prismatic Spring, pictured here, is the largest hot spring in the United States. The geysers and thermal features of this area draw over 3 million visitors each year.

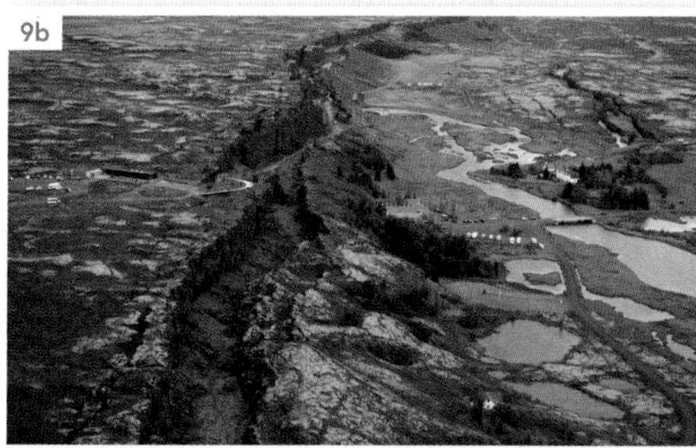

9b

The Mid-Atlantic Ridge system surfaces at Thingvellir, Iceland, now a tourist destination. The rifts mark the divergent boundary separating the North American and Eurasian plates.

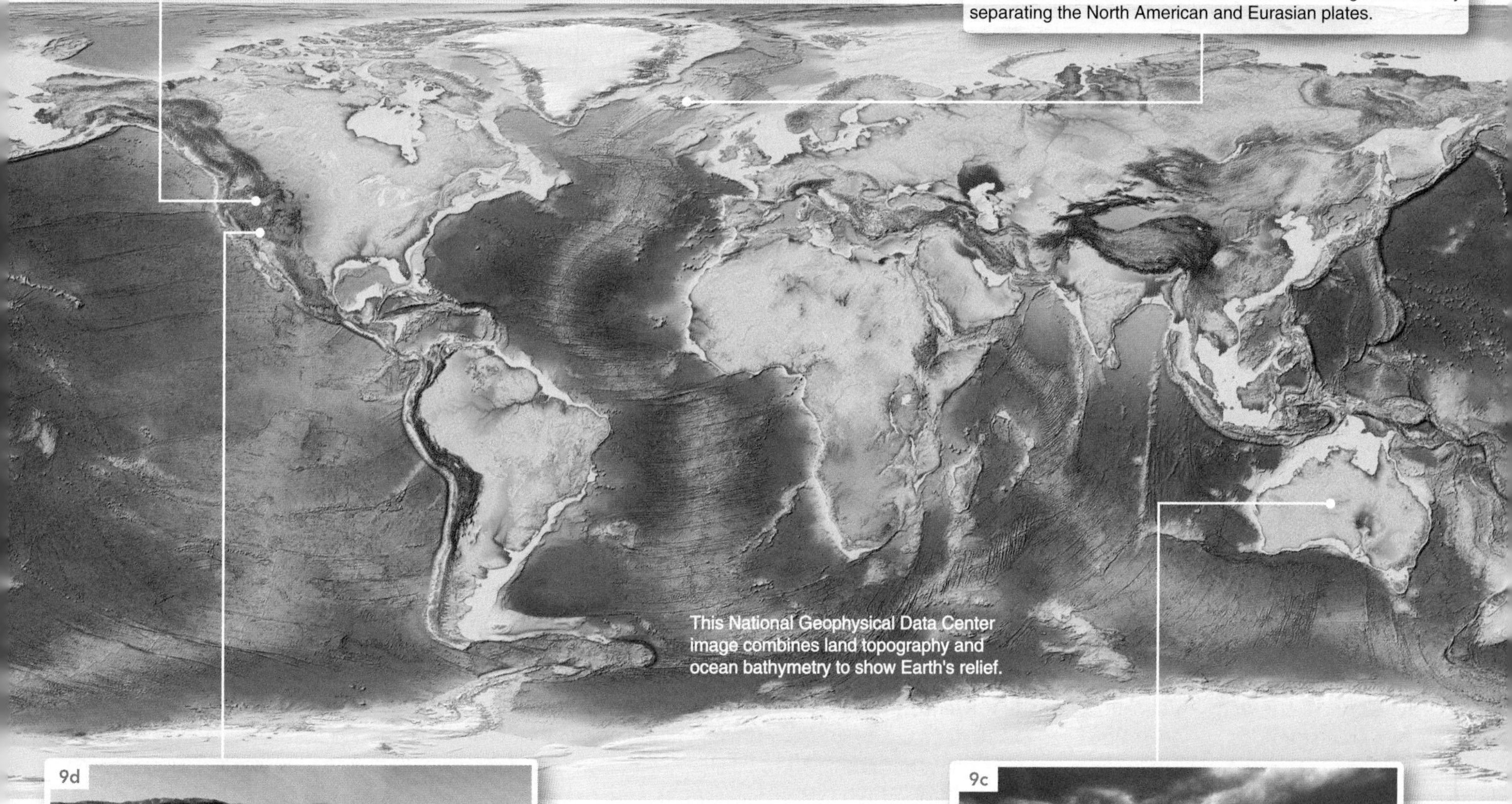

This National Geophysical Data Center image combines land topography and ocean bathymetry to show Earth's relief.

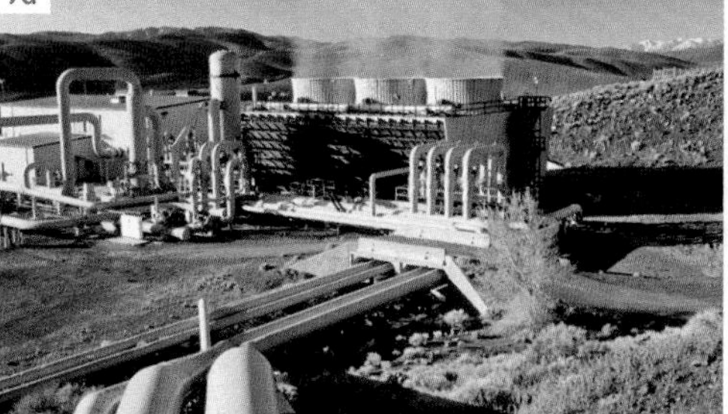

9d

In April 2013, the Nevada Desert Peak EGS became the first U.S. enhanced geothermal project to supply electricity to the power grid.

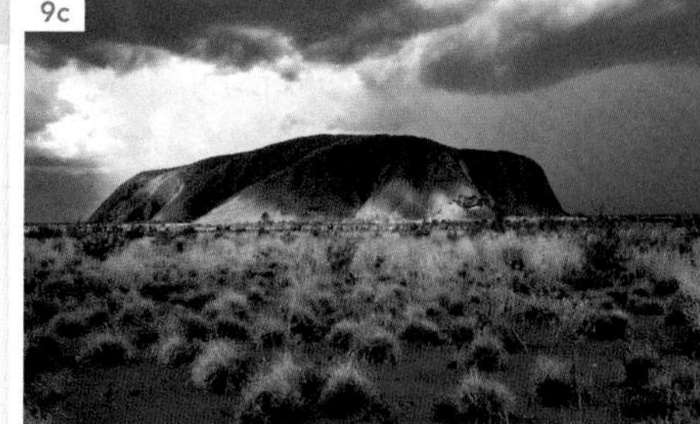

9c

Uluru, also known as Ayers Rock, is probably Australia's best-known landmark. This steep-sided isolated sandstone feature, about 3.5 km (2.2 mi) long and 1.9 km (1.2 mi) wide, was formed from endogenic and exogenic processes and has cultural significance for the Aboriginal peoples.

ISSUES FOR THE 21ST CENTURY

- Geothermal capacity will continue to be explored as an alternative energy source to fossil fuels.
- Mapping of tectonically active regions will continue to inform policy actions with regard to seismic hazards.

KEYLEARNINGconceptsreview

Distinguish between the endogenic and exogenic systems that shape Earth and *name* the driving force for each.

The Earth–atmosphere interface is where the **endogenic system** (internal), powered by heat energy from within the planet, interacts with the **exogenic system** (external), powered by insolation and influenced by gravity. These systems work together to produce Earth's diverse landscape. **Geomorphology** is the subfield within physical geography that studies the development and spatial distribution of landforms. Knowledge of Earth's endogenic processes helps us understand these surface features.

endogenic system (p. 284)
exogenic system (p. 284)
geomorphology (p. 284)

1. Define the endogenic and the exogenic systems. Describe the driving forces that energize these systems.

Explain the principle of uniformitarianism and *discuss* the time spans into which Earth's geologic history is divided.

The most fundamental principle of Earth science is **uniformitarianism**, which assumes that the same physical processes active in the environment today have been operating throughout geologic time. Dramatic, catastrophic events such as massive landslides or volcanic eruptions can interrupt the long-term processes that slowly shape Earth's surface. Scientists use the **geologic time scale** to organize the vast span of geologic time. Geologists assign *relative age*, based on the age of one feature relative to another in sequence, or *numerical age*, acquired from isotopic or other dating techniques. **Stratigraphy** is the study of layered rock strata, including their sequence (superposition), thickness, and spatial distribution, which yield clues to the age and origin of the rocks.

uniformitarianism (p. 284)
geologic time scale (p. 284)
stratigraphy (p. 284)

2. Explain the principle of uniformitarianism in the Earth sciences.
3. How is the geologic timescale organized? What era, period, and epoch are we living in today? What is the difference between the relative and numerical ages of rocks?

Depict Earth's interior in cross section and *describe* each distinct layer.

We have learned about Earth's interior indirectly, from the way its various layers transmit **seismic waves**. The **core** is differentiated into an inner core and an outer core, divided by a transition zone. Above Earth's core lies the **mantle**, differentiated into lower mantle and upper mantle. It experiences a gradual temperature increase with depth and flows slowly over time at depth, where it is hot and pressure is greatest. The boundary between the uppermost mantle and the crust is the **Mohorovičić discontinuity**, or **Moho**. The outer layer is the **crust**.

The outer part of Earth's crust is divided into two layers. The uppermost mantle, along with the crust, makes up the **lithosphere**. Below the lithosphere is the **asthenosphere**, or plastic layer. It contains pockets of increased heat from radioactive decay and is susceptible to slow convective currents in these hotter materials. The principles of buoyancy and balance produce the important principle of isostasy. **Isostasy** explains certain vertical movements of Earth's crust, such as isostatic rebound when the weight of ice is removed.

Earth's magnetic field is generated almost entirely within Earth's outer core. Polarity reversals in Earth's magnetism are recorded in cooling magma that contains iron minerals. The patterns of **geomagnetic reversal** in rock help scientists piece together the history of Earth's mobile crust.

seismic wave (p. 287)
core (p. 287)
mantle (p. 287)
Mohorovičić discontinuity (Moho) (p. 287)
crust (p. 287)
lithosphere (p. 288)
asthenosphere (p. 288)
isostasy (p. 288)
geomagnetic reversal (p. 289)

4. Make a simple sketch of Earth's interior, label each layer, and list the physical characteristics, temperature, composition, and depth of each on your drawing.
5. How does Earth generate its magnetic field? Is the magnetic field constant, or does it change? Explain the implications of your answer.
6. Describe the asthenosphere. Why is it also known as the plastic layer? What are the consequences of its convection currents?
7. What is a discontinuity? Describe the principal discontinuities within Earth.
8. Define isostasy and isostatic rebound, and explain the crustal equilibrium concept.
9. Diagram the uppermost mantle and crust. Label the density of the layers in grams per cubic centimeter. What two types of crust were described in the text in terms of rock composition?

Describe the three main groups of rock and *diagram* the rock cycle.

A **mineral** is an inorganic natural compound having a specific chemical formula and possessing a crystalline structure. A **rock** is an assemblage of minerals bound together (such as granite, a rock containing three minerals), or a mass of a single mineral (such as rock salt).

Igneous rock forms from **magma**, which is molten rock beneath the surface. **Lava** is the name for magma once it has emerged onto the surface. Magma either intrudes into crustal rocks, cools, and hardens, forming **intrusive igneous rock**, or extrudes onto the surface, forming **extrusive igneous rock**. The crystalline texture of igneous rock is related to the rate of cooling. **Granite** is a coarse-grained intrusive igneous rock; it is crystalline and high in silica, aluminum, potassium, calcium, and sodium. **Basalt** is a fine-grained extrusive igneous rock; it is granular and high in silica, magnesium, and iron. Intrusive igneous rock that cools slowly in the crust forms a **pluton**. The largest pluton form is a **batholith**.

Sedimentary rock is formed when loose *clasts* (grains or fragments) derived from several sources are compacted and cemented together in the process of **lithification**. Clastic sedimentary rocks are derived from the fragments of weathered and eroded rocks and the material that is transported and deposited as **sediment**. Chemical sedimentary rocks are formed either by biochemical processes or from the chemical dissolution of minerals into solution; the most common is **limestone**, which is lithified calcium carbonate, $CaCO_3$.

Any igneous or sedimentary rock may be transformed into **metamorphic rock** by going through profound physical or chemical changes under pressure and increased temperature. The **rock cycle** describes the three principal rock-forming processes and the rocks they produce.

mineral (p. 290)
rock (p. 290)
igneous rock (p. 290)
magma (p. 290)
lava (p. 290)
intrusive igneous rock (p. 290)
extrusive igneous rock (p. 290)
granite (p. 290)
basalt (p. 291)
pluton (p. 291)
batholith (p. 291)
sedimentary rock (p. 292)
sediment (p. 292)
lithification (p. 292)
limestone (p. 293)
metamorphic rock (p. 293)
rock cycle (p. 294)

10. What is a mineral? Name the most common minerals on Earth. What is a rock?
11. Describe igneous processes. What is the difference between intrusive and extrusive types of igneous rocks?
12. Explain what coarse- and fine-grained textures say about the cooling history of a rock.
13. Briefly describe sedimentary processes and lithification. Describe the sources and particle sizes of sedimentary rocks.
14. What is metamorphism, and how are metamorphic rocks produced? Name some original parent rocks and their metamorphic equivalents.

Describe Pangaea and its breakup and *explain* the physical evidence that crustal drifting is continuing today.

The present configuration of the ocean basins and continents is the result of tectonic processes involving Earth's interior dynamics and crust. **Pangaea** was the name Alfred Wegener gave to a single assemblage of continental crust existing some 225 m.y.a. that subsequently broke apart. Wegener coined the phrase *continental drift* to describe his idea that the crust is moved by vast forces within the planet. The theory of **plate tectonics** is that Earth's lithosphere is fractured into huge slabs or plates, each moving in response to gravitational pull and to flowing currents in the mantle that create frictional drag on the plate. Geomagnetic reversals along **mid-ocean ridges** on the ocean floor provide evidence of **seafloor spreading**, which accompanies the movement of plates toward the continental margins of ocean basins. At some plate boundaries, denser oceanic crust dives beneath lighter continental crust along **subduction zones**.

Pangaea (p. 295)
plate tectonics (p. 297)
mid-ocean ridge (p. 297)
seafloor spreading (p. 297)
subduction zone (p. 299)

15. Briefly review the history of the theory of plate tectonics, including the concepts of continental drift and seafloor spreading. What was Alfred Wegener's role?
16. What was Pangaea? What happened to it during the past 225 million years?
17. Describe the process of upwelling as it refers to magma under the ocean floor. Define subduction, and explain that process.

Draw the pattern of Earth's major plates on a world map and *relate* this pattern to the occurrence of earthquakes, volcanic activity, and hot spots.

Earth's lithosphere is made up of 14 large plates, and many smaller ones, that move and interact to form three types of plate boundaries: divergent, convergent, and transform. Along the offset portions of mid-ocean ridges, horizontal motions produce *transform faults*. Earthquakes and volcanoes often correlate with plate boundaries. As many as 50 to 100 **hot spots** exist across Earth's surface, where plumes of magma—some anchored in the lower mantle, others originating from shallow sources in the upper mantle—generate an upward flow. Some hot spots produce **geothermal energy**, or heat from Earth's interior, which may be used for direct geothermal heating or geothermal power. The **geologic cycle** is a model of the internal and external interactions that shape the crust—including the hydrologic, rock, and tectonic cycles.

hot spot (p. 302)
geothermal energy (p. 302)
geologic cycle (p. 303)

18. Characterize the three types of plate boundaries and the actions associated with each type.
19. What is the relation between plate boundaries and volcanic and earthquake activity?
20. What is geothermal energy?
21. Illustrate the geologic cycle, and define each component: rock cycle, tectonic cycle, and hydrologic cycle.

MasteringGeography™

Looking for additional review and test prep materials? Visit the Study Area in *MasteringGeography*™ to enhance your geographic literacy, spatial reasoning skills, and understanding of this chapter's content by accessing a variety of resources, including **MapMaster** interactive maps, geoscience animations, videos, *In the News* RSS feeds, flashcards, web links, self-study quizzes, and an eText version of *Elemental Geosystems*.

10 Tectonics, Earthquakes, and Volcanism

This comprehensive map of the ocean basins, published in 1977 by Marie Tharp and Bruce Heezen, gave scientists their first look at the global ocean floor, including the vast Mid-Atlantic Ridge, identified through Tharp and Heezen's work in the 1950s. See the tour of this ocean-floor map in Critical Thinking 10.2 at the end of this chapter. [Office of Naval Research.]

KEYLEARNING**concepts**

After reading the chapter, you should be able to:

- *Describe* first, second, and third orders of relief and *list* Earth's six major topographic regions.
- *Describe* the formation of continental crust and *define* displaced terranes.
- *Explain* the process of folding and *describe* the principal types of faults and their characteristic landforms.
- *List* the three types of plate collisions associated with orogenesis and *identify* specific examples of each.
- *Explain* earthquake characteristics and measurement, *describe* earthquake fault mechanics, and *discuss* the status of earthquake forecasting.
- *Describe* volcanic landforms and *distinguish* between an effusive and an explosive volcanic eruption.

The San Jacinto Fault Connection

In southern California, people live with earthquakes and with the ever-present question, "When will the 'Big One' occur?" The hundreds of faults that make up the San Andreas fault system in that region are produced by the relative horizontal motions, approximately 5 cm (2 in.) per year, of the northwestward-moving Pacific plate against the southeastward-moving North American plate. The San Jacinto fault, running from San Bernardino (just inland of Los Angeles) southward to the Mexican border, is an active part of this system. The San Jacinto runs somewhat parallel to the Elsinore fault and the Whittier fault, which crosses into Los Angeles. Numerous other related faults lace through the region with this same alignment (**Figure GN 10.1**).

Potential for a Major Earthquake In 1994, the Northridge earthquake in the San Fernando Valley north of Los Angeles caused 66 fatalities and set the record, which still stands today, for earthquake-related property damage in the United States at $30 billion. The U.S. Geological Survey (USGS) regards the San Jacinto fault as capable of an M 7.5 quake ("M" is the abbreviation for moment magnitude and refers to an earthquake rating scale discussed in this chapter). An M 7.5 would release almost 30 times more energy than that produced by the M 6.7 Northridge earthquake—thus, an M 7.5 is a major quake as compared to an M 6.7 strong quake.

Scientific evidence regarding the nature of faulting and crustal movement suggests that a major earthquake may be preceded by a number of small earthquakes that occur in a "wavelike pattern" as rupturing spreads along the fault. Recent earthquake activity along the San Jacinto and Elsinore faults may be following this pattern.

Records show that at least six quakes have occurred along the San Jacinto fault in the last 50 years: in addition to the M 7.5 in 1994, an M 5.8 and M 6.5 in 1968, an M 5.3 in 1980, an M 5.0 in 2005, and an M 4.1 in 2010, south of Palm Springs. Then in April 2010, an earthquake occurred along a nearby system of small faults that transferred strain to the San Jacinto; the M 7.2 El Mayor–Cucapah quake, located southeast of El Centro, in Baja, Mexico, was the largest to affect the region since 1994 (**Figure GN 10.2**). This temblor occurred along a complex, previously unknown fault system connecting the Gulf of California (see Figure 10.11a) to the Elsinore fault and caused large clusters of aftershocks toward the north along the San Jacinto fault structure. The M 5.4 Borrego quake occurred several months later, with aftershocks again spreading to the northwest. This pattern indicates that strain is moving northward along the system—a cause for concern that this sequence of seismic events may be leading to the "Big One."

▲**Figure GN 10.2 Land-surface shift of up to 3.0 m (9.8 ft) along the Borrego fault caused by the El Major–Cucapah quake.** [John Fletcher/CICESE/NASA.]

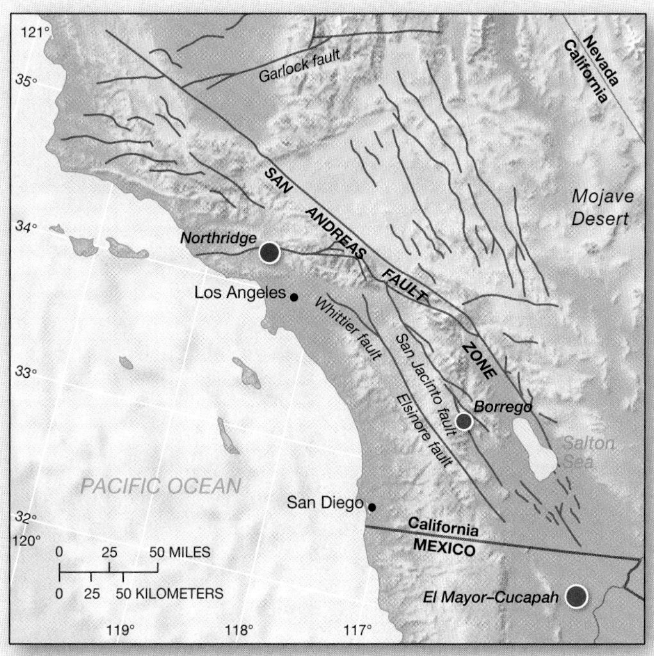

▲**Figure GN 10.1 Southern California seismic map sample, with locations of the 1994 Northridge quake, and 2010 El Mayor-Cucapah and Borrego quakes.** [Based on data from USGS and the California Geological Survey.]

Planning for Earthquakes The Global Positioning System (GPS) is now an essential part of earthquake forecasting, and a network of 100 GPS stations monitors crustal change throughout southern California. Given scientific advancements in earthquake analysis and forecasting, a major quake along the San Jacinto and related faults should not catch the region by surprise, assuming that proper planning, zoning, and preparation are put in place now. This chapter examines earthquakes and other tectonic processes that determine Earth's surface topography.

QUESTION AND EXPLORE For information and links regarding the Northridge quake of 1994, see http://earthquake.usgs.gov/earthquakes/states/events/1994_01_17.php, and for the 2010 El Mayor–Cucapah earthquake, see http://www.scsn.org/2010sierraelmayor.html. MG

The arrangement of continents and oceans, the topography of the land and the seafloor, the uplift and erosion of mountain ranges, and global patterns of earthquake and volcanic activity are all evidence of dynamic forces shaping the planet. Earth's endogenic systems send flows of heat and material toward the surface. These ongoing processes alter continental landscapes and produce oceanic seafloor crust, sometimes in dramatic events that make headline news.

Natural hazards such as earthquakes and volcanic eruptions near population centers pose threats to lives and property. The world was riveted to images of massive earthquakes in Haiti and Chile in 2010 and in New Zealand and Japan in 2011 as unstable plate boundaries snapped into new positions. (More on these events is in Focus Study 10.1 in this chapter.) Earth systems science is now providing analysis and warnings of seismic and volcanic activity to affected populations as never before.

Natural hazards such as earthquakes and volcanic eruptions near population centers pose threats to lives and property.

In this chapter: We examine processes that create the various landforms and crustal features that make up Earth's surface. Continental crust has been forming throughout most of Earth's 4.6-billion-year existence. Tectonic processes deform Earth's crust, which is then weathered and eroded into recognizable landforms: mountains, basins, faults and folds, and volcanoes. Such processes sometimes occur suddenly, as in the case of earthquakes, but more often the movements that shape the landscape are gradual, such as regional uplift and folding.

We begin our look at tectonics and volcanism on the ocean floor, where they are hidden from direct view. The map that opens this chapter and highlights the details of the ocean floor is a striking representation of the concepts learned in Chapter 9, which lay the foundation for this and subsequent chapters. Try to correlate this seafloor illustration with the map of crustal plates and plate boundaries shown in Figure 9.16.

Earth's Surface Relief

Landscapes across Earth occur at varying elevations; think of the low coastal plains of India and Bangladesh, the middle-elevation foothills and mountains of India and Nepal, and the high elevations of the Himalayas in Nepal and Tibet. These vertical elevation differences upon a surface are known as **relief**. The general term for the undulations and other variations in the shape of Earth's surface, including its relief, is **topography**—the lay of the land.

The relief and topography of Earth's landforms have played a vital role in human history: High mountain passes both protected and isolated societies, ridges and valleys dictated transportation routes, and vast plains encouraged the development of faster methods of communication and travel. Earth's topography has stimulated human invention and spurred adaptation.

Studying Earth's Topography

To study Earth's relief and topography, scientists use satellite radar, LiDAR systems (which use laser scanners), and tools such as GPS (which report location and elevation; review Chapter 1 for discussion of these tools). During an 11-day period in 2000, the Shuttle Radar Topography Mission (SRTM) instruments on board the Space Shuttle *Endeavor* surveyed almost 80% of Earth's land surface; **Figure 10.1** shows examples of SRTM images (see the image gallery at http://www2.jpl.nasa.gov/srtm). The data acquired from this mission comprise the most complete high-resolution topographic dataset available and are commonly used with a satellite image overlay for topographic display.

A recent advance in the study of topography is the development of digital elevation models (DEMs) to display elevation data in digital form. LiDAR, which provides the highest resolution for mapping Earth's surface,

▼Figure 10.1 Second and third orders of relief. [Shuttle Radar Topography Mission, courtesy of JPL/NGA/NASA–CalTech.]

(a) Second order of relief on the Kamchatka Peninsula, Russia.

(b) Third order of relief demonstrated by the local landscape near San Jose, Costa Rica, with the volcanoes Irazu (3401 m; 11,161 ft) and Turrialba (3330 m; 10,925 ft) in the distance.

is often used in conjunction with DEMs for scientific purposes. The USGS, known for its comprehensive topographic mapping program for the United States, is currently collaborating with NASA and the National Park Service to acquire LiDAR data for mapping U.S. National Parks (more information is available at http://nationalmap.gov/elevation.html).

In another USGS project, topography and geology are combined in a shaded relief map of the United States called "A Tapestry of Time and Terrain." This map is made up of 12 million spot elevations, with less than a kilometer between any two, offering a detailed composite color illustration of land surfaces and the ages of underlying rock formations (see http://tapestry.usgs.gov/).

Orders of Relief

For convenience of description, geographers group landscapes into three *orders of relief*. These orders classify landscapes by scale, from vast ocean basins and continents down to local hills and valleys. The first order of relief is the coarsest level of landforms, consisting of the continents and oceans. **Continental landmasses** are those portions of crust that reside above or near sea level, including the undersea continental shelves along the coastlines. **Ocean basins**, featured in the chapter-opening map, are portions of the crust that are entirely below sea level. Approximately 71% of Earth is covered by ocean.

The second order of relief is the intermediate level of landforms, both on continents and in ocean basins (Figure 10.1a). Continental features in the second order of relief include mountain ranges, plains, and lowlands. A few examples are the Alps, Canadian and American Rockies, west Siberian lowland, and Tibetan Plateau. This order includes the great rock "shields" that form the heart of each continental mass. In the ocean basins, the second order of relief includes continental rises and slopes, flat plains (called *abyssal plains*), mid-ocean ridges, submarine canyons, and oceanic trenches (subduction zones)—all visible in the seafloor illustration that opens this chapter.

The third and most detailed order of relief includes individual mountains, cliffs, valleys, hills, and other landforms of smaller scale (Figure 10.1b). These features characterize local landscapes.

Earth's Hypsometry

Hypsometry (from the Greek *hypsos*, meaning "height") is the measurement of land elevation relative to sea level (the measurement of underwater elevations is bathymetry). **Figure 10.2** is a hypsographic curve that shows the distribution of Earth's surface area according to elevation above and depth below sea level. Relative

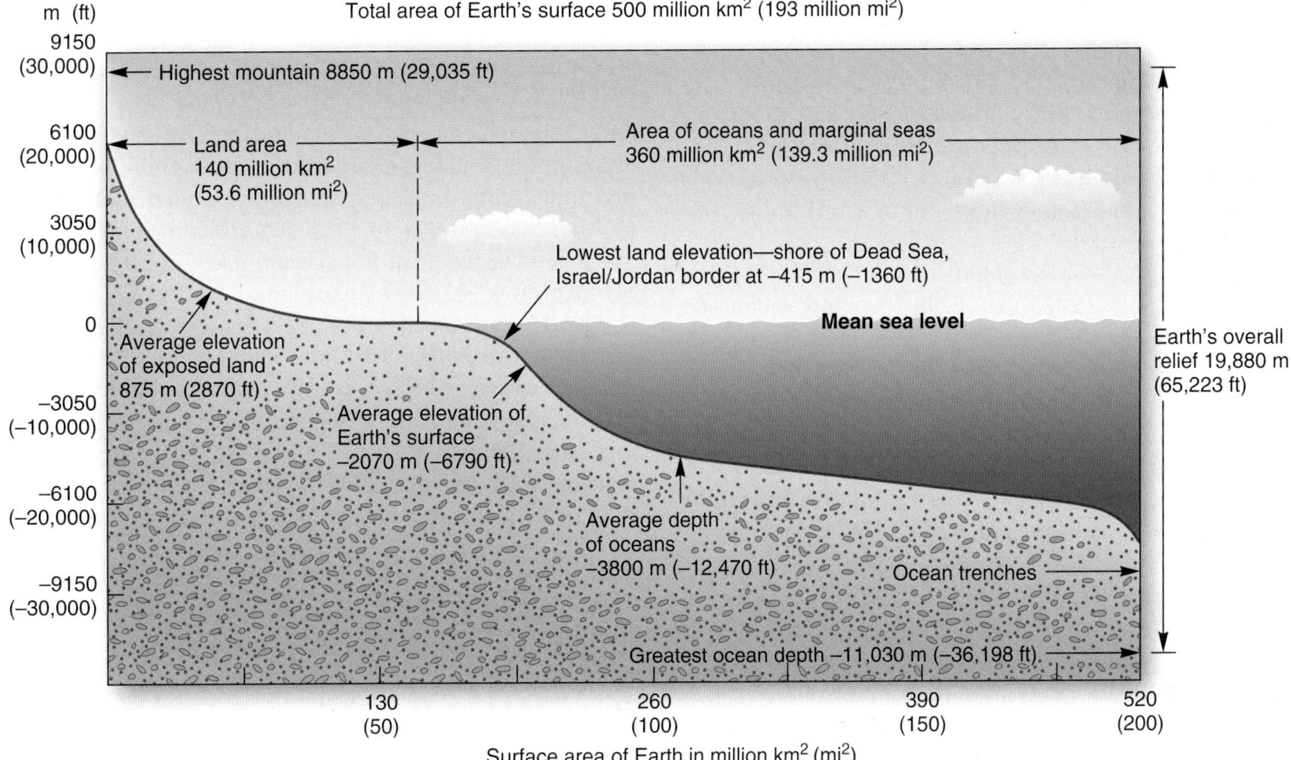

▲**Figure 10.2 Earth's hypsometry.** Hypsographic curve of Earth's surface area and elevation as related to mean sea level. From the highest point above sea level (Mount Everest) to the deepest oceanic trench (Mariana Trench), Earth's overall relief is almost 20 km (12.5 mi).

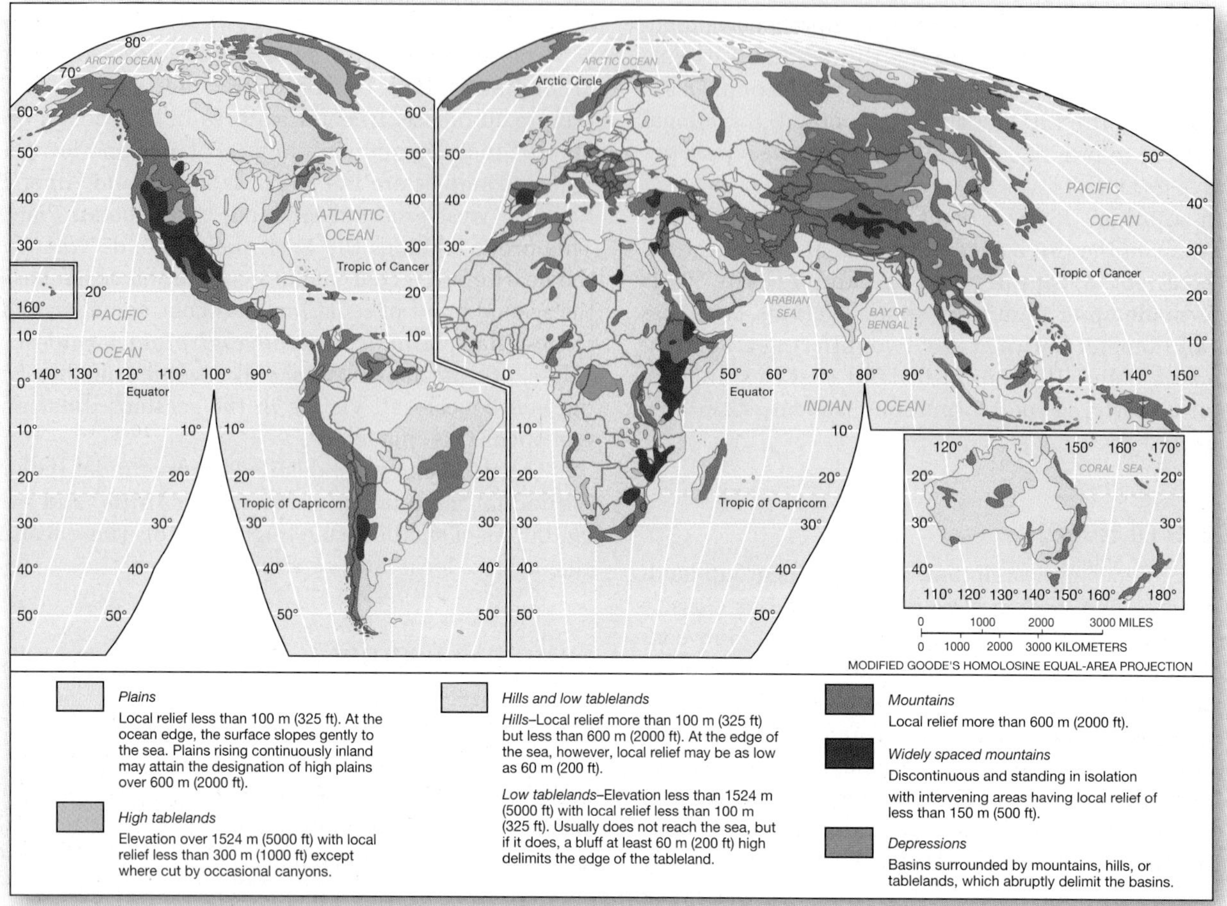

▲**Figure 10.3 Earth's topographic regions.** Compare the map and legend to the world physical map inside the back cover of this text. [R. E. Murphy, "Landforms of the world," *Annals of the Association of American Geographers* 58, 1 (March 1968). Adapted by permission.]

to Earth's diameter of 12,756 km (7926 mi), the surface has low relief—only about 20 km (12.5 mi) from highest peak to lowest oceanic trench. For perspective, Mount Everest is 8.8 km (5.5 mi) above sea level, and the Mariana Trench is 11 km (6.8 mi) below sea level.

The average elevation of Earth's solid surface is actually under water: –2070 m (–6790 ft) below mean sea level. The average elevation for exposed land is only 875 m (2870 ft). For the ocean depths, the average elevation is –3800 m (–12,470 ft). From this description, you can see that, on average, the oceans are much deeper than continental regions are high. Overall, the underwater ocean basins, ocean floor, and submarine mountain ranges form Earth's largest "landscape."

Earth's Topographic Regions

Earth's landscapes can be generalized into six types of topographic regions: plains, high tablelands, hills and low tablelands, mountains, widely spaced mountains, and depressions (**Figure 10.3**). An arbitrary elevation or other descriptive limit in common use defines each type of topography (see the map legend).

North and South America, Asia, and Australia possess extensive *plains. Hills* and *low tablelands* dominate Africa and part of Europe and Australia. The Colorado Plateau, Greenland, and Antarctica are notable *high tablelands* (the latter two composed of ice). *Mountains* occur on each continent; extensive *depressions*, or basins, occur only in Asia and Africa. Earth's relief and topography are

GEOreport 10.1 Mount Everest measured by GPS

In 1999, climbers determined the height of Mount Everest using direct GPS placement on the mountain's icy summit. The newly measured elevation of 8850 m (29,035 ft) replaced the previous official measure of 8848 m (29,028 ft) made in 1954 by the Survey of India. The 1999 GPS readings also indicated that the Himalayas are moving northeastward at a rate of up to 6 mm (0.25 in.) per year, as the mountain range is being driven farther into Asia by the continuing collision of the Indian and Asian landmasses.

undergoing constant change as a result of processes that form and rearrange crust.

CRITICAL**thinking 10.1**

Comparing Topographic Regions at Different Scales

Using the definitions in Figure 10.3, identify the type of topographic region represented by the area within 100 km (62 mi) of your campus, and then do the same for the area within 1000 km (620 mi) of your campus. Use Google Earth™ or consult maps and atlases to describe the topographic character and the variety of relief within these two regional scales. Do you perceive that the type of topographic region influences lifestyles? Economic activities? Transportation? Was topography influential in the history of the region?

Crustal Formation

How did Earth's continental crust form? What gave rise to the three orders of relief just discussed? Earth's surface is a battleground of opposing processes: On the one hand, tectonic activity, driven by our planet's internal energy, builds crust; on the other hand, the exogenic processes of weathering and erosion, powered by the Sun and occurring through the actions of air, water, waves, and ice, tear down crust.

Tectonic activity generally is slow, taking place over millions of years. Endogenic processes result in gradual uplift and new landforms, with major mountain building occurring along plate boundaries. The uplifted crustal regions are quite varied, but can be grouped into three general categories:

- Residual mountains and stable continental cratons, consisting of inactive remnants of ancient tectonic activity
- Tectonic mountains and landforms, produced by active folding, faulting, and crustal movements
- Volcanic landforms, formed by the surface accumulation of molten rock from eruptions of subsurface materials

The various processes mentioned in these descriptions operate in concert to produce the continental crust we see around us.

Continental Shields

All continents have a nucleus, called a *craton*, consisting of ancient crystalline rock on which the continent "grows" through the addition of crustal fragments and sediments. Cratons are generally old and stable masses of continental crust that have been eroded to a low elevation and relief. Most date to the Precambrian Eon and can be more than 2 billion years old. The lack of basaltic components in these cratons offers a clue to their stability. The lithosphere underlying a craton is often thicker than that underlying younger portions of continents and oceanic crust.

A **continental shield** is a large region where a craton is exposed at the surface (**Figure 10.4**). Layers of younger sedimentary rock—called continental platforms—surround these shields and appear quite stable over time. Examples of such stable platforms include the region from east of the Rockies to the Appalachians and northward into central and eastern Canada, a large portion of China, eastern Europe to the Ural Mountains, and portions of Siberia.

On the *MasteringGeography* website, you will find a map of seven world structural regions, including shields and their surrounding sedimentary deposits. Various mountain chains, rifted regions, and isolated volcanic areas are also noted on the map, which you can refer back to as you read through this chapter.

Building Continental Crust and Accretion of Terranes

The formation of continental crust is complex and takes hundreds of millions of years. It involves the entire sequence of seafloor spreading and formation of oceanic crust, eventual subduction and remelting of that oceanic crust, and the subsequent rise of remelted material as new magma, all summarized in **Figure 10.5**. In this process of crustal formation, you can literally follow the cycling of materials through the tectonic cycle.

To understand this process, study Figure 10.5 and the inset photos. Begin with the magma that originates in the asthenosphere and wells up along the mid-ocean ridges. Basaltic magma is formed from minerals in the upper mantle that are rich in iron and magnesium. Such magma contains less than 50% silica and has a low-viscosity (thin) texture—it tends to flow. This mafic material rises to erupt at spreading centers and cools to form new basaltic seafloor, which spreads outward to collide with continental crust along its far edges. The oceanic crust, being denser, plunges beneath the lighter continental crust, into the mantle, where it remelts. The new magma then rises and cools, forming more continental crust in the form of intrusive granitic igneous rock.

As the subducting oceanic plate works its way under a continental plate, it takes with it trapped seawater and sediment from eroded continental crust. The remelting incorporates the seawater, sediments, and surrounding crust into the mixture. As a result, the magma, generally called a *melt*, migrating upward from a subducted plate contains 50%–75% silica and aluminum. These give the melt a high-viscosity (thick) texture, and therefore it tends to block and plug conduits to the surface.

Bodies of such silica-rich magma may reach the surface in explosive volcanic eruptions, or they may stop short and become subsurface intrusive bodies in the crust, cooling slowly to form granitic crystalline plutons

◀Figure 10.4 Continental shields. [(a) Bobbé Christopherson. (b) Adapted from USGS Geologic Provinces map, available at http://earthquake.usgs.gov/data/crust/maps.php.]

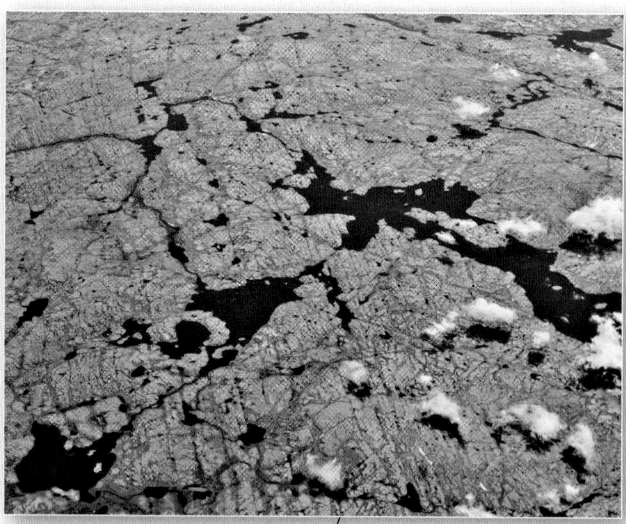

(b) Canadian shield landscape in northern Québec, stable for hundreds of millions of years, stripped by past glaciations and marked by intrusive igneous dikes (magmatic intrusions).

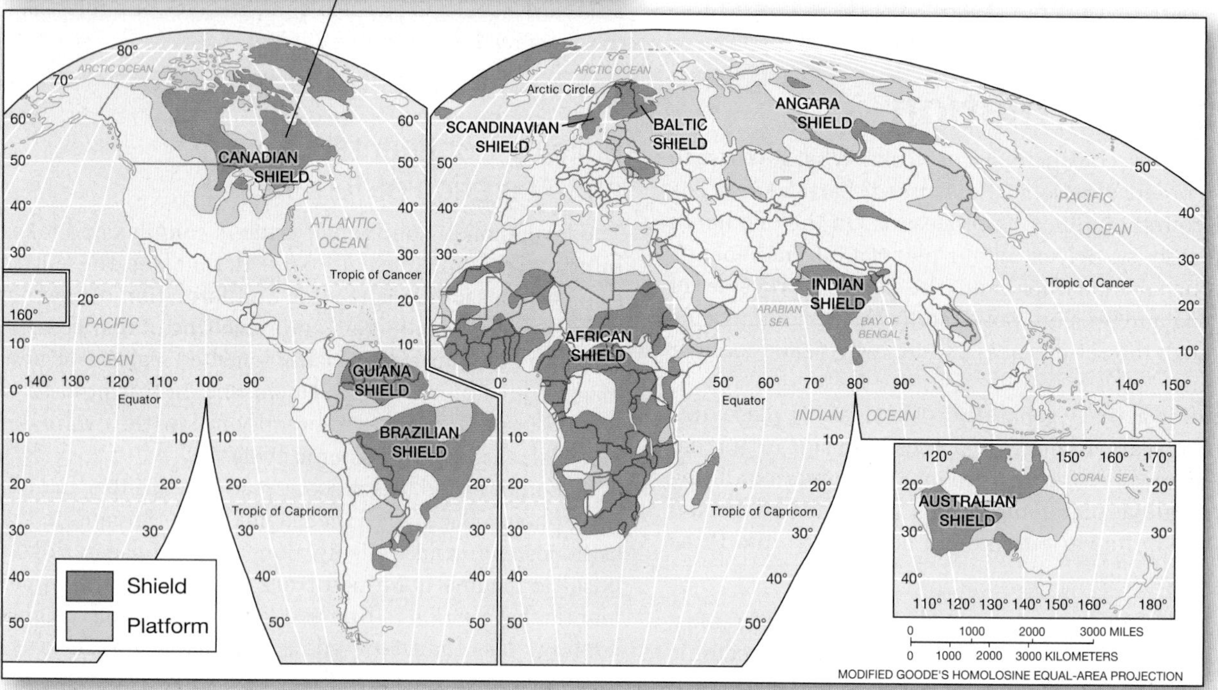

(a) Earth's major continental shields exposed by erosion. Continental platforms are the adjacent portions of these shields that remain covered by younger sedimentary layers.

such as batholiths (see Figure 9.5). As noted earlier, their composition is quite different from that of the magma that rises directly from the asthenosphere at seafloor spreading centers.

Each of Earth's major lithospheric plates actually is a collage of many crustal pieces acquired from a variety of sources. Over time, slowly migrating fragments of ocean floor, curving chains (or arcs) of volcanic islands, and pieces of crust from other continents all have been forced against the edges of continental shields and platforms. These varied crustal pieces that have become attached, or accreted, to the plates are **terranes** (not to be confused with *terrain*, which refers to the topography of a tract of land). Such displaced terranes, also known as *microplate*, or *exotic, terranes*, have histories different from those of the continents that capture them. They are usually framed by fault-zone fractures and differ in rock composition and structure from their new continental homes.

In the regions surrounding the Pacific Ocean, accreted terranes are particularly prevalent. At least 25% of the growth of western North America can be attributed to the accretion of at least 50 terranes since the early Jurassic Period (190 million years ago). A good example is the Wrangell Mountains, which lie just east of Prince William Sound and the city of Valdez, Alaska. The *Wrangellia terranes*—a former volcanic island arc and associated marine sediments from near the equator—migrated approximately 10,000 km (6200 mi) to form the Wrangell Mountains and three other distinct formations along the western margin of the continent (see a map on the *MasteringGeography* website).

Animation
Terrane Formation
http://goo.gl/s5qYzG
Basalt, from Hawai'i, is lower in silica
Dacite, from Mount St. Helens, is higher in silica
Spreading center
Magma with an andesitic-to-granitic composition derived from partial melting of subducted oceanic plate and remelting of continental crust
Oceanic ridge
Trench
Basaltic oceanic crust
Intrusive body
Continental crust
Subduction
Asthenosphere
Basaltic magma derived from partial melting of asthenosphere, or deeper plume
Oceanic crust: Material from the asthenosphere upwells along seafloor spreading centers as plates diverge.
Basaltic ocean floor is subducted beneath lighter continental crust, where it melts, along with its cargo of sediments, water, and minerals.
Continental crust: Melting generates magma, which makes its way up through the continental crust to form igneous intrusions and extrusive eruptions.

▲**Figure 10.5 Crustal formation processes, with examples of extrusive igneous rock types.** [Photos by Bobbé Christopherson.]

The Appalachian Mountains, extending from Alabama to the Maritime Provinces of Canada, possess bits of land once attached to ancient Europe, Africa, South America, Antarctica, and various oceanic islands. The discovery of terranes, which occurred as recently as the 1980s, revealed one of the ways continents are assembled.

Crustal Deformation

Rocks, whether igneous, sedimentary, or metamorphic, are subjected to powerful stress by tectonic forces, gravity, and the weight of overlying rocks. *Stress* is any force that affects an object, measured as force per unit area; note that these units are the same as for pressure (defined in Chapter 2). Three types of stress are important for crustal deformation: *tension*, which causes stretching; *compression*, which causes shortening; and *shear*, which causes twisting or tearing as objects slide parallel to one another (**Figure 10.6**).

Although stress is an important force in shaping Earth's crust, the landforms we see result from strain, which is how rocks respond to stress. *Strain* is, by definition, a dimensionless measure of the amount of deformation undergone by an object. Strain is the stretching, shortening, and twisting that result from stress and is expressed in rocks by *folding* (bending) or *faulting* (breaking). Whether a rock bends or breaks depends on several factors, including its composition and the amount of pressure it is undergoing. Figure 10.6 illustrates each type of stress and the resulting strain and surface expressions that develop.

Folding and Broad Warping

When rock strata that are layered horizontally are subjected to compressional forces, they become deformed (**Figure 10.7**). **Folding** occurs when rocks are deformed as a result of compressional stress and shortening. We can visualize this process by stacking sections of thick fabric on a table and slowly pushing on opposite ends of the stack. The cloth layers will bend and rumple into folds similar to those shown in the landscape of Figure 10.7a, with some folds forming arches (upward folds) and some folds forming troughs (downward folds).

An arch-shaped upward fold is an **anticline**; the rock strata slope downward away from an imaginary center

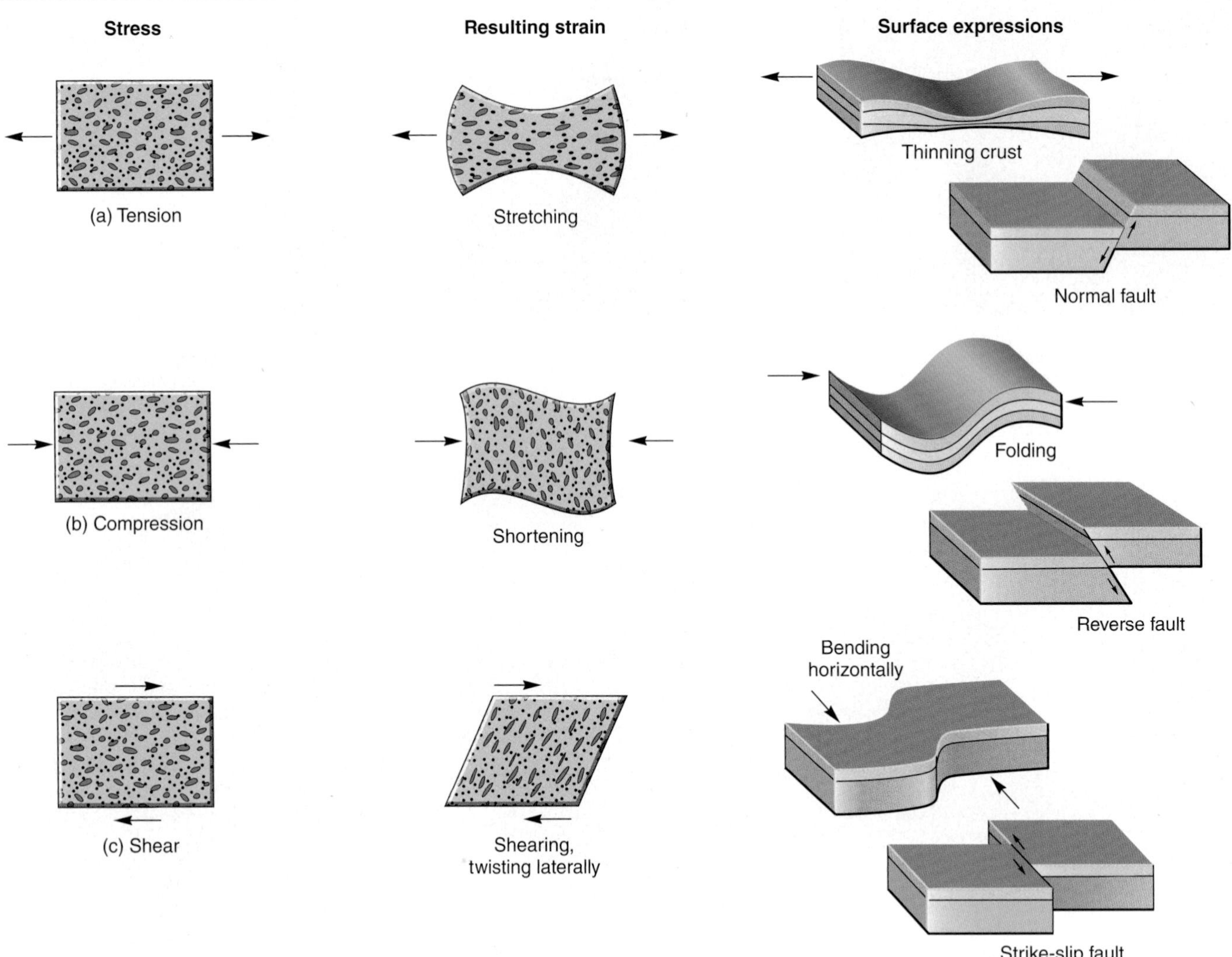

▲**Figure 10.6 Three kinds of stress and strain and the resulting surface expressions on Earth's crust.**

axis that divides the fold into two parts. A trough-shaped downward fold is a **syncline**; the strata slope upward away from the center axis. The erosion of a syncline may form a *synclinal ridge*, produced when the different rock strata offer different degrees of resistance to weathering processes (Figure 10.7b).

Figure 10.7a illustrates some of the features associated with folded landscapes. The *hinge* is the horizontal line that defines the part of the fold with the sharpest curvature. If the hinge is not horizontal, meaning that it is not "level" (parallel with Earth's surface), the fold is *plunging*, or dipped down (inclined) at an angle. If the *axial plane* of the fold, an imaginary surface that parallels the hinge, but descends downward through each layer, is inclined from vertical, the resulting configuration is an *overturned anticline*, in which folds have been compressed so much that they overturn upon their own strata. Further stress eventually fractures the rock strata along distinct lines, a process that forms a thrust fault (see Figure 10.7; faults are discussed ahead); some overturned folds are thrust upward, causing a considerable shortening of the original strata. Areas of intense stress, compressional folding, and faulting are visible along the San Andreas fault in southern California (Figure 10.7c).

Knowledge of folding and stratigraphy are important for the petroleum industry. For example, petroleum geologists know that oil and natural gas collect in the upper portions of anticlinal folds in permeable rock layers such as sandstone.

Over time, folded structures can erode to produce interesting landforms (**Figure 10.8**). An example is a *dome*, which is an area of uplifted rock strata resembling an anticline that has been heavily eroded over time (Figure 10.8a). Since an anticline is a fold that is convex in an upward direction, erosion exposes the oldest rocks in the center of a dome, which often have a circular pattern that resembles a bull's eye when viewed from the air—the Richat Structure in Mauritania is an example. The Black Hills of South Dakota are another dome structure. A *basin* forms when an area resembling a syncline is uplifted and then erodes over time; in this structure, the oldest rock strata are at the outside of the circular structure (Figure 10.8b). Since a syncline is concave when considered from above, erosion exposes the youngest rocks in the center of the structure.

Mountain ranges in North America, such as the Canadian Rockies and the Appalachian Mountains, and in the Middle East exhibit the complexity that folding

▲**Figure 10.7 Types of folds and their features.** [(b) Squirlgirl/Fotolia (c) Bobbé Christopherson.]

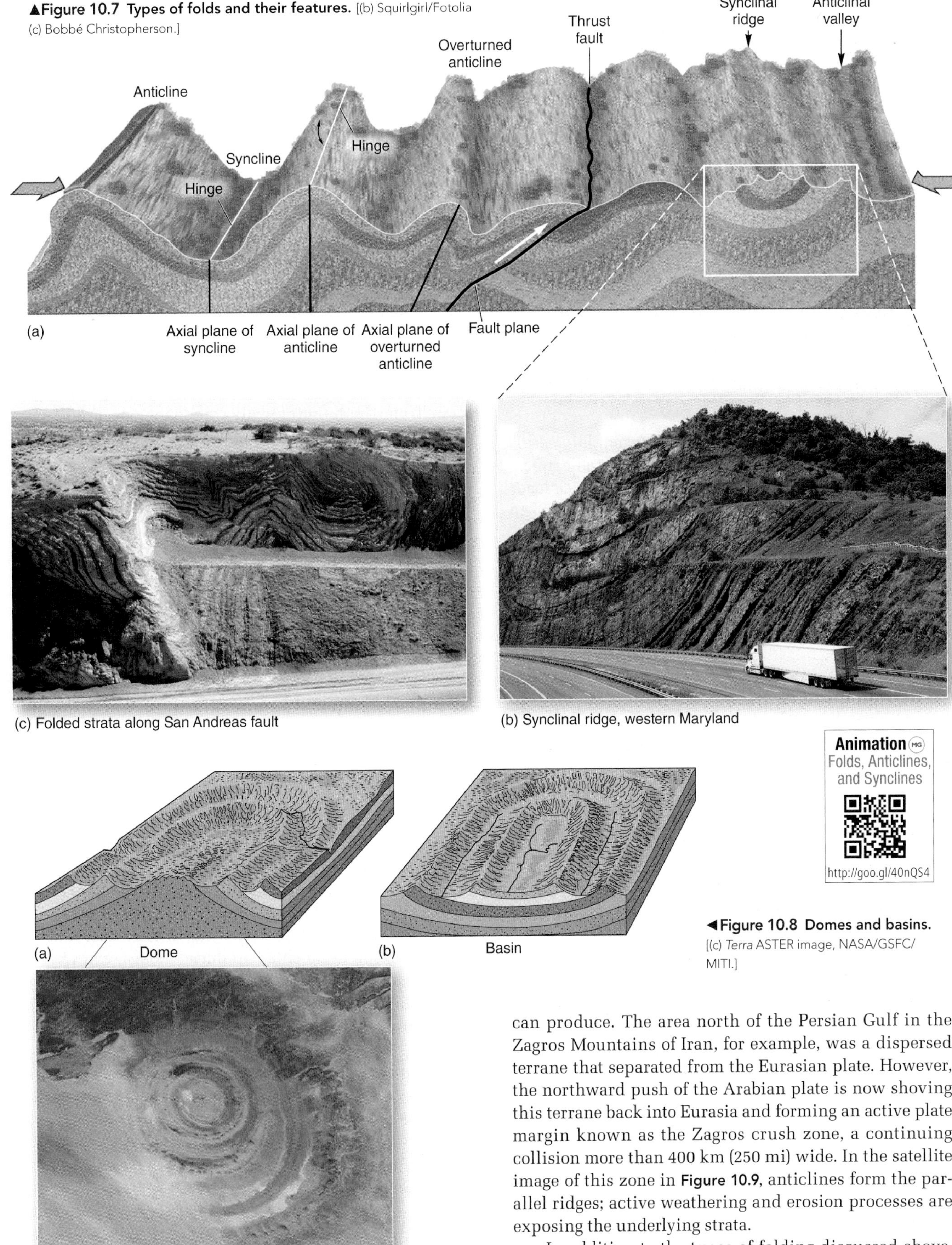

(c) Folded strata along San Andreas fault

(b) Synclinal ridge, western Maryland

◀**Figure 10.8 Domes and basins.** [(c) *Terra* ASTER image, NASA/GSFC/MITI.]

(c) The Richat dome, Mauritania; with sand dunes encroaching toward the dome.

can produce. The area north of the Persian Gulf in the Zagros Mountains of Iran, for example, was a dispersed terrane that separated from the Eurasian plate. However, the northward push of the Arabian plate is now shoving this terrane back into Eurasia and forming an active plate margin known as the Zagros crush zone, a continuing collision more than 400 km (250 mi) wide. In the satellite image of this zone in **Figure 10.9**, anticlines form the parallel ridges; active weathering and erosion processes are exposing the underlying strata.

In addition to the types of folding discussed above, broad warping actions are another cause of bending in continental crust. The bends produced by these actions, however, are far greater in extent than the folds produced

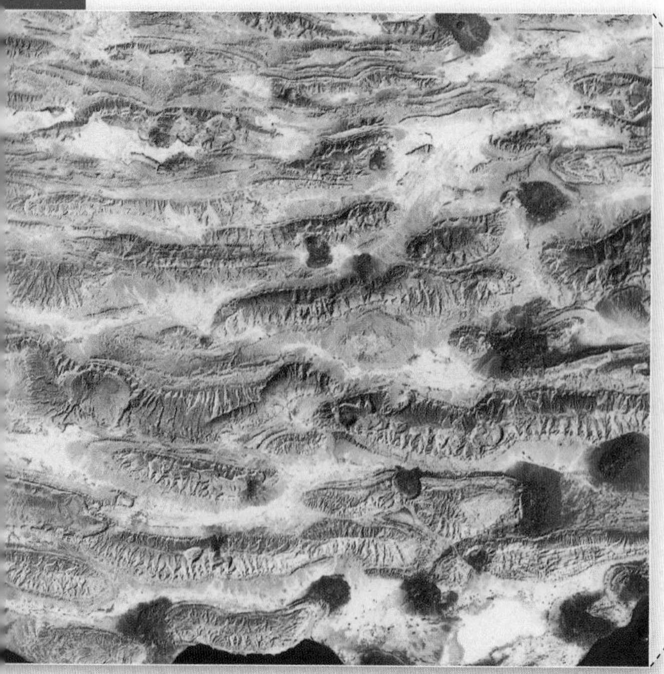

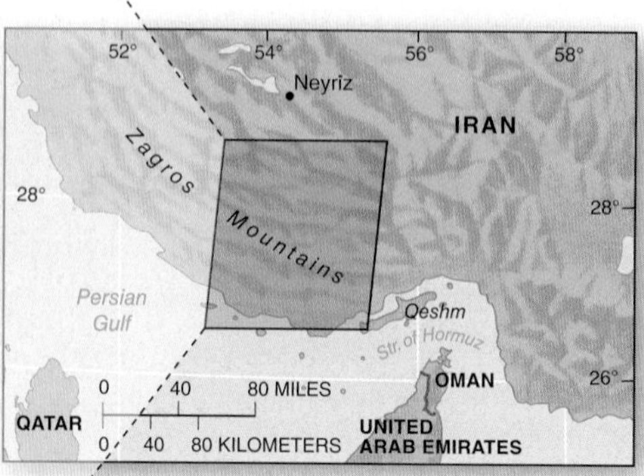

◀**Figure 10.9 Folded mountains in the Zagros crush zone, Iran.** The Zagros Mountains are a product of the Zagros crush zone, where the Arabian plate pushes northward into the Eurasian plate. [NASA.]

by compression. Forces responsible for such large-scale warping include mantle convection, isostatic adjustment (such as that caused by the weight of previous ice loads across northern Canada), and crustal swelling above an underlying hot spot.

Faulting

A freshly poured concrete sidewalk is smooth and strong. Adding stress to the sidewalk by driving heavy equipment over it may result in strain that causes a fracture. Pieces on either side of the fracture may move up, down, or horizontally, depending on the direction of stress. Similarly, when rock strata are stressed beyond their ability to remain a solid unit, they express the strain as a fracture. **Faulting** occurs when rocks on either side of the fracture shift relative to the other side. *Fault zones* are areas where fractures in the rock demonstrate crustal movement.

Types of Faults The fracture surface along which the two sides of a fault move is the *fault plane*; the tilt and orientation of this plane are the basis for differentiating the three main types of faults introduced in Figure 10.6: normal, reverse, and strike-slip, caused, respectively, by tensional stress, by compressional stress, and by lateral-shearing stress.

When forces pull rocks apart, the tensional stress causes a **normal fault**, in which rock on one side moves vertically along an inclined fault plane (**Figure 10.10a**). The downward-shifting side is the *hanging wall*; it drops relative to the *footwall block*. An exposed fault plane sometimes is visible along the base of faulted mountains, where individual ridges are truncated by the movements of the fault and end in triangular facets. A displacement of the ground surface caused by faulting is commonly called a *fault scarp*, or *escarpment*.

When forces push rocks together, such as when plates converge, the compression causes a **reverse fault**, in which rocks move upward along the fault plane (**Figure 10.10b**). On the surface, it appears similar to a normal fault, although more collapse and landslides may occur from the hanging-wall component. In England, when miners worked along a reverse fault, they would stand on the lower side (footwall) and hang their lanterns on the upper side (hanging wall), giving rise to these terms.

A **thrust fault**, or *overthrust fault*, occurs when the fault plane forms a low angle relative to the horizontal, so that the overlying block has shifted far over the underlying block (see Figure 10.7). Place your hands palms-down on your desk, with fingertips together, and slide one hand up over the other—this is the motion of a low-angle thrust fault, with one side pushing over the other.

In the Alps, several such overthrusts have resulted from compressional forces of the ongoing collision between the African and Eurasian plates. Beneath the Los Angeles Basin, overthrust faults caused numerous earthquakes in the twentieth century, including the $30 billion 1994 Northridge earthquake. Many of the faults beneath the Los Angeles region are "blind thrust faults," meaning that no evidence of rupture exists at the surface. Such faults are essentially buried under the crust, but remain a major earthquake threat.

When lateral shear causes horizontal movement along a fault plane, such as produced along a transform plate boundary and the associated transform faults, the fault is called a **strike-slip fault** (**Figure 10.10c**). The movement is right lateral or left lateral, depending on the direction of motion an observer on one side of the fault sees occurring on the other side.

The San Andreas fault system is a famous example of both a transform and a strike-slip fault. Recall from Chapter 9 that transform faults occur along transform plate boundaries; most are found in the ocean basins along mid-ocean ridges, but some cross continental crust. The crust on either side of a transform fault moves parallel to the fault itself; thus, transform faults are a type of strike-slip fault. However, since some strike-slip faults occur at locations away from plate boundaries, not all strike-slip faults are transform.

Animation MG
Fault Types, Transform Faults, Plate Margins
http://goo.gl/NMH7sr

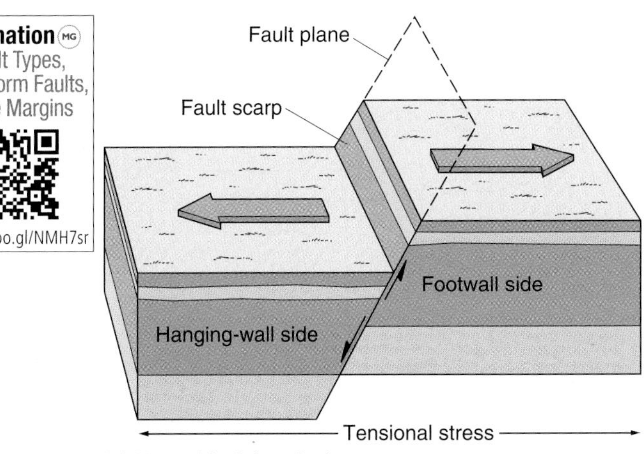

(a) Normal fault (tension)

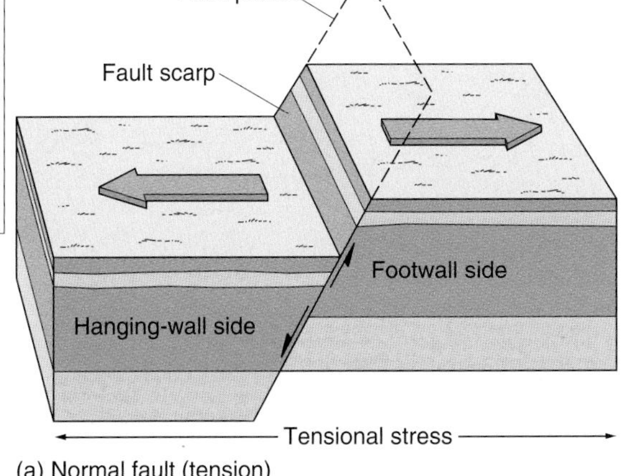

(a) A normal fault visible along the edge of mountain ranges in California and Utah.

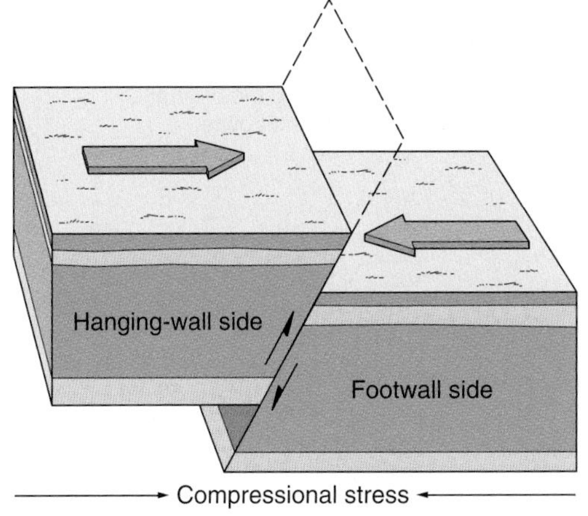

(b) Thrust or reverse fault (compression)

(b) A thrust, or reverse, fault visible in these offset strata in coal seams and volcanic ash in British Columbia.

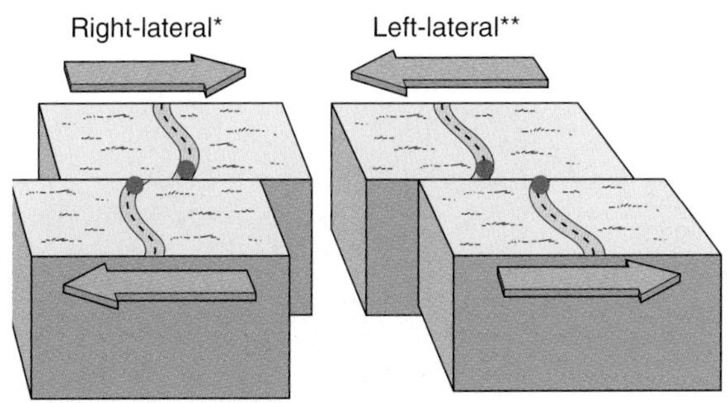

(c) Strike-slip fault (lateral shearing)

* Viewed from either dot on each road, movement of opposite side is *to the right*.
** Viewed from either dot on each road, movement of opposite side is *to the left*.

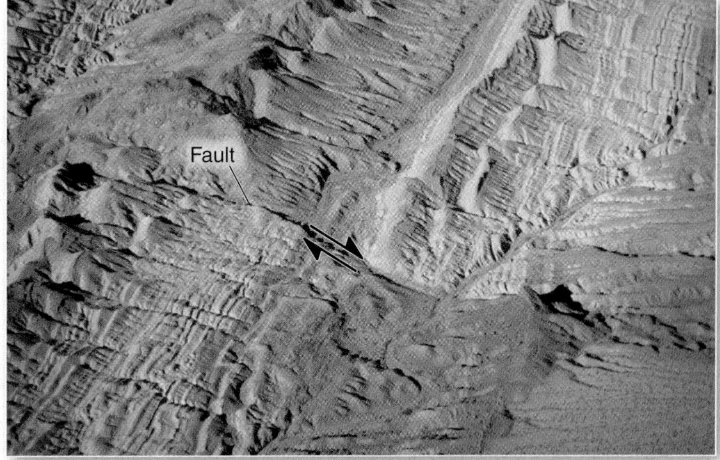

(c) Aerial view of a right-lateral strike-slip fault in southern Nevada.

▲**Figure 10.10 Types of faults.** [(a) Bobbé Christopherson. (b) Fletcher and Baylis/Science Source. (c) Marli Bryant Miller.]

Along the western margin of North America, plate boundaries take several forms. The San Andreas transform fault is the product of a continental plate (the North American plate) overriding an oceanic transform plate boundary. The San Andreas fault meets a seafloor spreading center and a subduction zone at the Mendocino Triple Junction (a *triple junction* is where three plates intersect). Each of these plate boundaries is illustrated in **Figure 10.11a.**

Strike-slip faults often create linear valleys, or troughs, along the fracture zone, such as those along the San Andreas (**Figure 10.11b**). Offset streams are another

▶Figure 10.11 Plate boundaries of western North America and the San Andreas fault. [(a) Communications and Education Division/NOAA. (b) Lloyd Cluff/Eureka Premium/Corbis.]

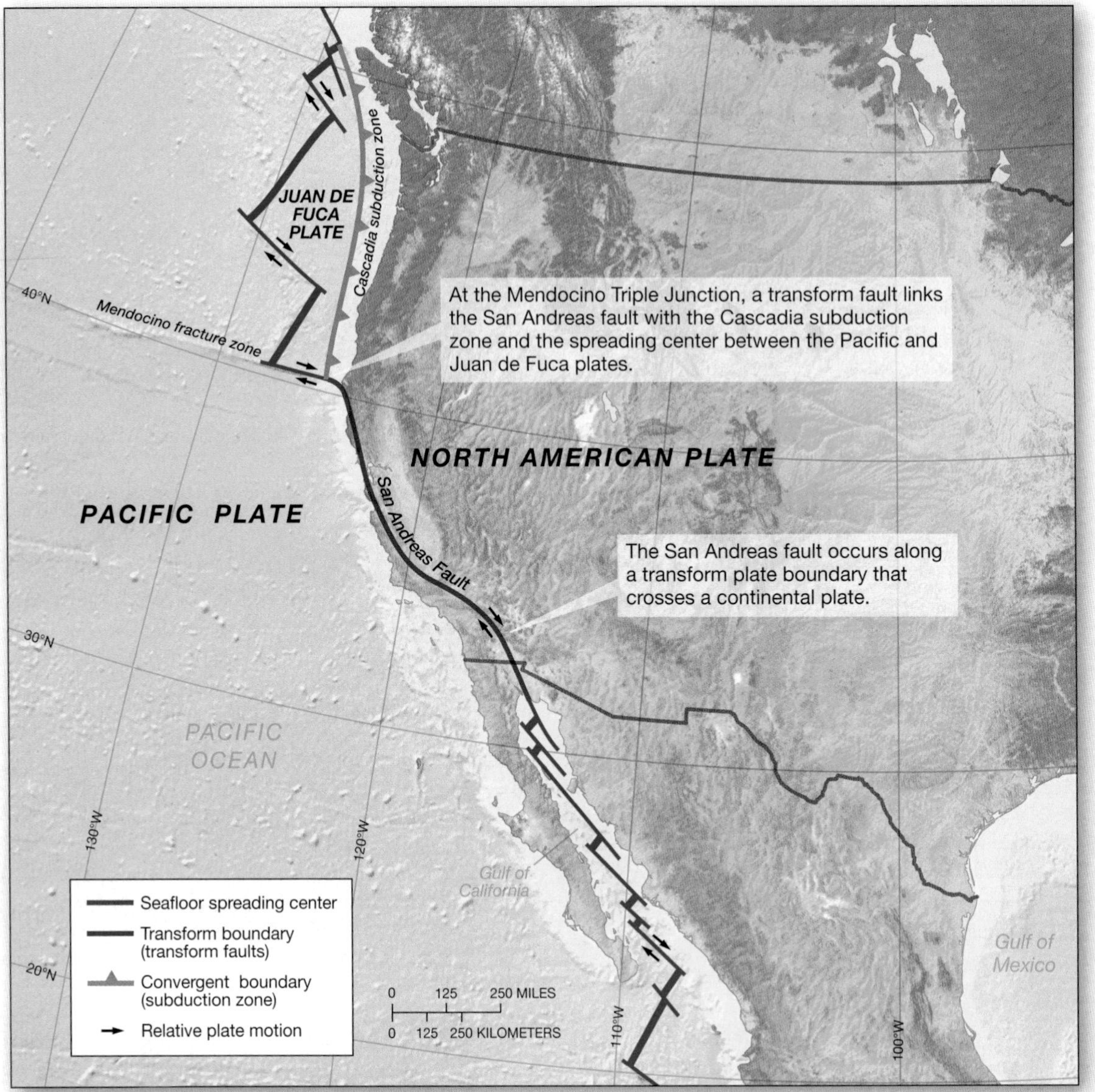

At the Mendocino Triple Junction, a transform fault links the San Andreas fault with the Cascadia subduction zone and the spreading center between the Pacific and Juan de Fuca plates.

The San Andreas fault occurs along a transform plate boundary that crosses a continental plate.

(a) The western margin of North America is the meeting point of three plates with different types of boundaries. Between the Juan de Fuca and Pacific plates is a spreading center with transform faults linking mid-ocean ridges. Between the Juan de Fuca and North American plates is the Cascadia subduction zone. The San Andreas transform fault separates the Pacific and North American plates. The meeting point of three plates is a "triple junction."

landform associated with strike-slip faults, characterized by an abrupt bend in the course of the stream as it crosses the fault.

Faulted Landscapes Across some landscapes, pairs of faults act in concert to form distinctive terrain. The term **horst** applies to upward-faulted blocks; **graben** refers to downward-faulted blocks (**Figure 10.12**). The Great Rift Valley of East Africa, associated with crustal spreading, is an example of such a horst-and-graben landscape. This rift extends northward to the Red Sea, which fills the rift formed by parallel normal faults. Lake Baikal in Siberia, discussed in the Chapter 6 Geosystems Now, is also a graben. This lake basin is the deepest continental "rift valley" on Earth and continues to widen at an average rate of about 2.5 cm (1 in.) per year.

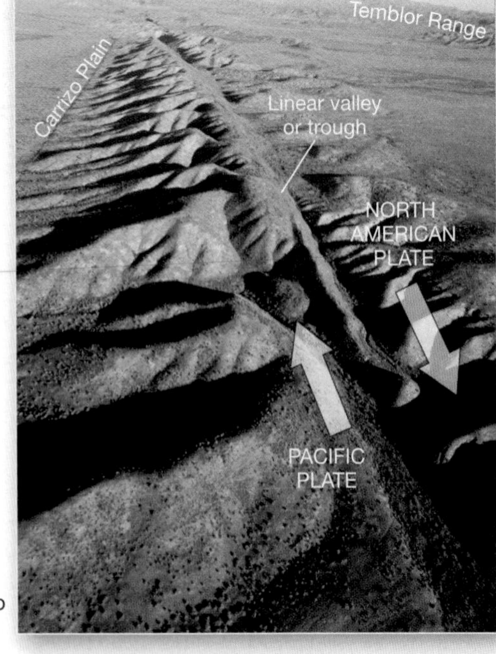

(b) The San Andreas fault, San Luis Obispo County, California.

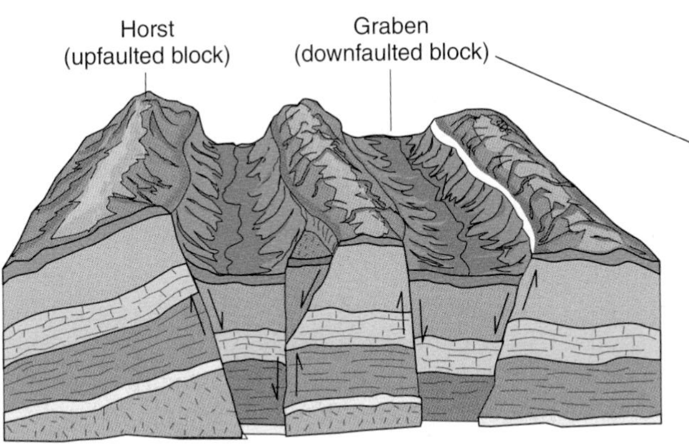

(a) Pairs of faults produce a horst-and-graben landscape.

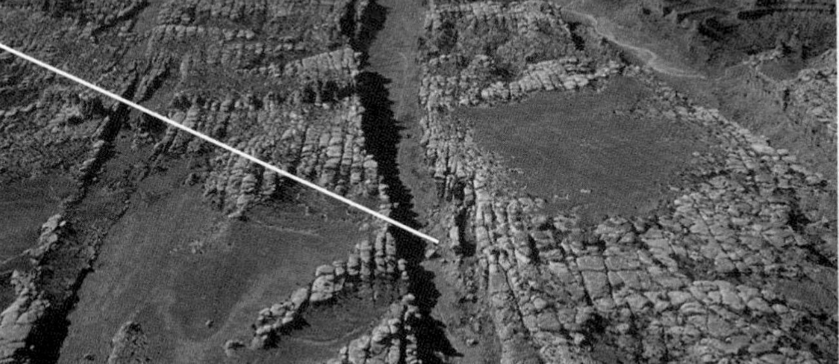

(b) Horsts and grabens result from normal faults in Canyonlands National Park, Utah.

▲**Figure 10.12 Faulted landscapes.** [(b) Airphotona–Jim Wark.]

A large region that is identified by several geologic or topographic traits is known as a *physiographic province*. In the U.S. interior west, the **Basin and Range Province** is a physiographic province recognized for its north-and-south-trending basins and mountains—the basins are low-elevation areas that dip downward toward the center; the ranges are interconnected mountains of varying elevations above the basins. These roughly parallel mountains and valleys (known as *basin-and-range topography*) are aligned pairs of normal faults, an example of a horst-and-graben landscape (**Figures 10.13a** and **b**).

The driving force for the formation of this landscape is the westward movement of the North American plate; the faulting results from tensional forces caused by the uplifting and thinning of the crust. Basin-and-range relief is abrupt, and its rock structures are angular and rugged. As the ranges erode, transported materials accumulate to great depths in the basins, gradually producing extensive plains. Basin elevations average roughly 1200–1500 m (4000–5000 ft) above sea level, with mountain crests rising higher by another 900–1500 m (3000–5000 ft).

Death Valley, California, is the lowest of these basins, with an elevation of –86 m (–282 ft). Directly to the west, the Panamint Range rises to 3368 m (11,050 ft) at Telescope Peak, producing almost 3.5 vertical kilometers (2.2 mi) of relief from the desert valley to the mountain peak.

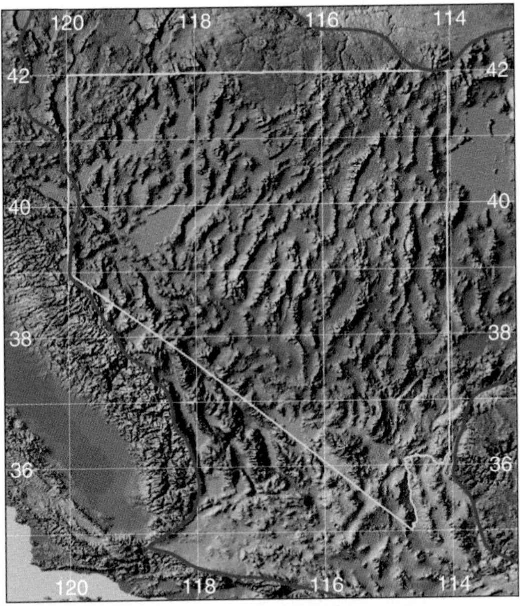

(a) DEM shaded relief map with the Basin and Range Province within the red outline.

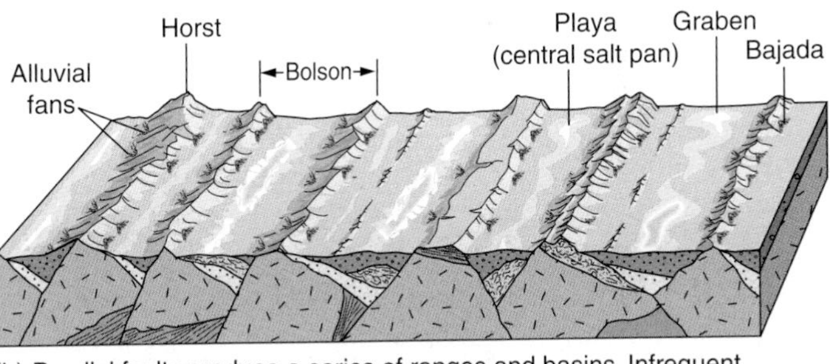

(b) Parallel faults produce a series of ranges and basins. Infrequent precipitation events leave alluvial fan deposits at the mouths of canyons; coalesced alluvial fans join to form a bajada.

(c) Parallel mountain ranges, bolsons, and playas in Nevada.

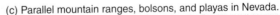

▲**Figure 10.13 Landforms of the Basin and Range Province.** [(a) GSFC/NASA. (c) Bobbé Christopherson.]

Several other landforms are associated with basin-and-range topography. The area composed of slopes and basin between the crests of two adjacent ridges in a dry region of internal drainage is a **bolson** (Figures 10.13b and c). A *playa* is a dry lakebed characterized by an area of salt crust left behind by evaporation of water in a bolson or valley (Figure 10.14c). Chapter 12 discusses other landforms associated with running water in this dry region.

Orogenesis (Mountain Building)

The geologic term for mountain building is **orogenesis**, literally meaning the birth of mountains (*oros* comes from the Greek for "mountain"). An *orogeny* is a mountain-building episode, occurring over millions of years, usually caused by large-scale deformation and uplift of the crust. An orogeny may begin with the capture of migrating exotic terranes and their accretion to the continental margins or with the intrusion of granitic magmas to form plutons. The net result of this accumulating material is a thickening of the crust. The next event in the orogenic cycle is uplift, which is followed by the work of weathering and erosion, exposing granite plutons and creating rugged mountain topography.

The locations of Earth's major chains of folded and faulted mountains, called *orogens*, are remarkably well correlated with the plate tectonics model. Two major examples are the Cordilleran mountain system in North and South America and the Eurasian–Himalayan system, which stretches from the Alps across Asia to the Himalayas. Go to the *Mastering Geography* website to view a map of world structural regions, including these mountain systems.

No orogeny is a simple event; many involve previous developmental stages dating back far into Earth's past, and the processes are ongoing today. For example, the Alps in Europe were formed as a result of continental plate convergence during the Alpine Orogeny, about 2 to 66 million years ago (**Figure 10.14**). Geosystems in Action 10.1 presents the major mountain ranges and the latest related orogenies that caused them (also review Figure 9.1 for orogeny dates within the context of the geologic time scale). The GIA illustration also shows the types of tectonic activity that form mountain ranges, with examples of plate interactions and correlated mountain chains.

Types of Orogenesis

Three types of tectonic activity cause mountain building along convergent plate margins. As discussed in Chapter 9, an *oceanic plate–continental plate collision* produces a subduction zone as the denser oceanic plate dives beneath the continental plate (Figure GIA 10.2a). This convergence creates magma below Earth's surface that is forced upward to become magma intrusions, resulting in granitic plutons and sometimes volcanic activity at the surface. Compressional forces cause the crust to uplift and buckle. This type of convergence is now occurring along the Cordilleran mountain system that follows the Pacific coast of the Americas and has formed the Andes, the Sierra Madre of Central America, and the Rockies (see the map in Figure GIA 10.1).

An *oceanic plate–oceanic plate collision* can produce curving belts of mountains called *island arcs* that rise from the ocean floor. When the plates collide, one is forced beneath the other, creating an oceanic trench. Magma forms at depth and rises upward, erupting as it

◀ **Figure 10.14 European Alps.** The Alps are some 1200 km (750 mi) in length, occupying a crescent of 207,000 km² (80,000 mi²) with western (France), central (Italy), and eastern (Austria) segments. Note the snow coverage in this December image. [*Terra* MODIS image, NASA/GSFC.]

reaches the ocean bottom and beginning the construction of a volcanic island. As the process continues along the trench, the eruptions and accumulation of volcanic material form a volcanic island arc (Figure GIA 10.2b). These processes formed the chains of island arcs and volcanoes that range from the southwestern Pacific into the western Pacific, the Philippines, the Kurils, and on through portions of the Aleutians. Some of the arcs are complex, such as Indonesia and Japan, which exhibit surface rock deformation and metamorphism of rocks and granitic intrusions.

These two types of plate collisions are active around the Pacific Rim, and each is part thermal in nature because the diving plate melts and migrates back toward the surface as molten rock. The region of active volcanoes and earthquakes around the Pacific is known as the *circum-Pacific belt* or, more popularly, the **Ring of Fire**.

The third type of orogenesis occurs during a *continental plate–continental plate collision*. This process is mainly mechanical, as large masses of continental crust are subjected to intense folding, overthrusting, faulting, and uplifting (Figure GIA 10.2c). The converging plates crush and deform both marine sediments and basaltic oceanic crust. The European Alps are a result of such compression forces and exhibit considerable crustal shortening in conjunction with great overturned folds, called *nappes*.

The collision of India with the Eurasian landmass, producing the Himalayas, is estimated to have shortened the overall continental crust by as much as 1000 km (about 600 mi) and to have produced telescoping sequences of thrust faults at depths of 40 km (25 mi). The Himalayas feature the tallest above-sea-level mountains on Earth, including all 10 of Earth's highest peaks.

The Tetons and the Sierra Nevada

Mountain landscapes can be altered when a normal fault along one side of a range produces a tilted linear landscape with dramatic relief known as a *tilted-fault-block* mountain range. The Tetons of Wyoming and the Sierra Nevada of California are recent examples of this stage of mountain building. In both these ranges, mountain building first began hundreds of millions of years ago with magma intrusions that cooled to form granitic cores of coarsely crystalline rock. Tectonic uplift followed, with subsequent faulting and tilting occurring less than 10 m.y.a. The removal of overlying material through weathering, erosion, and transport then exposed the granitic masses, leaving the rugged topography and steep vertical relief we see today (**Figure 10.15**).

Recent research in the Sierra Nevada disclosed that some of the uplift in this range was isostatic, in response to the erosion of overlying material and the melting of ice following the last ice age some 18,000 years ago. The accumulation of sediments in the adjoining valley to the west depressed the crust there, further enhancing the topographic relief.

(a) The east face of the Tetons, with 2130 m (7,000 ft) of vertical relief between the valley of Jackson Hole and the mountain summits.

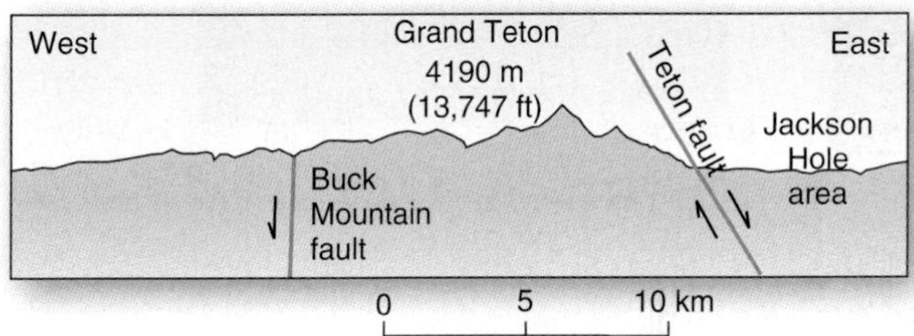

(b) Erosion of the upthrown footwall side of the 70 km (44 mi)-long Teton fault (a normal fault) causes the rugged topography and vertical relief of the Teton range.

▲**Figure 10.15 The Tetons of Wyoming, a tilted-fault-block mountain range.** [Robert Christopherson.]

The Appalachian Mountains

The origin of the Appalachian Mountains of the eastern United States and southeastern Canada dates to the formation of Pangaea and the collision of Africa with North America (250–300 m.y.a.). The complexity of the *Alleghany orogeny* derives from at least two earlier orogenic cycles of uplift and the accretion of several terranes.

Mountain ranges that were linked during the time of Pangaea, but that are now separated by the Atlantic Ocean are similar in both structure and composition. Such similarities indicate that the Lesser (or Anti-) Atlas Mountains of Mauritania and northwestern Africa were connected to the Appalachians in the past (Figure 9.11). Subsequent plate movement created active plate boundaries and several orogenic periods that gave rise to the mountains of today, stretching from Newfoundland, Canada, to central Alabama in the United States.

The central Appalachian Mountain region includes several landscape subregions. The Appalachian Plateau on the western edge is a plateau of eroded sedimentary rock; the Ridge and Valley Province consists of elongated sequences of folded sedimentary strata; the Blue Ridge Province is an area principally of crystalline rock, highest where North Carolina, Virginia, and Tennessee converge; the Piedmont is a region of hilly to gentle terrain along most of the eastern and southern margins of the

(*text continued on page 328*)

Orogenesis, or mountain building, is the result of plate interactions and related processes that thicken and uplift the crust, such as folding, faulting, and volcanism. Combined with weathering, erosion, and isostatic adjustment, these processes produce the striking landscapes of Earth's mountain ranges (GIA 10.1). Collisions of Earth's plates produce three distinct kinds of orogenesis (GIA 10.2).

10.1 Major Mountain Ranges and Orogenies

The mountain ranges we see today have roots deep in geologic time—some, such as the Appalachians, have repeatedly been formed, eroded away, and uplifted again as Earth's plates interacted over hundreds of millions of years.

Rocky Mountains: *Formed mainly during the **Laramide orogeny**, 40–80 m.y.a., but also during several earlier orogenies, beginning 170 m.y.a. (including the **Sevier orogeny**).*

Appalachian Mountains: *Formed during the **Alleghany orogeny**, 250–300 million years ago (m.y.a.), when Africa and North America collided. Includes folded Ridge and Valley Province of the eastern United States and extends into Canada's Maritime Provinces.*

Alps: *Formed during the **Alpine orogeny**, 2–66 m.y.a., and continuing to the present across southern Europe and the Mediterranean, with many earlier episodes (see Figure 10.14).*

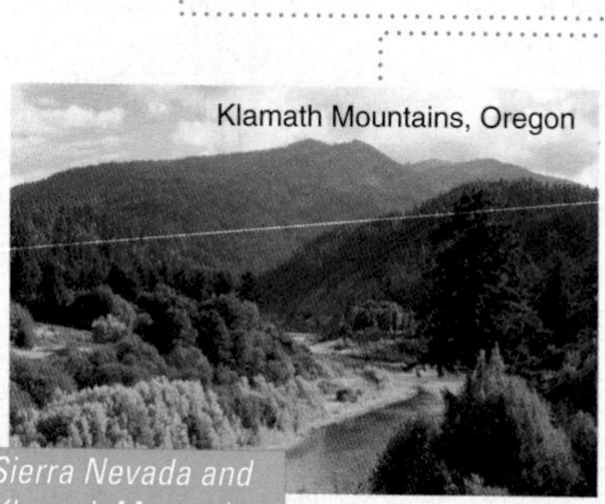

Sierra Nevada and Klamath Mountains: *Formed during the **Nevadan orogeny**, with faulting 29–35 m.y.a. (older batholithic intrusions date to 80 to 180 m.y.a.).*

Andes: *Formed during the **Andean orogeny** over the past 65 million years, the Andes are the South American segment of a vast north–south belt of mountains running along the western margin of the Americas from Tierra del Fuego to Alaska.*

Himalayas: *Formed during the **Himalayan orogeny**, 45–54 m.y.a., beginning with the collision of the Indian and Eurasian plates and continuing to the present.*

Identify: What geologic event triggered the Alleghany orogeny, which formed the Appalachians?

Animation Subduction Zones

http://goo.gl/oXhhXS

MasteringGeography™

Visit the Study Area in MasteringGeography™ to explore mountain building.

Visualize: Study geosciences animations of subduction zones and plate boundaries.

Assess: Demonstrate understanding of mountain building (if assigned by instructor).

Animation Plate Boundaries

http://goo.gl/r9mxVK

10.2 Mountain Building at Convergent Boundaries

Three different types of lithospheric plate collisions result in mountain building: (a) oceanic plate–continental plate, (b) oceanic plate–oceanic plate, (c) continental plate–continental plate. Each plate interaction leads to a different kind of orogenesis.

Oceanic plate–continental plate

Where a dense oceanic plate collides with a less-dense continental plate, a subduction zone forms and the oceanic plate is subducted. Magma forms above the descending plate. Where the magma erupts to the surface through the continental plate, volcanic mountains form. Magma may also harden beneath the surface, forming batholiths.

Example: *The Andes of South America formed as a result of the subduction of the oceanic Nazca plate beneath the continental South American plate.*

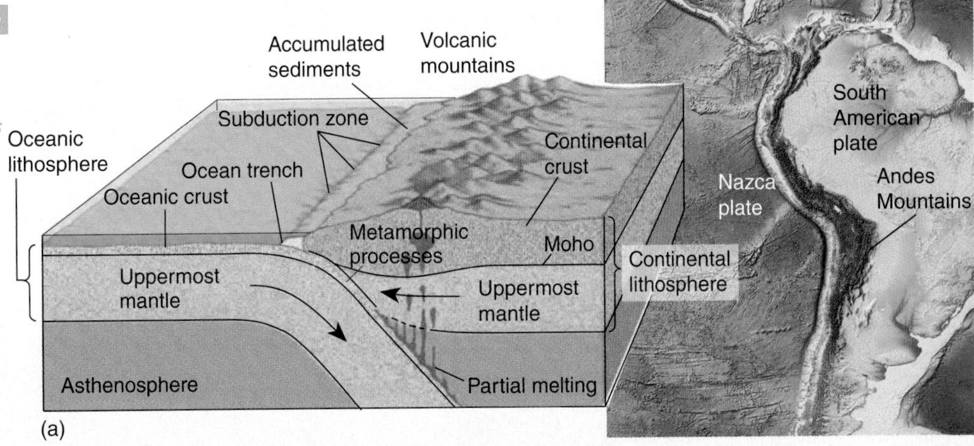

(a)

Oceanic plate–oceanic plate

Where two oceanic plates collide, one plate is subducted beneath the other. Magma forms above the descending plate, giving rise to a volcanic island arc.

Example: *As part of the "Ring of Fire," there are many volcanic island arcs where the Pacific plate interacts with other oceanic plates. These arcs extend from the southwestern Pacific (shown here) through Indonesia, the Philippines, and Japan to the Aleutians.*

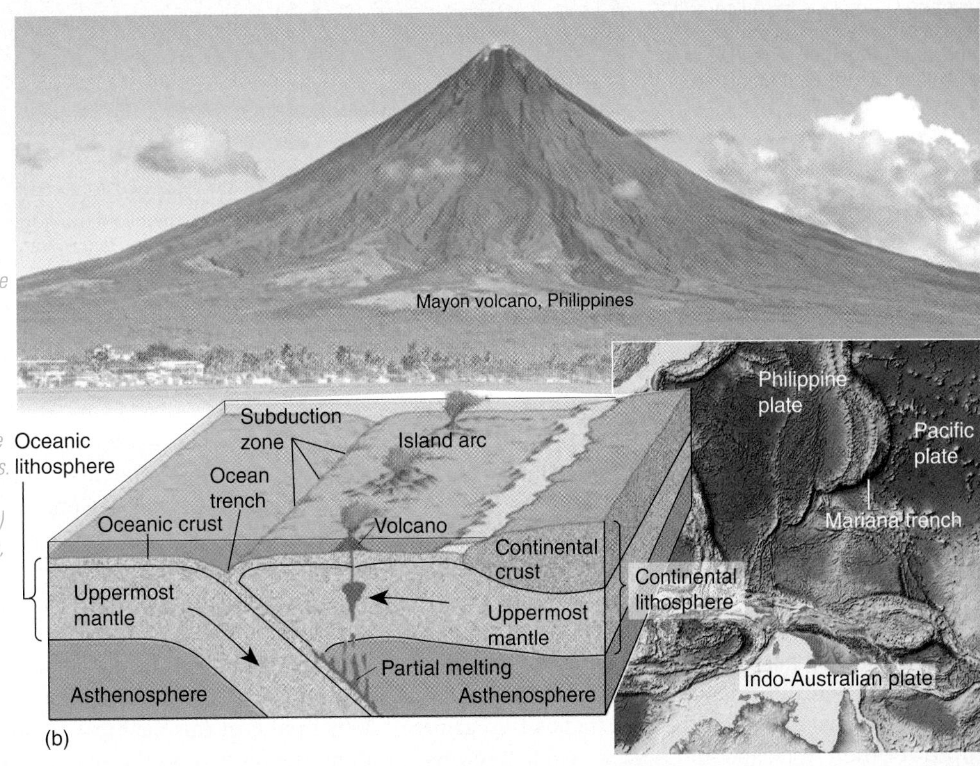

(b)

Continental plate–continental plate

Where two continental plates collide, neither plate is subducted. Instead, the collision subjects the plates to powerful compression forces that fold, fault, and uplift the crust, pushing up huge mountain ranges.

Example: *The Himalayas formed as a result of the ongoing collision of the Indian and Eurasian plates. The Himalayas are part of a long east–west mountain belt, stretching from Europe across Asia, formed by similar collisional processes.*

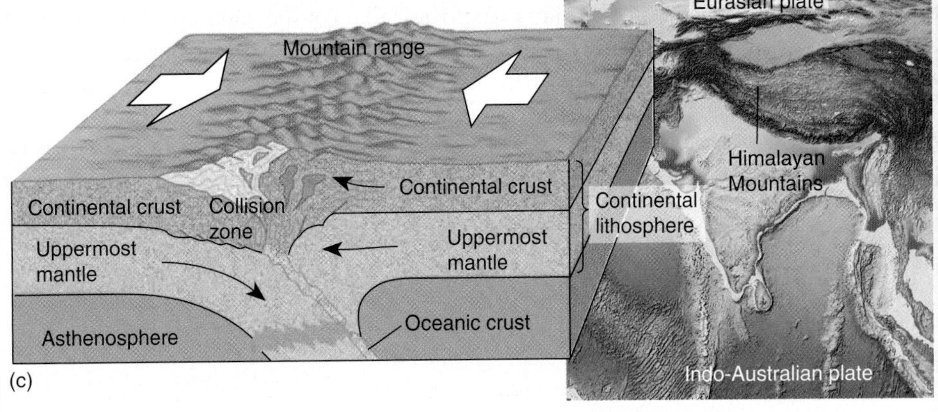

(c)

Infer: Why doesn't subduction occur when two continental plates collide?

GEOquiz

1. Predict: Will the Himalayas keep growing higher and higher indefinitely? Explain your answer.

2. Compare: In terms of orogenesis and plate tectonics, how are the Alps and the Andes similar? How are they different?

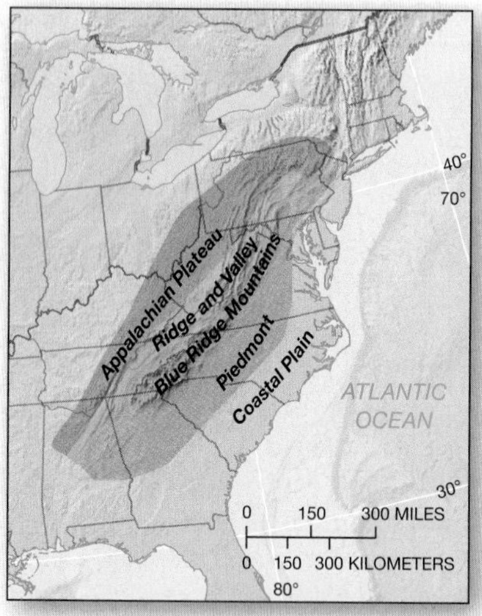

(a) Landscape subregions of the central Appalachian Mountains. The folded Ridge and Valley Province extends from Pennsylvania south through Maryland, Virginia, and West Virginia.

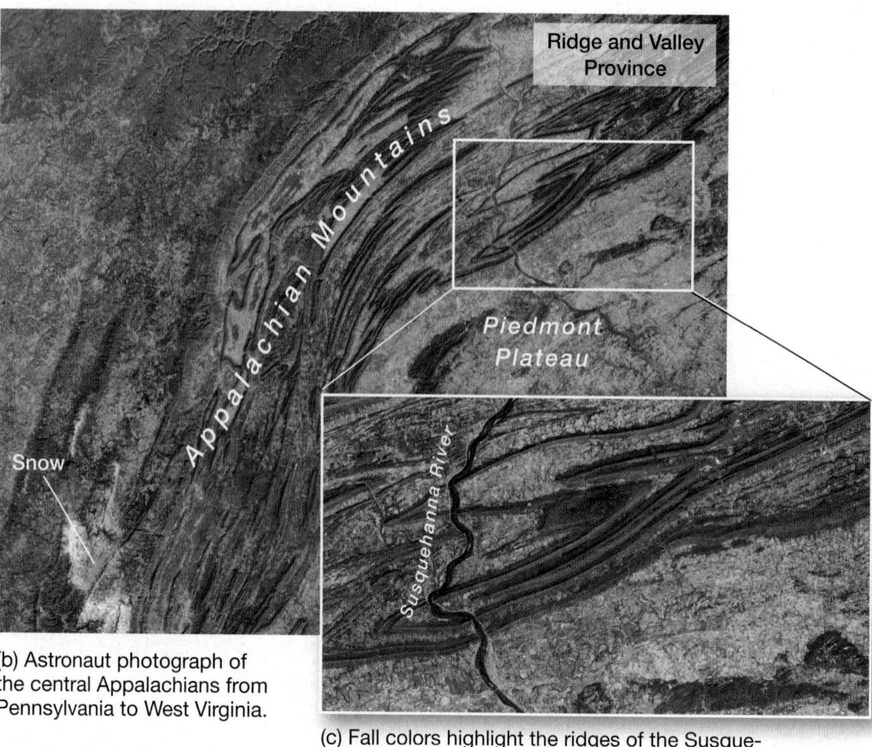

(b) Astronaut photograph of the central Appalachians from Pennsylvania to West Virginia.

(c) Fall colors highlight the ridges of the Susquehanna River Valley, Pennsylvania.

▲**Figure 10.16 The folded Ridge and Valley Province of the Appalachian Mountains.** [(a) USGS. (b) *ISS* Crew Earth Observations Experiment and Image Science & Analysis Laboratory/Johnson Space Center/NASA. (c) *Landsat-7*, NASA.]

mountains; and the coastal plain consists of gentle hills descending to flat plains that extend to the Atlantic coast (**Figure 10.16**).

In the Ridge and Valley Province, folded anticlines and synclines form prominent linear ridges. Rivers such as the Susquehanna in east-central Pennsylvania have carved *water gaps* where the watercourse flows through a mountain ridge. Water gaps usually indicate that the river is older than the mountain ridge through which it cuts, suggesting that the river had established its position prior to the uplift of the landscape and thus was able to erode through the uplift and maintain its course.

Water gaps in the rugged Appalachians were important breaks in topography that greatly influenced human migration, settlement patterns, and the diffusion of cultural traits in the 1700s. The initial flow of people, goods, and ideas toward the west was guided by these geomorphic features.

Earthquakes

Crustal plates do not glide smoothly past one another. Instead, tremendous friction exists along plate boundaries. The stress, or force, of plate motion builds strain, or deformation, in the rocks until friction is overcome and the sides along plate boundaries or fault lines suddenly break loose. The sharp release of energy that occurs at the moment of fracture, producing seismic waves, is an **earthquake**, or *quake*. The two sides of the fault plane then lurch into new positions, moving distances ranging from centimeters to several meters, and release enormous amounts of seismic energy into the surrounding crust. This energy radiates throughout the planet, diminishing with distance.

The plate collision in which India is moving northeastward at about 2 m (6.6 ft) a year creates disruption that has reached far under China, causing frequent earthquakes. As evidence of this ongoing strain, the October 2005 quake in the Kashmir region of Pakistan occurred along the fault zone that marks the meeting of the Eurasian and Indo-Australian plates. A 40-km (25-mi) segment of the 2500-km (1553-mi) fault snapped, causing an M 7.6 quake that killed more than 83,000 people.

Tectonic earthquakes are those quakes associated with faulting. Earthquakes can also occur in association with volcanic activity. Recent research suggests that the injection of wastewater from oil and gas drilling into subsurface areas is another cause, leading to episodes of *induced seismicity* (discussed with fault mechanics ahead).

Earthquake Anatomy

The subsurface area where the motion of seismic waves is initiated along a fault plane is the *focus*, or hypocenter, of an earthquake (see the example in **Figure 10.17a**). The area at the surface directly above the focus is the *epicenter*.

Shock waves produced by an earthquake radiate outward through the crust from the focus and epicenter. As discussed earlier, scientists use the seismic wave patterns and the nature of their transmission to learn about the deep layers of Earth's interior.

A *foreshock* is a quake that precedes the main shock. The pattern of foreshocks is now regarded as an important consideration in earthquake forecasting. An *aftershock* occurs after the main shock, sharing the same general area of the epicenter; some aftershocks rival the main tremor in magnitude. For instance, on the South Island of New Zealand an M 7.1 quake struck in September 2010 with an epicenter 45 km (30 mi) from Christchurch, causing USD$2.7 billion in damage and no deaths. Seventeen days later, a 6.3 aftershock with an epicenter just 6 km (3 mi) from the city produced building collapses, 350 deaths, and more than USD$15 billion in damage. These events show that the distance from the epicenter is an important factor in determining overall earthquake effects on population centers.

In 1989, the Loma Prieta earthquake hit south of San Francisco, California, east of Santa Cruz. Damage totaled $8 billion, 14,000 people were displaced from their homes, 4000 were injured, and 63 were killed. Unlike previous earthquakes—such as the San Francisco quake of 1906, when the plates shifted a maximum of 6.4 m (21 ft) relative to each other—no fault plane or rifting was evident at the surface in the Loma Prieta quake. Instead, the Pacific and North American plates moved horizontally approximately 2 m (6 ft) past each other deep below the surface, with the Pacific plate thrusting 1.3 m (4.3 ft) upward (Figure 10.17). This vertical motion is unusual for the San Andreas fault and indicates that this portion of the San Andreas system is more complex than previously thought.

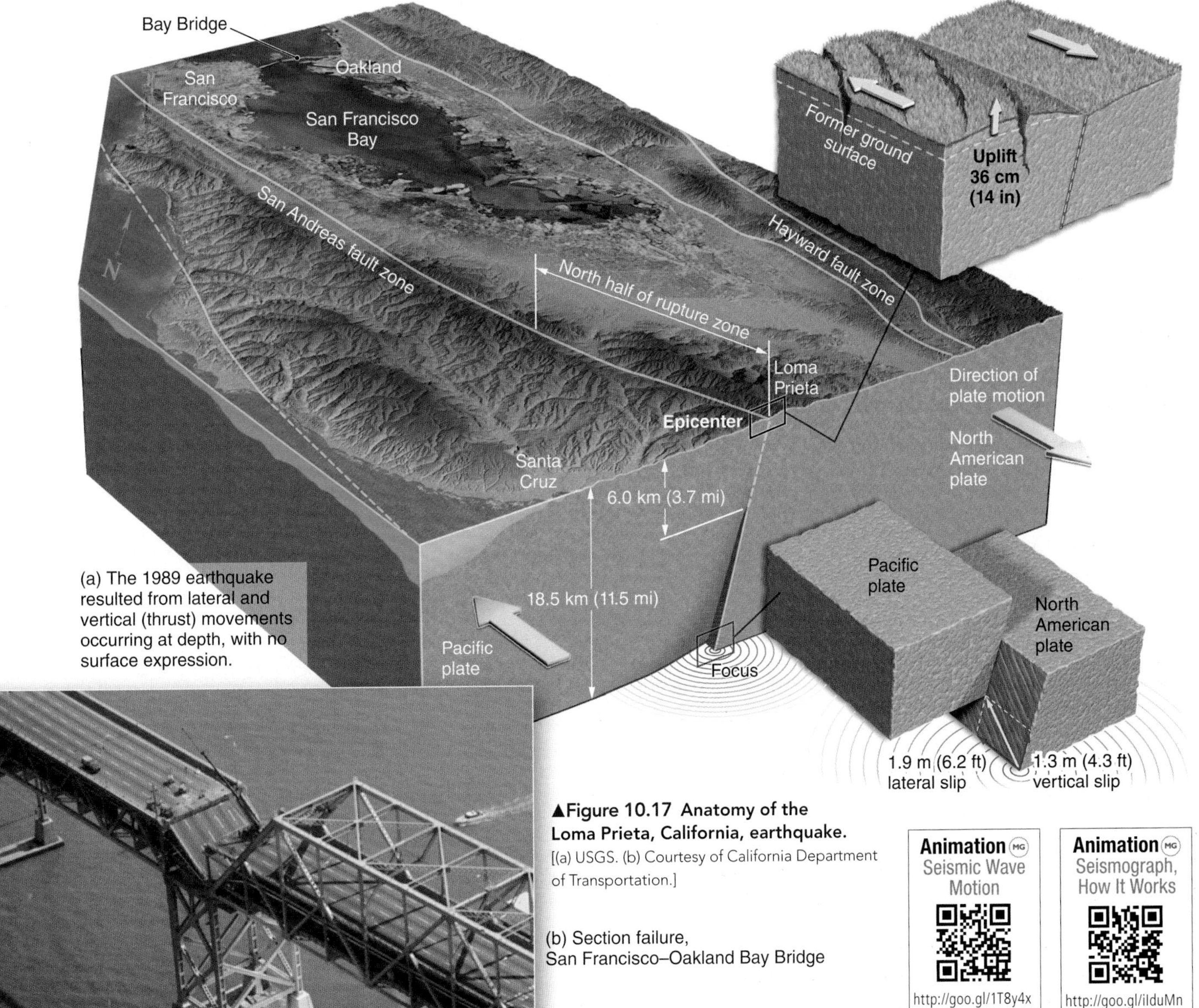

(a) The 1989 earthquake resulted from lateral and vertical (thrust) movements occurring at depth, with no surface expression.

(b) Section failure, San Francisco–Oakland Bay Bridge

▲**Figure 10.17 Anatomy of the Loma Prieta, California, earthquake.** [(a) USGS. (b) Courtesy of California Department of Transportation.]

Animation Seismic Wave Motion http://goo.gl/1T8y4x

Animation Seismograph, How It Works http://goo.gl/ilduMn

Earthquake Intensity and Magnitude

A **seismometer**, or seismograph, is an instrument used to detect and record the ground motion that occurs during an earthquake. This instrument records motion in only a single direction, so scientists use a combination of vertical-motion and horizontal-motion seismometers to determine the source and strength of seismic waves. The instrument detects body waves (traveling through Earth's interior) first, followed by surface waves, recording both on a *seismogram* in the form of a graph. Scientists use a worldwide network of more than 4000 seismometers to sense earthquakes, and these quakes are then classified on the basis of either damage intensity or the magnitude of energy released.

Before the invention of modern earthquake instrumentation, damage to terrain and structures and severity of shaking were used to assess the size of earthquakes. These surface effects are a measure of earthquake *intensity*. The *Modified Mercalli Intensity (MMI) scale* is a Roman-numeral scale from I to XII that ranges from earthquakes that are "barely felt" (lower numbers) to those that cause "catastrophic total destruction" (higher numbers; see **Table 10.1**). The scale was designed in 1902 and modified in 1931.

Earthquake *magnitude* is a measure of the energy released and provides a way to compare earthquake size. In 1935, Charles Richter designed a system to estimate earthquake magnitude based on measurement of maximum wave amplitude on a seismometer. *Amplitude* is the height of a seismic wave and is directly related to the amount of ground movement. The size and timing of maximum seismic wave height can be plotted on a chart called the **Richter scale**, which formerly provided a number for earthquake magnitude in relation to a station located more than 100 km (62 mi) from the epicenter of the quake. (For more on the Richter scale, see http://earthquake.usgs.gov/learn/topics/richter.php.)

The Richter scale is logarithmic: Each whole number on it represents a 10-fold increase in the measured wave amplitude. Translated into energy, each whole number signifies a 31.5-fold increase in energy released. Thus, a magnitude of 3.0 on the Richter scale represents 31.5 times more energy than a 2.0 and 992 times more energy than a 1.0. Although useful for measuring shallow earthquakes, the Richter scale does not properly measure or differentiate between quakes of high intensity.

The **moment magnitude (M) scale**, in use since 1993, is more accurate for large earthquakes than is Richter's amplitude magnitude scale. Moment magnitude considers the seismic moment, calculated using the amount of fault slippage produced by the earthquake, the size of the surface (or subsurface) area that ruptured, and the nature of the materials that faulted, including how resistant they were to failure. Technically, the M is equal to the rigidity of Earth multiplied by the average amount of slip on the fault and its area. This scale considers extreme ground acceleration (movement upward), which the Richter amplitude magnitude method underestimates.

TABLE 10.1 Magnitude, Intensity, and Expected Frequency of Earthquakes

Moment Magnitude Scale	Modified Mercalli Scale	Effects on Populated Areas	Number Expected per Year*
2–2.9	None to I	Instrumental. Not felt, but recorded.	1,300,000 (estimated)
3–3.9	II–III	Slight. Felt by some, especially on upper floors of buildings.	130,000 (estimated)
4–4.9	IV–V	Moderate. Felt by some to felt by many; some disturbance and vibration.	13,000 (estimated)
5–5.9	VI–VII	Strong. Felt by all, with slight building damage.	1319
6–6.9	VIII–IX	Destructive. Slight to considerable damage, depending on building design; buildings shifted off their foundations.	134
7–7.9	X–XI	Disastrous. Major damage; bridges destroyed, most structures partially collapsed; railroad tracks bent.	17
8.0 and higher	XII	Catastrophic. Damage nearly total.	1

*Based on observations since 1990.

Source: USGS Earthquake Hazards Program.

GEOreport 10.2 Ongoing earthquake activity in Sumatra, Indonesia

In 2009, an M 7.6 earthquake caused over 1000 fatalities in southern Sumatra, Indonesia, near the same plate boundary where six quakes greater than M 7.9 had already occurred since 1998. In 2010, two more quakes hit in the region just to the north. At this boundary, the Indo-Australian plate moves northeast, subducting beneath the Sunda plate at a relative speed of 6.6 cm/year (2.6 in./year). This is where the M 9.1 Sumatra–Andaman earthquake struck on December 26, 2004, triggering the devastating Indian Ocean tsunami (more on tsunami in Chapter 13); the quake and seismic sea wave took 228,000 lives. For complete listings of these and other earthquakes, go to http://earthquake.usgs.gov/earthquakes.

Table 10.1 shows the M and MMI scales and the expected number of quakes in each category in a year. In 1960, an M 9.5 earthquake in Chile produced Mercalli XII damage—this was the strongest earthquake in recorded history.

A reassessment of pre-1993 quakes using the moment magnitude scale has increased the rating of some and decreased that of others. As an example, the 1964 earthquake at Prince William Sound in Alaska had an amplitude magnitude of 8.6 (on the Richter scale), but on the moment magnitude scale, it increased to an M 9.2.

On the *MasteringGeography* website, you will find a sampling of significant earthquakes with their M and MMI ratings. For a range of information about earthquakes, see http://earthquake.usgs.gov/regional/neic/ or http://www.ngdc.noaa.gov/hazard/earthqk.shtml. Focus Study 10.1 offers more details on the quakes in Haiti, Chile, and Japan in 2010 and 2011.

Fault Mechanics

Earlier in the chapter, we described faulting, types of faults, and direction of faulting motions. The specific mechanics of how a fault breaks, however, remain under study. **Elastic-rebound theory** describes the basic process. Generally, two sides along a fault appear to be locked by friction, resisting any movement despite the powerful forces acting on the adjoining pieces of crust. Stress continues to build strain along the fault-plane surfaces, storing elastic energy like a wound-up spring. When the strain buildup finally exceeds the frictional lock, both sides of the fault abruptly move to a condition of less strain, releasing a burst of mechanical energy.

Think of the fault plane as a surface with irregularities that act as sticking points to prevent movement, similar to two pieces of wood held together by drops of glue of different sizes rather than an even coating of glue. These small areas are points of high strain, known as *asperities*—when these sticking points break, they release the sides of the fault.

If the fracture along the fault line is isolated to a small asperity break, the quake will be small in magnitude. As some asperities break (perhaps recorded as small foreshocks), the strain increases on surrounding asperities that remain intact (**Figure 10.18**). Thus, small earthquakes in an area may be precursors to a major quake. However, if the break involves the release of strain along several asperities, the quake will be greater in extent and will involve the shifting of massive amounts of crust. The latest evidence suggests that movement along the fault occurs in a wavelike pattern, as rupturing spreads along the fault plane, rather than the entire fault surface giving way at once.

Human activities can exacerbate the natural processes occurring along faults, causing *induced seismicity*, or human-induced earthquakes. For example, if the pressure on the pores and fractures in rocks is increased by the addition of fluids (called fluid injection), then earthquake activity may accelerate. The extraction of fluids, especially at a rapid rate, can also induce seismicity by

(*text continued on page 334*)

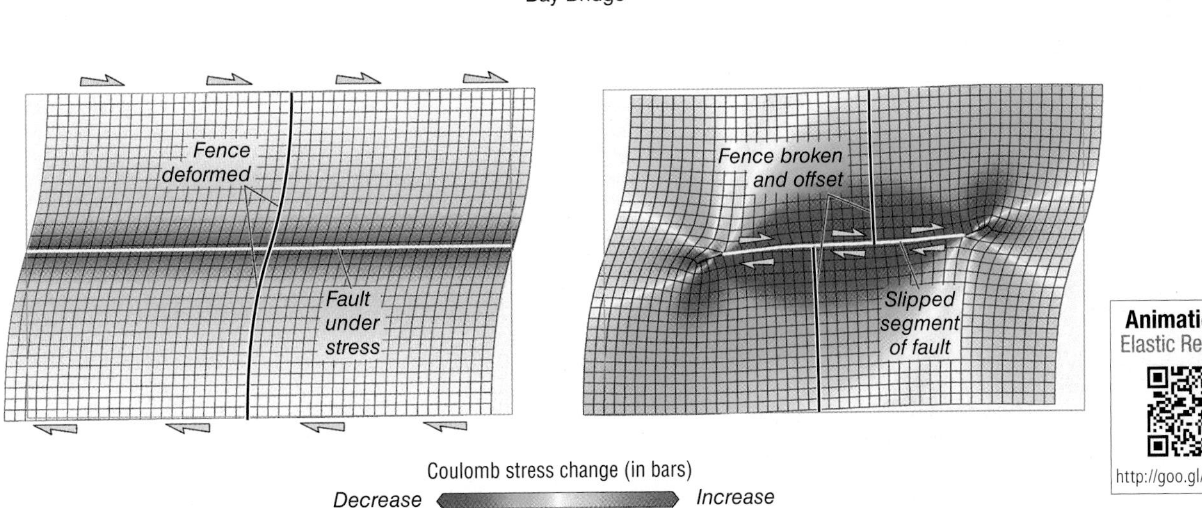

(a) Note the line denoting a fence that crosses the fault line. When stress on the fault has built to the break point, the two sides snap into new positions, strain is released, and the fence no longer forms a continuous line.

(b) The segments of the fault that did not move past each other, and instead remain locked, now have added strain.

▲**Figure 10.18 Buildup and release of stress and strain along a fault system.** A coulomb is a unit of shear-stress change on a fault, measured in bars (units of pressure; 1 bar is approximately equal to atmospheric pressure at sea level); the color scale ranges from blue (decreased stress) to red (increased stress). [Illustrations courtesy of Serkan Bozkurt, USGS.]

focusstudy 10.1 Natural Hazards

Earthquakes in Haiti, Chile, and Japan: A Comparative Analysis

In 2010 and 2011, three quakes struck areas near major population centers, causing massive destruction and fatalities. These earthquakes—in the countries of Haiti, Chile, and Japan—all occurred at plate boundaries and ranged in magnitude from M 7.0 to M 9.0 (**Figure 10.1.1** and **Table 10.1.1**).

The Human Dimension

The 2010 Haiti earthquake hit an impoverished country where little of the infrastructure was built to withstand earthquakes. Over 2 million people live in the capital city of Port-au-Prince, which has been destroyed by earthquakes several times, mostly notably in 1751 and 1770. The total damage there from the 2010 quake exceeded the country's $14 billion gross domestic product (GDP). In developing countries such as Haiti, earthquake damage is worsened by inadequate construction, lack of enforced building codes, and the difficulties of getting food, water, and medical help to those in need (Figure 10.1.1a).

The Maule, Chile, earthquake, which occurred just 6 weeks later, caused only minimal damage, in large part due to the fact that the country enacted strict building codes in 1985 (Figure 10.1.1b). The result was a fraction of the human cost compared to the Haiti earthquake.

The Japan quake resulted in an enormous and tragic human fatality count (Figure 10.1.1c), mainly due to the massive Pacific Ocean tsunami (defined as a set of seismic sea waves; discussed in Chapter 13). When an area of ocean floor some 338 km (N–S) by 150 km (210 mi by 93 mi) snapped and was abruptly lifted as much as 80 m

(a) Destruction in Port-au-Prince, Haiti, in 2010. The quake epicenter was along multiple surface faults and a previously unknown subsurface thrust fault.

(b) A collapsed bridge in Santiago, Chile, after the M8.8 earthquake hit Maule, 95 km (60 mi) away. The epicenter was on a convergent plate boundary between the Nazca and South American plates.

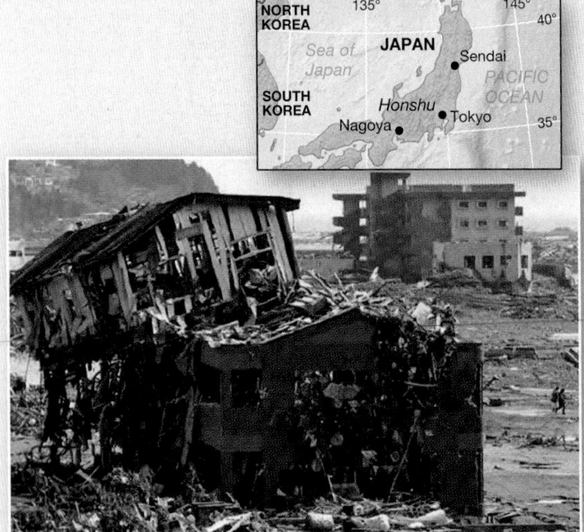

(c) Honshu Island, Japan, after the quake and tsunami. The epicenter was on a convergent plate boundary between the Pacific and North American plates.

(d) Tsunami moves ashore, Iwanuma, Japan. Iwanuma is 20 km (12.4 mi) south of Sendai, the city closest to the epicenter.

▲**Figure 10.1.1 The 2010–2011 Haiti, Chile, and Japan earthquakes and the 2011 Japan tsunami.** [(a) Julie Jacobson/AP Images. (b) Martin Bernetti/Getty Images. (c) and (d) Kyodo/Reuters.]

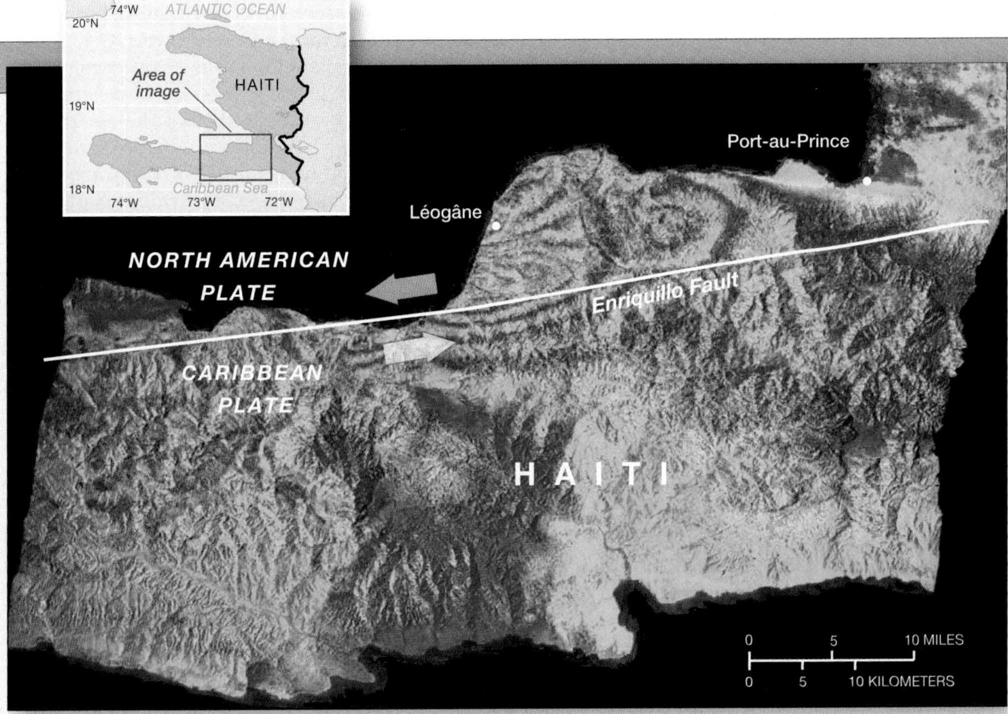

◀**Figure 10.1.2 Radar image of Haiti earthquake faults.** Synthetic-aperture radar image shows ground deformation near Léogâne, west of Port-au-Prince; narrow bands of color are contours, each representing 11.8 cm, or 4.6 in., of ground motion. This radar interferogram combines data from topographic surveys before and after the earthquake. [NASA/JPL/JAXA/METI.]

(260 ft), the ocean was displaced above it. This disturbance caused the tsunami, in which the largest wave averaged 10 m (33 ft) along the coast near Iwanuma (Figure 10.1.1d). Where it entered narrow harbors and embayments, wave height reached nearly 30 m (98 ft). Although Japan's tsunami warning system sent out immediate alerts, there was not enough time for evacuation (see Focus Study 13.1). This event illustrates the damage and human cost associated with an earthquake and tsunami, even in a country with strict and extensive earthquake preparedness standards.

Faulting and Plate Interactions

The Chile and Japan quakes both occurred along subduction zones. Along the coast of Chile, the Nazca plate is moving eastward beneath the westward-moving South American plate at a relative speed of 7 to 8 cm (2.7 to 3.1 in.) per year. This is the same subduction zone that produced the M 9.6 that hit Chile in 1960, the largest earthquake of the 20th century. Off the coast of Japan, the Japan Trench defines the subduction zone in which the westward-moving Pacific plate is pulled beneath a segment of the North American plate at a rate averaging 8.3 cm/year (3.5 in./year). Several microplates form this plate boundary, visible on the ocean-floor map that begins this chapter and in Figure 9.16.

The Haiti earthquake involved more complex fault interactions. Scientists first thought that this earthquake occurred along a 50-km section of the Enriquillo–Plantain Garden strike-slip fault, where the Caribbean plate moves eastward relative to the North American plate's westward shift. After extensive analysis, experts now think that the quake resulted from slip along multiple faults, primarily along a previously unknown subsurface thrust fault.

Key data for the analysis came from radar *interferograms*, remotely sensed images produced by comparing radar topography measurements before and after earthquake events. The Haiti interferogram shows surface deformation in the area of the fault rupture; the narrow rings of color represent contours of ground motion (**Figure 10.1.2**). Overall, the earthquake displaced Léogâne upward about 0.5 m (20 in.). Scientists found no evidence of surface rupture after a field survey along the Enriquillo fault. Because the slip was not near the surface, scientists believe that strain is continuing to accumulate, making future rupture at the surface likely.

For a listing and details of the 10 biggest earthquakes in history, including the Chile (ranked 6th) and Japan (ranked 4th) events, go to http://earthquake.usgs.gov/earthquakes/world/10_largest_world.php.

1. Four commercial nuclear power plants were damaged by the Japanese tsunami and suffered core meltdowns. What planning considerations should be in force for coastal locations on Honshu Island?

TABLE 10.1.1 Summary of Three Major Earthquakes in 2010 and 2011

Location, date, and local time	Moment magnitude*	Focus depth	Epicenter distance to nearest city	Human dimension	Damage cost (USD)
Port-au-Prince, Haiti, Jan. 12, 2010 4:53 P.M.	M 7.0	13 km (8 mi) Ocean	15 km (10 mi) southwest from Port-au-Prince	222,570 killed, 300,000 injured, 1.3 million displaced	$25 billion
Maule, Chile, Feb. 27, 2010 3:34 A.M.	M 8.8	35 km (22 mi) Ocean	95 km (60 mi) from Santiago	521 killed, 12,000 injured, 800,000 displaced	$30 billion
Tohoku, Honshu, Japan, Mar. 11, 2011 2:46 P.M.	M 9.0	32 km (20 mi) Ocean	129 km (80 mi) from Sendai	15,885 deaths, 6148 injured, 2623 missing (as of April 2014)	~$325 billion (maybe as high as $500 billion)

*Reported by USGS.

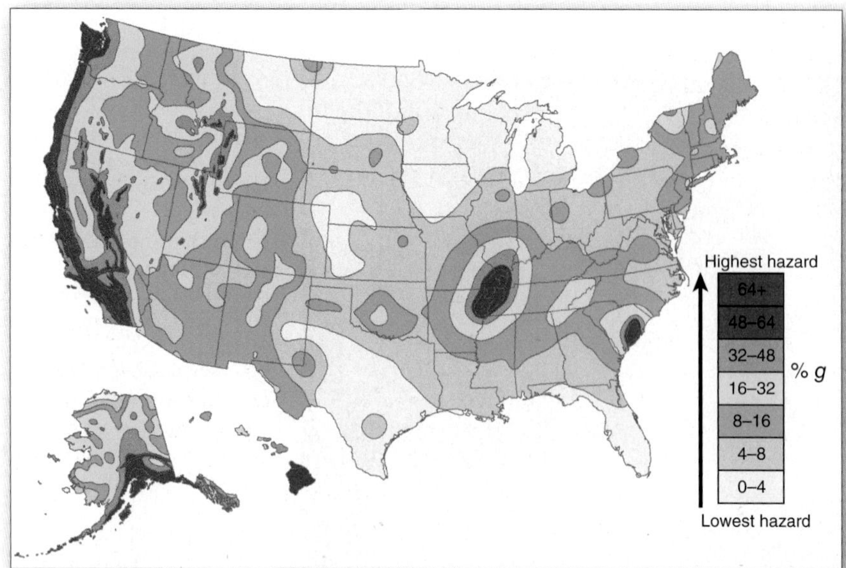

◀**Figure 10.19 Earthquake hazard map for the United States.** Colors on the map show the levels of horizontal shaking that have a 2-in-100 chance of being exceeded during a 50-year period. Shaking is expressed as a percentage of *g* (the acceleration of a falling object with gravity), with red being the highest shaking. Active seismic regions include the West Coast, the Wasatch Front of Utah northward into Canada, the central Mississippi Valley, the southern Appalachians, and portions of South Carolina, upstate New York, and Ontario. [USGS; see http://earthquake.usgs.gov/hazards/products/.]

MG MapMaster
North America Physical Environment
Earthquake Hazard Areas

causing subsidence of the ground and enhancing slippage along faults.

Both fluid injection and fluid extraction are common activities associated with oil and natural gas drilling and with geothermal energy production. Hydraulic fracturing, or fracking, associated with shale gas extraction injects large quantities of fluid to break up subsurface rock, making this process a probable cause for induced seismicity (review the Chapter 1 Geosystems Now, and see The Human Denominator 10 at the end of this chapter). In 2013, scientists linked increased earthquake activity in Colorado, New Mexico, and Oklahoma to fluid injection associated with fracking. In the Los Angeles region, fracking near active fault zones is cause for concern. Enhanced geothermal systems, discussed in Focus Study 9.1, also use fracking, which has resulted in seismic activity at several locations, including The Geysers Geothermal Field in California.

Earthquake Forecasting and Planning

The probability of earthquakes varies with location. In the United States, regions having a particularly high risk include California and the Yellowstone area of Wyoming, Idaho, and Montana. The map in **Figure 10.19** plots the earthquake hazard for the United States in terms of the probability of ground motion; it was developed using the most recent seismic, geologic, and geodetic information regarding earthquakes and ground shaking. The National Earthquake Hazards Reduction Program is a multiagency program that includes the Advanced National Seismic System, which provides key data for the hazard maps (see http://earthquake.usgs.gov/monitoring/anss/).

A major challenge for scientists is to predict earthquake occurrences. One approach to earthquake forecasting is the science of *paleoseismology*, which studies the history of plate boundaries and the frequency of past earthquakes. Paleoseismologists construct maps that estimate expected earthquake activity based on past performance. An area that is quiet and overdue for an earthquake is a *seismic gap*; such an area possesses accumulated strain. The area along the Aleutian Trench subduction zone had three such gaps until the great 1964 Alaskan earthquake filled one of them. The areas around San Francisco and northeast and southeast of Los Angeles represent other such seismic gaps along the San Andreas fault system.

A second approach to forecasting is to observe and measure phenomena that might precede an earthquake. *Dilatancy* refers to the slight increase in rock volume produced by small cracks that form under stress and accumulated strain. One indication of dilatancy is a tilting and swelling in the affected region in response to strain, as measured by *tiltmeters*. Another indicator of dilatancy is an increase in the amount of radon (a naturally occurring, slightly radioactive gas) dissolved in groundwater. At present, earthquake hazard zones have thousands of radon monitors taking samples in test wells.

Both tiltmeters and gas-monitoring wells are used for earthquake monitoring at the most intensely studied seismic area in the world, along the San Andreas fault

GEOreport 10.3 Large earthquakes affect Earth's axial tilt

Scientific evidence is mounting that Earth's largest earthquake events have a global influence. Both the 2004 Sumatran–Andaman quake and the 2011 Tohoku quake in Japan caused Earth's axial tilt to shift several centimeters. NASA scientists estimate that the redistribution of mass in each quake shortened daylength by 6.8 millionths of a second for the 2004 event and 1.8 millionths of a second for the 2011 event.

outside Parkfield, California. The area also features a newly completed drill hole, the San Andreas Fault Observatory at Depth, that allows instruments to be placed deep into the fault (between 2 km and 3 km, or 1.2 mi and 1.9 mi, down) with the goal of measuring the physical and chemical processes occurring within an active fault. Research sites such as this provide critical data for predicting future seismic events.

Although scientists are not yet able to accurately forecast earthquakes, they have made strides in predicting earthquake probabilities over periods of decades. For example, in 2008, a working group of scientists and engineers reported that the probability of an M 6.7 earthquake along the San Andreas fault system in the San Francisco Bay Area between 2007 and 2030 is 63%. Adding to the risk presented by such a quake is the extent of landfill in the Bay Area, where about half the original bay is now filled and occupied with buildings. In an earthquake, this type of landfill fails in a process of *liquefaction*, in which shaking brings water to the surface and liquefies the soil.

Earthquake warning systems have been successfully implemented in some countries. A Mexico City warning system provides 70-second notice of arriving seismic waves. The system was effective in March 2012, when a senate hearing at the capitol was interrupted by the sirens indicating an imminent earthquake. Shaking began about a minute later. In Japan, a warning system was activated during the Tohoku earthquake, sending alerts to televisions and cell phones and automatically shutting down some transportation and industrial services. (The tsunami warning system in the Pacific is discussed in Chapter 13.) In the United States, an earthquake early warning system is still in development. See the Southern California Seismographic Network at http://www.scsn.org/ for more information.

Someday accurate earthquake forecasting may be a reality, but the actual implementation of an action plan to reduce death, injury, and property damage from earthquakes is difficult to achieve. For example, such a plan is likely to be unpopular politically, since it involves large expenditures of money before a quake has even hit. Moreover, the negative image created by the possibility of earthquakes in a given municipality is not likely to be welcomed by local businesses, banks, and politicians. These factors work against the adoption of effective prediction methods and planning.

Another barrier to effective earthquake planning is that *humans and their institutions seem unable or unwilling to perceive hazards in a familiar environment.* In other words, people tend to feel secure in their homes, even in communities known to be sitting on a quiet fault zone. Such an axiom of human behavior certainly helps explain why large populations continue to live and work in earthquake-prone settings. Similar statements also can be made about populations in areas vulnerable to floods, hurricanes, and other natural hazards. (See the Natural Hazards Center at the University of Colorado at http://www.colorado.edu/hazards/index.html.)

Volcanism

Volcanic eruptions across the globe remind us of Earth's tremendous internal energy and of the dynamic forces shaping the planet's surface. The distribution of ongoing volcanic activity matches the distribution of plate boundaries, as shown on the map in Figure 9.17, as well as indicating the location of hot spots. Over 1300 identifiable volcanic cones and mountains exist on Earth, although fewer than 600 are active.

An *active* volcano is defined as one that has erupted at least once in recorded history. In an average year, about 50 volcanoes erupt worldwide, varying from small-scale venting of lava or fumes to major explosions. North America has about 70 volcanoes (mostly inactive) along the western margin of the continent. The Global Volcanism Program lists information for more than 8500 eruptions at http://www.volcano.si.edu/, and the USGS provides extensive information about current volcanic activity at http://volcanoes.usgs.gov/.

Eruptions in remote locations and at depths on the seafloor go largely unnoticed, but the occasional eruption of great magnitude near a population center makes headlines. Even a distant eruption has global atmospheric effects. For example, in April 2010, the eruption of the Eyjafjallajökull volcano in southern Iceland garnered world attention for its effects on air transportation (**Figure 10.20**). The first eruption of this volcano since the 1820s produced an ash cloud that rose to 10,660 m (35,000 ft) and quickly dispersed toward Europe and commercial airline corridors. Airspace was closed for 5 days, canceling more than 100,000 flights. When flights resumed, routes were changed to avoid lingering ash.

▼Figure 10.20 The Eyjafjallajökull eruption in Iceland, May 10, 2010. The ash plume is seen rising to between 5 and 6 km (3.1 and 3.7 mi). [*Aqua*, MODIS sensor, NASA/GSFC.]

Iceland's Meteorological Office monitored the eruption with its 56-station seismic network.

Settings for Volcanic Activity

Volcanic activity occurs in three settings, listed below with representative examples and illustrated in **Figure 10.21**:

- Along *subduction boundaries* at continental plate–oceanic plate convergence (Mount St. Helens; Kliuchevskoi, Siberia) or oceanic plate–oceanic plate convergence (the Philippines; Japan)
- Along *seafloor spreading centers* on the ocean floor (Iceland, on the Mid-Atlantic Ridge; off the coast of Oregon and Washington) and along areas of rifting on continental plates (the rift zone in East Africa)
- At *hot spots*, where individual plumes of magma rise to the crust (Hawai'i; Yellowstone National Park)

Volcanic Materials

A **volcano** is the structure in the Earth's crust containing an opening at the end of a central vent or pipe through which magma rises from the asthenosphere and upper mantle. Magma rises and collects in a magma chamber deep below the volcano until conditions are right for an eruption. This subsurface magma emits tremendous heat; in some areas, it boils groundwater, as seen in the thermal springs and geysers of Yellowstone National Park and at other locations with surface expressions of geothermal energy.

Various materials pass through the central vent to the surface to build volcanic landforms, including lava (magma that has cooled to form rock), gases, and **pyroclastics**—pulverized rock and clastic materials of various sizes ejected violently during an eruption (also called *tephra*). These materials may emerge explosively, or they may emerge effusively (flowing gently) from the vent (eruption types are discussed ahead).

As discussed in Chapter 9, solidified magma forms igneous rock. When magma emerges at the surface, it is *lava*. The chemistry of lava determines its behavior (whether it is thin and liquid or is thick and forms a plug).

Geologists classify lava depending on its chemical composition. Basaltic lava, which is low in silica and high in magnesium and iron, has two principal forms, both known by Hawaiian names (**Figure 10.22**). The composition of both these forms of lava is the same; the texture difference results from the manner in which the lava flows while it cools. Rough and jagged basalt with sharp edges is **aa**; it forms as a thick skin over the surface of a slowing lava flow, cracking and breaking as it cools and solidifies. Shiny and smooth basalt that resembles coiled, twisted rope is **pahoehoe**; it forms as a thin crust that develops folds as the lava cools. Both forms can come from the same eruption, and sometimes pahoehoe becomes aa as the flow progresses. Other types of basaltic magma are described later in this section.

During a single eruption, a volcano may behave in several different ways, which depend primarily on the chemistry and gas content of the lava. These factors determine the lava's *viscosity*, or resistance to flow. Viscosity can range from low (very fluid) to high (thick and flowing slowly). For example, pahoehoe has lower viscosity than aa.

Volcanic Landforms

Volcanic eruptions result in structures that range among several forms, such as hill, cone, and mountain. In a volcanic mountain, a *crater*, or circular surface depression, is usually found at or near the summit.

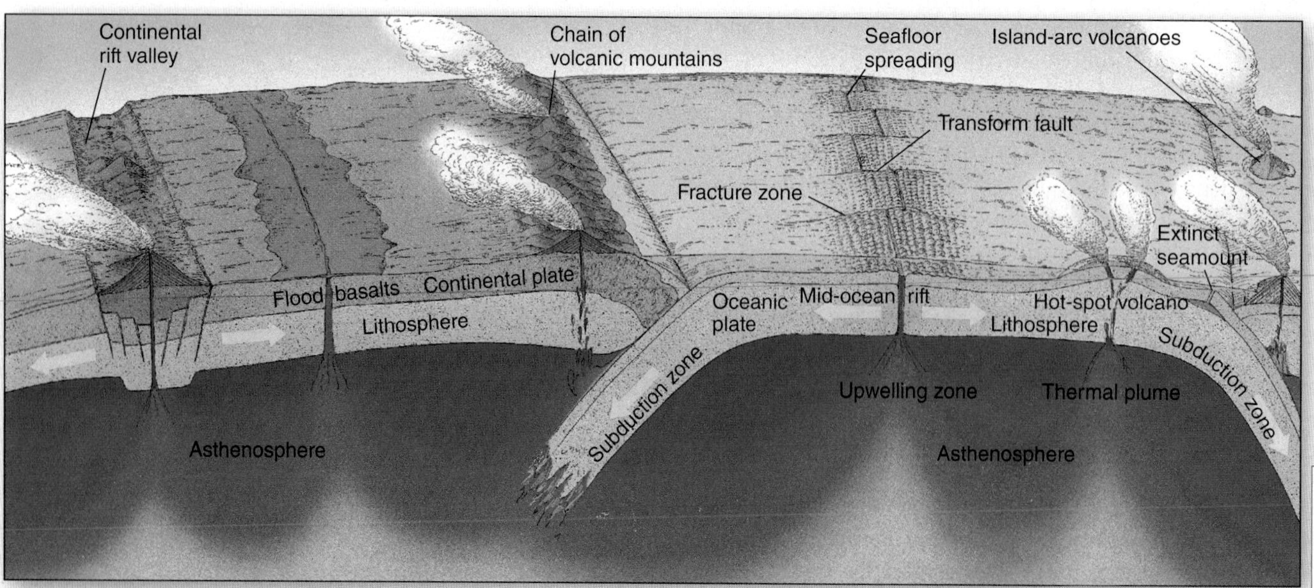

▲**Figure 10.21 Tectonic settings of volcanic activity.** Magma rises and lava erupts from rifts, through crust above subduction zones, and where thermal plumes at hot spots break through the crust. [Adapted from U.S. Geological Survey, *The Dynamic Planet* (Washington, DC: Government Printing Office, 1989).]

Animation Forming Types of Volcanoes

http://goo.gl/a7OlaJ

(a) Aa is a rough, sharp-edged lava said to get its name from the sounds people make if they attempt to walk on it.

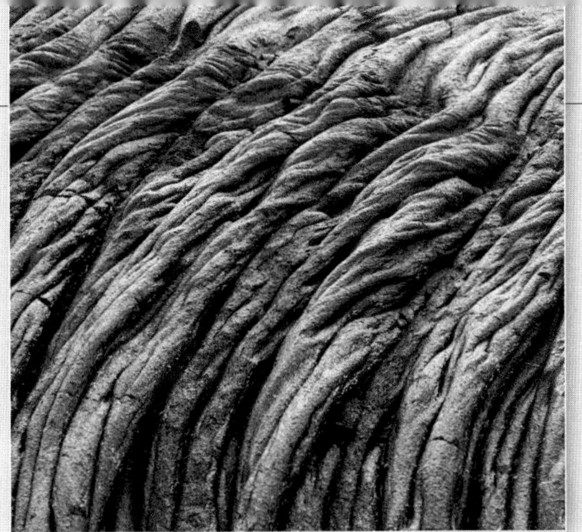

(b) Pahoehoe forms ropy cords in twisted folds.

◀**Figure 10.22 Two types of basaltic lava—Hawaiian examples, close up.** [Bobbé Christopherson.]

A **cinder cone** is a small, cone-shaped hill usually less than 450 m (1500 ft) high, with a truncated top formed from cinders that accumulate during moderately explosive eruptions. Cinder cones are made of pyroclastic material and *scoria* (cindery rock, full of air bubbles). Several notable cinder cones are located on the San Francisco volcanic field of northern Arizona. Ascension Island, at about 8° S latitude in the Atlantic Ocean, has over 100 cinder cones and craters to mark its volcanic history (**Figure 10.23**).

A **caldera** (Spanish for "kettle") is a large, basin-shaped depression that forms when summit material on a volcanic mountain collapses inward after an eruption or other loss of magma (**Figure 10.24**). A caldera may fill with rainwater to form a lake, such as Crater Lake in southern Oregon and Mount Pinatubo Lake in the Philippines (see Chapter 1, GIA 1, on page 12).

The Long Valley Caldera, near the California–Nevada border, was formed by a powerful volcanic eruption 760,000 years ago. The area is characterized today by hydrothermal activity such as hot springs and fumaroles that fuel the Casa Diablo geothermal plant, which supplies power to about 40,000 homes. About 1200 tons of carbon dioxide are coming up through the soil in the caldera each day, killing acres of forests in six different areas of the caldera floor. These gas emissions signal volcanic activity—in this case, active and moving magma at a depth of some 3 km (1.86 mi)—and are useful indicators of potential eruptions (go to *MasteringGeography* for photos of the caldera).

▼**Figure 10.23 Cinder cones on Ascension Island.** Ascension Island in the south Atlantic Ocean is a massive composite volcano that rises over 3000 m (9842 ft) from the ocean floor, with 858 m (2815 ft) above sea level. [Bobbe' Christopherson.]

Effusive Eruptions

Effusive eruptions are outpourings of low-viscosity magma that produce enormous volumes of lava annually on the seafloor and in places such as Hawai'i and Iceland. These eruptions flow directly from the asthenosphere and upper mantle, releasing fluid magma that cools to form a dark, basaltic rock low in silica (less than 50%) and rich in iron and magnesium. Gases readily escape from this magma because of its low viscosity. Effusive eruptions pour out on the surface with relatively small explosions and few pyroclastics. However, dramatic fountains of basaltic lava sometimes shoot upward, powered by jets of rapidly expanding gases.

An effusive eruption may come from a single vent or from the flank of a volcano through a side vent. If such vent openings are linear in form, they are *fissures*, which sometimes erupt in a dramatic "curtain of fire" as sheets of molten rock spray into the air.

On the island of Hawai'i, the continuing Kīlauea eruption is the longest in recorded history—active since January 3, 1983 (**Figure 10.25a**). Although this eruption is located on the slopes of the massive Mauna Loa volcano, scientists have determined that Kīlauea has its own magma system extending down some 60 km (37 mi) into Earth. To date, the active crater on Kīlauea (called Pu'u O'o) has produced more lava than any other in recorded history—some 3.1 km^3 (0.7 mi^3). To see a series of photographs showing the actively changing Pu'u O'o crater from 1999 to 2011, go to Chapter 10 on the *MasteringGeography* website.

Prior to 2011, massive flows of basaltic lava from the Kilauea volcano moved southward, toward the ocean. Kilauea's entire south flank is in long-term motion toward the sea, along a low-angle fault at a rate of about 7 cm (2.75 in.) per year. In 2011, lava flows changed course as new eruptions began west of the Pu'u O'o crater. In the summer of 2014, new active flows moved northeastward into the town of Pāhoa, Hawai'i (Figure 10.25b).

A typical mountain landform built from effusive eruptions is gently sloped, gradually rising from the surrounding landscape to a summit crater. The shape is similar in

▲**Figure 10.24 Tambora caldera, Sumbawa Island, Indonesia.** The caldera, formed during the 1815 eruption (the largest in recorded history), is 6 km (3.7 mi) in diameter and 1100 m (0.7 mi) deep. [2009 astronaut photograph ISS020-E-6563, *ISS* Crew Earth Observations experiment and Image Science & Analysis Laboratory, Johnson Space Center, NASA.]

(a) Basaltic lava flows from the Kīlauea volcano flow southward to the sea, Hawai'i Volcanoes National Park.

(b) In 2014, active flows began in June and reached private property near the town of Pāhoa in late October.

▲**Figure 10.25 Kīlauea landscape and 2014 lava flow.** [(a) Bobbé Christopherson. (b) USGS.]

GEOreport 10.4 Mount Ontake's deadly 2014 eruption in Japan

On September 27, 2014, in central Japan, as hundreds of people hiked toward the 3067 m (10,062 ft) summit, Mount Ontake erupted. The surprise eruption triggered a pyroclastic flow—a fast-moving, billowing mixture of hot steam, gases, and ash—that killed more than 50 people. Although the Japan Meteorological Association detected harmonic (volcanic) tremors on the mountain early in September, scientists did not raise the volcano alert level, nor did they detect rising subsurface magma. Mount Ontake's shallow steam eruption was mainly water, gases, and heat emerging through surface vents, pulverizing rock in the process. This is a phreatic eruption that scientists cannot accurately predict. Mount Ontake's last phreatic eruption was in 2007; the volcano's last explosive eruption was in 1979.

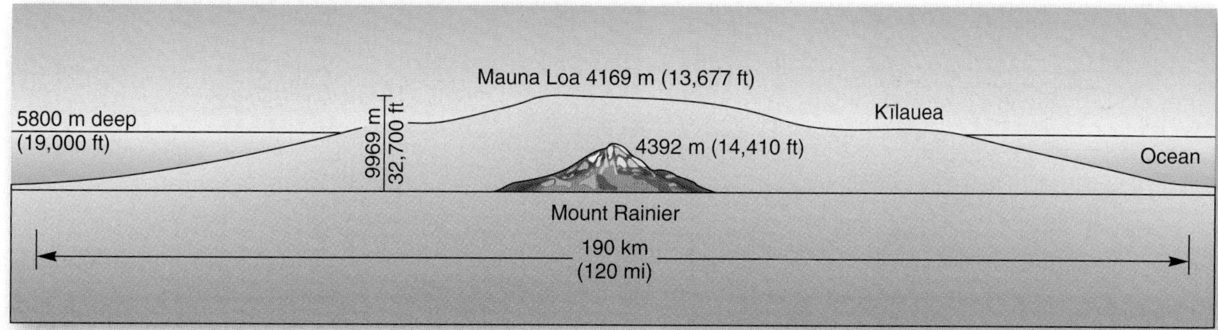

(a) Comparison of Mauna Loa in Hawai'i, a shield volcano, and Mount Rainier in Washington State, a composite volcano. Their strikingly different profiles reveal their different tectonic origins.

(b) Mauna Loa's gently sloped shield shape dominates the horizon.

▲**Figure 10.26 Shield and composite volcanoes compared.** [(a) After USGS, *Eruption of Hawaiian Volcanoes*, 1986. (b) Bobbé Christopherson.]

outline to a shield of armor lying face up on the ground and therefore is called a **shield volcano.** Mauna Loa is one of five shield volcanoes that make up the island of Hawai'i. The height of the Mauna Loa shield is the result of successive eruptions, flowing one on top of another. At least 1 million years were needed to accumulate this shield volcano, forming the most massive single mountain on Earth (although Mauna Kea, also located on Hawai'i, is slightly taller). The shield shape and size of Mauna Loa are distinctive when compared with Mount Rainier in Washington, which is a different type of volcano (explained shortly) and the largest in the Cascade Range (**Figure 10.26**).

In volcanic settings above hot spots and in continental rift valleys, effusive eruptions send material out through elongated fissures, forming extensive sheets of basaltic lava on the surface (see Figure 10.21). The Columbia Plateau of the northwestern United States, some 2–3 km thick (1.2–1.8 mi), is the result of the eruption of these **flood basalts** (sometimes called *plateau basalts*), which formed volcanic strata now exposed by rivers throughout the region (**Figure 10.27**).

▼**Figure 10.27 Flood basalt on the Columbia Plateau, Washington.** Formed by effusive eruptions, flood basalt is exposed by erosion along the Columbia River, Washington; the Mount Hood composite volcano, formed by explosive eruptions, is in the background. [Danita Delimont/Alamy.]

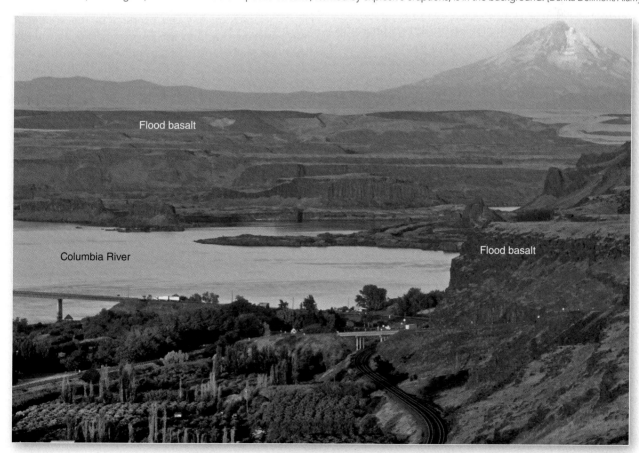

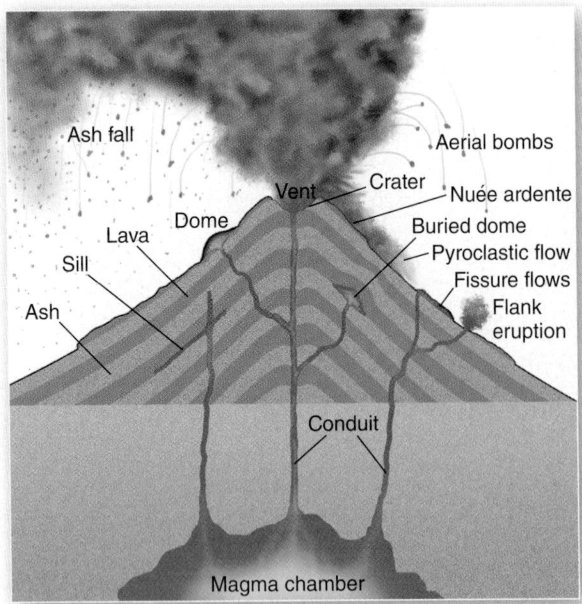

(a) A typical composite volcano with its cone-shaped form in an explosive eruption.

(b) Mount Redoubt, Alaska, erupts in 2009.

▲**Figure 10.28 A composite volcano.** [(b) Game McGimsey, USGS.]

Explosive Eruptions

Violent explosions of magma, gas, and pyroclastics driven by the buildup of pressure in a magma conduit form **explosive eruptions**. This buildup occurs because magma produced by the melting of subducted oceanic plate and other materials is thicker (more viscous) than magma that forms effusive volcanoes. Consequently, it tends to block the magma conduit by forming a plug near the surface. The blockage traps and compresses gases (so much so that they remain liquefied) until their pressure is great enough to cause an explosive eruption.

Such an explosion is equivalent to megatons of TNT blasting the top and sides off the mountain. This type of eruption produces much less lava than effusive eruptions, but larger amounts of pyroclastics, which include volcanic ash (<2 mm, or <0.08 in., in diameter), dust, cinders, scoria (dark-colored, cindery rock with holes from gas bubbles), pumice (lighter-colored, less-dense rock with holes from gas bubbles), and *aerial bombs* (explosively ejected blobs of incandescent lava). A *nuée ardente*, French for "glowing cloud," is an incandescent, hot, turbulent cloud of gas, ash, and pyroclastic that can jet across the landscape in these kinds of eruptions (**Figure 10.28**).

A mountain produced by a series of explosive eruptions is a **composite volcano**, formed by multiple layers of lava, ash, rock, and pyroclastics. These landforms are sometimes called *stratovolcanoes* to describe the alternating layers of ash, rock, and lava, but shield volcanoes also can exhibit a stratified structure, so composite is the preferred term. Composite volcanoes tend to have steep sides and a distinct conical shape and therefore are also known as *composite cones*. If a single summit vent erupts repeatedly, a remarkable symmetry may develop as the mountain grows in size, as demonstrated by Popocatépetl in Mexico (see Figure HD 10d, on page 345).

Mount St. Helens Probably the most studied and photographed composite volcano on Earth is Mount St. Helens (**Figure 10.29**), the youngest and most active of the Cascade Range of volcanoes, which extend from Mount Lassen in California to Mount Meager in British Columbia. The Cascade Range is the product of the subduction zone between the Juan de Fuca and North American plates (see Figure 10.11). Today, more than 1 million tourists visit the Mount St. Helens Volcanic National Monument each year.

In 1980, after 123 years of dormancy, Mount St. Helens erupted. As the contents of the mountain exploded, a surge of hot gas (about 300°C, or 570°F), steam-filled ash, pyroclastics, and a nuée ardente moved northward, hugging the ground and traveling at speeds up to 400 kmph (250 mph) for a distance of 28 km (17 mi). A series of photographs, taken at 10-second intervals from the east looking west, records the sequence of the eruption, which continued with intensity for 9 hours and then blasted new material intermittently for days (Figure 10.29).

The slumping that occurred along the north face of the mountain produced the greatest landslide witnessed in recorded history; about 2.75 km^3 (0.67 mi^3) of rock, ice, and trapped air, all fluidized with steam, surged at speeds approaching 250 kmph (155 mph). Landslide materials traveled for 21 km (13 mi) into the valley, blanketing the forest, covering a lake, and filling the rivers below.

As destructive as such eruptions are, they also are constructive, for this is the way in which a volcano

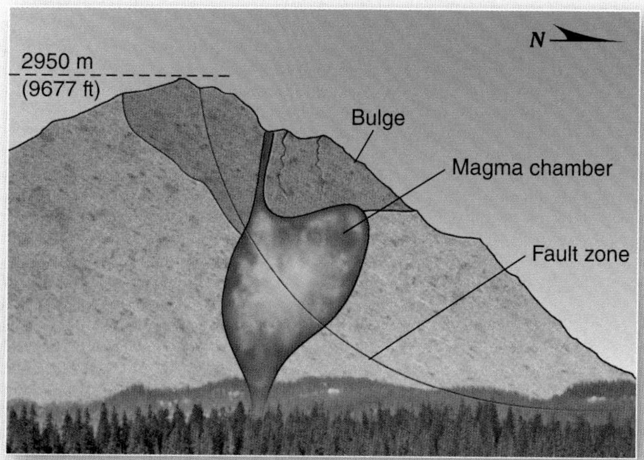

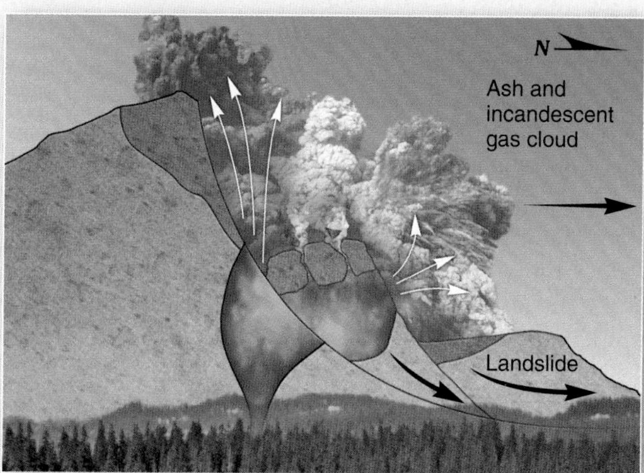

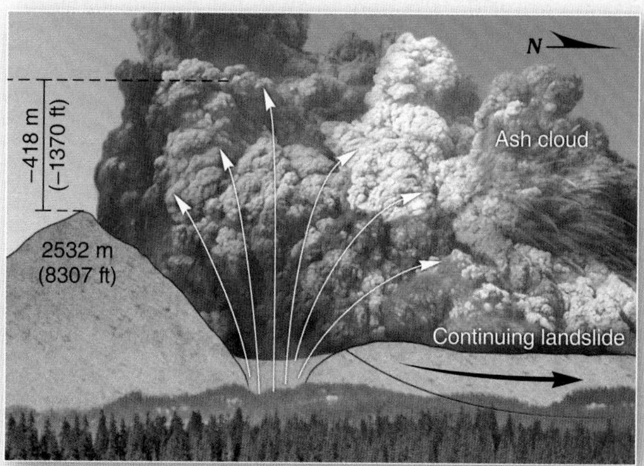

▲**Figure 10.29 The Mount St. Helens eruption sequence and corresponding schematics.** [Photo sequence by Keith B. Ronnholm. All rights reserved.]

eventually builds its height. Before the eruption, Mount St. Helens was 2950 m (9677 ft) tall; the eruption blew away 418 m (1370 ft). Today, Mount St. Helens is building a lava dome within its crater (see the post-eruption photo in **Figure 10.30**). The thick lava rapidly and repeatedly plugs and breaks in a series of lesser dome eruptions that may continue for several decades. The buildup of the lava dome is now more than 300 m (1000 ft) high, so a new mountain is being born from the eruption of the old.

◀**Figure 10.30 Mount St. Helens after the 1980 eruption.** [Images & Volcans/Science Source.]

Animation MG
Debris Avalanche and Eruption of Mount St. Helens
http://goo.gl/yilZQJ

Mount Pinatubo The 1991 eruption of Mount Pinatubo in the Philippines was the second largest of that century (the largest was Novarupta on the Katmai Peninsula in Alaska in 1912) and the largest to affect a densely populated area. The eruption produced 15 to 20 million tons of ash and 12 km^3 (3.0 mi^3) of magma, ash, and pyroclastics—about 12 times the volume of material produced by Mount St. Helens. The loss of this vast amount of material caused the summit of the volcano to collapse, forming a caldera 2.5 km (1.6 mi) in diameter. The eruption killed 800 people and devastated many surrounding villages. However, accurate prediction of this event saved many lives, as approximately 60,000 evacuated their homes prior to the eruption.

Although volcanoes are local events, they have global effects. As discussed in Chapters 1 and 4, the Mount Pinatubo eruption affected Earth's climate, releasing an aerosol cloud that changed atmospheric albedo, impacted atmospheric absorption of insolation, and altered net radiation at Earth's surface (review Chapter 1 Geosystems in Action and Figure 4.1).

Volcano Forecasting and Planning

After 23,000 people died in the 1985 eruption of Nevado del Ruiz in Colombia, the USGS and the Office of Foreign Disaster Assistance established the Volcano Disaster Assistance Program (VDAP; see http://vulcan.wr.usgs.gov/Vdap/). In the United States, VDAP helps local scientists forecast eruptions by setting up mobile volcano-monitoring systems at sites with activity or with vulnerable populations. A number of "volcano cams" are positioned around the world for 24-hour surveillance (go to http://vulcan.wr.usgs.gov/Photo/volcano_cams.html).

At Mount St. Helens, a dozen survey benchmarks and several tiltmeters have been placed within the crater to monitor the building lava dome. The monitoring, accompanied by intensive scientific research, has paid off, as every eruption since 1980 was successfully forecasted from days to as long as 3 weeks in advance (with the exception of one small eruption in 1984). Swarms of minor earthquakes along the north flank of the mountain occurred in 2001, and dome eruptions of varying intensities occurred through 2007.

Early warning systems for volcanic activity are now possible through integrated seismographic networks and monitoring. In addition, satellite remote sensing allows scientists to monitor eruption cloud dynamics and the climatic effects of volcano emissions and to estimate volcanic hazard potential. In 2005, the USGS identified 57 priority volcanoes in the United States in need of improved monitoring as part of the National Volcano Early Warning System.

CRITICAL**thinking 10.2**

Ocean-Floor Tectonics Tour

Using the chapter-opening map, follow the ocean ridge and spreading center known as the East Pacific Rise northward as it trends beneath the west coast of the North American plate, disappearing under earthquake-prone California. Locate continents, offshore submerged continental shelves, and expanses of sediment-covered abyssal plain on the map.

On the floor of the Indian Ocean, you see the wide track along which the Indo-Australian plate traveled northward to its collision with the Eurasian plate. Vast deposits of sediment cover the Indian Ocean floor, south of the Ganges River and to the east of India. Sediments derived from the Himalayan Range blanket the floor of the Bay of Bengal (south of Bangladesh) to a depth of 20 km (12.4 mi). These sediments result from centuries of soil erosion in the land of the monsoons.

In the Pacific, a chain of islands and seamounts marks the hot-spot track on the Pacific plate from Hawai'i to the Aleutians. Visible as dark trenches are subduction zones south and east of Alaska and Japan and along the western coast of South and Central America. Follow the Mid-Atlantic Ridge spreading center the full length of the Atlantic to where it passes through Iceland, sitting astride the ridge. Take time with this map and find other examples in it of the many concepts discussed in Chapters 9 and 10.

THE**human**DENOMINATOR 10 Tectonics

TECTONIC PROCESSES IMPACT HUMANS

- Earthquakes cause damage and human casualties; destruction is amplified in developing countries, such as Haiti.
- Volcanic eruptions can devastate human population centers, disrupt human transportation, and affect global climate.

In 1959, an M 7.5 earthquake hit near West Yellowstone, Montana, fracturing highways along the shores of Hebgen Lake. This quake caused a landslide that dammed the Madison River, discussed in Chapter 11.

HUMANS IMPACT TECTONIC PROCESSES

- Human activity such as subsurface fluid injections associated with gas drilling and geothermal energy use can cause earthquakes.

In 2012, the government approved exploratory shale gas drilling in Great Britain, despite environmental concerns. Recent research has linked oil and gas injection wells to increased earthquake activity in several U.S. states.

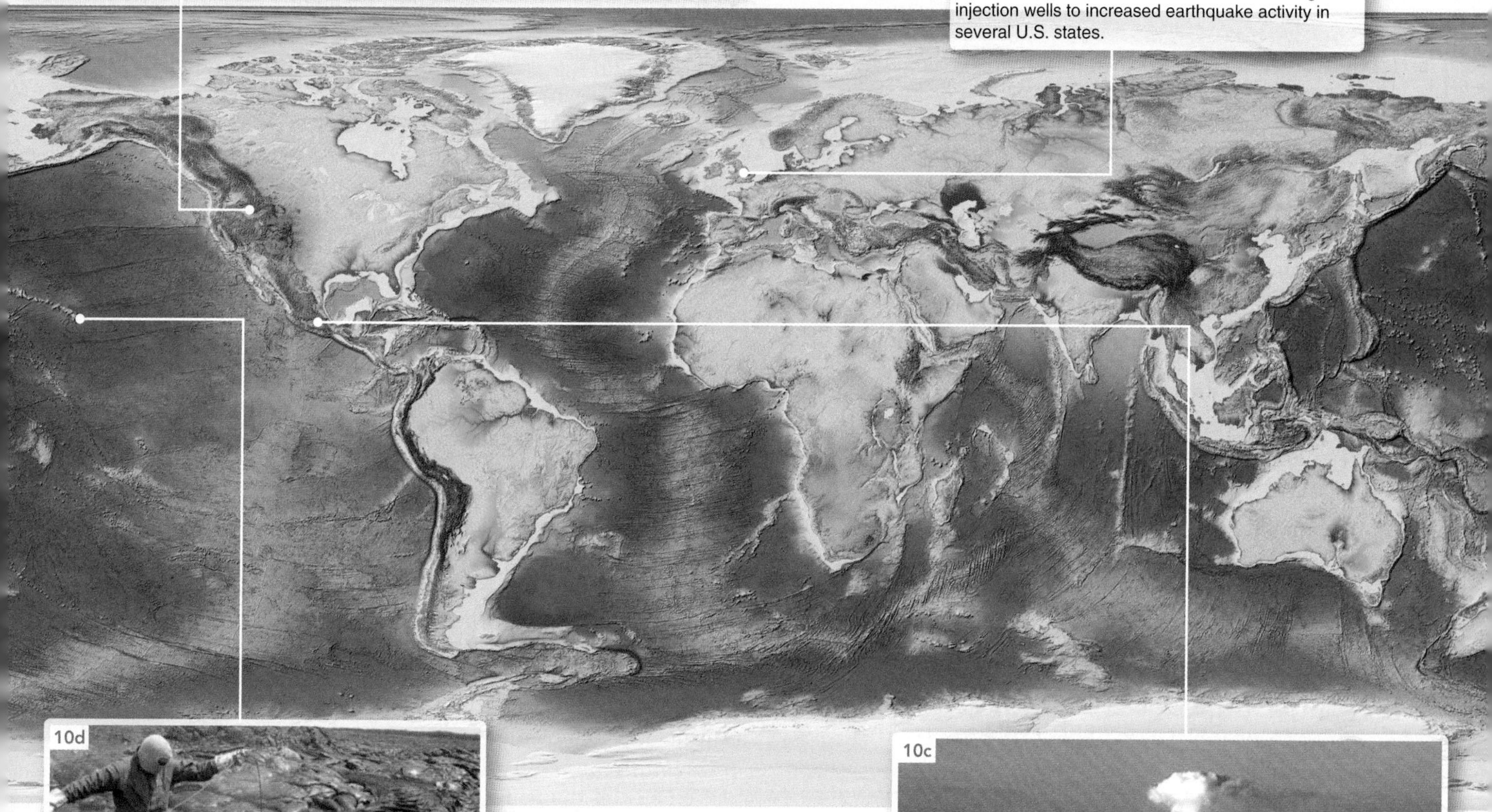

10d

A scientist at the Hawaiian Volcano Observatory takes a sample of lava at Kilauea, part of an effort to understand changes in lava chemistry on Mauna Loa.

Mexico's Popocatépetl is an active composite volcano about 70 km (45 mi) from Mexico City. Ongoing activity since 1994 includes growth of the lava dome within the crater, episodic steaming and ash emission, and ejection of material. Evacuation routes and shelters are ready for another eruption, which could affect millions of people living nearby.

ISSUES FOR THE 21ST CENTURY

- Growth of human population centers in regions prone to seismic activity and near active volcanoes will increase the hazard.
- Scientific research is needed for earthquake prediction and volcano forecasting.

KEYLEARNINGconceptsreview

Describe first, second, and third orders of relief and *list* Earth's six major topographic regions.

Tectonic forces generated within the planet dramatically shape Earth's surface. **Relief** is the vertical elevation difference in a local landscape. **Topography** is the general term for all the variations in the physical surface of Earth, including relief. *Orders of relief* are convenient descriptive categories for landforms; the coarsest (first) level includes the **continental landmasses** (portions of crust that reside above or near sea level) and **ocean basins** (portions of the crust that are entirely below sea level), and the finest (third) level comprises local hills and valleys.

relief (p. 312)
topography (p. 312)
continental landmass (p. 313)
ocean basin (p. 313)

1. How does the map of the ocean floor in the chapter-opening illustration exhibit the principles of plate tectonics? Briefly analyze.
2. What is meant by an order of relief? Give an example from each order.
3. Explain the difference between relief and topography.

Describe the formation of continental crust and *define* displaced terranes.

A continent has a nucleus of ancient crystalline rock called a *craton*. A region where a craton is exposed is a **continental shield**. As continental crust forms, it is enlarged through accretion of dispersed **terranes**. An example is the Wrangellia terrane of the Pacific Northwest and Alaska.

continental shield (p. 315)
terrane (p. 316)

4. What is a craton? Describe the relationship of cratons to continental shields and platforms, and describe these regions in North America.
5. What is an accreted terrane, and how does it add to the formation of continental landmasses? Briefly describe the journey and current location of the Wrangellia terrane.

Explain the process of folding and *describe* the principal types of faults and their characteristic landforms.

Folding, broad warping, and faulting deform the crust and produce characteristic landforms. Compression causes rocks to deform in a process known as **folding**, during which rock strata bend and may overturn. Along the ridge of a fold, layers slope downward away from the axis, forming an **anticline**. In the trough of a fold, however, layers slope downward toward the axis; this is a **syncline**.

When rock strata are stressed beyond their ability to remain a solid unit, they express the strain as a fracture. Rocks on either side of the fracture are displaced relative to the other side in a process known as **faulting**. Thus, fault zones are areas where fractures in the rock demonstrate crustal movement.

When forces pull rocks apart, the tension causes a **normal fault**, sometimes visible on the landscape as a scarp, or escarpment. Compressional forces associated with converging plates force rocks to move upward, producing a **reverse fault**. A low-angle fault plane is referred to as a **thrust fault**. Horizontal movement along a fault plane, often producing a linear rift valley, is a **strike-slip fault**. The term **horst** is applied to upward-faulted blocks; **graben** refers to downward-faulted blocks. In the U.S. interior west, the **Basin and Range Province** is an example of aligned pairs of normal faults and a distinctive horst-and-graben landscape. A **bolson** is the slope-and-basin area between mountain ridges in this type of arid region.

folding (p. 317)
anticline (p. 317)
syncline (p. 318)
faulting (p. 320)
normal fault (p. 320)
reverse fault (p. 320)
thrust fault (p. 320)
strike-slip fault (p. 320)
horst (p. 322)
graben (p. 322)
Basin and Range Province (p. 323)
bolson (p. 324)

6. Diagram a simple folded landscape in cross section, and identify the features created by the folded strata.
7. Define the four basic types of faults. How are faults related to earthquakes and seismic activity?
8. How did the Basin and Range Province evolve in the western United States? What other examples exist of this type of landscape?

List the three types of plate collisions associated with orogenesis and *identify* specific examples of each.

Orogenesis is the birth of mountains. An *orogeny* is a mountain-building episode, occurring over millions of years, that thickens continental crust. It can occur through large-scale deformation and uplift of the crust. It also may include the capture and cementation of migrating terranes to the continental margins and the intrusion of granitic magmas to form plutons.

Three types of tectonic activity cause mountain building along convergent plate margins. *Oceanic plate–continental plate collisions* are now occurring along the Pacific coast of the Americas, forming the Andes, the Sierra Madre of Central America, the Rockies, and other western mountains. *Oceanic plate–oceanic plate collisions* produce volcanic island arcs such as Japan, the Philippines, the Kurils, and portions of the Aleutians. The region around the Pacific contains expressions of each type of collision in the *circum-Pacific belt*, or the **Ring of Fire**. In a *continental plate–continental plate collision*, large masses of continental crust, such as the Himalayan Range, are subjected to intense folding, overthrusting, faulting, and uplifting.

orogenesis (p. 324)
Ring of Fire (p. 325)

9. Define orogenesis. What is meant by the birth of mountain chains?
10. Name some significant orogenies.

11. Identify on a map several of Earth's mountain chains. What processes contributed to their development?

12. How are plate boundaries related to episodes of mountain building? Explain how different types of plate boundaries produce differing orogenic episodes and different landscapes.

13. Relate tectonic processes to the formation of the Appalachians and the Alleghany orogeny.

Explain earthquake characteristics and measurement, *describe* earthquake fault mechanics, and *discuss* the status of earthquake forecasting.

An **earthquake** is the release of energy that occurs at the moment of fracture along a fault in the crust, producing seismic waves. Earthquakes generally occur along plate boundaries. Seismic motions are measured with a **seismometer**, also called a seismograph.

Scientists measure earthquake magnitude using the **moment magnitude scale**, a more precise and quantitative scale than the **Richter scale**, which was mainly an effective measure for small-magnitude quakes. The **elastic-rebound theory** describes the basic process of how a fault breaks, although the specific details are still under study. The small areas that are sticking points along a fault are points of high strain, known as *asperities*—when these sticking points break, they release the sides of the fault. When the elastic energy is released abruptly as the rock breaks, both sides of the fault return to a condition of less strain. Earthquake forecasting remains a major challenge for scientists.

earthquake (p. 328)
seismometer (p. 330)
Richter scale (p. 330)
moment magnitude (M) scale (p. 330)
elastic-rebound theory (p. 331)

14. What is the relationship between an epicenter and the focus of an earthquake? Give an example from the Loma Prieta, California, earthquake.

15. Differentiate among the Mercalli, moment magnitude (M), and amplitude magnitude (Richter) scales. How are these used to describe an earthquake? Reference some recent quakes in your discussion.

16. How do the elastic-rebound theory and asperities help explain the nature of faulting? In your explanation, relate the concepts of stress (force) and strain (deformation) along a fault. How does this lead to rupture and earthquake?

17. Describe the San Andreas fault and its relationship to ancient seafloor spreading movements along transform faults.

18. How are paleoseismology and the seismic gap concept related to expected earthquake occurrences?

19. What do you see as the biggest barrier to effective earthquake prediction?

Describe volcanic landforms and *distinguish* between an effusive and an explosive volcanic eruption.

A **volcano** forms at the end of a central vent or pipe that rises from the asthenosphere through the crust. Eruptions produce lava (molten rock), gases, and **pyroclastics** (pulverized rock and clastic materials ejected violently during an eruption) that pass through the vent to openings and fissures at the surface and build volcanic landforms. Basaltic lava flows occur in two principal textures: **aa**, rough and sharp-edged lava, and **pahoehoe**, smooth, ropy folds of lava.

Landforms produced by volcanic activity include **cinder cones**, which are small conical-shaped hills, and **calderas**, large basin-shaped depressions caused by the collapse of a volcano's summit.

Volcanoes are of two general types, based on the chemistry and gas content of the magma involved. An **effusive eruption** produces a **shield volcano** (such as Kīlauea in Hawai'i) and extensive deposits of **flood basalts**, or *plateau basalts*. **Explosive eruptions** (such as Mount Pinatubo in the Philippines) produce a **composite volcano**. Volcanic activity has produced some destructive moments in history, but constantly creates new seafloor, land, and soils.

volcano (p. 336)
pyroclastics (p. 336)
aa (p. 336)
pahoehoe (p. 336)
cinder cone (p. 337)
caldera (p. 337)
effusive eruption (p. 337)
shield volcano (p. 339)
flood basalt (p. 339)
explosive eruption (p. 340)
composite volcano (p. 340)

20. What is a volcano? In general terms, describe some volcanic features.

21. Where do you expect to find volcanic activity in the world? Why?

22. Compare effusive and explosive eruptions. Why are they different? What distinct landforms are produced by each type? Give examples of each.

23. Describe several recent volcanic eruptions, such as in Hawai'i and Iceland. What is the present status in each place? Specifically, what changes are occurring in Hawai'i?

MasteringGeography™

Looking for additional review and test prep materials? Visit the Study Area in *MasteringGeography*™ to enhance your geographic literacy, spatial reasoning skills, and understanding of this chapter's content by accessing a variety of resources, including **MapMaster** interactive maps, geoscience animations, videos, *In the News* RSS feeds, flashcards, web links, self-study quizzes, and an eText version of *Elemental Geosystems*.

11 Weathering, Karst Landscapes, and Mass Movement

The North Fork of the Stillaguamish River valley in western Washington, one day after a massive landslide and mudflow buried part of the town of Oso in March 2014. Note the landslide scarp on the right side and the blue water (in the foreground) of the temporary lake formed by the slide debris. Over 30 homes were buried by the main portion of the slide. [Ted S. Warren/AP Images.]

KEYLEARNING**concepts**

After reading the chapter, you should be able to:

- ***Describe*** the dynamic equilibrium approach to the study of landforms and ***illustrate*** the forces at work on materials residing on a slope.
- ***Define*** weathering and ***explain*** the importance of parent rock and joints and fractures in rock.
- ***Describe*** the physical weathering processes of frost wedging, salt-crystal growth, and pressure-release jointing.
- ***Explain*** the chemical weathering processes of hydration, hydrolysis, oxidation, carbonation, and dissolution.
- ***Review*** the processes and features associated with karst topography.
- ***Categorize*** the various types of mass movements and ***identify*** examples of each by moisture content and speed of movement.

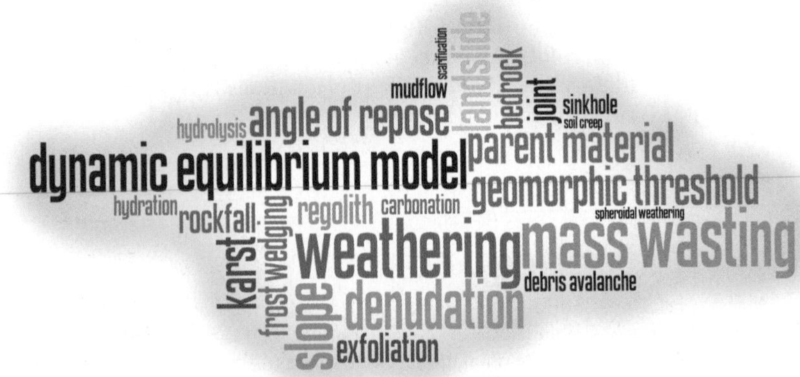

GEOSYSTEMS**now**

The Oso, Washington, Landslide

On the morning of March 22, 2014, residents in a riverside neighborhood just east of Oso, Washington, about 80 km (50 mi) northeast of Seattle, went about their usual weekend activities. Around 11 A.M., with no warning to those in the homes below, the mountainside above the North Fork of the Stillaguamish River gave way, unleashing an estimated 11.5 million m^3 (15 million yd^3) of material. The block of earth slid rapidly down to the valley floor, breaking into pieces and picking up debris as it fell, and then flowed 1.1 km (0.7 mi) across the valley, damming the river channel and burying a portion of Oso and State Route 530 with mud, rock, trees, and other wreckage. The slide—ultimately covering 2.6 km^2 (1 mi^2) of the valley floor—destroyed more than 35 houses and caused 41 fatalities (**Figure GN 11.1** and chapter-opening photo).

Landslides represent one type of mass movement, or mass wasting, process in which large bodies of earth materials move downslope with gravity. Although mass-movement events are natural occurrences, especially frequent in mountain environments, their effects can be disastrous in populated areas.

Conditions for Mass Movement On the western slopes of the Cascade Range in Washington, the winter of 2013–2014 was wetter than normal, with precipitation in February and March at 150 to 200% of the long-term average. In this region of steep slopes and heavy rainfall, landslides are not uncommon. In fact, the slope above Oso, known as the Hazel landslide, had a well-known history of significant mass-movement events, including episodes in 1951, 1961, 1988, and, most recently, 2006 (**Figure GN 11.2**).

▼**Figure GN 11.1 Destroyed house in the slide path, with headscarp in background.** [Genna Martin/The Herald/AP Images.]

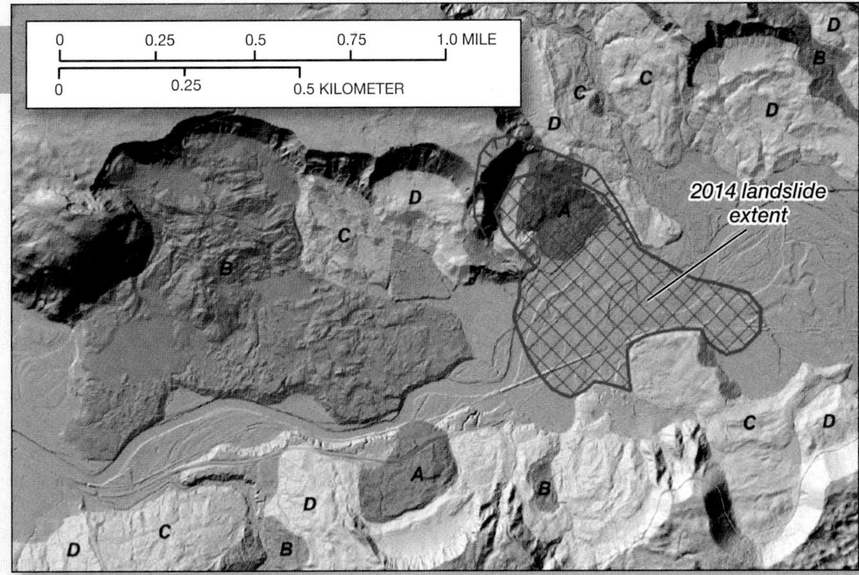

▲**Figure GN 11.2 Map of landslide deposits near Oso.** Shaded relief image from a 2013 LiDAR survey shows older landslide deposits (colored areas) ranging from youngest (A) to oldest (D). Red cross-hatching marks the extent of the 2014 event; the red line with tick marks shows the approximate headscarp. [Ralph Haugerud, 2014, Preliminary Interpretation of Pre-2014 Landslide Deposits in the Vicinity of Oso, Washington; USGS Open File Report 2014–1065, p. 4.]

According to a 1999 report by an environmental consulting firm for the Army Corps of Engineers, two main factors contribute to ongoing slope instability at the Hazel landslide: erosion by the Stillaguamish River, which causes oversteepening of the toe of the slope, and water saturation of the unconsolidated slope materials, which can cause the material to flow. The report warned of the potential for a "large, catastrophic" slope failure. Under the reported geomorphic conditions, high streamflow or large amounts of rainfall could potentially increase the landslide hazard. Tree removal associated with logging on mountain slopes could also increase landslide risk; past logging around the Hazel slide area may have helped trigger the 2014 event.

Over the years, despite the history of mass-movement activity, people built houses closer to the toe of the slope. Prior to and just after the 2006 slide, the state spent millions of dollars on reinforcements to the riverbanks and slope toe, all of which created a false sense of security for residents in the slide path.

Anatomy of the Landslide Initial observations indicate that the Oso event was a complex mix of rotational slide and mudflow. These different classes are based on the rate of movement and the water content of the material, discussed in this chapter. Just below the headscarp—the top of the slide, where the material initially broke loose—the stepped appearance of the new mountainside suggests a rotational slumping that occurs when a sliding block of earth turns on its side. At the toe, the slurry of mud, rock, and debris resembles a mudflow, a fluidized mass that can move long distances and pick up materials the size of large boulders. This particular landslide was unusual in its extensive path across the valley.

The force of the falling and flowing material in Oso that morning caused ground vibrations large enough to register on regional seismographs operated by the University of Washington Pacific Northwest Seismic Network. However, the seismic readings show no evidence that an earthquake triggered the mass-movement event.

Recovery The initial rescue and recovery effort involved over 600 personnel, many of them volunteers. Rescuers used helicopters, heat-sensing equipment, and rescue dogs to search through a slide area 2.6 km^2 (1 mi^2) in size with mud and debris up to 6 m (20 ft) deep, in places contaminated by chemicals and bacteria.

The question remains whether many of the consequences of this disaster might have been avoided if officials and residents had heeded earlier warnings of the landslide hazard.

QUESTION AND EXPLORE Go to the USGS Landslide Hazards Program at http://landslides.usgs.gov/current/ to find out more about current landslide activity and efforts at landslide monitoring. MG

As mentioned in earlier chapters, the exogenic processes at work on Earth's landscapes include weathering, erosion, and deposition of materials. In this chapter and the three chapters that follow, we look at exogenic agents and their handiwork—weathering and mass-movement processes, river systems and their landforms, landscapes shaped by waves and wind, and landforms worked by ice and glaciers. All of these are subjects of geomorphology, the science of the origin, development, and spatial distribution of landforms.

We begin our study of Earth's exogenic systems with weathering, the process that breaks down rock by disintegrating it into mineral particles or dissolving it into water. Weathering produces an overall weakening of surface rock, which makes it more susceptible to other exogenic processes. The difference between weathering and erosion is important: *Weathering* is the breakdown of materials, whereas *erosion* includes the transport of weathered materials to different locations.

In addition to earthquakes and volcanic eruptions... many events related to exogenic processes are often in the news...

In addition to the earthquakes and volcanic eruptions that were the focus of Chapter 10, many events related to exogenic processes are often in the news: for example, debris avalanches in Pakistan, landslides in Turkey, rockfalls in the Utah canyon country, and mudflows in the southern California suburbs. In 2008, the rainfall from three hurricanes in Haiti caused massive landslides and mudflows on deforested mountain slopes; in 2010, more landslides were caused by the earthquake described in Focus Study 10.1.

In this chapter: We look at physical (mechanical) and chemical weathering processes that break up, dissolve, and generally reduce the landscape. Such weathering releases essential minerals from bedrock for soil formation and enrichment. In limestone regions, chemical weathering produces sinkholes, caves, and caverns. In these karst environments, water has dissolved enormous underground areas that are still being discovered by scientists and explorers. In addition, we examine types of mass movements and discuss the processes that cause them.

Landmass Denudation

Denudation is any process that wears away or rearranges landforms. The principal denudation processes affecting surface materials include *weathering*, *mass movement*, *erosion*, and *deposition*, as produced by moving water, air, waves, and ice—all influenced by the pull of gravity.

Interactions between the structural elements of the land and the processes of denudation are complex. They represent an ongoing opposition between the forces of weathering and erosion and the resistance of Earth materials.

The iconic 15-story-tall Delicate Arch in Utah is dramatic evidence of this conflict (**Figure 11.1**). Various weathering processes have worked in combination with the differing resistances of the rocks to produce this delicate sculpture—an example of **differential weathering**, where a more resistant cap rock protects supporting strata below.

The buttes, pinnacles, and mesas of the U.S. Southwest are other examples of resistant horizontal rock strata that have eroded differentially. Removal of strata that are less resistant produces unusual desert sculptures—arches, windows, pedestals, and delicately balanced rocks. For an idea of the quantity of material removed by weathering and erosion to produce these landscapes, imagine a line intersecting the tops of the Mitten Buttes shown in **Figure 11.2**. These buttes exceed 300 m (1000 ft) in height, which is similar to the Chrysler Building in New York City or the U.S. Bank Tower (Library Tower) in Los Angeles.

As portrayed in earlier chapters, endogenic processes, such as tectonic uplift and volcanic activity, build landforms into *initial landscapes*, whereas exogenic processes tear landforms down, developing *sequential landscapes* characterized by lower relief, gradual change,

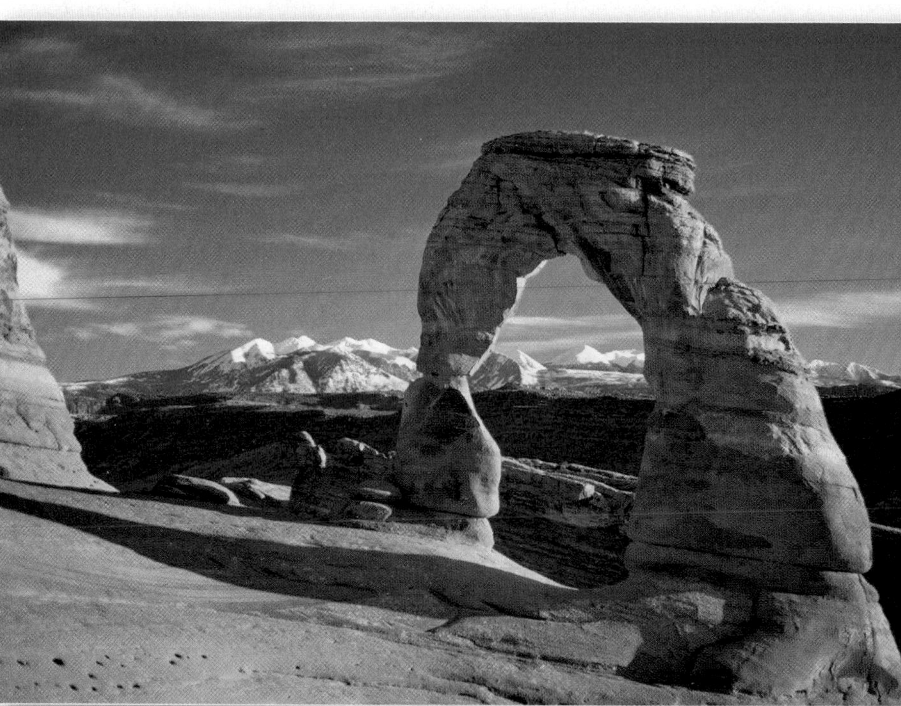

►**Figure 11.1 Delicate Arch, Arches National Park, Utah.** Resistant rock strata at the top of the structure helped preserve the arch beneath as surrounding rock eroded away. In the distance are the snow-covered La Sal Mountains, an example of a laccolith (a type of igneous intrusion) exposed by erosion. [Bobbé Christopherson.]

(a)

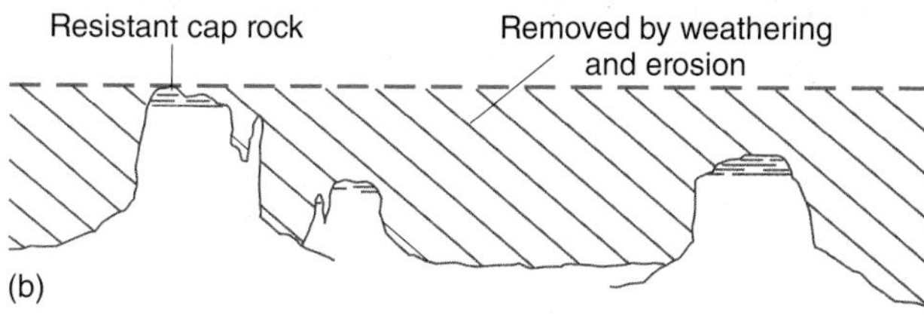

(b)

◀Figure 11.2 Monument Valley landscape. (a) A rainbow over Mitten Buttes and Merrick Butte in Monument Valley, Navajo Tribal Park along the Utah–Arizona border. (b) A schematic of the tremendous removal of material by weathering, erosion, and transport. [Robert Christopherson.]

and stability. However, these countering sets of processes happen simultaneously. Scientists have proposed several hypotheses to model denudation processes and to account for the appearance of the landscape.

Dynamic Equilibrium Approach to Understanding Landforms

A landscape is an open system, with highly variable inputs of energy and materials. The Sun provides radiant energy that converts into *heat energy* that drives the hydrologic cycle and other Earth systems. The hydrologic cycle imparts *kinetic energy* through the mechanical motion of moving air and water. *Chemical energy* is available from the atmosphere and various reactions within the crust. In addition, uplift of the land by tectonic processes creates *potential energy of position* as land rises above sea level. Remember from Chapter 3 that potential energy is stored energy that has the capacity to do work under the right conditions, such as the pull of gravity down a hillslope.

As landscapes and the forces acting on them change, the surface constantly responds in search of equilibrium. Every change produces compensating actions and reactions. Tectonic uplift creates disequilibrium, an imbalance, between relief and the energy required to maintain stability. The idea of landscape formation as a balancing act between uplift and reduction by weathering and erosion is the **dynamic equilibrium model**. Landscapes in a dynamic equilibrium show ongoing adaptations to the ever-changing conditions of local relief, rock structure, and climate.

Endogenic events, such as faulting or a volcanic eruption, or exogenic events, such as a heavy rainfall or a forest fire, may change the relationships between landscape elements and within landscape systems. During or following a destabilizing event, a landform system sometimes arrives at a **geomorphic threshold**, or tipping point, where the system lurches to a new operational level. This threshold is reached when a geomorphic system moves from the slow accumulation of small adjustments (as occurs in a steady-state equilibrium) to a point of abrupt change that takes it to a new system state (as occurs in a dynamic equilibrium)—such as when a flood establishes a new river channel or a hillslope adjusts after a landslide. Such a threshold can also occur at the precise moment when force overcomes resistance within a system; for example, when slope stability fails and movement ensues in a downhill direction (as during a landslide). After crossing this threshold, the system establishes a new set of equilibrium relationships. (Review Figure 1.8 in Chapter 1.)

The dynamic equilibrium model encompasses a series of steps that usually follow a sequence over time. First is equilibrium stability, in which the system fluctuates around some average. Next is a destabilizing event, followed by a period of adjustment. Last is arrival at a new and different condition of equilibrium stability. Slow, continuous-change events, such as soil development and erosion, tend to maintain a near-equilibrium condition in the system. Dramatic events such as a major landslide require longer recovery times before equilibrium is reestablished. Figure GIA 11.1 provides an example, in which the failure of saturated slopes caused a landslide that brought sediment and debris into a river and introduced a disequilibrium condition.

Slopes

Material loosened by weathering is susceptible to erosion. However, for material to move downslope, the forces of erosion must overcome other forces: friction, inertia (the resistance to movement), and cohesion among particles. If the angle is steep enough for gravity to overcome frictional forces or if the impact of raindrops or moving animals or even wind dislodges material, then erosion of particles and deposition in a new location downslope can occur.

(text continued on page 352)

A slope, like the recently disturbed slope in GIA 11.1, is an open system that tends toward dynamic equilibrium. If the forces acting on slope materials-shown in GIA 11.2—are balanced, the slope remains stable. If the forces become unbalanced, the slope changes until a new equilibrium is reached. Over time, this equilibrium-seeking process gives slopes a characteristic structure, or "anatomy" (GIA 11.3).

11.1 A Slope in Disequilibrium

Unstable, saturated soils gave way on this hillslope, leaving a debris dam partly blocking the river. The hillslope, river, and forest ecosystem are in disequilibrium as adjustments to new conditions proceed.

The Greys River in the Wyoming Range, western Wyoming

11.2 Forces on a Slope

Directional forces (noted by arrows) act on materials along an inclined slope. If the force promoting motion (gravity, the driving force) exceeds the forces opposing the motion (the resisting force), the slope is destabilized and material moves downhill. A variety of events can destabilize a slope, including heavy rain, a wildfire that destroys protective plant cover, or an earthquake.

Potential energy: Particles on a hillslope have potential energy because of their position.

Exogenic processes

Forces opposing motion: Friction, cohesion of particles, inertia

Weathered materials added to slope

Endogenic processes

Potential energy becomes kinetic energy

Push of surface

Frictional resistance

Weathered materials removed from slope

Movement at geomorphic threshold

Degree of cohesion

Weight of rock

Forces promoting motion: Gravity, aided by endogenic and exogenic events that disturb slope equilibrium

Gravity

Infer: What events or processes could reduce the degree of cohesion of particles on a slope?

Animation MG Mass Movements

http://goo.gl/CWFyUr

MasteringGeography™

Visit the Study Area in MasteringGeography™ to explore slopes and the dynamic equilibrium model.

Visualize: Study a geosciences animation of mass movement.

Assess: Demonstrate understanding of slopes and the dynamic equilibrium model (if assigned by instructor).

11.3 Anatomy of a Slope

Hillslopes typically develop a structure made up of several elements: a convex *waxing slope*, rock outcrop, debris slope, and concave *waning slope*. One main process predominates on each part of a hillslope: physical and chemical weathering on the upper slope, transportation on the debris slope, and deposition on the lower, waning slope.

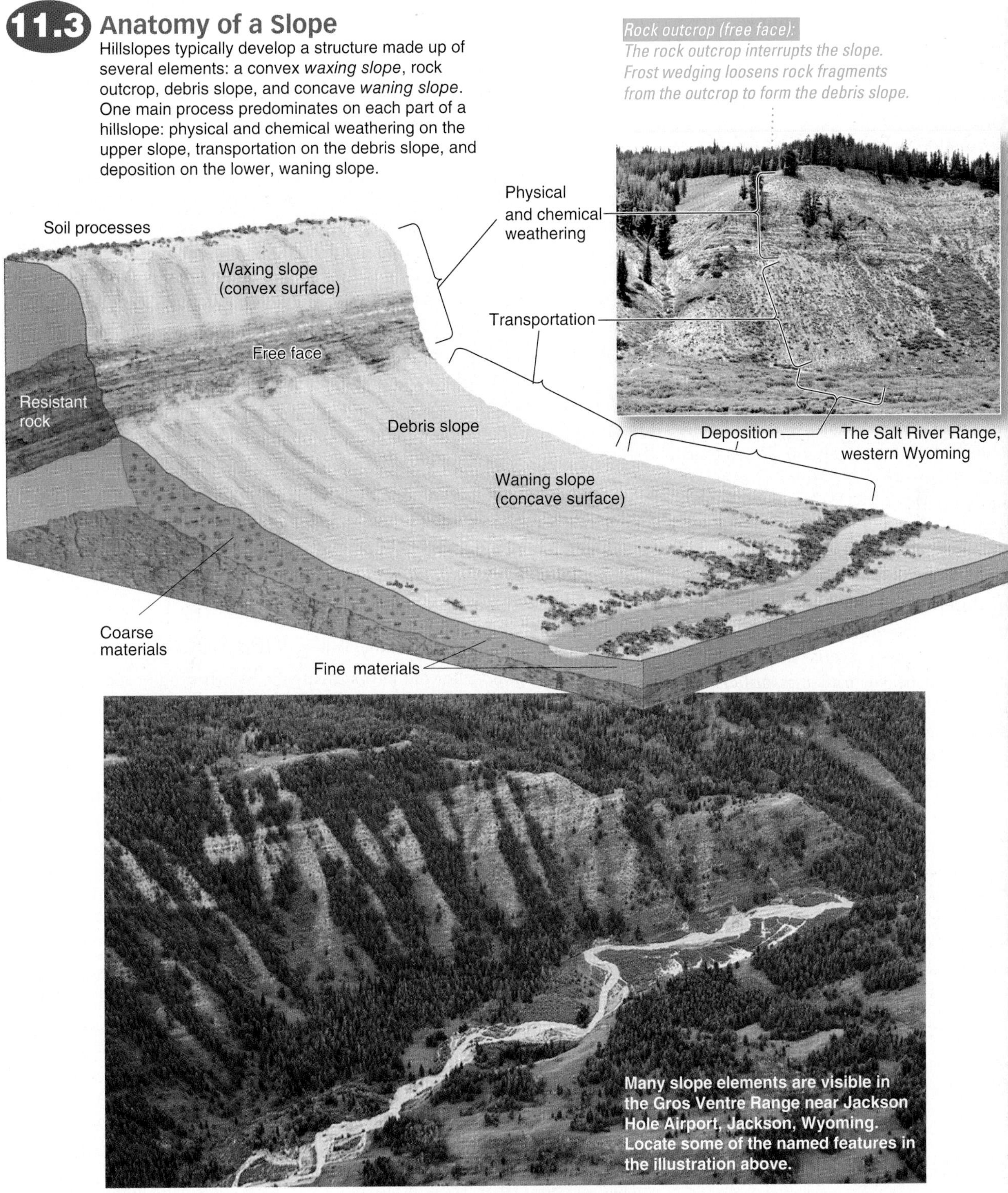

Many slope elements are visible in the Gros Ventre Range near Jackson Hole Airport, Jackson, Wyoming. Locate some of the named features in the illustration above.

Predict: What will eventually happen to the coarse materials on the debris slope?

GEOquiz

1. Explain: Explain how an exogenic event results in a rock particle's movement down a hillslope. Refer to the forces and energy types shown in GIA 11.2 in your answer.

2. Apply concepts: Is the slope in GIA 11.3 at its angle of equilibrium? Explain your answer, referring to specific parts of the slope and the processes that affect them.

Slopes, or *hillslopes*, are curved, inclined surfaces that form the boundaries of landforms. The basic components of a slope, illustrated in Geosystems in Action 11, vary with conditions of rock structure and climate. Slopes generally feature an upper *waxing slope* near the top (*waxing* means increasing). This convex surface curves downward and may grade into a *free face* below, a steep scarp or cliff whose presence indicates an outcrop of resistant rock.

Downslope from the free face is a *debris slope*, which receives rock fragments and materials from above. The condition of a debris slope reflects the local climate. In humid climates, continually moving water carries material away, lowering the angle of the debris slope. But in arid climates, debris slopes accumulate material. A debris slope grades into a *waning slope*, a concave surface along the base of the slope. You can identify these slope components and conditions on the actual hillslope shown in Figure GIA 11.3.

Slopes are open systems and seek an *angle of equilibrium* among the forces described here. Conflicting forces work simultaneously on slopes to establish a compromise incline that balances these forces optimally. When any condition in the balance is altered, all forces on the slope compensate by adjusting to a new dynamic equilibrium.

In summary, the rates of weathering and breakup of slope materials, coupled with the rates of mass movement and material erosion, determine the shape and stability of the slope. A slope is *stable* if its strength exceeds these denudation processes and *unstable* if its materials are weaker than these processes. Why are hillslopes shaped in certain ways? How does slope anatomy evolve? How do hillslopes behave during rapid, moderate, or slow uplift? These are topics of active scientific study and research.

CRITICAL**thinking** 11.1

Find a Slope; Apply the Concepts

Locate a slope, possibly near campus, your home, or exposed in a local road cut. Using GIA 11, can you identify the different parts of the hillslope? What forces act on the hillslope, and what is the evidence of their activity? How would you go about assessing the stability of the slope? Do you see evidence of slope instability near your campus or the region in which you are located—perhaps at a construction site or other disturbed area?

Weathering Processes

Weathering is the process that breaks down rock at Earth's surface and slightly below, either disintegrating rocks into mineral particles or dissolving it into water. Weathering weakens surface rock, making it more susceptible to the pull of gravity. Weathering processes are both physical (mechanical), such as the wedging action of frost in the cracks of a rock surface, and chemical, such as the dissolution of minerals into water. The interplay of these two broad types of weathering is complex; in many cases, the suite of processes combines synergistically to produce unique landforms such as Delicate Arch in Figure 11.1.

On a typical hillside, loose surface material such as gravel, sand, clay, or soil overlies consolidated, or solid, **bedrock**. In most areas, the upper surface of bedrock undergoes continual weathering, creating broken-up **regolith**. As regolith continues to weather, or is transported and deposited, the loose surface material that results becomes the basis for soil development (**Figure 11.3**). In some areas, regolith may be missing or undeveloped, exposing an outcrop of unweathered bedrock.

As a result of this process, bedrock is known as the *parent rock* from which weathered regolith and soils develop. Wherever a soil is relatively young, its parent rock is traceable through similarities in composition. For example, in the canyon country of the U.S. Southwest, sediments derive their color and character from the parent rock that is the substance of the cliffs seen in Figure 11.3c. **Parent material** is the consolidated or unconsolidated material from which soils develop, ranging from unconsolidated sediments and weathered rock (the fragments in Figure 11.5) to bedrock (the cliff in Figure 11.3c). We discuss soils in Chapter 15.

Factors Influencing Weathering Processes

A number of factors influence weathering processes.

- **Rock composition and structure (jointing).** The character of the bedrock (hard or soft, soluble or insoluble, broken or unbroken) and its mineral composition (different minerals weather at different rates) influence the rate of weathering. **Joints** are fractures or separations in rock that occur without displacement of the rock on either side (in contrast with faulting). Jointing increases the surface area of rock exposed to both physical and chemical weathering.
- **Climate (precipitation and temperature).** Wetter, warmer environments speed up chemical weathering processes; colder environments have freeze–thaw cycles that cause physical weathering. Rocks that weather rapidly in warm, humid climates may be resistant to weathering in dry climates (an example is limestone).
- **Slope orientation.** Whether a slope faces north, south, east, or west controls the slope's exposure to Sun, wind, and precipitation. Slopes facing away from the Sun's rays tend to be cooler, moister, and more vegetated than are slopes in direct sunlight. This effect of orientation is especially noticeable in the middle and higher latitudes.
- **Subsurface water.** The position of the water table and water movement within soil and rock structures influence weathering.

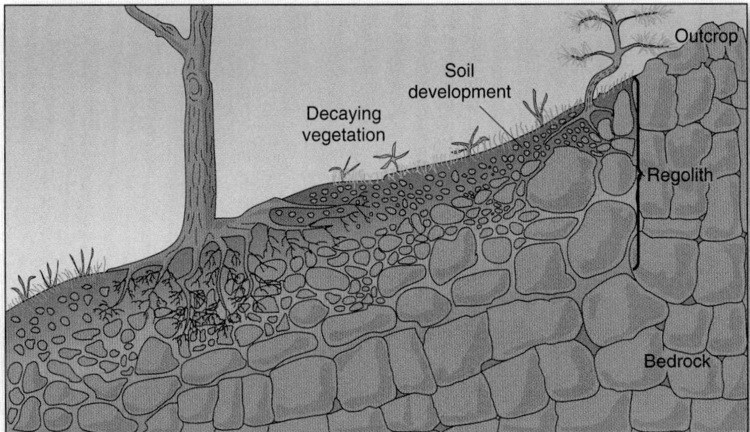

(a) A cross section of a typical hillside.

(b) A cliff exposes hillside components.

(c) Reddish-colored dunes in the Navajo Tribal Park, near the Utah–Arizona border, derive their color from the red-sandstone parent materials in the background.

▲**Figure 11.3 Regolith, soil, and parent materials.** [(b) and (c) Robert Christopherson.]

- **Vegetation.** Although vegetative cover can protect rock by shielding it from raindrop impact and providing roots to stabilize soil, it also produces organic acids, from the partial decay of organic matter, that contribute to chemical weathering. Moreover, plant roots can enter crevices and mechanically break up a rock, exerting enough pressure to force rock segments apart, thereby exposing greater surface area to other weathering processes (**Figure 11.4**). You may have observed how tree roots can heave the sections of a sidewalk or driveway sufficiently to raise and crack concrete.

Weathering processes occur on micro- as well as macroscopic scales. In particular, research at *microscale* levels reveals a more complex relationship between climate and weathering than previously thought. At the small scale of actual reaction sites on the rock surface, both physical and chemical weathering processes can occur over a wide range of climate types. At this scale, soil moisture (hygroscopic water and capillary water) activates chemical weathering processes even in the driest landscape. (Review the types of soil moisture in Figure 6.8.) Similarly, the role of bacteria in weathering is an important new area of research, with these organisms potentially affecting physical processes as they colonize rock surfaces and chemical processes as they metabolize certain minerals and secrete acids.

Keep in mind that, in the complexity of nature, all these factors influencing weathering rates are operating in concert and that physical and chemical weathering processes usually operate together. *Time* is the final critical factor affecting weathering, for these processes require long periods. Usually, the longer the duration of exposure for a particular surface, the more it will be weathered.

Animation (MG) Physical Weathering

http://goo.gl/9qHlwK

▼**Figure 11.4 Physical weathering by tree roots.** [Bobbé Christopherson.]

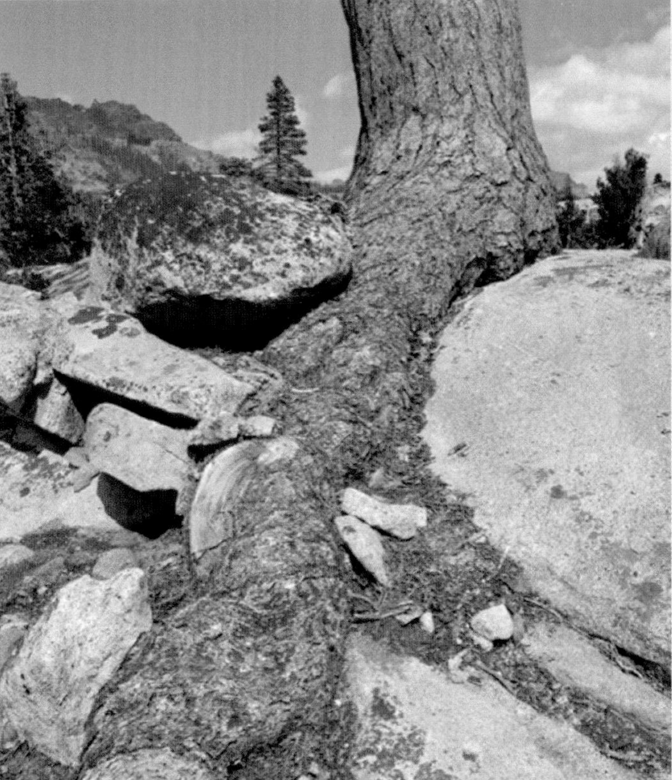

Physical Weathering Processes

Physical weathering, or *mechanical weathering*, is the disintegration of rock without any chemical alteration. By breaking up rock, physical weathering produces more surface area on which all weathering may operate. For example, breaking a single stone into eight pieces exposes double the surface area susceptible to weathering processes. Physical weathering occurs primarily by frost wedging, salt-crystal growth, and exfoliation.

Frost Wedging When water freezes, its volume expands as much as 9% (see Chapter 5). This expansion produces a powerful mechanical force that can overcome the tensional strength of rock. Repeated freezing (expanding) and thawing (contracting) of water is *frost action*, or *freeze–thaw*, which breaks rocks apart in the process of **frost wedging** (Figure 11.5).

The work of ice begins in small openings along existing joints and fractures, gradually expanding them and cracking or splitting the rock in varied shapes, depending on the rock structure. Sometimes frost wedging results in blocks of rock, or *joint-block separation* (Figure 11.6).

Frost wedging is an important weathering process in the humid microthermal climates (*humid continental* and *subarctic*) and the polar climates and in the highland climates at high elevations in mountains worldwide. At high latitudes, frost action is important in soils affected by permafrost (discussed in further detail in Chapters 14 and 15).

As winter ends and temperatures warm in mountainous terrain, the falling of rocks from cliff faces occurs more frequently. The rising temperatures that melt the winter's ice cause newly fractured pieces to fall without warning and sometimes start rockslides. Many such incidents are reported in the European Alps, and they appear to be on the increase. The falling rock pieces shatter on impact—another form of physical weathering (look ahead to Figure 11.20).

▼**Figure 11.5 Physical weathering by frost wedging.** Ice expansion in freeze–thaw activity broke this marble (a metamorphic rock) apart. [Bobbé Christopherson.]

(a) Physical weathering along joints in sandstone produces discrete blocks in Canyonlands National Park, Utah. Note the differential weathering, as the softer supporting rock underneath the slabs has already weathered and eroded.

(b) Joint-block separation in slate at Alkenhornet, Isfjord, on Spitsbergen Island in the Arctic Ocean, where freezing is intense.

▲**Figure 11.6 Physical weathering along joints.** [(a) Robert Christopherson. (b) Bobbé Christopherson.]

Salt-Crystal Growth (Salt Weathering) Especially in arid climates where heating is intense, evaporation draws moisture to the surface of rocks, leaving behind previously dissolved minerals in the form of crystals (the process of crystallization). Over time, as the crystals accumulate and grow, they exert a force great enough to separate the grains making up the rock and begin breaking the rock to pieces, a process known as *salt-crystal growth*, or *salt weathering*.

In many areas of the U.S. Southwest, groundwater that meets an impermeable rock layer, such as shale, within sandstone rock strata will flow laterally until it emerges at a surface. The water then evaporates and leaves salt crystals that loosen the sand grains within the rock. Subsequent erosion of the grains by water and wind complete the sculpting process, forming alcoves at the base of sandstone cliffs. More than 1000 years ago, Native Americans built entire villages in these weathered niches, as in Mesa Verde in Colorado and Arizona's Canyon de Chelly (pronounced "canyon duh shay"; Figure 11.7).

◀Figure 11.7 Physical weathering in sandstone. [(a) Bobbé Christopherson.]

(a) Ancient cliff dwelling in a niche formed partially by salt weathering, Canyon de Chelly, Arizona. The dark streaks on the cliff are thin coatings of desert varnish, composed of manganese that is taken up and metabolized by microbes transformed into oxide minerals.

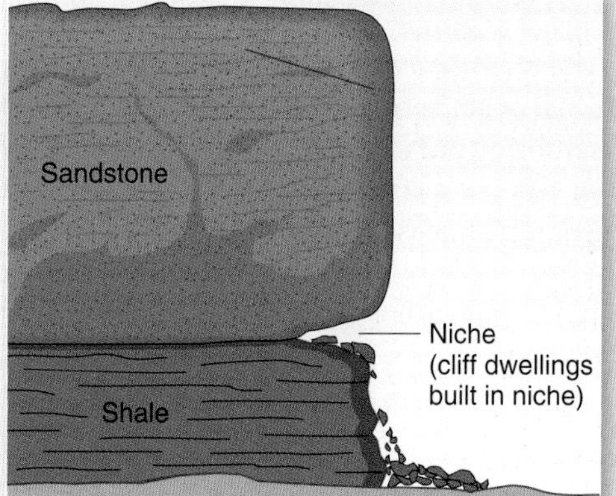

(b) Water and an impervious rock layer helped concentrate weathering processes in a niche in the overlying sandstone.

Exfoliation The process whereby rock peels or slips off in sheets instead of breaking up into grains is **exfoliation**, a term that generally refers to the removal or shedding of an outer layer. This process is also known as *sheeting*. Exfoliation creates arch-shaped and dome-shaped features on the exposed landscape. These *exfoliation domes* are probably the largest weathering features, in areal extent, on Earth (**Figure 11.8**).

Exfoliation is thought to occur as pressure is released from the removal of overlying rock. Recall from Chapter 9 how magma that rises into the crust and then remains deeply buried under high pressure forms intrusive igneous rocks called plutons. These plutons cool

▼Figure 11.8 Exfoliation in granite. Exfoliation loosens slabs of rock, freeing them for further weathering and downslope movement. [(a) Bobbé Christopherson. (b) Robert Christopherson.]

(a) Exfoliated granite, White Mountains, New Hampshire.

(b) Exfoliation forms characteristic granite domes such as Half Dome in Yosemite, California.

slowly into coarse-grained, crystalline, granitic rocks that may then be uplifted and subjected to weathering and erosion. As the tremendous weight of overlying material is removed from a granite pluton, the pressure of deep burial is relieved. Over millions of years, the granite slowly responds with an enormous physical heave, initiating a process known as *pressure-release jointing*, in which the rock cracks into joints. Exfoliation is the mechanical weathering that separates the joints into layers resembling curved slabs or plates, often thinner at the top of the rock structure and thicker at the sides. Recent research suggests that exfoliation may also result from the force of gravity working a curved surface, creating tension beneath a dome that augments pressure-release processes.

Chemical Weathering Processes

Chemical weathering refers to the chemical breakdown, always in the presence of water, of the constituent minerals in rock. The chemical decomposition and decay become more intense as both temperature and precipitation increase. Although individual minerals vary in susceptibility, all rock-forming minerals are responsive to some degree of chemical weathering. An example of chemical weathering is the eating away of cathedral façades and the etching of tombstones by acid precipitation. In Europe, where increasingly acidic rains resulted from the burning of coal, chemical weathering processes are visible on many buildings. (see GeoReport 11.1).

Spheroidal weathering is chemical weathering that softens and rounds the sharp edges and corners of jointed rock (thus the name *spheroidal*) as water penetrates the joints and dissolves weaker minerals or cementing materials (**Figure 11.9**). A boulder can be attacked from all sides by such weathering, shedding spherical shells of decayed rock like the layers of an onion. Spheroidal weathering of rock resembles exfoliation, but it does not result from pressure-release jointing.

Hydration and Hydrolysis Chemical decomposition of rock by water can result from the simple combination of water with a mineral, in the process of *hydration*, and from the chemical reaction of water with a mineral, in the process of *hydrolysis*. **Hydration**, meaning "combination with water," involves little chemical change (it does not form new chemical compounds) but does involve a change in structure. Water becomes part of the chemical composition of the mineral, forming a hydrate. One such hydrate is gypsum, which is hydrous calcium sulfate ($CaSO_4 \cdot 2H_2O$).

When some minerals undergo hydration, they expand, creating a strong mechanical wedging effect that stresses the rock, forcing grains apart in a physical weathering process. A cycle of hydration and dehydration can lead to granular disintegration and further susceptibility of the rock to chemical weathering. Hydration also works with other processes to convert feldspar, a common mineral in many rocks, into clay minerals. The hydration process is also at work on the sandstone niches shown in Figure 11.7.

Hydrolysis is the decomposition of a chemical compound by reaction with water. In geomorphology, hydrolysis is of interest as a process that breaks down silicate minerals in rocks. In contrast with hydration, in which water merely combines with minerals in the rock, hydrolysis chemically breaks down a mineral, thereby producing a different mineral through the chemical reaction.

For example, the weathering of feldspar minerals in granite can occur by reaction with the normal mild acids dissolved in precipitation:

feldspar (K, Al, Si, O) + carbonic acid and water →
residual clays + dissolved minerals + silica

The products of chemical weathering of feldspar in granite include clay (such as kaolinite) and silica. The particles of quartz (silica, or SiO_2) formed in this process are resistant to further chemical breakdown and may wash downstream, eventually becoming sand on some distant beach. Clay minerals become a major component in soil and in shale, a common sedimentary rock.

(a) Chemical weathering processes act on the joints in granite to dissolve weaker minerals, leading to a rounding of the edges of the cracks in the Alabama Hills. Mount Whitney is visible on the crest of the Sierra Nevada in the background.

(b) Rounded granite outcrop demonstrates spheroidal weathering and the disintegration of rock. The surface is actually crumbly.

◀**Figure 11.9 Spheroidal weathering, a chemical process.** [Bobbé Christopherson.]

When minerals in rock are changed by hydrolysis, the interlocking crystal network consolidating the rock breaks down, and *granular disintegration* takes place. Such disintegration in granite may make the rock appear corroded and even crumbly (Figure 11.9b).

Oxidation Another type of chemical weathering occurs when certain metallic elements combine with oxygen to form oxides. This process is known as **oxidation**. Perhaps the most familiar oxidation is the "rusting" of iron to produce iron oxide (Fe_2O_3). You see the result of this oxidation after leaving a tool or nails outside, only to find them, weeks later, coated with a crumbly reddish-brown substance. Its rusty color is visible on the surfaces of rock and in heavily oxidized soils such as those in the humid southeastern United States, the arid U.S. Southwest, and the tropics. Here is a simple oxidation reaction in iron:

iron (Fe) + oxygen (O_2) → iron oxide (hematite; Fe_2O_3)

When oxidation reactions remove iron from the minerals in a rock, the disruption of the crystal structures makes the rock more susceptible to further chemical weathering and disintegration.

Dissolution of Carbonates Chemical weathering also occurs when a mineral dissolves into solution—for example, when sodium chloride (common table salt) dissolves in water. Remember, water is called the universal solvent because it is capable of dissolving at least 57 of the natural elements and many of their compounds.

Water vapor readily dissolves carbon dioxide, thereby yielding precipitation containing carbonic acid (H_2CO_3). This acid is strong enough to dissolve many minerals, especially limestone, by a **carbonation** reaction. This type of chemical weathering breaks down minerals that contain calcium, magnesium, potassium, or sodium. When rainwater attacks formations of limestone (mainly calcium carbonate, $CaCO_3$), the constituent minerals dissolve and wash away with the mildly acidic rainwater:

calcium carbonate + carbonic acid and water →
calcium bicarbonate ($Ca_2^{2+}CO_2H_2O$)

The dissolution of marble, a metamorphic form of limestone, is apparent on tombstones in many cemeteries (**Figure 11.10**). In environments where adequate water is available for dissolution, weathered limestone and marble take on a pitted and worn appearance. Acid precipitation also enhances carbonation processes (see Focus Study 2.1, Acid Deposition: Damaging to Ecosystems).

▲**Figure 11.10 Dissolution of limestone.** A marble tombstone is chemically weathered beyond recognition in a Scottish churchyard. Marble is a metamorphic form of limestone. Readable dates on surrounding tombstones suggest that this one is about 228 years old. [Bobbé Christopherson.]

Karst Topography

In certain areas of the world with extensive limestone formations, chemical weathering involving dissolution of carbonates dominates entire landscapes (**Figure 11.11**). These areas are characterized by pitted, bumpy surface topography, poor surface drainage, and well-developed *solution channels* (dissolved openings and conduits) underground. In landscapes of this type, weathering and erosion caused by groundwater may result in remarkable mazes of underworld caverns.

These are the hallmark features and landforms of **karst topography**, named for the Krš Plateau in Slovenia (formerly Yugoslavia), where karst processes were first studied. Approximately 15% of Earth's land area has some karst features, with outstanding examples found in southern China, Japan, Puerto Rico, Jamaica, the Yucatán of Mexico, Kentucky, Indiana, New Mexico, and Florida.

GEOreport 11.1 Weathering on bridges in Central Park, NYC

In New York City's Central Park, 36 bridges are built out of various rock types from sources across the U.S. Northeast and Canada. For more than 140 years, physical and chemical processes have weathered these bridges. As air pollution from the burning of fossil fuels has increased, acidity in rain and snow has hastened weathering rates, a problem compounded by the use in winter of salt on the roads crossing the bridges. Decorative design elements on the bridges are now disappearing as weathering tears at the surface rock. Some heavily weathered sandstone blocks have had to be replaced by cast concrete.

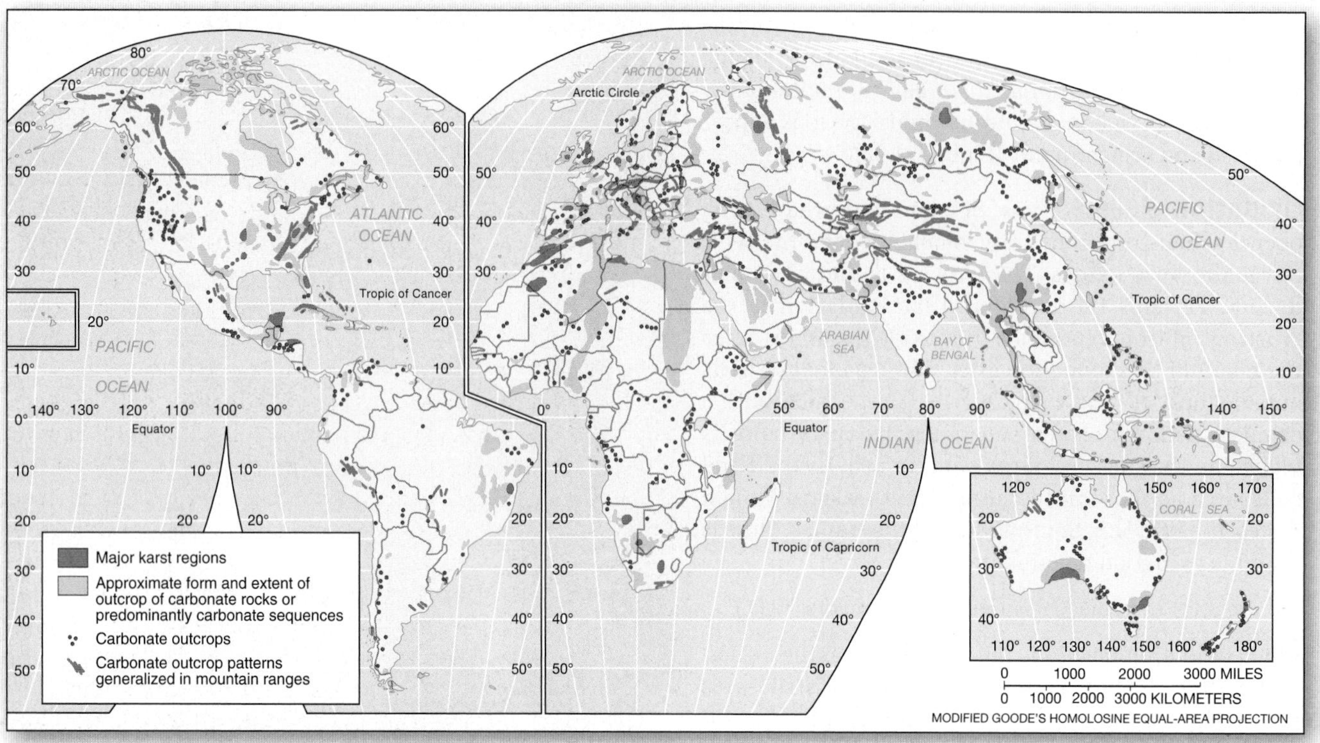

▲**Figure 11.11 Karst landscapes and limestone regions.** Major karst regions exist on every continent except Antarctica. The outcrops of carbonate rocks or predominantly carbonate sequences are limestone and dolomite (calcium magnesium carbonate), but may contain other carbonate rocks. [Map adapted by Pam Schaus, after USGS sources, and D. C. Ford and P. Williams, *Karst Geomorphology and Hydrology*, p. 601. © 1989 by Kluwer Academic Publishers. Adapted by permission.]

MapMaster: World Physical Environment: Karst Landscapes

Formation of Karst

For a limestone landscape to develop into karst topography, several conditions are necessary:

- The limestone formation must contain 80% or more calcium carbonate for dissolution processes to proceed effectively.
- Complex patterns of joints in the otherwise impermeable limestone are needed for water to form routes to subsurface drainage channels.
- An aerated (air-containing) zone must exist between the ground surface and the water table.
- Vegetation cover is needed to supply varying amounts of organic acids that enhance the dissolution process.

The role of climate in providing optimum conditions for karst processes remains under debate, although the amount and distribution of rainfall appear important. The karst features found today in arid regions were formed during past climatic conditions of greater humidity. Karst is rare in the Arctic and Antarctic regions because subsurface water, although present there, is generally frozen.

As with all weathering processes, time is an important factor. Early in the 20th century, scientists proposed that karst landscapes progress through identifiable stages of development, from youth to old age. Evidence has not supported this idea, and today karst landscapes are thought to be locally unique, a result of site-specific conditions. Nonetheless, mature karst landscapes display certain characteristic forms.

Features of Karst Landscapes

Several landforms are typical of karst landscapes. Each form results to some extent from the interaction among surface weathering processes, underground water movement, and processes occurring in subterranean cave networks, described just ahead.

Sinkholes The weathering by dissolution of limestone landscapes creates **sinkholes**, or *dolines*, which are circular depressions in the ground surface that may reach 600 m (2000 ft) in depth. Two types of sinkholes are most prominent in karst terrain. A *solution sinkhole* forms by the slow subsidence of surface materials along joints or at an intersection between joints. These sinkholes typically have depths of 2–100 m (7–330 ft) and diameters of 10–1000 m (33–3300 ft; **Figure 11.12**).

A *collapse sinkhole* develops over a period of hours or days and forms when a solution sinkhole collapses through the roof of an underground cavern (**Figures 11.13** and 11.17). These sinkholes can have dramatic features, not all of which are associated with karst processes. Human activities cause many of these sinkhole subsidence events, as described in GeoReport 11.2.

Karst Valleys Through continuing dissolution and collapse, sinkholes may coalesce to form a *karst valley*—an elongated depression up to several kilometers long. Such a valley may have bogs or ponds in sinkhole depressions and unusual drainage patterns. Surface streams may even

◄**Figure 11.12 Buraco das Araras, a solution sinkhole near Goiás, Brazil.** [Guilherme de Carvalho/Moment Open/Getty Images.]

dive underground to join the subterranean water flow typical of karst landscapes; these "disappearing" streams may join subsurface flows by way of joints or holes linking to cavern systems or may flow directly into caves.

The area southwest of Orleans, Indiana, shown in **Figure 11.14** has an average of 1022 sinkholes per 2.6 km^2 (1 mi^2). In this area, the Lost River, a disappearing stream, flows from the surface into more than 13 km (8 mi) of underground solution channels before it resurfaces in a spring, or "rise." A topographic map of this karst region is on the *MasteringGeography* website.

◄**Figure 11.13 Collapse sinkhole in limestone landscape.** Collapse of this sinkhole near Frederick, Maryland, in 2003 was likely made worse by runoff from the highway (note the storm drain pipe under the highway in the photo). [Randall Orndorff/USGS.]

Tropical Karst In tropical climates, karst topography includes two characteristic landforms—cockpits and cones—with prominent examples found in the Caribbean region (Puerto Rico, Jamaica) and southeast Asia (China, Vietnam, and Thailand). Weathering in these wet climates, where thick beds of limestone are deeply jointed (exposing a large surface area for dissolution processes), forms a complex topography called *cockpit karst*, resembling the shape of an egg-carton (**Figure 11.15**). The "cockpits" are steep-sided, star-shaped hollows in the landscape with water draining by percolation from the bottom of the cockpit to the underground water flow. Sinkholes may form in the cockpit bottoms, and according to some theories, solution sinkhole collapse is an important cause of cockpit karst topography.

Dissolution weathering in the tropics also leaves isolated resistant limestone blocks that form cones known as *tower karst*. These resistant cones and towers are most remarkable in several areas of China, where towers up to 200 m (660 ft) high interrupt an otherwise flat, low-elevation plain (**Figure 11.16**).

Caves and Caverns

Caves are defined as natural underground areas large enough for humans to enter. Caves form in limestone because it is so easily dissolved by carbonation; any large cave formed by chemical processes is a *cavern*. The largest limestone caverns in the United States are Mammoth Cave in Kentucky (also the longest surveyed cave in the world at 560 km, or 350 mi), Carlsbad Caverns in New Mexico, and Lehman Cave in Nevada.

Carlsbad Caverns are in 200-million-year-old limestone formations deposited when shallow seas covered the area. Regional uplifts associated with the building of the Rockies (the Laramide orogeny, 40–80 million years ago) elevated the region above sea level, subsequently leading to active cave formation.

Caves generally form just beneath the water table, where later lowering of the water level exposes them to

GEOreport 11.2 Sinkholes caused by human activities

Along Bushkill Creek, downstream from the Hercules mining quarry enterprise, several dozen sinkholes have collapsed since 2000, taking down a bridge from State Route 33 and threatening neighborhoods in Stockertown, Northampton County, Pennsylvania. Sinkhole development correlated with groundwater pumping at the nearby quarry, which lowered water tables. In Chicago in 2013, a sinkhole opened in the middle of a street, swallowing three cars. A burst water main caused the collapse, which led to only minor injuries. (See the *MasteringGeography* website for other examples of sinkhole collapse from groundwater removal.)

▲**Figure 11.14 Features of karst topography.** [(map) Mitchell, Indiana quadrangle, USGS. (b) and (c) Bobbé Christopherson.]

further development (**Figure 11.17**). As discussed in Chapter 8, speleothems are formations consisting of mineral deposits inside caves and occur in various characteristic shapes (look back to Figure 8.10). *Dripstones* are speleothems formed as water containing dissolved minerals slowly drips from the cave ceiling. Calcium carbonate precipitates out of the evaporating solution, literally one molecular layer at a time, and accumulates on a spot below on the cave floor. Thus, dripstones are depositional features—*stalactites* growing from the ceiling and *stalagmites* building from the floor. For more on caves and their related formations, see http://www.goodearthgraphics.com/virtcave/virtcave.html.

Speleology is the exploration and scientific study of caves. Scientists and explorers estimate that some 90% of caves worldwide still lie undiscovered; in addition, more than 90% of known caves have not been biologically surveyed, making this a major research frontier.

Mass-Movement Processes

In the South American country of Colombia, Nevado del Ruiz is the northernmost of two dozen dormant (not extinct, sometimes active) volcanic peaks in the Cordillera Central. This volcano erupted six times during the past 3000 years, killing 1000 people during its eruption in 1845. On November 13, 1985, at 11 P.M., after a year of earthquakes and harmonic tremors (seismic energy releases associated with volcanoes), a growing bulge on its northeast flank, and months of small summit

◀**Figure 11.15 Deep-space research using cockpit karst topography.** Cockpit karst topography near Arecibo, Puerto Rico, is the setting for Earth's largest radio telescope. The discoloration of the dish does not affect telescope reception. The suspended movable receivers where the signals focus are 168 m (550 ft) above the dish. [Bobbé Christopherson; (inset) Cornell University.]

▲**Figure 11.16 Tower karst, Li River valley, China.** [Keren Su/Terra/Corbis.]

eruptions, Nevado del Ruiz violently erupted in a lateral explosion and triggered a mudflow down its slopes toward the sleeping city and villages below.

The mudflow was a mixture of liquefied mud and volcanic ash that developed as the hot eruption melted ice on the mountain's snowy peak. This *lahar*, an Indonesian word referring to mudflows of volcanic origin, moved rapidly down the Lagunilla River toward the villages below. The wall of mud was at least 40 m (130 ft) high as it approached Armero, a regional center with a population of 25,000. The lahar buried the sleeping city: 23,000 people were killed; thousands were injured; 60,000 were left homeless across the region. The debris flow generated by the 1980 eruption of Mount St. Helens was also a lahar.

Landslides are another type of mass movement that poses a major hazard, killing 8000 people on average every year worldwide, with about 12 fatalities each year in the United States. For current information on global landslide activity, see the American Geophysical Union's landslide blog at http://blogs.agu.org/landslideblog/.

Mass-Movement Mechanics

Mass movement, or **mass wasting**, is the downslope movement of a body of material made up of soil, sediment, or rock propelled by the force of gravity. Mass movements can occur on land, or they can occur beneath the ocean as submarine landslides. The term **landslide** refers to any sudden rapid movement of a cohesive mass of soil, regolith, or bedrock. In a landslide, a large amount of material—either saturated or unsaturated—fails simultaneously. Surprise creates the danger, for the downward pull of gravity wins the struggle for equilibrium in an instant.

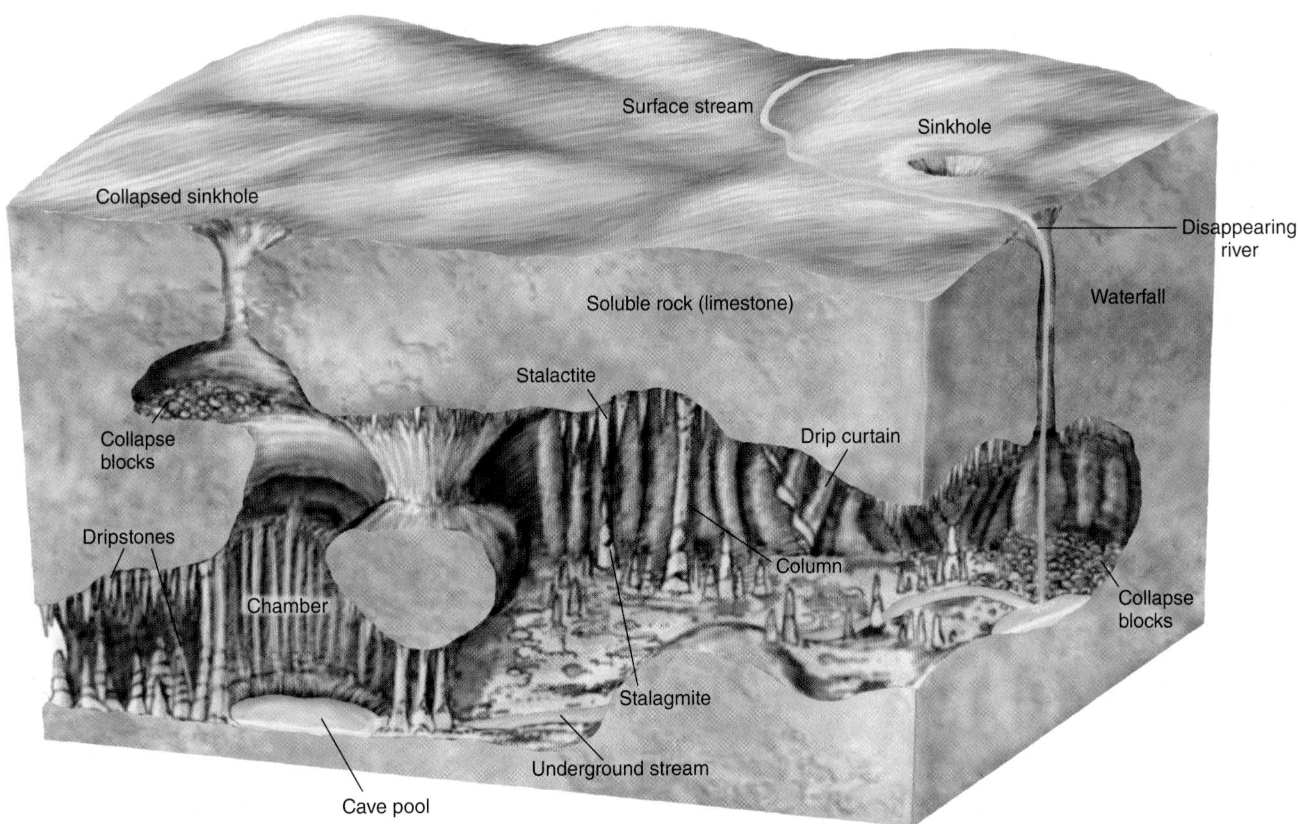

▲**Figure 11.17 An underground cavern and related forms in limestone.** A column is created when stalactites from the ceiling and stalagmites from the floor connect.

To eliminate the surprise element, scientists are using the Global Positioning System (GPS) to monitor landslide movement. With GPS, scientists measure slight land shifts in vulnerable areas for clues to an impending danger of mass wasting. At two sites in Japan, GPS effectively identified pre-landslide movements of 2–5 cm per year, providing information to expand the area of hazard concern and warning.

Slope Angle and Forces All mass movements occur on slopes under the influence of gravitational stress. If we pile dry sand on a beach, the grains will flow downslope until equilibrium is achieved. The steepness of the resulting slope, called the *angle of repose*, depends on the size and texture of the grains. This angle represents a balance of the driving force (gravity) and the resisting force (friction and shear). The angle of repose for various materials ranges between 33° and 37° (from horizontal) and between 30° and 50° for snow avalanche slopes.

As noted, the *driving force* in mass movement is gravity. It works in conjunction with the weight, size, and shape of the surface material; the degree to which the slope is oversteepened (how far it exceeds the angle of repose); and the amount and form of moisture available (frozen or fluid). The greater the slope angle, the more susceptible the surface material is to mass-wasting processes.

The *resisting force* is the shear strength of the slope material—that is, its cohesiveness and internal friction, which work against gravity and mass wasting. To reduce shear strength is to increase shear stress, which eventually reaches the point at which gravity overcomes friction, initiating slope failure.

Conditions for Slope Failure Several conditions can lead to the slope failure that causes mass movement. Failure can occur when a slope becomes saturated by a heavy rainfall; when a slope becomes oversteepened (40° to 60° slope angle), such as when river or ocean waves erode the base; when a volcanic eruption melts snow and ice, as happened on Nevado del Ruiz and Mount St. Helens; or when an earthquake shakes debris loose or fractures the rock that stabilizes an oversteepened slope.

Water content is an important factor for slope stability; an increase in water content may cause rock or regolith to begin to flow. Clay surfaces are highly susceptible to hydration (physical swelling in response to the presence of water). When clay surfaces are wet, they deform slowly in the direction of movement; when saturated, they form a viscous fluid that fails easily with overlying weight. The 1995 La Conchita mudslide in California (seen ahead in Figure 11.19a) occurred during an unusually wet year. The same slope failed again in 2005, after a 2-week period of near-record rainfall.

The shocks and vibrations associated with earthquakes often cause mass movement, as happened in the Madison River Canyon near West Yellowstone, Montana. Around midnight on August 17, 1959, an M 7.5 earthquake broke a dolomite (a type of limestone) block along the foot of a deeply weathered and oversteepened slope (the white area in **Figure 11.18**), releasing 32 million m^3 (1.13 billion ft^3) of mountainside. The material moved downslope at 95 kmph (60 mph), causing gale-force winds through the canyon. Momentum carried the material more than 120 m (about 400 ft) up the opposite side of the canyon, trapping several

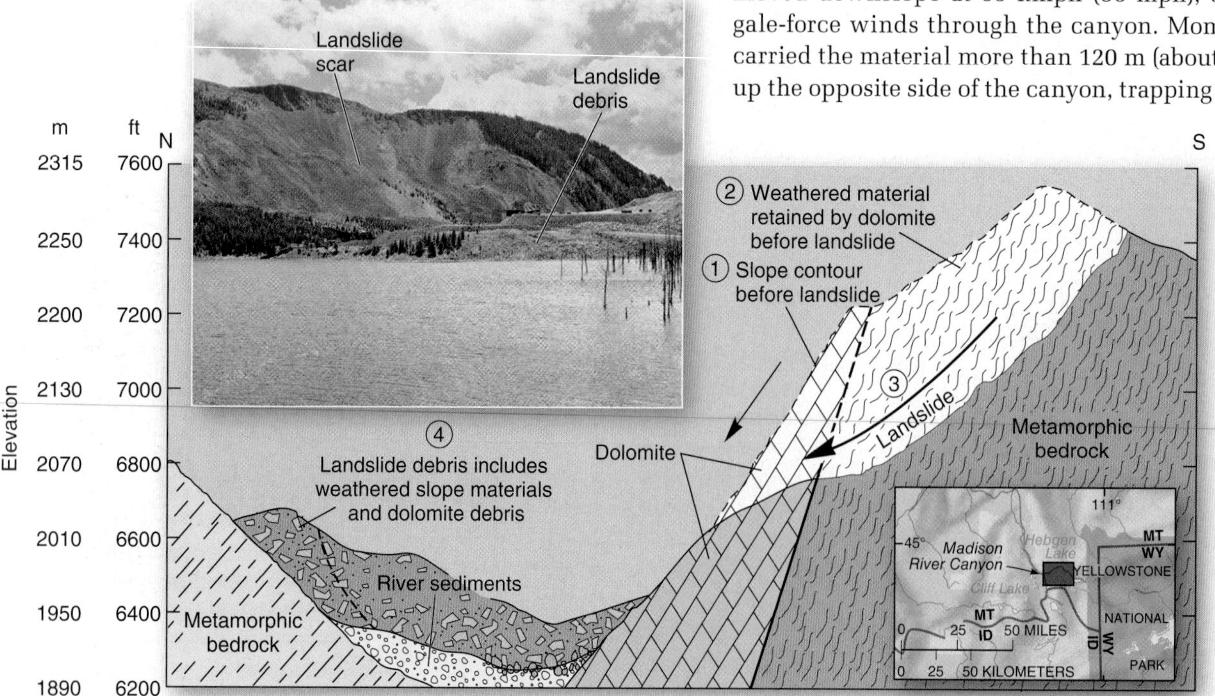

▲Figure 11.18 Madison River landslide. Cross section showing geologic structure of the Madison River Canyon in Montana, where an earthquake triggered a landslide in 1959. Numbers indicate (1) pre-landslide topography; (2) area of weathered rock that moved during the slide; (3) direction of landslide; and (4) landslide debris that dammed the Madison River, visible in the inset photo. [USGS Professional Paper 435-K, August 1959, p. 115. (inset photo) Bobbé Christopherson.]

hundred campers with about 80 m (260 ft) of rock and killing 28 people.

The mass of material that dammed the Madison River as a result of this event created a new lake, dubbed Quake Lake. To prevent overflow and associated erosion and flooding downstream, the U.S. Army Corps of Engineers excavated a channel through which the lake could drain.

The M 8.0 earthquake in the Sichuan Province of China in 2008 caused thousands of landslides throughout the region, many of which created dams on rivers and earthquake lakes. At the largest of these landslide dams on the Qianjiang River, channel dredging successfully prevented overtopping, which can lead to dam failure and associated downstream flooding. In 2010 in northern Pakistan, a massive landslide dammed the Hunza River. In this case, dredging was impossible due to muddy conditions at the site. The dam survived repeated overtoppings; then, in 2012, a spillway was blasted to reduce the water level of the lake.

Classes of Mass Movements

In any mass movement, gravity pulls on a mass of material until the critical shear-failure point is reached—a geomorphic threshold. The material then can *fall*, *slide*, *flow*, or *creep*—the four classes of mass movement. These classes range in volume of material (small to massive), moisture content (dry to wet), and rate of movement (rapid free-falling rock to slow-moving creep). **Figure 11.19** displays the specific types of mass movement discussed ahead according to the moisture and speed categories.

Rockfalls and Debris Avalanches Rockfalls and debris avalanches are types of mass movement that occur at faster rates and in materials that have little to intermediate water content. A **rockfall** is simply a volume of rock that falls through the air and hits a surface (**Figure 11.20**). During a rockfall, individual pieces fall independently and characteristically form piles of irregular broken rocks called *talus*. These cone-shaped piles, known

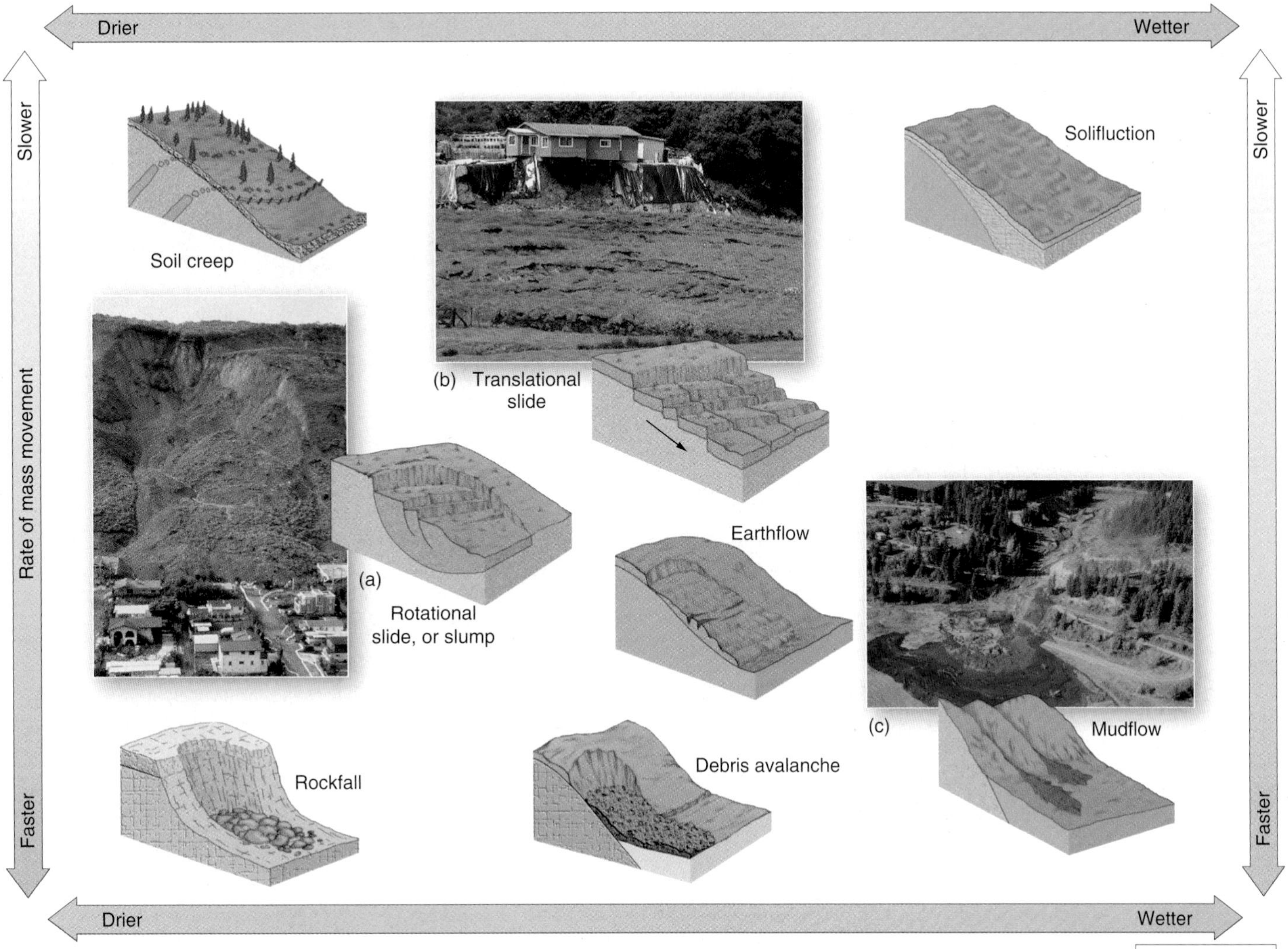

▲Figure 11.19 Mass-movement classification. Principal types of mass movement produced by variations in water content and rates of movement. (a) A 1995 slide in La Conchita, California, also the site of a 2005 mudslide event. (b) Saturated hillsides fail, Santa Cruz County, California. (c) A 1998 mudflow buried part of a railroad track and highway near Bonner's Ferry in northern Idaho. [(a) Robert L. Schuster/USGS. (b) Alexander Lowry/Science Source. (c) D. Krammer/Disaster Services Boundary County, Idaho/NOAA/NGDC.]

Animation Mass Movements

http://goo.gl/CWFyUr

▲**Figure 11.20 Rockfall.** Shattered rock debris from a large rockfall in Rockville, Utah, in February 2010 damaged outbuildings and part of a home. The largest boulder (red arrow) measures about 6.4 m (21 ft) in length and weighed an estimated 450 tons. Note the lighter color of the freshly exposed rocks and the person for scale (white arrow). [Utah Geological Survey.]

as talus cones, often coalesce in a *talus slope* at the base of a steep incline (**Figure 11.21**).

A **debris avalanche** is a mass of falling and tumbling rock, debris, and soil traveling at high velocity owing to the presence of ice and water that fluidize the debris. The extreme danger of a debris avalanche results from its tremendous speed. In 1962 and again in 1970, debris avalanches roared down the west face of Nevado Huascarán, the highest peak in the Peruvian Andes. An earthquake initiated the 1970 event, in which upward of 100 million m^3 (3.53 billion ft^3) of debris traveling at 300 kmph (185 mph) buried the city of Yungay, killing 18,000 people.

Slides There are two basic forms of slides: translational or rotational (see Figure 11.19 for a photo and idealized view of each). *Translational slides* involve movement along a planar (flat) surface roughly parallel to the angle of the slope, with no rotation. The Madison Canyon landslide described earlier was a translational slide. Flow and creep patterns also are considered translational in nature.

Rotational slides, also called *slumps*, occur when surface material moves along a concave surface. Frequently, underlying clay presents an impervious barrier to percolating water. As a result, water flows along the clay's surface, undermining the overlying block. The overlying material may rotate as a single unit, or it may acquire a stepped appearance. Continuing rotational mudslides in response to heavy rainfall plague La Conchita, California (Figure 11.19a). In 1995, a slump landslide buried homes there, and in January 2005, a mudslide episode following a period of heavy rains buried 30 homes and took 10 lives.

In October 2007, a rotational slump occurred in La Jolla, California, damaging more than 100 homes along Soledad Mountain Road. The area is inherently unstable, having experienced three other collapse events since 1961. The 2007 slide is attributed to unrestricted irrigation of lawns and gardens, feeding drainage runoff water into subsurface strata and, as a result, increasing instability and lubricating slides.

One of the worst landslide and dam disasters in history occurred in 1963 at Vaiont Canyon in Italy. A large landslide into a reservoir caused water to overtop Vaiont Dam, producing a 69-m (226-ft) wave of water that killed 3000 people in a town downstream (read more about this event on the *MasteringGeography* website).

On May 5, 2014, a large landslide in northeastern Afghanistan buried 700 homes in the village of Abi Barak, causing hundreds of fatalities (**Figure 11.22**). The cause of the slide, which also had characteristics of a mudflow, was prolonged heavy rainfall occurring on loess soils, which are prone to failure when saturated (see the discussion in Chapter 15).

▲**Figure 11.21 Talus slope.** Rockfall and talus deposits at the base of a steep slope along Duve Fjord, Nordaustlandet Island. Can you see the lighter rock strata above that are the source for the three talus cones? [Bobbé Christopherson.]

GEOreport 11.3 Rockfalls in Yosemite

Records indicate that in the past 150 years, at least 600 rockfalls have occurred in Yosemite Valley, located in the Sierra Nevada of California. In July 1996, a 162,000-ton granite slab dropped 670 m at 260 kmph (2200 ft at 160 mph), felling more than 500 trees before pulverizing into a light dust that covered 50 acres. In 2006, a large rockfall occurred on Half Dome (see Figure 11.8b). A National Park Service (NPS) map of rockfalls from 1857 to 2011 is at http://www.nps.gov/yose/nature-science/rockfall.htm. Note from the NPS map that winter and spring events dominate the record, although large rockfalls can occur during the warmer months as well.

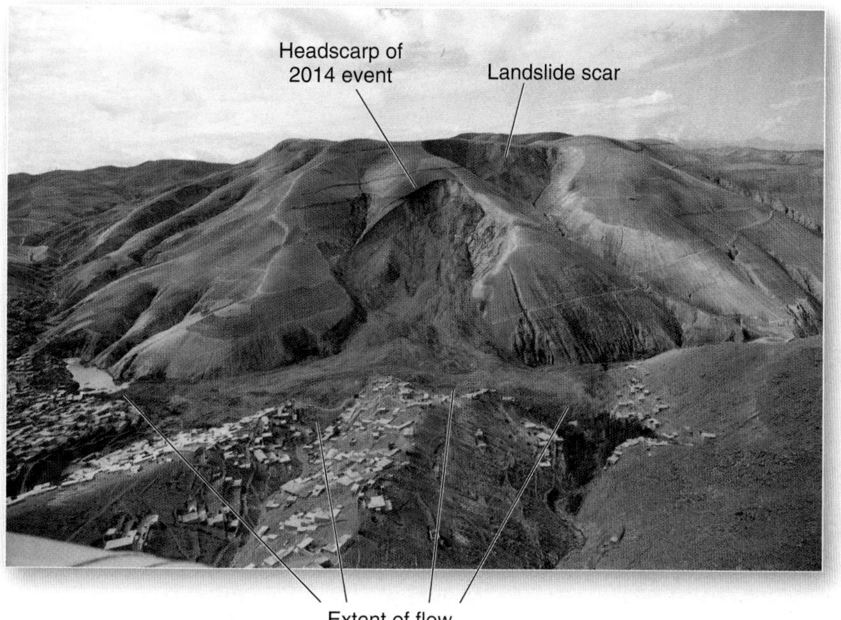

◀**Figure 11.22 Landslide in northeast Afghanistan, May 2014.** The landslide occurred after prolonged heavy rainfall saturated the fine-grained loess soils (discussed in Chapter 15) typical of this region. Note the scar from a previous landslide on the upper hillslope. [Rahmat Gul/AP Images.]

Flows When the moisture content of moving material is high, the suffix *-flow* is used, as in *earthflows* and more fluid **mudflows**. Heavy rains can saturate barren mountain slopes and set them moving, as was the case in the Gros Ventre River valley east of Jackson Hole, Wyoming, in the spring of 1925. About 37 million m^3 (1.3 billion ft^3) of wet soil and rock moved down one side of the canyon and surged 30 m (100 ft) up the other side, damming the river and forming a lake. The water content of this mass-wasting event was great enough to classify it as a flow. It originated when sandstone formations resting on weak shale and siltstone became moistened and soft and then eventually failed with the weight of the overlying strata. In 1925, equipment was not available to excavate a channel to drain the water collecting behind the earthflow dam. Two years later the water broke through, transporting a tremendous quantity of debris over the region downstream.

The Oso, Washington, mass movement event described in Geosystems Now had characteristics of both a slide and a flow (see the chapter-opening photo). Near the top of the hillslope, the remaining materials resemble a rotational slide that broke free as a single unit. Toward the bottom, the landscape shows the signs of a mudflow—a fast-moving slurry of mud, rock, and water.

Creep A persistent, gradual mass movement of surface soil is **soil creep**. In creep, individual soil particles are lifted and disturbed, whether by the expansion of soil moisture as it freezes, by cycles of moistness and dryness, by diurnal temperature variations, or by grazing livestock or digging animals.

In the freeze–thaw cycle, particles are lifted at right angles to the slope by freezing soil moisture, as shown in **Figure 11.23**. When the ice melts, however, the

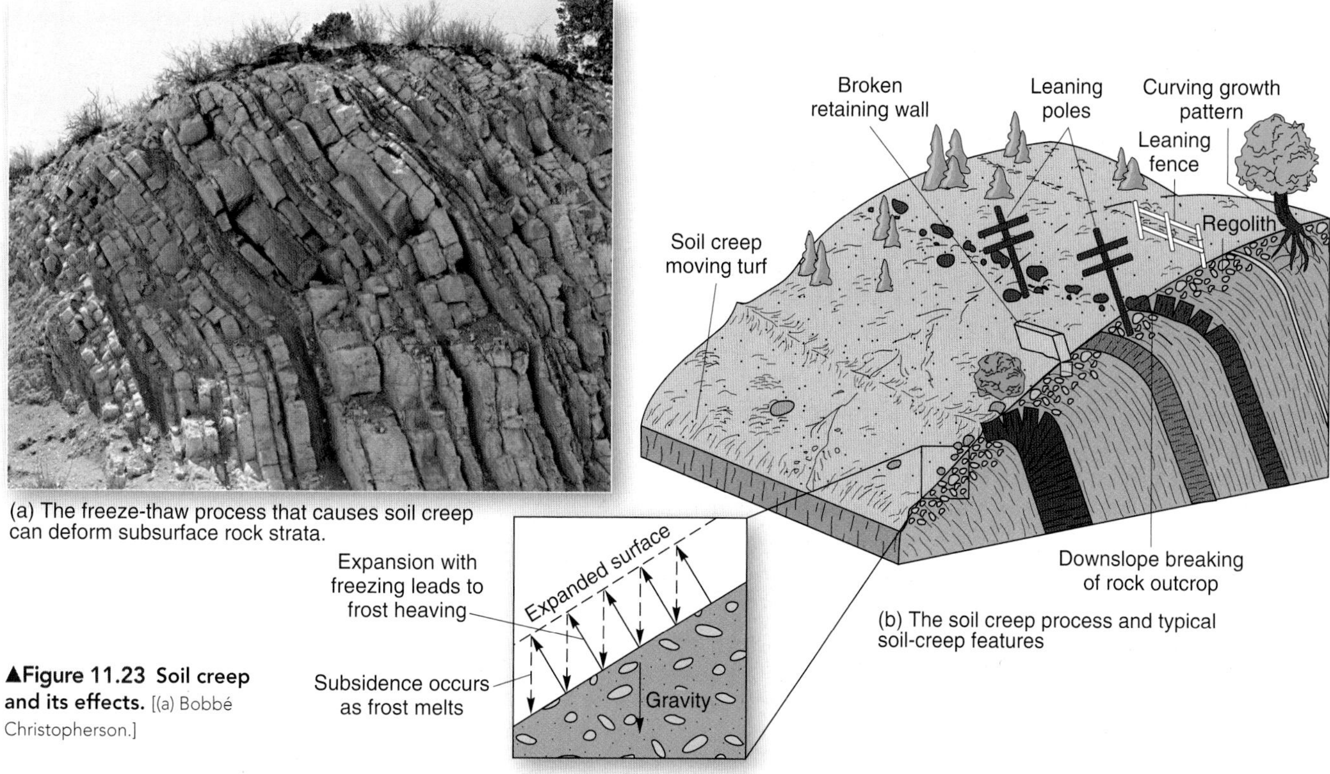

(a) The freeze-thaw process that causes soil creep can deform subsurface rock strata.

(b) The soil creep process and typical soil-creep features

▲**Figure 11.23 Soil creep and its effects.** [(a) Bobbé Christopherson.]

focusstudy 11.1 Natural Hazards

Human-Caused Mass Movement at the Kingston Steam Plant, Tennessee

Located near the town of Kingston in eastern Tennessee, the Kingston Steam Plant (KSP) is a coal-fired power plant that burns 14,000 tons of pulverized coal a day. Built by the Tennessee Valley Authority (TVA) in the 1950s to provide power for the atomic energy installations at nearby Oak Ridge, this plant has nine generating units capable of producing 1400 MW of electricity by heating water in a boiler to produce steam, which then moves turbines for power production. The plant burns a low-sulfur blend of coal, with smoke as a by-product. Before the exhaust smoke leaves the 305-m (1000-ft) smokestacks, fly ash is extracted from it (to reduce air pollution), fluidized with water, and moved as slurry to ash ponds (**Figure 11.1.1a**). In these ponds,

▲**Figure 11.1.1 Before and after the TVA ash slurry spill disaster.** (a) The Emory River enters from the north and flows around the dredge cells, main ash pond, and stilling pond, all of which are on the river floodplain. The power plant itself is off the photo's lower edge. (b) On December 23, the day after the spill, the extent of the contaminated wastage is clearly visible. [Courtesy of TVA.]

particles fall straight downward in response to gravity. As the process repeats, the surface soil gradually creeps its way downslope.

The overall wasting of a creeping slope may cover a wide area and may cause fence posts, utility poles, and even trees to lean downslope. Various strategies are used to arrest the mass movement of slope material—grading the terrain, building terraces and retaining walls, planting ground cover—but the persistence of creep often renders these strategies ineffective.

In polar regions and at high elevations, freeze–thaw processes are a key factor in mass wasting. During the summer when the upper layers of soil thaw and become saturated, slow downslope movement occurs, called *solifluction* (shown in Figure 11.19 and discussed with periglacial environments in Chapter 14).

CRITICAL**thinking 11.2**

Compare Two Mass-Movement Events

Compare the chapter-opening photo of the Oso landslide with the photo of the 2014 Afghanistan landslide in Figure 11.22, and review the descriptions of each mass-movement event. What factors contributed to instability on each slope? How are these landslides similar? How are they different?

Humans as a Geomorphic Agent

Any human disturbance of a slope—highway road cutting, surface mining, or construction of a shopping mall, housing development, or home—can hasten mass wasting.

the solids settle and are gradually collected in dredge holding cells constructed along the Emory River floodplain.

Embankments surrounding the dredge cells (labeled in the aerial photo) consisted originally of clay and later were built up with materials derived from the ash-waste product, without the benefit of engineering design specifications. As more waste ash was added, the walls eventually rose to 18 m (59 ft) in height. Over the years, published reports mentioned seepage and leaking at the site.

Containment Pond Failure

During the first three weeks of December 2008, above-normal rainfall of more than 16 cm (6.5 in.) fell throughout Roane County, Tennessee, and the surrounding region, saturating soils and sediments. In the early morning hours of December 22, the entire northwest corner and sides of the ash-pond embankment failed, triggering a mass-wasting event that released fly-ash slurry onto the landscape, destroying homes and infrastructure (Figure 11.1.1b). The volume of the spill was equal to 1.1 billion gallons, or about 6 times the total amount of the 2010 *Deepwater Horizon* oil spill in the Gulf of Mexico. Worse, the slurry contained harmful metals and other pollutants, such as arsenic, copper, barium, cadmium, chromium, lead, mercury, nickel, and thallium. These contaminants pose a significant risk for wildlife and human health, especially when found in high concentrations.

Massive in force and extent, the wave of slow-moving sludge and polluted water snapped tree trunks and knocked several nearby houses off their foundations. Toxic ash was found on the bed of the Emory River more than 9.6 km (6 mi) from the spill.

Cleanup and Recovery

Almost a year after the disaster, the TVA had removed about two-thirds of the ash in the Emory River, moving it by train to a landfill in Alabama. The next cleanup phase—in which the TVA began to permanently store on-site all of the ash released into the embayment, thus reducing the hazards of transport—was completed in 2010. The final phase, to be completed in 2015, includes ash excavation from the embayment to an on-site landfill and restoration of the aquatic and riparian ecosystems, with a total cost over $1.1 billion.

The Tennessee Department of Environment and Conservation (TDEC) later criticized the TVA Kingston plant in a 2009 "lessons learned" report, citing critical structural stability deficiencies in the dredge cells. Worsening the problem was the lack of oversight as the years passed and the embankments grew in size.

This human-caused mass-movement event illustrates the hazards of ignoring scientific and engineering principles, in both natural and human-modified environments. In 2010, a similar event occurred in western Hungary when a retaining wall around a toxic holding pond broke at an aluminum oxide plant, sending a torrent of chemical waste over land and into waterways (see **http://www.npr.org/blogs/thetwo-way/2010/10/05/130351938/red-sludge-from-hungarian-aluminum-plant-spill-an-ecological-disaster**).

In 2014, leaks from ash ponds and spills from slurry lines occurred at coal-fired power plants in North Carolina and West Virginia. These events illustrate the environmental problems with aging coal power facilities and the methods used to store waste; improved planning, regulation, and oversight is clearly needed.

1. After the Kingston spill, what forces of erosion dispersed the pollutants across the landscape? (Think of the exogenic processes mentioned in this chapter, such as rivers, wind, and waves.) How fast and in which direction might they have moved?
2. The concept of "externalities" can be applied to pollution and environmental damage that occurs beyond the boundaries of corporate property and is sometimes considered outside of corporate financial responsibility. What kind of externalities occurred with the Kingston event, and who is responsible for the related costs?

Large open-pit surface mines—such as the Bingham Canyon Copper Mine west of Salt Lake City; the abandoned Berkeley Pit in Butte, Montana; several iron mines in the Brazilian rain forest; and numerous large coal surface mines in the eastern and western United States (such as Black Mesa, Arizona)—are examples of human impacts that move sediment, soil, and rock material, a process known as **scarification**.

At the Bingham Canyon Copper Mine, a mountain literally was removed since mining began in 1906, forming a pit 4 km wide and 1.2 km deep, or 2.5 mi wide and 0.75 mi deep. This is easily the largest human-made excavation on Earth. In April 2013, a large landslide occurred within the open pit on an unstable slope that was being closely monitored for safety reasons (**Figure 11.24a**). No fatalities occurred.

The disposal of tailings (mined ore of little value) and waste material is a significant problem at any mine. Such large excavations produce tailing piles that are unstable and susceptible to further weathering, mass wasting, or wind dispersal. Additionally, the leaching of toxic materials from tailings and waste piles poses an ever-increasing problem for streams, aquifers, and public health across the country.

Where underground mining is common, particularly for coal in the Appalachians, land subsidence and collapse may produce mass movement on hillslopes. Homes, highways, streams, wells, and property values are severely affected. A controversial form of mining called *mountaintop removal* is done by removing ridges and summits and dumping the debris into stream valleys, thereby exposing the coal seams for mining, but burying the stream

(a) Large 2013 landslide within Bingham Canyon Mine outside Salt Lake City, Utah.

(b) Mountaintop removal on Kayford Mountain, West Virginia.

◀Figure 11.24 Scarification. [(a) Ravell Call/Deseret News/AP Images. (b) Dr. Chris Mayda, Eastern Michigan University, all rights reserved.]

channels as a consequence. Mountaintop removal on Kayford Mountain, West Virginia, and elsewhere in the region has flattened more than 500 mountains, removing an estimated 1.2 million acres and filling some 2000 km (1245 mi) of streams with tailings (**Figure 11.24b**). These valley fills affect downstream water quality with concentrations of potentially toxic nickel, lead, cadmium, iron, and selenium that generally exceed government standards.

In areas where humans have disturbed the landscape, mass movement may occur more frequently than in natural environments, with disastrous consequences. Focus Study 11.1 describes a catastrophic displacement of soil and sediment that occurred in 2008 at the containment ponds of the Kingston coal-fired power plant in Tennessee. This single event, in which the embankment of a fly-ash holding pond was breached, released 4.13 million m^3 (5.4 million yd^3) of toxic ash laced with an array of potentially harmful pollutants into the Emory River and over the surrounding area.

Scientists have made informal, but impressive, quantitative comparisons between scarification and natural denudation processes. Geologist R. L. Hooke used estimates of U.S. excavations for new housing, mineral production (including the three largest types—stone, sand and gravel, and coal), and highway construction. He then prorated these quantities of moved earth for all countries, based on their gross domestic product, energy consumption, and agriculture's effect on river sediment loads. From these, he calculated a global estimate for human earth moving. Later researchers confirmed and expanded on these findings.

Hooke estimated for the early 1990s that humans, as a geomorphic agent, annually moved 40–45 Gt, or 40–45 billion tons, of the planet's surface. Compare this quantity with the material moved by natural processes, such as 14 Gt/year of river sediment, or 1.25 Gt/year of wave action and erosion along coastlines, or 7 Gt/year of deep-ocean sedimentation. In 2005, geologist Bruce Wilkinson corroborated these measurements, concluding that humans are 10 times more active in shaping the landscape than are Earth's natural processes.

VISUALanalysis 11 Processes at Work on a Sandstone Cathedral

Saint Magnus Cathedral, in Kirkwell, Scotland, built almost 9 centuries ago, today shows signs of wear as the sandstone features appear out-of-focus. [Bobbé Christopherson.]

1. What type of exogenic processes have caused the sandstone to "melt" over this long period of time?
2. Do local atmospheric conditions (such as weather or pollution) play a role in these processes?

GEOMORPHIC PROCESSES IMPACT HUMANS

- Chemical weathering processes break down carvings made by humans in rock, as on tombstones, cathedral facades, and bridges.
- Sudden sinkhole formation in populated areas can cause damage and human casualties.
- Mass movements cause human casualties and sometimes catastrophic damage, burying cities, damming rivers, and sending flood waves downstream.

HUMANS IMPACT GEOMORPHIC PROCESSES

- Mining causes scarification, often moving contaminated sediments into surface water systems and groundwater.
- Removal of vegetation on hillslopes may lead to slope failure, destabilizing streams and associated ecosystems.
- Lowering of water tables from groundwater pumping causes sinkhole collapse in population centers.

11a

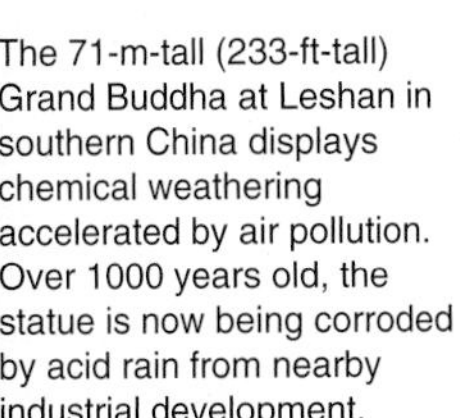

The 71-m-tall (233-ft-tall) Grand Buddha at Leshan in southern China displays chemical weathering accelerated by air pollution. Over 1000 years old, the statue is now being corroded by acid rain from nearby industrial development.

11c

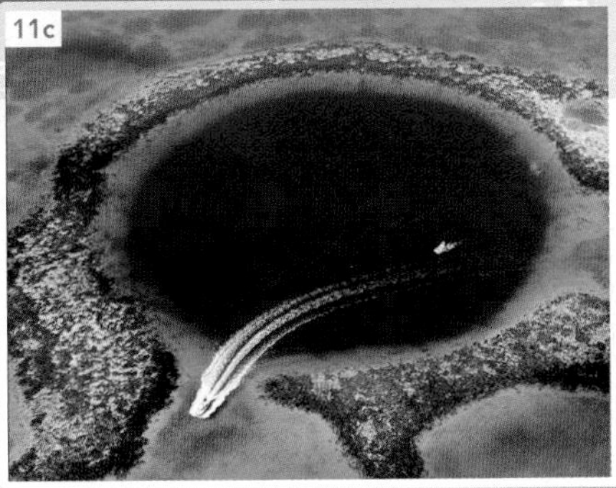

Blue holes are typical karst sinkholes. Lying offshore today, they formed on land during times when sea level was lower. The Great Blue Hole near Belize is in the Belize Barrier Reef Reserve System, a United Nations World Heritage site.

11b

In April 2010, a massive translational landslide covered parts of a highway near Taipei, Taiwan. The cause is uncertain but apparently not related to earthquake activity or excessive rainfall.

ISSUES FOR THE 21ST CENTURY

- Global climate change will affect forest health; declining forests (from disease or drought) will increase slope instability and mass-movement events.
- Open-pit mining worldwide will continue to move massive amounts of Earth materials, with associated impacts on ecosystems and water quality.
- Failures of containment ponds holding industrial by-products will spread toxic materials onto landscapes and into downstream areas.

KEYLEARNINGconceptsreview

Describe the dynamic equilibrium approach to the study of landforms and *illustrate* the forces at work on materials residing on a slope.

Geomorphology is the science that analyzes and describes the origin, evolution, form, and spatial distribution of landforms. Earth's exogenic system, powered by solar energy and gravity, tears down the landscape through processes of landmass **denudation** involving weathering, mass movement, erosion, transportation, and deposition. Different rocks offer differing resistance to these weathering processes and produce a pattern on the landscape of **differential weathering**.

Agents of change include moving air, water, waves, and ice. Since the 1960s, research and understanding of the processes of denudation have moved toward the **dynamic equilibrium model**, which considers slope and landform stability to be consequences of the resistance of rock materials to the attack of denudation processes. When a destabilizing event occurs, a landform or landform system may reach a **geomorphic threshold**, where force overcomes resistance and the system moves to a new level and toward a new equilibrium state.

Slopes are shaped by the relation between the rate of weathering and breakup of slope materials and the rate of mass movement and erosion of those materials. Slopes that form the boundaries of landforms have several general components: *waxing slope, free face, debris slope*, and *waning slope*. Slopes seek an *angle of equilibrium* among the operating forces.

denudation (p. 348)
differential weathering (p. 348)
dynamic equilibrium model (p. 349)
geomorphic threshold (p. 349)
slope (p. 352)

1. Define landmass denudation. What processes are included in the concept?
2. What is the interplay between the resistance of rock structures and differential weathering?
3. Describe what is at work to produce the landform in Figure 11.1.
4. What are the principal considerations in the dynamic equilibrium model?
5. Describe conditions on a hillslope that is right at the geomorphic threshold. What factors might push the slope beyond this point?
6. Given all the interacting variables, do you think a landscape ever reaches a stable, old-age condition? Explain.
7. What are the general components of an idealized slope?
8. Relative to slopes, what is meant by an *angle of equilibrium*? Can you apply this concept to the photograph in Figure GIA 11.3?

Define weathering and *explain* the importance of parent rock and joints and fractures in rock.

Weathering processes disintegrate both surface and subsurface rock into mineral particles or dissolve them in water. On a typical hillside, loose surface material overlies consolidated, or solid, rock called **bedrock**. In most areas, the upper surface of bedrock undergoes continual weathering, creating broken-up rock called **regolith**. The unconsolidated, fragmented material that is carried across landscapes by erosion, transportation, and deposition is sediment, which along with weathered rock forms the **parent material** from which soil evolves.

Important in weathering processes are **joints**, the fractures and separations in the rock. Jointing opens up rock surfaces on which weathering processes operate. Factors that influence weathering include the character of the bedrock (hard or soft, soluble or insoluble, broken or unbroken), climatic elements (temperature, precipitation, freeze–thaw cycles), position of the water table, slope orientation, surface vegetation and its subsurface roots, and time.

weathering (p. 352)
bedrock (p. 352)
regolith (p. 352)
parent material (p. 352)
joint (p. 352)

9. Describe weathering processes operating on an open expanse of bedrock. How does regolith develop? How is sediment derived?
10. Describe the relationship between climate and weathering at microscale levels.
11. What is the relationship between parent rock, parent material, regolith, and soil?
12. What role do joints play in the weathering process? Give an example from this chapter.

Describe the physical weathering processes of frost wedging, salt-crystal growth, and pressure-release jointing.

Physical weathering, or mechanical weathering, refers to the breakup of rock into smaller pieces with no alteration of mineral identity. The physical action of water when it freezes (expands) and thaws (contracts) causes rock to break apart in the process of **frost wedging**. Working in joints, expanded ice can produce *joint-block separation* through this process. Another physical weathering process is *salt-crystal growth* (*salt weathering*); as crystals in rock grow and enlarge over time by crystallization, they force apart mineral grains and break up rock.

Removal of overburden from a granitic batholith relieves the pressure of deep burial, producing joints. **Exfoliation**, or *sheeting*, occurs as mechanical forces enlarge the joints, separating the rock into layers of curved slabs or plates (rather than granular disintegration that occurs with many weathering processes). The resulting arch-shaped or dome-shaped feature is an *exfoliation dome*.

physical weathering (p. 354)
frost wedging (p. 354)
exfoliation (p. 355)

13. What is physical weathering? Give an example.
14. Why is freezing water such an effective physical weathering agent?
15. What weathering processes produce a granite dome? Describe the sequence of events.

Explain the chemical weathering processes of hydration, hydrolysis, oxidation, carbonation, and dissolution.

Chemical weathering is the chemical decomposition of minerals in rock. It can cause **spheroidal weathering**, in which chemical weathering that occurs in cracks in the rock removes cementing and binding materials, so that the sharp edges and corners of rock disintegrate and become rounded. **Hydration** occurs when a mineral absorbs water and expands, thus changing the mineral structure. This process also creates a strong mechanical (physical weathering) force that stresses rocks. **Hydrolysis** breaks down silicate minerals in rock through reaction with water, as in the chemical weathering of feldspar into clays and silica. **Oxidation** is a chemical weathering process in which oxygen reacts with certain metallic elements, the most familiar example being the rusting of iron to produce iron oxide. The *dissolution* of materials into solution is also considered chemical weathering. An important type of dissolution is **carbonation**, resulting when carbonic acid in rainwater reacts to break down certain minerals, such as those containing calcium, magnesium, potassium, or sodium.

chemical weathering (p. 356)
spheroidal weathering (p. 356)
hydration (p. 356)
hydrolysis (p. 356)
oxidation (p. 357)
carbonation (p. 357)

16. What is chemical weathering? Contrast this set of processes to physical weathering.
17. What is meant by the term *spheroidal weathering*? How does spheroidal weathering occur?
18. What is hydration? What is hydrolysis? Differentiate between these processes. How do they affect rocks?
19. Iron minerals in rock are susceptible to which form of chemical weathering? What characteristic color is associated with this type of weathering?
20. With what kind of minerals does carbonic acid react, and what circumstances bring this type of reaction about? What is this weathering process called?

Review the processes and features associated with karst topography.

Karst topography refers to distinctively pitted and weathered limestone landscapes. **Sinkholes** are circular surface depressions that may be *solution sinkholes* formed by slow subsidence or *collapse sinkholes* formed in a sudden collapse through the roof of an underground cavern below. In tropical climates, karst landforms include *cockpit karst* and *tower karst*. The creation of caverns is a result of karst processes and groundwater erosion. Limestone caves feature many unique erosional and depositional features.

karst topography (p. 357)
sinkhole (p. 358)

21. Describe the development of limestone topography. What is the name applied to such landscapes? From what area was this name derived?
22. Explain and differentiate among the formation of sinkholes, karst valleys, cockpit karst, and tower karst. Which forms are found in the tropics?
23. In general, how would you characterize the region southwest of Orleans, Indiana?
24. What are some of the characteristic erosional and depositional features you find in a limestone cavern?

Categorize the various types of mass movements and *identify* examples of each by moisture content and speed of movement.

Any movement of a body of material, propelled and controlled by gravity, is **mass movement**, or **mass wasting**. **Landslide** is the general term for a large amount of soil, regolith, or bedrock that fails as a unit. The *angle of repose* of loose sediment grains represents a balance of driving and resisting forces on a slope. Mass movement of Earth's surface produces some dramatic incidents, including **rockfalls** (volumes of falling rocks), which can form a *talus slope* of loose rock along the base of the cliff; **debris avalanches** (masses of tumbling, falling rock, debris, and soil moving at high speed); *slides* and *slumps* (large amounts of material failing simultaneously); **mudflows** (material in motion with a high moisture content); and **soil creep** (persistent movement of individual soil particles that are lifted by the expansion of soil moisture as it freezes, by cycles of wetness and dryness, by temperature variations, or by the impact of grazing animals). In addition, human mining and construction activities have created massive **scarification** of landscapes.

mass movement (p. 361)
mass wasting (p. 361)
landslide (p. 361)
rockfall (p. 363)
debris avalanche (p. 364)
mudflow (p. 365)
soil creep (p. 365)
scarification (p. 367)

25. Define the role of slopes in mass movements, using the terms *angle of repose, driving force, resisting force*, and *geomorphic threshold*.
26. What events occurred in the Madison River Canyon in 1959?
27. What are the classes of mass movement? Describe each briefly and differentiate among these classes.
28. Name and describe the type of mudflow associated with a volcanic eruption.
29. Describe the difference between a rotational slide, or slump, and what happened on the slopes of Nevado Huascarán.
30. What is scarification, and how does it relate to mass movement? Give several examples of scarification. Why are humans a significant geomorphic agent?

MasteringGeography™

Looking for additional review and test prep materials? Visit the Study Area in *MasteringGeography*™ to enhance your geographic literacy, spatial reasoning skills, and understanding of this chapter's content by accessing a variety of resources, including **MapMaster** interactive maps, geoscience animations, videos, *In The News* RSS feeds, flashcards, web links, self-study quizzes, and an eText version of *Elemental Geosystems*.

12 River Systems

Five Finger Rapids on the Yukon River in Yukon, Canada, is formed by four basalt islands that divide the river channel into five narrow passages, with only one easily passable. The rapids were a major obstacle to poorly constructed rafts and boats during the Klondike Gold Rush of 1898, claiming many lives. [Bobbé Christopherson.]

KEYLEARNING**concepts**

After reading the chapter, you should be able to:

- ***Sketch*** a basic drainage basin model and ***identify*** different types of drainage patterns by visual examination.
- ***Explain*** the concepts of stream gradient and base level and ***describe*** the relationship between stream velocity, depth, width, and discharge.
- ***Explain*** the processes involved in fluvial erosion and sediment transport.
- ***Describe*** common stream channel patterns and ***explain*** the concept of a graded stream.
- ***Describe*** the depositional landforms associated with floodplains and alluvial fan environments.
- ***List*** and ***describe*** several types of river deltas and ***explain*** flood probability estimates.

Proposed Dams on the Nu River in China

In the United States, the razing of dams and restoration of rivers has become a multibillion dollar industry, discussed in Focus Study 12.1 in this chapter. However, in China the trend is quite different. There, and in certain other countries, dam building and hydropower development continue in order to meet increasing energy demands. In 2013, the Chinese government announced plans to build a series of large dams on the Nu River—Southeast Asia's longest free-flowing watercourse.

The Nu River, known as the Salween in Thailand and Burma, flows from the mountains of Tibet, through the Yunnan Province of southwestern China, and into the Andaman Sea (**Figure GN 12.1**). The river's headwaters lie adjacent to those of the Mekong and Yangtze Rivers within the Three Parallel Rivers World Heritage Site, famed for its biological diversity. The upper watershed is home to people from 13 ethnic groups, many relying on subsistence farming as a way of life (**Figure GN 12.2**).

The Chinese government is proposing to relocate some 60,000 people from these communities to make way for the reservoirs that are part of the hydropower development. In some areas, the relocation has already begun as dam sites are being prepared for construction.

▲**Figure GN 12.2 Locals crossing a suspension bridge spanning the Nu River, Yunnan, China.** [Redlink/Encyclopedia/Corbis.]

Interruptions to Water and Sediment Flows Rivers move both water and sediment, a process that builds fertile soils on valley floors and in the flatlands where rivers meet the sea. Dams interrupt this process, starving downstream areas of sediment and nutrients that naturally replenish farmland in the cycle of annual spring floods. Farmers in the Nu River's lower reaches stand to suffer soil degradation and crop losses if the dams move forward as planned.

Sediment is also critical for maintaining stream habitat as well as coastal wetlands near the river's mouth. When sediment is trapped behind a dam, excessive erosion often results downstream, leading to degradation of banks and the riverbed. Alterations to water and sediment movement also have detrimental effects on fisheries, which are critical food resources for populations in the downstream portions of the river system.

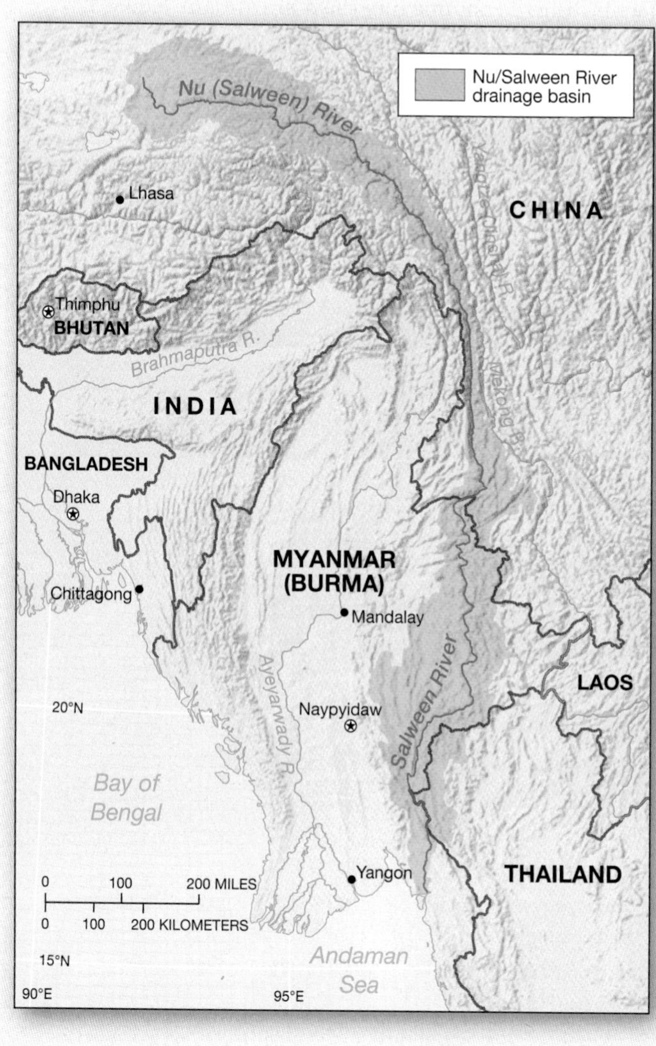

◄**Figure GN 12.1 Map of the Nu/Salween River system, Southeast Asia.**

Induced Seismicity Recently, scientists have warned that reservoirs may be connected to earthquake activity in tectonically active southwest China. Although the idea of *reservoir-induced seismicity* (earthquakes induced by the location of large reservoirs along fault lines) is not new, the proposed dams on the Nu River have prompted scientists to take a fresh look at this phenomenon. The weight of a large reservoir creates pressure that forces water into cracks and fissures in the ground beneath, increasing instability and possibly lubricating fault zones. Seismic events induced by large reservoirs may damage the dams that impound them, increasing the risk of catastrophic flooding in the event of dam failure.

First proposed almost 10 years ago, the Nu River dams were delayed owing to environmental concerns, primary among which were the high numbers of sensitive species in the watershed and the potential earthquake hazard. However, development along the river has been under way since 2006 in preparation for dam construction.

With air quality worsening owing to industrial activity, China must use alternative energy to alleviate air pollution. As power demand increases, the government continues to develop hydropower on its rivers despite the environmental risks. This chapter examines stream and river systems—their natural processes and the role of humans in altering them.

QUESTION AND EXPLORE For a recent study on the impacts of small dams in southwestern China, see http://www.nsf.gov/news/news_summ.jsp?cntn_id=128073.

MG

Earth's rivers and waterways form vast arterial networks that drain the continents, and at any moment, approximately 1250 km^3 (300 mi^3) of water is flowing through them. Even though this volume is only 0.003% of all freshwater, the work performed by this energetic flow makes it a dominant natural agent of landmass denudation. Rivers shape the landscape by removing the products of weathering, mass movement, and erosion and transporting them downstream. Rivers also serve society in many ways. They not only provide us with essential water supplies, but also receive, dilute, and transport wastes; provide critical cooling water for industry; and form critical transportation networks.

Rivers shape the landscape . . . and also serve society in many ways.

Of the world's rivers, those with the greatest *discharge* (the streamflow volume past a point in a given unit of time, discussed in this chapter) are the Amazon of South America, and the Congo of Africa. In North America, the greatest discharges are from the Missouri–Ohio–Mississippi, Saint Lawrence, and Mackenzie River systems (**Table 12.1**).

Remember from Chapter 6 that *hydrology* is the science of water at and below Earth's surface. Processes that are related expressly to streams and rivers are termed **fluvial** (from the Latin *fluvius*, meaning "river"). There is some overlap in usage between the terms *river* and *stream*. Specifically, the term *river* is applied to the trunk or main stream of the network of tributaries forming a *river system*. *Stream* is a more general term for water flowing in a channel and is not necessarily related to size. Fluvial systems, like all natural systems, have characteristic processes and produce recognizable landforms, yet also can behave with randomness and seeming disorder.

In this chapter: We begin by examining the organization of river systems into drainage basins and surveying the types of drainage patterns. With this foundation, we examine gradient, base level, and stream discharge. We then discuss factors that affect flow characteristics and the work performed by flowing water, including erosion and transport. We also examine the effects of urbanization on stream hydrology and the impacts of dams on sediment regimes. Depositional features are illustrated with a detailed look at floodplains and the Mississippi River delta. Finally, we examine floods, floodplain management, and river restoration.

Drainage Basins and Drainage Patterns

Streams, which come together to form river systems, lie within drainage basins, the portions of landscape from which they receive their water. Every stream has its own **drainage basin**, or *watershed*, ranging in size from tiny to vast. A major drainage basin system is made up of many smaller drainage basins, each of which gathers and delivers its runoff and sediment to a larger basin, eventually concentrating the volume into the main stream. **Figure 12.1** illustrates the drainage basin of the Amazon River, from headwaters to the river's mouth (where the river meets the ocean). The Amazon has an average flow greater than 175,000 m^3/s (or cms, cubic meters per second; equivalent to 6.2 million ft^3/s or cfs, cubic feet per second) and moves millions of tons of sediment through the drainage basin, which is as large as the Australian continent.

TABLE 12.1 Largest Rivers on Earth Ranked by Discharge

Rank by Volume	Average Discharge at Mouth in Thousands of m^3/s (ft^3/s)	River (Tributaries)	Outflow (Location)	Length, km (mi)	Rank by Length
1	180 (6350)	Amazon	Atlantic Ocean (Amapá-Pará, Brazil)	6800 (4225)	1*
2	41 (1460)	Congo	Atlantic Ocean (Angola, DR Congo)	4630 (2880)	10
3	34 (1201)	Yangtze or Chàng Jiang	East China Sea (Kiangsu, China)	6300 (3915)	3
4	30 (1060)	Orinoco	Atlantic Ocean (Venezuela)	2737 (1700)	27
5	21.8 (779)	Rio de la Plata	Atlantic Ocean (Argentina)	3945 (2450)	16
6	19.6 (699)	Ganges (Brahmaputra)	Bay of Bengal (India)	2510 (1560)	23
7	19.4 (692)	Yenisey	Gulf of Kara Sea (Siberia)	5870 (3650)	5
8	18.2 (650)	Mississippi (Missouri, Ohio, Tennessee, Jefferson)	Gulf of Mexico (Louisiana)	6020 (3740)	4
9	16.0 (568)	Lena	Laptev Sea (Siberia)	4400 (2730)	11
17	9.7 (348)	St. Lawrence	Gulf of St. Lawrence (Canada and United States)	3060 (1900)	21
36	2.83 (100)	Nile	Mediterranean Sea (Egypt)	6690 (4160)	2*

*Measurement in 2007 places the Amazon first in length, replacing the Nile as the world's longest river (see Figure 12.1)

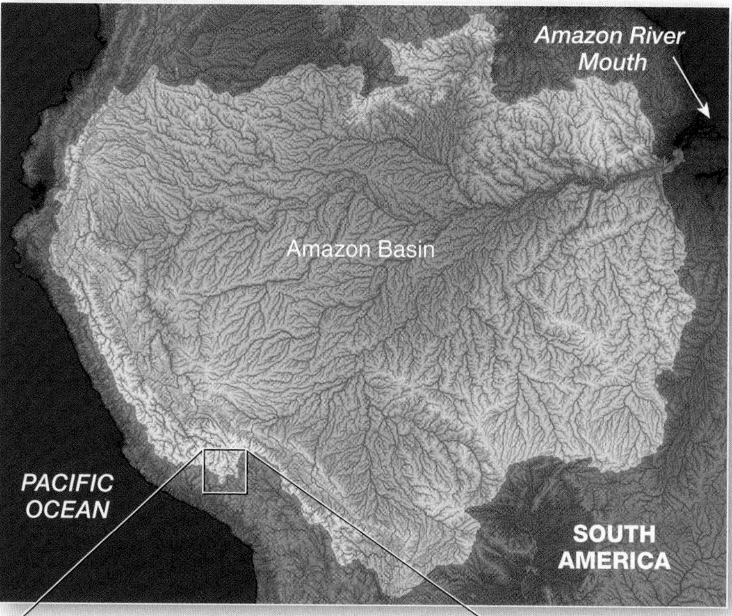

(a) Radar images showing elevation are combined with digitally mapped stream channels in this view of the Amazon River basin. Elevations range from sea level in green to above 4500 m (14,764 ft) in white. In 2007, Brazilian researchers reported finding a new source for the Amazon (white box), near Mount Mismi in southern Peru; the new length measurement of 6800 km (4225 mi), makes it longer than the Nile.

(b) The mouth of the Amazon is 160 km (100 mi) wide and discharges a fifth of all the freshwater that enters the world's oceans. Large islands of sediment are deposited where the flow enters the Atlantic.

◀**Figure 12.1 Amazon River drainage basin and mouth.** [(a) NASA SRTM image by Jesse Allen, University of Maryland, Global Land Cover Facility; stream data World Wildlife Fund, HydroSHEDS project (see http://hydrosheds.cr.usgs.gov/). (b) *Terra* image, NASA/GSFC/JPL.]

Drainage Divides

In any drainage basin, water initially moves downslope as *overland flow*, which takes two forms: It can move as **sheetflow**, a thin film spread over the ground surface; and it can concentrate in *rills*, small-scale grooves in the landscape made by the downslope movement of water. Rills may develop into deeper *gullies* and then into stream channels leading to the valley floor.

The high ground that separates one valley from another and directs sheetflow is called an *interfluve* (**Figure 12.2**). Ridges act as *drainage divides* that define the *catchment*, or water-receiving, area of every drainage basin; such ridges are the dividing lines that control into which basin the surface runoff drains.

A special class of drainage divides, **continental divides**, separate drainage

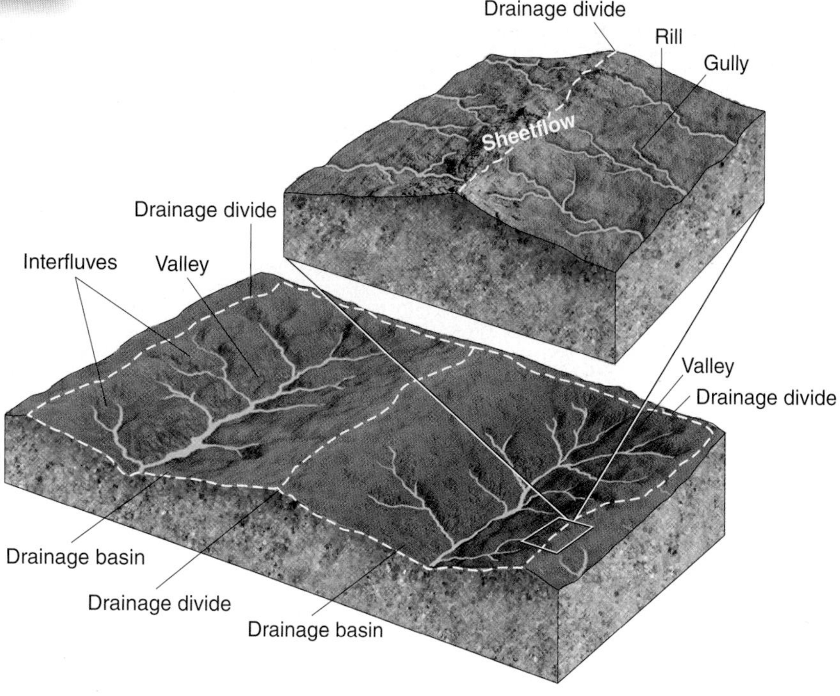

▲**Figure 12.2 Drainage basins.** A drainage divide separates drainage basins.

basins that empty into different bodies of water surrounding a continent; for North America, these bodies are the Pacific Ocean, the Gulf of Mexico, the Atlantic Ocean, Hudson Bay, and the Arctic Ocean. The principal drainage divides and drainage basins in the United States and Canada are mapped in **Figure 12.3**. These divides form water-resource regions and provide a spatial framework for water-management planning.

In North America, the great Mississippi–Missouri–Ohio River system drains some 3.1 million km² (1.2 million mi²), or 41% of the continental United States (Figure 12.3). Within this basin, rainfall in northern Pennsylvania feeds hundreds of small streams that flow into the Allegheny River. At the same time, rainfall in western Pennsylvania feeds hundreds of streams that flow into the Monongahela River. The two rivers then join at Pittsburgh to form the Ohio River. The Ohio flows southwestward and at Cairo, Illinois, connects with the Mississippi River, which eventually flows on past New Orleans and disperses into the Gulf of Mexico. Each contributing tributary, large or small, adds its discharge, pollution, and sediment load to the larger river. In our example, sediment weathered and eroded in Pennsylvania is transported thousands

CRITICAL**thinking 12.1**

Locate Your Drainage Basin

Determine the name of the drainage basin within which your campus is located. Where are its headwaters? Where is the river's mouth? If you are in the United States or Canada, use Figure 12.3 to locate the larger drainage basins and divides for your region, and then take a look at this region on Google Earth™. Does any regulatory organization oversee planning and coordination for the drainage basin you identified? Can you find topographic maps online that cover this region?

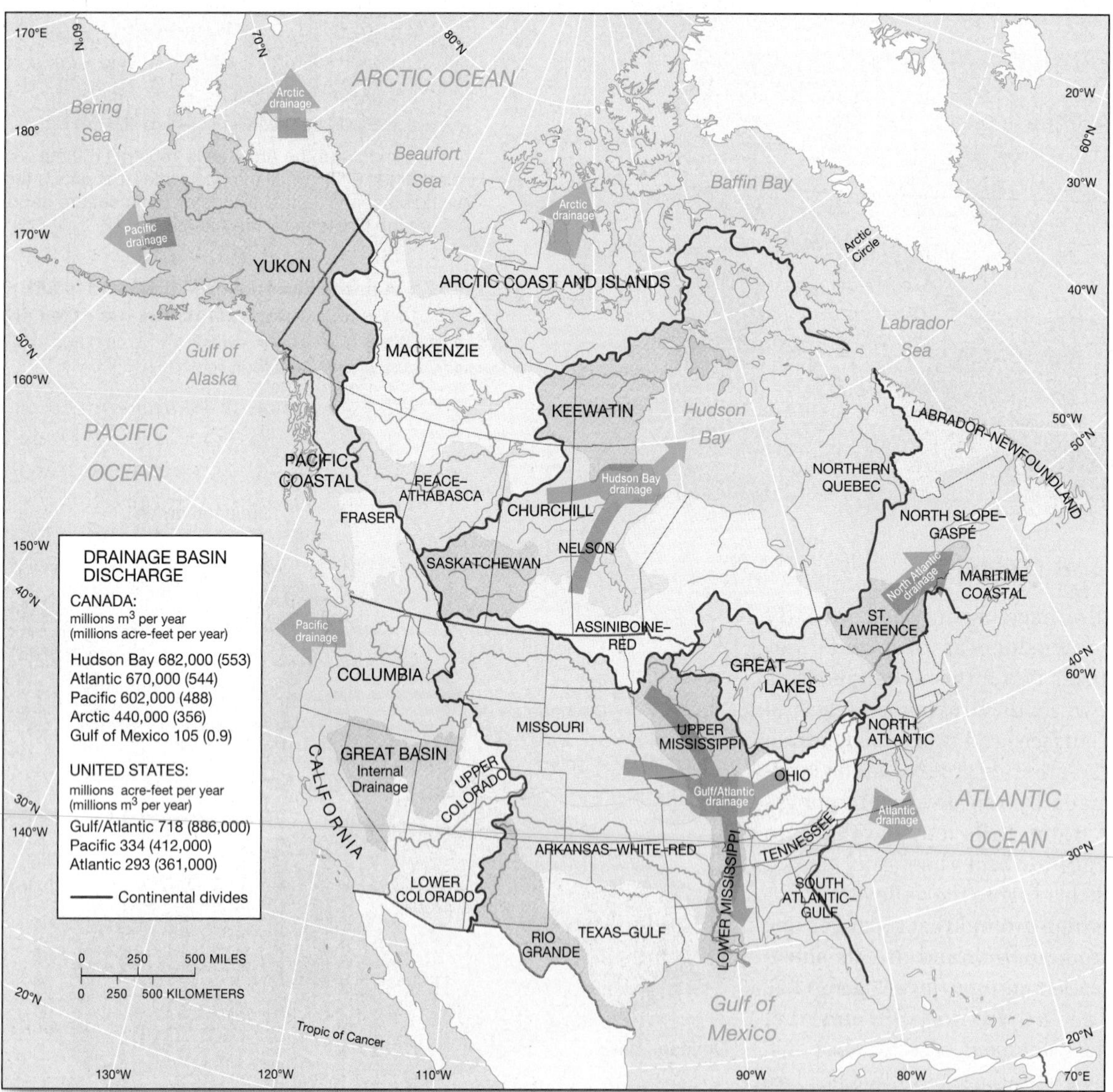

▲**Figure 12.3 Drainage basins and continental divides.** Continental divides (red lines) separate the major drainage basins that empty through the United States into the Pacific Ocean, Atlantic Ocean, and Gulf of Mexico and, to the north, through Canada into Hudson Bay and the Arctic Ocean. Subdividing these major drainage basins are major river basins. [After U.S. Geological Survey; *The National Atlas of Canada*, 1985, "Energy, Mines, and Resources Canada"; and Environment Canada, *Currents of Change—Inquiry on Federal Water Policy—Final Report 1986*.]

of kilometers and accumulates on the floor of the Gulf of Mexico, where it forms the Mississippi River delta.

The ultimate outlet for most drainage basins is the ocean. In some regions, however, stream drainage does not reach the ocean. Instead, the water leaves the drainage basin by means of evaporation or subsurface gravitational flow. Such basins are described as having *internal drainage*. Regions of internal drainage occur in Asia, Africa, Australia, Mexico, and the western United States, such as in the the Basin and Range Province in Nevada and Utah, shown in Figure 10.13 and Figure 12.3. An example within this region is the Humboldt River, which flows westward across Nevada and eventually disappears into the Humboldt Sink as a result of evaporation and seepage losses to groundwater.

Drainage Basins as Open Systems

Drainage basins are open systems. Inputs include precipitation and the minerals and rocks of the regional geology. Energy and materials are redistributed as the stream constantly adjusts to its landscape. System outputs of water and sediment disperse through the mouth of the stream or river into a lake, another stream or river, or the ocean, as shown in Figure 12.1.

Change that occurs in any portion of a drainage basin can affect the entire system. If a stream is brought to a geomorphic threshold where it can no longer maintain its present form, the river system may become destabilized, initiating a transition period to a more stable condition. A river system constantly strives for equilibrium among the interacting variables of discharge, channel steepness, channel shape, and sediment load, all of which are discussed in the chapter ahead.

International Drainage Basins

The Danube River in Europe, which flows 2850 km (1770 mi) from western Germany's Black Forest to the Black Sea, exemplifies the political complexity of an international drainage basin. The river crosses or forms part of a border of 19 countries (**Figure 12.4**). A total area of 817,000 km^2 (315,000 mi^2) falls within the drainage basin, including some 300 tributaries.

The Danube serves many economic functions: commercial transport, municipal water source, agricultural irrigation, fishing, and hydroelectric power production. An international struggle is under way to save the river from its burden of industrial and mining wastes, sewage, chemical discharge, agricultural runoff, and drainage from ships. The many shipping canals actually spread pollution and worsen biological conditions in the river. All of this pollution passes through Romania and the deltaic ecosystems in the Black Sea. The river is widely regarded as one of the most polluted on Earth.

Political changes in Europe in 1989 allowed the first scientific analysis of the entire Danube River system. The United Nations Environment Programme (UNEP) and the European Union, along with other organizations, are now dedicated to improving the Danube's water quality and restoring its floodplain and delta ecosystems; see http://www.icpdr.org/.

Drainage Patterns

A primary feature of any drainage basin is its *drainage density*, determined by dividing the total length of all stream channels in the basin by the area of the basin. The number and length of channels in a given area reflect the landscape's regional geology and topography.

The **drainage pattern** is the arrangement of channels in an area. Patterns are quite distinctive and are determined by a combination of regional steepness and relief; variations in rock resistance, climate, and hydrology; and structural controls imposed by the underlying rocks. Consequently, the drainage pattern of any land area on Earth is a remarkable visual summary of every geologic and climatic characteristic of that region.

The seven most common types of drainage patterns are shown in **Figure 12.5**. A most familiar pattern is

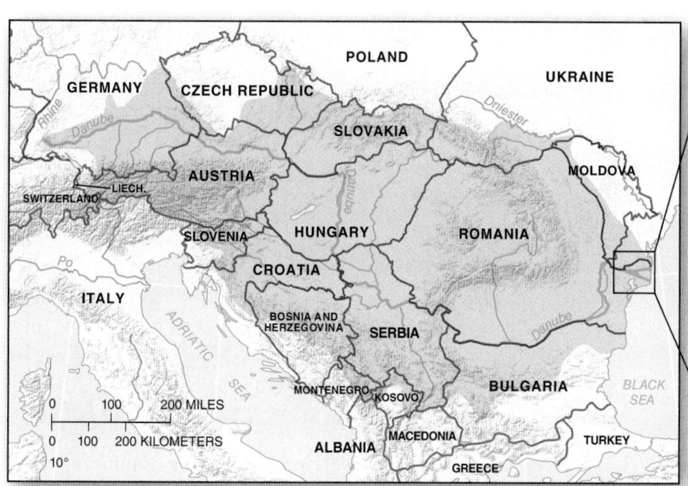

(a) The Danube crosses or forms part of a border of 19 countries as it flows across Europe to the Black Sea.

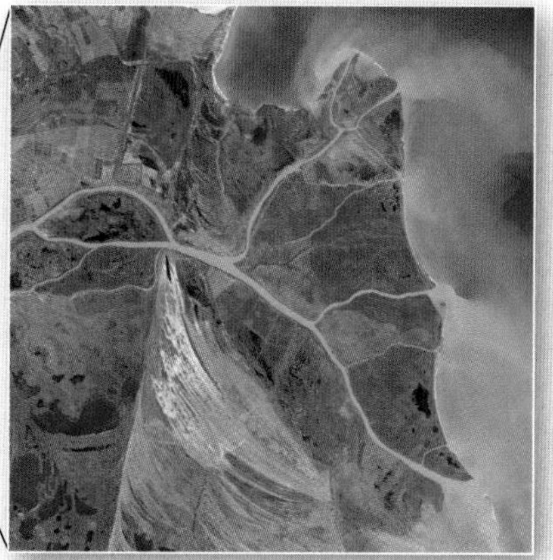

(b) Often called the Everglades of Europe, the Danube delta provides wetland habitat for over 300 bird species and 45 species of freshwater fish.

◄Figure 12.4 An international drainage basin—the Danube River. [(b) Advanced Land Imager, *EO–1* satellite, February 2013, NASA/GSFC.]

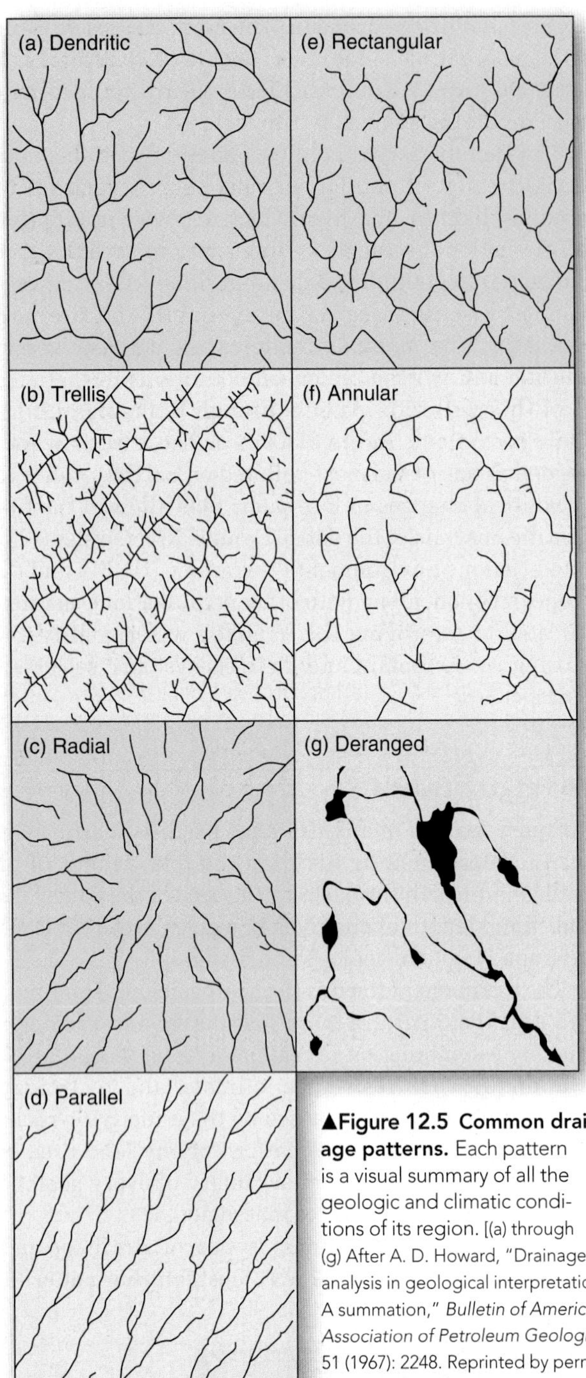

▲Figure 12.5 Common drainage patterns. Each pattern is a visual summary of all the geologic and climatic conditions of its region. [(a) through (g) After A. D. Howard, "Drainage analysis in geological interpretation: A summation," *Bulletin of American Association of Petroleum Geologists* 51 (1967): 2248. Reprinted by permission of AAPG whose permission is required for further use.]

dendritic drainage (Figure 12.5a). This treelike pattern (from the Greek word *dendron*, meaning "tree") is similar to that of many natural systems, such as capillaries in the human circulatory system, or the veins in leaves, or the roots of trees. Energy expenditure in the moving of water and sediment through this drainage system is efficient because the total length of the branches is minimized.

The *trellis* drainage pattern (Figure 12.5b) is characteristic of dipping or folded topography. Such drainage is seen in the nearly parallel mountain folds of the Ridge and Valley Province in the eastern United States (shown in Figure 10.16). Here drainage patterns are influenced by folded rock structures that vary in resistance to erosion. Parallel structures direct the principal streams, while smaller dendritic tributary streams are at work on nearby slopes, joining the main streams at right angles, as in a plant trellis.

The remaining drainage patterns in Figures 12.5c–g are responses to other specific structural conditions:

- A *radial* drainage pattern (c) results when streams flow off a central peak or dome, such as occurs on a volcanic mountain.
- *Parallel* drainage (d) is associated with steep slopes.
- A *rectangular* pattern (e) is formed by a faulted and jointed landscape, which directs stream courses in patterns of right-angle turns.
- *Annular* patterns (f) occur on structural domes, with concentric patterns of rock strata guiding stream courses (discussed in Chapter 10).
- A *deranged* pattern (g) with no clear geometry and no true stream valley occurs in areas such as the glaciated shield regions of Canada, northern Europe, and some parts of Michigan and other states.

Occasionally, drainage patterns occur that seem discordant with the landscape through which they flow. For example, a drainage system may initially develop over horizontal strata that have been deposited on top of uplifted, folded structures. As the streams erode into the older folded strata, they keep their original course, downcutting into the rock in a pattern contrary to its structure.

CRITICAL**thinking 12.2**

Identifying Drainage Patterns

Examine the photograph in **Figure CT 12.2.1**, where you see two distinct drainage patterns. Of the seven types illustrated in Figure 12.5, which two patterns are most like those in the aerial photo? Looking back to Figure 12.1a, which drainage pattern is prevalent in the area around Mount Mismi in Brazil? Explain your answer. The next time you fly in an airplane, look out the window to observe the various drainage patterns across the landscape.

▲Figure CT 12.2.1 Two drainage patterns dominate this scene from central Montana, in response to rock structure and local relief. [Bobbé Christopherson.]

Such a stream is a *superposed stream*, in which a preexisting channel pattern has been imposed upon older underlying rock structures. A few examples are Wills Creek, presently cutting a water gap through Haystack Mountain at Cumberland, Maryland; the Columbia River flowing through the Cascade Mountains of Washington; and the River Arun, which cuts across the Himalayas.

Basic Fluvial Concepts

In general, streams, a mixture of water and solids, provide resources and shape landforms. They create fluvial landscapes through the ongoing erosion, transport, and deposition of materials in a downstream direction. The energy of a stream to accomplish this geomorphic work depends on a number of factors, including gradient, base level, and volume of flow (discharge), all discussed in this section.

Gradient

Within its drainage basin, every stream has a degree of inclination or gradient, which is also known as the channel slope. The **gradient** of a stream is defined as the drop in elevation per unit of distance, usually measured in meters per kilometer or feet per mile. Characteristically, a river has a steeper slope nearer the headwaters and a more gradual slope downstream. A stream's gradient affects its energy and ability to move material; in particular, it affects the velocity of the flow (discussed just ahead).

Base Level

The level below which a stream cannot erode its valley is **base level**. In general, the *ultimate base level* is sea level, the average level between high and low tides. Base level can be visualized as a surface extending inland from sea level, inclined gently upward under the continents. In theory, this is the lowest practical level for all denudation processes (**Figure 12.6a**).

American geologist and explorer John Wesley Powell, leader of the first expedition on the Colorado River through the Grand Canyon, put forward the idea of base level in 1875. Powell recognized that not every landscape has degraded all the way to sea level; clearly, other intermediate base levels are in operation. A *local base level*, or temporary one, may determine the lower limit of local or regional stream erosion. A river or lake is a natural local base level; the reservoir behind a dam is a human-caused local base level (**Figure 12.6b**). In arid landscapes with internal drainage, valleys, plains, or other low points act as local base level.

Stream Discharge

A mass of water situated above base level in a stream has potential energy. As the water flows downslope, or downstream, under the influence of gravity, this energy becomes kinetic energy. The rate of this conversion from potential to kinetic energy determines the ability of the stream to do geomorphic work and depends in part on the volume of water involved.

A stream's volume of flow per unit of time is its **discharge** and is calculated by multiplying three variables measured at a given cross section of the channel. It is summarized in the simple expression

$$Q = wdv$$

where Q = discharge, w = channel width, d = channel depth, and v = stream velocity. Discharge is expressed in either cubic meters per second (m^3/s or cms) or cubic feet per second (ft^3/s or cfs). According to this equation, as Q

(a) The ultimate base level is sea level. Note how base level curves gently upward from the sea as it is traced inland; this is the theoretical limit for stream erosion. The reservoir behind a dam is a local base level.

(b) Glen Canyon Dam impounds Lake Powell, forming a local base level on the Colorado River.

▲**Figure 12.6 Ultimate and local base levels.** [(b) Bobbé Christopherson.]

increases, one or more of the other variables—channel width, channel depth, and stream velocity—must also increase. How these variables interact depends on the climate and geology of the fluvial system.

Changes in Discharge with Distance Downstream In most river basins in humid regions, discharge increases in a downstream direction. The Mississippi River is typical, beginning as many small streams that merge successively with tributaries to form a large-volume river ending in the Gulf of Mexico. However, if a stream originates in a humid region and subsequently flows through an arid region, this relationship may change. High potential evapotranspiration rates in arid regions can cause discharge to decrease with distance downstream, a process that is often exacerbated by water removal for irrigation (**Figure 12.7**). This type of stream is an *exotic stream*.

The Nile River, one of Earth's longest rivers, drains much of northeastern Africa. But as it flows through the deserts of Sudan and Egypt, it loses water, instead of gaining it, because of evaporation and withdrawal for agriculture. By the time it empties into the Mediterranean Sea, the Nile's flow has dwindled so much that it ranks only 36th in discharge.

In the United States, discharge decreases on the Colorado River with distance from its source; in fact, the river no longer produces enough natural discharge to reach its mouth in the Gulf of California—only some agricultural runoff remains at its delta. The river is depleted by high evapotranspiration and removal of water for agriculture and municipal uses; shifting climatic patterns are adding to the river's water losses (review Focus Study 6.1).

As discharge increases in a downstream direction, velocity usually increases. Stream velocity is affected by friction between the flow and the roughness of the channel bed and banks. Friction is highest in shallow mountain streams with boulders and other obstacles that add roughness and slow the flow. In streams where friction is high (more contact with the bed and banks and/or obstacles in the channel), as in a section of rapids, *turbulent flow* occurs, and most of the stream's energy is expended in turbulent eddies (see Figure 12.10 just ahead). In deep, lowland rivers, where the flow has less contact with the bed and banks and the channel has fewer obstacles that create roughness, friction is reduced; however, the apparent smoothness and quietness of the flow mask the increased velocity. The energy of these rivers is enough to move large amounts of sediment, discussed in the next section.

Changes in Discharge over Time Discharge varies throughout the year for most streams, depending on precipitation and temperature. Rivers and streams in arid and semiarid regions may have perennial, ephemeral, or intermittent discharge. *Perennial streams* flow all year, fed by snowmelt, rainfall, groundwater, or some combination of those sources. *Ephemeral streams* flow only after precipitation events and are not connected to groundwater systems. Years may pass between flow events in these usually dry stream channels. *Intermittent streams* flow for several weeks or months each year and may have some groundwater inputs.

Discharge changes over time at any given channel cross section. A graph of stream discharge over time for a specific location is a **hydrograph**. The time scale of a hydrograph can vary. For example, *annual hydrographs* show discharge over the course of an entire year, usually with the highest discharge occurring during the spring snowmelt season. *Storm hydrographs* may cover only a period of days, reflecting changes in discharge caused by specific precipitation events that lead to local flooding. The hydrograph in **Figure 12.8a** shows the relation between precipitation input (the bar graphs) and stream discharge (the curves). During dry periods, the low discharge is described as *base flow* (dark blue line) and is largely maintained by input from local groundwater (review the discussion in Chapter 6).

When rainfall occurs in some portion of the watershed, the runoff is concentrated in streams and tributaries in that area. The amount, location, and duration of the rainfall episode determine the *peak flow*, the highest discharge that occurs during a precipitation event. The nature of the surface in a watershed, whether permeable or impermeable, affects peak flow and the timing of changes recorded in the hydrograph. In deserts, where surfaces have thin, impermeable soils and little vegetation, runoff can be high during rainstorms. A rare or large precipitation event in a desert can fill a stream channel with a

◀**Figure 12.7 Declining discharge with distance downstream.** The Virgin River in southwest Utah, a tributary of the Colorado River, is a perennial stream in which discharge decreases in the lower reaches as water is removed for irrigation, is transpired by riparian vegetation (water-loving plants), and is lost to evapotranspiration in this semiarid climate. [Bobbé Christopherson.]

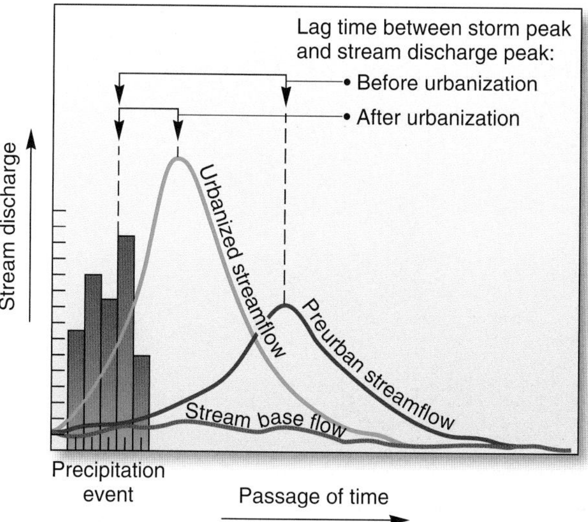

(a) Normal base flow is indicated with a dark blue line. The purple line indicates post-storm discharge prior to urbanization. Following urbanization, stream discharge dramatically increases, as shown by the light blue line.

(b) Increasing urbanization has worsened flooding in many parts of Asia, including Bangkok, Thailand, pictured here when flooding submerged part of the highway system in 2011.

▲**Figure 12.8 Effect of urbanization on a typical stream hydrograph.** [(b) Apichart Weerawong/AP Images.]

torrent known as a **flash flood**. These channels may fill in a few minutes and surge briefly during and after a storm.

Human activities have enormous impact on patterns of discharge in a drainage basin. A hydrograph for a specific portion of a stream changes after a disturbance such as a forest fire or urbanization of the watershed, with peak flows occurring sooner during the precipitation event. The effects of urbanization are quite dramatic, both increasing and hastening peak flow, as you can see by comparing discharge prior to an area's urbanization (purple curve) and discharge after urbanization has occurred (light blue curve) in Figure 12.8a. In fact, urban areas produce runoff patterns quite similar to those of deserts, since the sealed surfaces of the city drastically reduce infiltration and soil-moisture recharge. These issues will intensify as urbanization continues (**Figure 12.8b**).

Measuring Discharge Measurements of width, depth, and velocity are needed at a stream cross section in order to calculate discharge. Field measurements of these variables may be difficult to obtain, depending on a stream's size and flow. The common practice is to measure velocity for different subsections of the stream cross section, using a movable current meter (**Figure 12.9a**). Width and depth for each subsection are then combined with velocity to compute subsection discharge, and then all the subsection discharges for the cross section are totaled. Since channel beds are often composed of soft sediments that may change over short time periods, stream depth is measured as the height of the stream surface above a constant reference elevation (a datum) and is called the *stage*. Scientists may use a *staff gage* (a pole marked with water levels) or a *stilling well* on the stream bank with a gage mounted in it to measure stage (**Figures 12.9b** and **12.9c**).

Approximately 11,000 stream-gaging stations are in use in the United States (an average of more than 200 per state). Of these, 7500 are operated by the U.S. Geological Survey and have continuous recorders for stage and discharge (see http://pubs.usgs.gov/circ/circ1123/). Many of these stations automatically send telemetry data to satellites, from which information is retransmitted to regional centers. The gaging station on the Colorado River at Lees Ferry, just south of Glen Canyon Dam, was established in 1921 and was used to determine flows for the Colorado River Compact, discussed in Focus Study 6.1 (**Figure 12.9d**).

Fluvial Processes and Landforms

The ongoing interaction between erosion, transportation, and deposition in a river system produces fluvial landscapes. **Erosion** in fluvial systems is the process by which water dislodges, dissolves, or removes weathered surface material. This material is then transported to new locations, where it is laid down in the process of **deposition**. Erosion, transport, and deposition are affected by discharge and channel gradient. Running water is an important erosional force; in fact, in desert landscapes it is the most significant agent of erosion even though precipitation events are infrequent. We discuss processes of erosion and deposition, and their characteristic landforms, in this section.

Stream Channel Processes

The geomorphic work performed by a stream includes erosion and deposition, and depends on the volume of water and the total amount of sediment in the flow.

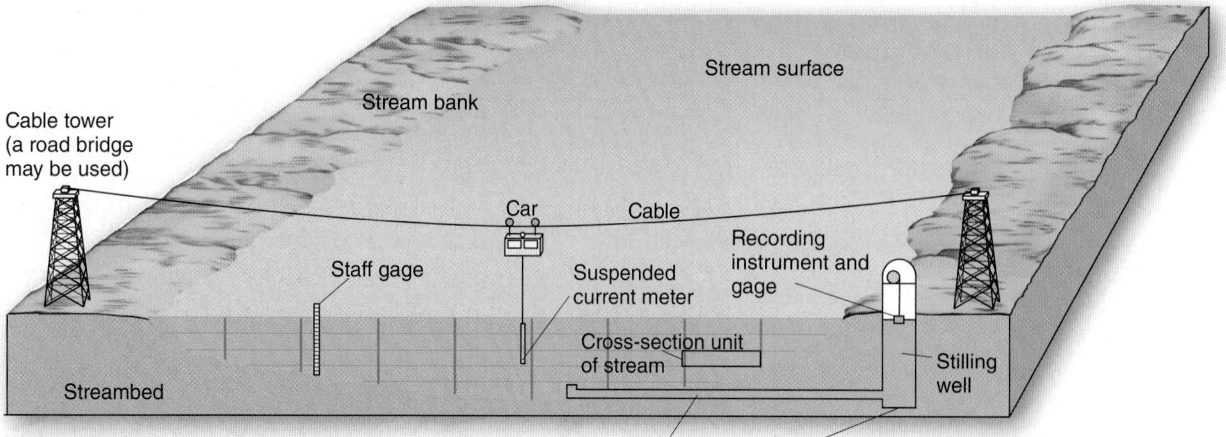

(a) A typical flow-measurement installation

(b) An automated hydrographic station

(c) A stilling well

(d) Cable towers and cable from which current meters are lowered, Lees Ferry, Arizona

▲**Figure 12.9 Stream-discharge measurement.** [(b) California Department of Water Resources. (c) and (d) Bobbé Christopherson.]

Hydraulic action is a type of erosive work performed by flowing water alone, a squeeze-and-release action that loosens and lifts rocks. Hydraulic action is at a maximum in upstream tributaries of a drainage basin, where sediment load is small and flow is turbulent (**Figure 12.10**). The downstream portions of a river, however, move much larger volumes of water past a given point and carry larger amounts of sediment. As this debris moves along, it mechanically erodes the streambed further through the process of **abrasion**, with rock and sediment grinding and carving the streambed like liquid sandpaper.

Fluvial erosion by hydraulic action and abrasion causes streams to erode downward (deepen), erode laterally (widen), and erode in an upstream direction (lengthen). The process whereby streams deepen their channel is known as *channel incision* (an example on the San Juan River is discussed ahead). The process of lateral erosion is discussed in the next section with meandering river channels. The process whereby streams lengthen their channels upstream is called *headward erosion*. This type of erosion occurs when the flow entering a main channel has enough power to downcut, such as occurs at the break in slope where a gully enters a deep valley.

►**Figure 12.10 A turbulent stream.** The high-gradient, turbulent Maligne River flows through a bedrock canyon in the Canadian Rockies. [Ashley Cooper/Encyclopedia/Corbis.]

Sediment Load When stream energy is high and a supply of sediment is present, streamflow propels sand, pebbles, gravel, and boulders downstream in the process known as **sediment transport**. The material carried by a stream is its *sediment load*, and the sediment supply is determined by topographic relief, the nature of rock and soil through which the stream flows, climate, vegetation, and human activity in a drainage basin. Discharge is also closely linked to sediment transport—increased discharge moves a greater amount of sediment, often causing streams to change from clear to murky brown after a heavy or prolonged rainfall. Sediment is moved as dissolved load, suspended load, or bed load by four primary processes: solution, suspension, saltation, and traction (**Figure 12.11**).

The **dissolved load** of a stream is the material that travels in solution, especially the dissolved chemical compounds derived from minerals such as limestone or dolomite or from soluble salts. The main process contributing material in solution is chemical weathering. Along the San Juan and Little Colorado Rivers, which flow into the Colorado River near the Utah–Arizona border, the salt content of the dissolved load is so high that human use of the water is limited.

The **suspended load** consists of fine-grained clastic particles (bits and pieces of rock). They are held aloft in the stream until the stream velocity slows nearly to zero, at which point even the finest particles are deposited. Turbulence in the water, with random upward motion, is an important mechanical factor in holding a load of sediment in suspension.

Bed load refers to coarser materials that are moved by **traction**, which is the rolling or dragging of materials along the streambed, or by **saltation**, a term referring to the way particles may bounce along in short hops and jumps (from the Latin *saltim*, which means "by leaps or jumps"). Particles transported by saltation are too large to remain in suspension, but are not confined to the sliding and rolling motion of traction (see Figure 12.11). Stream velocity affects these processes, particularly the stream's ability to retain particles in suspension. With increased kinetic energy in a stream, parts of the bed load are rafted upward and become suspended load.

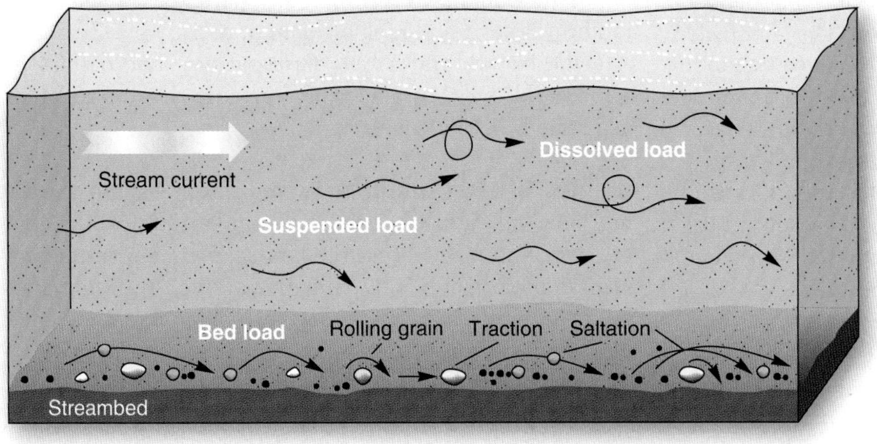

During a flood (a high flow that overtops the channel banks), a river may carry an enormous sediment load, as larger material is picked up and carried by the enhanced flow. The *competence* of a stream is its ability to move particles of a specific size and is a function of stream velocity and the energy available to move materials. The *capacity* of a stream is the total possible sediment load that it can transport and is a function of discharge; thus, a large river has higher capacity than a small stream. As flood flows build, stream energy increases and the competence of the stream becomes high enough that sediment transport occurs. As a result, the channel erodes, a process known as **degradation**. With the return of flows to normal, stream energy is reduced, and the sediment transport slows or stops. If the load exceeds a stream's capacity, sediment accumulates in the stream bed, building up the channel through deposition; this is the process of **aggradation**.

Sediment Transport during a Flood We saw in the previous section that discharge can change quickly in response to precipitation events in a watershed. Greater discharge increases flow velocity and therefore the competence of the river to transport sediment as the flood progresses. As a result, the river's ability to scour materials from its bed is enhanced.

As an example, **Figure 12.12** shows changes in the San Juan River channel in Utah that occurred during a flood. The channel was deepest on October 14, when floodwaters were highest (blue line plotted in Figure 12.12a). During this time, the channel bed eroded. The erosive action of the flood, known as *scouring*, moved a depth of about 3 m (10 ft) of sediment from the depicted cross section. By October 26, with the discharge returning to normal, the energy of the river was reduced, and the bed again filled as sediment redeposited. This type of channel adjustment is ongoing, as the system continuously works toward equilibrium, maintaining a balance between discharge, sediment load, and channel form.

Effects of Dams on Sediment Transport As discussed in the chapter-opening Geosystems Now, dams disrupt natural river discharge and sediment regimes, usually with detrimental effects on river systems. For example, Glen Canyon Dam on the Colorado River near the Utah–Arizona border controls discharge and blocks sediment from flowing into the Grand Canyon downstream (see Figure 12.6 and the map in Focus Study 6.1). Consequently, over the years, the river's sediment supply was cut off,

◀**Figure 12.11 Fluvial transport.** Eroded materials move downstream as dissolved load, suspended load, and bed load.

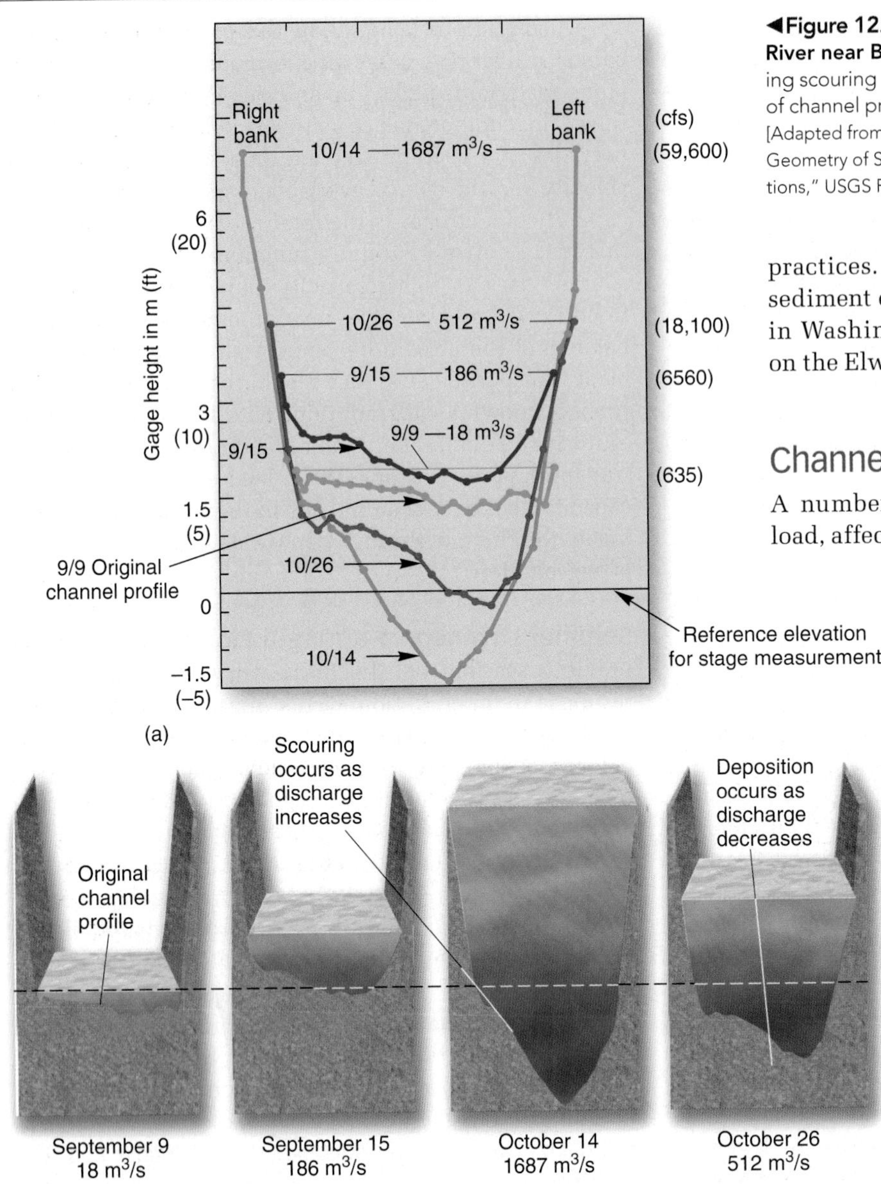

◄Figure 12.12 The effects of a flood on the San Juan River near Bluff, Utah. (a) Channel cross sections showing scouring and filling of the stream channel. (b) Details of channel profiles during the four stages of the flood. [Adapted from L. Leopold and T. Maddock, "The Hydraulic Geometry of Stream Channels and Some Physiographic Implications," USGS Professional Paper 252, p. 32, 1941.]

starving the river's beaches for sand, disrupting fisheries, and depleting backwater channels of nutrients.

In 1996, 2004, 2008, and 2012, the Grand Canyon was artificially flooded with dam-controlled releases in an unprecedented series of scouring–redistribution–deposition experiments for sediment movement. The later tests, with flows lasting several days, were timed to coincide with floods in tributaries that supplied fresh sediment to the system. The results were mixed—the flood releases disrupted ecosystems and eroded some sediment deposits even while building up others. With such a limited sediment supply, not enough sediment is present in the system to build beaches and improve habitat even when high discharge occurs (more information is at http://www.gcmrc.gov/).

Recent dam removals have allowed scientists to study post-dam sediment redistribution. Focus Study 12.1 discusses dam deconstruction and other stream restoration practices. See Figure 12.1.2 for a photo of the sediment outflow into the Strait of Juan de Fuca in Washington following removal of two dams on the Elwha River.

Channel Patterns

A number of factors, including the sediment load, affect the channel pattern. Multiple-thread channels have several interconnected channels in a braided pattern and tend to occur in areas with abundant sediment or in the lowest reaches of large river systems. Single-thread channels have one channel and are either straight or meandering. Straight channels tend to occur in headwater areas, where gradient is high. In lower-gradient areas with finer sediments, meandering is more common; this is the classic river pattern in which a single channel curves from side to side in a valley or canyon.

Multiple-Thread Channels

With excess sediment, a stream might become a maze of interconnected channels that form a **braided stream** pattern (**Figure 12.13**). Braiding often occurs when reduced discharge lowers a stream's transporting ability, such as after flooding, or when a landslide occurs upstream, or when sediment load increases in channels that have weak banks of sand or gravel. Braided rivers commonly occur in glacial environments, where coarse sediment is abundant and slopes are steep, as in New Zealand, Alaska, Nepal, and Tibet. This pattern also occurs in wide, shallow channels with variable discharge, such as in the U.S. Southwest.

Single-Thread Channels Where channel slope is gradual, streams develop a sinuous (snakelike) form, weaving back and forth across the landscape in a **meandering stream** pattern and acquiring distinctive flow and channel characteristics. The tendency to meander is evidence of a river system's propensity (like any natural system) to find the path of least effort toward a balance between self-equilibrating order and chaotic disorder.

▲**Figure 12.13 A braided stream.** The braided Sanctuary River channel flows through the glaciated landscape of the Alaska Range, Denali National Park, Alaska. [Bobbé Christopherson.]

Geosystems in Action 12 illustrates some of the processes associated with meandering streams. A cross-sectional view of a meandering stream channel shows the flow characteristics that produce the channel deposits typical of these streams. In a straight channel or section of channel, the greatest flow velocities are near the surface at the center, corresponding to the deepest part of the stream (Figure GIA 12.1a). Velocities decrease closer to the sides and bottom of the channel because of the frictional drag on the water flow. As the stream flows around a meander curve, the maximum flow velocity shifts from the center of the stream to the outside of the curve. As the stream then straightens, the maximum velocity shifts back to the center, until the next bend, where it shifts to the outside of that meander curve. Thus, the portion of the stream flowing at maximum velocity moves diagonally across the stream from bend to bend.

Because the outer portion of each meandering curve is subject to the fastest water velocity, it undergoes the greatest scouring. This erosive action can form a steep **undercut bank**, or *cutbank* (Figure GIA 12.1b). In contrast, the inner portion of a meander experiences the slowest water velocity and thus is a zone of fill (or aggradation) that results in a **point bar**, an accumulation of sediment on the inside of a meander bend. As meanders develop, these scour-and-fill processes gradually work at stream banks, causing them to move laterally across a valley—this is the process of lateral erosion. As a result, the landscape near a meandering river bears marks called *meander scars* that are the residual deposits from previous river channels (seen in the map and image of the Mississippi River's meanders in Figure 12.20).

Meandering streams create a remarkable looping pattern on the landscape, as shown in Figure GIA 12.2. Actively meandering streams erode their outside banks as they migrate, often forming a narrow neck of land that eventually erodes through and forms a *cutoff*. A cutoff marks an abrupt change in the stream's lateral movements—the stream becomes straighter.

After the former meander becomes isolated from the rest of the river, the resulting **oxbow lake** may gradually fill with organic debris and silt or may again become part of the river when it floods. The Mississippi River is many miles shorter today than it was in the 1830s because of artificial cutoffs that were dredged across meander necks to improve navigation and safety. How many of these stream features—meanders, oxbow lakes, cutoffs—can you spot in Figure 12.20 just ahead?

Streams often form natural political boundaries, as we saw with the Danube River earlier. Yet problems may arise when boundaries are based on river channels that change course. For example, the Ohio, Missouri, and Mississippi Rivers, which form boundaries of several states, can shift their positions quite rapidly during times of flood. Consider the Nebraska–Iowa border, which was originally placed mid-channel in the Missouri River. In 1877, the river cut off the meander loop around a town, leaving the town "captured" by Nebraska (**Figure 12.14**). The new

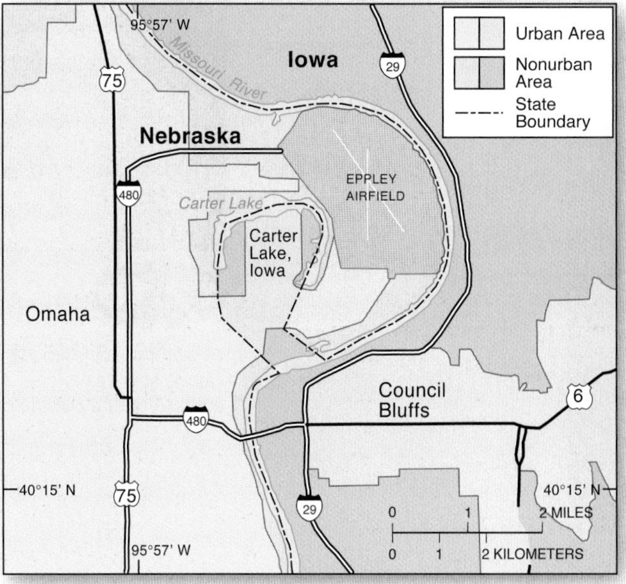

▲**Figure 12.14 A town left stranded by shifting meanders.** Carter Lake, Iowa, sits within a curve of a former meander that was cut off by the Missouri River. The city and oxbow lake remain part of Iowa even though they are now mostly surrounded by Nebraska.

(*text continued on page 390*)

Meandering channels curve from side to side in a snakelike pattern and usually occur where low-gradient streams flow through fine sediments. *Meanders* form because the portion of the stream with maximum velocity shifts from one side of the stream to the other as the stream bends, thus affecting erosion and deposition along the stream's banks (GIA 12.1). Through these "scour-and-fill" processes, a meandering stream moves position laterally across its valley and creates a distinctive landscape (GIA 12.2).

12.1a Profile of a Meandering Stream

The cross sections show how the location of maximum flow velocity shifts from the center along a straight stretch of the stream channel to the outside bend of a meander. The oblique view shows how the stream erodes, or "scours," an *undercut bank* on the outside of a bend, while depositing a *point bar* on the inside of the bend.

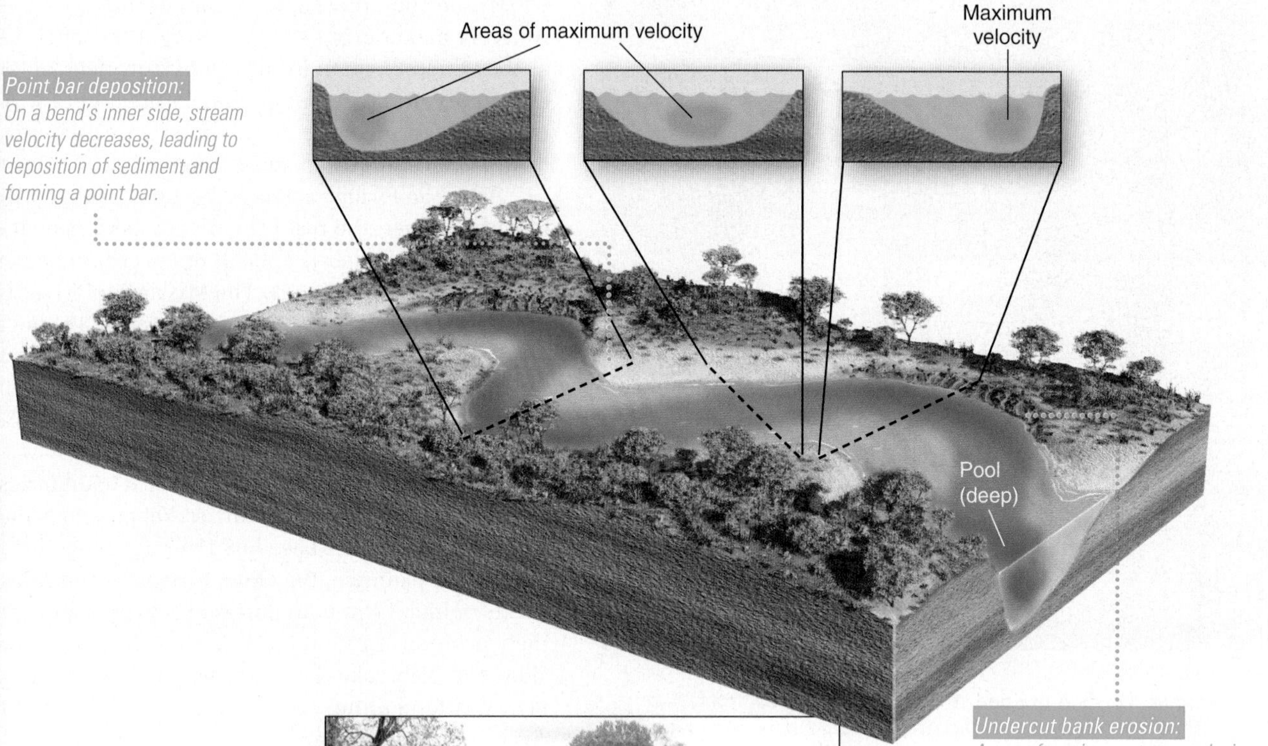

Areas of maximum velocity

Maximum velocity

Point bar deposition: On a bend's inner side, stream velocity decreases, leading to deposition of sediment and forming a point bar.

Pool (deep)

Undercut bank erosion: Areas of maximum stream velocity (darker blue) have more power to erode, so they undercut the stream's banks on the outside of a bend.

Cutbank

12.1b Active Erosion Along a Meander

Notice how this stream in Iowa has eroded a steep cutbank on the outside of a bend.

Explain: Explain the relationship between stream velocity, erosion, and deposition in the formation of a meander.

MasteringGeography™

Visit the Study Area in MasteringGeography™ to explore meander and oxbow lake formation.

Visualize: Study a geosciences animation of meander and oxbow lake formation.

Assess: Demonstrate understanding of meander and oxbow lake formation (if assigned by instructor).

Animation MG
Meandering Streams

http://goo.gl/ySMJp5

12.2a Stream Meandering Process

Over time, stream meanders migrate laterally across a stream valley, eroding the outside of bends and filling the insides of bends. Narrow areas between meanders are *necks*. When discharge increases, the stream may scour through the neck, forming a *cutoff*.

Stream valley landscape: A neck has recently been eroded, forming a cutoff and straightening the stream channel. The bypassed portion of the stream may become a meander scar or an oxbow lake.

A cutoff forms on the Itkillik River, north slope of the Brooks Range, Alaska.

12.2b Formation of an Oxbow Lake

The diagrams below show the steps often involved in forming an oxbow lake; this photo corresponds to Step 3, the formation of a cutoff. As stream channels shift, these processes leave characteristic landforms on a floodplain.

Step 1: A neck is forms where a lengthening meander loops back on itself.

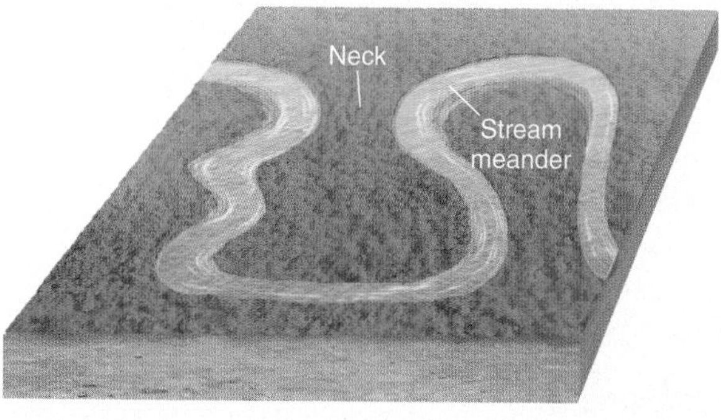

Step 2: Over time, the neck narrows as erosion undercuts the banks.

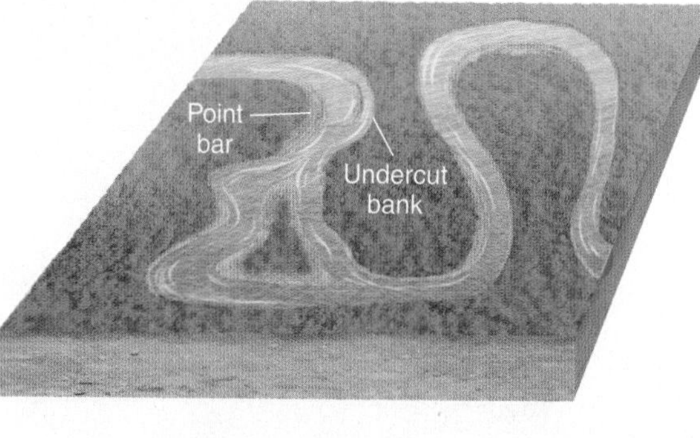

Step 3: Eventually, the stream erodes through the neck, forming a cutoff.

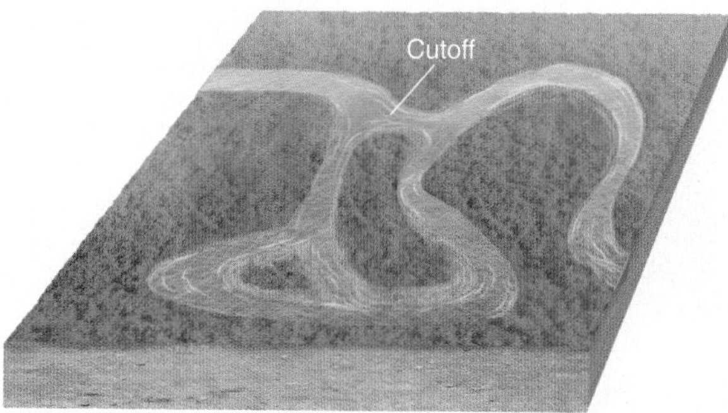

Step 4: An oxbow lake forms as sediment fills the area between the new stream channel and its old meander.

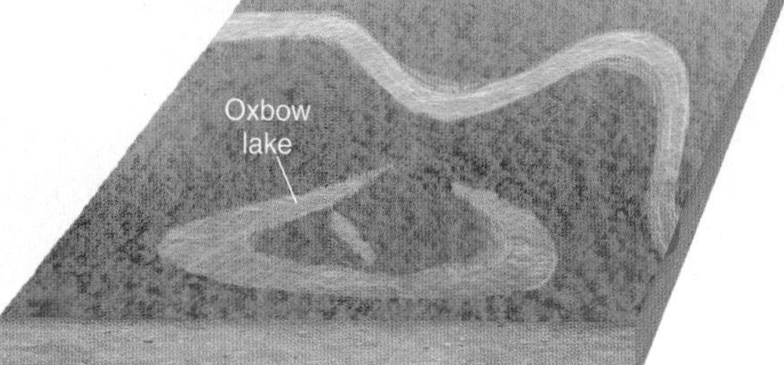

Follow up: In your own words, describe the sequence of steps in the process that forms an oxbow lake.

GEOquiz

1. Explain: Explain the processes that cause a gentle bend along a stream to become a deeply looping meander.

2. Summarize: Summarize the process by which a stream, over time, could produce the landscape in the GIA12.2a photograph.

focusstudy 12.1 Environmental Restoration

Stream Restoration: Merging Science and Practice

As mentioned in Chapter 1, "basic" science is designed mainly to advance knowledge and build scientific theories. "Applied" science solves real-world problems and, by doing so, often advances new technologies and develops natural resource management strategies. Beginning in the late 1980s, the restoration of rivers and streams has become a focus for both basic and applied geomorphology.

Stream restoration, also called *river restoration*, is the process that reestablishes the health of a fluvial ecosystem, including channel processes and form, riparian vegetation, and fisheries. Every stream restoration project has a particular focus, which varies with the problems and impacts on that particular stream. Common restoration goals are to reinstate instream flows, restore fish passage, prevent bank erosion, and reestablish vegetation along the channel or on the floodplain. The scale of a stream restoration varies from short local stretches of stream to hundreds of kilometers of river to an entire watershed.

Dam Removals

As many small dams overseen by the Federal Energy Regulatory Commission (FERC) have come up for relicensing over the past 25 years, scientists and environmental groups have worked with city, state, and federal agencies to identify dams for removal. Numerous dams that were deemed unsafe or outdated, or whose original purpose was no longer valid, have since been deconstructed. In 1999, Edwards Dam was deconstructed from the Kennebec River in Augusta, Maine, marking the first dam removal in the United States for ecological reasons (in this case, primarily to restore passage between the river and sea for migratory fish).

In 2013, the deconstruction of the Elwha and Glines Canyon Dams (both over 80 years old) in northwest Washington became the largest dam removal in U.S. history, restoring fish passage and associated river ecosystems on the 72-km-long (45-mi-long) Elwha River (**Figure 12.1.1**). A free-flowing Elwha River enables the return of five species of Pacific salmon to the watershed, with fish numbers already on the rise and expected to increase from 3000 to 390,000 over the next 30 years. Such species are *anadromous* (from the Greek *anadromos*, "running up"), meaning they migrate upstream from the sea into freshwater rivers to spawn.

A year after the Elwha dam removals began, scientists reported that native steelhead, as well as chinook, coho, and pink salmon, were already making their way into previously inaccessible stream reaches on the former lakebed. Willow and cottonwood saplings were beginning to establish in the newly exposed, silt-laden river channel. In that first year, an estimated half million tons of sediment, previously trapped behind the dams, began moving downstream and exiting at the river's mouth (**Figure 12.1.2**). For more information, see http://www.nps.gov/olym/naturescience/elwha-restoration-docs.htm.

(a) Sites of former dams on the Elwha River.

(b) A barge-mounted hydraulic hammer chips away at the top of the Glines Canyon Dam in 2012.

(c) Glines Canyon Dam removal in progress, 2012.

▲**Figure 12.1.1 Glines Canyon Dam removal, Elwha River.** [(a) NPS/USGS. (b) NPS. (c) Brian Cluer/NOAA.]

A Cooperative Process

Stream restoration involves the cooperation of numerous landowners and regulating agencies within a watershed. For instance, bank erosion at a given location may be linked to processes occurring upstream and, in turn, can affect downstream processes. Thus, restoring a stream to its natural state involves the entire system rather than just a single, isolated segment. Restoration also involves balancing different water use needs within a drainage basin.

In Maine's largest watershed, the Penobscot River restoration project is attempting to restore fisheries, while at the same time maintaining hydropower production. The Penobscot restoration project involves a large coalition of interest groups, including six environmental

◀**Figure 12.1.2 Sediment flowing from the mouth of the Elwha River after dam removal.** [Tom Roorda/AP Images.]

groups, the Penobscot Indian Nation, the State of Maine, the U.S. Department of the Interior, the National Oceanic and Atmospheric Administration, and hydropower companies. Restoration includes removing two dams, building a fish lift at another dam, and building a fish bypass around a fourth dam, thereby restoring fish access along hundreds of miles of streams. The estimated cost for the entire project is $62 million. In 2012 and 2013, the Great Works Dam (built in 1887) and Veazie Dam (built in 1913) were removed, completing the first phase.

Smaller stream restoration projects may be part of larger restoration efforts involving estuaries, bays, and harbors. Near New Bedford Harbor, Massachusetts, state, federal, and local agencies implemented several small stream projects as part of a larger effort to clean up pollution and restore migratory fish passage. In 2007, restoration specialists partially breached the Sawmill Dam and constructed a passage structure, or "fishway," consisting of a stone step-pool system designed to mimic natural conditions (**Figure 12.1.3**). Data collected from 2007 to 2011 show that river herring (alewives and blueback herring) increased over 1000% as fish passage around Sawmill and another nearby dam allowed access to prime spawning grounds.

Stream Restoration Science

Stream restoration practices have become a lucrative business for hundreds of companies throughout the United States, with Americans spending an estimated $1 billion annually on stream projects. However, the science of stream restoration is still in its infancy. At the University of California at Berkeley, scientists are experimenting with a scale model of a meandering gravel-bed river in a laboratory to understand interactions among gravel, sand, vegetation, and meander erosion and deposition processes—a project whose results will find useful application in restoration practices. At the multidisciplinary National Center for Earth Surface Dynamics at the University of Minnesota, one research goal is to develop a set of free, downloadable scientifically based tools for restoration methodology (see **http://www.nced.umn.edu/content/streams-science-restoration**).

Given the complexities of streams and their ecosystems, some intuitive and artistic license is often used when designing a stream, and not all designs withstand the test of time. Furthermore, the intensive monitoring needed to evaluate success or failure after a project's completion is often neglected due to lack of funds. One example of the long-term ecological studies that are necessary to advance and improve stream restoration science is the Baltimore Ecosystem Study by the Long Term Ecological Research Network, funded by the National Science Foundation (**http://www.lternet.edu/sites/bes**).

Ongoing dam removals and continued societal and scientific emphasis on ecosystem health have made stream restoration science a growing field of applied fluvial geomorphology—and one to which geographers and other Earth systems scientists are poised to contribute.

1. What stream restoration projects are occurring near your campus or home? Summarize the restoration goals and the degree of success achieved.
2. Where is the closest dam in your region, and what is its age? Do you recommend restoration of this stream? Explain.

(a) Sawmill Dam, before it was partially breached during fishway construction.

(b) Step-pool fish passage structure.

▲**Figure 12.1.3 Step-pool fishway construction on the Acushnet River, Massachusetts.** [Steve Block/NOAA.]

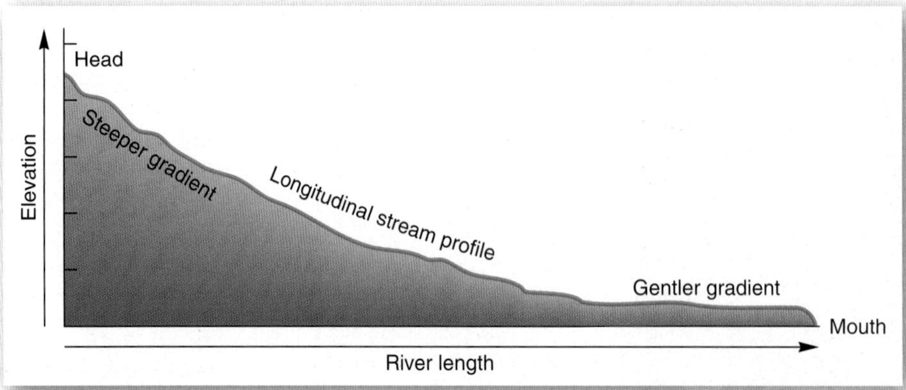

▲**Figure 12.15 A characteristic longitudinal profile.** The characteristic sloping profile of a stream from headwaters to mouth. Upstream segments of the profile have a steeper gradient; downstream the gradient is gentler.

oxbow lake was called Carter Lake and remains the state boundary. Today, the city of Carter Lake is the only part of Iowa that lies west of the Missouri River. Other states have taken precautions against such events. To avoid boundary disputes along the Rio Grande near El Paso, Texas, and along the Colorado River between Arizona and California, surveys have permanently established political boundaries independent of changing river locations.

Graded Streams

The changes in a river's gradient from its headwater to its mouth are usually represented in a side view called a *longitudinal profile.* The curve of a river's overall gradient is generally concave (**Figure 12.15**). As mentioned earlier, a river characteristically has a steeper slope nearer the headwaters and a more gradual slope downstream. The causes of this shape are related to the energy available to the stream for transporting the load it receives.

The tendency of natural systems, including streams, to move toward a state of equilibrium causes stream channels, over a period of years, to adjust their channel characteristics so that the flow is able to move the sediment supplied from the drainage basin. A **graded stream** is one in which the channel slope has adjusted, given the discharge and channel conditions, so that stream velocity is just enough to transport the sediment load.

A graded stream has the characteristic longitudinal profile illustrated in Figure 12.15. Any variation, or bump, in the profile, such as the steep drop of a waterfall, will be smoothed out over time as the stream adjusts toward a graded condition. Attainment of a graded condition does not mean that the stream is at its lowest gradient, but rather that it has achieved a state of *dynamic equilibrium* between its gradient and its sediment load. This balance depends on many factors that work together on the landscape and within the river system.

An individual stream can have both graded and ungraded portions, and it can have graded sections without having an overall graded slope. In fact, variations and interruptions are the rule rather than the exception. Disturbances in a drainage basin, such as mass wasting on hillslopes that carries material into stream channels or overgrazing of riparian vegetation and associated streambank instability, can cause disruptions to this equilibrium condition. The concept of stream gradation is intimately tied to stream gradient; any change in the characteristic longitudinal profile of a river causes the system to respond, seeking a graded condition. The following discussions of tectonic uplift and of nickpoints delve further into this concept.

Tectonic Uplift A graded stream can be affected by tectonic uplift that changes the elevation of the stream relative to its base level. Such lifting of the landscape increases the stream gradient, stimulating erosional activity. A previously low-energy river flowing through the newly uplifted landscape becomes *rejuvenated*; that is, the river gains energy and actively returns to downcutting. The associated degradation of the channel can eventually form *entrenched meanders* that are deeply incised in the landscape (**Figure 12.16**). Such a stream is called an *antecedent stream* (from the Greek *ante*, meaning "before") because it downcuts at the same rate at which the uplift occurs, thus maintaining its course. Note that superposed streams, mentioned earlier, do not downcut as uplift occurs; instead, they superpose their original course on older rock strata that become exposed by erosion.

Nickpoints When the longitudinal profile of a stream contains an abrupt change in gradient, such as at a waterfall or an area of rapids, the point of interruption is a **nickpoint** (also spelled *knickpoint*). Nickpoints can result when a stream flows across a resistant rock layer or a recent fault line or area of surface deformation. Temporary blockage in a channel, caused by a landslide or a logjam, also could be considered a nickpoint; when the logjam breaks, the stream quickly readjusts its channel to its former grade. Thus, a nickpoint is a relatively temporary and mobile feature on the landscape.

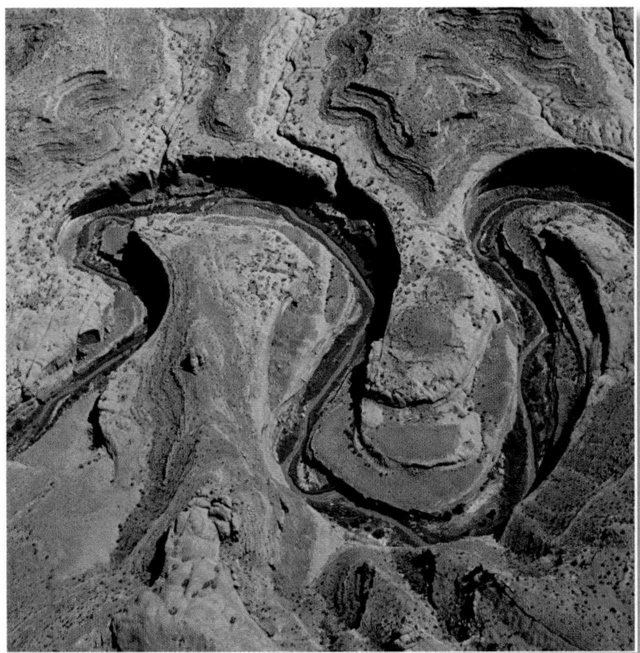

▲**Figure 12.16 Aerial view of entrenched meanders.** Aerial view of entrenched meanders of the Escalante River, Utah, on the Colorado Plateau, a high tableland that was uplifted during the Laramide orogeny. [James Kay/SCPhotos/Alamy.]

Figure 12.17 shows two nickpoints— an area of rapids (with an increased gradient) and a waterfall (with an even steeper gradient). At a waterfall, the conversion of potential energy in the water at the lip of the falls to concentrated kinetic energy at the base works to eliminate the nickpoint interruption and smooth out the gradient. At the edge of a waterfall, a stream is free-falling, moving at high velocity under the acceleration of gravity, and causes abrasion and hydraulic action in the channel below. Over time, the increased erosive action slowly undercuts the waterfall. Eventually, the rock ledge at the lip of the fall collapses, and the height of the waterfall is gradually reduced as debris accumulates at its base. Thus, a nickpoint migrates upstream, sometimes for kilometers, until it becomes a series of rapids and is eventually eliminated.

In the region of Niagara Falls on the Ontario–New York border, glaciers advanced and then receded some 13,000 years ago. In doing so, they exposed resistant rock strata that are underlain by less resistant shales. The resulting tilted formation is a *cuesta*, which is a ridge with a steep slope on one side (called an escarpment) and beds gently sloping away on the other side (**Figure 12.18a**). The Niagara escarpment actually stretches across more than 700 km (435 mi); from east of the falls, it extends northward through Ontario, Canada, and the Upper Peninsula of Michigan and then curves south through Wisconsin along the western shore of Lake Michigan and the Door Peninsula. As the less resistant material continues to weather, the overlying rock strata collapse, and Niagara Falls erodes upstream toward Lake Erie (this is the process of headward erosion, described earlier in the chapter). Engineers occasionally use control facilities upstream to reduce flows over the American Falls at Niagara in order to inspect cliff erosion, which has moved the location of the falls more than 11 km (6.8 mi) upstream from the steep face of the Niagara escarpment (**Figures 12.18b** and **12.18c**).

Depositional Landforms

The general term for the unconsolidated clay, silt, sand, gravel, and mineral fragments deposited by running water is **alluvium**, which may accumulate as sorted or semisorted sediment. The process of *fluvial deposition* occurs when a stream deposits alluvium, thereby creating depositional landforms, such as bars, floodplains, terraces, and deltas.

Floodplains The flat, low-lying area adjacent to a channel and subjected to recurrent flooding is a **floodplain**. It is the area that is inundated when the river overflows its channel during times of high flow. When

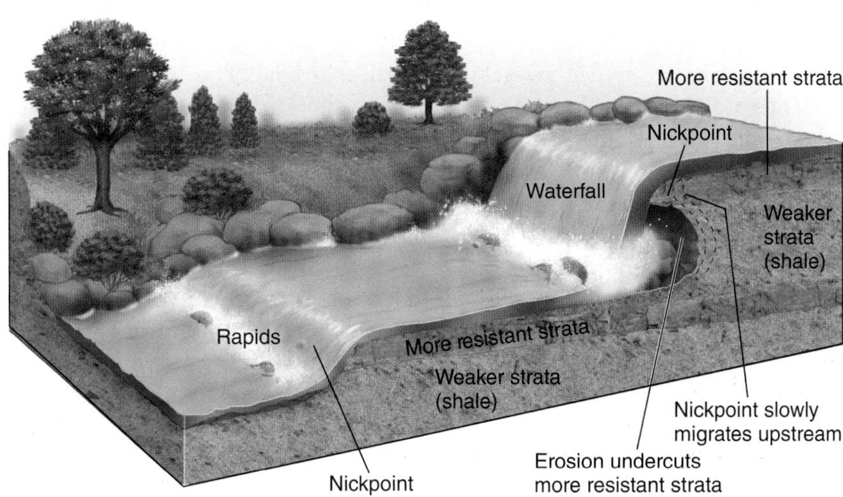

◀**Figure 12.17 Nickpoints interrupting a stream profile.** Longitudinal profile of a stream section shows nickpoints produced by resistant rock strata. Stream energy is concentrated at the nickpoint, accelerating erosion, which will eventually eliminate the feature.

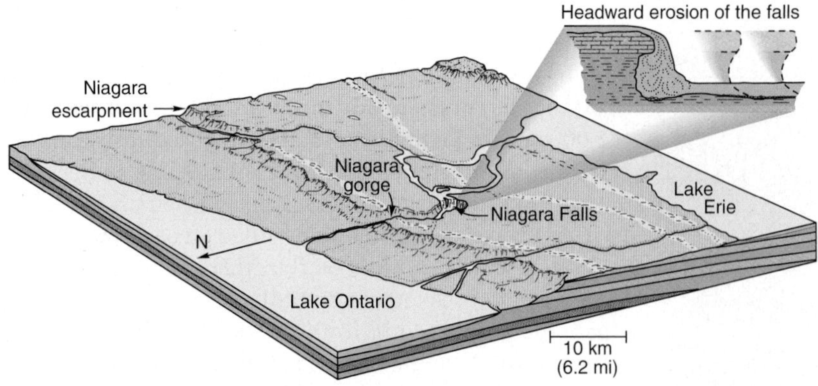

(a) Headward retreat of Niagara Falls from the Niagara escarpment has been ongoing for about 12,000 years, at a pace of about 1.3 m (4.3 ft) per year.

(b) Niagara Falls, with the American Falls portion shut off for engineering inspection. Horseshoe Falls in the background is still flowing over its 57-m (188-ft) plunge.

(c) American Falls at full release.

◄Figure 12.18 Retreat of Niagara Falls. [(a) After W. K. Hamblin, *Earth's Dynamic Systems*, 6th ed., Pearson Prentice Hall, Inc. © 1992, Figure 12.15, p. 246. (b) Courtesy of the New York Power Authority. (c) Bobbé Christopherson.]

the water recedes, it leaves behind alluvial deposits that generally mask the underlying rock with their accumulating thickness. The present river channel is embedded in these alluvial deposits. As discussed earlier, stream meanders tend to migrate laterally across a valley; over time, they produce characteristic depositional landforms in the floodplain, some of which are portrayed in **Figure 12.19**.

On either bank of some rivers, low ridges of coarse sediment known as **natural levees** are formed as by-products of flooding. As discharge increases during a flood, the river overflows its banks, loses stream competence and capacity as it spreads out, and drops a portion of its sediment load. Coarser, sand-sized particles (or larger) are deposited first, forming the principal component of the natural levees; finer silts and clays are deposited farther from the river. Successive floods increase the height of the natural levees (*levée* is French for "raising"). These may grow in height until the river channel becomes elevated, or *perched*, above the surrounding floodplain.

On meandering river floodplains, wetlands known as *riparian marshes* (sometimes called backswamps) often form in the poorly drained fine sediments deposited by overbank flows (Figure 12.19b). Another floodplain feature is *yazoo streams*, also known as *yazoo tributaries*, which flow parallel to the main river, but are blocked from joining it by the presence of natural levees. (These streams are named after the Yazoo River in the southern part of the Mississippi River floodplain.)

Low-lying ridges of alluvium that accumulate on the inside of meander bends as they migrate across a floodplain often form a landscape referred to as *bar and swale topography* (the bars form the higher areas, while swales are the low areas). The map and image in **Figure 12.20** illustrate the changing landforms over time along a portion of the meandering Mississippi River floodplain.

Stream Terraces As noted earlier, an uplifting of the landscape or a lowering of base level may rejuvenate stream energy, so that a stream again scours downward with increased erosion. The resulting entrenchment of the river into its own floodplain can produce **alluvial terraces** on both sides of the valley, which look like topographic steps above the river. Alluvial terraces generally

Animation (MG) Stream Processes, Floodplains
http://goo.gl/IdctHL

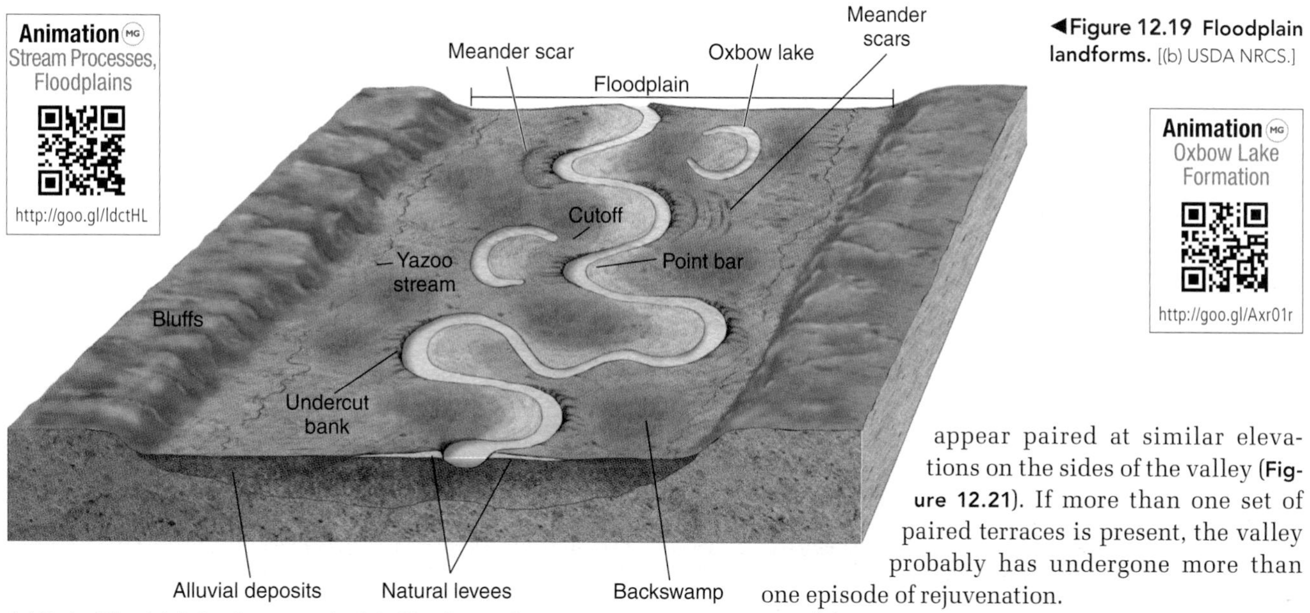

(a) Typical floodplain landscape and related landscape features.

◀**Figure 12.19 Floodplain landforms.** [(b) USDA NRCS.]

Animation (MG) Oxbow Lake Formation
http://goo.gl/Axr01r

(b) Riparian marshes, or backswamps, are floodplain wetlands that store floodwaters and provide habitat for wildlife. Humans filled many such wetlands for development during the 20th century; restoration is now a priority, since wetland water storage feeds streamflow during drought conditions.

appear paired at similar elevations on the sides of the valley (**Figure 12.21**). If more than one set of paired terraces is present, the valley probably has undergone more than one episode of rejuvenation.

If the terraces on the sides of the valley do not match in elevation, then entrenchment actions must have been continuous as the river meandered from side to side, with each meander cutting a terrace slightly lower in elevation. Thus, alluvial terraces represent an original depositional feature, a floodplain, that is subsequently eroded by a stream that has experienced a change in gradient and is downcutting.

Alluvial Fans In arid and semiarid climates, **alluvial fans** are prominent cone-shaped, or fan-shaped, deposits of fluvial sediments. They commonly occur at the mouth of a canyon where an ephemeral stream channel exits the mountains into a flatter valley (**Figure 12.22**). Alluvial fans are produced when flowing water (such as a flash

▼**Figure 12.20 Historical shifting of the Mississippi River.** The map and image show the portion of the river north of the Old River Control Structure (see Figure 12.25c). [(a) Army Corps of Engineers, *Geological Investigation of the Alluvial Valley of the Lower Mississippi*, 1944. (b) *Landsat* image, NASA.]

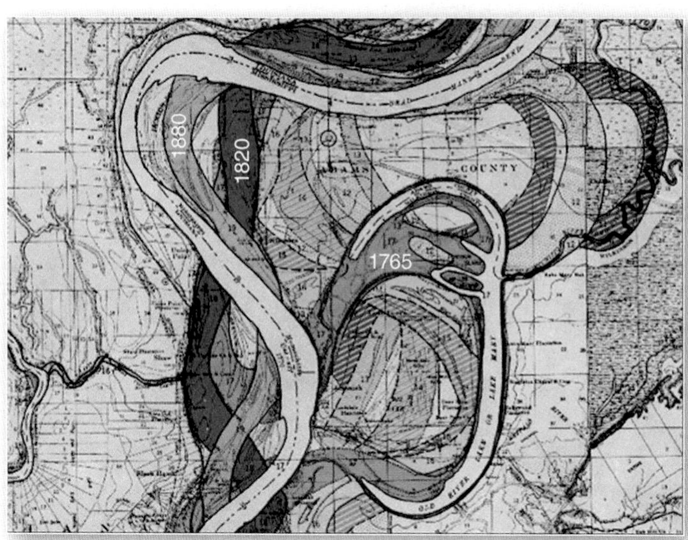

(a) Map of the 1944 channel (white) with former channels for 1765 (blue), 1820 (red), and 1880 (green).

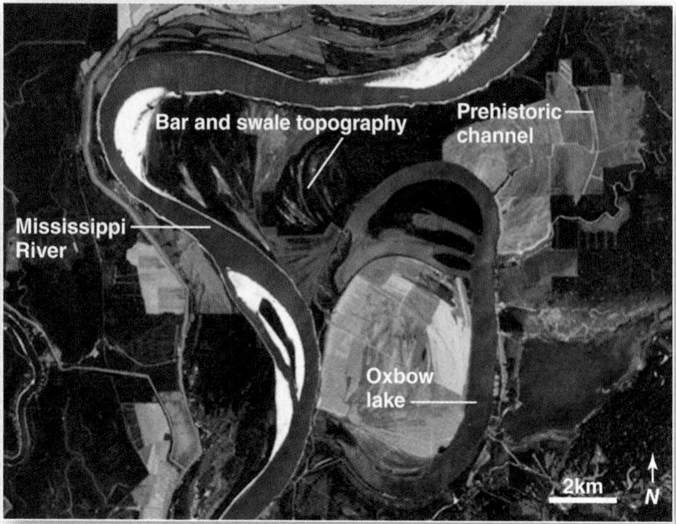

(b) Image of the same portion of the river channel in 1999.

Animation (MG) Stream Terrace Formation http://goo.gl/Y6hJIZ

▼Figure 12.21 Alluvial stream terraces. [(a) After W. M. Davis, *Geographical Essays* (New York: Dover, 1964 [1909]), p. 515. (b) Bill Bachman/Science Source.]

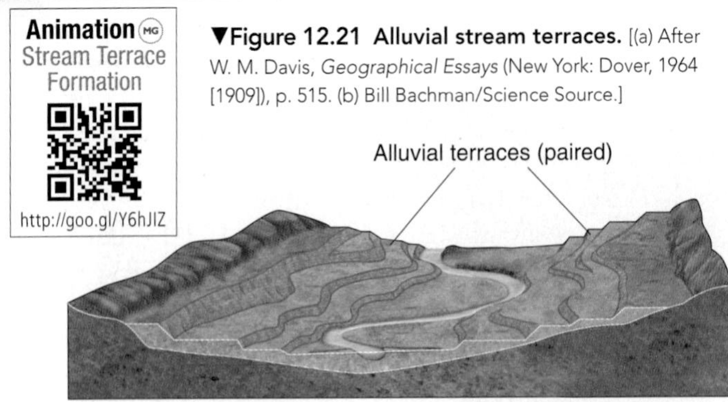

(a) Alluvial terraces are formed as a stream cuts into a valley.

(b) Alluvial terraces along the Rakaia River in New Zealand.

flood) abruptly loses velocity as it leaves the constricted channel of a canyon and therefore drops layer upon layer of sediment along the base of the mountain block. Water then flows over the surface of the fan and produces a braided drainage pattern, sometimes shifting from channel to channel. A continuous apron, or **bajada** (Spanish for "slope"), may form if individual alluvial fans coalesce into one sloping surface (see Figure 10.13b). Alluvial fans also can occur in humid climates along mountain fronts, such as in Japan, Nepal, and Venezuela.

The sediment composing alluvial fans is naturally sorted by size. The coarsest materials (gravels) are deposited near the mouth of the canyon at the apex of the fan, grading slowly to pebbles and finer gravels, and then to sands and silts, with the finest clays and dissolved salts carried in suspension and solution all the way to the valley floor. As water evaporates, salt crusts may be left behind on the desert floor in a **playa** (see Figure 10.13c). This intermittently wet and dry lowest area of a closed drainage basin is the site of an *ephemeral lake* when water is present.

Well-developed alluvial fans also can be a major source of groundwater. Some cities—San Bernardino, California, for example—are built on alluvial fans and extract their municipal water supplies from them. In other parts of the world, such water-bearing alluvial fans and water channels are known as *qanat* (Iran), *karex* (Pakistan), or *foggara* (western Sahara).

River Deltas The mouth of a river is where the river reaches a base level. There the river's velocity rapidly decelerates as it enters a larger, standing body of water. The reduced stream energy causes deposition of the

◄**Figure 12.22 Badwater alluvial fan, Death Valley, California.** [USGS.]

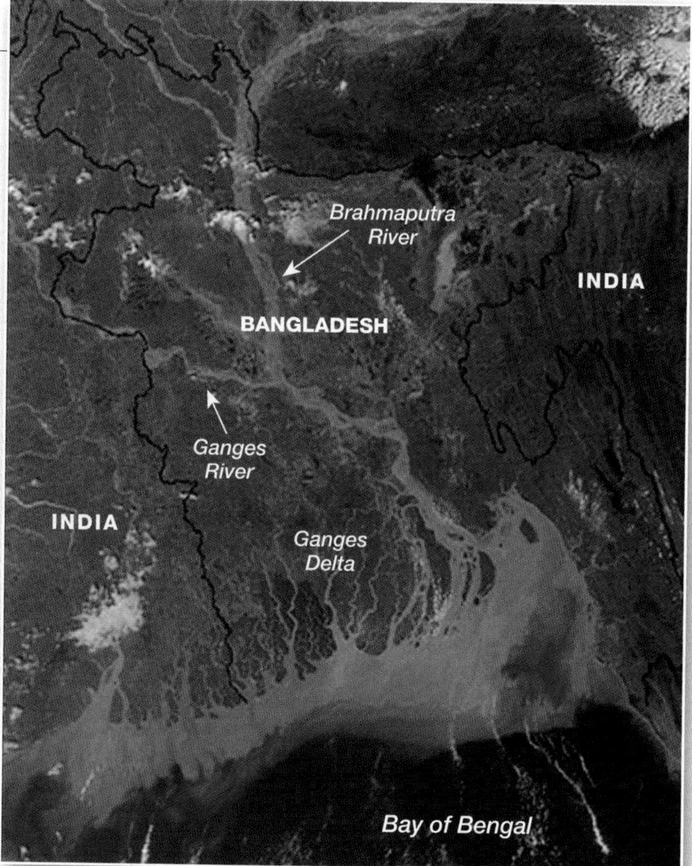

▲**Figure 12.23 The Ganges River delta.** The "Mouths of the Ganges" in South Asia, also known as the Ganges–Brahmaputra delta or the Sundarbands delta, is the world's largest delta and the largest tract of mangrove forest remaining on Earth. The Sundarbands National Park is a UNESCO World Heritage site, home to Bengal tigers, Ganges and Irrawaddy dolphins, and a rare finless porpoise; go to **http://whc.unesco.org/en/list/452** for more information. [Jacques Descloitres/NASA/*Terra* MODIS, NASA.]

sediment load. Coarse sand is deposited closest to the river's mouth. Finer materials, such as silty mud and clays, are carried farther and form the extreme end of the deposit, which may be *subaqueous*, or underwater, even at low tide. The level or nearly level depositional plain that forms at the mouth of a river is a **delta**, named for its characteristic triangular shape, after the Greek letter delta (Δ).

Each flood deposits a new layer of alluvium over portions of the delta, extending the delta outward. As in braided rivers, channels running through the delta divide into smaller courses known as *distributaries*, which appear as a reverse of the dendritic drainage pattern discussed earlier.

The combined delta complex of the Ganges and Brahmaputra Rivers in South Asia is the largest in the world at some 60,000 km^2 (23,165 mi^2). This delta features an extensive lower plain covered by an intricate maze of distributaries formed in an *arcuate* (arc-shaped) pattern (**Figure 12.23**). Owing to the high sediment load of these rivers, deltaic islands are numerous.

The Nile River delta is another arcuate delta (**Figure 12.24** and GeoReport 12.1), as are the Danube River delta in Romania, where the river enters the Black Sea, and the Indus River delta in Pakistan. The Tiber River in Italy has an *estuarine delta*, one that is in the process of filling an **estuary**, the body of water at a river's mouth where freshwater flow encounters seawater.

Numerous rivers throughout the world lack a true delta. In fact, Earth's highest-discharge river, the Amazon, carries sediment far into the deep Atlantic offshore, but lacks a delta. Its mouth, 160 km (100 mi) wide, has formed a subaqueous deposit on a sloping continental shelf. As a result, the river ends by braiding into a broad maze of islands and channels (see Figure 12.1).

▲**Figure 12.24 The arcuate Nile River delta.** Intensive agricultural activity and small settlements are visible on the delta and along the Nile River floodplain. The two main distributaries are Damietta to the east and Rosetta to the west (see arrows). [*Terra* image, NASA/GSFC/JPL.]

GEOreport 12.1 The disappearing Nile River delta

Over several centuries, more than 9000 km (5500 mi) of canals were built in Egypt's Nile River delta to augment the natural distributary system carrying water and sediment to the sea. Yet as river discharge enters the network of canals, flow velocity is reduced, stream competence and capacity are decreased, and sediment load is deposited far short of where the delta touches the Mediterranean Sea. In 1964, completion of the Aswân High Dam blocked sediment movement downstream, further decreasing the sediment supply to the delta. Today, the delta coastline is receding at an alarming 50 to 100 m (165 ft to 330 ft) per year. Seawater is intruding inland into both surface water and groundwater. Rising sea level also threatens the delta, which provides the fertile soils that produce 60% of the country's food; a 1-m rise, considered likely during the next 100 years, would inundate one-third of the delta and displace about 8 million people.

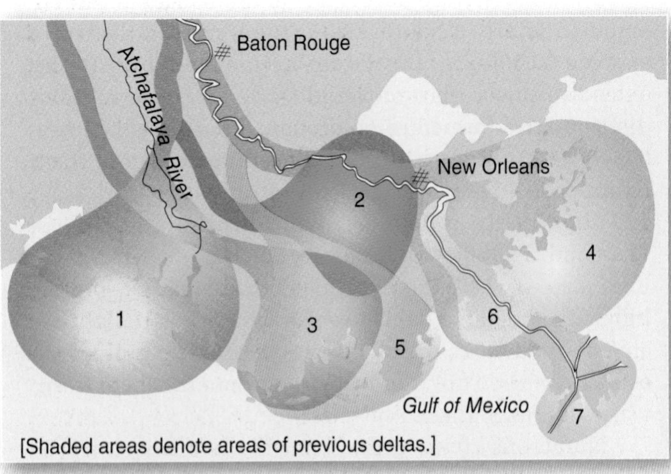

(a) Evolution of the present delta, from 5000 years ago (1) to the present (7).

(b) The bird's-foot delta of the Mississippi River receives a continuous sediment supply, focused by controlling levees, although subsidence of the delta and rising sea level have diminished the overall surface area.

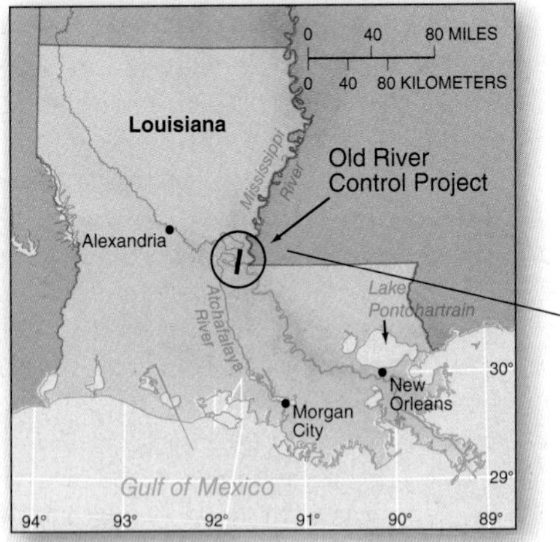

(c) Location of the Old River Control Structures and potential capture point where the Atchafalaya River may one day divert the present channel.

(d) Old River Control Auxilliary Structure, one of the dams to keep the Mississippi in its channel.

▲**Figure 12.25 The Mississippi River delta.** [(a) Adapted from C. R. Kolb and J. R. Van Lopik, "Depositional Environments of the Mississippi River Deltaic Plain," in *Deltas in Their Geologic Framework* (Houston, TX: Houston Geological Society, 1966). (b) *Terra* image courtesy of Liam Gumley, Space Science and Engineering Center, University of Wisconsin, and NASA. (d) Bobbé Christopherson.]

Other rivers that lack deltas include the Rio de la Plata in Argentina and the Sepik River of Papua New Guinea. Deltaic formations are also absent on rivers that do not produce significant sediment or that discharge into strong erosive currents. The Columbia River of the U.S. Northwest lacks a delta because offshore currents remove sediment as quickly as it is deposited.

Mississippi River Delta Over the past 120 million years, the Mississippi River has transported alluvium throughout its vast basin into the Gulf of Mexico. During the past 5000 years, the river has formed a succession of seven distinct deltaic complexes along the Louisiana coast. Each new complex formed after the river changed course, probably during an episode of catastrophic flooding. The first of these deltas was located near the mouth of the Atchafalaya River. The seventh and current delta has been building for at least 500 years and is a classic example of a *bird's-foot delta*—a long channel with many distributaries, carrying sediments beyond the tip of the delta into the Gulf of Mexico (**Figure 12.25**).

The history of the Mississippi River delta shows a dynamic system with inputs and outputs of sediment and shifting distributaries. The 3.25-million-km^2 (1.25-million-mi^2) Mississippi drainage basin produces 550 million metric tons of sediment annually—enough to extend the Louisiana coast 90 m (295 ft) a year. However, several factors are causing losses to the area of the delta each year.

Compaction and the tremendous weight of the sediment in the Mississippi River create isostatic adjustments in Earth's crust. These adjustments are causing the entire delta region to subside, a natural process that has occurred throughout the evolution of the river basin. In the past, subsidence was balanced by additions of sediment that caused areal growth of the delta. With the onset of human activities such as upstream dam construction and the excavation of canals and waterways through the delta for shipping and oil and gas exploration, the supply of alluvial sediment has decreased. The delta is now subsiding without sediment replenishment. Activities such as the pumping of oil and gas from thousands of onshore and offshore wells, and thousands of kilometers of canals built by the oil and gas industry, are thought to be an additional cause of regional land subsidence.

The present main channel of the Mississippi River persists in large part from the effort and expense directed at maintaining the extensive system of artificial levees. As in the past, a worst-case flood scenario could cause the river to break from its existing channel and seek a new route to the Gulf of Mexico. This process, called *channel avulsion*, occurs as a river suddenly changes its channel—usually to one with a shorter and more direct course—during a flood.

The Atchafalaya River, shown on the map in Figure 12.25c, is an alternative course to the Mississippi's present channel. The Atchafalaya has a steeper gradient than the Mississippi and would provide a much shorter route to the Gulf of Mexico—less than half the present distance from where the rivers separate. Currently, this distributary carries about 30% of the Mississippi's total discharge; note the Atchafalaya's sediment plume to the west of the main Mississippi delta in the Figure 12.25b satellite image. If the Mississippi were to shift to this alternative course, it would bypass New Orleans entirely, removing the flood threat to that urban area. However, this shift would be a financial disaster, as a major U.S. port would consequently fill with silt and seawater would intrude into freshwater resources.

At present, artificial barriers block the Atchafalaya from reaching the Mississippi at the point shown in Figure 12.25c. The Old River Control Project (1963) maintains three structures and a lock about 320 km (200 mi) from the Mississippi's mouth to keep these rivers in their channels (Figure 12.25d). But another major flood—one that might cause the river channel to change back into the Atchafalaya—is only a matter of time.

Floods and River Management

A **flood** is defined as a high water flow that passes over the natural bank along any portion of a stream. As discussed earlier, floods in a drainage basin are strongly connected to precipitation and snowmelt, which are, in turn, connected to weather patterns. Floods can result from periods of prolonged rainfall over a broad region, from intense rainfall associated with short-lived thunderstorms, from rapid melting of the snowpack, or from rain-on-snow events that accelerate snowpack melting. Floods vary in magnitude and frequency, and their effects depend on many factors.

In September 2013, flooding from an unusually heavy rainfall event occurred in Colorado along the Rocky Mountain front from the central to northern part of the state. During a 7-day period, over 43 cm (17 in.) of rain fell, shattering precipitation records in Boulder and in other parts of the region. Extensive flooding resulted along the mountain front and further east onto the plains of the Platte River watershed, displacing over 12,000 people and causing several fatalities and billions of dollars in damage.

Humans and Floodplains

Throughout history, civilizations have settled on floodplains and deltas, especially since the agricultural revolution of 10,000 years ago, when the fertility of floodplain soils was discovered. Villages generally were built away from the area of flooding, or on stream terraces, because the floodplain was dedicated exclusively to farming. Over time, as commerce grew and river transportation became more important, development near rivers increased. Also, water is a basic industrial raw material used for cooling and for diluting and removing wastes; thus, industrial sites along rivers became desirable—and remain so. In short, despite our historical knowledge of flood events and their effects, floodplains continue to be important sites of human activity and settlement. These activities place lives and property at risk during floods.

The effects of flooding are especially disastrous in less-developed regions of the world. Bangladesh is perhaps the most persistent example: It is one of the most densely populated countries on Earth, and more than three-fourths of its land area is a floodplain and delta complex. The country's vast alluvial plain sprawls over an area the size of Alabama (130,000 km^2, or 50,000 mi^2).

In Bangladesh, the severe effects of flooding, both in damage costs and in human fatalities, are a consequence of human economic activities, along with heavy precipitation episodes. Excessive forest harvesting throughout the 20th century in the upstream portions of the Ganges–Brahmaputra River watersheds increased runoff and sediment load. Over time, the increased sediment load was deposited in the Bay of Bengal, creating new islands. These islands, barely above sea level, became sites for

GEOreport 12.2 America's levees

By several estimates, over 100,000 miles of artificial levees exist along rivers and streams in the United States, the vast majority of them privately owned. The U.S. population living in areas protected by levees is estimated to be in the tens of millions; some major urban areas with levee systems are New Orleans, Sacramento, Dallas–Fort Worth, St. Louis, Portland, and Washington, D.C. In fact, over 30 major cities in America are located on floodplains. Currently, no national policy exists concerning the safety of levees. For more information, see http://www.leveesafety.org/docs/NCLS-Recommendation-Report_012009_DRAFT.pdf.

(a) In 2011, floodwaters flow over part of an intentional breach in the Bird's Point levee in Missouri.

(b) Sheep graze on the slopes of an artificial levee along the Sacramento River in California. Note that the agricultural fields are lower in elevation than the river, caused by subsidence of the Sacramento River delta.

▲**Figure 12.26 Artificial levees.** [(a) Scott Olson/Getty Images News/Getty Images. (b) California Department of Water Resources.]

farms and villages. As a result of the 1988 and 1991 floods and storm surges, about 150,000 people in this region perished (revisit Figure 12.23).

Flood Protection

In the United States, floods cause an average of about $6 billion in annual losses. The catastrophic floods along the Mississippi River and its tributaries in 1993 and 2011 produced damage that exceeded $30 billion in each occurrence. In 2010, floods occurred in 30 U.S. states and in at least as many countries in the world, as record land and ocean temperatures energized air masses, producing excessive rainfall totals. Flood protection, when in place, generally takes the form of dams (discussed in Chapter 6), spillways, and artificial levee construction along river channels.

Usually, the term *levee* connotes an element of human construction, and these engineered features are common across the United States and throughout the world. **Artificial levees** are earthen embankments, often built on top of natural levees. They run parallel to the channel (rather than across it, like a dam) and increase the capacity in the channel by adding to the height of the banks (**Figure 12.26**). For efficient use of time and materials, channels are often straightened during levee construction. Levees are intended to hold floods within the channel, but not prevent them completely. Eventually, given severe enough conditions, an artificial levee will be overtopped or damaged in a flood. When overtopping (known as levee breaching) or levee failure occurs, extensive flood damage and erosion can result downstream. In the United States, nearly 85% of levees are locally owned, with the remaining 15% maintained by the U.S. Army Corps of Engineers or other state or federal agencies.

The 2011 Mississippi River floods broke records dating to back 1927. Record rainfall throughout the watershed in April coupled with the timing of snowmelt to cause the flood (rated as having a probability of happening only once every 500 years in that region). During the flooding, which extended throughout the Mississippi River basin across the central United States, some artificial levees were intentionally breached, with the aim of lowering the flood peaks moving downstream toward cities. In Mississippi County, Missouri, near the confluence of the Ohio and Mississippi Rivers, engineers blew a hole in the Bird's Point levee in order to relieve the flood threat in nearby Cairo, Illinois. The levee breach resulted in the flooding of over 100 homes and 518 km^2 (200 mi^2) of farmland (Figure 12.26a).

As the water levels peaked in Mississippi and Louisiana, the Morganza Spillway (just south of the Old River Control Project shown in Figure 12.25) was opened for only the second time in 40 years. The floodplain below this structure is a *bypass channel*, designed to carry discharge from seasonal floods. When not flooded, the bypass channel is forest or farmland, often benefiting from the occasional soil-replenishing inundation. When the river reaches flood stage, large gates are opened, allowing the water to enter the bypass channel. In 2011, the Morganza Spillway gates were opened over a period of days, flooding rural areas in the bypass channel, but reducing the downstream flood crest for the cities of Baton Rouge and New Orleans (**Figure 12.27**).

In many instances, flood protection structures have not protected floodplains as designed—levees, spillways, and even dams themselves have failed. For example, in 2006, the Ka Loko Dam on the island of Kauai, Hawai'i, failed suddenly after several weeks of heavy rains; the floodwaters killed seven people. Levee failures are more common, as discussed in Chapter 5 regarding the inundation of New Orleans after Hurricane Katrina (see the Visual Analysis activity at the end of the chapter).

▲**Figure 12.27 Opening of the Morganza Spillway, Louisiana.** In May 2011, the U.S. Army Corps of Engineers partially opened the Morganza Spillway to divert water into the Atchafalaya River and alleviate flooding on the Mississippi. [U.S. Army Corps of Engineers New Orleans District.]

On Asia's Indus River, which flows through Pakistan into the Arabian Sea, heavy monsoon rains in July 2010 increased the flow of the river and its many tributaries, leading to levee and dam failures, and associated channel avulsion, that caused extreme flooding in downstream areas (see a time series of satellite images of the flooding on the *MasteringGeography* website). Damage from this event was greater than that from the 2004 Indian Ocean tsunami, as floods inundated entire cities and 3.6 million hectares (8.9 million acres) of productive farmland. More than 2000 people died, and 20 million were left homeless. In addition, more than 5.4 million agricultural workers were left unemployed for the 2010–2011 season.

Flood Probability

Maintaining extensive historical records of discharge during precipitation events is critical for predicting the behavior of present streams under similar conditions. The U.S. Geological Survey has detailed records of stream discharge at stream-gaging stations for only about 100 years—in particular, since the 1940s. On the basis of these relatively short-term historical data, flood discharges are rated statistically according to the time intervals expected between discharges of similar size. Thus, a "10-year flood" has a recurrence interval of 10 years, a "50-year flood" has a recurrence interval of 50 years, and so on. In other words, a 10-year flood has a discharge that is statistically likely to occur once every 10 years, based on discharge data for that particular stream. This also means that a flood of this size has only a 10% likelihood of occurring in any one year and is likely to occur about 10 times each century. The use of historical data works well where available; however, complications are introduced by urbanization and dam construction, which can change the magnitude and frequency of flood events on a stream or in a watershed.

These statistical estimates are probabilities that events will occur randomly during a specified period; they do not mean that events will occur regularly during that time period. For example, 2 decades might pass without a 50-year flood, or a 50-year level of flooding could occur 3 years in a row. The record-breaking Mississippi River Valley floods in 2011 exceeded a 1000-year flood probability.

Floodplain Management

The flood-recurrence interval is useful for floodplain management and hazard assessment. A 10-year flood indicates a moderate threat to a floodplain. A 50-year or 100-year flood is of greater and perhaps catastrophic consequence, but it is also less likely to occur in a given year. For a particular river system, or portion of a river system, flood-recurrence intervals can be mapped and used to define floodplains according to flood probability, such as a "50-year floodplain" or a "100-year floodplain." In this way, scientists and engineers can develop the best possible flood-management strategy. Restrictive zoning using these floodplain designations is an effective way of avoiding potential flood damage. Flood hazard mapping shows the different degrees of risk for parts of the floodplain and is used to determine costs for flood insurance (see http://www.fema.gov/national-flood-insurance-program-flood-hazard-mapping).

Restrictive zoning based on flood hazard mapping is not always enforced, and the scenario sometimes goes like this: (1) Minimal zoning precautions are not carefully supervised, (2) a flooding disaster occurs, (3) the public is outraged at being caught off guard, (4) businesses and homeowners are surprisingly resistant to stricter laws and enforcement, and (5) eventually another flood refreshes the memory and promotes more planning meetings and questions. As strange as it seems, human risk perception does not appear to improve as the risk increases.

For information on floods worldwide, see the Dartmouth Flood Observatory at http://floodobservatory.colorado.edu/. For weather and flood warnings, go to http://www.noaawatch.gov/floods.php.

GEOreport 12.3 Another measure of statistical flood probability

Increasingly, scientists are describing floods and precipitation events using the annual exceedance probability (AEP) to represent the statistical likelihood of occurrence. By this measure, a 100-year flood has a 1% annual exceedance probability.

Note that the AEP of a precipitation event does not necessarily match the AEP of the resultant flood. For the September 2013 rainfall and flooding event in Colorado that caused extensive flooding along the Rocky Mountain front near Boulder, scientists estimate that the 7-day rainfall event had an AEP of 0.1% (a 1000-year event). However, the AEP of the resultant flooding in Boulder was 5% (only a 50-year event). Had the rain fallen in springtime and accelerated snowmelt, the flood severity would have been much greater.

THE**human**DENOMINATOR 12 Rivers, Floodplains, and Deltas

RIVER SYSTEMS IMPACT HUMANS

- Humans use rivers for recreation and have farmed fertile floodplain soils for centuries.
- Flooding affects human settlements on floodplains and deltas.
- Rivers are transportation corridors and provide water for municipal and industrial use.

HUMANS IMPACT RIVER SYSTEMS

- Dams and diversions alter river flows and sediment loads, affecting river ecosystems and habitat. River restoration efforts include dam removal to restore ecosystems and threatened species.
- Urbanization, deforestation, and other human activities in watersheds alter runoff, peak flows, and sediment loads in streams.
- Levee construction affects floodplain ecosystems; levee failures cause destructive flooding.

12a In June 2013, floodwaters following days of heavy rainfall inundated Germany, Austria, Slovakia, Hungary, and the Czech Republic. According to local residents, water levels in Passau, Germany, were higher than any recorded in the past 500 years.

12b Monsoon rains in August 2013 caused flooding across Pakistan, damaging over 80,000 homes, affecting over a million people, and causing more than 200 fatalities. The Swat Valley in northern Pakistan, pictured here, had the worst flooding in over a decade.

12c In 2011, Americans spent $42 billion on fishing-related activities. Streams in Montana, Missouri, Michigan, Utah, and Wisconsin are designated "blue ribbon fisheries" based on sustainability criteria such as water quality and quantity, accessibility, and the presence of certain species.

ISSUES FOR THE 21ST CENTURY

- Increasing population will intensify human settlement on floodplains and deltas worldwide, especially in developing countries, making more people vulnerable to flood impacts.
- Stream restoration will continue, including dam decommissioning and removal, flow restoration, vegetation reestablishment, and restoration of stream geomorphology.
- Global climate change may intensify storm systems, including hurricanes, increasing runoff and flooding in affected regions. Rising sea level will make delta areas more vulnerable to flooding.

KEYLEARNINGconceptsreview

Sketch a basic drainage basin model and *identify* different types of drainage patterns by visual examination.

Fluvial processes are stream-related. The basic fluvial system is a **drainage basin**, or *watershed*, which is an open system. *Drainage divides* define the catchment (water-receiving) area of a drainage basin. In any drainage basin, water initially moves downslope in a thin film of **sheetflow**, or *overland flow*. This surface runoff concentrates in *rills*, or small-scale downhill grooves, which may develop into deeper *gullies* and a stream course in a valley. High ground that separates one valley from another and directs sheetflow is an *interfluve*. Extensive mountain and highland regions act as **continental divides** that separate major drainage basins. Some regions, such as the Great Salt Lake Basin, have *internal drainage* that does not reach the ocean, the only outlets being evaporation and subsurface gravitational flow.

Drainage density is determined by the number and length of channels in a given area and is an expression of a landscape's topographic surface appearance. **Drainage pattern** refers to the arrangement of channels in an area as determined by the steepness, variable rock resistance, variable climate, hydrology, relief of the land, and structural controls imposed by the landscape. Seven basic drainage patterns are generally found in nature: dendritic, trellis, radial, parallel, rectangular, annular, and deranged.

fluvial (p. 374)
drainage basin (p. 374)
sheetflow (p. 375)
continental divide (p. 375)
drainage pattern (p. 377)

1. Define the term *fluvial*. What is a fluvial process?
2. What role is played by rivers in the hydrologic cycle?
3. What are the five largest rivers on Earth in terms of discharge? Relate these to the weather patterns in each area and to regional potential evapotranspiration (PE) and precipitation (P)—concepts discussed in Chapter 6.
4. What is the basic organizational unit of a river system? How is it identified on the landscape? Define the several relevant key terms used.
5. In Figure 12.3, follow the Allegheny–Ohio–Mississippi river system to the Gulf of Mexico. Analyze the pattern of tributaries, and describe the channel. What role do continental divides play in this drainage?
6. Describe drainage patterns. Define the various patterns that commonly appear in nature. What drainage patterns exist in your hometown? Where you attend school?

Explain the concepts of stream gradient and base level and *describe* the relationship between stream velocity, depth, width, and discharge.

The **gradient** of a stream is the slope, or the stream's drop in elevation per unit distance. **Base level** is the lowest-elevation limit of stream erosion in a region. A *local base level* occurs when something interrupts the stream's ability to achieve base level, such as a dam or a landslide that blocks a stream channel.

Discharge, a stream's volume of flow per unit of time, is calculated by multiplying the velocity of the stream by its width and depth for a specific cross section of the channel. Streams may have *perennial*, *ephemeral*, or *intermittent* flow regimes. Discharge usually increases in a downstream direction; however, in rivers in semiarid or arid regions, discharge may decrease with distance downstream as water is lost to evapotranspiration and water diversions.

A graph of stream discharge over time for a specific place is called a **hydrograph**. Precipitation events in urban areas result in higher peak flows during floods. In deserts, a torrent of water that fills a stream channel during or just after a rainstorm is a **flash flood**.

gradient (p. 379)
base level (p. 379)
discharge (p. 379)
hydrograph (p. 380)
flash flood (p. 381)

7. Explain the base level concept. What happens to a stream's base level when a reservoir is constructed?
8. What was the impact of flood discharge on the channel of the San Juan River near Bluff, Utah? Why did these changes take place?
9. Differentiate between a natural stream hydrograph and one from an urbanized area.

Explain the processes involved in fluvial erosion and sediment transport.

Water dislodges, dissolves, or removes surface material and moves it to new locations in the process of **erosion**. Sediments are laid down by the process of **deposition**. **Hydraulic action** is the erosive work of water caused by hydraulic squeeze-and-release action to loosen and lift rocks and sediment. As this debris moves along, it mechanically erodes the streambed further through a process of **abrasion**. Streams may deepen their valley by channel incision, they may lengthen in the process of headward erosion, or they may erode a valley laterally in the process of meandering.

When stream energy is high, particles move downstream in the process of **sediment transport**. The sediment load of a stream can be divided into three primary types. The **dissolved load** travels in solution, especially the dissolved chemicals derived from minerals such as limestone or dolomite or from soluble salts. The **suspended load** consists of fine-grained, clastic particles held aloft in the stream, with the finest particles not deposited until the stream velocity slows nearly to zero. **Bed load** refers to coarser materials that are dragged and pushed and rolled along the streambed by **traction** or that bounce and hop along by **saltation**.

Degradation occurs when sediment is eroded and channel incision occurs. If the load in a stream exceeds its capacity, **aggradation** occurs as sediment accumulates on the bed of the stream channel.

erosion (p. 381)
deposition (p. 381)
hydraulic action (p. 382)
abrasion (p. 382)
sediment transport (p. 383)
dissolved load (p. 383)
suspended load (p. 383)
bed load (p. 383)
traction (p. 383)
saltation (p. 383)
degradation (p. 383)
aggradation (p. 383)

10. What is the sequence of events that takes place as a stream dislodges material?
11. How does stream discharge do its erosive work? What are the processes at work in the channel?
12. Differentiate between stream competence and stream capacity.
13. How does a stream transport its sediment load? What processes are at work?

Describe common stream channel patterns and *explain* the concept of a graded stream.

With excess sediment, a stream may become a maze of interconnected channels that form a **braided stream** pattern. Where the slope is gradual, stream channels develop a sinuous form called a **meandering stream**. The outer portion of each meandering curve is subject to the fastest water velocity and can be the site of a steep **undercut bank**. The inner portion of a meander experiences the slowest water velocity and forms a **point bar** deposit. When a meander neck is cut off as two undercut banks merge, the meander becomes isolated and forms an **oxbow lake**.

The drop in elevation along a river from headwaters to mouth is usually represented in a side view called a *longitudinal profile*. A **graded stream** condition occurs when the slope is adjusted so that a channel has just enough energy to transport its sediment load; this represents a balance between slope, discharge, channel characteristics, and the load supplied from the drainage basin. Tectonic uplift may cause a stream to develop *entrenched meanders* as it carves the landscape during uplift. An interruption in a stream's longitudinal profile is called a **nickpoint**. This abrupt change in slope can occur as the stream flows across hard, resistant rock or after tectonic uplift episodes.

braided stream (p. 384)
meandering stream (p. 384)
undercut bank (p. 385)
point bar (p. 385)
oxbow lake (p. 385)
graded stream (p. 390)
nickpoint (p. 390)

14. Describe the flow characteristics of a meandering stream. What is the pattern of flow in the channel? What are the erosional and depositional features and the typical landforms created?
15. Explain these statements: (a) All streams have a gradient, but not all streams are graded. (b) Graded streams may have ungraded segments.
16. Why is Niagara Falls an example of a nickpoint? Without human intervention, what do you think will eventually take place at Niagara Falls?

Describe the depositional landforms associated with floodplains and alluvial fan environments.

Alluvium is the general term for the clay, silt, sand, gravel, or other unconsolidated rock and mineral fragments deposited by running water. The flat, low-lying area adjacent to a stream channel that is subjected to recurrent flooding is a **floodplain**. On either bank of some streams, **natural levees** develop as by-products of flooding. On a floodplain, riparian marshes are common, and *yazoo streams* may develop, which flow parallel to the river channel, but are separated from it by natural levees. Entrenchment of a river into its own floodplain forms **alluvial terraces**.

Along mountain fronts in arid climates, **alluvial fans** develop where ephemeral stream channels exit from canyons into the valley below. A **bajada** may form where individual alluvial fans coalesce along a mountain block. Runoff may flow all the way to the valley floor, where it forms a **playa**, a low, intermittently wet area in a region of internal drainage.

alluvium (p. 391)
floodplain (p. 391)
natural levee (p. 392)
alluvial terrace (p. 392)
alluvial fan (p. 393)
bajada (p. 394)
playa (p. 394)

17. Describe the formation of a floodplain. How are natural levees, oxbow lakes, backswamps, and yazoo tributaries produced?
18. Describe any floodplains near where you live or where you go to college. Have you seen any of the floodplain features discussed in this chapter?
19. What processes are involved in the formation of an alluvial fan? What is the arrangement, or sorting, of alluvial material on the fan?

List and *describe* several types of river deltas and *explain* flood probability estimates.

A depositional plain formed at the mouth of a river is called a **delta**. Deltas may be arcuate or bird's foot in shape, or estuarine in nature. Some rivers have no deltas. When the mouth of a river enters the sea and is inundated by seawater in a mix with freshwater, it is called an **estuary**. Despite historical devastation by floods, floodplains and deltas are important sites of human activity and settlement. Efforts to reduce flooding include the construction of artificial levees, bypasses, straightened channels, diversions, dams, and reservoirs.

A **flood** occurs when high water overflows the natural bank along any portion of a stream. Human-constructed **artificial levees** are common features along many rivers of the United States where flood protection is needed for developed floodplains. Both floods and the floodplains they occupy are rated statistically for the expected time interval between floods of given discharges. For example, a 10-year flood has a statistical probability of happening once every 10 years. Flood probabilities are useful for floodplain zoning.

delta (p. 395)
estuary (p. 395)
flood (p. 397)
artificial levee (p. 398)

20. What is a river delta? What are the various deltaic forms? Give some examples.

21. Describe the Ganges River delta. What factors upstream explain its form and pattern? Assess the consequences of settlement on this delta.
22. What is meant by this statement: "The Nile River delta is disappearing"?
23. Specifically, what is a flood? How are such flows measured and tracked, and how are they used in floodplain management?

VISUALanalysis 12 Levee Breaks in New Orleans after Hurricane Katrina

In August 2005, Hurricane Katrina caused severe flooding in the city of New Orleans on the Mississippi River delta. The city's canals, built throughout the 20th century for drainage and navigation, were reinforced with levees and concrete floodwalls that failed during Katrina's heavy rainfall and storm surge. Study the "before" and "after" images and the map of New Orleans, which shows the area below sea level, the systems of levees and floodwalls, and the four major levee breaches. [(a) and (b) USGS Landsat Image Gallery. (d) U.S. Coast Guard—digital ve/Science Faction/Encyclopedia/Corbis.]

1. How does subsidence of the Mississippi River delta worsen flooding in New Orleans during storms?
2. How will the city's need for flood protection change during the next century, with rising sea level and increased intensity of coastal storms? Who should be responsible for the costs of future storm-related damage?
3. How does urbanization affect runoff and streamflow? Did these effects play a role in the 2005 flooding in New Orleans?

(a) Part of New Orleans on April 24, 2005, before Hurricane Katrina.

(b) Flooded portions of the city on August 30, after Hurricane Katrina.

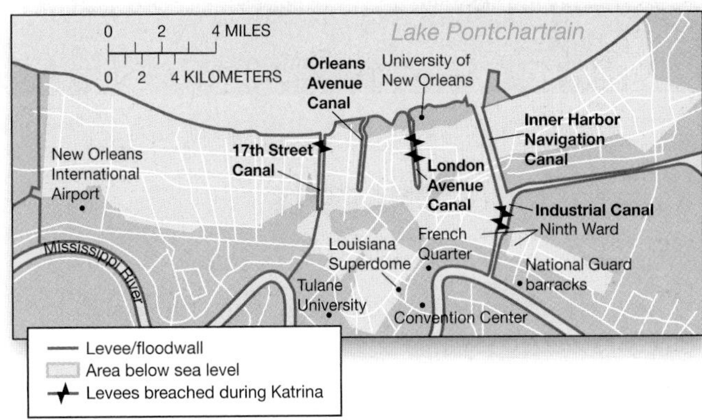

(c) Location of levee breaks.

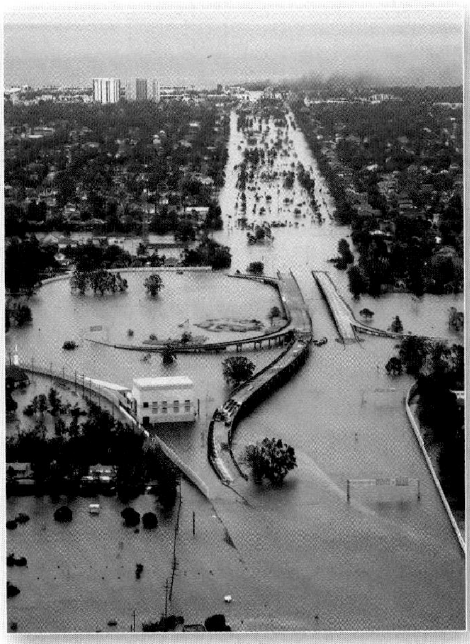
(d) New Orleans on August 29, looking toward Lake Pontchartrain with Interstate 10 at West End Boulevard in the foreground. The 17th Street Canal is just to the left, off the photo.

MasteringGeography™

Looking for additional review and test prep materials? Visit the Study Area in *MasteringGeography*™ to enhance your geographic literacy, spatial reasoning skills, and understanding of this chapter's content by accessing a variety of resources, including MapMaster™ interactive maps, geoscience animations, videos, *In the News* RSS feeds, flashcards, web links, self-study quizzes, and an eText version of *Elemental Geosystems.*

13 Oceans, Coastal Systems, and Wind Processes

Waves break west of Yiti beach, near Muscat, Oman, along the coastline of the Gulf of Oman (see location on Figure 13.1). [Ivan Pavlov/Shutterstock.]

KEYLEARNING**concepts**

After reading the chapter, you should be able to:

- *Describe* the chemical composition and physical structure of the ocean.
- *Identify* the components of the coastal environment and *explain* the actions of tides.
- *Describe* wave motion at sea and near shore and *explain* coastal straightening and coastal landforms.
- *Describe* barrier beaches and islands and their hazards as they relate to human settlement.
- *Describe* the nature of coral reefs and coastal wetlands and *assess* human impacts on these living systems.
- *Describe* eolian erosion and deposition and the resultant landforms.

GEOSYSTEMSnow

Sand Dunes Protect Coastlines during Hurricane Sandy

During the winter of 2013, several months after Hurricane Sandy, many residents along New Jersey's coastline added their discarded Christmas trees to carefully stacked lines of trees acting as "seeds" for new sand dune formation along several area beaches. The trees were intended to catch windblown sand to begin the dune formation process, in one of many such restoration efforts along the Atlantic coast. In the face of Sandy's winds, houses and neighborhoods with protective dunes in place experienced less damage than those that were more exposed to and closer to the ocean.

Dune Protection versus Ocean Views The effectiveness of dune systems as protection from wave erosion and storm surge during Hurricane Sandy, far from being a subtle statistical phenomenon, was easily observed by local residents. However, the fostering of large and sometimes obtrusive sand dunes near the shoreline is controversial in coastal communities with million-dollar homes. For such dunes to function as barriers to erosion, they must sit between oceanfront property and the sea, thus blocking ocean views and decreasing property values (**Figure GN 13.1**). For many landowners, establishing dunes for storm protection means financial loss in the short term, even if long-term protection is the result.

Video (MG)
The Making of a Superstorm
tp://goo.gl/k6HaNa

Coastal Dune Geomorphology Coastal sand dunes consist of sediment supplied by the work of ocean waves and by fluvial processes that move sediment onto deltas and estuaries. Once sand is deposited on shore, it is reworked by wind processes into the shape of dunes. Dunes along seacoasts are either *foredunes*, where sand is pushed up the seaward-facing slope, or *backdunes*, which form farther away from the beach and are protected from onshore winds (blowing toward the beach); backdunes are more stable and may be hundreds of years old. Most areas of coastal dunes are relatively small in size (especially when compared with desert dune fields that may cover large portions of continents).

Along the Atlantic coast, foredunes are moving inland as sea level rises and storm energy increases with climate change. In developed areas, this landward retreat of foredunes impinges on human development. When storms occur, dune movement is intensified, and either dune erosion or sand deposition, or both, occurs within the developed area of the coast (**Figure GN 13.2**).

Video (MG)
Hurricane Sandy
http://goo.gl/Yj3FWj

Dune Restoration Efforts The establishment of new foredunes replenishes the sand supply and protects structures and infrastructure, making this a potentially worthwhile investment of money and effort for communities along the New Jersey shoreline. Many experts point out that dunes are *not* a guarantee of storm protection and that Sandy's winds and storm surge were strong enough to erode some large natural dune systems along the Atlantic Seaboard. However, in Bradley Beach, New Jersey, where the storm eroded several miles of restored dunes about 4.6 m (15 ft) in height, the community still escaped excessive damage, since the dunes absorbed much of the storm's impact.

Thus, many local communities are supporting dune restoration, as evidenced by the 2013 Christmas tree initiative. Because vegetation is important for dune stabilization, the planting of grasses is another protective strategy being embraced by New Jersey residents. In this chapter, we discuss coastal systems, wind processes, and dune formation.

▲**Figure GN 13.2 Coastal damage from Sandy in Mantoloking, New Jersey.** View looking west before and after Hurricane Sandy. The yellow arrow points to the same feature in each image. [USGS.]

QUESTION AND EXPLORE For information and links to research on dunes in New Jersey and along the Atlantic coast, see **http://marine.rutgers.edu/geomorph/geomorph/_pages/dunes.html**. More on coastal dune geomorphology is at **http://www.nature.com/scitable/knowledge/library/coastal-dunes-geomorphology-25822000**. (MG)

◀**Figure GN 13.1 Constructed dunes.** Restored sand dunes shield homes in Mantoloking, New Jersey, from an incoming nor'easter a few weeks after Hurricane Sandy. [Sharon Karr/FEMA.]

Earth's vast oceanic, atmospheric, and lithospheric systems reach a meeting point along seacoasts. At times, the ocean attacks the coast in a stormy rage of erosive power; at other times, the moist sea breeze, salty mist, and repetitive motion of the water are gentle and calming. The coastlines are areas of dynamic change and beauty.

Commerce and access to sea routes, fishing, and tourism prompt many people to settle near the ocean. In fact, about 40% of Earth's population lives within 100 km (62 mi) of an ocean coast. In the United States, about 50% of the people live in areas designated as *coastal* (this includes the Great Lakes). A 2007 study determined that, globally, 634 million people live in low-elevation coastal areas that are less than 30 m (98 ft) above sea level, meaning that 1 in 10 people on Earth live in a zone that is highly vulnerable to tropical storm damage, flooding, and rising sea level. Given this population distribution, an understanding of coastal processes and landforms is important for planning and development.

1 in 10 people on Earth live in a zone that is highly vulnerable to tropical storm damage, flooding, and rising sea level.

Pollution is also a major concern in coastal areas. According to the United Nations Environment Program (UNEP), about 6 trillion gallons of sewage are discharged into coastal waters each year, along with about 50,000 tons of toxic organic chemicals and 68,000 tons of toxic metals. Aside from the potentially dangerous biological hazards it poses, coastal and marine pollution affects coastal tourism, which is a large component of the economy in many coastal cities.

Wind is an important geomorphic agent along coastlines as well as in other environments. Although wind's ability to erode, transport, and deposit materials is small compared to that of water and ice, wind processes can move significant quantities of sand and shape landforms. Wind contributes to soil formation (discussed in Chapter 15), fills the atmosphere with dust that crosses the oceans between continents (discussed in Chapter 2), and spreads living organisms.

In this chapter: After beginning with a brief look at our global oceans and seas, we discuss the physical and chemical properties of seawater. Next, we look at coastal systems, discussing tides, waves, coastal erosion, and depositional landforms such as beaches and barrier islands. A systems framework focusing on inputs (components and driving forces), actions (movements and processes), and outputs (results and consequences) organizes our discussion. We also look at the important organic processes that produce corals, salt marshes, and mangroves. Lastly, we examine wind processes—first, wind erosion and the resulting landforms, and then wind deposition, sand dunes, and sand seas.

Global Oceans and Seas

The oceans are one of Earth's last great scientific frontiers. Remote sensing from orbiting spacecraft and satellites, aircraft, surface vessels, and submersibles now provides a wealth of data and a new capability for understanding oceanic systems. Earlier chapters have touched on a number of topics related to oceans. We discussed sea-surface temperatures in Chapter 3 (review Figure 3.18) and ocean currents, both surface and deep, in Chapter 4 (Figures 4.17 and 4.19). The surface area of the world's oceans is discussed in Chapter 6 (Figure 6.3). The National Ocean Service coordinates many scientific activities related to oceans; information is available at http://www.nos.noaa.gov/.

A *sea* is generally smaller than an ocean and tends to be associated with a landmass. **Figure 13.1** shows the world's principal oceans and seas. The term *sea* may also refer to a large, inland, salty body of water, such as the Black Sea in Europe.

Properties of Seawater

As mentioned in Chapter 11, water dissolves at least 57 of the 92 elements found in nature and is known as the "universal solvent." In fact, most natural elements and the compounds they form are found in the world's oceans and seas as dissolved solids, or *solutes*. Thus, seawater is a solution, and the concentration of dissolved solids in that solution is known as **salinity**, commonly expressed as dissolved solids per volume. Water, you recall, moves continuously through the hydrologic cycle, driven by energy from the Sun, but the dissolved solids remain in the ocean. The water you drink today may have water molecules in it that not long ago were in the Pacific Ocean, in the Yangtze River, in groundwater in Sweden, or airborne in the clouds over Peru.

Chemical Composition The uniform chemical composition of seawater was first demonstrated in 1874 by scientists sampling seawater as they sailed around the world aboard the British HMS *Challenger*. The ocean continues to be a remarkably homogeneous mixture today—the ratio of individual salts does not change, despite minor fluctuations in overall salinity.

The chemical composition of seawater is affected by the atmosphere, minerals, bottom sediments, and living organisms. For example, the flows of mineral-rich water from hydrothermal (hot water) vents in the ocean floor ("black smokers," as seen in Figure 9.8) alter ocean chemistry in that area. However, the continuous mixing among the interconnected ocean basins keeps the overall chemical composition mostly uniform. Until recently, experts thought that the chemistry of seawater has been fairly constant over the past 500 million years. However, samples of ancient seawater gathered from fluid inclusions in marine formations, such as limestone and evaporite deposits, suggest that slight chemical variations in seawater have occurred over time. The variations are consistent with changes in seafloor spreading rates, volcanic activity, and sea level.

Seven elements account for more than 99% of the dissolved solids in seawater. In solution, they take their ionic

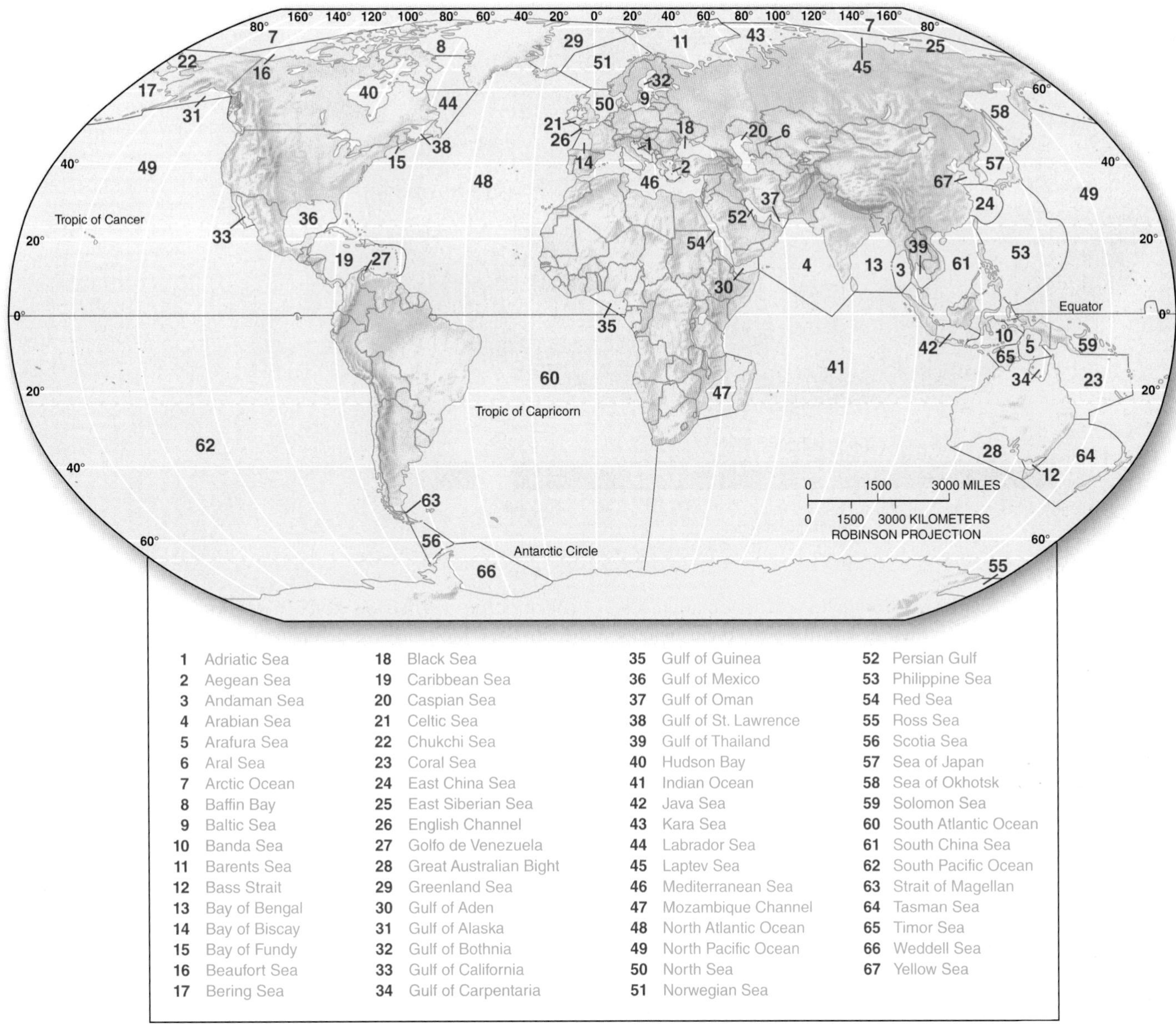

▲**Figure 13.1 Principal oceans and seas of the world.**

form (shown here in parentheses): chlorine (as chloride ions, Cl^-), sodium (as Na^+), magnesium (as Mg^{2+}), sulfur (as sulfate ions, SO_4^{2-}), calcium (as Ca^{2+}), potassium (as K^+), and bromine (as bromide ions, Br^-). Seawater also contains dissolved gases (such as carbon dioxide, nitrogen, and oxygen), suspended and dissolved organic matter, and a multitude of trace elements.

Commercially, only sodium chloride (common table salt), magnesium, and bromine are extracted in any significant amount from the ocean. Mining of minerals from the seafloor is technically feasible, although it remains uneconomical.

Average Salinity Scientists express the worldwide average salinity of seawater in several ways:

- 3.5% (parts per hundred)
- 35,000 ppm (parts per million)
- 35,000 mg/L
- 35 g/kg
- 35‰ (parts per thousand); this is the most common notation

Salinity worldwide normally varies between 34‰ and 37‰; variations are attributable to atmospheric conditions above the water and to the volume of freshwater inflows. **Figure 13.2** shows an image of global variations in salinity. High annual precipitation over equatorial oceans leads to slightly lower than average salinity values in those regions of about 34.5‰ (note the lower values in the Pacific Ocean along the Intertropical Convergence Zone in Figure 13.2). In subtropical oceans—where evaporation rates are greatest because of the influence of hot, dry subtropical high-pressure cells—salinity is more concentrated. In these regions, salinity is presently increasing as rising temperatures lead to increased evaporation rates.

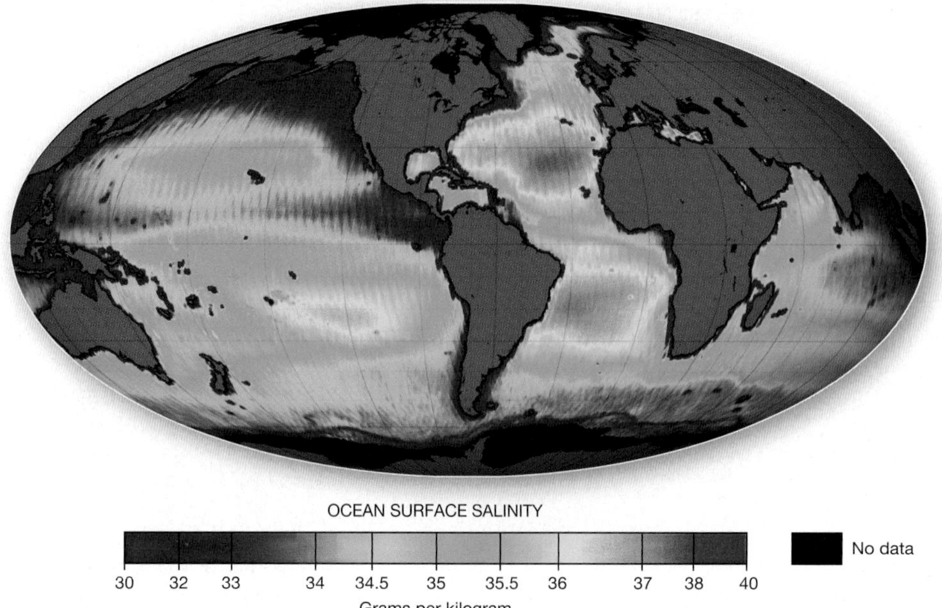

◀Figure 13.2 Ocean salinity. Composite image of global ocean surface salinity from August 2011 to July 2012 using data from the *Aquarius* satellite, in orbit since 2011. See **http://aquarius.nasa.gov/**. [NASA.]

In general, oceans are lower in salinity near landmasses because of freshwater inputs. The term **brackish** applies to water that is less than 35‰ salts. Extreme examples include the Baltic Sea (north of Poland and Germany) and the Gulf of Bothnia (between Sweden and Finland), which average 10‰ or less salinity because of heavy freshwater runoff and low evaporation rates. In general, the high-latitude oceans have been freshening over the past decade with increased melting of glaciers and ice sheets, as mentioned in Chapter 4.

In contrast, the Sargasso Sea, within the North Atlantic subtropical gyre, averages 38‰ (Figure 13.2). The Persian Gulf has a salinity of 40‰ as a result of high evaporation rates in a nearly enclosed basin. The term **brine** is applied to water that exceeds the average of 35‰ salinity. Deep pockets, or "brine lakes," along the floor of the Red Sea and the Mediterranean Sea register up to a salty 225‰.

Physical Structure and Human Impacts

The basic physical structure of the ocean consists of three horizontal layers (**Figure 13.3**). In the surface layer, warmed by the Sun, mixing is driven by winds. In this *mixing zone*, which represents only 2% of the oceanic mass, variations in water temperature and solutes are blended rapidly. Below the mixing zone is the *thermocline transition zone*, a region more than 1 km deep that lacks the motion of the surface and has a gradient in temperature that decreases with depth. Friction at these depths dampens the effect of surface currents. In addition, colder water temperatures at the thermocline transition zone's lower margin tend to inhibit any convective movements.

In the top two layers of the ocean, average temperature, salinity, dissolved carbon dioxide, and dissolved oxygen all vary with increasing depth. In contrast, from a depth of 1–1.5 km (0.6–0.9 mi) to the ocean floor, temperature and salinity values are quite uniform. Temperatures in this *deep cold zone* are near 0°C (32°F), and the coldest water is generally along the ocean bottom. However, seawater in the deep cold zone does not freeze because the freezing point of seawater is lower than that of plain water, owing to the presence of dissolved salts. (At the surface, seawater freezes at about –2°C, or 28.4°F.)

Ocean Acidification The ocean also reflects the changing composition of Earth's atmosphere. As the oceans absorb excess carbon dioxide from the atmosphere, the process of carbonation (discussed in Chapter 11) forms carbonic acid in seawater, resulting in a lowering of the ocean pH—an acidification. A more acid ocean will cause certain marine organisms such as corals and some plankton to have difficulty maintaining external

GEOreport 13.1 The Mediterranean Sea is getting saltier

The Mediterranean Sea is warming at a faster rate than the oceans—notice the high salinity levels in Figure 13.2. Increased salinity and temperatures are found in the deep layers, below 600 m (1968 ft) in depth. Saltier conditions change the water density and cause net outflows past the Strait of Gibraltar, thus blocking natural mixing with the Atlantic Ocean. As climate changes, warming is disrupting the natural mixing in large water bodies, including lakes as discussed in Chapter 6.

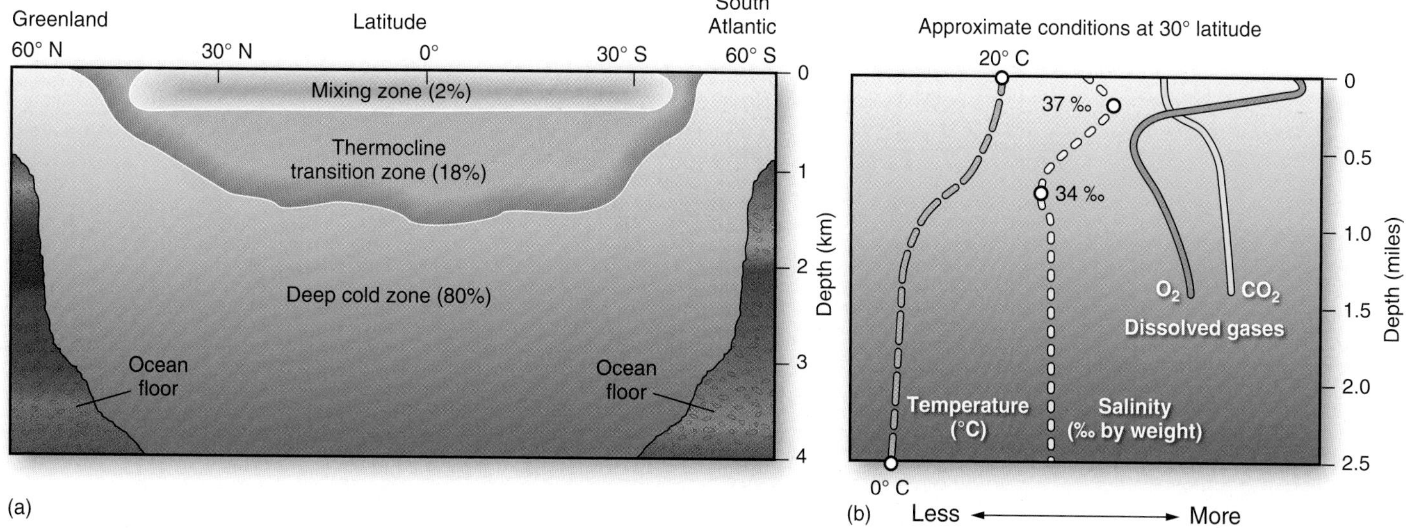

▲**Figure 13.3 The ocean's physical structure.** (a) Schematic of the average physical structure observed throughout the ocean's vertical profile as sampled along a line from Greenland to the South Atlantic. (b) Temperature, salinity, and dissolved gases are shown plotted by depth.

Animation Midlatitude Productivity

http://goo.gl/ZSXufh

calcium carbonate structures. The ocean's average pH today is 8.1, down from 8.2 at the beginning of the Industrial Revolution. Scientists think that ocean pH could decrease by 0.4 to 0.5 units this century as atmospheric CO_2 increases. The pH scale is logarithmic, so a decrease of 0.1 equals a 30% increase in acidity (see the pH scale in Chapter 15, Figure 15.8). Oceanic biodiversity and food webs will respond to this change in unknown ways.

Pollution and Oil Spills The world's oceans have become repositories for much of the world's waste, whether discarded intentionally into the ocean or accidentally leaked or spilled. Marine and terrestrial oil pollution is a continuing problem in coastal regions as waste oil seeps and leaks into oceans from improper disposal and spills into oceans from offshore drilling and transportation problems. On average, 27 oil-releasing accidents occur every day, totaling 10,000 a year worldwide and ranging from a few disastrous spills to numerous small ones (**Figure 13.4a**).

The largest oil spill in U.S. history occurred in 2010 in the Gulf of Mexico (**Figure 13.4b**), surpassing the 1989 *Exxon Valdez* spill in Prince William Sound, Alaska, in volume. Somewhere between 50,000 and 95,000 barrels of oil a day, for 86 days, exploded from a broken wellhead on the seafloor; this is 2.1 to 4.0 million gallons a day, equivalent to an *Exxon Valdez* spill every 4 or 5 days for 3 months. The *Deepwater Horizon* well, at an ocean depth of 1.6 km (1 mi), was one of the deepest drilling attempts ever made, and much of the technology of the operation remains untested or unknown. Scientists are analyzing many aspects of the tragedy to determine the extent of the biological effects on the open water, beaches, wetlands, and wildlife of the Gulf (**Figure 13.4c**).

When oil spills into seawater, it first spreads out on the surface, forming an oil slick that may be cohesive or may be broken up by rough seas. The slick may drift over large areas of open ocean, affecting marine habitat, or toward shorelines, impacting coastal wetlands and associated wildlife. The oil may partially evaporate, making the remaining slick denser; it may partially dissolve into the water; or it may combine with particulate matter and sink to the bottom. Over the long term, some of the oil breaks down through processes driven by sunlight and through decomposition by microorganisms—the rate of this deterioration depends on temperature and the availability of oxygen and nutrients. Along a coastline, oil spreads over beach sediments and drifts into coastal wetlands, contaminating and poisoning aquatic organisms and wildlife and disrupting human activities such as fishing and recreation.

Coastal restoration in the Gulf is ongoing, even though the most immediate and dramatic effects of the 2010 oil spill have subsided. Oil has the potential to persist in the environment for decades, coating sandy beach sediments and sinking into the muddy bottoms of salt marshes. In May 2013, almost 3 years after the initial Gulf spill, the long-term restoration of Gulf ecosystems and economies was still in the planning stages, with an emphasis on future protection and revitalization.

Coastal System Components

Although many of Earth's surface features, such as mountains and crustal plates, were formed over millions of years, most of Earth's coastlines are relatively young and undergoing continuous change. Land, ocean, atmosphere, Sun, and Moon interact to produce the tides, currents, and waves responsible for the erosional and depositional features along the continental margins.

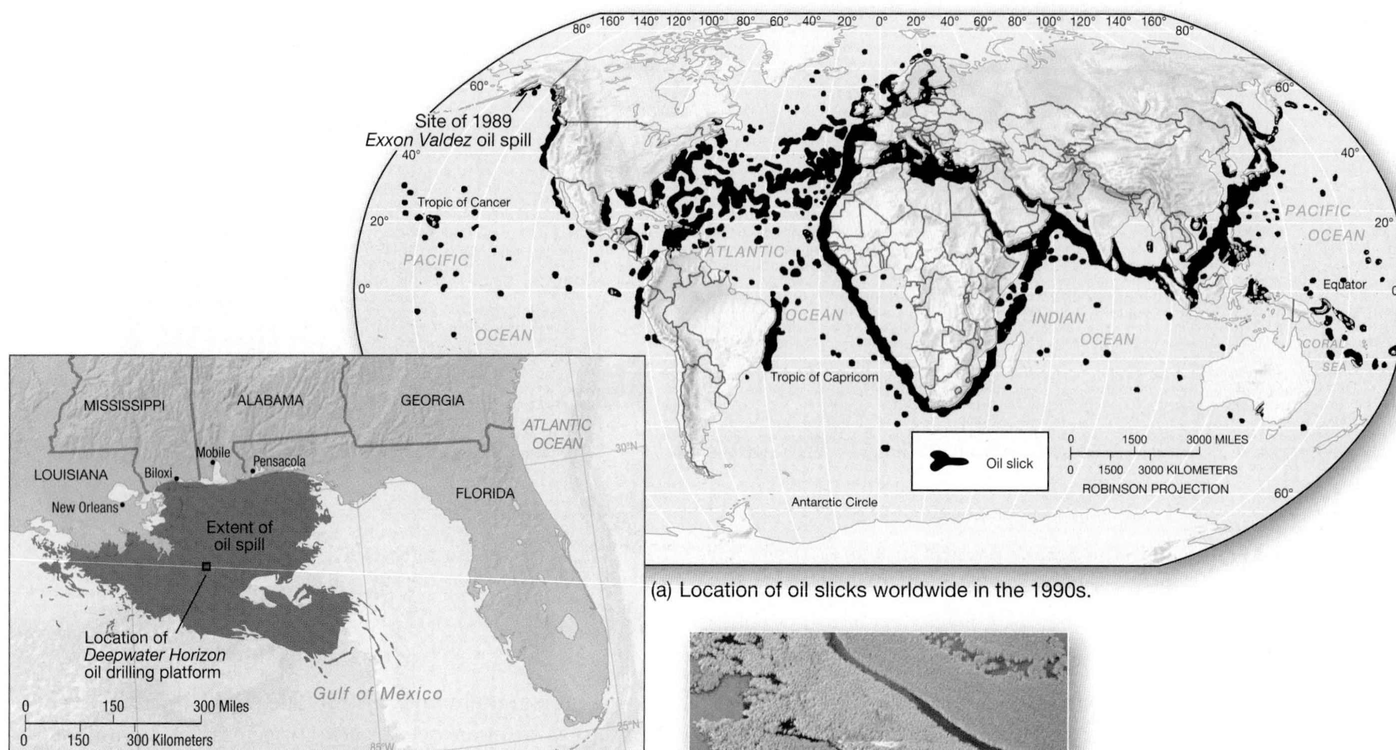

(a) Location of oil slicks worldwide in the 1990s.

(b) The extent of spreading oil in the Gulf of Mexico on May 24, 2010, just over a month after the *Deepwater Horizon* spill.

(c) Oil within a Louisiana coastal wetland after the Gulf spill.

▲Figure 13.4 Worldwide oil spills and the 2010 *Deepwater Horizon* disaster. [(a) Data from Organization for Economic Cooperation and Development. (b) and (c) NOAA.]

Inputs to the coastal environment include many elements discussed in previous chapters:

- *Solar energy* input drives the atmosphere and the hydrosphere. Conversion of insolation to kinetic energy produces prevailing winds, weather systems, and climate.
- *Atmospheric winds*, in turn, generate ocean currents and waves, key inputs to the coastal environment.
- *Climatic regimes*, which result from insolation and moisture, strongly influence coastal geomorphic processes.
- Local characteristics of *coastal rock* and coastal geomorphology are important in determining rates of erosion and sediment production.
- *Human activities* are an increasingly significant input producing coastal change.

All these inputs occur within the ever-present influence of gravity's pull—exerted not only by Earth, but also by the Moon and Sun. Gravity provides the potential energy of position and produces the tides. A dynamic equilibrium among all these components produces coastline features.

The Coastal Environment

The coastal and shallow offshore areas make up the **littoral zone**, from the Latin word *litoris*, for "shore." **Figure 13.5** illustrates the littoral zone and includes specific components discussed later in the chapter. The littoral zone spans land as well as water. Landward, it extends to the highest waterline reached on shore during a storm. Seaward, it extends to where water is too deep for storm waves to move sediments on the seafloor—usually around 60 m, or 200 ft, in depth. The line of actual contact between the sea and the land is the *shoreline*, and it shifts with tides, storms, and sea-level adjustments. The *coast* continues inland from high tide to the first major landform change and may include areas considered to be part of the coast in local usage. The foreshore is often called the *intertidal zone*.

Because the level of the ocean varies, the littoral zone naturally shifts position from time to time. A rise in sea level causes submergence of land, whereas a drop in sea level exposes new coastal areas. In addition, uplift and subsidence of the land itself initiate changes in the littoral zone.

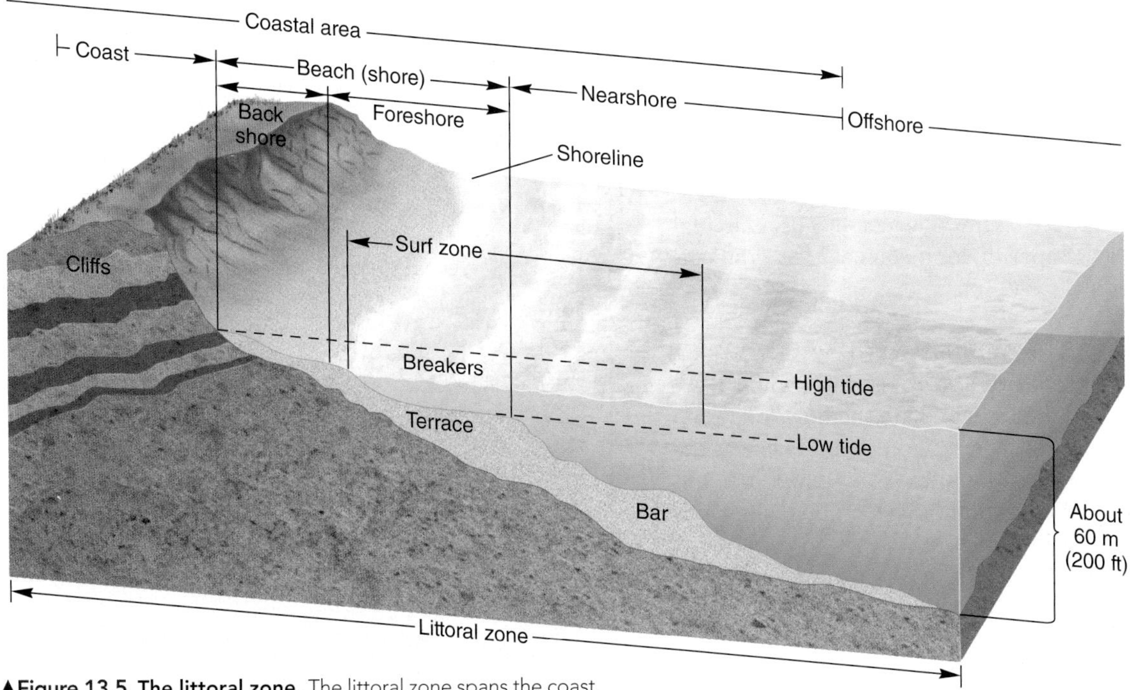

▲**Figure 13.5 The littoral zone.** The littoral zone spans the coast, beach, nearshore, and part of the offshore environment.

Sea Level

Average sea level changes daily with the tides and over the long term with changes in climate, tectonic plate movements, and glaciation. Thus, *sea level* is a relative term. At present, no international system exists to determine exact sea level over time. The Global Sea Level Observing System (GLOSS) is an international group actively working on sea-level issues and is part of the larger Permanent Service for Mean Sea Level (see http://www.psmsl.org/). Over the long term, sea-level fluctuations expose a range of coastal landforms to tidal and wave processes.

As discussed in Chapter 8, elevation on Earth is referenced to mean sea level (MSL), a value based on average tidal levels recorded hourly at a given site over many years. At present, the overall U.S. MSL is calculated at approximately 40 locations along the coastal margins of the continent. At a given instant, sea level varies along the full extent of North American shorelines, as measured by the height of the water relative to a specific point on land. The MSL of the U.S. Gulf coast is about 25 cm (10 in.) higher than that of Florida's east coast, which is the lowest in North America. MSL values rise as one moves northward along the east coast, being 38 cm (15 in.) higher in Maine than in Florida. Along the U.S. west coast, MSL is higher than Florida's by about 58 cm (23 in.) in San Diego and by about 86 cm (34 in.) in Oregon. Overall, North America's Pacific coast MSL averages about 66 cm (26 in.) higher than the Atlantic coast MSL. For the United States, see "Sea Level Trends" at http://tidesandcurrents.noaa.gov/sltrends/index.shtml.

CRITICAL**thinking 13.1**

Thinking Through a Rising Sea Level

NOAA provides an interactive map for viewing potential sea-level rise and coastal flooding at http://www.csc.noaa.gov/slr/viewer/#. Use the "Sea-Level Rise and Coastal Flooding Impacts Viewer" to observe coastal inundation in parts of the United States under different scenarios. Adjust the height of sea-level rise using the slider on the left side. Briefly analyze what you find. Can the extra cost of developing alternative energy to slow greenhouse gas emissions credit favorably against the damage estimates from such coastal inundation?

Coastal System Actions

The coast is the scene of complex tidal fluctuations, winds, waves, ocean currents, and occasional storms. These forces shape landforms ranging from gentle beaches to steep cliffs and at the same time sustain delicate ecosystems.

Tides

Tides are complex, usually twice-daily oscillations in sea level, ranging worldwide from barely noticeable to a rise and fall of several meters. They are experienced to varying degrees along every ocean shore around the world. Tidal action is a relentless and energetic agent of geomorphic change, causing a daily migration of the shoreline landward and seaward that affects sediment erosion and transportation.

Tides are important in human activities, including navigation, fishing, and recreation. They are of special concern to ships because the entrance to many ports is limited by shallow water, and thus high tide is required for passage. Conversely, tall-masted ships may need a low tide to clear overhead bridges. Tides also occur in large lakes, but are difficult to distinguish from changes caused by wind in those bodies of water because the tidal range is small. Lake Superior, for instance, has a tidal variation of only about 5 cm (2 in.).

Causes of Tides Tides are produced by the gravitational pull of both the Sun and the Moon (**Figure 13.6**). Chapter 2 discusses Earth's relation to the Sun and Moon and the reasons for the seasons. Figure 13.6 illustrates the relationship between the Moon, the Sun, and Earth and the generation of variable tidal bulges on opposite sides of the planet.

The gravitational pull of the Moon tugs on Earth's atmosphere, oceans, and lithosphere. The Sun's gravitational pull is only about half that of the Moon's because of the Sun's greater distance from Earth, although it is still a significant force. Earth's solid and fluid surfaces all experience some stretching as a result of these forces. The stretching raises large *tidal bulges* in the atmosphere (which we cannot see), smaller tidal bulges in the ocean, and very slight bulges in Earth's rigid crust. Our concern here is the tidal bulges in the ocean.

Gravity and inertia are essential elements in understanding tides. *Gravity* is the force of attraction between two bodies. *Inertia* is the tendency of objects to stay still if motionless or to keep moving in the same direction if in motion. The gravitational effect on the side of Earth facing the Moon or Sun is greater than that experienced by the far side, where inertial forces are slightly greater. Because of inertia, as the nearside water and Earth are drawn toward the Moon or Sun, the farside water is left behind because of the slightly weaker gravitational pull. This arrangement produces opposing tidal bulges on opposite sides of Earth.

Tides appear to move in and out along the shoreline, but they do not actually do so. Instead, Earth's surface rotates into and out of the relatively "fixed" tidal bulges as Earth changes its position in relation to the Moon and Sun. Every 24 hours and 50 minutes, any given point on Earth rotates through two bulges as a direct result of this rotational positioning. Thus, every day, most coastal locations experience two high (rising) tides, known as *flood tides*, and two low (falling) tides, known as *ebb tides*. The difference between consecutive high and low tides is considered the *tidal range*.

Spring and Neap Tides The combined gravitational effects of the Sun and Moon are strongest in the conjunction alignment—when they are on the same side of Earth—and result in the greatest tidal range between high and low tides, known as *spring tides* (Figure 13.6a). (Spring means to "spring forth"; it has no relation to the season of the year.) Figure 13.6b shows the other alignment that gives rise to spring tides, when the Moon and Sun are at *opposition*—on opposite sides of Earth. In this arrangement, the Moon and Sun cause separate tidal bulges, as each celestial body affects the water nearest to it. In addition, the left-behind water resulting from the pull of the body on the opposite side augments each bulge.

When the Moon and Sun are neither in conjunction (Figure 13.6a) nor in opposition (Figure 13.6b), but are more or less in the positions shown in Figures 13.6c and d,

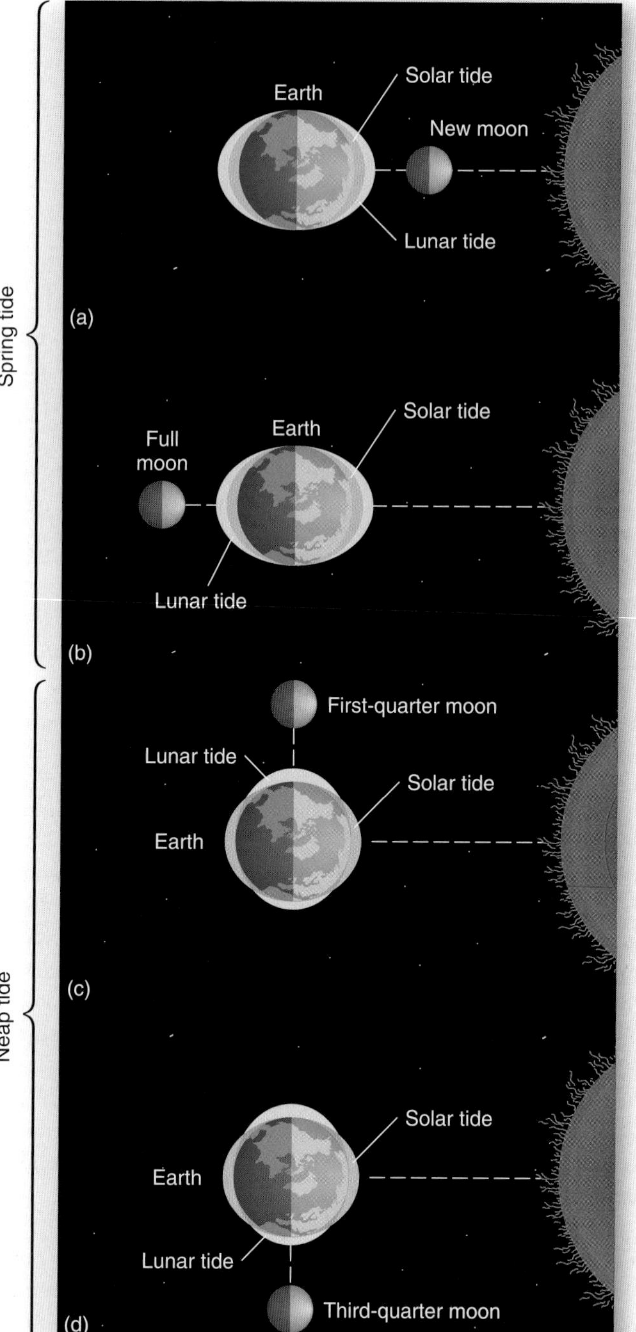

▲**Figure 13.6 The cause of tides.** Gravitational relations of Sun, Moon, and Earth combine to produce spring tides (a, b) and neap tides (c, d). (Tides are greatly exaggerated for illustration.)

Animation (MG) Monthly Tidal Cycles
http://goo.gl/KYR2Pr

(a) Flood tide at Halls Harbor, Nova Scotia, Canada (near the Bay of Fundy).

(b) Ebb tide at Halls Harbor.

(c) The Annapolis Tidal Generating Station in the Bay of Fundy harnesses tidal energy using a tidal barrage, similar to a hydroelectric dam.

▲**Figure 13.7 Tidal range and tidal power generation.** [(a)–(c) Bobbé Christopherson.]

their gravitational influences are offset and counteract each other, producing a lesser tidal range known as *neap tide*. (*Neap* means "without the power of advancing.")

Tides also are influenced by other factors, including ocean-basin characteristics (size, depth, and topography), latitude, and shoreline shape. These factors cause a great variety of tidal ranges. For example, some locations may experience almost no difference between high and low tides. The highest tides occur when open water is forced into partially enclosed gulfs or bays. The Bay of Fundy in Nova Scotia records the greatest tidal range on Earth, a difference of 16 m (52.5 ft) (**Figure 13.7**). For tide predictions in the United States and Caribbean region, see http://tidesandcurrents.noaa.gov/tide_predictions.shtml.

Tidal Power The fact that sea level changes daily with the tides suggests an opportunity: Could these predictable flows be harnessed to generate electricity? The answer is yes, given the right conditions. Bays and estuaries tend to focus tidal energy, concentrating it in a smaller area than in the open ocean. Power generation can be achieved in such locations through the building of a dam, called a tidal barrage, that creates a difference in height by holding water at flood tide and releasing it at ebb tide. The first tidal power plant was built on the Rance River estuary on the Brittany coast of France in 1967 using this method of power production. The tides in the La Rance estuary fluctuate up to 13 m (43 ft), providing an electrical-generating capacity of a moderate 240 MW (about 12% of the possible capacity of Hoover Dam). The first tidal power generation in North America also uses a tidal barrage, at the Annapolis Tidal Generating Station in the Bay of Fundy in Nova Scotia, Canada, built in 1984 (Figure 13.7c). Nova Scotia Power Incorporated operates this 20-MW plant.

Tidal power generation can also be achieved through the use of tidal stream generators, underwater turbines that are powered by the movement of flood and ebb tides to produce electricity. This is a more sustainable method with fewer environmental impacts because a dam is not built within the tidal estuary. The first tidal stream generator was completed in 2007 at Strangford Lough in Northern Ireland. In 2013, the first underwater turbines in the United States began generating power near Eastport, Maine, at the mouth of the Bay of Fundy. The main limitation of tidal power is the tidal energy required; only about 30 locations in the world have the tidal energy needed to turn the turbines. However, many scientists suggest that this energy resource has huge potential in some regions.

Waves

Friction between moving air (wind) and the ocean surface generates undulations of water in **waves**, which travel in groups known as *wave trains*. Waves vary widely in scale: On a small scale, a moving boat creates a wake of small waves; at a larger scale, storms generate large wave trains. At the extreme is the wind wake produced by the presence of the Hawaiian Islands, traceable westward across the Pacific Ocean surface for 3000 km (1865 mi). This is a consequence of the islands' disruption of the steady trade winds, which also causes changes in surface temperature.

A stormy area at sea can be a *generating region* for large wave trains, which radiate outward in all directions. The ocean is crisscrossed with intricate patterns of these multidirectional waves. The waves seen along a coast may be the product of a storm center thousands of kilometers away.

Regular patterns of smooth, rounded waves, the mature undulations of the open ocean, are **swells**. As these swells, and the energy they contain, leave the generating region, they can range from small ripples to very large, flat-crested waves. A wave leaving a deep-water generating region tends to extend its wavelength horizontally for many meters (remember from Chapter 2 that wavelength is the distance between corresponding points on any two successive waves). Tremendous energy occasionally accumulates to form unusually large waves. One moonlit night in 1933, the U.S. Navy tanker *Ramapo* reported a wave in the Pacific higher than its mainmast, at about 34 m (112 ft)!

Wave movement in open water suggests to an observer that the water is migrating in the direction of wave travel, but in reality only a slight amount of water is actually advancing. The appearance of movement is produced by the *wave energy* that is moving through the flexible medium of water. The water within a wave in the open ocean is transferring energy from molecule to molecule in simple cyclic undulations known as *waves of transition* (**Figure 13.8**). Individual water particles move forward only slightly, in a vertical pattern of circles. The diameter of the paths traced by the orbiting water particles decreases with depth.

As a deep-ocean wave approaches the shoreline and enters shallower water (10–20 m, or 30–65 ft), the orbiting water particles are vertically restricted, causing elliptical, flattened orbits of water particles to form near the bottom. This change from circular to elliptical orbits slows the entire wave, although more waves keep arriving. The result is closer-spaced waves, growing in height and steepness, with sharper wave crests. As the crest of each wave rises, a point is reached when its height exceeds its vertical stability, and the wave falls into a characteristic **breaker**, crashing onto the beach (Figure 13.8b).

►Figure 13.8 Wave formation and breakers. [(b) and (c) Bobbé Christopherson.]

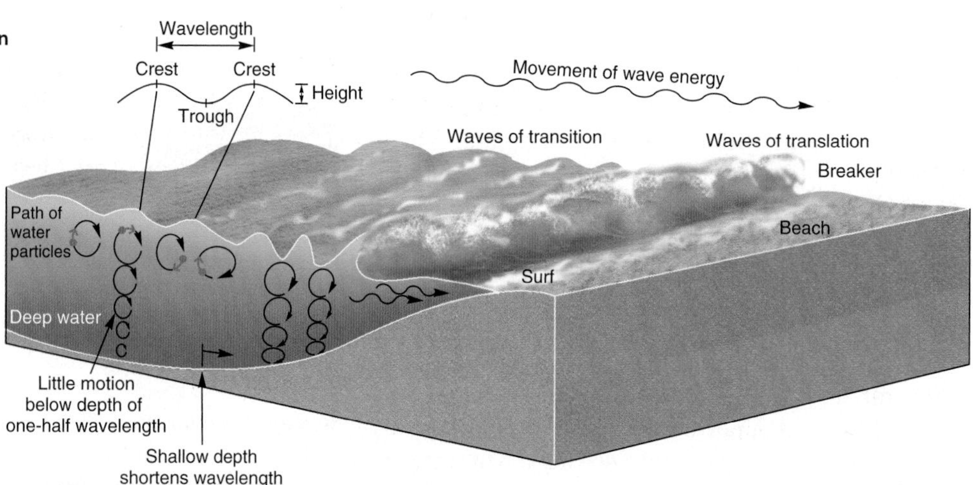

(a) The orbiting tracks of water particles change from circular motions and swells in deep water (waves of transition) to more eliptical orbits near the bottom in shallow water (waves of translation).

(b) Breakers along the coast of Baja California, Mexico.

(c) A dangerous rip current interrupts approaching breakers. Note the churned-up water where the rip current enters the surf.

(b) Headland

(c) Cove

(d) Lighthouse on headland bluff on Farne Island, England.

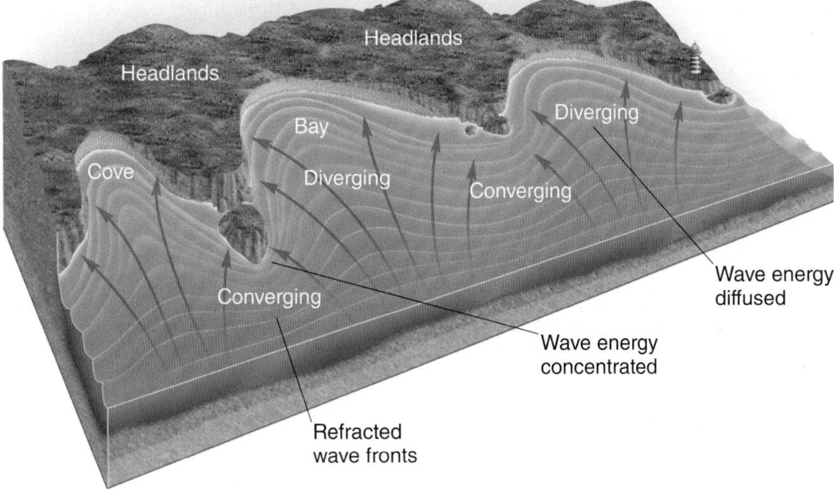

(a) Wave energy is concentrated as it converges on headlands and is diffused as it diverges in coves and bays.

▲**Figure 13.9 Wave refraction and coastal straightening.** [(b)–(d) Bobbé Christopherson.]

In a breaker, the orbital motion of transition gives way to elliptical *waves of translation*, in which both energy and water move toward shore. The slope of the shore determines wave type. Plunging breakers indicate a steep bottom profile, whereas spilling breakers indicate a gentle, shallow bottom profile. In some areas, high waves can arise suddenly, creating unexpected dangers along shorelines.

Another potential danger is the brief, short torrent called a *rip current*, created when the backwash of water produced by breakers flows to the ocean from the beach in a concentrated column, usually at a right angle to the line of breakers (Figure 13.8c). A person caught in one of these can be swept offshore, but usually only a short distance. However, drownings in rip currents are a continuing threat; in Australia, rip currents were a factor in an average 21 deaths per year from 2004 to 2011, with 59% of these occurring on beaches patrolled by lifeguards. In Florida, rip currents played a role in 297 fatalities between 1999 and 2013.

As various wave trains move along in the open sea, they interact by *interference*. When these interfering waves are in alignment, or in phase, so that the crests and troughs from one wave train are in phase with those of another, the height of the waves becomes amplified, sometimes dramatically. The resulting waves, called "killer," "sleeper," "rogue," or "sneaker" waves, can sweep in unannounced and overtake unsuspecting victims. Signs along portions of the California, Oregon, Washington, and British Columbia coastline warn beachgoers to watch for such waves. In November 2012 in northern California, three people were drowned in an incident that began when a family dog was carried away by a sleeper wave. A little over a month later, another person and her dog perished in Shelter Cove, California, victims of a sleeper wave. In 2009, a person was killed as several giant waves hit the shoreline in Maine; in this case, the source of the wave energy was Hurricane Bill offshore in the Atlantic.

In contrast, out-of-phase wave trains will dampen wave energy at the shore. When you observe the breakers along a beach, the changing beat of the surf actually is produced by the patterns of wave interference that occurred in far-distant areas of the ocean.

Wave Refraction In general, wave action tends to straighten a coastline. Where waves approach an irregular coast, the submarine topography refracts, or bends, approaching waves around headlands, which are protruding landforms generally composed of resistant rocks (**Figure 13.9**). The refracted energy becomes focused around the headlands and dissipates in coves, bays, and

GEOreport 13.2 Surprise waves flood a cruise ship

On March 3, 2010, a large cruise ship in the western Mediterranean Sea, off the coast of Marseilles, France, was struck by three surprise waves about 7.9 m (26 ft) in height. Two passengers were killed and many injured as windows shattered and water flooded parts of the ship's interior. Rescue personnel took the injured to hospitals in Barcelona, Spain. Scientists are studying what causes such abnormal waves, which tend to happen in open ocean; elements include strong winds and wave interference.

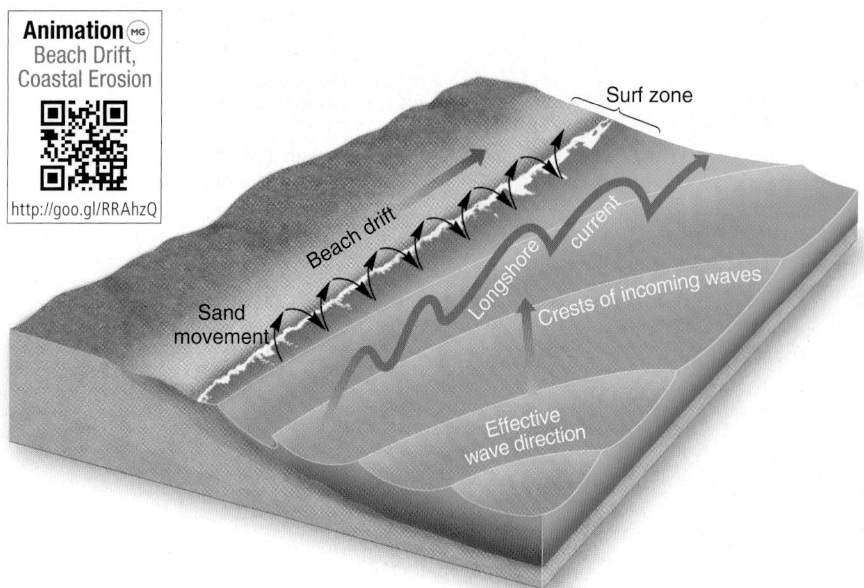

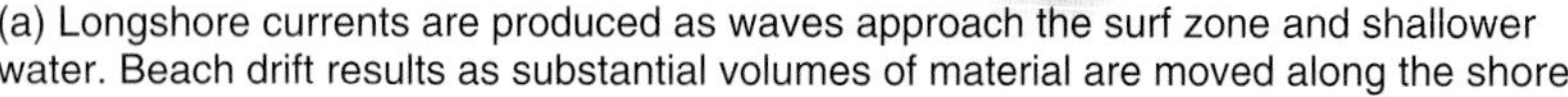

(a) Longshore currents are produced as waves approach the surf zone and shallower water. Beach drift results as substantial volumes of material are moved along the shore.

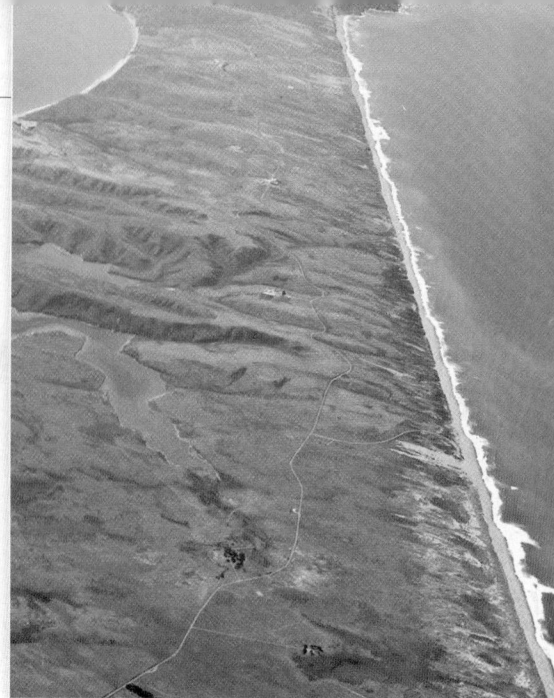

(b) Processes at work along Point Reyes Beach, Point Reyes National Seashore, California (aerial view to the south).

▲**Figure 13.10 Longshore current and beach drift.** [(b) Bobbé Christopherson.]

the submerged coastal valleys between headlands. Thus, headlands receive the brunt of wave attack along a coastline. The result of **wave refraction** is a redistribution of wave energy, so that different sections of the coastline vary in erosion potential, with the long-term effect of straightening the coast.

Waves usually approach the coast at a slight angle (Figure 13.10). In consequence, as the shoreline end of the wave enters shallow water and slows down, the portion of the wave in deeper water continues to move at a faster speed. The velocity difference refracts the wave, producing a current that flows parallel to the coast, zigzagging in the prevalent direction of the incoming waves. This **longshore current**, or *littoral current*, depends on wind direction and the resultant wave direction. A longshore current is generated only in the surf zone and works in combination with wave action to transport large amounts of sand, gravel, sediment, and debris along the shore. This process, called **beach drift**, moves particles along a beach with the longshore current by shifting them back and forth between water and land with each *swash* and *backwash* of surf. **Littoral drift** is the term for the combined actions of the longshore current and beach drift. The particles dislodged and transported by littoral drift can represent a significant volume of sediment that is eventually deposited in coves, inlets, and other low-energy areas along the coast.

Tsunami A series of waves generated by a large undersea disturbance is known as a **tsunami**, Japanese for "harbor wave" (named for the large size and devastating effects of the waves when their energy is focused in harbors). Often, tsunami are reported incorrectly as "tidal waves," but they have no relation to the tides. Sudden, sharp motions in the seafloor, caused by earthquakes, submarine landslides, eruptions of undersea volcanoes, or meteorite impacts in the ocean, produce tsunami. They are also known as *seismic sea waves*, since about 80% of tsunami occur in the tectonically active region associated with the Pacific Ring of Fire. However, tsunami can also be caused by nonseismic events. Often, the first wave of a tsunami is the largest, fostering the misconception that a tsunami is a single wave. However, successive waves may be larger than the first wave, and tsunami danger may last for hours after the first wave's arrival.

Tsunami generally exceed 100 km (60 mi) in wavelength (crest to crest), but are only a meter (3 ft) or so in height. They travel at great speeds in deep-ocean water—velocities of 600–800 kmph (375–500 mph) are not uncommon—but often pass unnoticed on the open sea because their long wavelength makes the rise and fall of water hard to observe.

As a tsunami approaches a coast, the increasingly shallow water forces the wavelength to shorten. As a result, the wave height may increase up to 15 m (50 ft) or more, potentially devastating a coastal area far beyond the tidal zone and taking many human lives. In 1992, a 12-m (39-ft) tsunami wave killed 270 people in Casares, Nicaragua. A 1998 Papua New Guinea tsunami, launched by a massive undersea landslide of some 4 km^3 (1 mi^3), killed 2000. During the 20th century, global records show 141 damaging tsunami and perhaps 900 smaller ones, with a total death toll of about 70,000. No warning system was in place when these tsunami occurred.

On December 26, 2004, the M 9.3 Sumatra–Andaman earthquake struck off the west coast of northern Sumatra

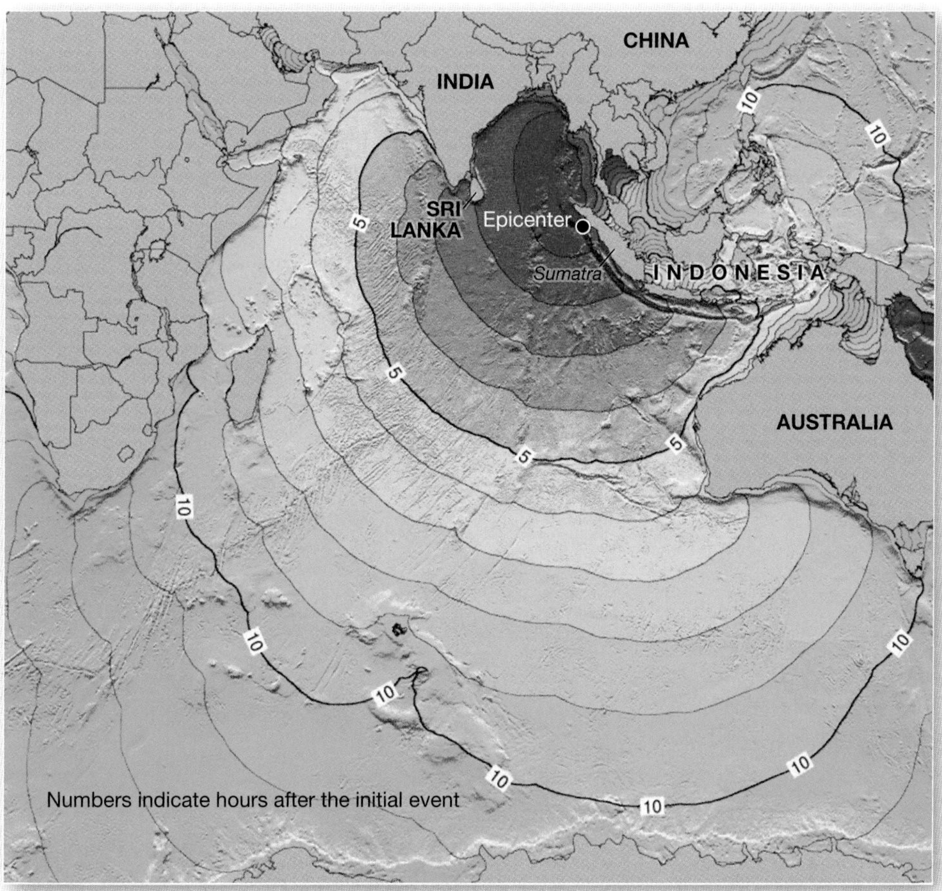

◀Figure 13.11 Travel times for the 2004 Indian Ocean tsunami. Black circle indicates the earthquake epicenter, located 250 km (155 mi) off the west coast of northern Sumatra, Indonesia. Contour lines represent hour intervals. Red indicates 1–4 hour arrival time; yellow is 5–6 hours; green is 7–14 hours; blue is 15–21 hours. Map compiled with integrated data from several sources. [NOAA.]

MG **MapMaster**
World Physical Environment
Tsunami Hazard

along the subduction zone formed where the Indo-Australian plate moves beneath the Burma plate along the Sunda Trench. (Review the Chapter 10 opening map to find this trench along the coast of Indonesia.) The earthquake caused the island of Sumatra to spring up about 13.7 m (45 ft) from its original elevation, triggering a massive tsunami that traveled across the Indian Ocean (**Figure 13.11**). Energy from the tsunami waves traveled around the world several times through the global ocean basins before dissipating.

The total human loss from the Indonesian quake and tsunami exceeded 150,000 people. After this event, the Indian Ocean Tsunami Warning and Mitigation System was created as part of the ongoing United Nations tsunami-warning-system project (see http://itic.ioc-unesco.org/). This event also prompted the addition of 32 ocean stations as part of the Deep-Ocean Assessment and Reporting of Tsunamis (DART), a global tsunami warning system developed by NOAA in the United States. (For NOAA's tsunami research program, see http://nctr.pmel.noaa.gov/.)

The 2011 Tohoku earthquake in Japan triggered a tsunami that killed over 15,000 people. Despite warning systems in what is one of the most technologically advanced countries in the world, there was little time for evacuation. Focus Study 13.1 describes the tsunami and its effects through the Pacific Ocean basin. Revisit the photos in Focus Study 10.1 to see tsunami-related damage in Japan and the wave as it moved inland.

For Hawai'i and nations surrounding the Pacific, the Pacific Tsunami Warning Center (PTWC) issues tsunami warnings. Alaska and the U.S. West Coast rely on the West Coast/Alaska Tsunami Warning Center. These warning centers, and others throughout the world, use the DART network of 39 stations in the Pacific, Indian, and Atlantic Oceans, discussed in Focus Study 13.1. When a tsunami triggers the DART sensors on the ocean floor, data relays to surface buoys and then to regional warning centers, which issue bulletins to areas likely to be affected. The effectiveness of these warnings varies; for those closest to the undersea disturbance, even the most accurate warning cannot help when there are only minutes to reach safety.

Coastal System Outputs

Coastlines are active, energetic places, with sediment being continuously delivered and removed. The action of tides, currents, wind, waves, and changing sea level produces a variety of erosional and depositional landforms. We look first at erosional coastlines, such as the U.S. West Coast, where in general more sediment is removed than is deposited. We then look at depositional coastlines, such as the U.S. East and Gulf Coasts, where in general more sediment is deposited, primarily from streams, than eroded. In this era of rising sea level, coastlines are becoming even more dynamic.

focusstudy 13.1 Natural Hazards

The 2011 Japan Tsunami

On March 11, 2011, just minutes after the Tohoku earthquake hit Japan, its epicenter about 129 km (80 mi) offshore of the island of Honshu (discussed in Focus Study 10.1), tsunami warnings went out across the country. Eight to 10 minutes after the quake, the first tsunami wave hit the northeastern coast of Honshu, the closest shoreline to the epicenter.

Tsunami wave heights averaged 10 m (33 ft) in some areas and reached 30 m (98 ft) in narrow harbors. At Ofunato, the tsunami traveled 3 km (1.8 miles) inland; in other areas, waves reached 10 km (6.2 miles) inland. Although seawalls and breakwaters designed for typhoon and tsunami waves guard about 40% of Japan's coastline, the deep coastal embayments seaward of the walls worked to magnify the tsunami energy to the point that the walls offered little protection (**Figure 13.1.1**). In Kamaishi, the $1.5 billion tsunami seawall, anchored to the seafloor and extending 2 km (1.2 mi) in length, was breached by a 6.8-m (22-ft) wave, submerging the city center.

Japan's tsunami early warning system is activated by an earthquake and uses the seismic signals measured during the first minute of the quake as input for computer models designed to estimate the size of the tsunami wave. The Japan Meteorological Agency (JMA) then issues

▲**Figure 13.1.1 Tsunami wave breaks over a seawall, Miyako, Japan.** A tsunami wave, triggered by the M 9.0 Tohoku earthquake of March 11, 2011, breaks over a protective wall onto the streets of Miyako, Iwate Prefecture, in northeastern Japan. Buildings, cars, houses, and victims were carried far inland. Miyako is about 120 km (75 mi) north of the quake epicenter. [Mainichi Shimbun/Reuters.]

Coastal Erosion

The active margin of the Pacific Ocean along North and South America is a typical erosional coastline. *Erosional coastlines* tend to be rugged, of high relief, and tectonically active, as expected from their association with the leading edge of drifting lithospheric plates (review the plate tectonics discussions in Chapters 9 and 10). **Figure 13.12** presents features commonly observed along an erosional coast. Some of the landforms within this setting may be formed from depositional processes, despite the erosional nature of the overall landscape.

Sea cliffs are formed by the undercutting action of the sea. As indentations slowly grow at water level, a sea cliff becomes notched and eventually will collapse and

(a) Conventional DART buoy.

(b) DART ETD buoy.

◀**Figure 13.1.2 NOAA's DART buoys.** The sea-surface buoy is anchored above a bottom pressure recorder, the two linked by acoustic telemetry for real-time communication. The buoy transmits readings from the seafloor recorder to land-based surface stations through the *Iridium* satellite system. See **http://www.ndbc.noaa.gov/dart/dart.shtml** for more information. [NOAA.]

warnings that include the forecasted tsunami wave size for each prefecture.

Moments after the Tohoku quake, JMA issued a tsunami warning that we now know was an underestimation of the actual wave size. The quake continued for over 2 minutes after the tsunami model calculations began, and during this time, the tsunami energy increased. JMA issued a corrected warning, but not until 20 minutes after the quake and too late for evacuation.

Nine minutes after the initial earthquake, the Pacific Tsunami Warning Center (PTWC) issued tsunami warnings to the Pacific islands and continents around the Pacific basin. The tsunami warning process used by the PTWC begins when ocean-bottom sensors register a change in pressure associated with an ocean disturbance. Data are relayed to a surface buoy and then transmitted via satellite to the PTWC. The network of 32 Pacific Ocean stations, including sensors and buoys, is part of the Deep-Ocean Assessment and Reporting of Tsunamis (DART) that monitors tsunami wave heights. These stations include conventional DART buoys—relatively heavy and difficult to deploy in high seas—and new, lightweight Easy-to-Deploy (ETD) buoys (**Figure 13.1.2**).

Over the next hour, tsunami forecasts and warnings continued for the Pacific region, and NOAA issued wave-height predictions. The tsunami moved across the Pacific, its energy guided and deflected by seafloor topography. Four hours after the quake, the tsunami overwashed portions of the Midway Islands, northwest of Hawai'i. Seven hours after the quake, waves ranging from 1 to 2.2 m (3.3 to 7.2 ft) hit Oahu, Maui, and Hawai'i. Finally, nearly 12 hours after the Tohoku quake, waves 2.1 m (7 ft) high reached the northern and central California shorelines, causing several million dollars in damage to harbors, boats, and piers. Waves 30 to 70 cm (1.0 to 2.3 ft) high arrived at New Zealand.

The tsunami warnings generally failed to help the Japanese during this huge-wave event. The people in Japan not only had too little time to flee from vulnerable coastal areas, but also expected that the breakwaters and tsunami walls would protect them. In hindsight, these structures may have provided a false sense of security. However, the warnings were effective in preparing other Pacific regions for the waves. At the same time, despite warnings in Hawai'i and along the U.S. mainland, some people actually went down to the shorelines with cameras in hand to capture images of the incoming danger.

1. After reviewing Focus Study 10.1 on pages 332-333, explain the faulting and tectonic plate interaction that caused the 2011 Tohoku earthquake and tsunami.
2. Do you favor continued funding and expansion of the DART station network? Explain your answer.

retreat (Figure 13.12d). Other erosional forms that evolve along cliff-dominated coastlines include *sea caves* and *sea arches* (Figure 13.12a). As erosion continues, arches may collapse, leaving isolated *sea stacks* in the water (Figure 13.12c).

Wave action can cut a horizontal bench in the tidal zone, extending from the foot of a sea cliff out into the sea. Such a structure is a **wave-cut platform**, or *wave-cut terrace*. In places where the elevation of the land relative to sea level has changed over time, multiple platforms or terraces may rise like stair steps back from the coast; some terraces may be more than 370 m (1200 ft) above sea level. A tectonically active region, such as the California coast, has many examples of multiple wave-cut platforms, which at times can be unstable and prone to mass wasting (Figures 13.12b and e).

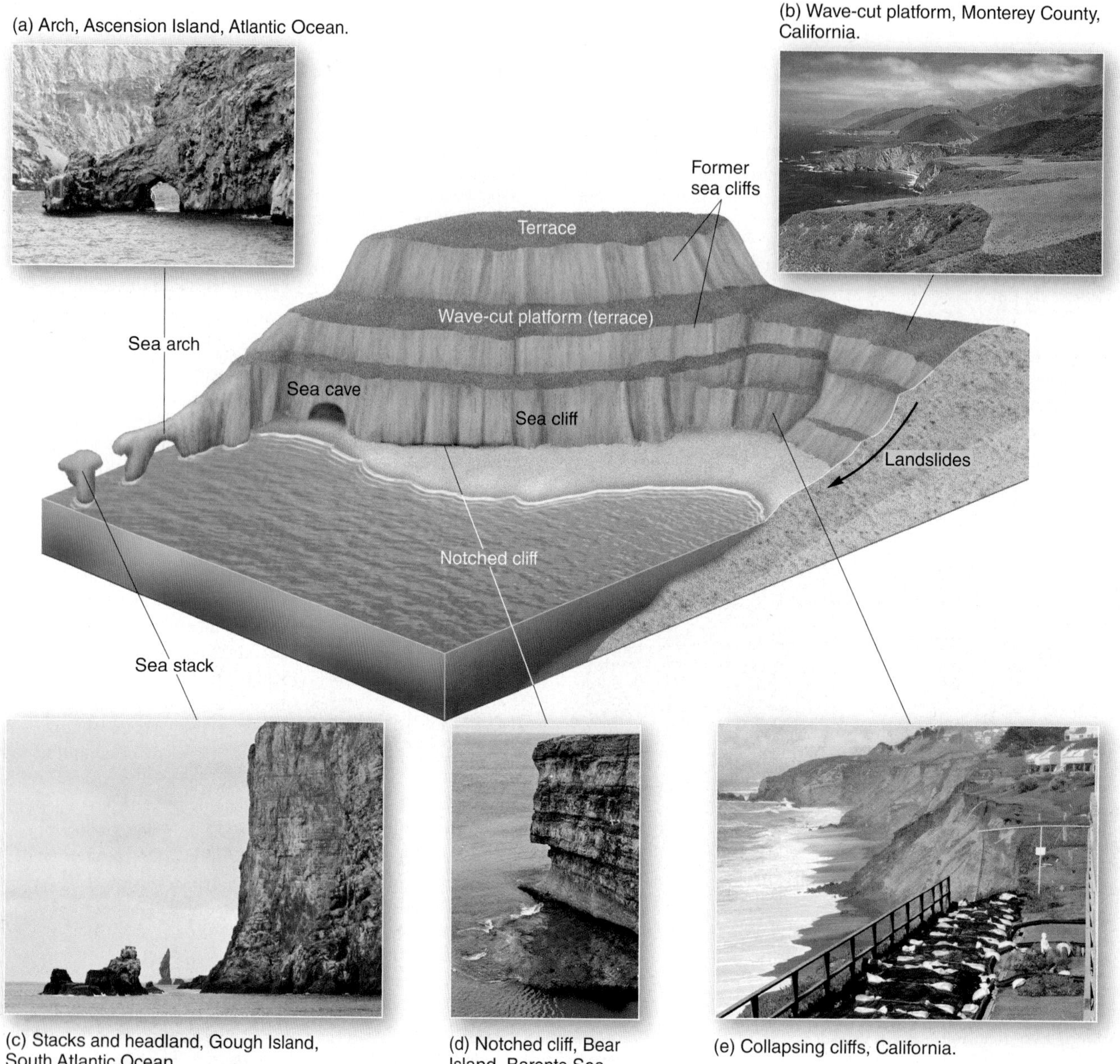

(a) Arch, Ascension Island, Atlantic Ocean.

(b) Wave-cut platform, Monterey County, California.

(c) Stacks and headland, Gough Island, South Atlantic Ocean.

(d) Notched cliff, Bear Island, Barents Sea.

(e) Collapsing cliffs, California.

▲**Figure 13.12 Erosional coastal landforms.** [(a)–(e) Bobbé Christopherson.]

Coastal Deposition

Depositional coasts generally occur along coastlines where relief is gentle and lots of sediment is available from river systems. Such is the case with the Atlantic and Gulf coastal plains of the United States, which lie along the relatively passive, trailing edge of the North American lithospheric plate, as well as along portions of the U.S. Pacific coast. Although the landforms are generally classified as depositional along such coastlines, erosional processes are also at work, especially during storms.

Figure 13.13 illustrates characteristic landforms deposited by waves and currents. **Barrier spits** consist of material deposited in a long ridge extending out from a coast, sometimes partially crossing and blocking the mouth of a bay. A classic barrier spit is Sandy Hook, New Jersey (south of New York City). Such barrier spit formations are also found at Point Reyes (Figure 13.13a) and Morro Bay (Figure 13.13b) in California.

If a spit grows to completely cut off the bay from the ocean, it becomes a **bay barrier**, or *baymouth bar*. Spits and barriers are made up of materials transported by littoral drift. For sediment to accumulate, offshore currents must be weak, since strong currents carry material away before it can be deposited. Bay barriers often surround an inland **lagoon**, a shallow saltwater body that is cut off from the ocean. A **tombolo** occurs when sediment deposits connect the shoreline with an offshore island or sea stack by accumulating on an underwater wave-built terrace (Figure 13.13c).

Beaches Of all the depositional landforms along coastlines, beaches probably are the most familiar. Technically,

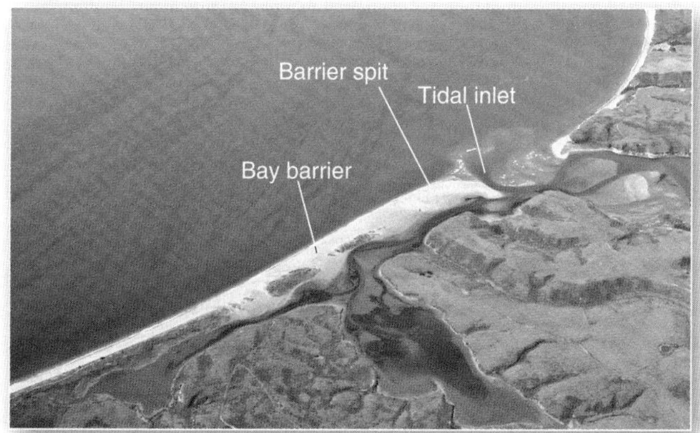

(a) The Limantour barrier spit nearly blocks the entrance to Drakes Estero, along Point Reyes.

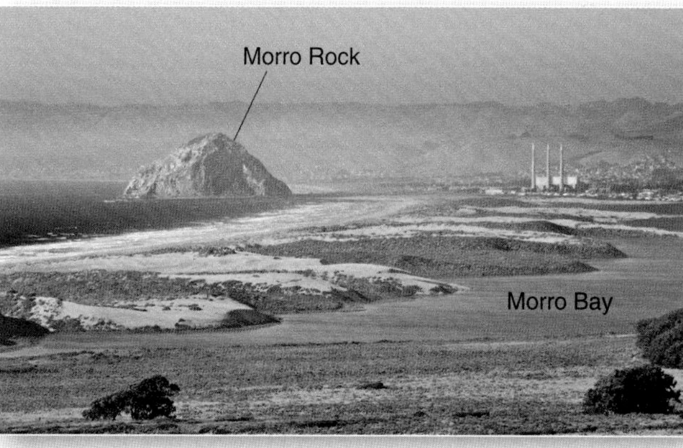

(b) A barrier spit forms Morro Bay, with the sound opening to the sea near 178-m (584-ft) Morro Rock, a volcanic plug.

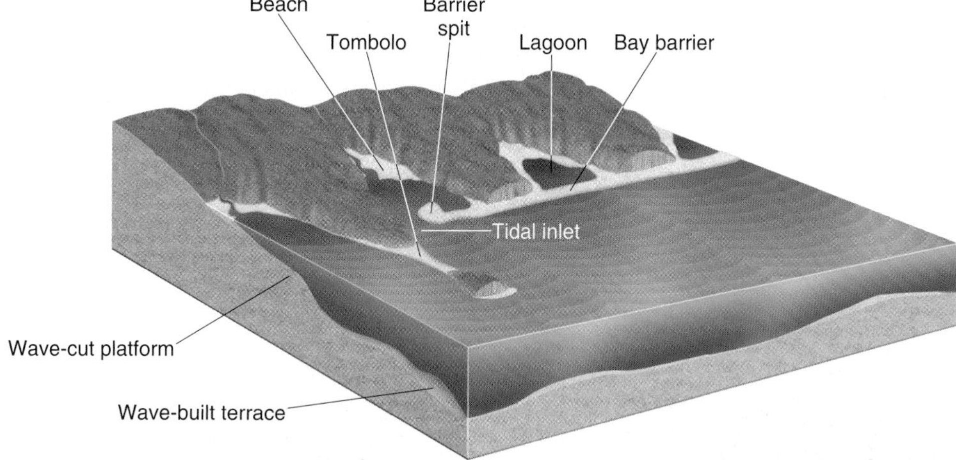

(c) A tombolo at Point Sur along the central California coast, where sediment deposits connect the shore with an island.

(d) A shell beach along the U.S. Atlantic coast.

▲**Figure 13.13 Depositional coastal landforms: barrier spits, lagoons, tombolos, and beaches.** [(a)–(d) Bobbé Christopherson.]

a **beach** is the relatively narrow strip along a coast where sediment is reworked and deposited by waves and currents. Sediment temporarily resides on the beach while in active transit along the shore. Beaches occur along seacoasts, lakeshores, and rivers. Not all the beaches of the world are composed of sand, for they can be made up of *shingles* (beach gravel) and shells, among other materials (Figure 13.13d). Gravels reflect the contribution of stream sediments into coastal areas; shells reflect the contribution of materials from oceanic sources. Beaches vary in type and permanence, especially along coastlines dominated by wave action.

On average, the beach zone spans the area from about 5 m (16 ft) above high tide to 10 m (33 ft) below low tide (see Figure 13.5). However, the size and location of the beach zone varies greatly along individual shorelines. Worldwide, quartz (SiO_2) dominates beach sands because it resists weathering and therefore remains after other minerals are removed. In volcanic areas, beaches are derived from wave-processed lava. Hawai'i and Iceland, for example, feature some black-sand beaches.

Many beaches, such as those in southern France and western Italy, lack sand and are composed of pebbles and cobbles—a type of *shingle beach*. Some shores have no beaches at all, but are lined with boulders and cliffs. The coasts of Maine and portions of Canada's Atlantic Provinces are classic examples. These coasts, composed of resistant granite rock, are scenically rugged and have few beaches.

A beach acts to stabilize a shoreline by absorbing wave energy, as is evident from the amount of material that is in almost constant motion (see "Sand movement" in Figure 13.10a). Some beaches are stable; others have seasonal cycles of deposition, erosion, and redeposition. Many beaches accumulate during the summer; are moved offshore by winter storm waves, forming a submerged bar; and are redeposited onshore the following summer. Protected areas along a coastline tend to accumulate sediment, which can lead to large coastal sand dunes. Prevailing winds and storms often drag such coastal dunes inland, sometimes burying trees, highways, and housing developments, as described in Geosystems Now.

Beach Protection Changes in coastal sediment transport can disrupt human activities as beaches are lost, harbors are closed, and coastal highways and beach houses are inundated with sediment. Thus, people use various strategies to interrupt littoral drift (**Figure 13.14**). The goal is either to halt sand accumulation or to force a more desirable type of accumulation through construction of engineered structures, or "hard" shoreline protection. Common approaches include the building of *groins* to slow drift action along the coast, *jetties* to block material from harbor entrances, and *breakwaters* to create zones of still water near the coastline. However, interrupting the littoral drift disrupts the natural beach replenishment process and may lead to unwanted changes in sediment distribution in areas nearby. Careful planning and impact assessment should be part of any strategy for preserving or altering a beach.

In contrast to "hard" protection, the hauling of sand to replenish a beach is considered "soft" shoreline protection,

Animation Coastal Stabilization Structures
http://goo.gl/9CrVbS

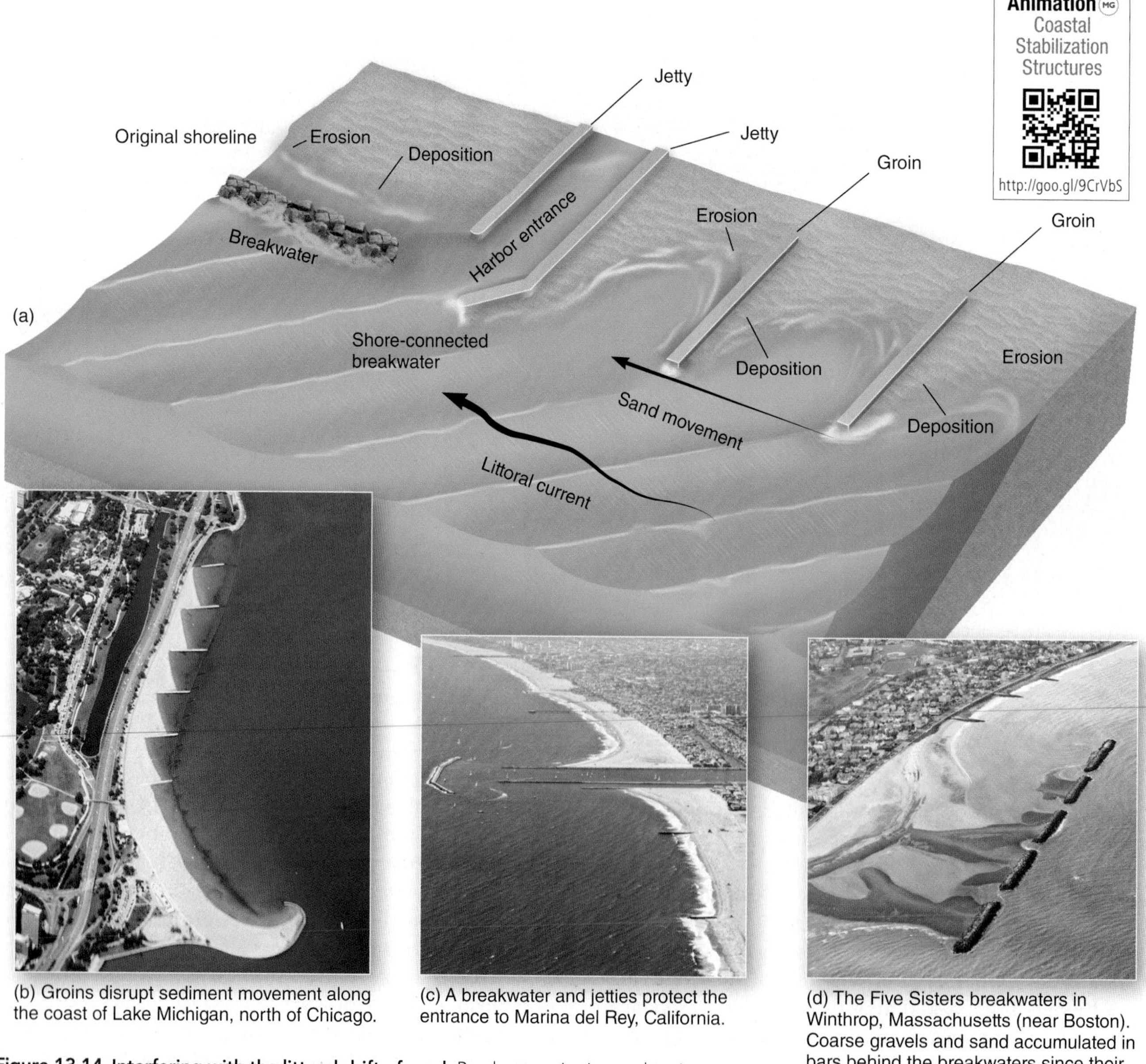

(b) Groins disrupt sediment movement along the coast of Lake Michigan, north of Chicago.

(c) A breakwater and jetties protect the entrance to Marina del Rey, California.

(d) The Five Sisters breakwaters in Winthrop, Massachusetts (near Boston). Coarse gravels and sand accumulated in bars behind the breakwaters since their construction in the 1930s.

▲**Figure 13.14 Interfering with the littoral drift of sand.** Breakwaters, jetties, and groins are constructions that attempt to control littoral drift along a coast. [(b)–(d) Bobbé Christopherson.]

a category that includes nonstructural stabilization methods. *Beach nourishment* refers to the artificial replacement of sand along a beach. Theoretically, through such efforts, a beach that normally experiences a net loss of sediment will be fortified with new sand. However, years of human effort and expense to build beaches can be erased by a single storm. In addition, disruption of marine and littoral zone ecosystems may occur if the new sand does not physically and chemically match the existing sand.

In Florida, local, state, and federal agencies spend over $100 million annually on replenishment projects and manage over 200 miles of restored beaches. Until recently, sand was pumped from offshore onto the beach. However, over 30 years of dredging for sand has depleted offshore sand supplies, and now sand transport from faraway source areas is necessary. In Virginia Beach, Virginia, a $9 million beach replenishment project in 2013 rebuilt a strip of sand for the 49th time since 1951. The Army Corps of Engineers, which typically executes such projects on the U.S. East Coast, states that beach replenishment saves money in the long run by preventing damage to coastal development. Others, including scientists and politicians, disagree. At present, the federal government pays for about 65% of all beach replenishment projects, with the remaining cost picked up by state and local communities. As discussed with regard to the impacts of Hurricane Sandy in *Geosystems Now*, the controversy is ongoing.

CRITICAL**thinking 13.2**

Examining Hard versus Soft Shoreline Protection

The two general categories of shoreline stabilization methods are "hard" (structural, such as sea walls and jetties) and "soft" (nonstructural, such as organic plantings or beach nourishment). What are the drawbacks and benefits of each? In what type of coastal environment is hard protection appropriate? Which method requires more long-term maintenance? Go to NOAA's Ocean and Coastal Resource management page, **http://coastalmanagement.noaa.gov/initiatives/definitions.html**, for help in assessing shoreline protection and answering these questions.

Barrier Beaches and Islands

Barrier beaches are long, narrow depositional features, generally of sand, that form offshore roughly parallel to the coast. When these features are broader and more extensive, they form **barrier islands**. The sediment supplied to these beaches often comes from alluvial coastal plains, and tidal variation near these features usually is moderate to low. Barrier beaches and islands are quite common worldwide, lying offshore of nearly 10% of Earth's coastlines. Examples are found off Africa, India's eastern coast, Sri Lanka, Australia, and Alaska's northern slope, as well as offshore in the Baltic and Mediterranean Seas. Earth's most extensive chain of barrier islands is along the U.S. Atlantic and Gulf Coasts, extending some 5000 km (3100 mi) from Long Island to Texas and Mexico.

▲**Figure 13.15 Barrier island chain along North Carolina coast.** The Outer Banks of North Carolina are presently designated as one of 10 national seashore reserves supervised by the National Park Service. [*Terra* MODIS, NASA/GSFC.]

North Carolina's famed Outer Banks are a 200-mile-long string of barrier islands and peninsulas that separate the Atlantic Ocean from the mainland. The Outer Banks stretch southward from Virginia Beach, Virginia, to Cape Lookout and are separated from the mainland by Pamlico Sound (*sound* is a general term for a body of water forming an inlet) and two other sounds to the north (**Figure 13.15**). Mud flats (also called tidal flats) and salt marshes (a type of coastal wetland) are characteristic low-relief environments on the landward side of a barrier formation, where tidal influence is greater than wave action. Typical landforms are foredunes on the seaward side of the formation and backdunes and lagoons on the landward side. **Figure 13.16** shows landforms and associated vegetation, along with basic human usage and recommendations from a planning perspective, for a typical barrier island along the U.S. East Coast.

Barrier Island Processes Various hypotheses explain the formation of barrier islands. They may begin as offshore bars or low ridges of submerged sediment near shore and then gradually migrate toward shore with wave

Ocean	Beach	Foredunes	Trough	Backdunes	Mud flats and wetlands	Lagoon
Subject to pollution controls	Intolerant of construction	Fragile, easily disturbed	Plants stabilize sand surfaces	Intolerant of construction and recreation on seaward-facing side of dunes	Filling not allowed	Subject to recreation
Tolerant of recreation	Tolerant of recreation	Intolerant of construction and recreation	Tolerant of limited construction and recreation	Tolerant of construction and recreation on inland-facing side of dunes	Intolerant of construction and recreation	Tolerant of recreation

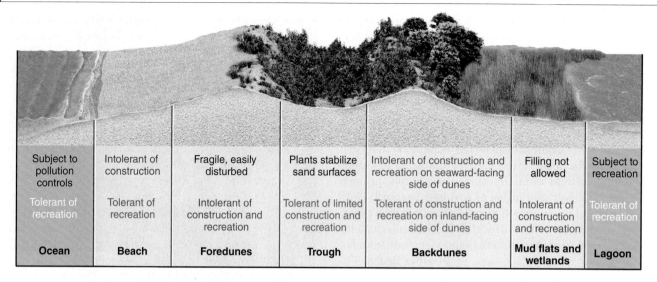

▲**Figure 13.16 Barrier island landforms and ecosystems, with planning guidelines based on the New Jersey coastal environment.** [Planning content after Ian McHarg, *Design with Nature*, Copyright © 1969.]

action or rising sea level. Barrier beaches naturally shift position in response to wave action and longshore currents. The name "barrier" is appropriate, for these formations take the brunt of storm energy, migrating over time with erosion and redeposition. For example, during Hurricane Sandy in 2012, Fire Island, a barrier island and popular summer destination off the southern coast of Long Island, New York, expanded 19 to 25 m (65 to 85 ft) toward the mainland (**Figure 13.17**). As of 2013, the new inlet had allowed seawater to flush out a polluted section of Great South Bay; however, the barrier island breach makes the mainland more vulnerable to the effects of future storms. The processes at work at Fire Island were typical of the effects of storms on barrier islands: erosion on the beach and foredune, deposition in the backdune area and in the lagoon, formation of new inlets, and a general shifting of the barrier formation toward shore in response to waves and storm surge.

(a) Pre-Sandy LiDAR elevations along a narrow portion of the island.

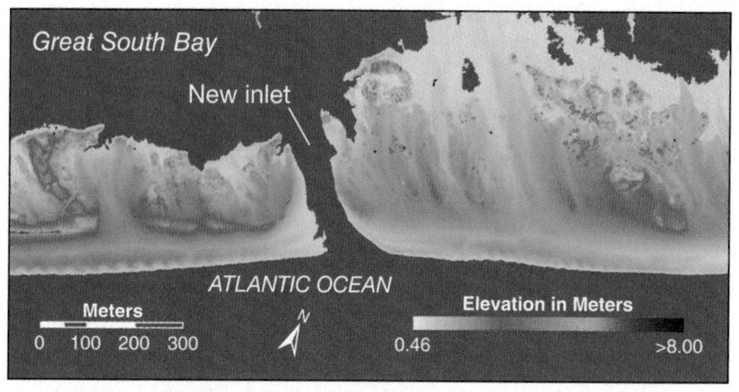

(b) Post-Sandy LiDAR elevations, showing beach erosion through 4-m-high sand dunes, forming a new inlet.

(c) Changes in elevation related to Sandy. Red-orange colors indicate loss of sand; blue-green colors indicate sand accumulation caused by waves and surge.

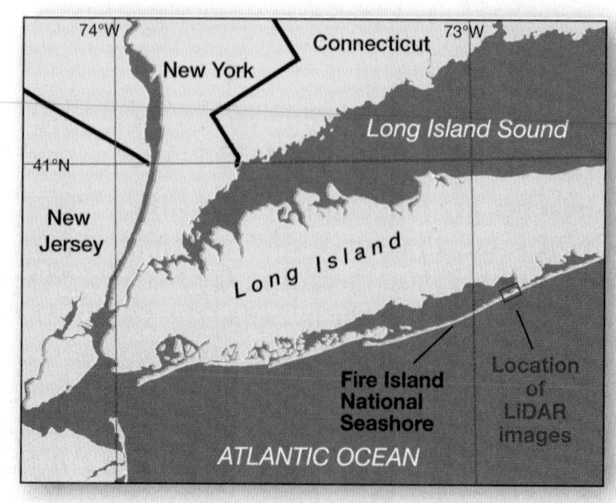

▲**Figure 13.17 Coastal change at Fire Island, National Seashore New York, after Hurricane Sandy.** [(a)–(c) USGS.]

Animation Movement of Barrier Island in Response to Rising Sea Level

http://goo.gl/WqJoKR

Video Making of a Superstorm

http://goo.gl/k6HaNa

Development on Barrier Islands Human-built structures on barrier islands are vulnerable to erosion and redeposition of coastal sediments by tropical storms and rising sea level. As proven again in the aftermath of Hurricane Sandy, the effects of hurricanes on barrier islands have inflicted tremendous economic losses, human hardship, and fatalities.

Several hurricanes were notable for their destruction and impacts on barrier island geomorphology. In 1989, Hurricane Hugo hit the South Carolina coast, sweeping away barrier island developments and millions of tons of sand; the hurricane destroyed up to 95% of the single-family homes in one community. In 1998, Hurricane Georges destroyed large tracts of the Chandeleur Islands offshore from the Louisiana–Mississippi Gulf Coast, and then Hurricane Katrina, and to a lesser extent Hurricane Dennis, in 2005 swept away much of what remained, leaving only sand bars. In 2008, Hurricane Ike struck the Texas–Louisiana Gulf Coast, including Galveston Island and the Bolivar Peninsula, a barrier spit near Galveston. In this area, $30 billion in structures were swept away (80 to 95% of homes), and 195 lives were lost. (See photos of changes to the Chandeleur Islands in the Visual Analysis activity at the end of this chapter.)

Our understanding of beach and barrier island migration and of the effects of storms has improved with continuing scientific research, and as a result, coastal development now often includes precautions for limiting erosion. As just one example among many, along the Mid-Atlantic U.S. coast, residents are encouraged to plant native species when landscaping their seaside homes because these species are tolerant of flooding and saline conditions and have root systems that help stabilize dunes.

Coral Formations

Not all coastlines form by purely physical processes. Some form as the result of biological processes, such as coral growth. A **coral** is a simple marine animal with a small, cylindrical, saclike body called a *polyp*; it is related to other marine invertebrates such as anemones and jellyfish. Corals secrete calcium carbonate ($CaCO_3$) from the lower half of their bodies, forming a hard, calcified external skeleton.

Corals and algae live together in a *symbiotic* relationship, an overlapping arrangement in which each depends on the other for survival. Corals cannot photosynthesize, but they do obtain some of their nourishment from their relationship with photosynthesizing algae, which by converting solar energy to chemical energy provide corals with about 60% of their nutrition. Algae also assist corals with the calcification process. In return, corals provide algae with certain nutrients. Coral reefs are the most diverse marine ecosystems. Preliminary estimates of species living in coral reefs place the number at a million worldwide, yet, as in most ecosystems in water or on land, biodiversity is declining in these communities.

Figure 13.18 shows the global distribution of living coral formations. Corals mostly thrive in warm tropical oceans, so the difference in ocean temperature between the western coasts and eastern coasts of continents is critical to their distribution. Western coastal waters tend to be cooler, thereby discouraging coral activity, whereas eastern coastal currents are warmer and thus enhance coral growth.

Living colonial corals range in distribution from about 30° N to 30° S latitude. Corals occupy a very specific ecological zone: 10- to 55-m (30- to 180-ft) depth, 27‰ to 40‰ salinity, and 18°C to 29°C (64°F to 85°F) water temperature. Their upper threshold for water temperature is 30°C (86°F); above that limit, corals begin to bleach and die. Corals require clear, sediment-free water and consequently do not locate near the mouths of sediment-charged freshwater streams. For example, note the lack of these structures along the U.S. Gulf Coast. Corals have low genetic diversity worldwide and long generation times, which together mean that corals are slow to adapt and vulnerable to changing conditions.

Coral Reefs Corals exist as both solitary and colonial formations. The colonial corals produce enormous structures, formed by the accumulation of their calcium

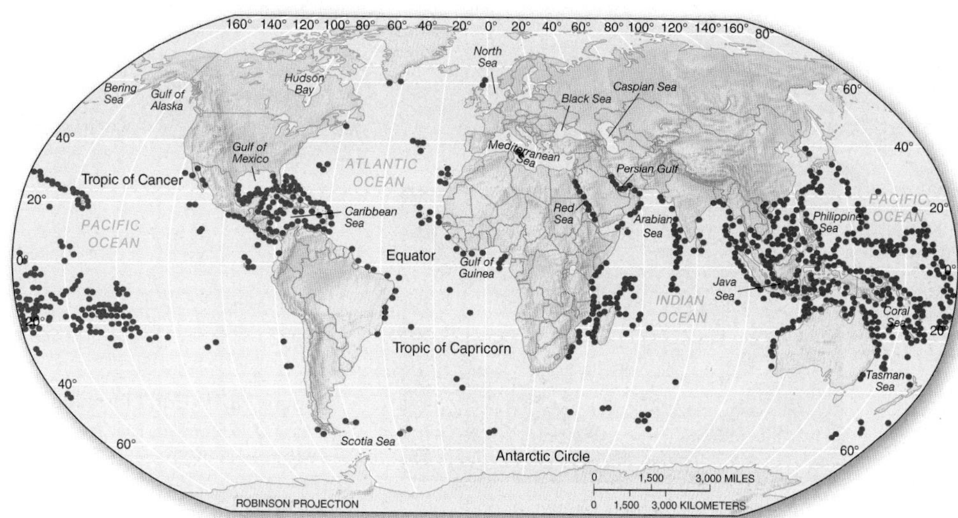

◄**Figure 13.18 Worldwide distribution of living coral formations.** The red dots represent major reef-forming coral colonies. Colonial corals range in distribution from about 30° N to 30° S latitude. [NOS/NOAA, 2011.]

carbonate skeletons, which is lithified into rock. *Coral reefs* form through many generations, with live corals near the ocean's surface building on the foundation of older coral skeletons, which, in turn, may rest on a volcanic seamount or some other submarine feature built up from the ocean floor. Thus, a coral reef is a biologically derived sedimentary rock that can assume one of several distinctive shapes.

In 1842, Charles Darwin proposed a hypothesis for reef formation. He suggested that, as reefs develop around a volcanic island and the island itself gradually subsides, equilibrium is maintained between the subsidence of the island and the upward growth of the corals (to keep the living corals at their optimum depth, not too far below the surface). This idea, generally accepted today, is portrayed in **Figure 13.19**. Note the specific examples of each reef stage: *fringing reefs* (platforms of surrounding coral rock), *barrier reefs* (reefs that enclose lagoons), and *atolls* (circular, ring-shaped reefs).

Earth's most extensive fringing reef is the Bahama Platform in the western Atlantic, covering some 96,000 km^2 (37,000 mi^2). The Bahama archipelago is made up of two carbonate platforms consisting of shallow-water limestone formations. The largest barrier reef, the Great Barrier Reef along the shore of the state of Queensland, Australia, exceeds 2025 km (1260 mi) in length, is 16–145 km (10–90 mi) wide, and includes at least 700 coral-formed islands and keys (coral islets or barrier islands).

Coral Bleaching As mentioned previously, coral reefs may experience a phenomenon known as *bleaching*, in which normally colorful corals turn stark white by expelling their own nutrient-supplying algae. Exactly why corals eject their symbiotic partner is unknown, for without

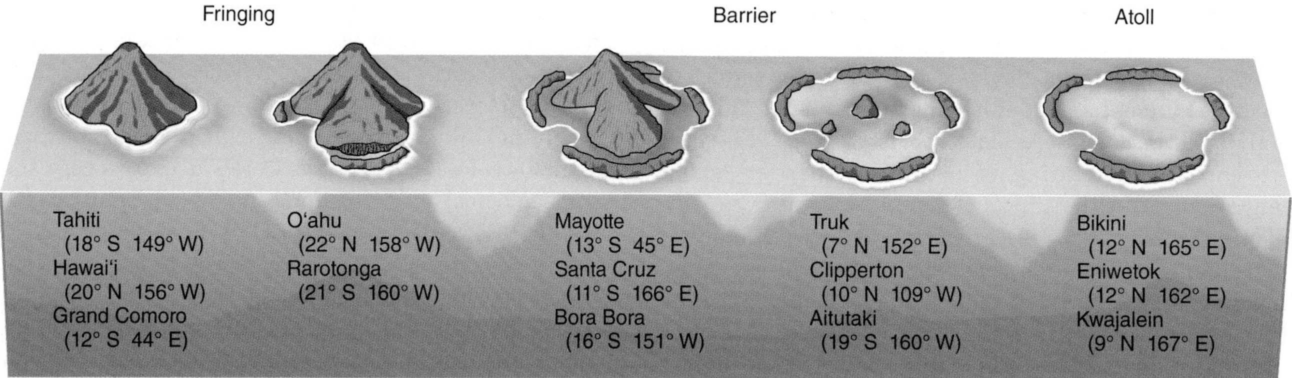

(a) Common coral formations in a sequence of reef growth around a subsiding volcanic island: fringing reefs, barrier reefs, and an atoll.

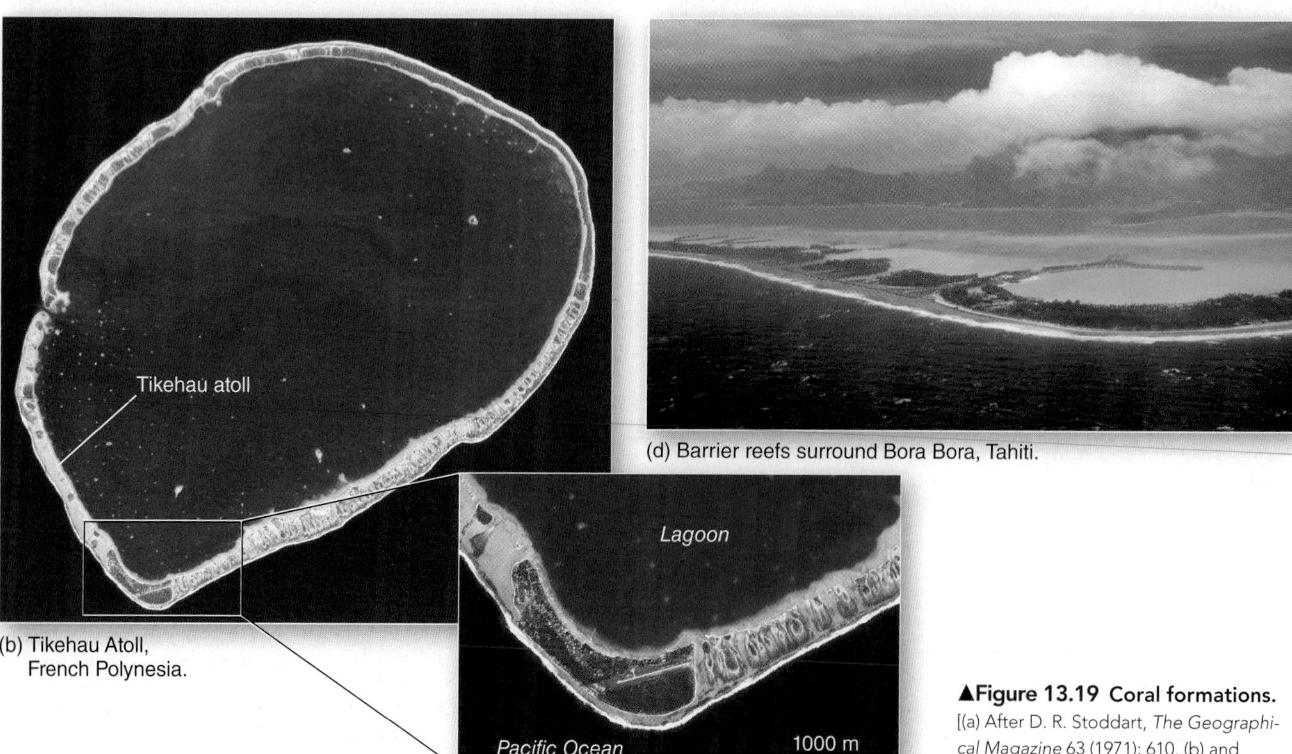

(b) Tikehau Atoll, French Polynesia.

(c) Tuherahera village and Tikehau airport.

(d) Barrier reefs surround Bora Bora, Tahiti.

▲**Figure 13.19 Coral formations.** [(a) After D. R. Stoddart, *The Geographical Magazine* 63 (1971): 610. (b) and (c) *EO-1* image, NASA. (d) Wilar/Shutterstock.]

algae they die. Scientists are currently tracking this worldwide phenomenon, which is occurring in the Caribbean Sea and the Indian Ocean as well as off the shores of Australia, Indonesia, Japan, Kenya, Florida, Texas, and Hawai'i. Possible causes include local pollution, disease, sedimentation, changes in ocean salinity, and increasing oceanic acidity.

Since 2000, scientists have acknowledged that the warming of sea-surface temperatures, linked to greenhouse warming of the atmosphere, is a greater threat to corals than local pollution or other environmental problems. Although a natural process, coral bleaching is now occurring at an unprecedented rate as average ocean temperatures climb higher with climate change. The 1998 record El Niño event caused the die-off of perhaps 30% of the world's reefs. In 2010, scientists reported one of the most rapid and severe coral bleaching and mortality events on record near Aceh, Indonesia, on the northern tip of the island of Sumatra. Some species declined 80% in just a few months, in response to increased sea-surface temperatures across the region. Many of these corals previously were resilient in the face of other ecosystem disruptions, including the Sumatra–Andaman tsunami in 2004.

As sea-surface temperatures continue to rise and ocean acidification worsens, coral losses will continue. For more information and Internet links, see the Global Coral Reef Monitoring Network at http://www.gcrmn.org/.

Coastal Wetlands

In some coastal areas, sediments are rich in organic matter, leading to lush plant growth and spawning grounds for fish, shellfish, and other organisms. A coastal marsh environment of this type provides optimal habitat for varied wildlife. Unfortunately, these wetland ecosystems are quite fragile and are threatened by human development (Figure 13.20).

▲**Figure 13.20 Coastal salt marsh.** This wetland along the Long Island coast, New York, is protected from development by a private land trust. Land trusts are nonprofit, independent organizations that work with landowners to conserve natural resources and open space. Since the vast majority of coastal areas are privately owned, land trusts have become critical tools for wetland protection. [Brooks Kraft/Corbis.]

As discussed in Chapter 6, wetlands are permanently or seasonally saturated with water, and as such, they have hydric soils (with anaerobic, or oxygen-free, conditions) and support *hydrophytic vegetation* (plants that grow in water or wet soil). Coastal wetlands are of two general types—mangrove swamps (occurring between 30° N and 30° S latitude) and salt marshes (occurring at latitudes of 30° and higher). This distribution is dictated by temperature—specifically, the occurrence of freezing conditions.

In tropical regions, sediment accumulation on coastlines provides sites for mangroves, the name for the trees, shrubs, palms, and ferns that grow in these intertidal areas as well as for the habitat, which is known as a **mangrove swamp** (Figure 13.21). These ecosystems have a high diversity of species that are tolerant of saltwater inundation, but generally intolerant of freezing temperatures (especially as seedlings). Mangrove roots are typically visible above the waterline, but the root portions that reach below the water surface provide a habitat for a multitude of specialized life forms. The root systems maintain water quality by trapping sediment and taking up excess nutrients and prevent erosion by stabilizing accumulated sediments.

Mangrove ecosystems are threatened by ongoing removal, owing to falsely conceived fears that they harbor disease or pestilence; to pollution, especially from agricultural runoff; to overharvesting, especially in developing countries where they supply firewood; to storm surges in areas where protective barrier islands and coral reefs have disappeared; and to climate change, since mangroves require a stable sea level for long-term survival. According to the Food and Agriculture Organization of the United Nations, 20% of the world's mangroves were lost from 1980 to 2005. A 2011 study using satellite data reported that the remaining extent of global mangroves

GEOreport 13.3 Ocean acidification impacts corals

As the oceans absorb more excess carbon dioxide, their acidity increases and potentially damages coral formations, an interaction that scientists are actively researching. A 2013 study examined Mediterranean red coral (*Corallium rubrum*) colonies under more acidic conditions in a laboratory and discovered reduced growth rates of 59% and abnormal skeleton development when compared with colonies growing under current ocean conditions. The test conditions were at a pH of 7.8 (which would occur with CO_2 levels of 800 ppm, forecasted for the year 2100) as compared to recent conditions of pH 8.1 (380 to 400 ppm).

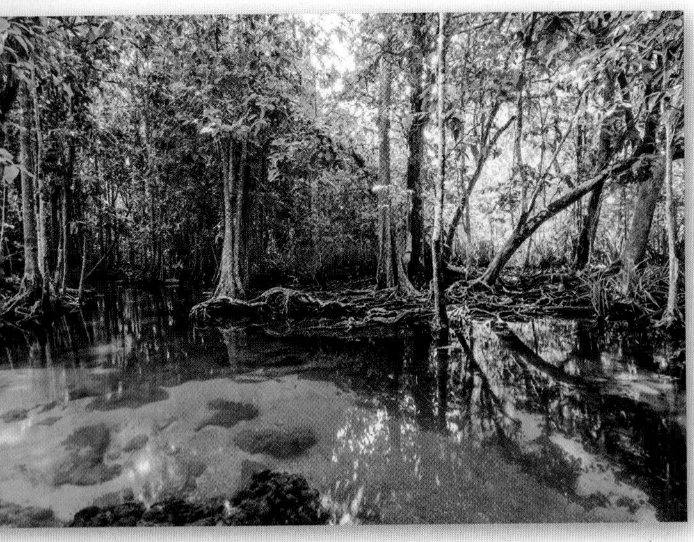

▲**Figure 13.21 Mangrove forest, Thailand.** Corals, sponges, anemones, fish, and invertebrates live among the roots of some mangrove forests. Development and aquaculture such as shrimp farming are two of many threats to mangrove ecosystems. [Nature Capture Realfoto/Shutterstock.]

is 12% less than previously thought. Loss of these ecosystems also affects climate, since mangroves store carbon in greater amounts than other tropical forests.

Salt marshes consist mainly of halophytic (salt-tolerant) plants (mainly grasses) and usually form in estuaries and in the tidal mud flats behind barrier beaches and spits. These marshes occur in the intertidal zone and are often characterized by sinuous, branching water channels produced as tidal waters flood into and ebb from the marsh. Marsh vegetation traps and filters sediment, spreads out floodwaters, and buffers coastlines from storm surges associated with hurricanes. However, in many regions these coastal wetlands are threatened by human activities and the effects of climate change.

Most of coastal Louisiana, which includes about 40% of the coastal marshes in the United States, is profoundly altered and disrupted by dam and levee construction, flow alterations, oil and gas exploration and pumping, pipelines, and dredging for navigation and industrial needs. Wetlands in the Mississippi delta are disappearing at the rate of 65 km^2 (25 mi^2) per year. On the *MasteringGeography* website, you will find a discussion of the impacts that wetland removal, storm surge, and rising sea level have had on Bayou Lafourche in southern Louisiana.

Wind Processes

The effects of wind as an agent of geomorphic change are most easily visualized in coastal and desert environments. Like water, moving air is a fluid, and like moving water, it transports materials such as dust, sand, and snow, creating erosional and depositional landforms. The work of wind is **eolian** (also spelled *aeolian*, for Aeolus, ruler of the winds in Greek mythology).

Since the viscosity and density of air are much lower than those of other transporting agents such as water and ice, the ability of wind to move materials is correspondingly weaker. Yet, over time, wind accomplishes enormous work. For example, consistent local wind can prune and shape vegetation (**Figure 13.22**).

Eolian Transport of Dust and Sand

Just like water in a stream picking up sediment, wind exerts a drag, or frictional pull, on surface particles until they become airborne. Grain size, or particle size, is important in wind erosion. Intermediate-sized grains move most easily, whereas movement of the largest and the smallest sand particles requires the strongest winds. Stronger wind is needed for the large particles because they are heavier and for the small particles because they are mutually cohesive and because they usually present a smooth (aerodynamic) surface that minimizes frictional pull. Eolian processes work only on dry surface materials, since wet soils and sediments are too cohesive for movement to occur.

The mechanisms for wind transport include suspension, saltation, and surface creep (**Figure 13.23**). The distance that wind is capable of transporting particles in *suspension* varies with particle size (for comparison, Figure 12.11 shows the transport of stream sediment in suspension, a similar process). In a dust storm, fine materials are lifted higher and travel farther, a condition known as long-term suspension. In a sand storm, slightly larger sand particles remain lower to the ground in short-term suspension. As discussed in previous chapters, atmospheric circulation can transport fine material, such as volcanic debris, fire soot and smoke, and dust, worldwide within days. In some arid and semiarid regions, winds associated with thunderstorms can cause dramatic dust storms (**Figure 13.24**) consisting of fine particles that infiltrate even the smallest cracks of homes and businesses.

▼**Figure 13.22 Wind-sculpted tree near South Point, Hawai'i.** Nearly constant tradewinds cause the distinct shape of this tree, with branches elongated in the downwind direction. [Bobbé Christopherson.]

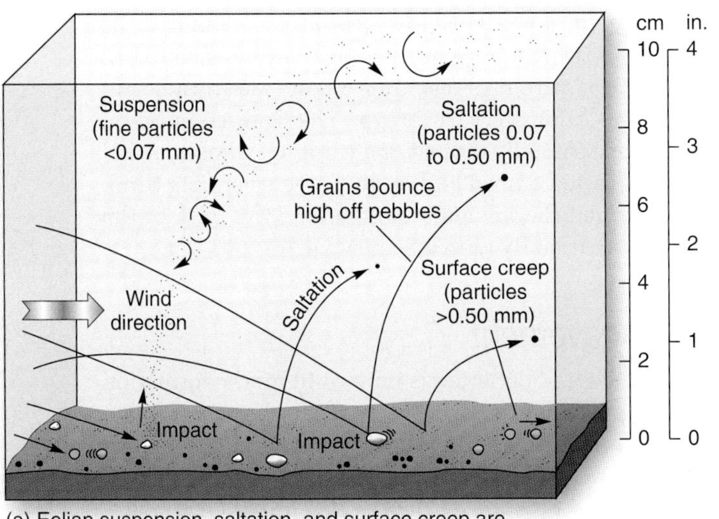

(a) Eolian suspension, saltation, and surface creep are transportation mechanisms.

(b) Sand grains saltating along the surface in the Stovepipe Wells dune field, Death Valley, California.

▲**Figure 13.23 How the wind moves sand.** [(b) Robert Christopherson.]

Animation MG How Wind Moves Sand http://goo.gl/6p3mSB

Eolian processes transport particles between 0.07 and 0.50 mm (0.0027 and 0.02 in.) along the ground by *saltation*, the bouncing and skipping action of particles that accounts for about 80% of wind transport of particles (Figure 13.23). In fluvial transport, saltation is accomplished by hydraulic lift; in eolian transport, saltation occurs as a result of aerodynamic lift, elastic bounce, and impact with other particles (compare Figure 13.23a with Figure 12.11).

Particles larger than about 0.50 mm (0.02 in.) slide and roll along the ground surface, a type of movement called **surface creep**. Saltating particles may collide with sliding and rolling particles, knocking them loose and forward in this process, which affects about 20% of the material transported by wind. In a desert or along a beach, sometimes you can hear a slight hissing sound, almost like steam escaping, produced by the myriad saltating grains of sand as they bounce along and collide with surface particles. Once particles are set in motion, the wind velocity need not be as high to keep them moving.

British Army Major Ralph Bagnold, an engineering officer stationed in Egypt in 1925, pioneered studies of wind transport and authored a classic work in geomorphology, *The Physics of Blown Sand and Desert Dunes*, published in 1941. Bagnold's studies of wind transport over the surface of a sand dune showed that at lower wind speeds, sand moves only in small amounts; however, beyond a wind speed of about 30 kmph (19 mph), the amount of sand moved increases rapidly. A steady wind of 50 kmph (30 mph) can move approximately one-half ton of sand per day over a 1-m-wide section of dune.

▼**Figure 13.24 Dust storm engulfing Phoenix, Arizona.** A massive dust storm known as a haboob passes through Phoenix, Arizona, in July 2011. In dry regions, such a wall of dust frequently precedes a thunderstorm, with winds traveling in the opposite direction of the oncoming storm. [Ross D. Franklin/AP Images.]

Eolian Erosion and Related Landforms

Erosion of the ground surface resulting from the lifting and removal of individual particles by wind is **deflation**. Wherever wind encounters loose sediment, deflation may remove enough material to form depressions in the landscape ranging in size from small indentations less than a meter wide up to areas hundreds of meters wide and many meters deep. The smallest of these are known as *deflation hollows*, or *blowouts*. They commonly occur in dune environments, where winds remove sand from specific areas, often in conjunction with the removal of stabilizing vegetation (possibly by fire, by grazing, or from drought). Large depressions in the Sahara Desert are at least partially formed by deflation, but are also affected by large-scale tectonic processes. The enormous Munkhafad el Qattâra (Qattâra Depression), which covers 18,000 km^2 (6950 mi^2) just inland from the Mediterranean Sea in the Western Desert of Egypt, is now about 130 m (427 ft) below sea level at its lowest point.

The grinding and shaping of rock surfaces by the "sandblasting" action of particles captured in the air is **abrasion**. Like the intentional sandblasting of streets and buildings for maintenance, this process is accomplished by a stream of compressed air filled with sand grains that quickly abrade the surface. Since sand grains are not lifted to great heights above the ground surface, abrasive action in nature usually is restricted to a distance of no more than a meter or two above the ground. Variables that affect natural abrasion rates include the hardness of surface rocks, wind velocity, and wind constancy.

Rocks that are pitted, fluted (grooved), or polished from eolian erosion are called **ventifacts** (literally, "artifacts of the wind," shown in **Figure 13.25**). They usually become aerodynamically shaped in a direction determined by the consistent flow of airborne particles in prevailing winds. On a larger scale, deflation and abrasion together are capable of streamlining multiple rock structures in a landscape in alignments parallel to the most effective wind direction, thus producing distinctive, elongated formations called **yardangs**. Abrasion is concentrated on the windward end of each yardang, with deflation operating on the leeward portions. These wind-sculpted features can range from meters to kilometers in length and up to many meters in height (**Figure 13.26**).

On Earth, some yardangs are large enough to be detected on satellite imagery. The Ica Valley of southern Peru contains yardangs reaching 100 m (330 ft) in height and several kilometers in length. The Sphinx in Egypt was perhaps partially formed as a yardang, whose natural shape suggested a head and body. Some scientists think this shape led the ancients to complete the bulk of the sculpture artificially with masonry.

Desert Pavement

The work of wind deflation is important for the formation of **desert pavement**, a hard, stony surface—as opposed to the usual sand—that commonly occurs in arid regions (**Figure 13.27a**). Scientists have put forth several explanations for the formation of desert pavement. One explanation is that deflation literally blows away loose or noncohesive sediment, eroding fine dust, clay, and sand and leaving behind a compacted concentration of pebbles and gravel (**Figure 13.27b**).

Another hypothesis that better explains some desert pavement surfaces states that deposition of windblown sediments, not removal, is the formative process. Windblown particles settle between and below coarse

▼Figure 13.25 A ventifact. One of the wind-eroded rocks in the Dry Valleys area of Antarctica, a snow-free polar desert with winds reaching speeds of 320 kmph (200 mph). [Scott Darsney/Lonely Planet Images/Getty.]

▼Figure 13.26 A field of yardangs. Abrasion from consistent, unidirectional winds shaped these yardangs in the Qaidam Basin in northwest China. [Xinhua/Photoshot.]

GEOreport 13.4 Human activities disturb eolian landforms

Recreational off-road vehicles (ORVs) and all-terrain vehicles (ATVs), which currently number more than 15 million in the Unites States, erode desert dunes, disrupt desert pavement, and create ruts that easily concentrate surface runoff into gullies that deepen with continuing erosion. Military activities such as explosions and the movement of heavy vehicles also destroy desert pavement, as in Iraq and Afghanistan, where the breakdown of thousands of square kilometers of stable desert pavement has sent dust and sand into nearby cities and onto farmland. In the Registan Desert of southern Afghanistan, south of the city of Kandahar, drought conditions were exacerbated by military activities. The disruption of desert pavement surfaces resulted in sand movement that has overtaken areas of sparse agricultural activity and has covered more than 100 villages with sand and dust.

(a) A typical desert pavement.

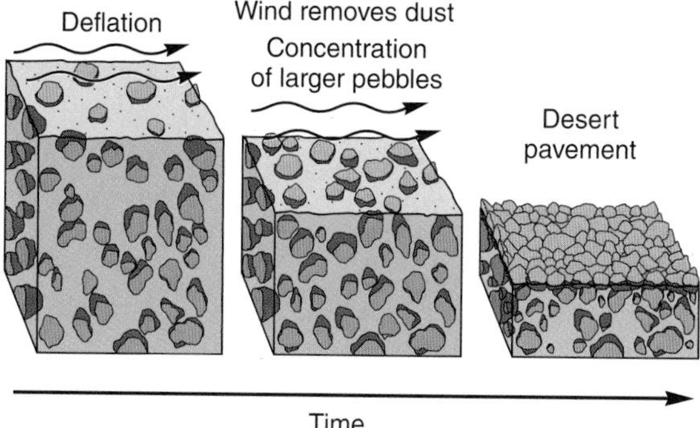

(b) The deflation hypothesis: Wind removes fine particles, leaving larger pebbles, gravels, and rocks, which become consolidated into desert pavement.

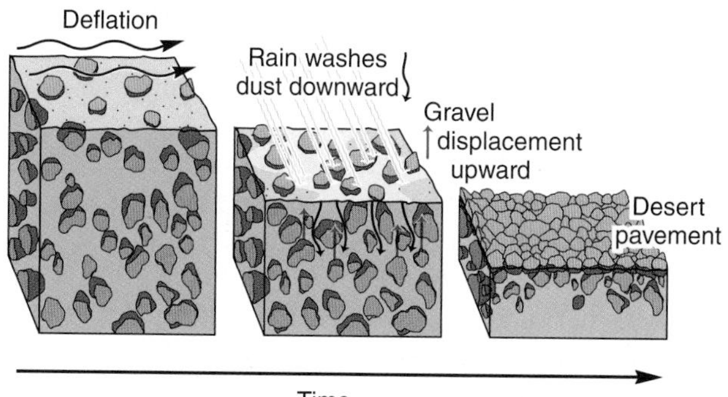

(c) The sediment-accumulation hypothesis: Wind delivers fine particles that settle and wash downward as cycles of swelling and shrinking cause gravels to migrate upward, forming desert pavement.

▲**Figure 13.27 Desert pavement.** [(a) Bobbé Christopherson.]

rocks and pebbles that are gradually displaced upward. Rainwater plays a part, as wetting and drying episodes swell and shrink clay-sized particles. The gravel fragments are gradually lifted to surface positions to form the pavement (**Figure 13.27c**).

Desert pavements are so common that many provincial names are used for them—for example, *gibber plain* in Australia; *gobi* in China; and in Africa, *lag gravels* or *serir*, or *reg* desert if some fine particles remain. Most desert pavements are strong enough to support human weight, and some can support motor vehicles, but in general, these surfaces are fragile. They are also of critical importance, since they protect underlying sediment from further deflation and water erosion.

Landforms of Eolian Deposition

An extensive area of windblown sand (usually larger than 125 km², or 48 mi²) is an **erg** (after the Arabic word for "dune field"), or a **sand sea**. The Grand Erg Oriental in the central Sahara, active for more than 1.3 million years, exceeds 1200 m (4000 ft) in depth and covers 192,000 km² (75,000 mi²), comparable to the area of Nebraska. Similar sand seas, such as the Grand Ar Rub'al Khālī Erg, are active in Saudi Arabia. In eastern Algeria, the Issaouane Erg covers 38,000 km² (14,673 mi²) of the Sahara Desert (**Figure 13.28a**). Extensive dune fields characterize sand seas, which are also present in semiarid regions such as the Great Plains of the United States (**Figure 13.28b**) as well as on the planet Mars (see photos on the *MasteringGeography* website).

The smallest features shaped by the movement of windblown sand are ripples, which form in crests and troughs, positioned transversely (at a right angle) to the direction of the wind. Larger deposits of sand grains form **dunes**, defined as wind-sculpted, transient ridges or hills of sand.

Dune Formation and Movement

When saltating sand grains encounter small patches of sand, their kinetic energy (motion) is dissipated, and they accumulate. Once the height of such accumulations increases above 30 cm (12 in.), a *slipface* and characteristic dune features form. Geosystems in Action 13 illustrates a dune profile and various dune forms.

A dune usually is asymmetrical in one or more directions. Winds characteristically create a gently sloping *windward side* (stoss side), with a more steeply sloped slipface on the *leeward side* (Figure GIA 13.1). The angle of a slipface is the steepest angle at which loose material is stable—its *angle of repose*. Thus, the constant flow of new material makes a slipface a type of avalanche slope: Sand builds up as it moves over the crest of the dune to the brink; then it avalanches, falling and cascading as the slipface continually adjusts, seeking its angle of repose (usually 30° to 34°). In this way, a dune migrates downwind, in the direction in which effective—that is, sand-transporting—winds are blowing, as suggested by the successive dune profiles in Figure GIA 13.1. (Stronger seasonal winds or winds from a passing storm may prove more effective in this regard than average prevailing winds.)

Active sand dunes cover about 10% of Earth's deserts, and dune migration can threaten populated areas (see The Human Denominator 13d, ahead). Dune fields are also present in humid climates, such as along coastal

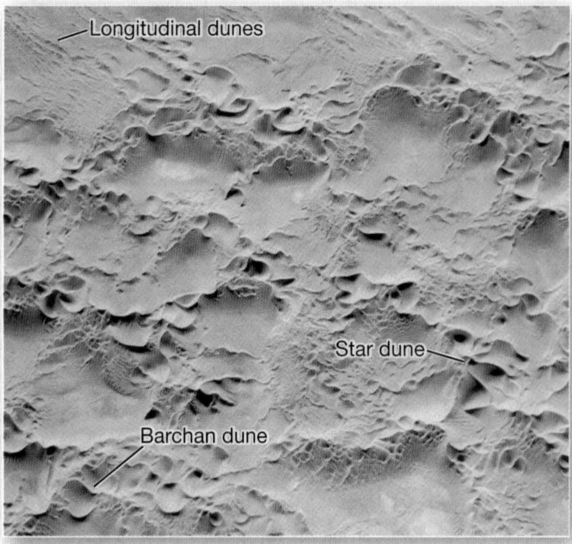

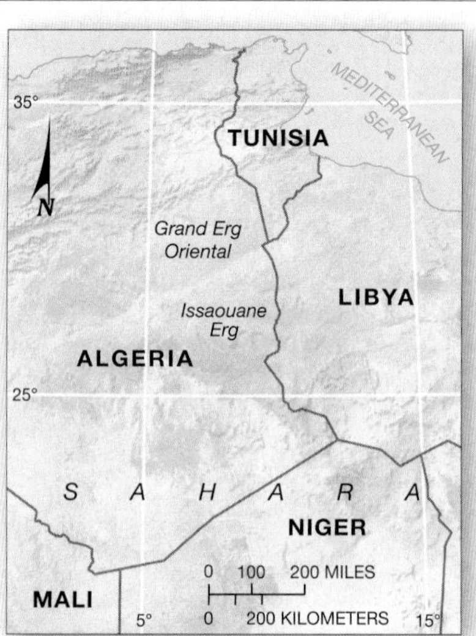

◀Figure 13.28 Examples of sand seas, or ergs. [(a) ISS astronaut photo, NASA/GSFC. (b) NASA.]

(a) The Issaouane Erg of eastern Algeria consists of star dunes, barchan dunes, and longitudinal dunes, disclosing the prevailing wind history of the region.

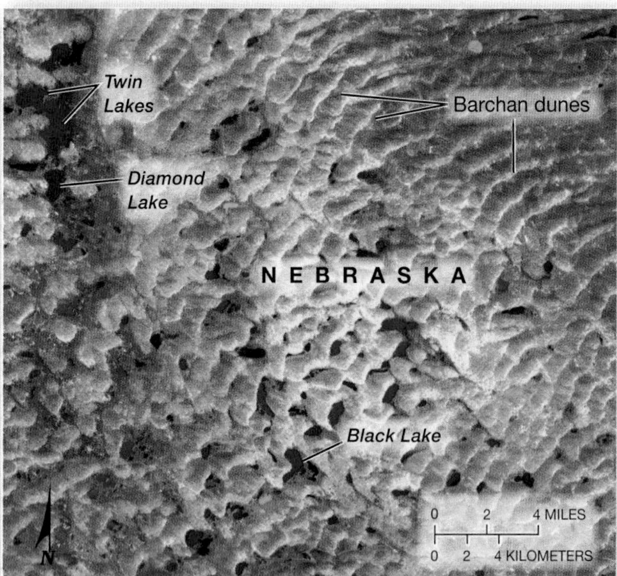

(b) The Sand Hills in central Nebraska are sand and silt deposits derived from glaciated regions to the north and west. These densely packed barchan dunes, inactive for at least 600 years, are now stabilized by vegetation (green). Water is in blue.

Oregon, the south shore of Lake Michigan, and the U.S. Gulf and Atlantic coastlines.

These same dune-forming principles and dune terminology apply to snow-covered landscapes. *Snow dunes* are formed as wind deposits snow in drifts. In semiarid farming areas, drifting snow captured by fences and by tall stubble left in fields contributes significantly to soil moisture when the snow melts.

Desert Dune Classification Dunes have many wind-produced shapes that make classification difficult. Scientists generally classify dunes according to three general shapes—*crescentic* (crescent, curved shape), *linear* (straight form), and massive *star dunes*. Figure GIA 13.2 shows four types of dunes that fall within these classes or are a complex mix of these general shapes. The crescentic class includes *barchan* and *parabolic* dunes. Linear dunes include *longitudinal* dunes. Star dunes are the largest in size. In some ergs, winds from varying directions produce star dunes with multiple slipfaces (Figure 13.28a). They are pinwheel-shaped, with several radiating arms rising and joining to form a common central peak that can approach 200 m (650 ft) in height. Figure 13.28a also shows crescentic dunes, suggesting that the region has experienced changing wind patterns over time, as, in contrast to star dunes, crescentic dunes form from a single principal wind flow.

Ancient sand dunes can be lithified into sedimentary rock that carries patterns of cross bedding, or *cross stratification*. As the ancient dune was accumulating, the sand that cascaded down its slipface established distinct bedding planes (layers) that remained as the dune lithified. These layers are now visible as cross bedding, so named because they form at an angle to the horizontal layers of the main strata (look back to Figure 9.6a on page 292). Ripple marks, animal tracks, and fossils also are found preserved in these desert sandstones.

CRITICAL**thinking** 13.3

The Nearest Eolian Features

What eolian features are nearest to your present location? Are they coastal, lakeshore, or desert dunes? Which causative factors discussed in this chapter explain the location or form of these features? Visit the site in person or on Google Earth™ to help with your answers.

The dramatic, sculptural shapes of dunes occur in a variety of settings: along shorelines, in sandy parts of deserts, and in semiarid regions. Wherever there is a sufficient supply of loose, dry sand or other fine particles unprotected by plant cover, wind erosion and deposition can build dunes (GIA 13.1). Prevailing winds, along with other factors, create dunes of many sizes and shapes (GIA 13.2).

13.1 Dune Profile

Wind erosion and deposition work together to build a dune's characteristic profile. A dune grows as wind-borne particles accumulate on the gentler, windward slope and then cascade down the steep slipface of the leeward slope.

Angle of repose:
The loose particles on the slipface tend to slip and slide downhill until the slope stabilizes at its angle of repose—about 30°–34°—the steepest angle at which the particles are stable.

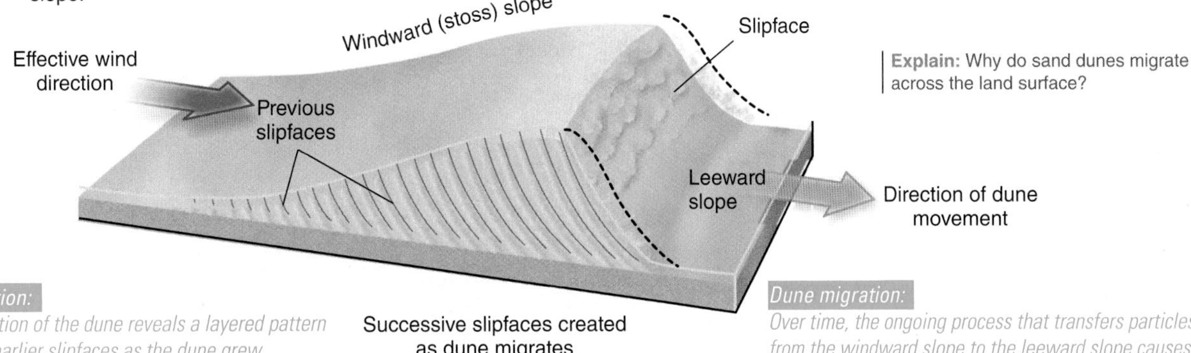

Explain: Why do sand dunes migrate across the land surface?

Cross section:
A cross section of the dune reveals a layered pattern formed by earlier slipfaces as the dune grew.

Dune migration:
Over time, the ongoing process that transfers particles from the windward slope to the leeward slope causes the entire dune to migrate downwind.

13.2 Dune Forms

The different types of sand dunes vary in shape and size depending on several factors including:
- directional variability and strength (or "effectiveness") of the wind
- whether the sand supply is limited or abundant
- presence or absence of vegetation

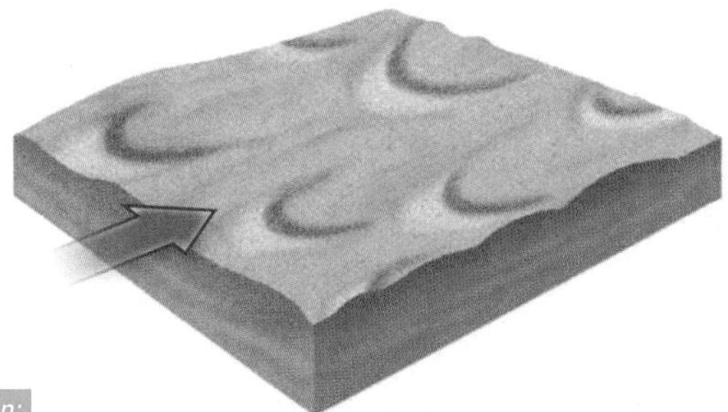

Barchan:
Crescent-shaped dune with horns pointed downwind; found in areas with constant winds and little directional variability, and where limited sand is available.

Parabolic:
Crescent-shaped dune with opening end facing upwind; U-shaped "blowout" and arms anchored by vegetation, which stabilizes dune form.

Longitudinal:
Linear, slightly sinuous, ridge-shaped dune, aligned parallel with the wind direction. Averages 100 m (328 ft) high and 100 km (63 mi) long but can reach to 400 m (1312 ft) high.

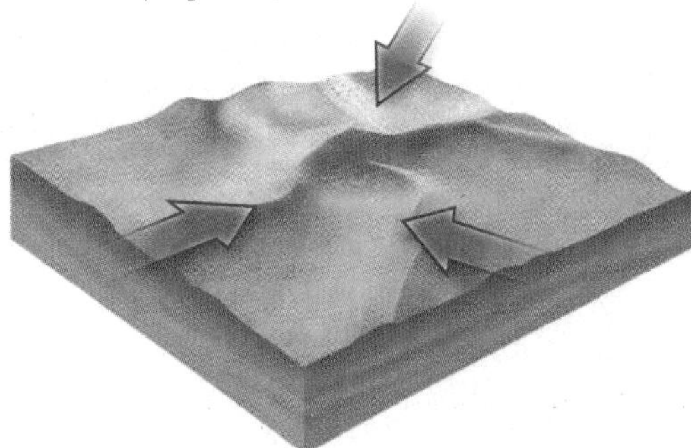

Star:
Pyramidal-shaped structure with three or more sinuous, radiating arms extending outward from a central peak; results from effective winds shifting in all directions.

Compare: How are barchan and parabolic dunes similar? How are they different?

GEOquiz

1. Summarize: Describe the growth, structure, and migration of a sand dune beginning with a small obstacle that intercepts sand particles and assuming a relatively constant wind direction.

2. Infer: Give one reason that star dunes and longitudinal dunes are often taller than other types of dunes.

MasteringGeography™

Visit the Study Area in MasteringGeography™ to explore dunes.

Visualize: Study a geosciences animation of dunes.

Assess: Demonstrate understanding of dunes (if assigned by instructor).

COASTAL SYSTEMS IMPACT HUMANS

- Rising sea level has potential to inundate coastal communities.
- Tsunami cause damage and loss of life along vulnerable coastlines.
- Coastal erosion changes coastal landscapes, affecting developed areas; human development on depositional features such as barrier island chains is at risk from storms, especially hurricanes.

HUMANS IMPACT COASTAL SYSTEMS

- Rising ocean temperatures, pollution, and ocean acidification impact corals and reef ecosystems.
- Human development drains and fills coastal wetlands and mangrove swamps, thereby removing their buffering effect during storms.

13a A tanker ran aground on Nightingale Island, Tristan da Cunha, in the South Atlantic in 2011, spilling an estimated 800 tons of fuel and coating endangered penguins with oil.

13b Dredgers pump sand through a hose to replenish beaches on Spain's Mediterranean coast, a popular tourist destination. Near Barcelona, pictured here, sand is frequently eroded during storms; natural replenishment is limited by structures that block longshore currents.

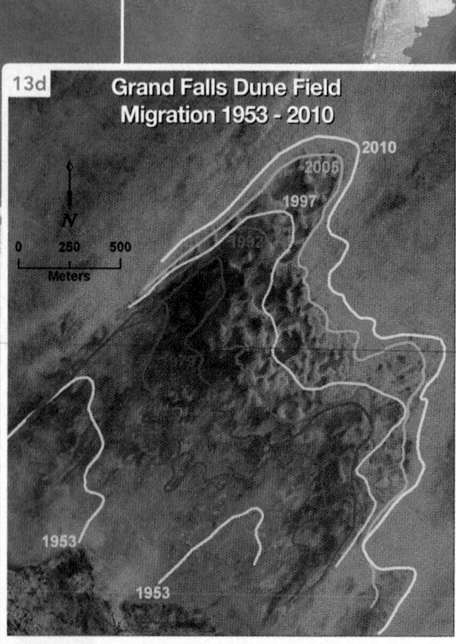

13d On Navajo Nation lands in the U.S Southwest, dune migration is threatening houses and transportation, and affecting human health. The Grand Falls dune field in northeast Arizona grew 70% in areal extent from 1997 to 2007. The increasingly dry climate of this region has accelerated dune migration and reactivated inactive dunes.

ISSUES FOR THE 21ST CENTURY

- Degradation and loss of coastal ecosystems-wetlands, corals, mangroves—will continue with coastal development and climate change.
- Continued building on vulnerable coastal landforms will necessitate expensive recovery efforts, especially as storm systems become more intense with climate change.

13c Mangrove planting: In Aceh, Indonesia, near the site of the 2004 Indian Ocean tsunami, authorities encourage local people to plant mangroves for protection against future tsunami.

KEYLEARNINGconceptsreview

Describe the chemical composition and physical structure of the ocean.

Because water is the "universal solvent," dissolving at least 57 of the 92 elements found in nature, seawater is a solution, and the concentration of dissolved solids is its **salinity**. **Brackish** water has less than 35‰ (parts per thousand) salinity; **brine** exceeds the average 35‰. The ocean is divided by depth into the narrow mixing zone at the surface, the thermocline transition zone, and the deep cold zone.

salinity (p. 406)
brackish (p. 408)
brine (p. 408)

1. Describe the salinity and composition of seawater and the distribution of its solutes.
2. Analyze the latitudinal distribution of salinity discussed in the chapter. Why is salinity less along the equator and greater in the subtropics?
3. What are the three general zones in the physical structure of the ocean? Characterize each by temperature, salinity, dissolved oxygen, and dissolved carbon dioxide.

Identify the components of the coastal environment and *explain* the actions of tides.

The coastal environment is the **littoral zone** and exists where the tide-driven, wave-driven sea confronts the land. System inputs to the coastal environment include solar energy, wind and weather, climatic variation, coastal geomorphology, and human activities. Mean sea level (MSL) varies over space and is rising worldwide in response to global warming of the atmosphere and oceans.

Tides are complex daily oscillations in sea level, ranging worldwide from barely noticeable to many meters. Tides are produced by the gravitational pull of both the Moon and the Sun. Most coastal locations experience two high (rising) *flood tides* and two low (falling) *ebb tides* every day. The difference between consecutive high and low tides is the tidal range. *Spring tides* exhibit the greatest tidal range, when the Moon and the Sun are in either conjunction or opposition. *Neap tides* produce a lesser tidal range.

littoral zone (p. 410)
tide (p. 411)

4. What are the key terms used to describe the coastal environment?
5. How is mean sea level determined? Is it constant or variable around the world? Explain.
6. What interacting forces generate the pattern of tides?
7. What characteristic tides are expected during a new Moon and a full Moon? During the first-quarter and third-quarter phases of the Moon? What is meant by a flood tide? An ebb tide?
8. Explain briefly how tidal power is used to produce electricity. Are there any tidal power plants in North America? If so, briefly describe where they are and how they operate.

Describe wave motion at sea and near shore and *explain* coastal straightening and coastal landforms.

Friction between moving air (wind) and the ocean surface generates undulations of water that we call **waves**. Wave energy in the open sea travels through water, but the water itself stays in place. Regular patterns of smooth, rounded waves—the mature undulations of the open ocean—are **swells**. Near shore, the restricted depth of water slows the wave, forming *waves of translation*, in which both energy and water move forward toward shore. As the crest of each wave rises, the wave falls into a characteristic **breaker**.

Wave refraction redistributes wave energy along a coastline. Headlands are eroded, whereas coves and bays are areas of deposition, with the long-term effect of these differences being a straightening of the coast. As waves approach a shore at an angle, refraction produces a **longshore current** of water moving parallel to the shore. Particles move along the beach as **beach drift**, shifting back and forth between water and land. The combined action of these processes produces the **littoral drift** of sand, sediment, gravel, and assorted materials along the shore. A **tsunami** is a seismic sea wave triggered by an undersea landslide or earthquake. It travels at great speeds in the open sea and gains height as it comes ashore, posing a coastal hazard.

An *erosional coast* features wave action that cuts a horizontal bench in the tidal zone, extending from a sea cliff out into the sea. Such a structure is a **wave-cut platform**, or *wave-cut terrace*. In contrast, *depositional coasts* generally are located along land of gentle relief, where depositional sediments are available from many sources. Characteristic landforms deposited by waves and currents are the **barrier spit** (material deposited in a long ridge extending out from a coast); the **bay barrier**, or *bay-mouth bar* (a spit that cuts the bay off from the ocean and forms an inland **lagoon**); the **tombolo** (where sediment deposits connect the shoreline with an offshore island or sea stack); and the **beach** (land along the shore where sediment is in motion, deposited by waves and currents).

wave (p. 413)
swell (p. 414)
breaker (p. 414)
wave refraction (p. 416)
longshore current (p. 416)
beach drift (p. 416)
littoral drift (p. 416)
tsunami (p. 416)
wave-cut platform (p. 419)
barrier spit (p. 420)
bay barrier (p. 420)
lagoon (p. 420)
tombolo (p. 420)
beach (p. 421)

9. What is a wave? How are waves generated, and how do they travel across the ocean? Does the water travel with the wave? Discuss the process of wave formation and transmission.
10. Describe the refraction process that occurs when waves reach an irregular coastline. Why is the coastline straightened?
11. Describe the process of beach drift and the movement of longshore currents to produce littoral drift.
12. Explain how a seismic sea wave attains such tremendous velocities. Why is it given the name *tsunami*?

13. What is meant by an erosional coast? What are the expected features of such a coast?
14. What is meant by a depositional coast? What are the expected features of such a coast?
15. How do people attempt to modify littoral drift? What strategies do they use?
16. Describe a beach—its form, composition, function, and evolution.
17. Is beach replenishment a practical strategy?

Describe barrier beaches and islands and their hazards as they relate to human settlement.

Barrier chains are long, narrow depositional features, generally of sand, that form offshore roughly parallel to the coast. Common forms are **barrier beaches** and the broader, more extensive **barrier islands**. Barrier formations are transient coastal features, constantly on the move, and they are a poor, but common, choice for development.

barrier beach (p. 423) **barrier island (p. 423)**

18. What types of impacts did Hurricane Sandy have on barrier beaches and islands along the Atlantic coast?
19. On the basis of the information in the text and any other sources at your disposal, do you think barrier islands and beaches should be used for development? If so, under what conditions? If not, why not?

Describe the nature of coral reefs and coastal wetlands and *assess* human impacts on these living systems.

A **coral** is a simple marine invertebrate that forms a hard, calcified, external skeleton. Over generations, corals accumulate in large reef structures. Corals live in a *symbiotic* (mutually helpful) relationship with algae; each is dependent on the other for survival.

Wetlands are lands saturated with water that support specific plants adapted to wet conditions. Coastal wetlands form as **mangrove swamps** equatorward of the 30th parallel in each hemisphere and as **salt marshes** poleward of these parallels.

coral (p. 425) **salt marsh (p. 428)**
mangrove swamp (p. 427)

20. How are corals able to construct reefs and islands?
21. Describe a trend in corals that is troubling scientists, and discuss some possible causes.
22. Why are the coastal wetlands poleward of 30° N and S latitude different from those that are equatorward? Describe the differences.

Describe eolian erosion and deposition and the resultant landforms.

Eolian, or wind, processes modify and move sand accumulations along coastal beaches and deserts. Wind exerts a drag or frictional pull on surface particles until they become airborne. The finer material suspended in a dust storm is lifted much higher than are the coarser particles of a sandstorm; only the finest dust particles travel significant distances. Saltating particles crash into other particles, knocking them both loose and forward. The motion of **surface creep** slides and rolls particles too large for saltation.

Erosion of the ground surface from the lifting and removal of particles by wind is **deflation**. Wherever wind encounters loose sediment, deflation may remove enough material to form depressions called *deflation hollows*, or *blowouts*, ranging in size from small indentations less than a meter wide up to areas hundreds of meters wide and many meters deep. **Abrasion** is the "sandblasting" of rock surfaces with particles captured in the air. Rocks that bear evidence of eolian abrasion are **ventifacts**. On a larger scale, deflation and abrasion are capable of streamlining rock structures, leaving behind distinctive rock formations or elongated ridges called **yardangs**. **Desert pavement** is the name for the hard, stony surface that forms in some deserts and protects underlying sediment from erosion.

Dunes are wind-sculpted accumulations of sand that form in arid and semiarid climates and along some coastlines where sand is available. An extensive area of dunes, such as that found in North Africa, is an **erg**, or **sand sea**. When saltating sand grains encounter small patches of sand, kinetic energy is dissipated, and the grains start to build into a dune. As the height of the sand pile increases above 30 cm (12 in.), a steeply sloping *slipface* on the lee side and characteristic dune features are formed. Dune forms are broadly classified as *crescentic*, *linear*, and *star*.

eolian (p. 428) **yardang (p. 430)**
surface creep (p. 429) **desert pavement (p. 430)**
deflation (p. 429) **erg (p. 431)**
abrasion (p. 430) **sand sea (p. 431)**
ventifact (p. 430) **dune (p. 431)**

23. Explain the term *eolian*. How would you characterize the ability of the wind to move material?
24. What is the difference between eolian saltation and fluvial saltation?
25. Explain the concept of surface creep.
26. Explain deflation. What role does deflation have in the formation of desert pavement?
27. How are ventifacts and yardangs formed by wind processes?
28. What is an erg? Name an example of a sand sea. Where is the example located?
29. What are the three classes of dune forms? Describe an example within each class. What do you think is the major shaping force for sand dunes?

MasteringGeography™

Looking for additional review and test prep materials? Visit the Study Area in *MasteringGeography*™ to enhance your geographic literacy, spatial reasoning skills, and understanding of this chapter's content by accessing a variety of resources, including MapMaster interactive maps, geoscience animations, videos, *In The News* RSS feeds, flashcards, web links, self-study quizzes, and an eText version of *Elemental Geosystems*.

VISUALanalysis 13 Coastal Processes and Barrier Islands

Over the past century, the Chandeleur Islands, an uninhabited barrier chain in the Gulf of Mexico, have been migrating toward the mainland and shrinking in areal extent, largely as a result of coastal storms. Study the satellite images showing changes to these islands before and after Hurricane Katrina (2005). [(a) USGS. (b) Erik Zobrist/NOAA Restoration Center Collection. (c), (d) *Landsat-5*, NASA.]

1. How do erosion and deposition of coastal sediments reshape barrier islands during a hurricane? Explain the exogenic processes causing the changes observed in these images.
2. What geomorphic features associated with barrier islands attract wildlife, allowing the designation of this area as a national wildlife refuge?
3. Where does the sediment eroded from these islands accumulate? What are two sources of sediment that could potentially rebuild the island chain? How will changes in sea level affect these islands in future decades?

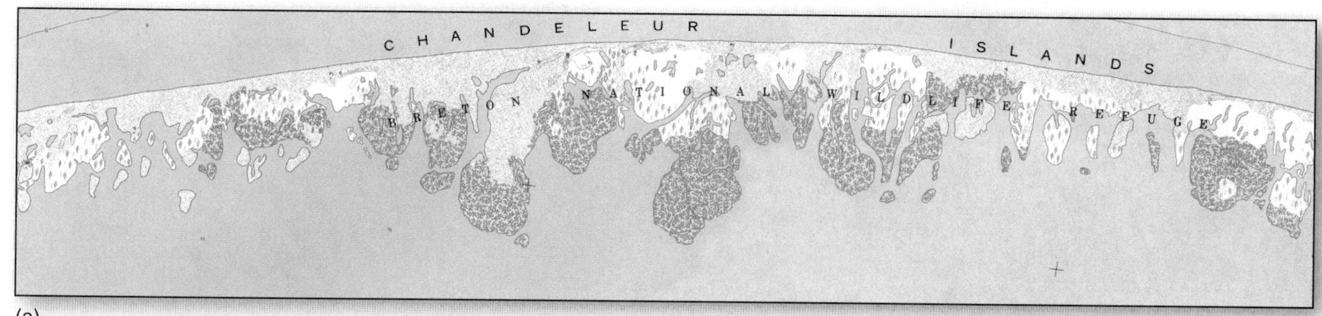

(a)

(b) Chandeleur Islands, June 2001, before Hurricane Katrina.

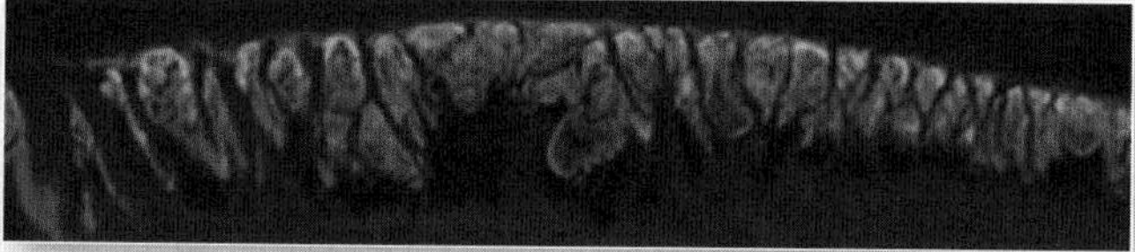

(c) October 2004, before Katrina.

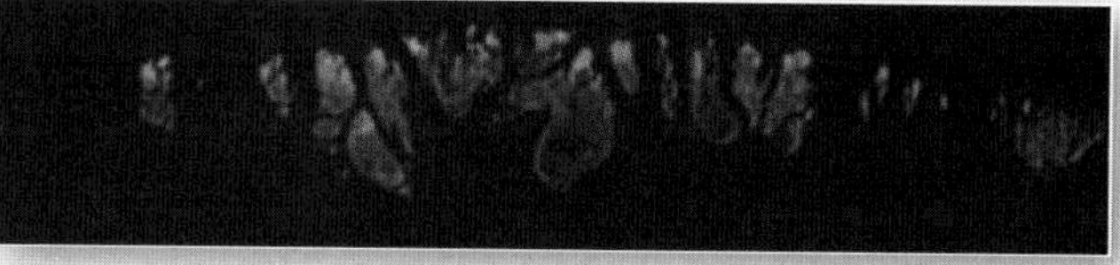

(d) September 2005, after Katrina.

14 Glacial and Periglacial Landscapes

Shaped by glacial action, the dramatic Grande Jorasses peaks near Chamonix, France, reach 4000 m (13,123 ft) in elevation above the Mer de Glace, the longest glacier in the French Alps. A wild goat, the alpine ibex (*Capra ibex*), scouts the scene. [Rafael Rojas Photography/The Image Bank/Getty Images.]

KEYLEARNING**concepts**

After reading the chapter, you should be able to:

- ***Explain*** the process by which snow becomes glacial ice.
- ***Differentiate*** between alpine glaciers and continental ice sheets and ***describe*** ice caps and ice fields.
- ***Illustrate*** the mechanics of glacial movement.
- ***Describe*** characteristic erosional and depositional landforms created by glaciation.
- ***Discuss*** the distribution of permafrost and ***explain*** several periglacial processes.
- ***Describe*** landscapes of the Pleistocene ice-age epoch and ***list*** changes occurring today in the polar regions.

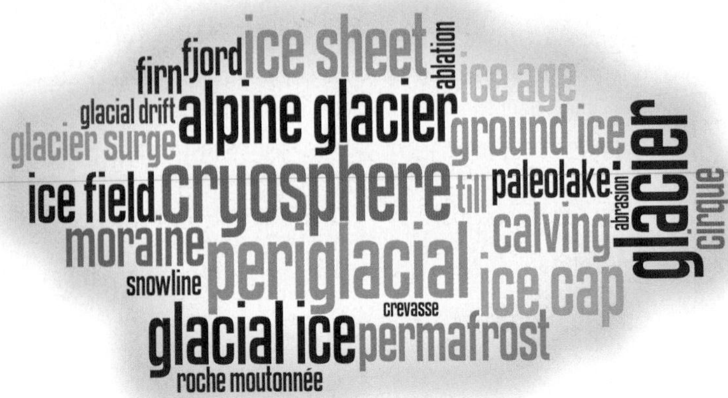

Tidewater Glaciers and Ice Shelves Give Way to Warming

Warming air and ocean temperatures are causing changes to snow and ice features across the globe, and these changes are perhaps most visible along the coasts of the Arctic region, Greenland, and Antarctica. With ongoing warming, tidewater glaciers—large masses of glacial ice flowing downhill toward the sea—are increasing their flow rate and calving more frequently, breaking off large icebergs into the surrounding ocean. Ice shelves—thick, floating platforms of ice that extend over the sea while still attached to continental ice—are thinning and breaking up, forming large icebergs equivalent in size to small U.S. states. Let us look at some notable examples of these effects.

Petermann Glacier, Greenland In northwest Greenland, calving of the Petermann Glacier has released huge chunks of ice into the sea in recent years. In August 2010, an island of ice measuring 251 km^2 (97 mi^2) broke loose, forming the largest iceberg in the Arctic in a half century (equivalent to 25% of this glacier's entire floating ice shelf). Then in July 2012, another large iceberg broke off the tongue of the glacier, upstream of the 2010 event (**Figure GN 14.1**).

With warmer air melting ice from above and higher sea temperatures melting ice from below, the rate of glacial loss increases. Scientists are studying how these processes apply to the Petermann Glacier. New cracks are opening upstream on the ragged edges of the glacier, demonstrating forward-moving stress. Data show that the Greenland Ice Sheet as a whole, which covers about 80% of the landmass, is now melting at a rate three times faster than in the 1990s. Glaciers such as Petermann along the edge of the ice sheet are melting more rapidly than the ice sheet itself.

Ward Hunt Ice Shelf, Canada Along the northern coast of Canada's Ellesmere Island is the Ward Hunt Ice Shelf, largest in the Arctic (see the location of Ellesmere Island on Figure 14.27a). After remaining stable for at least 4500 years, this ice shelf began to break up in 2003 and broke into several pieces in 2011.

The breakup of an ice shelf does not directly influence sea level because the ice shelf mass has already displaced its own volume in seawater. However, ice shelves hold back flows of grounded ice that do not yet displace ocean water, but are moving toward the sea. As the ice shelves disappear, their buttressing effect is lost, allowing the glaciers to flow more rapidly. This region of the Canadian Arctic Archipelago ranks third behind the Antarctic and Greenland ice sheets in terms of ice-mass loss on Earth, and this melting ice is making a significant contribution to global sea-level rise.

Pine Island Glacier, Antarctica To the west of the Antarctic Peninsula, the Pine Island Glacier flows from the West Antarctic Ice Sheet to the Amundsen Sea (as noted on Figure 14.8). This glacier is one of Antarctica's largest ice streams, a type of glacier that flows at a faster rate than the surrounding ice mass. The flow rate of the Pine Island Glacier is accelerating, increasing by 30% in the last 10 years (it is also shown in Figure 8.19).

The Pine Island Glacier's 40-km-wide (25-mi-wide) ice shelf is also calving and thinning at higher rates than previously recorded. This small ice shelf and glacier help buttress downslope movement of the West Antarctic Ice Sheet, which already contributes 0.15 to 0.30 mm/year to sea-level rise.

The warming trends demonstrated in these examples continued through 2014, promoting the rise of sea level across the globe. This chapter examines snow, ice, and frozen ground and the rapid changes that are occurring in these environments with climate change.

QUESTION AND EXPLORE For more information on melting ice shelves and glaciers, go to the National Snow and Ice Data Center at http://nsidc.org/. For the latest ice conditions in Canada, go to http://www.ec.gc.ca/glaces-ice/default.asp?lang=En&n=D32C361E-1. What positive feedback mechanisms are accelerating ice melt in the polar regions? (Review Chapter 3 Geosystems Now.) MG

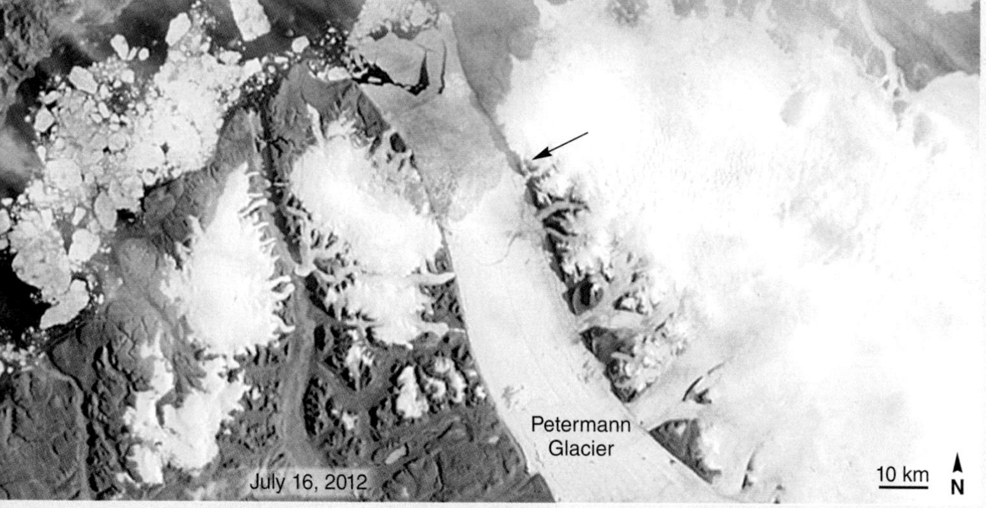

◀**Figure GN 14.1 Greenland tidewater glacier breakup, 2012.** An iceberg breaks off the Petermann Glacier. Notice at least five tributary glaciers. [*Aqua* MODIS, NASA.]

About three-quarters of Earth's freshwater is frozen. Currently, more than 32.7 million km³ (7.8 million mi³) of water are tied up as ice: in Greenland, Antarctica, and ice caps and mountain glaciers worldwide. The bulk of that snow and ice sits in just two places—Greenland (2.4 million km³, or 0.6 million mi³) and Antarctica (30.1 million km³, or 7.2 million mi³). The remaining snow and ice (180,000 km³, or 43,184 mi³) covers other near-polar regions and various mountains and alpine valleys (**Figure 14.1**).

Earth's **cryosphere** consists of the portions of the hydrosphere and lithosphere that are perennially frozen, including the freshwater making up snow, ice, glaciers, and frozen ground and the frozen saltwater in sea ice. These cold regions are generally found at high latitudes and, worldwide, at high elevations on mountains. The extent of the cryosphere changes on a seasonal basis, given that more snow accumulates and more soil and freshwater freeze during the winter.

With rising temperatures causing worldwide glacial and polar ice melts, the cryosphere today is in a state of dramatic change.

With rising temperatures causing worldwide glacial and polar ice melts, the cryosphere today is in a state of dramatic change. In 2012, Arctic air temperatures set records of more than 5 C° (9 F°) above normal, and Arctic Ocean sea ice decreased to its smallest areal extent in the past century. The surface ice loss in 2007 was second to this record, with 2008 third.

In this chapter: We focus first on snow and the processes by which permanent snow forms glacial ice. We then look at Earth's extensive ice deposits—their formation, their movement, and the ways in which they produce various erosional and depositional landforms. Glaciers, transient landforms themselves, leave in their wake a variety of landscape features. Glacial processes are intricately tied to changes in global temperature and rising or falling sea level. We also examine the freezing conditions that create permafrost and the periglacial processes such as frost action that shape landscapes. The chapter ends with a look at the changing polar regions.

▼Figure 14.1 Rivers and sheets of ice. [(a) *Terra* MODIS, NASA. (b) Bobbé Christopherson.]

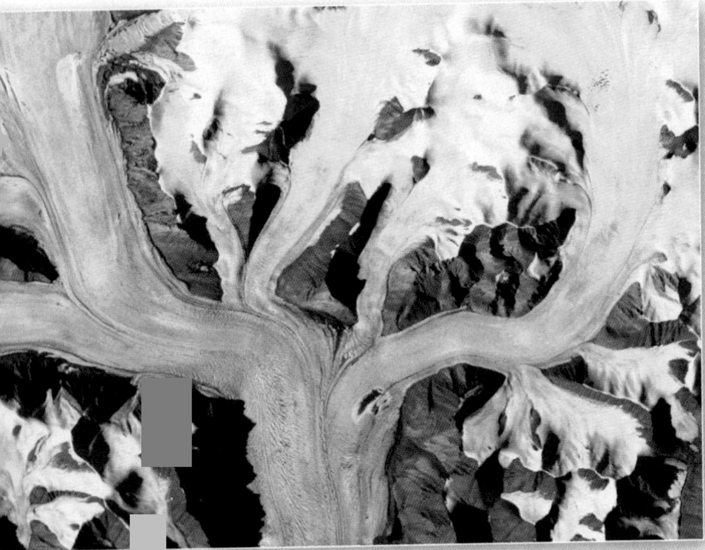

(a) Satellite view of alpine glaciers merging from adjoining glacial valleys in the northeast region of Ellesmere Island in the Canadian Arctic.

(b) Cracks indicate movement of the Greenland Ice Sheet, an accumulation of ice perhaps 100,000 years in the making. The peaks rising above the snow are known as *nunataks*.

Snow into Ice—The Basis of Glaciers

In previous chapters, we discussed some of the important aspects of seasonal and permanent snow cover on Earth. Water stored as snow is released gradually during the summer months, feeding streams and rivers and the resources they provide (discussed in Chapter 6). For example, many western states rely heavily on snowmelt for their municipal water supplies. At the same time, snow can create a hazard in mountain environments (discussed ahead).

Another role of the seasonal snowpack is that it increases Earth's albedo, or reflectivity, affecting the Earth–atmosphere energy balance (discussed in Chapter 3). As temperatures increase with climate change, seasonal snow cover decreases, creating a positive feedback loop in which decreasing snow cover lowers the global albedo, leading to more warming and, in turn, further decreasing the seasonal snow cover.

Properties of Snow

When conditions are cold enough, precipitation falls to the ground as snow. As discussed in Chapter 5, all ice crystals have a six-sided preference owing to the molecular structure of water. Snowflakes, which are made up of ice crystals, also have six sides, yet each snowflake is unique because its growth is dictated by the temperature and humidity conditions in the cloud in which it forms. As snowflakes fall through layers of clouds, their growth follows different patterns, resulting in the intricate shapes that arrive at Earth. Because the temperature at which snowflakes exist is very near their melting point, the flakes can change rapidly once they are on the ground, in a process known as *snow metamorphism*.

When snow falls to Earth, it either accumulates or melts. During the winter in high latitudes or at upper elevations, cold temperatures allow the snow to accumulate seasonally. Each storm is unique, so the snowpack is deposited in distinguishable layers, much like the layered sedimentary rock strata of the Grand Canyon.

The properties of each layer and the relationship between them determine the susceptibility of a mountain slope to a *snow avalanche*, the sudden release and movement of massive amounts of snow down a steep slope. The snowpack normally consists of both stronger and weaker layers; when a stronger layer, called a slab, overlies a weaker layer, avalanches are possible. Snow avalanches claim about 30 lives each year in the United States and can sometimes be large enough to destroy forests or entire mountain communities. These natural hazards can leave visible evidence of their repeated occurrence in some mountain regions (**Figure 14.2**).

Formation of Glacial Ice

In some regions on Earth, snow is permanent on the landscape, and it is in those regions—both at high latitudes and at high elevations at any latitude—that glaciers form. As mentioned in Chapter 3, a **snowline** is the lowest elevation where snow remains year-round; specifically, it is the lowest line where winter snow accumulation persists throughout the summer. On equatorial mountains, the snowline is around 5000 m (16,400 ft) above sea level; on midlatitude mountains, such as the European Alps, snowlines average 2700 m (8850 ft); and in southern Greenland, snowlines are as low as 600 m (1970 ft).

Glaciers form by the continual accumulation of snow that recrystallizes under its own weight into an ice mass. Ice, in turn, is both a mineral (an inorganic natural compound of specific chemical makeup and crystalline structure) and a rock (a mass of one or more minerals). As mentioned earlier, the accumulation of snow in layered deposits is similar to the layering in sedimentary rock. To give birth to a glacier, snow and ice are transformed under pressure, recrystallizing into a type of metamorphic rock.

Consider that as snow accumulates during the winter, the increasing thickness results in increased weight and pressure on the underlying layers. In summer, rain and snowmelt contribute water, which stimulates further melting, and this meltwater seeps down into the snowfield and refreezes. Air spaces between ice crystals are compressed as the snow packs to a greater density, recrystallizing and consolidating as the pressure continues to increase. Through this process, snow that survives the summer and is still present the following winter begins a slow transformation into glacial ice. In a transition step, the snow becomes **firn**, a granular, partly compacted snow that is intermediate between snow and ice.

Dense **glacial ice** is produced over a period of many years as this process continues. In Antarctica, glacial ice formation may take 1000 years because of the dryness of the climate and minimal snowfall, whereas in wet climates, the time is reduced to several years because of constant heavy snowfall.

Types of Glaciers

A **glacier** is defined as a large mass of ice resting on land or floating in the sea attached to a landmass (the latter is an ice shelf, discussed in Geosystems Now and later in the chapter). Glaciers are not stationary; they move under the pressure of their own great weight and the pull of gravity. In fact, they move in streamlike patterns, merging as tributaries into large rivers of ice that slowly flow outward toward the ocean (see Figure 14.1a). For an inventory of world glaciers, go to http://glims.colorado.edu/glacierdata/db_summary_stats.php.

Although glaciers are as varied as the landscape itself, they fall within two general groups, based on their form, size, and flow characteristics: alpine glaciers and continental ice sheets (also called continental glaciers), both of which we describe below. Today, alpine glaciers and ice sheets cover about 10% of Earth's land area, ranging from the polar regions to midlatitude mountain ranges to some of the high mountains along the equator, such as in the Andes Mountains of South America and on Mount Kilimanjaro in Tanzania, Africa. During colder climate episodes in the past, glacial ice covered as much as 30% of continental land. Throughout these "ice ages," below-freezing temperatures occurred for extended periods at lower latitudes than they do today, allowing snow to accumulate and persist year after year.

◀**Figure 14.2 Avalanche paths in the Madison Range near Hebgen Lake, southwest Montana.** In certain mountain regions, snow avalanches occur repeatedly, so that avalanche paths are visible features of the landscape. On forested slopes, trees are sometimes completely cleared from these paths; continued avalanche activity prevents new trees from establishing. [Karl Birkeland.]

Alpine Glaciers

With few exceptions, a glacier in a mountain range is an **alpine glacier**, or *mountain glacier.* The name comes from the Alps of central Europe, where such glaciers abound. Alpine glaciers have several subtypes. *Valley glaciers* are masses of ice confined within a valley that originally was formed by stream action. These glaciers range in length from as little as 100 m (325 ft) to more than 100 km (60 mi). How many valley glaciers do you see joining the main glacier in Figure 14.1a? **Figure 14.3** shows a valley glacier in the Tien Shan in central Asia, one of the largest continuous mountain ranges in the world. The two highest peaks in the central part of this range, both shown in the photo, are Xuelian Feng at 6527 m (21,414 ft) and Peak 6231, aptly named at 6231 m (20,443 ft) above sea level.

A glacier that forms within the snow filling a **cirque**, or bowl-shaped recess at the head of a valley, is a *cirque glacier.* Several cirque glaciers may jointly feed a valley glacier (Figure 14.3). A *piedmont glacier* is formed wherever several valley glaciers pour out of their confining valleys and coalesce at the base of a mountain range. A piedmont glacier spreads freely over the lowlands; an example is the Malaspina Glacier, which flows into Yakutat Bay, Alaska (see the NASA image at http://earthobservatory.nasa.gov/IOTD/view.php?id=3421).

As a valley glacier flows slowly downhill, it erodes the mountains, canyons, and river valleys beneath its mass, transporting material within or along its base. A portion of the transported debris may also be carried on its icy surface, visible as dark streaks and bands. This surface material is known as *supraglacial debris*, which originates either from rockfalls and other gravity-driven processes that carry material downward from above or from processes that float material upward from the glacier's bed.

A *tidewater glacier*, or *tidal glacier*, ends in the sea. Such glaciers are characterized by **calving**, a process in which pieces of ice break free to form floating ice masses known as *icebergs*, which are usually found wherever glaciers meet an ocean, bay, or fjord (**Figure 14.4**). Icebergs are inherently unstable, as their center of gravity shifts with melting and further breakup (review the iceberg discussion in Chapter 5).

▲**Figure 14.3 Glaciers in the Tien Shan, central Asia, 2011.** The area shown is in the central Tien Shan, north of the Himalayas and just east of the meeting of the borders of China, Kazakhstan, and Kyrgyzstan. [*ISS* Astronaut photo, NASA/GSC.]

▲**Figure 14.4 Glacial calving.** Active calving fills the sea with icebergs along the edge of the Austfonna Ice Cap on Nordaustlandet Island in the archipelago of Svalbard, Norway. The glacial front retreated about 2 km (12.4 mi) from 2012 to 2013. [Bobbé Christopherson.]

Continental Ice Sheets

An **ice sheet** is an extensive, continuous mass of ice that may occur on a continental scale. Most of Earth's glacial ice exists in the ice sheets that blanket 81% of Greenland—1,756,000 km^2 (678,000 mi^2) of ice—and 90% of Antarctica—14.2 million km^2 (5.48 million mi^2) of ice. Antarctica alone contains 92% of all the glacial ice on the planet (review the ice volumes in the chapter introduction).

The ice sheets of Antarctica and Greenland have such enormous mass that large portions of each landmass beneath the ice are isostatically depressed (pressed down by weight) below sea level. Each ice sheet reaches thicknesses of more than 3000 m (9800 ft), with average thickness around 2000 m (6500 ft), burying all but the highest peaks of land.

Where a continental ice sheet meets the coast, the ice may extend out over the sea as an *ice shelf.* These shelves are often found in protected inlets and bays, cover thousands of square kilometers, and reach thicknesses of 1000 m (3280 ft).

Ice caps and ice fields are two additional types of glaciers with continuous ice cover, on a slightly smaller scale than an ice sheet. An **ice cap** is roughly circular and, by definition, covers an area of less than 50,000 km^2 (19,300 mi^2), completely burying the underlying landscape.

The volcanic island of Iceland features several ice caps; an example is Vatnajökull in **Figure 14.5**. Volcanoes lie beneath these icy surfaces. Iceland's Grímsvötn Volcano erupted in 1996 and 2004, producing large quantities of melted glacial water in a sudden flood called a *jökulhlaup*, an Icelandic term that is now widely used to describe a glacial outburst flood. The most

▲**Figure 14.5 Ice caps.** The Vatnajökull in southeastern Iceland is the largest of four ice caps on the island (*jökull* means "ice cap" in Danish). Note the ash on the ice cap from the 2004 Grímsvötn eruption [NASA/GSFC.]

recent eruption in 2011 was the largest in a century, but did not produce an outburst flood.

An **ice field** extends in a characteristic elongated pattern over a mountainous region and is not large enough to form the dome of an ice cap. The Patagonian ice field of Argentina and Chile is one of Earth's largest. It is only 90 km (56 mi) wide, but stretches 360 km (224 mi), from 46° to 51° S latitude (**Figure 14.6**).

Ice sheets and ice caps may be drained by rapidly moving *ice streams*, made up of solid ice that flows at a faster rate than the main ice mass toward lowland areas or the sea. For example, a number of ice streams flow through the periphery of Greenland and Antarctica. An *outlet glacier* is a stream of ice flowing out from an ice sheet or ice cap, usually constrained on each side by the bedrock of a mountain valley.

▼**Figure 14.6 The Patagonian ice fields and major glacial lakes of Argentina and Chile.** [NASA/GSFC.]

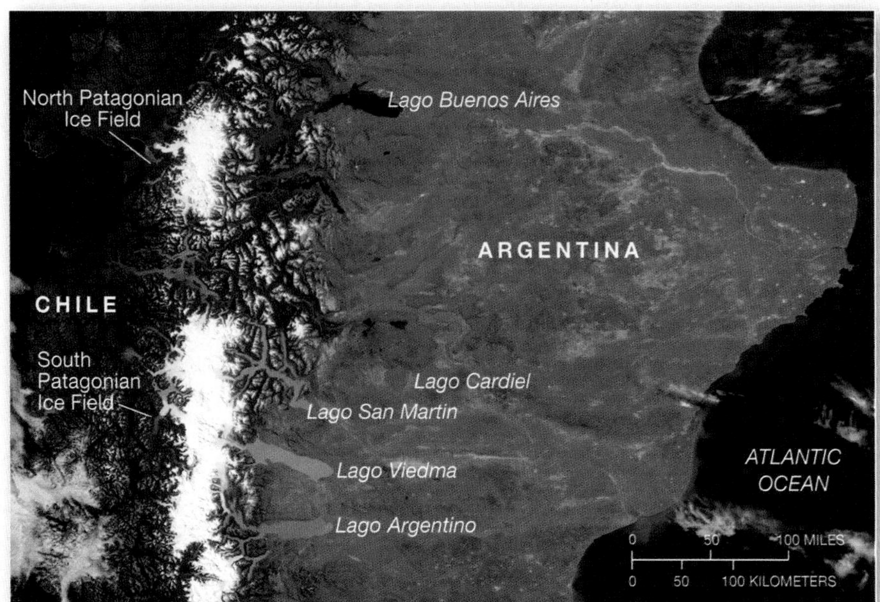

Glacial Processes

A glacier is a dynamic body, moving relentlessly downslope at rates that vary within its mass, shaping the landscape through which it flows. Like so many of the systems described in this text, glacial processes are linked to the concept of equilibrium. A glacier at equilibrium maintains its size because the incoming snow is approximately equal to the melt rate. In a state of disequilibrium, the glacier either expands (causing its terminus to move downslope) or retreats (causing its terminus to move upslope).

Glacial Mass Balance

A glacier is an open system, with *inputs* of snow and *outputs* of ice, meltwater, and water vapor, as illustrated in Geosystems in Action 14. Glaciers acquire snow in their accumulation zone, a snowfield at the highest elevation of an ice sheet or ice cap or at the head of a valley glacier, usually in a cirque (Figure GIA 14.1). Snow avalanches from surrounding steep mountain slopes can add to the snowfield depth. The accumulation zone ends at the **firn line**, which marks the elevation above which the winter snow and ice remained intact throughout the summer melting season, but below which melting occurs. At the lower end of the glacier, far below the firn line, the glacier undergoes wasting (reduction) through several processes: melting on the surface, internally, and at the base; ice removal by deflation from wind; the calving of ice blocks; and sublimation (recall from Chapter 5 that this is the phase change of solid ice directly into water vapor). Collectively, these processes cause losses to the glacier's mass, known as **ablation**.

These gains (accumulation) and losses (ablation) of glacial ice determine the glacier's *mass balance*, the property that decides whether the glacier will advance (grow larger) or retreat (grow smaller). During cold periods with adequate precipitation, a glacier has a *positive net mass balance* and advances. In warmer times, a glacier has a *negative net mass balance* and retreats. Internally, gravity continues to move a glacier forward even though its lower terminus might be in retreat owing to ablation. Within the glacier is a zone where accumulation balances ablation; this is known as the *equilibrium line* (Figure GIA 14.2), and it generally coincides with the firn line.

(*text continued on page 446*)

As an open system, a glacier is in equilibrium if it is neither advancing nor retreating. But if inputs of snow are greater than losses through melting, deflation by wind, sublimation, and calving, the glacier will expand. If ice losses exceed inputs, the glacier will retreat (GIA 14.1). Whether a glacier is in equilibrium can be determined from its mass balance (GIA 14.2). Today, many alpine glaciers worldwide are retreating as they melt because of warming related to climate change (GIA 14.3).

14.1 Cross Section of a Typical Retreating Alpine Glacier

The diagram shows the relationship between the zone of accumulation, the equilibrium line, and the zone of ablation in a retreating glacier. Ice continues to slide downhill as the glacier's terminus retreats upslope, depositing terminal and recessional moraines. Additional inputs of ice can come from tributary glaciers as glaciers merge.

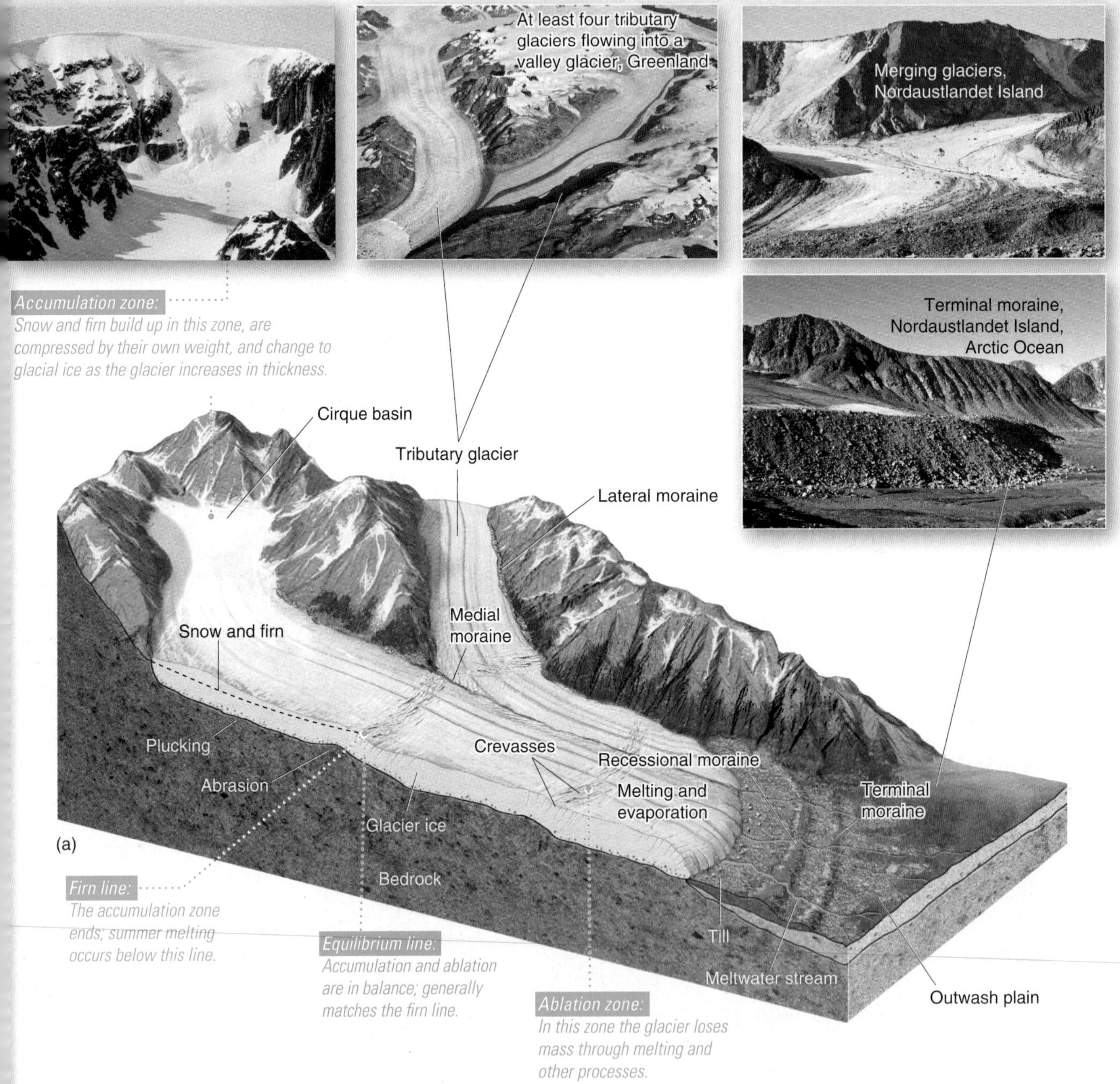

At least four tributary glaciers flowing into a valley glacier, Greenland

Merging glaciers, Nordaustlandet Island

Terminal moraine, Nordaustlandet Island, Arctic Ocean

Accumulation zone: Snow and firn build up in this zone, are compressed by their own weight, and change to glacial ice as the glacier increases in thickness.

Cirque basin

Tributary glacier

Lateral moraine

Snow and firn

Medial moraine

Plucking

Abrasion

Crevasses

Recessional moraine

Melting and evaporation

Terminal moraine

Glacier ice

Bedrock

Till

Meltwater stream

Outwash plain

(a)

Firn line: The accumulation zone ends; summer melting occurs below this line.

Equilibrium line: Accumulation and ablation are in balance; generally matches the firn line.

Ablation zone: In this zone the glacier loses mass through melting and other processes.

Compare: How are the accumulation zone and the ablation zone similar? How are they different?

Animation Glacial Processes

http://goo.gl/OzhTkq

MasteringGeography™

Visit the Study Area in MasteringGeography™ to explore glacial mass balance.

Visualize: Study a geosciences animation of glacial processes.

Assess: Demonstrate understanding of a glacier's mass balance (if assigned by instructor).

Animation A Tour of the Cryosphere

http://goo.gl/SjvDGd

14.2 Glacial Mass Balance

The diagram shows the annual mass balance of a glacial system, which determines the location of the equilibrium line. Generally, a glacier with a positive mass balance will advance, while a glacier with a negative mass balance will retreat.

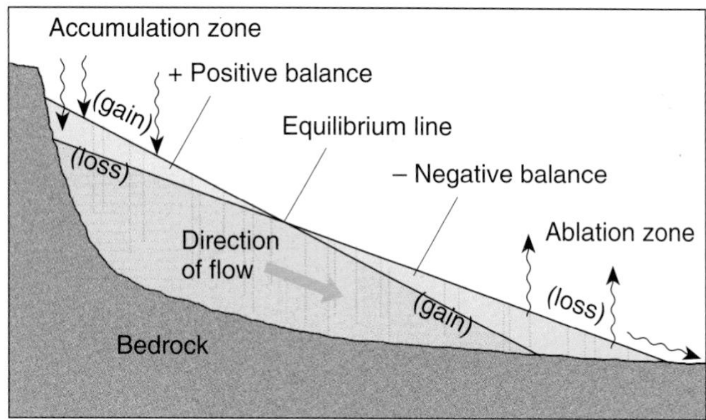

14.3 Portrait of a Retreating Glacier, 1979–2010

Photographs and ground measurements reveal that the South Cascade Glacier in Washington is retreating and that its mass balance is declining. This glacier is one of several being intensively monitored by USGS scientists to assess the effects of climate change.

Infer: Based on what you can see in the photos, outline the largest area formerly occupied by South Cascade Glacier. What evidence helped you arrive at this conclusion?

Animation (MG) Operation Ice Bridge

http://goo.gl/qyNp0D

GEOquiz

1. Predict: How would the position of the firn line change if a glacier receives more snowfall at higher elevations for several years in a row? Explain.

2. Explain: Thinking of a glacier as a system, explain how changes to inputs and outputs result in a glacier's having a positive or negative mass balance.

Illustrating the global trend, the net mass balance of the South Cascade Glacier in Washington State demonstrated significant losses between 1955 and 2010. As a result of this negative mass balance, in some years the terminus retreated tens of meters, and it has retreated every year in the record except 1972. Figure GIA 14.3 presents a photo comparison of the South Cascade Glacier between 1979 and 2010. The USGS is tracking glacial changes in a Repeat Photography Project (see http://nrmsc.usgs.gov/repeatphoto/).

A comparison of the trend of this glacier's mass balance with that of others in the world shows that temperature changes apparently are causing widespread reductions in middle- and lower-elevation glacial ice. The present wastage (ice loss) from alpine glaciers worldwide is thought to contribute over 25% to the measured rise in sea level.

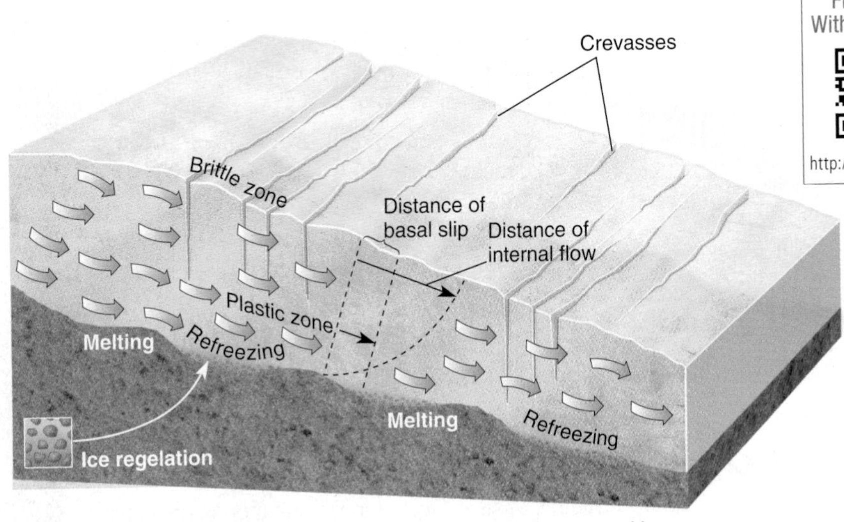

(a) Cross section of a glacier, showing its forward motion, brittle cracking at the surface, and flow along its basal layer.

(b) Surface crevasses are evidence of forward movement on the Fox Glacier, South Island, New Zealand.

▲**Figure 14.7 Glacial movement.** [(b) David Wall/Alamy.]

Glacial Movement

Glacial ice is quite different from the small, brittle cubes of ice we find in our freezer. In particular, glacial ice behaves in a plastic (pliable) manner; it distorts and flows in its underlying portions in response to the weight and pressure of overlying snow and the degree of slope below. In contrast, the glacier's upper-surface portions are quite brittle. Rates of flow range from almost no movement to a kilometer or two of movement per year on a steep slope. The rate of accumulation of snow in the glacier's formation area is critical to the speed of forward motion.

Glaciers, then, are not rigid blocks that simply slide downhill. The greatest movement within a valley glacier occurs *internally*, below the rigid surface layer, which fractures as the underlying plastic zone moves forward (**Figure 14.7a**). At the same time, the base creeps and slides along, varying its speed with temperature and the presence of any lubricating water beneath the ice. This *basal slip* usually is much less rapid than the internal plastic flow of the glacier, so the upper portion of the glacier flows ahead of the lower portion.

Animation (MG) Flow of Ice Within a Glacier
http://goo.gl/8TBHLV

Unevenness in the landscape beneath the ice may cause the pressure to vary, melting some of the basal ice by compression at one moment, only to have it refreeze later. This process is *ice regelation*, meaning to refreeze, or re-gel. Such melting/refreezing action incorporates rock debris into the glacier. Consequently, the basal ice layer, which can extend tens of meters above the base of the glacier, has a much higher debris content than the ice above.

A flowing alpine glacier or ice stream can develop vertical cracks known as **crevasses** (Figure 14.7). Crevasses result from friction with valley walls, from tension due to stretching as the glacier passes over convex slopes, or from compression as the glacier passes over concave slopes. Traversing a glacier, whether an alpine glacier or an ice sheet, is dangerous because a thin veneer of snow sometimes masks the presence of a crevasse.

Scientists recently completed a map of ice movement speed on the Antarctic continent based on satellite radar measurements from 1996 to 2009 (**Figure 14.8**). The map reveals that many of the tributaries around ice shelves extend surprisingly far inland and are moving by basal slip (sliding

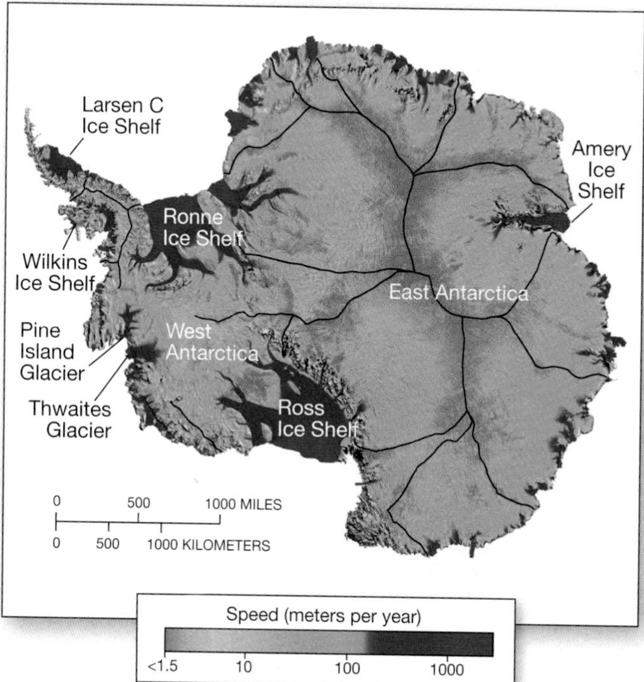

▲**Figure 14.8 First complete map of ice movement speed in Antarctica.** The black lines show ice divides, similar to drainage divides. Colors indicate the speed of ice movement; fastest movement is in red and purple. Note that the fast-flowing ice channels extend far inland, a surprise to scientists. The tributaries shown in blue are moving faster than the ice sheet around them, but do not move as quickly as an ice stream. This map was created using data from a group of international satellites from the Canadian, Japanese, and European Space Agencies. [*RADARSAT–SAR*, NASA/JPL.]

on the ground) rather than slowly deforming under the weight of the ice. Identifying the areal extent of this type of motion on the ice sheet is important because a loss of ice at the coasts as ice shelves break up may open the tap for massive amounts of ice to flow more quickly from the interior, with implications for sea-level rise.

Glacier Surges Although glaciers flow plastically and predictably most of the time, some will advance rapidly at speeds much faster than normal, in a **glacier surge**. A surge is not quite as abrupt as it sounds; in glacial terms, a surge can be tens of meters per day. The Jakobshavn Glacier on the western Greenland coast, for example, is one of the fastest moving, at between 7 and 12 km (4.3 and 7.5 mi) a year. In 2012, scientists reported that although the overall trend in Greenland was toward glacial surging, in some regions glaciers slowed between 2005 and 2010, pointing to the complexity of glacial behavior.

Scientists are investigating the exact causes of glacier surges. Some surge events result from a buildup of water pressure under the glacier—sometimes enough to actually float the glacier slightly, detaching it from its bed during the surge. Another cause of glacier surges is the presence of a water-saturated layer of sediment, a *soft bed*, beneath the glacier. This is a deformable layer that cannot resist the tremendous sheer stress produced by the moving ice of the glacier. In Antarctica, scientists examining cores taken from several ice streams now accelerating through the West Antarctic Ice Sheet think they have identified the occurrence there of this kind of glacial surge—although water pressure is still important. As any type of surge begins, ice quakes are detectable, and ice faults are visible.

Scientists think that glacial surges in Greenland are related to the meltwater that works its way to the basal layer, lubricating the interface between the glacier and the underlying bedrock. In addition, the warmer surface waters draining beneath the glacier deliver heat that increases basal melt rates. However, a 2013 study reported that the meltwater flows in distinct channels under the ice, affecting the channels but not necessarily lubricating wide areas of the ice sheet basal layer.

Glacial Erosion The process by which a glacier erodes the landscape is similar to a large excavation project, with the glacier hauling debris from one site to another for deposition. The passing glacier mechanically picks up rock material and carries it away in a process known as *glacial plucking*. Debris is carried on its surface and is also transported internally, or *englacially*, embedded within the glacier itself.

When a glacier retreats, it can leave behind cobbles or boulders (sometimes house-sized) that are "foreign" in composition and origin to the ground on which they are deposited. These *glacial erratics*, lying in strange locations with no obvious sign of how they got there, were an early clue to the glacial plucking that occurred during times when blankets of ice covered the land (pictured ahead in Figure 14.12).

The rock pieces frozen to the basal layers of the glacier enable the ice mass to scour the landscape like sandpaper as it moves. This process, called **abrasion**, produces a smooth surface on exposed rock, which shines with *glacial polish* when the glacier retreats (**Figure 14.9**). Larger rocks in the glacier act much like chisels, gouging the underlying surface and producing glacial striations parallel to the flow direction.

GEOreport 14.1 Greenland Ice Sheet melting

The Greenland Ice Sheet is experiencing a greater amount of ice loss and a greater area of surface melting than at any time since systematic satellite monitoring started in the 1970s. Scientists calculated that 98% of the ice sheet's surface melted in July 2012, an occurrence never before seen in the satellite record (see Figure 14.29b). A typical summer melt is 50%. Near-surface air temperatures at the highest and coldest station on the ice sheet have increased 0.22 F° per year since 1992, six times faster than the global average temperature rise. In response, the equilibrium line (at which accumulation balances ablation) has been moving up the ice sheet on average 35 m/year (115 ft/year).

◀Figure 14.9 Glacial sandpapering of rock. Glacial polish and striations are examples of glacial abrasion and erosion. The polished, marked surface is seen beneath a glacial erratic—a rock left behind by a retreating glacier. [Bobbé Christopherson.]

Glacial Landforms

Glacial erosion and deposition produce distinctive landforms that differ greatly from those existing before the ice came and went. Alpine glaciers and continental ice sheets each produce characteristic landscapes, although some landforms exist in either type of glacial environment.

Erosional Landforms

A landscape feature produced by both glacial plucking and abrasion is a **roche moutonnée** ("sheep rock" in French), an asymmetrical hill of exposed bedrock. This landform has a characteristic gently sloping upstream side (stoss side) that is polished smooth by glacial action and an abrupt and steep downstream side (lee side) where the glacier plucked rock pieces (**Figure 14.10**).

Glacial Valleys The effects of alpine glaciation created the dramatic landforms of the Canadian Rockies, the Swiss Alps, and the Himalayan peaks. Geomorphologist William Morris Davis depicted the stages of a valley glacier in drawings published in 1906 and redrawn here in **Figures 14.11** and **14.12**. Study of these figures reveals the handiwork of ice as sculptor in mountain environments.

Figure 14.11a shows the **V** shape of a typical stream-cut valley as it existed before glaciation. Figure 14.11b shows the same landscape during subsequent glaciation. Glacial erosion actively removes much of the regolith (weathered bedrock) and the soils that covered the stream-valley landscape. When glaciers erode parallel valleys, a thin, sharp ridge forms between them, known as an **arête** ("knife-edge" in French). Arêtes can also form between adjacent cirques as they erode in a headward direction. Two eroding cirques may reduce an arête to a saddlelike

◀Figure 14.10 Roche moutonnée. [(a) Robert Christopherson.]

(a) Lembert Dome in the Tuolumne Meadows area of Yosemite National Park, California.

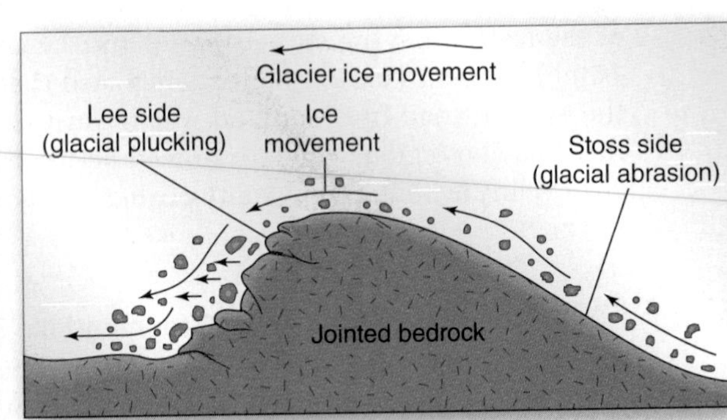

(b) The erosional formation processes at work on Lembert Dome (the bluish/whitish color represents glacial ice).

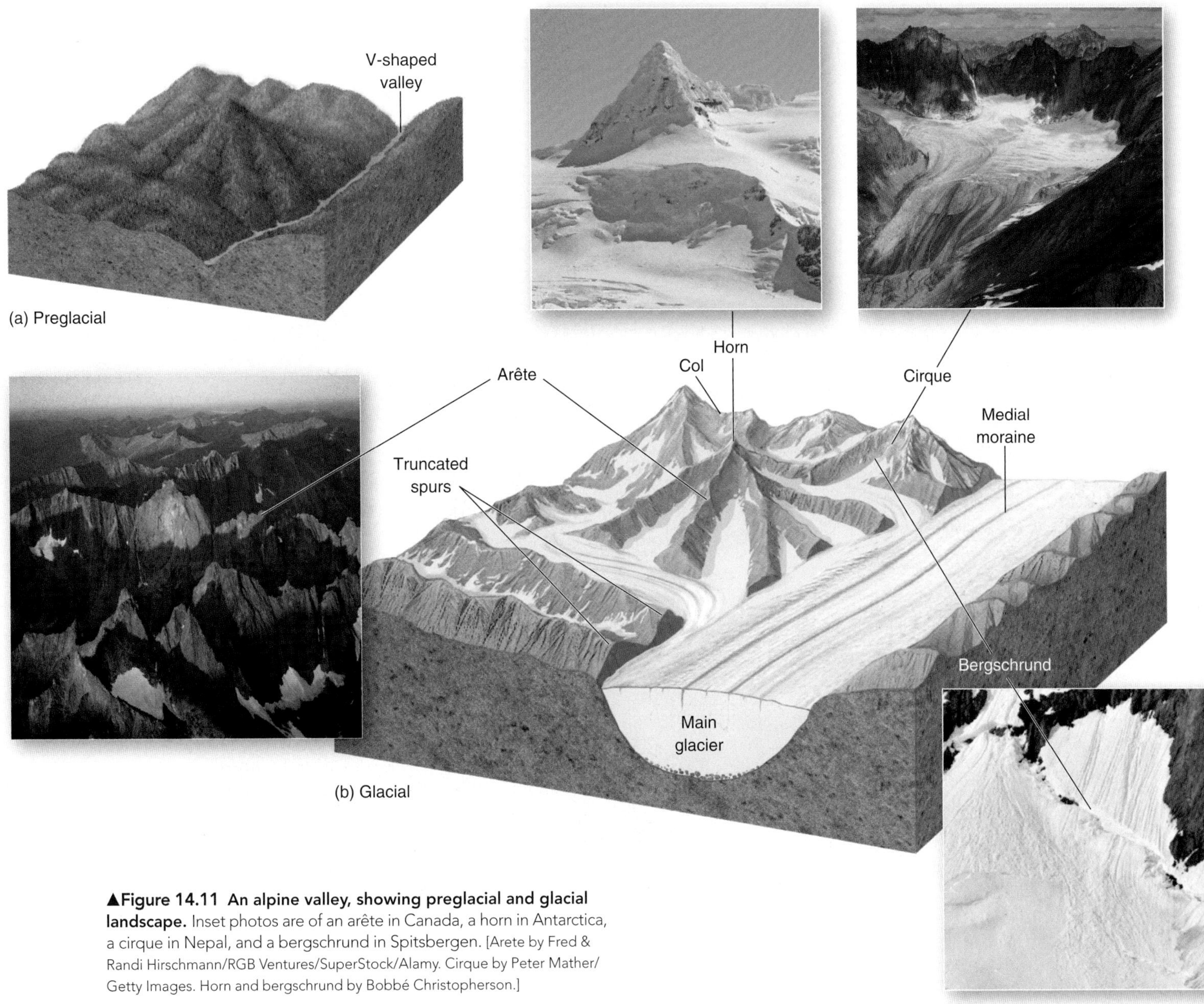

▲**Figure 14.11 An alpine valley, showing preglacial and glacial landscape.** Inset photos are of an arête in Canada, a horn in Antarctica, a cirque in Nepal, and a bergschrund in Spitsbergen. [Arete by Fred & Randi Hirschmann/RGB Ventures/SuperStock/Alamy. Cirque by Peter Mather/Getty Images. Horn and bergschrund by Bobbé Christopherson.]

depression or pass, forming a **col**. A **horn**, or pyramidal peak, results when several cirque glaciers gouge an individual mountain summit from all sides. Most famous is the Matterhorn in the Swiss Alps, but many others occur worldwide. A *bergschrund* is a crevasse, or wide crack, that separates flowing ice from stagnant ice in the upper reaches of a glacier or in a cirque. Bergschrunds are often covered in snow in winter, but become apparent in summer when this snow cover melts.

Figure 14.12 shows the same landscape at a time of warmer climate, when the ice retreated. The glaciated valleys now are **U**-shaped, greatly changed from their previous stream-cut **V** form. Physical weathering from the freeze–thaw cycle has loosened rock along the steep cliffs, and it has fallen to form *talus slopes* along the valley sides. In the cirques where the valley glaciers originated, small mountain lakes called **tarns** have formed. Some cirques contain small, circular, stair-stepped lakes, called **paternoster** ("our father") **lakes** for their resemblance to rosary (religious) beads. Paternoster lakes may form from the differing resistance of rock to glacial processes or from damming by glacial deposits.

In some cases, valleys carved by tributary glaciers are left stranded high above the main valley floor because the primary glacier eroded the main valley so deeply. These *hanging valleys* are the sites of spectacular waterfalls. How many of the erosional forms from Figures 14.11 and 14.12 can you identify in **Figure 14.13**? (Look for arêtes, cols, horns, cirques, cirque glaciers, **U**-shaped valleys, and tarns.)

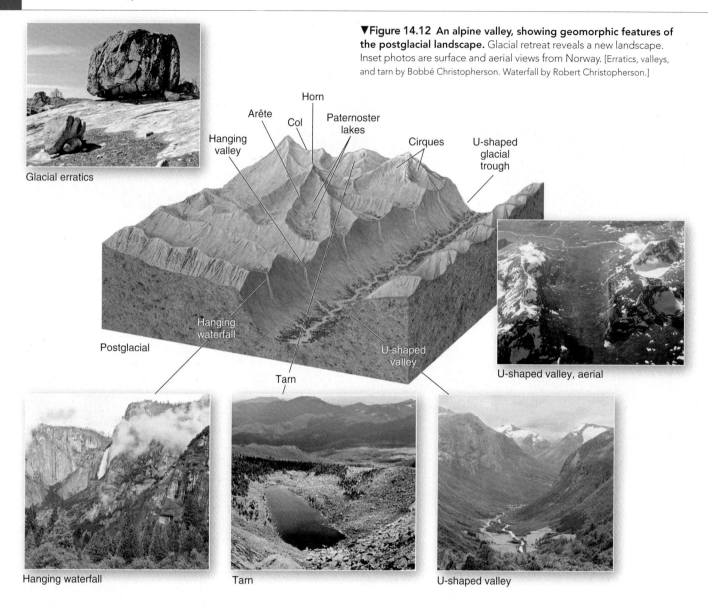

▼Figure 14.12 An alpine valley, showing geomorphic features of the postglacial landscape. Glacial retreat reveals a new landscape. Inset photos are surface and aerial views from Norway. [Erratics, valleys, and tarn by Bobbé Christopherson. Waterfall by Robert Christopherson.]

Glacial erratics

Horn
Arête
Col
Paternoster lakes
Hanging valley
Cirques
U-shaped glacial trough
Hanging waterfall
Postglacial
U-shaped valley
Tarn

U-shaped valley, aerial

Hanging waterfall

Tarn

U-shaped valley

▼Figure 14.13 Erosional features of alpine glaciation. How many erosional glacial features can you find in this photo of the Chugach Mountains in Alaska? See Critical Thinking 14.1. [Bruce Molnia, USGS.]

Fjords Where a glacial trough encounters the ocean, the glacier can continue to erode the landscape, even below sea level. As the glacier retreats, the trough floods and forms a deep **fjord** in which the sea extends inland, filling the lower reaches of the steep-sided valley (**Figure 14.14**). The fjord may be flooded further by rising sea level or by changes in the elevation of the coastal region. All along the glaciated coast of Alaska, retreating alpine glaciers are opening many new fjords that previously were

CRITICAL**thinking** 14.1

Looking for Glacial Features

Go back to the photos in the chapter opener and Figures 14.1 and 14.3, and then examine Figure 14.13 again. List all the glacial formations that you can identify in these photos. Are there any erosional landforms you find on all the photos other than the glaciers themselves?

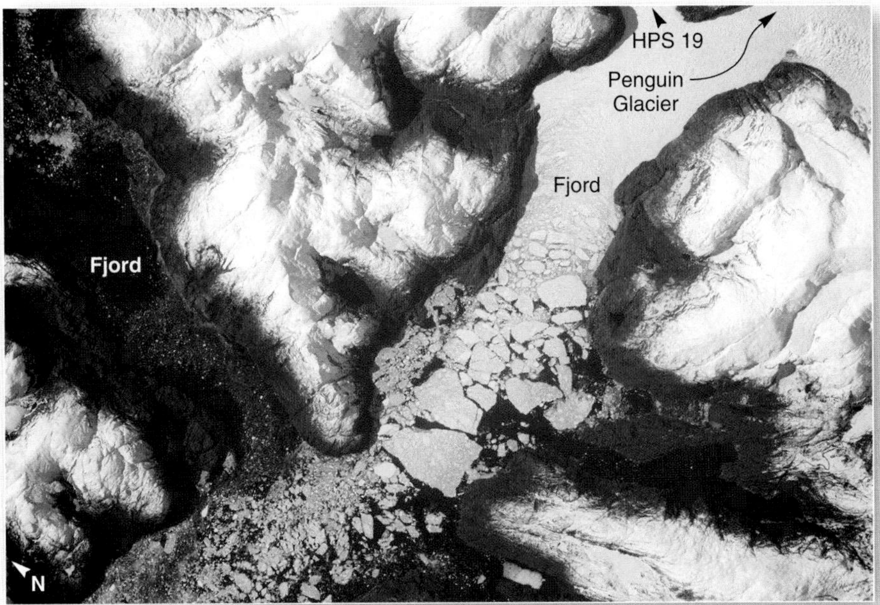

◀**Figure 14.14 Fjords on the Pacific Ocean side of the South Patagonian Ice Field, Chile.** As ice from the Penguin Glacier and HPS 19 flows into fjords, it calves and forms icebergs. (HPS stands for Hielo Patagónico Sur, or South Patagonian Ice Field, in the numbering system for glaciers with no geographic name.) The largest iceberg in the image is about 2 km (1.2 mi) wide. [NASA *ISS* Astronaut photo.]

blocked by ice. Coastlines with notable fjords include those of Norway (**Figure 14.15**), Chile, the South Island of New Zealand, Alaska, and British Columbia.

Fjords also occur along the edges of Earth's ice sheets. In Greenland, rising water temperatures in some of the longest fjord systems in the world appear to be accelerating melt rates where the glaciers meet the sea. In Antarctica, recent use of ice-penetrating radar identified numerous fjords beneath the Antarctic ice sheet, indicating that the present ice sheet was smaller in areal extent in the past.

Depositional Landforms

Glaciers transport materials upon and within the ice, producing unsorted sediment deposits, as well as by the actions of meltwater streams at the glacier's downstream end, producing sorted deposits. The general term for all glacial deposits, both unsorted and sorted, is **glacial drift**.

▼**Figure 14.15 Norwegian fjord.** Sediment carried in runoff is visible in this fjord, which fills a U-shaped, glacially carved valley. [Bobbé Christopherson.]

Moraines As mentioned earlier, as a glacier flows to a lower elevation, a wide assortment of rock fragments become *entrained* (carried along) on its surface or embedded within its mass or in its base. As the glacier melts, this unsorted and unstratified debris is deposited on the ground as **till**, usually marking the glacier's former margins.

The deposition of glacial sediment also produces a class of landform called a **moraine**, which may take several forms. In areas that have undergone alpine glaciations, **lateral moraines** are lengthy ridges of till along each side of a glacier. If two glaciers with lateral moraines join, a **medial moraine** may form (see Figure 14.1 and GIA 14.1). In areas that were formerly covered by single, large ice sheets, lateral moraines and medial moraines are lacking.

End moraines accumulate at the glacier's *terminus*, or endpoint, and are associated with both alpine and continental-scale glaciation. Eroded debris that is dropped at the glacier's farthest extent is a **terminal moraine** (**Figure 14.16**). *Recessional moraines* may also be present, having formed at other points where a glacier paused after reaching a new equilibrium between accumulation and ablation.

Till Plains When the ice sheets retreated from their maximum extent, about 18,000 years ago, during the most recent glaciation in North America and Europe (portrayed in Figure 14.25), they left distinct landscapes that we see today. A **till plain**, also called a *ground moraine*, is a deposition of till that forms behind a terminal moraine as the glacier retreats. The till in such cases (as in parts of the U.S. Midwest) is generally spread widely across the ground surface, usually hiding the former landscape and creating irregular topography, but not the characteristic ridges of other moraines. **Figure 14.17** illustrates common depositional features associated with the retreat of a continental ice sheet.

Till plains are composed of coarse till, with low and rolling relief, and a deranged drainage pattern that

▲**Figure 14.16 Terminal moraine.** A terminal moraine of unsorted till forms Isispynten Island, part of the Svalbard archipelago in the Arctic Ocean; the moraine is separated from the present ice cap by more than a kilometer. [Bobbé Christopherson.]

includes scattered wetlands (Figure 14.17b; see also Figure 12.5g). Common features of till plains are **drumlins**, hills of deposited till that are streamlined in the direction of ice sheet movement, with blunt end upstream and tapered end downstream. The shape of a drumlin sometimes resembles an elongated teaspoon bowl, lying face down. Multiple drumlins, known as *drumlin swarms*, occur across the landscape in portions of New York and Wisconsin, among other areas (**Figure 14.18**).

Drumlins may attain lengths of 100–5000 m (330 ft–3.1 mi) and heights up to 200 m (650 ft). Although similar in shape to an erosional roche moutonnée, a drumlin is a depositional feature with tapered end downstream. Figure 14.18a shows a portion of a topographic map for the area south of Williamson, New York. Can you identify the numerous

▼**Figure 14.17 Landforms associated with ice sheets.** [(b) Bobbé Christopherson.]

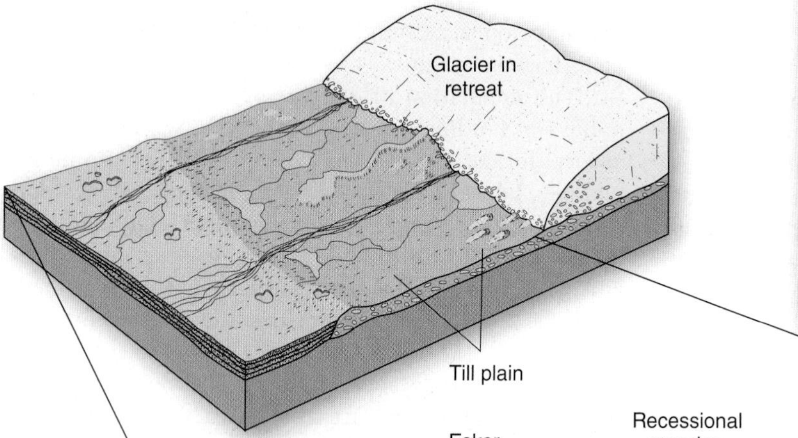

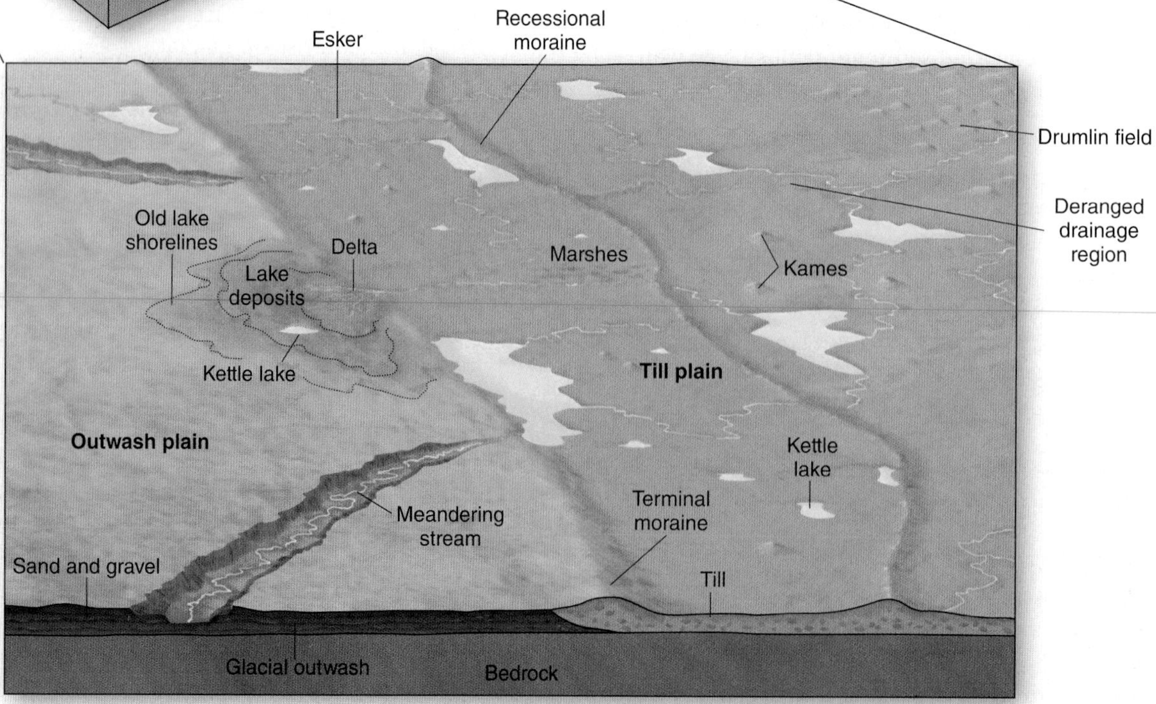

(b) Deranged drainage, central Saskatchewan, Canada.

(a) Common depositional landforms produced by continental glaciation.

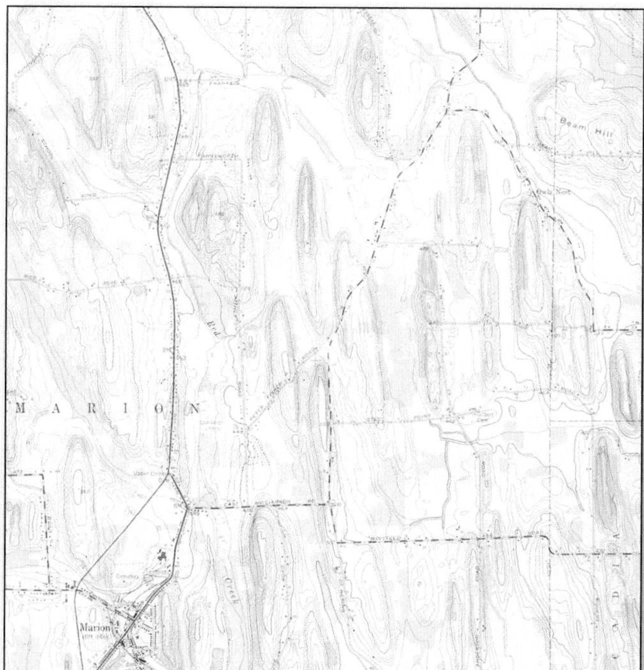

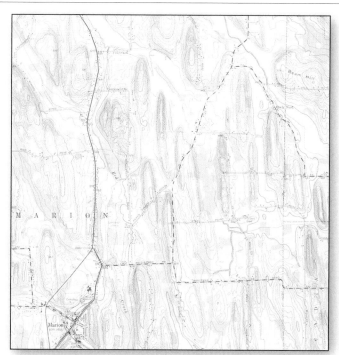

(a) Topographic map south of Williamson, near Marion, New York, featuring numerous drumlins (7.5-minute series quadrangle map, originally produced at a 1:24,000 scale; 10-ft contour interval).

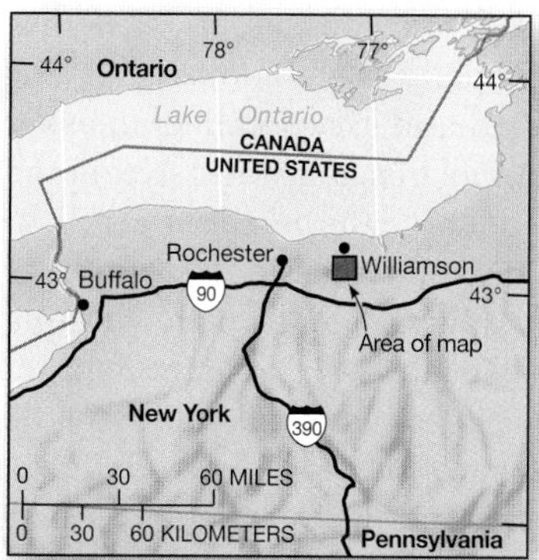

(b) Aerial view of drumlin swarm; drumlins with vegetation cover are most visible.

▲**Figure 14.18 Drumlins.** [(a) USGS map. (b) Bobbé Christopherson.]

drumlins on the map? In what direction do you think the ice sheets moved across this region?

Glacial Outwash Beyond the glacial terminus, meltwater flows downstream and is typically milky in color owing to the sediment load of fine-grained materials, known as "rock flour." This meltwater flow occurs when a glacier is retreating or during any period of ablation; flow volumes are highest during the warm summer months.

Sediments deposited by glacial meltwater are sorted by size, becoming **stratified drift**. The sorting comes from the combined effect of *glaciofluvial* (glacial and fluvial) processes—flowing water sorts sediments according to size, often with the largest particles dropped out of the sediment load closest to the glacial terminus (forming an alluvial fan) and the smaller particles carried farthest downstream. These glaciofluvial sediments are also stratified, with sediments laid down in layers.

The area of sediment deposition beyond the glacial terminus can form an extensive **outwash plain**, or *sandur* (a term that originated in Iceland). Outwash plains feature braided stream channels, which typically form when streams carry a large sediment load. When material is moved and deposited by glacial streams in a valley, such as at the terminus of valley glaciers, the outwash forms a *valley train deposit.* Peyto Glacier in Alberta, Canada, produced such a deposit, made up primarily of sand and gravel. This glacier experienced massive ice losses since 1966 and is now actively retreating from Peyto Lake due to increased ablation and decreased accumulation related to climate change (the glacier is at the far left in **Figure 14.19**).

▼**Figure 14.19 A valley train deposit.** Note the distributary channels of the braided stream and milky-colored glacial meltwater below Peyto Glacier in Alberta, Canada. [Robert Christopherson.]

A typical landform that is composed of glacial outwash, but located on a till plain is a sinuously curving, narrow ridge of coarse sand and gravel called an **esker**. Eskers form along the channel of a meltwater stream that flows beneath a glacier, in an ice tunnel, or between ice walls. As a glacier retreats, the steep-sided esker is left behind in a pattern roughly parallel to the path of the glacier (Figure 14.17). The ridge may not be continuous and in places may even appear to be branched, following the path set by the subglacial watercourse. Commercially valuable deposits of sand and gravel are quarried from some eskers.

Another landform composed of glaciofluvial deposits is a **kame**, a small hill, knob, or mound of sorted sand and gravel that is deposited by water on the surface of a glacier (for example, after having collected in a crevasse) and then is left on the land surface after the glacier retreats. Kames also can be found in deltaic forms—made of material originally deposited as deltas at the edges of glacial lakes—and in terraces along valley walls.

Sometimes an isolated block of ice, perhaps more than a kilometer across, remains on a ground moraine, on an outwash plain, or on a valley floor after a glacier has retreated. As much as 20 to 30 years is required for it to melt. In the interim, material continues to accumulate around the melting ice block. When the block finally melts, it leaves behind a steep-sided hole that then frequently fills with water, forming a **kettle**, also known as a *kettle lake*. Thoreau's famous Walden Pond in Massachusetts is such a glacial kettle.

Periglacial Landscapes

In 1909, Polish geologist Walery von Lozinski coined the term **periglacial** to describe processes of frost-action weathering and freeze–thaw rock shattering in the Carpathian Mountains. The term now is used to describe places where geomorphic processes related to freezing water occur. These periglacial regions occupy over 20% of Earth's land surfaces. At high latitudes, they have a near-permanent ice cover; at high elevation in lower latitudes, they are seasonally snow-free. Periglacial landscapes occur in the *subarctic* and *polar* climate zones, especially in *tundra* climate regions either at high latitude or at high elevation in lower-latitude mountains (review climate types in Chapter 7).

Permafrost and Its Distribution

When soil, sediment, or rock temperatures remain below 0°C (32°F) for at least 2 years, **permafrost** (perennially frozen ground) develops. An area of permafrost that is not covered by glaciers is considered periglacial; the largest extent of such lands is in Russia (**Figure 14.20**). Approximately 80% of Alaska has permafrost beneath its surface, as do parts of Canada, China, Scandinavia, Greenland, and Antarctica, in addition to alpine mountain regions of the world. Note that the criterion for a permafrost designation is based solely on *temperature* and has nothing to do with how much or how little water is present. Two factors other than temperature also contribute to permafrost conditions and occurrence: the presence of fossil permafrost from previous ice-age conditions and the insulating effect of snow cover or vegetation that inhibits heat loss.

Continuous and Discontinuous Zones Permafrost regions are divided into two general categories, continuous and discontinuous, which merge along a general transition zone. *Continuous permafrost* occurs in the region of severest cold and is perennial, roughly poleward of the −7°C (19°F) mean annual temperature isotherm (white area in

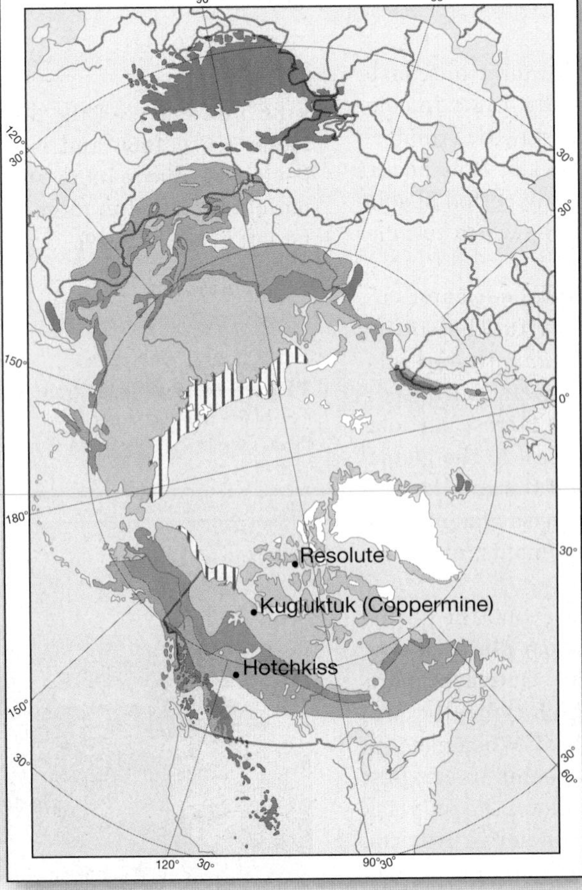

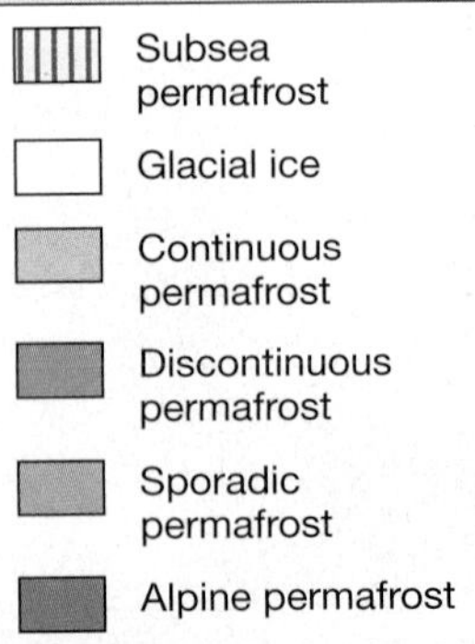

▶Figure 14.20 Permafrost distribution in the Northern Hemisphere. Alpine permafrost is noted except for small occurrences in Hawai'i, Mexico, Europe, and Japan. Subsea permafrost occurs in the ground beneath the Arctic Ocean along the margins of the continents, as shown. Note the towns of Resolute and Kugluktuk (Coppermine) in Nunavut (formerly part of Northwest Territories) and Hotchkiss in Alberta. A cross section of the permafrost beneath these towns is shown in Figure 14.21. [Adapted from USGS, 2007, *Circumpolar permafrost extent, based on J. Brown et al., 1997, Circum-Arctic Map of Permafrost and Ground Ice Conditions*, NSIDC (http://nsidc.org/data/ggd318).]

Figure 14.20). Continuous permafrost affects all surfaces except those beneath deep lakes or rivers. The depth of continuous permafrost averages approximately 400 m (1300 ft) and may exceed 1000 m (3300 ft).

Unconnected patches of *discontinuous permafrost* gradually coalesce poleward of the −1°C (30.2°F) mean annual temperature isotherm (light purple area in Figure 14.20), toward the continuous zone. In contrast, equatorward of this isotherm, permafrost becomes scattered or sporadic until it gradually disappears. In the discontinuous zone of the Northern Hemisphere, permafrost is absent on sun-exposed south-facing slopes, in areas of warm soil, and in areas insulated by snow. In the Southern Hemisphere, north-facing slopes experience increased warmth.

Discontinuous permafrost zones are the most susceptible to thawing with climate change. Their peat-rich soils (Gelisols and Histosols, discussed in Chapter 15) contain roughly twice the amount of carbon as is currently in the atmosphere, and as they thaw, the release of carbon dioxide creates a powerful positive feedback that accelerates warming (review Geosystems Now in Chapter 8 and Figure 8.1.2).

Scientists also suggest that thawing methane hydrates, also called gas hydrates, in permafrost on land and under the seafloor are releasing methane, another important greenhouse gas, as discussed in Chapter 8. Focus Study 14.1 examines thawing methane hydrates in the Arctic and the potential effects on global climate change.

Permafrost Behavior Figure 14.21 shows a cross section of a periglacial region in northern Canada, extending from approximately 75° N to 55° N latitude through the three sites located on the map in Figure 14.20. The zone of seasonally frozen ground that exists between the subsurface permafrost layer and the ground surface is called the **active layer** and is subjected to consistent daily and seasonal freeze–thaw cycles. This cyclic thawing of the active layer affects as little as 10 cm (4 in.) of depth in the north of the periglacial region (Ellesmere Island, 78° N), up to 3 m (9.8 ft) in the southern margins (55° N) of the periglacial region and 15 m (50 ft) in the alpine permafrost of the Colorado Rockies (40° N).

Permafrost actively adjusts to changing climatic conditions: Higher temperatures reduce permafrost thickness and increase the thickness of the active layer; lower

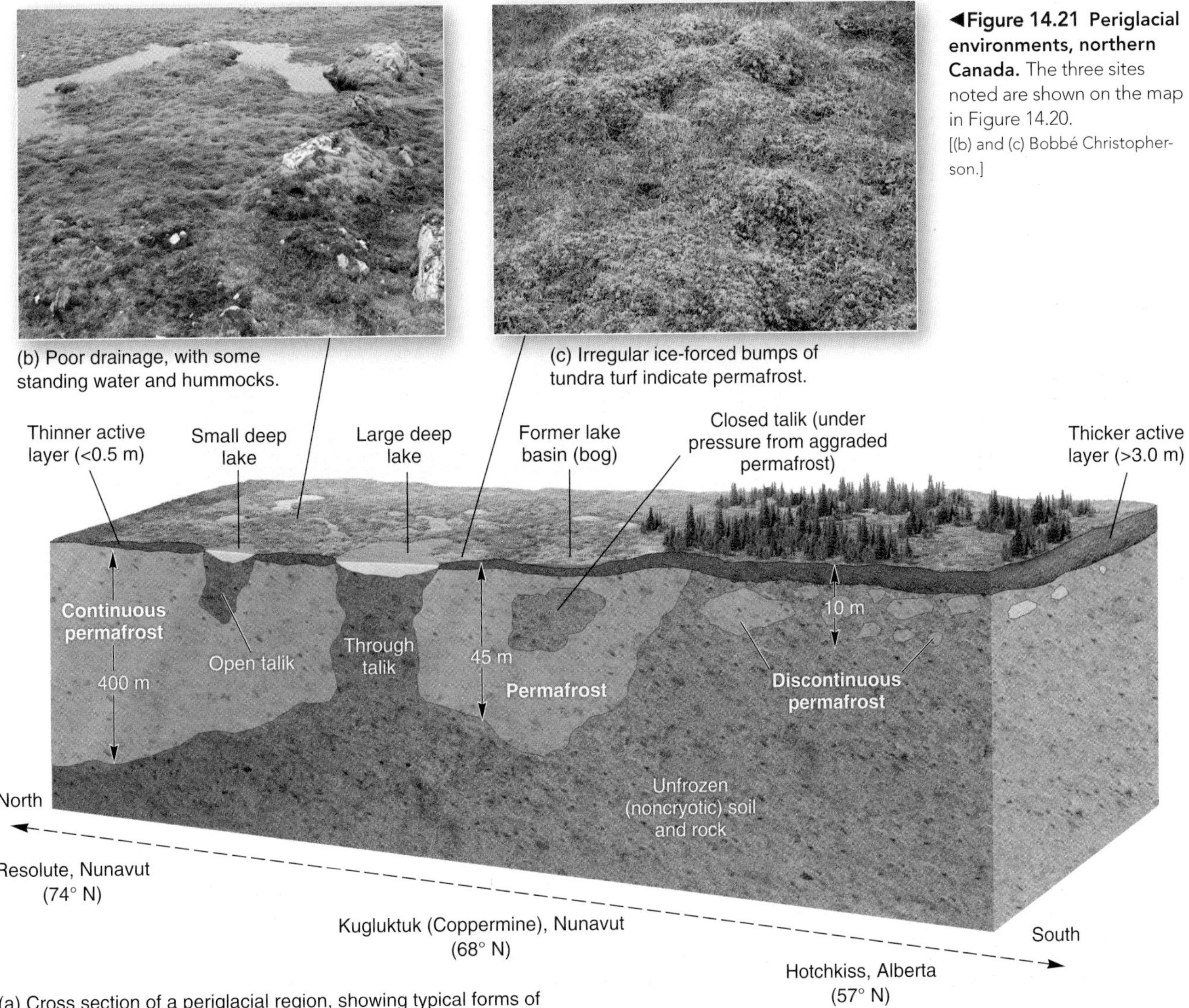

◀**Figure 14.21 Periglacial environments, northern Canada.** The three sites noted are shown on the map in Figure 14.20. [(b) and (c) Bobbé Christopherson.]

focusstudy 14.1 Climate Change

Threat of Thawing Methane Hydrates in Arctic Permafrost

In the Chapter 8 Geosystems Now, we discussed the release of greenhouse gases—CO_2 and methane—into the atmosphere as permafrost thaws in Arctic regions. This process is biogenic (performed by living organisms), a result of bacterial action breaking down organic matter in shallow soils and sediments. Meanwhile, methane also exists there in another form—that of gas hydrates, specifically *methane hydrates*, stored in natural deposits deep beneath areas of permafrost on land and in sediments on the ocean floor (**Figure 14.1.1**).

Methane hydrates consist of methane molecules encased in ice and are destabilized by warming. Melting causes them to release bursts of methane—Earth's most potent greenhouse gas—into the oceans and atmosphere. Multiplied over a large area, these bursts could increase atmospheric methane concentrations enough to accelerate global warming.

Methane Hydrate Essentials

Methane hydrate is a solid, icy compound in which each methane molecule is surrounded by a structure, or "cage," of interconnected water molecules. Methane hydrates exist only under conditions of cold temperature and high pressure, usually in subsurface deposits of sedimentary rock. The methane in the gas hydrate is formed by the deep burial and heating of organic matter, a thermogenic (heat-related) process similar to that which forms oil.

As temperatures rise in the ground and oceans, methane hydrate deposits are at risk of dissociation, or melting, which would release high concentrations of methane gas to the atmosphere. For example, melting 1 m^3 (35 ft^3) of methane hydrate releases about 160 m^3 (5650 ft^3) of methane gas. If all of the gas hydrates in the Arctic were to thaw, the result could be a pulse of methane so large that it would almost certainly trigger abrupt climate change. Scientists think that a massive release of carbon observed in climate records from ocean sediment cores about 55 million years ago may be related to a gas hydrate dissolution event (see the temperature spike called the PETM in Chapter 8, Figure 8.7).

Causes of Methane Hydrate Thaw

Under today's conditions of atmospheric warming, scientists propose two possible pathways for methane hydrate thaw (**Figure 14.1.2**). On land, at high latitudes in the Arctic, permafrost could thaw to depths of 180 m (600 ft), causing methane hydrates in rock to dissociate. In the Arctic Ocean, below subsea permafrost at shallow depths along continental shelves, rising ocean and land temperatures could also thaw permafrost to depths that would compromise hydrate structures. In the East Siberian Sea, off the shore of northern Russia, scientists suggest that an estimated 50 billion tons of methane stored in the form of hydrates are already beginning to dissociate, producing rising plumes of methane that reach the atmosphere. The process, they think, is triggered by changes in ocean temperatures, which recently warmed up to 7 C° (3.9 F°), according to satellite data. Summer sea ice declined so much above the Siberian shelf that additional warming is occurring as sunlight reaches more open water. The warming extends downward about 50 m (164 ft) to the shallow seafloor, melting the frozen sediments. In areas where

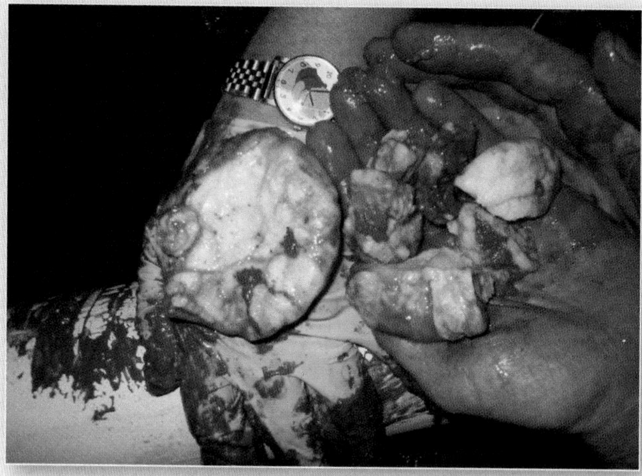

◀**Figure 14.1.1 Solid methane hydrate.** Scientists extracted this sample from the shallow sediments below the sea floor in the northern Gulf of Mexico. As methane hydrate warms, it releases enough methane to sustain a flame. [USGS.]

temperatures gradually increase permafrost thickness and reduce active-layer thickness. Although somewhat sluggish in response, the active layer is a dynamic, open system driven by energy gains and losses in the subsurface environment.

With the warming temperatures recorded in the Canadian and Siberian Arctic since 1990, more disruption of permafrost surfaces is occurring—leading to highway, railway, and building damage. In Siberia, many lakes have disappeared in the discontinuous permafrost region as thawing of permafrost opens the way for subsurface drainage; yet in the continuous region, new lakes have formed as a result of thawed soils becoming waterlogged. In Canada, hundreds of lakes have disappeared from excessive evaporation into the warming air. These trends are measurable from satellite imagery.

A *talik* is an area of unfrozen ground that may occur above, below, or within a body of discontinuous permafrost or beneath a water body in regions of continuous permafrost. Taliks occur beneath deep lakes and may extend to bedrock and noncryotic soil beneath large, deep lakes (see Figure 14.21). Taliks in areas of discontinuous

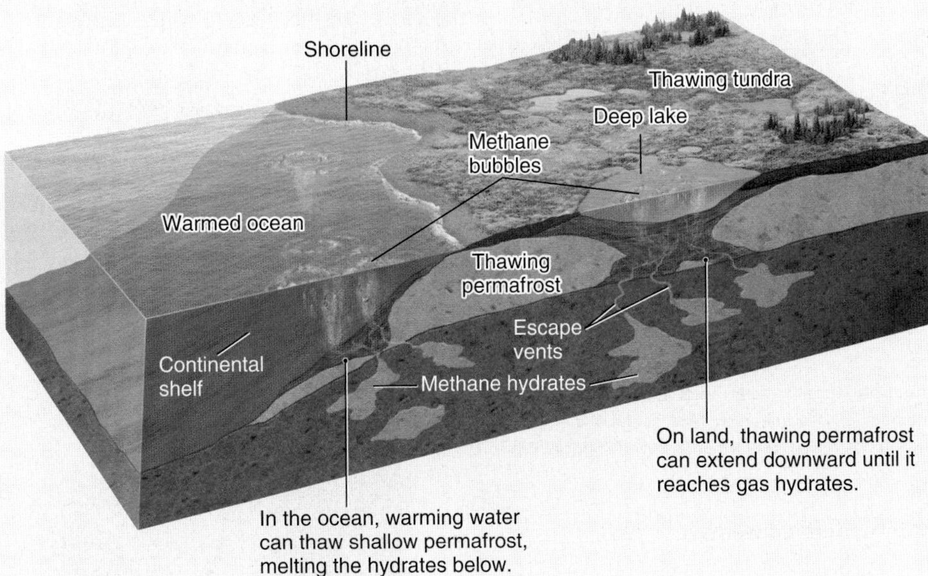

▲Figure 14.1.2 Theoretical pathways for the thaw of methane hydrate deposits in arctic permafrost and under continental shelves. [Adapted from K. Walter Anthony, "Methane: A menace surfaces," *Scientific American* 301 (2009): 68–75.]

the seabed is deeper along continental slopes, gas hydrates may dissociate if ocean warming continues, but scientists do not yet know whether the methane released would reach the atmosphere.

Implications for Climate Change

Several dangers exist with regard to the dissociation of methane hydrates and its effect on climate change. One is the possibility of a destabilizing event causing a sudden release of enough methane to accelerate global warming. For example, the dissociation of large gas hydrate deposits—the breakdown of the solids into liquids and gases—can destabilize seafloor sediments, causing a loss of structural support that can lead to subsidence and collapse in the form of submarine landslides. This type of major landslide could release large quantities of methane. A second danger is the potential for massive methane release as a by-product of energy extraction.

Methane hydrates are now thought to be the world's largest reserve of carbon-based fuel—scientists think that 10,000 gigatonnes (Gt) of methane are trapped in gas hydrates worldwide, an amount that exceeds the energy available in coal, oil, and other natural gas reserves combined. These deposits occur at depths greater than about 900 m (3000 ft) under seafloor sediments, making the extraction process difficult and expensive. Several countries are exploring the use of methane hydrates as an energy source. In 2013, Japan's deep-water ocean drilling rig, *Chikyu*, successfully extracted gas hydrates from a depth of 1000 m (3280 ft) in the Pacific Ocean. The country's goal is to achieve commercial production of methane hydrates within 6 years. However, the possibility of accidental uncontrolled methane releases during extraction is an important concern.

The processes and environmental effects of methane hydrate thaw are a focus of ongoing research. For more information, see the article "Good Gas, Bad Gas" at **http://ngm.nationalgeographic.com/2012/12/methane/lavelle-text** and the U.S. Geological Survey Gas Hydrates Project page at **http://woodshole.er.usgs.gov/project-pages/hydrates/**.

1. Explain the difference between methane stored in arctic soils and permafrost and methane stored as gas hydrates. (Hint: Review the Chapter 8 Geosystems Now.)
2. What type of climate feedback—positive or negative—is initiated as methane hydrate deposits thaw? Explain. (Review the discussion of climate feedbacks in Chapter 8 and Focus Study 8.1.)

permafrost form connections between the active layer and groundwater, whereas in continuous permafrost, groundwater is essentially cut off from surface water. In this way, permafrost disrupts aquifers and taliks, leading to water-supply problems.

Periglacial Processes

In regions of permafrost, frozen subsurface water forms **ground ice**. The amount of ground ice present varies with moisture content, ranging from only a small percentage in drier regions to almost 100% in regions with saturated soils. The presence of frozen water in the soil initiates geomorphic processes associated with *frost action.*

Frost Action Processes The 9% expansion of water as it freezes produces strong mechanical forces that fracture rock and disrupt soil at or below the surface. If sufficient water freezes, the saturated soil and rocks are subjected to *frost heaving* (vertical movement) and *frost thrusting* (horizontal movement). Boulders and rock slabs may be thrust to the surface. Soil horizons (layers) may be disrupted by frost action and appear to be stirred or churned. Frost action also can produce contractions

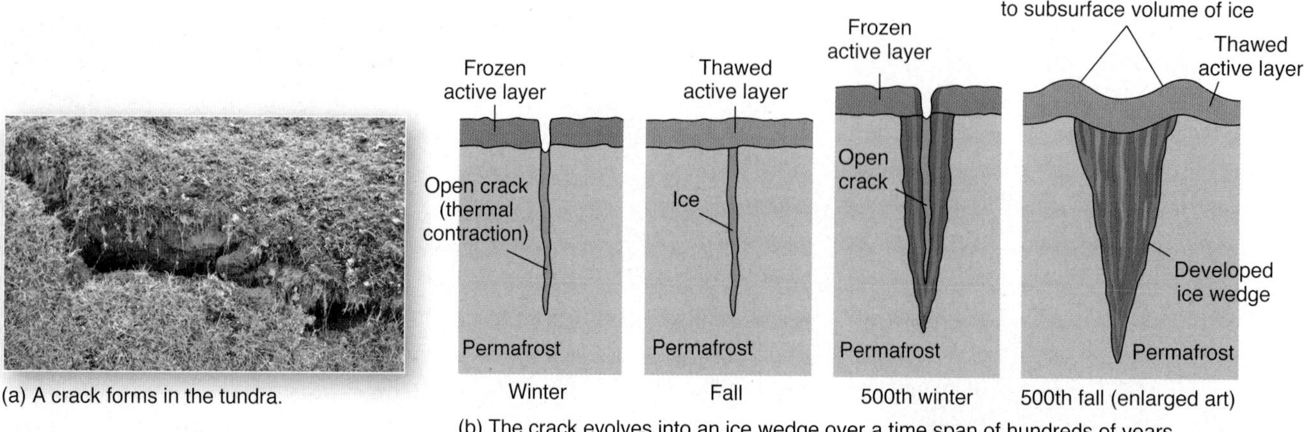

(a) A crack forms in the tundra.

(b) The crack evolves into an ice wedge over a time span of hundreds of years.

(c) An example of an ice wedge and ground ice in northern Canada.

▲**Figure 14.22 Evolution of an ice wedge.** Sequential illustration of ice-wedge formation. [(a) Bobbé Christopherson. (b) Illustration adapted from A. H. Lachenbruch, "Mechanics of thermal contraction and ice-wedge polygons in permafrost," *Geological Society of America Bulletin Special Paper 70* (1962). (c) Hugh MIceWedge French.]

in soil and rock, opening up cracks in which ice wedges can form.

An *ice wedge* develops when water enters a crack in the permafrost and freezes (**Figures 14.22a** and **b**). Thermal contraction in ice-rich soil forms a tapered crack—wider at the top, narrowing toward the bottom. Repeated seasonal freezing and thawing progressively enlarge the wedge, which may widen from a few millimeters to 5–6 m (16–20 ft) and deepen up to 30 m (100 ft). Widening may be small each year, but after many years, the wedge can become significant, as in **Figure 14.22c**.

In some periglacial regions, the expansion and contraction of frost action result in the movement of soil particles, stones, and small boulders into distinct shapes known as **patterned ground** (**Figure 14.23**). This freeze–thaw process brings about a self-organization in which stones move toward stone domains (stone-rich areas) and soil particles move toward soil domains (soil-rich areas). The stone-centered polygons in Figure 14.23b indicate higher stone concentrations, and the soil-centered polygons in Figure 14.23c indicate higher soil-particle concentrations with lesser availability of stones. Patterned ground may take centuries to form. Slope angle also affects the arrangement—greater slopes produce striped patterns, whereas lesser slopes result in sorted polygons.

Such polygon nets in patterned ground provide vivid evidence of frozen subsurface water on Mars (Figure 14.23d). In 2008, when the *Phoenix* lander set down in the middle of a Martian arctic plain covered with polygonal forms, the craft dug into the Martian surface and verified the presence of water in the form of ground ice.

Hillslope Processes: Gelifluction and Solifluction

Soil drainage is poor in areas of permafrost and ground ice. The active layer of soil and regolith is saturated with soil moisture during the thaw cycle (summer), and the whole layer commences to flow from higher to lower elevation if the landscape is even slightly inclined. This flow of soil is generally called *solifluction*. In the presence of ground ice or permafrost, the more specific term *gelifluction* is applied. In this ice-bound type of soil

GEOreport 14.2 Feedback loops from fossil-fuel exploration to permafrost thawing

The lengthening periods of thaw in the active layer of the Alaskan tundra have shortened the annual number of days that oil exploration equipment can operate. Previously, the frozen ground lasted more than 200 days, permitting the heavy rigs and trucks to operate on the solid surface. With the increased thawing and unstable soft surfaces, exploration is now restricted to only 100 days a year. Consider this trend from a systems approach: The exploration is for fossil fuels, which, when burned, increase the carbon dioxide levels in the atmosphere, which enhance greenhouse warming, which increases temperatures and permafrost thawing, which decrease the number of days to explore for fossil fuels—a negative feedback into the system.

(a) Patterned ground in Beacon Valley of the McMurdo Dry Valleys of East Antarctica.

(b) Polygons and circles (about a meter across) in a stone-dominant area, Nordaustlandet Island, Arctic Ocean.

(c) Polygons and circles in a soil-dominant area, Spitsbergen Island, northern Norway.

(d) On Mars, polygons 100 m (300 ft) across in the northern plains.

▲**Figure 14.23 Patterned-ground phenomena.** [(a) Courtesy of Joan Myers. (b) and (c) Bobbé Christopherson. (d) Malin Space Science Systems.]

flow, movement up to 5 cm (2 in.) per year can occur on slopes as gentle as a degree or two.

The cumulative effect of this flow can be an overall flattening of a rolling landscape, combined with visibly sagging surfaces and scalloped and lobed patterns in the downslope soil movements. Other types of periglacial mass movement include failure in the active layer, producing translational and rotational slides and rapid flows associated with melting ground ice. Periglacial mass-movement processes are related to slope dynamics and processes discussed in Chapter 11.

Humans and Periglacial Landscapes

In areas of permafrost, people face certain problems related to periglacial landforms and phenomena. Because thawed ground above the permafrost zone frequently shifts, highways and rail lines may warp or twist, and utility lines are disrupted. In addition, any building placed directly on frozen ground will "melt" (subside) into the defrosting soil (**Figure 14.24**).

In periglacial regions, structures must be suspended slightly above the ground to allow air circulation beneath. The airflow permits the ground to cycle through its normal annual temperature pattern. Utilities such as water and sewer lines must be enclosed aboveground to protect them from freezing and thawing ground. The trans-Alaska oil pipeline was constructed aboveground on racks for 675 km of its 1285-km length (420 mi of its 800-mi length) to avoid thawing the frozen ground and causing shifting that could rupture the line (look ahead to Figure HD 14a). Where it runs underground, the pipeline uses a cooling system to keep the permafrost around the pipeline stable.

◀**Figure 14.24 Permafrost thawing and structure collapse.** (a) An improperly constructed building conducts heat to the ground and causes permafrost thaw. (b) A cabin sinks and eventually collapses as permaforst thaws south of Fairbanks, Alaska. [Adapted from USGS: photo by Steve McCutcheon/Anchorage Museum; based on U.S. Geological Survey pamphlet "Permafrost" by L. L. Ray.]

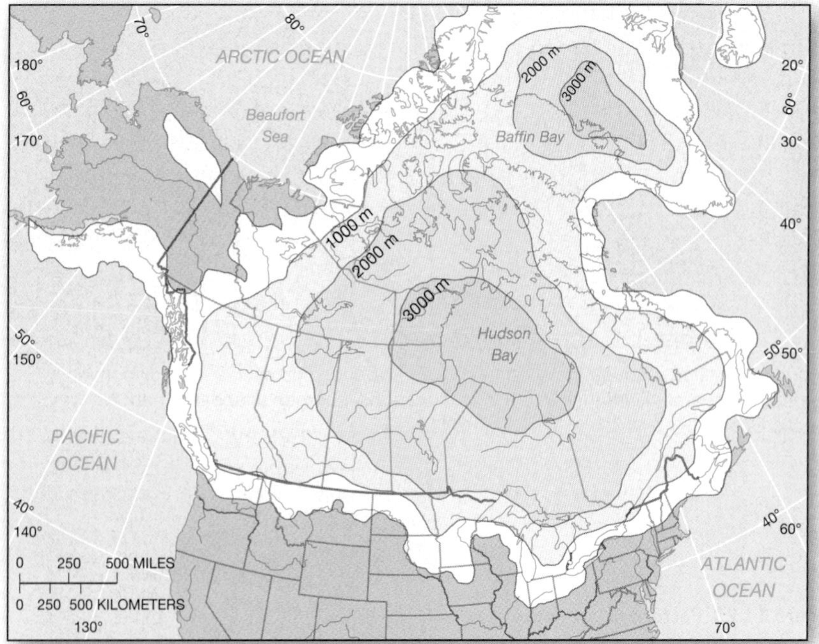

(a) Ice-sheet extent 18,000 years ago over North America, with ice-sheet thickness (in meters).

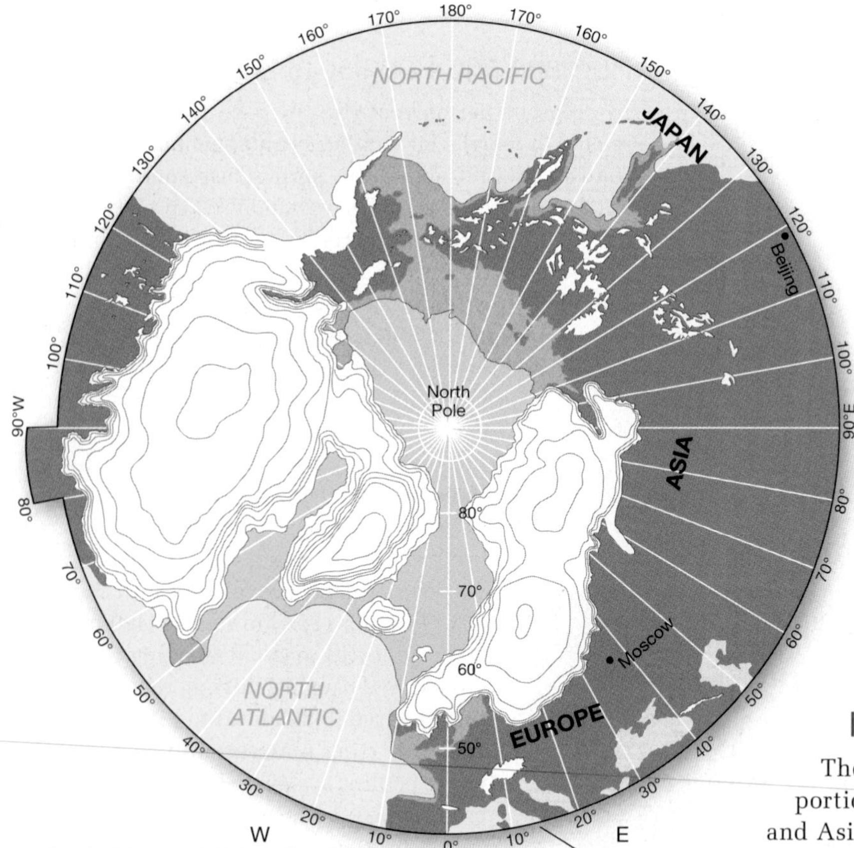

(b) Polar perspective, 18,000 years ago.

◄**Figure 14.25 Extent of Pleistocene glaciation.** Earlier episodes produced ice sheets of slightly greater extent. [From A. McIntyre, *CLIMAP* (Climate: Long-Range Investigation, Mapping, and Prediction) Project, Lamont–Doherty Earth Observatory. © 1981 by the GSA. Adapted by permission.]

The Pleistocene Epoch

Imagine almost a third of Earth's land surface buried beneath ice sheets and glaciers—most of Canada, the northern Midwest, England, and northern Europe, with many mountain ranges beneath thousands of meters of ice. This occurred at the height of the Pleistocene Epoch of the late Cenozoic Era (see Chapter 9, Figure 9.1). During this last ice age, periglacial regions along the margins of the ice covered about twice the areal extent of periglacial regions today.

The Pleistocene Epoch, thought to have begun about 2.5 million years ago, was one of the more prolonged cold periods in Earth's history. As discussed in Chapter 8, the term **ice age**, or *glacial age*, is applied to any extended period of cold (not a single brief cold spell), in some cases lasting several million years. An ice age includes one or more *glacials*, characterized by glacial advance, interrupted by brief warm spells known as *interglacials*. The Pleistocene featured not just one glacial advance and retreat, but at least 18 expansions of ice over Europe and North America. Glaciation can take about 100,000 years, whereas deglaciation is rapid, requiring less than about 10,000 years for the ice accumulation to melt away.

Ice-Age Landscapes

The continental ice sheets that covered portions of Canada, the United States, Europe, and Asia about 18,000 years ago are illustrated on the maps in **Figure 14.25.** Ice sheets ranged in thickness to more than 2 km (1.2 mi). In North America, the Ohio and Missouri River systems mark the southern terminus of continuous ice at its greatest extent during the Pleistocene Epoch. The ice sheet disappeared by 7000 years ago.

As the glaciers of the last ice age retreated, they exposed a drastically altered landscape: the rocky soils of New England, the polished and scarred surfaces of Canada's Atlantic Provinces, the sharp crests of the Sawtooth Range and Tetons of Idaho and Wyoming, the scenery of the Canadian Rockies and the Sierra Nevada, the Great Lakes of the United States and Canada, the Matterhorn of Switzerland, and much more. In the Southern Hemisphere, evidence of this ice age exists in the form of fjords and sculpted mountains in New Zealand and Chile.

Sea levels 18,000 years ago were approximately 100 m (330 ft) lower than they are today because so much of Earth's water was frozen in glaciers. Imagine the coastline of New York being 100 km farther east, Alaska and Russia connected by land across the Bering Strait, and England and France joined by a land bridge.

Paleolakes

From 12,000 to 30,000 years ago, the American West was dotted with large, ancient lakes—**paleolakes**, or *pluvial lakes* (**Figure 14.26**). The term *pluvial* (from the Latin word for "rain") describes any extended period of wet conditions, such as occurred during the Pleistocene Epoch. During pluvial periods in arid regions, lake levels increase in closed basins with internal drainage. The drier periods between pluvials, called *interpluvials*, are often marked by **lacustrine deposits**, the name for lake sediments that form terraces, or benches, along former shorelines. Except for the Great Salt Lake in Utah (a remnant of the former Lake Bonneville; Figure 14.26a) and a few smaller lakes, only dry basins, ancient shorelines, and lake sediments remain today.

Scientists have attempted to correlate pluvial and glacial events, given their coincidence during the Pleistocene. However, few sites demonstrate a direct relationship. Recent evidence suggests that the occurrence of these lakes in North America was related to specific changes in the polar jet stream that steered storm tracks across the region, creating pluvial conditions. The continental ice

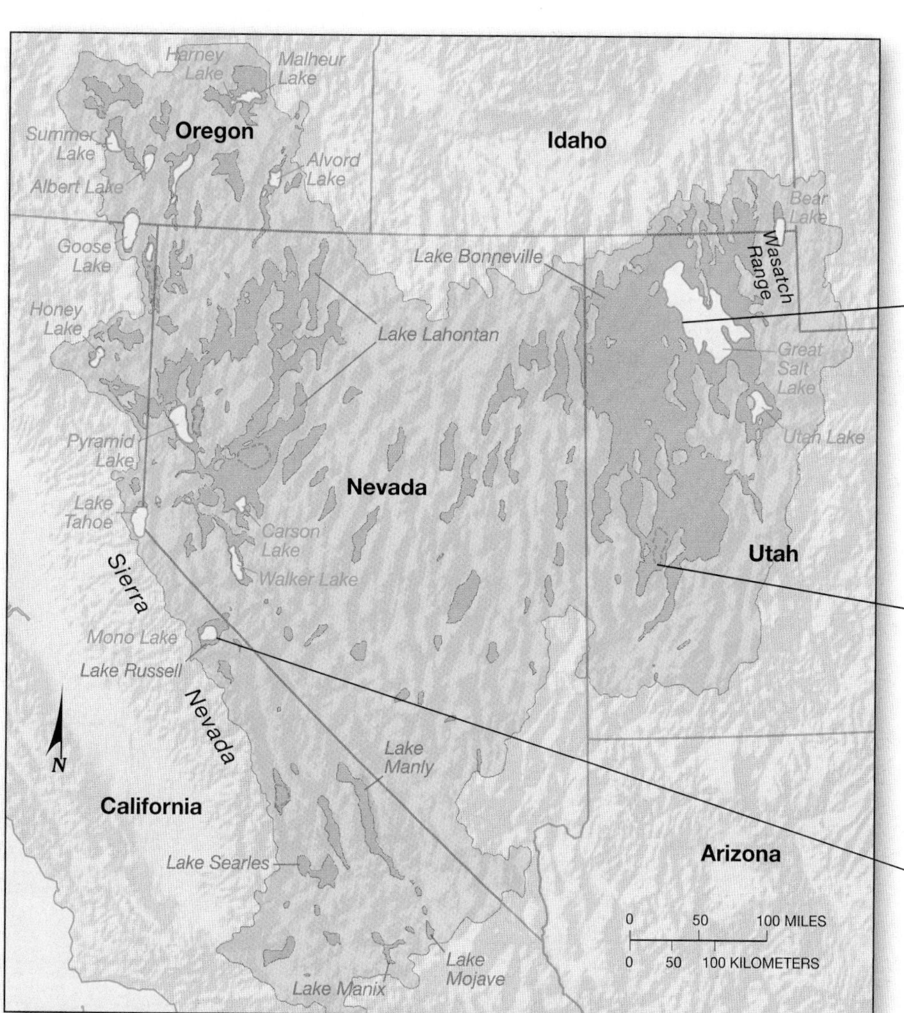

(a) Paleolakes at their greatest extent 12,000 to 30,000 years ago, a recent pluvial period. Lake Lahontan and Lake Bonneville were the largest. Pluvial lakes are purple, present-day lakes are blue, and the region of interior drainage is green.

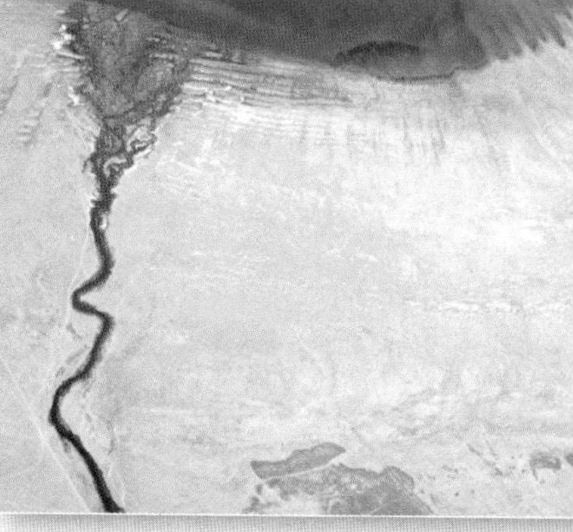

(b) Great Salt Lake shoreline and salt flats.

(c) Sevier Dry Lake, another remnant of Lake Bonneville.

(d) Mono Lake in California, a remnant of pluvial Lake Russell.

▲**Figure 14.26 Paleolakes in the western United States.** [(a) After USGS. (b)–(d) Bobbé Christopherson.]

sheet evidently influenced changes in the position of the jet stream.

Paleolakes existed in North and South America, Africa, Asia, and Australia. Today, the Caspian Sea in Kazakhstan and southern Russia has a level 30 m (100 ft) below global mean sea level, but ancient shorelines are visible about 80 m (265 ft) above the present lake level. In North America, the two largest late Pleistocene paleolakes were Lake Bonneville and Lake Lahontan, located in the Basin and Range Province in the western United States. These two lakes were much larger than their present-day remnants.

The Great Salt Lake, near Salt Lake City, Utah, and the Bonneville Salt Flats in western Utah are remnants of Lake Bonneville; today, the Great Salt Lake is the fourth largest saline lake in the world. At its greatest extent, this paleolake covered more than 50,000 km^2 (19,500 mi^2) and reached depths of 300 m (1000 ft), spilling over into the Snake River drainage to the north. Now, it is a closed-basin terminal lake with no drainage except an artificial outlet to the west, where excess water from the Great Salt Lake can be pumped during rare floods. Lake levels continue to decline in response to climate change to drier conditions.

(a) Note the 10°C (50°F) isotherm in midsummer, which designates the Arctic region, dominated by pack ice.

(b) Arctic sea ice about 965 km (600 mi) from the North Pole.

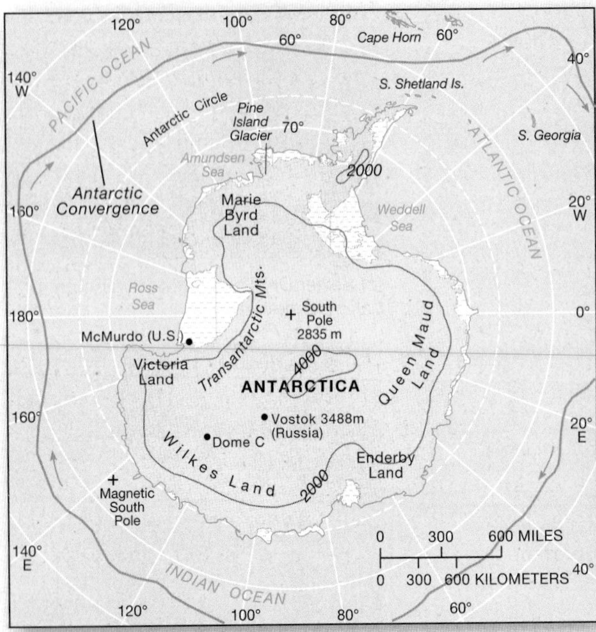

(c) The Antarctic convergence designates the Antarctic region.

(d) Iceberg and ship for scale (at lower left), Antarctic Sound near the tip of the Antarctic Peninsula and the South Shetland Islands.

▲**Figure 14.27 The Arctic and Antarctic regions.** [(b) and (d) Bobbé Christopherson.]

Arctic and Antarctic Regions

Climatologists use environmental criteria to designate the Arctic and the Antarctic regions. The 10°C (50°F) isotherm for July defines the Arctic region (green line on the map in **Figure 14.27a**). This line coincides on land with the visible tree line—the boundary between the northern forests and tundra. On the sea, the Arctic region is characterized by the presence of *pack ice* (masses of drifting ice, unattached to shore), which occurs as two general types: *floating sea ice* (frozen seawater; **Figure 14.27b**) and *glacier ice* (frozen freshwater). This pack ice thins in the summer months and sometimes breaks up.

The Antarctic region is defined by the Antarctic convergence, a narrow zone that marks the boundary between colder Antarctic water and warmer water at lower latitudes. This boundary extends around the continent, roughly following the 10°C (50°F) isotherm for February, in the Southern Hemisphere summer, and is located near 60° S latitude (green line in **Figure 14.27c**). The part of the Antarctic region covered just with sea ice represents an area greater than North America, Greenland, and Western Europe combined.

The Antarctic landmass is surrounded by ocean and is much colder overall than the Arctic, which is an ocean surrounded by land. In simplest terms, Antarctica can be thought of as a continent covered by a single enormous glacier, although it contains distinct regions such as the East Antarctic and West Antarctic Ice Sheets, which respond differently to slight climatic variations. These ice sheets are in constant motion.

The fact that Antarctica is so remote from civilization makes it an excellent laboratory for sampling past and present evidence of human and natural variables that are transported by atmospheric and oceanic circulation to this pristine environment. High elevation, winter cold and darkness, and distance from pollution sources make this polar region an ideal location for certain astronomical and atmospheric observations.

CRITICAL**thinking 14.2**

A Sample of Life at the Polar Station

Read some of the posts at **http://www.snowbetweenmytoes.blogspot.com/** regarding life at the Amundsen–Scott South Pole Station, Antarctica. Then explore "Life on the Ice" reports at the U. S. Antarctic Program website (**http://antarcticsun.usap.gov/**). Of the approximately 50 people who winter over at the station (from the last airplane's departure in mid-February to the next scheduled flight arrival in mid-October), many serve as scientists, technicians, and support staff. What are some of the unique aspects of life at the South Pole? What do you see as the positives and negatives of living and working there? How would you combat the elements, the isolation, and the dark conditions?

Recent Polar Region Changes

As mentioned earlier, the smallest extent of Arctic sea ice on record occurred in the year 2012. About half of Arctic sea-ice volume has disappeared since 1970 due to warming throughout the region. As discussed in Chapter 3 Geosystems Now, the fabled Northwest Passage across the Arctic from the Atlantic to the Pacific is now ice-free for a portion of the summer as the Arctic ice continues to melt. The Northeast Passage, north of Russia, has been ice-free for the past several years. These changes affect surface albedo, with impacts on global climate (review the Chapter 3 Geosystems Now).

Ice-Sheet Darkening Satellite measurements show that on the Greenland Ice Sheet, the reflectivity of the snow and ice decreased over the past decade as the surface darkened. Along the outer edges, ice melt exposed darker land, vegetation, and water surfaces. On the interior, black carbon from wildfires in Asia and North America accumulated on the ice and may be contributing to the overall darkening (**Figure 14.28a**). Another factor may be related to basic processes of snow metamorphism: As temperatures rise, snow crystals clump together in the snow pack, reflecting less light than the smaller, faceted individual crystals. The overall effect is that the ice sheet now absorbs more sunlight, which speeds up melting and causes a positive feedback that accelerates warming.

Meltponds and Supraglacial Lakes Another indicator of changing surface conditions is an increase in meltponds across the polar regions. Meltponds are pools of water that form on sea ice, glaciers, and ice shelves as ice melts. In the polar regions, these meltponds are part of the albedo positive feedback loop—meltponds provide a darker surface than snow and ice, which causes them to absorb more insolation and become warmer, which, in turn, melts more ice, making more meltponds, and so forth. Both satellites and aircraft have identified an increase in meltpond occurrence on glaciers, icebergs, ice shelves, and the Greenland Ice Sheet. In July 2012, a record 97% of the Greenland Ice Sheet was covered with meltwater (see **Figure 14.28b**).

In western Greenland, increasing numbers of meltponds and areas of water-saturated ice enlarged the extensive melt zone at the edge of the ice sheet. The meltponds look like small blue dots across the ice (**Figures 14.29a** and **b**). Melt streams also are common during periods of warmer temperatures in glaciated environments, especially in summer (**Figure 14.29c**). The streams can melt through the ice sheet, forming *moulins*, or drainage channels, that work their way to the base of the glacier (**Figure 14.29d**).

Multiple streams can flow together in summer to form a *supraglacial lake* on top of the ice. When the water pressure builds to a high enough level, the ice below the lake fractures and drains the lake through a near-vertical

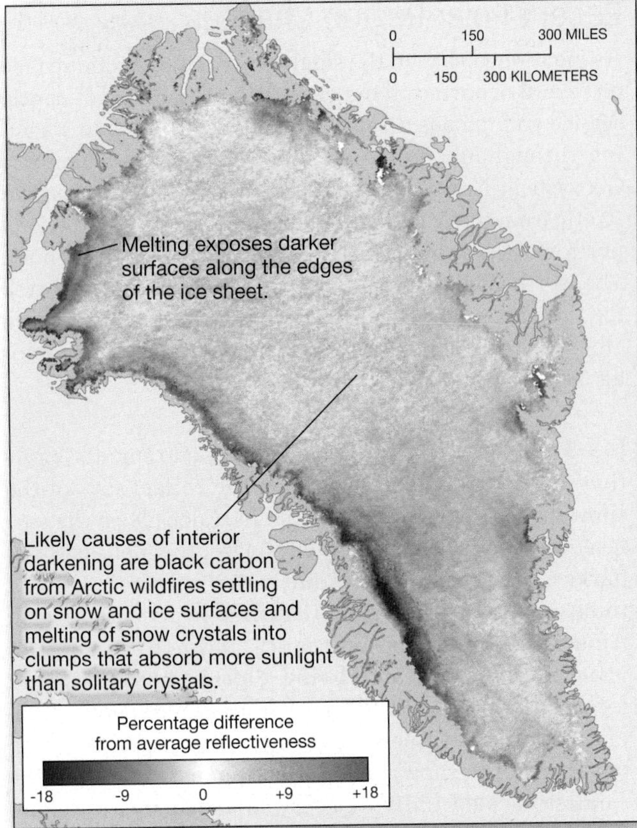

(a) Data from this 2011 image indicate that some areas of the ice sheet reflect 20% less sunlight than just a decade ago.

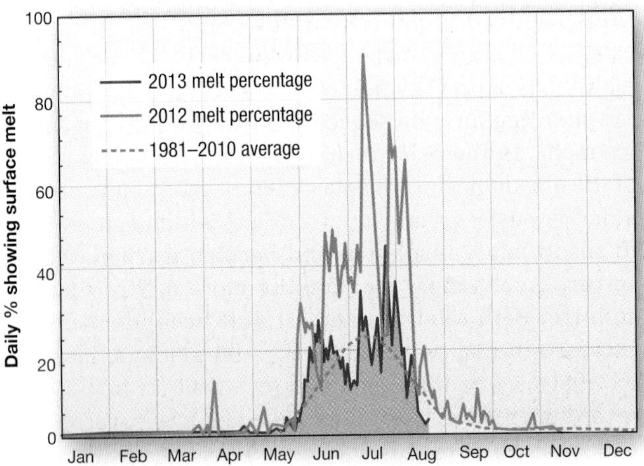

(b) Surface melt on the Greenland Ice Sheet in 2012 reached its greatest extent in the satellite record since 1979. Melt during 2013 was closer to average (dotted line).

◀ **Figure 14.28 Darkening of Greenland ice surfaces and recent ice-sheet melting.** [(a) *Terra/Aqua* MODIS, NASA. (b) Data courtesy NSIDC/Thomas Mote, University of Georgia.]

moulin to the glacier's bed. This drainage may result in a large volume of water arriving suddenly at the base of the glacier. Scientists have witnessed such events and are studying the effects on glacial movement.

Ice Shelves Another recent change in the polar regions is the breakup of ice shelves, as discussed in Geosystems Now. Ice shelves surround the margins of Antarctica and constitute about 11% of its surface area (see Figure 14.8 for some of the major ice shelves). Although ice shelves constantly break up to produce icebergs, more large sections have broken free in the past two decades than expected. For example, in March 2000, an iceberg tagged B-15, measuring twice the area of Delaware (300 km by 40 km, or 190 mi by 25 mi), broke off the Ross Ice Shelf (some 3027 km, or 1900 mi, west of the Antarctic Peninsula). In 2013, the Wilkins Ice Shelf underwent further disintegration after major breakup events in 2008 and 2009. Scientists think that the recent breakups made the remaining ice more vulnerable, especially in places where the shelf remnants are in direct contact with open water and the force of ocean waves.

Since 1993, seven ice shelves have disintegrated in Antarctica. More than 8000 km^2 (3090 mi^2) of ice shelf are gone, requiring significant revision of maps, freeing up islands to circumnavigation, and creating thousands of icebergs. The Larsen Ice Shelf, along the east coast of the Antarctic Peninsula, was retreating slowly for years. Larsen A suddenly disintegrated in 1995. Then, in only 35 days in early 2002, Larsen B collapsed into icebergs (**Figure 14.30**). Larsen B was at least 11,000 years old.

Larsen C, the next segment to the south, is losing mass from both the ocean and the atmosphere faces. Since the water temperature is warmer by 0.65 C° (1.17 F°) than the melting point for ice at a depth of 300 m (984 ft), this ice loss is likely a result of warmer water as well as of the air temperature increase in the peninsula region during the last 50 years. In response to the increasing warmth, the Antarctic Peninsula is also experiencing previously unseen vegetation growth, reduced sea ice, and disruption of penguin feeding, nesting, and fledging activities. (Among many changes, ticks are a new problem for these animals.)

GEOreport 14.3 Glacial ice might protect underlying mountains

Researchers are studying how glacial ice affected the underlying topography during the last glacial maximum. The temperature at the base of the ice was a determining factor. In the southernmost Patagonian Andes, conditions were so cold that the glacial ice froze to the bedrock. Evidence suggests that this protected the bedrock from erosion and typical glacial excavation, resulting in higher mountain peaks and a wider mountain belt in the southern Andes than in the northern part of the range, where mountain surfaces were ground down and narrowed by glacial action.

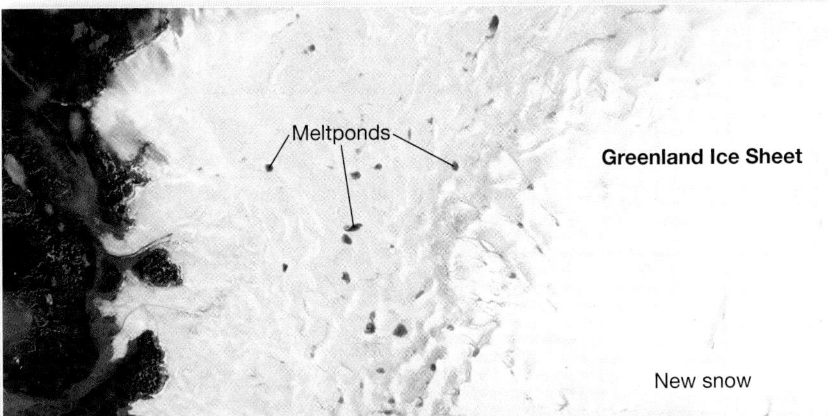

(a) Meltponds are increasing in number on the Greenland Ice Sheet (shown), as on icebergs and ice shelves throughout the Arctic.

(b) Close-up of meltpond.

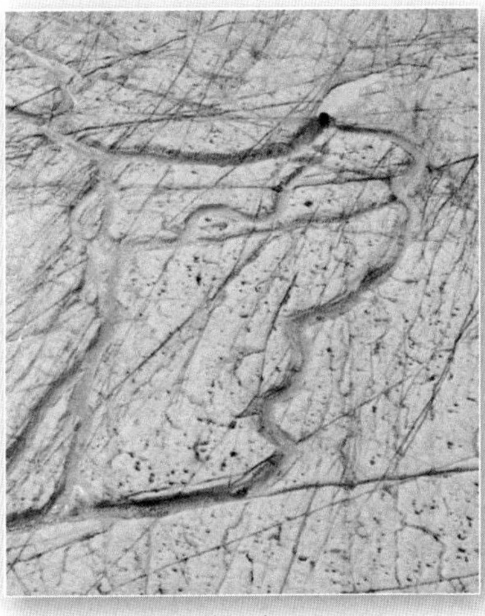

(c) Meltponds and melt streams, southwest Greenland, 2008.

(d) Meltwater flows into a moulin.

◀**Figure 14.29 Meltponds, melt streams, and moulins on the increase in Greenland.** Why are meltponds positive feedback climate indicators? [(a) *Landsat 8* image, June 2013, NASA/GSFC. (b) Bobbé Christopherson. (c) and (d) Courtesy of JPL/NASA.]

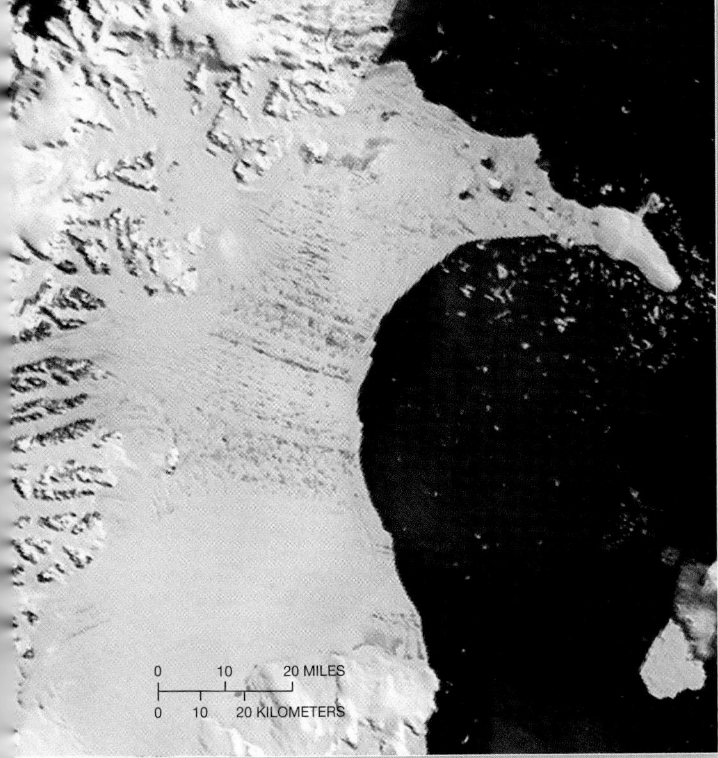

January 31, 2002

March 7, 2002

▲**Figure 14.30 Disintegrating ice shelves along the Antarctic coast.** Breakup and retreat of the Larsen B ice shelf between January and March 2002 caused a sixfold increase in the flow speed of glaciers that feed the ice shelf. Note the meltponds in the January image prior to breakup. [*Terra* images, NASA.]

GLACIAL ENVIRONMENTS IMPACT HUMANS

• Glacial ice is a freshwater resource; ice masses affect sea level, which is linked to security of human population centers along coastlines.
• Snow avalanches are a significant natural hazard in mountain environments.
• Permafrost soils are a carbon sink, estimated to contain half the pool of global carbon.

HUMANS IMPACT GLACIAL ENVIRONMENTS

• Rising temperatures associated with human-caused climate change are accelerating ice sheet losses and glacial melting, and hastening permafrost thaw.
• Particulates in the air from natural and human sources darken snow and ice surfaces, which accelerates melting.

14a A 675-km (420-mi) section of the trans-Alaska oil pipeline was constructed above the ground to prevent permafrost thaw. The pipeline is 1.2 m (4 ft) in diameter, and throughout this distance is supported on racks that average 1.5 to 3.0 m (5 to 10 ft) high.

14b A USGS scientist photographs Grinnell Glacier in Glacier National Park, Montana, as part of a repeat photography project to document the effects of climate change on glacial retreat.

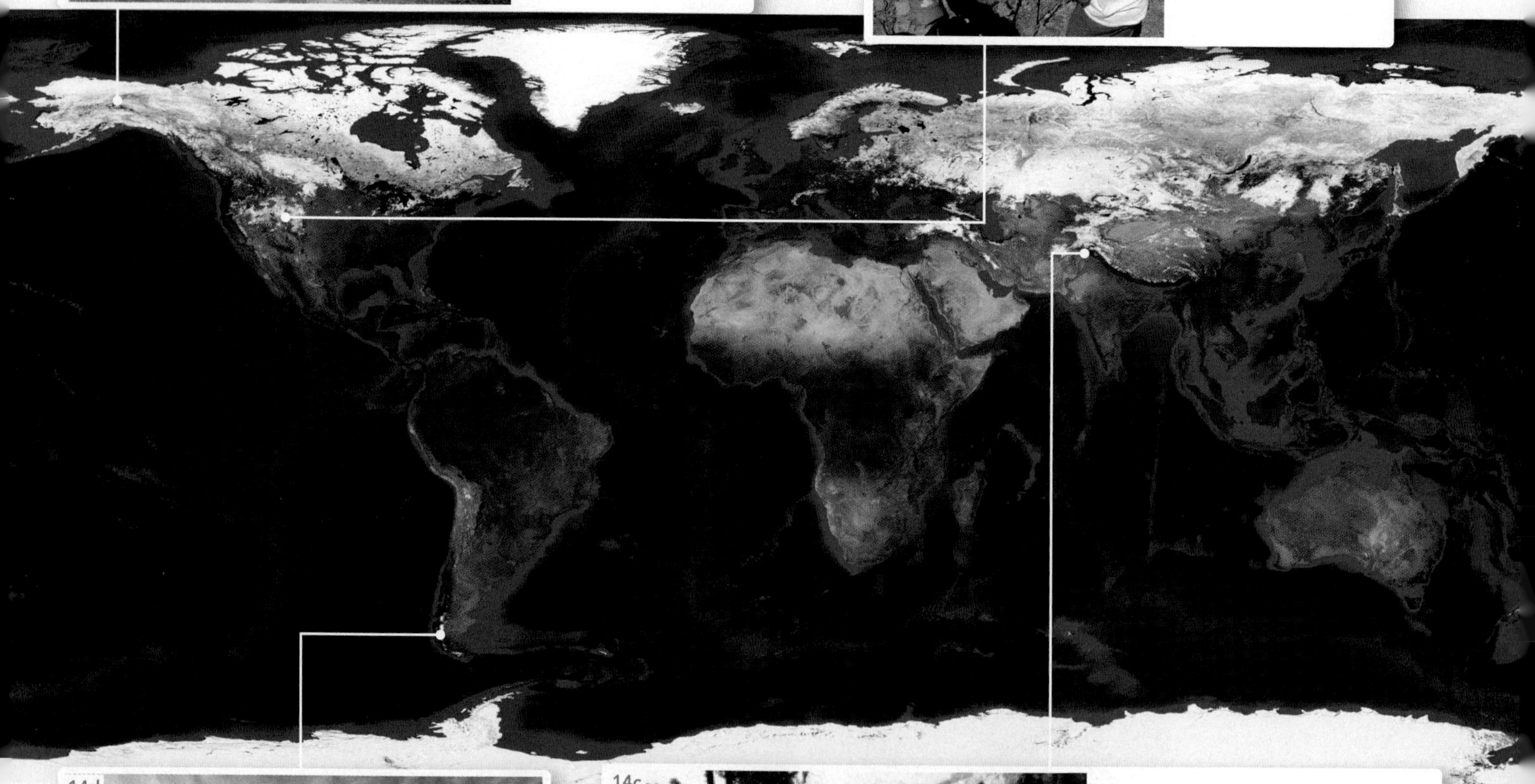

14d Argentina's Perito Moreno Glacier on the South Patagonian Ice Field in Los Glaciares National Park is a premier tourist destination. Recent research found that glaciers in this region are thinning at a rate of about 1.8 m (5.9 ft) per year. These freshwater losses will impact regional water supplies.

14c In the Indian-controlled region of Kashmir, avalanches buried a military camp and killed 16 Indian soldiers in February 2012. Three months later, 100 Pakistani soldiers were killed nearby. Large snowfall volumes and frequent winds combine with steep Himalayan slopes to create dangerous avalanche conditions in this area.

ISSUES FOR THE 21ST CENTURY

• Melting of glaciers and ice sheets will continue to raise sea level, with potentially devastating consequences for coastal communities and low-lying island nations.
• Thawing of permafrost in response to climate change will release vast amounts of carbon into the atmosphere, accelerating global warming.

KEYLEARNING**conceptsreview**

Explain the process by which snow becomes glacial ice.

More than 77% of Earth's freshwater is frozen, and ice covers about 11% of Earth's surface. Earth's **cryosphere** is the portion of the hydrosphere and ground that is perennially frozen, generally at high latitudes and elevations.

A **snowline** is the lowest elevation where snow occurs year-round, and this elevation varies by latitude—higher near the equator, lower poleward. Snow becomes glacial ice through stages of accumulation, increasing thickness, pressure on underlying layers, and recrystallization. Snow progresses through transitional steps from **firn** (compact, granular) to a denser **glacial ice** after many years.

cryosphere (p. 440)
snowline (p. 441)
firn (p. 441)
glacial ice (p. 441)

1. Describe the location of most freshwater on Earth today.
2. Trace the evolution of glacial ice from fresh fallen snow.

Differentiate between alpine glaciers and continental ice sheets and *describe* ice caps and ice fields.

A **glacier** is a mass of ice sitting on land or floating as an ice shelf in the ocean next to land. Glaciers form in areas of permanent snow. A glacier in a mountain range is an **alpine glacier**. If confined within a valley, it is termed a *valley glacier*. The area of origin is a snowfield, usually in a bowl-shaped erosional landform called a **cirque**. Where alpine glaciers flow down to the sea, the process of **calving** occurs as masses of ice break off the glacier into the sea and form *icebergs*. An **ice sheet** is an extensive, continuous mass of ice that may occur on a continental scale. An **ice cap** is a smaller, roughly circular ice mass, less than 50,000 km^2 (19,300 mi^2) in size. An ice mass covering a mountainous region is an **ice field**.

glacier (p. 441)
alpine glacier (p. 442)
cirque (p. 442)
calving (p. 442)
ice sheet (p. 442)
ice cap (p. 442)
ice field (p. 443)

3. What is a glacier? What can we learn about existing climate patterns from conditions in glacial regions and glacial mass balances?
4. Differentiate between an alpine glacier, an ice sheet, an ice cap, and an ice field. Which occurs in mountains? Which covers Antarctica and Greenland?
5. How are icebergs generated? Describe their buoyancy characteristics using this chapter's discussion and the section on ice in Chapter 5.

Illustrate the mechanics of glacial movement.

A glacier is an open system. The **firn line** is the elevation above which the winter snow and ice remain intact throughout the summer melting season, but below which melting occurs. A glacier is fed by snowfall and is wasted by **ablation** (losses from its upper and lower surfaces and along its margins). Accumulation and ablation achieve a mass balance in each glacier.

As a glacier moves downhill, vertical **crevasses** may develop. Sometimes a glacier will move rapidly, an event known as a **glacier surge**. The presence of water along the basal layer appears to be important in glacial movements. As a glacier moves, it plucks rock pieces and debris, incorporating them into the ice, and this debris scours and sandpapers underlying rock through **abrasion**.

firn line (p. 443)
ablation (p. 443)
crevasse (p. 446)
glacier surge (p. 447)
abrasion (p. 447)

6. What is meant by glacial mass balance? What are the basic inputs and outputs contributing to that balance?
7. What is meant by a glacier surge? What do scientists think produces surging episodes?

Describe characteristic erosional and depositional landforms created by glaciation.

A **roche moutonnée** is an erosional landform produced by plucking and abrasion. It is an asymmetrical hill of exposed bedrock, gently sloping on the upstream end and abruptly sloping on the downstream end.

Extensive valley glaciers have profoundly reshaped mountains worldwide, transforming **V**-shaped stream valleys into **U**-shaped glaciated valleys and producing many other distinctive erosional and depositional landforms. As cirque walls erode away, sharp **arêtes** (sawtooth, or serrated, ridges) form, dividing adjacent cirque basins. Two eroding cirques may reduce an arête to a saddlelike **col**. A **horn** results when several cirque glaciers gouge an individual mountain summit from all sides, forming a pyramidal peak. An ice-carved rock basin left as a glacier retreats may fill with water to form a **tarn**; tarns in a string separated by moraines are **paternoster lakes**. Where a glacial trough joins the ocean and the glacier retreats, the sea extends inland to form a **fjord**.

All glacial deposits, whether ice-borne or meltwater-borne, constitute **glacial drift**. Direct deposits from ice consist of unstratified and unsorted **till**. Specific landforms produced by the deposition of till at glacial margins are **moraines**. A **lateral moraine** forms along each side of a glacier; lateral moraines of converging glaciers can merge to form a **medial moraine**; and eroded debris dropped at the farthest extent of a glacier's terminus is a **terminal moraine**. Recessional moraines mark temporary endpoints as the glacier advances and retreats over time.

A **till plain**, which forms behind a terminal moraine, features unstratified coarse till, low and rolling relief, and deranged drainage. **Drumlins** are elongated hills of deposited till, streamlined in the direction of continental ice movement (blunt end upstream and tapered end downstream).

Glacial meltwater deposits are sorted and stratified and called **stratified drift**, forming **outwash plains** featuring braided stream channels that carry a heavy sediment load. An **esker** is a sinuously curving, narrow ridge of coarse sand and gravel that forms along the channel of a meltwater stream beneath a glacier. A **kame** is a small hill, knob, or mound of poorly sorted sand and gravel that is deposited directly on top of glacial ice and then deposited on the ground when the glacier melts. An isolated block of ice left by a retreating glacier becomes surrounded by debris; when the block finally melts, it leaves a steep-sided depression called a **kettle** that, when filled with water, forms a *kettle lake*.

roche moutonnée (p. 448)
arête (p. 448)
col (p. 449)
horn (p. 449)
tarn (p. 449)
paternoster lake (p. 449)
fjord (p. 450)
glacial drift (p. 451)
till (p. 451)
moraine (p. 451)
lateral moraine (p. 451)
medial moraine (p. 451)
terminal moraine (p. 451)
till plain (p. 451)
drumlin (p. 452)
stratified drift (p. 453)
outwash plain (p. 453)
esker (p. 454)
kame (p. 454)
kettle (p. 454)

8. How does a glacier accomplish erosion?
9. Describe the transformation of a V-shaped stream valley into a U-shaped glaciated valley. What features are visible after the glacier retreats?
10. How is an arête formed? A col? A horn? Briefly differentiate among them.
11. Differentiate between two forms of glacial drift—till and glacial outwash.
12. What is a morainal deposit? What specific moraines are created by alpine glaciers?
13. What is a common depositional feature encountered in a till plain?
14. Contrast a roche moutonnée and a drumlin with regard to appearance, orientation, and the way each forms.

Discuss the distribution of permafrost and *explain* several periglacial processes.

The term **periglacial** describes cold-climate processes, landforms, and topographic features that exist along the margins of glaciers, past and present. When soil or rock temperatures remain below 0°C (32°F) for at least 2 years, **permafrost** (perennially frozen ground) develops. Note that this defining criterion for permafrost is based solely on temperature and has nothing to do with how much or how little water is present. The **active layer** is the zone of seasonally frozen ground that exists between the subsurface permafrost layer and the ground surface. In regions of permafrost, frozen subsurface water forms **ground ice**. **Patterned ground** forms in the periglacial environment where freezing and thawing of the ground create polygonal forms of circles, polygons, stripes, and nets.

periglacial (p. 454)
permafrost (p. 454)
active layer (p. 455)
ground ice (p. 457)
patterned ground (p. 458)

15. In terms of climatic types, describe the areas on Earth where periglacial landscapes occur.
16. Define two types of permafrost. What are the characteristics of each, and where does each occur on Earth?
17. Describe the active zone in permafrost regions, and relate its differing thickness to specific latitudes.
18. What is the difference between permafrost and ground ice?
19. Describe the role of frost action in the formation of various landform types in the periglacial region, such as patterned ground.
20. Explain some of the specific problems humans encounter in building on periglacial landscapes.

Describe landscapes of the Pleistocene ice-age epoch and *list* changes occurring today in the polar regions.

An **ice age** is any extended period of cold. The late Cenozoic Era featured pronounced ice-age conditions during the Pleistocene. Beyond the ice, **paleolakes** formed because of wetter conditions. **Lacustrine deposits** are lake sediments that form terraces along former shorelines.

The 10°C (50°F) isotherm for July, coinciding with the visible tree line separating northern forests and tundra, defines the Arctic region. The Antarctic convergence defines the Antarctic region in a narrow zone located near 60° S latitude that extends around the continent as a boundary between colder Antarctic water and warmer water at lower latitudes. Changes occurring in the polar regions are causing positive feedback loops related to changes in surface albedo. Warming temperatures are causing the collapse of ice shelves.

ice age (p. 460)
paleolake (p. 461)
lacustrine deposit (p. 461)

21. Define an ice age. When was the most recent ice age? Explain the terms *glacial* and *interglacial* in your answer.
22. What is the relationship between the criteria defining the Arctic and Antarctic regions? Is there any coincidence between the Arctic criteria and the distribution of Northern Hemisphere forests?
23. Based on information in this chapter and elsewhere in *Elemental Geosystems*, summarize a few of the changing conditions under way in each polar region.

VISUALanalysis 14 Glacial Processes and Landforms

This August 2013 photo shows a glacier located along the coast of Svalbard, Norway, at 80.5° N latitude. The water body in the foreground is the Arctic Ocean. Study the character of the ice, the adjacent landforms, and the overall setting. Twenty years ago, glacial ice covered most of this landscape and formed a shelf off the coast. [Bobbé Christopherson.]

1. What is the name for this type of glacier (for example, cirque glacier, piedmont glacier, or tidewater glacier).
2. What characteristic of the ice indicates glacial movement toward the sea? What glacial landforms can you identify?
3. Based on your observation, would you say that this glacier is advancing or retreating? Explain.
4. What processes related to climatic warming are potentially affecting the mass balance of this glacier?

MasteringGeography™

Looking for additional review and test prep materials? Visit the Study Area in *MasteringGeography*™ to enhance your geographic literacy, spatial reasoning skills, and understanding of this chapter's content by accessing a variety of resources, including **MapMaster** interactive maps, geoscience animations, videos, *In the News* RSS feeds, flashcards, web links, self-study quizzes, and an eText version of *Elemental Geosystems.*

PART 4 Soils, Ecosystems, and Biomes

Earth is the home of the Solar System's only known biosphere—a uniquely complex system of interacting abiotic (nonliving) and biotic (living) components working together to sustain a tremendous diversity of life. Energy enters the biosphere through conversion of solar energy by photosynthesis in the leaves of plants. Energy then moves through a feeding hierarchy from producers to consumers, ending with decomposers. Together, these varied organisms, in concert with the Earth's abiotic components, produce aquatic and terrestrial ecosystems, generally organized into various biomes. Soil is the essential link connecting the living world to the lithosphere and the rest of Earth's physical systems. Thus, soil is the appropriate bridge between Part 3 and Part 4 of this text.

Today, we face the crucial issue of how to preserve the diversity of life in the biosphere with increasing human population and a changing global climate, including shifts in patterns of land and ocean temperatures, precipitation, and extreme weather phenomena, all of which impact Earth's living systems. The resilience of the biosphere as we know it is being tested in a real-time, one-time experiment. These important issues of biogeography are considered in Part 4.

INPUTS → ACTIONS → OUTPUTS

INPUTS
Insolation
Abiotic and biotic elements
Ecosystem components

ACTIONS
Photosynthesis/respiration
Biogeochemical cycling
Trophic relations, food webs
Evolution, succession

OUTPUTS
Soil, plants, animals, life
Ecosystems
Biodiversity
Biomes: marine and terrestrial

HUMAN-EARTH CONNECTIONS
Soil degradation
Desertification
Biodiversity losses
Carbon sinks

The forested banks of the Arthur River in the Tarkine wilderness in western Tasmania, Australia's largest remaining temperate rainforest. [Nature Connect/Corbis.] ▶

Atmosphere
Biosphere
Lithosphere
Hydrosphere

15 The Geography of Soils

Terraced fields of rice, ready for harvest, in northern Vietnam. Depletion of soil nutrients and recent droughts associated with climate change threaten production of this water-intensive crop. [Cristal Tran/Shutterstock.]

KEYLEARNINGconcepts

After reading the chapter, you should be able to:

- *Define* soil and soil science and *list* four components of soil.
- *Describe* the principal soil-formation factors and *describe* the horizons of a typical soil profile.
- *Describe* the physical properties used to classify soils: color, texture, structure, consistence, porosity, and soil moisture.
- *Explain* basic soil chemistry, including cation-exchange capacity, and *relate* these concepts to soil fertility.
- *Discuss* human impacts on soils, including desertification.
- *Describe* the 12 soil orders of the Soil Taxonomy classification system and *explain* their general distribution across Earth.

GEOSYSTEMS**now**

Desertification: Declining Soils in Earth's Drylands

▲**Figure GN 15.1 Trees stabilize soils and slow land degradation.** Poplar trees stabilize soils at the edge of the Taklamakan Desert in China. These trees help slow desertification, but are declining after years of drought. [TAO Images Limited/Getty Images.]

In September 2012, on the edge of the Gobi Desert in the Inner Mongolia Autonomous Province of China, a group of volunteers planted the millionth tree in an attempt to fight desertification, the degradation of drylands. In a region devastated by sandstorms and deteriorating land, this forest restoration effort, funded by a private organization since 2007, plants trees (mainly from the genus *Populus*, or poplars), monitors water availability for tree growth, and educates communities about the importance of trees for preventing erosion, producing oxygen, and storing carbon dioxide. To the west, in the Taklamakan Desert of central Asia, native poplar trees are declining with ongoing drought (**Figure GN 15.1**).

Desertification is defined by the United Nations (UN) as "the persistent degradation of dryland ecosystems by human activities and climate change." This process along the margins of semiarid and arid lands is caused in part by human abuse of soil structure and fertility—one of the subjects of this chapter.

Central Asia Throughout central Asia, overexploitation of water resources has combined with drought to cause desertification. The Aral Sea, formerly one of the four largest lakes in the world, has steadily shrunk in size since the 1960s, when inflowing rivers were diverted for irrigation (see The Human Denominator 15 at the end of this chapter). Fine sediment and alkali dust blanketing the former lakebed are subject to wind deflation, leading to massive dust storms. This sediment contains fertilizers and other pollutants from agricultural runoff, so its mobilization and spread over the land causes crop damage and human health problems, including increased cancer rates.

Africa's Sahel In Africa, the Sahel is the transition region between the Sahara Desert in the subtropics and the wetter equatorial regions. The southward expansion of desert conditions through portions of the Sahel region has left many African peoples on land that no longer experiences the rainfall of just three decades ago. Yet climate change is only part of the story: Other factors contributing to desertification in the Sahel are population increases, land degradation from deforestation and overgrazing, poverty, and the lack of a coherent environmental policy.

A Growing Problem The UN estimates that degraded lands worldwide cover some 1.9 billion hectares (4.7 billion acres) and affect 1.5 billion people; many millions of additional hectares are added each year (**Figure GN 15.2**). The primary causes of desertification are overgrazing, unsustainable agricultural practices, and forest removal. However, desertification is a complex phenomenon related, as noted earlier, to population issues, poverty, resource management, and government policies.

Initiatives to promote sustainable land management began in 1994 with the UN Convention to Combat Desertification (see http://www.unccd.int/), yet desertification continues to threaten livelihoods and food resources in many areas of the world. Delays in addressing the problem will result in far higher costs when compared to the cost of taking action now. Further discussion is on pages 490–91 in this chapter.

QUESTION AND EXPLORE For more information on desertification, see the UN website at http://www.un.org/en/events/desertificationday/background.shtml. Perspectives on China's ongoing reforestation effort to combat desertification are at http://e360.yale.edu/feature/chinas_reforestation_programs_big_success_or_just_an_illusion/2484/ and http://www.chinadaily.com.cn/business/greenchina/2014-03/11/content_17340458.htm. MG

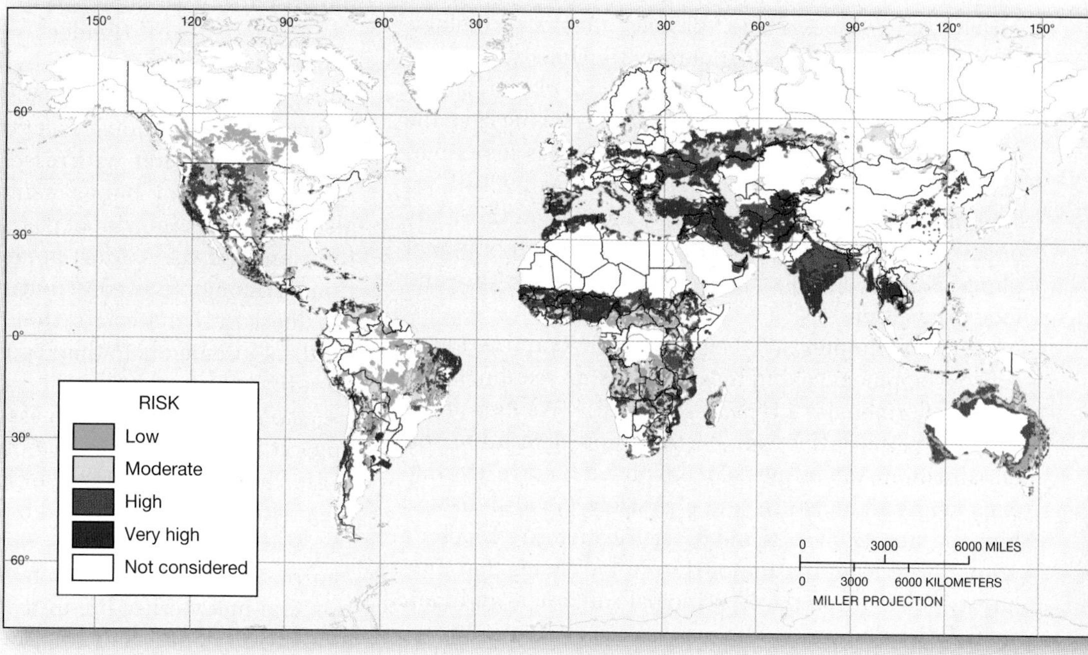

►**Figure GN 15.2 Areas at risk of desertification.** [Map prepared by USDA–NRCS, Soil Survey Division; includes consideration of population densities in affected regions provided by the National Center for Geographic Information Analysis at University of California, Santa Barbara.]

MG MapMaster
World Physical Environment: Desertification

Earth's landscape generally is covered with **soil**, a dynamic natural material composed of water, air, and fine particles—both mineral fragments (sands, silts, clays) and organic matter—in which plants grow. Soil is the basis for functioning ecosystems: It retains and filters water; is habitat for a host of microbial organisms, many of which produce antibiotics that fight human diseases; serves as a source of slow-release nutrients; and stores carbon dioxide and other greenhouse gases. Nearly 80% of terrestrial organic and inorganic carbon is stored in soil, and about a quarter of this amount is stored in wetlands, which are defined by the presence of hydric soils (waterlogged soils, discussed in Chapter 6 and later in this chapter). The soil carbon pool is about three times larger than the atmospheric carbon pool; only the ocean stores more carbon than soil. Remember from Chapter 8 that although about two-thirds of the recent increase in atmospheric carbon dioxide comes from fossil-fuel burning, one-third comes from the loss of soil associated with land-use changes.

Soils do not reproduce, nor can they be re-created—they are a nonrenewable natural resource.

Soils develop over long periods of time; in fact, many soils bear the legacy of climates and geological processes during last 15,000 years or more. Soils do not reproduce, nor can they be re-created—they are a nonrenewable natural resource. This fact means that human use and abuse of soils is happening at rates much faster than those at which soils form or can be replaced.

Soil is a complex substance whose characteristics vary from kilometer to kilometer—and even centimeter to centimeter. Physical geographers are interested in the spatial distributions of soil types and the physical factors that interact to produce them. **Soil science**, the interdisciplinary study of soil as a natural resource on Earth's surface, draws on aspects of physics, chemistry, biology, mineralogy, hydrology, taxonomy, climatology, and cartography. *Pedology* deals with the origin, classification, distribution, and description of soils—*ped* being from the Greek *pedon*, meaning "soil" or "earth." Soil is sometimes called the edaphosphere, as *edaphos* means "soil" or "ground." *Edaphology* specifically focuses on the study of soil as a medium for sustaining the growth of higher plants. Knowledge of soils is critical for agriculture and food production.

In this chapter: We begin with an examination of soil development, using loess soils as an example, and the soil horizons of a typical soil profile. We look at the properties that affect soil fertility and determine soil classification, including color, texture, structure, consistence, porosity, moisture, and chemistry. We also discuss human impacts on soils and desertification. We conclude with a brief examination of the United States Soil Taxonomy, focusing on the 12 principal soil orders and their spatial distribution.

Soil Development and Soil Profiles

Soil is composed of about 50% mineral and organic matter; the other 50% is air and water stored in the pore spaces between soil particles. The organic matter, although making up only about 5% of a given soil volume, is critical for soil function and includes living microorganisms and plant roots, dead and partially decomposed plant matter, and fully decomposed plant material that forms a nutrient-rich mixture called humus (discussed ahead).

A soil body is an open system with physical inputs of insolation, water, rock and sediment, and microorganisms and outputs of improved air and water quality and plant ecosystems that sustain animals and human societies. Soil scientists recognize five primary natural soil-forming factors: parent material, climate, organisms, topography and relief, and time. Human activities, especially those related to agriculture and livestock grazing, also affect soil development and are discussed later in the chapter. Soils are assessed and classified using soil cross sections, usually extending from the ground surface to the bedrock or sediments beneath.

Natural Soil-Formation Factors

As discussed in Chapter 11, physical and chemical weathering of rocks in the upper lithosphere provides the raw mineral ingredients for soil formation. Bedrock, rock fragments, and sediments are the *parent material*, and their composition, texture, and chemical nature help determine the type of soil that forms. Clay minerals are the principal weathered by-products in soil.

Climate also influences soil development; in fact, soil types correlate closely with climate types worldwide. The temperature and moisture regimes of climates determine the chemical reactions, organic activity, and movement of water within soils. The present-day climate is important, but as mentioned earlier, many soils also exhibit the imprint of past climates, sometimes over thousands of years. Most notable is the effect of glaciations. Among other contributions, glaciation produced the loess soil materials that were windblown thousands of kilometers to their present locations (discussed ahead).

Biological activity is an essential factor in soil development (see Geosystems in Action 15 on page 481). Vegetation and the activities of animals and bacteria—all the organisms living in, on, and over the soil, such as algae, fungi, worms, and insects—determine the organic content of soil. The chemical characteristics of the vegetation and many other life forms contribute to the acidity or alkalinity of the soil solution (soil pH is discussed in

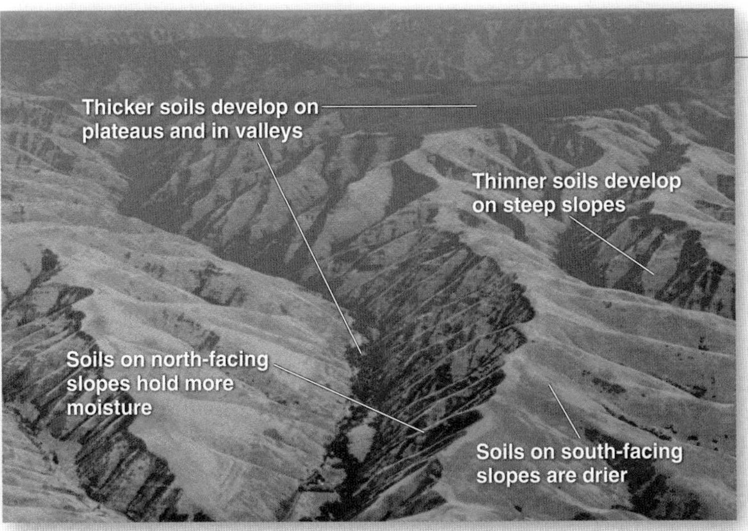
Thicker soils develop on plateaus and in valleys
Thinner soils develop on steep slopes
Soils on north-facing slopes hold more moisture
Soils on south-facing slopes are drier

▲**Figure 15.1 Topography and soil development, Blue Mountains, Oregon.** [Kevin Ebi/Alamy.]

the next section). For example, broadleaf trees tend to increase alkalinity, whereas needleleaf trees tend to produce higher acidity. When humans move into new areas and alter natural vegetation by logging or plowing, the affected soils are likewise altered, often permanently.

Relief and topography also affect soil formation (**Figure 15.1**). Slopes that are too steep cannot have full soil development because gravity and erosional processes remove materials. Lands that are level or nearly level tend to develop thicker soils, but may be subject to soil drainage issues such as waterlogging. The orientation of slopes relative to the Sun is also important because it controls exposure to sunlight. In the Northern Hemisphere, south-facing slopes are warmer overall through the year because they receive higher-angle direct sunlight. North-facing slopes are colder, causing slower snowmelt and a lower evaporation rate, thus providing more moisture for plants than is available on south-facing slopes, which tend to dry out faster.

All of the identified natural factors in soil development require *time* to operate. The rate of soil development is closely tied to the nature of the parent material (soils develop more quickly from sediments than from bedrock) and to climate (soils develop at a faster rate in warm, humid climates). Over geologic time, plate tectonics has redistributed landscapes and thus subjected soil-forming processes to diverse conditions.

Loess Deposits

The parent materials of soils are variable, ranging from residual materials that have remained in place to transported materials, such as the sediments carried by glaciers, rivers, gravity, or wind. Many soils have more than one parent material. One example is the fine-grained sediment derived from glacial activity and subsequently carried to new locations by wind.

About 15,000 years ago, near the end of the Pleistocene, retreating glaciers in many parts of the world left behind fine-grained sediment (clays, silts, and fine sand) from glacial outwash deposits. Wind then transported these sediments (remember from Chapter 13 that wind can transport dust and silt long distances), redepositing them in unstratified, homogeneous (evenly mixed) accumulations of **loess** (pronounced "luss"), originally named by peasants working along the Rhine River Valley in Germany. In some regions, loess deposits form a blanket of material that covers previously existing landforms. Over time, loess soils have developed, today forming a thin layer in many of the world's soils (described later in the chapter). **Figure 15.2** shows the worldwide distribution of these accumulations, which underlay some of Earth's most productive agricultural regions.

The loess deposits in Europe and North America are thought to be derived mainly from glacial and periglacial sources. In the United States, significant loess accumulations with glacial origins occur throughout the Mississippi and Missouri River Valleys, forming continuous deposits 15–30 m (50–100 ft) thick. The Loess Hills of Iowa reach heights of about 61 m (200 ft) above the nearby prairie farmlands and run north–south for more than 322 km (200 mi). Only China has deposits that exceed these areal dimensions.

The vast deposits of loess in China, covering more than 300,000 km^2 (116,000 mi^2), are derived from windblown desert sediment. Accumulations in the Loess Plateau of China are more than 300 m (1000 ft) thick, forming complex weathered badlands and good agricultural land; in some areas, dwellings are carved into the strong vertical structure of loess cliffs. Loess deposits also cover much of Ukraine, central Europe, the Pampas region of Argentina, and New Zealand.

Because of its binding strength and internal coherence, loess weathers and erodes into steep bluffs, or vertical faces. When a bank is cut into a loess deposit, it generally will stand vertically, although it can fail if saturated. Loess deposits are well drained, can be easily tilled, and have excellent moisture retention. The soils derived from loess are the basis for some of Earth's "breadbasket" farming regions, especially in North America, Asia, and South America (**Figure 15.3**).

Soil Horizons

As a book cannot be judged by its cover, so soils cannot be evaluated at the ground surface only. Instead, scientists evaluate soils using a **soil profile**, a vertical section of soil that extends from the surface to the deepest extent of plant roots or to the point where regolith or bedrock is encountered. Soil profiles may be exposed by human activities, such as at a construction site or excavation or along a highway road cut. When soil is not exposed by natural processes or human activity, scientists dig soil pits to expose a soil profile for analysis.

For soil classification, pedologists use a three-dimensional representation of the soil profile, known as a *pedon*. A soil pedon is the smallest unit of soil that displays all the characteristics and properties used for

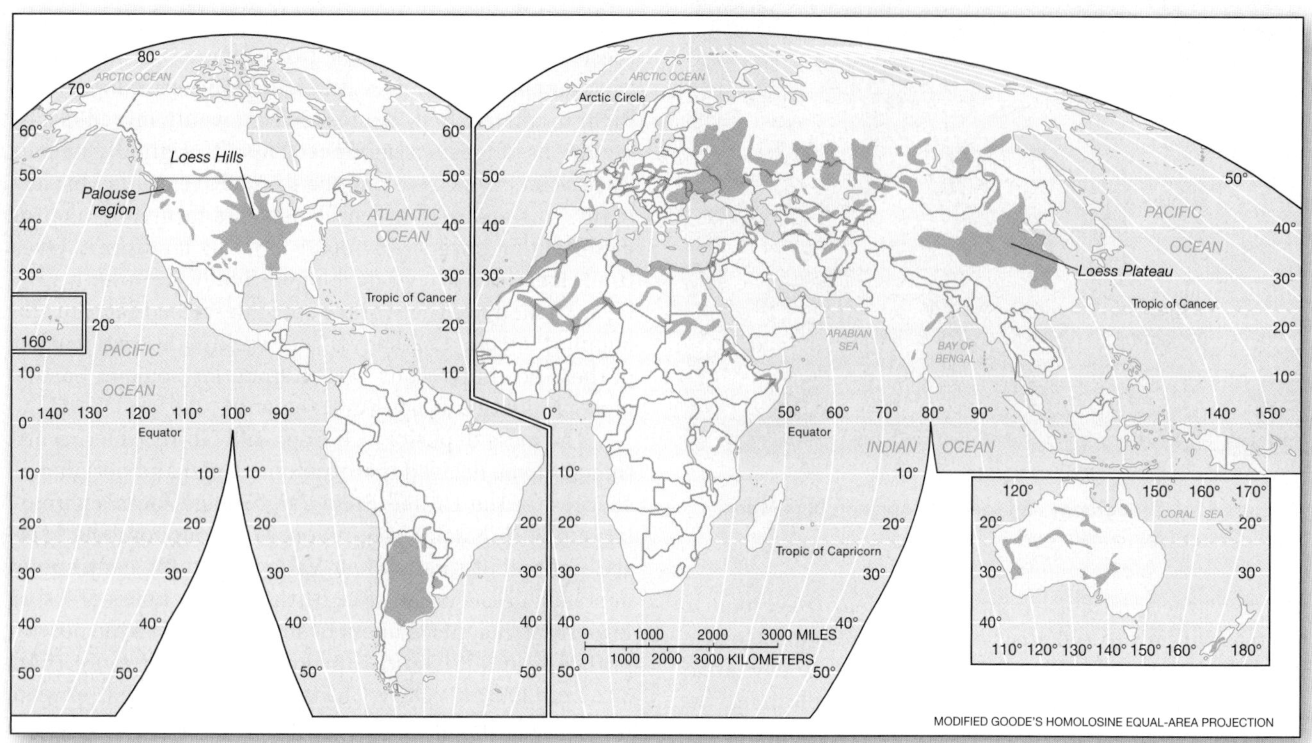

▲**Figure 15.2 Global loess deposits.** [Adapted from NRCS, FAO, and USGS data.]

classification (discussed later in the chapter). A soil profile represents one side of a pedon, as shown in Figure 15.4a.

Within a soil profile, soils are generally organized into distinct horizontal layers known as **soil horizons**. These horizons are roughly parallel to the land surface, and each has characteristics recognizably different from those of horizons directly above or below. The four "master" horizons in most agricultural soils are known as the O, A, B, and C horizons (**Figure 15.4**).

The boundary between horizons usually is distinguishable when viewed in profile, owing to differences in one or more physical soil characteristics, such as color, texture, structure, consistence (meaning soil consistency or cohesiveness), porosity, and moisture. These and other soil properties, which all affect soil function, are discussed in the next section.

O Horizon At the top of the soil profile is the *O horizon*, named for its *o*rganic composition, derived from plant and animal litter that was deposited on the surface and transformed into **humus**, a mixture of decomposed and synthesized organic materials that is usually dark

▼**Figure 15.3 Loess soils and agriculture, North America and China.** [(a) Clint Farlinger/Alamy. (b) Dennis Cox/Alamy.]

(a) Agricultural fields in the Loess Hills of western Iowa. Terraces provide flat surfaces for planting crops.

(b) Terraced farming near the Yellow River on the Loess Plateau in northern China.

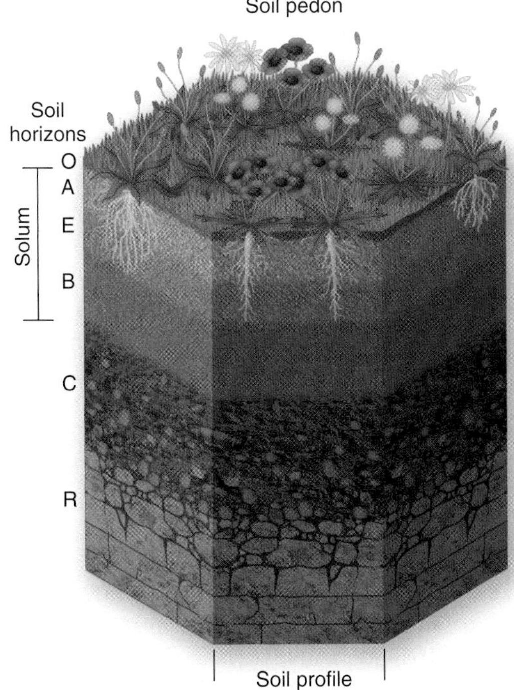

(a) An idealized soil profile within a pedon.

(b) Profile of a well-drained soil with till as parental material (a Mollisol) in southeastern South Dakota. Carbonate nodules are visible in the lower B and upper C horizons.

◀Figure 15.4 A typical soil profile within a pedon, and example. [(b) Marbut Collection, Soil Science Society of America, Inc.]

in color. Microorganisms work busily on this organic debris, performing a portion of the *humification* (humus-making) process. The O horizon is 20%–30% or more organic matter, which is important because of its ability to retain water and nutrients and because of the way its behavior complements that of clay minerals.

The A, E, B, and C horizons extend below the O horizon to the R horizon, which is composed of sediment or bedrock. These middle layers are composed of sand, silt, clay, and other weathered by-products.

A Horizon In the *A horizon*, humus and clay particles are particularly important, as they provide essential chemical connections between soil nutrients and plants. This horizon usually is richer in organic content, and hence darker, than lower horizons. Human disruption through plowing, pasturing, and other activities takes place in the A horizon. This horizon is commonly called *topsoil*.

E Horizon The A horizon grades downward into the *E horizon*, which is made up mainly of coarse sand, silt, and leaching-resistant minerals. From the lighter-colored E horizon, silicate clays and oxides of aluminum and iron are leached (removed by water) and carried to lower horizons with water as it percolates through the soil. This process of removing fine particles and minerals by water, leaving behind sand and silt, is **eluviation**—thus, the E designation for this horizon. As precipitation increases, so does the rate of eluviation.

B Horizon In contrast to the A and E horizons, *B horizons* accumulate clays, aluminum, and iron. B horizons are dominated by **illuviation**, in which materials leached by water from one layer enter and accumulate in another. Both eluviation and illuviation are types of *translocation*, in which material (such as nutrients, salts, and clays) is moved downward in the soil. In contrast to eluviation, which removes material, illuviation is a depositional process. B horizons may exhibit reddish, yellowish, or white hues because of the presence of illuviated minerals (silicate clays, iron and aluminum, carbonates, and gypsum) and organic oxides. Some materials occurring in the B horizon may have formed in place from weathering processes rather than arriving there by translocation, especially in the humid tropics. In dry climates, calcium carbonate commonly forms the cementing material that causes hardening of this layer.

Together, the A, E, and B horizons are designated the **solum**, considered the true definable soil of the profile (and labeled in Figure 15.4a). The horizons of the solum experience active soil processes.

C Horizon Below the solum is the *C horizon*, made up of weathered bedrock or weathered parent material. This zone is identified as *regolith* (although the term sometimes is used to include the solum as well). The C horizon is not much affected by soil operations in the solum and lies outside the biological influences experienced in the shallower horizons. Plant roots and soil microorganisms are rare in the C horizon.

R Horizon At the bottom of the soil profile is the *R* (rock) *horizon*, consisting of either unconsolidated (loose) material or consolidated bedrock. When bedrock physically and chemically weathers into regolith, it may or may not contribute to overlying soil horizons.

Along with the O, A, E, B, C, and R designations, soil scientists using the U.S. soil classification system (discussed later in the chapter) employ lowercase letters to designate subhorizons within each master horizon, indicating particular conditions. For example, the Ap horizon refers to an A horizon that has undergone plowing; the Bh horizon refers to the presence of organics (humic material).

Soil Characteristics

A number of physical and chemical characteristics differentiate soils and affect their fertility and resistance to erosion. **Soil fertility** is the ability of soil to sustain plants. Billions of dollars are expended to create fertile soil conditions, yet the future of Earth's most fertile soils is threatened because soil erosion is on the increase worldwide.

Here, we discuss the most widely applicable properties for describing and classifying soils; however, other properties exist and may be of value depending on the particular site. Chapter 3 in the U.S. Department of Agriculture, Natural Resources Conservation Service (NRCS) *Soil Survey Manual* presents additional information on soil properties (**http://www.nrcs.usda.gov/wps/portal/nrcs/detail/soils/survey/publication/?cid=nrcs142p2_054262**).

Physical Properties

The physical properties that distinguish soils and can be observed in soil profiles are color, texture, structure, consistence, porosity, and moisture.

Soil Color Color is important because it suggests the composition and chemical makeup of a soil. Among the many possible hues are the reds and yellows found in soils of the southeastern United States (high in iron oxides), the blacks of prairie soils in portions of the U.S. grain-growing regions and in Ukraine (richly organic), and the white to pale hues found in soils containing carbonates. Color may be the most obvious trait in an exposed soil. All the same, color can be deceptive: Soils with high humus content are often dark, yet clays of warm temperate and tropical regions with less than 3% organic content are some of the world's blackest soils.

Soil Texture *Texture* refers to the mixture and proportions of different particle sizes and is perhaps a soil's most permanent attribute. Soil texture is classified according to the relative amounts of different-sized particles smaller in diameter than 2 mm (0.08 in.), ranging from coarse sand to clay. Sands are graded from coarse to medium to fine, down to 0.05 mm; silt is finer, to 0.002 mm; and clay is finer still, at less than 0.002 mm.

Figure 15.5 is a *soil texture triangle* showing the relation of sand, silt, and clay concentrations in soils.

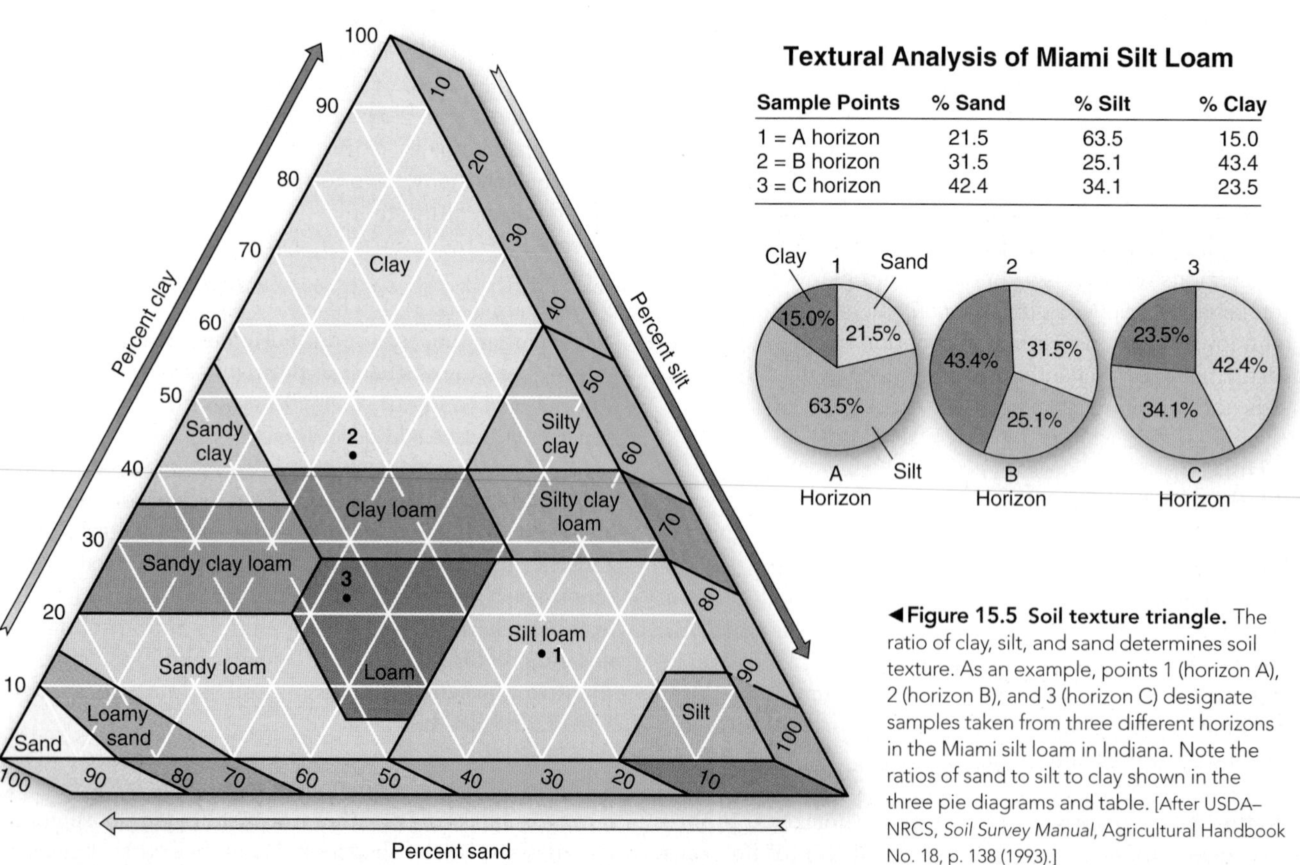

Textural Analysis of Miami Silt Loam

Sample Points	% Sand	% Silt	% Clay
1 = A horizon	21.5	63.5	15.0
2 = B horizon	31.5	25.1	43.4
3 = C horizon	42.4	34.1	23.5

◄**Figure 15.5 Soil texture triangle.** The ratio of clay, silt, and sand determines soil texture. As an example, points 1 (horizon A), 2 (horizon B), and 3 (horizon C) designate samples taken from three different horizons in the Miami silt loam in Indiana. Note the ratios of sand to silt to clay shown in the three pie diagrams and table. [After USDA–NRCS, *Soil Survey Manual*, Agricultural Handbook No. 18, p. 138 (1993).]

Each corner of the triangle represents a soil consisting solely of the particle size noted (although rarely are true soils composed of a single separate). Every soil on Earth is defined somewhere in this triangle.

Loam is the common designation for the balanced mixture of sand, silt, and clay that is beneficial to plant growth (Figure 15.5). Farmers consider a sandy loam with clay content below 20% (lower left) as the ideal soil because of its water-holding characteristics and ease of cultivation. Soil texture is important in determining water-retention and water-transmission traits.

To see how the soil texture triangle works, consider *Miami silt loam*, a soil type that is common in Indiana. Samples from this soil type are plotted on the soil texture triangle in Figure 15.5 as points 1, 2, and 3. Point 1 describes a sample taken near the surface in the A horizon, point 2 describes a sample taken from the B horizon, and point 3 describes a sample from the C horizon. Textural analyses of these samples are summarized in the table and in the three pie diagrams to the right of the triangle. Note that silt dominates the surface, clay the B horizon, and sand the C horizon. The *Soil Survey Manual* presents guidelines for estimating soil texture by feel, a relatively accurate method when used by an experienced person. However, laboratory methods using graduated sieves and separation by mechanical analysis in water allow more precise measurements.

Soil Structure Soil texture describes the size of soil particles, but soil *structure* refers to the size and shape of the aggregates of particles in the soil. Structure can partially modify the effects of soil texture. The smallest natural lump or cluster of particles is a *ped*. The shape of soil peds determines which of the structural types the soil exhibits: crumb or granular, platy, blocky, or prismatic or columnar (**Figure 15.6**).

Peds separate from each other along zones of weakness, creating voids, or pores, that are important for moisture storage and drainage. Rounded peds have more pore space between them, resulting in greater permeability than occurs with other shapes. They are therefore better for plant growth than are blocky, prismatic, or platy peds, despite comparable fertility. Terms used to describe soil structure include *fine*, *medium*, and *coarse*.

◀Figure 15.6 Types of soil structure. Structure is important because it controls drainage, rooting of plants, and how well the soil delivers nutrients to plants. The shape of individual peds, shown here, controls a soil's structure. [USDA–NRCS, National Soil Survey Center.]

GEOreport 15.1 Soil compaction—causes and effects

Soil compaction is the physical consolidation of the soil that destroys soil structure and reduces porosity. The increasing weight of today's heavy agricultural machinery, in addition to earlier planting and the conventional arrangement of row crops, tends to increase soil compaction and can result in a 50% reduction in crop yields owing to restricted root growth, poor aeration of the root zone, and poor drainage. Scientists now suggest that no-till agricultural practices (in which plowing does not occur), combined with maintaining a continuous cover of actively growing plants, is the best way to reduce soil compaction, since roots increase porosity and water availability, preserve organic matter content, and reduce surface erosion.

Adhesion among peds ranges from weak to strong. The work of soil organisms, illustrated in Figure GIA 15.1, affects soil structure and increases soil fertility.

Soil Consistence In soil science, the term *consistence* is used to describe the consistency of a soil or cohesion of its particles. Consistence is a product of texture (particle size) and structure (ped shape). Consistence reflects a soil's resistance to breaking and manipulation under varying moisture conditions:

- A *wet soil* is sticky between the thumb and forefinger, ranging from a little adherence to either finger, to sticking to both fingers, to stretching when the fingers are moved apart. Wet soils also exhibit *plasticity*, the quality of being moldable, roughly measured by rolling a piece of soil between fingers and thumb to see whether it rolls into a thin strand.
- A *moist soil* is filled to about half of field capacity (the usable water capacity of soil), and its consistence grades from loose (noncoherent) to *friable* (easily pulverized) to firm (not crushable between the thumb and forefinger).
- A *dry soil* is typically brittle and rigid, with consistence ranging from loose to soft to hard to extremely hard.

Soil Porosity *Porosity* refers to the available air spaces within a material; **soil porosity** denotes the part of a volume of soil that is filled with air, gases, or water (as opposed to soil particles or organic matter). We discussed soil porosity, permeability, and moisture storage in Chapter 6.

Pores in the soil horizon control the movement of water—its intake, flow, and drainage—and air ventilation. Important porosity factors are pore *size*, pore *continuity* (whether pores are interconnected), pore *shape* (whether pores are spherical, irregular, or tubular), pore *orientation* (whether pore spaces are vertical, horizontal, or random), and pore *location* (whether pores are within or between soil peds).

Porosity is improved by the presence of plant roots; by animal activity, such as the tunneling actions of gophers or worms (see Geosystems in Action 15); and by human actions, such as supplementing the soil with humus or sand or planting soil-building crops. Much of the soil-preparation work done by farmers before they plant—and by home gardeners as well—is done to improve soil porosity.

Soil Moisture As discussed in Chapter 6 and shown in Figure 6.8, plants operate most efficiently when the soil is at *field capacity*, which is the maximum water available for plant roots after large pore spaces have drained of gravitational water. Soil type determines field capacity. If soil moisture is below field capacity, plant roots may be unable to access available water, and the plant will eventually reach the wilting point. Beyond this point, plants are unable to extract the water they need, and they die. More than any other factor, soil moisture regimes shape the biotic and abiotic properties of the soil.

Chemical Properties

Recall that soil pores may be filled with air, water, or a mixture of the two. Consequently, soil chemistry involves both air and water. The atmosphere within soil pores is mostly nitrogen, oxygen, and carbon dioxide. Nitrogen concentrations are about the same as in the atmosphere, but oxygen is less and carbon dioxide is greater because of ongoing respiration processes in the ground.

Water present in soil pores is called the *soil solution* and is the medium for chemical reactions in soil. This solution is a critical source of nutrients for plants, providing the foundation of soil fertility. Carbon dioxide combines with the water to produce carbonic acid, and various organic materials combine with the water to produce organic acids. These acids are then active participants in soil processes, as are dissolved alkalis and salts.

A brief review of chemistry basics helps us understand how the soil solution behaves. An *ion* is an atom or group of atoms that carries an electrical charge (examples: Na^+, Cl^-, HCO_3^-). An ion has either a positive charge or a negative charge. For example, when NaCl (sodium chloride) dissolves in solution, it separates into two ions: Na^+, which is a *cation* (positively charged ion), and Cl^-, which is an *anion* (negatively charged ion). Some ions in soil carry single charges, whereas others carry double or even triple charges (e.g., sulfate, SO_4^{2-}, and aluminum, Al^{3+}).

Soil Colloids and Mineral Ions The tiny particles of clay or organic material (humus) suspended in the soil solution are **soil colloids**. Because they carry a negative electrical charge, they attract any positively charged ions in the soil (**Figure 15.7**). The positive ions, many metallic, are critical to plant growth. If it were not for the negatively charged soil colloids, the positive ions would be

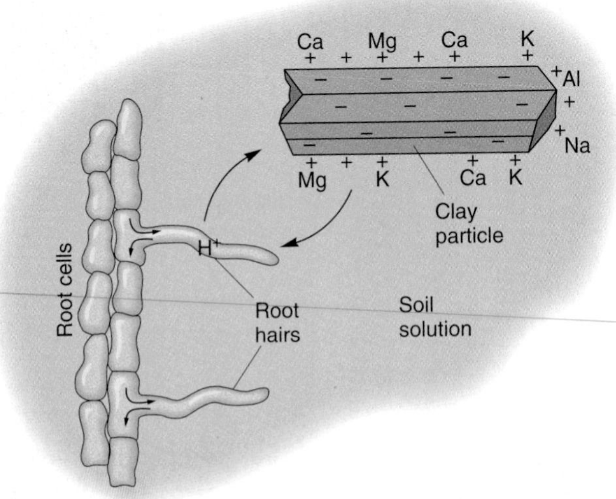

▲**Figure 15.7 Soil colloids and cation-exchange capacity (CEC).** A soil colloid, such as this clay particle, retains mineral ions by adsorption to its surface (opposite charges attract). This process holds the ions until they are absorbed by root hairs.

A diverse collection of organisms inhabits soil environments. Organisms play a vital role in soil-forming processes, helping to weather rock both mechanically and chemically, breaking up and mixing soil particles, and enriching soil with organic matter from their remains and wastes.

Moles can cause extensive soil disturbances.

15.1 Soil Organisms

Soil organisms range in size from land mammals that burrow into the ground, such as badgers, prairie dogs, and voles; to earthworms that ingest and secrete soil; to microscopic organisms that break down organic matter. The actions of these living organisms help maintain soil fertility.

Mammals: Mammals cause mechanical disturbances that mix soil, a process known as **bioturbation**.

Earthworms: Earthworms increase soil porosity, breaking up organic matter and then recycling soil aggregates to new locations (upward or downward in the soil column) by ingesting and secreting soil material.

Plant litter: The remains of plants, from leaves and stems to tree trunks, accumulate on the surface and as they decay gradually add organic matter to the soil.

Insects and other invertebrates: A wide range of insects, including ants and beetles, inhabit soil, along with spiders, mites, and many other invertebrates. All contribute to soil-forming processes.

Plant roots: Plant roots provide channels for water and air movement within the soil; these channels remain intact even after the root decomposes. The area around plant roots is biologically active and contains nutrients from root secretions and sloughed-off root cells.

Fungi: Fungi have threadlike extensions (called **mycelia**) that extend beneath the soil surface and that bind soil particles together.

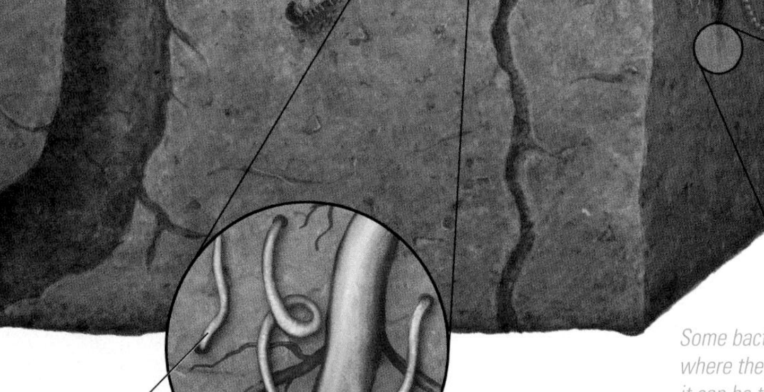

Some bacteria live on root nodes, where they “fix” nitrogen so that it can be taken up by plants.

Describe: How do earthworms affect soil?

Microorganisms: Soil bacteria and other microorganisms such as protozoa (single-celled organisms) and nematodes (non-segmented roundworms) help to break down the remains of organisms in the soil or release wastes other organisms can use.

Animation (MG)
The Soil Moisture (SMAP) Mission
http://goo.gl/h11xOB

Soil Science of America

http://goo.gl/Sc1S4O

MasteringGeography™

Visit the Study Area in MasteringGeography™ to explore biological activity in soil.
Visualize: Study a video of NASA's Soil Moisture (SMAP) Mission.
Assess: Demonstrate understanding of biological activity in soil. (if assigned by instructor).

GEOquiz

1. **Compare:** How are the effects of mammals and plant roots on soil similar? How are they different?
2. **Explain:** Explain three ways in which organisms improve soil fertility.

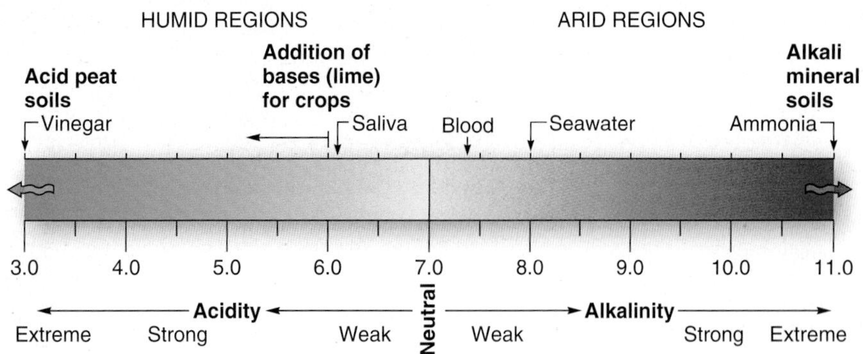

◀**Figure 15.8 pH scale.** The pH scale measures acidity (lower pH) and alkalinity (higher pH). (The complete pH scale ranges between 0 and 14.)

leached away in the soil solution and thus would be unavailable to plant roots.

Individual clay colloids are thin and platelike, with parallel surfaces that are negatively charged. They are more chemically active than silt and sand particles, but less active than organic colloids. Metallic cations attach to the surfaces of the colloids by *adsorption* (not *ab*sorption, which means "to enter"). **Cation-exchange capacity (CEC)** is the total number of cations that the soil is capable of adsorbing and exchanging. A high CEC means that the soil colloids can store or exchange a relatively large amount of cations from the soil solution. These cations then become available to plants through their roots. Thus, a high CEC indicates good soil fertility (unless a complicating factor exists, such as a soil that is too acidic). Soil is fertile when it contains organic substances and clay minerals that *absorb* water and *adsorb* certain elements needed by plants.

Soil Acidity and Alkalinity A soil solution may contain a significant amount of hydrogen ions (H^+), the cations that stimulate acid formation. The result is a soil rich in hydrogen ions, or an *acid soil.* A soil high in base cations (calcium, magnesium, potassium, and sodium) is a *basic* or *alkaline soil.* Such acidity or alkalinity is expressed on the pH scale (**Figure 15.8**).

Pure water has close to a neutral pH of 7.0. Readings below 7.0 represent increasing acidity. Readings above 7.0 indicate increasing alkalinity. Acidity usually is regarded as strong at 5.0 or lower on the pH scale, whereas 10.0 or above is considered strongly alkaline.

One contributor to soil acidity in this modern era is acid precipitation (rain, snow, fog, or dry deposition), as discussed in Chapter 2. Scientists have measured acid precipitation values below pH 2.0 (the acidity of lemon juice)—incredibly low for natural precipitation. Increased acidity in the soil solution reduces the CEC (H^+ ions attach to colloids, pushing other cations into the soil solution) and can accelerate the chemical weathering of minerals, either of which can reduce soil fertility. Because most crops are sensitive to specific pH levels, acid soils below pH 6.0 require treatment to raise the pH. This soil treatment is accomplished by the addition of bases in the form of minerals that are rich in base cations, usually lime (calcium carbonate, $CaCO_3$).

Human Impacts on Soils

Unlike living species, soils do not propagate themselves. Furthermore, owing to their complexity and long developmental histories, all soils are unique and cannot be duplicated. A few centimeters' thickness of prime farmland soil may require 500 years to mature. Yet this same thickness is being lost annually through soil erosion that occurs when humans remove vegetation and plow the land, whether on a mountainside or on a valley floor (**Figure 15.9**). Additional losses occur when flood control structures block fluvial sediments and their nutrients from replenishing floodplain soils. As a result of human intervention and unsustainable agricultural practices, some 35% of farmlands are losing soil faster than it can form—a loss exceeding 23 billion metric tons (25 billion tons) per year. Soil depletion (such as the loss of fertility that occurs when soils are leached of cations) and soil loss are at record levels from Iowa to China, Peru to Ethiopia, and the Middle East to the Americas. The impact on society is potentially disastrous as population and food demands increase.

▲**Figure 15.9 Soil degradation.** An example of soil loss through sheet and gully erosion on a northwest Iowa farm. One millimeter of soil lost from an acre weighs about 5 tons. [USDA–NRCS, National Soil Survey Center.]

Soil Erosion

The NRCS describes *soil erosion* as "the breakdown, detachment, transport, and redistribution of soil particles by forces of wind, water, or gravity." Overcultivation and excessive tilling, overgrazing, and the clearing of forested slopes are some of the main human activities that make soils more prone to erosion. Soil erosion removes topsoil, the layer that is richest in organic matter and nutrients. Millennia ago, farmers in most cultures learned to plant slopes "on the contour"—to sow seeds in rows or mounds that run around a slope at the same elevation rather than vertically up and down the slope. Planting on the contour prevents water from flowing straight down the slope and thus reduces soil erosion. Contour farming on gradually sloping land and terracing (cutting level platforms into steep terrain) in mountainous regions are used today to combat erosion (see the chapter-opening photo).

An expanding practice for slowing soil erosion is *no-till agriculture* (also called no-till farming; see GeoReport 15.1). In this approach, farmers no longer till, or plow, the soil after a harvest. Instead, they leave crop residue on the field between plantings, thus preventing soil erosion by wind and water. Seeds are then inserted into the ground without disturbing the soil. Planting the new crop on top of the old crop also preserves moisture. In Texas, where severe drought conditions have persisted in recent years, some farmers are successfully using no-till practices. The photos in **Figure 15.10** compare roots of wheat planted using no-till practices with those of wheat planted using conventional agriculture. Because the soil is less compacted, roots in the untilled fields can grow longer, reaching moisture and nutrients farther below the surface.

The Dust Bowl Large-scale removal of native vegetation associated with the expansion of farming into the American Great Plains in the late 1800s and early 1900s led to a catastrophic soil erosion event known as the Dust Bowl. Intensive agriculture and overgrazing combined with reduced precipitation and above-normal temperatures to trigger a multiyear period of severe wind erosion and loss of farmlands.

The deflation of soil—in some places as much as 10 cm (4 in.) over several years—occurred mainly in southern Nebraska, Kansas, Oklahoma, Texas, and eastern Colorado, but also extended into southern Canada and northern Mexico. The transported dust darkened the skies of midwestern cities (requiring streetlights to stay on throughout the day) and drifted over farmland, accumulating in depths that covered failing crops. By 1940, 2 million people had moved out of the Plains states—the largest migration in American history. The recent prolonged drought through 2012 in the American Southwest and into west and central Texas and Oklahoma is similar climatically to the conditions that led up to the Dust Bowl (see http://www.pbs.org/wgbh/americanexperience/films/dustbowl/ for more information).

◄Figure 15.10 Roots of wheat plants in tilled and untilled soils. [USDA.]

(a) No-till farming leads to greater moisture retention and looser soil, allowing wheat to develop longer root systems that access moisture and nutrients farther below the surface.

(b) Conventional farming leads to soil compaction and shorter plant root systems.

GEOreport 15.2 Slipping through our fingers

The U.S. Department of Agriculture estimated that more than 5 million acres of prime farmland are lost each year in the United States through mismanagement or conversion to nonagricultural uses. About half of all cropland in the United States and Canada (two of the few countries that monitor loss of topsoil) is experiencing excessive rates of soil erosion. Worldwide, about one-third of potentially farmable land has been lost to erosion, much of that in the past 40 years. The causes for degraded soils, in order of severity, include overgrazing, vegetation removal, agricultural practices, conversion to nonagricultural activities, overexploitation, and industrial and bioindustrial use.

▲**Figure 15.11 Desertification in Africa's Sahel region.** Herders carry straw to cattle outside a village in Mali. Ethnic tensions in this west African country are interfering with agricultural activities, worsening food shortages, and slowing efforts aimed toward sustainable land stewardship. [Nic Bothma/epa/Corbis.]

Erosion Rates and Costs In 2007, the NRCS reported a 43% decrease in soil erosion from water and wind on U.S. cropland between 1982 and 2007. Most of this decline occurred between 1982 and 1992, with erosion rates showing less variation since 1992. The study also revealed that erosion by water in rills and gullies in the United States varies geographically, with the majority (54%) concentrated in the Corn Belt, stretching from Ohio in the east to Iowa in the west, and in the northern Plains, stretching from Nebraska in the south into North Dakota. Ninety-seven percent of soil erosion from wind occurred in the Great Plains, Rocky Mountain Region, and Lake Region of Minnesota and Wisconsin.

In 2010, the Environmental Working Group reported that, according to scientists at Iowa State University, soil erosion rates are far higher than the NRCS estimates. According to these new studies, the effects of individual storm events are more significant for erosion than the long-term, statewide averages calculated by the NRCS. As the intensity of storm events increases with climate change, soil erosion may accelerate.

One recent study tabulated the monetary impact of lost soil nutrients and of other variables affected by erosion, estimating the sum of direct damage (to agricultural land) and indirect damage (to streams, society's infrastructure, and human health) to be more than $25 billion a year in the United States and hundreds of billions of dollars worldwide. However, this assessment remains controversial in the agricultural industry. The cost to bring erosion under control in the United States is estimated at approximately $8.5 billion, or about 30 cents on every dollar of damage and loss.

Desertification

Land degradation that occurs in dry regions is known as **desertification**, the expansion of deserts. As discussed in Geosystems Now, this worldwide phenomenon along the margins of semiarid and arid lands results from a combination of factors: poor agricultural practices, such as overgrazing and activities that abuse soil structure and fertility; improper soil-moisture management; salinization (the accumulation of salts on the soil surface, discussed later in the chapter) and nutrient depletion; and deforestation. A worsening causative force is global climate change, which is shifting temperature and precipitation patterns and causing poleward movement of Earth's subtropical high-pressure systems, discussed in previous chapters. Desertification is now affecting over a billion people worldwide, leading to losses of topsoil and declines in food production (**Figure 15.11**).

The map of desertification risk in Geosystems Now shows that many of the highest-risk lands are in India and central Asia. In fact, a 2009 mapping project showed

GEOreport 15.3 Overgrazing on Argentina's grasslands

Overgrazing occurs when the number of grazing animals is greater than the productive capacity of the land. The resulting reduction in plant leaf area weakens plants and leads to deterioration of vegetation and soils. In southern Argentina, sheep ranching is the primary economic activity in the expansive grasslands, once home to only one native grazing mammal: the guanaco, a relative of the llama. Although sheep numbers have declined since the 1950s, overgrazing over the past century has led to widespread desertification. Sustainable grazing practices are becoming a priority as this region seeks to preserve its economic base of wool and meat production and reverse the desertification trend.

that 25% of India is undergoing desertification. The severity of this problem is magnified by poverty in many of the affected areas, since most people lack the capital to change agricultural practices and implement conservation strategies.

CRITICAL**thinking 15.1**

Soil Losses—What to Do?

Using the information presented in the section "Human Impacts on Soils," break down the issue of soil loss into the forcing causes, impacts produced, and possible actions to slow soil degradation and loss. Next, consider the possible actions in terms of scale, moving from individual to local to regional to state and finally to national in scope. Given the problem and the scale you select, which solutions are best implemented, what actions do you suggest to reverse the situation of soil degradation here and abroad?

Soil Classification

Soil classification is complicated by the variety of interactions that create thousands of distinct soils—well over 15,000 soil types in the United States and Canada alone. A number of different classification systems are in use worldwide, including those from the United States, Canada, the United Kingdom, Germany, Australia, Russia, and the United Nations Food and Agricultural Organization (FAO). Each system reflects the environment of the country or countries in which it originated. Because of the involvement of interacting variables, classifying soils is similar to classifying climates.

Soil Taxonomy

The U.S. soil classification system, the **Soil Taxonomy**, was first developed by the NRCS in 1975. Information in this chapter is based on the publication *Keys to Soil Taxonomy*, now in its 12th edition (2014), available for free download at http://www.nrcs.usda.gov/wps/portal/nrcs/detail/national/nedc/training/soil/?cid=nrcs142p2_053580. Soil surveys and local soil maps for most U.S. counties are available from the NRCS (see http://www.nrcs.usda.gov/wps/portal/nrcs/main/national/soils/).

The basis for the Soil Taxonomy system is field observation of soil properties and morphology (appearance, form, and structure). The smallest unit of soil used in soil surveys is a **pedon**, a hexagonal column measuring 1 to 10 m^2 in top surface area (see Figure 15.4a). A pedon is considered a soil individual, and a soil profile within it is used to evaluate its soil horizons. In the Soil Taxonomy, pedons with similar characteristics are grouped together to form a *soil series*, the lowest and most precise level of the classification system.

The Soil Taxonomy is a sorted hierarchy with six levels, or categories, beginning with 15,000 *soil series* classifications. Sequentially higher-level categories are *soil families* (6000), *soil subgroups* (1200), *soil great groups* (230), *soil suborders* (47), and finally, the 12 *soil orders* discussed in this section.

Diagnostic Soil Horizons Soil scientists use diagnostic soil horizons to group soils into each soil series. A *diagnostic horizon* has distinctive physical properties (color, texture, structure, consistence, porosity, and moisture) or a dominant soil process (discussed below with the soil types). A diagnostic horizon that occurs at the surface or just below it is an **epipedon**. It may extend downward through the A horizon and may even include all or part of an illuviated B horizon. It is visibly darkened by organic matter and sometimes is leached of minerals. Excluded from consideration as part of the epipedon are alluvial deposits, eolian deposits, and cultivated areas because these are relatively short-lived surfaces that soil-forming processes would eventually erase. A diagnostic horizon that forms below the soil surface at varying depths is a **diagnostic subsurface horizon**. It may include part of the A or B horizon or both.

Pedogenic Regimes Prior to the U.S. Soil Taxonomy system, scientists used **pedogenic regimes** to describe soils. These regimes attach specific soil-forming processes to climatic regions. Although such climate-based regimes are convenient for relating climate and soil processes, the use of climatic variables as the sole basis of soil classification leads to uncertainty and inconsistency. In this chapter, we discuss each pedogenic regime with the soil order in which it most commonly occurs, even though each pedogenic process may be active in several soil orders and in different climates.

The five pedogenic regimes are:

- **Laterization**—a process that leaches most cations and silica (SiO_2) in humid and warm climates (discussed with Oxisols and shown in Figure 15.14)
- **Calcification**—a process that produces an illuviated accumulation of calcium carbonates in arid and semiarid deserts and grasslands (discussed with Aridisols and shown in Figure 15.16)
- **Salinization**—a process that concentrates salts in soils in climates with high potential evapotranspiration (PE) rates (discussed with Aridisols)
- **Podzolization**—a process of eluviation–illuviation of iron and aluminum oxides in an acid regime, associated with forest soils in cool climates (discussed with Spodosols and shown in Figure 15.22)
- **Gleization**—a process that results in an accumulation of humus and a thick, water-saturated gray layer of clay beneath, associated with poor drainage conditions, usually in cold, wet climates

Soil Orders of the Soil Taxonomy

The Soil Taxonomy includes 12 general soil orders, listed with a brief description in **Figure 15.12** (left side). Their worldwide distribution is shown on the map in

SOIL ORDER	DESCRIPTION/LOCATION
Oxisols	Tropical soils; hot, humid areas
Aridisols	Desert soils; hot, dry areas
Mollisols	Grassland soils; subhumid, semiarid lands
Alfisols	Moderately weathered forest soils; humid temperate forests
Ultisols	Highly weathered forest soils; subtropical forests
Spodosols	Northern conifer forest soils; cool, humid forests
Entisols	Recent soils; profile undeveloped, all climates
Inceptisols	Weakly developed soils; humid regions
Gelisols	Permafrost-affected soils; high latitudes and mountains
Andisols	Volcanic soils; areas of volcanic activity, especially Pacific Rim
Vertisols	Expandable clay soils; subtropics, tropics with sufficient dry period
Histosols	Organic soils; wetlands

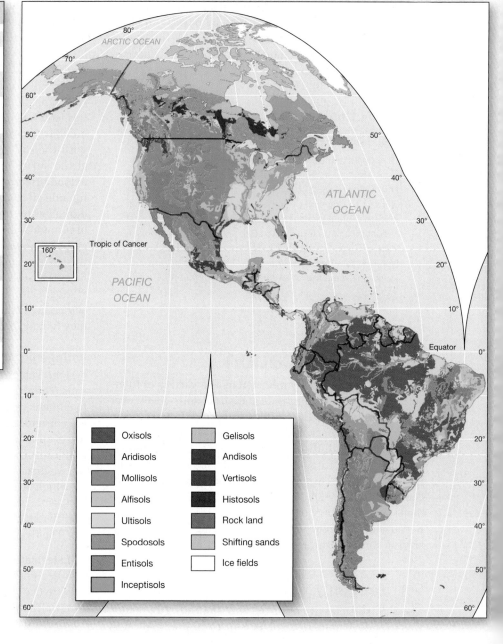

▲**Figure 15.12 Soil Taxonomy.** Worldwide distribution of the Soil Taxonomy's 12 soil orders, with each order listed and briefly described at left. [Adapted from Natural Resources Conservation Service maps, 1999, 2006.]

Figure 15.12 and in individual maps provided with the soil discussions that follow. Consult the maps as you read the descriptions; further information on each soil order is at http://soils.ag.uidaho.edu/soilorders/. Because the Soil Taxonomy evaluates each soil order on the basis of its particular characteristics, there is no priority to the classification. However, we use a progression arranged loosely by latitude; we begin, as in Chapter 7 (on climates) and Chapter 17 (on terrestrial biomes), along the equator.

Oxisols The intense moisture, high temperature, and uniform daylength of equatorial latitudes profoundly affect soils. In these generally old landscapes, exposed to tropical conditions for millennia or hundreds of millennia, soils are well developed, and their minerals are altered (except in certain newer volcanic soils in Indonesia—the Andisols). Thus, Oxisols are among the most mature soils on Earth. Distinct horizons usually are lacking where these soils are well drained (**Figure 15.13a**). Related vegetation is the luxuriant and diverse tropical and equatorial rain forest.

Oxisols (tropical soils) are so named because they have a distinctive horizon of iron and aluminum oxides. The concentration of oxides results from heavy precipitation, which leaches soluble minerals and soil constituents from the A horizon. Typical Oxisols are reddish (from

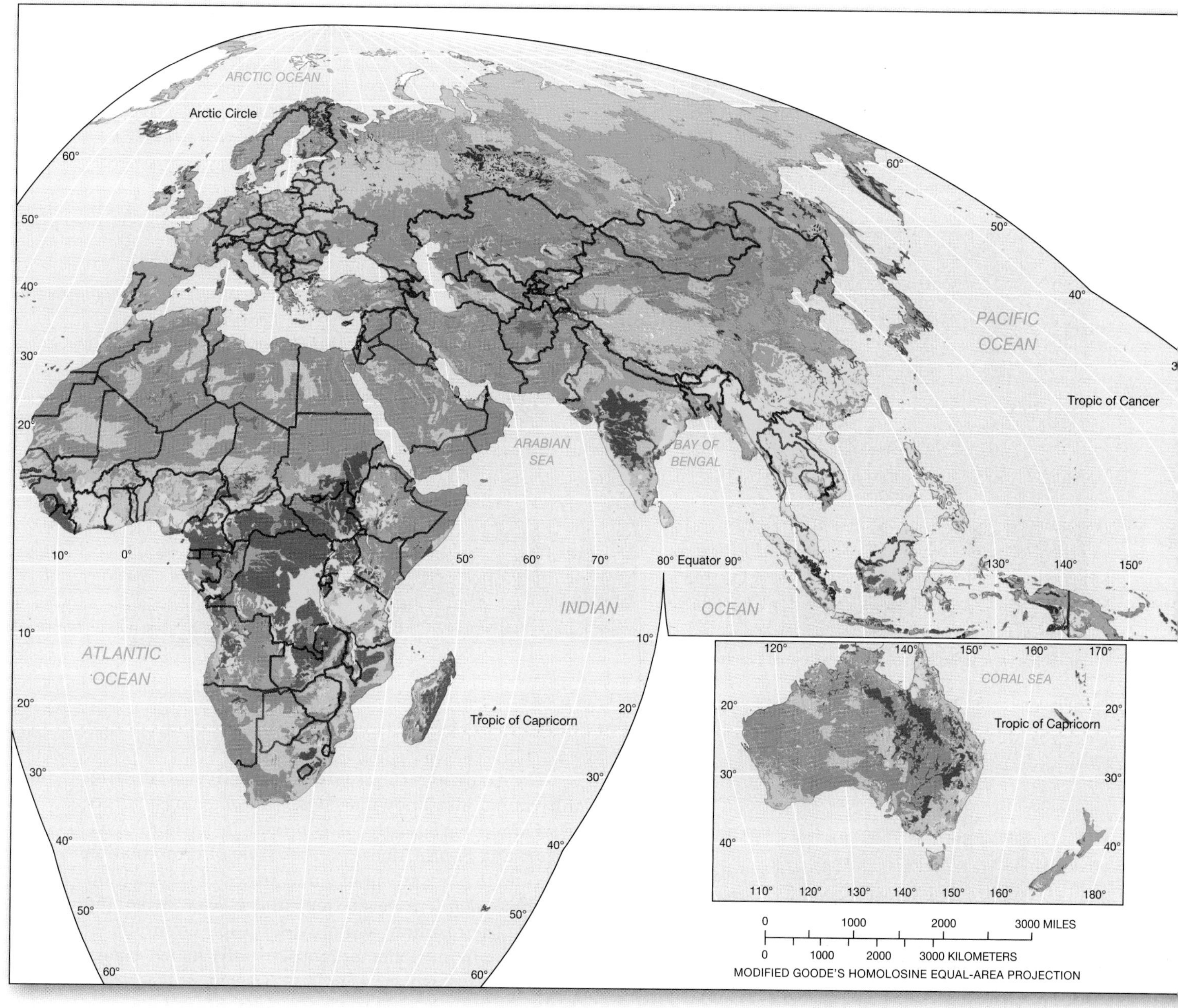

the iron oxide) or yellowish (from the aluminum oxides), with a weathered claylike texture, sometimes in a granular soil structure that is easily broken apart. The high degree of eluviation removes basic cations and colloidal material to lower illuviated horizons. Thus, Oxisols are low in CEC and fertility, except in regions augmented by alluvial or volcanic materials. In short, Oxisols have a diagnostic subsurface horizon that is highly weathered, contains iron and aluminum oxides, is at least 30 cm (12 in.) thick, and lies within 2 m (6.5 ft) of the surface (see **Figure 15.13**).

The world's lush rain forests are found in regions of Oxisols, even though these soils are poor in inorganic nutrients. This forest system relies on the recycling of nutrients from soil organic matter to sustain fertility; however, this nutrient-recycling ability is quickly lost when the ecosystem is disturbed.

Figure 15.14 illustrates *laterization*, the leaching process that operates in well-drained soils in warm, humid tropical and subtropical climates. If the soils are subjected to repeated wetting and drying, a *hardpan* (a hardened soil layer)—in this case, an iron-rich and humus-poor clay with quartz and other minerals—develops in the lower A or in the B horizon. This process forms *plinthite* (from the Greek *plinthos*, meaning "brick"), also known as a *laterite*, which can be quarried in blocks and used as a building material (**Figure 15.13c**).

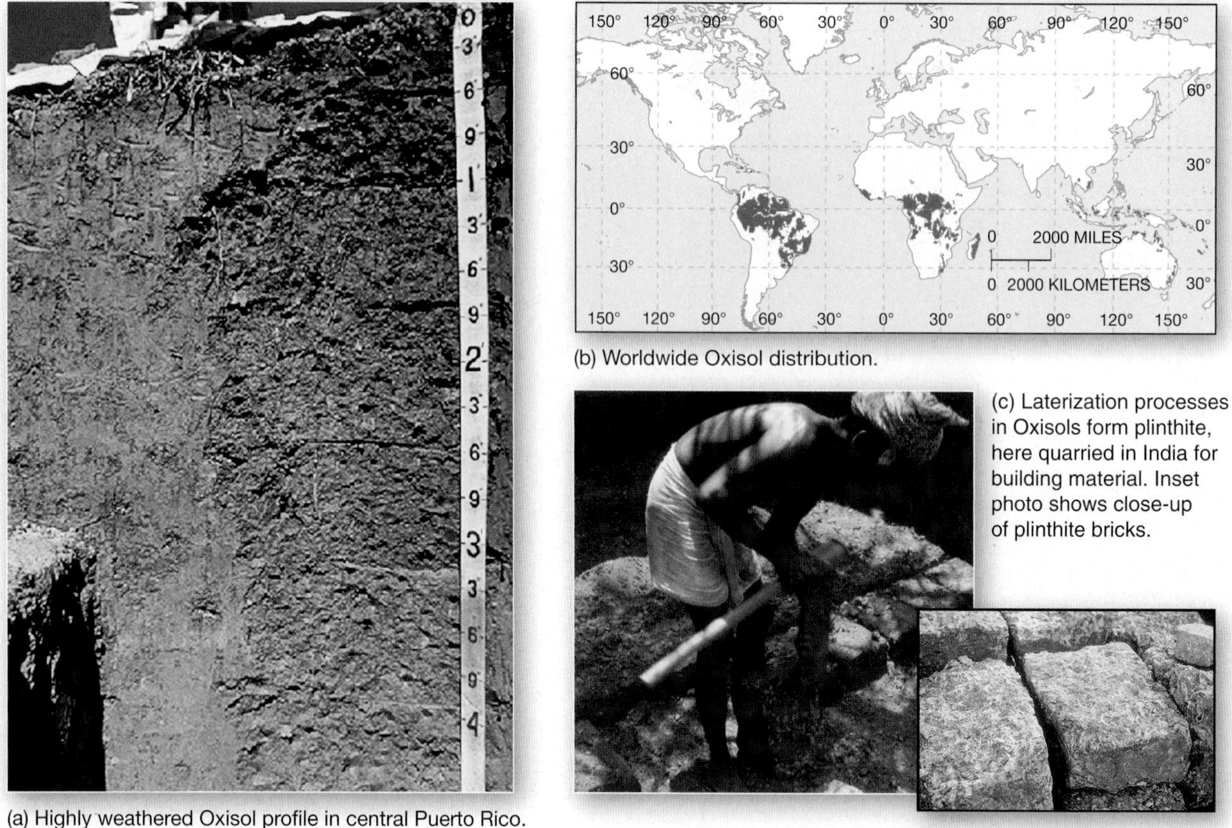

(a) Highly weathered Oxisol profile in central Puerto Rico.

(b) Worldwide Oxisol distribution.

(c) Laterization processes in Oxisols form plinthite, here quarried in India for building material. Inset photo shows close-up of plinthite bricks.

▲Figure 15.13 Oxisols. [(a) Marbut Collection, Soil Science Society of America, Inc. (c) Satprem Maïni/Auroville Earth Institute. (inset) USDA.]

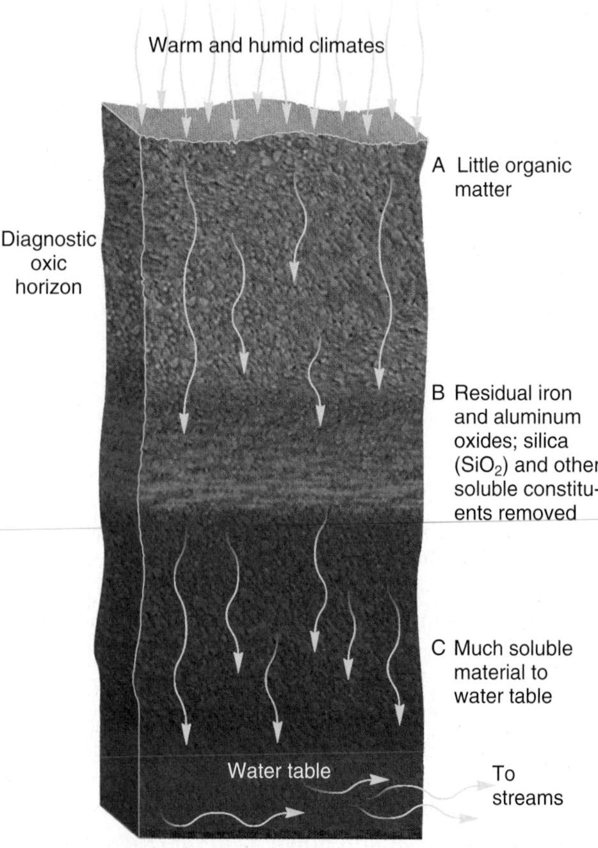

▲Figure 15.14 A soil undergoing laterization. Leaching occurs as water moves downward through the soil.

The traditional agricultural practice of shifting cultivation, also known as *slash-and-burn agriculture* or *swidden agriculture*, is common in parts of Asia, Africa, and South America. This style of crop rotation begins with the cutting of small tracts of tropical forests into *slash* (cut vegetation) that is then dried and burned. The resultant ash provides a soil environment that is rich in nutrients for crops, usually maize, beans, and squash. However, after 3 to 5 years, soil fertility declines through leaching by intense rainfall, causing farmers to shift cultivation to another tract, where the process is repeated. After a period of recovery, a previously used tract can again be cut and burned as the cycle repeats.

Although this practice has occurred for thousands of years, the orderly land rotation inherent to its success is now disrupted by the influx of foreign plantation interests, development by local governments, vastly increased population pressures, and conversion of vast forest tracts to pasturage. Permanent tracts of cleared land, taken out of the former rotation mode, have been severely eroded. When Oxisols are disturbed, soil loss can exceed 1000 tons per square kilometer per year, not to mention the greatly increased extinction rates of plant and animal species that accompany soil depletion and rain forest destruction. The regions dominated by the Oxisols and rain forests are rightfully the focus of much worldwide environmental attention.

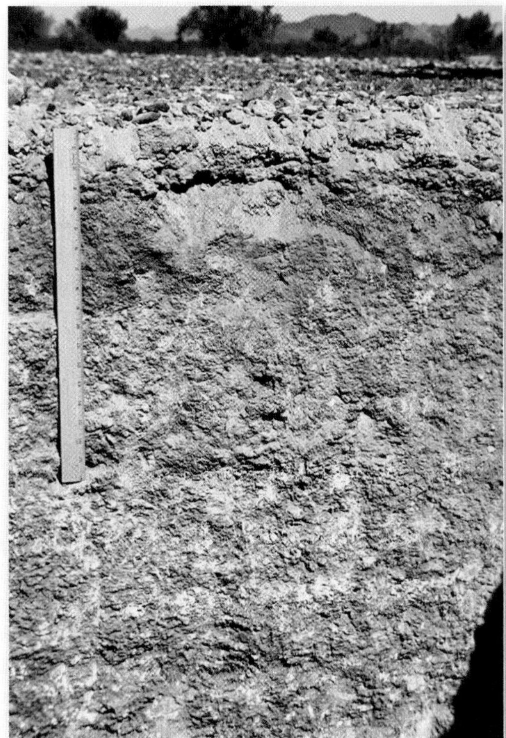

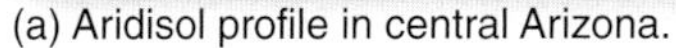

(a) Aridisol profile in central Arizona.

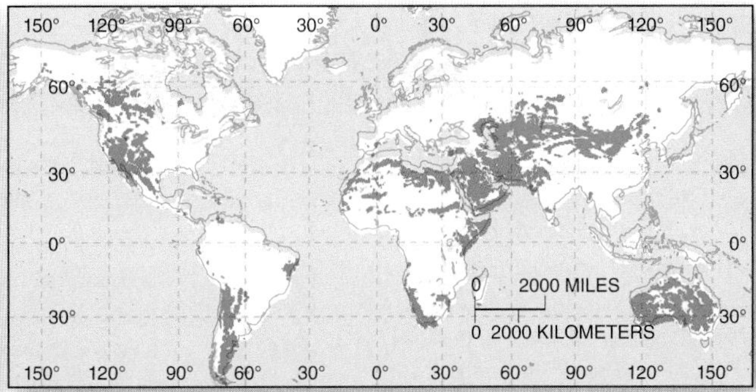

(b) Worldwide Aridisol distribution.

(c) Irrigated cropland and surrounding desert, Imperial Valley, southern California.

▲**Figure 15.15 Aridisols.** [(a) Marbut Collection, Soil Science Society of America, Inc. (c) Bobbé Christopherson.]

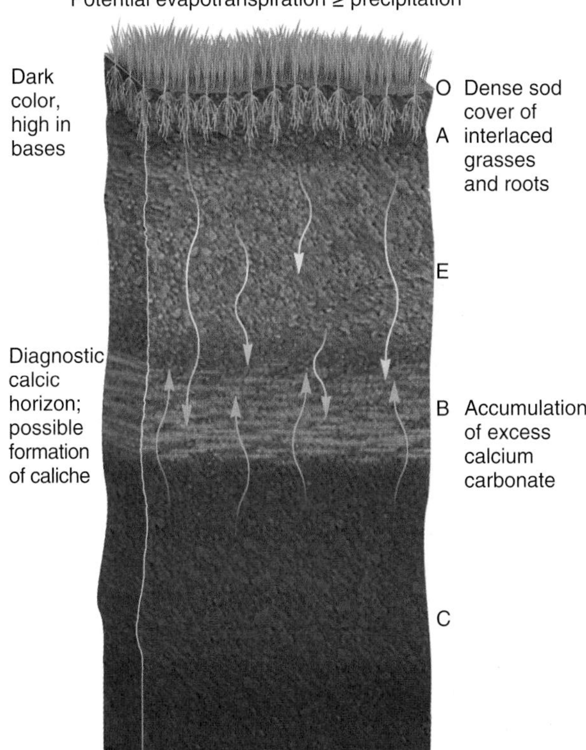

◄**Figure 15.16 A soil undergoing calcification.** This process occurs in desert and grassland soils in climatic regimes that have potential evapotranspiration equal to or greater than precipitation.

Aridisols The largest single soil order occurs in the world's dry regions. **Aridisols** (desert soils) occupy approximately 19% of Earth's land surface (see Figure 15.12). A pale, light soil color near the surface is diagnostic (**Figure 15.15a**).

Not surprisingly, the water balance in Aridisol regions is characterized by periods of soil-moisture deficit and generally inadequate soil moisture for plant growth. High potential evapotranspiration and low precipitation produce very shallow soil horizons. Usually, these soils have adequate moisture for only 3 months a year. Lacking water and therefore lacking vegetation, Aridisols also lack organic matter of any consequence. Low precipitation means infrequent leaching.

Calcification is a soil process characteristic of Aridisols and some Mollisols (discussed ahead) in which calcium carbonate or magnesium carbonate accumulates in the B and C horizons. Calcification by calcium carbonate ($CaCO_3$) forms a diagnostic calcic subsurface horizon (**Figure 15.16**).

focusstudy 15.1 Pollution

Selenium Concentration in Soils: The Death of Kesterson

About 95% of the irrigated acreage in the United States lies west of the 98th meridian, on lands that are increasingly troubled with salinization and waterlogging problems. In these semiarid and arid regions, river discharge is inadequate to dilute and remove wastewater from the fields, which are often purposely overwatered to keep salts away from the effective rooting depth of the crops. One solution is to place field drains beneath the soil to collect gravitational water (**Figure 15.1.1**). But the water must then go somewhere, and for the San Joaquin Valley of central California, this problem triggered a 25-year controversy surrounding toxic levels of selenium in the wetland ecosystem of Kesterson Reservoir.

Selenium Toxicity

Selenium is a trace element that occurs naturally in bedrock, particularly Cretaceous shales found throughout the U.S. West. Toxic effects of selenium were reported during the 1980s in some domestic animals grazing on grasses grown in selenium-rich soils in the Great Plains.

In California, the coastal mountain ranges are a significant source region for selenium. As parent materials weather, selenium-rich alluvium washes into valleys, forming Aridisols that become productive with the addition of irrigation water. Selenium then becomes concentrated by evaporation in farmlands and from there may be transported by irrigation drainage into wetlands, where it bioaccumulates to toxic levels. California's western San Joaquin Valley is one of at least nine sites in the western United States experiencing contamination from increasing selenium concentrations.

Contamination at Kesterson

Central California's potential drain outlets for agricultural wastewater are limited. Yet by the late 1970s, about 80 miles of a drain had been built in the western San Joaquin Valley, without an outlet or even a formal plan to complete the drain. Large-scale irrigation of corporate-owned farms continued in the area, supplying the field drains with salty, selenium-laden runoff that flowed through the unfinished drain, which stopped abruptly at the boundary of the Kesterson National Wildlife Refuge (**Figure 15.1.2**).

The selenium-tainted drainage took only 3 years to contaminate the wildlife refuge, which subsequently was officially declared a toxic waste site. Selenium was first taken in by aquatic life forms (e.g., marsh plants, plankton, and insects) and then made its way up the food chain and into the diets of higher life forms in the refuge. According to U.S. Fish and Wildlife Service scientists, the toxicity causes genetic abnormalities and death in wildlife, including all varieties of birds that nested at Kesterson; approximately 90% of the exposed birds perished or suffered abnormalities. Because this refuge was a major migration flyway and stopover point for birds from throughout the Western Hemisphere, its contamination also violated several multinational wildlife protection treaties.

Restoration Efforts

The field drains were sealed and removed in 1986, following a court order that forced the federal government to uphold existing laws. Irrigation water then immediately began backing up in the corporate farmlands, producing waterlogged and selenium-contaminated soils. The Kesterson Unit became part of the San Luis National Wildlife Refuge—and selenium control and restoration became a priority.

Frustrated, large-scale corporate agricultural interests pressured the federal government to finish the drain, extending it either to San Francisco Bay or to the ocean. In 1996, the Grasslands Bypass Project was implemented by the U.S. Bureau of Reclamation to prevent the discharge of agricultural drainage water into the wetlands and wildlife refuges of central California. Thus, agricultural drain water now moves through the old San Luis Drain to Mud Slough, a natural waterway through the San Luis National Wildlife Refuge, and then on to the San Joaquin River, the San Joaquin–Sacramento delta, and eventually San Francisco Bay. Initially, selenium levels increased in those channels, although fluctuations downward in concentrations were noted as well. Biological monitoring continues today.

The Kesterson tragedy provided important lessons regarding irrigation practices and the movement of selenium from sedimentary rock formations into aquatic ecosystems. The pathway of selenium from geologic source through agricultural drainage and ultimately into waterfowl is today known as the "Kesterson Effect."

▲**Figure 15.1.1 Drainage canal.** A drainage canal collects contaminated water from field drains and directs it into the Salton Sea. Such soil-moisture tile drains and collection channels are also in use in the San Joaquin Valley. [Robert Christopherson.]

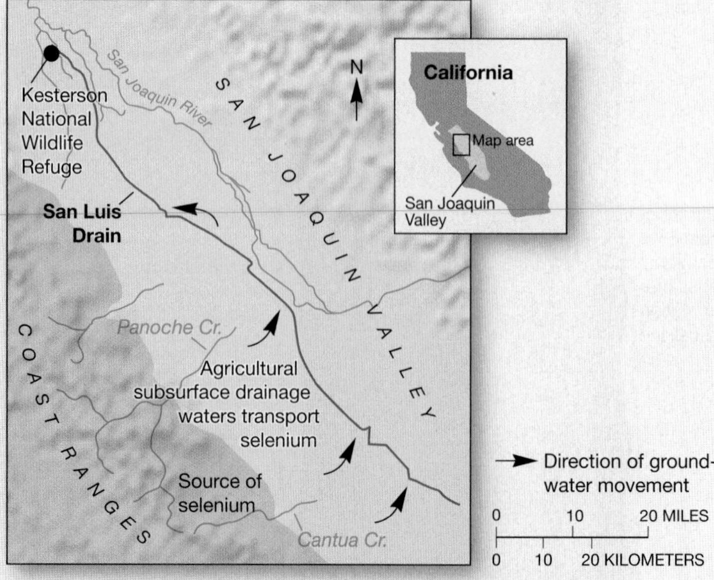

▲**Figure 15.1.2 Kesterson locator map.** The source of selenium is the Coast Ranges; surface runoff delivered this trace element over thousands of years to the soils of the region. The agricultural drains complete the delivery to the wildlife refuge. [USGS.]

Aridisols can be made productive for agriculture using irrigation. Two related problems common in irrigated lands are salinization and water logging. *Salinization* occurs as salts dissolved in soil water migrate to surface horizons and are deposited as the water evaporates. These deposits appear as subsurface salty horizons, which will damage or kill plants if the horizons occur near the root zone. Salinization is common in Aridisols and results from the excessive potential evapotranspiration rates in arid and semiarid regions. Waterlogging (saturation of the soil that interferes with plant growth) occurs with the introduction of irrigation water for farming, especially in soils that are poorly drained.

Irrigated agriculture has increased greatly since 1800, when only 8 million hectares (about 20 million acres) were irrigated worldwide. Today, approximately 255 million hectares (about 630 million acres) are irrigated, many of them Aridisols, and this figure is on the increase in some parts of the world (Figure 15.15c). However, in many of these areas, crop production has decreased and even ended because of salt buildup in the soils. Examples include areas along the Tigris and Euphrates Rivers in Iraq, the Indus River Valley in Pakistan, sections of South America and Africa, and the western United States.

In California, the former Kesterson National Wildlife Refuge, located on Aridisols, was reduced to a toxic waste dump in the early 1980s by contaminated agricultural drainage. Focus Study 15.1 elaborates on the Kesterson tragedy.

Mollisols Some of Earth's most significant agricultural soils are **Mollisols** (grassland soils). This group includes seven recognized suborders that vary in fertility. The dominant diagnostic horizon is a dark, organic surface layer some 25 cm (10 in.) thick (**Figure 15.17**). As the Latin origin of the name implies (*mollis*, meaning "soft," is the root of *mollify* and *emollient*), Mollisols are soft, even when dry. They have granular or crumbly peds, loosely arranged when dry. These humus-rich soils are high in basic cations (calcium, magnesium, and potassium) and have a high CEC and therefore high fertility. In soil moisture, these soils are intermediate between humid and arid. The B horizon can have clay accumulation and can be enriched in calcium carbonate in drier climates. The carbonate-enriched B horizon is thickest along the boundary between dry and humid climates (**Figure 15.18**).

Mollisols include soils of the steppes and prairies—the North American Great Plains, the Palouse of Washington State, the Pampas of Argentina, and the region stretching from Manchuria in China through to Europe. Agriculture in these areas ranges from large-scale commercial grain farming to grazing along the drier portions. With fertilization or soil-building practices, high crop

(a) Mollisol profile in eastern Idaho, from loess that is high in calcium carbonate, related to the soils of the Palouse agricultural region.

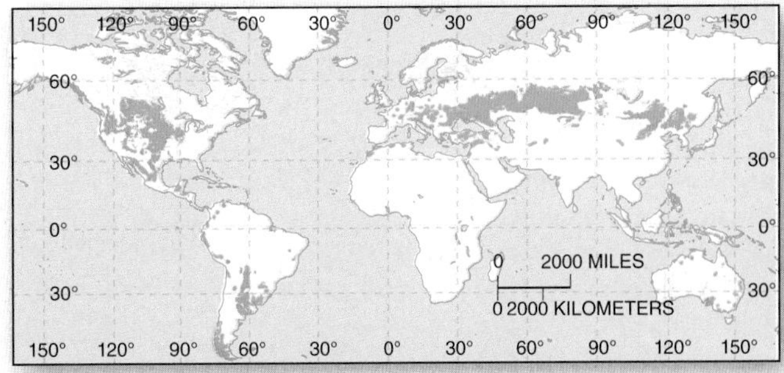

(b) Worldwide Mollisol distribution.

(c) Wheat flourishes in the fertile Palouse of eastern Washington.

▲**Figure 15.17 Mollisols.** [(a) Marbut Collection, Soil Science Society of America, Inc. (c) Bobbé Christopherson.]

yields are common. The "fertile triangle" of Ukraine, Russia, and western portions of the former Soviet Union is of this soil type.

In North America, the Great Plains straddle the 98th meridian, which is coincident with the 51-cm (20-in.) isohyet of annual precipitation—wetter to the east and drier to the west. The Mollisols here mark the historic division between the short- and tall-grass prairies.

Alfisols Spatially, **Alfisols** (moderately weathered forest soils) are the most widespread of the soil orders, extending in five suborders from near the equator to high latitudes. Representative Alfisol areas include Boromo and Burkina Faso (interior western Africa); Fort Nelson, British Columbia; the states near the Great Lakes; and the valleys of central California. Most Alfisols are grayish brown to reddish and are considered moist versions of the Mollisol soil group. Moderate eluviation is present as well as a subsurface horizon of illuviated clays and clay formation because of a pattern of increased precipitation (**Figure 15.19**).

Alfisols have moderate to high reserves of basic cations and are fertile. However, productivity depends on moisture and temperature. Alfisols usually are supplemented by a moderate application of lime and fertilizer in areas of active agriculture.

Some of the best U.S. farmland occurs in the humid continental, hot summer climates surrounding the Great Lakes. Alfisols in this region produce grains, hay, and dairy products. The moist winter, dry summer pattern of the

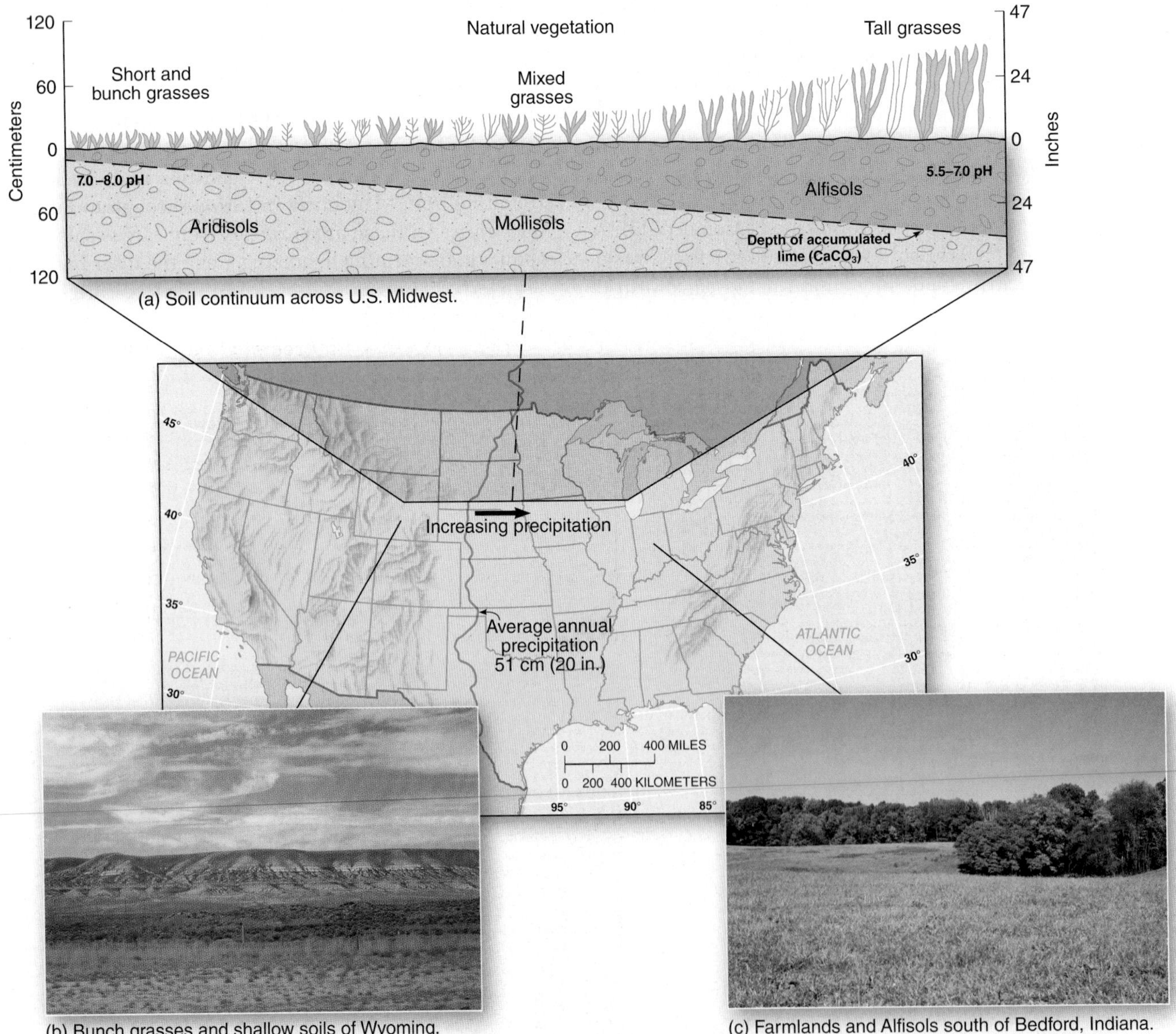

▲**Figure 15.18 Soils of the Midwest.** Aridisols (to the west), Mollisols (central), and Alfisols (to the east) are part of a soil continuum in the north-central United States and southern Canadian prairies. Note the changes that occur in soil pH and the depth of accumulated calcium carbonate. Note the 51-cm isohyet of annual precipitation on the map, roughly along the 98th meridian—drier to the west and wetter to the east. [(a) Illustration adapted from N. C. Brady, *The Nature and Properties of Soils*, 10th ed., © 1990 by Macmillan Publishing Company, adapted by permission. (b) Robert Christopherson. (c) Bobbé Christopherson.]

(a) Alfisol profile in northern Idaho loess.

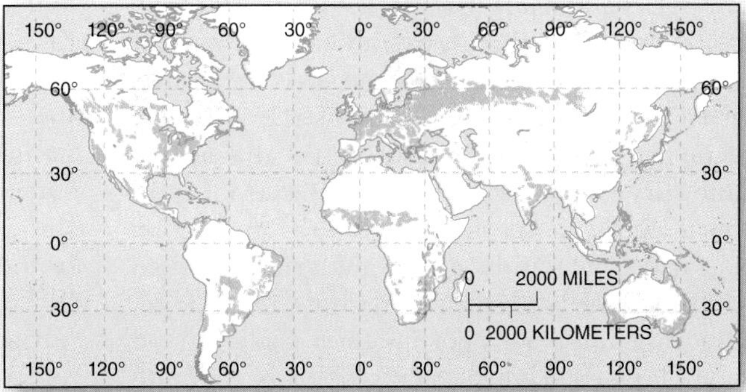

(b) Worldwide Alfisol distribution.

(c) An olive orchard in northern California, where virtually all U.S. olive production occurs.

▲**Figure 15.19 Alfisols.** [(a) Marbut Collection, Soil Science Society of America, Inc. (c) Bobbé Christopherson.]

Mediterranean climate also produces Alfisols. These naturally productive soils are farmed intensively for subtropical fruits, nuts, and special crops that grow in only a few locales worldwide—for example, California olives, grapes, citrus, artichokes, almonds, and figs (Figure 15.19c).

Ultisols Farther south in the United States are the **Ultisols** (highly weathered forest soils). An Alfisol might evolve into an Ultisol, given time and exposure to increased weathering under moist conditions. These soils tend to be reddish because of residual iron and aluminum oxides in the A horizon (**Figure 15.20**).

The relatively high precipitation in Ultisol regions causes greater mineral alteration and more eluvial leaching than in other soils. Therefore, the level of basic cations is lower, and the soil fertility is lower. Fertility is further reduced by certain agricultural practices and the effect of soil-damaging crops such as cotton and tobacco, which deplete nitrogen and expose soil to erosion. These soils respond well to good management—for example, crop rotation restores nitrogen, and certain cultivation practices prevent the washing action of rain that leads to soil erosion. Peanut plantings assist in nitrogen restoration.

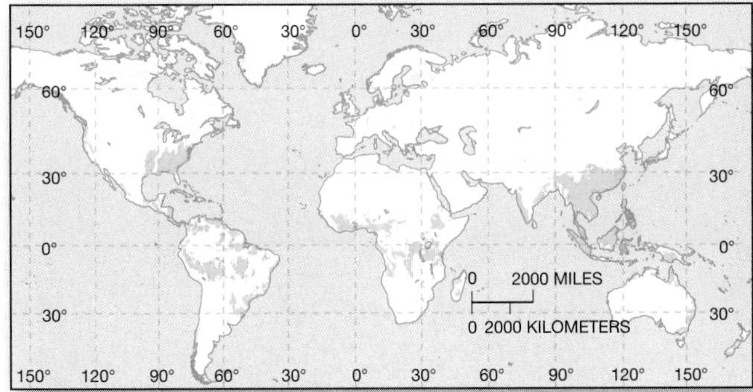

(a) Worldwide Ultisol distribution.

▲**Figure 15.20 Ultisols.** [(b) Bobbé Christopherson.]

(b) Ultisols planted with rows of peanuts in west-central Georgia have the characteristic reddish color.

Spodosols The **Spodosols** (northern coniferous forest soils) occur generally to the north and east of the Alfisols, mainly in forested areas in the humid continental mild-summer climates of northern North America and Eurasia, Denmark, the Netherlands, and southern England. Because comparable climates are rare in the Southern Hemisphere, this soil type is rare there. Spodosols form from sandy parent materials, shaded under evergreen forests of spruce, fir, and pine. Spodosols with more moderate properties form under mixed or deciduous forests. An ashen-gray color is common in these subarctic forest soils (**Figure 15.21**). Agricultural use of Spodosols may require the addition of a soil amendment such as limestone to increase crop production by raising the pH of these acidic soils.

The colors of a Spodosol profile display the eluvial–illuvial relationship in soils produced by *podzolization*. These soils commonly have an O horizon, and some have an A horizon below the O. Beneath that is the light-colored E horizon, characterized by eluviated iron and aluminum oxides and bases leached downward through the soil profile (**Figure 15.22**). Beneath is the B horizon containing illuviated organic matter and iron and aluminum oxides. Podzolization is most prominent in sandy parent materials and in the low-pH soil solution produced by the decomposition of base-poor, acid-rich evergreen tree litter.

Entisols The **Entisols** (recent, undeveloped soils) lack vertical development of their horizons and occur in many climates worldwide. Entisols are true soils, but they have not had sufficient time to generate the usual horizons.

Entisols generally are poor agricultural soils. The same conditions that inhibit complete development—too much or too little water, poor structure, and insufficient accumulation of weathered nutrients—also prevent adequate fertility. The exception is Entisols formed from river silt deposits, which are quite fertile. Entisols are

▼Figure 15.21 Spodosols. [(a) Marbut Collection, Soil Science Society of America, Inc. (c) and (d) Bobbé Christopherson.]

(a) Spodosol profile from northern New York.

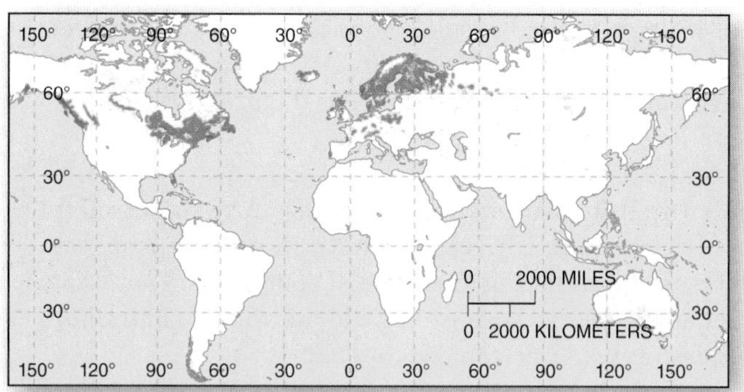

(b) Worldwide Spodosol distribution.

(c) Characteristic temperate forest and Spodosols in the cool, moist climate of central Vancouver Island.

(d) Freshly plowed Spodosols (Podzolic soils, in the Canadian System) near Lakeville, Nova Scotia. The soils are formed beneath coniferous forest before the land is cleared for agriculture.

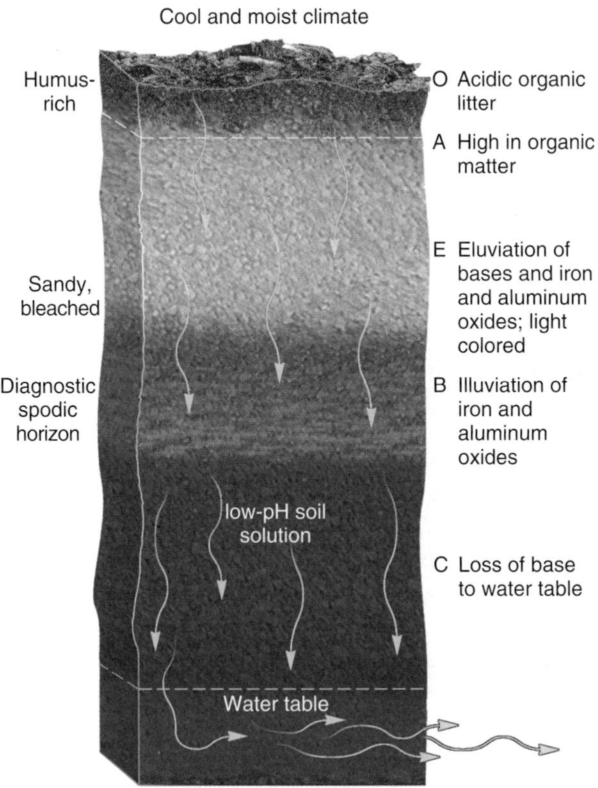

▲**Figure 15.22 A soil undergoing podzolization.** This process is typical in cool and moist climatic regimes and Spodosols.

characteristically found on active slopes, floodplain alluvium, poorly drained tundra, tidal mudflats, dune sands and ergs, and plains of glacial outwash. **Figure 15.23** shows a landscape of Entisols in a desert climate where shales formed the parent material.

Inceptisols Although more developed than the Entisols, **Inceptisols** (weakly developed soils) are young, infertile soils. This order includes a wide variety of different soils, all having in common a lack of maturity and most showing only the beginning stages of weathering.

Inceptisols are associated with moist soil regimes and are regarded as eluvial because they demonstrate a loss of soil constituents throughout their profile; however, they do retain some weatherable minerals. This soil group has no distinct illuvial horizons. Most of the glacially derived till and outwash materials from New York down through the Appalachians are Inceptisols, as is the alluvium on the Mekong and Ganges floodplains.

Gelisols The **Gelisols** (cold and frozen soils) contain permafrost within 2 m (6.5 ft) of the surface and are found at high latitudes (Canada, Alaska, Russia, Arctic Ocean islands, and the Antarctic Peninsula) and high elevations (mountains). Temperatures in these regions are at or below 0°C (32°F) , making soil development a slow process and disturbances of the soil long-lasting. Cold temperatures slow the decomposition of materials in the soil, so Gelisols can store large amounts of organic matter; thick O horizons are common (**Figure 15.24**). Only Histosols (discussed ahead) have as high a content of organic matter as Gelisols.

Gelisols contain about half of the pool of global carbon. The latest estimate of the carbon contained in these periglacial soils is 1.7 trillion tons. When permafrost thaws, substantial amounts of greenhouse gases are released into the atmosphere. Warming in the higher latitudes begins the process; Gelisols can quickly become wet and soggy with only a slight shift in their thermal balance. As thawing progresses, the poorly decomposed organic content in the soil begins to decay, and its decomposition releases enormous quantities of carbon dioxide into the atmosphere through increased respiration. Another greenhouse gas, methane, is released as well (discussed in Chapter 8).

Gelisols are subject to *cryoturbation* (frost churning and mixing) in the freeze–thaw cycle in the active layer (see Chapter 14). This process disrupts soil horizons, pulling organic material to lower layers and drawing rocky C-horizon material to the surface, a process that often forms patterned ground.

◀**Figure 15.23 Entisols.** A landscape showing Entisols—undeveloped soils forming in the shales of the Anza–Borrego Desert, California. [Bobbé Christopherson.]

◄**Figure 15.24 Gelisols.** [(b) and (c) Bobbé Christopherson.]

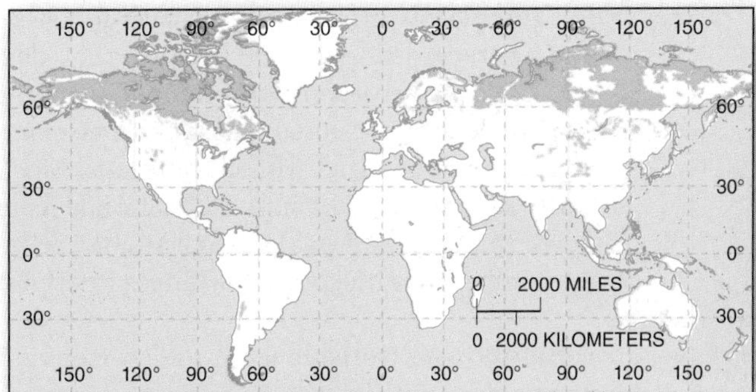

(a) Worldwide Gelisol distribution.

(b) The tundra is green in the brief summer season on Spitsbergen Island, northern Norway, as the active layer thaws.

(c) Fibrous organic content exposed on the underside of a soil clod, Spitsbergen.

Andisols Areas of volcanic activity feature **Andisols** (soils formed from volcanic parent materials). Andisols are derived from volcanic ash and glass and frequently bury previous soil horizons with materials from repeated eruptions. Volcanic soils have high mineral content because they are recharged by eruptions.

Weathering and mineral transformations are important in this soil order. For example, volcanic glass weathers readily into a clay colloid and oxides of aluminum and iron. Andisols have a high CEC and high water-holding ability and develop moderate fertility, although phosphorus availability is an occasional problem. In Hawai'i, fields of Andisols produce coffee, pineapples, macadamia nuts, and small amounts of sugar cane as important cash crops. Andisol distribution is small in areal extent; however, such soils are locally important in regions associated with the volcanic Pacific Rim, discussed in Chapter 9 (**Figure 15.25**).

►**Figure 15.25 Andisols in agricultural production.** An onion plantation in the Chiriquí Province on the west coast of Panama in Central America. [Alfredo Maiquez/Getty Images.]

Vertisols Soils high in expandable clays are **Vertisols**. Diagnostic horizons are usually absent, and an A horizon is common (**Figure 15.26**). Vertisols are located in regions experiencing highly variable soil-moisture balances through the seasons. These soils occur in areas of subhumid to semiarid moisture and moderate to high temperature. Vertisols frequently form in savannas and grasslands of tropical and subtropical climates and are sometimes associated with a distinct dry season following a wet season. Although widespread in their distribution, individual Vertisol units are limited in extent.

These deep clay soils swell when moistened and shrink when dried. They contain more than 30% swelling clays (clays that swell significantly when they absorb water), such as *montmorillonite*. In the drying process, they may form vertical cracks as wide as 2–3 cm (0.8–1.2 in.) and up to 40 cm (16 in.) deep. Loose material falls into these cracks, only to disappear when the soil again expands and the cracks close. After many such cycles, soil contents tend to invert, or mix vertically, bringing lower horizons to the surface.

Despite the fact that clay soils become plastic and heavy when wet and leave little soil moisture available for plants, Vertisols are high in bases and nutrients and thus are some of the better farming soils where they occur. Vertisols often are planted with grain sorghums, corn, and cotton (Figure 15.26c).

CRITICAL**thinking** 15.2

Soil Observations

Select a small soil sample from your campus or an area near where you live. Based on the sections in this chapter on soil characteristics, properties, and formation, describe the sample as completely as you can. Using the general soil map and any other sources available (e.g., local agriculture extension service, Internet, related department on campus), are you able to roughly place this sample in one of the soil orders?

(a) Vertisol profile in the Lajas Valley of Puerto Rico.

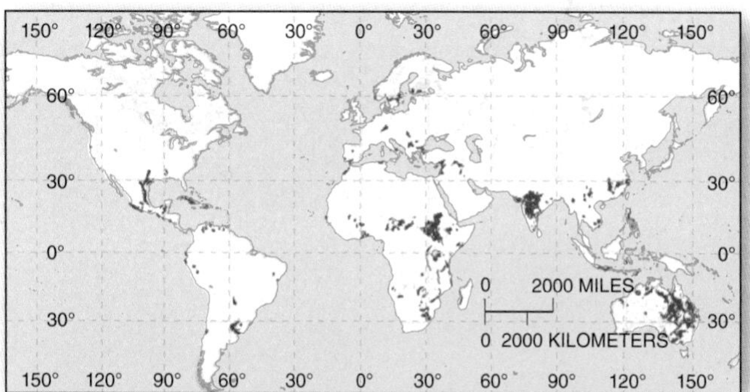

(b) Worldwide Vertisol distribution.

(c) Commercial sorghum crop planted in Vertisols on the Texas coastal plain, northeast of Palacios. Note the characteristic dark soil color.

▲**Figure 15.26 Vertisols.** [(a) Marbut Collection, Soil Science Society of America, Inc. (c) Bobbé Christopherson.]

GEO**report** 15.4 Biological soil crusts

In arid and semiarid regions, where vegetation is sparse or absent, soil surfaces are host to a community of organisms that glue soil particles together, forming a crust several centimeters thick. Such a biological soil crust, also known as a cryptobiotic crust, helps stabilize soils and prevent wind and water erosion. The organisms in these crusts include cyanobacteria (discussed in Chapter 16), algae, lichens, mosses, fungi, and other bacteria, all of which grow on the soil surfaces between vascular plants. Such crusts trap and store water, nutrients, and organic matter for vegetation growth, but are easily disturbed by humans and animals. For photos and more information, see http://www.nps.gov/cany/naturescience/soils.htm.

Histosols Accumulations of thick organic matter can form **Histosols** (organic soils). In the midlatitudes, when conditions are right, beds of former lakes may turn into Histosols, with water gradually replaced by organic material to form a bog. (We discuss bogs and lake succession in Chapter 16.) Histosols also form in small, poorly drained depressions, where conditions can be ideal for significant deposits of sphagnum peat to form (**Figure 15.27**).

Peat beds, often more than 2 m (6.5 ft) thick, can be cut by hand with a spade into blocks, which are then dried, baled, and sold as a soil amendment (Figure 15.27a). Once dried, the peat blocks burn hot and smoky. Peat is the first stage in the natural formation of lignite, an intermediate step toward coal. The Histosols that formed in lush swamp environments in the Carboniferous Period (359 to 299 million years ago) eventually underwent coalification to become coal deposits.

Most Histosols are **hydric soils**, defined as soils that are saturated or flooded for long enough periods of time to develop anaerobic (oxygen-free) conditions during the growing season. The presence of hydric soils is the basis for the legal delineation of wetlands, which are protected from dredging, filling, and the discharge of pollutants under the U.S. Clean Water Act. Bogs are a type of wetland, and many Histosols develop in wetland environments. Entisols are another soil order that frequently develops as hydric soils in large river valleys and along coastlines.

When wetlands containing organic soils are drained for agriculture or other purposes, land subsidence can occur through compaction. Additionally, oxidation and the action of soil microbes break down organic matter, releasing carbon dioxide gas. Rapid land subsidence related to the breakdown of Histosols is happening in two large U.S. wetland ecosystems—the Florida Everglades and California's Sacramento–San Joaquin River Delta (look back to Figure 12.26b on page 398). In the Everglades, some areas have subsided 1.5 m (5.0 ft), or more, since the early 1900s, as a result of water diversion and wetland drainage.

(a) A Histosol profile on Mainland Island in the Orkneys, north of Scotland. The inset photo shows drying blocks of peat, used as fuel. Note the fibrous texture of the sphagnum moss growing on the surface and the darkening layers with depth in the soil profile as the peat is compressed and chemically altered.

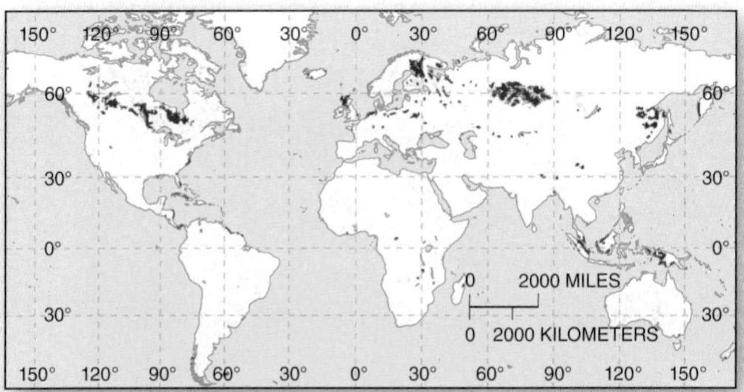

(b) Worldwide Histosol distribution.

(c) A bog in coastal Maine, near Popham Beach State Park.

▲**Figure 15.27 Histosols.** [(a) and (c) Bobbé Christopherson.]

GEOreport 15.5 Huge tropical peat bog discovered in Africa

In 2014, a team of scientists confirmed the presence of a massive peat bog in the Congo River basin in west–central Africa. The Congo Basin bog, first observed in satellite images and later confirmed by a research team on the ground, covers some 100,000 to 200,000 km^2 (38,000 to 76,000 mi^2), with the peat layer reaching a depth of 7 m (23 ft). The discovery is unusual, not only for the sheer size of the peatland, but also for its presence in a tropical climate—peat is more often found in colder areas where vegetation decomposition happens slowly. Scientists are dating and analyzing vegetation in peat samples from the bog to understand past climate in this little-studied region of Africa.

SOILS IMPACT HUMANS

- Soils are the foundation of basic ecosystem function and are a critical resource for agriculture.
- Soils store carbon dioxide and other greenhouse gases in soil organic matter.

HUMANS IMPACT SOILS

- Humans have modified soils through agricultural activities. Recently, fertilizer use, nutrient depletion, and salinization have increased soil degradation.
- Poor land-use practices are combining with changing climate to cause desertification, soil erosion, and the loss of prime farmland.

15a

Grapevines grow in the Andisols of Lanzarote in the Canary Islands, producing wines from the fertile black ash of some of the most isolated vineyards in the world. Stone walls protect plants from the Atlantic winds.

Nigerian women dig a trench to collect rainwater in the Sahel region of Africa. Although above-average rainfall in 2012 led to a successful harvest, the effects of desertification are ongoing throughout the region.

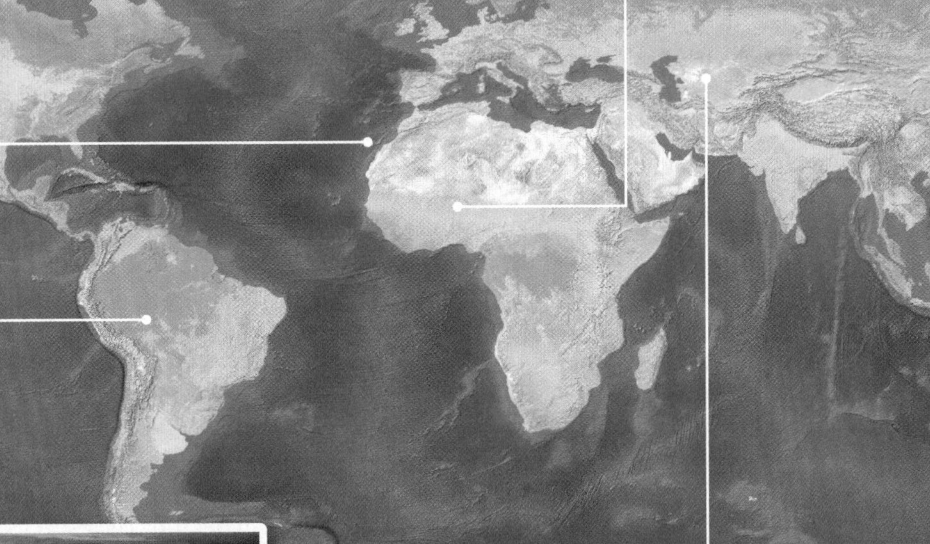

Soybean fields are readied for planting in Rondônia, Brazil, surrounded by the Amazon rain forest. Oxisols, the soils of the tropics, are less fertile than most soils and obtain their red color from iron minerals.

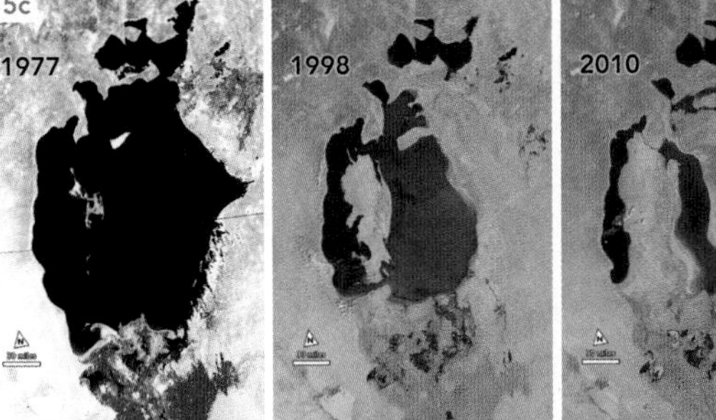

Desiccation of the Aral Sea began when rivers were diverted to irrigate cotton fields. The shrinking lake has accelerated desertification in the Aral basin of Kazakhstan and Uzbekistan and affected local climate, now hotter in summer without the water's moderating influence.

ISSUES FOR THE 21ST CENTURY

- Continued soil erosion and degradation will cause lowered agricultural productivity worldwide and possible food shortages.
- Thawing of frozen soils (Gelisols) in the northern latitudes emits carbon dioxide and methane into the atmosphere, creating a positive feedback loop that leads to further warming.

KEYLEARNING**concepts**review

Define soil and soil science and *list* four components of soil.

Soil is a dynamic natural mixture of fine materials, including both mineral and organic matter. **Soil science** is the interdisciplinary study of soils involving physics, chemistry, biology, mineralogy, hydrology, taxonomy, climatology, and cartography. *Pedology* deals with the origin, classification, distribution, and description of soil. *Edaphology* specifically focuses on the study of soil as a medium for sustaining the growth of plants. Soil is composed of about 50% mineral and organic matter and 50% water and air contained in pore spaces between the soil particles.

soil (p. 474) **soil science (p. 474)**

1. Soils provide the foundation for animal and plant life and therefore are critical to Earth's ecosystems. Why is this true?
2. What are the differences among soil science, pedology, and edaphology?

Describe the principal soil-formation factors and *describe* the horizons of a typical soil profile.

Environmental factors that affect soil formation include parent materials, climate, biological activity, topography, and time. **Loess** deposits consist of fine-grained sediments from glacial or fluvial environments that were redeposited by wind. Loess accumulations occur worldwide and develop into good agricultural soils.

To evaluate soils, scientists use a **soil profile**, a vertical section of soil that runs from the surface to the deepest extent of plant roots or to the point where regolith or bedrock is encountered. Each discernible layer in a soil profile is a **soil horizon**. The horizons are designated O (contains **humus**, a complex mixture of decomposed and synthesized organic materials), A (rich in humus and clay, darker), E (zone of **eluviation**, the removal of fine particles and minerals by water), B (zone of **illuviation**, the deposition of clays and minerals translocated from elsewhere), C (*regolith*, weathered bedrock), and R (bedrock). Soil horizons A, E, and B experience the most active soil processes and together are designated the **solum**.

loess (p. 475)
soil profile (p. 475)
soil horizon (p. 476)
humus (p. 476)
eluviation (p. 477)
illuviation (p. 477)
solum (p. 477)

3. Briefly describe the contributions of the following factors and their effects on soil formation: parent material, climate, vegetation, landforms, time, and humans.
4. Where does the sediment that forms the loess deposits of China come from? What is the origin of loess in Iowa? Name several other significant loess deposits on Earth.
5. Characterize the principal aspects of each soil horizon. Where does the main accumulation of organic material occur? Where does humus form? Which horizons constitute the solum?
6. Explain the difference between the processes of eluviation and illuviation.

Describe the physical properties used to classify soils: color, texture, structure, consistence, porosity, and soil moisture.

We use several physical properties to assess **soil fertility** (the ability of soil to sustain plants) and classify soils. Color suggests composition and chemical makeup. Soil texture refers to the size of individual mineral particles and the ratios of different sizes. For example, **loam** is a balanced mixture of sand, silt, and clay. Soil structure refers to the shape and size of the soil *ped*, which is the smallest natural cluster of particles in a given soil. The cohesion of soil particles to each other is called soil consistence. **Soil porosity** refers to the size, alignment, shape, and location of spaces in the soil that are filled with air, gases, or water. Soil moisture refers to water in the soil pores and its availability to plants.

soil fertility (p. 478)
loam (p. 479)
soil porosity (p. 480)

7. How can soil color be an indication of soil qualities? Give a couple of examples.
8. What are the various sizes of particles in soil? What is loam? Why is loam regarded so highly by agriculturists?
9. What is a quick, hands-on method for determining soil consistence?

Explain basic soil chemistry, including cation-exchange capacity, and *relate* these concepts to soil fertility.

Particles of clay and organic material form negatively charged **soil colloids** that attract and retain positively charged mineral ions in the soil. The capacity to exchange ions between colloids and roots is called the **cation-exchange capacity (CEC)**.

soil colloid (p. 480) **cation-exchange capacity (CEC) (p. 482)**

10. What are soil colloids? How are they related to cations and anions in the soil? Explain cation-exchange capacity.
11. What is meant by the concept of soil fertility, and how does soil chemistry affect fertility?

Discuss human impacts on soils, including desertification.

Essential soils for agriculture and their fertility are threatened by human activities and mismanagement. *Soil erosion* is the breakdown and redistribution of soils by wind, water, and gravity. To slow soil erosion, farmers in the United States and elsewhere use *no-till agriculture*, a practice in which the land is not plowed after a harvest. **Desertification** is the ongoing degradation of drylands caused by human activities and climate change; presently, this process affects some 1.5 billion people.

desertification (p. 484)

12. What is meant by desertification? What world regions are affected by this phenomenon?
13. Explain some of the details that support the concern over loss of our most fertile soils. What cost estimates have been placed on soil erosion?

Describe the 12 soil orders of the Soil Taxonomy classification system and *explain* their general distribution across Earth.

The U.S. **Soil Taxonomy** classification system is built around an analysis of various diagnostic horizons and 12 soil orders, as actually seen in the field. The basic sampling unit used in soil surveys is the **pedon**. The system divides soils into six hierarchical categories. From smallest to largest, they are series, families, subgroups, great groups, suborders, and orders. The Soil Taxonomy system uses two diagnostic horizons to identify soils: the **epipedon**, or the surface soil, and the **diagnostic subsurface horizon**, or the soil layer below the surface (at various depths) having properties specific to the type of soil.

Specific soil-forming processes keyed to climatic regions (not a basis for classification) are called **pedogenic regimes**. These include **laterization** (leaching in warm and humid climates), **calcification** (accumulation of carbonates in the B and C horizons in drier continental climates), **salinization** (collection of salt residues in surface horizons in hot, dry climates), **podzolization** (soil acidification in forest soils in cool climates), and **gleization** (humus and clay accumulation in cold, wet climates with poor drainage).

The 12 soil orders are **Oxisols** (tropical soils), **Aridisols** (desert soils), **Mollisols** (grassland soils), **Alfisols** (moderately weathered, temperate forest soils), **Ultisols** (highly weathered, subtropical forest soils), **Spodosols** (northern conifer forest soils), **Entisols** (recent, undeveloped soils), **Inceptisols** (weakly developed, humid-region soils), **Gelisols** (cold soils underlain by permafrost), **Andisols** (soils formed from volcanic materials), **Vertisols** (expandable clay soils), and **Histosols** (organic soils). Soils saturated for long enough periods to develop anaerobic, or "oxygen-free," conditions are **hydric soils**.

Soil Taxonomy (p. 485)
pedon (p. 485)
epipedon (p. 485)
diagnostic subsurface horizon (p. 485)
pedogenic regime (p. 485)
laterization (p. 485)
calcification (p. 485)
salinization (p. 485)
podzolization (p. 485)
gleization (p. 485)
Oxisols (p. 486)
Aridisols (p. 489)
Mollisols (p. 491)
Alfisols (p. 492)
Ultisols (p. 493)
Spodosols (p. 494)
Entisols (p. 494)
Inceptisols (p. 495)
Gelisols (p. 495)
Andisols (p. 496)
Vertisols (p. 497)
Histosols (p. 498)
hydric soil (p. 498)

14. What is the basis of the Soil Taxonomy system? What is the number of classifications in each of the following: soil orders, suborders, great groups, subgroups, families, and series?
15. Define an epipedon and a diagnostic subsurface horizon. Give a simple example of each.
16. Locate each soil order on the world map and on the U.S. map as you give a general description of it.
17. How was slash-and-burn shifting cultivation, as practiced in the past, a form of crop and soil rotation and conservation of soil properties?
18. Describe the salinization process in arid and semiarid soils. What associated soil horizons develop?
19. Which of the soil orders are associated with Earth's most productive agricultural areas?
20. Why is the 51-cm (20-in.) isohyet of annual precipitation in the Midwest significant to plants? How do the pH and lime content of soils change on either side of this isohyet?
21. Describe the podzolization process associated with northern coniferous forest soils. What characteristics are associated with the surface horizons? What strategies might enhance these soils?
22. Describe the location, nature, and formation processes of Gelisols. What is the linkage between these soils and climate change?
23. What type of soil is used to define wetlands?
24. Why has a selenium contamination problem arisen in some western U.S. soils? Explain the impact of agricultural practices on selenium concentrations.

16 Ecosystem Essentials

Aerial view of Aparamán-tepui in the Aparamán range in Bolivar State, southern Venezuela. These sandstone plateaus, known as tepuis, are isolated ecosystems surrounded by sheer vertical cliffs rising thousands of meters above the lowland rain forests. [Fabian Michelangeli/Age Fotostock.]

KEYLEARNING**concepts**

After reading the chapter, you should be able to:

- ***Define*** ecology, biogeography, and ecosystem.
- ***Explain*** photosynthesis and respiration and ***describe*** the world pattern of net primary productivity.
- ***Discuss*** the oxygen, carbon, and nitrogen cycles and ***explain*** trophic relationships.
- ***Describe*** communities and ecological niches and ***list*** several limiting factors on species distributions.
- ***Outline*** the stages of ecological succession in both terrestrial and aquatic ecosystems.
- ***Explain*** how biological evolution led to the biodiversity of life on Earth.

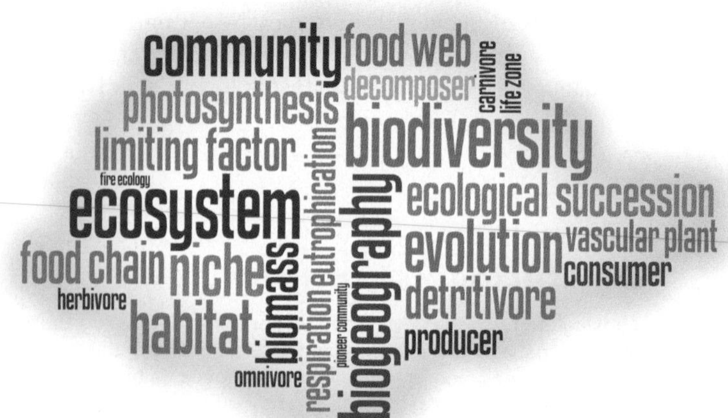

Species' Distributions Shift with Climate Change

Every plant or animal species in nature has a range of tolerance for variations in the physical characteristics of its environment, and this range of tolerance affects its geographical distribution. In particular, temperature and moisture requirements are often critical for determining a species' range. This is one reason global climate change can have a huge effect on biological communities. As environmental conditions shift (with temperatures becoming too high or too low and rainfall too much or too little), species must adapt, move to new habitat, or become extinct.

Scientists reported in 2011 that terrestrial species distributions are shifting higher in altitude at an average rate of 11 m (36 ft) per decade and higher in latitude at an average rate of 19.9 km (10.5 mi) per decade. These changes are happening two to three times faster than previously thought.

Range Changes by Elevation Some species in tropical and temperate mountains are adapting to climate change by moving to higher elevations. A long-term study in Yosemite National Park, California, found that small-mammal communities shifted their distributions in response to rising temperatures—notably the 3 C° (5.5 F°) increase in minimum temperature—during the last century. Half the species monitored showed substantial movement toward cooler temperatures at higher elevations. Species formerly found at low elevations expanded their ranges higher, and high-elevation species contracted their ranges away from lower areas. These species risk mountaintop extinction as warming pushes climatically suitable conditions beyond the reaches of mountain summits.

This study is consistent with others suggesting that high-elevation animal species are losing available habitat as temperatures increase, a situation that ultimately threatens these species' survival. In southern California, the endangered Inyo chipmunk (*Tamias umbrinus inyoensis*), a subspecies of the Uinta chipmunk, has not been seen for more than 4 years in the Sierra Nevada, raising fears of extinction. Throughout the intermountain western United States, species of voles, bats, and pikas, as well as other squirrels, are at risk of extinction as climates shift (**Figure GN 16.1**).

Plant distributions are also changing. A 2013 study reported that almost 90% of native plants in the Indian Himalayas shifted their ranges upward in elevation over the last century. Low-elevation species shifted upward to a greater extent than high-elevation species, suggesting that high-elevation species are already reaching the limits of available mountain habitat.

Range Changes by Latitude As temperatures increase, many plants and animals are shifting their distributions into higher-latitude areas with more favorable temperature conditions. Studies spanning the past 40 years show that maximum range shifts varied from 200 to 1000 km (125 to 620 mi); a more recent study documented range shifts averaging 6.1 km (3.8 mi) per year.

In general, plant communities are slower than animal species to respond to environmental change; however, global climate change is already impacting forest distributions. A recent study of 130 species of North American trees suggests that ranges will shift northward between 330 and 700 km (205 and 435 mi), depending on the success of dispersal into new habitats. Thus, deciduous forests that are now common in the United States would be located in Canada by century's end, and their present range would be occupied by grasslands in some areas and by a different mix of tree species in other regions.

To illustrate the magnitude of these shifts, **Figure GN 16.2** shows the predicted "migration" of what is now Illinois during this century based on forecasted changes in temperature and precipitation—in summer conditions, in particular. By mid-century, Illinois' summers will be similar to those of Arkansas and northern Louisiana; by 2090, Illinois' climate will be similar to that of Texas and Louisiana. The plants and animals that live in Illinois today will have to either shift northward to stay within their tolerance limits or adapt quickly to survive in the new temperature and moisture regime. We can expect present Illinois environmental conditions to be in central Manitoba and Ontario, Canada, by century's end.

▲**Figure GN 16.1 Pikas at risk of extinction.** Pikas, which inhabit cold climates near mountain summits, have disappeared from some areas of Nevada and Utah in recent decades. [Imagebroker/SuperStock.]

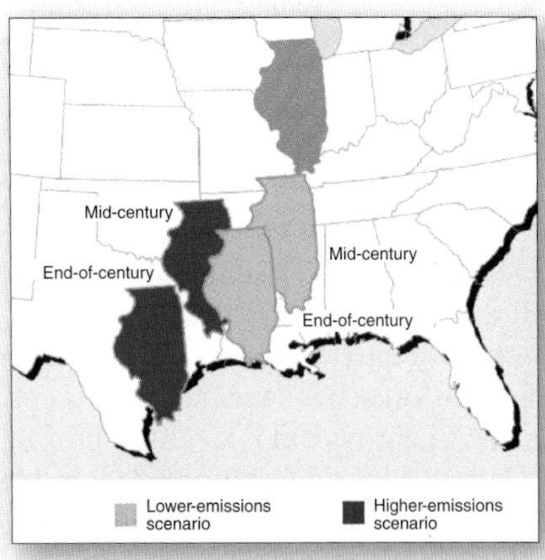

▲**Figure GN 16.2 Climatic shifts forecasted for the Midwest.** The relative future climatic conditions of Illinois forecasted by 2090 for two scenarios. [U.S. Global Change Research Program, 2009.]

Scientists suggest that a warming of 1.9 to 3.0 C° (3.5 to 5.5 F°) would leave more than 30% of species outside of their historic range, placing them at risk of extinction if they are unable to adapt or shift their ranges northward or upslope. A physical geography text written 20 to 70 years from now may have different vegetation maps from the ones depicting distributions and vegetation patterns today. In this chapter, we discuss ecosystems and species distributions; world vegetation patterns are the focus of Chapter 17.

QUESTION AND EXPLORE For more information on changing species distributions in California, see the U.C. Berkeley News Center at http://newscenter.berkeley.edu/2012/08/15/climate-change-range-shift/. For a study on the effects of climate change on genetic variation (discussed in this chapter), go to http://evolution.berkeley.edu/evolibrary/news/120301_chipmunks. MG

The diversity of organisms on the living Earth is one of our planet's most impressive features. This diversity is a response to the interaction of the atmosphere, hydrosphere, and lithosphere, which produces a variety of conditions within which the biosphere exists. The diversity of life also results from the intricate interplay of living organisms themselves. Each species uses strategies that maintain biodiversity and species coexistence.

The diversity of life results from the intricate interplay of living organisms.

The biosphere, the sphere of life and organic activity, extends from the ocean floor to an altitude of about 8 km (5 mi) into the atmosphere. It consists of myriad ecosystems, from simple to complex, each operating within general spatial boundaries.

An **ecosystem** is a self-sustaining association of living plants and animals and their nonliving physical environment. Earth's natural ecosystems are open systems with regard to both solar energy and matter, with almost all ecosystem boundaries functioning as transition zones rather than as sharp demarcations. Ecosystems vary in size from micro-scale, such as in a drop of pond water, to small-scale, such as the ecosystem of a city park, to mid-scale, such as a mountaintop or beach, to large-scale, such as a forest or desert. Internally, every ecosystem is a complex of many interconnected variables, all functioning independently yet in concert, with complicated flows of energy and matter.

Ecology is the study of the relationships between organisms and their environment and among the various ecosystems in the biosphere. The word *ecology*, developed by German naturalist Ernst Haeckel in 1869, is derived from the Greek *oikos* ("household" or "place to live") and *logos* ("study of"). **Biogeography** is the study of the distribution of plants and animals, the diverse spatial patterns they create, and the physical and biological processes, past and present, that produce Earth's species richness.

Earth's most influential biotic agents are humans. From the time humans first developed agriculture, tended livestock, and used fire, the influence of humans over Earth's physical systems has been increasing. For example, the Gulf Coast wetlands and associated coastal habitat bore the brunt of the 2010 BP oil spill; restoration of coastal marshes is ongoing. The degree to which modern society understands Earth's biogeography and conserves Earth's living legacy will determine the extent of our success as a species and the long-term survival of a habitable planet.

In this chapter: We explore the methods by which plants use photosynthesis and respiration to translate solar energy into usable forms to energize life. We then examine relevant nonliving systems and important biogeochemical cycles and look at the organization of living ecosystems into complex food chains and webs. We also examine communities and species interactions. Next, we consider how the biodiversity of living organisms results from biological evolution over the past 3.6+ billion years. We conclude with a discussion of ecosystem stability and resilience and of how living landscapes change over space and time through the process of succession, now influenced by the effects of global climate change.

Energy Flows and Nutrient Cycles

By definition, an ecosystem includes both biotic and abiotic components. Chief among the abiotic components is the direct input of solar energy, on which nearly all ecosystems depend. (The few, limited ecosystems that exist in dark caves, in wells, or on the ocean floor depend instead on chemical reactions—chemosynthesis—for energy.)

Ecosystems are divided into subsystems. The biotic tasks are performed by primary producers (plants, cyanobacteria, and some other unicellular organisms), consumers (animals), and detritus feeders and decomposers (worms, mites, bacteria, and fungi). The abiotic processes include gaseous, hydrologic, and mineral cycles. **Figure 16.1** illustrates these essential elements of an ecosystem and how they operate together.

Converting Energy to Biomass

The energy that powers the biosphere comes primarily from the Sun. Solar energy enters the ecosystem energy flow by way of photosynthesis; heat energy is dissipated from the system, as an output, at many points. Of the total energy intercepted at Earth's surface and available for work, only about 1.0% is actually fixed by photosynthesis as carbohydrates in plants, which then become the source of energy or the construction materials for the rest of the ecosystem. "Fixed" means chemically bound into plant tissues.

Plants (in terrestrial ecosystems) and algae (in aquatic ecosystems) are the critical biotic link between solar energy and the biosphere. Organisms that are capable of using the Sun's energy directly to produce their own food (using carbon dioxide, CO_2, as their sole source of carbon) are *autotrophs* (self-feeders), or **producers**. These include plants, algae, and cyanobacteria (a type of blue-green algae). Autotrophs accomplish this transformation of light energy into chemical energy by the process of photosynthesis, as previously mentioned. Ultimately, the fate of all members of the biosphere, including humans, rests on the success of these organisms and their ability to turn sunlight into food.

The oxygen gas in Earth's atmosphere was produced as a by-product of photosynthesis. The first photosynthesizing bacteria to produce oxygen appeared in oceans on Earth about 2.7 billion years ago. These *cyanobacteria*—microscopic, usually unicellular, blue-green algae that can form large colonies—were fundamental to the creation of Earth's modern atmosphere. These organisms were also critical in the origin of plants, since free-living cyanobacteria eventually became the chloroplasts used in plant photosynthesis. Although these bacteria are

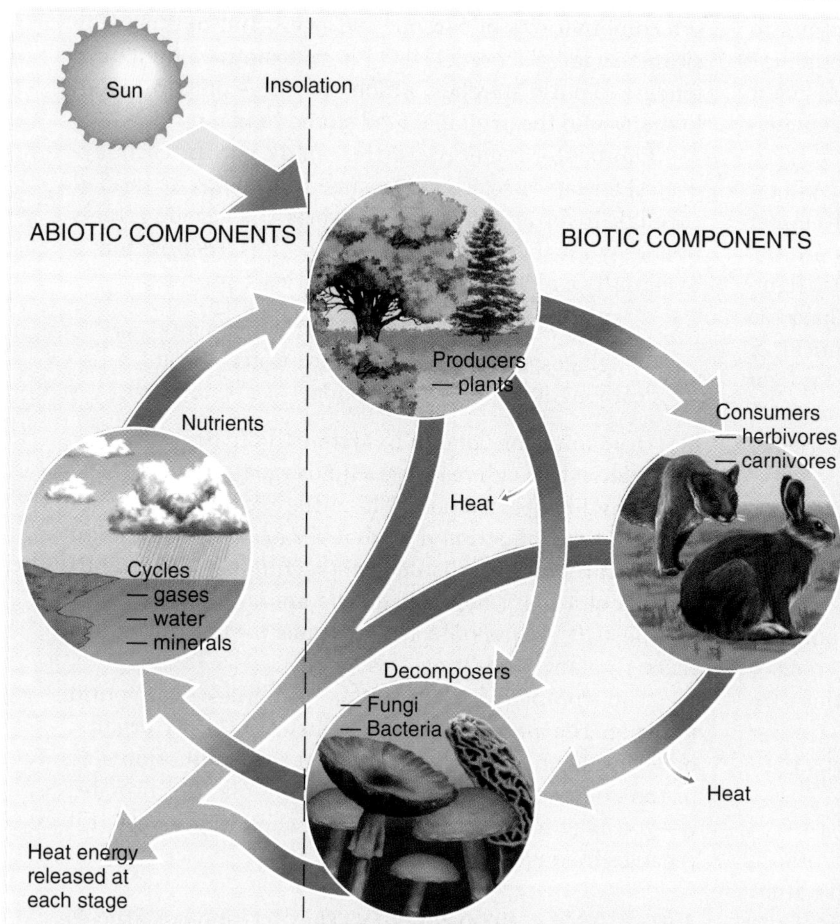

(a) Solar energy input drives biotic and abiotic ecosystem processes. Heat energy and biomass are the outputs from the biosphere.

(b) Biotic and abiotic ingredients operate together to form this rain forest floor ecosystem in Puerto Rico.

(c) Five or six species of lichen live in extreme Arctic climate conditions on Bear Island in the Barents Sea. Each little indentation in the rock provides some advantage to the lichen.

(d) Brain coral in the Caribbean Sea, at a 3-m (9.8-ft) depth, lives in a symbiotic relationship with algae.

▲Figure 16.1 Biotic and abiotic components of ecosystems. [Bobbé Christopherson.]

called blue-green algae (mainly because they are photosynthetic and aquatic), they are not related to other organisms we know as algae. True *algae* are a large group of single-celled or multi-celled photosynthetic organisms that range in size from microscopic diatoms (a type of phytoplankton) to giant sea kelp.

Land plants (and animals) became common about 430 million years ago, according to fossilized remains. **Vascular plants** are land plants that have conductive tissues and true roots for internal transport of fluid and nutrients. (*Vascular* is from a Latin word for "vessel-bearing," referring to the conducting cells.)

In vascular plants, leaves are solar-powered chemical factories wherein photochemical reactions take place. Veins in the leaf bring in water and nutrient supplies and carry off the sugars (food) produced by photosynthesis. The veins in each leaf connect to the stems and branches of the plant and to the main circulation system.

Flows of CO_2, water, light, and oxygen enter and exit the surface of each leaf. Gases move into and out of a leaf through small pores, the **stomata** (singular: *stoma*), which usually are most numerous on the lower side of the leaf. Each stoma is surrounded by guard cells that open and close the pore, depending on the plant's changing needs. Water that moves through a plant exits the leaves through the stomata in the process of transpiration, thereby assisting the plant's temperature regulation. As water evaporates from the leaves, a pressure gradient is created that allows atmospheric pressure to push water up through the plant all the way from the roots, in the same manner that a soda straw works.

Photosynthesis and Respiration Powered by energy from certain wavelengths of visible light, **photosynthesis** unites CO_2 and hydrogen (hydrogen is derived from water in the plant). The term is descriptive: *photo-* refers to sunlight and *-synthesis* describes the "manufacturing" of starches and sugars through reactions within plant leaves. The process releases oxygen and produces energy-rich food for the plant (**Figure 16.2**).

The largest concentration of light-responsive, photosynthetic structures in leaf cells is below the leaf's upper layers. These specialized units within the cells are the *chloroplasts*, and each chloroplast contains a green, light-sensitive pigment called **chlorophyll**. Light stimulates the molecules of this pigment, producing a photochemical, or light-driven, reaction. Consequently, competition for light is a dominant factor in the formation of plant communities. This competition is expressed in the height, orientation, distribution, and structure of plants.

Only about one-quarter of the light energy arriving at the surface of a leaf is useful to the light-sensitive chlorophyll. Chlorophyll absorbs only the orange-red and violet-blue wavelengths for photochemical operations, and it reflects predominantly green hues (and some yellow). That is why trees and other vegetation look green.

Photosynthesis essentially follows this equation:

$$\underset{\text{(Carbon dioxide)}}{6CO_2} + \underset{\text{(water)}}{6H_2O} + \underset{\text{(solar energy)}}{\text{Light}} \rightarrow \underset{\text{(glucose, carbohydrate)}}{C_6H_{12}O_6} + \underset{\text{(oxygen)}}{6O_2}$$

From the equation, you can see that photosynthesis removes carbon (in the form of CO_2) from Earth's atmosphere. The quantity is enormous: approximately 91 billion metric tons (100 billion tons) of CO_2 per year. Carbohydrates, the organic result of the photosynthetic process, are combinations of carbon, hydrogen, and oxygen. The simple sugar *glucose* ($C_6H_{12}O_6$) is an example. Plants use glucose to build starches, which are more-complex carbohydrates and the principal food stored in plants.

Plants store energy (in the bonds within carbohydrates) for later use. They consume this energy as needed through respiration, which converts the carbohydrates to energy for their other operations. Thus, **respiration** is essentially a reverse of the photosynthetic process:

$$\underset{\text{(glucose, carbohydrate)}}{C_6H_{12}O_6} + \underset{\text{(oxygen)}}{6O_2} \rightarrow \underset{\text{(carbon dioxide)}}{6CO_2} + \underset{\text{(water)}}{6H_2O} + \underset{\text{(heat energy)}}{\text{Energy}}$$

In respiration, plants oxidize carbohydrates (break them down through reaction with oxygen), releasing CO_2, water, and energy as heat. The difference between photosynthetic production of carbohydrates and respiration loss of carbohydrates is *net photosynthesis*. The overall growth of a plant depends on the amount of net photosynthesis, a surplus of carbohydrates beyond those lost through plant respiration.

The *compensation point* is the break-even point between the production and consumption of organic material. Each leaf must operate on the production side of the compensation point, or else the plant eliminates it—you may have observed a plant shedding leaves if it receives inadequate water or light.

Net Primary Productivity The net photosynthesis for an entire ecosystem is its **net primary productivity**. This is the amount of stored chemical energy that the

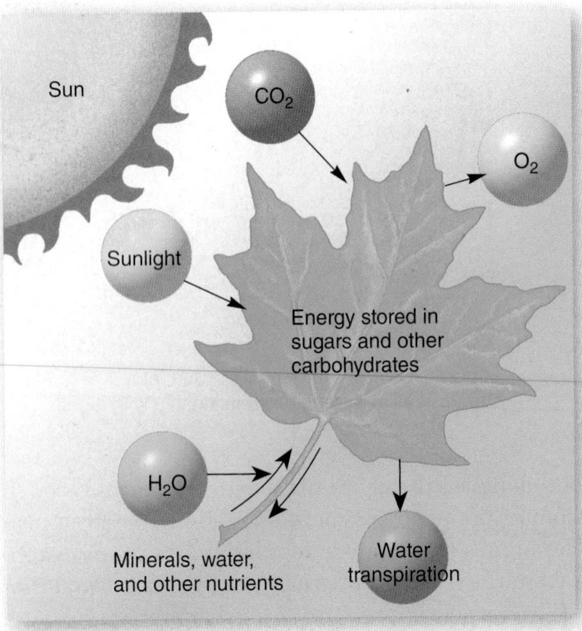

(a) Plant photosynthesis

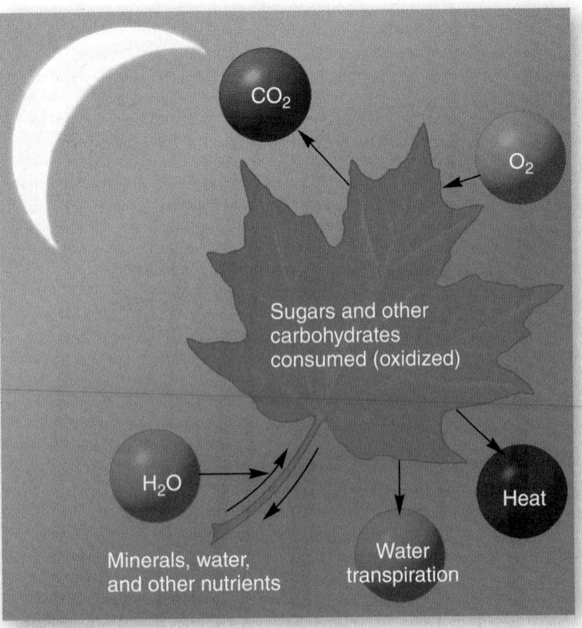

(b) Plant respiration

▲**Figure 16.2 Photosynthesis and respiration.** In the process of photosynthesis, plants consume light, carbon dioxide (CO_2), nutrients, and water (H_2O) and produce outputs of oxygen (O_2) and carbohydrates (sugars) as stored chemical energy. Plant respiration, illustrated here at night, approximately reverses this process. The balance between photosynthesis and respiration determines net photosynthesis and plant growth.

ecosystem generates. The total organic matter (living and recently living, both animal and plant) in an ecosystem, with its associated chemical energy, is the ecosystem's **biomass** and is often measured as the net dry weight of all organic material. Net primary productivity is an important factor in any type of ecosystem because it determines the biomass available for consumption by *heterotrophs*, or **consumers**—organisms that feed on organic matter for energy. The distribution of productivity over Earth's surface is an important aspect of biogeography.

Net primary productivity is measured as fixed carbon per square meter per year. The map in **Figure 16.3** shows that on land, net primary production tends to be highest between the Tropics of Cancer and Capricorn at sea level and decreases toward higher latitudes and elevations. Productivity levels are tied to both sunlight and precipitation, as evidenced by the correlations of abundant precipitation with high productivity adjacent to the equator and reduced precipitation with low productivity in the subtropical deserts. Even though deserts receive high amounts of solar radiation, water availability and other controlling factors, such as soil conditions, limit productivity.

In temperate and high latitudes, the rate at which carbon is fixed by vegetation varies seasonally. It increases in spring and summer as plants flourish with increasing solar input and, in some areas, with more available (nonfrozen) water, and it decreases in late fall and winter. In contrast, productivity rates in the tropics are high throughout the year, and turnover in the photosynthesis–respiration cycle is faster, exceeding by many times the rates experienced in a desert environment or in the far northern limits of the tundra. A lush hectare (2.5 acres) of sugarcane in the tropics might fix 45 metric tons (50 tons) of carbon in a year, whereas desert plants in an equivalent area might achieve only 1% of that amount.

In the oceans, differing nutrient levels control and limit productivity. Regions with nutrient-rich upwelling currents off western coastlines generally are the most productive. Figure 16.3 shows that the tropical oceans and areas of subtropical high pressure are quite low in productivity.

Table 16.1 on the *MasteringGeography* website lists the net primary productivity of various ecosystems and provides an estimate of net total biomass worldwide. Compare the productivity of the various ecosystems in the table, noting especially how the productivity of cultivated land compares with that of natural communities.

Elemental Cycles

Numerous abiotic physical and chemical factors support the living organisms of each ecosystem. Some of these abiotic components, such as light, temperature, and water, are critical for ecosystem operation. Nutrients (the chemical elements essential for life) are also necessary; however, those that accumulate as pollutants can have negative effects on ecosystem function.

The cycling of nutrients and flow of energy between organisms determines the structure of an ecosystem. As energy cascades through the system, it is constantly replenished by the Sun. But nutrients and minerals cannot be replenished from an external source, so they constantly cycle within each ecosystem and through the biosphere.

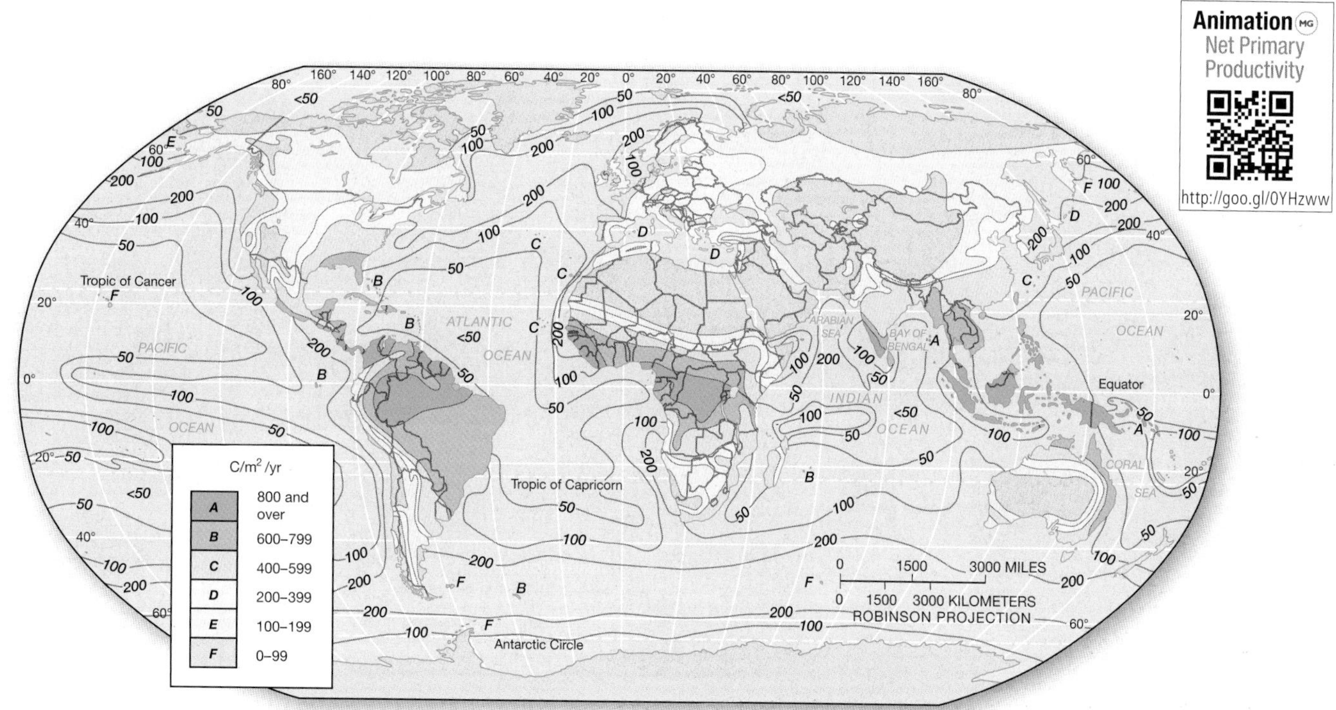

▲**Figure 16.3 Net primary productivity.** Worldwide net primary productivity in grams of carbon per square meter per year (approximate values). [Adapted from D. E. Reichle, *Analysis of Temperate Forest Ecosystems* (Heidelberg, Germany: Springer, 1970).]

The most abundant natural elements in living matter are hydrogen (H), oxygen (O), and carbon (C). Together, these elements make up more than 99% of Earth's biomass; in fact, all life (being composed of organic molecules) contains hydrogen and carbon. In addition, nitrogen (N), calcium (Ca), potassium (K), magnesium (Mg), sulfur (S), and phosphorus (P) are significant nutrients, elements necessary for the growth of a living organism.

These key elements flow through the natural world in various chemical cycles. Oxygen, carbon, and nitrogen each have *gaseous cycles*, parts of which take place in the atmosphere. Other major elements, including phosphorus, calcium, potassium, and sulfur, have *sedimentary cycles*, which principally involve mineral and solid phases. Some elements cycle through both gaseous and sedimentary stages. The recycling of gases and nutrient sedimentary materials forms Earth's **biogeochemical cycles**, so called because they involve chemical reactions necessary for growth and development of living systems. The chemical elements themselves recycle over and over again in life processes.

Oxygen and Carbon Cycles We consider the oxygen and carbon cycles together because they are so closely intertwined through photosynthesis and respiration (**Figure 16.4**). The atmosphere is the principal reservoir of available oxygen. Larger reserves of oxygen exist in Earth's crust, but they are unavailable, being chemically bound with other elements, especially in the silicate (SiO_2) and carbonate (CO_3) mineral families. Unoxidized reserves of fossil fuels and sediments also contain oxygen.

As discussed in Chapter 8, the oceans are enormous pools of carbon; however, all of this carbon is bound chemically in CO_2, calcium carbonate, and other compounds. The ocean initially absorbs CO_2 by means of the photosynthesis carried on by phytoplankton; it becomes part of the living organisms and through them is fixed in certain carbonate minerals, such as limestone ($CaCO_3$). The ocean water can also absorb CO_2 directly from the atmosphere, resulting in ocean acidification (discussed in Chapter 13).

The atmosphere, which is the integrating link between photosynthesis (fixation) and respiration (release) in the carbon cycle, contains only about 800 billion metric tons of carbon (as CO_2) at any moment. This is far less carbon than is stored in fossil fuels and oil shales (as hydrocarbon molecules) or in living and dead

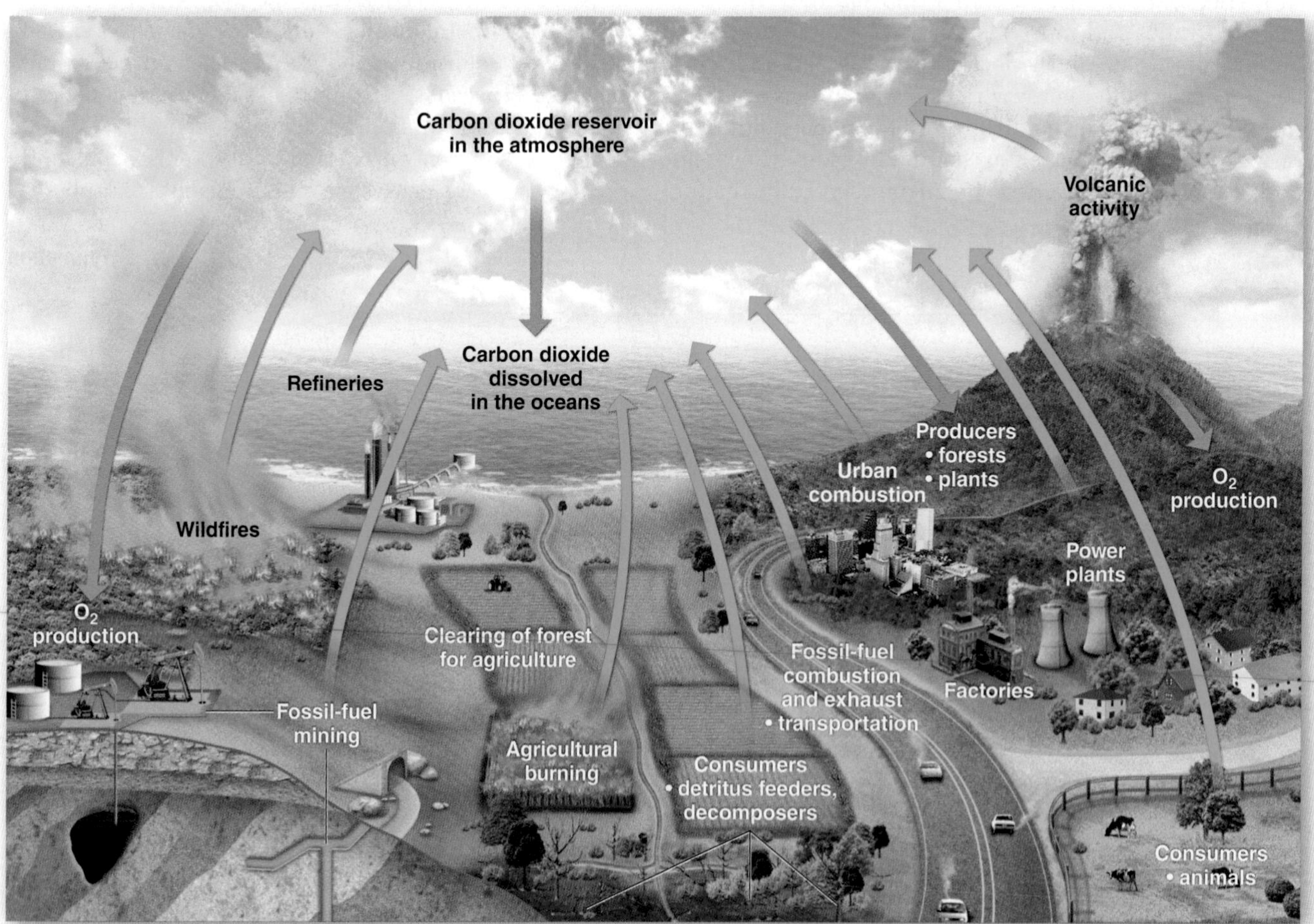

▲**Figure 16.4 The carbon and oxygen cycles.** Carbon is fixed (orange arrows) through photosynthesis, with oxygen as a by-product. Respiration by living organisms, the burning of forests and grasslands, and the combustion of fossil fuels release carbon to the atmosphere (blue arrows). These cycles are greatly influenced by human activities.

organic matter (as carbohydrate molecules). In addition to being released into the atmosphere through the respiration of plants and animals, CO_2 is released through the burning of grasslands and forests, volcanic activity, land-use changes, and fossil-fuel combustion by industry and transportation (review Geosystems in Action 8 on pages 258–259).

Carbon Cycle Response to the Mount Pinatubo Eruption One month after the 1991 Mount Pinatubo eruption, the second largest volcanic eruption of the 20th century, temperatures decreased in the Northern Hemisphere, and global carbon dioxide levels declined sharply.

Scientists initially thought that the CO_2 decrease was caused by a decline in plant respiration linked to cooling temperatures. However, research now suggests that the globally spread atmospheric aerosols from the eruption caused an increase in diffuse light, as opposed to direct sunlight that creates shadows and areas of concentrated heat that cause plant stress. This change increased plant photosynthesis and removed more CO_2 from the air. In one deciduous forest, photosynthesis increased by 23% in 1992 and 8% in 1993 under cloudless conditions. Thus, the eruption's aerosols affected the global carbon cycle, lowering atmospheric carbon levels and enhancing the terrestrial carbon sink for a brief period. (Review other effects of the eruption in Chapter 1, Geosystems in Action 1.)

Nitrogen Cycle Nitrogen, which accounts for 78.084% of each breath we take, is the major constituent of the atmosphere. Nitrogen also is important in the makeup of organic molecules, especially proteins, and therefore is essential to living processes. A simplified view of the nitrogen cycle is portrayed in **Figure 16.5**.

▲**Figure 16.5 The nitrogen cycle.** The atmosphere is the reservoir of gaseous nitrogen. Atmospheric nitrogen gas is chemically fixed by bacteria in producing ammonia. Lightning and forest fires produce nitrates, and fossil-fuel combustion forms nitrogen compounds that are washed from the atmosphere by precipitation. Plants absorb nitrogen compounds and incorporate the nitrogen into organic material.

Nitrogen-fixing bacteria, which live principally in the soil and are associated with the roots of certain plants, are critical for bringing atmospheric nitrogen into living organisms. Colonies of these bacteria reside in nodules on the roots of legumes (plants such as clover, alfalfa, soybeans, peas, beans, and peanuts) and chemically combine the nitrogen from the air into nitrates (NO_3) and ammonia (NH_3). Plants use the nitrogen from these molecules to produce their own organic matter. Anyone or anything feeding on the plants thus ingests the nitrogen. Finally, the nitrogen in the organic wastes of the consuming organisms is freed by denitrifying bacteria, which recycle it to the atmosphere.

To improve agricultural yields, many farmers enhance the available nitrogen in the soil by means of synthetic inorganic fertilizers as opposed to soil-building organic fertilizers (manure and compost). Inorganic fertilizers are chemically produced through artificial nitrogen fixation at factories. Humans presently fix more nitrogen as synthetic fertilizer per year than is found in all terrestrial sources combined.

This surplus of usable nitrogen accumulates in Earth's ecosystems. Some is present as excess nutrients, washed from soil into waterways and eventually to the ocean. This excess nitrogen load begins a water pollution process that feeds an excessive growth of algae and phytoplankton, increases biochemical oxygen demand, diminishes dissolved oxygen reserves, and eventually disrupts the aquatic ecosystem. In addition, excess nitrogen compounds in air pollution are a component in acid deposition, further altering the nitrogen cycle in soils and waterways.

Dead Zones The Mississippi River receives runoff from 41% of the area of the continental United States. It carries agricultural fertilizers, farm sewage, and other nitrogen-rich wastes to the Gulf, causing huge spring blooms of phytoplankton: an explosion of primary productivity. By summer, the biological oxygen demand of bacteria feeding on the decay of the spring bloom exceeds the dissolved oxygen content of the water; hypoxia (oxygen depletion) develops, killing any fish that venture into the area. These low-oxygen conditions create **dead zones** that limit marine life. Geosystems in Action 16 features the Gulf of Mexico dead zone. The agricultural, feedlot, and fertilizer industries dispute the connection between their nutrient input and this extensive dead zone. The human-caused creation of dead zones in water bodies is cultural eutrophication, discussed later in the chapter.

Similar coastal dead zones occur as the result of nutrient outflows from more than 400 river systems worldwide, affecting almost 250,000 km^2 (94,600 mi^2) of offshore oceans and seas. In Sweden and Denmark, however, a concerted effort to reduce nutrient flows into rivers reversed hypoxic conditions in the Kattegat strait (between the Baltic and North Seas). Also, fertilizer use has decreased more than 50% in the former Soviet Republics since the fall of state agriculture in 1990. The Black Sea no longer undergoes year-round hypoxia at river deltas, as the dead zones in those areas now disappear for several months each year.

Dead zones are occurring in lakes as well, such as those that appeared in Lake Erie, one of the Great Lakes, in the 1960s. In 2011, the dead zone in this lake reached its largest extent in recorded history, caused by fertilizers (mainly phosphorus) flowing into the lake combined with slower natural mixing attributed to climate change.

Energy Pathways

The feeding relationships among organisms make up the energy pathways in an ecosystem. These *trophic relationships*, or feeding levels, consist of food chains and food webs that range from simple to complex. As discussed earlier, autotrophs are the producers. Organisms that depend on producers as their carbon source are heterotrophs, or consumers, and are generally animals.

Trophic Relationships The producers in an ecosystem capture sunlight and convert it to chemical energy, incorporating carbon, forming new plant tissue and biomass, and freeing oxygen. From the producers, which manufacture their own food, energy flows through the system along an idealized unidirectional pathway called a **food chain**. Solar energy enters each food chain through the producers, either plants or phytoplankton, and subsequently flows to higher and higher levels of consumers. Organisms that share the same feeding level in a food chain are said to be at the same *trophic level*. Food chains usually have between three and six levels, beginning with primary producers and ending with *detritivores*, which break down organic matter and are the final link in the theoretical chain (**Figure 16.6**).

The actual trophic relationships between species in an ecosystem are usually more complex than the simple food chain model might suggest. The more common arrangement of feeding relationships is a **food web**, a complex network of interconnected food chains with multidirectional branches. In a food web, consumers often participate in several different food chains.

Nutrient cycling is continuous within a food web, aided by **detritivores** (also known as detritus feeders), the organisms that feed on *detritus*—dead organic debris (dead bodies, fallen leaves, and waste products) produced by living organisms. Detritivores include worms, mites, termites, centipedes, snails, slugs, and crabs in terrestrial environments and bottom feeders in marine environments. These organisms renew the entire system by breaking down these organic materials and releasing simple inorganic compounds and nutrients. **Decomposers** are primarily bacteria and fungi that digest organic debris outside their bodies and absorb and release

Coastal ocean waters are often highly productive ecosystems teeming with marine life. Yet they can become dead zones where organisms die for lack of oxygen (GIA 16.1). The Gulf of Mexico dead zone results from a process that begins with agricultural runoff of fertilizers and farm-animal wastes (GIA 16.2). The size of dead zones can vary from year to year. Freshwater lakes are also subject to "blooms" of the algae that form dead zones.

16.1 Formation of a Dead Zone

In the water's surface layer, agricultural runoff delivers nitrogen and phosphorus, nutrients that greatly boost the growth of algae, producing an algal bloom. When the algae die, they sink into the bottom layer. Bacteria feed on the dead algae and deplete the water of oxygen, forming a dead zone. Marine organisms that cannot leave the dead zone will die.

Explain: How does the water in a dead zone become depleted of oxygen?

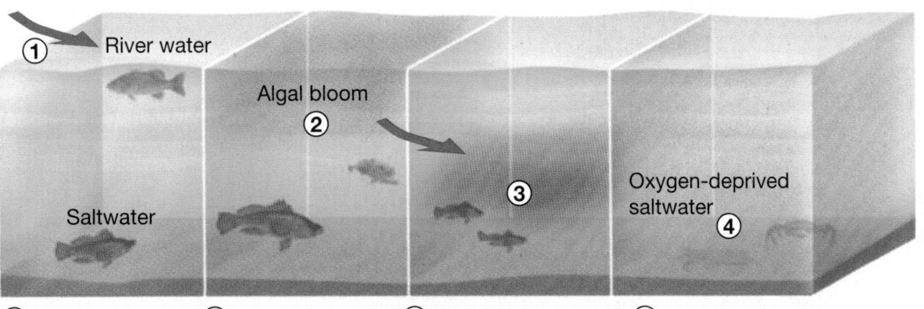

① *Agricultural runoff enters rivers, and then moves downstream to the ocean or to a lake.*

② *The nutrients, mainly nitrogen and phosphorus, cause algal blooms.*

③ *The algae die, sink into the bottom layer, and are decomposed by bacteria, using up the oxygen in the water.*

④ *A dead zone (defined as water with less than 2 mg/L dissolved oxygen) is formed, killing organisms that cannot flee.*

16.2 The Gulf of Mexico Dead Zone

Agricultural runoff from the Mississippi River watershed provides the nitrogen for the Gulf of Mexico dead zone (GIA 16.2a). In 2013, the dead zone extended along much of the Louisiana coast (GIA 16.2b).

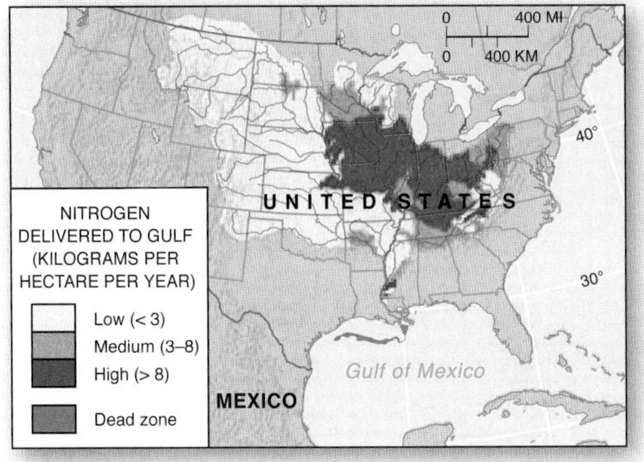

16.2a *The map shows total nitrogen in the upstream portion of the Mississippi River watershed.*

Bottom-water dissolved oxygen across the Louisiana shelf from July 22–28, 2013

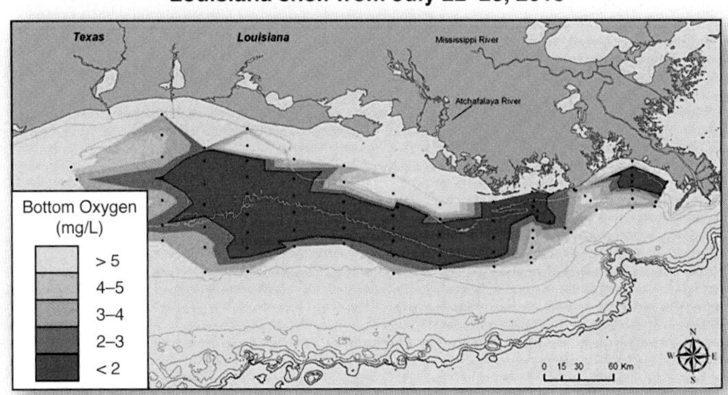

16.2b *Nutrients from the Mississippi River enrich the offshore waters of the Gulf, causing huge algal blooms in early spring that later form the dead zone (red areas).*

16.2c

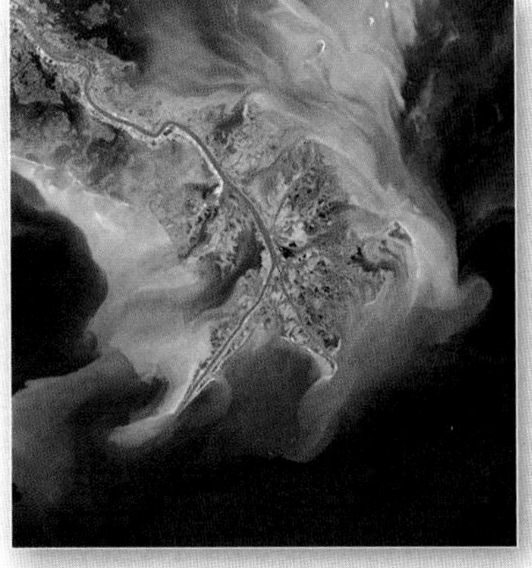

Gulf of Mexico algal bloom: Channels in the Mississippi River's delta bring nutrients that fuel the green algal blooms seen in this image and help to form the Gulf's large, and expanding, dead zone.

Video (MG) The Ocean's Green Machines

http://goo.gl/MKr4vJ

GEOquiz

1. Explain: The Gulf dead zone varies in size from year to year. Explain how changes in annual precipitation in the Mississippi River watershed could affect the delivery of nitrogen to the Gulf of Mexico.

2. Solve Problems: Suppose you are a member of a commission charged with developing a plan to reduce the size of the Gulf of Mexico dead zone. Describe strategies you would suggest and the changes needed to achieve this goal.

MasteringGeography™

Visit the Study Area in MasteringGeography™ to explore dead zones.

Visualize: Study the video of phytoplankton.

Assess: Demonstrate understanding of dead zones (if assigned by instructor).

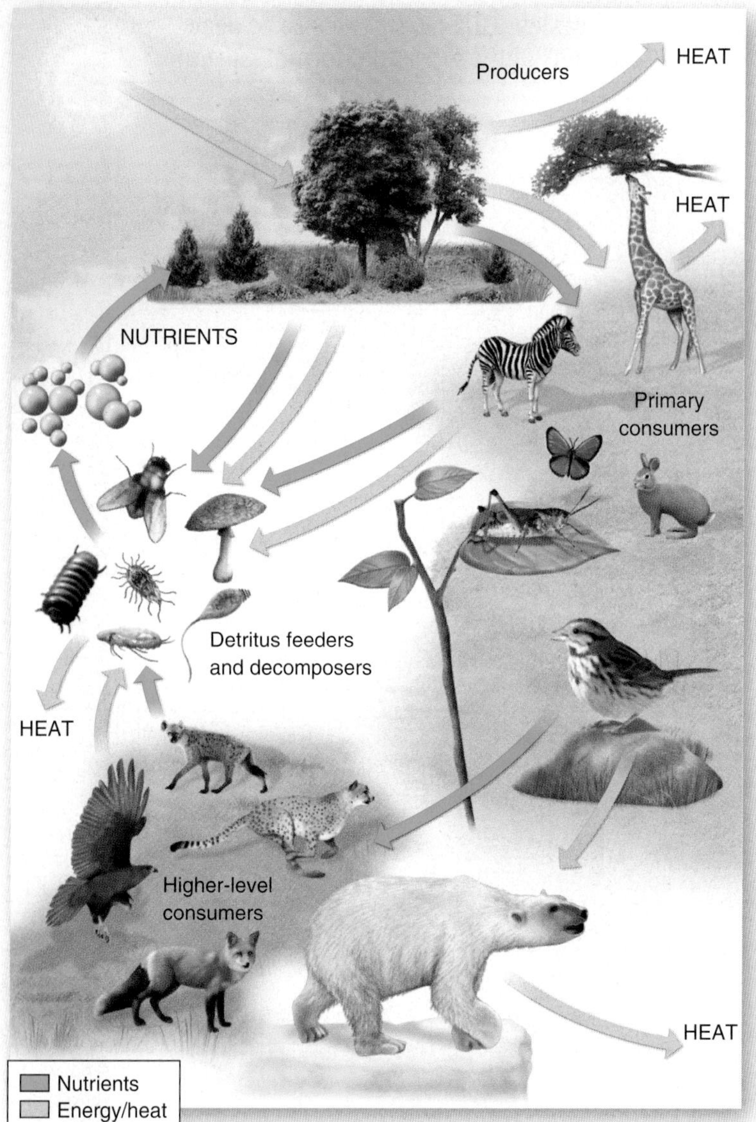

(a) The flow of energy, cycling of nutrients, and trophic (feeding) relationships portrayed for a generalized ecosystem. The operation is fueled by radiant energy supplied by sunlight and first captured by the plants.

(b) A bearded seal on a bergy bit in the Arctic Ocean.

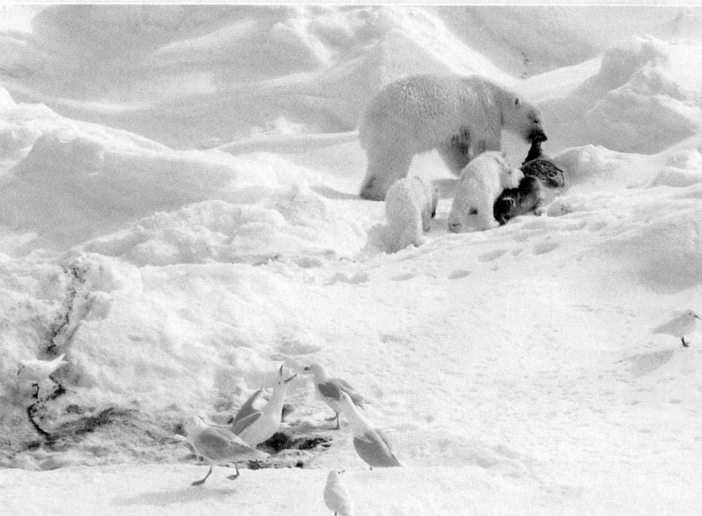

(c) A mother polar bear and cubs eat a seal on an iceberg. Glaucous Gulls and Ivory Gulls consume part of the leftovers.

▲**Figure 16.6 Energy, nutrient, and food pathways in the environment.** [(b) and (c) Bobbé Christopherson.]

nutrients in the process. The metabolic work of microbial decomposers produces the "rotting" action that breaks down detritus. Detritus feeders and decomposers, although operating differently, have a similar function in an ecosystem.

In a food web, the organisms that feed on producers are *primary consumers*. Because producers are always plants, the primary consumer is a **herbivore**, or plant eater. A *secondary consumer* mainly eats primary consumers (herbivores) and is therefore a **carnivore**. A *tertiary consumer* eats primary and secondary consumers and is referred to as the "top carnivore" in the food chain; examples are the polar bear in the Arctic and the leopard seal and orca in Antarctica. The orca, an oceanic dolphin, feeds on fish, seals, penguins, and other whales in both Arctic and Antarctic waters. A consumer that feeds on both producers (plants) and consumers (meat) is an **omnivore**—a category occupied by humans, among other animals.

Several examples illustrate food webs. In the Arctic waters, bearded seals (*Erignathus barbatus*), with body fat often exceeding 30%, are consumers that feed on fish and clams (Figure 16.6b). In turn, the seal is preyed on by the polar bear (*Ursus maritimus*), another marine mammal and the dominant Arctic predator. Polar bears consume most of the seal except for the bones and intestines, which are eaten by scavenging birds (Figure 16.6c).

In the Antarctic region, the food web begins with phytoplankton, the microscopic algae that harvest solar energy in photosynthesis (**Figure 16.7**). Herbivorous

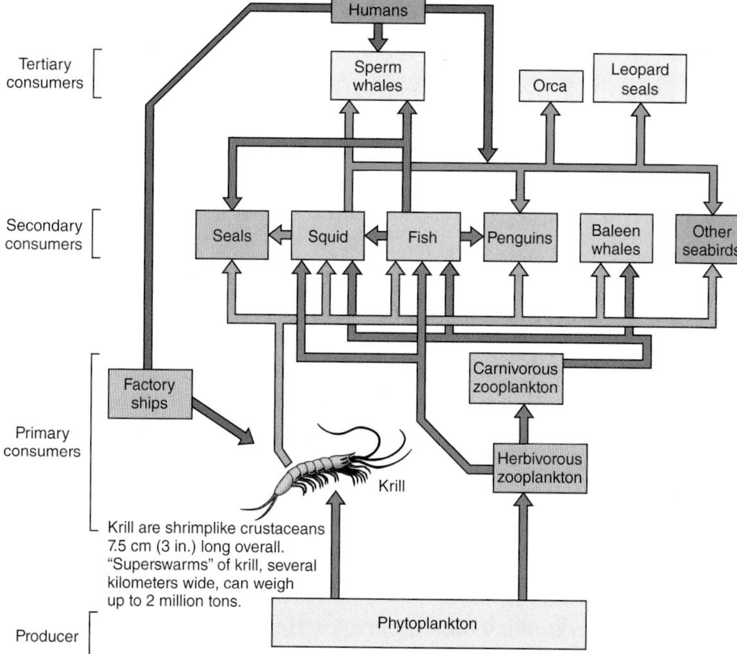

◀**Figure 16.7 A simplified Antarctic Ocean food web.** Phytoplankton (bottom), the producers, use solar energy for photosynthesis. Krill and other herbivorous zooplankton eat the phytoplankton, and are then consumed by organisms at the next trophic level.

zooplankton, such as the shrimplike crustaceans called krill (*Euphausia*), eat phytoplankton and are thus the primary consumers. Secondary consumers such as whales, fish, seabirds, seals, and squid eat krill, forming the next trophic level. Many Antarctic-dwelling seabirds depend on krill and on fish that eat krill. All of these organisms participate in other food chains, some as consumers and some being consumed.

Figure 16.8 shows part of a temperate forest food web in eastern North America. Like the previous diagrams, the figure is simplified compared to the actual complexity of nature.

▲**Figure 16.8 Temperate forest food web.** Based on the text discussion, can you find the primary producers and then locate the primary, secondary, and tertiary consumers in this web? What role do the earthworms and bacteria play?

Energy Pyramids The overall amount of energy moving through trophic levels decreases from lower to higher levels, a pattern that can be illustrated in an *energy pyramid* in which horizontal bars represent each trophic level. (Ecological pyramids also include *biomass pyramids*, discussed ahead.)

At the bottom of the pyramid are the producers, which have the most energy and usually (but not always) the highest biomass and numbers of organisms. The next level, primary consumers, represents less energy because energy is used up by metabolism and given off as heat as one organism eats another. Energy decreases again at the next level (secondary consumers), with each trophic level having (usually) less biomass and fewer organisms than the one beneath (**Figure 16.9a**). Although the pattern generally holds for numbers of organisms and biomass, exceptions exist, and pyramids can be inverted, such as when the number of large trees (producers) is less than the number of small insects (primary consumers) or when the biomass of phytoplankton (which have short life spans) is less than that of the zooplankton that eat them. Only energy consistently decreases between lower and higher trophic levels, maintaining the true pyramid shape.

Food Web Efficiency In terms of energy, only about 10% of the kilocalories (food calories, not heat calories) in plant matter are passed from primary producers to primary consumers. In turn, only about 10% of the energy for primary consumers is passed to secondary consumers, and so on. Thus, the most efficient consumption of resources happens at the bottom of the food chain, where plant biomass is higher and the energy input toward food production is lowest.

This concept applies to human eating habits and, on a broader scale, to world food resources. If humans take the role of herbivores, or primary consumers, they eat food with the highest energy available in the food chain. If humans take the role of carnivores, or secondary consumers, they eat food in which the available energy has been cut by 90% (the grain is fed first to cattle, and then the cattle are consumed by humans). In terms of biomass, 810 kg of grain is reduced to 81 kg of meat. In terms of the numbers of organisms, if 1000 people can be fed as primary consumers, only 100 people can be fed as secondary consumers. By the latter analysis, far more people can be fed from the same land area if it is producing grain than if it is producing meat (**Figure 16.9b**).

Today, approximately half of the cultivated acreage in the United States and Canada is planted for animal consumption—beef and dairy cattle, hogs, chickens, and turkeys. Much of U.S. grain production goes to livestock feed rather than to human consumption. In some areas of the world, forests are being cleared and converted to pasture for beef production—in most cases for export to developed countries. Thus, dietary patterns in North America and Europe are perpetuating inefficiency, since consumption of animal products requires much more energy for each calorie produced than consumption of plant products.

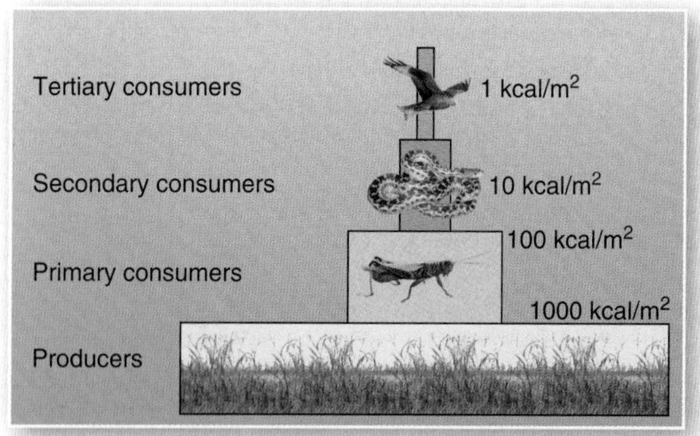

(a) A pyramid shape illustrates the decrease in energy between lower and higher trophic levels. Kilocalorie amounts are idealized to show the general trend of the energy decrease.

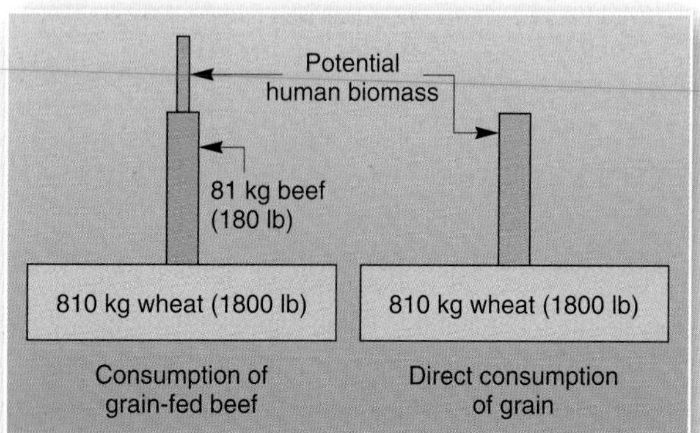

(b) Biomass pyramids illustrate the difference in efficiency between direct and indirect consumption of grain.

▲**Figure 16.9 Pyramids of energy and biomass.**

Biological Amplification When chemical pesticides are applied to an ecosystem of producers and consumers, the food web concentrates some of these chemicals. Many chemicals are degraded or diluted in air and water and thus are rendered relatively harmless. Other chemicals, however, are long-lived, stable, and soluble in the fatty tissues of consumers. They become increasingly concentrated at each higher trophic level. This is called *biological amplification*, or *biomagnification*. In the 1970s, scientists determined that the pesticide DDT was biomagnifying, especially in birds, building up in their fat tissues and causing a thinning of eggshells that caused hatchling mortality. The subsequent ban on DDT for agricultural use is now credited by many experts as saving the Brown Pelican and Peregrine Falcon from extinction.

Thus, pollution in a food web can efficiently poison the organism at the top. The polar bears of the Barents Sea near northern Europe have some of the highest levels of *persistent organic pollutants* (POPs) in any animal in the world, despite their remoteness from civilization. Many species are threatened in this manner (see the orcas in The Human Denominator 16 on page 527), and, of course, humans are at the top of many food chains and therefore at risk of ingesting chemicals concentrated in this way.

Communities and Species Distributions

The levels of organization within ecology and biogeography range from the biosphere, at the top, encompassing all life on Earth, down to single living organisms at the bottom. The biosphere can be broadly divided into ecosystems (including biomes, discussed in Chapter 17), each of which can then be divided into **communities**, made up of interacting populations of living plants and animals in a particular place. A community may be identified in several ways—by its physical appearance, by the species present and the abundance of each, or by the complex patterns of their interdependence, such as the trophic (feeding) structure.

For example, in a forest ecosystem, a specific community may exist on the forest floor, while another community may function in the canopy of leaves high above. Similarly, within a lake ecosystem, the plants and animals that flourish in the bottom sediments form one community, whereas those near the surface form another.

Whether viewed in terms of its ecosystem or in terms of its community within an ecosystem, each species has a **habitat**, defined as the environment in which an organism resides or is biologically adapted to live. A habitat includes both biotic and abiotic elements of the environment, and habitat size and character vary with each species' needs. For example, Great Blue Herons (*Ardia herodias*) are large wading birds that occupy shoreline habitats (riverbanks, freshwater marshes, tidal flats) throughout North America. They frequently nest in the tops of trees near their preferred foraging areas, thereby keeping their young safe from terrestrial predators and humans (**Figure 16.10**).

The Niche Concept

An **ecological niche** (from the French word *nicher*, meaning "to nest") is the function, or occupation, of a life form within a given community. A niche is determined by the physical, chemical, and biological needs of the organism. This is not the same concept as habitat. Niche and habitat are different in that habitat is an environment that can be shared by many species, whereas niche is the specific, unique role that a species performs within that habitat.

▼**Figure 16.10 Great Blue Heron with chicks in a treetop nest.** [Wolf Mountain Images/Shutterstock.]

▲**Figure 16.11 White-breasted Nuthatch in its ecological niche.** [Voyager Images/Alamy.]

For example, the White-breasted Nuthatch (*Sitta carolinensis*) is a small bird that occurs throughout the United States and in parts of Canada and Mexico in forest habitats, especially in *deciduous forests* (those that drop their leaves in winter). Like other nuthatches, this species occupies a particular ecological niche by foraging for insects up and down tree trunks, probing into the bark with their sharp bills and often turning upside down and sideways as they move (**Figure 16.11**). This behavior enables them to find and extract insects that are overlooked by other birds. They also jam nuts and acorns into the bark, and then bang on them with their bill to extract the seeds. Although nuthatches and woodpeckers occupy a similar habitat, the nuthatch's distinctive foraging behavior causes it to occupy a specific niche that is different from a woodpecker's.

The *competitive exclusion principle* states that no two species can occupy the same niche (using the same food or space) because one species will always outcompete the other. Thus, closely related species are spatially separated either by distance or by species-specific strategies. In other words, each species operates to reduce competition and to maximize its own reproduction rate—because, literally, species survival depends on successful reproduction. This strategy, in turn, leads to greater diversity as species shift and adapt to fill different niches.

Species Interactions

Within communities, some species are *symbiotic*—that is, have some type of overlapping relationship. One type of symbiosis, *mutualism*, occurs when each organism benefits and is sustained over an extended period by the relationship. For example, lichen (pronounced "liken") is made up of algae and fungi living together (Figure 16.1c). The alga is the producer and food source for the fungus,

◀**Figure 16.12 Epiphytes using a tree trunk for support, Washington.** Epiphytic club mosses are common in the temperate rain forest of Olympic National Park. [Don Johnston/Alamy.]

and the fungus provides structure and physical support. Their mutualism allows the two to occupy a niche in which neither could survive alone. Lichen developed from an earlier parasitic relationship in which the fungi broke into the algal cells. Today, the two organisms have evolved into a supportive and harmonious symbiotic relationship. The partnership of corals and algae discussed in Chapter 13 is another example of mutualism in a symbiotic relationship (Figure 16.1d).

Another form of symbiosis is *parasitism*, in which one species benefits and another is harmed by the association. Often this association involves a parasite living off a host organism, such as a flea living on a dog. A parasitic relationship may eventually kill the host—an example is parasitic mistletoe (*Phoradendron*), which lives on and can kill various kinds of trees.

A third form of symbiosis is *commensalism*, in which one species benefits and the other experiences neither harm nor benefit. An example is the remora (a sucker fish) that lives attached to sharks and consumes the waste produced as the shark eats its prey. Epiphytic plants, such as orchids, are another example; these "air plants" grow on the branches and trunks of trees, using them for physical support (**Figure 16.12**).

A final symbiotic relationship is *amensalism*, in which one species harms another but is not affected itself. This typically occurs either when two organisms are in competition and one deprives the other of food or habitat or when a plant produces chemical toxins that damage or kill other plants. For example, black walnut trees excrete a chemical toxin through their root systems into the soil that inhibits the growth of other plants beneath them.

CRITICAL**thinking** 16.1

Mutualism? Parasitism? Where Do We Fit In?

Some scientists are asking whether our human society and the physical systems of Earth constitute a global-scale symbiotic relationship of mutualism, which is sustainable, or of parasitism, which is unsustainable. After reviewing the definitions of these terms, what is your response to that statement? How well do our human economic systems coexist with the need to sustain the planet's life-supporting natural systems? Do you characterize this as mutualism, parasitism, or something else?

Abiotic Influences

A number of abiotic environmental factors influence species distributions, interactions, and growth. For example, the distribution of some plants and animals depends on *photoperiod*, the duration of light and dark over a 24-hour period. Many plants require longer days for flowering and seed germination, such as ragweed (*Ambrosia*). Other plants require longer nights to stimulate seed production, such as the poinsettia (*Euphorbia pulcherrima*), which needs at least 2 months of 14-hour nights to start flowering. These species cannot survive in equatorial regions with little daylength variation; they are instead restricted to latitudes with appropriate photoperiods, although other factors may also affect their distribution.

In terms of entire ecosystems, air and soil temperatures are important, since they determine the rates at which chemical reactions proceed. Precipitation and water availability are also critical, as is water quality—its mineral content, salinity, and levels of pollution and toxicity. All of these factors work together to determine the distributions of species and communities in a given location.

Pioneering work in the study of species distribution was done by geographer and explorer Alexander von Humboldt (1769–1859), the first scientist to write about the distinct zonation of plant communities with changing elevation. After several years of study in the Andes Mountains of Peru, von Humboldt hypothesized that

GEO**report** 16.1 Sea turtles navigate using Earth's magnetic field

The fact that birds and bees can detect the abiotic influence of Earth's magnetic field and use it for finding direction is well established. Small amounts of magnetically sensitive particles in the skull of the bird and the abdomen of the bee provide compass directions. Recently, scientists found that sea turtles detect magnetic fields of different strengths and inclinations (angles). This means that the turtles have a built-in navigation system that helps them find certain locations on Earth. Loggerhead turtles hatch in Florida, crawl into the water, and spend the next 70 years traveling thousands of miles between North America and Africa around the subtropical high-pressure gyre in the Atlantic Ocean. The females return to where they were hatched to lay their eggs. In turn, the hatchlings are imprinted with magnetic data unique to the location of their birth and then develop a more global sense of position as they live a life swimming across the ocean.

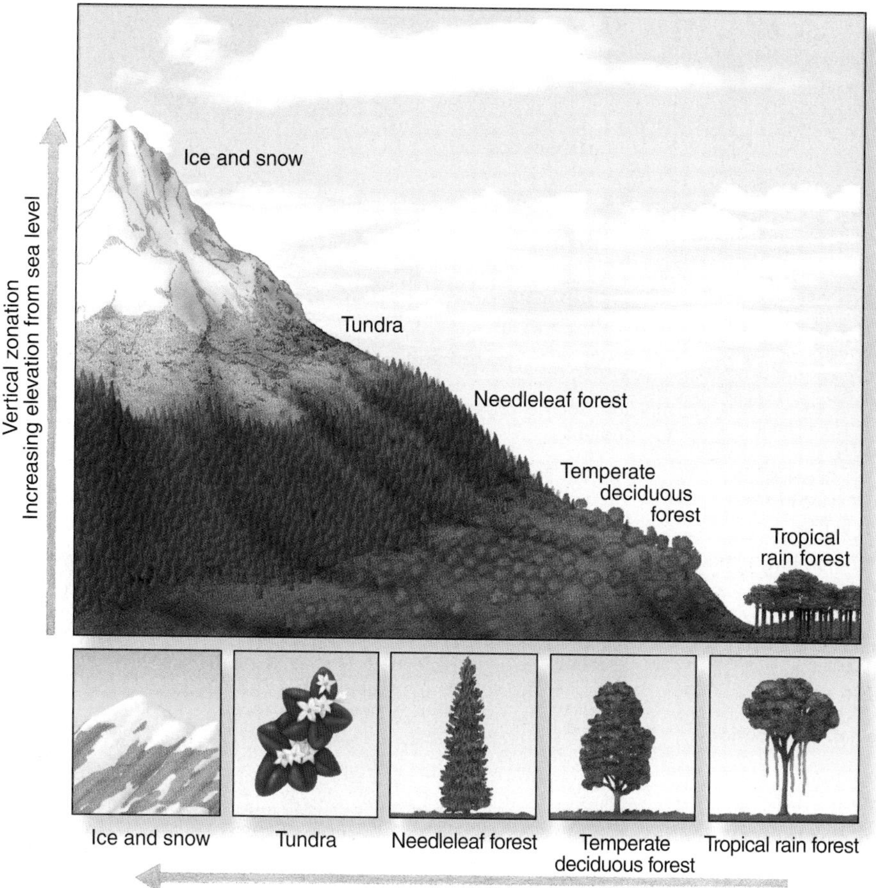

(a) Progression of plant community life zones with changing elevation or latitude.

(b) Treeline for a needleleaf forest in the Canadian Rockies marks the point above which trees cannot grow.

◄**Figure 16.13 Vertical and latitudinal zonation of plant communities.** [Robert Christopherson.]

plants and animals occur in related groupings wherever similar climatic conditions occur. His ideas were the basis for the *life zone concept*, which describes this zonation of flora and fauna along an elevational transect (**Figure 16.13**). Each **life zone** possesses its own temperature and precipitation regime and therefore its own biotic communities.

The life zone concept became prominent in the 1890s with the work of ecologist C. Hart Merriam, who mapped 12 life zones with distinct plant associations in the San Francisco Peaks in northern Arizona. Merriam also expanded the concept to include the changing zonation from the equator toward higher latitudes. Chapter 17 further discusses plant associations in relationship to climatic conditions.

As discussed in this chapter's Geosystems Now, recent scientific studies show that climate change is causing plants and animals to move their ranges to higher elevations with more suitable climates as established life zones shift. Evidence exists that some species have run out of space on mountains, as environmental conditions are pushing them to elevations beyond their mountains' reach, essentially taking them "out of bounds," forcing them either to move elsewhere or into extinction.

Limiting Factors

The term **limiting factor** refers to physical, chemical, or biological characteristics of the environment that determine species distributions and population size. For example, in some ecosystems, precipitation is a limiting factor on plant growth, through either its lack or its excess. Temperature, light levels, and soil nutrients all affect vegetation patterns and abundance:

- Low temperatures limit plant growth at high elevations.
- Lack of water limits growth in a desert; excess water limits growth in a bog.
- Changes in salinity levels affect aquatic ecosystems.
- Low phosphorus content of soils limits plant growth.
- The general lack of active chlorophyll above 6100 m (20,000 ft) limits primary productivity.

For animal populations, limiting factors may be the number of predators, availability of suitable food and habitat, availability of breeding sites, and prevalence of disease. The Snail Kite (*Rostrhamus sociabilis*), a tropical raptor with a small habitat in the Florida Everglades, is a specialist that feeds on only one specific type of snail. In contrast, the Mallard Duck (*Anas platyrhynchos*) is a generalist, feeds from a variety of widely diverse sources, is easily domesticated, and is found throughout most of North America (**Figure 16.14a**).

For some species, one critical limiting factor determines survival and growth; for other species, a combination of factors is at play, with no one single factor being dominant. When taken together, limiting factors determine the *environmental resistance*, which eventually stabilizes populations in an ecosystem.

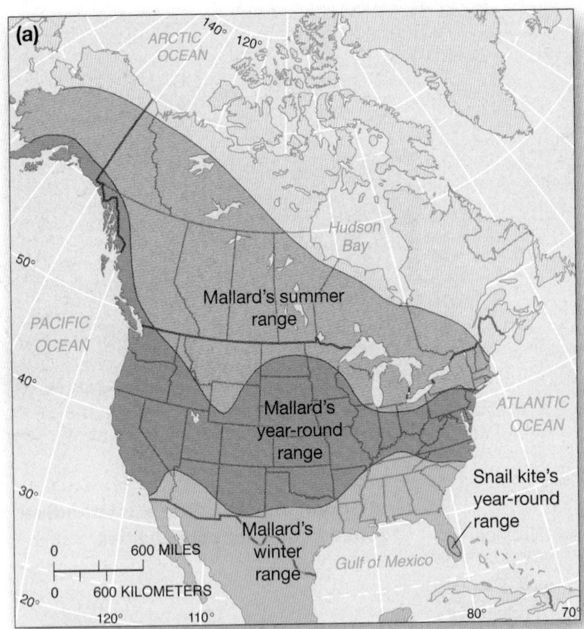

(a) The Snail Kite's small range in North America depends on a single food source; the Mallard Duck is a generalist and feeds widely.

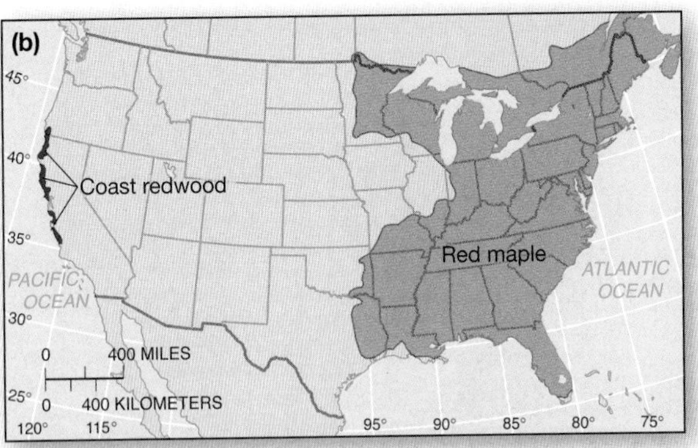

(b) The coast redwood is limited by the need for fog as a moisture source; red maple tolerates a variety of environmental conditions.

▲Figure 16.14 Limiting factors affecting species' distributions.

Each organism possesses a *range of tolerance* for physical and chemical environmental characteristics. Within that range, species abundance is high; at the edges of the range, the species is found infrequently; and beyond the range limits, the species is absent. For example, the coast redwood (*Sequoia sempervirens*) is abundant within a narrow range along the California and Oregon coast where foggy conditions provide condensation to meet the tree's water needs. Redwoods at the limit of their range—for example, at higher elevations above the fog layer—are shorter, smaller, and less abundant. The red maple (*Acer rubrum*) has a wide tolerance range and is distributed over a large area with varying moisture and temperature conditions (**Figure 16.14b**).

Disturbance and Succession

Over time, communities undergo natural disturbance events such as windstorms, severe flooding, a volcanic eruption, or an insect infestation (**Figure 16.15**). Human activities, such as the logging of a forest or the overgrazing of a rangeland, also create disturbance. Such events damage or remove existing organisms, making way for new communities.

Wildfires are a natural component of many ecosystems and a common cause of ecosystem disturbance. The science of **fire ecology** examines the role of fire in ecosystems, including the adaptations of individual plants to the effects of fire and the human management of fire-adapted ecosystems. Focus Study 16.1 takes a look at this important subject.

When a community is disturbed enough that most, or all, of its species are eliminated, a process known as **ecological succession** occurs, in which the cleared area undergoes a series of changes in species composition as

(a) Damage from a debris flow in North Carolina, triggered by the rainfall associated with Hurricane Ivan in 2004.

(b) Thunderstorm winds damaged forests in eastern Minnesota and northwest Wisconsin in July 2011; wind speeds reached over 160 kmph (100 mph).

▲Figure 16.15 Ecosystem disturbance, making way for new communities. [NOAA.]

newer communities of plants and animals replace older ones. Each successive community modifies the physical environment in a manner that favors a different community. During the transitions between communities, species having an adaptive advantage, such as the ability to produce lots of seeds or disperse them over great distances, will outcompete other species for space, light, water, and nutrients. Successional processes occur in both terrestrial and aquatic ecosystems.

Terrestrial Succession An area of bare rock or a disturbed site with no vestige of a former community can be a site for **primary succession**, the beginning stage of an ecosystem. Primary succession can occur on new surfaces created by mass movement of land, glacial retreat, volcanic eruptions, surface mining, clear-cut logging, or the movement of sand dunes. In terrestrial ecosystems, primary succession begins with the arrival of organisms that are well adapted for colonizing new substrates, forming a **pioneer community**. For example, a pioneer community of lichens, mosses, and ferns may establish on bare rock (**Figure 16.16**). These early inhabitants prepare the way for further succession: Lichens secrete acids that break down rock, which begins the process of soil formation, which enhances habitat for other organisms. As new organisms colonize soil surfaces, they bring nutrients that further change the habitat, eventually leading to the growth of grasses, shrubs, and trees.

More commonly encountered in nature is **secondary succession**, which occurs when some aspect of a previously functioning community is still present: for example, a disturbed area where the underlying soil remains intact. As secondary succession begins, new plants and animals having niches that differ from those of the previous community colonize the area; species assemblages may shift as soil develops, habitats change, and the community matures.

▲**Figure 16.16 Primary succession.** Plants establishing on recently cooled lava flows from the Kīlauea volcano in Hawai'i illustrate primary succession. [Bobbé Christopherson.]

Most of the areas affected by the Mount St. Helens eruption and blast in 1980, which burned or blew down about 38,450 hectares (95,000 acres) of trees, underwent secondary succession (**Figure 16.17**). Some soils, young trees, and plants were protected under ash and snow, so community development began almost immediately after the event. The areas completely destroyed near the Mount St. Helens volcano and those buried beneath the massive

(a) Mount St. Helens, 2008.

(b) Repeat photography of post-eruption recovery at Meta Lake, 1983 and 1999.

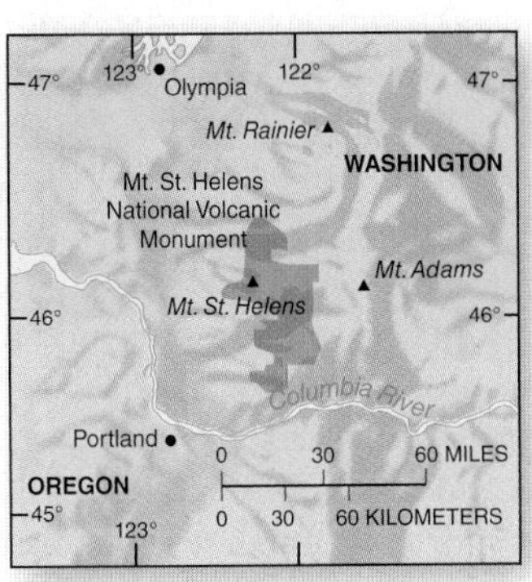

(c) Repeat photography showing secondary succession, 1983 and 1999.

▲**Figure 16.17 The pace of change in the region of Mount St. Helens.** [(a) *ISS* astronaut photo, NASA/GSFC; (b) and (c) 1983 photos by Robert Christopherson; 1999 photos by Bobbé Christopherson.]

focusstudy 16.1 Natural Hazards

Wildfire and Fire Ecology

Fire is one of Earth's significant natural hazards, and damage from wildfire has become an economic burden to human societies in some parts of the world. In the United States, wildfires burned over 9 million acres in 2006 and 2007 and again in 2012. In Australia, the "Black Saturday" fires in 2009, the most destructive in the country's history, destroyed more than 2000 homes and claimed 173 lives. According to the National Interagency Fire Center (http://www.nifc.gov/fireInfo/fireInfo_main.html), the cost of fire suppression in the United States reached almost $2 billion in 2012; other estimates place annual average fire-fighting costs around $3 billion since 2000, as compared to $1 billion in the 1990s.

Lightning-caused wildfire is a natural disturbance, with a dynamic role in community succession. Many ecosystems have properties that influence the intensity and size of wildfires, which in turn create a mosaic of habitats, ranging from totally burned to partially burned to unburned areas. This patchwork of habitats ultimately benefits biodiversity. Fire affects soils, making them more nutrient-rich in some cases, yet more susceptible to erosion in cases of intensely hot fires. Fire also affects plants and animals; in fact, some species are adapted to, even dependent on, frequent fire occurrence.

▲**Figure 16.1.1 Landscape recovery after 1988 wildfires in Yellowstone National Park, Wyoming.** Decades of fire suppression in Yellowstone fueled the 1988 fires. Ten years later, young lodgepole pine, a fire-adapted species, grow among the burned stands. [Jim Peaco, NPS.]

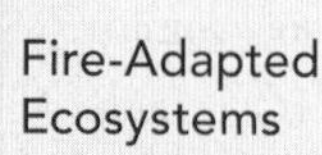

Fire-Adapted Ecosystems

A number of Earth's grasslands, forests, and scrublands have evolved through interaction with fire and are known as *fire-adapted ecosystems.* Plant species in such environments may have dense bark, which protects them from heat, or lack lower branches, which protects them from ground fires. Fire-adapted species typically resprout quickly after fire destroys their branches or trunks.

Several North American tree species depend on fire for reproduction. For example, lodgepole pine and jack pine rely on fire to crack and open the resin that otherwise seals their cones and keeps seeds from being released. Seedlings of giant sequoia grow best on open, burned sites, without grasses or other vegetation competing for resources. Fire-disturbed areas quickly recover with stimulated seed production, protein-rich woody growth, and young plants that provide abundant food for animals.

Fire Management

Modern society's demand for fire prevention to protect property began with European forestry practices of the 1800s and carried over into forest management in North America. Since then, however, forestry experts have learned that when fire-prevention strategies are rigidly followed, they can lead to a buildup of forest undergrowth that fuels major fires. For example, in Yellowstone National Park in the 1970s, after decades of fire suppression, forest managers began a new policy

landslide north of the mountain became candidates for primary succession.

Traditionally, communities of plants and animals were thought to pass through several successional stages, eventually reaching a mature state with a predictable *climax community*—a stable, self-sustaining assemblage of species that would remain until the next major disturbance. However, contemporary biogeography and ecology assume that disturbances constantly disrupt the sequence and that a community may never reach what would be considered a climax stage. Mature communities are in a state of constant adaptation—a dynamic equilibrium—sometimes with a lag time in their adjustment to environmental changes. Scientists now know that successional processes are driven by a dynamic set of interactions with sometimes unpredictable outcomes.

Disturbance often occurs in discrete spatial units across the landscape, creating habitats, or *patches,* at different successional stages. The concept of *patch dynamics* refers to the interactions between and within this mosaic of habitats, which add to complexity across the landscape. The overall biodiversity of an ecosystem is in part the result of such patch dynamics.

Aquatic Succession Aquatic ecosystems occur in lakes, estuaries, and wetlands and along shorelines, and the communities in these systems also undergo succession. For example, lakes and ponds exhibit successional stages as they fill with sediment and nutrients and as aquatic plants take root and grow. The plant growth captures more sediment and adds organic debris to the system (**Figure 16.18**). This gradual enrichment in water of letting natural fires burn; 18 years later, in 1988, after one of the driest summers on record, massive fires burned through the park, destroying buildings and about 1.2 million acres of forest and grassland. Twenty-five years later, vegetation regrowth is ongoing, a slow process in the short growing seasons on this high-elevation plateau (**Figure 16.1.1**).

Today, following the principles of fire ecology, fire specialists worldwide use controlled ground fires, deliberately set to prevent undergrowth accumulation and maintain ecosystem health. These controlled "cool fires" remove fuel and prevent catastrophic and destructive "hot fires" that burn through the forest crown. Scientists and forest managers also use such prescribed burns to control invasive species and restore natural habitat (**Figure 16.1.2**).

Wildfire, Climate Change, and Urban Development

With recent, ongoing climate change, the wildfire threat is worsening. Scientists have linked record wildfires in the American West since 2000 to increased spring and summer temperatures and an earlier spring snowmelt. Perhaps more important is the fact that these climatic changes are occurring after 150 years or more of fire suppression across the United States, which has resulted in a buildup of undergrowth as fuel. Lightning-caused fires related to more intense weather systems are also on the increase in some regions. In June 2013, the West Fork Complex fire, ignited by lightning, burned explosively through the rugged terrain of southwest Colorado, fueled by forests desiccated from drought and from extensive die-off caused by spruce beetle infestations.

▲**Figure 16.1.2 Prescribed burn for grassland restoration.** Near Fort Lewis, Colorado, nearly 12,000 acres of prairie were burned in 2009 to eliminate invasive plant species. [Ingrid Barrantine/U.S. Department of Defense.]

The destruction caused by wildfires is increasing as urban development encroaches on forests, putting homes at risk and threatening public safety. In 2013, the Black Forest Fire became the most destructive fire in Colorado's history, burning over 500 homes north of Colorado Springs. Wildfires have devastated communities in southern California, especially those developed in the chaparral country, a vegetation community characterized by its fire adaptations. In 2007, fire destroyed more than 2000 homes in that region and burned over 202,340 hectares (500,000 acres) in two dozen wildfires. This is part of the overall pattern continuing today (look back to the Chapter 4 Geosystems Now, focusing on the effects of the Santa Ana winds in southern California).

Recently, *pyrogeography* has become a growing geographic subfield studying the spatial distribution and ecological effects of fire across Earth. As fires intensify, the connections between fire, ecosystem processes, climate, and human health and property are gaining significance, calling for increased scientific study.

1. What vegetation characteristics are present in fire-adapted ecosystems? Describe some fire adaptations of North American plant species.
2. Using the principles of fire ecology, assess the effectiveness of total fire suppression in forest ecosystems.

bodies is known as **eutrophication** (from the Greek *eutrophos*, meaning "well nourished").

In moist climates, a lake will develop a floating mat of vegetation that grows outward from the shore to form a bog. Cattails and other marsh plants become established, and partially decomposed organic material accumulates in the basin, with additional vegetation bordering the remaining lake surface. Vegetation and soil and a meadow may fill in as water is displaced; willow trees follow, and perhaps cottonwood trees; eventually, the lake may evolve into a forest community. Thus, when viewed across geologic time, a lake or pond is really a temporary feature on the landscape.

Even large bodies of water may have eutrophic areas along the shore. As humans dump sewage, agricultural runoff, and pollution into waterways, the nutrient load is enhanced beyond the cleansing ability of natural biological processes. This human-caused eutrophication, known as *cultural eutrophication*, hastens succession in aquatic systems.

Biodiversity, Evolution, and Ecosystem Stability

Far from being static, Earth's ecosystems have been dynamic—vigorous, energetic, and ever-changing—from the beginning of life on the planet. Over time, communities of plants and animals have adapted and evolved to produce great diversity and, in turn, have shaped their environments. Each ecosystem is constantly adjusting to changing conditions and disturbances. Ironically, the concept of change is key to understanding ecosystem stability.

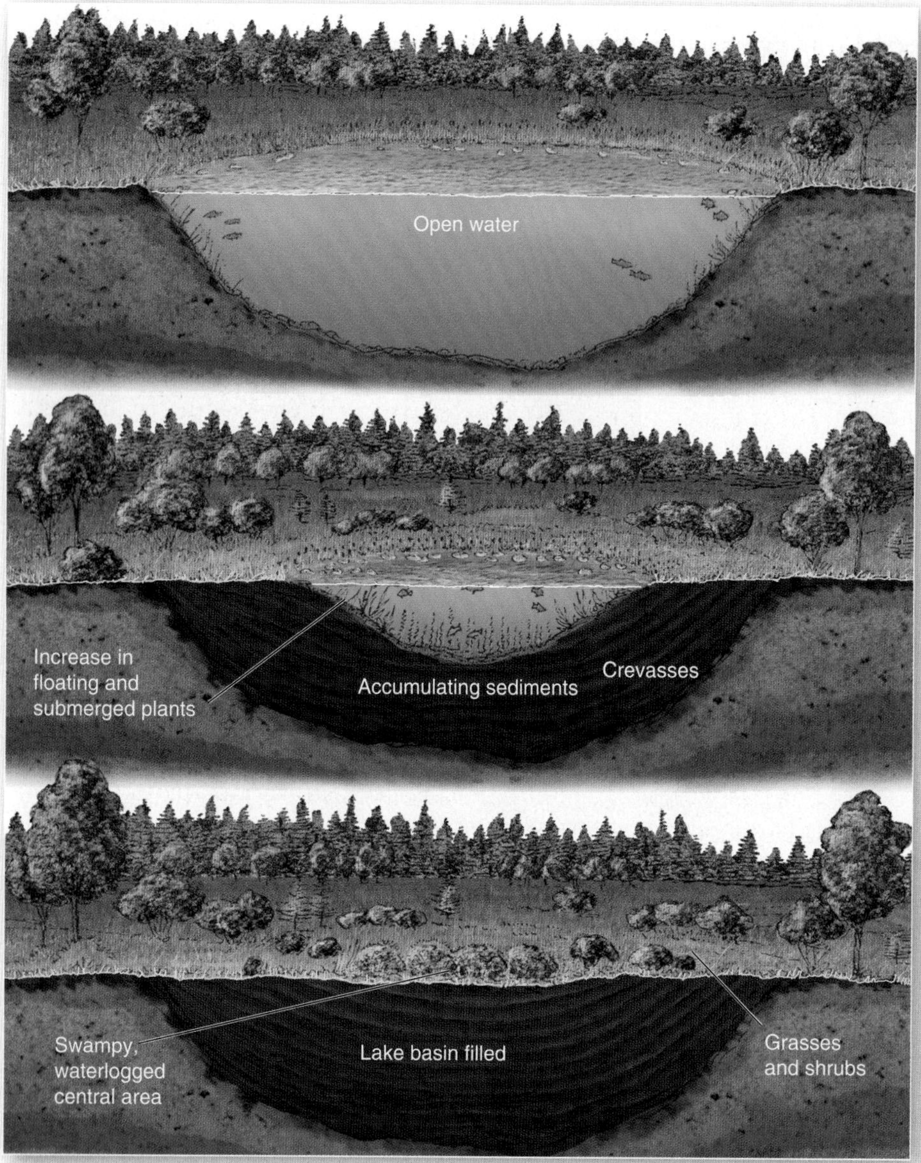

Open water

Increase in floating and submerged plants

Accumulating sediments

Crevasses

Swampy, waterlogged central area

Lake basin filled

Grasses and shrubs

(a) A lake gradually fills with organic and inorganic sediments, shrinking the area of open water. A bog forms, then a marsh, and finally a meadow, the last of the successional stages.

(b) Spring Mill Lake, Indiana

(c) Organic content increases as succession progresses in a western N.A. mountain lake.

(d) Peat bog with acidic soils, Richmond Nature Park, near Vancouver, British Columbia.

▲**Figure 16.18 Idealized lake–bog–meadow succession in temperate conditions, with real-world examples.** [Bobbé Christopherson.]

The dynamics of change in natural ecosystems can range from gradual transitions between equilibrium states to abrupt changes caused by extreme catastrophes such as an asteroid impact or severe volcanism. For most of the last century, scientists thought that an undisturbed ecosystem—whether a forest, a grassland, or a lake—would progress to a stage of equilibrium, a stable point, with maximum chemical storage and biomass. Modern research has determined, however, that ecosystems do not progress to some static conclusion, but instead reflect a constant interplay of physical, chemical, and living factors in a dynamic equilibrium.

A critical aspect of ecosystem stability and vitality is **biodiversity**, or variation of life (a combination of

GEOreport 16.2 Another take on lake–bog succession

In areas that have been recently deglaciated, scientists have uncovered a pattern that seems the opposite of lake–bog succession, alerting them to gaps in the understanding of successional processes in aquatic ecosystems. Evidence from lakes in the Glacier Bay, Alaska, area suggests that these water bodies became more dilute, acidic, and unproductive—in other words, less eutrophic—over the past 10,000 years. Successional changes in the surrounding vegetation and soils seem to be linked to these changes in the aquatic ecosystem. The studies suggest that in various cool, moist, temperate rainforest climates with landscapes created by glacial retreat, different processes are at work in lakes than the ones described as typical in this chapter.

the terms *bio*logical and *diversity*). The concept of biodiversity encompasses species diversity, the number and variety of different species; genetic diversity, the amount of genetic variation within these species; and ecosystem diversity, the number and variety of ecosystems, habitats, and communities on a landscape scale.

Biological Evolution

The origin of Earth's biodiversity is laid out in the *theory of evolution*. (The definition of a scientific theory is given in Chapter 1.) **Evolution** is the process in which the first, single-celled organisms adapted, modified, and passed along inherited changes to descendants, eventually producing the world's diverse species of organisms, many of which are multicellular. A *species* is a population that can reproduce sexually and produce viable offspring. By this definition, each species is reproductively isolated from other species.

The genetic makeup of successive generations is shaped by environmental factors, physiological functions, and behaviors that lead to greater rates of survival and reproduction in some members of a population than in others. Traits that help a species survive and reproduce—especially the traits that are most successful at exploiting niches different from those of other species or that help the species adapt to environmental changes—are passed along to offspring and their descendants more frequently than those that do not. Such differential reproduction and adaptation is known as *natural selection* and is the basis of evolutionary change. The process continues generation after generation, tracing the passage of inherited characteristics that were successful—the failures pass into extinction. Thus, today's humans are the result of billions of years of affirmative natural selection.

Inherited traits are encoded by an array of genes, part of an organism's primary genetic material—*DNA* (deoxyribonucleic acid)—which resides in the nest of chromosomes in every cell nucleus. New genes in the *gene pool*, the collection of all genes possessed by individuals in a given population, result from *mutation*, a process in which a random occurrence, perhaps an error as the DNA reproduces, alters the genetic material. Mutation can introduce new traits to be selected for or against in the process of natural selection.

Geography also comes into play in natural selection, since spatial variation in physical environments affects survival and reproductive success. For example, a species may disperse through migration, such as across ice bridges or land connections at times of low sea level, to a different environment where new traits are favored. A species may also be separated from other species by a natural *vicariance* event (a fragmentation of the environment). An example is continental drift, which establishes natural barriers to species movement and results in the evolution of new species. The physical and chemical evolution of Earth's systems is therefore closely linked to the biological evolution of life.

Ecosystem Stability and Resilience

In the context of ecosystems, "stable" does not mean unchanging; stable ecosystems are constantly changing. A stable ecosystem is one that does not deviate greatly from its original state despite changing environmental conditions (the environmental resistance, mentioned earlier). *Resilience* is the ecosystem's ability to recover from disturbance quickly and return to its original state.

In the 1990s, field experiments in the prairie ecosystems of Minnesota began to confirm an important scientific assumption: Greater biological diversity in an ecosystem leads to greater resilience. For instance, during a drought, some species of plants will decline from water stress. In a diverse ecosystem, however, other species with deeper roots and better water-obtaining ability will thrive, thus acting to preserve the stability and productivity of the system as a whole. Ongoing experiments also suggest that a more diverse plant community retains and uses soil nutrients more efficiently than one with less diversity. (More about this research at the Cedar Creek Ecosystem Science Reserve is at http://www.cedarcreek.umn.edu/about/.)

Some disturbances are too extreme for even a highly resilient ecosystem. For example, several of the dramatic asteroid-impact episodes that triggered partial extinctions over the past 440 million years overcame the resilience of plant and animal communities, destabilizing the ecosystem. When an ecosystem crosses such a threshold, it moves toward a new stable state.

An ecosystem can be stable yet not resilient. A tropical rain forest is a diverse, stable community that can withstand most natural disturbance. Such an ecosystem has *inertial stability*, the ability to resist some low-level disturbance. Yet this ecosystem has low resilience in terms of severe events; a cleared tract of rain forest will recover at a slower rate than many other communities because most of the nutrients are stored in the vegetation rather than in the soil. Furthermore, changes in microclimates may make regrowth of the same species difficult. In contrast, a midlatitude grassland, although less diverse than a rain forest, has high resilience because the system can cope with a range of disturbances and recover quickly. For example, after a fire, rapid regrowth occurs from the extensive root systems of grassland species.

In reference to ecosystem stability and resilience, consider the elimination of a full section of forest ecosystem on private land in southern Oregon, south-southeast of Crater Lake, shown in **Figure 16.19**. The practice of clear-cutting (the complete removal of timber) can cause a disturbance that overcomes a forest community's resilience and prevents it from returning to its natural stable state. Adjacent lands administered by the U.S Forest Service use more sustainable harvesting regimes, including partial tree removal and forest thinning, that are not as likely to destabilize forest communities.

◀**Figure 16.19 Disruption of a forest community.** An example of clear-cut timber harvesting that devastated a stable forest community and produced drastic changes in microclimatic conditions. About 10% of the Northwest's old-growth forests remain, as identified through satellite images and GIS analysis. [Bobbé Christopherson.]

When humans purposely eliminate biodiversity from an area, as they do in most agricultural practices, the area becomes more vulnerable to disturbance. An artificially produced monoculture community, such as a field of wheat or a tree plantation, is vulnerable to insect infestations or plant diseases (**Figure 16.20**). In some regions, simply planting multiple crops brings more stability to the ecosystem—this is an important principle of sustainable agriculture.

Biodiversity on the Decline

Human activities have great impact on global biodiversity; the present loss of species is irreversible and is accelerating. We are now facing a loss of genetic diversity that may be unparalleled in Earth's history, even compared with the major extinctions that punctuate the geologic record.

Since life arose on the planet, six major mass extinctions have occurred. The fifth one was 65 million years ago, whereas the sixth is happening over the present decades (see Figure 9.1). Of all these extinction episodes, this is the only one of biotic origin, caused for the most part by human activity. According to a 2014 study, species are now disappearing at a rate 1000 times faster than natural, pre-human extinction rates.

Presently, about 270,000 species of plants are known to exist, with many more species yet to be identified. They represent a great untapped resource base. Only about 20 species of plants provide 90% of food for humans; just three—wheat, maize (corn), and rice—make up half of that supply. Plants are also a major source of new medicines and chemical compounds that benefit humanity.

Table 16.1 summarizes the numbers of known and estimated species on Earth. Scientists have classified only 1.75 million species of plants and animals. The wide range of estimates for the count of total species is between a low of 3.6 million and a high of 111.7 million. This figure represents an increase in what scientists once thought to be the diversity of life on Earth. Estimates of annual species loss range between 1000 and 30,000 species, although this range might be conservative. The possibility exists that over half of Earth's present species could be extinct within the next 100 years.

◀**Figure 16.20 Tree plantation, southern Georgia.** [Bobbé Christopherson.]

TABLE 16.1 Known and Estimated Species on Earth

Categories of Living Organisms	Number of Known Species	Estimated Number of Species High (x1000)	Low (x1000)	Working Estimate (x1000)	Accuracy
Viruses	4000	1000	50	400	Very poor
Bacteria	4000	3000	50	1000	Very poor
Fungi	72,000	27,000	200	1500	Moderate
Protozoa	40,000	200	60	200	Very poor
Algae	40,000	1000	150	400	Very poor
Plants	270,000	500	300	320	Good
Nematodes	25,000	1000	100	400	Poor
Arthropods:					
Crustaceans	40,000	200	75	150	Moderate
Arachnids	75,000	1000	300	750	Moderate
Insects	950,000	100,000	2000	8000	Moderate
Mollusks	70,000	200	100	200	Moderate
Chordates	45,000	55	50	50	Good
Others	115,000	800	200	250	Moderate
Total	**1,750,000**	**111,655**	**3635**	**13,620**	**Very poor**

Source: United Nations Environment Programme, *Global Biodiversity Assessment* (Cambridge, England: Cambridge University Press, 1995), Table 3.1–3.2, p. 118, used by permission.

Five categories of human impact represent the greatest threat to biodiversity:

- Habitat loss, degradation, and fragmentation as natural areas are converted for agriculture and urban development
- Pollution of air, water, and soils
- Resource exploitation and harvesting of plants and animals at unsustainable levels
- Human-induced climate change, discussed in this chapter's Geosystems Now and in Chapter 8
- Introduction of non-native plants and animals, discussed in Chapter 17

The World Conservation Monitoring Centre and its International Union for Conservation of Nature (IUCN) maintain a global "Red List" of endangered species at http://www.iucnredlist.org/. See also the endangered species home page of the Fish and Wildlife Service at http://www.fws.gov/endangered/. Let us now look at some specific examples of species in decline.

Threatened Species—Examples Amphibians have a higher risk of extinction than mammals, fish, and birds because they are vulnerable to changes in both terrestrial and aquatic ecosystems, such as habitat destruction, pollution, invasive species, and changing climate. Although amphibian declines can also be attributed to natural causes such as competition, predation, and disease, the bottom line is that these species are not evolving fast enough to keep up with the rate of environmental change.

In the Arctic region, the polar bear (*Ursus maritimus*) faces melting sea-ice habitat associated with climate change. The IUCN in 2006 listed the species as "vulnerable" to extinction, and it was designated as "threatened" under the U.S. Endangered Species Act (ESA) in 2008. Research released by the U.S. Geological Survey in September 2007 predicted that with the loss of Alaskan, Canadian, and Russian sea-ice habitat, some two-thirds of the world's 23,000 polar bears will die off by 2050 or earlier. The remaining 7500 bears will be struggling.

In Africa, black rhinos (*Diceros bicornis*) and white rhinos (*Ceratotherium simum*) exemplify species in jeopardy from declining habitat and overharvesting. Rhinos once grazed over much of the savannas and woodlands.

GEOreport 16.3 Will species adapt to climate change?

A 2013 study reveals that in order for vertebrate species to adapt to projected changes in climate by the year 2100, they will need to evolve their niche requirements 10,000 times faster than rates in the past. Using genetic data for over 500 species of terrestrial vertebrates, including frogs, snakes, birds, and mammals, spread out over 17 evolutionary trees, the scientists examined how long each species took to shift its climatic niche under past environmental conditions. They found that over about a million years, species were able to adapt to a temperature difference of 1 C°. These results suggest that adaptation may not be an option for species survival in today's rapidly warming climate.

Today, they survive only in protected districts in heavily guarded sanctuaries. Consider these statistics:

- Black rhinos: The population of 70,000 in 1960 dropped to 2599 in 1998—a decline of 96%. South Africa guards about 50% of the herd. Slow recovery is under way; numbers rose to 4880 in 2010. The western black rhino, a subspecies, has not been seen since 2006 and is considered extinct.
- White rhinos: The 11 northern white rhinos surviving in 1984 increased to over 25 by 1998 but then dropped as political unrest in the Congo slowed protection efforts. In 2014, only 6 were left in the Ol Pejeta Conservancy in Kenya. The southern white rhinos are on the increase; their population topped 20,000 in 2014 (**Figure 16.21**).

Rhinoceros horn sells for $29,000 per kilogram as an aphrodisiac (but in reality has no medicinal effect). These large land mammals are nearing extinction and will survive only as a dwindling zoo population. The limited genetic pool that remains complicates further reproduction.

Species and Ecosystem Restoration Since the 1990s, species restoration efforts in North America have focused on returning predators such as wolves and condors to parts of the American West and, recently, jaguars to the Southwest. Other efforts have resulted in rising populations of black-footed ferrets and Whooping Cranes in the prairie regions and shortnose sturgeon along the Atlantic seaboard. These projects have reintroduced captive-bred animals or relocated wild animals into their former habitats, while at the same time limiting practices such as hunting that once caused species decline. The preservation of large habitats has also played a critical role in restoring these, and other, endangered species worldwide.

Efforts to restore entire ecosystems began over thirty years ago. For example, restoration of the Great Lakes ecosystems started in the 1970s and is ongoing. For maps, lake levels, and the latest restoration information, see Chapter 16 on the *MasteringGeography* website.

Recent efforts at ecosystem restoration have had some success in restoring or preserving biodiversity, although questions remain about the effects of such work on overall ecosystem functioning. Numerous river restoration projects, such as the dam removals discussed in Chapter 12, are successfully restoring natural conditions for fisheries and riparian wetlands in the short term. In the Florida Everglades, a $9.5 billion restoration project began in 2000 and is ongoing. The goal is to return freshwater flow into the south Florida swamplands to revive the dying ecosystem. The Everglades restoration is the largest and most ambitious watershed restoration project in history (see http://www.evergladesplan.org/index.aspx).

A question that is raised in regard to restoration of these and many other ecosystems is "What is natural?"—especially considering the frequent involvement of human activity as a factor in ecosystem changes. The goal of returning ecosystems to the conditions that prevailed before human intervention is now being expanded to include the possibility of creating "novel ecosystems," human-built or human-modified ecosystems that may have species and habitats that have never occurred together. These novel systems have no natural analogs on which to base scientific hypotheses or restoration strategies—and yet, to sustain biodiversity and ecosystem function in our changing world, humans may need to understand and manage such ecosystems.

CRITICAL**thinking** 16.2

Observe Ecosystem Disturbance and Recovery

Over the next several days, observe the landscape as you travel between home and campus, a job, or other localities. What types of ecosystem disturbances do you see? Are the disturbances natural or anthropogenic (human-induced)? Do you see evidence that natural recovery is occurring? Finally, look for evidence of environmental restoration occurring in your area, noting that restoration can occur on many scales, from a small plot of land to an entire ecosystem.

◀**Figure 16.21 The rhinoceros in Africa.** White rhinoceros with young, from the southern population, Lake Nakuru National Park, Kenya. [Pal Taravagimov/Shutterstock.]

ECOSYSTEM PROCESSES IMPACT HUMANS

- All life depends on healthy, functioning ecosystems, which provide the food and all other natural resources that humans use.

HUMANS IMPACT ECOSYSTEM PROCESSES

Human activities cause declining biodiversity. For example,

- Habitat loss occurs as natural areas are converted for agriculture and urban development.
- Pesticides and other pollutants poison organisms in food webs.
- Climate change affects plant and animal distributions and overall ecosystem function.
- Fertilizer use and industrial activities alter biogeochemical cycles, as when dead zones disrupt the nitrogen cycle.

16a

Hunted to near-extinction by the early 1900s, the Eurasian beaver (*Castor fiber*) was successfully reintroduced throughout most of its former range. The North American beaver (*Castor canadensis*) also declined but has now recovered in most regions. Beaver are large, semi-aquatic rodents whose dams create wetland habitat for many plants and other animals.

16b

Scientists successfully outfitted baby loggerhead sea turtles with satellite tracking tags in 2012. The tags will allow experts to follow migration routes throughout all life stages, providing critical information for sea turtle conservation. (See GeoReport 16.1.)

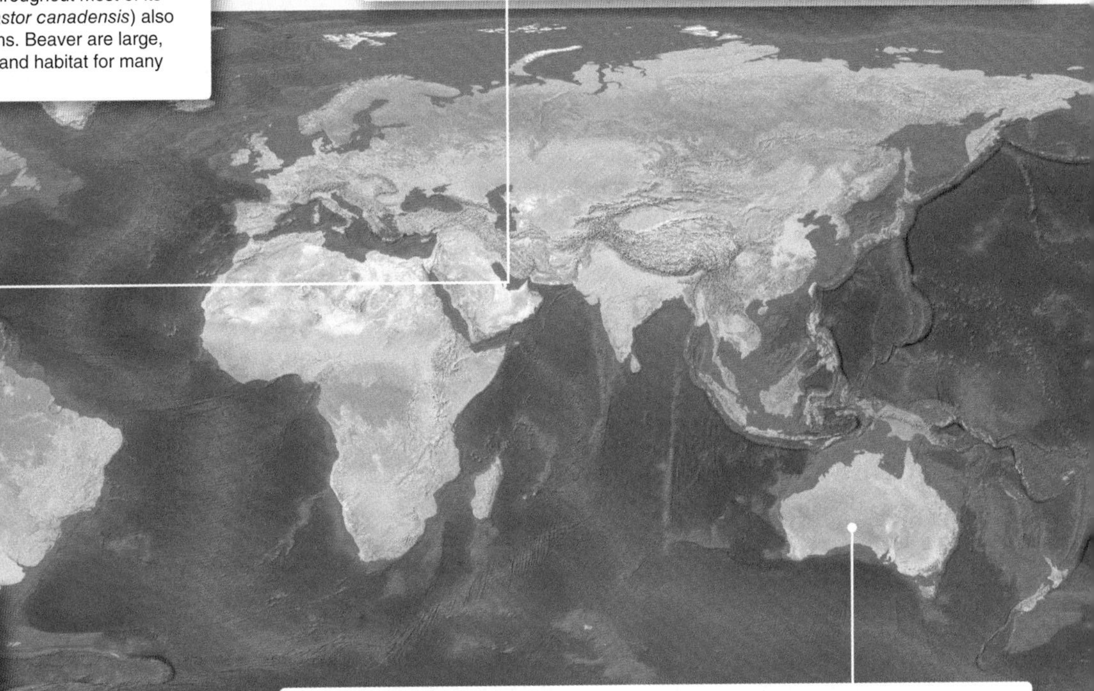

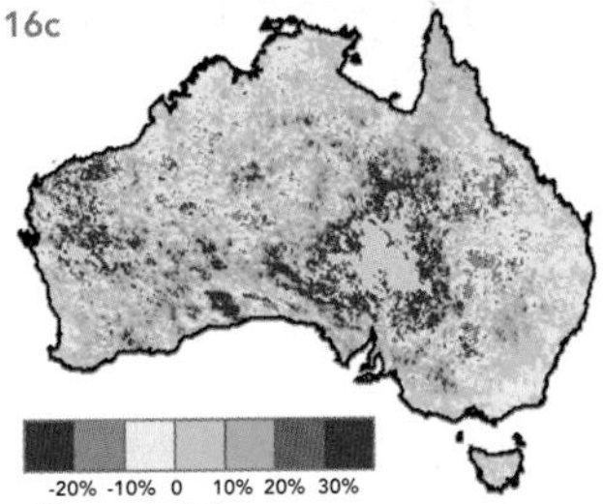

16c

-20% -10% 0 10% 20% 30%
Change in foliage cover

Scientists attribute increased foliage cover since 1982 in parts of Australia to the "CO_2 fertilization effect"—enhanced photosynthesis caused by rising atmospheric CO_2 levels. In Australia's warm, dry climates, leaves drawing in extra CO_2 lose less water, enabling plants to put out even more leaves and producing a "greening" that shows in satellite images. Other warm, arid regions of the world show the same trend. (See http://www.csiro.au/Portals/Media/ Deserts-greening-from-rising-CO2.aspx.)

16d

Orcas (*Orcinus orca*), also known as killer whales, are threatened by high levels of polychlorinated biphenyls (PCBs), as well as other contaminants, in Puget Sound, Washington. Persistent organic pollutants are stored in the whale's tissues and may be a primary cause for declining resident populations of these marine mammals.

ISSUES FOR THE 21ST CENTURY

- Species and ecosystem conservation and restoration will be essential to save species from extinction.
- Fire ecology will become increasingly important as climate change leads to prolonged drought in some areas and as human populations spread farther into wildlands.
- Addressing and mitigating climate change may become essential to preserving a future for all species, including humans.

KEYLEARNINGconceptsreview

Define ecology, biogeography, and ecosystem.

Earth's biosphere is made up of **ecosystems**, self-sustaining associations of living plants and animals and their nonliving physical environment. **Ecology** is the study of the relationships between organisms and their environment and among the various ecosystems in the biosphere. **Biogeography** is the study of the distribution of plants and animals and the diverse spatial patterns they create.

ecosystem (p. 504)
ecology (p. 504)
biogeography (p. 504)

1. Define ecosystem, and give some examples.
2. What does biogeography include? Describe its relationship to ecology.

Explain photosynthesis and respiration and *describe* the world pattern of net primary productivity.

Producers, which fix the carbon they need from CO_2, are the plants, algae, and cyanobacteria (a type of blue-green algae). As plants evolved, the **vascular plants** developed conductive tissues. **Stomata** on the underside of leaves are the portals through which the plant participates with the atmosphere and hydrosphere. Plants (primary producers) perform **photosynthesis** as sunlight stimulates a light-sensitive pigment called **chlorophyll**. This process produces food sugars and oxygen to drive biological processes. **Respiration** is essentially the reverse of photosynthesis and is the way the plant derives energy by oxidizing carbohydrates. **Net primary productivity** is the net photosynthesis (photosynthesis minus respiration) of an entire community. **Biomass** is the total organic matter derived from all living and recently living organisms and is measured as the net dry weight of organic material. Net primary productivity produces the energy needed for **consumers**—generally animals (including zooplankton in aquatic ecosystems)—that depend on producers as their carbon source.

producer (p. 504)
vascular plant (p. 505)
stomata (p. 505)
photosynthesis (p. 505)
chlorophyll (p. 506)
respiration (p. 506)
net primary productivity (p. 506)
biomass (p. 507)
consumer (p. 507)

3. Define a vascular plant. How many plant species are there on Earth?
4. How do plants function to link the Sun's energy to living organisms? What is formed within the light-responsive cells of plants?
5. Compare photosynthesis and respiration with regard to the concept of net photosynthesis, which is the result of deducting respiration from photosynthesis. What is the importance of knowing the net primary productivity of an ecosystem and how much biomass an ecosystem has accumulated?
6. Briefly describe the global pattern of net primary productivity.

Discuss the oxygen, carbon, and nitrogen cycles and *explain* trophic relationships.

Life is sustained by **biogeochemical cycles**, through which circulate the gases and nutrients necessary for growth and development of living organisms. Excessive nutrient inputs into oceans or lakes can create **dead zones** in the water, areas with low-oxygen conditions that limit underwater life.

Energy in an ecosystem flows through *trophic levels*, or feeding levels, which are the links that make up a **food chain**, the linear energy flow from producers through various consumers. Producers, at the lowest trophic level, build sugars (using sunlight, carbon dioxide, and water) to use for energy and tissue components. Within ecosystems, the feeding relationships are arranged in a complex network of interconnected food chains called a **food web**.

Herbivores (plant eaters) are primary consumers. **Carnivores** (meat eaters) are secondary consumers. A consumer that eats both producers and other consumers is an **omnivore**—a role occupied by humans. **Detritivores** are detritus feeders (including worms, mites, termites, and centipedes) that ingest dead organic material and waste products and release simple inorganic compounds and nutrients. **Decomposers** are the bacteria and fungi that process organic debris outside their bodies and absorb nutrients in the process, producing the rotting action that breaks down detritus. Energy and biomass pyramids illustrate the flow of energy between trophic levels; energy always decreases with movement from lower to higher feeding levels in an ecosystem.

biogeochemical cycle (p. 508)
dead zone (p. 510)
food chain (p. 510)
food web (p. 510)
detritivore (p. 510)
decomposer (p. 510)
herbivore (p. 512)
carnivore (p. 512)
omnivore (p. 512)

7. What are biogeochemical cycles? Describe several of the essential cycles.
8. What roles are played in an ecosystem by producers and consumers?
9. Describe the usual trophic relationships between producers, consumers, and detritivores in an ecosystem. What is the place of humans in a trophic system?
10. What is an energy pyramid? Describe how it relates to the nature of trophic levels.

Describe communities and ecological niches and *list* several limiting factors on species distributions.

A **community** is formed by the interactions among populations of living animals and plants. Within a community, a **habitat** is the specific environment in which an organism resides, analogous to its address. An **ecological niche** is the function or operation of a life form within a given community—its occupation.

Light, temperature, water, and nutrients constitute the life-supporting abiotic components of ecosystems. The zonation of plants and animal communities with altitude underlies the **life zone** concept, based on visible differences between ecosystems at different elevations. Each species has a *range of tolerance* that determines distribution. Species populations are stabilized by **limiting factors**, which may be physical, chemical, or biological characteristics of the environment.

community (p. 515)
habitat (p. 515)
ecological niche (p. 515)
life zone (p. 517)
limiting factor (p. 517)

11. Define a community within an ecosystem.
12. What do the concepts of habitat and niche involve? Relate them to some specific plant and animal communities.
13. Describe these four types of symbiotic relationships: mutualism, parasitism, commensalism, and amensalism.
14. Discuss several abiotic influences on the function and distribution of species and communities.
15. Describe what Alexander von Humboldt found that led him to propose the life zone concept. What are life zones?
16. What is a limiting factor? How does it function to control populations of plant and animal species?

Outline the stages of ecological succession in both terrestrial and aquatic ecosystems.

Natural and anthropogenic disturbance are common in most ecosystems. Wildfire can have far-ranging effects on communities; the science of **fire ecology** examines the role of fire in ecosystem maintenance. **Ecological succession** describes the process whereby communities of plants and animals change over time, often after an initial disturbance. An area of bare rock and soil with no trace of a former community can be a site for **primary succession**. The species that first establish in a disturbed area make up the **pioneer community** that then alters the habitat such that different species arrive. **Secondary succession** begins in an area that has a vestige of a previously functioning community in place. Rather than progressing smoothly to a definable stable endpoint, ecosystems tend to operate in a dynamic condition, with intermittent disturbance that forms a mosaic of habitats at different successional stages. Aquatic ecosystems also undergo succession; **eutrophication** is the gradual enrichment of water bodies that occurs with nutrient inputs, either natural or human-caused.

fire ecology (p. 518)
ecological succession (p. 518)
primary succession (p. 519)
pioneer community (p. 519)
secondary succession (p. 519)
eutrophication (p. 521)

17. How does ecological succession proceed? Describe the character of a pioneer community. What is the difference between primary and secondary succession?
18. How are wildfires important for ecological succession? How have species and ecosystems adapted for frequent wildfires?
19. Assess the impact of climate change on natural communities and ecosystems. Possible examples are changes in species' distributions or the changes and effects of wildfire.
20. Summarize the process of succession in a body of water. What is meant by eutrophication?

Explain how biological evolution led to the biodiversity of life on Earth.

Biodiversity refers to the number and variety of different species, the genetic diversity within species, and ecosystem and habitat diversity. The greater the biodiversity within an ecosystem, the more stable and resilient the system is and the more productive it will be.

Evolution states that the original, single-cell organisms adapted, modified, and passed along inherited changes that eventually led to the development of diverse multicellular organisms. The genetic makeup of successive generations is shaped by environmental factors, physiological functions, and behaviors that result in greater rates of survival and reproduction. This so-called natural selection determines the traits that are passed along to offspring and their descendants.

biodiversity (p. 522)
evolution (p. 523)

21. Give some of the reasons why biodiversity makes ecosystems more stable, efficient, and sustainable.
22. Referring back to Chapter 1, define the scientific method and a theory, and describe the progressive stages that lead to the development of a theory.
23. What is meant by ecosystem stability?
24. What do prairie ecosystems teach us about communities and biodiversity?

MasteringGeography™

Looking for additional review and test prep materials? Visit the Study Area in *MasteringGeography*™ to enhance your geographic literacy, spatial reasoning skills, and understanding of this chapter's content by accessing a variety of resources, including MapMaster interactive maps, geoscience animations, videos, *In the News* RSS feeds, flashcards, web links, self-study quizzes, and an eText version of *Elemental Geosystems.*

17 Terrestrial Biomes

Rhinoceros Hornbills (*Buceros rhinoceros*) are one of the largest birds of the tropical rain forest biome, pictured here on the island of Borneo, Indonesia. The structure on top of the beak, the casque, occurs in both males and females and amplifies the sound of the bird's calls. [Timothy Laman/National Geographic/Getty Images.]

KEYLEARNING**concepts**

After reading the chapter, you should be able to:

- *Locate* the world's biogeographic realms and *discuss* the basis for their specification.
- *Explain* the basis for grouping plant communities into biomes and *list* the major terrestrial biomes on Earth.
- *Explain* the potential impact of non-native species on biotic communities, using several examples, and *discuss* strategies for biodiversity conservation.
- *Summarize* the characteristics of Earth's 10 major terrestrial biomes and *locate* them on a world map.

Invasive Species Arrive at Tristan da Cunha

In 2006, as an oil-drilling platform was being towed westward across open ocean on its way from Brazil to Singapore, an accident cut it loose from its towing vessel, leaving the oil rig adrift in the South Atlantic Ocean. Nearly a month later, carried by the currents of the West Wind Drift, the rig ran aground on Tristan, the largest island in the Tristan da Cunha archipelago, located some 2775 km (1725 mi) from Africa and 3355 km (2085 mi) from South America (**Figure GN 17.1**).

The Brazilian owners of the drilling platform had neglected to clean it in preparation for towing. (Clean rigs move through the water with less friction, resulting in lower fuel and labor costs.) This oversight meant that the rig carried new organisms into an existing marine ecosystem, potentially disrupting plant and animal communities (**Figure GN 17.2**).

An Isolated Island Ecosystem Only 267 people live on Tristan. This unique, small society practices subsistence farming and depends on rich marine life that the people manage carefully. The Tristan rock lobster (a crawfish) is harvested and exported to all parts of the world, forming the island's main source of income. Although several ships a year transport the island's commodities to a global market, Tristan has no pier, port, or airport.

A non-native species, also known as an exotic or alien species, is one that originates in a different ecosystem from where it is now found. If a non-native species becomes invasive in a new environment, it outcompetes native species for resources and can introduce new predators, pathogens, or parasites into an ecosystem. Invasive species can devastate biodiversity, especially in isolated island ecosystems. The arrival of an exotic marine community on the drilling platform provided an opportunity for scientists to assess a potential biological invasion.

▼**Figure GN 17.1 The Brazilian oil-drilling platform aground in Trypot Bay Tristan.** [Sue Scott. All rights reserved.]

The Scientific Assessment After the platform made landfall on Tristan, scientists checked it for new organisms. Although the living quarters inside the rig showed no rodents or other terrestrial animals, the underwater portion carried a virtually intact subtropical reef community of 62 species, all non-native to the island.

Scientists made numerous dives to survey the newly arrived organisms. They developed a system of four assessed risk levels for a potential invasion: (1) no threat, from species that perished in transit; (2) low threat, from species that persisted on the rig alone; (3) medium threat, from species that could spread from the rig; and (4) high threat, from breeding species with strong invasive potential.

At level 1, scientists found corals that died in transit, providing skeleton microhabitats for various non-native worms, small crabs, amphipods, and other species that posed a level-2 threat. Also present were barnacles; the living acorn barnacles, the largest on the rig, were assessed at level 3. Among the shells left by the dead barnacles (assessed at level 1) lived small sponges, brown mussels, and urchins, assessed at level 2 (**Figure GN 17.3**).

A population of free-swimming finfish species was found around the rig, apparently having swum along with the rig as it drifted. Two of these species, the silver porgy (with more than 60 counted around the rig) and the variable blenny (having a reproductive doubling time of 15 months), pose the greatest threat to native communities—a level-4 risk. Scientists also found porcelain crabs and balanidae (a type of barnacle), both assessed as presenting a level-4 invasion risk.

Effects and Lessons Learned In 2007, to prevent invasive species from threatening the rock lobster industry, the drilling platform was salvaged and then towed to distant deep water and sunk, at a total cost of $20 million. Nine months after the rig's removal, scientists failed to find any exotic species at the grounding site. However, the risk of invasion will continue for an unknown period. The scientific team concluded that the towing of rigs that have not been properly cleaned presents "unexcelled opportunities for invasion to a wide diversity of marine species."

(a) Natural kelp forest.

(b) Native Tristan rock lobster.

▲**Figure GN 17.2 Native marine environment offshore from Tristan da Cunha.** [Sue Scott. All rights reserved.]

The arrival of the oil platform and its associated species into Tristan's waters demonstrates how globalization affects even the most distant archipelago. Terrestrial biomes and the effects of invasive species are the subjects of this chapter.

QUESTION AND EXPLORE For more about environmental issues in Tristan, including a March 2011 oil and soybean spill on Nightingale Island just south of Tristan, see http://www.tristandc.com/. Also see R. M. Wanless et al., "Semi-submersible Rigs: A Vector Transporting Entire Marine Communities around the World," *Biological Invasions* 10, no. 8 (2009): 2573–2583. MG

▲**Figure GN 17.3 Coral skeletons and dead barnacle shells on the submerged portion of the oil-drilling rig.** [Sue Scott. All rights reserved.]

The patterns of species distributions on Earth are important subjects of biogeography. Earth's biodiversity is spread unevenly across the planet and is related to geology, climate, and the evolutionary history of particular species and species assemblages. The branch of biogeography that is concerned with the past and present distributions of animals is called *zoogeography*; the corresponding branch for plants is *phytogeography*.

Plant and animal communities are commonly grouped into *biomes*, also known as *ecoregions*, representing the major ecosystems of Earth. A biome is a large, stable community of plants and animals whose boundaries are closely linked to climate. In theory, biomes are defined by mature, natural vegetation; however, most of Earth's biomes have been affected by human activities, and many are now experiencing accelerated rates of change that could produce dramatic alterations in the biosphere within our lifetime.

Most of Earth's biomes have been affected by human activities, and many are now experiencing accelerated rates of change that could produce dramatic alterations in the biosphere within our lifetime.

In this chapter: We begin with a discussion of Earth's biogeographic realms, the broadest geographic assemblages of species. We then examine biomes, explaining the basis for their classification and considering invasive species and their impacts on plant and animal communities within biomes. The bulk of this chapter explores Earth's 10 major terrestrial biomes, including their location, community structure, and sensitivity to human impacts. Table 17.1 on page 539 summarizes the connections among vegetation, climate, soils, and water-budget characteristics for each biome, drawing together the chapters of this text.

Biogeographic Divisions

Earth's biosphere can be divided geographically based on assemblages of similar plant and animal communities. One class of geographic division—the biogeographic region, or realm—is determined by species distributions and their evolutionary history. Another class—the biome—is based on plant communities; it is determined mainly according to vegetation growth forms and community characteristics as they relate to climate and soils.

Biogeographic Realms

The recognition that distinct regions of broadly similar flora (plants) and fauna (animals) exist was the earliest beginning of *biogeography* as a discipline. (*Flora* and *fauna* are general terms for the typical collections of plants and animals throughout a region or ecosystem.) A **biogeographic realm** (sometimes called an *ecozone*) is a geographic region where a group of associated plant and animal species evolved. Alfred Wallace (1823–1913), the first scholar of zoogeography, developed a map delineating six zoogeographical regions in 1860, building on earlier work by others regarding bird distributions (**Figure 17.1a**). Wallace's realms correspond generally to the continental plates, although Wallace knew nothing of the theory of plate tectonics at the time. Today's biogeographic realms, originally defined on the basis of plant associations and modified over time, are similar to Wallace's realms, though slightly more specific, as shown in **Figure 17.1b**.

Species interactions occurred as continents collided and accreted; species became separated when continents drifted apart. Consequently, the organisms within each realm are a product of plate tectonics and evolutionary processes. For example, the Australian realm is unique for the approximately 450 species of *Eucalyptus* among its plants and for its 125 species of marsupials—animals, such as kangaroos, that carry their young in pouches, where gestation is completed. The presence of monotremes, egg-laying mammals such as the platypus, adds further distinctiveness to this realm.

Australia's unique native flora and fauna are the result of its early isolation from the other continents. During critical evolutionary times, Australia drifted away from Pangaea (see Chapter 9, Figure 9.11) and never again was reconnected by a land bridge, even when sea level lowered during repeated glacial ages. New Zealand, although relatively close in location, was isolated from Australia, explaining why it has no native marsupials. However, other factors resulted in the grouping of New Zealand within the Australian realm in the most recent classification of biogeographic realms.

Wallace noted the stark contrast in animal species between several of the islands of present-day Indonesia—Borneo and Sulawesi, in particular—and those of Australia. This led him to draw a dividing line between the Oriental and Australian realms over which he believed species did not cross. A deep water barrier existed here even during the lower sea levels of the last glacial maximum, when land connections existed

GEOreport 17.1 A new look at Wallace's zoogeographic regions

In 2013, a group of scientists published a new map of zoogeographic realms based on the present distributions of amphibians, birds, and nonmarine mammals as well as their phylogeny (the evolutionary relationships between organisms based on their ancestors and descendants). The research group identified 11 zoogeographic realms, which are roughly similar to but more detailed than Wallace's original six realms. This updated map provides a baseline for a variety of biogeographical and conservation-oriented studies; see the map, published in the journal *Science*, at **http://macroecology.ku.dk/resources/wallace/credit_journal_science_aaas.jpg/**.

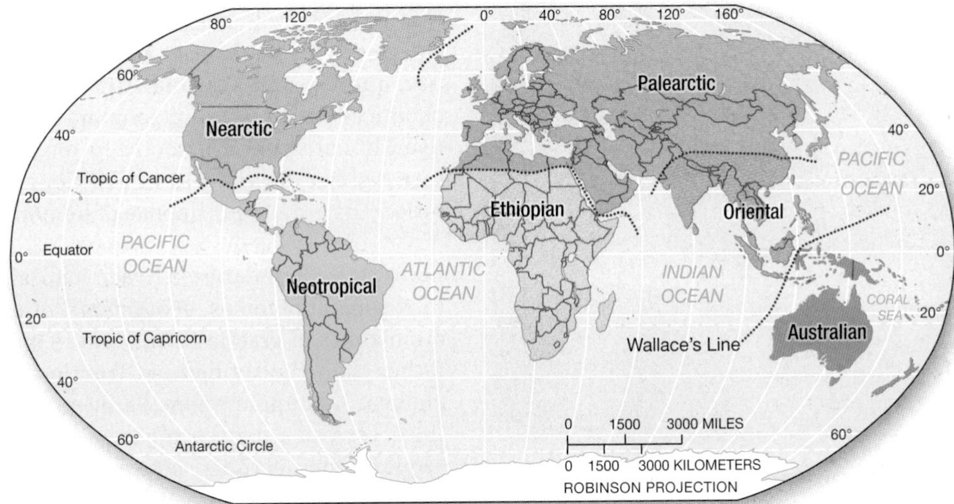

(a) The six animal realms as defined by biogeographer Alfred Wallace in 1860.

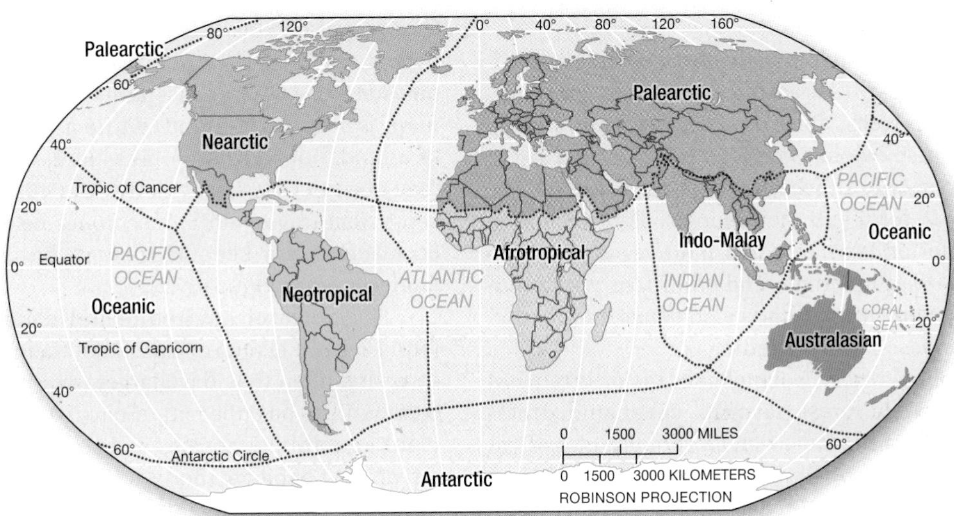

(b) The eight realms recognized today, based on plant and animal associations and evolution.

▲**Figure 17.1 Biogeographic realms.** [(b) After D. M. Olsen et al., "Terrestrial Ecoregions of the World: A New Map of Life on Earth," *Bioscience* 51 (2004): 933–938; modified by UNEP/WCMC, 2011.]

elsewhere in the Indonesian archipelago. His boundary is today known as "Wallace's line." Modern biogeographers have modified this line so that it now encircles the island region between Java and Papua New Guinea, an area that never had a land connection to the mainland and is now sometimes referred to as *Wallacea*.

Biomes

A **biome** is defined as a large, stable, terrestrial or aquatic ecosystem classified according to the predominant vegetation type and the adaptations of particular organisms to that environment. Although scientists identify and describe aquatic biomes (the largest of which are separated into freshwater and marine), biogeographers have applied the biome concept much more extensively to *terrestrial ecosystems*, associations of land-based plants and animals and their abiotic environment.

Biomes are defined by species that are native to a region, meaning that their occurrence is a result of natural processes. Today, few natural communities of plants and animals remain; most biomes have been greatly altered by human intervention. Thus, the "natural vegetation" identified on many biome maps reflects idealized potential mature vegetation, given the environmental characteristics in a region. For example, in Norway, old-growth forested landscapes are today a mix of second-growth forests, farmlands, and altered landscapes (**Figure 17.2**). However, the forest biome designation for this region remains, based on idealized conditions before human impacts (discussed later in the chapter).

Vegetation Types *Vegetation* refers to the entire flora of a region. Scientists determine biomes based on easily identifiable vegetation characteristics.

Earth's vegetation types can be grouped according to the *growth form* (sometimes called *life form*) of the

▲**Figure 17.2 Boreal forest landscape modified by human activity, Norway.** So-called edge species often occupy the varied border zones where natural habitat adjoins disturbed land. [Bobbé Christopherson.]

dominant plants. Growth forms are based on size, woodiness, life span, leaf traits, and general plant morphology (for example, trees, shrubs, vines, and epiphytes). Vegetation can also be characterized by the structure of the canopy, especially in forested regions. Together, the dominant growth form and the canopy structure characterize the vegetation type; the dominant vegetation type then characterizes the biome. The dominant vegetation type extending across a region is also sometimes called the *formation class.*

Biogeographers often designate six major groups of terrestrial vegetation: forest, savanna, shrubland, grassland, desert, and tundra. However, most biome classifications are more specific, with the total number of biomes usually ranging from 10 to 16, depending on the particular classification system being used. The specific vegetation types of each biome have related animal associations that also help define its geographic area.

For example, forests can be subdivided into several biomes—rain forests, seasonal forests, broadleaf and mixed forests, and needleleaf forests—based on moisture regime, canopy structure, and leaf type. *Rain forests* occur in areas with high rainfall; tropical rain forests are composed of mainly evergreen *broadleaf trees* (having broad leaves, as opposed to needles), and temperate rain forests are composed of both broadleaf and *needleleaf trees* (having needles as leaves). *Seasonal forests,* also known as dry forests, are characterized by distinct wet and dry seasons during the year, with trees that are mainly *deciduous* (shedding their leaves for some season of the year) during the dry season. *Broadleaf mixed forests* occur in temperate regions and include broadleaf deciduous trees as well as needleleaf trees. *Needleleaf forests* are the coniferous forests of Earth's high-latitude and high-elevation mountain regions. *Coniferous forests* are cone-bearing trees with needles or scaled evergreen leaves, such as pines, spruces, firs, and larches.

In their form and distribution, plants reflect Earth's physical systems (the abiotic factors discussed in Chapter 16), including its energy patterns; atmospheric composition; temperature and winds; precipitation quantity, quality, and seasonal timing; soils and nutrients; chemical pathways; and geomorphic processes. Biomes usually correspond directly to moisture and temperature regimes (**Figure 17.3**). In addition, plant communities reflect the growing influence of humans.

Ecotones Boundaries between natural systems, whether they separate biomes, ecosystems, or small habitats, are often zones of gradual transition in species composition rather than rigidly defined frontiers marked by abrupt change. A boundary zone between different, but adjoining ecosystems at any scale is an **ecotone**. These are often "zones of shared traits" between different communities.

Ecotones are defined by physical factors, and they vary in width. Ecosystems separated by different climatic conditions usually have gradual ecotones, whereas those separated by differences in soils or topography may have more abrupt boundaries. For example, the climatic boundary between grasslands and forests can occupy many kilometers of land, while a boundary in the form of a landslide, a river, a lakeshore, or a mountain ridge may occupy only a few meters. As human impacts cause ecosystem fragmentation, ecotones between habitats and ecosystems are becoming more numerous across the landscape (see Figure 17.2).

The range of environmental conditions frequently found within ecotones can make them areas of high biodiversity; often they have larger population densities than communities on either side. Scientists have defined certain plant and animal species as having a range of tolerance for varying habitats; these "edge" species are often able to occupy territory within and on either side of the ecotone.

Conservation Biogeography

With the increasing influence of human activity on natural species distributions, conservation has become a focus for scientists and the public. In the early 2000s, biogeographers defined the new, emerging scientific field of *conservation biogeography.* This subdiscipline applies biogeographic principles, theories, and analyses to solve problems in biodiversity conservation. Among the hot research topics in this field are the impacts of rapid climate change on biodiversity (discussed in Chapter 16), the distribution and effects of invasive species, and the implementation of conservation planning and establishment of protected areas.

Invasive Species

The native species of natural biomes have come to inhabit those areas as a consequence of the evolutionary and physical factors discussed previously in this chapter and in Chapter 16. However, communities, ecosystems, and biomes can also be inhabited by species that are

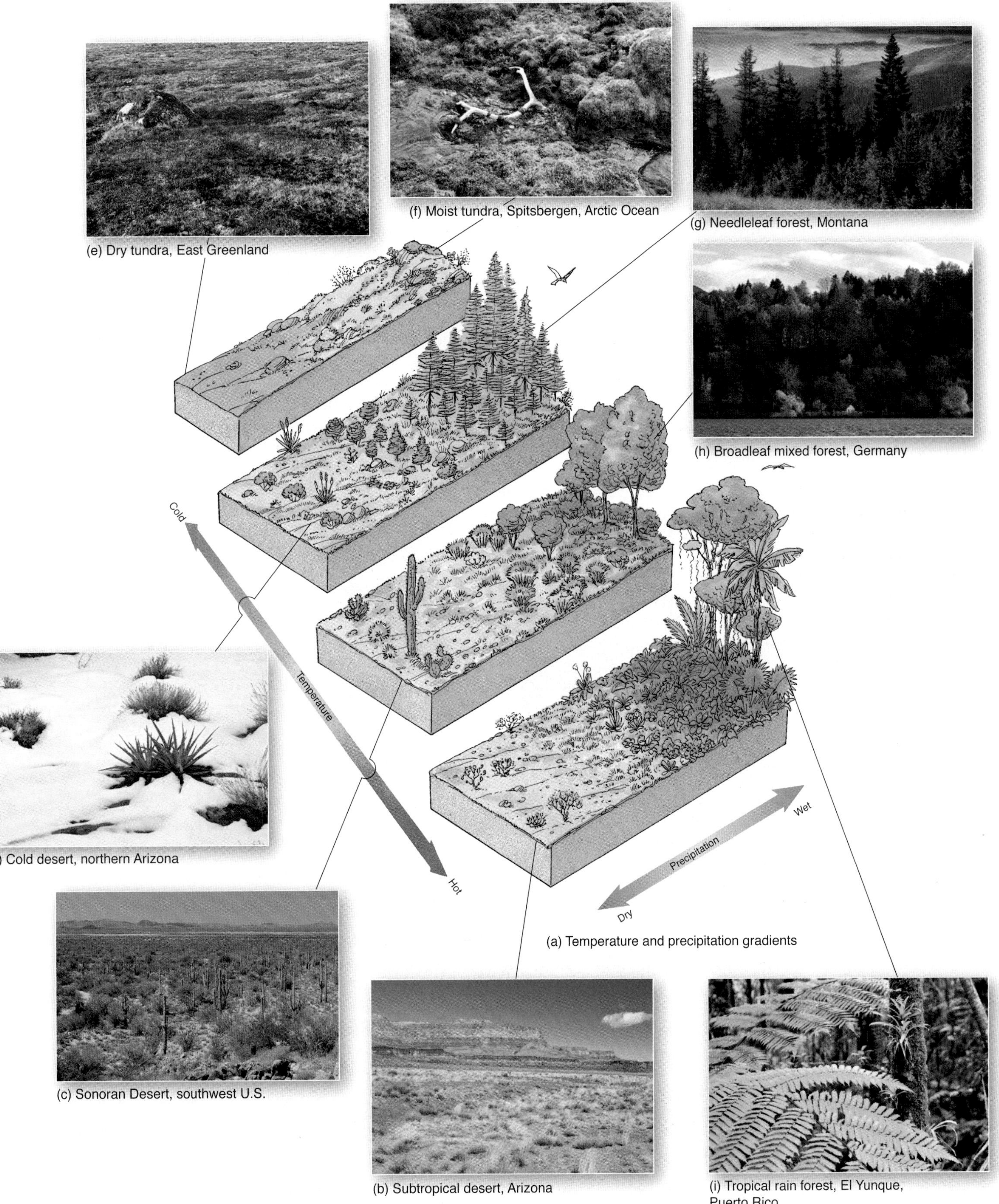

▲**Figure 17.3 Vegetation patterns in relationship to temperature and precipitation.** [(b), (d)–(f), and (i) Bobbé Christopherson. (c) Robert Christopherson. (g) Snehit/Shutterstock. (h) Blickwinkel/Hartl/Alamy.]

introduced from elsewhere by humans, either intentionally or accidentally, as described for Tristan da Cunha in Geosystems Now. Such non-native species are also known as *exotic species*, or *aliens*.

After arriving from a different ecosystem, an estimated 90% of introduced non-native species fail to move into established niches in their new community or habitat. However, some species are able to do so, taking over niches already occupied by native species and thus becoming **invasive species**. The 10% that become invasive can alter community dynamics and lead to declines in native species. Prominent examples are Africanized "killer bees" in North and South America; brown tree snakes in Guam; zebra and quagga mussels in the Great Lakes (**Figure 17.4a**); kudzu in the U.S. Southeast (**Figure 17.4b**); and Russian olive and tamarisk trees along streams in the U.S. Southwest (**Figure 17.4c**). For information on invasive species prevention and management, see http://www.invasivespecies.gov/.

Consider the example of Purple loosestrife (*Lythrum salicaria*), which was introduced from Europe in the 1800s as a desirable ornamental plant with some medicinal applications. The plant's seeds also arrived in soil that ships were using for ballast. This hardy *perennial*, meaning a plant that lives for more than 2 years, escaped cultivation and invaded wetlands across the eastern portions of the United States and Canada, through the upper Midwest, and as far west as Vancouver Island, British Columbia, replacing native plants on which wildlife depend (**Figure 17.4d**). The plant's invasive characteristics are its ability to produce vast quantities of seed during an extended flowering season and to spread vegetatively through underground stems as well as its tendency to form dense stands once established.

Invasive species can alter the dynamics of entire biomes. In the United States and Canada, humans are perpetuating a new type of terrestrial plant community in developed areas. This new community, a mix of native and non-native species used for landscaping, is somewhere between a grassland and a forest. Investments of water, energy, and capital are required to sustain the new species. Additionally, on rangelands and in agricultural

(a) Zebra mussels cover most hard surfaces in the Great Lakes; they rapidly colonize on any surface, even sand, in freshwater environments.

(b) Kudzu, originally imported for cattle feed, spread from Texas to Pennsylvania; here, it overruns pasture and forest in western Georgia.

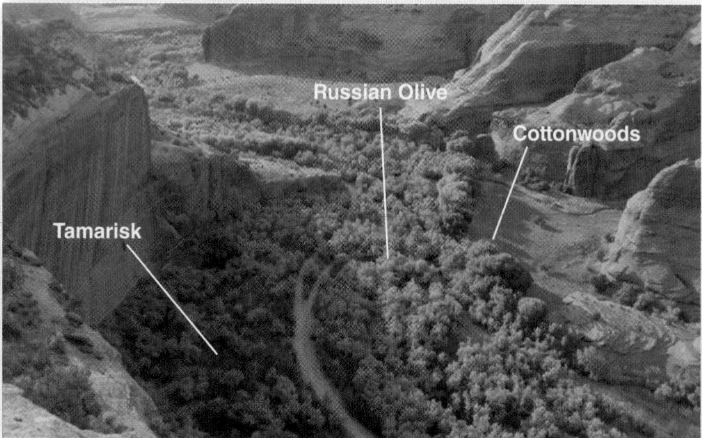

(c) Invasive Russian olive (green-gray color) and tamarisk (dark green color in the shade) along Chinle Wash, New Mexico, in riparian habitat formerly occupied by native cottonwoods.

(d) Purple loosestrife has invaded wetland habitats throughout much of the United States and Canada; shown here is southern Ontario.

▲**Figure 17.4 Exotic species.** [(a) Purestock/Alamy. (b) Bobbé Christopherson. (c) Lindsay Reynolds, Colorado State University/USGS. (d) Gaertner/Alamy.]

areas, humans alter natural biomes by grazing non-native animals and planting crops from other regions (we discuss anthropogenic biomes further at the end of the chapter). Whether the land would return to its natural vegetation if human influences were removed is unknown.

Island Biogeography for Species Preservation

When the first European settlers landed on the islands of Hawai'i in the late 1700s, they counted 43 species of birds. However, as these settlers introduced rabbits, goats, rats, and other non-native species into island ecosystems, native species declined. Today, 15 of Hawai'i's native bird species are extinct, and 19 more are threatened or endangered. In most of Hawai'i, native birds no longer exist below elevations of 1220 m (4000 ft) because of an introduced avian virus (**Figure 17.5**). This is just one example of declining biodiversity on islands, which are particularly vulnerable to species losses because their unique ecosystems evolved in isolation from mainland species.

The principles developed in the study of isolated species' evolution on islands and of the decline of those species with the introduction of non-native species have become useful in global conservation efforts. One strategy for conservation of species is to focus on habitat preservation, such as setting aside parks and wildlife refuges. Yet these protected areas are often of limited value in species preservation, being surrounded by human development and disconnected from other natural habitat. Such habitat fragmentation is problematic for species requiring a large range for survival. In the 1980s, researchers discovered that a number of U.S. national parks had become isolated "islands" of biodiversity and some species within them were declining or disappearing completely.

A key conceptual model for understanding the effects of habitat fragmentation is Robert MacArthur and E. O. Wilson's theory of **island biogeography**, published as a book of the same name in 1967. The theory, based on scientific work on small, isolated mangrove islands in the Florida Keys, links the number of species on an island to the island's size and distance from the mainland.

The theory summarized three patterns of species distributions on islands: (1) The number of species increases with island area, (2) the number of species decreases with island isolation (distance from the mainland), and (3) the number of species on an island represents an equilibrium between the rates of immigration and extinction. Larger islands have a wider variety of habitat and niches and thus lower extinction rates. This theory provided the foundation for understanding "islands" of fragmented habitat, inspired thousands of studies in biogeography and ecology, and increased awareness of the importance of landscape-scale thinking for species preservation. Although present research goes beyond the original theory, the basic conceptual ideas inform conservation science, especially with regard to proper formation of parks and reserves.

Focus Study 17.1 discusses specific efforts to preserve biodiversity, all of which are based loosely on the concept of natural biomes and principles of island biogeography.

Earth's Terrestrial Biomes

Given that extensive transition zones separate many of Earth's biomes, the classification of biomes according to distinct vegetation associations is difficult and somewhat arbitrary. The result is that a number of classification systems—similar in concept, but different in detail—are used. Here, we describe 10 biomes that are common to most of these classification systems: tropical rain forest, tropical seasonal forest and scrub, tropical savanna, midlatitude broadleaf and mixed forest, boreal and montane forest, temperate rain forest, Mediterranean shrubland, midlatitude grassland, desert, and arctic and alpine tundra.

The global distribution of these biomes is summarized in **Table 17.1**—which also includes pertinent information regarding climate, soils, and water availability—and portrayed on the map in **Figure 17.6**. The following pages provide descriptions of each biome, synthesizing all we have learned in previous chapters about the interactions of atmosphere, hydrosphere, lithosphere, and biosphere. Because plant distributions respond to environmental conditions and reflect variations in climate and soil, the world climate map in Chapter 7, Figure 7.2, is a helpful reference for this discussion.

(text continued on page 540)

◀**Figure 17.5 The threatened Hawaiian I'iwi, a Honeycreeper.** Once found throughout the Hawaiian Islands and prized for its striking plumage, the I'iwi is now extinct on Lana'i and extremely rare on O'ahu and Moloka'i. On the other islands, the bird is still relatively common above 1000 m (3280 ft), beyond the reach of mosquitos that transmit disease. [Chris Johns/National Geographic/Getty Images.]

focusstudy 17.1 Environmental Restoration

Global Conservation Strategies

One goal of conservation biogeography, restoration ecology, and other related scientific fields is the preservation of biodiversity through habitat conservation. Habitat fragmentation is a major cause of species decline and extinction, and protecting and restoring habitat has become a conservation focus. Climate change is an important variable to consider in setting aside protected areas, since temperature and precipitation regimes in parks and reserves could eventually end up outside the natural range of the species being protected.

Biodiversity Hot Spots

Several concepts are used as the basis for conservation strategies for maintaining biodiversity. First implemented by Conservation International in 1989, the idea of biodiversity "hot spots" has provided a focus for conservation efforts and has received scientific attention and financial support. To qualify as a hot spot, a community or ecosystem must contain at least 1500 endemic (native) plant species, and it must have lost at least 70% of its original habitat (more information is at **http://www.conservation.org/How/Pages/Hotspots.aspx**).

Global 200 Ecoregions

The World Wildlife Fund (WWF) uses the concept of *ecoregions* as the basis for its conservation strategies, with the goal of implementing conservation on the scale of large natural habitats similar to biomes. In 2000, a team of WWF-sponsored scientists identified 238 ecoregions, known as the "Global 200," as the focus of conservation efforts. The protection of these representative habitats could save a broad diversity of Earth's species (**Figure 17.1.1**).

Biosphere Reserves

The United Nations' Man and the Biosphere Program is an integrated approach to species conservation and sustainable resource use, ongoing since 1971. The program focuses on biological assets and human activity, establishing biosphere reserves to preserve biodiversity as well as promote economic and social development and maintain the cultural values of local communities. Its world network of reserves ranges from relatively undisturbed ecosystems, such as Glacier Bay in Alaska, to the mixing of town life and green space in southern Germany.

The intent of the UN's biosphere reserves is to promote sustainable development by establishing a central region, or core, in which natural features are protected from outside disturbances. This protected core is surrounded by zones of local development, natural and cultural resource management, and scientific experimentation. Some reserves remain in the planning stage, although they are officially designated. In the United States, the designated biosphere reserves include Everglades National Park in Florida and Olympic National Park in Washington.

The ultimate goal, about half achieved, is to create at least one reserve in each of the 194 distinctive biogeographic communities presently identified. Scientists predict that by about 2025, designating new, undisturbed reserves may no longer be possible because pristine areas will be gone. More than 621 biosphere reserves now exist in 117 countries (see **http://www.unesco.org/new/en/natural-sciences/environment/ecological-sciences/**).

1. In your opinion, should developing countries consider the WWF Global 200 Ecoregions concept in economic planning? Why or why not?
2. How is the preservation of "biodiversity hot spots" important to your daily life? If the concept is not important, explain your reasoning.

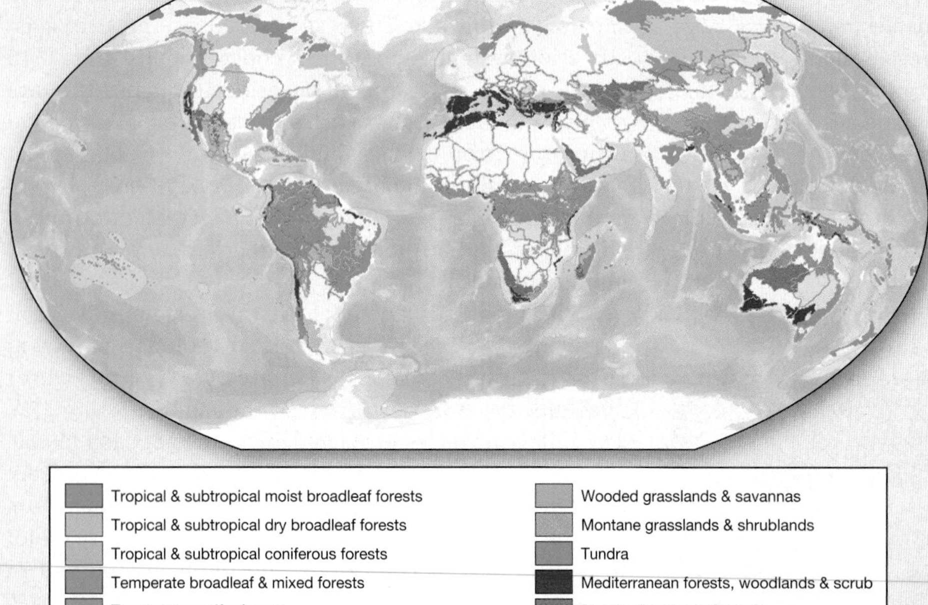

MapMaster
World Physical Environment Vegetation

▲**Figure 17.1.1 Biomes containing the WWF "Global 200" ecoregions important for biodiversity preservation.** The 14 terrestrial biomes shown, plus the freshwater and marine biomes, are the broad divisions containing a total of 238 specific ecoregions that, if protected, could preserve a large percentage of Earth's biodiversity. [World Wildlife Fund; **http://www.worldwildlife.org/science/ecoregions/global200.html**.]

TABLE 17.1 Terrestrial Biomes and Their Characteristics

Biome and Ecosystems	Vegetation Characteristics	Soil Orders	Climate Type	Annual Precipitation	Temperature Patterns	Water Budget Characteristics
Tropical Rain Forest Evergreen broadleaf forest Selva	Leaf canopy thick and continuous; broadleaf evergreen trees, vines (lianas), epiphytes, tree ferns, palms	Oxisols Ultisols (on well-drained uplands)	*Tropical rain forest*	180–400 cm (>6 cm/mo)	Always warm (21°–30°C; avg. 25°C)	Surpluses all year
Tropical Seasonal Forest and Scrub Tropical monsoon forest; Tropical deciduous forest; Scrub woodland and thorn forest	Transitional between rain forest and grassland; broadleaf, some deciduous trees; open parkland to dense undergrowth; acacias and other thorn trees	Oxisols Ultisols Vertisols (in India) Some Alfisols	*Tropical monsoon* *Tropical savanna*	130–200 cm (>40 rainy days during 4 driest months)	Variable, always warm (>18°C)	Seasonal surpluses and deficits
Tropical Savanna Tropical grassland Thorn tree scrub Thorn woodland	Transitional between seasonal forests, rain forests, and tropical steppes and desert; trees with flattened crowns, clumped grasses, and bush thickets; fire adaptations	Alfisols Ultisols Oxisols	*Tropical savanna*	9–150 cm, seasonal	No cold-weather limitations	Tending toward deficits; therefore, fire- and drought-susceptible
Midlatitude Broadleaf and Mixed Forest Temperate broadleaf Midlatitude deciduous Temperate needleleaf	Mixed broadleaf and needleleaf trees; deciduous broadleaf trees, losing leaves in winter; southern and eastern evergreen pines are fire-adapted	Ultisols; Some Alfisols	*Humid subtropical* *Humid continental* (hot summer)	75–150 cm	Temperate with cold season	Seasonal pattern with summer-maximum P and PE; no irrigation needed
Boreal and Montane Forest Taiga	Needleleaf conifers, mostly evergreen pine, spruce, fir; Russian larch, a deciduous needleleaf	Spodosols Histosols Inceptisols Alfisols	*Humid continental* (mild summer) *Subarctic* *Highland*	30–100 cm	Short summer, cold winter	Low PE, moderate P; moist soils, some waterlogged and frozen in winter; no deficits
Temperate Rain Forest West Coast forest U.S. coast redwoods	Narrow margin of lush evergreen and deciduous trees on windward slopes; redwoods, tallest trees on Earth	Spodosols Inceptisols (mountainous environs)	*Marine west coast*	150–500 cm	Mild summer and mild winter for latitude	Large surpluses and runoff
Mediterranean Shrubland Sclerophyllous shrub Australian eucalyptus forest	Short shrubs, drought-adapted, tending to grassy woodlands and chaparral; fire adaptations	Alfisols Mollisols	*Mediterranean* (dry summer)	25–65 cm	Hot, dry summers; cool winters	Summer deficits, winter surpluses
Midlatitude Grassland Temperate grassland Sclerophyllous shrub	Tallgrass prairies and shortgrass steppes, highly modified by human activity; major areas of commercial grain farming; plains, pampas, and veld; fire adaptations	Mollisols Aridisols	*Humid subtropical* *Humid continental* (hot summer)	25–75 cm	Temperate continental regimes	Soil-moisture utilization and recharge balanced; irrigation and dry farming in drier areas
Warm Desert and Semidesert Subtropical desert and scrubland	Bare ground graduating into xerophytic plants, including cacti, creoste, and acacia trees	Aridisols Entisols (sand dunes)	*Arid desert*	< 2 cm	Average annual temperature around 18°C; highest temperatures on Earth	Chronic deficits, irregular precipitation events, P < 1/2 PE
Cold Desert and Semidesert Midlatitude desert, scrubland, and steppe	Grasses and shrubs adapted to dry conditions	Aridisols Entisols	*Semiarid steppe*	2–25 cm	Average annual temperature around 18°C	P >1/2 PE
Polar Desert	Mosses, lichens	(permafrost)	*Ice sheet, ice cap*	<25 cm	Warmest months <10°C	Not applicable
Arctic and Alpine Tundra	Treeless; dwarf shrubs, stunted sedges, mosses, lichens, and short grasses; alpine, grass meadows	Gelisols Histosols Entisols (permafrost)	*Tundra* *Subarctic* (cold winter)	15–180 cm	Warmest months >10°C; only 2 or 3 months above freezing	Not applicable most of the year, poor drainage in summer

Tropical Rain Forest

The lush biome covering Earth's equatorial regions is the **tropical rain forest**. In the tropical climates of these forests, with consistent year-round daylength (12 hours), high insolation, average annual temperatures around 25°C (77°F), and plentiful moisture, lives the most diverse collection of plants and animals on the planet. Rainforest species evolved during the long-term residence of the continental plates near equatorial latitudes. Although this biome is stable in its natural state, undisturbed tracts of rain forest are becoming increasingly rare; deforestation is perhaps the most pervasive human impact.

The largest tract of tropical rain forest occurs in the Amazon region, where it is called the *selva*. Tropical rain forests also cover the equatorial regions of Africa, parts of Indonesia, the margins of Madagascar and Southeast Asia, the Pacific coast of Ecuador and Colombia, and the east coast of Central America, with small discontinuous patches elsewhere. The cloud forests of western Venezuela are high-elevation tropical rain forests, perpetuated by high humidity and cloud cover. Rain forests occupy about 7% of the world's total land area, but represent approximately 50% of Earth's species and about half of its remaining forests.

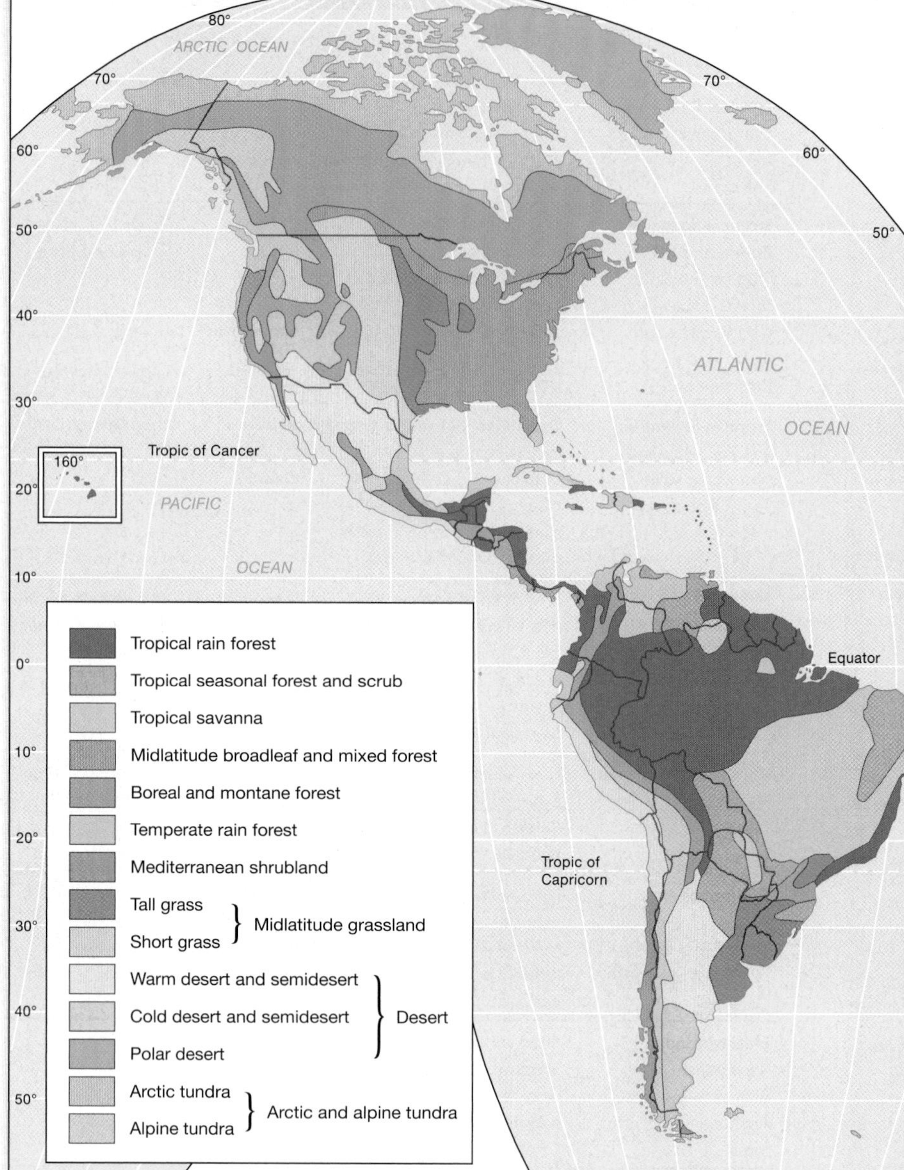

▲**Figure 17.6 The 10 major global terrestrial biomes.** These biomes are described in Table 17.1.

Rain Forest Flora and Fauna The structure of a rain forest includes four levels, illustrated in Geosystems in Action 17. The upper level, called the *overstory*, or *emergent layer*, is not continuous, but features the crowns of the tallest trees, which rise above the continuous *canopy* beneath. Biomass in a rain forest is concentrated in the dense mass of overhead leaves in these two upper levels. Beneath the canopy is the *understory*, made up of shade-tolerant shrubs, herbs, and small trees. The *forest floor* receives only about 1% of the sunlight arriving at the canopy. This lowest level of vegetation includes seedlings and ferns on a litter-strewn ground surface in deep shade.

The high humidity, odors of mold and rotting vegetation, strings of thin roots and vines dropping down from above, windless air, and echoing sounds of life in the trees together create a unique environment.

Rain forests feature ecological niches that are distributed vertically rather than horizontally because of the competition for light. The canopy is filled with a rich variety of plants and animals. *Lianas* (woody vines that are rooted in the soil) stretch from tree to tree, entwining them with cords that can reach 20 cm (8 in.) in diameter. Epiphytes flourish there, too; these plants, such as orchids, bromeliads, and ferns, live entirely aboveground, supported physically, but not nutritionally, by the structures of other plants. On the forest floor, the smooth, slender trunks of rainforest trees are

CRITICAL**thinking** 17.1

Reality Check

Using the map in Figure 17.6, the information in Table 17.1, and the discussion in this chapter, describe the biome in which you are located. What changes in the natural vegetation do you see, as we all live in altered environments brought on by human activities? Consider the climate classification information in Chapter 7 as you evaluate your biome. What generalizations can you make?

MG **MapMaster**
World Physical Environment
Vegetation

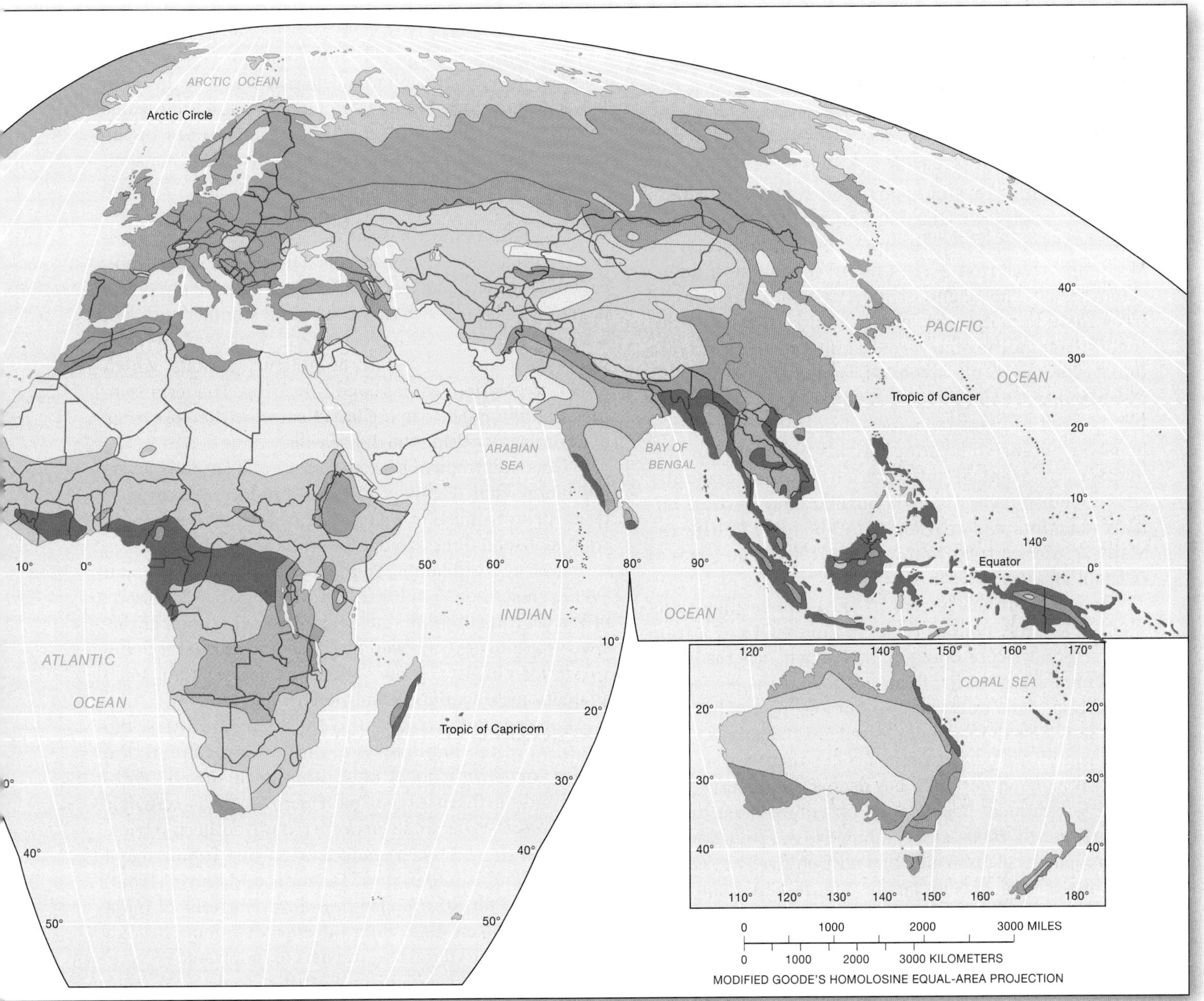

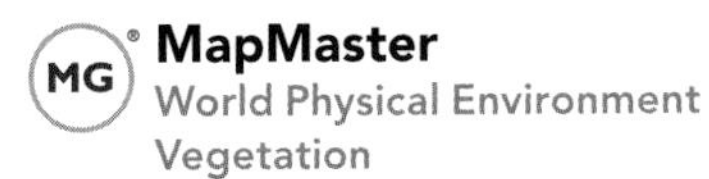

covered with thin bark and buttressed by large, wall-like flanks that grow out from the trees to brace the trunks. These buttresses form angular hollows that are ready habitat for various animals. Branches are usually absent on at least the lower two-thirds of the tree trunks.

The animal and insect life of the rain forest is diverse, ranging from animals living exclusively in the upper stories of the trees to decomposers (bacteria) working the ground surface. *Arboreal* (from the Latin word meaning "tree") species, those dwelling in the trees, include sloths, monkeys, lemurs, parrots, and snakes. Throughout the canopy are multicolored birds, tree frogs, lizards, bats, and a rich insect community that includes more than 500 species of butterflies. On the forest floor, animals include pigs (the bushpig and giant forest hog in Africa, wild boar and bearded pig in Asia, and peccary in South America), small antelope, and mammalian predators (the tiger in Asia, jaguar in South America, and leopard in Africa and Asia).

Deforestation of the Tropics Clearing of Earth's old-growth tropical rain forest to make way for agriculture has occurred for thousands of years, but with growing population, economic development, and globalization, the scale of deforestation has increased. For the past several decades, tropical forests have been cleared at alarming rates for farming, fuel wood, cattle ranching, timber export, and most recently, palm oil production. By continent, total rainforest losses are now estimated at more than 50% in

Africa, more than 40% in Asia, and 40% in Central and South America. Tropical deforestation is threatening native rainforest species, including potential sources of valuable pharmaceuticals and new foods—so much is still unknown and undiscovered. As discussed in Chapter 8, forest clearing and burning release millions of metric tons of carbon into the atmosphere each year.

Worldwide, an area nearly the size of Wisconsin is cleared each year (169,000 km^2, or 65,000 mi^2), and about a third more is disrupted by selective cutting of canopy trees that occurs along the edges of deforested areas. The economically valuable varieties of trees include mahogany, ebony, and rosewood. Additional commodities harvested and exported from rain forests include beef, soybeans, rubber, and coffee. As discussed in Chapter 15 (in the discussion of Oxisols), fire is used to clear land for subsistence agriculture; however, intensive farming quickly exhausts the productivity of tropical soils, which are then generally abandoned in favor of newly burned lands (unless fertility is maintained artificially by chemical fertilizers). Many rainforest trees require from 100 to 250 years to reestablish after a major disturbance.

Scientists are able to track tropical deforestation using satellite images, such as those in Figure GIA 17.2 from Rondônia in western Brazil. In this region, new roads and forest removal have significantly changed the landscape. In addition to the tracts of clear-cut logging and burning, the edges of every road and cleared area combined represent a significant portion of the habitat disturbance.

In Brazil, deforestation has decreased in recent years as the government has stepped up enforcement to preserve the forest; 2009–2010 combined losses were down to approximately 18,000 km^2 (6950 mi^2), equivalent to about 80% of the area of New Jersey (Figure GIA 17.2). This effort to reduce deforestation is a highly charged issue, especially for Brazil's growing cattle industry, which uses deforested lands for pasture. Cattle herds reached over 60 million head in Brazil by 2010, generating $3 billion in revenue. Among many available websites, see the Tropical Rainforest Coalition at http://www.rainforest.org/ and Rainforest Action Network at http://www.ran.org/.

CRITICAL**thinking** 17.2

Tropical Forests: A Global or Local Resource?

Given the information presented in this chapter about deforestation in the tropics and in the previous chapter about declining biodiversity, assess the present controversy over rainforest resources. What are the main issues? How do developing countries, which possess most of the world's rain forests, view rainforest destruction? How do developed countries, with their transnational corporations, view rainforest destruction? How do concerns for planetary natural resources balance against the needs of local peoples and sovereign state rights? How is climate change related to these issues? What kind of action plan would you develop to accommodate all parties?

Tropical Seasonal Forest and Scrub

At the margins of the world's rain forests are areas of seasonal changes in precipitation, characterized by the **tropical seasonal forest and scrub** biome. These are regions of lower and more erratic rainfall than occurs in the equatorial zone. The biome includes tropical monsoon and tropical deciduous forest as well as scrub woodland and thorn forest.

Vegetation in this biome is adapted to climatic conditions with a distinct dry season. The shifting intertropical convergence zone (ITCZ) affects precipitation regimes bringing moisture with the high Sun of summer and then a season of dryness with the low Sun of winter. This shift produces a seasonal pattern of moisture deficits, which affects vegetation leaf loss and flowering. The term *semideciduous* applies to many broadleaf trees that lose some of their leaves during the dry season.

Thus, the tropical seasonal forest and scrub is a varied biome that occupies a transitional area from wetter to drier tropical climates. Natural vegetation ranges from monsoon forests to open woodlands to thorn forests to semiarid shrublands. The monsoonal forests have an average height of 15 m (50 ft) with no continuous canopy of leaves, transitioning into drier areas with open grassy spaces or into areas choked by dense undergrowth. *Scrub vegetation* consists of low shrubs and grasses with some adaptations to semiarid conditions.

Local names are given to these communities: the *Caatinga* of the Bahia State of northeastern Brazil; the *Chaco* (or *Gran Chaco*) of southeastern Brazil, Paraguay, and northern Argentina (**Figure 17.7**); the *brigalow* scrub of Australia; and the *dornveld* of southern Africa. In Africa, this biome extends west to east from Angola through Zambia into parts of Tanzania and Kenya. Tropical seasonal forests are also present in portions of India and in Southeast Asia, from interior Myanmar through northeastern Thailand and in parts of Indonesia.

The trees throughout most of this biome make poor lumber, but some, especially teak, may be valuable for fine cabinetry and furniture. In addition, some of the plants with

▼Figure 17.7 Tropical seasonal forest and scrub, Gran Chaco, Paraguay. Trumpet trees (*Tabebuia caraiba*) are common dry-season deciduous trees in the Gran Chaco. [Thomas Vinke/ImageBroker/Alamy.]

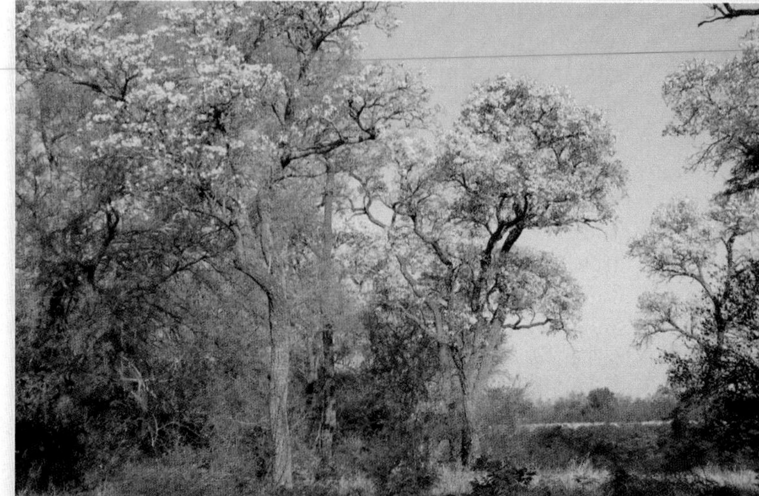

dry-season adaptations produce usable waxes and gums, such as the carnauba wax produced by the Brazilian palm tree. Animal life includes the koalas and cockatoos of Australia and the antelope, large cats, anteaters, rodents, and ground-dwelling birds in other examples of this biome. Worldwide, humans use these areas for ranching; in Africa, this biome includes numerous wildlife parks and preserves.

Tropical Savanna

The **tropical savanna** biome consists of large expanses of grassland, either treeless or interrupted by scattered trees and shrubs (**Figure 17.8**). Tropical savannas receive precipitation during approximately 6 months of the year, when they are influenced by the shifting ITCZ. The rest of the year they are under the drier influence of shifting subtropical high-pressure cells. This is a transitional biome between the tropical seasonal forests and the semiarid tropical steppes and deserts.

Shrubs and trees of the savanna biome are adapted to drought, grazing by large herbivores, and fire. Most species are *xerophytic*, or drought resistant, with various adaptations to help them conserve moisture during the dry season—for example, small, thick leaves or waxy leaf surfaces (other xerophytic adaptations are discussed with the desert biomes). In the vast savannas of east Africa, a common tree is the acacia, with its flat top, thorny stems, and small leaves that reduce moisture loss.

Savanna vegetation is maintained by fire, both a natural and a human-caused disturbance in this biome. During the wet season, grasses flourish, and as rainfall diminishes, this thick growth provides fuel for fires, which are often intentionally set to maintain the open grasslands. Hot-burning dry-season fires kill trees and seedlings and deposit a layer of nutrient-rich ash over the landscape. These conditions foster the regrowth of grasses, which again grow vigorously as the wet season returns, sprouting from extensive underground root systems that are an adaptation for surviving fire disturbance. In northern Australia, the aboriginal people are credited with creating and maintaining many of the region's tropical savannas; as the traditional practice of setting annual fires declines, many savannas are reverting to forest.

Africa has the largest area of tropical savanna on Earth, including the famous Serengeti Plains of Tanzania and Kenya and the Sahel region, south of the Sahara. Portions of Australia, India, and South America also are part of the savanna biome. Local names for tropical savannas include the *Llanos* in Venezuela, stretching along the coast and inland east of Lake Maracaibo and the Andes; the *Campo Cerrado* of Brazil and Guiana; and the *Pantanal* of southwestern Brazil.

Particularly in Africa, savannas are the home of large land mammals—zebra, giraffe, buffalo, gazelle, wildebeest, antelope, rhinoceros, and elephant. These animals graze on savanna grasses, while others (lion, cheetah) feed upon the grazers themselves. Birds include the Common Ostrich, Martial Eagle (largest of all eagles), and Secretary Bird. Many species of venomous snakes, as well as the crocodile, are present in this biome.

▲Figure 17.8 Elephants and acacias in the tropical savanna of southern Africa. [Franz Aberham/Stockbyte/Getty Images.]

Midlatitude Broadleaf and Mixed Forest

Moist continental climates support a mixed forest in areas of warm to hot summers and cool to cold winters. This **midlatitude broadleaf and mixed forest** biome includes several distinct communities in North America, Europe, and Asia. In the United States, relatively lush evergreen broadleaf forests occur along the Gulf of Mexico. To the north are the mixed deciduous broadleaf and needleleaf trees associated with sandy soils and frequent fires—pines (longleaf, shortleaf, pitch, loblolly) predominate in the southeastern and Atlantic coastal plains. In areas of this region protected from fire, broadleaf trees are dominant. Into New England and westward in a narrow belt to the Great Lakes, white and red pines and eastern hemlock are the principal conifers, mixed with broadleaf deciduous oak, beech, hickory, maple, elm, chestnut, and many others (**Figure 17.9**).

(*text continued on page 546*)

►Figure 17.9 Mixed broadleaf forest, southeastern United States. Great Smokey Mountains National Park in the southern Appalachian Mountains contains one of the largest remaining tracts of old-growth forest in North America, including nearly 100 native tree species, 66 mammal species, and over 200 species of birds. [Sean Lema/Shutterstock.]

arth's tropical rain forests are a vast reservoir of biodiversity. The rain forest's layered structure reflects intense competition for sunlight and space among numerous species of trees and other plants (GIA 17.1). During the past several decades, humans have cleared over half of Earth's old-growth rain forests for agriculture, cattle ranching, timber export, and palm oil production (GIA 17.2).

Rain forest in the mountains of Costa Rica

17.1 Vertical Structure of a Rain Forest

The structure of a tropical rain forest includes the overstory (also known as the emergent layer), the middle canopy, the understory, and the forest floor, shown below. Long vines called lianas, rooted in the soil, connect these layers, while dead leaves form litter on the deeply shaded forest floor.

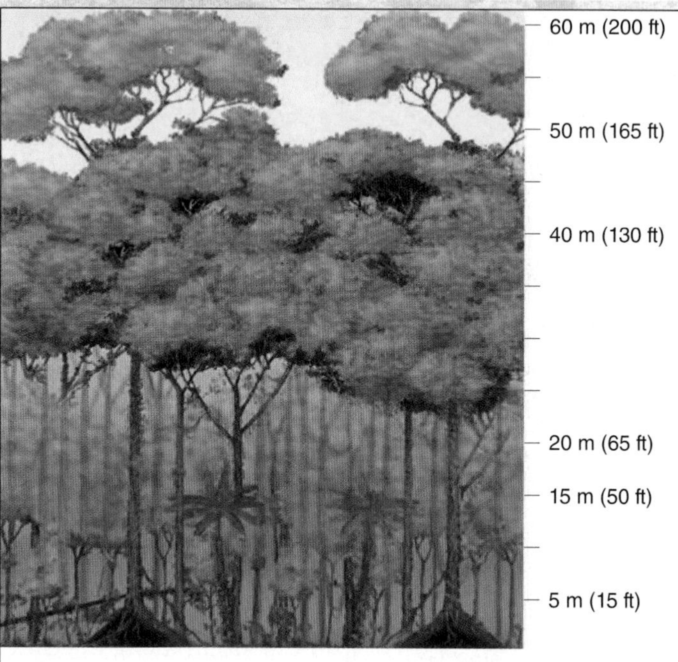

Overstory, or Emergent Layer: The overstory, or emergent layer, consists of the tallest trees, whose tops "emerge" from the main canopy, jutting above the surrounding forest.

Middle canopy: Formed of the interlocking crowns of mature trees, the middle canopy is home to a variety of animals and plants.

Understory: Between the middle canopy and the forest floor, the understory consists of shade-tolerant shrubs and trees and woody vines that clumb up tree trunks toward sunlight.

Forest floor: The forest floor is a deeply shaded area of ferns and litter of dead leaves and other plant material.

Describe: What are the characteristics of the four main layers of the rain forest?

Rainforest soil: Rainforest soil is poor in nutrients. Most soil nutrients have been taken up to help form the biomass of trees and other rainforest organisms. These nutrients are recycled rapidly as plant and animal remains decay on the forest floor and are reabsorbed by tree roots.

Leaf litter covers the rainforest floor, seen here with a typical buttressed tree trunk and lianas in the background.

Animation Plant Productivity in a Warming World

http://goo.gl/rwC5xC

MasteringGeography™

Visit the Study Area in MasteringGeography™ to explore rain forests.

Visualize: Study a video of plant productivity in a warming world.

Assess: Demonstrate understanding of rain forests (if assigned by instructor).

Animation Amazon Deforestation

http://goo.gl/a5gKav

17.2 Amazon Rain Forest Destruction

In Brazil, the vast Amazon rain forest is being cleared to make way for agriculture and ranching, and for selective timber export, some illegal, of species such as mahogany. Roads that penetrate undeveloped areas increase the habitat fragmentation that hastens biodiversity losses. Satellite images show the changes in one area between 2000 and 2009. During roughly the same time span, Brazil lost rain forest equal in area to all of the New England states plus New Jersey.

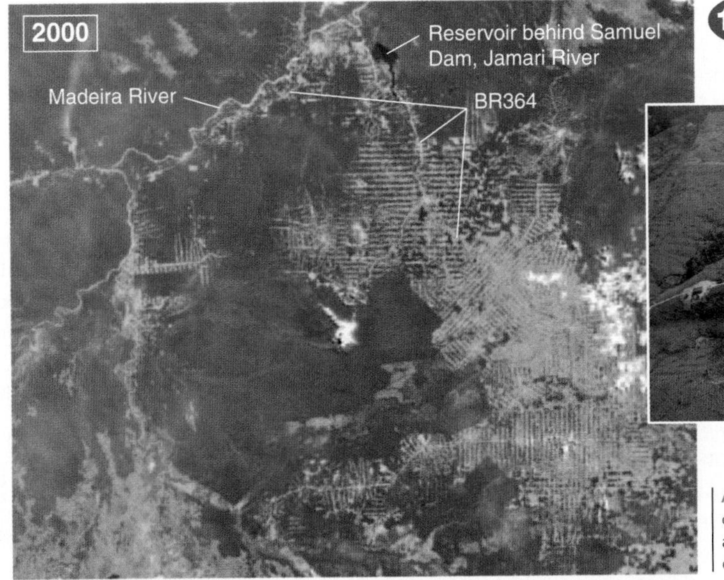

17.2a *True-color image of Rondônia in western Brazil in 2000 shows deforestation along highway BR364, the main artery of the region.*

Analyze: Refer to the satellite images in GIA 17.2 to compare conditions in the area between the Madeira River and highway BR364 in 2000 and in 2009. How might these changes have affected wildlife populations? Explain.

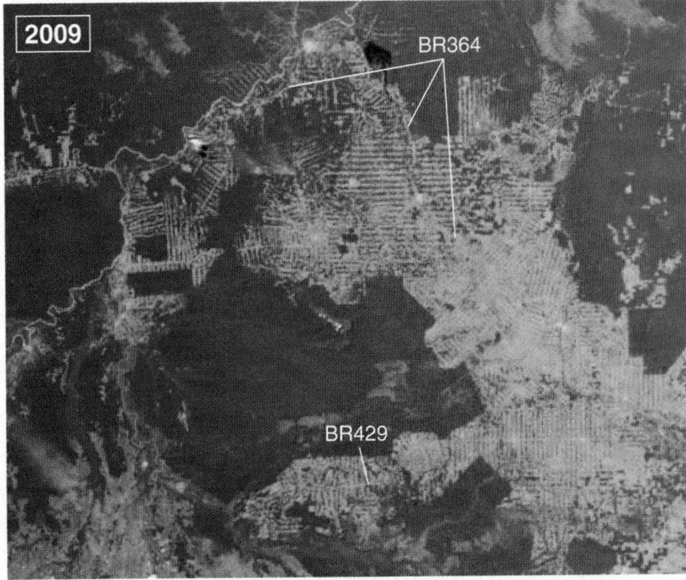

17.2b *The same region in 2009. Note the increased amount of deforested land and the branching pattern of feeder roads.*

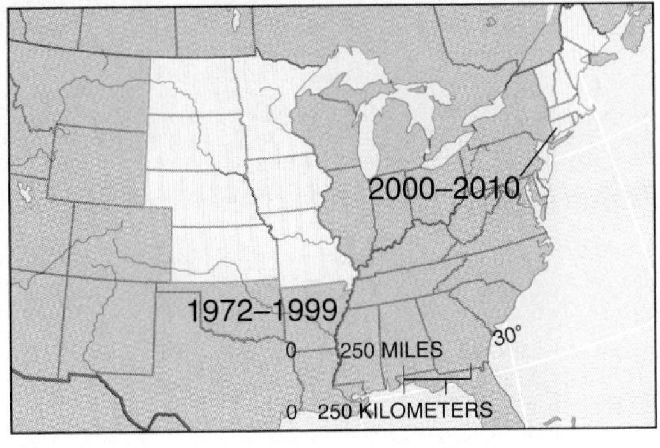

17.2c *Extent of deforestation in Brazil (yellow) shown relative to the equivalent U.S. area.*

GEOquiz

1. Infer: How does the physical structure of the rain forest help to account for the great variety of organisms found there?

2. Predict: Identify an area of rain forest on the 2009 satellite image in GIA 17.2b that is likely to be deforested in the near future and explain how and why the area will change.

These mixed stands contain valuable timber, and logging has altered their distribution. Native stands of white pine in Michigan and Minnesota were removed before 1910, although reforestation sustains their presence today. In northern China, these forests have almost disappeared as a result of centuries of harvest. The forest species that once flourished in China are similar to species in eastern North America: oak, ash, walnut, elm, maple, and birch. This biome is quite consistent in appearance from continent to continent and at one time represented the principal vegetation of the humid subtropical (hot summer) regions of North America, Europe, and Asia.

A wide assortment of mammals, birds, reptiles, and amphibians is distributed throughout this biome. Representative animals (some migratory) include red fox, white-tailed deer, southern flying squirrel, opossum, bear, and a great variety of birds, including Tanager and Cardinal. To the west of this biome in North America are the rich soils and midlatitude climates that favor grasslands, and to the north is the gradual transition to the poorer soils and colder climates that favor the coniferous trees of the northern boreal forests.

Boreal and Montane Forest

Stretching from the east coast of Canada and the Atlantic Provinces westward to the Canadian Rockies and portions of Alaska and from Siberia across the entire extent of Russia to the European Plain is the **boreal forest** biome, also known as the northern **needleleaf forest** (Figure 17.10). The northern, less densely forested part of this biome, transitional to the arctic tundra biome, is called the **taiga**. This biome is characteristic of microthermal climates (having a cold winter season and also some summer warmth); the Southern Hemisphere has no such biome except in a few mountainous locales. The needleleaf forests at high elevations on mountains worldwide are the **montane forests**.

Boreal forests of pine, spruce, fir, and larch occupy most of the subarctic climates on Earth that are dominated by trees. Although these forests have similar vegetation life forms, individual species vary between North America and Eurasia. The larch (*Larix*) is one of only a few needleleaf trees that drop needles in the winter months, perhaps as a defense against the extreme cold of its native Siberia (see the Verkhoyansk climograph and photograph in Figure 7.14). Larches are also found in North America.

This biome also occurs at high elevations at lower latitudes, such as in the Sierra Nevada, Rocky Mountains, Alps, and Himalayas. Douglas fir and white fir grow in the western mountains of the United States and Canada. Economically, these forests are important for lumber in the southern margins of the biome and for pulpwood throughout the middle and northern portions. Present logging practices and the sustainability of these yields are issues of increasing controversy.

Representative fauna in this biome include wolf, elk, moose (the largest member of the deer family), bear, lynx, beaver, wolverine, marten, small rodents, and migratory birds during the brief summer season. Birds include hawks and eagles, several species of grouse, Pine Grosbeak, Clark's Nutcracker, and several species of owls. About 50 species of insects particularly adapted to the presence of coniferous trees inhabit the biome.

Temperate Rain Forest

The lush forests in wet, humid regions make up the **temperate rain forest** biome. These forests of broadleaf and needleleaf trees, epiphytes, huge ferns, and thick undergrowth correspond generally to marine west coast climates (occurring along middle- to high-latitude west coasts), with precipitation approaching 400 cm (160 in.) per year, moderate air temperatures, summer fog, and an overall maritime influence. In

Animation (MG) End of the Last Ice Age

http://goo.gl/XB2LMA

▼Figure 17.10 Boreal forest of Canada (*boreal* means "northern"). [Robert Christopherson.]

North America, this biome occurs only along narrow margins of the Pacific Northwest. Similar temperate rain forests exist in southern China, small portions of southern Japan, New Zealand, and a few areas of southern Chile.

The biome is home to bear, badger, deer, wild pig, wolf, bobcat, fox, and numerous bird species, including the Northern Spotted Owl (**Figure 17.11b**). In the 1990s, this owl became a symbol for the conflict between species-preservation efforts and the use of resources to fuel local economies. In 1990, the U.S. Fish and Wildlife Service listed the owl as a "threatened" species under the U.S. Endangered Species Act, citing the loss of old-growth forest habitat as the primary cause for its decline. The next year, logging practices in areas with spotted owl habitat were halted by court order. The ensuing controversy pitted conservationists against loggers and other forest users, with the end result being large-scale changes in forest management throughout the Pacific Northwest.

Later research by the U.S. Forest Service and independent scientists noted the failing health of temperate rain forests and suggested that timber-management plans balance resource use with ecosystem preservation. Sustainable forestry practices emphasize the continuing health and productivity of forests into the future and are increasingly based on a multi-use ethic that serves local, national, and global interests.

The tallest trees in the world occur in this biome—the coast redwoods (*Sequoia sempervirens*) of the California and Oregon coasts. These trees can exceed 1500 years in age and typically range in height from 60 to 90 m (200 to 300 ft), with some exceeding 100 m (330 ft). Virgin stands of other representative trees, such as Douglas fir, spruce, cedar, and hemlock, have been reduced by timber harvests to a few remaining valleys in Oregon and Washington—less than 10% of the original forest that existed when Europeans first arrived. Most forests in this biome are secondary-growth forests, having regrown from a major disturbance, usually human-caused.

Mediterranean Shrubland

The **Mediterranean shrubland** biome, also referred to as a temperate shrubland, occupies temperate regions that have dry summers, generally corresponding to the Mediterranean climates. The dominant shrub formations that occupy these regions are low growing and able to withstand hot-summer drought. The vegetation is *sclerophyllous* (from *sclero*, for "hard," and *phyllos*, for "leaf"). Most shrubs average a meter or two in height, with deep, well-developed roots; leathery leaves; and uneven low branches.

Typically, the vegetation varies between woody shrubs covering more than 50% of the ground and grassy woodlands covering 25%–60% of the ground.

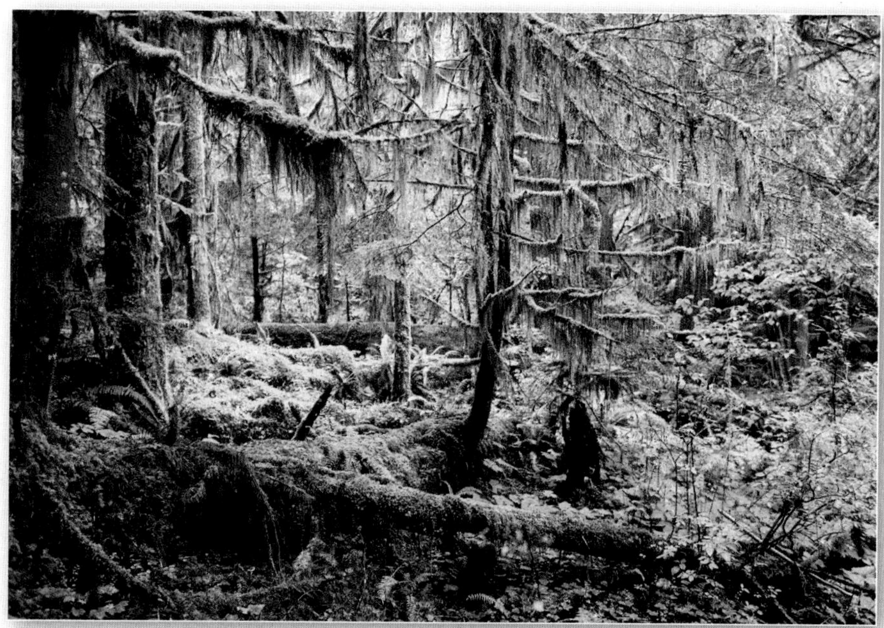

(a) Old-growth Douglas fir, redwoods, cedars, and a mix of deciduous trees, ferns, and mosses in the Gifford Pinchot National Forest, Washington. Only a small percentage of these old-growth forests remain in the Pacific Northwest.

(b) The Northern Spotted Owl is an "indicator species" representing the health of the temperate rainforest ecosystem.

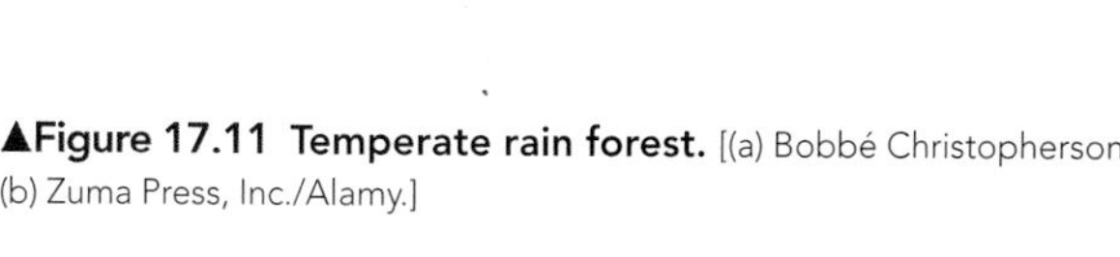

▲**Figure 17.11 Temperate rain forest.** [(a) Bobbé Christopherson. (b) Zuma Press, Inc./Alamy.]

In California, the Spanish word *chaparro* for "scrubby evergreen" gives us the name **chaparral** for this vegetation type (**Figure 17.12a**). This scrubland includes species such as manzanita, toyon, red bud, ceanothus, mountain mahogany, blue and live oaks, and the dreaded poison oak.

This biome is located poleward of the shifting subtropical high-pressure cells in both hemispheres. The stable high pressure produces the characteristic dry-summer climate and establishes conditions conducive to fire. The vegetation is adapted for rapid recovery after fire—many species are able to resprout from roots or burls after a burn or have seeds that require fire for germination (Figure 17.12b).

In the Mediterranean shrubland of southern California, invasive species have altered plant community dynamics in this fire-adapted ecosystem. Although the native vegetation is adapted for wildfire, non-native species often are able to colonize burned areas more efficiently; thus exotic plants are changing the successional processes in this biome. The establishment of non-natives leads to thick undergrowth, providing more fuel for fires that are increasing in frequency. Native vegetation is adapted for fires that occur at intervals of 30 to 150 years; the increase in fire frequency with climate change puts these species at a disadvantage. More frequent fires in the region combine with the increasing numbers of non-native species to cause the conversion of southern California's shrubland to grassland.

A counterpart to the California chaparral in North America is the *maquis* of the Mediterranean region of Europe, which includes live and cork oak trees (the source of cork) as well as pine and olive trees. In Chile, this biome is known as the *mattoral*, and in southwestern Australia, it is *mallee scrub*. In Australia, the bulk of the eucalyptus species are sclerophyllous in form and structure in whichever area they occur.

As described in Chapter 7, commercial agriculture of the *Mediterranean* climates includes subtropical fruits, vegetables, and nuts, with many food types (e.g., artichokes, olives, almonds) produced only in these climates. Animals include several types of deer, coyote, wolf, bobcat, various rodents and other small animals, and various birds. In Australia, this biome is home to Malleefowl (*Leipoa ocellata*), a ground-dwelling bird, and numerous marsupials.

Midlatitude Grassland

Of all the natural biomes, the **midlatitude grassland** is the most modified by human activity. This biome includes the world's "breadbaskets"—regions that produce bountiful grain (wheat and corn), soybeans, and livestock (hogs and cattle). In these regions, the only naturally occurring trees are deciduous broadleaf trees along streams and other limited sites. These regions are called grasslands because of the predominance of grass-like plants before human intervention (Figure 17.6 shows the natural location of this biome).

In North America, tallgrass prairie vegetation once grew to heights of 2 m (6.5 ft) and extended westward to about the 98th meridian, with shortgrass prairies in the drier lands farther west. The 98th meridian is roughly the location of the 51-cm (20-in.) isohyet, with wetter conditions to the east and drier conditions to the west (see Figure 15.18).

The climate and deep, tough sod of these grasslands posed problems for the first European settlers. The self-scouring steel plow, introduced in 1837 by John Deere, allowed the interlaced grass sod to be broken apart, freeing the soils for agriculture. Other inventions were also critical to opening this region and solving its unique spatial problems: barbed wire (the fencing material for a treeless prairie); well-drilling techniques developed by Pennsylvania

(a) Chaparral vegetation, southern California.

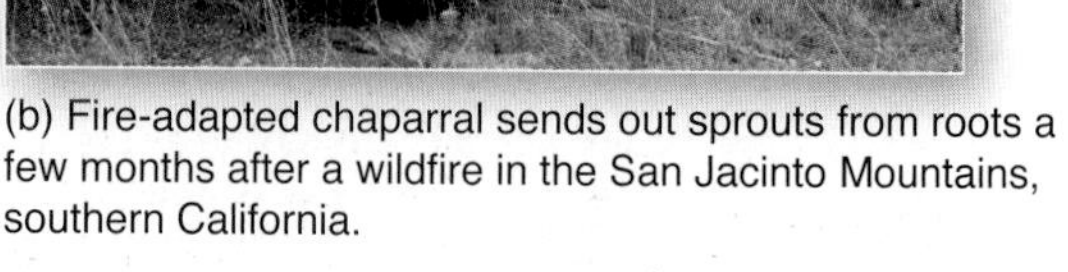

(b) Fire-adapted chaparral sends out sprouts from roots a few months after a wildfire in the San Jacinto Mountains, southern California.

▲**Figure 17.12 Mediterranean chaparral and fire adaptations.** [Bobbé Christopherson.]

▲Figure 17.13 Protected grasslands in the United States. Buffalo Gap National Grassland in western South Dakota is one of 20 protected national grasslands (see http://www.fs.fed.us/grasslands/). [Jason Patrick Ross/Shutterstock.]

oil drillers, but used for water wells; windmills for pumping; and railroads to transport materials.

Few patches of the original prairies (tall grassland) or steppes (short grassland) remain within this biome (**Figure 17.13**). In the prairies alone, the natural vegetation was reduced from 100 million hectares (250 million acres) down to a few areas of several hundred hectares each. Characteristic midlatitude grasslands outside North America are the *Pampas* of Argentina and Uruguay and the grassland of Ukraine. In most regions where these grasslands were the natural vegetation, human development of them was critical to territorial expansion.

This biome is the home of large grazing animals, including deer, pronghorn, and bison (**Figure 17.14**). Gophers, prairie dogs, ground squirrels, Turkey Vultures, grouse, and Prairie Chickens are common, as are grasshoppers and other insects. Predators include the coyote, black-footed ferret (see GeoReport 17.2), badger, and birds of prey—hawks, eagles, and owls.

Deserts

Earth's desert biomes cover more than one-third of its land area (Figure 17.6). We subdivide the desert biomes into **warm desert and semidesert**, caused by the dry air and low precipitation of subtropical high-pressure cells, and **cold desert and semidesert**, which tend toward higher latitudes, where subtropical high pressure affects climate for less than 6 months of the year. A third subdivision, Earth's **polar deserts**, occurs in high-latitude regions, including most of Antarctica and Greenland, with very cold, dry climates. Vegetation, sparse in these predominantly ice- and rock-covered regions, is mainly lichens and mosses.

Desert vegetation includes numerous *xerophytes*, plants that have adapted to dry conditions by evolving mechanisms to prevent water loss; for example, cacti and other succulents store water in their thick and fleshy tissues. Other xerophytic adaptations include long taproots to access groundwater (mesquite trees); shallow, spreading root systems to maximize water uptake (palo verde trees); small leaves to minimize surface area for water loss (acacia); waxy leaf coatings to retard water loss (creosote bush); and leaf drop during dry periods (ocotillo). A number of xerophytic plants have also developed spines, thorns, or bad-tasting tissue to discourage herbivory.

Some desert plants are *ephemeral*, or short-lived, an adaptation that takes advantage of a short wet season or even a single rainfall event in desert environments. The seeds of desert ephemerals lie dormant on the ground until a rainfall stimulates the seed germination. Seedlings grow rapidly, mature, flower, and produce large numbers of new seeds, which are then dispersed long distances by wind or water. Seeds then go dormant until the next rainfall event. Some plants that grow along desert washes

▲Figure 17.14 Bison in the Big Basin Prairie Preserve, western Kansas. Inset shows a male and female shedding winter coats. [Bobbé Christopherson.]

GEOreport 17.2 Black-footed ferrets return from the edge of extinction

The black-footed ferret (*Mustela nigripes*), a member of the weasel family, is the only native North American ferret. Once numbering in the tens of thousands and ranging throughout the grasslands from Canada to northern Mexico, this species was down to 18 individuals by 1986, a result of introduced diseases and habitat destruction. Today, after years of captive breeding, reintroduction, and habitat preservation, the black-footed ferret population has reached an estimated 1000 in the wild, including self-sustaining populations in three U.S. states and at least one in Canada; many more individuals are in captive breeding facilities. The species remains listed as endangered, but its promising future exemplifies a conservation success story.

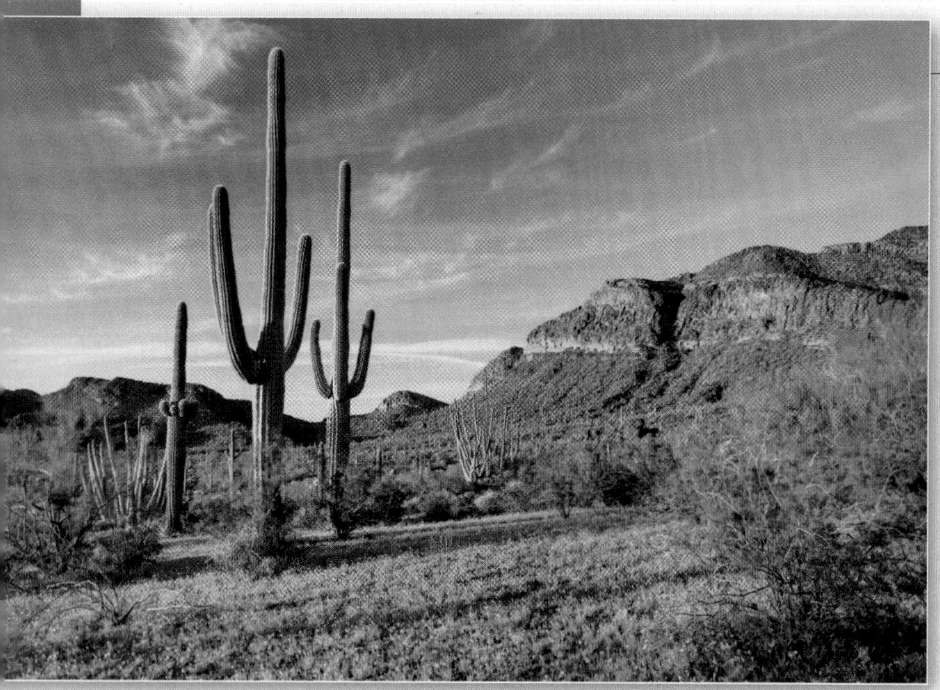

◀ Figure 17.15 Saguaro cacti in the Sonoran Desert. Saguaro cacti in a field of Mexican poppies, with smaller organ pipe cacti in the distance, Organ Pipe Cactus National Monument, Arizona. [Alan Majchrowicz/Photolibrary/Getty Images.]

produce seeds that require *scarification*—abrasion or weathering of the surface—for the seed to open and germinate. This can occur from the tumbling, churning action of a flash flood flowing down a desert wash, an event that also produces the moisture for seed germination.

The vegetation of the Sonoran Desert of southern Arizona is an example of the warm desert biome (**Figure 17.15**). This landscape features the unique saguaro cactus (*Carnegiea gigantea*), which grows to many meters in height and up to 200 years in age if undisturbed. First blooms do not appear until it is 50 to 75 years old. In cold deserts, where precipitation is greater and temperatures are colder, characteristic vegetation includes grasses and woody shrubs, such as sagebrush (*Artemisia tridentata*). Succulents that hold large amounts of water, such as the saguaro cactus, cannot survive in cold deserts that experience consecutive days or nights with freezing winter temperatures.

The faunas of both warm and cold deserts are limited by the extreme conditions and include only a few resident large animals. Camels, which still remain in the wild in the Gobi Desert of central Asia, are well adapted to the extreme daily temperature range of cold deserts as well as limited water availability. These animals can lose up to 30% of their body weight in water without harm (for humans, a 10%–12% loss is dangerous). Desert bighorn sheep are another large animal, occurring in scattered populations in inaccessible mountains and canyons, such as the inner Grand Canyon, but not at the rim. Desert bighorn declined precipitously from about 1850 to 1900 due to competition with livestock for food and water as well as exposure to parasites and disease. In an effort to reestablish bighorn populations, several states are transplanting the animals to their former ranges.

Other representative desert animals are the ring-tailed cat, kangaroo rat, lizards, scorpions, and snakes. Most of these animals become active only at night, when temperatures are lower. In addition, various birds have adapted to desert conditions and available food sources—for example, roadrunners, thrashers, ravens, wrens, hawks, grouse, and nighthawks.

Arctic and Alpine Tundra

The **arctic tundra** biome is located in the extreme northern area of North America and Russia, bordering the Arctic Ocean and generally north of the 10°C (50°F) isotherm for the warmest month. Daylength varies greatly throughout the year, seasonally changing from almost continuous day to continuous night. The region, except for a few portions of Alaska and Siberia, was covered by ice during all of the Pleistocene glaciations.

This biome corresponds to the tundra climates; winters are cold and long; summers are cool and brief. A growing season of sorts lasts only 60–80 days, and even then frosts can occur at any time. Soils are poorly developed and underlain by permafrost. In the summer months, thawing permafrost produces a mucky surface of poor drainage (**Figure 17.16a**). Roots can penetrate only to the depth of thawed ground, usually about a meter (3 ft). With recent climate change, these regions have been warming at more than twice the rate of the rest of the planet over the past few decades.

Arctic tundra vegetation consists of low, ground-hugging herbaceous plants such as sedges, mosses,

GEOreport 17.3 Plant communities survive under glacial ice

Glacial retreat has exposed communities of bryophytes (nonflowering, spore-producing plants, such as mosses) that lived 400 years ago, during the warmer interglacial period known as the Little Ice Age. Recently, scientists collected and dated samples of these communities in the Canadian Arctic. They also successfully cultured the plants in a laboratory, using a single cell of the exhumed material to regenerate the entire original organism. Thus, bryophytes can survive long periods of burial under thick glacial ice and, under the right conditions, potentially recolonize a landscape after glaciation.

(a) Tundra mosses with a glacially eroded roche moutonnée in the background (shape denotes glacial movement from left to right).

(b) Grasses, mosses, and dwarf willow flourish in the cold high-latitude climates.

▲**Figure 17.16 Arctic tundra.** [Bobbé Christopherson.]

arctic meadow grass, and snow lichen and some woody species such as dwarf willow (**Figure 17.16b**). Owing to the short growing season, some perennials form flower buds one summer and open them for pollination the next. Animals of the tundra biome include musk ox, caribou, reindeer, rabbit, Ptarmigan, lemming, and other small rodents, which are important food for the larger carnivores—the wolf, fox, weasel, Snowy Owl, polar bear, and, of course, mosquito. The tundra is an important breeding ground for geese, swans, and other waterfowl.

Alpine tundra is similar to arctic tundra, but it can occur at lower latitudes because it is associated with high elevations. This biome usually occurs above the treeline (the elevation above which trees cannot grow), which shifts to higher elevations closer to the equator. Alpine tundra communities occur in the Andes near the equator, the White Mountains and Sierra of California, the American and Canadian Rockies, the Alps, and Mount Kilimanjaro of equatorial Africa as well as in mountains from the Middle East to Asia.

Alpine tundra features ground-hugging grasses and herbs, lichens, mosses, and low-growing woody shrubs, such as willows and heaths. In many alpine locations, plants have forms that are shaped by frequent winds. Alpine tundra can also experience permafrost conditions. Characteristic fauna include mountain goats, Rocky Mountain bighorn sheep, elk, and voles (**Figure 17.17**).

Vegetation of the tundra biome is slow-growing, has low productivity, and is easily disturbed. Hydroelectric projects, mineral exploitation, and even tire tracks leave marks on the landscape that persist for hundreds of years. With rising population and energy demand, the region will face even greater challenges from the environmental impacts of petroleum resource development. The possibility of drilling for shale gas and methane hydrates, as described in Chapters 1 and 14, is a new threat to this biome.

CRITICAL**thinking** 17.3

A Shifting-Climate Hypothetical

Using Figure 17.6 (biomes), Figure 7.2 (climates), Figures 6.6 and 7.1 (precipitation), and Figure 5.20 (air masses) and noting the printed graphic scales on these maps, consider the following hypothetical situation. Assume a northward climatic shift in the United States and Canada of 500 km (310 mi); in other words, imagine moving North America 500 km south to simulate climatic categories shifting north. Describe your analysis of conditions through the Midwest from Texas to the prairies of Canada. Describe your analysis of conditions from New York through New England and into the Maritime Provinces. How will biomes change? What economic relocations do you envision? Extend your thinking to another region of the world: If the subtropical high-pressure cell over Australia expanded and intensified, consider the new pattern of climate categories and ecosystems.

▲**Figure 17.17 Mountain goats, Montana.** Mountain goats (*Oreamnos americanus*) inhabit the rocky cliffs and alpine tundra of Glacier National Park. [Universal Images Group/SuperStock.]

Anthropogenic Biomes

Even in many of the most pristine ecosystems on Earth, evidence of early human settlement exists. Today, we are the most powerful biotic agent on Earth, influencing all ecosystems on a planetary scale (**Figure 17.18**). Scientists are measuring ecosystem properties and building elaborate computer models to simulate the evolving human–environment experiment on our planet—in particular, the shifting patterns of environmental factors (temperatures and changing frost periods; precipitation timing and amounts; air, water, and soil chemistry; and nutrient redistribution) wrought by human activities.

In 2008, two geographers presented the concept of "anthropogenic biomes," based on today's human-altered ecosystems, as an updated and more accurate portrayal of the terrestrial biosphere than the "pristine" natural vegetation communities described in most biome classifications. Their map, shown in The Human Denominator 17, shows five broad categories of human-modified landscapes: settlements, croplands, rangelands, forested lands, and wildlands. Within these categories, the scientists defined 21 biomes, which summarize the current mosaic of landscapes in terms of common combinations of land uses and land cover.

Anthropogenic biomes result from ongoing human interaction with ecosystems, linked to land-use practices such as agriculture, forestry, and urbanization. The most extensive anthropogenic biome is rangelands, covering about 32% of Earth's ice-free land; croplands, forested lands, and wildlands each cover about 20%, and settlements take up about 7%.

The concept of anthropogenic biomes does not replace terrestrial biome classifications, but instead presents another perspective. Understanding of the natural biomes presented in this chapter is essential for the advancement of basic and applied sciences as they relate to conservation biogeography and ecosystem and species restoration.

▲**Figure 17.18 Freeway through the Puerto Rican rain forest.** Humans are Earth's most powerful agent of geomorphic and biotic change. The human denominator influences all biomes and all Earth systems. [Bobbé Christopherson.]

GEOreport 17.4 Aquatic biomes and marine ecosystem management

Human activities have affected freshwater and marine biomes in roughly similar ways to terrestrial biomes. Coastal ocean waters, in particular, continue to deteriorate from pollution and habitat degradation, as well as unsustainable fishing practices. Declines in aquatic species, such as the precipitous drop of the herring population in the Georges Bank fishing area of the Atlantic in the 1970s, highlight the need for an ecosystem approach to understanding and managing these international waters.

This need was partly met by the designation of large marine ecosystems (LMEs), distinctive oceanic regions identified on the basis of organisms, ocean-floor topography, currents, areas of nutrient-rich upwelling circulation, or areas of significant predation, including human. Examples of identified LMEs include the Gulf of Alaska, California Current, Gulf of Mexico, Northeast Continental Shelf, and Baltic and Mediterranean Seas. Some 64 LMEs, each encompassing more than 200,000 km^2 (77,200 mi^2), are presently defined worldwide (see the list at **http://www.lme.noaa.gov/**). A number of these LMEs include government-protected areas, such as the Monterey Bay National Marine Sanctuary within the California Current LME and the Florida Keys Marine Sanctuary within the Gulf of Mexico LME (see **http://sanctuaries.NOAA.gov/**).

THE**human**DENOMINATOR 17 Anthropogenic Biomes

BIOMES IMPACT HUMANS

- Natural plant and animal communities are linked to human cultures, providing resources for food and shelter.
- Earth's remaining undisturbed ecosystems are becoming a focus for tourism, recreation, and scientific attention.

HUMANS IMPACT BIOMES

- Invasive species, many introduced by humans, disrupt native ecosystems.
- Tropical deforestation is ongoing, with more than half of Earth's original rain forest already cleared.

17a **Residential irrigated cropland**. Prince Edward Island, Canada.

17b **Urban settlement.** London, England.

17c **Irrigated village**. Satpara, Pakistan.

Settlements
- Urban
- Dense settlement
- Rice villages
- Irrigated villages
- Cropland and pastoral
- Pastoral villages
- Rain-fed villages
- Rain-fed mosaic villages

Croplands
- Residential irrigated cropland
- Residential rain-fed mosaic
- Populated irrigated cropland
- Populated rain-fed cropland
- Remote cropland

Rangelands
- Residential rangelands
- Populated rangelands
- Remote rangelands

Forested lands
- Populated forest
- Remote forest

Wildlands
- Wild forest
- Sparse trees
- Barren or ice-covered

17e **Remote rangelands**. Northern Chile.

17d **Populated forest**. Raja Ampat Islands, Indonesia.

Map courtesy of Erle Ellis, University of Maryland, Baltimore County, and Navin Ramankutty, McGill University/NASA; available at: http://earthobservatory.nasa.gov/IOTD/view.php?id=40554

ISSUES FOR THE 21ST CENTURY

- Management of species and ecosystems must become a priority to avoid extinctions and loss of diversity.
- Shifting of species distributions in response to environmental factors will continue with ongoing climate change.
- Population control and global education (including education for women and disadvantaged minorities in all countries) are critical for sustaining natural and anthropogenic biomes.

KEYLEARNINGconceptsreview

Locate the world's biogeographic realms and *discuss* the basis for their specification.

The interplay of evolutionary and abiotic factors within Earth's ecosystems determines biodiversity and the distribution of plant and animal communities. A **biogeographic realm** is a major geographic region in which certain groups of associated plant and animal species evolved. This recognition laid the groundwork for understanding communities of flora and fauna known as biomes.

biogeographic realm (p. 532)

1. What is a biogeographic realm? What are the zoological realms? What is Wallace's line?

Explain the basis for grouping plant communities into biomes and *list* the major terrestrial biomes on Earth.

A **biome** is a large, stable, terrestrial or aquatic ecosystem classified according to the predominant vegetation type and the adaptations of particular organisms to that environment. Biomes carry the name of the dominant vegetation because it is the most easily identified feature. The six main terrestrial vegetation classifications are forest, savanna, grassland, shrubland, desert, and tundra. Within these general groups, biome designations are based on more-specific growth forms; for example, forests are subdivided into rain forests, seasonal forests, broadleaf mixed forests, and needleleaf forests. Ideally, a biome represents a mature community of natural vegetation. A boundary transition zone between adjoining ecosystems is an **ecotone**.

biome (p. 533) **ecotone (p. 534)**

2. Define biome. What is the basis for the designation?
3. Give some examples of vegetation growth forms.
4. Describe a transition zone between two ecosystems. How wide is an ecotone? Explain.

Explain the potential impact of non-native species on biotic communities, using several examples, and *discuss* strategies for biodiversity conservation.

Communities, ecosystems, and biomes can be affected by species that are introduced from elsewhere by humans, either accidentally or intentionally. These non-native species are also called *exotic species* or *aliens*. After arriving in the new ecosystem, some species may disrupt native ecosystems and become **invasive species**.

Efforts are under way worldwide to set aside and protect remaining representative sites within most of Earth's principal biomes. Principles of **island biogeography** used in the study of isolated ecosystems are important in setting up biosphere reserves. Island communities are special places for study because of their spatial isolation and the relatively small number of species present.

invasive species (p. 536) **island biogeography (p. 537)**

5. Give several examples of invasive species described in the text, and describe their impact on natural systems.
6. What happened in the waters of Tristan da Cunha? What economic damage might evolve from a biological invasion in Tristan's marine ecosystems?
7. Describe the theory of island biogeography. How has this theory been important for preserving biodiversity? What are the goals of a biosphere reserve?

Summarize the characteristics of Earth's 10 major terrestrial biomes and *locate* them on a world map.

For an overview of Earth's 10 major terrestrial biomes and their vegetation characteristics, soil orders, climate-type designations, annual precipitation ranges, temperature patterns, and water-balance characteristics, review Table 17.1. The tropical rainforest biome is undergoing rapid deforestation. Because the rain forest is Earth's most diverse biome and is important to the climate system, this loss is creating great concern. In reality, few undisturbed biomes exist in the world, for most have been modified by human activity. The new concept of **anthropogenic biomes** considers the impacts of human settlement, agriculture, and forest practices on vegetation patterns.

tropical rain forest (p. 540)
tropical seasonal forest and scrub (p. 542)
tropical savanna (p. 543)
midlatitude broadleaf and mixed forest (p. 543)
boreal forest (p. 546)
needleleaf forest (p. 546)
taiga (p. 546)
montane forest (p. 546)
temperate rain forest (p. 546)
Mediterranean shrubland (p. 547)
chaparral (p. 548)
midlatitude grassland (p. 548)
warm desert and semidesert (p. 549)
cold desert and semidesert (p. 549)
polar desert (p. 549)
arctic tundra (p. 550)
alpine tundra (p. 551)
anthropogenic biome (p. 552)

8. Using the integrative chart that is Table 17.1 and the world map in Figure 17.6, select any two biomes and study the correlation of vegetation characteristics, soil, moisture, and climate with their spatial distribution. Then contrast the two using each characteristic.
9. Describe the tropical rain forests. Why is the rain-forest floor somewhat clear of plant growth? Why is logging of individual tree species so difficult there?
10. What issues surround the deforestation of the rain forest? What is the impact of these losses on the rest of the biosphere? What new threat to the rain forest has emerged?
11. What do *Caatinga, Chaco, brigalow*, and *dornveld* refer to? Explain.
12. Describe the role of fire in the tropical savanna biome and in the midlatitude broadleaf and mixed forest biome.
13. Why does the boreal forest biome not exist in the Southern Hemisphere, except in mountainous regions? Where is this biome located in the Northern Hemisphere, and what is its relationship to climate type?

14. In which biome do we find Earth's tallest trees? Which biome is dominated by small, stunted plants, lichens, and mosses?
15. What type of vegetation predominates in the Mediterranean (dry summer) climate? Describe the adaptations necessary for these plants to survive.
16. What is the significance of the 98th meridian in terms of North American grassland? What types of inventions enabled agriculture in this grassland?
17. Describe some of the unique adaptations of xerophytes.
18. What types of plants and animals are found in the tundra biome?
19. Describe the concept of anthropogenic biomes. According to the categories presented on the map in Human Denominator 17, how would you classify the area in which you live?
20. As an example of shifting-climate impacts, we tracked temperature and precipitation conditions for Illinois in Geosystems Now in Chapter 16. What impacts do you think climate change will have on biomes in the United States and in other countries?

VISUALanalysis 17 Seasonal Changes

Study the seasonal changes in this ornamental pear tree (*Pyrus calleryana*), a species native to China and Vietnam and now planted widely across North America. [Robert Christopherson.]

1. As illustrated by these photos, explain the connections between day length, Sun angle, and net photosynthesis as they change throughout the four seasons.
2. Applying your observations of this tree to an entire natural ecosystem, assess changes in net primary productivity on a seasonal basis. In which season is net productivity highest? What environmental factors affect net primary productivity throughout the year? Explain.
3. In which anthropogenic biomes might this pear tree be found?
4. Thinking back to all you have learned about present-day climate change, summarize the impacts of global warming and climate change on the timing of seasons. Among the various biomes, how are such changes in seasonal timing becoming apparent?

(a) Spring (b) Summer (c) Fall (d) Winter

MasteringGeography™

Looking for additional review and test prep materials? Visit the Study Area in *MasteringGeography*™ to enhance your geographic literacy, spatial reasoning skills, and understanding of this chapter's content by accessing a variety of resources, including MapMaster interactive maps, geoscience animations, videos, *In the News* RSS feeds, flashcards, web links, self-study quizzes, and an eText version of *Elemental Geosystems*.

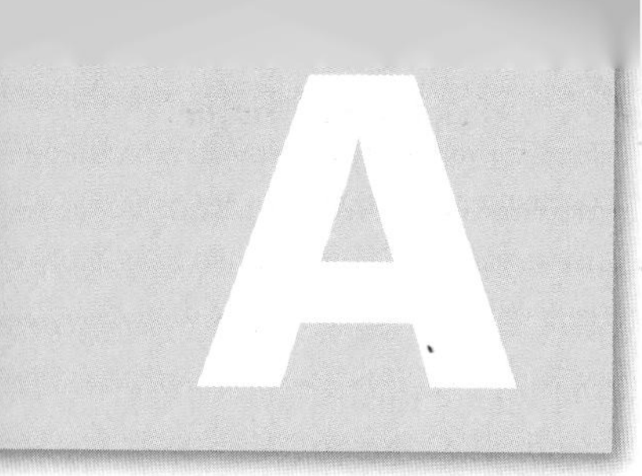

Maps in This Text and Topographic Maps

Maps in This Text

Elemental Geosystems uses several map projections to present different types of data: for example, Goode's homolosine, Robinson, and Miller cylindrical. **Goode's homolosine projection** is an interrupted world map designed in 1923 by Dr. J. Paul Goode of the University of Chicago and first used in the Rand McNally *Goode's Atlas* in 1925. This equal-area map projection (**Figure A.1**) is a combination of two oval projections, which together make the projection excellent for mapping spatial distributions when interruptions of oceans or continents do not pose a problem.

In the Goode's homolosine projection, two equal-area projections are cut and pasted together to improve the rendering of landmass shapes. A *sinusoidal projection* is used between 40° N and 40° S latitude. Its central meridian is a straight line; all other meridians are drawn as sinusoidal curves (based on sine-wave curves), and parallels are evenly spaced. A *Mollweide projection*, also called a *homolographic projection*, is used from 40° N latitude to the North Pole and from 40° S latitude to the South Pole. Its central meridian is a straight line; all other meridians are drawn as elliptical arcs, and parallels are unequally spaced—farther apart at the equator, closer together poleward. This technique of combining two projections preserves areal size relationships.

Examples of the Goode's homolosine projection in *Elemental Geosystems* include the world climate maps in Chapter 7, the topographic regions and continental shield maps in Chapter 10 (Figures 10.3 and 10.4), the world karst map in Chapter 11 (Figure 11.11), the world loess deposits map in Chapter 15 (Figure 15.2), and the terrestrial biomes map in Chapter 17 (Figure 17.6).

This text also uses the **Robinson projection**, designed by Arthur Robinson in 1963. This projection is neither equal area nor true shape, but is a compromise between the two (**Figure A.2**). The North and South Poles appear as lines slightly more than half the length of the equator; thus, higher latitudes are exaggerated less than on other oval and cylindrical projections.

Examples of the Robinson projection in *Elemental Geosystems* include the latitudinal geographic zones map in Chapter 1 (Figure 1.11), the daily net radiation map in Chapter 2 (Figure 2.8), the world temperature range map in Chapter 3 (Figure 3.23), the maps of lithospheric plates and volcanoes and earthquakes in Chapter 9 (Figures 9.16 and 9.17), and the global oil spills map in Chapter 13 (Figure 13.4).

The **Miller cylindrical projection** is another compromise map used in this text (**Figure A.3**). This projection, which today frequently appears in world atlases, was first developed by Osborn Miller and presented by The American Geographical Society in 1942. This projection is neither true shape nor true area, but is a compromise that avoids the severe scale distortion of the Mercator. Examples of the Miller cylindrical projection in *Elemental Geosystems* include the world time zone map in Chapter 1 (Figure 1.15), global temperature maps

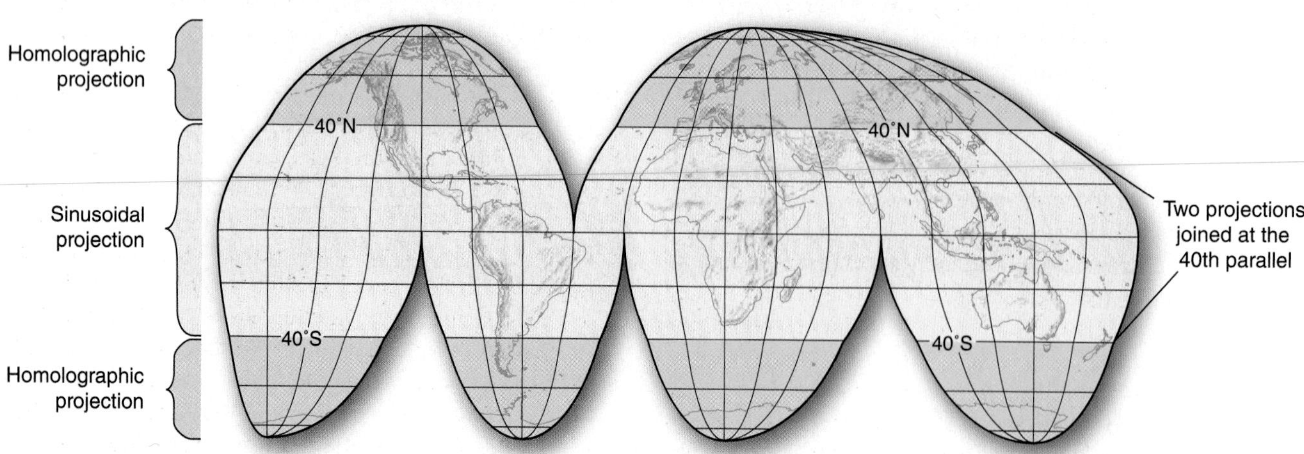

Figure A.1 Goode's homolosine projection.
An equal-area projection.

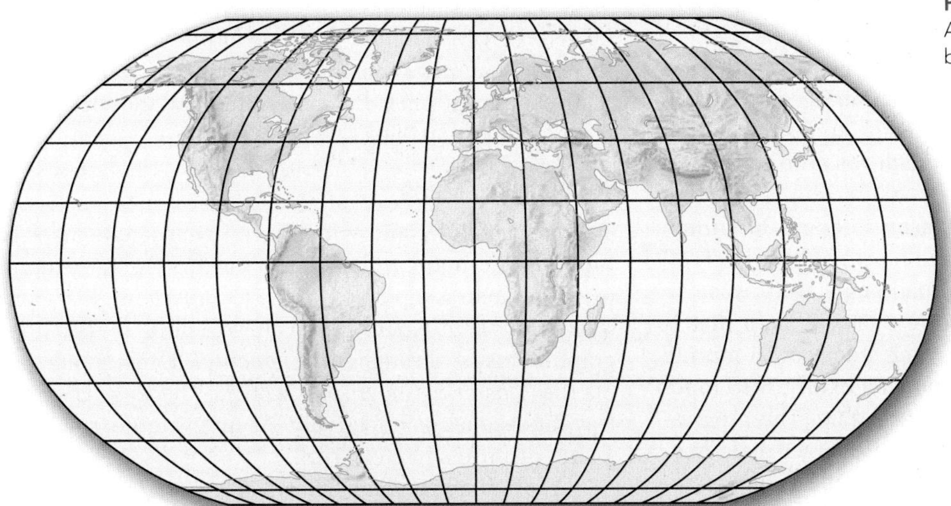

Figure A.2 Robinson projection. A compromise map projection between equal area and true shape.

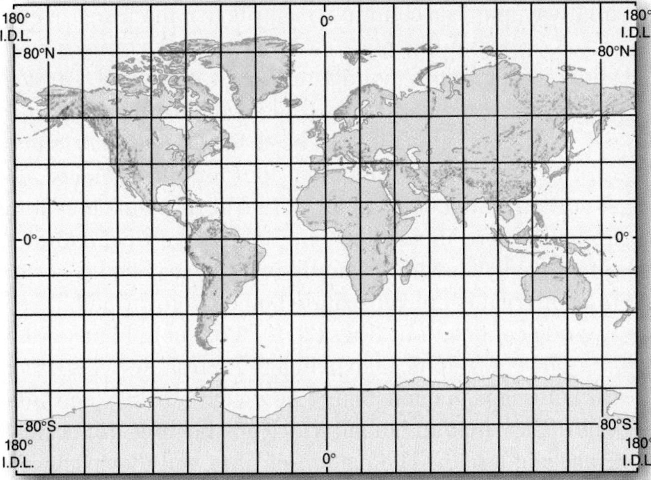

Figure A.3 Miller cylindrical projection. A compromise map projection between equal area and true shape.

in Chapter 3 (Figures 3.21 and 3.22), and the two global pressure maps in Chapter 4 (Figure 4.9).

Quadrangles and Topographic Maps

The westward expansion across the vast North American continent demanded a land survey for the creation of accurate maps. Maps were needed to subdivide the land and to guide travel, exploration, settlement, and transportation. In 1785, the Public Lands Survey System began surveying and mapping government land in the United States. In 1836, the Clerk of Surveys in the Land Office of the Department of the Interior directed public-land surveys. The Bureau of Land Management replaced the Land Office in 1946. The actual preparation and recording of survey information fell to the U.S. Geological Survey (USGS), also a branch of the Department of the Interior (see http://www.usgs.gov/pubprod/maps.html).

In Canada, National Resources Canada conducts the national mapping program. Canadian mapping includes base maps, thematic maps, aeronautical charts, federal topographic maps, and the National Atlas of Canada, now in its fifth edition (see http://atlas.nrcan.gc.ca/).

Quadrangle Maps

The USGS depicts survey information on quadrangle maps, so called because they are rectangular maps with four corner angles. The angles are junctures of parallels of latitude and meridians of longitude rather than political boundaries. These quadrangle maps utilize the Albers equal-area projection, from the conic class of map projections.

The accuracy of conformality (shape) and scale of this base map is improved by the use of not one, but two standard parallels. (Remember from Chapter 1 that standard lines are where the projection cone touches the globe's surface, producing greatest accuracy.) For the conterminous United States (the "lower 48"), these parallels are 29.5° N and 45.5° N latitude (noted on the Albers projection shown in Figure 1.19). The standard parallels shift for conic projections of Alaska (55° N and 65° N) and for Hawai'i (8° N and 18° N).

Because a single map of the United States at 1:24,000 scale would be more than 200 m wide (more than 600 ft), some system had to be devised for dividing the map into a manageable size. Thus, a quadrangle system using latitude and longitude coordinates was developed. Note that these maps are not perfect rectangles because meridians converge toward the poles. The width of quadrangles narrows noticeably as you move north (poleward).

Quadrangle maps are published in different series, covering different amounts of Earth's surface at different scales. You see in **Figure A.4** that each series is referred to by its angular dimensions, which range from 1° × 2° (1:250,000 scale) to 7.5′ × 7.5′ (1:24,000 scale). A map that is one-half of a degree (30′) on each side is a 30-minute quadrangle, and a map that is one-fourth of a degree (15′) on each side is a 15-minute quadrangle (this was the USGS standard size from 1910 to 1950). A map that is one-eighth of a degree (7.5′) on each side is a 7.5-minute quadrangle, the most widely produced of all USGS topographic maps and the standard since 1950. The progression toward more-detailed maps and a larger-scale map standard through the years reflects the continuing refinement of geographic data and new mapping technologies.

The USGS National Mapping Program has completed coverage of the entire country (except Alaska) on 7.5-minute maps (1 in. to 2000 ft, a large scale). It takes 53,838 separate 7.5-minute quadrangles to cover the lower 48 states, Hawai'i, and the U.S. territories. A series of smaller-scale, more-general 15-minute topographic maps offers Alaskan coverage.

In the United States, most quadrangle maps remain in English units of feet and miles. The eventual changeover to the metric system requires revision of the units used on all maps, with the 1:24,000 scale eventually changing to a scale of 1:25,000. However, after completing only a few metric quads, the USGS halted the program in 1991. In Canada, the entire country is mapped at a scale of 1:250,000, using metric units (1.0 cm to 2.5 km). About half the country also is mapped at 1:50,000 (1.0 cm to 0.50 km).

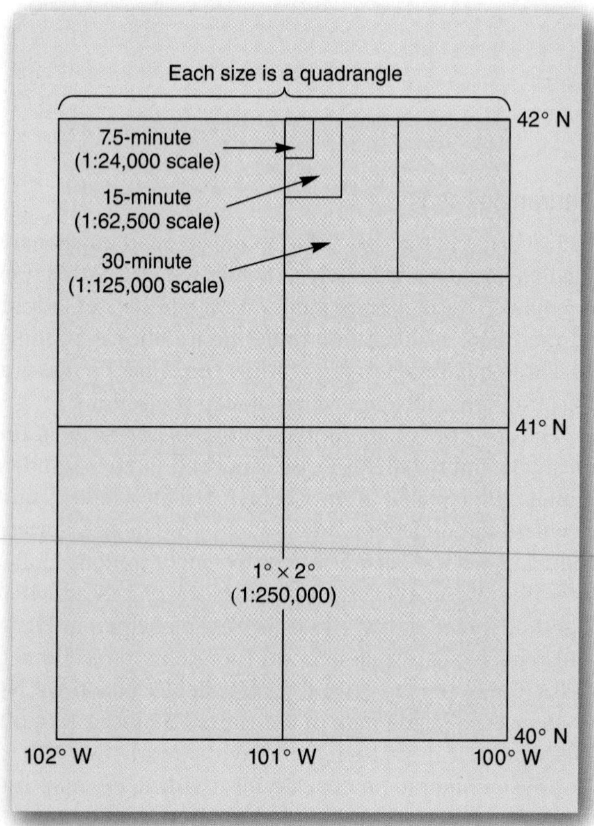

Figure A.4 Quadrangle system of maps used by the USGS.

Topographic Maps

The most popular and widely used quadrangle maps are **topographic maps** prepared by the USGS. An example of such a map is a portion of the Cumberland, Maryland, quad shown in **Figure A.5**. You will find several topographic maps throughout *Elemental Geosystems* (and on the *MasteringGeography* website) because they portray landscapes so effectively. As an example, see Figure 14.18, drumlins in New York.

A **planimetric map** shows the horizontal position (latitude/longitude) of boundaries, land-use aspects, bodies of water, and economic and cultural features. A highway map is a common example of a planimetric map.

A topographic map adds a vertical component to show topography (configuration of the land surface), including slope and relief (the vertical difference in local landscape elevation). These fine details are shown through the use of elevation contour lines (**Figure A.6**). A *contour line* connects all points at the same elevation. Elevations are shown above or below a vertical datum, or reference level, which usually is mean sea level. The contour interval is the vertical distance in elevation between two adjacent contour lines (20 ft, or 6.1 m in Figure A.6b).

The topographic map in Figure A.6b shows a hypothetical landscape, demonstrating how contour lines and intervals depict slope and relief, which are the three-dimensional aspects of terrain. The pattern of lines and the spacing between them indicate slope. The steeper a slope or cliff, the closer together the contour lines appear—in the figure, note the narrowly spaced contours that represent the cliffs to the left of the highway. A wider spacing of these contour lines portrays a more gradual slope, as you can see from the widely spaced lines on the beach and to the right of the river valley.

Figure A.7 shows the standard symbols and colors used on USGS topographic maps: black for human constructions, blue for water features, brown for relief features and contours, pink for urbanized areas, and green for vegetation.

The margins of a topographic map contain information about its concept and content, including the quadrangle name, adjoining quad names, and quad series and type; the position in the latitude-longitude and other coordinate systems; the map title, legend, magnetic declination (alignment of magnetic north), and compass information; the datum plane; the symbols used for roads and trails; and the dates and history of the survey of that particular quadrangle.

Topographic maps are available from the USGS (http://nationalmap.gov/ustopo/index.html) or Centre for Topographic Information, NRC (http://maps.nrcan.gc.ca/). Many state geological survey offices, national and state park headquarters, outfitters, sports shops, and bookstores also sell topographic maps to assist people in planning their outdoor activities.

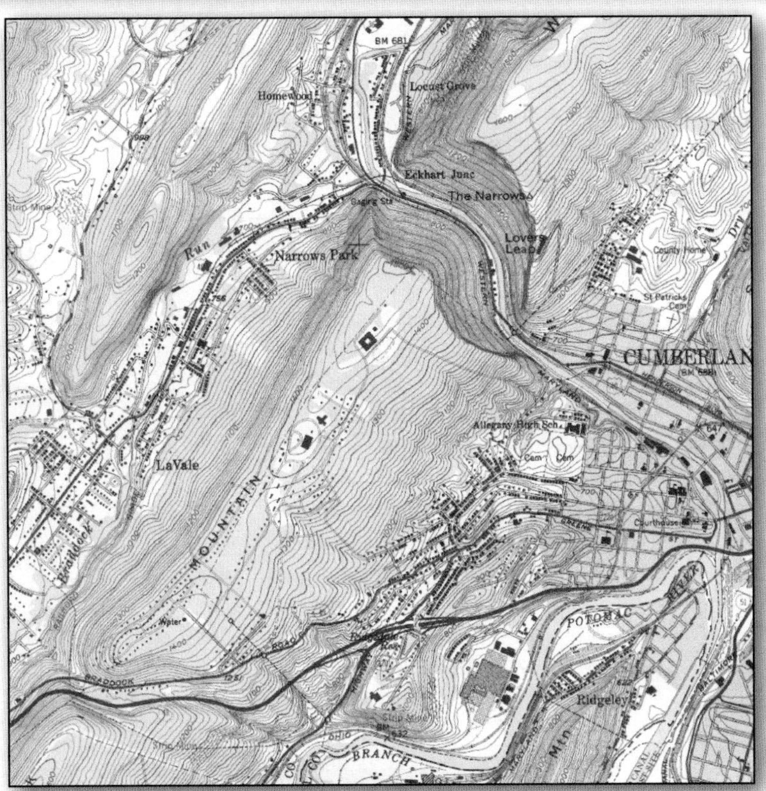

Figure A.5 An example of a topographic map from the Appalachians.
Cumberland, MD, PA, WV 7.5-minute quadrangle topographic map prepared by the USGS. In the *Applied Physical Geography*, 9/e lab manual, this topographic map is accessible through Google Earth™ topographic services, where you experience the map as a 3-D landscape and maneuver with your computer to see the topography at any angle or detail you choose.

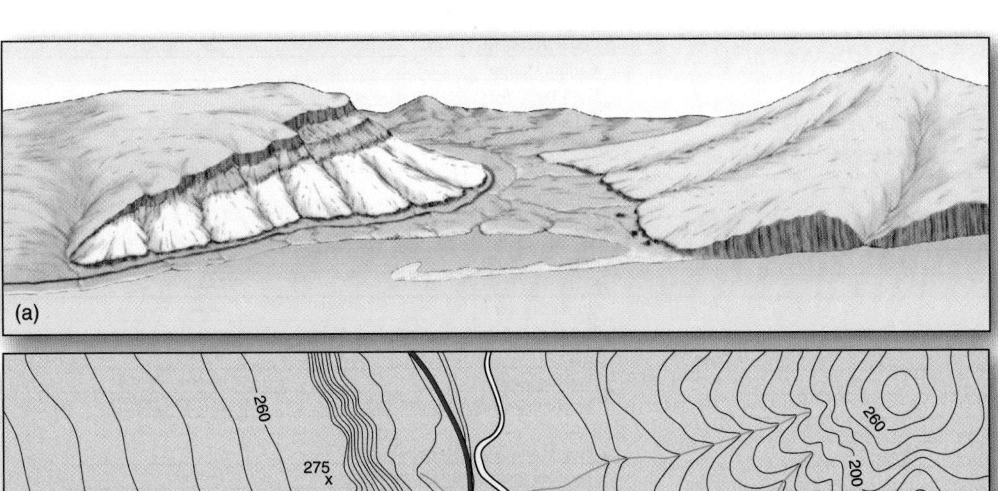

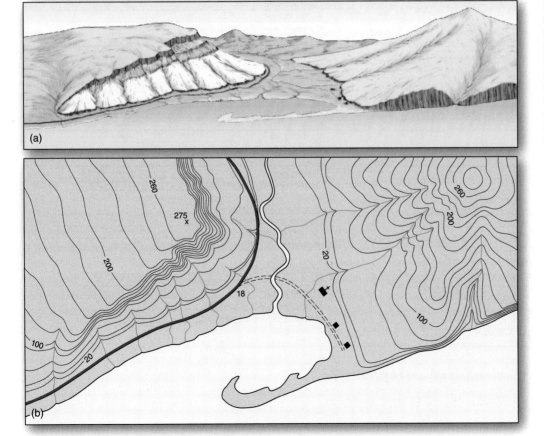

Figure A.6 Topographic map of a hypothetical landscape.
(a) Perspective view of a hypothetical landscape. (b) Depiction of that landscape on a topographic map. The contour interval on the map is 20 feet (6.1 m). [After the U.S. Geological Survey.]

Control data and monuments	
Vertical control	
Third order or better, with tablet	BM ×16.3
Third order or better, recoverable mark	× 120.0
Bench mark at found section corner	BM 18.6
Spot elevation	× 5.3

Contours	
Topographic	
Intermediate	
Index	
Supplementary	
Depression	
Cut; fill	
Bathymetric	
Intermediate	
Index	
Primary	
Index primary	
Supplementary	

Boundaries	
National	
State or territorial	
County or equivalent	
Civil township or equivalent	
Incorporated city or equivalent	
Park, reservation, or monument	

Surface features	
Levee	Levee
Sand or mud area, dunes, or shifting sand	Sand
Intricate surface area	Strip mine
Gravel beach or glacial moraine	Gravel
Tailings pond	Tailings pond

Mines and caves	
Quarry or open pit mine	
Gravel, sand, clay, or borrow pit	
Mine dump	Mine dump
Tailings	Tailings

Vegetation	
Woods	
Scrub	
Orchard	
Vineyard	
Mangrove	Mangrove

Glaciers and permanent snowfields	
Contours and limits	
Form lines	

Marine shoreline	
Topographic maps	
Approximate mean high water	
Indefinite or unsurveyed	
Topographic-bathymetric maps	
Mean high water	
Apparent (edge of vegetation)	

Coastal features	
Foreshore flat	Mud
Rock or coral reef	Reef
Rock bare or awash	
Group of rocks bare or awash	
Exposed wreck	
Depth curve; sounding	3
Breakwater, pier, jetty, or wharf	
Seawall	

Rivers, lakes, and canals	
Intermittent stream	
Intermittent river	
Disappearing stream	
Perennial stream	
Perennial river	
Small falls; small rapids	
Large falls; large rapids	
Masonry dam	
Dam with lock	
Dam carrying road	
Perennial lake; Intermittent lake or pond	
Dry lake	Dry lake
Narrow wash	
Wide wash	Wide wash
Canal, flume, or aquaduct with lock	
Well or spring; spring or seep	

Submerged areas and bogs	
Marsh or swamp	
Submerged marsh or swamp	
Wooded marsh or swamp	
Submerged wooded marsh or swamp	
Rice field	Rice
Land subject to inundation	Max pool 431

Buildings and related features	
Building	
School; church	
Built-up area	
Racetrack	
Airport	
Landing strip	
Well (other than water); windmill	
Tanks	
Covered reservoir	
Gaging station	
Landmark object (feature as labeled)	
Campground; picnic area	
Cemetery: small; large	Cem

Roads and related features

Roads on Provisional edition maps are not classified as primary, secondary, or light duty. They are all symbolized as light duty roads.

Primary highway	
Secondary highway	
Light duty road	
Unimproved road	
Trail	
Dual highway	
Dual highway with median strip	

Railroads and related features	
Standard gauge single track; station	
Standard gauge multiple track	
Abandoned	

Transmission lines and pipelines	
Power transmission line; pole; tower	
Telephone line	Telephone
Aboveground oil or gas pipeline	
Underground oil or gas pipeline	Pipeline

Figure A.7 Standardized topographic map symbols used on USGS maps.
English units still prevail, although a few USGS maps are in metric. [From USGS, Topographic Maps, 1969.]

The Köppen Climate Classification System

B

Over a century ago, German climatologist and botanist Wladimir Köppen (1846–1940) designed a system for classifying climate that is still today the most widely used in teaching and research. The Köppen system, well known for its ease of use, is based on empirical data that are standardized and readily available. The classification uses average monthly temperatures, average monthly precipitation, and total annual precipitation to define each climate region. The system is most useful for identifying general climate patterns rather than for delineating precise climate boundaries (remember that climate boundaries are zones of gradual change, not abrupt transitions). The emphasis on general trends is especially important given the small scales used on world maps.

After initial publication of his system, Köppen collaborated with German climatologist Rudolph Geiger (1894–1981) to modify the climate zones, producing the *Köppen–Geiger climate classification*, first mapped in 1923. This map was revised numerous times until Geiger's last version in 1961.

In 2007, a team of Australian scientists published a comprehensive update of the Köppen–Geiger climate map, using temperature and precipitation data spanning over 70 years from thousands of stations worldwide. We present this map in **Figure B.1**. On the world climate map in Chapter 7, Figure 7.2 on pages 222-23, we present the same map with the addition of the genetic, or causative, factors for each climate type (and without the Köppen lettering system). For additional maps and detailed information, see M. C. Peel, B. L. Finlayson, and T. A. McMahon, "Updated World Map of the Köppen–Geiger Climate Classification," *Hydrology and Earth System Sciences* 11 (2007): 1633–1644 (available at http://www.hydrol-earth-syst-sci.net/11/1633/2007/hess-11-1633-2007.pdf).

The Köppen Climate Types

The Köppen system uses capital letters (A, B, C, D, E) to designate primary climatic categories from the equator to the poles. Each category includes two or three subcategories with more specific climatic conditions. The guidelines for each of these categories and subcategories are in the margin of Figure B.1.

Four of the primary climates are based mainly on temperature characteristics:

A Tropical climates (rain forest, monsoon, and savanna)

C Mesothermal climates (humid subtropical, marine west coast, and Mediterranean)

D Microthermal climates (humid continental and subarctic)

E Polar climates (tundra and ice cap/ice sheet)

Only one primary climate is based mainly on moisture characteristics:

B Dry climates (deserts and semiarid steppes)

Within each capital letter climate category, additional lowercase letters designate specific temperature and precipitation conditions. For example, in a tropical rain forest (*Af*) climate, the *A* tells us that the average coolest month is above 18°C (64.4°F, average for the month), and the *f* indicates that the weather is constantly wet, with the driest month receiving at least 6 cm (2.4 in.) of precipitation. (The designation *f* is from the German *feucht*, for "moist.") The map shows the distribution of the *Af* climate along the equator and equatorial rain forest.

In a *Dfa* climate, the *D* means that the average warmest month is above 10°C (50°F), with at least 1 month falling below 0°C (32°F); the *f* says that at least 3 cm (1.2 in.) of precipitation fall during every month; and the *a* indicates a warmest summer month averaging above 22°C (71.6°F). Thus, a *Dfa* climate is a humid continental hot-summer climate category within the microthermal category.

Highland climates, abbreviated *H* and discussed in Chapter 7, were not part of the Köppen climate classification until the 1953 revision by Geiger and German climatologist Wolfgang Pohl. Because the 2007 update in Figure B.1 is based on the Köppen–Geiger system, it does not include the highland climate type. However, many modern climate classification schemes include highland climates to represent the effects of altitude in mountain ranges at all latitudes.

Köppen Guidelines and Map

Take a few minutes to examine the climate classifications on the map in Figure B.1 and the criteria and considerations for each principal climate category in the colored boxes. Remember that the modified Köppen–Geiger system does not consider winds, temperature extremes, precipitation intensity, quantity of sunshine, cloud cover, or net radiation.

As a way to work through the climate types and distributions, first check the margin boxes for a primary climate type and examine its subcategories. Then check the distribution of that climate on the map. As a next step, consider the causal elements that produce this climate; refer to Chapter 7—Figure 7.2 and the colored boxes summarizing each major climate category—for help.

Figure B.1 World climates and their classification guidelines according to the Köppen system.

Köppen Guidelines

Tropical Climates — A

Consistently warm with all months averaging above 18°C (64.4°F); annual water supply exceeds water demand.

Af — Tropical rain forest

f = All months receive precipitation in excess of 6 cm (2.4 in.).

Am — Tropical monsoon

m = A marked short dry season with 1 or more months receiving less than 6 cm (2.4 in.) precipitation; an otherwise excessively wet rainy season. ITCZ 6–12 months dominant.

Aw — Tropical savanna

w = Summer wet season, winter dry season; ITCZ dominant 6 months or less, winter water-balance deficits.

Mesothermal Climates — C

Warmest month above 10°C (50°F); coldest month above 0°C (32°F), but below 18°C (64.4°F); seasonal climates.

Cfa — Humid subtropical, moist all year

Cwa, Cwb, Cwc — Humid subtropical, winter dry

f = Year-round precipitation.

w = Dry winter; wettest summer month with 10 times more precipitation than driest winter month.

a = Hot summer; warmest month above 22°C (71.6°F).

b = Warmest month below 22°C (71.6°F) with 4 months above 10°C.

c = 1–3 months above 10°C.

Cfb, Cfc — Marine west coast, mild-to-cool summer

f = Year-round precipitation.

b = Warmest month below 22°C (71.6°F) with 4 months above 10°C.

c = 1–3 months above 10°C.

Csa, Csb — Mediterranean dry summer

s = Pronounced dry summer with 70% of winter precipitation.

a = Hot summer with warmest month above 22°C (71.6°F).

b = Mild summer; warmest month below 22°C.

Microthermal Climates — D

Warmest month above 10°C (50°F); coldest month below 0°C (32°F); cool-to-cold conditions; snow climates. In Southern Hemisphere, occurs only in mountains.

Dwa, Dfa, Dsa — Humid continental, hot summer

Dwb, Dfb, Dsb — Humid continental, mild summer

w = Dry winter.

f = Year-round precipitation.

s = Dry summer.

a = Hot summer; warmest month above 22°C (71.6°F).

b = Mild summer; warmest month below 22°C (71.6°F).

Dwc, Dfc, Dsc — Subarctic, cool summer

Dwd, Dfd, Dsd — Subarctic, cold winter

w = Dry winter.

f = Year-round precipitation.

s = Dry summer.

c = 1–4 months above 10°C.

d = Coldest month below −38°C (−36.4°F), in Siberia only.

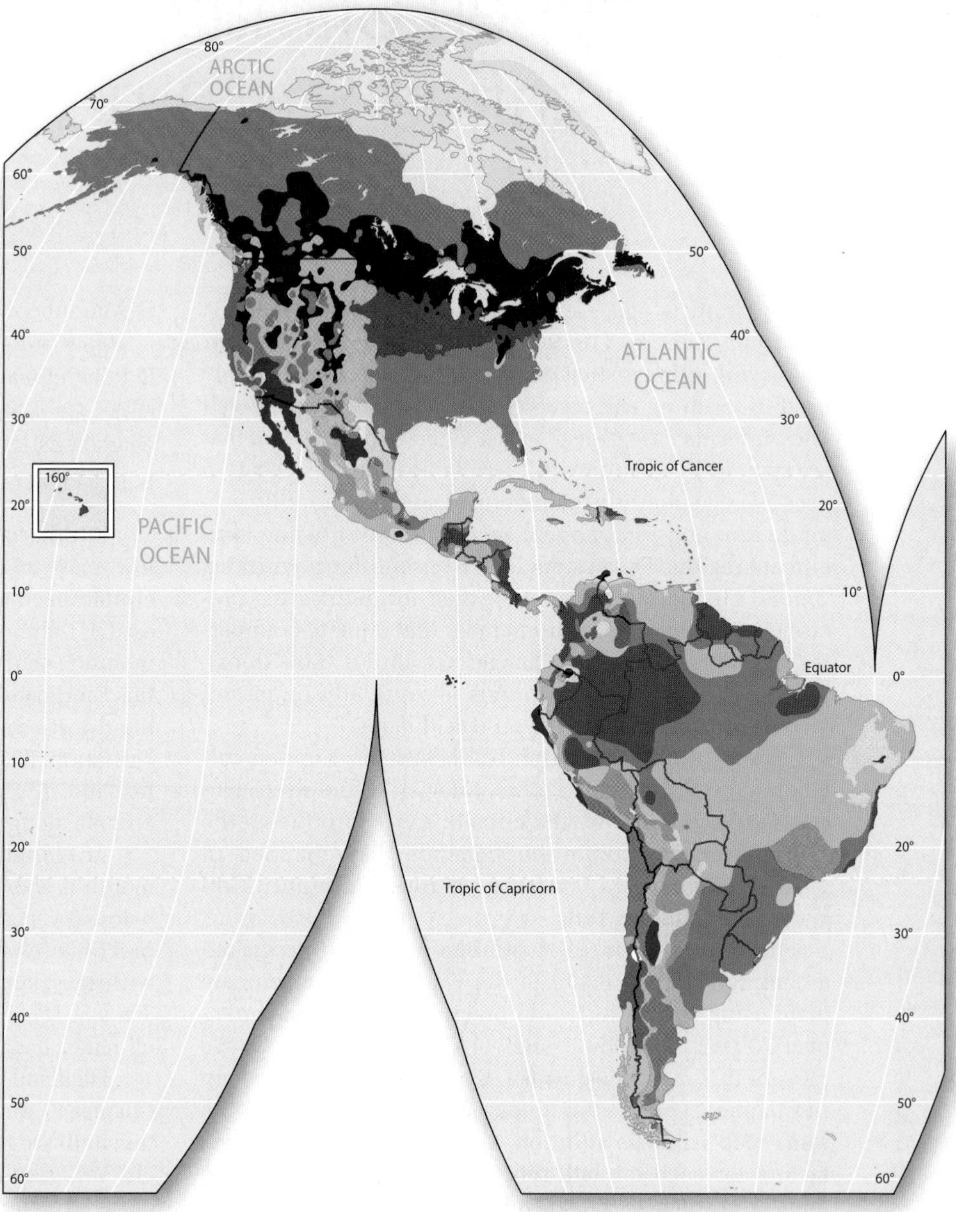

Arid and Semiarid Climates — B

Potential evapotranspiration* (natural moisture demand) exceeds precipitation (natural moisture supply) in all B climates. Subdivisions based on precipitation timing and amount and mean annual temperature.

Arid Climates:

BWh — Hot low-latitude desert

BWk — Cold midlatitude desert

BW = Precipitation less than 1/2 natural moisture demand.

h = Mean annual temperature >18°C (64.4°F).

k = Mean annual temperature <18°C.

Semiarid climates:

BSh — Hot low-latitude steppe

BSk — Cold midlatitude steppe

BS = Precipitation more than 1/2 natural moisture demand, but not equal to it.

h = Mean annual temperature >18°C.

k = Mean annual temperature <18°C.

Polar Climates — E

Warmest month below 10°C (50°F); always cold; ice climates.

ET — Tundra

Warmest month 0–10°C (32–50°F); precipitation exceeds small potential evapotranspiration demand;* snow cover 8–10 months.

EF — Ice cap and ice sheet

Warmest month below 0°C (32°F); precipitation exceeds a very small potential evapotranspiration demand;* the polar regions.

*Potential evapotranspiration = the amount of water that would evaporate or transpire if it were available—the natural moisture demand in an environment; see Chapter 6.

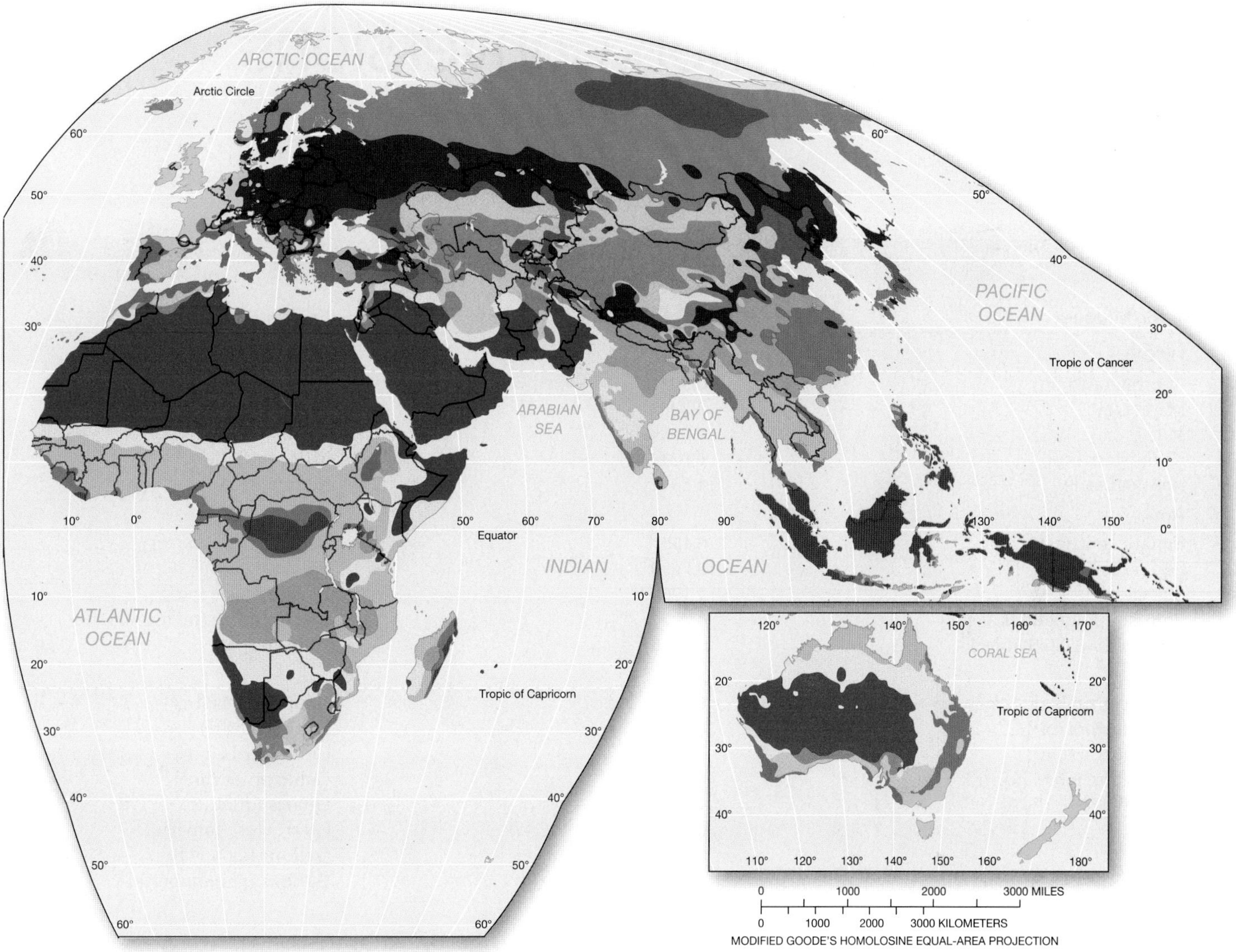

ARCTIC OCEAN
Arctic Circle
PACIFIC OCEAN
Tropic of Cancer
ARABIAN SEA
BAY OF BENGAL
Equator
INDIAN
OCEAN
ATLANTIC OCEAN
Tropic of Capricorn
CORAL SEA
Tropic of Capricorn
0 1000 2000 3000 MILES
0 1000 2000 3000 KILOMETERS
MODIFIED GOODE'S HOMOLOSINE EQUAL-AREA PROJECTION

A TROPICAL CLIMATES

- **Af** Tropical rain forest
- **Am** Tropical monsoon
- **Aw** Tropical savanna

B ARID AND SEMIARID CLIMATES

- **BWh** Tropical, subtropical hot desert
- **BWk** Midlatitude cold desert
- **BSh** Tropical, subtropical hot steppe
- **BSk** Midlatitude cold steppe

C MESOTHERMAL CLIMATES

- **Cfa** Humid subtropical, without dry season, hot summers
- **Cwa Cwb Cwc** Humid subtropical, winter-dry
- **Cfb Cfc** Marine west coast, without dry season, warm to cool summers
- **Csa Csb** Mediterranean summer-dry

D MICROTHERMAL CLIMATES

- **Dwa Dfa Dsa** Humid continental, hot summers
- **Dwb Dfb Dsb** Humid continental, warm summers
- **Dwc Dfc Dsc** Subarctic, cool summers
- **Dwd Dfd Dsd** Subarctic, very cold winter

E POLAR CLIMATES

- **ET** Tundra
- **EF** Ice cap and sheets

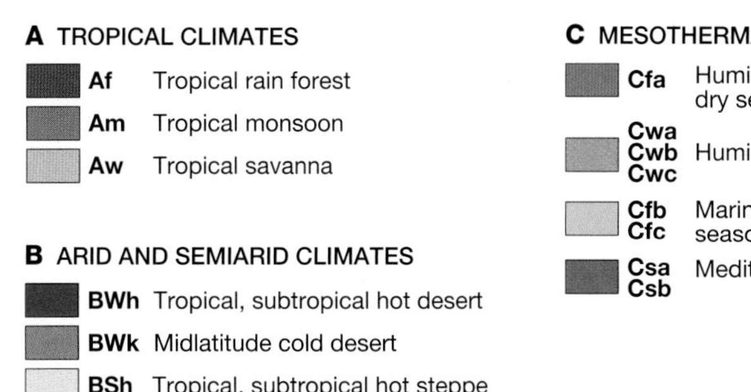

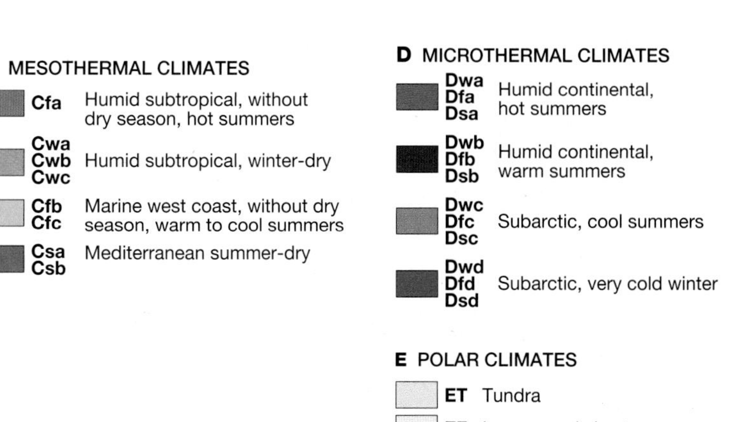

C Common Conversions

Metric to English

Metric Measure	Multiply by	English Equivalent
Length		
Centimeters (cm)	0.3937	Inches (in.)
Meters (m)	3.2808	Feet (ft)
Meters (m)	1.0936	Yards (yd)
Kilometers (km)	0.6214	Miles (mi)
Nautical mile	1.15	Statute mile
Area		
Square centimeters (cm^2)	0.155	Square inches ($in.^2$)
Square meters (m^2)	10.7639	Square feet (ft^2)
Square meters (m^2)	1.1960	Square yards (yd^2)
Square kilometers (km^2)	0.3831	Square miles (mi^2)
Hectare (ha) (10,000 m^2)	2.4710	Acres (a)
Volume		
Cubic centimeters (cm^3)	0.06	Cubic inches ($in.^3$)
Cubic meters (m^3)	35.30	Cubic feet (ft^3)
Cubic meters (m^3)	1.3079	Cubic yards (yd^3)
Cubic kilometers (km^3)	0.24	Cubic miles (mi^3)
Liters (l)	1.0567	Quarts (qt), U.S.
Liters (l)	0.88	Quarts (qt), Imperial
Liters (l)	0.26	Gallons (gal), U.S.
Liters (l)	0.22	Gallons (gal), Imperial
Mass		
Grams (g)	0.03527	Ounces (oz)
Kilograms (kg)	2.2046	Pounds (lb)
Metric ton (tonne) (t)	1.10	Short ton (tn), U.S.
Velocity		
Meters/second (mps)	2.24	Miles/hour (mph)
Kilometers/hour (kmph)	0.62	Miles/hour (mph)
Knots (kn) (nautical mph)	1.15	Miles/hour (mph)
Temperature		
Degrees Celsius (°C)	1.80 (then add 32)	Degrees Fahrenheit (°F)
Celsius degree (C°)	1.80	Fahrenheit degree (F°)
Additional water measurements		
Gallon (Imperial)	1.201	Gallon (U.S.)
Gallons (gal)	0.000003	Acre-feet

1 cubic foot per second per day = 86,400 cubic feet = 1.98 acre-feet

Additional Energy and Power Measurements

1 watt (W) = 1 joule/s

1 joule = 0.239 calorie

1 calorie = 4.186 joules

1 W/m^2 = 0.001433 cal/min

697.8 W/m^2 = 1 cal/cm^2min^{-1}

1 W/m^2 = 2.064 cal/cm^2day^{-1}

1 W/m^2 = 61.91 cal/cm^2month^{-1}

1 W/m^2 = 753.4 cal/cm^2year^{-1}

100 W/m^2 = 75 $kcal/cm^2year^{-1}$

Solar constant:
1372 W/m^2
2 cal/cm^2min^{-1}

English to Metric

English Measure	Multiply by	Metric Equivalent
Length		
Inches (in.)	2.54	Centimeters (cm)
Feet (ft)	0.3048	Meters (m)
Yards (yd)	0.9144	Meters (m)
Miles (mi)	1.6094	Kilometers (km)
Statute mile	0.8684	Nautical mile
Area		
Square inches ($in.^2$)	6.45	Square centimeters (cm^2)
Square feet (ft^2)	0.0929	Square meters (m^2)
Square yards (yd^2)	0.8361	Square meters (m^2)
Square miles (mi^2)	2.5900	Square kilometers (km^2)
Acres (a)	0.4047	Hectare (ha)
Volume		
Cubic inches ($in.^3$)	16.39	Cubic centimeters (cm^3)
Cubic feet (ft^3)	0.028	Cubic meters (m^3)
Cubic yards (yd^3)	0.765	Cubic meters (m^3)
Cubic miles (mi^3)	4.17	Cubic kilometers (km^3)
Quarts (qt), U.S.	0.9463	Liters (l)
Quarts (qt), Imperial	1.14	Liters (l)
Gallons (gal), U.S.	3.8	Liters (l)
Gallons (gal), Imperial	4.55	Liters (l)
Mass		
Ounces (oz)	28.3495	Grams (g)
Pounds (lb)	0.4536	Kilograms (kg)
Short ton (tn), U.S.	0.91	Metric ton (tonne) (t)
Velocity		
Miles/hour (mph)	0.448	Meters/second (mps)
Miles/hour (mph)	1.6094	Kilometers/hour (kmph)
Miles/hour (mph)	0.8684	Knots (kn) (nautical mph)
Temperature		
Degrees Fahrenheit (°F)	0.556 (after subtracting 32)	Degrees Celsius (°C)
Fahrenheit degree (F°)	0.556	Celsius degree (C°)
Additional water measurements		
Gallon (U.S.)	0.833	Gallons (Imperial)
Acre-feet	325,872	Gallons (gal)

Additional Notation

Multiples	Prefixes	
1,000,000,000 = 10^9	giga	G
1,000,000 = 10^6	mega	M
1,000 = 10^3	kilo	k
100 = 10^2	hecto	h
10 = 10^1	deka	da
1 = 10^0		
0.1 = 10^{-1}	deci	d
0.01 = 10^{-2}	centi	c
0.001 = 10^{-3}	milli	m
0.000001 = 10^{-6}	micro	μ

glossary

The chapter in which each term appears is **boldfaced** in parentheses and followed by a specific definition relevant to the term's usage in the chapter.

Aa (10) Rough, jagged, and clinkery basaltic lava with sharp edges. This texture is caused by the loss of trapped gases, a slow flow, and the development of a thick skin that cracks into a jagged surface.

Abiotic (1) Nonliving; Earth's nonliving systems of energy and materials.

Ablation (14) Loss of glacial ice through melting, sublimation, wind removal by deflation, or the calving of blocks of ice. (*See* Deflation.)

Abrasion (12, 13, 14) Mechanical wearing and erosion of bedrock accomplished by the rolling and grinding of particles and rocks carried in a stream, removed by wind in a "sandblasting" action, or imbedded in glacial ice.

Absorption (3) Assimilation and conversion of radiation from one form to another in a medium. In the process, the temperature of the absorbing surface is raised, thereby affecting the rate and wavelength of radiation from that surface.

Active layer (14) A zone of seasonally frozen ground that exists between the subsurface permafrost layer and the ground surface. The active layer is subject to consistent daily and seasonal freeze–thaw cycles. (*See* Permafrost, Periglacial.)

Actual evapotranspiration (6) ACTET; the actual amount of evaporation and transpiration that occurs; derived in the water balance by subtracting the deficit (DEFIC) from potential evapotranspiration (POTET). (*Compare* Potential evapotranspiration.)

Adiabatic (5) Pertaining to the cooling of an ascending parcel of air through expansion or the warming of a descending parcel of air through compression, without any exchange of heat between the parcel and the surrounding environment.

Advection (3) Horizontal movement of air or water from one place to another. (*Compare* Convection.)

Advection fog (5) Active condensation formed when warm, moist air moves laterally over cooler water or land surfaces, causing the lower layers of the air to be chilled to the dew-point temperature.

Aerosols (2) Small particles of dust, soot, and pollution suspended in the air.

Aggradation (12) The general building of land surface because of deposition of material; opposite of degradation. When the sediment load of a stream exceeds the stream's capacity to carry it, the stream channel becomes filled through this process.

Air mass (5) A distinctive, homogeneous body of air that has taken on the moisture and temperature characteristics of its source region.

Air pressure (2, 4) Pressure produced by the motion, size, and number of gas molecules in the air and exerted on surfaces in contact with the air; an average force at sea level of 1 kg/cm^3 (14.7 lb/in^2). Normal sea-level pressure, as measured by the height of a column of mercury (Hg), is expressed as 1013.2 millibars, 760 mm of Hg, or 29.92 inches of Hg. Air pressure can be measured with mercury or aneroid barometers (*see listings for both*).

Albedo (3) The reflective quality of a surface, expressed as the percentage of reflected insolation to incoming insolation; a function of surface color, angle of incidence, and surface texture.

Alfisols (15) A soil order in the Soil Taxonomy. Moderately weathered forest soils that are moist versions of Mollisols, with productivity dependent on specific patterns of moisture and temperature; rich in organics. Most wide-ranging of the soil orders.

Alluvial fan (12) Fan-shaped fluvial landform at the mouth of a canyon; generally occurs in arid landscapes where streams are intermittent. (*See* Bajada.)

Alluvial terraces (12) Level areas that appear as topographic steps above a stream, created by the stream as it scours with renewed downcutting into its floodplain; composed of unconsolidated alluvium. (*See* Alluvium.)

Alluvium (12) General descriptive term for clay, silt, sand, gravel, or other unconsolidated rock and mineral fragments transported by running water and deposited as sorted or semisorted sediment on a floodplain, delta, or streambed.

Alpine glacier (14) A glacier confined in a mountain valley or walled basin, consisting of three subtypes: valley glacier (within a valley), piedmont glacier (coalesced at the base of a mountain, spreading freely over nearby lowlands), and outlet glacier (flowing outward from a continental glacier; *compare* Ice sheet).

Alpine tundra (17) A biome found above treeline at high elevation in mountains, featuring ground-hugging grasses, herbs, lichens, mosses, and low-growing woody shrubs. (*See* Arctic tundra.)

Altitude (2) The angular distance between the horizon (a horizontal plane) and the Sun (or any point in the sky).

Altocumulus (5) Middle-level, puffy clouds that occur in several forms: patchy rows, wave patterns, a "mackerel sky," or lens-shaped "lenticular" clouds.

Andisols (15) A soil order in the Soil Taxonomy; derived from volcanic parent materials in areas of volcanic activity. A new order, created in 1990, of soils previously considered under Inceptisols and Entisols.

Anemometer (4) A device that measures wind velocity.

Aneroid barometer (4) A device that measures air pressure using a partially evacuated, sealed cell. (*See* Air pressure.)

Antarctic Circle (2) This latitude (66.5° S) denotes the northernmost parallel (in the Southern Hemisphere) that experiences a 24-hour period of darkness in winter or daylight in summer.

Antarctic high (4) A consistent high-pressure region centered over Antarctica; source region for an intense polar air mass that is dry and associated with the lowest temperatures on Earth.

Anthropogenic atmosphere (2) Earth's future atmosphere, so named because humans appear to be the principal causative agent.

Anthropogenic biome (17) A recent conceptual term for large-scale, stable ecosystems that result from ongoing human interaction with natural environments. Human modifications are often linked to land-use practices such as agriculture, forestry, and urbanization.

Anticline (10) Upfolded rock strata in which layers slope downward from the axis of the fold, or central ridge. (*Compare* Syncline.)

Anticyclone (4) A dynamically or thermally caused area of high atmospheric pressure with descending and diverging airflows that rotate clockwise in the Northern Hemisphere and counterclockwise in the Southern Hemisphere. (*Compare* Cyclone.)

Aphelion (2) The point of Earth's greatest distance from the Sun in its elliptical orbit; reached on July 4 at a distance of 152,083,000 km (94.5 million mi); variable over a 100,000-year cycle. (*Compare* Perihelion.)

Aquifer (6) A body of rock that conducts groundwater in usable amounts; a permeable rock layer.

Arctic Circle (2) This latitude (66.5° N) denotes the southernmost parallel (in the Northern Hemisphere) that experiences a 24-hour period of darkness in winter or daylight in summer.

Arctic tundra (17) A biome in the northernmost portions of North America and northern Europe and Asia, featuring low, ground-level herbaceous plants as well as some woody plants. (*See* Alpine tundra.)

Arête (14) A sharp ridge that divides two cirque basins. Derived from "knife edge" in French, these form sawtooth and serrated ridges in glaciated mountains.

Aridisols (15) A soil order in the Soil Taxonomy; largest soil order. Typical of dry climates; low in organic matter and dominated by calcification and salinization.

Artesian water (6) Pressurized gro-undwater that rises in a well or a rock structure above the local water table; may flow out onto the ground without pumping.

Artificial levee (12) Human-built earthen embankment along a river channel, often constructed on top of a natural levee.

Asthenosphere (9) Region of the upper mantle just below the lithosphere; the least rigid portion of Earth's interior and known as the plastic layer, flowing very slowly under extreme heat and pressure.

Atmosphere (1) The thin veil of gases surrounding Earth, which forms a protective boundary between outer space and the biosphere; generally considered to extend out about 480 km (300 mi) from Earth's surface.

Atmosphere–Ocean General Circulation Model (AOGCM) (8) A sophisticated general circulation model that couples atmosphere and ocean submodels to simulate the effects of linkages between specific climate components over different time frames and at various scales.

Aurora (2) A spectacular glowing light display in the ionosphere, stimulated by the interaction of the solar wind with principally oxygen and nitrogen gases at high latitudes; called *aurora borealis* in the Northern Hemisphere and *aurora australis* in the Southern Hemisphere.

Axial parallelism (2) Earth's axis remains aligned the same throughout the year (it "remains parallel to itself"); thus, the axis extended from the North Pole points into space always near Polaris, the North Star.

Axial tilt (2) Earth's axis tilts 23.5° from a perpendicular to the plane of the ecliptic (plane of Earth's orbit around the Sun).

Bajada (12) A continuous apron of coalesced alluvial fans, formed along the base of mountains in arid climates; presents a gently rolling surface from fan to fan. (*See* Alluvial fan.)

Barrier beach (13) Narrow, long, depositional feature, generally composed of sand, that forms offshore roughly parallel to the coast; may appear as barrier islands and long chains of barrier beaches. (*See* Barrier island.)

Barrier island (13) Generally, a broadened barrier beach offshore. (*See* Barrier beach.)

Barrier spit (13) A depositional landform that develops when transported sand or gravel in a barrier beach or island is deposited in long ridges that are attached at one end to the mainland and partially cross the mouth of a bay.

Basalt (9) A common extrusive igneous rock, fine-grained, comprising the bulk of the ocean-floor crust, lava flows, and volcanic forms; gabbro is its intrusive form.

Base flow (6) The portion of streamflow that consists of groundwater.

Base level (12) A hypothetical level below which a stream cannot erode its valley—and thus the lowest operative level for denudation processes; in an absolute sense, it is represented by sea level, extending under the landscape.

Basin and Range Province (10) A region of dry climates, few permanent streams, and interior drainage patterns in the western United States; a faulted landscape composed of a sequence of horsts and grabens.

Batholith (9) The largest plutonic form exposed at the surface; an irregular intrusive mass; it invades crustal rocks, cooling slowly so that large crystals develop. (*See* Pluton.)

Bay barrier (13) An extensive barrier spit of sand or gravel that encloses a bay, cutting it off completely from the ocean and forming a lagoon; produced by littoral drift and wave action; sometimes referred to as a baymouth bar. (*See* Barrier spit, Lagoon.)

Beach (13) The portion of the coastline where an accumulation of sediment is in motion.

Beach drift (13) Material, such as sand, gravel, and shells, that is moved by the longshore current in the effective direction of the waves.

Bed load (12) Coarse materials that are dragged along the bed of a stream by traction or by the rolling and bouncing motion of saltation; involves particles too large to remain in suspension. (*See* Traction, Saltation.)

Bedrock (11) The rock of Earth's crust that is below the soil and is basically unweathered; such solid crust sometimes is exposed as an outcrop.

Biodiversity (16) A principle of ecology and biogeography: The more diverse the species population in an ecosystem (in number of species, quantity of members in each species, and genetic content), the more risk is spread over the entire community, which results in greater overall stability, greater productivity, and increased use of nutrients, as compared to a monoculture of little or no diversity.

Biogeochemical cycle (16) One of several circuits of flowing elements and materials (carbon, oxygen, nitrogen, phosphorus, water) that combine Earth's biotic (living) and abiotic (nonliving) systems; the cycling of materials is continuous and renewed through the biosphere and the life processes.

Biogeographic realm (17) One of eight regions of the biosphere, each representative of evolutionary core areas of related flora (plants) and fauna (animals); a broad geographical classification scheme.

Biogeography (16) The study of the distribution of plants and animals and related ecosystems; the geographical relationships with their environments over time.

Biomass (16) The total mass of living organisms on Earth or per unit area of a landscape; also the weight of the living organisms in an ecosystem.

Biome (17) A large-scale, stable, terrestrial or aquatic ecosystem classified according to the predominant vegetation type and the adaptations of particular organisms to that environment.

Biosphere (1) That area where the atmosphere, lithosphere, and hydrosphere function together to form the context within which life exists; an intricate web that connects all organisms with their physical environment.

Biotic (1) Living; referring to Earth's living system of organisms.

Bolson (10) The slope and basin area between the crests of two adjacent ridges in a dry region.

Boreal forest (17) *See* Needleleaf forest.

Brackish (13) Descriptive of seawater with a salinity of less than 35%; for example, the Baltic Sea. (*Compare* Brine.)

Braided stream (12) A stream that becomes a maze of interconnected channels laced with excess sediment. Braiding often occurs with a reduction of discharge that reduces a stream's transporting ability or with an increase in sediment load.

Breaker (13) The point where a wave's height exceeds its vertical stability and the wave breaks as it approaches the shore.

Brine (13) Seawater with a salinity of more than 35%; for example, the Persian Gulf. (*Compare* Brackish.)

Calcification (15) The illuviated (deposited) accumulation of calcium carbonate or magnesium carbonate in the B and C soil horizons.

Caldera (10) An interior sunken portion of a composite volcano's crater; usually steep-sided and circular, sometimes containing a lake; also can be found in conjunction with shield volcanoes.

Calving (14) The process in which pieces of ice break free from the terminus of a tidewater glacier or ice sheet to form floating ice masses (icebergs) where glaciers meet an ocean, bay, or fjord.

Capillary water (6) Soil moisture, most of which is accessible to plant roots; held in the soil by the water's surface tension and cohesive forces between water and soil. (*See also* Field capacity, Wilting point.)

Carbonation (11) A chemical weathering process in which weak carbonic acid (water and carbon dioxide) reacts with many minerals that contain calcium, magnesium, potassium, and sodium (especially limestone), transforming them into carbonates.

Carbon monoxide (CO) (2) An odorless, colorless, tasteless combination of carbon and oxygen produced by the incomplete combustion of fossil fuels or other carbon-containing substances; toxicity to humans is due to its affinity for hemoglobin, displacing oxygen in the bloodstream.

Carbon sink (8) An area in Earth's atmosphere, hydrosphere, lithosphere, or biosphere where carbon is stored; also called a *carbon reservoir.*

Carnivore (16) A secondary consumer that principally eats meat for sustenance. The top carnivore in a food chain is considered a tertiary consumer. (*Compare* Herbivore.)

Cartography (1) The making of maps and charts; a specialized science and art that blends aspects of geography, engineering, mathematics, graphics, computer science, and artistic specialties.

Cation-exchange capacity (CEC) (15) The ability of soil colloids to exchange cations between their surfaces and the soil solution; a measured potential that indicates soil fertility. (*See* Soil colloid, Soil fertility.)

Chaparral (17) Dominant shrub formations of *Mediterranean* (dry summer) climates; characterized by sclerophyllous scrub and short, stunted, tough forests; derived from the Spanish *chaparro*; specific to California. (*See* Mediterranean shrubland.)

Chemical weathering (11) Decomposition and decay of the constituent minerals in rock through chemical alteration of those minerals. Water is essential, with rates keyed to temperature and precipitation values. Chemical reactions are active at microsites even in dry climates. Processes include hydrolysis, oxidation, carbonation, and solution.

Chlorophyll (16) A light-sensitive pigment that resides within chloroplasts (organelles) in leaf cells of plants; the basis of photosynthesis.

Cinder cone (10) A volcanic landform of pyroclastics and scoria, usually small and cone-shaped and generally not more than 450 m (1500 ft) in height, with a truncated top.

Circle of illumination (2) The division between light and dark on Earth; a day–night great circle.

Cirque (14) A scooped-out, amphitheater-shaped basin at the head of an alpine glacier valley; an erosional landform.

Cirrus (5) Wispy, filamentous ice-crystal clouds that occur above 6000 m (20,000 ft); appear in a variety of forms, from feathery hairlike fibers to veils of fused sheets.

Classification (7) The process of ordering or grouping data or phenomena in related classes; results in a regular distribution of information; a taxonomy.

Climate (7) The consistent, long-term behavior of weather over time, including its variability, in contrast to weather, which is the condition of the atmosphere at any given place and time.

Climate change science (8) The interdisciplinary study of the causes and consequences of changing climate for all Earth systems and the sustainability of human societies.

Climate feedback (8) A process that either amplifies or reduces a climatic trend toward either warming or cooling.

Climatic region (7) An area of homogenous climate that features characteristic regional weather and air mass patterns.

Climatology (7) The scientific study of climate and climatic patterns and the consistent behavior of weather, including its variability and extremes, over time in one place or region; includes the effects of climate change on human society and culture.

Climograph (7) A graph that plots daily, monthly, or annual temperature and precipitation values for a selected station; may also include additional weather information.

Closed system (1) A system that is shut off from the surrounding environment, so that it is entirely self-contained in terms of energy and materials; Earth is a closed material system. (*Compare* Open system.)

Cloud (5) An aggregate of tiny moisture droplets and ice crystals; classified by altitude of occurrence and shape.

Cloud-albedo forcing (3) An increase in albedo (the reflectivity of a surface) caused by clouds due to their reflection of incoming insolation.

Cloud-condensation nuclei (5) Microscopic particles necessary as matter on which water vapor condenses to form moisture droplets; can be sea salts, dust, soot, or ash.

Cloud-greenhouse forcing (3) An increase in greenhouse warming caused by clouds because they can act like insulation, trapping longwave (infrared) radiation.

Col (14) Formed by two headward-eroding cirques that reduce an arête (ridge crest) to form a high pass or saddle-like narrow depression.

Cold desert and semidesert (17) A type of desert biome found at higher latitudes than warm deserts. Interior location and rain shadows produce these cold deserts in North America.

Cold front (5) The leading edge of an advancing cold air mass; identified on a weather map as a line marked with triangular spikes pointing in the direction of frontal movement. (*Compare* Warm front.)

Community (16) A convenient biotic subdivision within an ecosystem; formed by interacting populations of animals and plants in an area.

Composite volcano (10) A volcano formed by a sequence of explosive volcanic eruptions; steep-sided and conical in shape; sometimes referred to as a stratovolcano, although composite is the preferred term. (*Compare* Shield volcano.)

Conduction (3) The slow molecule-to-molecule transfer of heat through a medium, from warmer to cooler portions.

Cone of depression (6) The depressed shape of the water table around a well after active pumping. The water table adjacent to the well is drawn down by the water removal.

Confined aquifer (6) An aquifer that is bounded above and below by impermeable layers of rock or sediment. (*See* Artesian water; *compare* Unconfined aquifer.)

Constant isobaric surface (4) An elevated surface in the atmosphere on which all points have the same pressure, usually 500 mb. Along this constant-pressure surface, isobars mark the paths of upper-air winds.

Consumer (16) An organism in an ecosystem that depends on producers (organisms that use carbon dioxide as their sole source of carbon) for its source of nutrients; also called a *heterotroph*. (*Compare* Producer.)

Consumptive use (6) A use that removes water from a water budget at one point and makes it unavailable farther downstream. (*Compare* Water withdrawal.)

Continental divide (12) A ridge or elevated area that separates drainage on a continental scale; specifically, that ridge in North America that separates drainage to the Pacific Ocean on the west side from drainage to the Atlantic Ocean and the Gulf of Mexico on the east side and to Hudson Bay and the Arctic Ocean in the north.

Continental effect (3) A quality of regions that lack the temperature-moderating effects of the ocean and that exhibit a greater range of minimum and maximum temperatures, both daily and annually, than do marine stations. (*See* Marine effect, Land–water heating difference.)

Continental landmasses (10) The broadest category of landform, including those masses of crust that reside above or near sea level and the adjoining undersea continental shelves along the coastline; sometimes synonymous with *continental platforms*.

Continental shield (10) Generally, old, low-elevation heartland regions of continental crust; various cratons (granitic cores) and ancient mountains are exposed at the surface.

Convection (3) Transfer of heat from one place to another through the physical movement of air; involves a strong vertical motion. (*Compare* Advection.)

Convectional lifting (5) Air passing over warm surfaces gains buoyancy and lifts, initiating adiabatic processes.

Convergent lifting (5) Air flowing from different directions forces lifting and displacement of air upward, initiating adiabatic processes.

Coordinated Universal Time (UTC) (1) The official reference time in all countries, formerly known as Greenwich Mean Time; now measured by primary standard atomic clocks, the time calculations are collected in Paris at the International Bureau of Weights and Measures (BIPM); the legal reference for time in all countries and broadcast worldwide.

Coral (13) A simple, cylindrical marine animal with a saclike body that secretes calcium carbonate to form a hard external skeleton and, cumulatively, landforms called reefs; lives symbiotically with nutrient-producing algae; presently in a worldwide state of decline due to bleaching (loss of algae).

Core (9) The deepest inner portion of Earth, representing one-third of its entire mass; differentiated into two zones—a solid-iron inner core surrounded by a dense, molten, fluid metallic-iron outer core.

Coriolis force (4) The apparent deflection of moving objects (wind, ocean currents, missiles) from traveling in a straight path, in proportion to the speed of Earth's rotation at different latitudes. Deflection is to the right in the Northern Hemisphere and to the left in the Southern Hemisphere; maximum at the poles and zero along the equator.

Crevasse (14) A vertical crack that develops in a glacier as a result of friction between valley walls, or tension forces of extension on convex slopes, or compression forces on concave slopes.

Crust (9) Earth's outer shell of crystalline surface rock, ranging from 5 to 60 km (3 to 38 mi) in thickness from oceanic crust to mountain ranges. Average density of continental crust is 2.7g/cm^3, whereas oceanic crust is 3.0g/cm^3.

Cryosphere (1, 14) The frozen portion of Earth's waters, including ice sheets, ice caps and fields, glaciers, ice shelves, sea ice, and subsurface ground ice and frozen ground (permafrost).

Cumulonimbus (5) A towering, precipitation-producing cumulus cloud that is vertically developed across altitudes associated with other clouds; frequently associated with lightning and thunder and thus sometimes called a *thunderhead.*

Cumulus (5) Bright and puffy cumuliform clouds up to 2000 m (6500 ft) in altitude.

Cyclone (4) A dynamically or thermally caused area of low atmospheric pressure with ascending and converging airflows that rotate counterclockwise in the Northern Hemisphere and clockwise in the Southern Hemisphere. (*Compare* Anticyclone; *see* Midlatitude cyclone, Tropical cyclone.)

Daylength (2) Duration of exposure to insolation, varying during the year depending on latitude; an important aspect of seasonality.

Daylight saving time (1) Time is set ahead 1 hour in the spring and set back 1 hour in the fall in the Northern Hemisphere. In the United States and Canada, time is set ahead on the second Sunday in March and set back on the first Sunday in November—except in Hawai'i, Arizona, and Saskatchewan, which exempt themselves.

Dead zone (16) Low-oxygen conditions and limited marine life caused by excessive nutrient inputs in coastal oceans and lakes.

Debris avalanche (11) A mass of falling and tumbling rock, debris, and soil; can be dangerous because of the tremendous velocities achieved by the onrushing materials.

December solstice (2) The time when the Sun's declination is at the Tropic of Capricorn, at 23.5 S latitude, on December 21–22 each year (also known as *winter solstice*). The day is 24 hours long south of the Antarctic Circle. The night is 24 hours long north of the Arctic Circle. (*Compare* June solstice.).

Declination (2) The latitude that receives direct overhead (perpendicular) insolation on a particular day; the subsolar point migrates annually through 47° of latitude between the Tropics of Cancer (23.5° N) and Capricorn (23.5° S).

Decomposers (16) Bacteria and fungi that digest organic debris outside their bodies and absorb and release nutrients in an ecosystem. (*See* Detritivores.)

Deficit (6) DEFIC; in a water balance, the amount of unmet (unsatisfied) potential evapotranspiration (POTET, or PE); a natural water shortage. (*See* Potential evapotranspiration.)

Deflation (13) A process of wind erosion that removes and lifts individual particles, literally blowing away unconsolidated, dry, or noncohesive sediments.

Degradation (12) The process occurring when sediment is eroded along a stream, causing channel incision.

Delta (12) A depositional plain formed where a river enters a lake or an ocean; named after the triangular shape of the Greek letter delta, Δ .

Dendroclimatology (8) The study of past climates using tree rings. The dating of tree rings by analysis and comparison of ring widths and coloration is *dendrochronology.*

Denudation (11) A general term that refers to all processes that cause degradation of the landscape: weathering, mass movement, erosion, and transport.

Deposition (12) The process whereby weathered, wasted, and transported sediments are laid down by air, water, and ice.

Derechos (5) Strong linear winds in excess of 26 m/sec (58 mph), associated with thunderstorms and bands of showers crossing a region.

Desalination (6) In a water resources context, the removal of organics, debris, and salinity from seawater through distillation or reverse osmosis to produce potable water.

Desertification (15) The expansion of deserts worldwide, related principally to poor agricultural practices (overgrazing and inappropriate agricultural practices), improper soil-moisture management, erosion and salinization, deforestation, and the ongoing climatic change; an unwanted semipermanent invasion into neighboring biomes.

Desert pavement (13) On arid landscapes, a surface formed when wind deflation and sheetflow remove smaller particles, leaving residual pebbles and gravels to concentrate at the surface; an alternative sediment-accumulation hypothesis explains some desert pavements; resembles a cobblestone street. (*See* Deflation, Sheetflow.)

Detritivores (16) Detritus feeders and decomposers that consume, digest, and destroy organic wastes and debris. *Detritus feeders*—worms, mites, termites, centipedes, snails, crabs, and even vultures, among others—consume detritus and excrete nutrients and simple inorganic compounds that fuel an ecosystem. (*Compare* Decomposers.)

Dew-point temperature (5) The temperature at which a given mass of air becomes saturated, holding all the water it can hold. Any further cooling or addition of water vapor results in active condensation.

Diagnostic subsurface horizon (15) A soil horizon that originates below the epipedon at varying depths; may be part of the A and B horizons; important in soil description as part of the Soil Taxonomy.

Differential weathering (11) The effect of different resistances in rock, coupled with variations in the intensity of physical and chemical weathering.

Diffuse radiation (3) The downward component of scattered incoming insolation from clouds and the atmosphere.

Discharge (12) The measured volume of flow in a river that passes by a given cross section of a stream in a given unit of time; expressed in cubic meters per second or cubic feet per second.

Dissolved load (12) Materials carried in chemical solution in a stream, derived from minerals such as limestone and dolomite or from soluble salts.

Downwelling current (4) An area of the sea where a convergence or accumulation of water thrusts excess water downward; occurs, for example, at the western end of the equatorial current or along the margins of Antarctica. (*Compare* Upwelling current.)

Drainage basin (12) The basic spatial geomorphic unit of a river system; distinguished from a neighboring basin by ridges and highlands that form divides, marking the limits of the catchment area of the drainage basin.

Drainage pattern (12) A distinctive geometric arrangement of streams in a region, determined by slope, differing rock resistance to weathering and erosion, climatic and hydrologic variability, and structural controls of the landscape.

Drawdown (6) *See* Cone of depression.

Drought (6) Does not have a simple water-budget definition; rather, it can occur in at least four forms: *meteorological drought, agricultural drought, hydrologic drought,* and/or *socioeconomic drought.*

Drumlin (14) A depositional landform related to glaciation that is composed of till (unstratified, unsorted) and is streamlined in the direction of continental ice movement—blunt end upstream and tapered end downstream with a rounded summit.

Dry adiabatic rate (DAR) (5) The rate at which an unsaturated parcel of air cools (if ascending) or heats (if descending); a rate of 10 C° per 1000 m (5.5 F° per 1000 ft). (*See* Adiabatic; *compare* Moist adiabatic rate.)

Dune (13) A depositional feature of sand grains deposited in transient mounds, ridges, and hills; extensive areas of sand dunes are called sand seas.

Dust dome (3) A dome of airborne pollution associated with every major city; may be blown by winds into elongated plumes downwind from the city.

Dynamic equilibrium (1) Increasing or decreasing operations in a system demonstrate a trend over time, a change in average conditions.

Dynamic equilibrium model (11) The balancing act between tectonic uplift and erosion, between the resistance of crust materials and the work of denudation processes. Landscapes evidence ongoing adaptation to rock structure, climate, local relief, and elevation.

Earthquake (10) A sharp release of energy that sends waves traveling through Earth's crust at the moment of rupture along a fault or in association with volcanic activity. The moment magnitude scale (formerly the Richter scale) estimates earthquake magnitude; intensity is described by the Mercalli scale.

Earth systems science (1) An emerging science of Earth as a complete, systematic entity. An interacting set of physical, chemical, and biological systems that produce the processes of a whole Earth system. A study of planetary change resulting from system operations; includes a desire for a more quantitative understanding among components rather than a qualitative description.

Ecological niche (16) The function, or operation, of a life form within a given ecological community.

Ecological succession (16) The process whereby different and usually more complex assemblages of plants and animals replace older and usually simpler communities; communities are in a constant state of change as each species adapts to changing conditions. Ecosystems do not exhibit a stable point or successional climax condition as previously thought. (*See* Primary succession, Secondary succession.)

Ecology (16) The science that studies the relations between organisms and their environment and among various ecosystems.

Ecosphere (1) Another name for the biosphere.

Ecosystem (16) A self-regulating association of living plants and animals and their nonliving physical and chemical environments.

Ecotone (17) A boundary transition zone between adjoining ecosystems that may vary in width and represent areas of tension as similar species of plants and animals compete for the resources. (*See* Ecosystem.)

Effusive eruption (10) A volcanic eruption characterized by low-viscosity basaltic magma and low-gas content, which readily escapes. Lava pours forth onto the surface with relatively small explosions and few pyroclastics; tends to form shield volcanoes. (*See* Shield volcano, Lava, Pyroclastic; *compare* Explosive eruption.)

Elastic-rebound theory (10) A concept describing the faulting process in Earth's crust, in which the two sides of a fault appear locked despite the motion of adjoining pieces of crust, but with accumulating strain, they rupture suddenly, snapping to new positions relative to each other, generating an earthquake.

Electromagnetic spectrum (2) All the radiant energy produced by the Sun placed in an ordered range, divided according to wavelengths.

El Niño–Southern Oscillation (ENSO) (4) Sea-surface temperatures increase, sometimes more than 8 C° (14 F°) above normal in the central and eastern Pacific, replacing the normally cold, nutrient-rich water along Peru's coastline. Pressure patterns and surface ocean temperatures shift from their usual locations across the Pacific, forming the Southern Oscillation.

Eluviation (15) The removal of finer particles and minerals from the upper horizons of soil; an erosional process within a soil body. (*Compare* Illuviation.)

Empirical classification (7) A climate classification based on weather statistics or other data; used to determine general climate categories. (*Compare* Genetic classification.)

Endogenic system (9) The system internal to Earth, driven by radioactive heat derived from sources within the planet. In response, the surface fractures, mountain building occurs, and earthquakes and volcanoes are activated. (*Compare* Exogenic system.)

Entisols (15) A soil order in the Soil Taxonomy. Specifically lacks vertical development of horizons; usually young or undeveloped. Found in active slopes, alluvial-filled floodplains, and poorly drained tundra.

Environmental lapse rate (5) The actual rate of temperature decrease with increasing altitude in the lower atmosphere at any particular time under local weather conditions; may deviate above or below the normal lapse rate of 6.4 C° per km, or 1000 m (3.5 F° per 1000 ft). (*Compare* Normal lapse rate.)

Eolian (13) Caused by wind; refers to the erosion, transportation, and deposition of materials; spelled *aeolian* in some countries.

Epipedon (15) The diagnostic soil horizon that forms at the surface; not to be confused with the A horizon; may include all or part of the illuviated B horizon.

Equal area (1) A trait of a map projection; indicates the equivalence of all areas on the surface of the map, although shape is distorted. (*See* Map projection.)

Equatorial low (4) A thermally caused low-pressure area that almost girdles Earth, with air converging and ascending all along its extent; also called the *intertropical convergence zone (ITCZ)*.

Erg (13) An extensive area of sand and dunes; from the Arabic word for "dune field." (*Compare* Sand sea.)

Erosion (12) Denudation by wind, water, or ice, which dislodges, dissolves, or removes surface material.

Esker (14) A sinuously curving, narrow deposit of coarse gravel that forms along a meltwater stream channel, developing in a tunnel beneath a glacier.

Estuary (12) The point at which the mouth of a river enters the sea, where freshwater and seawater are mixed; a place where tides ebb and flow.

Eustasy (6) Refers to worldwide changes in sea level that are related not to movements of land, but rather to changes in the volume of water in the oceans.

Eutrophication (16) The gradual enrichment of water bodies that occurs with nutrient inputs, either natural or human-caused.

Evaporation (6) The movement of free water molecules away from a wet surface into air that is less than saturated; the phase change of water to water vapor.

Evaporation fog (5) A fog formed when cold air flows over the warm surface of a lake, ocean, or other body of water; forms as the water molecules evaporate from the water surface into the cold, overlying air; also known as steam fog or sea smoke.

Evapotranspiration (6) The merging of evaporation and transpiration water loss into one term. (*See* Potential evapotranspiration, Actual evapotranspiration.)

Evolution (16) A theory that single-cell organisms adapted, modified, and passed along inherited changes to multicellular organisms. The genetic makeup of successive generations is shaped by environmental factors, physiological functions, and behaviors that created a greater rate of survival and reproduction and were passed along through natural selection.

Exfoliation (11) The physical weathering process that occurs as mechanical forces enlarge joints in rock into layers of curved slabs or plates, which peel or slip off in sheets; also called *sheeting*.

Exogenic system (9) Earth's external surface system, powered by insolation, which energizes air, water, and ice and sets them in motion, under the influence of gravity. Includes all processes of landmass denudation. (*Compare* Endogenic system.)

Exosphere (3) An extremely rarefied outer atmospheric halo beyond the thermopause at an altitude of 480 km (300 mi); probably composed of hydrogen and helium atoms, with some oxygen atoms and nitrogen molecules present near the thermopause.

Explosive eruption (10) A violent and unpredictable volcanic eruption, the result of magma that is thicker (more viscous), stickier, and higher in gas and silica content than that of an effusive eruption; tends to form blockages within a volcano; produces composite volcanic landforms. (*See* Composite volcano; *compare* Effusive eruption.)

Extrusive igneous rock (9) A rock such as basalt that solidifies and crystallizes from a molten state as it extrudes onto the surface.

Faulting (10) The process whereby displacement and fracturing occur between two portions of Earth's crust; usually associated with earthquake activity.

Feedback loop (1) Created when a portion of system output is returned as an information input, causing changes that guide further system operation. (*See* Negative feedback, Positive feedback.)

Field capacity (6) Water held in the soil by hydrogen bonding against the pull of gravity, remaining after water drains from the larger pore spaces; the available water for plants. (*See* Capillary water.)

Fire ecology (16) The study of fire as a natural agent and dynamic factor in community succession.

Firn (14) Snow of a granular texture that is transitional in the slow transformation from snow to glacial ice; snow that has persisted through a summer season in the zone of accumulation.

Firn line (14) The snow line that is visible on the surface of a glacier, where winter snows survive the summer ablation season; analogous to a snow line on land. (*See* Ablation.)

Fjord (14) A drowned glaciated valley, or glacial trough, along a seacoast.

Flash flood (12) A sudden and short-lived torrent of water that exceeds the capacity of a stream channel; associated with desert and semiarid washes.

Flood (12) A high water level that overflows the natural riverbank along any portion of a stream.

Flood basalt (10) An accumulation of horizontal flows formed when lava spreads out from elongated fissures onto the surface in extensive sheets; associated with effusive eruptions. (*See* Basalt.)

Floodplain (12) A flat, low-lying area along a stream channel, created by and subject to recurrent flooding; alluvial deposits generally mask underlying rock.

Fluvial (12) Stream-related processes; from the Latin *fluvius* for "river" or "running water."

Fog (5) A cloud, generally stratiform, in contact with the ground, with visibility usually reduced to less than 1 km (3300 ft).

Folding (10) The bending and deformation of beds of rock strata subjected to compressional forces.

Food chain (16) The circuit along which energy flows from producers (plants), which manufacture their own food, to consumers (animals); a one-directional flow of chemical energy, ending with decomposers.

Food web (16) A complex network of interconnected food chains. (*See* Food chain.)

Friction force (4) The effect of drag by the wind as it moves across a surface; may be operative through 500 m (1600 ft) of altitude. Surface friction slows the wind and therefore reduces the effectiveness of the Coriolis force.

Frost wedging (11) A mechanical force produced when water in a crack or cavity in rock expands as it freezes, shattering the rock when the force exceeds the rock's tensional strength.

Funnel cloud (5) The visible swirl extending from the bottom side of a cloud, which may or may not develop into a tornado. A tornado is a funnel cloud that has extended all the way to the ground. (*See* Tornado.)

Fusion (2) The process of forcibly joining positively charged hydrogen and helium nuclei under extreme temperature and pressure; occurs naturally in thermonuclear reactions within stars, such as our Sun.

Gelisols (15) A new soil order in the Soil Taxonomy, added in 1998, describing cold and frozen soils at high latitudes or high elevations; characteristic tundra vegetation.

General circulation model (GCM) (8) Complex, computer-based climate model that produces generalizations of reality and forecasts of future weather and climate conditions. Complex GCMs (three-dimensional models) are in use in the United States and in other countries.

Genetic classification (7) A climate classification that uses causative factors to determine climatic regions; for example, an analysis of the effect of interacting air masses. (*Compare* Empirical classification.)

Geodesy (1) The science that determines Earth's shape and size through surveys, mathematical means, and remote sensing. (*See* Geoid.)

Geographic information system (GIS) (1) A computer-based data processing tool or methodology used for gathering, manipulating, and analyzing geographic information to produce a holistic, interactive analysis.

Geography (1) The science that studies the interdependence and interaction among geographic areas, natural systems, processes, society, and cultural activities over space—a spatial science. The five themes of geographic education are location, place, movement, regions, and human–Earth relationships.

Geoid (1) A word that describes Earth's shape; literally, "the shape of Earth is Earth-shaped." A theoretical surface at sea level that extends through the continents; deviates from a perfect sphere.

Geologic cycle (9) A general term characterizing the vast cycling that proceeds in the lithosphere. It encompasses the hydrologic cycle, tectonic cycle, and rock cycle.

Geologic time scale (9) A depiction of eras, periods, and epochs that span Earth's history; shows both the sequence of rock strata and their absolute dates, as determined by methods such as radioactive isotopic dating.

Geomagnetic reversal (9) A polarity change in Earth's magnetic field. With uneven regularity, the magnetic field fades to zero and then returns to full strength, but with the magnetic poles reversed. Reversals have been recorded nine times during the past 4 million years.

Geomorphic threshold (11) The threshold up to which landforms change before lurching to a new set of relationships, with rapid realignments of landscape materials and slopes.

Geomorphology (9) The science that analyzes and describes the origin, evolution, form, classification, and spatial distribution of landforms.

Geostrophic wind (4) A wind moving between areas of different pressure along a path that is parallel to the isobars. It is a product of the pressure gradient force and the Coriolis force. (*See* Isobar, Pressure gradient force, Coriolis force.)

Geothermal energy (9) The energy in steam and hot water heated by subsurface magma near groundwater. Geothermal energy literally refers to heat from Earth's interior, whereas *geothermal power* relates to specific applied strategies of geothermal electric or geothermal direct applications. This energy is used in Iceland, New Zealand, Italy, and northern California, among other locations.

Glacial drift (14) The general term for all glacial deposits, both unsorted (till) and sorted (stratified drift).

Glacial ice (14) A hardened form of ice, very dense in comparison to normal snow or firn.

Glacier (14) A large mass of perennial ice resting on land or floating shelflike in the sea adjacent to the land; formed from the accumulation and recrystallization of snow, which then flows slowly under the pressure of its own weight and the pull of gravity.

Glacier surge (14) The rapid, lurching, unexpected forward movement of a glacier.

Gleization (15) A process of humus and clay accumulation in cold, wet climates with poor drainage.

Global carbon budget (8) The exchange of carbon between sources and sinks in Earth's atmosphere, hydrosphere, lithosphere, and biosphere.

Global dimming (3) The decline in sunlight reaching Earth's surface due to pollution, aerosols, and clouds.

Global Positioning System (GPS) (1) Latitude, longitude, and elevation are accurately calibrated using a handheld instrument that receives radio signals from satellites.

Goode's homolosine projection (Appendix A) An equal-area projection formed by splicing together a sinusoidal and a homolographic projection.

Graben (10) Pairs or groups of faults that produce downward-faulted blocks; characteristic of the basins of the interior western United States. (*Compare* Horst; *see* Basin and Range Province.)

Graded stream (12) An idealized condition in which a stream's load and the landscape mutually adjust. This forms a dynamic equilibrium among erosion, transported load, deposition, and the stream's capacity.

Gradient (12) The drop in elevation from a stream's headwaters to its mouth, ideally forming a concave slope.

Granite (9) A coarse-grained (slow-cooling) intrusive igneous rock of 25% quartz and more than 50% potassium and sodium feldspars; characteristic of the continental crust.

Gravitational water (6) That portion of surplus water that percolates downward from the capillary zone, pulled by gravity to the groundwater zone.

Gravity (2) The mutual force exerted by the masses of objects that are attracted one to another and produced in an amount proportional to each object's mass.

Great circle (1) Any circle drawn on a globe with its center coinciding with the center of the globe. An infinite number of great circles can be drawn, but only one parallel of latitude—the equator—is a great circle. (*Compare* Small circle.)

Greenhouse effect (3) The process whereby radiatively active gases (carbon dioxide, water vapor, methane, and CFCs) absorb and emit energy at longer wavelengths, which are retained longer, delaying the loss of infrared to space. Thus, the lower troposphere is warmed through the radiation and re-radiation of infrared wavelengths. The approximate similarity between this process and that of a greenhouse explains the name.

Greenhouse gases (3) Gases in the lower atmosphere that delay the passage of longwave radiation to space by absorbing and re-radiating specific wavelengths. Earth's primary greenhouse gases are carbon dioxide, water vapor, methane, nitrous oxide, and fluorinated gases, such as chlorofluorocarbons (CFCs).

Greenwich Mean Time (GMT) (1) Former world standard time, now reported as Coordinated Universal Time (UTC). (*See* Coordinated Universal Time.)

Ground ice (14) The subsurface water that is frozen in regions of permafrost. The moisture content of areas with ground ice may vary from nearly 0% in regions of drier permafrost to almost 100% in saturated soils.

Groundwater (6) Water beneath the surface that is beyond the soil-root zone; a major source of potable water.

Groundwater mining (6) Pumping an aquifer beyond its capacity to flow and recharge; an overuse of the groundwater resource.

Gulf Stream (3) A strong, northward-moving, warm current off the east coast of North America, which carries its water far into the North Atlantic.

Habitat (16) A physical location to which an organism is biologically suited. Most species have specific habitat parameters and limits. (*Compare* Ecological niche.)

Hail (5) A type of precipitation formed when a raindrop is repeatedly circulated above and below the freezing level in a cloud, with each cycle freezing more moisture onto the hailstone until it becomes too heavy to stay aloft.

Heat (3) The flow of kinetic energy from one body to another because of a temperature difference between them.

Heat wave (3) A prolonged period of abnormally high temperatures, usually, but not always, in association with humid weather.

Herbivore (16) The primary consumer in a food web, which eats plant material formed by a producer (plant) that has photosynthesized organic molecules. (*Compare* Carnivore.)

Heterosphere (2) A zone of the atmosphere above the mesopause, from 80 km (50 mi) to 480 km (300 mi) in altitude; composed of rarefied layers of oxygen atoms and nitrogen molecules; includes the ionosphere.

Histosols (15) A soil order in the Soil Taxonomy. Formed from thick accumulations of organic matter, such as beds of former lakes, bogs, and layers of peat.

Homosphere (2) A zone of the atmosphere from Earth's surface up to 80 km (50 mi), composed of an even mixture of gases, including nitrogen, oxygen, argon, carbon dioxide, and trace gases.

Horn (14) A pyramidal, sharp-pointed peak that results when several cirque glaciers gouge an individual mountain summit from all sides.

Horst (10) Upward-faulted blocks produced by pairs or groups of faults; characteristic of the mountain ranges of the interior of the western United States. (*See* Graben, Basin and Range Province.)

Hot spot (9) An individual point of upwelling material originating in the asthenosphere, or deeper in the mantle; tends to remain fixed relative to migrating plates; some 100 are identified worldwide, exemplified by Yellowstone National Park, Hawai'i, and Iceland.

Human–Earth relationships (1) One of the oldest themes of geography (the human–land tradition); includes the spatial analysis of settlement patterns, resource utilization and exploitation, hazard perception and planning, and the impact of environmental modification and artificial landscape creation.

Humidity (5) Water vapor content of the air. The capacity of the air for water vapor is mostly a function of the temperature of the air and the water vapor.

Humus (15) A mixture of organic debris in the soil worked by consumers and decomposers in the humification process;

characteristically formed from plant and animal litter deposited at the surface.

Hurricane (5) A tropical cyclone that is fully organized and intensified in inward-spiraling rainbands; ranges from 160 to 960 km (100 to 600 mi) in diameter, with wind speeds in excess of 119 kmph (65 knots, or 74 mph); a name used specifically in the Atlantic and eastern Pacific. (*Compare* Typhoon.)

Hydration (11) A chemical weathering process involving water that is added to a mineral, which initiates swelling and stress within the rock, mechanically forcing grains apart as the constituents expand. (*Compare* Hydrolysis.)

Hydraulic action (12) The erosive work accomplished by the turbulence of water; causes a squeezing and releasing action in joints in bedrock; capable of prying and lifting rocks.

Hydric soil (15) A soil that is saturated for long enough periods to develop anaerobic, or "oxygen-free," conditions. Hydric soils are characteristic of wetlands.

Hydrograph (12) A graph of stream discharge (in m^3/s or ft^3/s) over a period of time (minutes, hours, days, years) at a specific place on a stream. The relationship between stream discharge and precipitation input is illustrated on the graph.

Hydrologic cycle (6) A simplified model of the flow of water, ice, and water vapor from place to place. Water flows through the atmosphere and across the land, where it is stored as ice and as groundwater. Solar energy empowers the cycle.

Hydrology (6) The science of water, including its global circulation, distribution, and properties—specifically water at and below Earth's surface.

Hydrolysis (11) A chemical weathering process in which minerals chemically combine with water; a decomposition process that causes silicate minerals in rocks to break down and become altered. (*Compare* Hydration.)

Hydropower (6) Electricity generated using the energy of moving water, usually flowing downhill through the turbines at a dam; also called *hydroelectric power.*

Hydrosphere (1) An abiotic open system that includes all of Earth's water.

Ice age (14) A cold episode, with accompanying alpine and continental ice accumulations, that has repeated roughly every 200 to 300 million years since the late Precambrian Era (1.25 billion years ago); includes the most recent episode during the Pleistocene Ice Age, which began 1.65 million years ago.

Ice cap (14) A large, dome-shaped glacier, less extensive than an ice sheet, although it buries mountain peaks and the local landscape; generally, less than 50,000 km^2 (19,300 mi^2).

Ice field (14) The least extensive form of a glacier, with mountain ridges and peaks visible above the ice; less than an ice cap or ice sheet.

Ice sheet (14) A continuous mass of unconfined ice, covering at least 50,000 km^2 (19,500 mi^2). The bulk of glacial ice on Earth covers Antarctica and Greenland in two ice sheets (*Compare* Alpine glacier.)

Igneous rock (9) One of the basic rock types; it has solidified and crystallized from a hot molten state (either magma or lava). (*Compare* Metamorphic rock, Sedimentary rock.)

Illuviation (15) The downward movement and deposition of finer particles and minerals from the upper horizon of the soil; a depositional process. Deposition usually is in the B horizon, where accumulations of clays, aluminum, carbonates, iron, and some humus occur. (*Compare* Eluviation; *see* Calcification.)

Inceptisols (15) A soil order in the Soil Taxonomy. Weakly developed soils that are inherently infertile; usually, young soils that are weakly developed, although they are more developed than Entisols.

Industrial smog (2) Air pollution associated with coal-burning industries; it may contain sulfur oxides, particulates, carbon dioxide, and exotics.

Infiltration (6) Water access to subsurface regions of soil moisture storage through penetration of the soil surface.

Insolation (2) Solar radiation that is incoming to Earth systems.

Interception (6) A delay in the fall of precipitation toward Earth's surface caused by vegetation or other ground cover.

International Date Line (IDL) (1) The 180° meridian, an important corollary to the prime meridian on the opposite side of the planet; established by an 1884 treaty to mark the place where each day officially begins.

Intertropical convergence zone (ITCZ) (4) *See* Equatorial low.

Intrusive igneous rock (9) A rock that solidifies and crystallizes from a molten state as it intrudes into crustal rocks, cooling and hardening below the surface, such as granite.

Invasive species (17) Species that are brought, or introduced, from elsewhere by humans, either accidentally or intentionally. These non-native species are also known as *exotic species* or *alien species.*

Ionosphere (2) A layer in the atmosphere above 80 km (50 mi) where gamma rays, X-rays, and some ultraviolet radiation are absorbed and converted into longer wavelengths and where the solar wind stimulates the auroras.

Island biogeography (17) Island communities are special places for study because of their spatial isolation and the relatively small number of species present. Islands resemble natural experiments because the impact of individual factors, such as civilization, can be more easily assessed on islands than over larger continental areas.

Isobar (4) An isoline connecting all points of equal atmospheric pressure.

Isostasy (9) A state of equilibrium in Earth's crust formed by the interplay between portions of the less-dense lithosphere and the more-dense asthenosphere and the principle of buoyancy. The crust depresses under weight and recovers with its removal—for example, with the melting of glacial ice. The uplift is known as isostatic rebound.

Isotherm (3) An isoline connecting all points of equal temperature.

Isotope analysis (8) A technique for long-term climatic reconstruction that uses the atomic structure of chemical elements, specifically the relative amounts of their isotopes, to identify the chemical composition of past oceans and ice masses.

Jet contrails (3) Condensation trails produced by aircraft exhaust, particulates, and water vapor can form high cirrus clouds, sometimes called *false cirrus clouds.*

Jet stream (4) The most prominent movement in upper-level westerly wind flows; irregular, concentrated, sinuous bands of geostrophic wind, traveling at 300 kmph (190 mph).

Joint (11) A fracture or separation in rock that occurs without displacement of the sides; increases the surface area of rock exposed to weathering processes.

June solstice (2) The time when the Sun's declination is at the Tropic of Cancer, at 23.5 N latitude, on June 20–21 each year (also known as *summer solstice*). The day is 24 hours long north of the Arctic Circle. The night is 24 hours long south of the Antarctic Circle. (*Compare* December solstice.).

Kame (14) A depositional feature of glaciation; a small hill of poorly sorted sand and gravel that accumulates in crevasses or in ice-caused indentations in the surface.

Karst topography (11) Distinctive topography formed in a region of chemically weathered limestone with poorly developed surface drainage and solution features that appear pitted and bumpy; originally named after the Krš Plateau in Slovenia.

Katabatic winds (4) Air drainage from elevated regions, flowing as gravity winds. Layers of air at the surface cool, become denser, and flow downslope; known worldwide by many local names.

Kettle (14) Forms when an isolated block of ice persists in a ground moraine, an outwash plain, or a valley floor after a glacier retreats; as the block finally melts, it leaves behind a steep-sided hole that frequently fills with water.

Kinetic energy (2) The energy of motion in a body; derived from the vibration of the body's own movement and stated as temperature.

Lacustrine deposit (14) Lake sediments that form terraces, or benches, along former lake shorelines and often mark lake-level fluctuations over time.

Lagoon (13) An area of coastal seawater that is virtually cut off from the ocean by a bay barrier or barrier beach; also, the water surrounded and enclosed by an atoll.

Land–sea breeze (4) Wind along coastlines and adjoining interior areas created by different heating characteristics of land and water surfaces—onshore (landward) breeze in the afternoon and offshore (seaward) breeze at night.

Landslide (11) A sudden rapid downslope movement of a cohesive mass of regolith and/or bedrock in a variety of mass-movement forms under the influence of gravity; a form of mass movement.

Land–water heating difference (3) Differences in the degree and way that land and water heat, as a result of contrasts in transmission, evaporation, mixing, and specific heat capacities. Land surfaces heat and cool faster than water and have continentality, whereas water provides a marine influence.

Latent heat (3, 5) Heat energy is stored in one of three states—ice, water, or water vapor. The energy is absorbed or released in each phase change from one state to another. Heat energy is absorbed as the latent heat of melting, vaporization, or evaporation. Heat energy is released as the latent heat of condensation and freezing (or fusion).

Latent heat of condensation (5) The heat energy released to the environment in a phase change from water vapor to liquid; under normal sea-level pressure, 540 calories are released from each gram of water vapor that changes phase to water at boiling, and 585 calories are released from each gram of water vapor that condenses at 20°C (68°F).

Latent heat of sublimation (5) The heat energy absorbed or released in the phase change from ice to water vapor or water vapor to ice—no liquid phase. The change from water vapor to ice is also called deposition.

Latent heat of vaporization (5) The heat energy absorbed from the environment in a phase change from liquid to water vapor at the boiling point; under normal sea-level pressure, 540 calories must be added to each gram of boiling water to achieve a phase change to water vapor.

Lateral moraine (14) Debris transported by a glacier that accumulates along the sides of the glacier and is deposited along these margins.

Laterization (15) A pedogenic process operating in well-drained soils that occurs in warm and humid regions; typical of Oxisols. Plentiful precipitation leaches soluble minerals and soil constituents. Resulting soils usually are reddish or yellowish.

Latitude (1) The angular distance measured north or south of the equator from a point at the center of Earth. A line connecting all points of the same latitudinal angle is a parallel. (*Compare* Longitude.)

Lava (9) Magma that issues from volcanic activity onto the surface; the extrusive rock that results when magma solidifies. (*See* Magma.)

Life zone (16) A zonation by altitude of plants and animals that form distinctive communities. Each life zone possesses its own temperature and precipitation relations.

Lightning (5) Flashes of light caused by tens of millions of volts of electrical charge heating the air to temperatures of 15,000°–30,000°C (27,000°–54,000°F).

Limestone (9) The most common chemical sedimentary rock (nonclastic); it is lithified calcium carbonate; very susceptible to chemical weathering by acids in the environment, including carbonic acid in rainfall.

Limiting factor (16) The physical or chemical factor that most inhibits biotic processes, through either lack or excess.

Lithification (9) The compaction, cementation, and hardening of sediments into sedimentary rock.

Lithosphere (1, 9) Earth's crust and that portion of the uppermost mantle directly below the crust, extending down about 70 km (45 mi). Some sources use this term to refer to the entire Earth.

Littoral drift (13) Transport of sand, gravel, sediment, and debris along the shore; a more comprehensive term that considers *beach drift* and *longshore drift* combined.

Littoral zone (13) A specific coastal environment; that region between the high-water line during a storm and a depth at which storm waves are unable to move seafloor sediments.

Loam (15) A soil that is a mixture of sand, silt, and clay in almost equal proportions, with no one texture dominant; an ideal agricultural soil.

Location (1) A basic theme of geography dealing with the absolute and relative positions of people, places, and things on Earth's surface.

Loess (15) Large quantities of fine-grained clays and silts left as glacial outwash deposits; subsequently blown by the wind great distances and redeposited as a generally unstratified, homogeneous blanket of material covering existing landscapes; in China, loess originated from desert lands.

Longitude (1) The angular distance measured east or west of a prime meridian from a point at the center of Earth. A line connecting all points of the same longitude is a meridian. (*Compare* Latitude.)

Longshore current (13) A current that forms parallel to a beach as waves arrive at an angle to the shore; generated in the surf zone by wave action, transporting large amounts of sand and sediment. (*See* Beach drift.)

Magma (9) Molten rock from beneath Earth's surface; fluid, gaseous, under tremendous pressure, and either intruded into existing crustal rock or extruded onto the surface as lava. (*See* Lava.)

Magnetosphere (2) Earth's magnetic force field, which is generated by dynamo-like motions within the planet's outer core; deflects the solar wind flow toward the upper atmosphere above each pole.

Mangrove swamp (13) A wetland ecosystem between 30° N and 30° S; tends to form a distinctive community of mangrove plants. (*Compare* Salt marsh.)

Mantle (9) An area within the planet representing about 80% of Earth's total volume, with densities increasing with depth and averaging 4.5g/cm^3; occurs between the core and the crust; is rich in iron and magnesium oxides and silicates.

Map (1) A generalized view of an area, usually some portion of Earth's surface, as seen from above at a greatly reduced size. (*See* Scale, Map projection.)

Map projection (1) The reduction of a spherical globe onto a flat surface in some orderly and systematic realignment of the latitude and longitude grid.

March equinox (2) The time around March 20–21 when the Sun's declination crosses the equatorial parallel (0° latitude) and all places on Earth experience days and nights of equal length (also known as *vernal equinox*). The Sun rises at the North Pole and sets at the South Pole. (*Compare* September equinox.)

Marine effect (3) A quality of regions that are dominated by the moderating effect of the ocean and that exhibit a smaller range of minimum and maximum temperatures, both daily and annually, than do continental stations. (*See* Continental effect, Land–water heating difference.)

Mass movement (11) All unit movements of materials propelled by gravity; can range from dry to wet, slow to fast, small to large, and free-falling to gradual or intermittent.

Mass wasting (11) Gravitational movement of nonunified material downslope; a specific form of mass movement.

Meandering stream (12) The sinuous, curving pattern common to graded streams, with the energetic outer portion of each curve subjected to the greatest erosive action and the lower-energy inner portion receiving sediment deposits. (*See* Graded stream.)

Mean sea level (MSL) (8) The average of tidal levels recorded hourly at a given site over a long period, which must be at least a full lunar tidal cycle.

Medial moraine (14) Debris transported by a glacier that accumulates down the middle of the glacier, resulting from two glaciers merging their lateral moraines; forms a depositional feature following glacial retreat.

Mediterranean shrubland (17) A major biome dominated by the *Mediterranean* (dry summer) climate and characterized by sclerophyllous scrub and short, stunted, tough forests. (*See* Chaparral.)

Mercator projection (1) A true-shape projection, with meridians appearing as equally spaced straight lines and parallels appearing as straight lines that are spaced closer together near the equator. The poles are infinitely stretched, with the 84th north parallel and 84th south parallel fixed at the same length as that of the equator. It presents false notions of the size (area) of midlatitude and poleward landmasses, but presents true compass direction. (*See* Rhumb line.)

Mercury barometer (4) A device that measures air pressure using a column of mercury in a tube; one end of the tube is sealed, and the other end is inserted in an open vessel of mercury. (*See* Air pressure.)

Meridian (1) A line designating an angle of longitude. (*See* Longitude.)

Mesocyclone (5) A large, rotating atmospheric circulation, initiated within a parent cumulonimbus cloud at midtroposphere elevation; generally produces heavy rain, large hail, blustery winds, and lightning; may lead to tornado activity.

Mesosphere (2) The upper region of the homosphere from 50 to 80 km (30 to 50 mi) above the ground; designated by temperature criteria; atmosphere extremely rarified.

Metamorphic rock (9) One of three basic rock types, it is existing igneous and sedimentary rock that has undergone profound physical and chemical changes under increased pressure and temperature. Constituent mineral structures may exhibit foliated or nonfoliated textures. (*Compare* Igneous rock, Sedimentary rock.)

Meteorology (5) The scientific study of the atmosphere, including its physical characteristics and motions; related chemical, physical, and geological processes; the complex linkages of atmospheric systems; and weather forecasting.

Microclimatology (3) The study of local climates at or near Earth's surface or up to that height above the Earth's surface where the effects of the surface are no longer determinative.

Midlatitude broadleaf and mixed forest (17) A biome in moist *continental* climates in areas of warm-to-hot summers and cool-to-cold winters; relatively lush stands of broadleaf forests trend northward into needleleaf evergreen stands.

Midlatitude cyclone (5) An organized area of low pressure, with converging and ascending airflow producing an interaction of air masses; migrates along storm tracks. Such lows or depressions form the dominant weather pattern in the middle and higher latitudes of both hemispheres.

Midlatitude grassland (17) The major biome most modified by human activity; so named because of the predominance of grasslike plants, although deciduous broadleafs appear along streams and other limited sites; location of the world's breadbaskets of grain and livestock production.

Mid-ocean ridge (9) A submarine mountain range that extends more than 65,000 km (40,000 mi) worldwide and averages more than 1000 km (600 mi) in width; centered along sea-floor spreading centers. (*See* Seafloor spreading.)

Milankovitch cycles (8) The consistent orbital cycles—based on the irregularities in Earth's orbit around the Sun, its rotation on its axis, and its axial tilt—that relate to climatic patterns and may be an important cause of glacials and interglacials. Milutin Milankovitch (1879–1958), a Serbian astronomer, was the first to correlate these cycles to changes in insolation that affected temperatures on Earth.

Milky Way Galaxy (2) A flattened, disk-shaped mass in space estimated to contain up to 400 billion stars; a barred-spiral galaxy; includes our Solar System.

Miller cylindrical projection (Appendix A) A compromise map projection that avoids the severe distortion of the Mercator projection. (*See* Map projection.)

Mineral (9) An element or combination of elements that forms an inorganic natural compound; described by a specific formula and crystal structure.

Model (1) A simplified version of a system, representing an idealized part of the real world.

Mohorovičić discontinuity, or Moho (9) The boundary between the crust and the rest of the lithospheric upper mantle; named for the Yugoslavian seismologist Mohorovičić; a zone of sharp material and density contrasts.

Moist adiabatic rate (MAR) (5) The rate at which a saturated parcel of air cools in ascent; a rate of 6 C° per 1000 m (3.3 F° per 1000 ft). This rate may vary, with moisture content and temperature, from 4 C° to 10 C° per 1000 m (2 F° to 6 F° per 1000 ft). (*See* Adiabatic; *compare* Dry adiabatic rate.)

Moisture droplet (5) A tiny water particle that constitutes the initial composition of clouds. Each droplet measures approximately 0.002 cm (0.0008 in.) in diameter and is invisible to the unaided eye.

Mollisols (15) A soil order in the Soil Taxonomy. These have a mollic epipedon and a humus-rich organic content high in alkalinity. Some of the world's most significant agricultural soils are Mollisols.

Moment magnitude (M) scale (10) An earthquake magnitude scale. Considers the amount of fault slippage, the size of the area that ruptured, and the nature of the materials that faulted in estimating the magnitude of an earthquake—an assessment of the seismic moment. Replaces the Richter scale (amplitude magnitude); especially valuable in assessing larger-magnitude events.

Monsoon (4) An annual cycle of dryness and wetness, with seasonally shifting winds produced by changing atmospheric pressure systems; affects India, Southeast Asia, Indonesia, northern Australia, and portions of Africa. From the Arabic word *mausim*, meaning "season."

Montane forest (17) Needleleaf forest associated with mountain elevations. (*See* Needleleaf forest.)

Moraine (14) Marginal glacial deposits (lateral, medial, terminal, ground) of unsorted and unstratified material.

Mountain–valley breeze (4) A light wind produced as cooler mountain air flows downslope at night and as warmer valley air flows upslope during the day.

Movement (1) A major theme in geography involving migration, communication, and the interaction of people and processes across space.

Mudflow (11) Fluid downslope flows of material containing more water than earthflows.

Natural levee (12) A long, low ridge that forms on both sides of a stream in a developed floodplain; a depositional product (coarse gravels and sand) of river flooding.

Needleleaf forest (17) Consists of pine, spruce, fir, and larch and stretches from the east coast of Canada westward to Alaska and continuing from Siberia westward across the entire extent of Russia to the European Plain; called the *taiga* (a Russian word) or the *boreal forest*; principally in the microthermal climates. Includes montane forests that may be at lower latitudes at higher elevations.

Negative feedback (1) Feedback that tends to slow or dampen responses in a system; promotes self-regulation in a system; far more common than positive feedback in living systems. (*See* Feedback loop; *compare* Positive feedback.)

Net primary productivity (16) The net photosynthesis (photosynthesis minus respiration) for a given community; considers all growth and all reduction factors that affect the amount of useful chemical energy (biomass) fixed in an ecosystem.

Net radiation (NET R) (3) The net all-wave radiation available at Earth's surface; the final outcome of the radiation balance process between incoming shortwave insolation and outgoing longwave energy.

Nickpoint (knickpoint) (12) The point at which the longitudinal profile of a stream is abruptly broken by a change in gradient; for example, a waterfall, rapids, or cascade.

Nimbostratus (5) Rain-producing, dark, grayish stratiform clouds characterized by gentle drizzle.

Nitrogen dioxide (2) A noxious (harmful) reddish-brown gas produced in combustion engines; can be damaging to human respiratory tracts and to plants; participates in photochemical reactions and acid deposition.

Normal fault (10) A type of geologic fault in rocks. Tension produces strain that breaks a rock, with one side moving vertically relative to the other side along an inclined fault plane. (*Compare* Reverse fault.)

Normal lapse rate (2) The average rate of temperature decrease with increasing altitude in the lower atmosphere; an average value of 6.4 C° per km, or 1000 m (3.5 F° per 1000 ft). (*Compare* Environmental lapse rate.)

Occluded front (5) In a cyclonic circulation, the overrunning of a surface warm front by a cold front and the subsequent lifting of the warm air wedge off the ground; initial precipitation is moderate to heavy.

Ocean basin (10) The physical container (a depression in the lithosphere) holding an ocean.

Omnivore (16) A consumer that feeds on both producers (plants) and consumers (meat)—a role occupied by humans, among other animals. (*Compare* Consumer, Producer.)

Open system (1) A system with inputs and outputs crossing back and forth between the system and the surrounding environment. Earth is an open system in terms of energy. (*Compare* Closed system.)

Orogenesis (10) The process of mountain building that occurs when large-scale compression leads to deformation and uplift of the crust; literally, the birth of mountains.

Orographic lifting (5) The uplift of a migrating air mass as it is forced to move upward over a mountain range—a topographic barrier. The lifted air cools adiabatically as it moves upslope; clouds may form and produce increased precipitation.

Outgassing (6) The release of trapped gases from rocks, forced out through cracks, fissures, and volcanoes from within Earth; the terrestrial source of Earth's water.

Outwash plain (14) Area of glacial stream deposits of stratified drift with meltwater-fed, braided, and overloaded streams; occurs beyond a glacier's morainal deposits.

Overland flow (6) Surplus water that flows across the land surface toward stream channels. Together with precipitation and subsurface flows, it constitutes the total runoff from an area.

Oxbow lake (12) A lake that was formerly part of the channel of a meandering stream; isolated when a stream eroded its outer bank, forming a cutoff through the neck of the looping meander (*see* Meandering stream). In Australia, known as a *billabong* (the Aboriginal word for "dead river").

Oxidation (11) A chemical weathering process in which oxygen dissolved in water oxidizes (combines with) certain metallic elements to form oxides; most familiar is the "rusting" of iron in a rock or soil (Ultisols, Oxisols), which produces a reddish-brown stain of iron oxide.

Oxisols (15) A soil order in the Soil Taxonomy. Tropical soils that are old, deeply developed, and lacking in horizons wherever well drained; heavily weathered, low in cation-exchange capacity, and low in fertility.

Ozone layer (2) *See* Ozonosphere.

Ozonosphere (2) A layer of ozone occupying the full extent of the stratosphere (20 to 50 km, or 12 to 30 mi, above the surface); the region of the atmosphere where ultraviolet wavelengths of insolation are extensively absorbed and converted into heat.

Pahoehoe (10) Basaltic lava that is more fluid than aa. Pahoehoe forms a thin crust that forms folds and appears "ropy," like coiled, twisted rope.

Paleoclimatology (8) The science that studies the climates, and the causes of variations in climate, of past ages, throughout historic and geologic time.

Paleolake (14) An ancient lake, such as Lake Bonneville or Lake Lahonton, associated with former wet periods when the lake basins were filled to higher levels than today.

Pangaea (9) The supercontinent formed by the collision of all continental masses approximately 225 million years ago; named in the continental drift theory by Wegener in 1912. (*See* Plate tectonics.)

Parallel (1) A line, parallel to the equator, that designates an angle of latitude. (*See* Latitude.)

Parent material (11) The unconsolidated material, from both organic and mineral sources, that is the basis of soil development.

Particulate matter (PM) (2) Dust, dirt, soot, salt, sulfate aerosols, fugitive natural particles, or other material particles suspended in air.

Paternoster lake (14) One of a series of small, circular, stair-stepped lakes formed in individual rock basins aligned down the course of a glaciated valley; named because they look like a string of rosary (religious) beads.

Patterned ground (14) Areas in the periglacial environment where freezing and thawing of the ground create polygonal forms of arranged rocks at the surface; can be circles, polygons, stripes, nets, and steps.

Pedogenic regime (15) A specific soil-forming process keyed to a specific climatic regime: laterization, calcification, salinization, and podzolization, among others; not the basis for soil classification in the Soil Taxonomy.

Pedon (15) A soil profile extending from the surface to the lowest extent of plant roots or to the depth where regolith or bedrock is encountered; imagined as a hexagonal column; the basic soil sampling unit.

Percolation (6) The process by which water permeates the soil or porous rock into the subsurface environment.

Periglacial (14) Cold-climate processes, landforms, and topographic features along the margins of glaciers, past and present; periglacial characteristics exist on more than 20% of Earth's land surface; includes permafrost, frost action, and ground ice.

Perihelion (2) The point of Earth's closest approach to the Sun in its elliptical orbit, reached on January 3 at a distance of 147,255,000 km (91,500,000 mi); variable over a 100,000-year cycle. (*Compare* Aphelion.)

Permafrost (14) Forms when soil or rock temperatures remain below 0°C (32°F) for at least 2 years in areas considered periglacial; criterion is based on temperature and not on whether water is present. (*See* Periglacial.)

Permeability (6) The ability of water to flow through soil or rock; a function of the texture and structure of the medium.

Peroxyacetyl nitrate (PAN) (2) A pollutant formed from photochemical reactions involving nitric oxide (NO) and volatile organic compounds (VOCs). PAN produces no known human health effect, but is particularly damaging to plants.

Phase change (5) The change in phase, or state, among ice, water, and water vapor; involves the absorption or release of latent heat. (*See* Latent heat.)

Photochemical smog (2) Air pollution produced by the interaction of ultraviolet light, nitrogen dioxide, and hydrocarbons; produces ozone and PAN through a series of complex photochemical reactions. Automobiles are the major source of the contributive gases.

Photosynthesis (16) The process by which plants produce their own food from carbon dioxide and water, powered by solar energy. The joining of carbon dioxide and hydrogen in plants, under the influence of certain wavelengths of visible light; releases oxygen and produces energy-rich organic material, sugars, and starches. (*Compare* Respiration.)

Physical geography (1) The science concerned with the spatial aspects and interactions of the physical elements and process systems that make up the environment: energy, air, water, weather, climate, landforms, soils, animals, plants, microorganisms, and Earth.

Physical weathering (11) The breaking up and disintegrating of rock without any chemical alteration; sometimes referred to as *mechanical* or *fragmentation weathering.*

Pioneer community (16) The initial plant community in an area; usually is found on new surfaces or those that have been stripped of life, as in beginning primary succession, and includes lichens, mosses, and ferns growing on bare rock.

Place (1) A major theme in geography, focused on the tangible and intangible characteristics that make each location unique; no two places on Earth are alike.

Plane of the ecliptic (2) A plane (flat surface) intersecting all the points of Earth's orbit.

Planetesimal hypothesis (2) Proposes a process by which early protoplanets formed from the condensing masses of a nebular cloud of dust, gas, and icy comets; a formation process now being observed in other parts of the galaxy.

Planimetric map (Appendix A) A basic map showing the horizontal position of boundaries; land-use activities; and political, economic, and social outlines.

Plate tectonics (9) The conceptual model and theory that encompass continental drift, seafloor spreading, and related aspects of crustal movement; accepted as the foundation of crustal tectonic processes.

Playa (12) An area of salt crust left behind by evaporation on a desert floor, usually in the middle of a desert or semiarid bolson or valley; intermittently wet and dry.

Pluton (9) A mass of intrusive igneous rock that has cooled slowly in the crust; forms in any size or shape. The largest partially exposed pluton is a batholith. (*See* Batholith.)

Podzolization (15) A pedogenic process in cool, moist climates; forms a highly leached soil with strong surface acidity because of humus from acid-rich trees.

Point bar (12) In a stream, the inner portion of a meander, where sediment fill is redeposited. (*Compare* Undercut bank.)

Polar easterlies (4) Variable, weak, cold, and dry winds moving away from the polar region; an anticyclonic circulation.

Polar desert (17) A type of desert biome found at higher latitudes than cold deserts, occurring mainly in the very cold, dry climates of Greenland and Antartica.

Polar front (4) A significant zone of contrast between cold and warm air masses; roughly situated between 50° and 60° N and S latitudes.

Polar high (4) Weak, anticyclonic, thermally produced pressure systems positioned roughly over each pole; that over the South Pole is the region of the lowest temperatures on Earth. (*See* Antarctic high.)

Pollutants (2) Natural or human-caused gases, particles, and other substances in the troposphere that accumulate in amounts harmful to humans or to the environment.

Positive feedback (1) Feedback that amplifies or encourages responses in a system. (*Compare* Negative feedback; *see* Feedback loop.)

Potential evapotranspiration (6) POTET, or PE; the amount of moisture that would evaporate and transpire if adequate moisture were available; it is the amount lost under optimum moisture conditions, the moisture demand. (*Compare* Actual evapotranspiration.)

Precipitation (6) Rain, snow, sleet, and hail—the moisture supply; called PRECIP, or P, in the water balance.

Pressure gradient force (4) Causes air to move from an area of higher barometric pressure to an area of lower barometric pressure due to the pressure difference.

Primary succession (16) Succession that occurs among plant species in an area of new surfaces created by mass movement of land, cooled lava flows and volcanic eruption landscapes, or surface mining and clear-cut logging scars; exposed by retreating glaciers, or made up of sand dunes, with no trace of a former community.

Prime meridian (1) An arbitrary meridian designated as 0° longitude, the point from which longitudes are measured east or west; established at Greenwich, England, by international agreement in an 1884 treaty.

Process (1) A set of actions and changes that occur in some special order; analysis of processes is central to modern geographic synthesis.

Producer (16) Organism (plant) in an ecosystem that uses carbon dioxide as its sole source of carbon, which it chemically fixes through photosynthesis to provide its own nourishment; also called an *autotroph.* (*Compare* Consumer.)

Proxy method (8) Information about past environments that represent changes in climate, such as isotope analysis or tree ring dating; also called a *climate proxy.*

Pyroclastic (10) An explosively ejected rock fragment launched by a volcanic eruption; sometimes described by the more general term *tephra.*

Radiation fog (5) Formed by radiative cooling of a land surface, especially on clear nights in areas of moist ground; occurs when the air layer directly above the surface is chilled to the dew-point temperature, thereby producing saturated conditions.

Radiative forcing (8) The amount by which some perturbation causes Earth's energy balance to deviate from zero; a positive forcing indicates a warming condition, while a negative forcing indicates cooling; also called *climate forcing.*

Radioactive isotope (8) An unstable isotope that decays, or breaks down, into a different element, emitting radiation in the process. The unstable isotope carbon-14 has a constant rate of decay known as a *half-life* that can be used to date plant material in a technique called *radiocarbon dating.*

Rain shadow (5) The area on the leeward slope of a mountain range where precipitation receipt is greatly reduced compared to the windward slope on the other side. (*See* Orographic lifting.)

Reflection (3) The portion of arriving insolation that is returned directly to space without being absorbed and converted into heat and without performing any work. (*See* Albedo.)

Refraction (3) The bending effect on electromagnetic waves that occurs when insolation enters the atmosphere or another medium; the same process disperses the component colors of the light passing through a crystal or prism.

Region (1) A geographic theme that focuses on areas that display unity and internal homogeneity of traits; includes the study of how a region forms, evolves, and interrelates with other regions.

Regolith (11) Partially weathered rock overlying bedrock, whether residual or transported.

Relative humidity (5) The ratio of water vapor actually in the air (content) to the maximum water vapor possible in the air (capacity) at that temperature; expressed as a percentage. (*Compare* Vapor pressure, Specific humidity.)

Relief (10) Elevation differences in a local landscape; an expression of local height differences of landforms.

Remote sensing (1) Information acquired from a distance, without physical contact with the subject—for example, photography, orbital imagery, and radar.

Respiration (16) The process by which plants oxidize carbohydrates to derive energy for their operations; essentially, the reverse of the photosynthetic process; releases carbon dioxide, water, and heat energy into the environment. (*Compare* Photosynthesis.)

Reverse fault (10) Compressional forces produce strain that breaks a rock so that one side moves upward relative to the other side; also called a *thrust fault.* (*Compare* Normal fault.)

Revolution (2) The annual orbital movement of Earth about the Sun; determines the length of the year and the seasons.

Rhumb line (1) A line of constant compass direction, or constant bearing, that crosses successive meridians at the same angle; appears as a straight line only on the Mercator projection.

Richter scale (10) An open-ended, logarithmic scale that estimates earthquake magnitude based on measurement of the maximum seismic wave amplitude; designed by Charles Richter in 1935; now replaced by the moment magnitude scale. (*See* Moment magnitude scale.)

Ring of Fire (10) A tectonically and volcanically active region encircling the Pacific Ocean; also known as the circum-Pacific belt.

Robinson projection (Appendix A) A compromise (neither equal area nor true shape) oval projection developed in 1963 by Arthur Robinson.

Roche moutonnée (14) A glacial erosion feature; an asymmetrical hill of exposed bedrock; displays a gently sloping upstream side that has been smoothed and polished by a glacier and an abrupt, steep downstream side.

Rock (9) An assemblage of minerals bound together, or sometimes a mass of a single mineral.

Rock cycle (9) A model representing the interrelationships among the three rock-forming processes: igneous, sedimentary, and metamorphic; shows how each can be transformed into another rock type.

Rockfall (11) Free-falling movement of debris from a cliff or steep slope, generally falling straight or bounding downslope.

Rossby wave (4) An undulating horizontal motion in the upper-air westerly circulation at middle and high latitudes.

Rotation (2) The turning of Earth on its axis, averaging about 24 hours in duration; determines day–night relation; counterclockwise when viewed from above the North Pole and from west to east, or eastward, when viewed from above the equator.

Salinity (13) The concentration of natural elements and compounds dissolved in solution, as solutes; measured by weight in parts per thousand (‰) in seawater.

Salinization (15) A pedogenic process that results from high potential evapotranspiration rates in deserts and semiarid regions. Soil water is drawn to surface horizons, and dissolved salts are deposited as the water evaporates.

Saltation (12) The transport of sand grains (usually larger than 0.2 mm, or 0.008 in.) by stream or wind, bouncing the grains along the ground in asymmetrical paths.

Salt marsh (13) A wetland ecosystem characteristic of latitudes poleward of the 30th parallel. (*Compare* Mangrove swamp.)

Sand sea (13) An extensive area of sand and dunes; characteristic of Earth's erg deserts. (*Compare* Erg.)

Saturation (5) State of air that is holding all the water vapor that it can hold at a given temperature, known as the dew-point temperature.

Scale (1) The ratio of the distance on a map to that in the real world; expressed as a representative fraction, graphic scale, or written scale.

Scarification (11) Human-induced mass movement of Earth materials, such as large-scale open-pit mining and strip mining.

Scattering (3) Deflection and redirection of insolation by atmospheric gases, dust, ice, and water vapor; the shorter the wavelength, the greater the scattering; thus, skies in the lower atmosphere are blue.

Scientific method (1) An approach that uses applied common sense in an organized and objective manner; based on observation, generalization, formulation, and testing of a hypothesis, ultimately leading to the development of a theory.

Seafloor spreading (9) As proposed by Hess and Dietz, the mechanism driving the movement of the continents; associated with upwelling flows of magma along the worldwide system of mid-ocean ridges. (*See* Mid-ocean ridge.)

Secondary succession (16) Succession that occurs among plant species in an area where vestiges of a previously functioning community are present; an area where the natural community has been destroyed or disturbed, but where the underlying soil remains intact.

Sediment (9) Fine-grained mineral matter that is transported and deposited by air, water, or ice.

Sedimentary rock (9) One of the three basic rock types; formed from the compaction, cementation, and hardening of sediments derived from other rocks. (*Compare* Igneous rock, Metamorphic rock.)

Sediment transport (12) The movement of rocks and sediment downstream when energy is high in a river or stream.

Seismic wave (9) The shock wave sent through the planet by an earthquake or underground nuclear test. Transmission varies according to temperature and the density of various layers within the planet; provides indirect diagnostic evidence of Earth's internal structure.

Seismometer (10) An instrument used to detect and record the ground motion during an earthquake caused by seismic waves traveling through Earth's interior to the surface; the instrument records the waves on a graphic plot called a *seismogram.*

Sensible heat (3) Heat that can be measured with a thermometer; a measure of the concentration of kinetic energy from molecular motion.

September equinox (2) The time around September 22–23 when the Sun's declination crosses the equatorial parallel (0° latitude) and all places on Earth experience days and nights of equal length (also known as *autumnal equinox*). The Sun rises at the South Pole and sets at the North Pole. (*Compare* March equinox.).

Sheetflow (12) Surface water that moves downslope in a thin film as overland flow; not concentrated in channels larger than rills.

Shield volcano (10) A symmetrical mountain landform built from effusive eruptions (low-viscosity magma); gently sloped and gradually rising from the surrounding landscape to a summit crater; typical of the Hawaiian Islands. (*Compare* Effusive eruption, Composite volcano.)

Sinkhole (11) Nearly circular depression created by the weathering of karst landscapes with subterranean drainage; also known as a *doline* in traditional studies; may collapse through the roof of an underground space. (*See* Karst topography.)

Slope (11) A curved, inclined surface that bounds a landform.

Small circle (1) A circle on a globe's surface that does not share Earth's center—for example, all parallels of latitude other than the equator. (*Compare* Great circle.)

Snowline (14) A temporary line marking the elevation where winter snowfall persists throughout the summer; seasonally, the lowest elevation covered by snow during the summer.

Soil (15) A dynamic natural body made up of fine materials covering Earth's surface in which plants grow, composed of both mineral and organic matter.

Soil colloid (15) A tiny clay and organic particle in soil; provides a chemically active site for mineral ion adsorption. (*See* Cation-exchange capacity.)

Soil creep (11) A persistent mass movement of surface soil where individual soil particles are lifted and disturbed by the expansion of soil moisture as it freezes or by grazing livestock or digging animals.

Soil fertility (15) The ability of soil to support plant productivity when it contains organic substances and clay minerals that absorb water and certain elemental ions needed by plants through adsorption. (*See* Cation-exchange capacity.)

Soil horizons (15) The various layers exposed in a pedon; roughly parallel to the surface and identified as O, A, E, B, C, and R (bedrock).

Soil-moisture recharge (6) Water entering available soil storage spaces.

Soil-moisture storage (6) STRGE; the retention of moisture within soil; it is a savings account that can accept deposits (soil-moisture recharge) or allow withdrawals (soil-moisture utilization) as conditions change.

Soil-moisture utilization (6) The extraction of soil moisture by plants for their needs; efficiency of withdrawal decreases as the soil-moisture storage is reduced.

Soil-moisture zone (6) The area of water stored in soil between the ground surface and the water table. Water in this zone may be available or unavailable to plant roots, depending on soil texture characteristics.

Soil porosity (15) The total volume of space within a soil that is filled with air, gases, or water (as opposed to soil particles or organic matter).

Soil profile (15) A vertical section of soil extending from the surface to the deepest extent of plant roots or to regolith or bedrock.

Soil science (15) Interdisciplinary science of soils. Pedology concerns the origin, classification, distribution, and description of soil. Edaphology focuses on soil as a medium for sustaining higher plants.

Soil Taxonomy (15) A soil classification system based on observable soil properties actually seen in the field; published in 1975 by the U.S. Soil Conservation Service and revised in 1990 and 1998 by the Natural Resources Conservation Service to include 12 soil orders.

Solar constant (2) The amount of insolation intercepted by Earth on a surface perpendicular to the Sun's rays when Earth is at its average distance from the Sun; a value of 1372 W/m^2 (1.968 $calories/cm^2$) per minute; averaged over the entire globe at the thermopause.

Solar wind (2) Clouds of ionized (charged) gases emitted by the Sun and traveling in all directions from the Sun's surface. Effects on Earth include auroras, disturbance of radio signals, and possible influences on weather.

Solum (15) A true soil profile in the pedon; ideally, a combination of O, A, E, and B horizons. (*See* Pedon.)

Spatial (1) The nature or character of physical space, as in an area; occupying or operating within a space. Geography is a spatial science; spatial analysis is its essential approach.

Spatial analysis (1) The examination of spatial interactions, patterns, and variations over area and/or space; a key integrative approach of geography.

Specific heat (3) The increase of temperature in a material when energy is absorbed; water has a higher specific heat (can store more heat) than a comparable volume of soil or rock.

Specific humidity (5) The mass of water vapor (in grams) per unit mass of air (in kilograms) at any specified temperature. The maximum mass of water vapor that a kilogram of air can hold at any specified temperature is termed its maximum specific humidity. (*Compare* Vapor pressure, Relative humidity.)

Speed of light (2) Specifically, 299,792 km (186,282 mi) per second, or more than 9.4 trillion km (5.9 trillion mi) per year—a distance known as a light-year; at light speed, Earth is 8 minutes and 20 seconds from the Sun.

Speleothem (8) A calcium carbonate mineral deposit in a cave or cavern, such as a stalactite or stalagmite, that forms as water drips or seeps from rock and subsequently evaporates, leaving behind a residue of calcium carbonate that builds up over time.

Spheroidal weathering (11) A chemical weathering process in which the sharp edges and corners of boulders and rocks are weathered in thin plates that create a rounded, spheroidal form.

Spodosols (15) A soil order in the Soil Taxonomy. Occurs in northern coniferous forests; best developed in cold, moist, forested climates; lacks humus and clay in the A horizon, with high acidity associated with podzolization processes.

Squall line (5) A zone slightly ahead of a fast-advancing cold front where wind patterns are rapidly changing and blustery and precipitation is strong.

Stability (5) The condition of a parcel of air with regard to whether it remains where it is or changes its initial position. The parcel is stable if it resists displacement upward and unstable if it continues to rise.

Steady-state equilibrium (1) The condition that occurs in a system when the rates of input and output are equal and the amounts of energy and stored matter are nearly constant around a stable average.

Steppe (7) A regional term referring to the vast semiarid grassland biome of Eastern Europe and Asia; the equivalent biome in North America is shortgrass prairie, and in Africa, it is the savanna. Steppe in a climatic context is considered too dry to support forest, but too moist to be a desert.

Stomata (16) Small openings on the undersides of leaves through which water and gasses pass.

Storm surge (5) A large quantity of seawater pushed inland by the strong winds associated with a tropical cyclone.

Stratified drift (14) Sediments deposited by glacial meltwater that appear sorted; a specific form of glacial drift. (*Compare* Till.)

Stratigraphy (9) A science that analyzes the sequence, spacing, geophysical and geochemical properties, and spatial distribution of rock strata.

Stratocumulus (5) A lumpy, grayish, low-level cloud, patchy with sky visible, sometimes present at the end of the day.

Stratosphere (2) That portion of the homosphere that ranges from 20 to 50 km (12.5 to 30 mi) above Earth's surface, with temperatures ranging from −57°C (−70°F) at the tropopause to 0°C (32°F) at the stratopause. The functional ozonosphere is within the stratosphere.

Stratus (5) A stratiform (flat, horizontal) cloud generally below 2000 m (6500 ft).

Strike-slip fault (10) Horizontal movement along a fault line—that is, movement in the same direction as the fault; also known as a *transcurrent* fault. Such movement is described as right lateral or left lateral, depending on the relative motion observed across the fault.

Subduction zone (9) An area where two plates of crust collide and the denser oceanic crust dives beneath the less dense continental plate, forming deep oceanic trenches and seismically active regions.

Sublimation (5) A process in which ice evaporates directly to water vapor or water vapor freezes directly to ice (deposition).

Subpolar low (4) A region of low pressure centered approximately at 60° latitude in the North Atlantic near Iceland and in the North Pacific near the Aleutians as well as in the Southern Hemisphere. Airflow is cyclonic; it weakens in summer and strengthens in winter. (*See* Cyclone.)

Subsolar point (2) The only point receiving perpendicular insolation at a given moment—that is, the Sun is directly overhead. (*See* Declination.)

Subtropical high (4) One of several dynamic high-pressure areas covering roughly the region from 20° to 35° N and S latitudes; responsible for the hot, dry areas of Earth's arid and semiarid deserts. (*See* Anticyclone.)

Sulfur dioxide (SO_2) (2) A colorless gas detected by its pungent odor; produced by the combustion of fossil fuels, especially coal, that contain sulfur as an impurity; can react in the atmosphere to form sulfuric acid, a component of acid deposition.

Sunspots (2) Magnetic disturbances on the surface of the Sun, occurring in an average 11-year cycle; related flares, prominences, and outbreaks produce surges in solar wind.

Surface creep (13) A form of eolian transport that involves particles too large for saltation; a process whereby individual grains are impacted by moving grains and slide and roll.

Surface runoff (6) Surplus water that flows across the ground surface toward stream channels when soils are saturated or when the ground is impermeable; also called *overland flow.*

Surplus (6) SURPL; the amount of moisture that exceeds potential evapotranspiration; moisture oversupply when soil-moisture storage is at field capacity; extra or surplus water.

Suspended load (12) Fine particles held in suspension in a stream. The finest particles are not deposited until the stream velocity nears zero.

Sustainability science (1) An emerging, integrated scientific discipline based on the concepts of sustainable development related to functioning Earth systems.

Swell (13) Regular patterns of smooth, rounded waves in open water; can range from small ripples to very large waves.

Syncline (10) A trough in folded strata, with beds that slope toward the axis of the downfold. (*Compare* Anticline.)

System (1) Any ordered, interrelated set of materials or items existing separate from the environment or within a boundary; energy transformations and energy and matter storage and retrieval occur within a system.

Taiga (17) *See* Needleleaf forest.

Tarn (14) A small mountain lake, especially one that collects in a cirque basin behind risers of rock material or in an ice-gouged depression.

Temperate rain forest (17) A major biome of lush forests at middle and high latitudes; occurs along narrow margins of the Pacific Northwest in North America, among other locations; includes the tallest trees in the world.

Temperature (3) A measure of sensible heat energy present in the atmosphere and other media; indicates the average kinetic energy of individual molecules within a substance.

Temperature inversion (2) A reversal of the normal decrease of temperature with increasing altitude; can occur anywhere from ground level up to several thousand meters; functions to block atmospheric convection and thereby trap pollutants.

Terminal moraine (14) Eroded debris that is dropped at a glacier's farthest extent.

Terrane (10) A migrating piece of Earth's crust, dragged about by processes of mantle convection and plate tectonics. Displaced terranes are distinct in their history, composition, and structure from the continents that accept them.

Thermal equator (3) The isoline on an isothermal map that connects all points of highest mean temperature.

Thermohaline circulation (4) Deep-ocean currents produced by differences in temperature and salinity with depth; Earth's deep currents.

Thermopause (2) A zone approximately 480 km (300 mi) in altitude that serves conceptually as the top of the atmosphere; an altitude used for the determination of the solar constant.

Thermosphere (2) A region of the heterosphere extending from 80 to 480 km (50 to 300 mi) in altitude; contains the functional ionosphere layer.

Threshold (1) A moment in which a system can no longer maintain its character, so it lurches to a new operational level, which may not be compatible with previous conditions.

Thrust fault (10) A reverse fault where the fault plane forms a low angle relative to the horizontal; an overlying block moves over an underlying block.

Thunder (5) The violent expansion of suddenly heated air, created by lightning discharges, which sends out shock waves as an audible sonic bang.

Tide (13) A pattern of twice-daily oscillations in sea level produced by astronomical relations among the Sun, the Moon, and Earth; experienced in varying degrees around the world.

Till (14) Direct ice deposits that appear unstratified and unsorted; a specific form of glacial drift. (*Compare* Stratified drift.)

Till plain (14) A large, relatively flat plain composed of unsorted glacial deposits behind a terminal or end moraine. Low-rolling relief and unclear drainage patterns are characteristic.

Tombolo (13) A landform created when coastal sand deposits connect the shoreline with an offshore island outcrop or sea stack.

Topographic map (Appendix A) A map that portrays physical relief through the use of elevation contour lines that connect all points at the same elevation above or below a vertical datum, such as mean sea level.

Topography (10) The undulations and configurations, including its relief, that give Earth's surface its texture, portrayed on topographic maps.

Tornado (5) An intense, destructive cyclonic rotation, developed in response to extremely low pressure; generally associated with mesocyclone formation.

Traction (12) A type of sediment transport that drags coarser materials along the bed of a stream. (*See* Bed load.)

Trade winds (4) Winds from the northeast and southeast that converge in the equatorial low-pressure trough, forming the intertropical convergence zone.

Transmission (3) The passage of shortwave and longwave energy through space, the atmosphere, or water.

Transparency (3) The quality of a medium (air, water) that allows light to easily pass through it.

Transpiration (6) The movement of water vapor out through the pores in leaves; the water is drawn by the plant roots from soil-moisture storage.

Tropical cyclone (5) A cyclonic circulation originating in the tropics, with winds between 30 and 64 knots (39 and 73 mph); characterized by closed isobars, circular organization, and heavy rains. (*See* Hurricane, Typhoon.)

Tropical rain forest (17) A lush biome of tall broadleaf evergreen trees and diverse plants and animals, roughly between 23.5° N and 23.5° S latitude. The dense canopy of leaves is usually arranged in three levels.

Tropical savanna (17) A major biome containing large expanses of grassland interrupted by trees and shrubs; a transitional area between the humid rain forests and tropical seasonal forests and the drier, semiarid tropical steppes and deserts.

Tropical seasonal forest and scrub (17) A variable biome on the margins of the rain forests, occupying regions of lesser and more erratic rainfall; the site of transitional communities between the rain forests and tropical grasslands.

Tropic of Cancer (2) The parallel that marks the farthest north the subsolar point migrates during the year; 23.5° N latitude. (*See* Tropic of Capricorn, June solstice.)

Tropic of Capricorn (2) The parallel that marks the farthest south the subsolar point migrates during the year; 23.5° S latitude. (*See* Tropic of Cancer, December solstice.)

Troposphere (2) The home of the biosphere; the lowest layer of the homosphere, containing approximately 90% of the total mass of the atmosphere; extends up to the tropopause; occurring at an altitude of 18 km (11 mi) at the equator, at 13 km (8 mi) in the middle latitudes, and at lower altitudes near the poles.

True shape (1) A map property showing the correct configuration of coastlines; a useful trait of conformality for navigational and aeronautical maps, although areal relationships are distorted. (*See* Map projection; *compare* Equal area.)

Tsunami (13) A seismic sea wave, traveling at high speeds across the ocean, formed by sudden motion in the seafloor, such as a seafloor earthquake, submarine landslide, or eruption of an undersea volcano.

Typhoon (5) A tropical cyclone with wind speeds in excess of 119 kmph (65 knots, or 74 mph) that occurs in the western Pacific; same as a hurricane except for location. (*Compare* Hurricane.)

Ultisols (15) A soil order in the Soil Taxonomy. Features highly weathered forest soils, principally in the humid subtropical climatic classification. Increased weathering and exposure can degenerate an Alfisol into the reddish color and texture of these Ultisols. Fertility is quickly exhausted when Ultisols are cultivated.

Unconfined aquifer (6) An aquifer that is not bounded by impermeable strata. It is simply the zone of saturation in water-bearing rock strata with no impermeable overburden, and recharge is generally accomplished by water percolating down from above. (*Compare* Confined aquifer.)

Undercut bank (12) A steep bank formed along the outer portion of a meandering stream; produced by lateral erosive action of a stream; sometimes called a *cutbank*. (*Compare* Point bar.)

Uniformitarianism (9) An assumption that physical processes active in the environment today are operating at the same pace and intensity that have characterized them throughout geologic time; proposed by Hutton and Lyell.

Upslope fog (5) Forms when moist air is forced to higher elevations along a hill or mountain and is thus cooled. (*Compare* Valley fog.)

Upwelling current (4) An area of the sea where cool, deep waters, which are generally nutrient-rich, rise to replace vacating water, as occurs along the west coasts of North and South America. (*Compare* Downwelling current.)

Urban heat island (3) An urban microclimate that is warmer on average than areas in the surrounding countryside because of the interaction of solar radiation and various surface characteristics.

Valley fog (5) The settling of cooler, more dense air in low-lying areas; produces saturated conditions and fog. (*Compare* Upslope fog.)

Vapor pressure (5) That portion of total air pressure that results from water vapor molecules, expressed in millibars (mb). At a given dew-point temperature, the maximum capacity of the air is termed its saturation vapor pressure. (*Compare* Relative humidity, Specific humidity.)

Vascular plant (16) A plant having internal fluid and material flows through its tissues; almost 270,000 species exist on Earth.

Ventifact (13) A piece of rock etched and smoothed by eolian erosion—that is, abrasion by windblown particles.

Vertisols (15) A soil order in the Soil Taxonomy. Features expandable clay soils; composed of more than 30% swelling clays. Occurs in regions that experience highly variable soil moisture balances through the seasons.

Volcano (10) A mountainous landform at the end of a magma conduit, which rises from below the crust and vents to the surface. Magma rises and collects in a magma chamber deep below, erupting effusively or explosively and forming composite, shield, or cinder-cone volcanoes.

Warm desert and semidesert (17) A desert biome caused by the presence of subtropical high-pressure cells; characterized by dry air and low precipitation.

Warm front (5) The leading edge of an advancing warm air mass, which is unable to push cooler, passive air out of the way; tends to push the cooler, underlying air into a wedge shape; identified on a weather map as a line marked with semicircles pointing in the direction of frontal movement. (*Compare* Cold front.)

Water budget (6) A water accounting system for an area of Earth's surface using inputs of precipitation and outputs of evapotranspiration (evaporation from ground surfaces and transpiration from plants) and surface runoff. Precipitation "income" balances evaporation, transpiration, and runoff "expenditures"; soil moisture storage acts as "savings" in the budget.

Waterspout (5) An elongated, funnel-shaped circulation formed when a tornado exists over water.

Water table (6) The upper surface of groundwater; that contact point between the zone of saturation and the zone of aeration in an unconfined aquifer. (*See* Zone of aeration, Zone of saturation.)

Water withdrawal (6) Sometimes called *offstream use*, the removal of water from the natural supply, after which it is used for various purposes and then is returned to the water supply.

Wave (13) An undulation of ocean water produced by the conversion of solar energy to wind energy and then to wave energy; energy produced in a generating region or a stormy area of the sea.

Wave-cut platform (13) A flat or gently sloping, table-like bedrock surface that develops in the tidal zone where wave action cuts a bench that extends from the cliff base out into the sea.

Wave cyclone (5) *See* Midlatitude cyclone.

Wavelength (2) A measurement of a wave; the distance between the crests of successive waves. The number of waves passing a fixed point in 1 second is called the frequency of the wavelength.

Wave refraction (13) A bending process that concentrates wave energy on headlands and disperses it in coves and bays; the long-term result is coastal straightening.

Weather (5) The short-term condition of the atmosphere, as compared to climate, which reflects long-term atmospheric conditions and extremes. Temperature, air pressure, relative humidity, wind speed and direction, daylength, and Sun angle are important measurable elements that contribute to the weather.

Weathering (11) The processes by which surface and subsurface rocks disintegrate, or dissolve, or are broken down. Rocks at or near Earth's surface are exposed to physical and chemical weathering processes.

Westerlies (4) The predominant surface and aloft windflow pattern from the subtropics to high latitudes in both hemispheres.

Western intensification (4) The piling up of ocean water along the western margin of each ocean basin, to a height of about 15 cm (6 in.); produced by the trade winds that drive the oceans westward in a concentrated channel.

Wetland (6) An area that is permanently or seasonally saturated with water and characterized by vegetation adapted to hydric soils; highly productive ecosystem with an ability to trap organic matter, nutrients, and sediment.

Wilting point (6) That point in the soil-moisture balance when only hygroscopic water and some bound capillary water remain. Plants wilt and eventually die after prolonged stress from a lack of available water.

Wind (4) The horizontal movement of air relative to Earth's surface; produced essentially by air pressure differences from place to place; turbulence, wind updrafts and downdrafts, adds a vertical component; its direction is influenced by the Coriolis force and surface friction.

Wind vane (4) A weather instrument used to determine wind direction; winds are named for the direction from which they originate.

Yardang (13) A streamlined rock structure formed by deflation and abrasion; appears elongated and aligned with the most effective wind direction.

Zone of aeration (6) A zone above the water table that has air in its pore spaces and may or may not have water.

Zone of saturation (6) A groundwater zone below the water table in which all pore spaces are filled with water.

Human Denominator & Geosystems in Action Credits

GIA1: (World map) NASA. (Sphere photos) USGS. (Mount Pinatubo left) Dave Harlow/USGS. (Mount Pinatubo right) Josef Beck/imagebroke/imagebroker.net/SuperStock.

GIA2: (Background images) Bobbé Christopherson.

HD2: (2a) Steve Bower/Shutterstock. (2b) EPA, data courtesy K.E. Kunkel 2012; www.epa.gov/climatechange/indicators. (2c) AP images/Steve Parsons. (2d) Per-Anders Pettersson/Contributor/Getty images News/Getty images.

HD3: (3a) Justin Kase zninez/Alamy. (3b) Ajit Solanki/AP Images. (3c) Joanne Giuliani/Handout/Reuters. (3d) Graph based on data from Columbia University and NASA Goddard Institute for Space Studies.

GIA4: (Background image) NASA.

HD4: (4a) Rick Bowmer/AP images. (4b) After C.H. Greene and B.C. Monger, 2012, Rip Current: An arctic wild card in the weather. Oceanography 25(2): 7–9.] (4c) Adrees Latif/Reuters. (4d) Hemis/Alamy.

GIA5: (5.3a) NASA. (5.3b) NOAA.

HD5: (5a) Fabrice Coffrini/AFP/Getty images. (5b) Yu Hyung-jae, Yonhap/AP Images. (5c) Jason Clark/Zuma Press/Newscom.

GIA6: (Background image) Gilles DeCruyenaere/Shutterstock. (6.2) Bobbé Christopherson.

HD6: (6a) Alba/Alamy. (6b) Shutterstock. (6c) NASA. (6d) Mike Goldwater/Alamy.

GIA7: (Background image) Cpphotoimages/Shutterstock.

HD7: (7a) Alx Yago/Shutterstock. (7b) Nigel Cattlin/Alamy. (7c) Robert Harding Picture Library Ltd/Alamy. (7d) Scott Olson/Getty images News/Getty Images.

GIA8: (8.2) Bobbé Christopherson.

HD8: (8a) U.S. Department of Agriculture . (8b) Pat Roque/AP Images. (8c) David Hill/Photolibrary/Getty Images. (8d) Charles Sturge/Alamy.

GIA9: (9.3a) Annie Owen/ Robert Harding World Imagery/Getty Image. (9.3b) Tom Grundy/Shutterstock. (9.3c) Somchai Buddha/Shutterstock.

HD9: (9a) Edward Fielding/Shutterstock. (9b) Ragnar Th Sigurdsson/Arctic Images/Alamy. (9c) Penny Tweedie/Alamy. (9d) Inga spence/Alamy.

GIA10: (Three sisters) Skylightpictures/123RF. (Mt. Katahdin) All Canada Photos/Alamy. (French Alps) Calin Tatu/Shutterstock. (Himalayas) Microstock Man/Shutterstock. (Chimborazo) Michael Mellinger/Getty Images. (Klamath) Visions of America/Shutterstock. (GIA10.2) Suronin/Shutterstock.

HD10: (10a & 10d) USGS. (10b) Christopher Furlong/Getty Images News/Getty Images. (10c) Stringer Mexico/Reuters.

GIA11: (11.1) Robert Christopherson. (11.3) Bobbé Christopherson. (11.3 Rock outcrop) Robert Christopherson.

HD11: (11a) Bennett Dean/Eye Ubiquitous/Documentary Value/Corbis. (11b) Patrick Lin/AFP/Getty Images. (11c) Schafer & Hill/The Image Bank/Getty Images.

GIA12: (12.1b) USDA/NRCS. (12.2) USGS National Centern.

HD12: (12a) Matthias Schrader/AP Images. (12b) European Pressphoto Agency b.v./Alamy. (12c) Karl Weatherly/Nomad/Corbis.

HD13: (13a) Trevor Glass, RSPB/AP Images. (13b) Imagebroker.net/Superstock. (13c) Nani Afrida/epa/Corbis. (13d) USGS.

GIA14: (Background image) Leksele/Shutterstock. (GIA14.1 photos) Bobbé Christopherson. (GIA14.3) USGS.

HD14: (14a) A96/Zuma Press/Newscom. (14b) Lisa McKeon/USGS. (14c) Dar Yasin/AP Images. (14d) Elnavegante/Shutterstock.

GIA15: D. Kucharski K. Kucharska/Shutterstock.

HD15: (15a) Raul Mateos Fotografia/Getty Images. (15b) Issouf Sanogo/Getty Images. (15c) USGS EROS Data Center. (15d) Nature Picture Library/Alamy.

GIA16: (16.2a) Adapted from R.B. Alexander, R.A. Smith, and G.E. Schwatz, 2000, "Effect of stream channel size on the delivery of nitrogen to the Gulf of Mexico," Nature 403: 761. (16.2b) Data source: N.N. Rabafais, Louisiana Universities Marine Consortium, R.E. Turner, Louisiana State University. Funded by: NOAA, Center for Sponsored Coastal Ocean Research. (16.2c) NASA.

HD16: (16a) Danita Delimont/Getty Images. (16b) Jim Abernathy/NOAA. (16c) © Copyright CSIRO Australia, 2013. Used by permission. (16d) Danita Delimont/Getty Images.

GIA17: (Background image) lvalin/Shutterstock. (17.1) Bobbé Christopherson. (17.2a & b) NASA. (17.2a inset) EcoImages/Getty.

HD17: (Map) Courtesy Erle Ellis, University of Maryland, Baltimore County, and Navin Ramankutty, McGill University/NASA. Map found at http://earthobservatory.nasa.gov/IOTD/view.php?id=40554. (17a) Barrett & MacKay Photo/All Canada Photos/Alamy. (17b) Justin Kase zsixz/Alamy. (17c) Dave Stamboulis/Alamy. (17d) Images & Stories/Alamy. (17e) John R. Kreul/Independent Picture Service/Alamy.

index

D

H

Q

R

S